W9-AEW-488

Revolutions in France, Belgium, Poland	1830
First Reform Bill in Britain: victory of middle-class liberalism	1832
Repeal of British Corn Laws: another liberal victory	1846
Wave of liberal and nationalistic revolutions in Europe	
The Communist Manifesto, by Marx and Engels	1848
(December 2) Coup d'état by Louis Napoleon in France	1851
"Opening" of Japan by U. S. Commodore Perry	1853
Origin of Species, by Darwin	
On Liberty, by J. S. Mill	1859
Civil War in the United States	
Emancipation of serfs by Tsar Alexander II	1861
British North America Act: Canada a dominion	
Ausgleich: Habsburg Empire reorganized as Dual Monarchy	1867
Franco-Prussian War: leading to completion of German and Italian unification and to Third French Republic	1870
Triple Alliance: Germany, Austria-Hungary, Italy	1882
Rerum Novarum by Pope Leo XIII: basis of modern Catholic social philosophy	1891
J'Accuse, by Zola: agitation over Dreyfus in France	
Spanish-American War: United States emerging as world power	1898
Boer War in South Africa	1899

A
HISTORY
OF
CIVILIZATION

CRANE

McLean Professor of Ancient and Modern History, Harvard University

JOHN B.

University of Rochester

ROBERT LEE

Harvard University

Englewood Cliffs, New Jersey

PRENTICE-HALL, INC.

A
BRINTON

HISTORY

CHRISTOPHER

OF

WOLFF

CIVILIZATION

VOLUME TWO: *1715 to the Present*

Second Edition

Grateful acknowledgment is made to the following publishers for granting permission to use the material quoted on the pages indicated: George Allen & Unwin, Ltd., 339; DAEDALUS, 685; E. P. Dutton & Co., Inc., 19, 50, 55, 60, 61, 86, 87, 122, 146, 147, 148, 154, 156, 200, 205; Hafner Publishing Company, 58, 59; Harcourt, Brace and Company, 679; Harper & Brothers, 17; Harvard University Press, 628; William Hodge & Co., Ltd., 355; Houghton Mifflin Company, 137, 470; Alfred A. Knopf, Inc., 626, 684; Macmillan Company, 196, 206; The Museum of Modern Art, 681; Oxford University Press (London), 326, 532; Oxford University Press (New York), 441; Princeton University Press, 516; Public Affairs Press, 636; Random House, Inc., 211, 214, 684; Charles Scribner's Sons, 320; Viking Press, Inc., 680.

"The White Man's Burden" on page 364 is from "The Five Nations" by Rudyard Kipling. Copyright 1903 by Rudyard Kipling, reprinted by permission of Mrs. George Bambridge, Doubleday & Company, Inc., and Methuen & Co., Ltd.

A History of Civilization: VOLUME TWO: *1715 to the Present,* Second Edition

Brinton, Christopher, and Wolff

Color plates by arrangement with Harry N. Abrams, Inc.

Design by Walter Behnke   APR. 3 1963 Cooper Union Library

38975-C

Preface

IN PREPARING this revised edition of *A History of Civilization* we have had a triple aim in view. We have sought to record and interpret the fast-moving events that have occurred since the publication of the first edition in 1955; to incorporate the new discoveries that continue to revolutionize man's knowledge of his past, notably the remote past; and to profit by the suggestions for improvement offered by readers of the first edition. The result represents not a mere tinkering with the original work but a thorough revision and, we hope, a better and more useful book.

In particular, in Volume I we have recast large sections treating the first civilizations and the ancient Greeks, and have extended the political narrative of the Medieval West over three chapters rather than two (see Chapters V, VII, and X). We have also rearranged the two chapters (VI and IX) on the Medieval East so that they come directly after their western counterparts. In Volume II, we have reorganized the chapters on developments since the First World War and have greatly expanded our accounts of the non-western world and of the intellectual and cultural history of the twentieth-century West. Throughout the two volumes we have endeavored to trim off some of the "fat" of the original book without, we trust, cutting into the meat or impairing the flavor. The reading suggestions have been brought up to date, and the maps and illustrations have been considerably changed, specifically by the addition of the new color plates.

A revision of these dimensions would never have been possible without the help of the large number of people who have contributed suggestions. We wish to thank all the teachers—and students—who have taken the trouble to write us. We wish to express our special appreciation to the following gentlemen for their critiques of the first edition: Professors Paul J. Alexander, University of Michigan; the Reverend John Francis Bannon, St. Louis University; William A. Baumgartner, Paterson State College; William Bouwsma, University of California, Berkeley; Roderic H. Davison, George Washington University; Harold S. Fink, University of Tennessee; Franklin L. Ford, Harvard University; Carl Hammond, Flint Junior College; Arthur R. Hogue, Indiana University; H. Stuart Hughes, Harvard University; and Dun Li, Benjamin Matelson, and Alfred Young, all Paterson State College. And, as the second edition goes to press, we thank again the expert readers who five years ago contributed so substantially to the improvement of the original manuscript: Professors Richard V. Burks, Wayne State University; Leland H. Carlson, Northwestern University; Myron P. Gilmore, Harvard University; E. H. Harbison, Princeton University; Harry Kimber, Michigan State University; Harry R. Rudin, Yale University; Kenneth Setton, University of Pennsylvania; Robert A. Spiller, University of Pennsylvania; and Henry R. Winkler, Rutgers University.

Finally, we wish to record our especially heavy debt to those with whom we have worked most closely: to the late Donald C. McKay of Amherst College, the editor of the parent volumes, whose untimely death occurred just as the revision was beginning to take shape; to the members of the staff both at Prentice-Hall, Inc., and at Harry N. Abrams, Inc., who have applied their skills and energies most generously and effectively; and to our families and colleagues whose sympathy, understanding, and aid have demonstrated anew that authors' tributes are no mere courteous gestures but are based on solid historical facts.

CRANE BRINTON · JOHN B. CHRISTOPHER · ROBERT L. WOLFF

Contents

Maps *by Vaughn Gray*

Illustrations

A
HISTORY
OF
CIVILIZATION

The

Eighteenth

Century:

International
Balance

CHAPTER XVI

I: Introduction:

The Prospect in 1715

Long years of peace and quiet appeared to be in prospect for Europe in 1715. In the Baltic, as we shall see, the protracted Great Northern War between Russia and Sweden was nearing a settlement. In the West, the Peace of Utrecht, signed in 1713, had restored the balance of power and had ended Louis XIV's attempt to extend French dominance. The death of the Sun King himself in 1715 gave fresh promise of international stability, for the crown of France passed to his great-grandson, Louis XV, a boy of five. A long regency was necessary, and a long regency meant that France would probably be too preoccupied with internal problems to play the aggressor. In many western states, moreover, government debts had mounted alarmingly. The great conflicts of Louis XIV had exhausted his own nation and had brought even his victorious opponents to the edge of bankruptcy.

In 1715 the forms of government in Europe ranged from absolute monarchy, as in France and Russia, to the constitutional monarchy of Britain and the republics of the Swiss and the Dutch. The differences among these forms are important, but they should not conceal the fact that all govern-

3

Ocean

Atlantic

NORWAY

Oslo

S W E

Stockholm

North Sea

Baltic

DENMARK

Copenhagen

SWEDISH POMERANIA

SCOTLAND

Edinburgh

Berwick

Danzig

ULSTER

IRELAND

Limerick

Drogheda

Boyne

Dublin

ENGLAND

KINGDOM OF GREAT BRITAIN

London

Hamburg

Fehrbellin

Berlin

B R A N D E N B U R G

THE

SAXONY

SILESIA

Prague

BOHEMIA

MORAVIA

AUSTRIA

Vienna

UNITED NETHERLANDS

Bremen

Ryswick

Utrecht

Nimwegen

Dover

Tor Bay

C. La Hogue

Oudenarde

AUSTRIAN NETHERLANDS

Ramillies

Aachen

WEST-PHALIA

EMPIRE

Mal-plaquet

Seine R.

Rhine R.

Verdun

Metz

Toul

LORRAINE

ALSACE

Rastadt

Strasbourg

Blenheim

Augsburg

BAVARIA

STIRIA

Paris

Versailles

Orleans

Blois

Nantes

Loire R.

FRANCE

FRANCHE COMTE

SWITZER-LAND

TYROL

CARINTHIA

CARNIOLA

H U N

Bordeaux

Geneva

Rhône R.

SAVOY

MILAN

Venice

VENETIAN

REPUBLIC

Adriatic Sea

Avignon (to the papacy)

Genoa

PORTUGAL

Burgos

Ebro R.

Marseilles

Florence

PAPAL STATES

Ragusa

Lisbon

Madrid

CORSICA (to Genoa)

Rome

NAPLES

Tagus R.

SPAIN

Barcelona

Valencia

BALEARIC IS.

MINORCA (Br.)

Naples

Guadalquivir R.

Seville

Granada

SARDINIA (to Austria, 1714; to Savoy, 1720)

Gibraltar (Br.)

Mediterranean

Palermo

SICILY (to Savoy, 1714 to Austria, 172

ALGERIA

TUNIS

MALTA

Miles

0   500

G.

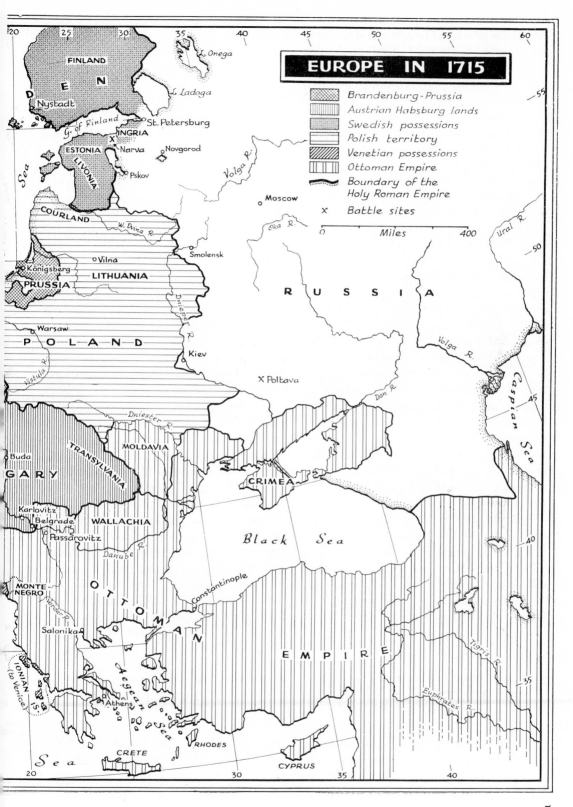

EUROPE IN 1715

Brandenburg-Prussia
Austrian Habsburg lands
Swedish possessions
Polish territory
Venetian possessions
Ottoman Empire
Boundary of the
Holy Roman Empire

x   Battle sites

0   Miles   400

FINLAND

L. Onega

DEN

Nystadt

L. Ladoga

G. of Finland

St. Petersburg

INGRIA

Narva   Novgorod

ESTONIA

LIVONIA

Sea

Pskov

COURLAND

W. Dvina R.

Volga R.

Moscow

Oka R.

Smolensk

Vilna

LITHUANIA

Königsberg

PRUSSIA

R U S S I A

Dnieper R.

Volga R.

Ural R.

Warsaw

P O L A N D

Kiev

Caspian Sea

Vistula R.

X Poltava

Don R.

Dniester R.

MOLDAVIA

CRIMEA

Black   Sea

Buda

TRANSYLVANIA

GARY

Karlovitz

Belgrade

WALLACHIA

Passarovitz

Danube R.

Constantinople

MONTE-
NEGRO

O T T O M A N

Vardar R.

Salonika

E M P I R E

Tigris R.

Aegean Sea

IONIAN
(to Venice)
IS.

Athens

Euphrates R.

RHODES

Sea

CRETE

CYPRUS

20   30   35   40

5

ments in those days represented the interests of the privileged few. We shall see that almost every European state showed some of the characteristics of oligarchy. In Britain, titled nobles, country squires, and rich merchants virtually monopolized the right to vote and to hold high office. Wealthy businessmen controlled the Dutch Republic. And the so-called absolute monarchs often wielded powers less absolute, in fact, than the theory of divine right suggested.

Historians use the term "Old Régime" to describe the oligarchical institutions of western Europe, especially France. It was the Old Régime of the eighteenth century in contrast to the "new" régime issuing from the French Revolution of 1789. In some respects, the Old Régime marked a radical change from the still older régime of the Middle Ages. Medieval Christian ideals had receded before the rationalism and balance of the seventeenth-century "classical spirit"; they would recede still further under the impact of the eighteenth-century intellectual movement of the Enlightenment, as the next chapter will show. In western Europe, the great majority of peasants had long ago cast off the bonds of serfdom, and the bourgeoisie had partly overcome the medieval prejudice against commoners.

And yet the Old Régime was often still close to the Middle Ages. Most Europeans of the eighteenth century lived in farming villages and retained their traditional parochial outlook; only a few had a real sense of nationalism, a sense of belonging to a larger entity transcending the local or pro-vincial unit. The Old Régime had its social foundations firmly based on the medieval division of society into the first estate of the clergy, the second estate of the nobility, and the third estate of everybody else. Peasants, merchants, craftsmen, and other members of the third estate had improved their lot since the Middle Ages, but most of them still remained within the great majority of the underprivileged. Only the wealthier bourgeois families enjoyed a voice in politics. Europe had always been in the main agrarian, parochial, and oligarchical; in 1715, it seemed likely to remain so forever.

The Old Régime, however, did not last forever. Its apparent stability was deceptive, and by the middle of the eighteenth century its foundations were beginning to crumble under the pressure of revolutionary economic changes. At the same time, the leaders of the Enlightenment were voicing the demands for reform that culminated in the great French Revolution of 1789.

The international stability promised by the Utrecht settlement also proved short-lived. The defeat of Louis XIV in the War of the Spanish Succession had not ended the world-wide rivalry of France and Britain, which again broke into war in 1740. Meantime, Russia was moving from semi-isolation to take an active and often an aggressive part in international affairs, and the once-obscure German state of Prussia was emerging as a first-rate military power, intent on expansion. Thus the balance of power established in 1713 survived uneasily for a generation and then dissolved.

II: The Economic Revolutions in the West

Three great sets of economic changes —in commerce, in agriculture, and in industry—helped to undermine the Old Régime and to alter the European balance. These were in fact economic revolutions, slower and less dramatic than political revolutions, but in the long run every bit as revolutionary in their effects upon human history. All three, of course, continued after the close of the eighteenth century, and we shall return to examine them again in the nineteenth century (see Chapter XX). Between 1715 and 1789 the commercial revolution was the most mature of the three. It extended to almost every European country, and it profoundly influenced war, politics, and society. In comparison, the agricultural and industrial revolutions were still in their infancy. Yet they were lusty infants, already providing farms and workshops with new techniques and lending new strength to Britain, France, and Prussia.

The Commercial Revolution

The basic institutions of the commercial revolution had developed before 1715. Banking and insurance houses dated back to the Renaissance and beyond, and chartered trading companies to the sixteenth century. Mercantilism, the philosophy underlying the policies of government toward commerce, had matured in the Spain of Philip II and the France of Louis XIV and Colbert. The steady growth of trade in the eighteenth century, however, quickened the pace of the commercial revolution.

The record-breaking volume of trade increased the demand for insurance on ships and cargoes. The insurance brokers of eighteenth-century London, like many other businessmen, often gathered in coffee houses to discuss business, news, and politics. Specialists in marine insurance gravitated to Edward Lloyd's coffee house in Lombard Street and continued to meet there after Lloyd himself died in 1713. Thus was born Lloyd's of London. The name stuck, even after the firm moved from the coffee house to more dignified quarters in the Royal Exchange in 1774.

Lloyd's developed the standard form of policy for marine insurance and published *Lloyd's List*, the first detailed and accurate shipping newspaper.

The informal atmosphere of the coffee house nurtured a second great London institution, the stock exchange. As the buying and selling of shares in joint-stock companies increased, traders began to gather at Jonathan's. In 1773, they changed the name of Jonathan's to the Stock Exchange Coffee House; thirty years later, they dropped "Coffee House" from the title and incorporated their business.

Meantime, the improvement of charts and the installation of lighthouses and buoys made navigation safer. At sea, captains learned to determine their geographical position by using two new instruments, the sextant and the chronometer. The sextant, an elaboration of the telescope, showed the altitude of the sun at noon and thus indicated the ship's latitude. The chronometer, an accurate "sea-going" clock unaffected by the motion of the ship, was kept on Greenwich Mean Time (the time at the meridian running through Greenwich near London). The two new instruments made it possible to calculate the ship's longitude, which represented the difference between Greenwich Mean Time and the local time aboard ship calculated with the sextant.

On land, the improvements in communication and transport came much more slowly than they did at sea. Except for the good highways of France, European roads were scarcely better than paths or trails. The shipment of goods overland remained slow, unsafe, and expensive until after 1750, when the construction of turnpikes and canals gradually eased the situation. The pioneer English canal, built in 1759-1761 by the Duke of Bridgewater, cut in half the cost of moving coal from the mines on his estate to the new factory town of Manchester. This was the beginning of the revolution in transport, which culminated after 1800 in the hard-surfaced highway and the railroad.

Businessmen also faced the handicaps resulting from restrictive guild regulations and from the inconvenience and profusion of local weights, measures, coins, and tolls. Sweden, for example, used copper for coins of all denominations, including a monstrosity weighing 43 pounds. Baden, one of the smaller German states, had 112 separate measures for length, 65 for dry goods, 123 for liquids, and 163 for cereals, not to mention 80 different pound weights! A German merchant who contracted to ship timber down the Elbe from Dresden in Saxony to Hamburg had to pay so many tolls to the towns and principalities along the way that of 60 planks floated at Dresden only six would reach Hamburg. Even in France, where Louis XIV had expected all things to be uniform and centralized, all sorts of local taxes and other obstacles to internal trade persisted.

Economic reformers attacked most of these anachronisms before 1789, but they won only an occasional victory, notably in standardizing and simplifying money. The success or failure of a state in its battle against guild restrictions and local taxes was an important matter, directly affecting its prosperity. In England, which had long been a unified national state, economic localism was dying, and trade thrived. In disunited Germany, on the other hand, commerce languished; presumably few merchants had the patience to master the weights and measures of Baden.

The survival of local vested interests showed the limitations of the power of the mercantilist state. Mercantilism meant that trade should be regulated on the national, rather than the local, level. But no eighteenth-century government, not even Britain's, possessed the staff of officials needed to make national regulation effective; states had to rely heavily on private companies and individuals to execute most of their policies. Thus the English East India Company exercised not only a trading monopoly in its colonial preserve but also virtual sovereign powers. Inventors worked on their own, not in government laboratories, although occasionally, under the pressure of business groups, the state offered prizes on matters of critical importance. The English Parliament promised £20,000 for the invention of a reliable "seagoing" clock; even so, the inventor of the chronometer had to wait twenty-five years to collect his prize money. Private enterprise, not sluggish governments, made the commercial revolution advance at a swift pace in the eighteenth century.

The Mississippi and South Sea Bubbles

The contrast between the initiative of businessmen and the inertia of statesmen is best illustrated by two speculative booms early in the century—the "Mississippi Bubble" in France and the "South Sea Bubble" in England. In 1715, hardly a state in Europe could manage the large debts that had piled up during the recent wars. Yet every state had to find some way of meeting at least a part of the large annual interest on its bonds and other debts, or else go bankrupt. The governments of France and England chose the way of experiment. They shifted responsibility for the management of state debts to joint-stock companies, which they rewarded with trading concessions. The commerce of the companies, it was hoped, would prove so lucrative that their profits would easily cover the interest charges on government bonds.

John Law (1671-1729), a Scottish mathematical wizard and an inveterate gambler, presided over the experiment in France. He studied monetary problems and banking methods in Amsterdam, then the commercial capital of Europe. Law was a mercantilist, but with a difference. He agreed with the doctrine that the strength of a state depended upon the quantity of money it possessed. But, he asserted, the limited supply of silver and gold made it difficult to increase the amount of specie circulating in any country and therefore difficult to promote business. Paper money, Law concluded, was the solution—paper money backed by a nation's wealth in land and in trade. The quantity of paper money in circulation could easily be raised or lowered in accordance with the needs of business. Trading companies would prosper as never before, the whole country would prosper, and, in the midst of the general prosperity, government debts would be paid off.

On the death of Louis XIV, Law secured an opportunity to try his "system." His old gambling crony, the Duke of Orléans, now Regent of France (1715-1723), permitted him to set up a central bank in Paris. The value of French money had been sinking steadily because the government was debasing the coinage. Law's bank, following the practice of the Bank of Amsterdam, issued paper notes of stable value; business activity was at once stimulated. Next, Law set up the Mississippi Company, which received a monopoly of commerce with the Louisiana colony and soon absorbed the other French colonial trading companies.

Law's system now reached to almost every corner of the French economy, and Law himself, appointed controller-general, became the economic dictator of the kingdom. His company took over the government debt, agreeing to accept government bonds in partial payment for shares of Mississippi stock. Many bondholders responded enthusiastically to Law's offer, for the bonds had depreciated to 20 per cent or less of their face value. Law, however, had to sell additional shares of Mississippi stock

Hogarth, "An Emblematical Print on the South Sea Bubble." The monument at right "was erected in memory of the destruction of the city by the South Sea in 1720." The women on the stair at left rear are entering the building in response to a sign announcing "Raffling for Husbands with Lottery Portions—in Here."

in order to obtain sufficient working capital for his company. To attract cash purchasers, he painted the company's prospects in brightest colors; in short, Law promoted a boom in Mississippi stock. Investors, large and small, caught the fever of speculation, and by the close of 1719 Mississippi stock was selling at forty times its par value.

The Mississippi Bubble soon burst, for Law's paper money could not stand the strain. As the price of Mississippi shares rose higher and higher, cautious investors became convinced that the boom could not last and decided to cash in. They sold their shares, received payment in banknotes, then took the notes to Law's bank and demanded their redemption in specie. The bank exhausted its reserves of gold and silver and suspended specie payments in February, 1720. Law was forced to relinquish the post of controller-general in May, 1720; he fled France shortly thereafter.

The explosion of the Mississippi Bubble had international repercussions, for within a few weeks of Law's resignation the South Sea Bubble burst in London. It might have been expected that management of the English government's debt would devolve upon the Bank of England. Founded in 1694 as a private institution (it was fully nationalized only after World War II), the Bank of England issued banknotes and performed other valuable services in the last wars against Louis XIV. The debt, however, was taken over not by the Bank but by the new South Sea Company, which paid the government the exorbitant sum of more than seven and a half million pounds. The resources of the South Sea Company were slim; they consisted largely of the right to exploit the trading concessions that Britain obtained under the Asiento agreement at the end of the War of the Spanish Succession. These privileges were limited to furnishing Spain's American colonies with 4800 slaves annually and to sending one ship a year to Panama for general trade.

The South Sea Company, like the Mis-

sissippi, invited government creditors to transfer their bonds into company stock. Its directors, like Law, created a boom in South Sea stock. They bought and sold shares secretly to create a more lively market, encouraged purchasers to buy stock with a down payment of only 10 per cent in cash, and spread false reports of forthcoming sailings by the company's ships on voyages of unparalleled promise. South Sea shares, with a par value of £100, sold for £129 in January of 1720, and for £1050 in June. Dozens of other promoters sprang into action, advertising schemes for wheels of perpetual motion, for making salt water fresh, "for carrying on an undertaking of great advantage, but nobody to know what it is." The gullibility of the investing public was remarkable, but it was not inexhaustible. South Sea shares fell to £880 in August, 1720, and £150 in September. Parliament now ordered an investigation and, to protect the company's creditors, seized the estates of its directors, who had meantime destroyed the company's books and fled the country.

The two bubbles produced some unfortunate results. The collapse of the Mississippi scheme ruined Law, whose talents, if used more discreetly, might have arrested the financial paralysis of the French government. In England, the South Sea fiasco long impeded the development of new stock companies, which were henceforth required to buy costly charters. It tarnished the reputations of many in high places. The mistresses of George I and the King himself had been "let in on the ground floor" and had endorsed the venture too enthusiastically. More than a hundred members of Parliament had borrowed money from the company in order to buy its shares on the installment plan.

The bubbles, however, were not unmitigated misfortunes. They were the growing pains of the European economy, of states groping for solutions to new and baffling financial problems. As Voltaire later declared, Law's "imaginary system gave birth to a real commerce," and released French business from the torpor induced by the defeats of Louis XIV. The Mississippi Company, reorganized after 1720, consistently made a handsome profit. In England, the South Sea Bubble scarcely affected the strongest institutions. The East India Company went right on paying an annual dividend of 5 to 10 per cent. The Bank of England, no longer competing with the South Sea Company for government favors, became more than ever the financial mainstay of the realm. In the political shake-up following the Bubble, the Whig statesman, Robert Walpole (see pp. 16-17), came to power with a program of honoring the debt as a *national* debt. This was a novel concept and a great step forward in fiscal morality in an age when most states still treated their debts as the monarch's personal obligation, to be recognized or repudiated as he saw fit.

The Agricultural Revolution

The agricultural revolution, the second of the great changes transforming the economy of the modern world, has centered on technological improvements that enable fewer farmers to produce more crops. The application of scientific discoveries to agriculture is actually an old story, as old as the irrigation ditches of ancient Mesopotamia and the improved plows and horse-collars of the Middle Ages. What was new and revolutionary in the eighteenth century was the tempo: for the first time the advance in farming techniques began to move at a rapid rate. The leaders of the movement were the "improving landlords" of England, notably Jethro Tull, Viscount Townshend, Robert Bakewell, and Arthur Young.

Jethro Tull (1674-1741) studied the painstaking methods used in French truck-gardens and vineyards, where farmers ob-

tained a heavy yield from small plots by planting seeds individually and by carefully hoeing the soil around each plant and vine. Tull adapted French methods to the much larger grain fields of England. In place of the inefficient custom of scattering seed broadcast, he planted it deeply in regular rows with a horse-drawn "drilling" machine, and he cultivated his crops with a horse-drawn hoe. The outstanding production record of Tull's test farm quickly justified his innovations.

Viscount Townshend (1674-1738) used his Norfolk estate to experiment with two valuable new crops brought in from Holland—turnips and clover. By storing sufficient turnips to feed all the livestock until the arrival of the spring pasturing season, Townshend avoided the customary slaughter of stock at the onset of winter. Clover, by fixing nitrogen in the soil, increased the fertility of the land and curtailed the wasteful practice of letting fields lie fallow every third year. "Turnip" Townshend's four-year rotation—planting the same field to turnips, barley, clover, and wheat, in successive years—soon became the standard procedure on many English estates.

Robert Bakewell (1725-1795) applied scientific principles to raising livestock. Before Bakewell's time, most farm animals were gaunt and tough creatures. Bakewell inbred selected strains of sheep, doubled the average weight of his stock, and marketed lamb and mutton of really appetizing quality. Although a critic complained that Bakewell's meat was "too expensive to buy and too fat to eat," his methods were widely copied.

Arthur Young (1741-1820) was the great publicist of the new agriculture. Gifted with a rare capacity for traveling, observing, and reporting, he made systematic trips through the farming districts of the British Isles and the Continent. In one five-year period, during the late 1760's and early '70's, he produced more than a dozen volumes on agrarian practices and economic problems. Campaigning for the innovations of Tull and Townshend, Young put his arguments so persuasively and entertainingly that he soon gained an international reputation. His admirers included George III, George Washington, Lafayette, and Catherine the Great.

Before 1789, the new agricultural techniques gained the support of only the most enterprising landlords. On the Continent, the leaders were to be found in France, Holland, and Prussia, where King Frederick the Great directed his subjects to breed livestock, grow fodder crops, and rotate plantings, all in the advanced English manner. In Britain itself, the new methods appealed chiefly to the holders of large estates, including George III, "Farmer George."

The agricultural revolution of the eighteenth century, halting and uneven though it was, marked an important stage in the gradual shift from the largely self-sufficient medieval manor to the modern capitalist farm producing specialized crops. The improving landlords used capitalistic methods which required large investments of money. They also required large plots of land that were not subject to such traditional practices as the utilization of fields in common by many individuals and the subdivision of fields into long, narrow strips. Since these old ways hampered the new agriculture, the improving landlords demanded that common fields be enclosed and fenced off as the private lands of single proprietors. In Tudor days enclosures had been used for the extension of privately owned sheep pastures. The new enclosure movement aimed to increase crop land. It reached its peak in the last decades of the eighteenth century and the first decades of the nineteenth, when Parliament passed hundreds of separate enclosure acts affecting several million acres. Rural England was assuming its modern aspect of large fields fenced by hedgerows.

From the standpoint of social welfare, enclosures brought unhappy results. In Georgian England, as in ancient Greece and Rome, the development of large capitalistic estates ruined many small farmers. They could not exist without their old rights in the common lands and could not afford to install fences, buy tools, and become improving landlords. Many of them, therefore, were forced to become hired hands on larger farms or to seek work in the towns. From the standpoint of agrarian productivity, however, enclosures marked a long step forward. They created large farms well suited to the application of drill-planting, horse-hoeing, and crop rotation. Britain, in consequence, as yet experienced no difficulty in feeding her growing population.

The Beginnings of the Industrial Revolution

By increasing farm output and at the same time releasing part of the labor force for jobs off the farm, the agricultural revolution was assisting the industrial revolution. Industry also required raw materials, markets for its manufactures, and capital to finance the building and equipment of factories. The raw materials and the markets were supplied in part by the colonies overseas, and the capital in part by merchants. Thus the commercial revolution, too, assisted the industrial revolution.

Some elements of industrial change had first appeared at the close of the Middle Ages. To take an example from textiles, the making of yarn and cloth had long been organized according to the "domestic system," in which spinners or weavers worked at home on simple wheels or looms. Many spinners and weavers, however, did not buy their own raw materials or market their finished products; rather, they worked as wage-laborers for a capitalist, an entrepreneur who furnished the raw materials and sold the finished yarn and cloth. In some industries, however, production was

Metal-planing and metal-cutting factory in the eighteenth century, as illustrated in the Encyclopédie.

organized not under the domestic system but under a primitive factory system. These early factories assembled many laborers in a large workshop, but still relied on hand processes rather than on machines. They were particularly common in enterprises utilizing expensive materials, as in the making of luxury cloth with gold or silver threads, or requiring close supervision for reasons of state, as in cannon foundries.

The industrial revolution made the domestic system obsolete and transformed the factory system. Machines superseded simple hand tools, like the spinning-wheel and the home loom, and water or steam replaced human muscles and animal energy as the source of power. Because the power-driven machines were often big, complicated, and costly, larger factories were

needed to house them. By 1789, these revolutionary changes had affected only a few industries; but those involved were key industries—mining, metallurgy, munitions, and textiles.

Coal-mining was becoming a big business in the eighteenth century, partly because of the increased demand for coal by iron-smelters. For centuries, the smelters had used charcoal to make iron from the raw ore, and they continued to do so in countries like Sweden that had abundant wood for charcoal. But in England, where almost all the great forests had been cut down, the price of charcoal rose so high that it constituted 80 per cent of the cost of producing iron. By 1750, despite the abundant native supply of ore, the output of English smelters was declining rapidly, and the country was relying more and more on imported iron. Ordinary coal could not replace charcoal as smelter fuel because the chemicals in coal made the iron too brittle. Here necessity mothered invention. The Darby family of Coalbrookdale in Shropshire discovered how to remove the chemical impurities from coal by converting it into coke through an oven process. Since coke was almost pure carbon, it produced iron of high quality.

In England, the Darbys and other private firms were the pioneers in metallurgy. On the Continent, governments took the lead—a significant exception to the rule about the inability of states to solve economic problems. Warfare required weapons and munitions in unprecedented quantities; France and Prussia met the demand by setting up state-financed and state-operated foundries and arms factories.

The revolution in textiles was focused on the cheaper production of cotton cloth. The "flying shuttle," a technical device first applied to the hand loom in England (1733), enabled a single weaver to do work that had previously required the services of two. The looms equipped with the flying shuttle used up the supply of hand-spun thread so rapidly that the London Society for the Encouragement of Arts, Manufactures, and Commerce offered a prize for improvement of the spinning process. James Hargreaves won the prize in 1764 with his "spinning jenny," a series of spinning wheels geared together which made eight threads simultaneously. Soon the jenny was adapted to water power, and its output was increased to a hundred or more threads at once. The eventual emancipation of industry from dependence on unreliable water power was foreshadowed in the 1760's when the Scotsman, James Watt, introduced the steam engine.

Although Britain had nearly 150 cotton mills in 1789, woolens and dozens of other basic commodities were still made by hand. The full sweep of industrial development would not appear until the canal and railroad permitted cheap transport of heavy freight and until the shortages of capital and skilled labor were overcome. A Swedish inventor of the early 1700's designed excellent machines for cutting wheels and files but could not raise the money to put them into operation. And in Britain the difficulty of making precisely fitting parts for Watt's engine held back its production. The eighteenth century had taken many of the initial steps in the industrial revolution; it remained for the nineteenth century to apply them on a truly revolutionary scale.

Hargreaves' spinning jenny, 1764.

III: The Western Powers

The Assets of Britain

Britain's leadership in the economic revolutions was making her the wealthiest nation in the world. British bankers, buttressed by the Bank of England and by the careful management of the national debt, extended credit to business enterprises at the relatively low interest rate of 5 per cent. The City, the square mile comprising the City of London proper and including the financial district, recovered quickly from the South Sea Bubble and challenged Amsterdam's position as the international capital of trade and finance. In the course of the eighteenth century, British merchants outdistanced their old trading rivals, the Dutch, and gradually took the lead over their new competitors, the French. Judged by the three touchstones of mercantilism—commerce, colonies, and sea power—Britain was the strongest state in Europe.

The British colonial empire, however, was not a mercantilist undertaking in the full sense. Supervision of the colonies rested with a government department, the Board of Trade, which followed an easygoing policy contrasting with the rigid controls exerted by other imperial powers over their possessions. This was the famous policy of "salutary neglect." In the long run, as the American Revolution was to show, "salutary neglect" did not satisfy the colonists, but in the short run it worked reasonably well, and the British Empire surpassed all others in prosperity and self-reliance.

The Royal Navy surpassed all others by virtue of its superior officer corps and its greater size. Future captains went to sea at the age of sixteen, or even younger, and passed through a long course of practical training before receiving commissions. The ships they commanded in the wars of the mid-eighteenth century were inferior in design to those of Britain's enemies, France and Spain; but there were more of them. Britain had a 2 to 1 advantage over France in number of warships, a 6 to 1 lead in merchant ships, and a 10 to 1 lead in total number of experienced seamen, merchant and naval. In wartime, the fleet could draw on the merchant marine for additional sailors and for transports and other auxiliary vessels.

Service on His Majesty's ships two hundred years ago was not exactly pleasant. The food doled out to the sailors was monotonous, wormy, and unhealthful. Captains frequently ordered the punishments of flogging and of keel-hauling, in which the offender was dragged under the barnacle-encrusted keel. These, however, were the common afflictions of all sailors in the eighteenth century; they did not put the British navy at a comparative disadvantage.

The British army, by contrast, was neither large nor impressive. Its officers were reputed to be the poorest in Europe, and its soldiers were in part mediocre mercenaries from the German state of Hesse-Cassel, the Hessians of the American Revolutionary War. Neglect of the army was a deliberate policy. The British Isles were relatively safe from invasion; moreover, statesmen feared that a standing army might become an instrument of potential absolutism, for they remembered the uses that Cromwell and James II had made of this weapon.

The Glorious Revolution, which had done so much to confirm distrust of the army, had also confirmed Britain's unique and greatest asset—the supremacy of Parliament over the king. Parliament had replaced James II with William and Mary; when Anne, the last Stuart monarch, died in 1714, Parliament had already arranged for the succession of the House of Hanover. Under the first kings of the new house—George I (1714-1727) and George II (1727-1760)—the institution that was to assure the everyday assertion of parliamentary supremacy was undergoing steady development. This was the cabinet.

Today the cabinet is a committee of the majority party in the House of Commons, headed by the prime minister; because it controls the executive branch of the government, the cabinet rules, the monarch merely reigns. Under the first two Hanoverians the cabinet was only beginning to accumulate this immense authority. George I and George II by no means abdicated all the old royal prerogatives. They took a direct interest in the South Sea Bubble and other financial matters, and they intervened in the conduct of war and diplomacy to a degree that would be unconstitutional today. George II was the last English monarch to command troops in person on the battlefield—in 1743 during the War of the Austrian Succession.

The two Georges chose their cabinet ministers from the Whig party, then in control of the House of Commons. They did so, however, not because they were obliged to, which would be the case today, but because it suited their convenience, and, even more, because they really had no choice. They thoroughly distrusted the other party, the Tories, some of whom were involved in futile Jacobite plots to restore to the English throne the descendants of James II (Jacobite from Jacobus, Latin for James). The Whigs, on the other hand, had engineered the Glorious Revolution and had arranged the Hanoverian succession. For two decades after the collapse of the South Sea Bubble, from 1721 to 1742, Robert Walpole, who led the Whigs in the Commons, headed the cabinet. Although the title was not yet official, he was in fact prime minister. And in 1733, when he forced the resignation of ministers who op-posed his plan for a drastic reduction of customs duties, he took a major step toward establishing the important principle of cabinet unanimity on a critical issue.

Thus, by the death of George II in 1760, it was *customary* for the king to select his ministers from the majority party in the House of Commons, but it was not yet *obligatory*. The next Hanoverian king, George III, tried vainly to change the custom (see Chapter XVII). The years preceding 1760 witnessed the shaping of the instrument that would one day assure the control of the executive branch by Parliament and thus by the people who elected the members of the Commons.

The Whig Oligarchy

The Whig party that ruled England under the first two Georges was a coalition of landed gentry and "funded" gentry, of land-owning nobles and squires and of businessmen from London and other towns. Thus the Whigs renewed a political alliance that had first appeared in the later Middle Ages when the knights of the shire had joined the burgesses to form the Commons. In the Whig parliaments the country gentlemen predominated by sheer numbers; in 1754, for instance, they outnumbered by 5 to 1 the merchants and lawyers sitting in the House of Commons. Family ties, common political aims, and a common reverence for property bound together the rural and urban members of the party. To consolidate the gains of the Glorious Revolution, the Whigs opposed Jacobite schemes and supported the unprepossessing Hanoverians. To protect their lands and other investments, they passed legislation making death the penalty for stealing livestock, for cutting down cherry trees, and for other relatively minor violations of the sanctity of property.

Robert Walpole himself exemplified the fusion of landed and funded elements in the party. He inherited his manners and his tastes from his father, a country squire. He fixed the English politician's tradition of the long country weekend in order to indulge his passion for hunting; he drank heavily and habitually told bawdy stories at mixed dinner parties. Like many Whig squires, Walpole married into the aristocracy of trade; his wife was the daughter of a well-to-do timber merchant and former Lord Mayor of London. As prime minister, Walpole, the country gentleman, promoted the interests of the City. His basic policy coincided with the City's program: financial stability through the gradual retirement of the national debt, political stability through Whig cabinets and the new Hanoverian dynasty.

Democracy scarcely existed in Walpole's England. In the professions, a social minority, the "gentlemen," alone could hope to become army and navy officers, lawyers, clergymen, and physicians. In politics, though the aristocracy of commerce gained admission to the Whig oligarchy, the millions of ordinary people were excluded. The landed gentry alone supplied the justices of the peace, who ran the local courts, fixed wage scales, superintended the relief of the poor, provided for the maintenance of bridges and highways, and were in general the despots of the English countryside. Fanatic defenders of the propertied classes, the justices of the peace represented the most unattractive side of oligarchy. The saying that "You may as well be hanged for [stealing] a sheep as a lamb" is a bitter reminder of their standards of justice.

In the main, only gentlemen had the right to vote for members of Parliament. The small number of voters in many constituencies encouraged corruption, particularly in the "rotten" or "pocket" boroughs, boroughs with such a tiny electorate that control of their vote reposed in the pocket of some wealthy lord. Politicians bribed the voters outright or else promised them places on the government payroll. An immensely rich Whig, the Duke of Newcastle, con-

"The House of Commons in Sir Robert Walpole's Administration," by Hogarth. Walpole is the gentleman in the left foreground.

trolled the outcome of elections in four counties and in seven pocket boroughs. Families with influential connections often obtained an immense amount of government patronage, as one tombstone records:

Here rest all that was mortal of Mrs. Elizabeth Bate,
Relict of the Reverend Richard Bate,
A woman of unaffected piety
    And exemplary virtue.
She was honourably descended
And by means of her Alliance to
The illustrious family of Stanhope
She had the merit to obtain
for her husband and children
Twelve separate employments
In Church and State.
She died June 9, 1751, in the 75th year of
    her age.*

---

* Quoted by G. M. Trevelyan, *England under Queen Anne* (New York, 1930-1934), III, 317.

In Britain, as on the Continent, the ruling classes governed the voteless masses. But there was an all-important difference between the island kingdom and the continental countries. The British ruling classes, selfish and narrow-minded though they often were, had at their best a sense of *noblesse oblige,* of public spirit and civic-mindedness. Within the aristocracy of land and trade there were fewer social barriers than on the Continent, and the doors were usually open to energetic newcomers from the lower classes. The English gentry were on the whole more responsive than their continental counterparts to the need for changes and reform. Disraeli, the great nineteenth-century Tory, dubbed the Whig cabinets of the first two Georges a "Venetian oligarchy," by which he meant that the wealthy ran the country for their private benefit, as in Renaissance Venice. And so they did; yet the Whigs, for all their oligarchy and corruption, provided the most enlightened government in eighteenth-century Europe.

The Liabilities of France

Where Britain was strong, France was weak. The France of Louis XV (1715-1774) suffered from the rigidity of its colonial system, the inferiority of its navy, and the very mediocre abilities of most of its statesmen. The Ministry of the Navy, which ruled the overseas empire, regarded these possessions as so many warships permanently at anchor. It refused to sanction any steps toward self-government and applied the same detailed regulations to colonies as different as the sugar islands of the West Indies and the wilderness of Canada. Under this régime, the mother country prospered, but the colonies languished. Commercial activity doubled in Nantes, Bordeaux, and other ports; refineries grew up to process the raw sugar imported from the plantations of Guadeloupe and Martinique. Overseas, however, the plethora of controls stifled the initiative of the colonists. The French imperial system lacked the elasticity and the energy to meet the test of war.

The French navy needed greater resources and better leadership. Its warships, though admirably designed, were inadequate in number. Since Dutch and British vessels carried much of French commerce, the merchant marine was too small to supplement the fleet. French naval officers, though rigorously trained in the classroom, lacked the experience gained by British captains in a lifetime at sea. Moreover, in a fashion characteristic of the Old Régime at its worst, officers from the aristocracy devoted much of their energies to thwarting the rise of officers from the middle class. In fairness, it must be added that French rulers were almost bound to neglect the navy in order to concentrate on the army. France was above all a land power, and its vulnerable northeastern frontier, lying across the Flemish plain, invited invasion.

Except in size, however, the army of Louis XV scarcely lived up to the great traditions of Louis XIV. The troops were poorly trained. The military organization was top-heavy with superfluous officers; there was one officer to fifteen men in the French army, compared with one to thirty-five in the more efficient Prussian army. As in the navy, aristocratic officers despised their bourgeois colleagues, and many of them regarded a commission simply as a convenient way of increasing their personal wealth.

Both the navy and the army underwent important reforms after 1763 and the defeats suffered by France in the Seven Years' War (see p. 43). The number of warships was increased, the officer corps of the army was cleared of much dead wood, and more aggressive military tactics were introduced. These improvements accounted in part for the excellent showing made by France in the American Revolutionary War and in the military campaigns resulting from her own revolution. They came too late, however, to save the vanishing prestige of the Old Régime.

The Old Régime was weakest at its very head, the monarchy itself. Successful divine-right monarchy required a perpetual series of able kings, ably assisted by men like Colbert and Richelieu. There were no "sun kings" in France after the death of Louis XIV, and few ministers of the caliber of their illustrious predecessors.

The Duke of Orléans, the Regent from 1715 to 1723, was a gambler, drunkard, and pervert, who popularized the word "roué" by remarking that his friends deserved to be broken on the wheel (roue is French for wheel). The Regent, however, did attempt two important administrative experiments. He allowed John Law to try out his "system," and, in place of Louis XIV's method of ruling through individual bourgeois ministers, he set up councils staffed by men from the most distinguished noble families of the realm. Although the first experiment produced some beneficial results, the second failed so completely that the Regent abandoned it after a three-year trial. The French second estate had outlived its usefulness. The Regency proved that the nobles were no longer able to govern; the mid-century wars proved that they were no longer able to lead French armies to victory.

Soon after the regency of Orléans, power passed to one of the few statesmen of pre-revolutionary France, Cardinal Fleury, the tutor of Louis XV and the chief minister from 1726 until his death in 1743 in his ninetieth year. Without attempting basic reforms, the aged Cardinal, in the words of Voltaire, "treated the state as a powerful and robust body which could cure itself." Fleury did not remedy the chronic and deep-seated injustice and inefficiency of French fiscal methods. But he did stabilize the coinage, and he put the farming of taxes on a more businesslike basis by allowing the tax-farmers the comparatively

modest profit of 7½ per cent. To make loans more readily available, he established state pawnshops in the chief cities of France. The success of Fleury's policies impressed Lady Mary Montagu, the wife of an English diplomat and one of the shrewdest observers of the century. Lady Mary wrote in 1739:

France is so much improved, it is not . . . the same country we passed through twenty years ago. Everything I see speaks in praise of Cardinal Fleury; the roads are all mended . . . and such good care taken against robbers, that you may cross the country with your purse in your hand. . . . The French are more changed than their roads; instead of pale, yellow faces, wrapped up in blankets, as we saw them, the villages are filled with fresh-coloured lusty peasants, in good cloth and clean linen. It is incredible the air of plenty and content that is over the whole country.*

The air of "plenty and content" remained after Louis XV began his personal rule in 1743, but the administrative stability achieved by Fleury soon vanished. Intelligent but timid and debauched, Louis XV did not have the interest or the patience to supervise the details of government. He appointed and dismissed ministers on a personal whim or at the bidding of his mistresses and favorites. Key ministers, like the controller-general or the foreign secretary, remained in office but two or three years on the average. Each change in personnel meant a shift in policy, and Louis aggravated the instability by conspiring against his own appointees. France had two conflicting foreign policies: that of the diplomatic corps; and the "King's Secret," conducted by royal agents who operated at cross purposes with the regular diplomats. Louis XV allowed the reins of government to go slack, yet refused to give them over to firmer hands.

Nevertheless, in spite of the deluge that Louis XV predicted would come after him,

---

* *Letters*, Everyman ed. (New York, 1906), 271-272.

France remained a great power. Her army, though enfeebled, was the largest in the world, and her navy was the second largest. She led the world in overseas trade until Britain forged ahead of her in the last quarter of the eighteenth century. French tastes, French thought, and the French language retained the international pre-eminence won in the age of Louis XIV. The misgovernment and the other weaknesses of the Old Régime were relative rather than absolute. They did not alter the fact that France was still the most populous country in Europe—a country that harbored almost inexhaustible reserves of strength.

The Other Western States

Spain was the only other state in western Europe with a claim to great-power status. War and the weaknesses induced by war had put an end to the major international roles played by Sweden and the Dutch Republic during the seventeenth century. The Great Northern War, as we shall see (below, pp. 29-31), ruined the Baltic empire of Sweden and killed off the flower of Swedish manhood. The Dutch, exhausted by their wars against Louis XIV, were losing their commercial leadership, and could no longer afford a large navy or an independent foreign policy. Eighteenth-century Holland, in the phrase of Frederick the Great, was often a "cockboat in the tow of the English frigate."

Spain, however, suffered little real damage from the great war over the succession to her throne that took place in the early 1700's. The loss of Belgium and parts of Italy at the Utrecht settlement of 1713 reduced the unwieldy Spanish domains to more manageable size. The new Bourbon kings were a marked improvement over the last Spanish Habsburgs. Philip V (1700-1746), the first of the Spanish Bourbons, infused fresh life into the country's fossilized institutions by importing French advisers schooled in the system of Louis XIV. He also enlisted the aid of two able adventurers, Alberoni and Ripperdá, whose fantastic careers almost outdid John Law's. Alberoni, the son of an Italian gardener, was successively a cook, a diplomat, the chief minister of Spain, and a cardinal. Ripperdá, a Dutch business expert and diplomat, ultimately lost the favor of Philip, entered the service of the Sultan of Morocco, and, after a lifelong alternation between the Protestant and Catholic faiths, died a Moslem. Philip and his remarkable advisers cut down the excessive formalities and endless delays of Spanish administration. They reasserted the authority of the monarchy over the traditionally powerful nobility and clergy. They improved the tax system, encouraged textiles and other new industries, built up the navy, and fortified strategic points in the Spanish empire in America.

The new dispensation, however, did not strike at the root causes of Spanish decline. The greed of governors and the restrictions of mercantilism still checked the progress of the colonies. The mother country remained impoverished, burdened with reactionary noble and clerical castes, and hampered by inadequate resources. Philip V himself was neurotic, refusing, for instance, to cut his toenails, which grew so long that he limped. He was dominated by his strong-willed second wife, Elizabeth Farnese, the patroness of Alberoni. Since Philip's son by his first marriage would inherit Spain, Elizabeth was determined to get thrones for her two sons, the issue of Philip's second marriage. Her persistent attempts to secure the succession of Italian states for them repeatedly threatened the peace of Europe.

IV: Italy and Germany

Disunited Italy

By 1715, the Italian states had lost much of the political and economic power they had enjoyed during the Renaissance. It is easy to see why. The opening of new worlds overseas and the rise of Spain, England, and the other Atlantic powers had diminished the importance of the Mediterranean. In the Mediterranean itself, the Ottoman Turks and their satellites in North Africa long menaced Italian shipping and trade. Moreover, beginning with the French invasion of 1494, Italy had been threatened with conquest by the new national monarchies.

The Spanish Habsburgs made the conquest. For almost two centuries Spain ruled Milan, Naples, and Sicily directly, and dominated the rest of the peninsula. Then, in the readjustment of the European balance in 1713, the Italians exchanged one foreign master for another. The Austrian Habsburgs took over the Italian possessions and the Italian hegemony of their Spanish cousins. On the completion of the readjustment in 1720, the political map of the peninsula (see pp. 4-5) showed Austria established in Lombardy. Flanking Lombardy were the two decaying commercial republics of Venice and Genoa, and in the mountainous northwest the small but rising state of Piedmont-Savoy (technically the Kingdom of Sardinia after its acquisition of that Mediterranean island in 1720). Further down the peninsula were the Grand Duchy of Tuscany (formerly the Republic of Florence), the Papal States, and the Austrian Two Sicilies. None of these states was more than a minor power.

Yet Italy could not be written off as a negligible quantity in the eighteenth century. Rome remained the capital of Catholicism, Venice still produced fine painters, and Naples was the schoolmaster of European musicians. Lombardy, Tuscany, and Naples contributed to the economic and intellectual advances of the century. Above all, Italy continued to be a stake in balance-of-power politics, a perennial source of dissension and spoils for the stronger European states. In 1720, to counter the ambitions of the Spanish queen, Elizabeth Farnese, the Austrian Habsburgs took over the island of Sicily, which had gone to Piedmont in the Utrecht settlement; in return, Piedmont secured Sardinia, originally assigned to Austria. In the 1730's, a series of exchanges gave the Two Sicilies to Elizabeth's elder son, "Baby Carlos," while the Austrians gained some minor bits of territory and the succession of Tuscany. In 1768, Genoa ceded the island of Corsica to France. Defenseless Italy was the natural victim of ambitious dynasts and empire-builders, not a nation-state but rather, in the old phrase, "a geographical expression."

Divided Germany: The Habsburg Domains

Germany, too, was "a geographical expression," divided into some three hundred states—large, small, and minute. The Peace of Westphalia in 1648 had added to the sovereign rights of the individual states and had reduced almost to zero the authority of their nominal overlord, the Holy Roman Emperor. Germany had also suffered from the blighting effects of the Thirty Years' War and the campaigns of Louis XIV. But Germany, unlike Italy, was not defenseless: it contained two considerable powers, Austria and Prussia.

The Austrian Habsburgs won a series of military and diplomatic victories in the two decades before 1715. In 1699, by the peace of Karlovitz, they recovered Hungary from the Turks, thereby advancing their own *Drang nach Osten* against the Ottoman Empire. In 1713, though they failed to keep the old Habsburg crown of Spain from going to the Bourbon Philip V, they received handsome compensation in Belgian and Italian territories. Yet these last acquisitions were distant from the central bloc of Habsburg lands in Austria, Hungary, Bohemia, and Silesia. The Emperor Charles VI (1711-1740) scarcely made a beginning at consolidating his rule over this disjointed empire. He spent much of his reign persuading his own noble subjects to ratify the Pragmatic Sanction, a constitutional agreement whereby, in the absence of sons, his daughter Maria Theresa would succeed him in all his territories. The empire thus carefully preserved was a dynastic creation, an assemblage of lands largely devoid of common interests or real unity. The Austrian, Bohemian, and Hungarian nobles kept most of their medieval prerogatives and, by controlling local estates and diets, controlled the grant of taxes and the appointment of officials. The other chief weaknesses of the Habsburg régime were financial and military. In 1740, when Charles VI died, the pay of the civil service and the army was more than two years in arrears. Small wonder that the army itself fell short of its paper strength of 100,000 men and was ill prepared for the great test of strength with Prussia that came in 1740.

The Rise of Prussia

Whereas Austria enjoyed the appearances rather than the realities of great-power status, Prussia possessed few of the appearances but a great many of the realities. Its territories were scattered across North Germany from the Rhine on the west to the Vistula and beyond on the east. Consisting largely of half-deserted tracts of sand and swamp, these lands had meager natural resources and carried on relatively little trade. With less than three million inhabitants, Prussia ranked only twelfth among the European states in population. Even her capital city, Berlin, located on the unimportant River Spree, had few of the obvious geographical advantages enjoyed by Constantinople, Paris, London, and the other great capitals. A wise prophet might well have foreseen that Catholic Austria would never unite a Germany in which Protestantism was so strong. But he would probably have predicted that a new Germany would center in Frankfurt in the heart of the Rhine country, or in Saxon Leipzig or Dresden; he would hardly have chosen the unpromising town of Berlin and the minor house of Hohenzollern.

The Hohenzollern house had been established since the fifteenth century as Electors of Brandenburg, which lay between the Elbe and Oder rivers. A Hohenzollern was the last Master of the Teutonic Knights, a crusading order which in the thirteenth century had pushed the Germanic frontier beyond the Vistula to a land called Prussia at the southeast corner of the Baltic Sea. In 1618, when this Prussian area fell to Brandenburg, it was separated from the center of Hohenzollern power by Polish territory and was still nominally a fief held from the Polish king. In western Germany, meantime (1614), the Hohenzollerns acquired Cleves, Mark, and some other parcels of land in the lower Rhine valley. Thus, when Frederick William, the Great Elector (1640-1688), succeeded to the Hohenzollern inheritance as the Thirty Years' War was drawing to a close, his lands consisted of a nucleus in Brandenburg with separate outlying regions to east and west. With extraordinary persistence, the rulers of Brandenburg-Prussia for the next two hundred years devoted themselves to the task of making a solid

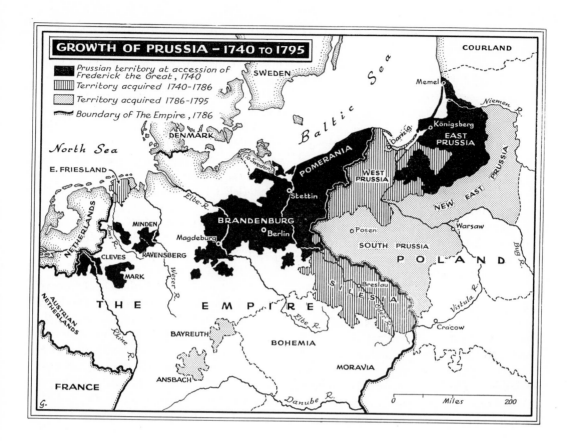

GROWTH OF PRUSSIA – 1740 to 1795

■ Prussian territory at accession of Frederick the Great, 1740
▥ Territory acquired 1740-1786
▦ Territory acquired 1786-1795
〰 Boundary of The Empire, 1786

COURLAND

SWEDEN

Baltic Sea

Memel

Niemen R.

Danzig

Königsberg

EAST PRUSSIA

North Sea

DENMARK

E. FRIESLAND

POMERANIA

WEST PRUSSIA

NEW EAST

To Sweden

Stettin

Elbe R.

NETHERLANDS

MINDEN

BRANDENBURG

Berlin

Posen

Warsaw

Magdeburg

CLEVES   RAVENSBERG

SOUTH PRUSSIA

P O L A N D

MARK

AUSTRIAN NETHERLANDS

T H E   E M P I R E

Weser R.

SILESIA

Breslau

Oder R.

Vistula R.

Bug R.

BAYREUTH

BOHEMIA

Rhine R.

Cracow

ANSBACH

Elbe R.

FRANCE

Danube R.

MORAVIA

0   Miles   200

G.

block of territory out of these scattered bits.

The Great Elector was the first in a line of able Hohenzollern rulers. In foreign policy, he won recognition from Poland as the full sovereign of Prussia, no longer subject to Polish overlordship. He also tried, with less success, to dislodge the Swedes from the Pomeranian territories, between Brandenburg and the Baltic, which they had acquired in 1648. Though he defeated the Swedes at Fehrbellin in 1675, he gained little, partly because of his own tortuous diplomatic maneuvers in the wars against Louis XIV. He shifted repeatedly from the French to the anti-French side and back again.

In his domestic accomplishments he fully merited the title "Great." He had found his lands largely ruined by the Thirty Years' War, the farms wasted, the popula-

tion cut in half, the army reduced to a disorderly rabble of a few thousand men. The Great Elector repaired the damage most thoroughly. To augment the population, he encouraged the immigration of Polish Jews and other refugees from religious persecution, notably 20,000 French Huguenots to whom he gave partial exemption from taxation. He built a small but efficient standing army that enabled Prussia to command large foreign subsidies for participating in the campaigns for or against Louis XIV. In peacetime, he assigned the soldiers to the construction of public works like the canal between the Elbe and the Oder.

In administration, the Great Elector fixed the Hohenzollern pattern of centralized absolutism, a policy in which he was assisted by a Lutheran state church that taught the virtues of obedience and discipline and by an educational tradition that did the same.

On his accession, he found that in all three territories—Prussia, Brandenburg, and Cleves-Mark—the authority of the ruler was limited by Estates, medieval assemblies representing the landed nobles and the townspeople. In all three territories he battled the Estates for supremacy and won, thereby delaying for two centuries the introduction of representative government into the Hohenzollern realm. He gradually gathered into his own hands the crucial power of levying taxes, which he collected through his appointees, the nucleus of the famous Prussian civil service. The money thus secured went to the army. Like Louis XIV, the Great Elector reduced the political power of the aristocracy, but, unlike Louis, he also cemented a working alliance with the landed gentry, particularly the celebrated Junkers of Prussia proper. He confirmed the Junkers' absolute authority over the serfs on their estates and their preponderance over the towns, and he encouraged them to serve the state, especially as army officers. In contrast to other monarchies, the absolutism of the Hohenzollerns rested on the co-operation of the sovereign and the aristocracy, not on their mutual antagonism.

Under the Great Elector's son, Frederick I (1688-1713), the house of Hohenzollern made a significant gain in prestige. The prestige was not military, for Prussia played only a minor role in the great wars that humbled Louis XIV and got only minor new territories in the Utrecht settlement. But in 1701 the Elector Frederick assumed the title "King in Prussia" and made international recognition of his new royal status the price for his entry into the War of the Spanish Succession. Though technically Frederick was king only in Prussia proper, which lay outside the boundaries of the Holy Roman Empire, even a limited royal title conferred new dignity on the dynasty. In trying to live up to his new eminence, however, King Frederick I nearly bankrupted his state with costly attempts to imitate the splendors of Versailles. Since he thought that a suggestion of marital infidelity enhanced the majesty of a king, he maintained an official mistress with whom he took decorous afternoon promenades. Actually, he was happily married, and his talented queen enlivened the provincial Hohenzollern court by inviting intellectuals and artists to Berlin. As Frederick the Great later remarked, under Frederick I Berlin was the "Athens of the north."

Frederick William I

But as Frederick the Great also remarked, under the next king, Frederick William I (1713-1740), Berlin became the "Sparta of the north." The flirtation with luxury and the finer things of life proved to be a passing exception to the usual Hohenzollern rule of austerity. Frederick William I returned with a vengeance to the policies of the Great Elector and devoted himself entirely to economy, absolutism, and the army. As soon as he had given his father a lavish funeral, he dismissed most of the officials and supernumeraries of the court and reduced governmental expenses to a fraction of what they had been. He reiterated the order *"Ein Plus Machen"* (make a surplus), and he bequeathed a full treasury to his son. His frugality enabled him to undertake the occasional project that he thought really worth while. Thus he financed the immigration of 12,000 South German Protestants to open up new farm lands in eastern Prussia.

To strengthen royal control over the apparatus of state, Frederick William I instituted a small board of experts and charged its members with administering both the provinces and the departments of the central government. This board had the explicit and resounding title of *Generaloberfinanzkriegsunddomänendirektorium* (General Superior Finance, War, and Domain Direc-

One of the giant soldiers of Frederick William I of Prussia.

tory—General Directory, for short). The King insisted on hard work and punctuality. He treated the counselors of the General Directory as he treated lesser officials, paying them meanly and belaboring them with his cane for slovenly performance of their duties. A late arrival at one of the daily sessions of the General Directory paid a severe fine; an unexcused absentee faced six months in jail.

Frederick William I doubled the size of the standing army, but he maintained the strength of the laboring force of his underpopulated state by furloughing troops for nine months a year to work on farms. To secure guns and uniforms, he established state factories. The army also prompted his

sole extravagance—a regiment of tall grenadiers, all six feet or over, who wore special caps more than a foot high to increase the impression of size. In recruiting his beloved "giants," the king threw economy to the winds, employing scores of scouts in other German states, paying exorbitant prices, and even trading royal musicians and prize stallions for especially tall specimens. Frederick William cherished his army too much to undertake an adventurous foreign policy. He engaged in but a single significant military campaign—against Sweden in the last phase of the Great Northern War. At the close of the war in 1720, Prussia obtained from Sweden part of Pomerania and also the important Baltic port of Stettin, thereby partially fulfilling the Great Elector's old aim of liquidating the Swedish possessions in Germany.

Eighteenth-century observers rightly called the Prussia of Frederick William an "armed camp" and berated its army for being a "gigantic penal institution" in which minor infractions of regulations entailed the death penalty. The King himself, obsessed with military matters, showed scant concern for culture, neglected the education of his subjects, and despised everything French. He carried parsimony to the extreme of refusing to raise the inadequate fees of judges and lawyers, so that corruption and lethargy obstructed the course of justice in Prussia. Yet this régime worked and, in terms of power, worked extremely well. The Junkers, for all their feudal outlook, were intensely loyal to the Hohenzollerns and made some of the best army officers of the century. The army itself, though smaller than those of France, Russia, and Austria, was the best drilled and the most rigorously disciplined in Europe. When Frederick William I died in 1740, the Prussian David was ready to fight the Austrian Goliath.

V: The Eastern Powers

The Early Years
of Peter the Great

Even more spectacular than the rise of Prussia was the emergence of Russia as a major power during the era of Peter the Great (1682-1725). In 1682, at the death of Tsar Fedor Romanov, Russia was still a backward eastern European country, with few diplomatic links with the West, and very little knowledge of the outside world. All contemporaries, Russians as well as foreigners, report on the brutality, the wide-spread immorality, the drunkenness, illiteracy, and filth prevalent among all classes of society. There was little education, even for the clergy, most of whom could not read, and who set no shining example to their flock by their mode of life. It is perhaps little wonder that students familiar with conditions in Russia before the advent of Peter the Great have saluted him as the great revolutionary who altered the face of his country. Yet the changes he made were neither so numerous nor so drastic as his admirers have often claimed. Moreover, the foundations for most of them were already present in the society he inherited. Finally, Russia would no doubt eventually have become a power of international importance without Peter, although it would have taken longer. Even if we accept all these dilutions of the usual estimate of his contribution, however, the fact remains that Peter was an awe-inspiring—and terror-inspiring—figure.

Tsar Fedor died childless in 1682, leaving a fifteen-year old brother, Ivan, who was partly blind and almost an idiot, and an ugly and capable sister, Sophia, both children of Tsar Alexis (1645-1676) by his first wife. The ten-year-old Peter was the half-brother of Ivan and Sophia, the son of Alexis by his second wife, and as bright and vigorous as Ivan was debilitated. A major court feud quickly developed between the partisans of the family of Alexis' first wife and those of the family of the second. At first the old Russian representative assembly, the *zemski sobor*, elected Peter as Tsar. But Sophia, as leader of the opposing faction, won the support of the *streltsy*, or musketeers, a special branch of the military, many of whom belonged to the conservative religious schismatics known as the Old Believers. Undisciplined, and angry with their officers, some of whom had indeed been cheating them, the *streltsy* were a menace to orderly government.

Sophia and her supporters encouraged the *streltsy* to attack the Kremlin, and the youthful Peter saw the infuriated troops murdering some of his mother's family and racing through the palace in pursuit of the rest, stabbing the furniture with swords and spears. For good measure, they killed many of the nobles living in Moscow, and pillaged the archives where the records of serfdom were kept. But, though their movement obviously had some social content, it was primarily a successful effort by Sophia to gain power. Sophia now became regent for both Ivan and Peter, who were hailed as joint Tsars.

But before her power was stabilized, she had to deal with the ungovernable *streltsy*, who terrorized the capital until threatened with open war by the regular army. Once the *streltsy* were calmed, Sophia moved to punish the Old Believers and any of the revolting serfs that could be captured. The first woman to govern Russia since Kievan times, Sophia was bound in any case to face severe opposition. She could not manage to get even her supporters to allow her to proclaim herself autocrat. And the maturing Peter, though out of favor and away from court, posed a threat to her position; in the end, the *streltsy* let her down. In 1689, Sophia was shut up in a convent, and Peter and Ivan ruled together until Ivan's death in 1696, although in practice Ivan never counted for anything.

The young Peter was almost seven feet tall, and extremely lively. Highly intelligent, he had learned to read and write (but never to spell) from a drunken tutor who was the only academic instructor the troubled times afforded. Even in his early years, Peter was fascinated by war and military games. He set up a play-regiment, staffed it with full-grown men, enlisted as a common soldier in its ranks (promoting himself from time to time), ordered equipment for it from the Moscow arsenals, and drilled it in war games with unflagging vigor, himself firing off cannon or pounding on a drum with equal enjoyment. He discovered a broken-down boat in a barn, and unraveled the mysteries of rigging and sail with the help of Dutch sailors settled in the foreigners' suburb of Moscow. Sailing remained one of his keenest passions. Though he married at the age of sixteen, Peter neglected his wife, and preferred working on his military maneuvers, sailing his boats, and relaxing with his peculiar circle of cronies.

This rowdy lot smoked huge quantities of tobacco (which horrified the conservative Muscovites, who believed that smoking was specifically forbidden by the Biblical text which says that what cometh out of the mouth defileth a man), and regularly got completely drunk. Then they would engage in obscene parodies of church services, or play elaborate and highly dangerous practical jokes on the unoffending citizenry, roaring about Moscow in winter late at night on sleighs and treating the sleeping populace to shrieking serenades. Masquerades and parties lasted for days; staid Moscow ladies, accustomed to almost harem-like seclusion, were commanded to put on low-necked evening dresses in the western style, and dance and engage in social chitchat. They were literally forced to drink with the Tsar and his friends: if a lady refused, Peter simply held her nose, and poured the wine down her throat. Peter spent enormous sums of state revenue on this sort of party, and richly endowed his boon companion Lefort, a young Swiss soldier of fortune who became Field Marshal, Grand Admiral and "chief diplomat."

The almost frantic energy that Peter devoted to pleasure reflected only part of his appetite for new experience. Just as he served in the ranks of his own play-regiment and sailed his boats himself, so he eagerly learned any new technique that came to his attention. At various times he took up carpentry, shoe-making, cooking, clock-making, ivory-carving, etching, and—worst of all—dentistry. Once he had acquired a set of dentist's tools, nobody was safe, since Peter did not care whether the intended victim had a toothache or not; whenever he felt the need to practice, he practiced—and those were the days before anesthetics. Preferring to wear shabby work clothes, driving his own horses, neglecting formal obligations and paying little attention to court and church ceremony, Peter in his own person was a shock to the Muscovites, and not in the least in keeping with their idea of a proper tsar.

After Lefort died in 1700, Peter's favorite was Menshikov, a man of low birth, who received high offices, the title of Prince, and a huge fortune. Unfortunately, like many of the public servants of the period, he was an unscrupulous grafter. Peter wrote to Menshikov as "my brother," and, though he came to distrust him, he never ruined him as he did many other favorites. Meantime, Peter had his first wife shut up in a convent and made a nun. He later took on as mistress a girl from the Baltic region, who had already passed through the hands of Menshikov and others, and after some years of liaison with her, during which she gave birth to two of Peter's children, he finally married her in 1712. This was the Empress Catherine, a simple, hearty, affectionate woman, long devoted to her difficult husband, and able to control him as no other human being could. But again, one can understand the horrified reaction of the old-fashioned Russian noble.

The Western Trip

In 1695, anxious to try his hand at war, Peter led a campaign against the Turks at Azov in the area of the Black Sea. He failed, but in the next year, with the help of Dutch experts, he assembled a fleet of river-boats on the Don, sailed them downriver, and defeated the Turks at Azov. Since the Habsburgs at the time were waging a long war against the Turks, this rather surprising Russian contribution aroused much interest and curiosity. The project of forming a league against the Turks with the states of western Europe now gave Peter the pretext for a trip outside Russia, the first undertaken by a Russian sovereign since the Kievan period.

Though ostensibly traveling incognito as a Russian noncommissioned officer, Peter naturally failed in his efforts to conceal his identity: after all, there were no other authoritarian seven-footers in the party. What fascinated him was western "know-how," especially naval. He planned to go to Holland, England, and Venice, where the best ships (in his opinion) were made, find out how they were made, and bring the knowledge back to Russia for the advancement of Russian aims. He hired several hundred technicians to work in Russia, raised money when he needed it by selling to an English peer the monopoly of tobacco sales in Russia, and visited every sort of factory or museum or printing press he could find. The huge Russian Tsar in all his vigor and crudity, emerging into the air of western Europe from his antiquated and stagnant country, made an unforgettable impression.

From the celebrated western trip many well-known pictures emerge: Peter laboring as a common hand on the docks in Holland; Peter and his suite, drunk and dirty, wrecking the handsome house and garden of the English diarist, John Evelyn, near London: "There is a house full of people," wrote Evelyn's harassed servant, "and that right nasty." Less well known perhaps are the spectacles of Peter dancing with a German princess, mistaking her whalebone corsets for her ribs, and commenting loudly that German girls have devilish hard bones; of Peter receiving an honorary degree at Oxford; of Peter deep in conversation (Dutch) with William Penn about the Quaker faith; of Peter gobbling his food without benefit of knife or fork, or asleep with a dozen or so of his followers on the floor of a tiny room in a London inn with no windows open.

Before Peter could get to Venice, the western trip was interrupted by news that the *streltsy* had revolted again (1698). Peter rushed home, and personally participated in the punishment of the alleged plotters; he and Menshikov rather enjoyed chopping off the heads of the victims. Though many innocent men suffered torture and death, Peter had broken the *streltsy* as a power in Russian domestic life.

From the West, Peter had returned more determined than ever to modernize his country and his countrymen. The very day of his return he summoned the court jester, and with his assistance went about with a great pair of shears, stopping his courtiers and clipping off their beards. Though this may seem a trivial joke, in fact it was an action full of symbolism. The tradition of the Orthodox Church held that God was bearded; if man was made in the image of God, man must also have a beard. Deprived of his beard, man was no longer made in God's image, and was a natural candidate for damnation. This was the way the Muscovite nobles and churchmen felt. Peter now decreed that Russian nobles must shave, or else pay a substantial tax for the privilege of wearing their beards. Bronze beard-tokens worn around the neck certified that the tax had been properly paid; without such a token a bearded man ran the risk of being clipped on sight.

Presently, Peter issued an edict commanding that all boyars, members of the gentry class, and the city population generally must abandon traditional Russian dress, which included long robes with flowing sleeves and tall bonnets, and adopt western-style costume. The manufacture of the old-fashioned clothes was made illegal, and Peter added point to his decree by taking up his shears again, and cutting off the sleeves of all the people he met wearing the forbidden robes. The enactments on the beards and on dress were regarded by the victims as an assault on precious customs and a forcible introduction of hated foreign ways.

Peter's Wars

War was Peter's greatest interest. We can understand his policies at home only after we realize how closely related they were to the virtually constant warfare of his reign, and to the ever-mounting need for money for fighting. On his way back to Russia in 1698, he discovered that the Austrians, instead of being eager to join him in a full-scale crusade against the Turks, were anxious to end their Turkish war. Irritated by the Austro-Turkish Peace of Karlovitz in 1699, which he felt to be a betrayal of Russia, Peter made a separate peace of his own with the Sultan in 1700. By this time, his plans for new aggression were already formed.

The victim was to be Sweden. Peter's allies, already signed up in 1699, were to be Denmark and Poland, the latter under its elected king, Augustus the Strong, who was also Elector of Saxony and who had quickly become an intimate of Peter after their first meeting in 1698. The real engineer of the alliance and moving spirit of the war against Sweden was a nobleman named Patkul from the Baltic shore, deeply resentful of measures taken by the Swedes against the feudal proprietors of that area. Patkul went from interview to interview, holding out to Augustus and Peter the glittering prospect that after they had defeated Sweden they might divide her Baltic territories. In 1697, the Swedish throne had descended to a youth of fifteen, King Charles XII, whom Peter, Augustus, and Patkul hoped they might easily overcome. They might have reconsidered had they seen Charles strengthening his sword-arm by beheading at a single stroke apiece whole flocks of sheep driven down his palace corridors in single file until the whole place swam in blood. The fact was that Peter the Great characteristically rushed unprepared into the Great Northern War (1700-1721).

Charles knocked Denmark out of the war before Russia even got in. He then frustrated Augustus' effort to take the Baltic port of Riga, and completely defeated a vastly larger Russian force at Narva (1700), capturing the entire supply of modern cannon of which Peter was so proud. Instead of taking advantage of Peter's helplessness, however, and marching into Russia, Charles detoured into Poland, where he spent seven years pursuing Augustus, sponsoring his own King of Poland, a noble named Stanislas Leszczynski, and eventually forcing Augustus to abandon the Polish crown to Leszczynski and to give up the Russian alliance. Charles then seized and executed Patkul.

During this interim, Peter had been busy rebuilding the shattered Russian armies, and had conquered from the Swedes the two Baltic provinces nearest to Russia, Ingria and Livonia. In the first he founded in 1703 a new city, St. Petersburg, soon to be the capital of Russia, and from the beginning the apple of Peter's eye. In 1708, Charles made the mistake of sweeping far to the south and east into the Ukraine in an effort to join forces with the Cossacks, whose leader Mazepa was an ally. Exhausted by the severe winter, the Swedish forces were finally defeated by the Russians in the decisive battle of Poltava (June 27, 1709). Charles managed to flee safely westward across the Dniester River and onto Turkish territory.

Peter was able to reinstate Augustus as King of Poland, but he was not able to force the Turks to surrender to him the refugee King of Sweden. Charles indeed had embarked on a series of intrigues designed to bring about a war between Turkey and Peter, and thus to enable him to avenge his defeat. So Peter in some dismay found himself embroiled in war against the Turks (1710-1711). Now for the first time in history the Russians made an appeal to the Balkan Christian subjects of the Turks on the ground of their common Orthodox faith. Bearing banners modeled on those of Constantine, first Emperor of Byzantium, and promising liberation from the Moslems, the Russian forces entered Turkish territory by crossing the river Pruth westward into the Danubian province of Moldavia (now a part of Rumania). Here the Turkish armies trapped Peter and forced him to surrender (1711).

The Turks could have dragged Peter off in captivity to Istanbul had they wanted, but they proved unexpectedly lenient. They required the surrender of Azov and the creation of an unfortified "no-man's land" between Russian and Ottoman territory. Furious with the Turks for not taking full advantage of Peter's discomfiture, Charles worked to bring about still another Russo-Turkish war. Although he came very close to success, the Turks eventually tired of their firebrand visitor and expelled him. Their own peace with Russia was secure, and Charles went sadly home (1714).

Still the Great Northern War dragged on for seven more years of diplomatic intrigue and military and naval action, involving the Prussians (see above, p. 25), and affecting the interests of all the western European powers. As Russian forces seized Finland, inflicted naval defeats on the Swedes in the Baltic, and occupied islands only a few miles from the Swedish coast, the Swedish empire was obviously dissolving, and the Russians were taking its place. To the last years of the Great Northern War belong a whole series of matrimonial and other alliances between Russia and the petty German courts, bringing the Russians deep into Central Europe, and embroiling them in questions in which Russia really had no national interest. From a remote and little-known state somewhere behind Poland, Russia had emerged as a major military power with enough might to affect the destiny of European states.

RUSSIAN EXPANSION IN EUROPE
1689 — 1796

Acquired by Peter the Great, 1689-1725
Acquired between 1730-1740
Acquired by Elizabeth, 1741-1762
Acquired by Catherine, 1762-1796
× Battle sites   0   Miles   400

CHAPTER XVI

The death of Charles XII in 1718 cleared the way for peace negotiations, but it took a Russian landing in Sweden proper (1719) to force a decision. At Nystadt (1721), Russia received all the former possessions of Sweden along the eastern shore of the Baltic. Peter returned Finland to Sweden and agreed to pay a substantial sum for the territories acquired. These Baltic lands were Peter's famous "window on the west," putting Russia into immediate contact with Europe, and ending the curious situation by which all seaborne traffic to Russia had had to sail around the northern edge of Europe and into the White Sea. Next, Peter undertook a brief campaign (1722-1723) against the Persians. At his death in 1725 Russia had been at war for almost the entirety of his thirty-five-year reign.

The Machinery of Peter's Government

Constant warfare requires constant supplies of men and money. Since the enlistment of volunteers provided cannon-fodder but not seasoned troops, Peter's government developed a crude form of draft system according to which a given number of households had to supply a given number of recruits. More men died of disease, hunger, and cold than at the hands of the enemy, and desertion was commonplace. But the very length of the Great Northern War meant that survivors served as a tough nucleus for a regular army. Though Peter built a Baltic fleet at the first opportunity, Russian naval tradition failed to strike deep roots. From 800 ships (mostly very small, of course) at the moment of his death, the fleet declined to fewer than twenty a decade later. And there was no merchant marine whatever. The apprehensions of the English and the Dutch that Russian emergence on the Baltic would create a new maritime nation proved unfounded.

To staff the military forces and the administration, Peter rigorously enforced the rule by which all landowners owed service to the state. He eventually decreed "civil death" for those who failed to register; this put them outside the protection of the law, and anyone could attack or kill them without fear of the consequences. State service became compulsory for life; at the age of fifteen, every male child of the service class was assigned to his future post, in the army, in the civil service, or at court. Peter often forced the gentry to do jobs they considered beneath them; he did not care whether they were interested in their work or even very much whether they had been trained for it. He filled their ranks with newcomers, who obtained grants of land, rank, and title. And he required that when a member of this class died he must leave his estate intact to one of his sons, not necessarily the eldest, so that it would not be divided anew in every generation.

Thus the class of service nobility—which now substantially included the survivors of the nobility of ancient birth, the old boyars—was brought into a position of complete dependence upon the tsar. The system threw open the possibility of a splendid career to men with talent. A person without estates or rank who reached a certain level in any branch of the service (for example, major in the army) automatically received lands and a title of nobility. The nobility of ancient birth viewed this as a cheapening of their position, and hated to see new recruits come into their own social order. But under Peter there was little they could do about it.

To raise cash, Peter tried all kinds of measures. He debased the currency; he taxed virtually everything—sales, rents, real estate, tanneries, baths, and beehives—and appointed special officials called "revenue-finders" to think up new levies. The government held a monopoly over a bewildering variety of important products, including salt and oil, coffins and caviar.

The basic tax on each individual household was not producing enough revenue, partly because the number of households had declined as a result of war and misery, and partly because households were combining in order to evade payment. Peter's government therefore substituted a head tax on every male—the "soul tax," as the Russians called it—making it useless for individuals to conceal themselves in households. This innovation required a new census, which produced a most important, and unintended, social result: the census-takers now classified as serfs a large number of floaters on the edge between freedom and serfdom, who thus found themselves and their children eternally labeled as unfree. At the cost of human misery, Peter's government managed in its later years to balance the budget.

In the administration, new ministries (*prikazy*) were first set up to centralize the handling of funds received from various sources. A system of army districts adopted for reasons of military efficiency led to the creation of the first Russian provinces, first eight, then nine, then twelve, embracing all Russia. Each province had its own governor; and many of the functions previously carried on inefficiently by the central government were thus decentralized. With the tsar often away from the capital, and many of the former *prikazy* abolished, decentralization had gone so far that Russia seemed at times to have little central government. But when Peter set out for the Pruth campaign in 1711, he created a nine-man "governing Senate," designed to exercise power in his absence. Later, Peter copied the Swedish system of central ministries to supersede the old *prikazy* and created nine "colleges"—for foreign affairs, army, navy, commerce, mines and manufactures, justice, income, expenditure, and control. Each "college" was administered not by a single minister but by a majority vote of an eleven-man board of directors or *collegium*. Corruption now became more

difficult, because the conduct of any one member of a college could be checked by his colleagues. On the other hand, the lengthy deliberations of so many directors often delayed final decisions.

The total picture of Peter's efforts to increase the efficiency of government is one of mixed success at best. Attempts to model Russian local government on Swedish practice broke down because of the enormous difference between the two countries in literacy, size, tradition, and attitude toward civic responsibility. Corruption still continued in high places; savage punishments were inflicted on some of those who were caught, while others, like Menshikov, were apparently immune. And yet the cumbrous machinery that Peter gradually established, hit or miss, to meet the immediate needs of his wars, was superior to any that Russia had previously known.

Other Innovations
of Peter the Great

Ever since 1703, Peter had been building a great city in the swamps he had seized from the Swedes. Thousands of men died in the effort to drain the marshes and create a seaport and a capital worthy of its imperial resident. Remote from the rest of Russia, St. Petersburg was frightfully expensive, because all food and building materials had to be transported great distances. It was also dangerous. When floods poured through the streets, Peter roared with laughter at the sight of furniture and household effects floating away. Wolves prowled the broad new boulevards and devoured a lady in front of Prince Menshikov's own house one fine day in June. But Peter made St. Petersburg his capital and commanded all members of the nobility to make it their home. Although palaces sprang up at the Tsar's command, the nobles complained bitterly about abandoning their beloved Moscow for this uncomfortable and costly town. Thus St. Petersburg became the symbol of Peter's war against his own gentry.

Peter also determined to disarm all possible future threats to his power from the Church. Knowing how the clergy loathed the new régime he was trying to impose, he simply failed to appoint a successor when the Patriarch of Moscow died in 1700. Eventually, in 1721, he extended the collegiate system of administration to the Church itself. He put it under an agency first called the "spiritual college," and later the Holy Directing Synod, headed by a Procurator who was a layman. Thus the Church became more than ever a department of state. Peter's own statement of his purpose is remarkably frank:

From the collegiate government of the church there is not so much danger to the country of disturbances and troubles as may be produced by one spiritual ruler. For the common people do not understand the difference between the spiritual power and that of the autocrat; but, dazzled by the splendor and glory of the highest pastor, they think that he is a second sovereign of like power with the autocrat or with even more, and that the spiritual power is that of another and better realm. If then there should be any difference of opinion between the Patriarch and the Tsar, it might easily happen that the people, perhaps misled by designing persons, should take the part of the Patriarch, in the mistaken belief that they were fighting for God's cause.[*]

The educational advances of the period reflected Peter's technological and military interests. Naval, military, and artillery academies were established to educate future officers and also many civil servants. When the government tried to institute compulsory education by requiring the establishment of two schools in each province (1714), it stressed mathematics and navigation, and the attempt failed. Part of the difficulty came from the reluctance of parents to see their children "waste time" in school, and part from the government's inexperience and its unwillingness to begin with primary education. Primary education was left to the church schools, which were few and on the whole not very competent. At all levels, foreigners had to be summoned to provide Russia with scholars. An Academy of Sciences founded just before Peter's death began with seventeen imported fellows, and eight students, also imported. Probably the mere presence in the new capital of these exotic academies helped to stimulate the native intellectual developments that would characterize the

[*] Quoted by E. Schuyler, *Peter the Great* (New York, 1884), II, 389.

Peter I striding along the dikes during the building of St. Petersburg. A painting by V. A. Serov.

next generation. Such tokens as the first Russian newspaper (1703) and the printing of occasional textbooks also augured well for the future.

Peter continued the practice, begun long before him, of importing foreign technicians and artisans to practice their crafts and teach them to Russians. Quite aware of the mercantilist ideas of the age, he offered such inducements as freedom from taxation and from government service, and all sorts of tariff protection, to develop manufacturing. Though sometimes employing a substantial number of laborers, industrial enterprise in Russia, chiefly textiles and iron, continued to be backward. The labor force was recruited among unwilling and badly treated serfs and criminals. Factory-owners were permitted to buy and sell serfs (otherwise a privilege restricted to the gentry), provided they were always bought or sold as a body together with the factory itself. This "possessional" industrial serfdom was hardly a system likely to provide much incentive for good work. Russian produce continued inferior to comparable goods manufactured abroad. In the commercial field, Peter's heavy protective tariffs discriminated against foreign goods, encouraging smuggling and false registration of foreign agents as Russian nationals. The effort to make Russia a manufacturing nation exporting its own produce was a failure. But Peter's conquests in the Baltic did give Russia the great port of Riga, and he successfully bent every effort to make St. Petersburg into a great trading center.

Peter the Great: A Final Evaluation

The records of Peter's secret police are full of the complaints his agents heard as they moved about listening for subversive remarks. The wives and children of the peasantry found themselves deserted by their men, who were snatched away to fight on distant battlefields or to labor in the swamps to build a city that nobody but Peter wanted. The number of serfs increased with the imposition of the new soul-tax and the multiplication of land-grants to service men. The tax burden was back-breaking. Service men found themselves in a kind of bondage of their own, condemned to work for the Tsar during the whole of their lives and seldom able to visit their estates. Nobles of ancient birth found themselves treated no differently from the upstarts who were flooding into their class from below. Churchmen of the conservative school were more and more convinced that Peter was the anti-Christ himself, as they beheld the increase of foreigners in high places, and saw the many innovations imported into the government and social life from the hated West. Rumors circulated that this was not the true Tsar at all, but a changeling somehow substituted for the real Peter by foreigners during the trip abroad, and sent back to persecute Russians and to ruin Russia.

Among the lower orders of society resistance took the usual form: peasant uprisings, punished with fantastic brutality. The usual allies of the peasant rebels, the Cossacks, suffered mass executions and sharp curtailment of their traditional independence. The leaders of the noble and clerical opposition focused their hopes on Peter's son by his first wife, the young heir to the throne, Alexis, who, they believed, would stop the expensive and (they felt) needless foreign wars, and move back to Moscow and comfortable Russian conservatism. Alexis, an alcoholic, was afraid of his father, and was early estranged from him. Though not stable enough to lead a true conspiracy against Peter, he fanned the hopes of the opposition by letting them know he shared their views. Eventually he caused a scandal by fleeing abroad and asking asylum from his brother-in-law, the Austrian Emperor Charles VI. Promising him fair treatment and forgiveness, Peter lured Alexis back to Russia and made him the show-piece of one of those horrible Russian investigations of nonexistent plots. Many were tortured, killed, and exiled; Alexis himself was tortured to death in his father's presence.

In the early nineteenth century, when the first self-conscious group of Russian intellectuals developed a keen interest in the past history of their country, they made a central figure of Peter. He had, they felt, intensified western influences on Russian society, and had thus turned his back on Russia's peculiarly Slavic character and her Byzantine heritage. One group hailed these actions as necessary to put Russia on her proper course. Its opponents damned Peter for having forced an unnatural development upon his country, and for having warped its social and political life by imposing an alien pattern. But both his friends and enemies among these later intellectuals believed, as most scholars have since argued, that what he did was drastic and revolutionary.

Yet we can see that Peter simply intensified the chief characteristics of Russian society. He made a strong autocracy even stronger, a universal service law for service men even more stringent, a serf more of a serf. His trip abroad, his fondness for foreign ways, his worship of advanced technology, his mercantilism, his wars, all had their precedents in the period of his forerunners. The Church, which he attacked, had already been weakened by the schism of the Old Believers, itself the result of western influences. Where Peter was radical was in the field of everyday manners and behavior. The attack on the beards, the dress, the calendar (he adopted the western dating from the birth of Christ and abandoned the traditional dating from a hypothetical year of the creation), his hatred of ceremony and fondness for manual labor—these things were indeed new. So too were the vigor and passion with which he acted. They were decisive in winning a revolutionary reputation for a monarch who in the major aspects of his reign was carrying out policies long since established.

Poland and Turkey

By the early eighteenth century, Russia was the only great power in eastern Europe. Poland and the Ottoman Empire still bulked large on the map, but their territories included lands they were soon to lose. Both states suffered from incompetent government, from a backward economy, and from the presence of large national and religious minorities. The Orthodox in Catholic Poland and Moslem Turkey were beginning to look to Russia for protection. In addition, the evident decay of both states stimulated the aggressive appetites of their stronger neighbors. Poland, consequently, was doomed to disappear as an independent power before the end of the century, the victim of partition by Russia, Austria, and Prussia. Turkey held on, but only just, and was already beginning to acquire the perilous reputation of being the "Sick Man of Europe."

The Polish government was a political curiosity shop. Its monarchy was elective; each time the throne fell vacant, the diet of the nobility chose a successor, usually the man who had offered the biggest bribes, sometimes a foreigner. Once elected, the kings were quite powerless, since they had already agreed to transfer their royal prerogatives to the diet, which cherished its famous institution of the *liberum veto*. Any one of its members could block any proposal by shouting "I do not wish it!" and then galloping off before his colleagues could catch up with him to make him change his mind. The diet was not a parliament in the western sense of the term, but an assembly of men, each of whom thought of himself as a power unto himself; unanimity was therefore necessary for all decisions. This loosely knit Polish national state had no regular army or diplomatic corps. Unlike the English gentry or Prussian Junkers, the dominant nobles had no concept of service to the Crown or indeed any sense of loyalty except to their own social class. They helped destroy a once-flourishing urban middle class by persecuting Jewish shopkeepers and foreign merchants. On their estates, the lot of the serfs was harsher than it was in Russia.

Compared with Poland, the Ottoman Empire was still a functioning state, yet it was falling farther and farther behind the major European powers, particularly in economics and technology. It had no Peter the Great to jar it out of isolation; with few exceptions, the sultans of the eighteenth century were captives of harem intrigue and bullied by the arrogant caste of Janissaries, who exploited their privileges to the neglect of their soldierly duties. This retrograde and corrupt government did at least govern, however, and showed considerable staying power in war. So the "Sick Man" was to linger on throughout the century, kept alive in part by the still unexhausted Ottoman reserves of vitality, and in part by the rivalry between the two would-be heirs of the Turkish inheritance, Russia and Austria.

VI: War and Diplomacy, 1713-1763

The Issues

From the survey just concluded of the European states in the early eighteenth century it is evident that the balance of power was at best precarious. Should the strong states prey upon the weak, the balance was certain to be upset. As we have seen, it was indeed upset as a result of the Great Northern War when Russia replaced Sweden as the dominant power in the Baltic. The expansion of Russia continued to be a major international issue throughout the eighteenth century, as Peter the Great's successors tried, with more or less success, to enlarge Russia's windows on the world (see Chapter XVII). In addition to Sweden, the chief victims of this expansion were Poland and Turkey. A second major issue at stake in the wars and diplomacy of the century was the expansion of Prussia; the chief victims of the Hohenzollerns were Austria, Sweden, and Poland. A third great issue was the colonial and commercial rivalry between Britain and the Bourbon monarchies of France and Spain.

All manner of secondary issues also entered into the play of international relations. The old competition between Austria and France, going back to the Habsburg-Valois wars of the 1500's, remained very lively. The family ambitions of Elizabeth Farnese added a new disturbing element and threatened the Austrian hegemony in Italy. And the Austrian Habsburgs themselves pursued the aim of driving the Turk from the Danube and extending their own domains southeast to the Black Sea. In the Austro-Turkish War of 1716-1718, the Habsburg Emperor Charles VI scored a major success and by the Treaty of Passarowitz in 1718 recovered the piece of Hungary still under Ottoman rule and secured parts of present-day Rumania and Yugoslavia. A second Turkish War, 1735-1739, however, revealed the infirmity of the Habsburg army and the mistrust between Austria and Russia. The two powers were allied in this war but soon fell to quarreling over the division of the prospective spoils. In the end there was almost nothing to divide, and Charles VI was obliged to hand back the Ottoman lands annexed in 1718. In the negotiations leading to the Austro-Turkish settlement of 1739, the Ottoman Empire received powerful support from France—an example of the way in which the French traditionally used the Turkish alliance to curb the expansion of the Habsburgs.

The War
of the Polish Succession

Meantime, in the early 1730's, another crisis in eastern Europe ranged Bourbon and Habsburg on opposing sides. This one concerned the crown of Poland. In the early stages of the Great Northern War, as we have seen, Charles XII of Sweden had unseated the Polish king, the Saxon Augustus the Strong, and had given the crown to a Polish nobleman, Stanislas Leszczynski; then, thanks to the support of Peter the Great, Augustus recovered the Polish throne. Stanislas, however, had by no means completed his historical role, for he eventually gave his daughter, Marie, in marriage to Louis XV of France. When Augustus the Strong died in 1733, French diplomats engineered the election of Stanislas to succeed him. But both Austria and Russia disliked the prospect of a French puppet on the Polish throne, and Russia sent 30,000 troops into Poland and convoked a rump session of the diet which elected a rival king, Augustus III, son of Augustus the Strong. The stage was set for the War of the Polish Succession, 1733-1735—Stanislas, France, and Spain *versus* Augustus III, Russia, and Austria.

After French and Austrian armies had fired away at each other for a while in the Rhine Valley and in northern Italy, hundreds of miles from Poland, the diplomats worked out a compromise settlement. To the satisfaction of Austria and Russia, Au-

gustus III secured the Polish throne. From the French standpoint, Stanislas Leszczynski was well compensated for his loss. He acquired the duchy of Lorraine, on the northeastern border of France, with the provision that when he died Lorraine would go to his daughter, Marie, and thence to the French crown. France would thus move one step closer toward filling out her "natural" frontiers. To be sure, Lorraine already had a duke, Francis, husband of the Habsburg heiress, Maria Theresa; the awkwardness was neatly resolved by transferring Francis to the Italian Grand Duchy of Tuscany, where the old line of rulers conveniently died out in 1737. Finally, as a by-product of the settlement, Elizabeth Farnese of Spain capped twenty years of maternal perseverance by procuring the Kingdom of Naples for "Baby Carlos," her elder and now grown-up son.

The War of the Polish Succession may well seem futile and trivial, much ado about a kingship possessing no real power. And the postwar settlement, which affected chiefly Italy and Lorraine, may seem to be a striking case of diplomatic irrelevance. Yet the whole Polish crisis is a most instructive example of the workings of dynastic politics and of the constant shifts in the balance of power. Certainly no great national issues were at stake, except for the rather nebulous ones of French, Russian, and Austrian prestige. The statesmen regarded thrones as the pawns of diplomacy, to be assigned without reference to the wishes of the populations involved. None of them contemplated canvassing Neapolitan sentiment on Carlos or holding a referendum to see whether the Poles preferred Stanislas or Augustus. None of them gave a thought to the welfare of Poland, which came out of the crisis weaker than ever.

The complicated arrangements of the 1730's preserved the balance of power by giving something to almost everybody involved. Although the diplomats could not prevent a little war over Poland, they did keep it from becoming a big one. Indeed, throughout the period from 1713 to 1739 the force of diplomacy operated to avoid or at least to localize wars. Britain and France took the lead in the campaign to keep any one power from upsetting the international apple-cart. For example, the British dispatched a squadron to the Baltic during the last part of the Great Northern War so that Tsar Peter's gains would not be too great. To prevent the dismemberment of Ottoman territories in Europe, Britain intervened in the negotiations between Turkey and Austria at Passarowitz in 1718, and the French revived their Ottoman alliance in the 1730's.

The War of Jenkins' Ear

The informal diplomatic partnership of Britain and France in the 1720's and 1730's reflected the basic policies of Walpole and Fleury, both of whom sought stability abroad to promote economic recovery at home. The partnership, however, collapsed in the face of the competition between the two Atlantic powers for commerce and empire. Neither Walpole nor Fleury could prevent the world-wide war between Britain and the Bourbon monarchies that broke out in 1739 and that lasted, with many intervals of peace, until the final defeat of Napoleon in 1815. This "Second Hundred Years' War" had, in fact, already begun half a century before 1739, in the days of Louis XIV. The Utrecht settlement of 1713 had not fully settled the rivalry between Britain and France (and France's Bourbon partner, Spain). Thus the war of 1739 was as much the renewal of an old struggle as the onset of a new one.

The specific issue behind the crisis of 1739 was the comparatively minor question of British chagrin at the disappointing results of the Asiento privilege. As the South Sea Company discovered, the Asiento gave Britain little more than a token share in the trade of the Spanish American colonies (see above, p. 10). What British captains could not get legitimately they got by smuggling. Spain retaliated by establishing a coast-guard patrol in American waters to ward off smugglers. British merchants complained of the rough treatment handed out by the Spanish guards, and in 1738 they exhibited to Parliament Captain Jenkins, who claimed that Spanish brutality had cost him an ear. Jenkins duly produced his severed ear, preserved in salt and cotton batting. Asked to state his reaction on losing the ear, he replied, "I commended my soul to God and my cause to my country." Walpole retorted that the protection of British smugglers against legitimate Spanish patrols did not give the government a very strong case. But Walpole could restrain neither the anti-Spanish fever sweeping the country to which Jenkins had commended his cause, nor the bellicose faction of "Boy Patriots" that had arisen within Walpole's own Whig party.

In October, 1739, to the joyful pealing of church bells, Britain began the War of Jenkins' Ear against Spain. "They are ringing their bells now," Walpole observed tartly. "They will be wringing their hands soon." As if to vindicate his prophecy, the British fleet promptly made a mess of the opening campaign in the Caribbean, and France showed every sign of coming to Spain's assistance. Dynastic ties had already brought the two Bourbon monarchies into alliance during the Polish war; now French economic interests were at stake, for France supplied the bulk of the wares which Spanish galleons carried to America, and which cheaper British contraband was driving out of the Spanish colonial market.

The War of the Austrian Succession, 1740-1748

In 1740, a chain of events linked the colonial war to a great continental conflict, the War of the Austrian Succession. On the death of the Emperor Charles VI in 1740,

The Battle of Culloden, 1746, showing the rigid battle formations used in the eighteenth century.

the Habsburg domains passed to his daughter, Maria Theresa, who was only twenty-three years old. Expecting to outwit Maria Theresa because of her youth, her sex, and her political inexperience, the German princes ignored the Pragmatic Sanction guaranteeing her succession and looked forward to the possible partition of the Habsburg lands. In addition, the Elector of Bavaria, a cousin of the Habsburgs, hoped to become Holy Roman Emperor, defeating Maria Theresa's candidate, her own husband, Francis of Lorraine and Tuscany. The first of the German princes to strike, however, was Frederick the Great (1740-1786), who had just inherited the Prussian throne from Frederick William I. In December, 1740, Frederick suddenly invaded Silesia, a Habsburg province (located in the upper

Oder valley to the southeast of Brandenburg) to which the Hohenzollerns had a tenuous family claim.

In the ensuing War of the Austrian Succession, England and Austria were ranged against France, Spain, Prussia, and Bavaria. Frederick won an emphatic victory in the campaigns on the Continent. The Prussian army astounded Europe by its long night marches, sudden flank attacks, and other tactics of surprise quite different from the usual deliberate warfare of sieges. Frederick, however, deeply antagonized his allies by repeatedly deserting them to make secret peace arrangements with Austria. And he did little to support the imperial aspirations of the Bavarian Elector, who enjoyed only a brief tenure as "Emperor Charles VII."

The Anglo-Austrian alliance worked no better than the Franco-Prussian one. Many Englishmen felt that George II was betraying their true interests overseas by entangling them in German politics and the defense of Hanover. Nevertheless, the British nation still preferred the Hanoverians to the Stuarts. In 1745, "Bonnie Prince Charles," the grandson of the deposed James II, secured French backing and landed in Britain. He won significant recruits only among the chronically discontented Scottish highlanders, and in 1746 he was thoroughly defeated at Culloden. Jacobitism, never a very important political threat, was dead.

Outside Europe, the fighting of the 1740's was quite indecisive. The New England colonists took Louisburg, the French naval base on Cape Breton Island commanding the approach to the St. Lawrence. On the other side of the world, the French took the port of Madras from the English East India Company. On the seas, the British fleet did not win a real victory until 1747, and by then British merchant ships had suffered numerous attacks from French privateering expeditions.

The peace settlement ending the War of the Austrian Succession faithfully reflected the outcome of the actual fighting. Overseas, the Treaty of Aix-la-Chapelle (1748) restored both Louisburg and Madras to their former owners, and Britain later agreed to give up the troublesome Asiento privilege. In Central Europe, the war made Prussia a first-rate power by confirming her acquisition of Silesia. The new province brought not only a large increase in the Prussian population but also an important textile industry and large deposits of coal and iron. Maria Theresa got scant compensation for the loss of Silesia. Although her husband, Francis, won recognition as Holy Roman Emperor, she had to surrender Parma and some other territorial crumbs in northern Italy to Philip, the second son of Elizabeth Farnese.

The Uneasy Peace, 1748-1756

The peace made in 1748 lasted only eight years. Then another and greater conflict, the Seven Years' War of 1756-1763, broke out, caused partly by old issues left unsettled at Aix-la-Chapelle and partly by new grievances arising from the War of the Austrian Succession. The world struggle between Britain and the Bourbons, in which the old war had been an indecisive preliminary engagement, kept right on in the undeclared warfare waged during the years of nominal peace after 1748. In Asia, the English and French East India companies fought each other once removed, so to speak, by taking sides in the rivalries of native princes in southern India. By 1751, the energetic French administrator, Dupleix, had won the initial round of this indirect fight. Then the English, led by the equally energetic Clive, seized the initiative, and in 1754 Dupleix was called back home by the directors of the French company, who were unwilling to back his aggressive policy. In North America, English colonists from the Atlantic seaboard had already staked out claims to the rich wilderness between the Appalachians and the Mississippi. But the French, equally intent on appropriating the area, stole a march on them and established a string of forts in western Pennsylvania from Presqu'Isle (later Erie) south to Fort Duquesne (later Pittsburgh). In 1754, a force of Virginians under the youthful George Washington tried unsuccessfully to dislodge the French from their strategic position at Fort Duquesne.

Colonists and mother country did not always see eye to eye on matters of basic policy. French recall of Dupleix is one example of such divergence. Another example is provided by the curious situation prevailing in the West Indies, then regarded as the greatest prizes of empire because they produced most of the world's sugar. New England traders could obtain sugar and its by-products (molasses and rum) more cheaply from the French plantations of Santo Domingo (Haiti), Guadeloupe, and Martinique than from Jamaica and other British sugar islands. French sugar made New England rum; New England rum besotted African Negroes; and, to complete this notorious "triangle trade," the sale of African slaves to French planters lined Yankee pockets—all in open violation of the mercantilist regulations that theoretically governed both the French and British empires.

In Europe, the dramatic shift of alliances called the Diplomatic Revolution immediately preceded the outbreak of the Seven Years' War. In the new war the fundamental conflicts were the same as in the old —Britain versus France, Prussia versus Austria—but the powers reversed their alliances. Britain, which had joined Austria *against* Prussia in the 1740's, now paired off *with* Frederick the Great. And, in the most revolutionary move of the Diplomatic Revolution, France, which had sided *with* Frederick before, not only stood *against* him but also joined *with* her hereditary enemy, Habsburg Austria. The Diplomatic Revolution reflected the resentment of the powers at the disloyal behavior of their old partners in the War of the Austrian Succession. The French had bitter memories of Frederick's repeated desertions and secret peace arrangements. Britain deplored Austrian reluctance to defend English continental interests, which included maintaining the territorial integrity of Hanover and excluding the French from the Austrian Netherlands. Austria, in turn, regarded Hanover and Belgium as peripheral to her main concern, the recovery of Silesia.

In 1755, the British almost unwittingly touched off the Diplomatic Revolution. In order to enlist a second power in the task of defending Hanover, they concluded a treaty with Russia. The Anglo-Russian treaty alarmed Frederick the Great, for he feared an eventual conflict with Russia for control of the Baltic and Poland. In January, 1756, the Prussian king concluded an alliance with Britain which detached her from Russia. The alliance between England and Prussia isolated France and gave the Austrian chancellor, Kaunitz, exactly the opportunity he had been waiting for. What Austria needed in order to avenge herself on Frederick and to regain Silesia was an ally with a large army; what Austria needed was the alliance of France, not Britain. Using the Anglo-Prussian alliance as an argument, Kaunitz convinced Louis XV and his mistress, Madame de Pompadour, to drop the traditional Bourbon-Habsburg feud in favor of a working partnership. The last act of the Diplomatic Revolution occurred when Russia joined the Franco-Austrian alliance. Russia had taken a minor part in the War of the Austrian Succession as an ally of England. In the new war the Russian Empress Elizabeth (1741-1762) entered as the full partner of Austria and France. Elizabeth hated Frederick the Great and feared his aggression all the more now that he had deprived her of her English ally.

The Seven Years' War, 1756-1763

The great coalition against Prussia was still in the process of formation when the war itself began. In May, 1756, Britain and France made official the state of hostilities already existing between them in North America. Three months later, Frederick the Great took the offensive against the coalition menacing him. Once more the powers were engaged in a war that was really two separate wars—one continental, the other naval and colonial.

In the European campaigns of the Seven Years' War, both Frederick the Great and the Hohenzollern system faced a most formidable test. Prussia confronted the forces of Austria, France, and Russia, whose combined population was more than fifteen times larger than her own. She had almost no allies except for the British, who supplied financial subsidies but little actual military assistance. The traditions established by the Great Elector and developed by Frederick William I and Frederick the Great enabled the nation to survive. The King himself set a commanding example. In 1757, he wrote to one of his French friends:

I am assaulted from every side. Domestic trials, secret afflictions, public misfortunes, approaching calamities—such is my daily bread. But do not imagine I am weakening. If everything collapses I should calmly bury myself beneath the ruins. In these disastrous times one must fortify oneself with iron resolutions and a heart of brass. It is a time for stoicism: the disciples of Epicurus would find nothing to say. . . .*

Frederick's "iron resolution" and "heart of brass" led him to adopt any expedient, fair or unfair, to gain his ends. To fill up the depleted ranks of his army, he ruthlessly violated international law by impressing soldiers from Prussia's smaller neighbors, Mecklenburg and Saxony. Since British subsidies covered only a fraction of his war expenses, he seized Saxon, Polish, and Russian coins. Then he melted them down, kept for Prussian use a large part of their precious metallic content, recast them with baser metals, and returned them to circulation.

A final factor, perhaps the most important one of all, in saving Prussia was the shakiness of the apparently formidable coalition arrayed against her. Most fortunately for Frederick, his enemies were never capable of exploiting their military successes to deliver a knock-out blow. Russia's generals were timid, and those of France and Austria were sometimes downright incompetent. Moreover, the French, the strongest of the allies, had to fight a two-front war, in Europe and overseas, and did not possess the financial resources to do both. The grand alliance created by Kaunitz suffered to an unusual extent from the friction, mistrust, and cross-purposes that customarily beset wartime coalitions. Indeed, his coalition did not last out the war. When Elizabeth of Russia died in January, 1762, she was succeeded by Tsar Peter III, a passionate admirer of Frederick the Great, who at once deserted Elizabeth's allies and placed Russia's forces at Frederick's disposal; no wonder the grateful Prussian king called him "a divine ruler to whom I ought to erect altars!" Although Peter III occupied the Russian throne for only a few months (see Chapter XVII), his brief rule marked a decisive turning in the Seven Years' War. In 1763 Prussia won her war, and Austria agreed to the Peace of Hubertusburg confirming the Hohenzollern retention of Silesia.

Meanwhile, Frederick's British partner was gaining a smashing victory abroad. Actually, Britain made a very lame start in the Seven Years' War, suffering setbacks on almost every front during the first year and a half of the fighting. At sea, the British lost the important Mediterranean base of Minorca in the Balearic Islands, a disaster to which the home government contributed by sending (too late) reinforcements (too few) under Admiral Byng (a poor choice). Byng was unfairly saddled with the whole blame and was executed—"in order to encourage the others," Voltaire observed ironically. In North America, the British lost the outpost of Oswego on Lake Ontario and fumbled an attack on Louisburg, the key to French Canada. The most dramatic of Britain's misfortunes occurred in India. In June, 1756, the Nawab of Bengal, a native ally of the French, crowded 146 British prisoners into one small room with only two windows. The result was the

---

* Quoted in G. P. Gooch, *Frederick the Great* (London, 1947), 41.

atrocious "Black Hole" of Calcutta, thus described by an officer of the English East India Company:

It was the hottest season of the year, and the night uncommonly sultry. . . . The excessive pressure of their bodies against one another, and the intolerable heat which prevailed as soon as the door was shut, convinced the prisoners that it was impossible to live through the night in this horrible confinement; and violent attempts were immediately made to force the door, but without effect, for it opened inward.

At two o'clock not more than fifty remained alive. But even this number were too many to partake of the saving air, the contest for which and for life continued until the morn. . . .

An officer, sent by the nawab, came . . . with an order to open the prison. The dead were so thronged, and the survivors had so little strength remaining, that they were employed near half an hour in removing the bodies which lay against the door before they could clear a passage to go out one at a time; when of one hundred and forty-six who went in no more than twenty-three came out alive, —the ghastliest forms that were ever seen alive.*

William Pitt turned the tide in favor of Britain. The "Great Commoner" (so named because of his long and able service in the House of Commons) was the most famous representative of the Whig oligarchy. In Parliament he sat for Old Sarum, a notorious "rotten" borough. The grandson of "Diamond" Pitt, a merchant prince who had made a fortune in India, Pitt consistently supported the interests of the City. In the late 1730's he had led the Whig rebels against Walpole's pacifistic policy, the "Boy Patriots" who forced Britain into the War of Jenkins' Ear. Now Pitt's great war ministry (1757-1761) organized victory from defeat. It ended the shilly-shallying policies of the cabinets that had held office since Walpole's downfall in 1742. Budget deficits rose higher and

higher, but Pitt used his personal and business connections with the City to assist the successful placement of government loans. He gave the Anglo-Prussian alliance meaning by sending Frederick substantial subsidies and placing English forces in Hanover under an able Prussian commander in place of the bungling Duke of Cumberland, a son of George II. Everywhere Pitt replaced blundering generals and admirals; everywhere he transformed the character of the naval and colonial war by his energetic measures. In 1759, the Royal Navy defeated both the Atlantic and Mediterranean squadrons of the French fleet.

Britain's overwhelming command of the seas enabled her to continue trading abroad at a prosperous pace, while French overseas trade rapidly sank to one-sixth of the prewar rate. And it prevented the French colonies abroad from receiving even the modest amount of money and meager reinforcements available for them at home. Cut off from significant aid and faced by generally superior British forces, the French outposts of empire fell in quick succession. In Africa, Britain's capture of the chief French slaving station ruined the slavers of Nantes in the mother country. In India, Clive and others avenged the "Black Hole" by punishing the Nawab of Bengal and capturing the key French posts. In the West Indies, the French lost all their sugar islands, except for Santo Domingo. In North America, the 65,000 French, poorly supplied and poorly led, were helpless against the million British colonists, fully supported by their mother country. Fort Duquesne was taken at last, and very appropriately renamed after Pitt, and the British went on to other triumphs in the war that the colonists called "French and Indian." In Canada, the English General Wolfe took Louisburg (1758) and in the next year, 1759, lost his life but won immortal fame in a great victory on the Plains of Abraham outside Quebec. When the remaining

_____
* R. Orme, *A History of the Transactions of the British Nation in Indostan* (London, 1778), II, sec. 1, 74 ff.

French stronghold, Montreal, fell in 1760, the doom of France's American empire was sealed.

This rain of victories led the British to expect sweeping gains in the postwar settlement; their expectation was soon disappointed. Pitt had won the war, but he did not make the peace: the accession of the obstinate and ambitious George III in 1760 led to the dismissal of the Prime Minister the next year. In the Peace of Paris, 1763, ending hostilities between Britain and France, the successors of Pitt allowed France to retain stations in India and on the African slave coast. Above all, they permitted the French to recover their islands in the West Indies. The restoration of the old order in the Caribbean was a great relief to British planters, whose markets had been flooded by sugar from the captured French island of Guadaloupe during the war. But to outraged patriots it seemed as though Britain had let the grand prize slip through her fingers.

Though France retained her Caribbean empire, she lost all her possessions on the mainland of North America. Britain secured both Canada and the vast disputed territories between the Appalachians and the Mississippi. Moreover, she also obtained Florida from Spain, which had committed the folly of joining France in 1762 when the war was already lost. And, though the French retained a few trading posts in India, they were not allowed to fortify them

or to continue their old policy of manipulating the politics and rivalries of native states. For Britain the Seven Years' War marked the beginning of a virtually complete ascendancy in India; for France it marked the end of an era of empire-building.

VII: Conclusion: The International Balance in Review

The peace settlements of Hubertusburg and Paris ended the greatest international crisis between the death of Louis XIV and the outbreak of the French Revolution. New crises were to arise soon after 1763, as the next chapter will show in detail —in 1768, a Russo-Turkish war; in 1772, the first partition of Poland; in 1775, the American War of Independence. The new crises in the East did not fundamentally alter the international balance; they accentuated shifts that had long been under way. And American independence, though it was the first step in the emergence of a great power, did not produce immediate world-shaking results. Britain lost the thirteen colonies, but otherwise maintained the maritime and imperial supremacy won in 1763.

The international balance established in 1763, then, remained largely unchanged down to 1789. In the incessant struggle for power during the eighteenth century the victorious states were the strongest states—Britain, Prussia, and Russia. The states that were less fit—France, Spain, Austria, Turkey—survived, though they sometimes suffered serious losses. The weakest units, Poland and Italy—as a Spanish diplomat observed early in the century—were being "pared and sliced up like so many Dutch cheeses."

The Duke of Choiseul, the foreign minister of Louis XV during the Seven Years' War, remarked that the "true balance of power resides in commerce." Choiseul's remark held a large measure of truth, but not the whole truth. The world struggle between Britain and the Bourbon empires did much to justify the mercantilist view that conceived of international relations in terms of incessant competition and strife. According to the mercantilist doctrine of the fixed amount of trade, a state could enlarge its share of the existing supply only if it reduced the shares held by rival states, either through war or, in time of peace, through smuggling and retaliatory legislation. All this was borne out by the War of Jenkins' Ear and by British success, and French failure, in maintaining overseas trade during the course of the Seven Years' War.

In the warfare of the eighteenth century, it is evident, economic motives and economic resources often played a more decisive role than they had played in the past. Yet the modern concept of economic warfare was only beginning to take shape. During the War of the Austrian Succession, London brokers supplied both insurance and information on naval movements to enemy shipowners. Moreover, economic factors did not fully explain all the changes in the international balance during the century. The stakes involved in the conquests of Peter the Great, or in the aggressions of Frederick, or in the strife over Poland and Italy, were not commercial. The stakes were the aggrandizement of Romanovs, Hohenzollerns, and Habsburgs, and of the nobles and Junkers supporting these dynasties. The stakes were on occasion as relatively trivial as the determination of Elizabeth Farnese to get royal, or at least ducal, thrones for Carlos and Philip.

War, of course, mirrors not only the economy but also all the other institutions of the society that wages it. Efficient utilization of Prussian economic resources played its part in the victories of Frederick the Great. But his success depended still more on qualities that had little to do with economics—his own brilliant and ruthless leadership, the discipline of the society that he headed. The case of Britain seemingly offers the most compelling evidence to support Choiseul's contention, as Pitt turned her formidable financial and commercial assets to practical advantage. Yet Pitt himself is not to be explained in simple economic terms. His accession as prime minister in the dark days of 1757, like that of Churchill in the dark days of 1940, was made possible by a political system that enabled the right man to come forward at the right time. And, like Churchill in the Second World War, like another capable British statesman, George Canning, in the 1820's, Pitt could have boasted that he had "called the New World into existence to redress the balance of the old."

To the Old World the eighteenth century, despite all its wars, brought an interlude of comparative calm between the age of religious strife that had preceded it and the storms of liberalism and nationalism that were to be loosed by the French Revolution. The prospect in 1715, the prospect of long years of peace and quiet, had not, after all, been wholly deceptive. The Seven

Years' War of the eighteenth century, for example, did not begin to equal in destructive force the Thirty Years' War of the seventeenth. Much more was involved here than the relative shortness of the Seven Years' War. Few of the combatants now had the feeling of fighting for a great cause, like Catholicism or Protestantism or national independence. The fighting itself was conducted in a more orderly fashion than it had been a hundred years before; soldiers were better disciplined, and armies were better supplied; troops lived off the land less often and no longer constituted such a menace to the lives and property of civilians. Even warfare indicated that this was the century of order and reason, the Age of the Enlightenment.

Reading Suggestions
on the International Balance in the Eighteenth Century

(Asterisk indicates paperbound edition.)

GENERAL ACCOUNTS

The following three volumes in the "Rise of Modern Europe" series (Harper) provide the best detailed introduction to eighteenth-century war and politics and have very full bibliographies: P. Roberts, *The Quest for Security, 1715-1740* (1947); W. L. Dorn, *Competition for Empire, 1740-1763* (1940); L. Gershoy, *From Despotism to Revolution, 1763-1789* (1944).

The New Cambridge Modern History, Vol. VII, *The Old Regime* (Cambridge Univ. Press, 1957). Useful chiefly for reference.

A. Sorel, *Europe under the Old Regime* (Ritchie, 1947). A celebrated and stimulating survey of the international balance in the eighteenth century.

SPECIAL STUDIES

E. F. Heckscher, *Mercantilism,* 2 vols., rev. ed. (Macmillan, 1955). The most famous work on the topic; controversial, but a mine of information on eighteenth-century economic developments.

H. Heaton, *Economic History of Europe,* rev. ed. (Harper, 1948), and S. B. Clough and C. W. Cole, *Economic History of Europe,* 3rd ed. (Heath, 1952). Two good general economic histories.

J. F. C. Fuller, *A Military History of the Western World* (Funk & Wagnalls, 1954-1956). The second volume of this helpful work covers the seventeenth and eighteenth centuries.

W. E. H. Lecky, *A History of England in the Eighteenth Century,* 8 vols. (Longmans, Green, 1883-1890). A celebrated detailed account.

B. Williams, *The Whig Supremacy, 1714-1760* (Clarendon, 1939). A competent modern survey.

J. H. Plumb, *England in the Eighteenth Century* (*Penguin, 1951). A good, brief, popular account. Plumb has also written several more specialized studies of eighteenth-century England, all of them very helpful: *Sir Robert Walpole: The Making of a Statesman* (Houghton, Mifflin, 1956); *The First Four Georges* (Macmillan, 1957); and *Chatham* (Macmillan, 1953), an account of the elder William Pitt.

H. Dodwell, *Dupleix and Clive* (Methuen, 1920). A balanced treatment of the imperial antagonists in India.

J. Lough, *An Introduction to Eighteenth Century France* (Longmans, Green, 1960). A first-rate general account.

A. M. Wilson, *French Foreign Policy during the Administration of Cardinal Fleury* (Harvard Univ. Press, 1936). A sound monograph, and one of the relatively few good books in English on the France of Louis XV.

G. P. Gooch, *Louis XV* (Longmans Green, 1956); and N. Mitford, *Madame de Pompadour* (Hamish, Hamilton, 1954). Recent but rather old-fashioned evaluations of these celebrities.

F. Ford, *Robe and Sword* (Harvard Univ. Press, 1953). An instructive study of the French aristocracy in the eighteenth century.

S. B. Fay, *The Rise of Brandenburg-Prussia to 1786* (Holt, 1937: A Berkshire study). An admirable little volume, packed with information.

F. L. Carsten, *The Origins of Prussia* (Clarendon, 1954). A monograph that carries the story through the reign of the Great Elector.

F. Schevill, *The Great Elector* (Univ. of Chicago, 1947). A helpful study of the founder of the Hohenzollern despotism.

R. R. Ergang, *The Potsdam Führer* (Columbia Univ. Press, 1941). A splendid study of Frederick William I of Prussia.

C. T. Atkinson, *A History of Germany, 1715-1815* (Methuen, 1908). An older but informative account, particularly full on war and diplomacy.

E. Schuyler, *Peter the Great*, 2 vols. (Scribner's, 1884). An old but excellent account by an American diplomat and scholar.

V. Klyuchevsky, *Peter the Great*, L. Archibald, trans. (St. Martin's, 1958). Translation of a famous account by a pre-revolutionary Russian scholar.

B. H. Sumner, *Peter the Great and the Emergence of Russia* (Macmillan, 1951). A very good introductory account.

B. H. Sumner, *Peter the Great and the Ottoman Empire* (Blackwell, 1949). A short and meaty monograph.

C. A. Petrie, *Diplomatic History, 1713-1933* (Hollis and Carter, 1946). A useful introductory manual.

J. A. Marriott, *The Eastern Question: An Historical Study in European Diplomacy*, 4th ed. (Clarendon, 1940). A standard survey.

A. Goodwin, ed., *The European Nobility in the Eighteenth Century* (Black, 1953). Very suggestive essays.

A. Young, *Tours in England and Wales* (London School of Economics and Political Science, 1932). A good selection from the reports of this prolific and perceptive observer.

Lady Mary W. Montagu, *Letters* (Dutton, 1906: Everyman edition). By perhaps the best of the century's letter-writers; particularly valuable on the Habsburg and Ottoman empires.

G. P. Gooch, *Courts and Cabinets* (Knopf, 1946). A graceful introduction to the memoirs of some of the great personages of the era.

H. Fielding, *Tom Jones* (many editions). The greatest of social novels on eighteenth-century England.

T. Smollett, *The Adventures of Roderick Random* (Oxford Univ. Press, 1952). A novel that provides a good contemporary account of life in His Majesty's Navy two centuries ago.

D. Merejkowski, *Peter and Alexis* (Putnam, 1905). A most interesting novel, dramatizing the conflict between the policies of the great Tsar and his son.

CHAPTER XVI

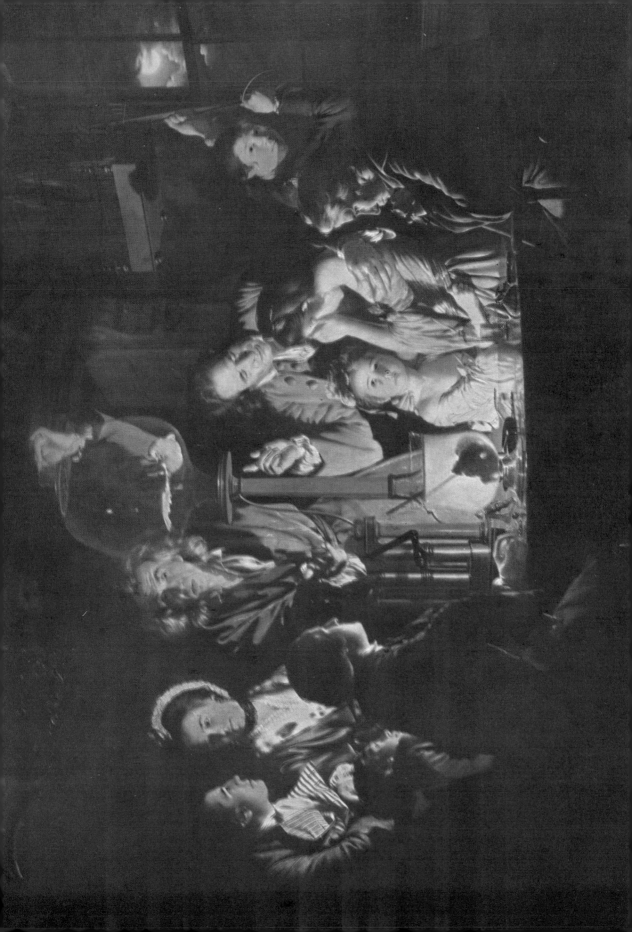

The Eighteenth Century: The Enlightenment

CHAPTER XVII

I: Basic Principles and Traits

REASON, NATURAL LAW, progress—these were the key words in the vocabulary of the eighteenth century, the Age of the Enlightenment. This was the age when many believed that human reason could free men of all their ills and lead them infallibly to perpetual peace, utopian government, and a perfect society. *Reason* would discover the *natural laws* regulating existence, thereby insuring the *progress* of the human race.

The prophets of this optimistic creed were known by the French name of *philosophes*, though they were not all French and few of them were philosophers in the strict sense. The *philosophes* were publicists, economists, political scientists, and social reformers. They derived their basic principles from the scientists and rationalists of the seventeenth century; their belief in the powers of human reason came largely from John Locke, their faith in natural law from Sir Isaac Newton.

The Inheritance from Locke and Newton

John Locke (1632-1704) wrote a celebrated defense of England's Glorious

49

Revolution, the *Two Treatises of Government* (1690). Men are, he contended, "by nature all free, equal, and independent"; they submit to government not because they acknowledge any divine right on the part of the monarch but because they find it convenient to do so. They make a compact or contract to be governed, a contract that they may break by revolutionary action if the monarch does not live up to his obligations, as James II had not lived up to his. To strengthen his case against absolute monarchy, Locke outlined a new psychology. Defenders of political and religious absolutism contended that the inclination to submit to absolute authority was present in men's minds when they were born. In the *Essay concerning Human Understanding* (1690), Locke denied the existence of innate ideas. He called the new-born mind a *tabula rasa*, a blank slate:

> Let us then suppose the mind to be . . . white paper, void of all characters, without any ideas. How comes it to be furnished? . . . To this I answer, in one word, from EXPERIENCE. . . . Our observation employed either about *external sensible objects, or about the internal operations of our minds perceived and reflected on by ourselves, is that which supplies our understandings with all the materials of thinking.* These two are the fountains of knowledge, from whence all the ideas we have, or can naturally have, do spring.*

In other words, the two "fountains of knowledge" were environment, rather than heredity, and reason, rather than faith. Locke's matter-of-fact outlook and his empiricism (reliance on experience) place him among the rationalists. He believed that human reason, though unable to account for everything in the universe, explains all that men need to know. "The candle that is set up in us," he wrote, "shines bright enough for all our purposes."

Locke pointed the way to a critical examination of the Old Régime. The *philosophes* read and admired both his political

---

* *Essay* (New York, 1947), Bk. II, Ch. I.

writings and his *Essay concerning Human Understanding*. They applied his test of common sense to existing social and economic institutions and found them complex and absurd. Locke's psychology suggested that teachers could make human institutions over by remolding the thinking of the rising generation. In effect, the *philosophes* sought the right kind of chalk to use on the "blank slates" of impressionable young minds; they found it in the concept of the Newtonian world-machine.

Indeed, the *philosophes* seized on Newton's scientific discoveries as revelations of ultimate truth. Those who could follow Newton's mathematical calculations read him in the original Latin or in translation; those who could not, turned to *Newtonianism for Ladies* or some other popularization. In the principle of gravitation, Newton had disclosed the natural force that held the universe together; he made the universe make sense. The eighteenth century believed that other Newtons would find comparable laws governing and explaining all phases of human activity. The *philosophes* pictured themselves as the Newtons of statecraft, justice, and economics who would reduce the most intricate institutions to formulas as neat as Sir Isaac's own mathematical laws and principles. The world, they concluded, resembled a giant machine. Hitherto, men had hampered its operations because they did not understand the machinery. Once they grasped the basic laws by which it ran, they would at last permit the "world-machine" to function smoothly and beneficently.

The optimism of the age was summed up in a book aptly entitled *The Progress of the Human Mind* (1794), written by the *philosophe* Condorcet when he was in hiding during the French revolutionary Reign of Terror. Condorcet asked:

> If men can predict, with almost complete assurance, the phenomena whose laws are known to them . . . , why should it be regarded as a vain enterprise to chart, with some

degree of probability, the course of the future destiny of mankind by studying the results of human history? Since the only basis of belief in the natural sciences is the idea that the general laws, known or unknown, regulating the phenomena of the universe are regular and constant, why should this principle be any less true for the development of the intellectual and moral faculties of man than for the other operations of nature? *

"Nature has placed no bounds on the perfecting of the human faculties," Condorcet concluded, "and the progress of this perfectibility is limited only by the duration of the globe on which nature has placed us." †

Eighteenth-century Science

The technological and scientific advances of the eighteenth century further strengthened the faith in natural law and progress. The *philosophes* hailed both the practical achievements in industry and agriculture and the rapidly expanding frontiers of the pure sciences. Biology and chemistry were now starting to acquire a modern look. Linnaeus (1707-1778), a Swede, demonstrated the natural laws of family relationships in biology. He took every known plant and animal, classified it by species, then bracketed several species together in a genus—and so on up the hierarchy of classification from genus through order to class. Thus arose a practice that biologists still follow in assigning every specimen two Latin names, that of its genus and that of its species.

The modern science of chemical analysis began with Black and Lavoisier. Joseph Black (1728-1799), a Scottish professor, exploded the old theory that air was composed of a single element. He proved the existence of several air-like substances or gases. Lavoisier (1743-1794), a French chemist and physicist, continued Black's study of gases, invented the name "oxygen," and demonstrated that water was made up of oxygen and hydrogen. He asserted that all substances were composed of a relatively few basic chemical elements, of which he identified twenty-three.

Meanwhile, astronomy and physics were consolidating the great advances they had made in the seventeenth century. Laplace (1749-1827), the "Newton of France," rounded out the great Isaac's investigation of celestial mechanics and explained the movement of the solar system in a series of mathematical formulas and theorems. The versatile American, Benjamin Franklin (1706-1790), showed that electricity and lightning were really the same thing. By flying a kite during a thunderstorm in Philadelphia, Franklin obtained an electrical charge in a key attached to the kite-string. This experiment aroused a lively interest across the Atlantic, and was repeated at Versailles for the instruction of the French royal family.

Almost everybody who was anybody attempted experiments. Voltaire made a serious hobby of chemistry; Montesquieu studied physics; and a noble French lady reportedly kept a cadaver in her carriage so that she might employ her travels profitably in dissection and the study of anatomy. Almost every state in Europe had its *philosophes* and its royal society or learned society to promote the progress of knowledge. Intellectual life was by no means limited to the capitals and big cities; France, for example, by the middle of the eighteenth century, possessed many provincial academies, well equipped with reading rooms and lending libraries. In those days, scientists and *philosophes* paid scant attention to national frontiers. Even when their countries were at war, they kept on visiting and corresponding—a striking example of the eighteenth century's disposition toward "business as usual."

---

* Condorcet, *Esquisse d'un Tableau Historique des Progrès de l'Esprit Humain* (Paris, n.d.), 203. Our translation.

† *Ibid.*, 5.

French Leadership

With roots reaching back into seventeenth-century England and with branches extending to Scotland, Germany, Italy, Spain, and the New World, the Enlightenment fully exhibited the cosmopolitan qualities of its century. Yet French leadership set an indelible stamp upon the whole Enlightenment. The Age of Reason marked the high point of French cultural hegemony, and it was the American *philosophe,* Thomas Jefferson, who maintained that every man had two homelands, "his own and France." The French language endowed the Enlightenment with its medium of communication; the *salons* of Paris did much to set the tone of enlightened writing; the great *Encyclopédie,* edited and published in France, provided the vehicle for enlightened thought.

By the eighteenth century, French was the accepted international language. Louis XIV had raised it to supremacy in diplomacy; Racine and the other great seventeenth-century writers had made it pre-eminent in literature. There was much justice in the claim that "a dangerous work written in French is a declaration of war on the whole of Europe." Almost everywhere in Europe, even in distant Russia, rulers, aristocrats, and intellectuals preferred French to their native tongues. In 1783, it was not a French society but the Academy of Berlin that conducted a competition for the best reply to the question, "What has made the French language universal?" The prize-winning essay furnished the answer in a single sentence: "Precise, popular, and reasonable, it is no longer just French; it is the language of humanity."

The Parisian *salons* taught writers precision, reasonableness, and the popular touch. The *salon* was the reception room of a large private home where guests assembled for a long afternoon or evening of conversation under the guidance of the hostess, usually a wealthy woman from the nobility or the upper bourgeoisie. Although the *salons* were sometimes snobbish and superficial, they often practiced a kind of democracy. They afforded young *philosophes* the opportunity to receive a hearing—and to obtain a square meal; they welcomed and, if the need arose, protected new men and new ideas. Their pressure affected the outcome of elections to the French Academy, which they helped to bring under the control of the *philosophes* in the 1760's.

The great organ of the *philosophes* was the *Encyclopédie,* which published the first of its many volumes in 1751. Its roster of 160 contributors amounted to a Who's Who of the Enlightenment; it included Voltaire, Montesquieu, Rousseau, Condorcet, Quesnay, and Turgot. For years the editor-in-chief, Denis Diderot (1713-1784), put in a fourteen-hour working day, every hour devoted to his crusade for reason and progress. He commissioned the drawing of superb plates showing the details of the new industrial machines and even learned to operate some of the machines himself. Diderot and his associates had no intention of issuing an objective compendium of information; their purpose was didactic: to expose what they judged to be the vices of the existing order, especially its superstition and intolerance, and to instruct the public in the virtues of natural law and the wonders of science. As Diderot explained in the article on the word "encyclopedia," they aimed to assemble knowledge

...in order that the labors of past centuries should not prove useless for succeeding centuries; that our descendants, by becoming better informed, will at the same time *become happier and more virtuous....* °

In the face of formidable opposition, the *Encyclopédie* accomplished its purpose. The Church condemned its materialism and its highly critical and skeptical articles on religious issues. Louis XV tried to keep it

---

° (Our italics. Our translation.)

from being printed and circulated. The publishers, without consulting Diderot, reduced some of the controversial articles to a meaningless hash by ordering the printers to cut out all passages likely to cause offense. The indignation of Diderot, the ridicule leveled by the *philosophes* at their detractors, the intense curiosity of the subscribers to the *Encyclopédie,* and the help extended to the editors by Choiseul, the foreign minister, and by Madame de Pompadour, herself an "enlightened" spirit —all frustrated the censors and facilitated the completion of publication. In the small provincial city of Dijon alone there were sixty copies of the *Encyclopédie* in 1768.

II: The Reform Program of the *Philosophes*

Laissez-Faire Economics

The articles written for the *Encyclopédie* by François Quesnay (1694-1774) announced the economic program of the Enlightenment. The versatile Quesnay, biologist, surgeon, and personal physician to Louis XV and Madame de Pompadour, headed a group of thinkers and publicists who adopted the name of Physiocrats, believers in the rule of nature. The new title revealed the basic outlook of the school. The Physiocrats felt certain that they would, as Quesnay claimed, discover natural economic laws "susceptible of a demonstration as severe and incontestable as those of geometry and algebra."

"The sovereign and the nation should never lose sight of the fact that the land is the only source of wealth, and that agriculture increases wealth." * Thus Quesnay introduced the new Physiocratic concept of natural wealth and attacked the mercantilist habit of equating money and wealth. "The riches which men need for their livelihood do not consist of money; they are rather the goods necessary both for life and for the annual production of these goods." Mercantilist states, Quesnay argued, committed a whole series of errors by placing excessive emphasis on specie. They tried to regulate commerce, when they should have allowed it free play. They made goods more expensive by levying tariffs and other indirect taxes, whereas they should have collected only a single, direct tax on the net income from land.

"*Laissez faire, laissez passer,*" the Physiocrats urged—live and let live, let nature take its course. They repudiated the controlled economy of mercantilism and enunciated the "classical" or "liberal" doctrine of the free economy. The state ought not interrupt the free play of natural economic forces. Most of all, it ought not to interfere with private property, so necessary for the production of agricultural wealth.

The classic formulation of laissez-faire was made by the Scotsman, Adam Smith (1727-1790), in his *Inquiry into the Nature and Causes of the Wealth of Nations* (1776). Adam Smith carried to vigorous completion the Physiocrats' attack on mercantilism. It was wrong to restrict imports by tariffs for the protection of home industries:

It is the maxim of every prudent master of a family never to attempt to make at home what it will cost him more to make than to buy. The tailor does not attempt to make his own shoes, but buys them of the shoemaker. The shoemaker does not attempt to make his own clothes, but employs a tailor. . . .

---

* Quesnay, "Maximes Générales du Gouvernement Economique d'un Royaume Agricole," in E. Daire, ed., *Physiocrates* (Paris, 1846), I, 82. Our translation.

What is prudence in the conduct of every private family, can scarce be folly in that of a great kingdom. If a foreign country can supply us with a commodity cheaper than we ourselves can make it, better buy it of them with some part of the produce of our industry. . . .*

Like the Physiocrats, Adam Smith attributed the wealth of nations to the production of goods; but, as befitted a citizen of Britain, the leading commercial and industrial state of the day, he took a less agrarian view of the matter. For Adam Smith, production depended less on the *soil* (the Physiocratic view) than on the *labor* of farmers, craftsmen, and mill-hands. Finally, in the most famous sentence of *The Wealth of Nations*, Adam Smith reduced government to the status of a passive policeman:

According to the system of natural liberty, the sovereign has only three duties to attend to; . . . first, the duty of protecting the society from the violence and invasion of other independent societies; secondly, the duty of protecting, as far as possible, every member of the society from the injustice and oppression of every other member of it, or the duty of establishing an exact administration of justice; and thirdly, the duty of erecting and maintaining certain public works and certain public institutions, which it can never be for the interest of any individual, or small number of individuals, to erect and maintain.†

The mercantilists had exalted the state over the individual and had declared a ceaseless trade warfare among nations. Adam Smith and the Physiocrats, reversing the emphasis, proclaimed both the economic liberty of the individual and free trade among nations to be natural laws. This laissez-faire program of the Enlightenment marked a revolutionary change in economic thought and foreshadowed the individualism of the industrial revolution in the nineteenth century (see Chapter XX). It did not, however, revolutionize the economic policies of the great powers. Mercantilism

retained much vitality, as we shall shortly see; Turgot, for instance, the chief practical exponent of Physiocratic doctrine, tried vainly to free French agriculture and French business from restrictions during his brief tenure as chief minister in the 1770's (see Chapter XVIII). The Physiocrats forgot what so many *philosophes* forgot. They overlooked the difficulty of adjusting the complexities of politics and the realities of human nature to the simple and reasonable dictates of natural law.

Justice

The attitude of letting nature take its course, so evident in laissez-faire economics, also determined the outlook of the Enlightenment on questions of justice. The *philosophes* believed that man-made legislation prevented the application of the natural laws of justice. They were horrified by the cumbersome judicial procedures of the Old Régime and by its unjust and antiquated statutes. New law-givers were needed to humanize and simplify the legal codes, and a new science was needed to make the punishment of crime both humane and effective.

The new science, which anticipated much of modern sociology, was promoted by Cesare Beccaria (1738-1794), an Italian *philosophe* and the author of the *Essay on Crimes and Punishments* (1764). Beccaria formulated three natural laws of justice. First, punishments should aim to

. . . prevent the criminal from doing further injury to society, and to prevent others from committing the like offence. Such punishments, therefore, . . . ought to be chosen, as will make the strongest and most lasting impressions on the minds of others, with the least torment to the body of the criminal.*

Second, justice should act speedily

. . . because the smaller the interval of time between the punishment and the crime, the

---

* *Wealth of Nations*, Bk. IV, Ch. 2.
† *Ibid.*, Bk. IV, Ch. 9.

* *Essay on Crimes and Punishments*, Ch. 12.

stronger and more lasting will be the association of the two ideas of *Crime* and *Punishment.* °

And last:

Crimes are more effectively prevented by the *certainty* than by the *severity* of the punishment. . . . The certainty of a small punishment will make a stronger impression than the fear of one more severe. . . . †

Beccaria attacked both torture and capital punishment because they diverged so sharply from these natural laws. Torture, he claimed, falsely assumed that "pain should be the test of truth, as if truth resided in the muscles and fibres of a wretch in torture." Jail sentences, not execution, should be imposed as punishments. Beccaria asserted, however, that punishment alone was not enough. The best method of preventing crime was to "let liberty be attended with knowledge," to "perfect the system of education."

Education

In education, too, the Old Régime failed to pass the tests of reason and natural law. The *philosophes* deplored both the almost universal ecclesiastical control of education and the heavy emphasis placed upon theology, Greek and Latin, and ancient history. They demanded more consideration of science, modern languages, and modern history. Diderot declared:

Under the name of rhetoric, is taught the art of speaking before teaching the art of thinking; and that of good expression before the students have any ideas to express.

. . .

Under the name of physics, are wearisome disputations about the elements of matter and the terrestrial systems; but not a word about natural history nor good chemistry, very little about the motion and fall of bodies, very few

experiments, still less anatomy and no geography.°

Jean-Jacques Rousseau (1712-1778) proposed the most drastic reform of education. Rousseau was a rebel. He rebelled against the strict and disciplined society of his birthplace, Calvinist Geneva. He rebelled against the intensive bookish studies he had been forced to pursue as a young boy, and against the polite conventions he later encountered in the Paris *salons*. The result of Rousseau's rebellion was *Emile* (1762), half treatise and half romance, a long and fervent plea for progressive education.

Emile had two heroes—Emile, the student, and Rousseau himself, the teacher. The training that Rousseau prescribed for his pupil departed in every particular from eighteenth-century practice:

Life is the trade I would teach him. When he leaves me, I grant you, he will be neither a magistrate, a soldier, nor a priest; he will be a man.†

Rousseau followed a policy of laissez-faire toward his pupil. He did not argue with Emile, or discipline him, or force him to learn reading at any early age. Emile observed the world of nature from first-hand experience, not in books. He learned geography by finding his own way in the woods (with his tutor's help), and agriculture by working in the fields. And when in his teens he was finally taught to read, his first assignment was Defoe's *Robinson Crusoe*, "the best treatise on an education according to nature."

Rousseau's educational program had many faults. It was impractical, for it assumed that every child should have the undivided attention of a tutor twenty-four hours a day. And it fostered the total and apparently permanent dependence of pupil upon teacher; when Emile married and be-

---

° *Ibid.*, Ch. 19.
† *Ibid.*, Ch. 27.

° Quoted in F. de la Fontainerie, *French Liberalism and Education in the Eighteenth Century* (New York, 1932), 208-209.
† *Emile*, Everyman ed. (New York, 1911), 9.

came a father, he implored his tutor to remain at his post: "I need you more than ever now that I am taking up the duties of manhood." And yet *Emile* was a most important book. Rousseau returned to some of the great ideas of the past—to the Renaissance concept of the universal man and to the ancient Greek ideal of the sound mind in the sound body. Pestalozzi (1746-1827), a Swiss educator and humanitarian, adapted the theoretical program of *Emile* to the practical requirements of the classroom and set a powerful example by teaching geography, drawing, and other useful novelties in his experimental school. Still more influential was the reaction of Pestalozzi against the barracks tradition of drilling lessons into the student through a combination of endless repetition and bodily punishment. Pupils of the twentieth century may thank the educational reformers of the eighteenth for having discovered the natural law that children should be treated as children, not as miniature adults.

Attitudes toward Religion

The attacks on clerical teaching methods formed part of a vigorous and growing body of criticism aimed at the role of the clergy in the Old Régime. The *philosophes* denounced what they regarded as fanaticism, intolerance, and superstition; their favorite target was the Jesuit Order, the symbol and instrument of militant Catholicism. Pressure for the dissolution of the Jesuits gained the support of Catholic monarchs and became so great that Pope Clement XIV yielded. In 1773, he dissolved the Society of Jesus, which was not to be revived until half a century later (see Chapter XIX).

Many *philosophes* not only championed tolerance but also adopted the religious attitude called *deism* (from the Latin *deus*, god). Deist doctrines arose in seventeenth-century England, the England of the Civil

Wars and Newtonian science, where the deists sought settlement of religious strife by the use of reason rather than by resort to arms. All men, they asserted, could agree on a few broad religious principles. Since the Newtonian world-machine implied the existence of a mechanic, the deists accepted God as the creator of the universe and as the ultimate judge of human conduct. But they denied, or at least doubted, that God answered prayer or extended grace. For the deists, the role of God lay in the dim past and the distant future, not the immediate present.

Voltaire (1694-1778) was the chief exponent of deism in France and the coiner of the anticlerical watchword, *"Ecrasez l'infâme!"*—crush the infamous thing, stamp out bigotry and superstition, perhaps even organized religion itself. Voltaire, indeed, was a one-man Enlightenment who devoted his prodigious energy and talent to the propagation of new ideas. Plays, tales, epic poems, histories, essays, and letters poured from his pen. Clear, witty, and often bitingly satirical, they were immensely popular, not least when they had to be printed outside France or under an assumed name in order to evade the censorship. Voltaire made Frenchmen aware of Newton, Locke, and Shakespeare. He set a new style in history-writing by discussing economics and culture as well as the usual politics and wars, thus foreshadowing the "new history" and the "surveys of civilization" of the twentieth century.

Voltaire experienced intolerance at first hand. As a young man he spent a year in the gloomy Paris prison, the Bastille, and three years of exile in England because he had criticized the French government and had offended a member of the privileged nobility. The relative religious and political freedom of Britain made an immense impression on the refugee:

If there were just one religion in England, despotism would threaten; if there were two religions, they would cut each other's throats;

Thirteen glimpses of Voltaire (from drawings by Hubert).

but there are thirty religions, and they live together peacefully and happily.*

Back in France, Voltaire carried on a lifelong crusade for toleration. In 1762, a Protestant merchant of Toulouse, Jean Calas, was accused of having murdered his son to prevent his conversion to Catholicism. Calas died in agony, his body broken on the wheel. Voltaire discovered that the accusation against Calas was based on rumor, and that the court condemning him had acted from an anti-Protestant hysteria that lumped all Huguenots together as enemies of the French state and willing tools of France's enemies. Voltaire campaigned for three years until the original verdict was reversed, and the name of Calas was cleared.

The existence of evil—of injustices like that which broke Calas—confronted the Age of Reason with a major problem. Few of the *philosophes* accepted the traditional Christian teaching that evil arose from original sin, from the fall of Adam and Eve. If God were purely benevolent, they asked,

---

* *Lettres Philosophiques,* Letter No. 6. Our translation.

why then had he created a world in which evil so often prevailed? Could a perfect God produce an imperfect creation? Alexander Pope, Voltaire's English contemporary, contended that this was the best of all possible worlds:

> All Nature is but Art, unknown to thee;
> All chance, direction which thou canst not see;
> All discord, harmony not understood;
> All partial evil, universal good:
> And, spite of Pride, in erring Reason's spite,
> One truth is clear, *Whatever is, is right.*

But Voltaire, in his most famous story, *Candide,* ridiculed the optimists and commented with bitter sarcasm on the disasters that abounded in the best of all possible worlds. A real disaster had inspired the writing of *Candide*—the great earthquake, tidal wave, and fire that engulfed the city of Lisbon on November 1, 1755, and killed upwards of 10,000 people.

Deism enabled Voltaire to effect a kind of reconciliation between a perfect God and the imperfect world. As a deist, Voltaire believed that God was indeed the Creator:

When I see a watch . . . , I conclude that an intelligent being arranged the springs of this mechanism so that the hand should tell the time. Similarly, when I see the springs of the human body, I conclude that an intelligent being has arranged these organs to be kept and nourished in the womb for nine months; that the eyes have been given for seeing, the hands for grasping, etc.*

But, Voltaire concluded, there was no way to determine whether or not God would attempt to perfect his creation. On one point Voltaire had no doubts: he never questioned the social usefulness of religion. "Man," he stated, "has always needed a brake." For the masses of people almost any religion, no matter how primitive, was better than atheism.

Baron d'Holbach (1723-1789), however, the most outspoken atheist of the Enlightenment, argued that men did not need the brake of religion; simple self-interest would suffice to make them behave morally. For Holbach, organized religions were sinister institutions that thwarted the benevolent operations of reason and natural law, and God was merely a "phantom of the imagination," whose existence was denied by the evils and imperfections of the world that he had supposedly created. A wealthy man, Holbach extended the hospitality of his *salon* to all comers, including Jesuit refugees from anticlerical persecution. His tolerance impressed his contemporaries more than his atheism did, and the *philosophes* continued to prefer deism, that halfway house between belief and disbelief.

Political Thought: Montesquieu

"In politics as in religion toleration is a necessity," decreed Voltaire. To him, therefore, tolerant Britain seemed utopia, and he paid the British constitution the

most flattering compliment at the command of his age when he claimed that it "might have been invented by Locke, Newton, or Archimedes." Montesquieu (1689-1755), a French lawyer and *philosophe*, set out to analyze the political virtues of Britain. In his major work, *The Spirit of the Laws* (1748), Montesquieu sought to define the principles underlying both the British constitution and governments in general. He began with the very sensible premise that no one system of government suited all countries. Laws, he wrote,

. . . should be in relation to the climate of each country, to the quality of its soil, to its situation and extent, to the principal occupation of the natives, whether husbandmen, huntsmen, or shepherds: they should have relation to the degree of liberty which the constitution will bear; to the religion of the inhabitants, to their inclinations, riches, numbers, commerce, manners, and customs.*

Montesquieu cautioned against supposing that old customs and traditions could simply be legislated out of existence, and he cited the telling example of Peter the Great's failure to establish western ways in Russia by decree.

In spelling out the influence of heredity and environment upon forms of government, Montesquieu concluded that republics were best suited to the small and barren countries, limited monarchies to the middle-sized and more prosperous, and despotisms to vast empires. Britain, being middle-sized and prosperous, was quite properly a monarchy limited by aristocracy. The hereditary nobility sat in the House of Lords; a kind of nobility of talent, the elected representatives, composed the Commons. All this was admirable in Montesquieu's view, for he pronounced the mass of people "extremely unfit" for government. If only France had let her aristocrats retain their old political functions, she would never have sunk to her present low state.

---

* *Le Traité de Métaphysique*, Ch. II. Our translation.

* *The Spirit of the Laws*, Thomas Nugent, trans. (New York, 1949), Bk. I, Ch. 3.

Montesquieu found another key to the political superiority of Britain in his famous concept of checks and balances. In Parliament, Lords and Commons checked each other. In the government as a whole, the balance was maintained by means of *the separation of powers:*

When the legislative and executive powers are united in the same person, or in the same body of magistrates, there can be no liberty; because apprehensions may arise, lest the same monarch or senate should enact tyrannical laws, to execute them in a tyrannical manner. Again, there is no liberty, if the judiciary power be not separated from the legislative and executive. Were it joined with the legislative the life and liberty of the subject would be exposed to arbitrary control; for the judge would be then the legislator. Were it joined to the executive power, the judge might behave with violence and oppression.*

Montesquieu, however, failed to see that the British constitution was moving, not toward the separation of powers, but toward their concentration in the House of Commons; the cabinet was becoming the instrument for the assertion of legislative supremacy over the executive. In fairness, it must be added that these developments were far from obvious in the mid-eighteenth century when *The Spirit of the Laws* appeared.

Montesquieu likewise ran into trouble when he tried to derive specific corollaries from his general theorem about the influence of climate and geography on human institutions. Autocracy and Catholicism, he asserted, flourish in the Mediterranean states because they are endowed with a warm climate and rich natural resources. Moderate government and Protestantism, conversely, are at home in the colder and harsher environment of northern Europe. The facts did not always confirm this rule about North and South. Freedom-loving Protestant Britain and Holland behaved in good northern fashion; but if Montesquieu

* *The Spirit of the Laws,* Bk. XXI, Ch. 6.

were correct, Prussia—barren, northern, Protestant Prussia—should have been a citadel of liberty, not the stronghold of Hohenzollern absolutism. By jumping to conclusions from insufficient evidence, Montesquieu committed a fault common in the Enlightenment. But he avoided another fault common to the age. He had too firm a grasp on political realities to assume that governments either were or should be the same everywhere. Later political thinkers made good use of the comparative methods introduced by *The Spirit of the Laws* and refined Montesquieu's judgments on the interrelationship of geography, religion, and politics.

Political Thought: Rousseau

From the standpoint of contributions to American history, as we shall see, Montesquieu and Locke proved to be the most important political thinkers of the Enlightenment. From the standpoint of European history, the most important is Jean-Jacques Rousseau, whose ideals inspired the radicals of the French Revolution. Rousseau started with a sweeping generalization very typical of the Enlightenment. Whereas nature dignifies man, he contended, civilization corrupts him; man would be corrupted less if civilized institutions followed nature more closely. This was the theme that ran through many of Rousseau's principal writings. In *Emile,* he placed it at the heart of his program for educational reform; in the *Discourse on the Moral Effects of the Arts and Sciences* (1750), he used it to win a competition set by the Academy of Dijon. The Academy asked: Has the restoration of the arts and sciences had a purifying effect upon morals? Certainly not, the prize-winner answered; it has nearly ruined them.

In a second discourse, *On the Origin of the Inequality of Mankind* (1755), Rousseau blamed the vices of civilization on private property:

The first man who, having enclosed a piece of ground, bethought himself of saying, 'This is mine,' and found people simple enough to believe him, was the real founder of civil society. From how many crimes, wars, and murders, from how many horrors and misfortunes might not any one have saved mankind, by pulling up the stakes, or filling up the ditch, and crying to his fellows: 'Beware of listening to this imposter; you are undone if you once forget that the fruits of the earth belong to us all, and the earth itself to nobody.' *

Men accepted laws and governors in order to protect their property:

... They had too many disputes among themselves to do without arbitrators, and too much ambition and avarice to go long without masters. All ran headlong to their chains, in hopes of securing their liberty; for they had just wit enough to perceive the advantages of political institutions, without experience enough to enable them to foresee their danger.†

Government was evil, Rousseau concluded, but a necessary evil. "What, then, is to be done? Must societies be totally abolished? ... Must we return again to the forest to live among bears?" No, civilized men could not return to a primitive existence, could "no longer subsist on plants or acorns, or live without laws and magistrates." **

Rousseau attempted a positive answer in his major political work, *The Social Contract* (1762), in which he strove to reconcile the liberty of the individual and the institution of government through a new and revolutionary version of the contract theory of government. Earlier theories of contract, from the Middle Ages to John Locke, had hinged on the agreement between the people to be governed, on the

one hand, and a single governor or small group of governors, on the other. Earlier theories postulated a political contract. Rousseau's contract, as the title of the book suggested, was social. A whole society agreed to be ruled by its *general will*:

Each of us puts his person and all his power in common under the supreme direction of the general will, and, in our corporate capacity, we receive each member as an indivisible part of the whole.*

"Each individual," Rousseau continued, "may have a particular will contrary or dissimilar to the general will which he has as a citizen." If the individual insists on putting self-interest above community interest, he should be obliged to observe the general will. "This means nothing less than that he will be forced to be free." † Thus, the general will was ethical as well as political in nature, for it represented what was best for the whole community, what the community *ought* to do.

Formulating the general will, Rousseau believed, was the business of everybody. The power of legislation, he stated, could never be properly transferred from the people to an institution like the British Parliament:

The deputies of the people ... are not and cannot be its representatives; they are merely its stewards, and can carry through no definitive acts. Every law the people has not ratified in person is null and void—is, in fact, not a law. The people of England regards itself as free; but it is grossly mistaken; it is free only during the election of members of Parliament. As soon as they are elected, slavery overtakes it, and it is nothing.**

Executing the general will, however, could legitimately be the business of a smaller group. Like Montesquieu, Rousseau believed that the number of governors should

---

* "Discourse on the Origin of Inequality," in *The Social Contract and Discourses,* Everyman ed. (New York, 1913), 192.
  † *Ibid.,* 205.
  ** *Ibid.,* 228.

---

* *The Social Contract,* Everyman ed. (New York, 1913), 13.
  † *Ibid.,* 15.
  ** *Ibid.,* 78.

vary inversely with the size and resources of the state—monarchy for the wealthy, aristocracy for the state "of middling size and wealth," and democracy for the small and poor. Rousseau doubted, however, that any state was ready for the absolute form of democracy in which the many actually execute the laws. "Were there a people of gods, their government would be democratic. So perfect a government is not for men." *

Rousseau was quite aware that *The Social Contract* was not a manual of practical politics. At another time, when he made suggestions for the reform of the Polish government, his counsels were distinctly moderate. While favoring the abolition of the liberum veto (see above, p. 35), he recommended that the elective monarchy be retained, that the nobles keep many of their privileges but acquire a new sense of duty, and that the serfs be liberated but only after they had been taught responsibility. The influence of Rousseau, however, has come from *The Social Contract;* it has not been exerted on the side of moderation. Almost every radical political doctrine in the past two centuries has owed something to Rousseau. Socialists justify collectivism on the basis of his attacks on the evils of private property and of his insistence that "the fruits of the earth belong to us all." Patriots and nationalists hail him as an early prophet of the creed that nations do—and should—differ. Throughout his writings he referred to "the dear love of country." In admonishing the Poles, he put great stress on the renewal of their national spirit through education and patriotic festivals; *The Social Contract* concluded with a plea for the establishment of a "civil religion." The moral code of early Christianity might be retained, Rousseau allowed, but the State should no longer have to compete with the Church for the allegiance of citizens.

* *The Social Contract*, 56.

Many have found in Rousseau a man who exalted the national welfare over particular individual wills, who indeed worshiped the State. Dictators have used the doctrine of the general will to sanction the methods of the police state. Without bothering about the niceties of ascertaining the general will, the dictator simply assumes that he has a special knowledge of it, as in the case of Hitler's celebrated "intuition." In forcing his subjects to obey his dictates, he is "forcing them to be free," in accordance with the precept of Rousseau.

But Rousseau was also the prophet of democracy and individualism. The authoritarian interpretation overlooks both his personal animosity toward the Old Régime and the strong idealistic tone of his writings. "Were there a people of gods, their government would be democratic." This declaration has inspired the democratic disciples of Rousseau from the French Revolution on down to the present. The people are not gods? Then they must be trained in godliness, and Rousseau himself suggested how this might come about. *Emile* showed how education could help, and *The Social Contract* implied that men might one day become so virtuous that they would always follow the general will naturally and would no longer have to be "forced to be free."

Enlightened Despotism

Many *philosophes*, however, sought a short cut to utopia, a political method that was more practicable than that of Rousseau or Montesquieu and that could operate within the framework of existing monarchical institutions. They found the answer in enlightened despotism. The Physiocrats, the chief theorists of enlightened despotism, had little sympathy with the concern of Montesquieu and Rousseau over the status of the legislative power. In the Physiocratic view, God was the legislator, nature preserved the divine legislation, and the sole duty of government lay in administering these natural laws. Democracy and aristocracy alike had the fatal weakness of delegating administrative authority to individuals whose transient selfish aims clashed with the permanent welfare of the nation. By contrast, the Physiocrats explained, the personal interests of hereditary monarchs coincided with national interests through their "co-ownership" of the territories under their rule. Because kings were best qualified to work for the true national interest, they should be despots, not in any sinister sense but on the model of the tyrants of ancient Greece or the best of the Renaissance despots. Like a new Solon, the enlightened despot should unearth the natural laws decreed by God and clear away the accumulation of artificial, man-made law that was choking progress.

This program of enlightened despotism won an immediate, enthusiastic response from European monarchs. And no wonder: it afforded them the chance to pose as the champions of reason and progress while pressing their age-old fight to make royal authority more absolute. In the late eighteenth century self-styled "enlightened despots" occupied many European thrones—in Prussia, Frederick the Great; in Austria, Joseph II; in Russia, Catherine the Great; in Spain, Charles III; in Sweden, Gustavus III; and still others. Their lands were proving-grounds not only for the theory of enlightened despotism but also for the whole reform program of the Enlightenment.

III: The Enlightened Despots

Prussia:
Frederick the Great

Of all the monarchs of eighteenth-century Europe, Frederick II, the Great, of Prussia (1740-1786), appeared best attuned to the Enlightenment. As a youth, he rebelled against the drill-sergeant methods of his father, Frederick William I (see Chapter XVI). He delighted in music, and played the flute, which he took with him everywhere, even on military campaigns. An attentive reader of the *philosophes,* he exchanged letters with them and brought Voltaire to live for a time as his pensioner in his palace at Potsdam near Berlin. He wrote a pamphlet, *Anti-Machiavel,* denouncing the immorality of *The Prince.* And he himself laid down the fundamental requirements for an enlightened despot:

Princes, sovereigns, kings are not clothed with supreme authority to plunge with impunity into debauchery and luxury. . . . [The prince] should often remind himself that he is a man just as the least of his subjects. If he is the first judge, the first general, the first financier, the first minister of the nation, . . . it is in order to fulfill the duties which these titles impose upon him. He is only the first servant of the state, obliged to act with fairness, wisdom, and unselfishness, as if at every instant he would have to render an account of his administration to his citizens.°

Frederick was indeed "the first servant of the state," shunning luxury, wearing stained and shabby clothing, and toiling long and hard at his desk. But did he also act with "fairness, wisdom, and unselfishness"? Despite his *Anti-Machiavel,* Frederick conducted foreign and military affairs in true Machiavellian style; his invasion of Silesia (see Chapter XVI) would have aroused the envy of Caesar Borgia. At

° "Essai sur les Formes de Gouvernement et sur les Devoirs des Souverains." *Oeuvres Posthumes* (Berlin, 1788), VI, 64, 83-84. Our translation.

home, closeted in his Potsdam palace where he conducted the business of state by correspondence, he drove his subordinates like slaves. Viewed as a general, a diplomat, and the master mechanic of Prussian administration, Frederick the Great was efficient and successful, but he was scarcely enlightened. His claim to be an enlightened despot must rise or fall on the record of his social and economic reforms.

No Physiocrat coud have done more than Frederick to improve Prussian agriculture. From England he imported clover, crop rotation, and the iron plow, which turned up the soil more effectively than the old wooden share. He drained the swamps of the lower Oder Valley, opened up farms in Silesia and elsewhere, and brought in 300,000 immigrants to populate the new lands. After the ravages of the Seven Years'

Frederick the Great of Prussia playing the flute at his Potsdam palace.

War, he gave the peasants tools, stock, and seed to repair their ruined farms. He nursed along the admirable German tradition of scientific forestry, then in its infancy.

Yet Frederick was hostile to the doctrine of laissez-faire and cut imports to the bone in order to save money for support of the army. His mercantilism stimulated the growth of Prussian industry, particularly the textiles and metals needed by the army. But it also placed a staggering burden of taxation on his subjects and produced several economic absurdities. For instance, Frederick tried to make Prussia grow its own tobacco, for which the climate was not suited. And, since the German taste for coffee required a large outlay of money abroad, he laid a heavy duty on imported coffee beans, and even established a special corps of French "coffee-smellers" to trap smugglers.

The religious and social policies of Frederick the Great likewise combined the Age of Reason at its most reasonable with the Old Régime at its least enlightened. A deist, Frederick prided himself on religious tolerance. He invited Jesuits to seek refuge in Prussia and protected the minority of Catholics in his predominantly Protestant kingdom, urging them to build their church steeples as high as they liked. He even boasted that he would build a mosque in Berlin if Moslems wanted to settle there. Yet the same Frederick consistently practiced anti-Semitism. He levied special heavy taxes on his Jewish subjects and tried to exclude them from the professions and from the civil service. Jews, he alleged, were "useless to the state."

Frederick the Great rendered Prussians a great service by his judicial reforms. He reduced the use of torture; he put an end to the curious custom of taking appeals from the ordinary courts to university faculties and instituted a regular system of appellate courts. He mitigated the venal practice of bribing judges by insisting that "tips" received from litigants be placed in common pool from which each judge should draw only his fair share.

Yet the same Frederick took a positively medieval view of the merits of social caste. He did nothing to loosen the bonds of serfdom that still shackled much of the Prussian peasantry. When he gave the peasants material assistance and urged them to learn the "three r's," his aims were severely utilitarian. Peasants were to learn nothing beyond the rudiments of reading and writing; otherwise, they might become discontented with their station in life. Regarding the middle class, too, with disdain, Frederick respected only the landed nobility and gentry. And even the favored Junkers did not escape Frederick's penny-pinching. Although he appointed only Junkers as army officers, he discouraged their marriage because every officer's wife represented a potential widow to whom the state would owe a pension.

An English diplomat who knew Frederick well observed:

I have seen him weep at tragedy, known him to pay as much care to a sick greyhound as a fond mother to a favourite child; yet the next day he has given orders for the devastation of a province or by a wanton increase of taxes made a whole district miserable. He is so far from being sanguinary that he scarce ever suffers a criminal to be punished capitally; yet in the last war he gave secret orders to . . . his army surgeons rather to run the risk of a wounded soldier dying than by the amputation of a limb increase the number and expense of his invalids.*

Frederick seemed constitutionally incapable of getting along with other people. Voltaire, the great French champion of toleration, could not tolerate the strain of daily association with Frederick. When the King requested Voltaire to edit his indifferent French poetry, Voltaire made a cutting remark about washing the dirty linen of royalty; Frederick retorted by comparing his

_____

* Sir James Harris, quoted in G. P. Gooch, *Frederick the Great* (New York, 1947), 142.

guest to an orange, to be sucked dry and thrown away. The two men eventually renewed their friendship through the less demanding medium of correspondence. Frederick despised and neglected his wife. His subjects sighed with relief at the news of his death, and his will directed that he be buried beside his pet dogs. "Such," remarked a French observer, "is the last mark of contempt which he thought proper to cast upon mankind."

This judgment is too harsh, or at least too one-sided. Actually, Frederick embodied two often conflicting political philosophies—the humane principles of the Enlightenment and the Spartan traditions of the Hohenzollerns. He was an enlightened despot only so far as the precepts of the Age of Reason could be reconciled to the realities of Hohenzollern kingship.

Austria: Maria Theresa and Joseph II

Frederick's decisive victory in the War of the Austrian Succession (see Chapter XVI) laid bare the basic weaknesses of the Habsburgs' dynastic empire. The Empress Maria Theresa (1740-1780) at once saw the need for reform and often took as her model the institutions of her hated but successful Hohenzollern rival. She increased taxes, especially on the nobility, strengthened the central government at the expense of local aristocratic assemblies, and obliged the non-German provinces to accept the hegemony of the German officials and the German language of Vienna. Maria Theresa employed both force and charm to get her way. The nobles of Hungary momentarily forgot their anti-German tradition when the beautiful and spirited empress, her infant son in her arms, personally appealed to their chivalry in the crisis of the War of the Austrian Succession.

The Empress was the first housewife of the realm as well as the first servant of the state. She was the mother of sixteen children, and she adored and respected Francis, her grasping, fickle husband. Francis' will provided a large bequest for his mistress; his widow executed its terms to the letter. Maria Theresa, however, was a devout Catholic, fundamentally out of sympathy with the Age of Reason. "Lady Prayerful," as Catherine the Great called her, banned the works of Rousseau and Voltaire and even forbade the circulation of the Catholic *Index*, lest that list of forbidden books pique the curiosity of her subjects.

The Habsburg representative of enlightened despotism was Joseph II, the eldest son of Maria Theresa, named by her to be emperor and co-regent on the death of Francis in 1765. Frederick the Great wrote Voltaire an estimate of the new emperor:

Born in a bigoted court, he has cast off its superstition; raised in magnificence, he has assumed simple manners; nourished on incense, he is modest; burning with a thirst for glory, he sacrifices his ambition to the filial duty which he executes scrupulously; and, having had only pedantic teachers, he still has enough taste to read Voltaire and to appreciate his merits.*

Frederick exaggerated only a little. Though Joseph complained that there were "too many notes" in Mozart's operas, he was a true disciple of the Age of Reason. Earnest and industrious in the highest degree, he promised to make "philosophy the legislator of my empire." Maria Theresa thwarted Joseph until her death in 1780; for fifteen years, mother and son had clashed, particularly over Joseph's anticlericalism. As a loving son Joseph mourned the passing of Maria Theresa, but as a *philosophe* he welcomed the release from her tutelage. The impatient emperor, now the sole ruler of Austria, plunged into activity; during his ten-year reign (1780-1790), eleven thousand laws and six thousand decrees issued from Vienna.

Joseph at once reversed his mother's religious policy. Calvinist, Lutheran, and Orthodox gained full toleration for the first time in the history of Catholic Austria. And, with a generosity unparalleled in Habsburg annals, the Emperor took measures to end the ghetto existence of the Jews. He exempted Jews from paying special taxes and from wearing the yellow patch as a badge of inferiority. Joseph brought the Catholic Church under strict state control, making himself rather than the pope the arbiter of church activities in Austria. He encouraged what he considered socially useful in Catholicism and dealt ruthlessly with what he judged superfluous and harmful. Thus he established hundreds of new churches and at the same time reduced the number of religious holidays. He called monks "the most dangerous and useless subjects in every state," and promised to convert "the monk of mere show into a useful citizen." He cut in half the number of monks and nuns and, of 2100 monasteries and nunneries, he suppressed 700, chiefly those run by the contemplative orders. Houses actively engaged in educational or charitable work were generally spared. The government sold or leased the lands of the suppressed establishments, applying the revenue to the support of the hospitals that were beginning to earn Vienna its reputation as a great medical center.

Unlike Frederick the Great, Joseph really believed in popular education and social equality. His government provided the teachers and textbooks for primary schools. More than a quarter of the school-age children in Austria actually attended school—the best record of any country in late eighteenth-century Europe. Everyone in Vienna, high and low, was invited to visit the Prater, the great public park of the capital, the entrance to which bore the inscription, "A place of pleasure for all men, prepared for them by their friend." The new Austrian

* "Correspondance avec les Souverains," *Oeuvres Complètes de Voltaire* (Paris, 1828), LXXIV, 37. Our translation.

Emperor Joseph II of Austria, working a plow.

legal code followed the recommendations of Beccaria in abolishing capital punishment and most tortures and in prescribing equality before the law. Aristocratic offenders, like commoners, were sentenced to stand in the pillory and to sweep the streets of Vienna. Joseph's peasant policy marked the climax of his equalitarianism. He freed the serfs, abolished most of their obligations to manorial lords, and deprived the lords of their traditional right of administering justice to the peasantry.

Joseph's economic policies incorporated both the new doctrines of the Physiocrats and the old practices of mercantilism. He levied high tariffs on imports, yet experimented with the collection of a single tax on land as recommended by Quesnay. In politics, however, Joseph adhered to his mother's Germanizing program. He customarily spoke German, patronized German writers, and made the French playhouse in Vienna a German-language theater. He attempted to terminate the autonomous rights of his non-German possessions, such as Bohemia, Hungary, and Belgium.

Both Joseph's enlightened reforms and his Germanizing policies aroused mounting opposition. Devout peasants, almost oblivious of his well-meaning attempts to improve their social and economic status, keenly resented his meddling with old religious customs. The nobility clamored against his equalitarian legislation; in the case of the single-tax experiment, their opposition was so violent that he had to revoke the decree a month after it was issued. Hungary and Belgium rose in open rebellion against his centralizing efforts and forced him to confirm their autonomous liberties. In foreign policy, too, the ambitious—and in this instance unenlightened—plans of Joseph II miscarried. By supporting Russian plans for the dismemberment of Turkey (see below, p. 79), Austria gained only a narrow strip of Balkan territory. Joseph also attempted to annex lands belonging to the important South German state of Bavaria, where the death of the ruling family opened another of those succession quarrels so common in the eighteenth century. He was thwarted by Frederick the Great, who was determined to check any advance of Habsburg power in Germany. In the late 1770's, Austria and Prussia fought a war—or, more exactly, glared at each other in the mismanaged "Potato War," in which the troops spent most of their time foraging for food. Joseph secured only a tiny fragment of the Bavarian inheritance.

Joseph II worked himself to death, as one of his friends observed, by "governing too much and reigning too little." The Emperor defended his habit of interfering personally in the details of government:

What else can I do in this country devoid of mind, without soul, without zeal, without heart in the work? I am killing myself because I cannot rouse up those whom I want to make work; but I hope I shall not die until I have so wound up the machine that others cannot put it out of order, even if they try to do so.*

Joseph never got the machine properly wound up; he could not implant in the Austrian bureaucracy the almost inhuman Prussian discipline that was needed to serve his purposes. Joseph II died unshaken in the conviction that he had pursued the proper course, yet believing that he had accomplished nothing. In the judgment of posterity, however, Joseph appears as the most truly enlightened despot. In ten years he attempted more than Frederick attempted in almost half a century. Though some of his major reforms, like the abolition of serfdom, were repealed soon after his death, others survived him, helping to transform the Habsburg lands into a more modern centralized state.

Sweden and Spain

Among the lesser enlightened despots, Gustavus III of Sweden and Charles III of Spain ranked high. Gustavus III (1771-1792), the nephew of Frederick the Great, was the most theatrical monarch of the century. While he distracted Swedish party leaders at the opera one evening, his soldiers staged a *coup* that enabled him to revive the royal authority and to dissolve the factions that dominated Swedish politics after Charles XII. Gustavus announced in ringing speeches his devotion to the Age of Reason. In economics and religion, his en-

* Quoted in Prince de Ligne, *His Memoirs, Letters, and Miscellaneous Papers* (Boston, 1902), II, 132.

lightenment outdistanced that of his uncle in Prussia, for he removed obstacles to both domestic and foreign trade and extended toleration to Jews as well as to the non-Lutheran Christian sects. Success, however, turned the head of Gustavus III. As he became more and more arbitrary, the nobles determined to recover their old power; in 1792, he was assassinated at a masquerade in Stockholm, and oligarchy resumed its feeble course in Sweden.

Charles III (1759-1788), Elizabeth Farnese's "Baby Carlos," inherited the Spanish crown on the death of his half-brother. He was a remarkably homely monarch, but he had already been seasoned in the struggle against feudal and clerical conservatism by a long and successful apprenticeship as King of Naples. In Spain, Charles III ener-

King Charles III of Spain in hunting costume, by Goya.

getically advanced the progressive policies begun by his father, Philip V (see Chapter XVI). Though a pious Catholic, he objected strongly to the political activities of the Church and even expelled the Jesuits from the native country of their founder, Loyola. He reduced the authority of the aristocracy, extended that of the Crown, and made Spain more nearly a centralized national state. He curbed the privileges of the great sheep-ranchers, whose almost unlimited grazing rights blighted Spanish agriculture. To enliven the torpid Spanish economy, he undertook irrigation projects, reclaimed waste lands, and established new roads, canals, banks, and textile mills. The results were astonishing: Spain's foreign commerce increased fivefold during the reign of Charles III. His successors, however, abandoned many of his forward-looking policies, and Spain soon began to slip back into her old ways, though the influence of the Enlightenment at least remained alive.

The Limitations of Enlightened Despotism

The problem of succession, in fact, sapped the whole structure of enlightened despotism. So long as monarchs came to the throne by the accident of their birth, there was nothing to prevent the unenlightened mediocrity from succeeding the enlightened despot. This happened in Spain, in Sweden, and in Prussia, where the great Frederick was followed by his nephew, Frederick William II (1786-1797), who was little better than a nincompoop. The principal exception occurred in Austria, where the enlightened Leopold II (1790-1792), fresh from an effective apprenticeship in Tuscany, salvaged some of the reforms of his brother, Joseph II.

Even the least of the enlightened despots improved a few of the bad features of the Old Régime. But not even the best of them struck a happy balance between enlightenment and despotism. Joseph II was too doctrinaire, too inflexible in his determination to apply the full reform program of the Age of Reason. Frederick, on the other hand, obsessed with the desire to strengthen the Crown, helped to entrench the power of the Junkers, who were hostile to the whole Enlightenment. And in Russia, the century after the death of Peter the Great provided another striking illustration of the limitations of enlightened despotism.

IV: Russia, 1725-1825

The Fate of the Autocracy, 1725-1762

When Peter the Great died, he left a tangled family situation in which nobody could truly decide who was his legitimate successor. Over the course of the next thirty-seven years, the throne changed hands seven times. The succession zigzagged across the family tree of the Romanovs: first to Peter's widow, who ruled as Empress Catherine I (1725-1727); then to Peter's young grandson, son of the murdered Alexis (see above, p. 34), who became Peter II (1727-1730); then to Peter's niece, who reigned as Empress Anne (1730-1740); then to Anne's great-nephew, Ivan VI, who was only eight weeks old when he began his one-year reign (1740-1741); then to Peter's own daughter by Catherine I, the Empress Elizabeth (1741-1762); then to Elizabeth's nephew, Peter III, who reigned only for six months in 1762;

and finally to Peter III's brilliant young widow, who became Catherine II, the Great (1762-1796), and dominated Russia as Peter I himself had done. More important than the individuals who governed Russia between Peter and Catherine the Great were the social forces contending for power, and the social processes at work in an autocracy suddenly deprived of its autocrat and for so long unable to produce a new one. In the series of palace overturns, the guards' regiments founded by Peter exercised a decisive influence. The service nobility, no longer restrained by the tsar, now entered into its era of dominance.

On the death of Peter the Great, his immediate circle, particularly Menshikov (see Chapter XVI), had every reason to fear the passage of the throne to the nine-year-old Peter, son of Alexis, and possible heir to the loyalties of the old nobility who had hated Peter the Great. Menshikov therefore strongly supported his one-time mistress, the Empress Catherine I, and succeeded in rallying to her side members of the guards who had come to like her while on campaigns. Catherine herself took little interest in affairs of state, and in practice Menshikov ran Russia during the two years of her reign. He tried to make himself secure by appointing a six-man "Supreme Privy Council" at the top of the administration, and to perpetuate his power he even planned to marry his daughter to the young heir, the future Peter II. On the death of Catherine I in 1727, he took the eleven-year-old boy into his house, where he proceeded to make him an alcoholic, as his father had been.

But Menshikov's arrogance had alienated even his followers. By 1728, the old boyars, led by the families of Dolgoruky and Galitsyn, had captured the throne, and Menshikov was exiled. Two Dolgoruky princes put themselves on the Supreme Privy Council, and the young Peter was engaged to a member of their family. The ascendancy of boyar families marked the return to supreme influence of a group that had been losing power ever since the days of Ivan the Terrible. Their plans were brought into crisis by the sudden death of Peter II on the very day scheduled for his coronation (January 19, 1730).

Their program can be studied in the conditions they submitted to the new candidate for the throne, Anne, the widow of the Duke of Courland. Summoning her from her petty Baltic principality, the Dolgoruky and the Galitsyns demanded that she sign these "Articles" before she take the throne. By their terms, she undertook never to marry or name an heir, and to continue the Supreme Privy Council, which by now had eight members, including four Dolgoruky and two Galitsyns. She further swore not to make peace or war, levy taxes, confer ranks in the army above that of colonel, or spend state funds without the specific consent of the Council. Moreover, the Councillors claimed for themselves supervision over the guards' regiments. This insistence on limiting the power of the new Empress reflected the outraged feelings of the old boyars, who had long been claiming the right to be consulted on all matters of state. The entire program was the most explicit constitutional destruction of all that Peter the Great had striven for. Anne signed the "Articles." Had she kept to their provisions, Russia would have embarked on an era of boyar oligarchy.

But the military-service nobility looked with horror at the prospect of taking orders indefinitely from the small group of old boyars. And the service gentry had the power, in the guards' regiments. What they wanted was an autocrat who would loosen the bonds that Peter the Great had forged for them. And so, when one of the Supreme Privy Councillors, the clever German Ostermann, convinced Anne that she need not abide by the Articles, the gentry in its armed might supported him. Anne simply tore up the Articles; thus, the attempt to creat an oligarchy of the two great families failed. The gentry now had the real power in Russia.

Anne allowed her lover, the German adventurer Biren, and a flock of Germans to obtain the most influential positions in the state. The secret police, briefly abolished after the death of Peter the Great, was now revived, and many thousands suffered torture, exile, and death at its hands. When Anne died, the German favorites fell out among themselves. Ostermann, a man of real ability, together with an excellent soldier, Marshal Münnich, brought about Biren's downfall and exile; then Ostermann forced Münnich out. Meanwhile, the tsar was the infant Ivan VI, whose mother, a German princess, acted as regent, and was so lazy that she lounged in her bedroom without the energy even to put on her clothes. Foreign intrigue produced the next shift in the imperial title. The French were deeply anxious to terminate the power of Ostermann, who had been instrumental in cementing an alliance between Russia and France's traditional enemy, Austria. A clever French ambassador played on the patriotic feelings of the guardsmen, disgusted with the behavior of the Germans at court. In 1741 a guards' *coup* brought to the throne the daughter of Peter the Great, Elizabeth. The infant Ivan VI vanished into a prison cell with his indolent mother.

Elizabeth inherited her father's lust for life but not his brains or interest in affairs of state. A succession of lovers had kept her busy all her life, and her habits did not change when she came to the throne. Though owning thousands of splendid dresses, she lived rather sluttishly in grubby palaces and enjoyed most of all a rousing peasant banquet with plenty to drink and lots of rustic music. Important state papers languished for days because the Empress could not be bothered to read them, much less sign them. Though she proclaimed her intention of restoring her father's methods of rule, she had no clear conception of what these had been. In an autocracy the autocrat has to take an interest in the affairs of state and assume responsibility for them; this Elizabeth did not do, and Russia drifted.

Soon after her accession, Elizabeth proclaimed her nephew, the half-mad Peter, heir to the throne. In 1745 he married a clever little German princess, the future Catherine II. Peter III, as he became after his succession in January, 1762, has had a bad "press"; he surely was not unusually intelligent, but was hardly the utter lunatic portrayed in the memoirs of his celebrated wife, who loathed him. The chief trouble with Peter seems to have been his great admiration for Prussia and his dislike of Russia. His effort to introduce rigid discipline on the Prussian model into the Russian army and his hatred for the influential guards' regiments cost him the friends he needed most. He could have played his war-games with his toy soldiers, held court-martials on rats whom he convicted of gnawing cardboard fortresses, and swilled his favorite English beer with impunity, and he would not have been any worse than many another tsar. But to drill the guards in the Prussian manner was unforgivable. So a new palace revolution took place, and Peter was eventually murdered by one of Catherine's lovers. The Empress' own role in his overthrow is still obscure.

Nobles and Serfs, 1730-1762

A deeply dissatisfied social group that had the power to make and unmake autocrats naturally had a program for the redress of its own grievances. Once the gentry had enabled Anne to tear up the Articles in 1730, it began strenuous efforts to realize the program and thus to emancipate itself from the servitude riveted upon it by Peter. Anne repealed the law requiring the noble to leave his estate intact to one of his sons. She founded a military school for noblemen's sons, graduation from which entitled one to a commission; no longer did young gentlemen have to start their careers in the ranks, as under Peter. Anne shortened the terms of service from life to twenty-five years, and exempted one son of every family with at least two sons, so that there would be one member of each generation able to look after the estate.

Simultaneously came a deepening of the authority of the nobles over the serfs. The proprietors became the government's agents for the collection of the poll tax. Serfs could no longer obtain their freedom by enlisting in the army and could not engage in trade or purchase land without written permission from their masters. Masters could deport their serfs to Siberia, and might punish them physically in any way they wished. Moreover, under Elizabeth, a series of laws restricted the right to own serfs to those who were already nobles. Thus the class that had been open to new recruits under Peter was closed by his daughter.

In 1762, finally, Peter III decreed that the nobles no longer need serve at all unless they wished to do so; except in the midst of a war, they might resign any time they chose. It was little wonder that some of the nobles proposed to erect a solid gold statue of Peter III. To understand the revolutionary nature of this liberation of the nobles from a duty to serve, we must remember that they had historically obtained their lands and serfs only on condition that they would serve. Now they kept their lands and serfs but had no obligations. Yet the service that had been hated when it was compulsory became fashionable now that it was optional; there was really little else for a Russian noble to do except serve the state. In contemplating all this, a great Russian historian remarked that the logic of history would have properly required that all serfs be liberated the day after the nobles were released from their duty to serve. But nothing could have been further

from the thoughts of Peter III or of any other Russian leader.

In these middle decades of the eighteenth century, successive waves of foreign influence affected the Russian nobility. It was not only the influx of foreigners that brought in western habits; it was also the involvement of Russia in the European wars of the period, and the increased travel abroad by Russians. Especially under Elizabeth, when the hated Germans disappeared from court, the way was clear for the French to exert their influence. With the French language came the literature, and many a Russian noble bought French books by the yard for his library because it was the thing to do. The champagne business boomed (the Russians liked the sweet kind that most Frenchmen despised); French styles of dress were slavishly copied by both men and women. Francomania took its extreme form among those Russians who were ashamed of being Russian and who would not fall in love with any girl unable to speak French. Indeed, the noble and the peasant no longer spoke the same language. This deep rift between the Frenchified nobles and the Russian people was to prove of critical importance for later Russian history.

Catherine the Great, 1762-1796

With the advent of Catherine II, we come to the most arresting personality to occupy the Russian throne since the death of Peter. Brought up in a petty German court, she found herself translated to St. Petersburg as a mere girl, living with a husband she detested, and forced to pick her way through the intrigues that flourished around the Empress Elizabeth. She managed to steer clear of trouble only by using her keen wits. Catherine fancied herself as an intellectual; she wrote plays, edited a satirical journal, and steeped herself in the literature of the Enlightenment. Both before and after ascending the throne she maintained a goodly supply of lovers, several of whom had important roles in affairs of state.

Catherine had a truly twentieth-century feeling for the importance of public relations, and cared deeply that leading spirits in the West should think well of her and of the state of Russia under her rule. Hence her voluminous correspondence with westerners. She invited Diderot to take up in Russia the task of editing the *Encyclopédie;* then she bought his library, but he kept his books, and received a pension—very favorable publicity for Russia and the Russian Empress. Diderot himself visited Russia in 1773; though he came back entranced with Catherine, who, he said, had the soul of Brutus and the charms of Cleopatra, the visit was not entirely a success. Catherine complained that in the excitement of conversation he pinched her legs until they were black and blue. Voltaire, though he judiciously stayed away from Russia, accepted Catherine's bounty, and in return poured out the praises that she yearned for, calling her "the north star" and "the benefactress of Europe."

Catherine would perhaps have liked to reform conditions in Russia; there was something of the enlightened despot about her "style." But as a woman and a foreigner and a usurper, owing the throne to a conspiracy, she could not act upon her principles. Depending as she did upon the good will of the nobility, she could not lay a finger on the institution of serfdom. She had to reward her supporters with vast grants of state land, inhabited by hundreds of thousands of state peasants, who once could not be sold but who now became privately owned serfs who could be sold. Even in theory, Catherine felt, Russia was so large that the only possible form of government was an autocracy. As an autocrat she was as arbitrary as any of her predecessors.

Once firmly established on the throne, however, Catherine decided to convoke a commission to codify the laws of Russia, a task that had not been accomplished since 1649. Catherine herself, with the help of advisers, spent three years composing the *Instruction* to the delegates, a long, rather windy document, full of abstract argument drawn from Montesquieu's *Spirit of the Laws* and Beccaria's *Crimes and Punishments* but altered to conform with the Empress' own beliefs. Here one can discern no intention to meddle with the fundamental institutions of Russia, but some concern for eliminating the worst abuses inherent in the institutions. The 564 delegates to the commission were elected by organs of the central government and by every social class in Russia except the serf peasants. Each delegate—noble, townsman, crown peasant, Cossack—was charged to bring with him a collection of written documents from his neighbors presenting their grievances and demands for change.

Many of these survive and teach us a great deal about the state of public opinion in Catherine's Russia. Nobody seems to have been dissatisfied with the autocracy; at least we find no requests that it modify its power or consult its subjects. People did seek more rights and duties for local government, and wanted their own obligations more clearly defined. Each class of representatives was eager to extend the rights of that class: the free peasants wanted to own serfs; the townsmen wanted to own serfs and be the only class allowed to engage in trade; the nobles wanted to engage in trade, and to have their exclusive right to own serfs confirmed. After 203 sessions lasting over a year and a half, devoted to inconclusive and sometimes heated debate, Catherine put an end to the labors of the commission in 1768. It had not codified the laws, but from Catherine's own point of view it had been a success; she knew that most of her subjects supported her as absolute autocrat. It is important to remember that the commission, with all its imperfections, was the last effort by the tsardom to consult the Russian people as a whole for 138 years—until revolution summoned the first Duma (parliament) into existence in 1906 (see Chapter XXII).

Catherine turned the spadework of the legislative commission to good advantage in her later reforms, which resulted from the great rebellion of the Cossacks under the leadership of Pugachev, 1773-1775. Pugachev roused the frontiersmen to revolt against Catherine's cancelation of their special privileges. Pretending to be Tsar Peter III, and promising liberty and land to the serfs who joined his forces, Pugachev swept over a wide area of southeastern Russia and finally marched toward Moscow. Like the disturbances of the seventeenth century, Pugachev's revolt revealed the existence of bitter discontent in Russia, a discontent directed not at the supreme autocrat but at the landlords and local officials.

The ramshackle structure of provincial administration almost collapsed under the strain of Pugachev's rebellion. Orders filtered down slowly to local officials, and the soldiers defending the government moved almost as slowly. When the rebels were finally suppressed, and Pugachev was traveling northward in an iron cage before being drawn and quartered, Catherine took action. Her reorganization of local government (1775) created fifty provinces where there had been twenty before. She thus replaced a small number of unwieldy units with a larger number of small provinces, each containing roughly 300,000 to 400,000 inhabitants. The reform of 1775 gave the nobles the lion's share of provincial offices but subjected them to the close direction of the central government, which had its own administrative, financial, and legal representatives in each province.

In the charter of 1785 the nobles received exemption from military service and taxation and secured absolute mastery over the fate of their serfs and their estates. A char-

ter to the towns in the same year (1785) disclosed Catherine's sympathy with the tiny but growing middle class. It established the principle of municipal self-government, but the principle remained a dead letter because of the rigorous class distinctions maintained in the backward urban centers of Russia. For the serfs, needless to say, there was no charter. Indeed, besides adding almost a million to their number by the gifts of state lands to private persons, Catherine increased still further the power of the proprietors. Long accustomed to selling the serfs without their land, the landlords now received the right to make such sales legally. Serf families were broken up, violent punishments and even torture employed (one notorious lady tortured seventy-five of her own serfs to death; but she was imprisoned for it), serfs were gambled away at cards, given as presents, and mortgaged for loans. All serf-owners were not cruel any more than all slave-owners in our own slave states, but both institutions tended to degrade both master and man. As in the American South, there was a distinction in Russia between field hands and household servants: great landowners often had hundreds of the latter, some of whom were formed into orchestras, gave dramatic performances, tutored the sons of the family, or acted as household poets and scientists.

The contrast between the climate of the Enlightenment which surrounded the court and the actual conditions in Russia was keenly felt by sensitive men. Foremost among them was a young noble, Alexander Radishchev, educated abroad and widely traveled. In his *Journey from St. Petersburg to Moscow* Radishchev included vivid and horrifying vignettes of serfdom and the abuses of the administration. Moreover, Radishchev's poetry praised Cromwell, the regicide. It is possible that the author's truly western culture might have enabled him to get away with this in the early days of Catherine's reign. But by 1790 the French

Revolution was under way, and Catherine had begun to hate the French and "their abominable bonfire" as much as she had formerly loved them. Proposing to burn the dangerous books of the Enlightenment, she could hardly overlook the subversive character of Radishchev's writings. Off he went into exile in Siberia. Similarly, the humanitarian freemason, Nicholas Novikov, manager of the newly active Moscow University Press, editor of newspapers, and sponsor of campaigns to raise money and food for famine-stricken peasants, also found himself jailed on flimsy charges. Though Novikov had done nothing against the régime, it could not tolerate the continuance of any enterprise it did not dominate. The two enlightened intellectuals, Radishchev and Novikov, not only serve as an illustration of the contrast between Catherine's professed principles and her actual conduct but also provide the first real examples of thoroughly westernized individual Russians.

Paul (1796-1801)

Catherine's son Paul (who may or may not have been the son of Catherine's husband Peter III) succeeded his mother in 1796 as a man of forty-two. All his life his mother had distrusted him, fearing that there might be a conspiracy to oust her and install Paul, ostensibly a legitimate Romanov. The best-educated Russian royal personage to date, active and eager to serve the state, Paul found himself given no duties, kept in the dark about the secrets of state, and even deprived of his two eldest children, Alexander and Constantine, whom Catherine insisted on educating herself. All he could do was drill a small garrison on his country estate and dress them in Prussian uniform.

Consequently, when Paul finally did succeed to the throne, he appeared to be motivated chiefly by a wish to undo his mother's work and act in every possible way contrary to the precedents she had set. He exiled some of Catherine's favorites, and released many of her prisoners, including Radishchev and Novikov. Paul believed in legality and system, and hoped to install a great deal more of both in Russia. He tried to restore more power and order to the central government by putting the colleges (see above, p. 32) under single ministers in place of the former boards of directors.

Paul's behavior, however, was spasmodic and eccentric. He forbade the importation of sheet-music because he feared that all music would be as revolutionary as the *Marseillaise*. He imposed a strict curfew on the capital. He issued a manifesto limiting to three the number of days per week a serf might be required to work on his master's land, but it is not clear whether this was a binding law or only a recommendation. In any case, he continued to give away state lands, and transformed some half a million state peasants into privately owned chattels. What was probably fatal to Paul was his policy of toughness toward the nobility. A noble, he is said to have remarked, is the man I am talking to at the moment, and he ceases to be a noble when I stop talking to him. This definition could hardly be expected to appeal to the privileged masters of Russia. Paul exacted compulsory service again, and in the provinces he curtailed the powers of the nobility. Nobles found themselves forced to meet the bills for public buildings, paying new taxes on their lands, and subjected to corporal punishments for crimes. Paul, like Peter III, wanted to Prussianize the army, and especially to inculcate in the officers a sense of responsibility for the men. In the guards' regiments such programs were detested, and a conspiracy of guardsmen ended in 1801 with Paul's murder and Alexander's succession. The forces behind the *coup* were the same as those that had engineered so many shifts of power during the preceding century. The precise degree to which

Alexander was informed of the *coup* in advance is sometimes debated, but he knew at least that the conspirators intended to force his father's abdication.

Alexander I (1801-1825)

In Alexander I there came to the throne an emperor whom historians usually call "enigmatic." Educated by a liberal

Tsar Alexander I of Russia.

Swiss tutor, he absorbed so much of the new eighteenth-century doctrines that he actually blossomed out with a red-white-and-blue ribbon, the colors of revolutionary France, on hearing of the fall of the Bastille to the Paris mob. Nothing could have been more unexpected of the eventual heir to the Russian throne. Yet the application of liberal principles in Russia would involve a direct challenge to all the most powerful forces in society. So, although Alexander

would occasionally say to his intimates that some day he would grant Russia a constitution and himself retire to a castle on the Rhine, in fact this was little but romantic twaddle. Tall and handsome, utterly devastating to the ladies, charming and cultivated, Alexander liked to please everybody; he vacillated, compromised, and in the end accomplished very little. Moreover, he loved power dearly, and always shied away from proposals to limit it.

The quarter-century of his reign was twice interrupted by major wars against Napoleon, in 1805-1807, and in 1812-1815 (see Chapter XVIII). In the first period of relative peace, 1801-1805, Alexander gathered round him a small group of youthful intimates, which he called the "unofficial committee." One of the members, Stroganov, had been an active member of the Jacobin Club in Paris during the revolution; two others greatly admired the English system of government. Meeting regularly after dinner over coffee and brandy, the unofficial committee had as its self-appointed task the preparation of a constitution for Russia, after due study of all known constitutions. But its discussions were little more than the unsystematic talk of pleasant, well-born young men who had dined well. A decree sponsored by the committee did abolish the system of colleges, and created eight new ministries to take their places; but this in fact had already been almost accomplished by Paul. When the committee stopped meeting in 1803, it had done nothing with regard to serfdom. The Tsar himself in these years passed two laws, whose very mildness shows how little he intended to disturb existing institutions. One of them forbade the public advertisement of sales of serfs without land, but the law was easily circumvented. The other created a new category of "free farmers," serfs who had been freed by their masters, and prescribed that if a proprietor freed an entire village of serfs he must confer their land upon them at the same time. Since this left the initiative for liberation entirely in the hands of the proprietor, fewer than 40,000 among all the millions of serfs in Russia actually received their freedom.

In the second period of peace, 1807-1811, Alexander had as his chief mentor a remarkable figure, Michael Speransky, son of a Russian priest, intelligent, well-educated, and conscientious. Utilizing Montesquieu's principle of the separation of powers, Speransky drafted for Alexander a constitutional project that would have made Russia a limited monarchy. A series of elected assemblies, beginning at the lowest level of administrative subdivision and continuing on up through district and province, would culminate in a great national assembly, the duma. A similar pyramid of courts was sketched, while a new set of executive institutions was also planned. The duma would have to approve any law promulgated by the Tsar and would have been a real Russian parliament. It is true that the franchise Speransky proposed would have enormously favored the nobility, while the serfs of course would not have participated in government. It is also true that Speransky did not include emancipation of the serfs in his proposal. None the less, the plan was decidedly advanced. Speransky was realistic, and knew that not everything could be accomplished at once. Indeed, as it turned out, Alexander balked at executing the plan that he himself had commissioned Speransky to draw up.

This is one of the most critical moments in all Russian history. Why did Speransky fail? He instituted a reform of the civil service, requiring examinations and a system of promotion by merit, which disturbed many of the almost illiterate and thoroughly incompetent men in high office. He even proposed that the nobility pay an income tax, a measure not likely to make its proposer popular. Friends and intimates of the Tsar spread slander about Speransky. But at bottom Alexander himself was at fault and unwilling to act on his own alleged

beliefs. Speransky's scheme was shelved, except for two elements that in no way diminished the power of the Tsar. A Council of State, which could advise the Tsar, was created, but he was not obliged to take its advice. Since he appointed and dismissed all members, the effect was simply to increase imperial efficiency, not to limit imperial authority. Further administrative efficiency was obtained through the reorganization of the ministries, whose duties were set out clearly for the first time, eliminating overlapping.

During the second war against Napoleon (1812-1815) Alexander fell under the influence of a Baltic Baroness named Madame de Krüdener, a mystical lady now repenting an ill-spent youth. She convinced the Tsar that he was a "man from the North" designed by destiny to overthrow Napoleon and institute a new order. At the Russian court an atmosphere of pious mysticism, deeply conservative, replaced the earlier flashes of liberal views. Although the leading spirits of the new religiosity were all nominally Orthodox, its character was rather Protestant. It was based upon assiduous reading of the Bible, and it also included a mixture of elements from Masonry, Pietism (see below, p. 87), and the more eccentric Russian sects. It aimed at the union of all Christendom in one new faith and thus aroused the fear and opposition of many Orthodox clerics. Its real importance, however, lay in its impact on Alexander, who was now convinced that as the bearer of a sacred mission all he needed to do was follow the promptings of his inmost feelings.

During the last decade of Alexander's reign, 1815-1825, the most important figure at court was Count Arakcheev, a competent but brutal officer, who once bit off the ear of one of his men as a punishment. The chief innovation of the decade, accomplished under Arakcheev's direction, was the hated system of "military colonies," the drafting of the population of whole districts to serve in the regiments quartered there. When not drilling or fighting, the soldiers were to work their farms, and their entire lives were subject to the whims of their officers. Far from being a kind of model community, the individual military colony was a wretched sort of concentration camp. By the end of Alexander's reign almost 400,000 soldiers were living in these dreaded places.

Though Alexander gave Russia no important reforms, he did act on liberal principles outside Russia, in Poland and in Finland. By the Vienna settlement of 1815 (see below, Chapter XIX), Alexander as King of Poland could give the Poles any form of government he chose. In fact, he gave the Poles an advanced constitution, with their own army, their own Polish officialdom, and the free use of their own language. He allowed the Finns, after their annexation by Russia in 1809, to preserve their own law codes and the system of local government introduced during the long preceding Swedish rule. But the "liberal Tsar" was liberal only outside his Russian dominions.

Russian Foreign Policy, 1725-1796

The motives of Russian foreign policy in the century between the death of Peter the Great and that of Alexander I were still the ancient ones of expansion against Sweden, Poland, and Turkey. But as a new member of the European power constellation, Russia found that pursuit of these old aims was now involving her in affairs that had primary significance for western Europe. The diplomatic pattern was set early in the period, when Ostermann concluded an alliance with the Habsburg Empire in 1726. This was to be a cornerstone of Russian foreign policy. Yet, especially in their joint undertakings against the Turks, the Russians and Austrians found, as early as the 1730's, that they had conflicting ambitions in southeast Europe. This early conflict of interests was a cloud, still no larger than a man's hand, but destined to swell into the colossal thunderhead that exploded in the World War of 1914-1918. To the eighteenth century also belong the first regular Russian diplomatic service, the first Russian participation in the international game of espionage and intrigue, and the first real Russian foreign ministers: Ostermann and his Russian successor Bestuzhev-Ryumin, men of enormous personal influence on the course of Russian foreign relations.

In the War of the Polish Succession (see above, p. 37) Russian forces took part in alliance with Austria in support of Augustus III and helped to force the abdication of Stanislas Leszczynski. Immediately, the Russians and Austrians became allies in a new war against the Turks, 1735-1739 (see above, p. 36). Though Marshal Münnich successfully invaded the Crimea, Russian gains at the Treaty of Belgrade in 1739 were limited to Azov. The Austrians failed to co-operate satisfactorily in an invasion of the Danubian principalities and made it clear that they did not relish a Russian advance into the principalities and thus to the Habsburg frontiers.

The War of the Austrian Succession, opening in 1740, found the Russians preoccupied with the dynastic problem at home. We have already seen how the French ambassador worked to assist the elevation of Elizabeth to the throne, and in this way to bring about the downfall of the pro-Austrian Ostermann. But, since Bestuzhev-Ryumin continued Ostermann's policies, French hopes were largely disappointed. Prussian (and therefore anti-Austrian) influence manifested itself with the appearance of Peter III as heir, and with the choice of the future Catherine II as his bride. Thus, during the War of the Austrian Succession, there was a good deal of rival jockeying for Russian assistance. Eventually, the advance of Frederick the

Great along the Baltic shore alarmed the Russians, and so, as the war ended, a Russian corps was leisurely pushing westward, intending to join the fighting in the Rhineland.

Russian anti-Prussian sentiment crystallized during the interval of peace before the outbreak of the Seven Years' War. Bestuzhev labored mightily to obtain an alliance with England, which he managed in 1755, the Russians accepting a large subsidy in exchange for a promise to keep troops in readiness against the Prussians. But the Diplomatic Revolution of 1756 (see Chapter XVI), making Prussia and England allies, negated this arrangement. The Russians thus remained loyal to Austria and fought the Prussians in the Seven Years' War. Once more Russian forces marched west, so slowly that there was suspicion of treason and the commander was removed. In 1758 the invasion of East Prussia began; and eventually in 1760 Russian forces entered Berlin. Elizabeth's death and the succession of the pro-Prussian Peter III led the Russians to change sides and join the Prussians briefly against the Austrians and French. Catherine, on her succession, withdrew the Russian forces, but did not again attack the Prussians. Thus Russia found herself excluded from the peace conferences of 1763.

In foreign policy, Catherine the Great was as vigorous and unscrupulous as she was at home. She concentrated on the traditional Russian anti-Polish and anti-Turkish aims. In 1763, only a year after she became Empress, the throne of Poland fell vacant, and Catherine secured the election of her protégé and former lover, a pro-Russian Pole, Stanislas Poniatowski. Frederick the Great joined with Catherine in a campaign to win rights for the persecuted Lutheran and Orthodox minorities in Catholic Poland. One party of Polish nobles, their national pride offended at foreign intervention, resisted, and secured the aid of France and Austria. These powers adopted the stratagem of pressing Turkey into war with Russia to distract Catherine from Poland.

In the first Russo-Turkish War (1768-1774), Catherine's forces won a series of victories. A Russian Baltic fleet, sent all the way around Europe and into the Mediterranean through the Straits of Gibraltar, destroyed the Turkish fleet in the Aegean (1770), largely owing to the superior seamanship of a few English officers who were advising the otherwise inefficient Russians. But the Russians failed to follow up their initial advantage by storming the Straits and attacking Istanbul, and operations shifted to the Crimea and the Danubian principalities. While the Russians and Turks were discussing peace terms, Frederick the Great had concluded that Russia had been too successful against the Turks, and might seize most of Poland for herself unless he acted quickly.

So Frederick took the leading part in arranging the first partition of Poland (1772). Poland lost to Russia, Prussia, and Austria almost one-third of her territory and one-half of her population in this act of international highway robbery. Frederick's share of the loot—the lands immediately to the west of East Prussia—was the smallest but the most strategic: it included the region that had previously separated Brandenburg from East Prussia. Maria Theresa, the Empress of Austria, abandoned her Turkish and Polish allies to participate. She did seem somewhat reluctant, but, as Frederick the Great observed caustically, "She wept, but she kept on taking." Russia received a substantial area of what is now known as Belorussia, or White Russia.

Two years later, the Russians imposed upon the Turks a most humiliating peace treaty, at Kutchuk Kainardji (1774). Catherine annexed much of the formerly Turkish stretch of Black Sea coast, and two places in the Crimea; the rest of the Crimea was separated from the Ottoman Empire as an independent Tartar state. She also obtained something the Russians had long coveted: freedom of navigation on the Black Sea and the right of passage through the Bosphorus and the Dardanelles. A vaguely worded clause gave her various rights to protect the Christian subjects of the sultan. This last provision gave the Russians a convenient excuse for intervening in Turkish affairs later on.

Catherine now began to dream of expelling the Turks from Europe, and reviving the Byzantine Empire at Istanbul under Russian protection. She saw to it that her younger grandson was christened Constantine and imported Greek-speaking nurses to train him in the language. She also proposed to set up a kingdom of Dacia (the Roman name for the area) in the Danubian principalities to be ruled by her lover and general, Potemkin. By way of preparation, in 1783, Catherine annexed the supposedly independent Tartar state of the Crimea, where she built a naval base at Sebastopol. To achieve these grandiose designs, Catherine sought the consent of Austria, and invited Joseph II on a famous tour by river-boat of the newly developed and annexed territories of the Russian southwest. On this tour, the Austrian Emperor was allegedly shown the famous "Potemkin villages," mere card-

PARTITIONS OF POLAND, 1772-1793-1795

	1772	1793	1795
To Prussia			
To Russia			
To Austria			

0   Miles   200

board facades facing the river to look like settlements but with nothing behind them; like so many other good stories, this one is untrue. At Sebastopol, however, signs pointed across the Black Sea, saying, "This way to Byzantium." In a second Russo-Turkish war (1787-1791), Catherine's allies, the Austrians, once again provided feeble assistance and made a separate peace. Again, a conflict of interests over the European lands of the Sultan precipitated Austro-Russian disagreement. In the end, Catherine had to abandon her Greek project and content herself with annexing the remaining Turkish lands along the northern coast of the Black Sea and securing recognition of Russian sovereignty over the Crimea.

Before her death, Catherine completed her work by participating in two more partitions of Poland. The second partition came as the result of a Polish constitutional movement, supported by the Prussians in opposition to Russian interest. Once Catherine's hands were free of her Turkish war, she intervened on the pretext of defending the established order in Poland and fighting the virus of revolution. In 1793, both she

and the Prussians took large new slices of Polish territories, the Austrians not participating. An attempted Polish revolution against the reduction of their state to a wretched remnant dominated by foreigners was followed by the third and final partition of 1795, by which Poland disappeared from the map. This time Austria joined the other two powers and obtained Cracow; Prussia got Warsaw, and Russia secured Lithuania and other Baltic and east Polish lands.

But the spectacular successes of Catherine meant the embodiment in Russia of millions of human beings—Poles, Lithuanians, Belorussians—who loathed the Russians, and left a legacy of trouble. It also meant that Russia had destroyed useful buffers in the shape of the Polish and Tartar states, and now had common frontiers with her potential enemies, Prussia and Austria. The last two partitions of Poland had been made possible by the preoccupation of the western powers with their war against revolutionary France; the story of Russian foreign policy after Catherine forms part of the larger story of this great war (see Chapter XVIII).

V: George III and the American Revolution

George III

Despite the fact that Catherine the Great failed to apply the ideas of the Age of Reason to practical politics, her name usually appears on lists of enlightened despots. Another name that might possibly be added to the list is George III, King of Great Britain (1760-1820). Actually, "Farmer George" showed very little enlightenment beyond taking an interest in the agrarian revolution and writing articles

on turnips for Arthur Young's *Annals of Agriculture* (see Chapter XVI). In politics, however, he did attempt a course that may, with some exaggeration, be termed a dilute form of enlightened despotism. The first of the Hanoverian monarchs born and bred in England, George III proposed to reassert some of the royal prerogatives that had lapsed under the first two Georges. He tried to wrest control of the House of Commons from the long-dominant Whig oligarchy and retain it by the Whig devices of patronage and bribery. He endeavored to beat the Whigs at their own parliamentary game.

Virtuous as a person, devoted as a family man, George as a monarch was stubborn, short-sighted, and in the long run unsuccessful. It was easy for him at first to exploit the factional strife among the Whigs, maneuver Pitt out of office in 1761, and make his friend and tutor, Lord Bute, the head of the cabinet. Bute and the King, however, found it hard to justify their failure to deprive France of the sugar-rich West Indies in the Peace of Paris, which brought the Seven Years' War to a conclusion (see Chapter XVI). The Commons ratified the treaty, but George dismissed Bute in 1763 in order to appease the critics of British diplomacy.

The harshest criticism came from John Wilkes, a member of the House of Commons, who dubbed the Peace of Paris "the peace of God, for it passeth all understanding." Wilkes' bitter attack on the treaty in his paper, the *North Briton*, infuriated the King. Bowing to the royal anger, the Commons ordered the offending issue of the *North Briton* to be burnt. Wilkes, who first fled to France, later ran for Parliament three separate times, and three times the Commons, under royal pressure, threw out his election. When Wilkes finally took his seat again in 1774, he was a popular hero, and riots had occurred in defense of "Wilkes and Liberty." A wise king would have reconsidered, but George III did not relax his determination to manage both Parliament and cabinet. After seven years of short-lived, unstable ministries (1763-1770), George finally cast Lord North in Bute's old role. During North's ministry (1770-1782), the policy of royal intervention first stiffened, then wavered, and at length collapsed entirely in the face of disaster. At home, the King unwittingly prepared the way for the increase of parliamentary authority; abroad, he lost the thirteen North American colonies.

Background of the Revolution

The breach between colonies and mother country first became serious at the close of the Seven Years' War when Britain began to retreat from the old policy of "salutary neglect" and to interfere more directly and more frequently in matters affecting the colonies. But, by 1763, the colonies had acquired the habit of regulating their own affairs, though the acts of their assemblies remained subject to the veto of royally appointed governors or the King himself. The vast territories in Canada and west of the Alleghenies acquired in 1763 brought Britain added opportunities for profitable exploitation and added responsibilities for government and defense. In 1763, an uprising of the Indians under Pontiac threatened frontier posts in the area of the Ohio Valley and the Great Lakes. In the absence of effective concerted action by colonial militias, British regulars were brought in to crush Pontiac. The continuing threat from the Indians prompted the royal proclamation of October, 1763, forbidding "all our loving subjects" to settle west of a line running along the summit of the Alleghenies. To His Majesty's "loving subjects" in the seaboard colonies, however, the proclamation seemed deliberately designed to exclude them from the riches of the West.

The colonies resented still more keenly the attempt by Parliament to raise more revenue in North America. The British government had very strong arguments for increasing colonial taxes. The national debt had almost doubled during the Seven Years' War; the colonies' reluctance to recruit soldiers and raise taxes themselves had increased the cost of the war to British taxpayers; now the mother country faced continued expense in protecting the frontier. Surely the Americans would admit the reasonableness of the case for higher taxes.

That, however, was precisely what the

Americans did *not* admit. The first of the new revenue measures, the Sugar Act of 1764, alarmed the merchants of the eastern seaboard because the customs officers actually undertook to collect duties on molasses, sugar, and other imports. Here was a departure from the comfortable laxity of salutary neglect. And here was a threat to the colonial economy, for the import duties had to be paid out of the colonies' meager supply of specie (metal coin). The second revenue measure, the Stamp Act of 1765, imposed a duty on a wide variety of items, including legal and commercial papers, liquor licenses, playing cards, dice, newspapers, calendars, and academic degrees. These duties, too, drained the supply of specie, which was now so low that some merchants faced bankruptcy.

The revenue measures touched off a major controversy. Indignant merchants in the New World boycotted all imports rather than pay the duties, and in October, 1765, delegates from nine of the thirteen colonies met in New York City as the "Stamp Act Congress." The Congress complained that the new duties had "a manifest tendency to subvert the rights and liberties of the colonists." The Congress resolved:

That His Majesty's liege subjects in these colonies are entitled to all the inherent rights and liberties of his natural born subjects within the kingdom of Great Britain.

That it is inseparably essential to the freedom of a people, and the undoubted right of Englishmen, that no taxes be imposed on them but with their own consent, given personally or by their own representatives.

That the people of these colonies are not, and from their local circumstances cannot be, represented in the House of Commons in Great Britain.

That the only representatives of these colonies are persons chosen therein by themselves, and that no taxes ever have been, or can be constitutionally imposed on them, but by their respective legislatures.*

* *Documents of American History*, H. S. Commager, ed. (New York, 1940), 58.

The Stamp Act Congress thus enunciated the celebrated principle of no taxation without representation. Britain surrendered on the practical issue, but did not yield on the principle. The appeals of London merchants, near ruin because of the American boycott against British goods, brought the repeal of the Stamp Act in 1765. Nevertheless, in the next year Parliament passed the Declaratory Act asserting that the King and Parliament could indeed make laws affecting the colonies.

For the next decade, Britain adhered firmly to the principles of the Declaratory Act, and colonial radicals just as firmly repeated their opposition to taxation without representation. Parliament again tried to raise revenue, this time by the Townshend duties (1767) on colonial imports of tea, paper, paint, and lead. Again the merchants of Philadelphia, New York, and Boston organized boycotts. In 1770, Lord North's cabinet withdrew the Townshend duties except for the three-penny tariff on a pound of tea, retained as a symbol of parliamentary authority over the colonies. Three years later, the English East India Company, reduced almost to bankruptcy by its own corrupt officials, took a calculated risk and attempted the sale of its surplus tea in North America. It hoped to overcome American opposition to the hated duty by making the retail price of East India tea, duty included, far cheaper than that of Dutch tea smuggled by the colonists. The result was the Boston Tea Party. On December 16, 1773, to the cheers of spectators lining the waterfront, a group of Bostonians, who had a large financial stake in smuggled tea, disguised themselves as redskins, boarded three East India ships, and dumped into the harbor tea chests worth thousands of pounds.

Britain answered defiance with coercion, and the colonists met coercion with resistance. The Quebec Act (1774), incorporating the lands beyond the Alleghenies into Canada, bolted the door to the westward expansion of colonial frontiers. The "Intolerable Acts" (1774) closed the port of Boston to trade and suspended elections in Massachusetts. At Lexington and Concord in April, 1775, the "embattled farmers" of Massachusetts fired the opening shots of the War of Independence. At Philadelphia on July 4, 1776, the delegates to the Continental Congress formally declared the American colonies independent of Great Britain.

Implications of the Revolution

For the mother country, the American Revolution implied more than the secession of thirteen colonies. It involved Britain in a minor world war that jeopardized her dominance abroad and weakened the power and prestige of King George III at home. The most crucial battle in North America came early in the war—Burgoyne's surrender of his British forces at Saratoga in 1777. Burgoyne had been marching south from Montreal with the aim of driving a wedge between New England and the other rebellious colonies. Not only did he fail completely, but his surrender convinced the French that support of the American colonists would give them an excellent chance to renew their world-wide struggle with Britain and avenge the humiliation of 1763. Entering the war in 1778, France soon gained the alliance of Spain and eventually secured the help, or at least the friendly neutrality, of most other European states. The intervention of the French prepared the way for the victory of George Washington's forces and the final British surrender at Yorktown in 1781. Meantime, the British lost 3,000 merchant vessels before the Royal Navy finally rallied. In the peace signed at Paris in 1783, Britain recognized the independence of her former colonies. To Spain she handed back Florida, which she had taken in 1763, and the

An English commentary on the Boston Tea Party and the tarring and feathering of a royal tax collector, who is forced to drink under a liberty tree.

strategic Mediterranean island of Minorca. But she kept Gibraltar, which the Spanish had also hoped to recover, and she ceded only minor territories to France.

During the early years of the war, the British public had generally been inclined to agree with Dr. Samuel Johnson that the Americans were "a race of convicts" and "ought to be thankful for anything we allow them short of hanging." But the temper of opinion changed as the strength of American resistance became evident, as instances of British mismanagement piled up, and as most of Europe rallied to the rebellious colonies. By 1780, George III and his policy were so unpopular that the House of Commons passed a resolution declaring that "the influence of the crown has increased, is increasing, and ought to be diminished."

The influence of the Crown *was* diminished. In 1782, Lord North, who had been imploring the King to accept his resignation for three years, finally stepped down. In the next year, the post of prime minister fell to William Pitt the Younger, son of the heroic Pitt of the Seven Years' War. The new minister, though only twenty-five years old, was already a seasoned parliamentarian and was to head the cabinet for the next eighteen years. With the advent of Pitt, control of British politics shifted away from the King and back to the professional politicians. George III briefly contemplated abdication and then gradually resigned himself to the role of constitutional monarch. The British flirtation (it was really no more than that) with enlightened despotism had come to an end.

In the rebelling colonies public opinion was by no means unanimous in support of the Revolution. Many colonists, including southern planters and well-to-do Pennsylvania Quakers, either backed the mother country or took a neutral position in the struggle; New York supplied more recruits to George III than to George Washington. Some of these "Loyalists" or "Tories" were to flee to Canada when independence became a fact. Scholars, however, now find that the traditional estimate—that only one-third of the colonists actively backed the Revolution—is too low. Revolutionary sentiment ran particularly high in Virginia and New England and among social groups who had the habit of questioning established authority—the pioneers living on the frontier, and the numerous Presbyterians, Congregationalists, and members of other strong-minded Protestant sects. Like adolescents everywhere, the colonists resented parental tutelage yet appealed to family precedent. They claimed that they were only following the example set by Englishmen in 1688 and defended by John Locke.

The ideas of Locke and Newton were as well known and as much respected in North America as they were in Europe. They underlay the Declaration of Independence:

When in the course of human events, it becomes necessary for one people to dissolve the political bands which have connected them with another, and to assume among the Powers of the earth, the separate and equal station to which the Laws of Nature and Nature's God entitle them, a decent respect to the opinions of mankind requires that they should declare the causes which impel them to the separation.

The opening paragraph of the Declaration thus expressed the concept of a world-machine ruled by the "Laws of Nature." The next paragraph applied to the colonies Locke's theory of contract and his justification of revolution:

We hold these truths to be self-evident, that all men are created equal, that they are endowed by their Creator with certain unalienable Rights, that among these are Life, Liberty and the pursuit of Happiness. That to secure these rights, Governments are instituted among Men, deriving their just power from the consent of the governed. That whenever any Form of Government becomes destructive of these ends, it is the Right of the People to alter or to abolish it, and to institute new Government. . . .

The Declaration of Independence revealed the debt of the American Revolution to the English prophets of the Enlightenment. The Constitution of the new republic was to show its indebtedness to the French *philosophes,* particularly Montesquieu. The delegates to the Constitutional Convention at Philadelphia in 1787 borrowed from *The Spirit of the Laws* the idea of separating the executive, legislative, and judicial powers. The president's check on the Congress through his veto power, the congressional check on the executive and judiciary through impeachment and the right of confirming appointments, and the check imposed on each house of Congress by the requirement that both houses consent to legislation—these familiar balancing devices were derived in part from Montesquieu. The recurrent tensions between President and Congress thus originated in the American adaptation of an eighteenth-century French misreading of British constitutional practice. The "Founding Fathers" also copied from the constitutions of the thirteen original states and from English precedents. The first ten amendments to the Constitution (1791), guaranteeing freedom of religion, freedom of the press, and other basic liberties, were taken mainly from the English Bill of Rights of 1689.

The Constitution abounded in compromises. It attempted a balance between states' rights and the central power of the federal government, and between the democratic principle of a directly elected House of Representatives and the aristocratic principle of an indirectly elected and conservative Senate. It was a compromise designed to win support from both rich and poor and from both the aristocratic opponents and the democratic supporters of the recent revolution. Like any compromise, it did not at first please all parties, but it worked well enough to make the new American republic a going concern. The "Founding Fathers" of the United States of America had succeeded perhaps better than any other statesmen of the century in adjusting the ideals of the *philosophes* to the realities of practical politics.

VI: The Culture of the Eighteenth Century

The Limitations of Reason

The Enlightenment, however, seldom produced such happy political results as it did in the United States. On the whole, the *philosophes* expected men to see reason when it was pointed out to them, to abandon the habits of centuries, and to revise their behavior in accordance with natural law. But men would not always see reason; as Joseph II discovered to his sorrow, they *would* cling perversely to irrational customs and unnatural traditions. The rationalism of the Enlightenment tended to omit the complexities of human nature from its calculation.

Responsibility for this major shortcoming lay partly with the "classical spirit" of the seventeenth century, inherited by the Enlightenment of the eighteenth. The writers of the Age of Louis XIV had found in their classical models, not a confirmation of existing standards, but a better, simpler set of standards that the eighteenth-century *philosophes* easily adapted to the concept of "nature's simple plan." The great writers achieve the miracle of giving life to these abstractions. But the lesser ones make only bloodless types, and encourage in their hearers and readers—the men and women who finally do work out social change—the belief that these easy mental images are somehow more real, and certainly more desirable, than the bewildering complexity of their concrete experiences. Like the "classical spirit," the spirit of natural science went too far when it was applied uncritically to problems of human relations. It gave men the illusion that what was going on in their minds would shortly go on in reality.

A minor *philosophe,* the Abbé Mably, got at this central problem by inquiring: "Is society, then, a branch of physics?" Most of the *philosophes* and their followers believed that it was. They applied to the unpredictable activities of man the mathematical methods used in the physical sciences. The Physiocrats, for example, tried to reduce the complexities of human economic activities to a few simple agricultural laws. Like the stars in their courses, human beings were thought to fit neatly into the Newtonian world-machine.

A few eighteenth-century minds disagreed. David Hume (1711-1776), the brilliant Scottish philosopher, doubted the wisdom of assuming that society was a branch of physics; indeed he doubted everything. Hume's skeptical mind insisted on submitting principles to the test of factual observation. The errors and illusions of the *philosophes*, he said, resulted from their failure to do this. They deduced untested conclusions from two great abstract principles—faith in natural law, belief in reason.

Hume made short work of the *philosophes'* appeals to nature. The laws of justice, he argued, were not the absolute and inflexible "Laws of Nature":

> . . . Suppose a society to fall into such want of all common necessaries, that the utmost frugality and industry cannot preserve the greater number from perishing, and the whole from extreme misery; it will readily, I believe, be admitted, that the strict laws of justice are suspended, in such a pressing emergence, and give place to the stronger motives of necessity and self-preservation. Is it any crime, after a shipwreck, to seize whatever means or instrument of safety one can lay hold of, without regard to former limitations of property? *

Nor could human conduct be analyzed "in the same manner that we discover by reason the truths of geometry or algebra."

> It appears evident that the ultimate ends of human actions can never, in any case, be accounted for by *reason*, but recommend themselves entirely to the sentiments and affections of mankind, without any dependance on the intellectual faculties. Ask a man *why he uses exercise:* he will answer, *because he desires to keep his health.* If you then enquire, *why he desires health,* he will readily reply, *because sickness is painful.* If you push your enquiries

farther, and desire a reason *why he hates pain,* it is impossible he can ever give any. . . . *

David Hume was among the first and most profound critics of the Age of Reason. The Romantics of the next generation would repeat his warnings against reason and his pleas on behalf of the "sentiments and affections of mankind" (see Chapter XIX). In Hume's own day, Rousseau and Kant were also worried by rather similar problems. Rousseau both represented the Enlightenment and foreshadowed the revolt against it. No *philosophe* defended natural law more ardently, yet no Romantic argued more convincingly in support of emotion and faith. "Too often does reason deceive us," Rousseau wrote in *Emile.* "We have only too good a right to doubt her; but conscience never deceives us; she is the true guide of man; . . . he who obeys his conscience is following nature and he need not fear that he will go astray." †

Immanuel Kant (1724-1804), who taught philosophy at the University of Königsberg in Prussia, raised Rousseau's argument to the level of metaphysics. Kant believed in a higher reality reaching ultimately to God. He called the eternal verities of the higher world "noumena," in contrast to the phenomena of the material world. Knowledge of the noumenal realm, Kant believed, reached men through reason—reason, however, not as the Enlightenment used the term, not as common sense, but as intuition. The highest expression of the Kantian reason was the "categorical imperative." This was the moral law within, the conscience implanted in man by God. It was the inescapable realization welling up in the individual that, when confronted with an ethical choice, he must choose the good and avoid the evil. Kant's redefinition of reason and his rehabilitation of conscience marked a high point in the philosophical re-

---

* *An Enquiry concerning the Principles of Morals,* L. A. Selby-Bigge, ed. (Oxford, 1902), 186.

* *Ibid.,* 293.
† *Emile,* Everyman ed. (New York, 1911), 249-250.

action against the dominant rationalism of the Enlightenment. The popular reaction took the very different form of the evangelical revival, which began with the German Pietists.

The Evangelical Revival

The Pietists were the spiritual descendants of the sixteenth-century Anabaptists. Deploring alike the growing Lutheran concern with the formal aspects of religion and the deists' emphasis on natural law, the Pietists asserted that religion came from the heart, not the head. For the Pietists God was far more than the watchmaker, the remote creator of the world-machine. One of the chief leaders of Pietism was a German nobleman, Count Zinzendorf (1700-1760), founder of the Moravian Brethren, who set up a model community based on Christian principles. Moravian emigrants to America planted a colony at Bethlehem, Pennsylvania, founding the "Pennsylvania Dutch" traditions of thrift, hard work, and strict living. In England, meanwhile, the example of Zinzendorf and other Pietists inspired John Wesley.

Ordained a priest of the Church of England, John Wesley (1703-1791) at first stressed the ritualistic aspects of religion. But the failure of his two-year ministry to the backward colony of Georgia (1736-1737) convinced him of the weakness of religious formalism. Disillusioned, Wesley felt his own faith evaporating: "I went to America, to convert the Indians: but Oh! who shall convert me! Who, what is he that will deliver me from this evil heart of unbelief?" * Pietism converted Wesley. Following the teachings of the Moravian Brethren, whom he met in England and America, he found faith through inner conviction.

---

* John Wesley, *Journal*, Everyman ed. (New York, 1907), I, 74.

For more than fifty years, Wesley labored tirelessly to share his discovery, traveling throughout the British Isles, and preaching in churches, in the fields, at the pitheads of coal mines, and even in jails. Angry crowds came to scoff but remained to pray. When Wesley died in 1791, his movement had already attracted more than a hundred thousand adherents. They were called Methodists, because of their methodical devotion to piety and to plain dressing and plain living. Though Wesley always considered himself a good Anglican, the Methodists eventually set up a separate organization—their nonconformist "Chapel" in contrast to the established Church of England. The new sect won its following almost entirely among the lower and middle classes, among people who sought the religious excitement and consolation that they did not find in the abstractions of deism or the austere formalism of the Church of England.

Although the beliefs of the Methodists diverged entirely from those of the enlightened rationalists, both groups worked in their different ways to improve the condition of society. Where the *philosophes* advised public reform, the Methodists favored private charity; and where the *philosophes* attacked the *causes* of social evils, the Methodists accepted these evils as part of God's plan and sought to mitigate their *symptoms*. They had in full measure the Puritan conscience of the nonconformists. They began agitation against drunkenness, the trade in slaves, and the barbarous treatment of prisoners, the insane, and the sick. John Wesley established schools for coalminers' children and opened dispensaries for the poor in London and Bristol. Part of the Methodists' success thus came from their social activities; part, too, came from the magnetism of Wesley and his talented associates. His brother, Charles Wesley, composed more than 6500 hymns, and in America Methodist missionaries flourished under the dynamic leadership of Francis Asbury (1745-1816). The number of colleges called Wesleyan and the number of churches and streets called Asbury testify to the significance of Methodism in American social history.

Literature

The middle-class public so strongly attracted to Methodism welcomed the novels of the Englishman, Samuel Richardson (1689-1761). A printer by trade, he turned to writing late in life and produced three gigantic novels in the form of letters by the chief characters. In *Clarissa Harlowe* (1748), for example, Richardson devoted 2400 pages of small print to the misfortunes of Clarissa, whose lover was a scoundrel, and whose relatives were a greedy pack, scheming to secure her considerable property. Whatever her distress,

Dr. Samuel Johnson, by Sir Joshua Reynolds.

Clarissa never lost the capacity to pour out her miseries on paper. If anyone missed the point of the story, he had only to turn to Richardson's preface:

What will be found to be more particularly aimed at in the following work is—to warn the inconsiderate and thoughtless of one sex, against the base arts and designs of specious contrivers of the other—to caution parents against the undue exercise of their natural authority over their children in the great article of marriage—to warn against preferring a man of pleasure to a man of probity upon that dangerous but too-commonly-received notion, *that a reformed rake makes the best husband* —but above all, to investigate the highest and most important doctrines not only of morality, but of christianity, by showing them thrown into action in the conduct of the *worthy* characters; while the *unworthy*, who set these doctrines at defiance, are condignly, and, as may be said, consequentially punished.

Although modern readers may find *Clarissa* tedious and sentimental, the eighteenth century was entranced. *Clarissa* was read aloud at family gatherings, it is said, and whenever some new disaster overwhelmed the heroine, the members separated for a good solitary cry. In spite of Richardson's exaggerations, his descriptions of the struggles of passion and conscience carried real conviction.

The novel as a literary form came into its own during the eighteenth century, particularly in England. By no means all the masters of English fiction were as sentimental as Richardson. In *Roderick Random* (1748), Tobias Smollett drew an authentic picture of life in the navy, with all its cruelty and hardship. Henry Fielding introduced a strong leaven of satire and burlesqued the excesses of Richardson. Fielding covered a broad social scene in his masterpiece, *Tom Jones* (1749), depicting both the hard-riding country squires and the low characters of the city slums. Richardson gave the English novel emotional and moral earnestness; Smollet and Fielding gave it vigorous realism.

Front drawing room of Home House, London, designed by Robert Adam (1772-1773).

On the whole, the eighteenth century was an age of prose and produced few poets of stature. Its literary monuments were the novels of Richardson and Fielding, the tales and essays of Voltaire, Gibbon's *History of the Decline and Fall of the Roman Empire* (1788), and Dr. Johnson's *Dictionary* (1755). Edward Gibbon utilized history for a sustained Voltairean attack on Christian fanaticism and employed a Ciceronian prose style which, by its balance and discipline, perfectly suited the classical temper of the Enlightenment. Dr. Samuel Johnson's dictionary also expressed the "style" of the age. He declared in the preface:

When I took the first survey of my undertaking, I found our speech copious without order and energetick without rules: wherever I turned my view, there was perplexity to be disentangled, and confusion to be regulated; choice was to be made out of a boundless variety, without any established principle of selection; adulterations were to be detected, without a settled test of purity; and modes of expression to be rejected or received, without the suffrages of any writers of classical reputation or acknowledged authority.

Pedantry and prejudice sometimes overcame the autocratic doctor. His definition of a cough—"a convulsion of the lungs, vellicated by some sharp serosity"—revealed the dangers of being too classical and resorting to little-known Latinisms. And, whenever he could, he aimed a volley at his favorite target, the Scots: thus he defined oats as "a grain, which in England is generally given to horses, but in Scotland supports the people." In the main, however, Dr. Johnson succeeded admirably in his aim of becoming a kind of Newton of the English language.

Art

The classicism of the century strongly affected its art. Gibbon's history, the researches of scholars and archaeologists, and the discovery in 1748 of the well-preserved ruins of Roman Pompeii, buried under lava from Vesuvius, raised the interest in antiquity to a high pitch. For the men of the Enlightenment, the balance and symmetry of Greek and Roman temples represented, in effect, the natural laws of building. Architects retreated somewhat from the theatricalism of the Baroque style and adapted classical models with great artistry and variety. We owe to them the elegance of the London town house, the monumental magnificence of the buildings flanking the Place de la Concorde in Paris, and the country-manor charm of Washington's Mount Vernon. They made Lisbon, rebuilt after its disastrous earthquake (see above, p. 57), a model of handsome town-planning. The twentieth-century vogue of the "colonial" and the "Georgian" testifies to the lasting influence of this neoclassical architecture.

In painting, neoclassicism reached a summit with Sir Joshua Reynolds (1723-1792), the first president of the Royal Academy and the artistic tsar of Georgian England.

Beauty, Sir Joshua told the academy, rested "on the uniform, eternal, and immutable laws of nature," which could be "investigated by reason, and known by study." Sir Joshua and his contemporaries, though preaching a coldly reasoned aesthetic, gave warmth to the actual portraits that they painted of wealthy English aristocrats, This was the golden age of English portraiture, the age of Reynolds, Lawrence, Gainsborough, and Romney.

And it was also the age of William Hogarth (1697-1764), who cast aside the academic restraints of neoclassicism to do in art what Fielding did in the novel. Instead of catering to a few wealthy patrons, Hogarth sought a mass market for the engravings that he turned out in thousands of copies. Instead of seeking proportion and harmony, as Reynolds advised, he sketched

Hogarth, "The Orgy," scene III from The Rake's Progress (about 1734).

Interior of Strawberry Hill, Twickenham, England, by Horace Walpole and others.

with brutal frankness the vices of London. *Marriage à la Mode, The Rake's Progress, The Harlot's Progress,* and *Gin Lane* were his satires on a licentious society (see also the illustration on p. 9).

The realism of Hogarth was far from being the only exception to the prevailing neoclassicism. The fashions for the oriental, the natural, and the Gothic, which were to be so important in the nineteenth century, were already beginning to catch on. The taste for the exotic produced Chinese wallpaper, the "Chinese" furniture of Thomas Chippendale, and the familiar Chinese pattern of "willow-ware" plates. Gardens were bestrewn with pagodas and minarets, and gardeners abandoned the tortured shrubs of Louis XIV's geometrical landscaping for the natural English garden. Even the dominance of neoclassical architecture was challenged. At Strawberry Hill near London, Horace Walpole, the son of the great Robert, concocted a curious house that had an abundance of Gothic "gloomth," as Horace himself boasted—battlements in the medieval style, and "lean windows fattened with rich saints in painted glass."

The Great Musicians

The crowning glory of eighteenth-century culture was its music. The first half of the century was the age of Bach and Handel, and the second half was the age of Haydn and Mozart. Johann Sebastian Bach (1685-1750) brought to perfection the Baroque techniques of seventeenth-century composers. He mastered the difficult art of the fugue, an intricate version of the round in which each voice begins the theme in turn while the other voices repeat and elaborate it. Bach also composed a wealth of material for the organ, the most Baroque and the most religious of instruments. Sacred themes inspired many of his cantatas, the Mass in B minor, and the two gigantic choral settings of the Passion of Christ according to St. John and St. Matthew. The religious music of Bach, dramatic and deeply felt, was a world apart from the anticlerical temper of the Enlightenment.

George Frederick Handel (1685-1759) had a stormy international career. Born in

Germany, Handel studied in Italy, then spent most of his adult years in England trying to run an opera company. The intrigues, the clashes of temperament, and the fiscal headaches inevitable in artistic enterprise nearly ruined him. Yet Handel wrote more than forty operas, including *Xerxes*, famous for "Handel's Largo." He used themes from the Bible for *The Messiah* and other vigorous oratorios directed at a mass audience and arranged for large choruses. These elaborate works differed greatly from the original oratorios of seventeenth-century Italy, written for the tiny prayer chapels called oratories.

Although Bach and Handel composed many instrumental suites and concertos, it was not until the second half of the century that orchestral music really came to the fore. New instruments then appeared, notably the piano, which greatly extended the limited range of the older keyboard instrument, the harpsichord. New forms also appeared, the sonata and the symphony, developed largely by Joseph Haydn (1732-1809). Haydn wrote more than fifty piano pieces in the form of the sonata, in which two contrasting themes are stated in turn, developed, interwoven, repeated, and finally resolved in a *coda* (the Italian for "tail"). Haydn then applied the sonata to the orchestra, grafting it on the Italian operatic overture, thus enlarging it into the first movement of the symphony.

The operatic landmark of the early century was John Gay's *Beggar's Opera* (1728). This tuneful work caricatured English society and politics in Hogarthian vein. Christoph Gluck (1714-1787) revolutionized the technique of the tragic opera. "I have striven," he said,

to restrict music to its true office of serving poetry by means of expression and by following the situations of the story, without interrupting the action or stifling it with a useless superfluity of ornaments. . . . I did not wish to arrest an actor in the greatest heat of dialogue . . . to hold him up in the middle of a word on a vowel favorable to his voice, nor to make display of the agility of his fine voice in some long-drawn passage, nor to wait while the orchestra gives him time to recover his breath for a cadenza.*

Gluck executed this declaration of operatic independence. His operas were well-constructed musical dramas, not just vehicles for the display of vocal pyrotechnics. Gluck kept to the old custom of taking heroes and heroines from classical mythology, but he invested shadowy figures like Orpheus, Eurydice, and Iphigenia with new vitality.

Opera, symphony, and chamber works all reached a climax in Wolfgang Amadeus Mozart (1756-1791). As a boy, Mozart was exploited by his father, who carted him all over Europe to show off his virtuosity on the harpsichord and his amazing talent for composition. Overworked throughout his life, and in his later years overburdened with debts, Mozart died a pauper at the age of thirty-five. Yet his youthful talent ripened steadily into mature genius, and his facility and versatility grew ever more prodigious. He tossed off the sprightly overture to *The Marriage of Figaro* in the course of an evening. In two months during the summer of 1788, he produced the three great symphonies familiar to concert audiences as No. 39 (E flat major), No. 40 (G minor), and No. 41 ("The Jupiter"). Mozart's orchestral works also included a long list of concertos, with the solo parts sometimes for piano or violin and sometimes, just to show that it could be done, for bassoon or French horn. In chamber music, Mozart experimented with almost every possible combination of instruments.

Three of Mozart's great operas were in the comic Italian vein of *opera buffa*. In *Così Fan Tutte* ("Thus Do All Women") he combined amorous farce with enchanting melodic duets. He derived his delight-

---

* Preface to *Alcestis*, as translated by Eric Blom and quoted in Curt Sachs, *Our Musical Heritage* (New York, 1948), 287.

ful *Marriage of Figaro* from Beaumarchais' famous satire of the caste system of the Old Régime, in which Figaro the valet outwits and outsings his noble employers. Tragic overtones appear in *Don Giovanni*, depicting the havoc wrought by Don Juan on earth before his eventual punishment in hell. Mozart composed with equal skill mournful and romantic arias for the Don's victims, elegantly seductive ballads for the Don himself, and a catalog of the Don's conquests for his valet ("A thousand and three in Spain alone"). The instruments in the pit dotted the "i's" and crossed the "t's" of the plot—scurrying violins to accompany characters dashing about the stage, portentous trombones to announce the entrance of the Devil. For the ballroom scene of *Don Giovanni*, Mozart accomplished the remarkable feat of employing three orchestras, playing simultaneously three different tunes for three different dances— a minuet for the aristocracy, a country dance for the middle class, a waltz for the lower orders. In his last opera, *The Magic Flute*, Mozart abandoned the usual Italian libretto and tried to create a consciously German work; but only the vaguest political significance emerged from the fantastic libretto, which apparently sought to vindicate the enlightened ideas of Joseph II and to decry the conservatism of Maria Theresa.

The Magic Flute was a rare exception to the generally cosmopolitan character of eighteenth-century music. The great composers with the German names had very little national feeling. Almost all of them felt equally at home in Vienna, Prague, Milan, Paris, and London, and they gratefully accepted patrons in any country. The fortunate Haydn moved from the princely estate of the Hungarian Esterhazy family to score an equal success with the paying public of the London concert-halls. Italian music was never totally eclipsed, nor was German dominance complete. Bach patterned his concertos on Italian models, Haydn borrowed Italian operatic overtures for his symphonies, and every operatic composer of the century profited from the labors of his Italian predecessors.

The great composers had the human touch so often lacking in the Age of Reason. They borrowed freely from folk-tunes and ballads, the popular music of their day, and were rewarded by having their themes whistled in the streets. Mozart's operas, Haydn's symphonies, and the great choral works of Bach and Handel have never lost this popular appeal. They have retained the capacity to engage the listener's emotions. In this sense, music probably came closest to resolving harmoniously the great conflict in eighteenth-century culture, the conflict between reason and emotion, between the abstractions of the Enlightenment and the flesh-and-blood realities of human existence.

In other realms, however, as the century drew toward its close, the lines were drawn for the vigorous prosecution of the conflict. In thought, the ideas of Kant and Hume were challenging the optimistic rationalism of the *philosophes*. Romantic artists and writers were soon to defy the defenders of classicism. And in politics, as the century ended, the European powers sought to check the French Revolution, the greatest effort to realize on earth the Enlightenment's dream of reason, natural law, and progress, "the heavenly city of the eighteenth-century philosophers."

Reading Suggestions
on the Enlightenment

(Asterisk indicates paperbound edition.)

GENERAL ACCOUNTS

W. L. Dorn, *Competition for Empire, 1740-1763* (Harper, 1940). Contains a meaty chapter on the Enlightenment and an excellent bibliography.

L. Gershoy, *From Despotism to Revolution, 1763-1789* (Harper, 1944). A comprehensive and rather caustic account of the Enlightened Despots.

G. Bruun, *The Enlightened Despots* (Holt, 1929). A first-rate brief account.

R. R. Palmer, *The Age of the Democratic Revolution,* Vol. I (Princeton Univ. Press, 1959). The first part of a projected two-volume work covering the political history of Europe and America, 1760-1800; by a very able scholar.

J. Bronowski and B. Mazlish, *The Western Intellectual Tradition from Leonardo to Hegel* (Harper, 1960). A survey stressing the correlations among economic, political, and intellectual history; the footnotes supply useful bibliographical information.

SPECIAL STUDIES: THE ENLIGHTENMENT

G. R. Havens, *The Age of Ideas: From Reaction to Revolution in Eighteenth-Century France* (Holt, 1955). A most useful volume, fully abreast of modern research.

P. Smith, *The History of Modern Culture, Vol. II* (Holt, 1934). A mine of information on details often neglected in intellectual histories.

E. Cassirer, *The Philosophy of the Enlightenment* (*Beacon, 1955). An important study of the great principles of 18th-century thought.

P. Hazard, *European Thought in the Eighteenth Century* (Hollis and Carter, 1954). A useful survey of some of the thinkers of the Enlightenment.

K. Martin, *The Rise of French Liberal Thought,* J. P. Mayer, ed. (New York Univ. Press, 1954). A brilliant and opinionated survey of the *philosophes.*

C. Becker, *The Heavenly City of the Eighteenth-Century Philosophers* (Yale Univ. Press, 1932; *1959). A delightful and influential essay, stressing the parallels between the medieval Age of Faith and the Age of Reason. May be coupled with R. O. Rockwood, ed., *Carl Becker's Heavenly City Revisited* (Cornell Univ. Press, 1958), a reappraisal.

J. B. Bury, *The Idea of Progress* (*Dover, 1955). A famous old pioneering study of enlightened optimism.

L. G. Crocker, *An Age of Crisis: Man and World in Eighteenth Century French Thought* (Johns Hopkins Univ. Press, 1959). An informative recent study.

A. Wilson, *Diderot: The Testing Years, 1713-1759* (Oxford Univ. Press, 1957). The first part of what promises to be a definitive biography.

N. L. Torrey, *The Spirit of Voltaire* (Columbia Univ. Press, 1938). A thoughtful study.

A. Cobban, *Rousseau and the Modern State* (Allen & Unwin, 1934). A good introduction to the implications of Rousseau's thought.

CHAPTER XVII

J. S. Schapiro, *Condorcet and the Rise of Liberalism* (Harcourt, Brace, 1934). A sympathetic study.

R. R. Palmer, *Catholics and Unbelievers in Eighteenth-Century France* (Princeton Univ. Press, 1939). A first-rate monograph.

T. D. Kendrick, *The Lisbon Earthquake* (Lippincott, 1957). An instructive account of the social and intellectual ramifications of the catastrophe.

M. F. Bukofzer, *Music in the Baroque Era* (Norton, 1947). Informative work on the period down to 1750. For more general accounts, see P. H. Láng, *Music in Western Civilization* (Norton, 1941), and C. Gray, *The History of Music*, 2nd ed. (Knopf, 1947).

F. Fosca, *The Eighteenth Century* (Skira, 1953). Superbly illustrated introduction to the painting of the century.

SPECIAL STUDIES: THE ENLIGHTENED DESPOTS

G. P. Gooch, *Frederick the Great* (Knopf, 1947) and F. J. P. Veale, *Frederick the Great* (Hamish, Hamilton, 1935). Two reasonable and balanced assessments of the great Hohenzollern.

W. H. Bruford, *Germany in the Eighteenth Century* (Cambridge Univ. Press, 1952). A valuable study, stressing social and intellectual history.

C. L. Morris, *Maria Theresa, The Last Conservative* (Knopf, 1937). Informative and sympathetic.

S. K. Padover, *The Revolutionary Emperor* (Ballou, 1934). Warmly favorable account of Joseph II.

G. Scott Thomson, *Catherine the Great and the Expansion of Russia* (Macmillan, 1950). A sound, brief introduction. Of the full biographies of Catherine, the best is perhaps still the old K. Walizewski, *The Romance of an Empress* (Appleton, 1894).

R. Herr, *The Eighteenth-Century Revolution in Spain* (Princeton Univ. Press, 1958). A full account of the reign of Charles III and of the impact of the Enlightenment.

SPECIAL STUDIES: GEORGE III AND THE AMERICAN REVOLUTION

J. C. Miller, *Origins of the American Revolution*, rev. ed. (Stanford Univ. Press, 1959). An excellent and balanced study.

L. H. Gipson, *The Coming of the Revolution, 1763-1775* (Harper, 1954); J. R. Alden, *The American Revolution, 1775-1783* (Harper, 1954). Full and up-to-date accounts in the "New American Nation" series.

E. S. Morgan, *The Birth of the Republic, 1763-1789* (*Univ. of Chicago Press, 1956). Another good introductory account.

C. Becker, *The Declaration of Independence*, new ed. (Knopf, 1948; *Vintage). An admirable monograph, analyzing the Declaration sentence by sentence and examining its European roots.

M. Beloff, *Thomas Jefferson and American Democracy* (Macmillan, 1949). A good introduction to one of the most versatile and intellectual of the Founding Fathers.

J. S. Watson, *The Reign of George III, 1760-1815* (Clarendon, 1960), Volume XII of *The Oxford History of England*. An up-to-date general account, incorporating recent scholarly reinterpretations of this important reign.

L. B. Namier, *The Structure of Politics at the Accession of George III*, 2 vols. (Macmillan, 1929), and *England in the Age of the American Revolution* (Macmillan, 1930). Detailed studies of English politics in the 1760's. For further works on 18th-century England, see the reading suggestions for Chapter XVI.

SOURCES

C. Brinton, ed., *The Portable Age of Reason Reader* (Viking, 1956). A good cross-section of the writing of the Enlightenment.

B. R. Redman, ed., *The Portable Voltaire* (*Viking, 1949). A well-chosen selection, prefaced by an informative introduction.

Montesquieu, *The Spirit of the Laws,* F. Neumann, ed. (Hafner, 1949). Excellent edition of a rambling classic.

Rousseau, *The Social Contract and Discourses* (Dutton, 1950; *The Social Contract* only, *Gateway), and *Emile* (Dutton, 1955; *Barron's). Handy editions of Jean-Jacques' famous writings.

F. de La Fontainerie, ed., *French Liberalism and Education in the Eighteenth Century* (McGraw-Hill, 1932). Proposals for educational reform by Diderot and others.

Beccaria, *Essay on Crimes and Punishments* (Academic Reprints, 1953). Short and pungent; a fine introduction to the thinking of the *philosophes.*

A. Smith, *Selections from "The Wealth of Nations"* (*Gateway). A convenient sample of this celebrated work.

B. Dobrée, ed., *The Letters of King George III* (Cassell, 1935). Most readable; full of the flavor of English politics.

M. Beloff, ed., *The Debate on the American Revolution, 1761-1783* (Kaye, 1949). Handy compilation of British speeches and writings for and against the rebels.

H. S. Commager, ed., *Documents of American History,* 6th ed. (Appleton-Century-Crofts, 1958). A useful collection.

HISTORICAL FICTION

S. Richardson, *Clarissa* (Modern Library, 1950). Abridgement of the celebrated marathon novel.

See also the works suggested for Chapter XVI.

CHAPTER XVII

The French Revolution and Napoleon

CHAPTER XVIII

I: The Causes
of the Revolution

In France, as in the thirteen North American colonies, a financial crisis produced a revolution. There was not only a parallel but also a direct connection between the revolution of 1776 and that of 1789. French participation in the War of American Independence increased an already excessive governmental debt by more than 1,500,000,000 *livres,** and the example of America fired the imagination of discontented Frenchmen. To them Benjamin Franklin, the immensely popular American envoy to France, was the very embodiment of the Enlightenment, and the new republic overseas promised to become the utopia of the *philosophes.* At most, however, the American precedent only speeded up developments in France. The forces causing the upheaval of 1789 were almost fully matured in 1776. And, just as the reasons for revolution were more deeply

---

* It is impossible to set a truly meaningful value for the pre-revolutionary French *livre* in terms of present-day money. It has been estimated that the *livre* may have been worth about $1.00 in terms of the 1960 dollar, or perhaps 20 cents in terms of the 1914 dollar, but such estimates are misleading because of the great increase in prices and the shifts in the proportionate cost of basic necessities during the two centuries since the Old Régime.

Opposite. NAPOLEON IN HIS STUDY, *by Jacques-Louis David (1748-1825); French, painted 1812; National Gallery of Art, Washington, D. C. David was the "painter laureate" of the Revolutionary and Napoleonic régimes. His portrait of Bonaparte not only exemplifies the prevailing neoclassicism in art (see below, p. 151) but also shows the revolutionary taste for sturdy furniture of ancient Roman design.*

rooted and more complicated in France than in America, so the Revolution itself was to be more violent and more sweeping.

The *immediate* cause of the great French Revolution, then, was financial. King Louis XVI vainly tried one expedient after another to avert bankruptcy and finally summoned the Estates General, the central representative assembly that had last met 175 years earlier. Once assembled, the deputies of the nation initiated the reforms that were to destroy the Old Régime in France. The *basic* causes of the Revolution, however, reached deep into France's society and economy and into her political and intellectual history. Behind the financial crisis of the 1780's lay many decades of fiscal mismanagement; the government had been courting insolvency since the last years of Louis XIV. The nobles and clergy, jealously guarding their traditional privileges, refused to pay a fair share of the taxes. Resentment against inequitable taxation and inefficient government built up among the unprivileged—the peasantry, the workers, and, above all, the bourgeoisie. The ideas of the *philosophes* translated bourgeois resentment into a program of active reform.

The Monarchy

France, the home of the Enlightenment, was never ruled by an enlightened despot until the advent of Napoleon. King Louis XV had refused to take decisive steps to remedy the abuses of the Old Régime (see Chapter XVI). What Louis XV would not do, his grandson and successor could not do. Louis XVI (1774-1792), unlike his grandfather, was earnest and pious, but he had a slow mind and was both irresolute and stubborn. Louis labored under the additional handicap of a politically unfortunate marriage. Marie Antoinette, his wife, was frivolous and ignorant; worse still, she was a Habsburg, the daughter of Maria Theresa, a constant reminder to French patriots of the Franco-Austrian alliance that had led so quickly to the humiliations of the Seven Years' War.

For want of a good mechanic, the machinery of centralized royal absolutism was gradually falling apart. The fact that it functioned at all could be credited to a relatively few capable administrators, notably the *intendants* who ran so much of provincial France. The best of the *intendants*, like the Physiocrat Turgot at Limoges, provided a welcome touch of enlightened despotism, but they could do little to stay the slow disintegration of the central government.

The whole legal and judicial system required reform. The law needed to be codified to eliminate obsolete medieval survivals and to end the overlapping of the two legal systems—Roman and feudal—that prevailed in France. The courts needed a thorough overhaul to make them swift, fair, and inexpensive. Many judges and lawyers purchased or inherited their offices and regarded them not as a public trust but as a means to private enrichment. Louis XV had permitted his ministers to attack the Parlement of Paris, the stronghold of these vested interests and the highest court in France. One of the last acts of his reign had been the cancellation of its privileges; one of the first moves taken by Louis XVI was the restoration of its full authority. Many Frenchmen regarded the Parlement of Paris as a kind of constitutional check on the absolutism of the monarchy, but the Parlement was also a formidable obstacle in the way of social and economic reform.

The First and Second Estates

Like the monarchy itself, the social and economic foundations of the Old Régime were beginning to crumble by the middle of the eighteenth century. The first estate, the clergy, occupied a position of conspicuous importance in France. Though forming less than one per cent of the total population, the clergy possessed extensive and lucrative lands and performed many functions that are normally undertaken by the state today. The Church kept records of vital statistics, dispensed relief to the poor, and ran the educational system, such as it was. The Gallican Church, however, was a house divided. The lower clergy came almost entirely from the third estate; humble, poorly paid, and generally hardworking, the priests resented the wealth and the arrogance of their ecclesiastical superiors. The bishops and abbots maintained the outlook of the noble class into which they had been born. Although some of them took their duties seriously, others regarded church office as a convenient means of securing a comfortable income. Dozens of prelates turned the administration of their bishoprics or monasteries over to subordinates, pocketed the revenue for themselves, and took up residence in Paris or Versailles.

The wealth and the lax discipline of the Church aroused criticism and envy. Good Catholics deplored the dwindling number of monks and nuns and their growing tendency to stress the exploitation of their properties. Well-to-do peasants and townspeople coveted these rich ecclesiastical estates. Taxpayers grumbled at the tithe levied by the Church, even though the full 10 per cent implied by the word "tithe" was seldom demanded. They complained still more about the Church's exemption from taxation and about the meager size of the "free gift" voted by the clergy to the government in lieu of taxes. The peasants on the whole remained moderately faithful Catholics and regarded the village priest, if not the bishop, with esteem and affection. The bourgeois, however, more and more accepted the anticlerical views of the *philosophes*. They interpreted Voltaire's plea to "crush the infamous thing" as a mandate to strip the Church of wealth and power.

Like the higher clergy, the nobles of the Old Régime, the second estate, enjoyed privilege, wealth—and unpopularity. Although forming less than 2 per cent of the population, they held about 25 per cent of the land. They had virtual exemption from taxation; they monopolized army commissions and appointments to high ecclesiastical office. The French aristocracy, however, comprised not a single social unit but a series of differing groups. At the top were the hereditary nobles, a few of them descended from royalty or from feudal lords of the Middle Ages, but more from families ennobled within the past two or three centuries. These "nobles of the sword" tended to view most of their countrymen, including the lesser nobility, as vulgar upstarts. In spite of their dismal failure during the regency of Orléans (see Chapter XVI), they dreamed of the day when they might rule France again, as the feudal nobles had ruled in the Middle Ages. Clustered at Versailles, they neglected their duties as the first landlords of the realm. Arthur Young, the observant English economist who made a tour of France in the late 1780's, commented on the uncultivated aristocratic lands he found:

Much of these wastes belonged to the Prince de Soubise, who would not sell any part of them. Thus it is whenever you stumble on a Grand Seigneur, even one that was worth millions, you are sure to find his property desert. The Duke of Bouillon's and this prince's are two of the greatest properties in France; and all the signs I have yet seen of their greatness, are wastes. . . . Oh! if I was the legislator of France for a day, I would make such great lords skip again! *

Below the nobility of the sword came the "nobility of the robe," including the robed justices of the Paris Parlement and other high courts and a host of other officials. The nobles of the robe, or their ancestors, had originally secured aristocratic

---

* *Travels in France,* Constantia Maxwell, ed. (Cambridge, England, 1929), 62.

status by buying their offices. But, since these dignities were then handed down from father to son, the mercenary origins of their status had become somewhat obscured with the passage of time. By the late eighteenth century there was often little practical distinction between the gentry of the robe and their brethren of the sword; marriages between members of the two groups were common. On the whole, the nobles of the robe were richer than the nobles of the sword, and they exerted more power and influence by virtue of their firm hold on key governmental positions. The ablest and most tenacious defenders of special privilege in the dying years of the Old Régime were the rich judges of Parlement, not the elegant but ineffectual courtiers of Versailles.

Many noblemen, however, had little wealth, power, or glamor. They belonged to the lowest level of French aristocracy—the *hobereaux*, the "little falcons" or "sparrow-hawks." They vegetated on their country estates, since they could afford neither the purchase of a government office nor the expensive pleasures of the court. In the effort to conserve at least part of their traditional status, almost all the *hobereaux* insisted on the meticulous collection of the surviving feudal and manorial dues from the peasantry. Their exhumation of old documents to justify levies sometimes long forgotten earned them the abiding hatred of the peasants and prepared the way for the document-burning that occurred during the Revolution.

Not every noble was a snobbish courtier or a selfish defender of the status quo. A few *hobereaux* calmly drifted down the social ladder to become simple farmers. Some nobles of the robe, attracted by the opportunities for wealth, took part in business enterprises. Even the loftiest noble families produced enlightened spirits, like the Marquis de Lafayette, like the young bloods who applauded the ingenious valet, Figaro, when he outwitted his social superiors in

Beaumarchais' satire on aristocracy, *The Marriage of Figaro*, first staged in 1784.

The Third Estate

The first two estates included only a small fraction of the French nation; at least 95 per cent of Frenchmen fell within the third estate in 1789. The great majority of these commoners were peasants. In some respects, the status of the peasantry was more favorable in France than it was anywhere else in Europe. Serfdom, which was still so prevalent in central and eastern Europe, had disappeared almost entirely except in Lorraine and the Franche Comté (County of Burgundy). While enclosures were gradually pushing small farmers off the land in England, small peasant holdings existed by the millions in France. Three out of every four adult peasants, it is estimated, held some land. Nevertheless, the observant eye of Arthur Young noted many signs of rural misery in 1787 and 1788. In southwestern France, for example:

> Pass Payrac, and meet many beggars, which we had not done before. All the country, girls and women, are without shoes or stockings; and the ploughmen at their work have neither sabots nor feet to their stockings. This is a poverty, that strikes at the root of national prosperity. . . . It reminded me of the misery of Ireland.[*]

Although the degree of agrarian distress varied greatly from province to province, the total picture was far from bright. The trouble came in part from three factors—backward methods of farming, the shortage of land, and overpopulation. The efficient techniques of the agricultural revolution made little headway in France before 1789. Vast areas were not cultivated at all or lay fallow every second or third year in accordance with medieval practice. The constantly increasing rural population sim-

---

[*] *Travels in France*, 23-24.

ply could not find full employment or a decent livelihood. Primitive farming required large tracts of land, but the property-holding three-quarters of the French peasantry controlled less than one-third of the land. The average holding was so small that even a propertied peasant might face starvation in poor crop years. The landless peasant turned to begging and sometimes to theft; the peasant who owned some land wanted more land and more "freedom."

Rising prices and heavy taxes also oppressed the peasants. The upward trend of prices in France throughout the eighteenth century brought prosperity to many towns, but to the backward rural economy it brought the new hardship of inflation. The price of the products sold by the farmer rose less swiftly than that of the goods which the farmer had to buy. To the Church the peasants paid the tithe, and to the nobility they paid the obsolete dues that the impecunious *hobereaux* demanded. To the state they owed a land tax, an income tax, a poll tax, and a variety of other duties, of which the most widely detested was the *gabelle*, the obligatory purchase of salt from government agents, usually at an exorbitant price.

France had a long history of agrarian unrest, going back to the *jacquerie*, the savage peasant uprising during the Hundred Years' War. In the decades before 1789 there was no new *jacquerie*, but unemployment and poverty had created a revolutionary temper among the peasants. They did not want a change in the form of government; they were ignorant of the reform program of the Enlightenment. But they most emphatically wanted more land, if need be at the expense of the clergy and the nobility; they wanted an end to manorial dues; and they wanted relief from a system of taxation that bore hardest upon those who could least afford to pay.

The other members of the third estate, the urban workers and the bourgeoisie, had little reason to cherish the Old Régime.

"Labor," in our modern sense of a large, self-conscious body of factory workers, hardly existed in pre-revolutionary France. Yet almost every sizable town had its wage-earners, employed chiefly in small businesses or workshops. These urban laborers felt with particular sharpness the pinch of rising prices. They were not, however, to take the commanding role in the Revolution itself; geographically scattered, lacking in class cohesiveness, they were ready to follow the lead of the bourgeoisie.

The bourgeoisie included Frenchmen of very divergent resources and interests—rich merchants and bankers in the cities, storekeepers and lawyers in country towns and villages, doctors and other professional men, and thousands upon thousands of craftsmen running their own little businesses. Implacable hostility to the privileged estates and warm receptiveness to the propaganda of the *philosophes* cemented this sprawling middle class into a political force. The bourgeoisie suffered fewer hardships than the peasants and workers did, but they resented the abuses of the Old Régime even more keenly. Though they paid a smaller proportion of their incomes in taxes, they violently denounced the inequality of assessments. While profiting by the rise in prices, the wealthier and more enterprising businessmen complained of guild regulations and other restrictions on free commercial activity. They found it galling to be snubbed by the nobility, treated as second-class subjects by the monarchy, and excluded from the better posts in government, Church, and army.

In sum, the men of the middle class fully realized their own growing economic importance, and they wanted social and political rights to match. Because they were wealthier, better educated, and more articulate than the peasants and wage-earners, they took the leading part in formulating the grievances of the entire third estate. These grievances were compiled in statements called *cahiers* and submitted to the Estates General in 1789.

The *cahier* of the third estate of the Longuyon district in Lorraine provides a good sample of the bourgeois reform program.* Sizable portions of this *cahier* dealt with local problems, like the destruction of the woods to supply fuel for iron-smelters. Other portions, however, showed a sharp awareness of the great issues of the day. The *cahier* prononunced the freedom of the press the "surest means of maintaining the freedom of the nation." It deplored the harshness of the criminal laws; they should conform to "the customs and the character of the French nation, the kindest people in the universe." It recommended "a social contract or act between the sovereign and his people," to safeguard "the personal freedom of all citizens" and "prevent the recurrence of those disastrous events which at present oppress the king and the nation." A spirited assertion of the sanctity of private property followed, a rebuke to Rousseau's economic principles thus accompanying the appeal to his political philosophy. The third estate of Longuyon, however, believed in a large measure of equality. It proposed that "all Frenchmen should have the right and the hope of securing any State office, of whatever grade, and all military and ecclesiastical dignities." Existing taxes should be swept away, to be replaced by levies on "all property without distinction as to owners, and on all persons without distinction of order and rank."

The Financial Crisis

The chronic financial difficulties of the French monarchy strengthened the hand of the middle-class reformers. The government debt, already large at the ac-

cession of Louis XVI, tripled between 1774 and 1789; about half the increase resulted from French participation in the American War of Independence. In 1789, the debt stood at 4,500,000,000 *livres*. The budget for 1788, the only one computed for the Old Régime, made alarming reading: *

Estimated Expenses	(In *livres*)
For debt service	318,000,000
For the court	35,000,000
For other purposes	276,000,000
Total	629,000,000
Estimated Revenues	503,000,000
Estimated Deficit	126,000,000

Note here the relatively modest cost of the court and the very high proportion of revenues consumed by interest payments on debts already contracted.

Louis XVI, in his feeble way, tried to cope with the growing emergency. On coming to the throne in 1774, he named as chief minister Turgot, a leading Physiocrat with a brilliant record as *intendant* of Limoges. Turgot temporarily reduced the deficit by imposing strict economies, particularly on the expenditures of the court. To increase prosperity and to propitiate the third estate, he curtailed the ancient guild monopolies, lifted restrictions on the internal shipments of grain, and replaced the *corvée*, the work on highways demanded of peasants, with a tax affecting nobles and commoners alike. At this the vested interests rebelled and, seconded by Marie Antoinette, secured Turgot's dismissal in 1776. The ousted minister admonished Louis XVI: "Remember, sire, that it was weakness which brought the head of Charles I to the block."

Louis ignored Turgot's warning. The government continued to raise new loans—653,000,000 *livres* between 1783 and 1786 alone. Then in 1786 the bankers refused to make new advances. The French government was caught between the irresistible

---

* The full text of this *cahier* is printed in B. F. Hyslop, *A Guide to the General Cahiers of 1789* (New York, 1936), 318-326. The quotations that follow are in our translation.

* Based on the figures in G. Lefebvre, *The Coming of the French Revolution*, R. R. Palmer, trans. (Princeton, 1947), 21-22.

CHAPTER XVIII

force of the third estate's demands for tax relief and the immovable object of the other estates' refusal to yield their fiscal exemptions. The monarchy had temporized and borrowed until it could afford neither fresh delays nor new loans. Calonne, the finance minister in 1786, proposed to meet the crisis by reviving Turgot's reforms. In the hope of persuading the first two estates to consent to heavier taxation, he convoked the Assembly of Notables, the chief aristocratic and ecclesiastical dignitaries of the kingdom. But the Notables declined to be persuaded.

Louis XVI dissolved the Notables and dismissed Calonne. Then, with unaccustomed firmness, he decided to levy a uniform tax on all landed property without regard to the social status of the holder. The clergy replied by reducing their "free gift" for 1788 to one-sixth of what it had previously been. The Parlement of Paris declared the new tax law illegal and asserted that only the nation as a whole assembled in the Estates General could make so sweeping a change. The King retreated and in the summer of 1788 announced that the Estates General would meet the following spring.

The Estates General

Louis XVI thus revived a half-forgotten institution which had represented the nation, after a fashion, but which scarcely seemed likely to enact drastic social and economic reforms. The three estates, despite their immense variation in size, had customarily received equal representation and equal voting power, so that the two privileged orders could outvote the commoners. The Estates General of 1789, however, met under unique circumstances.

In the first place, its election and subsequent meeting took place during an economic crisis that heightened the chronic social and financial tensions. In 1786, a trade treaty between France and Britain lowered French tariffs on British manufactures and allowed cheaper British textiles and metals to invade the French market. By 1789, thousands of French craftsmen were out of work; nor was this all: hail and drought ruined the harvest of 1788, and the winter of 1788-89 was so bitter that the Seine froze over at Paris, blocking shipments of grain by water. Half-starved and half-frozen, Parisians huddled around bonfires provided by the municipal government. In the spring of 1789, the price of grain rose to double the normal, and in some localities to quadruple.

France had survived depressions, bad weather, and poor harvests many times in the past without experiencing revolution. This time, however, the economic hardships were the last straw. Starving peasants begged, borrowed, and stole, poaching on the hunting preserves of the great lords and attacking their game wardens. The turbulence in Paris boiled over in a riot (April, 1789), witnessed by Thomas Jefferson, then the American minister to France:

... The Fauxbourg St. Antoine is a quarter of the city inhabited entirely by the class of day-laborers and journeymen in every line. A rumor was spread among them that a great paper manufacturer ... had proposed ... that their wages should be lowered to 15 sous a day [three-quarters of a *livre*]. ... They flew to his house in vast numbers, destroyed everything in it, and in his magazines and work shops, without secreting however a pin's worth to themselves, and were continuing this work of devastation when the regular troops were called in. Admonitions being disregarded, they were of necessity fired on, and a regular action ensued, in which about 100 of them were killed, before the rest would disperse.[*]

These disturbances impressed a sense of urgency on the deputies to the Estates General.

[*] *Autobiography of Thomas Jefferson,* P. L. Ford, ed. (New York, 1914), 133-134.

In the second place, the methods followed in electing the deputies aided the champions of reform. Contrary to precedent, and against the violent opposition of the Parlement, the third estate secured double representation, thus gaining as many seats as the clergy and the nobility combined. In each district of France, moreover, the third estate made its choice not by secret ballot but in a public meeting. Since this procedure greatly favored bourgeois orators over inarticulate farmers or workers, middle-class lawyers won control of the commoners' deputation. Finally, the radicals of the third estate found a few sympathizers in the second estate and many more in the first estate, where the discontented lower clergy had a large delegation:

THE ESTATES GENERAL, 1789

Estate	No. of Deputies
First:	
Higher Clergy	94
Lower Clergy	More than 200
Second	270
Third	578

A majority of the deputies were prepared to make drastic changes in the Old Régime.

But in all past meetings of the Estates General each estate, or order, had deliberated separately, with the consent of two estates and of the Crown required for the passage of a measure. In 1789, the King and the privileged orders favored retaining this "vote by order." The third estate, on the contrary, demanded "vote by head," with the deputies from all the orders deliberating together, each deputy having a single vote. Pamphleteers invoked Rousseau's concept of the general will. "What is the third estate?" wrote Abbé Siéyès in an influential broadside of the same name. "Everything."

...If votes are taken by order, five million citizens will not be able to decide anything for the general interest, because it will not please a couple of hundred thousand privileged individuals. The will of a single individual will veto and destroy the will of more than a hundred people.[*]

This crucial question of procedure came to a head soon after the Estates General convened on May 5, 1789, at Versailles. Siéyès and Mirabeau, a renegade nobleman, led the campaign for vote by head. On June 17, the third estate cut the Gordian knot of procedure by accepting Siéyès' invitation to proclaim itself the "National Assembly." It completed its revolutionary repudiation of the Old Régime by inviting the deputies of the other two estates to join its sessions.

A majority of the clerical deputies, chiefly parish priests, accepted; the nobility refused. The King barred the commoners from their meeting place, whereupon they assembled at an indoor tennis court on June 20 and solemnly swore never to disband until they had given France a constitution. To the "Tennis-Court Oath" Louis replied by commanding each estate to resume its separate deliberations. The third estate and some deputies of the first disobeyed. Louis, vacillating as ever, now gave in and on June 27 directed the noble and clerical deputies to join the National Assembly. The nation, through its representatives, had successfully challenged the King and the vested interests. The Estates General was dead, and in its place sat the National Assembly, pledged to reform French society and give the nation a constitution. The revolution was now under way.

---

[*] Emmanuel Siéyès, *Qu'est-ce Que le Tiers Etat?*, E. Champion, ed. (Paris, 1888), 82. Our translation.

II: The Dissolution of the Monarchy

Popular Uprisings
(July-October, 1789)

The National Assembly had barely settled down to work when a new wave of rioting swept over France, undermining further the position of the King. The economic depression grew more severe during the summer of 1789. Unemployment increased, and bread threatened to be scarce and expensive at least until after the autumn harvest. Meanwhile, the commoners feared that the King and the privileged orders might attempt a counter-revolution. Large concentrations of troops appeared in the Paris area early in July—to preserve order and protect the National Assembly, the King asserted. But the Parisians suspected that Louis was planning the forcible dissolution of the Assembly. Suspicion deepened into conviction after Louis dismissed Necker, the popular financier who had been serving as the chief royal adviser.

The reaction to Necker's dismissal was immediate and revolutionary. On July 12 and 13, the men who had elected the Paris deputies of the third estate formed a new municipal government and a new militia, both loyal to the National Assembly. Paris was forging the weapons that made it the leader of the Revolution. Mobs were roaming the streets, demanding cheaper bread, parading busts of Necker draped in mourning, and breaking into government buildings to obtain arms. On July 14, the armed mob stormed the Bastille, a fortress in the eastern part of the city, and massacred its garrison.

The fall of the Bastille had little practical significance, but its symbolic value was immense. The gloomy pile frowned like a monster sentry over a teeming and restless working-class quarter of Paris. Its capture and subsequent demolition symbolized the loosening of the shackles of the Old Régime. Further, the public imagined the Bastille to be crowded with innocent victims of royal tyranny. Actually, there were only seven prisoners to be liberated at the time of its capture—five criminals (mostly forgers) and two mental cases. But the anticlimactic facts have never destroyed the legend. Ever since 1789 the Fourteenth of July has been the great national holiday of Frenchmen, their counterpart of the American Fourth of July.

Rioting spread over much of France late in July, as the provincial population responded to the news from Paris or acted on its own. In town after town, mobs attacked the local version of the Bastille. Arthur Young, who was surveying the agriculture of Alsace, witnessed the scene at Strasbourg:

... The Parisian spirit of commotion spreads quickly; it is here; the troops ... are employed to keep an eye on the people who shew signs of an intended revolt. They have broken the windows of some magistrates that are no favourites; and a great mob of them is at this moment assembled, demanding clamourously to have meat at 5 *sous* a pound.*

The countryside, in the meantime, was experiencing the "Great Fear," one of the most extraordinary attacks of mass delusion on record. From village to village word spread that "brigands" were coming, aristocratic hirelings who would destroy crops and villages and force the National Assembly to preserve the status quo. There were in fact no brigands, only an occasional

---

* *Travels in France*, 181.

The Bastille, July 14, 1789.

starving farmhand trying to steal food. But the peasants in many districts went berserk, clutching hoes and pitchforks, anything resembling a weapon. When the brigands did not materialize, they attacked chateaux and broke into any building that might house a hoard of grain or the hated documents justifying collection of manorial dues. The wiser nobles voluntarily gave the peasants what they wanted; the others saw their barns and archives burnt. The Great Fear, beginning as a psychological aberration, ended as an uprising of the peasantry against its traditional oppressors.

By the end of July, 1789, four distinct sets of revolutionary events had taken place in France: (1) the constitutional revolution of June, resulting in the creation of the National Assembly; (2) the Paris revolution and the taking of the Bastille;

(3) the comparable outbreaks in provincial cities and towns; and (4) the Great Fear. Each of the four drove another nail into the coffin of the Old Régime. The transformation of the Estates General into the National Assembly and the creation of new local governments destroyed the political superiority of the first two estates. The Great Fear began the destruction of their social and economic privileges. Everywhere, legally constituted officials were turned out, taxes went unpaid, and valuable records were destroyed.

The "October Days," the last crisis of a momentous year, demonstrated anew the impotence of Louis XVI and the power of his aroused subjects. As the autumn of 1789 drew on, Parisians still queued for bread and still looked suspiciously at the royal troops stationed in the neighborhood of their city. Rumors of the Queen's behavior further incensed them. Marie Antoinette made a dramatic appearance at a banquet of royal officers, clutching the Dauphin (the heir to the throne) in her arms, striking the very pose that her mother, Maria Theresa, had employed so effectively to win the support of the Hungarians in the 1740's. And, on hearing that the people had no bread, she was said to have remarked callously: "Let them eat cake." This story was false, but it echoed and re-echoed in the lively new Paris papers that delighted in denouncing "l'Autrichienne."

The climax came on October 5, 1789, when an array of determined Paris housewives marched the dozen miles from Paris to Versailles in the rain. They disrupted the National Assembly and succeeded in extracting a kiss from a baffled Louis XVI. This bizarre demonstration had very significant consequences. On October 6, the women marched back to Paris, escorting "the baker, the baker's wife, and the baker's son"—in other words, the royal family—who took up residence in the Tuileries Palace. More important, the National Assembly, too, moved to Paris. The most revolutionary place in France had captured both the symbol of the Old Régime and the herald of the new.

The National Assembly (1789-1791)

The outlines of the new régime were already starting to take shape before the October Days. The Great Fear prompted the National Assembly to abolish in law what the peasants were destroying in fact. On the evening of August 4, 1789, the Viscount de Noailles, a liberal nobleman, addressed the deputies:

The kingdom at this moment hangs between the alternative of the destruction of society, and that of a government which will be the admiration and the exemplar of Europe.

How is this government to be established? By public tranquillity. . . . And to secure this necessary tranquillity, I propose:

(1) . . . That taxation will be paid by all the individuals of the kingdom, in proportion to their revenues;

(2) That all public expenses will in the future be borne equally by all.*

The deputies voted the proposals of Noailles. In addition, the clergy gave up its tithes, and the liberal minority of the second estate surrendered the nobility's game preserves, manorial dues, and other medieval rights. The assembly made it a clean sweep by abolishing serfdom, forbidding the sale of justice or of judicial office, and decreeing that "all citizens, without distinction of birth, can be admitted to all ecclesiastical, civil, and military posts and dignities." When the memorable session inaugurated by Noailles' speech ended at two o'clock on the morning of August 5, the Old Régime was dead.

Three weeks later, on August 26, 1789, the National Asssembly formulated the Declaration of the Rights of Man. "Men are born free and equal in rights," it asserted (Art. 1). "These rights are liberty, property, security and resistance to oppression" (Art. 2). Property it called "an inviolable and sacred right" (Art. 17), and liberty "the exercise of the natural rights of each man" within the limits "determined by law" (Art. 4). "Law," the Declaration stated, "is the expression of the general will. All citizens have the right to take part, in person or by their representatives, in its formation" (Art. 6). "Any society in which the guarantee of rights is not assured or the separation of powers not determined has no constitution" (Art. 16).†

The Declaration of the Rights of Man mirrored the political and economic attitudes of the middle class. It insisted on the

---

* *Archives Parlementaires*, Series 1, VIII, 343. Our translation.

† G. Lefebvre, *The Coming of the French Revolution* (Princeton, 1947), Appendix.

An assignat *for fifty* livres *(francs).*

sacredness of property. It committed the French to the creed of constitutional liberalism already affirmed by the English in 1688-89 and by the Americans in 1776, and it incorported the key phrases of the *philosophes:* natural rights, general will, and separation of powers. The National Assembly made a resounding statement of the ideals of the Enlightenment. Yet, as the subsequent history of the Revolution soon demonstrated, the Assembly found no magic formula by which to translate these ideals into practice. (ENFORCEMENT)

The economic legislation of the National Assembly provided a case in point. Belief in the theory of the equal taxation of all Frenchmen did not solve urgent financial problems. The new and just land tax imposed by the deputies simply could not be collected. Tax-collectors had vanished in the general liquidation of the Old Régime, and naive peasants thought that they owed nothing to a government turned revolutionary. Once again, the French state borrowed until its credit was exhausted, and then, in desperation, the National Assembly ordered the confiscation of church lands (November, 1789). "The wealth of the clergy is at the disposition of the nation," it declared, explaining that ecclesiastical lands fell outside the bounds of "inviolable" property as defined in the Declaration of the Rights of Man because they belonged to an institution and not to private individuals.

SAME EC. PROBLEMS

The government thus acquired an asset worth at least 2,000,000,000 *livres*. On the basis of this collateral it issued *assignats*, paper notes used to pay the government's debts. So far, so good: the *assignats* had adequate security behind them and temporarily eased the financial crisis. Unfortunately, the Revolution repeated the mistake of John Law (see Chapter XVI): it did not know when to stop. As the state sold parcels of confiscated land—that is, as it reduced the collateral securing its paper money—it should have destroyed *assignats* to the same amount. The temptation not to reduce the number of *assignats* proved too great to resist. Inflation resulted: the *assignats*, progressively losing their solid backing, depreciated until in 1795 they were worth less than 5 per cent of their face value.

This economic experiment resulted in the redistribution of some of the best farmland in France. Many peasants enlarged their holdings by purchasing former ecclesiastical property, and the bourgeoisie also invested heavily in land. The poor and landless peasants, however, gained nothing, since they did not have the money with which to buy. Following the doctrine of laissez-faire, the National Assembly made no move to help these marginal farmers. Following the same doctrine, it abolished the guilds and the irksome internal tariffs and tolls. And deeming the few primitive organizations of labor unnatural restrictions on economic freedom, it abolished them too. In June, 1791, after an outbreak of strikes, it passed the Le Chapelier Law banning both strikes and labor unions.

Since the suppression of tithes and the seizure of ecclesiastical property deprived the Church of its revenue, the National Assembly agreed to finance ecclesiastical salaries. The new arrangement virtually nationalized the Gallican Church and made it subject to constant government regulation. The Assembly's decision to suppress monasteries and convents caused little dif-

CHAPTER XVIII

ficulty; many of these establishments were already far gone in decay. But an uproar arose over the legislation altering the status of the secular hierarchy.

The Civil Constitution of the Clergy (June, 1790) redrew the ecclesiastical map of France. It reduced the number of bishoprics by more than one-third, making the remaining dioceses correspond to the new civil administrative units known as departments (see below). It transformed bishops and priests into civil officials, paid by the state and elected by the population of the diocese or parish; both Catholics and non-Catholics (the latter usually a small minority) could vote in these elections. A new bishop was required to take an oath of loyalty to the state, and the Civil Constitution stipulated that he might not apply to the Pope for confirmation, though he might write to him as the "Visible Head of the Universal Church."

These provisions stripped the "Visible Head of the Universal Church" of effective authority over the Gallican clergy and ran counter to the whole tradition of the Roman Church as an independent ecclesiastical monarchy. Naturally the Pope denounced the Civil Constitution. The National Assembly then required that every member of the French clergy take a special oath supporting the Civil Constitution, but only seven bishops and fewer than half of the priests complied. Thus a breach was opened between the Revolution and a large segment of the population. Good Catholics, from Louis XVI down to humble peasants, rallied to the non-juring clergy, those who refused the special oath. The Civil Constitution of the Clergy, supplying an issue for rebellion and civil war, was the first great blunder of the Revolution.

The Constitution of 1791

The major undertaking of the National Assembly was the Constitution of 1791. The Assembly devised a neat and orderly system of local government to replace the bewildering complex of provincial units that had accumulated under the Old Régime. It divided the territory of France into eighty-three departments of approximately equal size. Each department was small enough for its chief town to be within a day's journey of the outlying towns; each bore the name of a river, a mountain range, or some other natural landmark. The departments were subdivided into *arrondissements* or districts, and the districts into communes—that is, municipalities. The commune-district-department arrangement resembled, on a reduced scale, the American pattern of town-county-state. In the communes and departments, elected councils and officials enjoyed considerable rights of self-government. The administration of the new France, on paper anyhow, was to be far more decentralized than that of the Old Régime.

The principle of the separation of powers guided the reconstruction of the central government. The Constitution of 1791 established an independent hierarchy of courts staffed by elected judges. It vested legislative authority in a single elected chamber. Although the king still headed the executive branch, his actions now required approval by his ministers. But he was given the power of veto, a suspensive veto that could block legislation for four years. Louis XVI, no longer the absolute "King of France," acquired the new constitutional title, "King of the French."

The new constitution subscribed to many other principles issuing straight from the Enlightenment. It promised to give France a new law code, and it declared marriage a civil contract, not a sacrament. The state took over the old ecclesiastical functions of keeping records of vital statistics and providing charity and education. Indeed, the Constitution promised a system of free public education. In foreign policy revolutionary France would be more virtuous and less aggressive than autocratic France:

The French nation renounces the undertaking of any war with a view of making conquests, and it will never use its forces against the liberty of any people.[*]

The Constitution of 1791 went a long way toward instituting popular government, but it stopped well short of full democracy. Restricting the political equality promised by the Declaration of the Rights of Man, it divided Frenchmen into two classes of citizens, "active" and "passive." It limited the right of voting to "active" citizens, who paid annually in taxes an amount equal to at least three days' wages for labor in the locality. The "passive" citizens, numbering about one-third of the male population, enjoyed the full protection of the law but did not receive the franchise. Moreover, the new legislature was chosen by a process of indirect election. "Active" citizens did not vote for their deputies but for a series of electors, who were required to be men of substantial wealth, and who ultimately elected the deputies. The French middle class evidently assumed that the amount of worldly goods a man possessed determined the degree of his political wisdom.

The decentralized and limited monarchy established by the Constitution of 1791 was doomed to fail. It was too radical to suit the King and most of the aristocracy, and not radical enough for the many bourgeois who were veering toward republicanism. The majority in the National Assembly supporting the Constitution suffered the fate commonly experienced by the politically moderate in a revolution: they were squeezed out by the extremists. Despite their moderate intentions, they were driven to enact some drastic legislation, notably the Civil Constitution of the Clergy, which weakened their own position. And they

failed to develop an effective party organization at a time when the deputies of the radical minority were consolidating their strength.

These radicals were the Jacobins, so named because they belonged to the "Society of the Friends of the Constitution," which maintained its Paris headquarters in a former Jacobin monastery. The Jacobins were no true friends of the Constitution of 1791. They accepted it only as a stopgap until they might end the monarchy and set up a republic based on universal suffrage. To prepare for the millennium, the Jacobins used all the techniques of a political pressure group. They planted rabble-rousing articles in the press and manipulated the crowds of noisy and volatile spectators at the sessions of the National Assembly. Their network of political clubs extended throughout the provinces, providing the only nation-wide party organization in France. Almost everywhere, Jacobins captured control of the new department and commune councils. In local elections, as in the elections to the Estates General, an able and determined minority prevailed over a largely illiterate and politically inexperienced majority.

The defenders of the Old Régime played into the hands of the Jacobins. From the summer of 1789 on, alarmed nobles and prelates fled France, leaving behind more rich estates to be confiscated and giving Jacobin orators and editors a splendid opportunity to denounce the rats leaving a sinking ship. Many of these aristocratic *émigrés* gathered in the German Rhineland to intrigue for Austrian and Russian support of a counter-revolution. The King's grave misgivings about the Civil Constitution of the Clergy prompted his disastrous attempt to join the *émigrés* on the Franco-German frontier. In June, 1791, disguised as a valet and governess, Louis and Marie Antoinette left the Tuileries. But Louis unwisely showed his face in public, and a local official along the route recog-

---

[*] J. H. Stewart, A *Documentary Survey of the French Revolution* (New York, 1951), 260.

nized the royal profile from the portrait on the *assignats*. The alarm was sent ahead, and at Varennes in northeastern France a detachment of troops forced the royal party to return to Paris. After the abortive flight to Varennes, the revolutionaries viewed Louis XVI as a potential traitor and kept him closely guarded in the Tuileries. The experiment in constitutional monarchy began under most unfavorable auspices.

The Legislative Assembly
(October, 1791–September, 1792)

On October 1, 1791, the first and the only legislative assembly elected under the new constitution commenced its deliberations. No one faction commanded a numerical majority in the new assembly:

POLITICAL COMPLEXION OF THE
LEGISLATIVE ASSEMBLY, 1791

	Approximate No. of Seats
Right	
(Constitutional Monarchists)	265
Center (Plain)	345
Left (Jacobins)	130

(Here, as is still the practice in most continental European assemblies, the Right sat to the right of the presiding officer as he faced the assembly, the Left to his left, and the Center in between.)

The balance of political power rested with the timid and irresolute deputies of the Center, who were neither strong defenders of the Constitution nor yet convinced republicans. Since they occupied the lowest seats in the assembly hall, they received the derogatory nickname of the Plain or Marsh. The capable politicians of the Left soon captured the votes of the Plain, to demonstrate anew the power of a determined minority.

Leadership of this minority came from a small contingent of Jacobins known as Girondins because they clustered around the deputies from Bordeaux, in the Gironde

David, "The Death of Marat" (1793). *Jean Paul Marat was the popular editor of* Friend of the People, *a newspaper that appealed to the prejudices of the masses and urged direct action by the people. His assassination by Charlotte Corday, a revolutionist horrified by the excesses of the Terror, was cause for mourning.*

department. The Girondins specialized in patriotic oratory. They pictured revolutionary France as the intended victim of a great reactionary conspiracy, engineered by the *émigrés*, aided at home by the nonjuring clergy and the royal family, and abetted abroad by a league of monarchs under Leopold II, the Austrian emperor. But Louis XVI, despite the flight to Varennes, was no traitor, and Leopold II cautiously limited his aid to the *émigrés*. The sudden death of Leopold in March, 1792, and the accession of his inexperienced and less cautious son, Francis II, at once increased the Austrian threat. At the same time, belligerent Girondins secured control of French diplomacy. On April 20, 1792, the Legislative Assembly declared war on Austria. In the eyes of Frenchmen the war was defensive, not the campaign of conquest that the nation had forsworn in the fine phrases of its constitution.

The war went badly for France at the outset. Prussia soon joined Austria, and on July 25, 1792, the Prussian commander, the Duke of Brunswick, issued a manifesto drafted by an *émigré*. The manifesto stated the war aims of the allies:

> . . . To put a stop to the anarchy within France, to check the attacks delivered against throne and altar, to re-establish legal authority, to restore to the king the security and freedom of which he has been deprived, and to place him in a position where he may exercise the legitimate authority which is his due.

A threat followed. "If the Tuileries is attacked, by deed or word, if the slightest outrage or violence is perpetrated against the royal family, and if immediate measures are not taken for their safety, maintenance and liberty"—then Paris would witness "a model vengeance, never to be forgotten," and the persons responsible for the disorders would be handed over to the "tortures which they have richly deserved." [*]

The Duke of Brunswick's manifesto did not frighten the French, as it was intended

---

[*] *Le Moniteur Universel,* August 3, 1792. Our translation.

to do. On the contrary, it stiffened the already firm determination of republicans to do away with the monarchy. All through the early summer of 1792 the Jacobins of Paris had been plotting an insurrection. They won the support of a formidable following—patriotic army recruits, provincial radicals who had come to the capital to celebrate the third anniversary of the Bastille's taking, Paris workingmen angered by the depreciated value of the *assignats,* by a new food shortage, and by the government's failure to take decisive action against these economic hardships. One by one, the forty-eight *sections* or wards into which the city was divided came under the political control of the Jacobins. The climax came on the night of August 9-10, 1792, when the leaders of the *sections* ousted the regularly constituted authorities of the Paris municipal administration and installed a new and illegal Jacobin commune.

The municipal revolution in Paris at once produced decisive results. On the morning of August 10, the forces of the new commune attacked the Tuileries and massacred the King's Swiss guards. Though Louis XVI and the royal family found temporary safety with the Legislative Assembly, the uprising of August 10 sealed the doom of the monarchy. It demoralized the Assembly, thereafter little more than the errand boy of the illegal Paris commune. With most of the deputies of the Right and the Plain absent, the Assembly voted to suspend the King from office, to imprison the royal family, and to order the election of a constitutional convention. Until this new representative body should meet, a Jacobin committee was to run the government. The birth of the First French Republic was at hand.

III: The First Republic

The September Massacres
(1792)

The weeks between August 10 and the meeting of the Convention on September 21 were weeks of crisis and tension. The value of the *assignats* depreciated by 40 per cent during August alone. Rabble-rousing Jacobins continually excited the populace of Paris, already stirred by the economic difficulties and by the capture of the Tuileries. Excitement mounted still higher when the news arrived that Prussian troops had invaded northeastern France. In the emergency, Danton, the

Danton (1759-1794), in a sketch by David.

Jacobin minister of justice, won immortality by urging that the way to beat the enemy was *"de l'audace, encore de l'audace, toujours de l'audace"*—boldness, more boldness, always boldness.

In Paris, boldness took the form of the "September massacres," lynchings of supposed traitors and enemy agents. For five days, beginning on September 2, blood-thirsty mobs directed by Jacobin agents moved from prison to prison. At each stop they held impromptu courts and summary executions. The number of victims exceeded one thousand and included ordinary criminals as well as aristocrats and non-juring priests who were often quite innocent of the treason charged against them. The crowning horror was the mutilation of the Princesse de Lamballe, the Queen's maid of honor. The mob paraded her severed head on a pike before the window of the royal prison so that Marie Antoinette might see "how the people take vengeance on their tyrants." The September massacres foreshadowed the terror in store for France.

Later in the month (September 20, 1792), a rather minor French victory, grandly styled "the miracle of Valmy," turned the Duke of Brunswick and the Prussians back from the road to Paris; more solid French successes followed during the final months of 1792. Then the tide turned again, washing away the conquests of the autumn. By the summer of 1793 half-defeated France faced a hostile coalition including almost every major power in Europe. No wonder an atmosphere of perpetual emergency surrounded the Convention.

Gironde and Mountain

In theory, the election of deputies to the National Convention (August-September, 1792) marked the beginning of true political democracy in France. Both "active" and "passive" citizens were invited to the polls. In practice, however, only 10 per cent of the potential electorate of 7,000,000 actually voted. The others abstained or were turned away from the polls by the watchdogs of the Jacobin clubs, ever on the alert against "counter-revolutionaries." The result was a landslide for the republicans:

POLITICAL COMPLEXION OF THE CONVENTION, SEPTEMBER, 1792

	Approximate No. of Deputies
The Right (Gironde)	165
The Center (Plain)	435
The Left (Mountain)	150

The radicalism of the Convention was underlined by the Jacobin antecedents of both its Right and its Left. Many ties in common existed between the Gironde and the Mountain (so named because these left-wing deputies sat high up in the meeting hall). Both factions came from the middle class, both were steeped in the ideas of the *philosophes,* and both united to declare France a republic (September 21, 1792).

Rivalry, dissension, and bitter hostility, however, soon arose between the Gironde and the Mountain. As firm believers in laissez-faire, the Girondins favored a breathing spell in revolutionary legislation. They defended provincial interests against possible encroachments by Paris; as one of their deputies told the Convention (and his allusion to classical antiquity was most characteristic of the Revolution):

I fear the despotism of Paris. . . . I do not want a Paris guided by intriguers to become to the French Empire what Rome was to the Roman Empire. Paris must be reduced to its proper one-eighty-third of influence, like the other departments.[*]

---

[*] Lasource, September 25, 1792. *Archives Parlementaires,* Series 1. LII, 130. Our translation.

The political program of the Gironde, therefore, favored a large measure of "federalism," which meant decentralization in the Revolutionary vocabulary, and a government whose power would be limited by many checks and balances. The details of this program were set forth in a draft constitution completed early in 1793 by the distinguished Girondin deputy, Condorcet, the prophet of human progress (see Chapter XVII). In Condorcet's draft, the executive and the legislature would be independent of each other and separately elected, the results of elections would be adjusted according to proportional representation, projected laws would be submitted to a popular referendum, and voters would have the right to recall unworthy elected officials.

The leaders of the Mountain, in contrast, favored an all-powerful central government over federalism. Instead of Girondin laissez-faire, they demanded state intervention in economic affairs to appease their urban supporters. The chief spokesman of the Mountain was Maximilien Robespierre (1758-1794). This earnest young lawyer did not look like a revolutionary: he powdered his hair neatly and wore the light-blue coat and knee-breeches of the Old Régime. Yet Robespierre was a political fanatic whose speeches were lay sermons couched in the solemn language of a new revelation. He put his creed most forcefully in a discourse delivered in February, 1794:

What is the goal toward which we are striving? The peaceful enjoyment of liberty and equality: the rule of that eternal justice whose laws have been engraved . . . upon the hearts of men, even upon the heart of the slave who ignores them and of the tyrant who denies them.

We desire an order of things . . . where our country assures the welfare of each individual and where each individual enjoys with pride the prosperity and the glory of our country; where the souls of all grow through the constant expression of republican sentiments; where the arts are the ornament of the freedom which in turn ennobles them; and where commerce is the source of public wealth, not just of the monstrous opulence of a few houses.[*]

Robespierre really believed that he could translate the ideals of Rousseau's *Social Contract* into a practical political program. Like Rousseau, he had faith in the natural goodness of humanity, in "the laws of justice engraved upon the hearts of men." He was sure that he knew the general will, and that the general will demanded a Republic of Virtue. If Frenchmen would not be free and virtuous voluntarily, then, as Rousseau had recommended, they would be "forced to be free."

Robespierre and the Republic of Virtue triumphed. The Mountain won out over the Gironde in the competition for the votes of the relatively uncommitted deputies of the Plain in the Convention (see table on p. 114). In the early days of 1793, the Gironde suffered a significant defeat when, after one hundred hours of continuous voting, starting on January 15, 1793, the Convention declared "Citizen Louis Capet" guilty of treason and by a narrow margin sentenced him to the guillotine without delay. Louis XVI died bravely on January 21, 1793. Although the majority of the French population disapproved of the King's execution, the majority did not control the Convention. There some of the Girondin deputies had asserted that Louis did not deserve to die. They took a courageous stand in defense of the humanitarian principles of the Enlightenment, but they also exposed themselves to the charge of being "counter-revolutionaries."

A combination of events at home and abroad now soon destroyed the Gironde. In February, 1793, the Convention rejected Condorcet's draft constitution, and in the same month it declared war on Britain, Spain, and the Netherlands. France faced a formidable coalition of opponents, in-

cluding Austria and Prussia, already at war with her. In March, the army under Dumouriez, a Girondin general, suffered a series of defeats in the Low Countries, and in April Dumouriez deserted to the enemy. At home, in the face of unemployment, high prices, and food shortages, the Gironde had little to offer except laissez-faire. The leaders of the Mountain urged price controls and food requisitioning; they also pressed for the expulsion of Girondins from the Jacobin clubs. Finally, on June 2, 1793, the Jacobin *sections* of Paris, following the precedent of August, 1792, invaded the Convention and forced it to arrest twenty-nine Girondin deputies. Backed by these armed Parisians, the Mountain intimidated the Plain, and the Convention consigned the arrested Girondins to the guillotine. The Reign of Terror had begun.

The Reign of Terror (*June, 1793–July, 1794*)

How was it that the advocates of democracy now imposed a dictatorship on France? Here is Robespierre's explanation:

. . . To establish and consolidate democracy, to achieve the peaceful rule of constitutional laws, we must first finish the war of liberty against tyranny. . . . We must annihilate the enemies of the republic at home and abroad, or else we shall perish. . . .

If virtue is the mainstay of a democratic government in time of peace, then in time of revolution a democratic government must rely on *virtue* and *terror*. . . . Terror is nothing but justice, swift, severe and inflexible; it is an emanation of virtue. . . . It has been said that terror is the mainstay of a despotic government. . . . The government of the revolution is the despotism of liberty against tyranny.[*]

The Convention duly voted a democratic constitution, drawn up by the Mountain, granting universal manhood suffrage, and

[*] *Le Moniteur Universel,* February 7, 1794. Our translation.

[*] *Le Moniteur Universel,* February 7, 1794. Our translation.

"Government of Robespierre." The ex-ecutioner—having beheaded (from left to right) the clergy, the Parlement, the nobility, the Constituent Assembly, the Legislative Assembly, the Convention, and the people—guillotines himself.

and other stalwarts from the Mountain. Though nominally responsible to the Convention, the Committee of Public Safety enjoyed a large measure of independent authority and acted as a kind of war cabinet. A second group of deputies, the Committee of General Security, supervised police activities and turned suspected enemies of the Republic over to the new Revolutionary Tribunal, whose sixteen judges and sixty jurors were divided into several courts to speed the work of repression. At the local level, the Mountain scrapped much of the self-government inaugurated under the Constitution of 1791. Local Jacobin clubs purged department and commune administrations of political unreliables, while special local courts supplemented the grim labors of the Revolutionary Tribunal. To make sure that provincial France toed the line, the Mountain sent out trusted members of the Convention as its agents, the "deputies on mission." From the standpoint of administration, the Terror marked both an anticipation of twentieth-century dictatorship and a return to the age-old French principle of centralization. The deputies on mission were the successors of the *intendants* of Richelieu, the *enquêteurs* of St. Louis, and the *missi dominici* of Charlemagne.

The Record of the Terror

The "swift, severe, and inflexible justice" promised by Robespierre took the lives of 20,000 Frenchmen. Although the Terror claimed such social outcasts as criminals and prostitutes, its main purpose was military and political—to clear France of suspected traitors, including Marie Antoinette, and to purge the Jacobins of dissidents. It fell with the greatest relative severity on the clergy, the aristocracy, and the Girondins. Many of its victims came from the Vendée,

giving supreme power, unhampered by Girondin checks and balances, to a single legislative chamber. When the instrument was submitted to a referendum, less than 2,000,000 of the 7,000,000 qualified Frenchmen voted, and the ballots cast went almost unanimously for ratification. The Convention then postponed indefinitely the operation of this Constitution of 1793; as Robespierre had explained, "To establish and consolidate democracy, we must first finish the war of liberty against tyranny."

The actual government of the Terror centered on a twelve-man Committee of Public Safety, composed of Robespierre a strongly Catholic and royalist area in western France which had revolted against the Republic's attempts to recruit soldiers. The record of the Terror was bloody indeed, at least by eighteenth-century standards. And by any standard the Terror perpetrated some grisly deeds. In the *noyades* (drownings) at Nantes, more than 2,000 suspects were set adrift on the River Loire to perish in leaky boats.

The wartime hysteria that helped to account for the excesses of the Terror also inspired a very practical patriotism. On August 23, 1793, the Convention issued a decree epitomizing the democratic nationalism of the Jacobins:

From this moment, until the time when the enemy shall have been driven from the territory of the Republic, all Frenchmen are permanently requisitioned for the service of the armies.

Young men will go into combat, married men will manufacture arms and transport supplies; women will make tents and uniforms and will serve in the hospitals; children will make old linen into bandages; old men will be carried into the public squares to arouse the courage of the soldiers, excite hatred for kings and inspire the unity of the Republic.*

In an early, though limited, application of the modern principle of universal conscription, the army drafted all bachelors and widowers between the ages of eighteen and twenty-five. Hundreds of open-air forges were installed in Paris to manufacture weapons. Since the war prevented the importation of the saltpeter needed for gunpowder, the government sponsored a great campaign to scrape patches of saltpeter from cellars and stables.

By the close of 1793, the forces of the Republic had driven foreign troops off French soil. Credit for this new shift in the tide of battle did not rest solely with the Jacobins. The military successes of the Republic reflected in part the improvements

---

* *Le Moniteur Universel*, August 24, 1793. Our translation.

made in the army during the dying years of the Old Régime; they resulted still more from the weaknesses of the coalition aligned against France (see below, p. 123). Yet they could scarcely have been achieved without the new democratic spirit that allowed men of the third estate to become officers and that made the French army the most determined, the most enterprising—and, perhaps, the most idealistic—in Europe.

"Total" mobilization demanded an approximate equality of economic sacrifice. To

Sketch of Marie Antoinette on her way to the guillotine, by David.

exorcise the twin devils of inflation and food shortage, the Terror issued the *"maximum"* legislation, placing ceilings on prices and wages. In theory, at least, wages were halted at a maximum 50 per cent above the wage-rate of 1790, and prices were halted at 33 per cent above the price level of 1790. The government rationed scarce commodities, forbade the use of white flour, and directed all patriots to eat *pain d'égalité*—"equality bread," a loaf utilizing almost the whole of the wheat. Finally, early in 1794, the Convention passed the "Laws of Ventôse," named for a month in the revolutionary calendar (see below, p. 119). These laws authorized seizure of the remaining properties of the *émigrés* and other opponents of the Republic and recommended their distribution to landless Frenchmen.

Socialist historians have often found in the *maximum* and the Laws of Ventôse evidence that the Terror was moving from political to social democracy, that the Republic of Virtue was indeed beginning the socialist revolution. The *maximum,* however, resembled nothing so much as the economic controls employed in the non-socialist United States during World War II, right down to the provision permitting wages to rise proportionately more than prices. Though the *maximum* temporarily checked the depreciation of the *assignats,* black markets flourished during the Terror; even the government patronized them.

Although the redistribution of property foreseen by the Laws of Ventôse did anticipate socialism, the measure was never enforced. Furthermore, the Convention was assured that the Mountain did not intend a general assault on property:

The revolution leads us to recognize the principle that he who has shown himself the enemy of his country cannot own property. The properties of patriots are sacred, but the goods of conspirators are there for the unfortunate.[*]

To the thorough-going socialist not even the properties of patriots are sacred. The middle-class leaders of the Terror were not genuine socialists; only the emergencies of the Revolution forced them to abandon laissez-faire. They had to make food cheaper for townspeople—whence the *maxi-*

mum; and they had to promise men some hope of future well-being—whence the Laws of Ventôse.

The Terror presented its most revolutionary aspect in its drastic social and cultural reforms. "In our land," Robespierre announced, "we desire to substitute all the virtues and all the miracles of the Republic for all the vices and all the nonsense of monarchy." When Robespierre said "all," he meant "all"—clothing, the arts, amusements, the calendar, religion. The Republic of Virtue could tolerate nothing that smacked of the Old Régime. Even the traditional forms of address, "Monsieur" and "Madame," gave way to the newly orthodox "Citoyen" (citizen) and "Citoyenne" (citizeness).

Ever since 1789, revolutionaries had discarded elaborate gowns and knee-breeches (*culottes*) as symbols of idleness and privilege. With the exception of Robespierre, good republican men were *sans-culottes* (literally, without knee-breeches), attired in the long, baggy trousers of the humble peasant or workman. Women affected simple, high-waisted dresses, copied from the costumes of the ancient Romans. Rome became the model for behavior—the virtuous Rome of the Republic, of course, not the sordid Empire. Parents named their children Brutus or Cato or Gracchus, and the theater shelved the masterpieces of Racine and Corneille for stilted dramas glorifying Roman heroes. Cabinet-makers, deserting the graceful style of Louis XVI, produced sturdy neoclassical furniture decorated with Roman symbols. "The arts," said Robespierre, "are the ornament of the freedom which in turn ennobles them." Playwrights, authors, and editors who failed to ornament freedom properly experienced censorship or even the guillotine. The Jacobins reduced the lively newspapers of the early revolution to dull semi-official organs.

They also instituted a sweeping reform of the calendar (October, 1793). The first day of the Republic, September 22, 1792,

---

[*] Saint-Just, February 26, 1794, in *Le Moniteur Universel,* February 27, 1794. Our translation.

was designated the initial day of Year I, Roman numerals were assigned to the years, and the traditional classical names of the months were replaced by more "natural" ones:

THE MONTHS OF THE REVOLUTIONARY CALENDAR

Fall:	Vendémiaire (Grape-Harvest)
	Brumaire (Misty)
	Frimaire (Frosty)
Winter:	Nivôse (Snowy)
	Pluviôse (Rainy)
	Ventôse (Windy)
Spring:	Germinal (Seed)
	Floréal (Flowering)
	Prairial (Meadow)
Summer:	Messidor (Wheat-Harvest)
	Thermidor (Heat)
	Fructidor (Ripening)

Each month had thirty days, divided into three weeks of ten days. Every tenth day was set aside for rest and for the celebra- tion of one of the virtues so admired by Robespierre—Hatred of Tyrants and Traitors, Heroism, Frugality, Stoicism, not to mention two anticipations of Mother's Day, Filial Piety and Maternal Tenderness. The five days left over at the end of the year were holidays dedicated to Genius, Labor, Noble Actions, Awards, and Opinion. The revolutionary calendar, for all its sanctimonious touches, was worthy of the Enlightenment. Yet it antagonized workmen, who disliked laboring nine days out of ten, instead of six out of seven. It never really took root, and Napoleon scrapped it a decade later.

The Convention had better luck with another reform close to the spirit of the Age of Reason—the metric system. A special committee, including Condorcet, Laplace, Lavoisier, and other distinguished intellectuals, devised new weights and measures based on the uniform use of the decimal system rather than on illogical

The Goddess of Reason carried through the streets of Paris, 1793.

custom. In August, 1793, a decree made the meter the standard unit of length, and supplementary legislation in 1795 established the liter as the measure of volume and the gram as the unit of weight. The Anglo-Saxon countries have been the chief nations to cling to older and less rational weights and measures, and even in them scientists have adopted the metric system of revolutionary France.

By and large, however, the forces of tradition proved too strong for the Terror. Nowhere was this more evident than in the attempts to legislate a new religion. Many churches were closed and turned into barracks or administrative offices; often their medieval glass and sculpture were destroyed. Some of the Jacobins launched a "de-Christianization" campaign to make Catholics into *philosophes* and their churches into "temples of Reason." Robespierre, however, disliked the cult of Reason; the Republic of Virtue, he believed, should acknowledge an ultimate author of morality. The Convention therefore decreed (May, 1794) that "the French people recognize the existence of the Supreme Being and the immortality of the soul." At the festival of the Supreme Being, June 8, 1794, Robespierre set fire to three figures representing Vice, Folly, and Atheism. From the embers the statue of Wisdom emerged, but smudged with smoke because of a mechanical slip-up. The audience laughed. The deistic concept of the Supreme Being was too remote and the mechanics of the new worship too artificial to appeal to the religious emotions of Frenchmen.

The Thermidorean Reaction

Indeed, the Republic of Virtue was too abstract in ideals, and too violent in practice, to retain popular support. Like the Geneva of Calvin, the France of Robespierre demanded superhuman devotion to duty and inhuman indifference to bloodshed. During the first half of 1794, Robespierre pressed the Terror relentlessly; even the members of the Committees of Public Safety and General Security began to feel that they might be the next victims. Soon Robespierre lost his backing in the Convention. Shouts of "Down with the tyrant!" drowned out his attempts to address the deputies on the ninth of Thermidor, Year II (July 27, 1794). The Convention ordered Robespierre's arrest, and on the next day the great fanatic went to the guillotine.

The leaders of the Thermidorean Reaction, many of them former Jacobins, soon dismantled the machinery of the Terror. They disbanded the Revolutionary Tribunal, recalled the deputies on mission, and deprived the Committees of Public Safety and General Security of their independent authority. They closed the Paris Jacobin Club and invited the surviving Girondin deputies to resume their old seats in the Convention. They took the first step toward the restoration of Catholicism by permitting priests to celebrate Mass, though under state supervision and without state financial support. The press and the theater recovered their freedom. Pleasure-seekers again flocked to Paris, now that it was liberated from the somberness of the Republic of Virtue. France was resuming a normal existence.

Normality, however, exacted its price. In southern and western France a counter-revolutionary "White Terror," equalling the great Terror in fury, claimed many lives, not only supporters of the Mountain but also purchasers of former church and noble lands. The men of Thermidor caused an acute inflation by canceling the economic legislation of the Terror. No longer checked by the *maximum*, the prices of some foods rose to a hundred times the level of 1790, and the *assignats* sank so low in value that buinesssmen refused to accept them. Impoverished Parisians staged several demonstrations against the Thermidoreans in the course of 1795. Sometimes the rioters voiced their support of the discredited Mountain and its democratic Constitution of 1793 and sometimes they let themselves be used by royalist agents; but always they clamored for bread and lower prices.

The Thermidorean Reaction concluded with the passage of the Constitution of 1795, the last great act of the Convention. The men of Thermidor wanted both to retain the Republic and to assure the dominance of the propertied classes. The Constitution of 1795 therefore denied the vote to the poorest quarter of the nation and required that candidates for public office possess a considerable amount of property. It established two legislative councils, the Five Hundred and the Elders (who had to be at least forty years old and either married or widowed); both councils were to be elected piecemeal after the American practice of renewing one-third of the Senate every two years. The Council of Five Hundred nominated, and the Elders chose, five directors who headed the executive. Otherwise the Directory was almost totally independent of the legislative councils.

The Constitution of 1795 marked the third great effort of the Revolution to provide France with an enduring government. It followed in part a classical example, since the two councils were patterned on the Areopagus and the Five Hundred of ancient Athens; it also followed the American precedent of 1787, the French precedent of 1791, and the precepts of Montesquieu. It embodied the separation of powers and deferred to the aristocracy of wealth, though not to that of birth. By abandoning the political democracy of the still-born Constitution of 1793 and by reverting to the restricted suffrage of 1791, it demonstrated that the most radical phase of the Revolution had passed.

The Directory
(October, 1795–November, 1799)

The new regime of the Directory dealt harshly with the recurrent plots of royalists or Jacobin extremists. It suppressed with ease the "Conspiracy of the Equals" (1796-97), engineered by Gracchus Babeuf, the one undoubted socialist of the Revolution. Yet, in spite of these successes, political instability plagued the Directory. The directors and the legislative councils clashed repeatedly, each side seeking to turn the political balance in its own favor, and each, in consequence, violating the constitution. The councils sacked directors before their terms were finished; the directors refused to seat duly elected councilors in the legislature.

The Directory made a vigorous attack on economic problems. It levied high protective tariffs, both as a measure of war against England and as a concession to French businessmen. Again responding to business pressure, it destroyed the plates used to print the now almost worthless *assignats* and in 1797 withdrew paper money from circulation. The return to hard money required stringent governmental economies. The Directory instituted these economies, and it eased the crushing burden of the national debt by simply repudiating two-thirds of it. In short, the Directory brought at least a semblance of order out of the chronic financial chaos.

But it did not bring peace, and therein lay its downfall. The continuing war dominated all the other activities of the Directory; soon all French factions were maneuvering for the political support of the army. The result was the *coup d'état* of Brumaire in 1799 and the dictatorship of a general, Napoleon Bonaparte.

IV: The Rise of Napoleon

Edmund Burke, the British political philosopher, foresaw very early the whole long process that culminated in Napoleon's dominance of France and Europe. In 1790, Burke warned the French—and his own countrymen—in his *Reflections on the Revolution in France:*

> Everything depends on the army in such a government as yours; for you have industriously destroyed all the opinions, . . . all the instincts which support government. Therefore the moment any difference arises between your National Assembly and any part of the nation, you must have recourse to force. Nothing else is left to you. . . .
>
> It is besides to be considered, whether an assembly like yours . . . is fit for promoting the discipline and obedience of an army. It is known, that armies have hitherto yielded a very precarious and uncertain obedience to any senate, or popular authority. . . . The officers must totally lose the characteristic disposition of military men, if they see with perfect submission and due admiration, the dominion of pleaders; especially when they find that they have a new court to pay to an endless succession of those pleaders. . . . In the weakness of one kind of authority, and in the fluctuation of all, the officers of an army will remain for some time mutinous and full of faction, until some popular general who understands the art of conciliating the soldiery, and who possesses the true spirit of command, shall draw the eyes of all men upon himself. Armies will obey him on his personal account. There is no other way of securing military obedience in this state of things. But the moment in which that event shall happen, the person who really commands the army is your master; the master . . . of your king, the master of your assembly, the master of your whole republic.[*]

In 1790, Burke was a solitary prophet; no one else outside France paid much heed to the French army. Sovereigns and statesmen who deplored the Revolution believed that

_____
[*] Everyman ed. (New York, 1910), 217, 215-216.

the very intensity of domestic problems made France incapable of a vigorous foreign policy. Catherine the Great predicted as late as 1792 that ten thousand soldiers would be sufficient to conquer France. *Philosophes* and liberals hailed the peaceful promise of the Revolution. The capture of the Bastille delighted Charles James Fox, a leading English Whig: "How much the greatest event it is that ever happened in the world! and how much the best!"

The First Coalition (1792-1795)

The war that broke out in the spring of 1792 soon destroyed the illusions of French military weakness and French liberal purity. The war was to last continuously, save for a few intervals of peace, down to the final defeat of Napoleon. It deserves to be called the World War of 1792-1815, for almost all the European powers eventually participated, and the fighting itself ranged far beyond Europe. By the time the war was a year old Austria and Prussia, the charter members of the First Coalition against France, had been joined by Holland, Spain, and Great Britain. Both ideological and strategic factors brought Britain into the conflict early in 1793. She regarded the attack on the Tuileries, the September massacres, and the execution of Louis XVI as outrages against human decency and the institution of monarchy. And the French invasion of the Austrian Netherlands in the fall of 1792 raised the unpleasant prospect that this Belgian "cockpit of Europe" would fall under French control. The early campaigns of the war were indecisive. Late in 1792, the French followed up their success at

Valmy by the invasion of Belgium, only to lose ground again in 1793 after the defeat and desertion of Dumouriez (see above, p. 115). Then in 1794 the French definitely gained the advantage, and by 1795 French troops had occupied Belgium, Holland, and Germany west of the Rhine.

One reason for French success we have already seen—the Convention's energetic mobilization of national resources. Another reason, equally important yet easy to overlook, was the weakness of the First Coalition. The partners in the coalition had no first-rate commander, nor did they achieve effective co-ordination of their efforts. The Duke of Brunswick's failure to take Paris in 1792 resulted as much from his own deficient generalship as from the "miracle" of Valmy. Moreover, the partitions of Poland in 1793 and 1795 greatly assisted the French by distracting Prussia, Russia, and Austria. The pick of the Prussian army was diverted to occupation duty in newly annexed Polish provinces. By 1795, furthermore, things had come to such a pass that the Prussians did not dare attack the French for fear of being assaulted from the rear by their nominal Austrian ally!

Prussia was the first member of the coalition to make peace. In the Treaty of Basel (1795) she ceded to France the scattered Prussian holdings west of the Rhine on the understanding that she might seek compensation elsewhere in Germany. Spain and Holland soon deserted the coalition also. In 1795, then, France at last secured her "natural frontiers." In addition to Belgium and the Rhineland she had also annexed Savoy and Nice, thereby extending her southeastern border to the crest of the Alps. These conquests, however, belied the ideals of the Revolution. In declaring war on Austria in 1792 France had sworn to uphold the promise of the Constitution of 1791: that she would never undertake a war of conquest. This was to be "not a war of nation against nation, but the righteous defense of a free people against the unjust

aggression of a king." But the conquering armies of the First Republic brought closer the day when nation would fight nation—when the European nations would invoke "the righteous defense of a free people against the unjust aggression" not of a king, but of revolutionary France.

Napoleon's Early Career

At the close of 1795, only Britain and Austria remained officially at war with France. The Directory picked Austria as the first target and assigned Napoleon Bonaparte to lead the attack against the Habsburg forces in northern Italy. The youthful commander was at once a *philosophe*, a revolutionary, an inspired general, and a ruthlessly ambitious adventurer. He was born in Corsica in 1769, soon after the French acquisition of that Mediterranean island from Genoa. Napoleon retained throughout his life the strong family loyalty characteristic of Corsican society. From him the members of the Bonaparte clan were to receive all the spoils of conquest, even thrones.

As a youth, Napoleon attended military school in France. Largely cut off from his fellow students because he was a "foreigner," he devoted himself to his studies, read widely, especially in Rousseau, and dreamed of the day when he might liberate his native island from French control. Later, however, his zeal for Corsican independence faded. When the Revolution broke out, Napoleon helped to overthrow the Old Régime in Corsica but soon went back to France to resume his military career. The young officer defended the Convention, but more from expediency than from political conviction. He commanded the artillery when the forces of the Jacobin Convention recaptured the rebellious Mediterranean seaport of Toulon in December, 1793. In October, 1795, he delivered the famous "whiff of grapeshot" that saved the Thermidorean Convention from a rising of discontented Parisians. Next, he married Josephine de Beauharnais, a widow six years his senior and an intimate of the ruling clique of the Directory. Josephine's connections and Napoleon's own demonstrated talent as an artillery officer gained him the Italian command in 1796.

In the space of a year, Napoleon cleared the Austrians out of Italy and made them sue for peace. In this famous campaign he showed his remarkable ability to strike quickly and surprise his opponents before they could consolidate their defenses. He also demonstrated his flair for propaganda and "public relations." Witness the proclamation that he issued on April 26, 1796:

Soldiers! In two weeks you have won six victories; you have made 15,000 prisoners; you have killed or wounded more than 10,000 men.

Deprived of everything, you have accomplished everything. You have won battles without cannon, negotiated rivers without bridges, made forced marches without shoes, encamped without brandy, and often without bread. Only the phalanxes of the Republic, only the soldiers of Liberty, would have been capable of suffering the things that you have suffered.

You all burn to carry the glory of the French people; to humiliate the proud kings who dared to contemplate shackling us; to go back to your villages, to say proudly: 'I was of the conquering army of Italy!'

Friends, I promise you that conquest; but there is a condition you must swear to fulfill: to respect the people whom you are delivering; to repress horrible pillaging.

Peoples of Italy, the French army comes to break your chains; greet it with confidence; your property, religion and customs will be respected.*

Here was Napoleon's characteristic policy of promising all things to all men. He encouraged the nationalism of underpaid and underfed French soldiers; yet he appealed also to the nationalism of the Italians, promising them liberation from Austria and guaranteeing the orderly conduct of

the French army. He did not, of course, tell the Italians that they might be exchanging one master for another, nor did he publicize the money that he seized from Italian governments and the art treasures that he took from Italian galleries and shipped back to France.

In the Treaty of Campoformio (1797) terminating the Italian campaign, Austria acknowledged the loss of Belgium and Lombardy and recognized the two puppet states that Napoleon set up in northwestern Italy, the Ligurian Republic of Genoa and the Cisalpine Republic of Lombardy. In return, the Habsburgs received the Italian possessions of the Venetian Republic and a secret French assurance that, despite the specific promise made at Basel in 1795, Prussia would not be permitted to compensate for her losses in the Rhineland by lands elsewhere in Germany.

Napoleon now turned to Britain. He decided not to attack her directly, but rather to hit at her indirectly through Egypt, then a semi-independent vassal of the Ottoman Empire. This would-be Alexander the Great, seeking new worlds to conquer, talked grandly of digging a canal at Suez, giving French merchants the monopoly of a new short trade-route to India, and exacting belated retribution from Britain for Clive's victory in the Seven Years' War. Since Napoleon shared the passion of the Enlightenment for science and antiquity, he invited archaeologists and other experts to accompany him and thereby helped to found the study known as Egyptology. In the Nile Delta the French discovered the Rosetta Stone, the key to ancient Egyptian hieroglyphics, later deciphered by Champollion. Napoleon's experts established in Egypt an outpost of French cultural imperialism that lasted until the twentieth century.

From the military standpoint, however, the campaign failed totally. Having eluded the British Mediterranean fleet commanded by Nelson, Napoleon landed in Egypt in

---

* Abridged from *Le Moniteur Universel*, May 17, 1796. Our translation.

CHAPTER XVIII

July, 1798, and quickly routed the Mamluks, the ruling oligarchy. Then disaster struck. On August 1, 1798, Nelson discovered the French fleet anchored at Abukir Bay along the Egyptian coast and destroyed it before its captains had time to weigh anchor. Nelson's victory deprived the French of supplies, of reinforcements, and even of news from home. After a year of futile campaigning in the Near East, Napoleon suddenly left Egypt in August, 1799, and returned home to France. The soldiers whom he thus deserted were not so fortunate; they remained in Egypt until 1801, when arrangements were completed for their withdrawal.

Brumaire

Napoleon found the situation in France ripe for a decisive political stroke. During his absence Jacobinism had experienced a significant revival; several hundred members of the legislative councils belonged to the old Jacobin Club, now resurrected as the "Society of the Friends of Liberty and Equality." Abroad, the Directory had established four new satellite republics with classical names—the Roman, the Parthenopean in Naples, the Batavian in Holland, and the Helvetian in Switzerland. But this new success of French imperialism upset the European balance and provoked a renewal of war on the Continent. The Habsburgs resented the extension of French influence in their former Italian preserve, and Tsar Paul I (1796-1801) feared that Napoleon would harm Russia's Mediterranean interests. The eccentric Tsar was head of the Knights of Malta, a Catholic order of knighthood dating back to the time of the Crusades. Since Napoleon had expelled the Knights from their headquarters on the island of Malta, Paul joined with Austria and Britain in forming the Second Coalition (December, 1798). In the ensuing campaigns, Russian troops fought in Italy and Switzerland in alliance with the Austrians, in Holland in alliance with the English, and even in the Ionian islands off the western shores of Greece. The Russian General Suvorov, who defeated the French repeatedly, became the hero of western Europe. By August, 1799, the French had been expelled from Italy, and their puppet republics—Cisalpine, Roman, and Parthenopean—had been dismantled.

In these circumstances, patriotic Frenchmen were ready to welcome any military hero, and conservative Frenchmen were ready to welcome a champion of order against the new Jacobin threat. Napoleon got a rousing reception on his return from Egypt. Soon he was engaged in a plot to overthrow the Directory, with the complicity of two of the five directors, Roger-Ducos and Siéyès, the old champion of the third estate. On November 9 and 10, 1799 (18 and 19 Brumaire by the revolutionary calendar) the plot was executed. First, Napoleon forced the resignation of the three directors not in the plot; next, to win over the consent of the two legislative councils, he hinted at a dangerous Jacobin conspiracy. He gained the approval of the Elders, but in the Council of Five Hundred he ranted incoherently and fainted. His brother, Lucien, the presiding officer of the Council, saved the situation until a detachment of troops expelled a majority of the Five Hundred.

This almost comic *coup d'état* of Brumaire ended the Directory. The Bonapartist minority of the councilors entrusted both the government and the preparation of a new constitution to the victorious triumvirate of Roger-Ducos, Siéyès, and Napoleon, of whom only Napoleon really counted. It all happened just as Edmund Burke had predicted:

In the weakness of authority, . . . some popular general shall draw the eyes of all men upon himself. Armies will obey him on his personal account. . . . The person who really commands the army is your master.

V: Napoleon and France

Napoleonic Government

The Constitution of the Year VIII, drawn up after Brumaire, was based on the autocratic maxim, "Confidence from below, authority from above." It erected a very strong executive, somewhat disguised by terminology borrowed from the ancient Roman Republic. Three consuls shared the executive authority—or rather, Napoleon as First Consul took the lion's share, leaving his two colleagues only nominal power. Four separate bodies had a hand in legislation: (1) the Council of State proposed laws; (2) the Tribunate debated them but did not vote; (3) the Legislative Corps voted them but did not debate; (4) the Senate had the right to veto legislation. The members of all four bodies were either appointed by the First Consul or elected indirectly by a process so complex that Bonaparte had ample opportunity to manipulate candidates. The core of this system was the Council of State, staffed by Bonaparte's hand-picked choices, which served both as a sort of cabinet and as the highest administrative court in the land. The three remaining bodies were intended merely to go through the motions of enacting whatever the First Consul decreed. Even so, the debates of the Tribunate sometimes got in his way, and he finally abolished it in 1807.

Napoleon soon cast off the other restrictions imposed on his own authority by the constitution. In 1802, he persuaded the legislators to drop the original ten-year limitation on his term of office and make him First Consul for life, with the power to designate his successor and amend the constitution at will. In 1804, he took the next logical move and declared himself hereditary Emperor of the French. A magnificent coronation took place at Notre Dame in Paris on December 2. The Pope consecrated the Emperor, but Napoleon placed the crown on his own head.

Each time Napoleon revised the Constitution in a non-republican direction he made the republican gesture of submitting the change to the electorate. Each time, the results of the plebiscite were overwhelmingly favorable: in 1799-1800, the vote was 3,011,107 for Napoleon and the Constitution of the Year VIII, and 1,562 against; in 1802, it was 3,568,885 for Napoleon and the life Consulate, and 8,374 against; in 1804, it was 3,572,329 for Napoleon and the Empire, and 2,579 against. Although the voters were exposed to considerable official pressure and the announced results were perhaps rigged a little, the vast majority of Frenchmen undoubtedly supported Napoleon. His military triumphs appealed to their growing nationalism, and his policy of stability at home insured them against further revolutionary changes. Confidence did indeed seem to increase from below as authority increased from above.

If by any chance confidence failed to materialize below, Napoleon had the authority to deal with the recalcitrant. He wiped out the local self-government remaining from the early days of the Revolution. In place of locally elected officials he substituted those appointed by himself— prefects in departments, sub-prefects in *arrondissements*, mayors in communes—and all were instructed to enforce compliance with the Emperor's dictates. Napoleon, far more than the Jacobins, made France a highly centralized police state.

Men of every political background staffed the imperial administration. Napoleon cared little whether his subordinates were returned *émigrés* or ex-Jacobins, so long as they had ability. Besides, their varied antecedents reinforced the impression that narrow factionalism was dead and that the Empire rested on a broad political base. Napoleon paid officials well and offered the additional bait of high titles. With the establishment of the Empire he created dukes by the dozen and counts and barons by the hundred. He rewarded outstanding generals with the rank of Marshal and lesser civilian officials with the Legion of Honor. "Aristocracy always exists," Napoleon remarked. "Destroy it in the nobility, it removes itself to the rich and powerful houses of the middle class." * The imperial aristocracy gave the leaders of the middle class the social distinction that they felt to be rightfully theirs.

Law and Justice

Napoleon revived some of the glamor of the Old Régime, but not its glaring inequalities. His series of law codes, the celebrated *Code Napoléon* (1804-1810), declared all men equal before the law without regard to their rank and wealth. It extended to all the right to follow the occupation, and embrace the religion, of their choosing. It gave France the single coherent system of law which the *philosophes* had demanded and which the revolutionary governments had been too busy to formulate.

The *Code Napoléon* did not, however, embody the full judicial reform program of the Enlightenment; it incorporated from the old Roman law some practices that strengthened the absolutism of the Empire. In trial procedure, it permitted some use of torture; it favored the interests of the state over the rights of the individual. Though Napoleon confirmed the revolu-

tionary legislation permitting divorce by mutual consent, and though he himself divorced Josephine, he generally preserved the legal superiority of the man of the family. The code cancelled revolutionary legislation protecting the interests of wives, minors, and illegitimate children. Napoleon appointed judges himself and empowered the prefects to select jurors. Now confirming the principles of 1789, and now betraying them, Napoleonic law and justice offered a fair summary of the fate of the Revolution under the Empire.

A similar ambiguity clouded Napoleon's attitude toward civil liberties. He practiced religious toleration of a sort and welcomed former political heretics into his administration. But Napoleonic generosity stemmed always from expediency, never from any fundamental belief in liberty. If he failed to get his way by conciliation, then he used force. In the western departments, where royalist uprisings had become chronic since the revolt in the Vendée, he massacred the rebels who declined his offer of amnesty in 1800. In 1804, he kidnapped the Duke of Enghien from the neutral German state of Baden because the Duke was believed to be the choice of monarchists conspirators for the throne of France. Though Napoleon immediately discovered the Duke's innocence, he had him executed none the less.

Napoleon cared little for freedom of speech. In July, 1801, for example, he directed his librarian to read all the newspapers carefully and

. . . make an abstract of everything they contain likely to affect the public point of view, especially with regard to religion, philosophy, and political opinion. He will send me this abstract between 5 and 6 o'clock every day.

Once every ten days he will send me an analysis of all the books or pamphlets which have appeared . . . , calling attention to any passages that might bear on moral questions, or interest me in a political or moral connexion.

He will take pains to procure copies of all

---

* Quoted in H. A. L. Fisher, *Napoleon* (New York, 1913), Appendix I.

the plays which are produced, and to analyse them for me, with observations of the same character as those above mentioned. This analysis must be made, at latest, within 48 hours of the production of the plays.*

And so on through "bills, posters, advertisements, institutes, literary meetings, sermons and fashionable trials." No segment of public opinion escaped Napoleon's manipulation. He reduced by five-sixths the number of Paris newspapers and pestered theater managers with suggestions for improving the patriotic tone of plays. When he wanted to arouse French feelings, he simply started a press campaign, as in this instance from 1807:

A great hue and cry is to be raised against the persecutions experienced by the Catholics of Ireland at the hands of the Anglican Church. ... Bishops will be approached so that prayers will be offered entreating an end to the persecutions of the Anglican Church against the Irish Catholics. But the administration must move very delicately and make use of the newspapers without their realizing what the government is driving at.... And the term 'Anglican Church' must always be used in place of 'Protestants,' for we have Protestants in France, but no Anglican Church.†

Religion

Political considerations colored all Napoleon's decisions on religion. "I do not see in religion the mystery of the incarnation," he said, "but the mystery of the social order. It attaches to heaven an idea of equality which prevents the rich man from being massacred by the poor." ** Since French Catholics loathed the anticlericalism of the Revolution, Napoleon reasoned that he had everything to gain by

working out a reconciliation with Rome.

The Concordat that was negotiated in 1801 by Napoleon and Pope Pius VII (1800-1823) accomplished the reconciliation. The French state agreed to pay clerical salaries and to suppress the popular election of bishops and priests. The bishops were to be nominated by the government, and then consecrated by the Pope; the priests were to be appointed by the bishops. At this point Napoleon's concessions stopped. By declaring that Catholicism was the faith of the "majority of Frenchmen," rather than the state religion, the Concordat implicitly admitted the toleration of Protestants and Jews. Furthermore, it granted to the French government vague but extensive powers to regulate church activities. The Concordat of 1801 was a resounding confirmation of the principles of 1789, for it canceled only the most extreme provisions of the Civil Constitution of the Clergy. The Pope accepted such important measures of the Revolution as the abolition of the tithe and the confiscation of ecclesiastical lands. And, by granting Napoleon regulatory powers over the Gallican Church, he permitted that church to become in effect the ward of the French state.

So far as France was concerned, the Concordat worked reasonably well. It conciliated large numbers of Catholics, alienated only the relatively small group of determined anticlericals, and remained in force until 1905. The Concordat, however, did not bring complete peace between France and the Vatican, for Napoleon insisted that the Pope should render to Caesar the things that were Caesar's. When Pius VII objected to Napoleon's making a French satellite of the Papal states, the new Caesar lectured him on the proper division of authority between the spiritual and temporal powers. Pius VII passed the last years of the Napoleonic regime as Bonaparte's prisoner, first in northern Italy and then in France.

---

* Quoted in J. M. Thompson, ed., *Napoleon's Letters* (London, 1954), 93-94.

† *Lettres Inédites de Napoléon* (Paris, 1897), I, 93-94. Our translation.

** Quoted in H. A. L. Fisher, *Napoleon* (New York, 1913), Appendix I.

CHAPTER XVIII

Education

The Revolution and Napoleon cost the Church its monopoly over education. The Constitution of 1791 had promised France a system of state schools. The Convention, while doing little to apply this principle to primary education, did set up institutions for specialized training, like the famous Paris engineering school, the *Ecole Polytechnique.* In each department it established a "central school" to provide secondary education of high quality at relatively low cost. Napoleon abolished these flourishing central schools in 1802 and replaced them with a smaller number of *lycées* open only to the relatively few pupils who could afford the tuition or who received state scholarships. The change had a political motive. The *lycée* students wore uniforms and marched to military drums, and the curriculum, too, served the ends of patriotic indoctrination. To provide for the general supervision of the school system Napoleon founded in 1808 a governmental body with the misleading name of the "University," which controlled the institutions ordinarily called universities.

Napoleon, then, scarcely had the modern democratic belief that schools should provide free and, politically speaking, reasonably neutral training. He neglected primary schooling almost completely. Yet, building on the revolutionary base, he did advance the construction of a secular school system. The educational competition of Church and State, so often a bitter issue in modern French life, dates back to the Revolution and Napoleon.

Economics

Political aims likewise governed the economic program of an emperor determined to promote national unity. The French peasants wanted to be left alone to enjoy the new freedom acquired in 1789; Napoleon did not disturb them, except to raise army recruits. The middle class wanted a balanced national budget and the end of revolutionary experiments with paper currency and a controlled economy. Napoleon continued the sound money of the Directory and, unlike the Directory, balanced the budget, thanks to the immense plunder that he gained in war. He greatly improved the efficiency and probity of tax-collectors and established the semi-official Bank of France (1800) to act as the government's financial agent. He strengthened the curbs placed on labor by the Le Chapelier Law of 1791 (see above, p. 108) and obliged every workman to carry a written record listing his jobs and his general reputation. Rich war contracts and subsidies kept employment and profits high. As the war went on and on, however, Napoleon found it increasingly difficult to appease the peasantry and the bourgeoisie. Despite the levies on conquered countries, he had to draft more soldiers from the peasantry and increase the already unpopular taxes on salt, liquor, and tobacco.

In summary, the domestic policies of Napoleon I had something in common with the methods of all the celebrated one-man rulers. Like Caesar in Rome, Napoleon rendered lip-service to the Republic while subverting republican institutions; he used prefects to impose centralized authority as Louis XIV had used *intendants;* and, like modern dictators, he had only contempt for free speech. Yet Napoleon was also a genuine enlightened despot. His law code and some of his educational reforms would have delighted the *philosophes.* He ended civil strife without sacrificing the redistribution of land and the equality before the law gained in 1789 and the years following. Abandoning some revolutionary policies, modifying others, and completing still others, Napoleon regimented the Revolution, but he did not wholly destroy it.

VI: Napoleon and Europe

To many Frenchmen, Napoleon was the Man of Destiny, the most brilliant ruler in their country's long history. To most Europeans, on the other hand, Napoleon was the sinister Man on Horseback, the enemy of national independence, the foreigner who imposed French control and French reforms. As French conquests accumulated, and as nominally free countries became French puppets, Europe grew to hate the insatiable imperialism of Napoleon. Napoleonic France succeeded in building up a vast empire, but only at the cost of arousing the implacable enmity of the other European nations.

The War (1800-1807)

Napoleon had barely launched the Consulate when he took to the field again. The Second Coalition, which had reached the peak of its success in August, 1799, was now falling to pieces. The hot-headed Tsar Paul I had soon decided that his allies were more dangerous than his enemies and created a league of Russia, Sweden, Prussia, and Denmark against Britain. Paul now planned to defeat the English, to partition Turkey, and to conquer India, all in alliance with Napoleon. But these fantastic plans dissolved when Paul was murdered in 1801 and succeeded by Alexander I. Meanwhile, in 1800, Napoleon attacked the Austrians in Italy and forced them to sue for peace. The Treaty of Lunéville (1801) extended the gains that Napoleon had secured from Austria four years before at Campoformio. This time Austria had to agree that the German states which had lost territory to France west of the Rhine should be compensated to the east of the Rhine, and that France should

have a voice in allotting the compensations. Lunéville gave Napoleon the right to superintend the reshaping of Germany.

After Lunéville, as after Campoformio, Britain alone remained at war with France. British taxpayers, however, wanted relief from the heavy burden of war taxes; British merchants longed to resume trading with continental markets partially closed to them since 1793. Though Britain had been unable to check Napoleon's expansion in Europe, she had very nearly won the colonial and naval war by 1801. She had captured former Dutch and Spanish colonies, and Nelson's fleet had expelled the French from Egypt and Malta. The British cabinet was confident that it held a strong bargaining position and could obtain favorable terms from Napoleon. But in the Peace of Amiens (1802) the British promised to surrender almost all their colonial conquests and got nothing in return. The French refused either to reopen the Continent to British exports or to relinquish Belgium, which remained, in Napoleon's phrase, "a loaded pistol aimed at the heart of Britain."

The one-sided Peace of Amiens provided only a brief truce in the world-wide struggle of Britain and France. Napoleon had no intention of giving up the struggle permanently until he had destroyed British commercial and colonial supremacy. Meanwhile, he alarmed Austria and Prussia by using the right granted by Lunéville to revise the map of Germany. In 1803, more than a hundred German states were abolished, chiefly city-states and small ecclesiastical principalities. The chief beneficiaries of this territorial readjustment were the south German states of Bavaria, Württemberg, and Baden, which Napoleon clearly intended to make a "third" Germany dominated by France, as opposed to the "first"

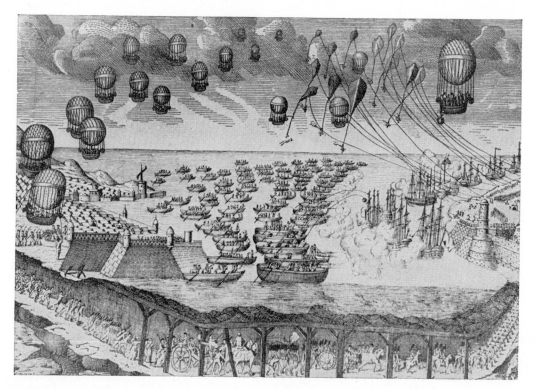

A Napoleonic scheme for the invasion of England in 1803. A diversion is being made by sea, but the main body of the army is marching into Dover Castle through a tunnel under the channel. Troop-carrying balloons are being met by a kite-borne defence.

and "second" Germanies, dominated by Austria and Prussia, respectively.

Britain he aroused by a new tariff law (1803) highly unfavorable to British exporters and by a grandiose project for an American colonial empire centering on the island of Haiti (Santo Domingo) and on the vast Louisiana territory that Spain had handed back to France in 1801. French soldiers wrested Haiti from the able Negro chieftain, Toussaint L'Ouverture. But the continued resistance of the Haitians and a virulent outbreak of yellow fever took a fearful toll of the French troops and forced Napoleon to abandon the American project. In 1803, therefore, he sold the whole of Louisiana to the United States for $11,000,000.

By the time the Louisiana Purchase was completed, Britain and France were again at war. From 1803 through 1805, Napoleon actively prepared to invade England. He assembled more than a hundred thousand troops and a thousand landing barges on the French side of the Straits of Dover. In 1805, he sent Admiral Villeneuve and the French fleet to the West Indies to lure the British fleet away from Europe. Then Villeneuve was to return post-haste to convoy the French invasion force across the Channel while Nelson was still vainly combing the Caribbean. Villeneuve failed to give Nelson the slip; back in European waters, he put in at a friendly Spanish port instead of heading directly for the Channel as Napoleon had ordered. Nelson engaged the combined French and Spanish fleets off Cape Trafalgar at the southwest corner of

"The Battle of Trafalgar," by Turner.

Spain (October, 1805). He lost his own life but not before he had destroyed half of his adversaries' ships without sacrificing a single one of his own. Trafalgar gave the British undisputed control of the seas for the balance of the war and blasted French hopes of a successful cross-Channel invasion.

By the time of Trafalgar, Austria and Russia had joined with Britain in the Third Coalition. Bonaparte routed his continental opponents in the most dazzling campaign of his career. At Ulm, on the upper Danube (October, 1805), he captured 30,000 Austrians who had moved westward without waiting for their Russian allies. He met the main Russian force and the balance of the Austrian army near the Moravian village

of Austerlitz. The ensuing battle (December 2, 1805) fittingly celebrated the first anniversary of Napoleon's coronation as emperor. Bringing up reinforcements secretly and with great speed, Napoleon completely surprised his opponents; their casualties were three times greater than his own. Within the month he forced the Habsburg emperor, Francis II, to sign the humiliating Treaty of Pressburg, giving the Austrian Tyrol to Bavaria and Venetia to the Napoleonic puppet kingdom of Italy.

A still harsher fate awaited the Prussians, brought back into the war for the first time since 1795 by Napoleon's repeated interventions in German affairs. The Prussian army, however, had not kept up with the military improvements introduced since the campaigns of Frederick the Great. In October, 1806, the French pulverized the main Prussian contingents in the twin battles of Jena and Auerstädt, and occupied Berlin. Napoleon decided to postpone a final settlement with Prussia until he had beaten his only remaining continental opponent. Russia went down at Friedland (June, 1807).

Napoleon's great string of victories against the Third Coalition resulted partly from the blunders of his enemies. The miscalculations of Austrian, Prussian, and Russian generals contributed to French successes at Austerlitz and at Jena. Further, the French army was the most seasoned force in Europe, its soldiers of every rank were well trained, and its officers were promoted because of ability rather than because of seniority or influence. Bonaparte seldom risked an engagement unless his forces were the numerical equal of the enemy's; then he staked everything on a dramatic surprise, as at Austerlitz. Yet even this almost invincible French army had defects. The pay was low and irregular, the medical services were a disgrace, and the supplies were so badly managed that French soldiers usually had to live off the land. Eventually, these shortcomings were to weaken French striking power; in 1807, however, they did not prevent the ascendancy of Napoleon in Europe.

The Empire at Its Height (1807-1812)

Napoleon reached the pinnacle of his career when he met his Russian adversary, Tsar Alexander I, on a raft anchored in the Niemen River at Tilsit in East Prussia. There, in July, 1807, the two emperors drew up a treaty dividing Europe between them. Alexander acknowledged France's hegemony over central and western Europe and secured in return the recognition of eastern Europe as the Russian sphere. Napoleon pledged Russia a share in the spoils if the Ottoman Empire should be dismembered. He demanded no territory from the defeated Tsar, only a commitment to cease trade with Britain and to join the war against her. The Tilsit settlement, however, made Alexander bitterly unpopular at home, where Russian propaganda had been denouncing Napoleon as anti-Christ.

Prussia was the chief victim at Tilsit. While the two emperors negotiated on the raft, Frederick William III (1797-1840), the Prussian king, nervously paced the banks of the Niemen. He had good cause to be nervous, for Tilsit cost him almost half his territory. Prussia's Polish provinces formed a new puppet state, the Grand Duchy of Warsaw, which Napoleon assigned to a French ally, the King of Saxony. Prussian territory west of the Elbe River went to Napoleon to dispose of as he wished. To complete the humiliation, Napoleon stationed occupation troops in Prussia and fixed the maximum size of its army at 42,000 men.

Under this latter-day Caesar almost all Europe could be divided into three parts. First came the French Empire, including France proper and the territories annexed since 1789. Second were the satellites, ruled in many cases by relatives of Napoleon. And third came Austria, Prussia, and Russia, forced by defeat to become the allies of France. Only Britain, Sweden, and Turkey remained outside the Napoleonic system.

The frontiers of the French Empire at their most extensive enclosed Belgium and Holland; the sections of Germany west of the Rhine and along the North Sea; the Italian lands of Piedmont, Genoa, Tuscany, and Rome; and finally, physically detached from the rest, the "Illyrian Provinces," stretching along the Dalmatian coast of the Adriatic, taken from Austria in 1809, and named after a province of the old Roman Empire. These annexed territories were usually subdivided into departments and

NAPOLEONIC EUROPE, 1812

Empire of France
States under French control
Allied with France
X Battle sites

Miles 0 ... 500

UNITED KINGDOM OF GREAT BRITAIN AND IRELAND

SCOTLAND

IRELAND

WALES ENGLAND

London

North Sea

SWEDEN

K. OF DENMARK & NORWAY

Baltic

Hamburg

Oldenburg

NETHERLANDS

Antwerp

K. of WESTPHALIA

Berlin

PRUSSIA

Auerstädt X X Leipzig

CONFEDERATION

Waterloo X

Amiens

Varennes

Jena X

SAXONY

Elbe R.

Prague

OF THE

Paris

Versailles

Valmy

Longuyon

Luneville

LORRAINE

Strasbourg

ALSACE

RHINE

BADEN

Austerlitz X

Pressburg

EMPIRE

Nantes

FRANCE

Limoges

Lyons

Basel

SWITZ.

Danube

Ulm

BAVARIA

Vienna

Loire R.

Gironde R.

Bordeaux

Payrac

PIED-MONT

TYROL

Campo formio

Milan

ILLYRIAN PROV.

AUSTRIA

Nice

Marengo X

Genoa

Venice

Adriatic Sea

Ebro R.

Madrid

PORTUGAL

SPAIN

Tagus R.

Guadalquivir R.

Atlantic Ocean

CORSICA

TUSCANY

ELBA

PAPAL STATES

Rome

K. OF ITALY

Po R.

Rhone R.

BALEARIC IS.

Mediterranean

SARDINIA

Naples

K. OF NAPLES

C. Trafalgar X

SICILY

MALTA (Br.)

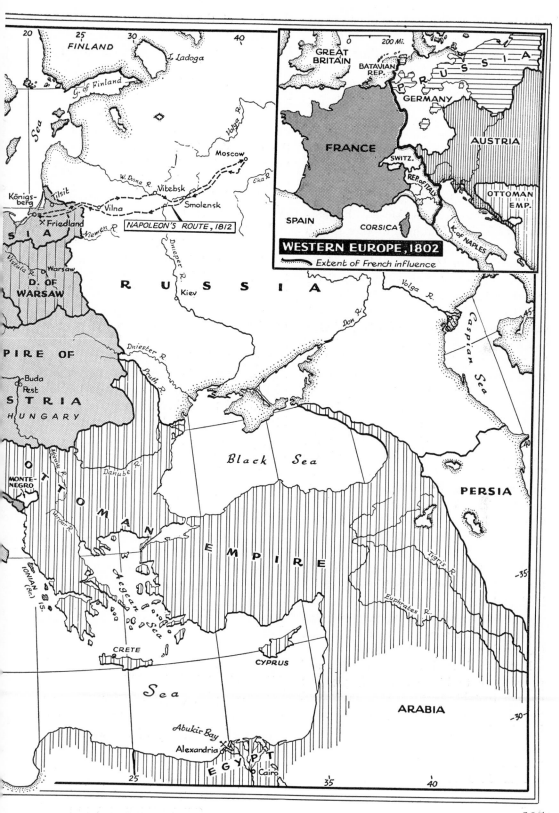

FINLAND

20 25 30 40

L. Ladoga

G. of Finland

Sea

Volga R.

Moscow

Königs-
berg

Tilsit

Vilna

W. Dvina R. Vitebsk

Oka R.

Smolensk

Friedland

Niemen R.

NAPOLEON'S ROUTE, 1812

D. OF
WARSAW

Vistula R.

Warsaw

R U S S I A

Dnieper R.

Kiev

Volga R.

PIRE OF

Dniester R.

Don R.

Caspian

STRIA

Buda
Pest

Pruth R.

Sea

HUNGARY

MONTE-
NEGRO

O T T O M A N

Morava R.

Danube R.

Black   Sea

PERSIA

Vardar R.

E M P I R E

Tigris R.

45

40

35

IONIAN
IS.

Aegean Sea

Euphrates R.

CRETE

CYPRUS

30

Sea

ARABIA

Abukir Bay

Alexandria

E G Y P T

Cairo

25 35 40

WESTERN EUROPE, 1802 (inset)

GREAT
BRITAIN

0 200 Mi.

R U S S I A

BATAVIAN
REP.

PRUSSIA

GERMANY

FRANCE

AUSTRIA

SWITZ.

REP. OF ITALY

OTTOMAN
EMP.

SPAIN

CORSICA

K. of NAPLES

WESTERN EUROPE, 1802

Extent of French influence

ruled by prefects, just like the departments of France proper.

The satellites flanked the French Empire. The Kingdom of Italy, an enlarged version of the Cisalpine Republic, included the northern and central Italian lands not directly annexed by France. Napoleon was the king, and his stepson, Eugene de Beauharnais, was viceroy. In southern Italy, Napoleon deposed the Bourbon king of Naples in 1805 and gave the crown first to his brother Joseph and then to his brother-in-law, Joachim Murat, the husband of his sister Caroline. Brother Joseph moved from Naples to Madrid in 1808 when Napoleon deposed the Spanish Bourbons in order to force the unwilling Spaniards to remain in the war against Britain.

In Central Europe, Napoleon energetically pursued his project of a "third" Germany. He decreed a further reduction in the number of German states, and in 1806 aided the dissolution of that venerable museum-piece, the Holy Roman Empire. Francis II, the reigning Habsburg, last of the Holy Roman Emperors, now styled himself Emperor of Austria. To replace the vanished Empire Napoleon created the Confederation of the Rhine, which included almost every German state except Austria and Prussia. At the heart of this confederation Napoleon carved out for his brother Jerome the Kingdom of Westphalia, which incorporated the Prussian holdings west of the Elbe seized at Tilsit. Two states outside the Confederation of the Rhine—Switzerland and the Grand-Duchy of Warsaw—completed the roster of French satellites. Europe had not seen such an empire since the heyday of imperial Rome.

Napoleon longed to give dignity and permanence to his creations. It was not enough that his brothers and his in-laws should sit on thrones; he himself must found a dynasty, must have the heir so far denied him in fifteen years of childless marriage. He divorced Josephine, therefore, and in 1810 married Marie-Louise, the daughter of the Habsburg Francis II. In due time, Marie-Louise bore a son, whom his father grandiloquently called "The King of Rome."

"Napoleon II," however, was never to rule in Rome or anywhere else. Throughout the new French acquisitions and the satellites Bonaparte and his relatives played the part of enlightened despots, curbing the power of the Church, abolishing serfdom, building roads, and introducing the new French law codes. Everywhere, however, they exacted a heavy toll of tribute and subjection. In the Kingdom of Italy, for instance, Napoleon doubled the tax rate previously levied by the Austrians; half the revenues of the kingdom went to defray the expenses of the French army and the French government. Napoleon flooded his relatives with instructions on the government of their domains and brought them abruptly to heel whenever they showed signs of putting local interests above those of France. When Louis Bonaparte in Holland dared to disobey the imperial orders, his brother delivered a crushing rebuke:

In ascending the throne of Holland, Your Majesty has forgotten that he is French and has stretched all the springs of his reason and tormented his conscience in order to persuade himself that he is Dutch. Dutchmen inclining toward France have been ignored and persecuted; those serving England have been promoted. . . . I have experienced the sorrow of seeing the name of France exposed to shame in a Holland ruled by a prince of my blood.[*]

Louis' boldness cost him his throne; his Dutch kingdom was annexed to France in 1810.

The Continental System

Nowhere was Napoleon's imperialism more evident than in his attempt to regulate the economy of the whole Con-

---

[*] *Lettres Inédites de Napoléon* (Paris, 1897), I, 382-383. Our translation.

tinent. The Continental System had a double aim: to build up the export trade of France and to cripple that of Britain. The collapse of Napoleon's cross-Channel invasion plans led him to expand the earlier tariff measures against Britain into a great campaign to bankrupt the nation of shopkeepers. The defeat of the Third Coalition gave him the opportunity to experiment with economic warfare on a continental scale and to carry to extremes the warlike implications of mercantilism.

The Berlin Decree, issued by Napoleon in November, 1806, forbade all trade with the British Isles and all commerce in British merchandise. It ordered the arrest of all Britons on the Continent and the confiscation of their property. Britain replied by requiring that neutral vessels wishing to trade with France put in first at a British port and pay duties. This regulation enabled Britain to share in the profits of neutral shipping to France. Napoleon retaliated with the Milan decree (December, 1807), ordering the seizure of all neutral ships that complied with the new British policy. The neutrals, in effect, were damned if they did and damned if they didn't.

Napoleon's vassals and allies had to support the Continental System or suffer the consequences. Of all the "un-French" activities countenanced by Louis Bonaparte

in Holland, the worst, in Napoleon's view, was his toleration of Dutch smuggling of English contraband. The Emperor likewise expected the satellites to contribute to French industrial prosperity. When the Italians objected to the regulation of their silk exports, Napoleon lectured his viceroy, Eugene, on the facts of economic life:

All the raw silk from the Kingdom of Italy goes to England. . . . It is therefore quite natural that I should wish to divert it from this route to the advantage of my French manufacturers: otherwise my silk factories, one of the chief supports of French commerce, would suffer substantial losses. . . . My principle is: France first. . . .
It is no use for Italy to make plans that leave French prosperity out of account; she must face the fact that the interests of the two countries hang together.*

The gigantic attempt to make "France first" failed almost totally. Only a few French industries benefited from the Continental System; the cessation of sugar imports from the West Indies, for example, promoted the cultivation of native sugar beets. But the decline of overseas trade greatly depressed Bordeaux and other French Atlantic ports. The increasing difficulty and expense of procuring raw

* Quoted in J. M. Thompson, ed., *Napoleon's Letters*, 241-242.

Gillray, "Tiddy-Dolly, the great French Gingerbread-Baker, drawing out a new Batch of Kings —his Man, Hopping-Talley, mixing up the Dough"—a British comment on Napoleon's imperialism.

materials like cotton caused widespread unemployment and produced a rash of bankruptcies. The new French markets on the Continent did not compensate for the loss of older markets overseas; the value of French exports declined by more than one-third between 1805 and 1813.

The Continental System did not ruin Britain, although it did confront the British with a severe economic crisis. Markets abroad for British exports were uncertain; food imports were reduced; and, while prices rose sharply, wages lagged behind. Both farm workers, already pinched by the enclosure movement (see Chapter XVI), and factory workers suffered acutely. Yet, fortified by her leadership in the economic revolutions and by the overwhelming superiority of her navy and merchant marine, Britain rode out the storm. Every tract of land at all capable of growing food was brought under the plow, and today one can see barren heights on Dartmoor that were last cultivated during the Napoleonic Wars. Exporters not only developed lucrative new markets in the Americas, the Ottoman Empire, and Asia but also continued to supply some of their old customers on the Continent. They smuggled their goods in neutral ships and with spurious "Made in France" labels. Napoleon lacked the vast naval force to apprehend smugglers at sea, and he lacked the large staff of incorruptible customs inspectors to control contraband in the ports. The most he could do was to confess his failure by confiscating and re-selling contraband *after* it had already been sold. Moreover, since the French army simply could not do without some items produced only in British factories, Napoleon violated his own decrees by authorizing secret purchases of British cloth and leather for uniforms.

The Continental System antagonized both the neutral powers and Napoleon's allies. French seizure of American vessels in European ports under the terms of the Milan Decree put a dangerous strain on Franco-American relations. But British restrictions likewise bore heavily on the Americans. British impressment of American seamen on the pretext that they were deserters from the Royal Navy, together with the designs of American expansionists on Canada, produced the indecisive Anglo-American War of 1812, which actually lasted until 1814.

The Downfall of Napoleon

In Europe, the political and military consequences of the Continental System formed a decisive and disastrous chapter in Napoleonic history. The chapter opened in 1807, when the Emperor declined to tolerate Portugal's economic ties with Britain. To impose the Continental System on Portugal, he suggested that France and Spain partition the country. The Spanish rulers agreed, not suspecting that Napoleon planned to use the Portuguese expedition as an excuse for French military occupation of Spain itself. In 1808 he lured the Spanish royal family away from Madrid and made his brother Joseph King of Spain. But every measure taken by Napoleon—the removal of the ineffectual Bourbons, the installation of a foreign monarch, the attempted enforcement of the Continental System, and, not least, the suppression of the Inquisition and the curtailment of noble and clerical privileges—violated Spanish tradition and offended Spanish nationalism. The irreconcilable Spaniards began fighting Napoleon in 1808.

This Peninsular War, named after the Iberian Peninsula, swiftly grew from a minor irritation to a deadly cancer on the body of the Napoleonic Empire. The Spaniards employed ambushes and poisoned wells, and used other guerrilla devices. The expedition that Britain sent to assist them upset all the rules about British inferiority in military, as opposed to naval, matters. It was ably commanded by Sir Arthur Welles-

Goya, "The Third of May, 1808" (1814-1815). Now in the Prado, Madrid.

ley (later the Duke of Wellington), generously supplied from home, and firmly based on Britain's unshakable command of the seas. Napoleon poured more than 300,000 troops into the Peninsular campaign, but his opponents gained the upper hand in 1812, when he detached part of his forces for the invasion of Russia. In 1813, King Joseph left Madrid forever, and Wellington, having liberated Spain, crossed into southern France.

Napoleonic imperialism also aroused a national spirit among the traditionally disunited Germans. Men of letters launched a campaign against the traditional influence of the French language and French culture.

Johann Grimm and his brother Wilhelm contributed not only their very popular—and very German—*Fairy Tales* (1812) but also philological researches designed to prove the innate superiority of the German language. The philosopher Fichte delivered at Berlin the highly patriotic *Addresses to the German Nation* (1807-08), claiming that German was the *Ursprache*, the fountainhead of language. And the Germans themselves, Fichte continued, were the *Urvolk*, the oldest and the most moral of nations.

Napoleon began to feel the impact of German nationalism when Austria re-entered the war in 1809. For the first time, the Habsburg monarchy now attempted a total mobilization comparable to that decreed by the French Convention in 1793. In spite of the new spirit, however, the Austrians lost the campaign and for the fourth time in a dozen years submitted to a peace dictated by Napoleon. The Treaty of Schönbrunn (1809) stripped them of the Illyrian Provinces and assigned their Polish territory of Galicia to the Grand Duchy of Warsaw. Francis II gave his daughter to Napoleon in marriage, and his defeated land became the unwilling ally of France. Leadership in the German revival passed to Prussia.

The shock of Jena and Tilsit jarred Prussia out of the lethargy that had overtaken her since the death of Frederick the Great in 1786. The new University of Berlin, founded in 1810, attracted Fichte and other prophets of German nationalism. Able generals and statesmen came to power. General Scharnhorst headed a group of officers who improved the efficiency of the army, abolished its inhuman discipline, and made all social classes liable to military service, even the previously exempted educated and well-to-do. The top limit of 42,000 soldiers imposed upon Prussia by Napoleon was evaded by the simple device of assigning recruits to the reserve after a fairly brief period of intensive training and then inducting another group of recruits. By 1813, Prussia had more than 150,000 trained men available for combat duty.

The social and administrative reorganization of the Prussian state was inspired by the energetic Stein—Baron vom und zum Stein, an enlightened aristocrat. Stein conciliated the middle class by granting towns and cities some self-government. To improve the status of the peasantry, he fostered the edict of October, 1807, at long last abolishing serfdom in Prussia. The edict, however, did not break up the large Junker estates or provide land for the liberated serfs; nor did it terminate the feudal rights of justice exercised by the Junker over his peasants. Stein and the others eliminated only the worst abuses of the Old Régime and left authority where it had traditionally rested—with the king, the army, and the Junkers. The Hohenzollern state was not so much reformed as restored to the traditions of absolutism and efficiency established by the Great Elector and Frederick the Great.

The event that enabled an aroused German nationalism to turn its full force against Napoleon was the French debacle in Russia. French actions after 1807 soon convinced Tsar Alexander that Napoleon was not keeping the Tilsit bargain and was intruding on Russia's sphere in eastern Europe. When Alexander and Napoleon met again at the German town of Erfurt in 1808, they could reach no agreement, though they concealed their differences by a show of great intimacy. French acquisition of the Illyrian provinces from Austria in 1809 raised the unpleasant prospect of French domination over the Balkans, and the simultaneous transfer of Galicia from Austria to the Grand Duchy of Warsaw suggested that this Napoleonic vassal might next seek to absorb the Polish territories of Russia. Meanwhile, Napoleon's insistent efforts to make Russia enforce the Continental System increasingly incensed Alexander. French annexations in northwest Germany completed the discomfiture of the Tsar, for they wiped out the state of Oldenburg, where his uncle was the reigning duke. All these factors caused an open break between the Tsar and the Emperor, and the famous invasion of Russia by the French in 1812.

For the invasion Napoleon assembled the *Grande Armée* of nearly 500,000 men. A large proportion of the Grand Army, however, were not Frenchmen but unwilling conscripts in the service of a foreign master. The supply system broke down almost immediately, and the Russian scorched-earth policy made it very hard for the soldiers to live off the land. As the Grand Army marched eastward, one of Napoleon's aides reported:

There were no inhabitants to be found, no prisoners to be taken, not a single straggler to be picked up. We were in the heart of inhabited Russia and yet we were like a vessel without a compass in the midst of a vast ocean, knowing nothing of what was happening around us.*

Napoleon marched all the way to Moscow without ever managing to strike a knockout blow. He remained in the burning city for five weeks (September-October, 1812) in the vain hope of bringing Tsar Alexander to terms. But Russian obduracy and the shortage of supplies forced him to begin a retreat that became a nightmare. Ill-fed and inadequately clothed and sheltered, the retreating soldiers suffered horribly from Russian attacks on stragglers, and from the deadly onslaughts of "General Winter." Less than a quarter of the Grand Army survived the retreat from Moscow; the rest had been taken prisoner or had died of wounds, starvation, disease, or the cold.

The Russian leaders had feared that Napoleon would liberate the serfs and turn them against their masters. Nevertheless, the peasants, despite the ill-treatment to which they had been subject for so long, formed guerrilla bands, harassed Napoleon's forces, and in every way proved that their patriotic sentiments outweighed their class grievances. Kutuzov, the victorious Russian commander, now wanted to allow Russia's allies to prosecute the war. But Alexander insisted on pursuing the French, and sent Russian armies westward beyond the Russian frontiers on the track of Napoleon's forces.

The British had been the first to resist

* A. A. L. de Caulaincourt, *With Napoleon in Russia* (New York, 1935), 62.

Napoleon successfully, at Trafalgar and on the economic battlefields of the Continental System. Then had come Spanish resistance, then Russian. Now in 1813 almost every nation in Europe joined the final coalition against the French. Napoleon raised a new army, but he could not replace so readily the equipment squandered in Russia. In October, 1813, he lost the "Battle of the Nations," fought at Leipzig in Germany, and by April, 1814, the forces of the coalition occupied Paris. The Emperor abdicated, to begin an honorable exile as ruler of the minute island of Elba not far from the western coast of Italy.

The statesmen of the victorious coalition gathered in the Congress of Vienna to draw up the terms of peace (see Chapter XIX). The Bourbons returned to France in the person of Louis XVIII, a younger brother of Louis XVI. Realizing that he could not revive the Old Régime intact, the new king issued the Charter of 1814 establishing a constitutional monarchy. The returned *émigrés*, however, showed no such good sense. They unleashed a new "White Terror" against the Revolution and all its works. Then, on March 1, 1815, Bonaparte pulled his last surprise: he landed on the Mediterranean coast of France.

For a hundred days, from March 20, 1815, when Napoleon re-entered Paris, the French Empire was reborn. Once again the Emperor rallied the French people, this time by promising a truly liberal regime. He never had time, however, to show the sincerity of his promise, for on June 18, 1815, the British under Wellington and the Prussians under Blücher delivered the final blow at Waterloo, near Brussels. Again Napoleon went into exile, to the remote British island of St. Helena in the South Atlantic. There, in 1821, he died of cancer.

VII: The Legacy of the Revolution and Napoleon

Bonapartism did not die in 1815 or 1821, any more than the Caesarism of ancient Rome had died on the Ides of March. A Napoleonic legend arose, glossing over the faults and failures of its hero, depicting him as the paladin of liberalism and patriotism, and paving the way for the advent of another Napoleon in 1848 (see Chapter XIX). This legend, with its overtones of hero-worship and belligerent nationalism, was one element in the legacy bequeathed by revolutionary and Napoleonic France. A second, and still more powerful, element was the great revolutionary motto—*Liberté, Egalité, Fraternité*. The motto lived on, to inspire later generations of Jacobins in France and elsewhere. And behind the motto was the fact that Frenchmen enjoyed a larger measure of liberty, equality, and fraternity in 1815 than they had ever known before 1789.

True, the Mountain's deputies on mission and Napoleon's censors and prefects gave new force to the old traditions of absolutism and centralization. But the Revolution founded a potent new tradition of liberty. The middle class had won its freedom from obsolete restraints, and Protestants, Jews, and free-thinkers had gained toleration both in France and in French-dominated countries. French institutions in 1815 by no means measured up to the liberal ideals expressed in the Declaration of the Rights of Man. Nevertheless, the ideals had been stated, and the campaign for their further implementation was to form the main theme of French domestic history in the nineteenth century.

The revolutionary and Napoleonic régimes introduced a large measure of equality. They established the principle of equal liability to taxation. They provided a greater degree of economic opportunity for large numbers of the third estate by breaking up the large land holdings of the clergy and nobility and by removing obstacles to the activity of businessmen, big and little. The *Code Napoléon* buried beyond all hope of exhumation the worst legal and social inequalities of the Old Régime. There was a good deal of truth in Napoleon's boast:

Whether as First Consul or as Emperor, I have been the people's king; I have governed for the nation and in its interests, without allowing myself to be turned aside by the outcries or the private interests of certain people.[*]

The Revolution and Napoleon promoted fraternity in the legal sense by making all Frenchmen equal in the eyes of the law. They advanced fraternity in a broader sense by encouraging nationalism, the feeling of belonging to the great corporate body of Frenchmen who were superior to all other nations. French nationalism had existed long before 1789; Joan of Arc, Henry IV, and Louis XIV had all been nationalists in their diverse ways. But it remained for the Convention to formulate a fervent new nationalistic creed in its decree of August 23, 1793, providing for the total mobilization of the French nation. The Napoleonic Empire then demonstrated how easily nationalism on an unprecedented scale could lead to imperialism of unprecedented magnitude. A century ago, Alexis de Tocqueville, the great French student of democracy, wrote:

The French Revolution was ... a political revolution, which in its operation and its aspect resembled a religious one. It had every peculiar and characteristic feature of a religious movement; it not only spread to foreign countries,

[*] Quoted in Caulaincourt, *With Napoleon in Russia*, 364.

but it was carried thither by preaching and by propaganda.

It roused passions such as the most violent political revolutions had never before excited. ... This gave to it that aspect of a religious revolution which so terrified its contemporaries, or rather ... it became a kind of new religion in itself—a religion, imperfect it is true, without a God, without a worship, without a future life, but which nevertheless, like Islam, poured forth its soldiers, its apostles, and its martyrs over the face of the earth.*

---

* A. de Tocqueville, *The State of Society in France Before the Revolution of 1789*, 3rd ed. (London, 1888), 9-11.

Its early adherents were fanatics—Robespierre and the Jacobins. Its later exponents —the men of Thermidor and Brumaire— modified the creed in the interests of practicality and moderation. Even in the hands of Napoleon, however, the Revolution remained a kind of religion, demanding political orthodoxy and punishing heretics, as Napoleon punished King Louis Bonaparte of Holland, by the political equivalent of excommunication. And after 1815, as we shall see in the next chapter, the Revolution continued to pour forth "its soldiers, its apostles, and its martyrs."

Reading Suggestions
on the French Revolution and Napoleon

(Asterisk indicates paperbound edition.)

GENERAL ACCOUNTS

C. Brinton, *A Decade of Revolution, 1789-1799* (Harper, 1934), and G. Bruun, *Europe and the French Imperium, 1799-1814* (Harper, 1938). Two highly useful volumes in the indispensable "Rise of Modern Europe" series.

L. Gershoy, *The French Revolution and Napoleon* (Appleton-Century-Crofts, 1934). A first-rate textbook account.

R. R. Palmer, *The Age of the Democratic Revolution*, Vol. I (Princeton Univ. Press, 1959). See comment on p. 94.

SPECIAL STUDIES: THE FRENCH REVOLUTION

H. A. Taine, *The Ancient Régime* (Holt, 1876), and *The French Revolution* (Holt, 1878-1887). The classic detailed account from the conservative point of view.

F. V. A. Aulard, *The French Revolution: A Political History* (Scribner's, 1910). The classic detailed account from the middle-of-the-road republican point of view.

A. Mathiez, *The French Revolution* (Knopf, 1928). The classic detailed account from a rather Marxian standpoint.

A. de Tocqueville, *The Old Régime and the Revolution* (*Anchor). A famous study, more than a century old, by a highly perceptive observer.

G. Lefebvre, *The Coming of the French Revolution* (*Vintage, 1957). A superlative short study of the causes and first months of the revolution.

G. Salvemini, *The French Revolution, 1788-1792* (Holt, 1954). A detailed and informative account by a distinguished Italian scholar.

G. Rudé, *The Crowd in the French Revolution* (Oxford Univ. Press, 1959). Enlightening study of the role of the popular masses; addressed to the general reader.

C. Brinton, *The Jacobins* (Macmillan, 1930). An instructive monograph.

R. R. Palmer, *Twelve Who Ruled*, rev. ed. (Princeton Univ. Press, 1958). Good short studies of the members of the Committee of Public Safety.

J. M. Thompson, *Robespierre and the French Revolution* (Macmillan, 1953), and *Leaders of the French Revolution* (Blackwell, 1948). Very useful introductions by a British scholar.

G. Brunn, *Saint-Just: Apostle of the Terror* (Houghton, Mifflin, 1932). Excellent brief biography.

C. Brinton, *The Anatomy of Revolution* (°Vintage, 1957). Compares the French Revolution with the English, American, and Russian revolutions.

SPECIAL STUDIES: NAPOLEON

F. M. Kircheisen, *Napoleon* (Harcourt, Brace, 1932). One of the best longer biographies.

H. A. L. Fisher, *Napoleon* (Oxford Univ. Press, 1945); A. L. Guérard, *Napoleon I* (Knopf, 1956). Good short biographies.

F. M. H. Markham, *Napoleon and the Awakening of Europe* (Macmillan, 1954). A useful popular introduction.

E. Heckscher, *The Continental System: An Economic Interpretation* (Clarendon, 1922). An important monograph.

J. Seeley, *The Life and Times of Stein: Germany and Prussia in the Napoleonic Age* (Roberts, 1879). An old detailed treatment, still worth reading.

W. C. Langsam, *The Napoleonic Wars and German Nationalism in Austria* (Columbia Univ. Press, 1930). An informative monograph.

H. A. L. Fisher, *Studies in Napoleonic Statesmanship: Germany* (Clarendon, 1903). A detailed and balanced evaluation of the impact of French reforms on German satellites.

P. Geyl, *Napoleon, For and Against* (Yale Univ. Press, 1949). A most interesting collection of judgments passed on Napoleon in later epochs.

SOURCES

J. H. Stewart, *A Documentary Survey of the French Revolution* (Macmillan, 1951). An ably edited collection of constitutional texts and other source materials.

A. Young, *Travels in France*, C. Maxwell, ed. (Cambridge Univ. Press, 1929). Fascinating reports by an English traveler on the eve of the revolution.

E. Higgins, *The French Revolution as Told by Contemporaries* (Houghton, Mifflin, 1938). Handy compendium of eye-witness reports.

E. Burke, *Reflections on the Revolution in France* (many editions). The celebrated diatribe against the Revolution.

R. M. Johnston, ed., *The Corsican* (Houghton, Mifflin, 1910). Napoleon's biography compiled from his own words.

J. M. Thompson, ed., *Napoleon's Letters* (Dutton, 1954). A most instructive and interesting collection.

A. A. L. de Caulaincourt, *With Napoleon in Russia* (Morrow, 1935; °Universal Library). Vivid recollections of one of Bonaparte's chief aides.

HISTORICAL FICTION

A. France, *The Gods Are Athirst* (Roy, 1953). Fascinating brief novel about a fanatical Jacobin; the best fictional treatment of the Revolution.

L. Tolstoy, *War and Peace* (many editions). The celebrated gargantuan novel about the Russian campaign.

144

Revolution and Counter-Revolution, 1815-1850

CHAPTER XIX

I: Introduction

THE HISTORY of the western world during the half-century after Napoleon's downfall is crammed with major events. Between 1815 and 1870 the industrial revolution came of age, modern doctrines of socialism were born, and Darwin brought a great revolution in science toward completion. In politics, during the same period, Great Britain and the United States moved steadily, and France more erratically, toward the practical establishment of democracy; Italy and Germany at last achieved national unification. All these developments, though they were well under way by 1850, reached a climax after the mid-century mark. Detailed treatment of them will therefore be postponed to subsequent chapters (XX-XXIII). The present chapter will be focused on the interaction of cultural and political forces, particularly in continental Europe, during the post-Napoleonic generation from 1815 to 1850.

One great thread through this period of European history is suggested by the terms "reaction" and "counter-revolution." By 1815, Europe was reacting strongly both against the French Revolution, which had made Napoleon possible, and against the Enlightenment, which had made the Revolution possible. The reaction against the

Opposite. LIBERTY LEADING THE PEOPLE, *by Eugène Delacroix (1798-1863); French, painted 1830; the Louvre, Paris. A celebrated evocation of the July Revolution in Paris, 1830 (p. 169). Delacroix stresses the Romantic qualities of vigor, color, and drama, in contrast to the more restrained and academic neoclassicism of David (see also below, p. 151).*

Enlightenment took the form of the Romantic movement. Romantic writers and artists protested against the omnipotent reason of the eighteenth century and championed faith, emotion, tradition, and other values that the Age of Reason had spurned. The political counter-revolution was very evident at the Congress of Vienna in 1814-1815, where the leaders of the last coalition against Napoleon re-established the European balance of power and repudiated the revolutionary principles that had shattered the eighteenth-century balance. Reason and natural law, in the judgement both of political leaders and of many Romantics, had led not only to progress but also to the Reign of Terror and Napoleonic imperialism.

But the spirit of 1789 did not die in 1815; the second great thread through the post-Napoleonic age is the persistence of revolution. Despite the ascendancy of counter-revolutionary forces, liberal and nationalistic ideas and aspirations still flourished. They were to produce new outbreaks of revolution in the 1820's, in 1830, and in 1848. Although none of these revolutions proved to be as formidable as the great upheaval of 1789, all of them threatened the status quo. In addition, the revolutions of 1848 marked the end of an era in European history, a great turning point in the evolution of liberalism and nationalism.

II: The Romantic Protest

The Romantic protest against reason reached its full force during the first third of the nineteenth century—the Romantic decades of 1800 to 1830 or 1840. Actually, as we have already seen in Chapter XVII, the reaction against the Enlightenment had set in much earlier. Before 1750 Wesley and the Pietists were challenging the deism of the *philosophes*. Soon Rousseau proclaimed conscience, not reason, the "true guide of man"; Hume fastened on men's "sentiments and affections," not their reason; and Kant exalted idealism and the eternal verities. Then in 1790 Edmund Burke's *Reflections on the Revolution in France* neatly turned against the *philosophes* their favorite appeal to the simple mathematical laws of Newtonian science. Natural rights, Burke argued,

... entering into common life, like rays of light which pierce into a dense medium, are, by the laws of nature, refracted from their straight line. Indeed in the gross and complicated mass of human passions and concerns, the primitive rights of men undergo such a variety of refractions and reflections, that it becomes absurd to talk of them as if they continued in the simplicity of their original direction. The nature of man is intricate; the objects of society are of the greatest possible complexity. . . .*

The protest against the oversimplification of man and society, and the insistence on the intricacy and complexity of humanity, formed a common denominator of the Romantic movement. Romanticism, however, was itself a complex phenomenon that cannot be defined by a simple formula. Other common denominators will emerge as we survey the achievements of the Romantics, beginning with their most characteristic and productive realm of activity —literature.

Literature:
The Revolt against Reason

Literary Romanticism may be traced back to the mid-eighteenth-century novels

---

* *Reflections on the Revolution in France*, Everyman ed. (New York, 1910), 59.

of sentiment and duty, like Richardson's *Clarissa*. Its immediate precursor was the German movement of the 1770's aptly named *Sturm und Drang* ("Storm and Stress") after a play by an obscure dramatist. The hero of the play, totally incapable of settling down, flees Europe to fight in the American Revolution:

Have been everything. Became a day-labourer to be something. Lived on the Alps, pastured goats, lay day and night under the boundless vault of the heavens, cooled by the winds, burning with an inner fire. Nowhere rest, nowhere repose. See, thus I am glutted by impulse and power, and work it out of me. I am going to take part in this campaign as a volunteer; there I can expand my soul, and if they do me the favour to shoot me down,—all the better.*

The most popular work of the *Sturm und Drang* period was *The Sorrows of Young Werther*, a lugubrious short novel by the youthful Goethe (1749-1832); even Napoleon claimed to have read it seven times over, weeping copiously each time at the hero's suicide. Restlessness, self-pity, and self-destruction—in fashionable twentieth-century terms, the sense of alienation, of being an "outsider"—were to be favorite themes of the Romantic writers, too. In contrast to the optimism of the *philosophes,* the Romantics sounded chords of pessimism and despair.

Goethe himself, whose long and productive career extended right through the Romantic era, was in some respects a good eighteenth-century man of reason. He was interested in natural science and settled happily at the enlightened court of a small German state at Weimar. Yet Romantic values lie at the very heart of his greatest work—many would say the greatest work in the German language—*Faust*. Begun when Goethe was in his twenties, and

---

* Klinger, *Sturm und Drang,* quoted in Kuno Francke, *A History of German Literature as Determined by Social Forces,* 4th ed. (New York, 1931), 309.

finished only when he was eighty, this long poetic drama was less a play in the conventional sense than a philosophical commentary on the main currents of European thought. According to the traditional legend, the aged Faust, weary of book learning and pining for eternal youth, sold his soul to the Devil, receiving back the enjoyment of his youth for an allotted time, and then, terror-stricken, went to the everlasting fires. Goethe transformed the legend. While Faust does indeed find intellectual pursuits disillusioning and profitless:

...Grey is all theory,
The golden tree of life is green!

he makes his infernal compact and is ultimately saved through his realization that he must sacrifice selfish concerns to the welfare of others. A drama of man's sinning, striving, and redemption, Goethe's *Faust* is a reaffirmation of the Christian way that the Enlightenment had belittled. The return to Christianity is a striking feature of Romanticism, as we shall see presently.

All over Europe, by the early 1800's, Romantic writers were following the example of the *Sturm und Drang* and rebelling against the reason and order of the "classical spirit." They decried what seemed to them the stilted and artificial verses of Racine and Pope, and praised the color and vigor of the Bible, Homer, and Shakespeare. They made impassioned pleas for a literary renaissance, a rebirth of imagination, feeling, and sensitivity. In consequence, the Romantic era was an age of poetry, in contrast to the eighteenth-century age of prose.

Britain produced a galaxy of Romantic poets—Byron, Shelley, Keats, Wordsworth, Coleridge, and still others. Of them all, Wordsworth (1770-1850) and Coleridge (1772-1834) perhaps pressed farthest in reaction against classicism and rationalism and may therefore serve to illustrate the Romantic outlook. In 1798 the two men published *Lyrical Ballads,* an early landmark in British Romanticism. As Coleridge later explained, their purpose was explicitly anti-classical:

In the present age the poet ... seems to propose to himself as his main object ... new and striking images; with incidents that interest the affections or excite the curiosity. Both his characters and his descriptions he renders, as much as possible, specific and individual, even to a degree of portraiture. In his diction and metre, on the other hand, he is comparatively careless.*

To *Lyrical Ballads* Wordsworth contributed this specific rejection of the Enlightenment:

Come forth into the light of things,
Let Nature be your teacher.

She has a world of ready wealth,
Our minds and hearts to bless—
Spontaneous wisdom breathed by health,
Truth breathed by cheerfulness.

One impulse from a vernal wood
May teach you more of man,
Of moral evil and of good,
Than all the sages can.

Sweet is the lore which Nature brings;
Our meddling intellect
Mis-shapes the beauteous forms of things:—
We murder to dissect.

Enough of Science and of Art;
Close up those barren leaves;
Come forth, and bring with you a heart
That watches and receives.†

Wordsworth transformed the old concept of nature; nature was no longer something to be analyzed and reduced to laws but a mysterious, vitalizing force that had to be sensed and experienced. Here, from his long autobiographical poem, *The Prelude,* are two passages that contain the essence of his belief:

Dust as we are, the immortal spirit grows
Like harmony in music; there is a dark
Inscrutable workmanship that reconciles

---

* *Biographia Literaria,* Everyman ed. (New York, 1908), 173.
† *The Tables Turned,* lines 15-32.

Discordant elements, makes them cling
    together
In one society.   . . .

Ye Presences of Nature in the sky
And on the earth! Ye Visions of the hills!
And Souls of lonely places! can I think
A vulgar hope was yours when ye
    employed
Such ministry, when ye, through many
    a year
Haunting me thus among my boyish
    sports,
On caves and trees, upon the woods and
    hills,
Impressed, upon all forms, the characters
Of danger or desire; and thus did make
The surface of the universal earth,
With triumph and delight, with hope
    and fear,
Work like a sea?*

"Visions," "Souls," "haunting"—these are surely Romantic words and concepts. In place of the light shed by Newton's laws, Wordsworth finds "a dark inscrutable workmanship," and in place of the *philosophes'* belief in the perfectibility of man through reason he puts his faith in the "immortal spirit" of the individual. Wordsworth in fact lived in France during the early years of the Revolution and witnessed the frustration of its high hopes for rational reform.

Literature:
The Return to the Past

It may seem a long leap from the mystical universe of Wordsworth to the Romantics' enthusiasm for the Middle Ages in general and for the earlier history of their own nations in particular. And yet nationalism is an irrational, almost mystical, force that in effect "reconciles discordant elements, makes them cling together in one society." The heightened sense of nationalism evident almost everywhere in Europe by 1815 was in part a matter of political

---

* *The Prelude,* Book I, lines 340-344, 464-475.

CHAPTER XIX

self-preservation. In the crisis of the Napoleonic wars, for example, the Spaniards became more aware of their Spanish heritage and the Germans of their Germanic one. The Romantic return to the past, however, though intensified by French imperialism, had begun before 1789 as part of the general retreat from the Enlightenment. The *philosophes* hated the Middle Ages, especially the medieval preoccupation with religion; naturally the pioneers of Romanticism tended to cherish what the *philosophes* detested.

The German writer, Herder (1744-1803) advanced a theory of cultural nationalism. Each separate nation, he argued, like any individual organism, had its own distinct personality, its *Volksgeist* or "folk spirit," and its own pattern of growth. The surest measure of a nation's growth was its literature—poetry in youth, prose in maturity. Stimulated by Herder, students of medieval German literature collected popular ballads, and the Grimms compiled their *Fairy Tales*. In 1782, the first complete text of the *Nibelungenlied* was published, a heroic saga of the nation's youth that had been much admired in the later Middle Ages only to be forgotten in succeeding centuries. By putting a new value on the German literature of the past, Herder helped to free the German literature of his own day from its bondage to French culture. Herder, however, was no narrow nationalist and asserted that the cultivated man should know cultures other than his own. So Herder also helped to loose the flood of translations that poured over Germany about 1800—translations of Shakespeare, of *Don Quixote*, of Spanish and Portuguese poetry, even of works in Sanskrit.

Some German Romantics, stirred by the patriotic revival after Jena and Tilsit, carried national enthusiasm to an extreme that Herder would have deplored. Thus the Grimms claimed pre-eminence for the German language (see Chapter XVIII), and the dramatist Kleist (1777-1811), in his *Battle of Arminius*, boasted of the prowess of the ancient Germans in defeating the Roman legions in 9 A.D. For the Romantic extremists the mere fact of being German appeared to be a cardinal virtue. Yet many German writers struck Herder's happy balance between national and cosmopolitan interests; Goethe, for example, prided himself on being a good European, not simply a German.

Many other nations experienced a notable revival of their older literature during the Romantic epoch. In Britain, Sir Walter Scott (1771-1832) assisted in collecting the vigorous folk ballads of the Middle Ages and went on to write more than thirty historical novels, of which *Ivanhoe*, set in the days of Richard Lionheart and the Crusades, is the best known. In France, the home of the "classical spirit," the Romantic reaction gathered slowly but reached full strength after 1825 with the vivid historical dramas of Victor Hugo (1802-1885) and his famous novel of fifteenth-century France, *Notre Dame de Paris*. In Russia, to cite a third example, the poet Pushkin (1799-1837) deserted the archaic Slavonic language of the Orthodox Church to write the first major literary works in the national vernacular. He introduced local color from Russian history and from the newly acquired provinces in the Crimea and the Caucasus, and he celebrated his own exotic grandfather, Hannibal, the African Negro slave of Peter the Great.

Music

Romantic musicians, too, sought out the popular ballads and tales of the national past. They, too, were inventive and imaginative, seeking to make their art more dramatic and flexible, less constrained by classical rules. To achieve color and drama, composers of opera and song turned frequently to the favorites of Romantic literature—Shakespeare's plays, Scott's novels, and the poems and tales of Goethe and Pushkin. In short, literature and music often followed parallel paths of development during the Romantic era. But the parallel was never complete, for Romantic musicians scarcely revolted against their great eighteenth-century predecessors in the sense that Romantic poets were revolting against the *philosophes*. Rather, Romantic music evolved peacefully out of the older classical school.

The composer who played the commanding part in this evolution was Beethoven (1770-1827), a Fleming by ancestry and a Viennese by adoption. Whereas Coleridge had said that the Romantic artist might be careless in matters of diction and meter, Beethoven showed a classical concern for the forms and techniques that were the musical counterparts of diction and meter. Yet he also reshaped the great tradition that he inherited from Bach, Haydn, and Mozart. For example, where Mozart and Haydn had used the courtly minuet for the third movement in a symphony, Beethoven introduced the more plebeian and rollicking *scherzo*. Where earlier composers had indicated the tempo with a simple *allegro* (fast) or *andante* (slow), Beethoven added such designations as *appassionato* and "Strife between Head and Heart." His compositions sometimes suggest vigorous conflicts and emotions: witness the opening chords of the Fifth Symphony, often compared to the rappings of fate. In good Romantic fashion, Beethoven drew inspiration from nature, as in the "Pastoral Symphony," with its musical thunderstorm and peaceful forest, complete with bird songs.

After Beethoven, orchestral works took on increasingly heroic dimensions. The pioneer was the Frenchman Berlioz (1803-1869), who projected an orchestra of 465 pieces, including 120 violins, 37 double-basses, and 30 each of pianos and harps. Although this utopian scheme remained on paper, Berlioz was virtually the first composer to utilize the full complement of instruments, especially winds and percussion, that make up the modern orchestra. His experiments with the theatrical potentialities of orchestral music created a landmark in musical history; the aptly named "Fantastic Symphony" (1830) was based, it is said, on Goethe's *Werther*.

Music for the human voice reflected both the increased enthusiasm for instruments, particularly the newly perfected piano, and the general Romantic nostalgia for the past. In composing songs and arias, Romantic musicians devoted as much skill to the accompaniment as to the voice part itself. Franz Schubert (1797-1826), Beethoven's Viennese contemporary, made a fine art of blending voice and piano in more than six hundred sensitive *Lieder* (songs), seventy of them musical settings of poems by Goethe. Meantime, Von Weber (1786-1826) was striving to create a truly German opera. He took an old legend as the libretto for *Der Freischütz* ("The Freeshooter," 1820), which ran the good Romantic gamut of an enchanted forest, a magic bullet, and an innocent maiden outwitting the Devil. For the choruses and marches of *Der Freischütz* he employed many folk-like melodies. Weber was by no means the only serious composer to utilize national folk tunes. The Russian Glinka (1804-1857) cast aside the Italian influences that had previously dominated the secular music of his country. He based his opera, *Russlan and Ludmilla* (1842), on a poem by Pushkin and embellished it with dances and choruses derived from the native music of Russia's Asiatic provinces.

The Arts

In the fine arts, the forces of Romanticism gained no such triumph as they won in literature and music. The virtual dictator of European painting during the first two decades of the nineteenth century

Romantic painting. Constable, "Stoke-by-Nayland" (1836).

was the French neoclassicist, David (1748-1825). The official painter of the French Jacobins, David depicted dramatic events like the Tennis-Court Oath but generally used traditional techniques. In the "Tennis-Court Oath," for example, he first drew the deputies naked, as if they were ancient athletes, and later painted in their clothes.

More direct and powerful—and much closer to the Romantic temper—were the works of the great Spanish painter, Goya (1746-1828). No one could have any illusions about Spanish royalty after looking at Goya's revealing portraits of the enlightened Charles III and his successors. After viewing Goya's etchings on the Peninsular War, no one could doubt the horrors of warfare (see illustration on p. 139). Goya is said to have made the sketches for these etchings in the very blood of the executed Spanish patriots whose agonies he was portraying. The outraged patriotism and frightening immediacy of Goya, however, attracted few imitators.

The two men responsible for establishing a Romantic school of painting were Constable and Delacroix. The lovely paintings of the English landscape by Constable (1776-1837) made nature artistically respectable once more. Delacroix (1799-1863), a Frenchman, insisted that color and light mattered more than classical purity of line; young painters, therefore, should study the flamboyant canvases of Rubens, whom David had banished from the ranks of orthodox artists. The purpose of art, Delacroix claimed in a good Romantic definition, was "not to imitate nature but to strike the imagination." His painting of "The Massacre of Scio" (1824), a bloody episode in the Greek War of Independence (see below, p. 165), was denounced as "barbarous, drunken, delirious"—the "massacre of painting." Today, however, the work of Delacroix seems conventional enough and less experimental than that of Goya (see also the illustration facing p. 145). By the 1830's, French painters were divided into opposing schools: the Romantic followers of Delacroix, and the still influential disciples of David.

In architecture, also, two schools flourished during the first half of the nineteenth century—the neoclassical, looking to Greek and Roman antiquity, and the neo-Gothic, or Gothic revival, looking to the Middle Ages. Significantly, the label "Gothic" was no longer derogatory, as it had once been when employed by rationalist haters of things medieval. While there were obvious differences between the two schools, the experts nowadays are inclined to minimize these contrasts. Many architects of the early 1800's mastered both styles; moreover, they did not so much copy ancient or medieval structures outright as adapt them to the needs and tastes of the day. Generally, the basic design was classical in its proportions, even if the external shell and decoration were medieval. The Houses of Parliament in London, rebuilt in the 1830's and '40's after a disastrous fire, seem very Gothic at a first glance, while a second shows that they embody classical principles of balance and symmetry. Romantic architecture anticipates the eclecticism, the wide range of inspiration and style, characteristic of the later nineteenth century (see Chapter XXIII).

As the nineteenth century began, the Roman vogue, so firmly set by the French Revolution, reached a peak in Napoleonic Paris with the *Arc de Triomphe* and with the Church of the Madeleine, patterned on an actual Roman temple (the *Maison Car-*

rée or "square house" at Nîmes). In America, the versatile Thomas Jefferson, who was a gifted designer, pronounced the *Maison Carrée* a perfect example of "cubical" architecture and adapted it to secular purposes for the Virginia capitol building at Richmond. At Charlottesville, about 1820, Jefferson provided the University of Virginia with a most distinguished group of academic buildings focused on a circular library, derived from the Roman Pantheon (the perfect example of "spherical" architecture). From the library, somewhat in the manner of a large Roman villa, he extended two rows of smaller structures, each recalling a different Roman temple, interconnected by colonnades. By the second quarter of the nineteenth century, neo-Roman was yielding place to the "Greek revival," stirred in part by the wave of Philhellenic enthusiasm then sweeping the western world (see below, p. 165). London's British Museum and Philadelphia's Girard College are two of many splendid reminders of the Greek revival.

Meantime, especially in Britain, the Gothic revival was gaining ground, stimulated by the wealth of medieval architectural lore in Scott's novels, by the revival of religion, and by buildings like Fonthill Abbey. This last, begun in 1797 at the

Neoclassical architecture. Girard College, Philadelphia, 1833-1847.

Gothic revival in architecture. The Houses of Parliament, London.

order of an eccentric millionaire, consisted mainly of immensely high and immensely long corridors. Though it cost £500,000, it was so shoddily built that the central tower collapsed twenty-five years later. Undeterred, British architects applied the Gothic manner to every kind of structure after 1820, public buildings like the Houses of Parliament, churches, elaborate villas, and modest cottages. Excessive "gloomth" often resulted, and the fad for "medieval" furniture, bristling with spikes, prompted one critic to warn that the occupant of a neo-Gothic room would be lucky to escape being "wounded by some of its minutiae." Though the Gothic revival prompted some monstrosities, it also fostered the preservation or restoration of medieval master-

pieces half ruined by neglect or by anti-clerical vandalism.

Religion and Philosophy

Neo-Gothic architecture was one sign of the Christian revival that formed part of the Romantic movement; another sign was the pope's re-establishment in 1814 of the Jesuit order, whose suppression had been one of the great victories of the Enlightenment. Most of the Romantics were horrified by the religious skepticism of the *philosophes;* an outspoken atheist like Shelley was an isolated exception to the general rule. In Germany, Catholicism gained many converts among Romantic writers, and in England Wordsworth and Coleridge vigorously defended the established Church. Coleridge declared:

... that the scheme of Christianity, as taught in the liturgy and homilies of our Church, though not discoverable by human reason, is yet in accordance with it; that link follows link by necessary consequence; that Religion passes out of the ken of Reason only where the eye of Reason has reached its own horizon; and that Faith is then but its continuation. . . .*

In philosophy, the outstanding Romantic was Hegel (1770-1831), a follower of Kant and a professor at the University of Berlin. Like his master, Hegel attacked the tendency of the Enlightenment to see in human nature and human history only what first met the eye. The history of mankind, properly understood, was the history of human efforts to attain the good, and this in turn was the unfolding of God's plan for the world. Good, he stated,

... is God. God governs the world; the actual working of his government—the carrying out of his plan—is the History of the World.†

For Hegel, history was a *dialectical* process, that is, a series of conflicts. The two elements in the conflict were the *thesis*, the established order of life, and the *antithesis*, the challenge to the old order. Out of the struggle of thesis and antithesis emerged the *synthesis*, no mere compromise between the two but a new and better way, another step in man's slow progression toward the best of all possible worlds. The synthesis, in turn, broke down; a new thesis and antithesis became locked in conflict; the dialectic produced another synthesis—and so on.

The death throes of the Roman Republic afforded Hegel an illustration of the dialectic at work. The thesis was represented by the decadent republic, the antithesis by

oriental despotism, and the synthesis by the Caesarism of the early Roman Empire. Hegel explained that "This important change must not be regarded as a thing of chance; it was *necessary*," a part of God's grand design. Julius Caesar himself Hegel called a "hero," one of the few "world-historical individuals" who "had an insight into the requirements of the time" and who knew "what was ripe for development." This concept of the hero as the agent of a cosmic process is another characteristic of the Romantic temper.

The dialectical philosophy of history was the most original and influential element in Hegel's thought, the antecedent of the dialectical materialism of Karl Marx (see Chapter XX). It is difficult for citizens of a twentieth-century democracy to appreciate that Hegel was once even more famous as a liberal idealist. His emphasis on duty, his choice of Alexander the Great, Caesar, and Napoleon as "world-historical" heroes, his assertion that the state "existed for its own sake"—all this suggests a direct link between Hegel and authoritarianism. In fairness, however, it should be pointed out that Hegel himself seems to have foreseen the final political synthesis not in a brutal police state but in a liberalized version of the Prussian monarchy.

The Romantic "Style"

Thus Hegel, too, believed in the perfectibility of man, though he also believed that the process would require far more time and struggle than a *philosophe* like Condorcet had ever imagined. Indeed the "style" of Romanticism by no means contrasted in every particular with that of the Enlightenment. Not only a modified doctrine of progress but also eighteenth-century cosmopolitanism lived on into the nineteenth. Homer, Cervantes, Shakespeare, and Scott won appreciative readers in many countries; the giants of the age, men like

---

* *Biographia Literaria*, Everyman ed., 334.
† *The Philosophy of History*, J. Sibree, trans. (New York, 1944), 36.

Beethoven and Goethe, were not merely Austrian or German but citizens of the world.

These similarities and continuities notwithstanding, Romanticism did have a decided style of its own—imaginative, emotional, and haunted by the past. To the Romantics history was no longer to be conceived in Gibbon's terms of an antique golden age followed by long centuries of benighted superstition; history was, rather, an organic process of growth and development in which the Middle Ages had made a major contribution with their magnificent Gothic buildings, religious enthusiasm, folk ballads, and heroic epics. To the Romantics the Newtonian world-machine was an entirely inadequate interpretation of the universe, too static, too drab and materialistic. In its place they put the neo-Gothic world of religious mystery, the Hegelian world of dialectic and heroes, the poetic and artistic world of feeling, color, and "impulses from the vernal wood." Perhaps the most conspicuous feature of the Romantic style was its insistence that society was more than a branch of physics and man more than a cog in a machine.

III: The Conservative Outlook and the Vienna Settlement

When we think of the Romantic political figure, the image of the rebel may well come to mind—Shelley preaching anarchism, Byron dying in the Greek War of Independence, revolutionaries protesting against the status quo. This stereotype, however, is misleading and incomplete. Romanticism by its stress on the individual did ultimately enrich the doctrines of liberalism, and by its emphasis on the national community it strengthened the force of nationalism. Yet the immediate political influence of Romanticism was more frequently counter-revolutionary. Shelley and Byron were exceptions; the rule was exemplified by Wordsworth and Coleridge who, in maturity, lost their youthful zeal for the French Revolution and adopted conservative political views.

Burke and Metternich

Edmund Burke (1729-1797) did much to shape the conservative outlook. As we have already noted (p. 146, above), Burke could not stomach the revolutionary assumptions of the simple goodness of man and the obvious evil of the Old Régime. Rather, he revered the social and political institutions so painstakingly built up over the centuries. Burke, however, did not believe these institutions were petrified; they had developed gradually in the past, they would develop gradually in the future. Political change was possible but difficult, Burke concluded. Reforms had to be introduced so that "the useful parts of the old establishment" might be preserved; they had to be managed slowly and "with circumspection and caution"—in a word, conservatively.

Burke approved of the American Revolution, for it was not so much a revolution as a reaffirmation of the glorious tradition of 1688. The same reasoning drove Burke to violent condemnation in his *Reflections on the Revolution in France* (1790). The men of 1789 destroyed everything, good, bad, and indifferent. Rage and frenzy, he observed, "pull down more in half an hour, than prudence, deliberation and foresight can build up in a hundred years;" * thereby the social contract itself is jeopardized. "Society is indeed a contract," Burke wrote, but he did not mean what Rousseau had meant:

The state ought not to be considered as nothing better than a partnership agreement in a trade of pepper and coffee, calico or tobacco, or some such other low concern, to be taken up for a little temporary interest, and to be dissolved by the fancy of the parties. It is to be looked on with other reverence, because it is not a partnership in things subservient only to the gross animal existence of a temporary and perishable nature. It is a partnership in all science; a partnership in all art; a partnership in every virtue, and in all perfection. As the ends of such a partnership cannot be obtained in many generations, it becomes a partnership not only between those who are living, but between those who are living, those who are dead, and those who are to be born.†

The force of tradition bore heavily upon the politics of post-Napoleonic Europe. For this was the Age of Metternich—Prince Clement Wenceslas Lothair Népomucène Metternich (1773-1859), Austrian foreign minister from 1809 to 1848, and the chief figure in European diplomacy during most of his long career. Handsome, dashing, an aristocrat through and through, Metternich retained some of the eighteenth century's belief in reform through enlightened despotism. But, he also believed, reform should proceed with Burkean conservatism, not at a revolutionary pace. His own family, living in the German Rhineland, had suffered directly from the French Revolution. Moreover, Metternich served a state that was particularly susceptible to injury by the liberal and nationalist energies released by the Revolution. Tradition was the cement that held together the differing parts of the Austrian Habsburg realm; it should be fortified, not overthrown.

---

* *Reflections*, Everyman ed., 164.
† *Ibid.*, 93.

The Congress of Vienna

In 1814 and 1815, Metternich was host to the Congress of Vienna, which approached its task of rebuilding Europe with truly conservative deliberateness. For the larger part of a year, the diplomats indulged to the full in balls and banquets, concerts and hunting parties. "Congress dances," remarked an observer, "but it does not march." Actually, the brilliant social life distracted the lesser fry while the important diplomats settled things in private conference.

Four men made most of the major decisions at Vienna—Metternich, Castlereagh, Talleyrand, and Tsar Alexander I. Viscount Castlereagh, the British foreign minister, shared the conservative outlook of Metternich. He was less concerned with punishing the French for their past sins than with preventing the appearance of new Robespierres and Bonapartes. Castlereagh announced that he went to Vienna "not to collect trophies, but to bring the world back to peaceful habits." Talleyrand, the foreign minister of Louis XVIII of France, scored at Vienna the greatest success of his long career. Originally a worldly bishop of the Old Régime, he had in succession rallied to the Revolution in 1789, supported the Civil Constitution of the Clergy (one of the very few bishops to do so), served as Napoleon's foreign minister, and intrigued against him during the years after Tilsit. Now he was serving the restored Bourbon king, and in his old age he would take an important part in the Revolution of 1830 (see below, p. 169). This supremely adaptable diplomat soon maneuvered himself into the inner circle at Vienna, and the representatives of the victorious powers accepted the emissary of defeated France as their equal. Talleyrand was particularly adept in exploiting his nuisance value—acting as the spokesman of lesser diplomats who resented being shoved aside, and making the most of the differences that divided the victors.

To these differences Alexander I contributed greatly. Metternich actually called the Tsar a Jacobin, although Alexander's reputation for enlightenment was only partially deserved (see Chapter XVII). By 1814 the Tsar had acquired a thoroughly Romantic enthusiasm for religion. For hours on end, he prayed and read the Bible in the company of Madame de Krüdener, and under her influence prepared a "Holy Alliance" whereby all states would regenerate their policies by following the teachings of Christ. In the first months at Vienna it was not Alexander's Romantic scheme of a Holy Alliance but rather his Polish policy that nearly disrupted the Congress. He proposed a partial restoration of pre-partition Poland, with himself as its monarch. Austria and Prussia would lose the Polish lands they had grabbed late in the preceding century. Alexander won the support of Prussia by backing her demands for the annexation of Saxony, whose king had remained loyal to Napoleon. Metternich, however, did not want Austria's traditional Prussian rival to make such a substantial gain. Moreover, both Metternich and Castlereagh disliked the prospect of a large, Russian-dominated Poland.

The dispute over Saxony and Poland gave Talleyrand a magnificent chance to fish in troubled waters. Thus it was that in January, 1815, the representative of defeated France joined Metternich and Castlereagh in threatening both Prussia and Russia with war unless they moderated their demands. The threat produced an immediate settlement. Alexander obtained Poland but agreed to reduce its size and allow Prussia and Austria to keep part of their loot from the partitions. Prussia took about half of Saxony; the King of Saxony retained the balance.

Once the Saxon-Polish question was out of the way, the Congress achieved a fairly amicable resolution of other important dynastic and territorial questions. Accord-ing to the doctrine that Talleyrand christened "the sacred principle of legitimacy," thrones and frontiers were to be re-established as they had existed in 1789. In practice, however, legitimacy was ignored almost as often as it was enforced. The diplomats at Vienna were statesmen enough to realize that they could not undo all the changes worked by the Revolution and Napoleon. Although they restored Bourbon dynasties to the thrones of France, Spain, and Naples in the name of legitimacy, they did not attempt to revive all the hundreds of German states that had vanished since 1789.

In Germany, the Congress provided for thirty-nine states, loosely grouped together in a confederation. The German Confederation came close to reincarnating the impotent Holy Roman Empire; its chief organ, the diet, was to be a council of diplomats from sovereign states rather than a representative national assembly. The most important members of the confederation were Prussia and Austria, for the German-speaking provinces of the Habsburgs were con-

Prince Talleyrand (1754-1838).

The statesmen of Europe at the Congress of Vienna, 1814-1815. Metternich is standing prominently at left front, Wellington at extreme left. Talleyrand is seated at right with his arm resting on the table.

sidered an integral part of Germany. Both states obtained important new territories at Vienna. Prussia, in addition to her Saxon annexation, expanded the old scattered Hohenzollern lands in western Germany into the imposing new Rhine Province. Austria lost Belgium, which was incorporated into the Kingdom of the Netherlands. But she recovered the old Habsburg territory of Lombardy in Italy, to which Venetia was now joined, and she also secured Napoleon's Illyrian Provinces along the eastern shore of the Adriatic.

In Italy, too, the Congress of Vienna confirmed the tradition of political disunity. It restored the Bourbon Kingdom of Naples in the south and the Papal States in the center. In the northwest it gave Genoa to the Kingdom of Piedmont-Sardinia. Austria was in a position to dominate Italy both by her possession of Lombardy-Venetia and by the close family ties between the Habsburgs and the ruling dynasties in the other Italian states. Elsewhere in Europe, the

Congress of Vienna restored and somewhat enlarged the independent Republic of Switzerland. It transferred Norway from the rule of Denmark to that of Sweden; Sweden, in turn, handed Finland over to Russia. Great Britain received Malta, controlling the "waist" of the Mediterranean, and, outside Europe, the former Dutch colonies of Ceylon and the Cape of Good Hope.

The Quarantine of France

France at first was given her boundaries of 1792, which included the minor territorial acquisitions made during the early days of the Revolution. Then came Napoleon's escape from Elba and the Hundred Days. The final settlement reached after Waterloo assigned France the frontiers of 1790, substantially those of the Old Régime. In addition, the French were to return Napoleon's art plunder to its rightful owners, pay the victorious allies an indemnity of 700,000,000 francs (roughly $140,000,000), and finance an allied army of occupation on their soil for not more than five years.

The Vienna diplomats did not so much punish France as take measures to quarantine any possible new French aggression. Castlereagh conceived the policy of strengthening France's neighbors so that they would be able to restrain the troublemaker in the future. Thus to the north the French faced the Belgians and the Dutch combined in the single Kingdom of the Netherlands. On the northeast they encountered the Rhine Province of Prussia, and on the east the expanded states of Switzerland and Piedmont. The Quadruple Alliance, signed in November, 1815, constituted the second great measure of quarantine. The four allies—Britain, Prussia, Austria, and Russia—agreed to use force, if necessary, to preserve the Vienna settlement. At Castlereagh's insistence, the allies further decided on periodic conferences to consider the measures "most salutary for the repose and prosperity of Nations, and the maintenance of the Peace of Europe." The Quadruple Alliance was to be both a watchdog against France and an experiment in government by international conference, a modest step along the road leading to the League of Nations and United Nations of the twentieth century.

Public opinion, especially in the English-speaking countries, unfortunately confused the Quadruple Alliance with Alexander's Holy Alliance scheme, which it identified with the blackest reaction. The Holy Alliance, signed in September, 1815, was actually a fairly harmless document dedicated to the proposition that "the policy of the powers . . . ought to be guided by the sublime truths taught by the eternal religion of God our Saviour." Although most of the major European rulers signed the Holy Alliance, only Tsar Alexander seems to have taken it seriously. Castlereagh called it "a piece of sublime mysticism and nonsense," and Britain declined to participate —the first sign of the rift that was to open between her and the continental powers. The Pope, refusing an invitation to join, remarked that the Vatican could very well dispense with interpretations of Christian doctrine by the laity.

Together with Westphalia (1648), Utrecht (1713), and Versailles (1919), the Vienna settlement of 1814-15 marked one of those rare attempts at the massive political reconstruction of Europe. Of the four, Vienna in many respects succeeded best. There was to be no major European war until the Crimean conflict of the 1850's, and none embroiling the whole of Europe until 1914. Most of the leading diplomats at Vienna could have said with Castlereagh that they acted "to bring the world back to peaceful habits." Seldom have victors treated the defeated aggressor more generously. Castlereagh, above all, deserved credit for his project of pacifying international disputes through conferences of the Quadruple Alliance. In operation, however, the Quadruple Alliance never fulfilled the noble aims of Castlereagh. Within five years of the Congress of Vienna, revolution broke out again in Europe, causing serious dissension within the Quadruple Alliance. And for these outbreaks the Congress of Vienna was itself partly responsible, because it attempted to stifle liberal and national aspirations.

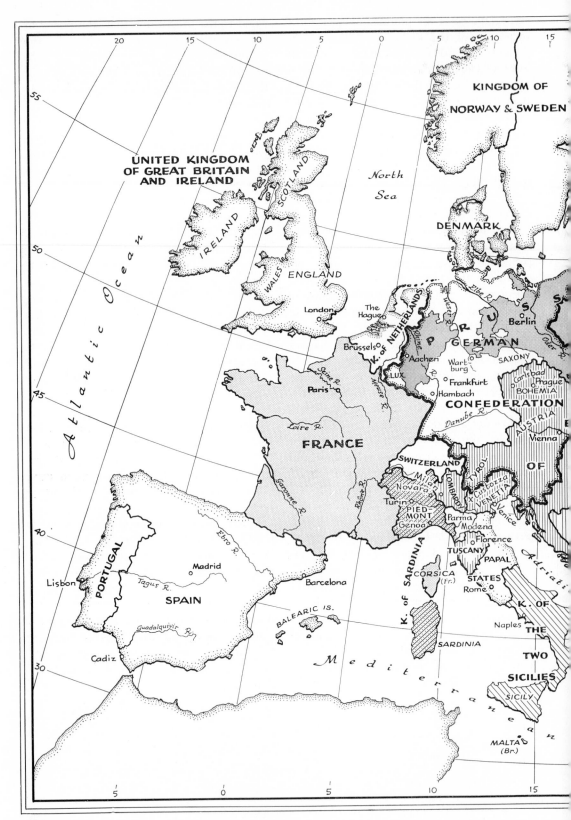

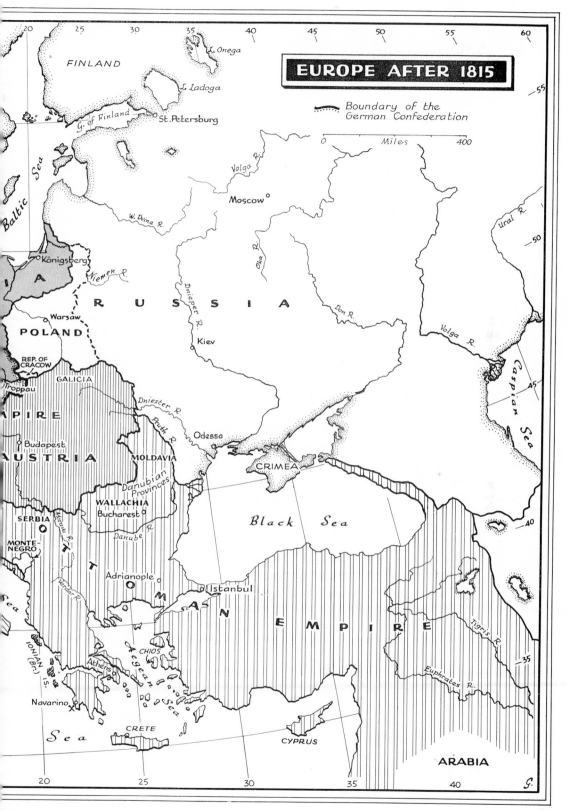

EUROPE AFTER 1815

Boundary of the
German Confederation

0   Miles   400

FINLAND

L. Onega

L. Ladoga

G. of Finland

St.Petersburg

Baltic Sea

Königsberg

Niemen R.

POLAND

Warsaw

REP. OF CRACOW

Troppau

GALICIA

Volga R.

Moscow

W. Dvina R.

R U S S I A

Dnieper R.

Oka R.

Don R.

Kiev

Volga R.

Ural R.

Caspian Sea

PIRE

Budapest

A U S T R I A

Dniester R.

Pruth R.

MOLDAVIA

Odessa

CRIMEA

Danubian Provinces

WALLACHIA

Bucharest

SERBIA

O

Morava R.

Danube R.

MONTE-NEGRO

T

Black   Sea

Vardar R.

Adrianople

T   O   M   A   N

Istanbul

E   M   P   I   R   E

Tigris R.

IONIAN (Br.) Is.

Athens

CHIOS

Aegean Sea

Euphrates R.

Navarino

Sea

CRETE

CYPRUS

ARABIA

G.

161

IV: The Revolutions of the 1820's

The Revolutionary Credo

The revolutionary leaders of the early nineteenth century despised the traditions so revered by conservatives. Opposing the counter-revolutionary alliance of Throne and Altar, they stood for Liberty, Equality, and Fraternity. In the revolutionary credo Liberty and Equality continued to mean the abolition of feudal and clerical privileges in society and, with few exceptions, laissez-faire in economics. They also meant the broadening of civil rights, the institution of representative assemblies, and the granting of constitutions—limited monarchies for most states, republics for the truly advanced, like France. For these aspects of the revolutionary program the best label is liberalism. Almost every leader of revolution proclaimed himself a liberal, although, as we shall soon see, the kind of liberalism actually practiced varied from the narrow to the sweeping.

The third word of the great revolutionary motto now came to have a more precise meaning. Fraternity, intensified by the Romantic cult of the nation, continued to evolve into the formidable doctrine of nationalism. The nationalists of the post-1815 generation dreamed of a world in which each nation would be free of domination by any other, and all nations would live together harmoniously. In terms of practical politics, this signified movements toward national unity and national independence. It meant growing pressure for the unification of Germany and Italy. And it inspired demands for freedom by peoples living under the control of a foreign power—by Belgians against their Dutch rulers, by Poles against Russians, by Greeks and Serbs against Turks, and by Italians, Hungarians, and Czechs against the Austrian Habsburg government in Vienna.

The Iberian States and Naples

The first revolutionary outbreaks after 1815 took place in Spain, Portugal, and the Kingdom of the Two Sicilies. In all three states the return to legitimacy restored the Old Régime at its least enlightened. The great majority of the population responded to the restoration calmly, even enthusiastically. The aristocracy were delighted to recover their ancient privileges; the poor and ignorant peasants welcomed the return of familiar traditions. But a small minority, drawn chiefly from the middle class, the intellectuals, and the army, dissented. In Spain and Italy, they greatly regretted the abrogation of the *Code Napoléon*, and of the anti-feudal and anticlerical legislation introduced by the French. In all three states the discontent of the liberal minority produced the revolutionary movement of 1820.

The trouble began in Spain. During the war against Napoleon, representatives from Cadiz and other commercial towns had framed the Constitution of 1812. This document, providing for universal suffrage and a severely limited monarchy, was very liberal—too liberal, in fact, to be workable in a country like Spain with deeply rooted feudal and clerical traditions. The Bourbon King Ferdinand VII, who resumed the Spanish crown in 1814, soon suspended the constitution, restored the social inequalities of the Old Régime, and re-established the twin instruments of Spanish clericalism, the Jesuits and the Inquisition. Finally, Ferdinand determined to recapture the rebellious Spanish colonies in the New World.

The colonial independence movement was caused directly by the refusal of the colonial populations either to recognize Napoleon's brother Joseph as their king or to accept the closer ties between colonies and mother country proposed by patriots in Spain. Behind the Spanish-American independence movement lay several other factors: the powerful examples of the American and French revolutions; the sympathetic interest of Great Britain, anxious to release lucrative markets from Spanish mercantilist restrictions; and the accumulated resentment of colonial peoples at the centuries of indifferent rule by Spanish governors. The colonial rebels won their initial success at Buenos Aires in 1810, and their movement spread rapidly to Spain's other American possessions. Ferdinand threatened to crush the rebels by force; to transport troops he augmented the small Spanish fleet with three leaky hulks purchased from Russia. At the end of 1819, this motley new armada, carrying 20,000 men, was about to sail from Cadiz. It never sailed, for on January 1, 1820, a mutiny broke out at Cadiz led by the liberal Colonel Riego. Uprisings soon followed in Madrid, in Barcelona, and in other Spanish cities. The revolutionaries sang "Riego's Hymn," with the refrain "Swallow it, you dog" (the "it" referred to the Constitution of 1812). Ferdinand surrendered.

The liberal minorities in Portugal and Naples followed the Spanish lead. An army faction seized control of the Portuguese government in 1820, abolished the Inquisition, and set up a constitution on the Spanish model of 1812. In Naples, the revolution was the work of the *Carbonari* (charcoal-burners), a secret society with a vaguely liberal program and a membership of more than 50,000. King Ferdinand I of the Two Sicilies, who was the uncle of the Spanish Ferdinand VII, gave in at the first sign of opposition in 1820 and accepted a constitution of the Spanish type.

The strength of the revolutionary move-ment of 1820 ebbed as quickly as it had risen. The reforms introduced precipitately by the inept liberal leaders in Spain and Naples alienated the bulk of the population at home and alarmed the conservative leaders of the great powers. Only in Portugal did the revolutionary régime survive for long, and there it inaugurated a long period of confusion and instability. The great Portuguese colony of Brazil profited by the confusion to declare itself independent of the mother country (1822).

The revolutions of 1820 tested both the stability of the Vienna settlement and the solidarity of the Quadruple Alliance of Britain, Prussia, Austria, and Russia. Legitimacy was again restored in Spain and Italy, but in the process the Quadruple Alliance was split in two. Britain increasingly moved toward a policy of non-intervention in the domestic affairs of other states; her three continental allies increasingly favored armed intervention to suppress revolution. The split became evident at the conference of the Quadruple Alliance meeting at Troppau in Silesia late in 1820. Castlereagh, the British foreign minister, knowing that the Neapolitan revolution threatened the Habsburg hegemony in Italy, was willing that Austria should intervene in Naples, but without the backing of the Alliance. The Alliance, Castlereagh declared, was never designed "for the superintendence of the internal affairs of other states." Metternich, on the other hand, was determined to secure a blanket commitment from the alliance. In spite of the protests of Britain, the Troppau Protocol (November, 1820) was signed by Austria, Prussia, and Russia. It declared that

States which have undergone a change of Government, due to revolution, the results of which threaten other states, *ipso facto* cease to be members of the European Alliance, and remain excluded from it until their situation gives guarantees for legal order and stability. If, owing to such alterations, immediate danger threatens other states, the Powers bind themselves, by peaceful means, or if need be by arms, to bring back the guilty state into the bosom of the Great Alliance.°

Under the terms of the Troppau Protocol, an Austrian army duly toppled the revolutionary government of Naples in 1821, and in 1823 a French army crossed the Pyrenees and restored the absolute authority of Ferdinand VII.

French intervention in Spain provoked the strong opposition of Great Britain and ended the Quadruple Alliance. Canning, who had succeeded Castlereagh as British Foreign Minister in 1822, suspected that the continental powers might now aid Spain to recover her former American colonies. So also did the United States, which had recognized the independence of the Latin-American republics. But America also feared both a possible Russian move southward from Alaska along the Pacific coast and an attempt by Britain to extend her sphere of control in the Caribbean. Therefore, when Canning proposed a joint Anglo-American statement to ward off any European interference in Latin America, the government of President Monroe refused the invitation.

In a message to the American Congress in December, 1823, President Monroe included the statement that is known to history as the Monroe Doctrine. Here are its key passages:

In the wars of the European powers, in matters relating to themselves, we have never taken any part, nor does it comport with our policy so to do. It is only when our rights are invaded, or seriously menaced, that we resent injuries or make preparation for our defence. With the movements in this hemisphere, we are, of necessity, more immediately connected, and by causes which must be obvious to all enlightened and impartial observers. The political system of the allied powers is essentially different, in this respect, from that of America. ... We owe it, therefore, to candor, and to the amicable relations existing between the United States and those powers, to declare, that we should consider any attempt on their part to extend their system to any portion of

° Quoted in W. A. Phillips, *The Confederation of Europe* (New York, 1920), 208-209.

this hemisphere, as dangerous to our peace and safety. With the existing colonies or dependencies of any European power, we have not interfered, and shall not interfere. But with the governments who have declared their independence, and maintained it, and whose independence we have, on great consideration, and on just principles, acknowledged, we could not view any interposition for the purpose of oppressing them, or controlling, in any other manner, their destiny, by an European power, in any other light than as the manifestation of an unfriendly disposition towards the United States.

This document marked an important assertion of policy on the part of the youthful American republic, but it had little immediate international significance. The European powers were not fully committed to the project of restoring Spain's American empire. And, so far as they were deterred from that venture, they were deterred less by the Monroe Doctrine than by the opposition of Canning and the potential opposition of the British fleet.

The Greek War of Independence

The British fleet was soon to take an important role in the Greeks' bid for national independence. The Greek revolt was part of the general movement of the Balkan nations for emancipation from their Turkish overlords. During the last quarter of the eighteenth century, the Christian peoples of the Balkan peninsula began to awaken to their national identities, to cherish their national past, and especially to put a high value on their native languages. The first outbreak against the Turkish authorities came in Serbia in 1804 and was led by a well-to-do pig-raiser named Karageorge. From the first, the Serb nationalists knew they would need outside help; some turned to Russia, others to Austria, thereby fixing a pattern of conflicting interests. Napoleon's venture in the Illyrian provinces (see above, p. 133) further stimulated the south

High-ranking officers at St. Petersburg secretly formed the Northern Society, which aimed to make Russia a limited, decentralized monarchy, with the various provinces enjoying rights somewhat like those of the states in the American republic. The serfs would receive their freedom but no land, and the whole series of reforms would be achieved by peaceful means. A second secret organization, the Southern Society, with headquarters at Kiev, included many relatively impoverished officers among its members; its leader was Colonel Pestel, a Jacobin in temperament and an admirer of Napoleon. On every main issue the program of the Southern Society went beyond that of the Petersburg group. It advocated a highly centralized republic, the granting of land to liberated serfs, and the use of violence—specifically, assassination of the Tsar—to gain its ends. Pestel himself planned to install a dictatorship, supported by secret police, as an interim government between the overthrow of the tsardom and the advent of the republic.

Both the Northern Society and the Southern Society tried to profit by the political confusion following the death of Alexander I. Since Alexander left no son, the crown would normally have passed to his younger brother, Constantine, his viceroy in Poland. Constantine, however, had relinquished his rights to a still younger brother, Nicholas, but in a document so secret that Nicholas never saw it. On the death of Alexander, Constantine declared that Nicholas was the legal tsar, and Nicholas declared that Constantine was. While the two brothers were clarifying their status, the Northern Society summoned the Petersburg garrison to revolt against Nicholas. Throughout the day of December 26, 1825, the rebels stood their ground in Russia's capital city until Nicholas subdued them. Two weeks later, the Southern Society launched a movement that was doomed from the start because its leader, Pestel, had already been arrested.

The Decembrist revolt, for all its ineffectiveness, was an important episode. It thoroughly alarmed Tsar Nicholas I (1825-1855), who now resolved to follow a severely autocratic policy (for details, see Chapter XXII). Although he dismissed the unpopular Arakcheev and put an end to the military colonies, he also had five of the Decembrists executed and exiled more than a hundred others to Siberia, where many of them contributed to the advance of local government and education. The Decembrists were the first in the long line of modern Russia's political martyrs, and the program of Pestel's Southern Society may now be seen as a kind of early blueprint for the revolutionary dictatorship that came to Russia with the Bolshevik uprising of 1917.

V: The Revolutions of 1830

France:
The July Revolution

The next wave of revolutions—that of 1830—arose in the traditional center of unrest, France. King Louis XVIII (1814-1824) had given the Bourbon restoration a promising start; aging, fat, gouty, and lethargic, but also moderate and sensible, Louis attempted a middle-of-the-road policy, exemplified by the Charter that he granted in 1814. Its preamble asserted the royal prerogative: "The authority in France resides in the person of the king." But the Charter then proceeded to establish a constitutional monarchy. The legislature was composed of a Chamber of Peers appointed by the king, and a Chamber of Deputies elected on a very restricted suffrage that allowed fewer than 100,000 of France's thirty millions the right to vote. "In the King alone is vested the executive power," the Charter stated, but in practice Louis followed the custom of limited monarchies by appointing ministers who were backed by a majority in the legislature. The Charter confirmed many of the decisive changes instituted in France since 1789. It guaranteed religious toleration, equality before the law, and equal eligibility to civil and military office; it likewise accepted the revolutionary property settlement and the *Code Napoléon*.

The Charter, however, greatly irritated the ultra-royalist faction, drawn from the noble and clerical *émigrés*, who had returned to France after their revolutionary exile. These "Ultras," grouped around the King's brother, the Count of Artois, were determined to recover both the privileges and the property they had lost during the Revolution. Louis XVIII held the Ultras at bay for five years. When the election of 1815 gave them control of the Chamber of Deputies, he dismissed the Chamber and held a new election, which returned a less fanatical majority. He chose moderate ministers who worked to pay off the indemnity to the victorious allies and, in general, to put French finances in good order. Events, however, soon strengthened the Ultras' hand. Anti-revolutionary fears swept France in the wake of the Spanish and Italian uprisings of 1820 and of the assassination of the Duke of Berri, the King's nephew (February, 1820). Louis XVIII was therefore obliged to appoint a reactionary ministry, which sent French troops to aid Ferdinand VII in Spain.

The tempo of the reaction quickened when Louis XVIII died and the Ultra leader, Artois, became King Charles X (1824-1830). Charles attempted to turn the clock back to the Old Régime. He allowed the Church greater influence by encouraging the activities of the Jesuits, who were still legally banned from France, and by appointing clerics as principals and administrators in the state school system. The *émigrés*, in compensation for their lost property, were granted state annuities; to help finance the annuities, the interest on government bonds was lowered. The indemnification of the *émigrés* could be defended as a sensible political move that lifted the last threat of confiscation from those who had acquired property during the Revolution. But the reduction of interest on government obligations infuriated many influential Parisian bourgeois and other bondholders.

Opposition to Charles X grew rapidly, nourished by two young historians who were to play an important part in French politics. Adolphe Thiers (1797-1877) published a popular and sympathetic *History of the French Revolution* and edited a liberal Paris newspaper. François Guizot (1787-1874) wrote a *History of Civilization*, an enthusiastic account of the rise of those wealthy bourgeois who detested the Ultras. Guizot also headed a nation-wide organization, *"Aide-toi, le ciel t'aidera!"* ("The Lord helps those who help themselves"), which urged Frenchmen to defend their legal rights against the encroachments of Charles X.

In 1829, Charles increased political tension by appointing as his chief minister the Prince of Polignac, an Ultra of Ultras, who claimed to have had visions in which the Virgin Mary promised him success. Polignac hoped to bolster the waning prestige of his monarch by scoring a resounding diplomatic victory. He therefore attacked the Dey of Algiers, a largely independent vassal of the Ottoman emperor, notorious for his collusion with the hated Barbary Pirates. The capture of Algiers (June, 1830) laid the foundation of the French empire in North Africa. Meanwhile, the liberal opposition in the Chamber of Deputies had pronounced Polignac's ministry unconstitutional because it had never received the approval of the legislature. In the hope of securing a more tractable chamber, Charles X held a new election in May, 1830, but the opposition won. On July 25, 1830, without securing the legislature's approval, Charles and Polignac issued ordinances muzzling the press, dissolving the newly elected Chamber, ordering a fresh election, and introducing new voting qualifications that would have disfranchised the bourgeois voters who were the mainstay of the opposition. The King and his chief minister believed that public opinion, mollified by the recent victory at Algiers, would accept these July Ordinances calmly. They miscalculated utterly.

Aroused by the protests of Thiers and other liberal journalists, and encouraged by the fine summer weather, the workers and students of Paris staged a riot. They threw up barricades and on July 28 captured the Paris City Hall. There they proclaimed their intention of making France a democratic republic with the Marquis de Lafayette, that aged symbol of revolution, as its president. The liberal leaders of the Chamber of Deputies, on the other hand, wanted a safe and sane constitutional monarchy. They wanted to make France's 1830 the counterpart of England's 1688. Headed by Thiers, Talleyrand, and the wealthy banker Laffitte, the liberals won handily. They had the money, they had the brains, and they had the perfect candidate for the throne—Louis Philippe, the Duke of Orléans.

Louis Philippe was a symbol of revolution at its most moderate. His father had participated in the Paris demonstrations of 1789 and had assumed the revolutionary name of *Philippe Egalité*, but, in spite of this, he had been guillotined during the Terror. Louis Philippe himself had fought in the revolutionary army at Valmy in 1792, then had emigrated in 1793 before the worst of the Terror. He had little use for the pomp of royalty; he dressed and acted like the sober and well-to-do businessman he was. At the close of July, 1830, the astute Louis Philippe persuaded the gullible Lafayette of his admiration for republicanism. Having won the support of the titular republican leader by this deception, the moderate deputies named Louis Philippe king in place of Charles X, who abdicated and fled to England. The July Monarchy, as the new régime was termed, retained most of the Charter of 1814, though it deleted references to royal absolutism and substituted the tricolor of the Revolution for the white flag of the Bourbons. The suffrage, though enlarged, was still highly restricted; slightly more than 200,000 Frenchmen had the right to vote. Thus the almost bloodless July Revolution left France a long way from democracy; the July Monarchy took a very narrow view of the great ideals of Liberty, Equality, and Fraternity.

Daumier, "The Legislative Belly" (1834). (Caricature of the rich and selfish French legislators under the July Monarchy.)

Belgium

Within a month of the July uprising in Paris, a nationalistic and liberal revolution began in Belgium. The union of Belgium and the Netherlands, decreed by the peacemakers of 1815, worked well only in economics. The commerce and colonies of Holland supplied raw materials and markets for the expanding manufactures of Belgium, at that time the most advanced industrial area of the Continent. In politics and religion, however, King William I of the Netherlands exerted arbitrary power where he might better have made tactful concessions. He made Dutch the official language throughout his realm and refused to grant special privileges to the Catholic Church in Belgium. He denied the pleas of Belgians for more equitable representation in the legislature, where the Dutch provinces had been given an unduly large number of seats. A common loyalty to the Catholic Church and a common concern for local rights and customs formed the foundation of Belgian nationalism. They brought together two different linguistic groups, the Flemish in the provinces north of Brussels and the French-speaking Walloons of the southern provinces.

The revolution broke out in Brussels on August 25, 1830, at a performance of a Romantic opera which depicted a revolt in Naples. Headed by students, inspired by the example of Paris—and perhaps incited by French agents—the audience rioted against Dutch rule. By the end of September, Dutch troops had been driven out of Brussels, and Dutch rule was collapsing. The insurgents recruited their fighters chiefly from the industrial workers, many of whom were victims of low pay and frequent unemployment. The Belgian workers, however, like the Parisian workers, lacked good leadership and a concrete political program. The better-organized middle-class liberals soon captured control of the revolutionary movement and predominated in the national Belgian congress that convened in November, 1830.

This congress proclaimed Belgium independent and made it a constitutional monarchy. The new constitution provided for much local self-government, put rigorous limits on the king's authority, and subordinated the executive to the legislature. Although it did not establish universal suffrage, the financial qualifications for voting were markedly lower in Belgium than they were in Britain or France, and the electorate was proportionately larger. The congress first chose as king the Duke of Nemours, a son of Louis Philippe. Britain protested violently, for this would have brought Belgium within the orbit of France. The congress then picked Leopold of Saxe-Coburg, a German princeling, and the widowed son-in-law of George IV of Britain. Leopold was admirably fitted for the exacting role of a constitutional monarch in a brand-new kingdom. He had already shown his political shrewdness by refusing the shaky new throne of Greece; he now demonstrated it by marrying a daughter of Louis Philippe, thus mitigating French disappointment over the aborted candidacy of the Duke of Nemours.

The Belgian revolution made the first permanent breach in the Vienna settlement. Although it aroused little enthusiasm among the great powers, representatives of Britain, France, Prussia, Austria, and Russia guaranteed both the independence and the neutrality of Belgium. King William, stubborn as the proverbial Dutchman, tried to retake Belgium by force in 1831-32. A French army and a British fleet successfully defended the Belgians, and negotiations finally resulted in Dutch recognition of Belgium's new status in 1839.

Poland

Revolution did not always succeed in 1830; the case of Poland contrasted tragically with that of Belgium. In 1815, the Kingdom of Poland possessed the most liberal constitution on the Continent; twenty years later, it had become a mere colony of the Russian Empire. The constitution given to the Poles by Tsar Alexander I preserved the *Code Napoléon* and endowed the diet with limited legislative power. A hundred thousand Poles received the franchise, more than the total number of voters in the France of Louis XVIII, which had a population ten times greater. In practice, however, difficulties arose. Many of the men chosen for official posts in Poland were not acceptable to the Poles; indeed, one may doubt that any government imposed by Russia would have satisfied them. Censorship, unrest, and police intervention developed during the last years of Alexander I.

The advent of the highly conservative Nicholas I in 1825 increased political friction, although the new tsar at first abided by the Polish constitution. Meantime, Romantic doctrines of nationalism made many converts at the Universities of Warsaw and Vilna (in Lithuania). Polish nationalists demanded the transfer from Russia to Poland of provinces that had belonged to the pre-partition Polish state—Lithuania, White Russia, and the Ukraine. Secret societies on the Carbonari model arose in these provinces and in the Kingdom of Poland.

The secret society of army cadets in Warsaw launched a revolution in November, 1830. The rebels were doomed from the start. They split into the two hostile camps of "Whites" and "Reds," the former representing the highly conservative aristocrats, the latter the somewhat less conservative gentry. Neither "Whites" nor "Reds" gained the support of the peasants, whom both factions had long oppressed. The misery of the Poles increased with a terrible epidemic of cholera, the first outbreak of that Asiatic scourge in Europe. Russian forces, at first taken off guard, were masters

of the situation by 1833. Nicholas I then scrapped the constitution, imposed a regime of permanent martial law, and closed the Universities of Warsaw and Vilna, the chief centers of Polish nationalist propaganda. To escape the vengeance of Nicholas, Polish intellectuals fled the country by the tens of thousands.

Italy and Germany

The liberals and nationalists of Italy and Germany likewise suffered defeat in the early 1830's. In 1831, Italian insurgents briefly controlled the little duchies of Parma and Modena and a sizable part of the Papal States. They counted on French assistance, but the July Monarchy had no intention of risking war with Austria by poaching on the Habsburg preserve. Again, as in 1821, Metternich sent troops to restore legitimacy in Italy.

Metternich did not require soldiers to preserve legitimacy in Germany; whenever a crisis arose, the Diet of the German Confederation obediently followed the Austrian lead. The poet Heine claimed to hear Germany snoring:

She slept peacefully under the protection of her thirty-six monarchs. In those days, crowns sat firmly on the princes' heads, and at night they just drew their night caps over them, while the people slept peacefully at their feet.*

In Prussia, King Frederick William III (1797-1840) had promised to grant a constitution but never made good his pledge. Mildly liberal constitutions, on the order of the French Charter of 1814, appeared only in Weimar and a few south German states. Political agitation came almost entirely from the small minority of intellectuals—journalists, Romantic writers, university professors, and students. After 1815, German university students formed a new organization, the *Burschenschaft* ("Students'

---

* Quoted by F. B. Artz, *Reaction and Revolution* (New York, 1934), 137.

Union"). In October, 1817, during a rally celebrating the tercentenary of Luther's Ninety-Five Theses, the *Burschenschaft* burned a wig, a Prussian officer's corset, and other symbols of reaction. In March, 1819, a demented theological student, perhaps influenced by *Burschenschaft* extremists, assassinated Kotzebue, a reactionary writer and a Russian agent. Metternich, already alarmed by the student prank of 1817, now got the Diet of the German Confederation to approve the Carlsbad Decrees (September, 1819), which stiffened press censorship, dissolved the *Burschenschaft,* and curtailed academic freedom.

Despite the Carlsbad Decrees, political ferment continued in Germany. In 1830 and the years following, a few rulers in northern Germany, notably in Saxony and Hanover, were forced to grant their subjects a constitution. Excited by these minor successes, twenty-five thousand revolutionary sympathizers gathered in May, 1832, to toast Lafayette and demand the union of the German states under a republic. Effective action for unification, however, was another matter. In 1833, the revolutionaries made a forlorn effort to seize Frankfurt, the seat of the Diet and capital of the German Confederation, and then relapsed into inactivity.

The Lessons of 1830

The European revolutionary movement of 1830 emphasized two great facts of political life. First, it widened the split between the West and the East. Britain and France were committed to support mild liberalism both at home and in neighboring Belgium. On the other hand, Russia, Austria, and Prussia were more firmly committed than ever to the counter-revolutionary principles of intervention set forth in the Troppau Protocol. In 1833, Tsar Nicholas I, Metternich, and King Frederick William III of Prussia formally pledged their joint assistance to any sovereign threatened by revolution.

Second, revolution succeeded in 1830 only in France and Belgium, only where it enlisted the support of a large segment of the population. It failed in every country where the revolutionaries represented only a fraction of the people. In Poland, the peasantry viewed both "Whites" and "Reds" as oppressors. Italian revolutionaries still relied on their Romantic Carbonari tradition and on flimsy hopes of foreign aid. In Germany, revolution was a matter of student outbursts, toasts to Lafayette, and other gestures by a small minority. Liberal and nationalist intellectuals needed to make their doctrines penetrate to the grass roots of society; they needed to develop able political leaders and to mature well-laid plans for political reform. These were the tasks they undertook after 1830; their success was to be tested in the most formidable and widespread political uprising in nineteenth-century Europe—the Revolutions of 1848.

VI: The Revolutions of 1848

Common Denominators

One of the common denominators of revolution in 1848 was nationalism, which prompted German and Italian attempts to gain political unification and also inspired the subject peoples of the Habsburg Empire to seek political and cultural autonomy. The Romantic movement had stimulated a nationalistic renaissance among most peoples in central and eastern Europe. For the national minorities within the Habsburg Empire, as for the Christian nationalities within the Ottoman Empire, the new nationalism tended to be focused on language. The Czech language, for example, was on the verge of extinction in the later eighteenth century; the population of Bohemia increasingly used the German of their Austrian rulers. By 1848, however, a Czech linguistic and literary revival was in full swing. Patriotic histories of Bohemia and collections of Czech folk-poetry kindled a lively interest in the national past and fostered dreams of a Pan-Slavic awakening in which the Czechs would lead their brother Slavs. Some nationalists in 1848 preached with Mazzini, the democratic Italian patriot, that each nation's "special mission" fulfilled the "general mission of humanity." Others, however, adopted more narrow views; John Stuart Mill, the English liberal (see Chapter XX), deplored the nationalists who ignored the welfare "of any portion of the human species, save that which is called by the same name and speaks the same language as themselves." *

---

* J. S. Mill, "The French Revolution and Its Assailants," *Westminster Review*, II (1849), 17.

CENTERS OF REVOLUTION, 1848-1849

There were many self-styled Chosen People in the revolutions of 1848.

Liberalism, the second common denominator of the revolutions, also encompassed a wide range of programs. In central and eastern Europe, where the Old Régime largely survived, liberals demanded constitutions to limit absolute monarchy and to liquidate feudal rights and manorial dues. In France, where constitutional monarchy had already been achieved, many liberals sought to replace the July Monarchy with a democratic republic. French liberalism, in fact, shaded into socialism; the Paris radicals of 1848 demanded the guarantee of the right to work and other advanced measures.

Finally, in the Europe of 1848, as in the France of 1789, an economic crisis helped to catalyze discontent into revolution. A blight ruined the Irish potato crop in 1845 and soon spread to the Continent. The grain harvest of 1846 failed in western Europe, resulting in a sharp rise in the price of bread and in bread riots and actual starvation. This agrarian crisis was accompanied by a severe industrial depression; the railroad-building boom of the early 1840's had collapsed by 1847 and produced a crop of business failures. The increase in the number of the unemployed coincided with the rise in food prices, thereby intensifying social misery.

France

The economic crisis hit France with particular severity. Railroad construction almost ceased, throwing more than half a million laborers out of work; coal mines and iron foundries, in turn, laid men off. Unemployment increased the discontent of French workers already embittered by their low wages and by the still lower esteem in which they were held by the government of Louis Philippe. The July Monarchy encouraged the rapid expansion of industry and trade but largely ignored the social misery that accompanied the new prosperity. In eighteen years, it took only two steps for the welfare of the industrial working class: an extension of the primary school system in 1833, and a laxly enforced law in 1841 limiting child labor. There was a great deal of truth in the famous judgment passed by de Tocqueville, an acute political observer—that "Government in those days resembled an industrial company whose every operation is undertaken for the profits which the stockholders may gain thereby."

The 200,000 landowners, investors, and businessmen who had the right to vote formed the "stockholders" of the July Monarchy. Those who demanded liberalization of the suffrage were answered by Guizot, a leader of the regime: "*Enrichissez-vous!*"—make yourself rich enough to meet the stiff property qualifications for voting. The government banned labor organizations and punished the workmen rioting in the early 1830's to demand a republic and higher wages. It imposed a censorship when the press caricatured the pear-shaped head and the inevitable umbrella of Louis Philippe.

Opposition to the July Monarchy, though stifled in the 1830's, revived rapidly during

Daumier, "It's Safe to Release This One" (1834). A bitter commentary on the repressive policies of the July Monarchy: the prisoner to be released is dead.

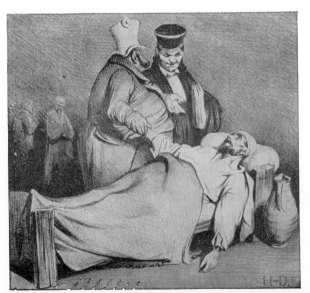

the 1840's. It was not a united opposition—a fact that goes far to explain the hectic course of the revolution it set off. Heading one group was Adolphe Thiers, a principal architect of the July Monarchy, who was shelved by Louis Philippe in favor of Guizot, the chief minister from 1840 until 1848. Thiers continued to support the principle of constitutional monarchy; the chief difference between him and Guizot was the fact that he was out of office while Guizot was in. The disappointed republicans of 1830 formed a second opposition group. The third, and smallest, group took in various socialists, who were to gain recruits from the economic depression of the late 1840's. Potentially more formidable than any of these, but as yet representing only a vague, unorganized sentiment, were the Bonapartists. The return of the Emperor's ashes from St. Helena to Paris in 1840 revived and renewed the legend of a glorious and warlike Napoleon, so different from the inglorious, peace-loving Louis Philippe.

In the summer of 1847, constitutional monarchists of the Thiers faction joined with republicans to stage a series of political banquets throughout France calling for reform and for the resignation of Guizot. This campaign appeared comparatively harmless until a particularly large banquet was announced for February 22, 1848, to be held in a radical quarter of Paris. When the Guizot ministry forbade the banquet, the Parisians substituted a large demonstration. On February 23, Louis Philippe dismissed Guizot and prepared to summon Thiers to the ministry. But his concessions came too late. Supported by workers, students, and the more radical republican leaders, the demonstration of February 22 turned into a riot on the 23rd. More than fifty of the rioters who attacked the residence of Guizot were killed or wounded. It has never been established who fired the first shots, but the casualties of February 23rd at once intensified the revolutionary atmosphere. On the next day, Louis Philippe abdicated.

As in July, 1830, so in February, 1848, working-class radicals and bourgeois moderates competed to fill the political vacuum created by the King's abdication. The radicals demanded a republic that would institute the social and economic changes summed up in the formula, the right to work. Thoroughly revolutionary in spirit, these radicals still lacked the organization to prosecute revolution successfully; their leaders were only slightly less gullible than Lafayette had been in 1830. The middle-class moderates were ready to grant universal suffrage but were determined to protect the rights of property and to keep social and economic concessions to a minimum.

The moderates secured the direction of the provisional government formed on February 24. As a sop to the aroused Parisians, they promised to guarantee the right to work and authorized the establishment in Paris of National Workshops, apparently inspired by the socialist, Louis Blanc (1811-1882). Louis Blanc had long advocated "social workshops," which the workers themselves would own and run with the financial assistance of the state. The National Workshops of 1848, however, were simply a relief project organized along semi-military lines, and enrolling more than 100,000 unemployed from Paris and the provinces. About 10,000 of the recruits received two francs (about 40 cents) a day for working on municipal improvements; the rest received a dole of one franc a day.

The moderates commanding the provisional government gained new strength as a result of the election of April, 1848—the first election in European history in which almost the entire adult male population of a country voted. Eight million Frenchmen elected members of the National Assembly that was to draw up a new constitution. The conservative peasants, who still made up the bulk of the population, approved the fall of the July Monarchy but dreaded anything resembling an attack on private property. Of the almost 900 deputies elected, therefore, only a hundred or so sympathized with the Paris radicals.

The latter, however, refused to accept the decision of the country. On May 15, a noisy mob invaded the meeting hall of the National Assembly and proposed the dissolution of the Assembly and the formation of a new provisional government at the Paris City Hall. The moderates, now thoroughly alarmed, decided that the National Workshops threatened law and order because they concentrated so many economically desperate men in Paris. The Assembly therefore dissolved the Workshops and gave the recruits the alternative of enlistment in the army or accepting work in the provinces. The workers of Paris resisted. From June 23 to June 26, 1848, the working-class districts of the capital rose in insurrection until they were finally subdued by the troops brought in by General Cavaignac, the energetic Minister of War.

These "June Days" were a landmark in modern history, the first large-scale outbreak of genuine class warfare, with both sides demonstrating a very strong class feeling. The specter of social revolution, for the moment a grim reality, terrified the propertied classes throughout France and throughout Europe. The spirit of panic accounted for the severe repression of the insurgents: nearly 1,500 were killed during the fighting; others were subsequently deported, chiefly to Algeria. All socialist clubs and newspapers were padlocked, and Louis Blanc fled to England. France became a virtual military dictatorship under General Cavaignac.

The fears of the moderates were evident in the formal constitution of the Second French Republic which the National Assembly completed in November, 1848. The Assembly declared property inviolable and rejected a motion to list the right to work among the fundamental rights of French citizens. In other respects, however, the constitution was a daring venture in representative democracy. It assigned legislative power to a single chamber, to be elected by universal male suffrage every three years. It gave executive authority to a President, to be chosen by popular election every four years. The French Constitution of November, 1848, thus inaugurated a régime based partly on Montesquieu's doctrine of the separation of powers and on the American type of presidential government. Circumstances, however, did not favor the success of this democratic experiment. The military rule exercised by Cavaignac while the Assembly was drafting the constitution was one ominous sign. Another was the outcome of the presidential election in December, 1848. Fewer than half a million votes were polled by the three genuinely republican candidates; a million and a half were cast for General Cavaignac; some five and a half million votes and the Presidency of the Republic went to Louis Napoleon Bonaparte, the nephew of the great Napoleon. President Bonaparte was to subvert the constitution in 1851 and then to proclaim himself Emperor Napoleon III (see Chapter XXI). The French Revolution of 1848, like that of 1789, had established a republic that ended in a Napoleonic empire.

Italy

In 1849, President Bonaparte sent French troops to Rome to defend the Pope against Italian radicals. By then the Italian revolutions were petering out. The Italian movement was ambitious, but weak and divided; it attempted to cast off the Austrian hegemony with only the slender military resources of the separate Italian states. Piedmont rejected the offer of assistance from revolutionary France in 1848 with the proud but unrealistic statement, *Italia farà da se*—Italy will do it alone.

Throughout the 1840's three schools of liberalism, none of them commanding really wide popular support, competed for leadership. The two moderate schools, while agreeing that political power in emancipated Italy should be limited to the nobility and the bourgeoisie, disagreed on the form that a united Italian nation should assume. One group of moderates, centered in the north, favored the domination of Piedmont. The other group called themselves "Neo-Guelfs" because, like the Guelf political faction of the Middle Ages, they expected the Pope to free Italy from the control of a German emperor. The Neo-Guelf leader, the priest Gioberti, declared that the future depended on "the union of Rome and Turin" (the Piedmontese capital). The Pope would head, and the army of Piedmont would defend, a federation of Italian states, each with its cautiously liberal constitution.

The third group of liberals, "Young Italy," asserted that Italy should be unified as a democratic republic. The founder of "Young Italy" was Mazzini (1805-1872), the great democratic idealist of modern Italian history. Here is a statement of Mazzini's political credo:

We believe, therefore, in the Holy Alliance of the Peoples as being the vastest formula of association possible in our epoch;—in the *liberty* and *equality* of the peoples, without which no true association can exist;—in *nationality*, which is the *conscience* of the peoples, and which, by assigning to them their part in the work of association, . . . constitutes their mission upon earth, that is to say, their *individuality*, without which neither liberty nor equality are possible;—in the sacred *Fatherland*, cradle of nationality; altar and workshop of the individuals of which each nation is composed.*

A good European as well as an ardent Italian nationalist, Mazzini inspired the formation of Young Germany, Young Poland, and similar movements, all joined together in a federation called "Young Europe."

Revolution struck first (January, 1848)

---

* "Faith and the Future," in *Life and Writings of Joseph Mazzini* (London, 1905), III, 129.

in Naples, where the king was obliged to grant a moderate constitution on the lines of the French Charter of 1814. During the next two months, King Charles Albert of Piedmont, the Grand Duke of Tuscany, and Pope Pius IX (1846-1878)—whose mild reforms had already aroused great liberal expectations—all followed suit. The news of the revolution in Vienna (see below, p. 182) provoked a successful insurrection

Joseph Mazzini (1805-1872).

in Milan, the capital of Austrian Lombardy (March 18-22). At the same time, Venice, the capital of Austria's other Italian province, proclaimed herself the independent Republic of St. Mark. The rapid collapse of Habsburg rule in Lombardy-Venetia touched off a national crusade against the Austrians. Charles Albert of Piedmont assumed command; Naples, Tuscany, and the Pope sent soldiers. For the moment, it seemed likely that both nationalism and liberalism would win in Italy.

But only for the moment. During the spring and early summer of 1848, Piedmont annexed Lombardy-Venetia and the two small North Italian duchies of Parma and Modena. The other Italian states, jealous of their particularist traditions, commenced to fear the imperialism of Piedmont more than they desired the unification of Italy. On April 29, 1848, Pope Pius IX announced that his "equal affection" for all peoples obliged him to adopt a neutral position in the war with Austria and to recall his soldiers. The Pope could not be both an Italian patriot and an international spiritual leader. Moreover, Pius was alarmed by the increasingly radical political temper of the Roman population and by the threats of German bishops to create an anti-pope. The Neo-Guelf cause had received a fatal blow. In May, 1848, the King of Naples withdrew his contingents from the war, and the Austrians, taking the offensive, crushed the forces of Charles Albert at Custozza (July, 1848). Italy had not been able to do it alone.

A few months later, the revolutionary movement got a brief second wind. Roman radicals, dissatisfied with the mildly liberal constitution of March, rose up in November, 1848. After Pius IX had fled to Neapolitan territory, they transformed the Papal States into a democratic Roman Republic, headed by Mazzini. In March, 1849, radicals in Piedmont forced the reluctant Charles Albert to renew the war with Austria, but at the battle of Novara (March 22) Austria again overwhelmed Piedmont. In August, 1849, the Austrians put an end to the Republic of St. Mark after a prolonged siege and bombardment of Venice. Meanwhile, besieged by French troops, Mazzini's Roman Republic had surrendered (July, 1849).

Again subdivided into many sovereign states, again dominated by the Habsburgs, Italy returned almost completely to its prerevolutionary status. The only bright spot in the picture was the emergence of Piedmont as the natural leader of Italian nationalism and liberalism. Despite the defeats at Custozza and Novara, despite the loss of the territories momentarily annexed in 1848, Piedmont enjoyed the prestige of having twice defied the hated Austrians.

Germany

The course of the German revolutions in 1848 roughly paralleled that of the Italian. In Germany, too, liberalism and nationalism won initial victories and then collapsed in the face of internal dissension and Austrian resistance. The failure in Germany was the more surprising—and ominous—since the revolutionary movement had begun to recruit support among industrial workers and among peasants who wished to abolish the relics of manorialism. Liberal and nationalist agitation, however, centered in the well-to-do bourgeoisie and in the professional classes, especially university professors, who enjoyed more influence and respect in Germany than anywhere else in Europe. Except for a few republicans and socialists, the German liberals were moderates. They wanted constitutional monarchies in the various German states, the strengthening of the German Confederation, and an end to the repressive hegemony of Metternich.

The hero of German liberals was King Frederick William IV of Prussia (1840-1861). Attractive and cultivated, but unstable and infatuated with divine-right concepts of kingship, Frederick William promised much and delivered little. He promised to carry out his father's unhonored pledge to give Prussia a constitution and a representative assembly. But the diet that he convoked at last in 1847 was neither popularly elected nor allowed the initiative in legislation.

Not this royal knight-errant, but rather the *Zollverein* (customs union) constituted Prussia's most solid contribution to German unification before 1848. In 1818, Prussia had abolished internal tariffs within its scattered territories and applied a uniform tariff schedule to imports. The innovation so stimulated commerce that by 1844 almost all the German states, except for Austria, had joined the customs union. The *Zollverein* liberated Germany from an oppressive burden of local tolls and taxes and cleared the way for her phenomenal economic development later in the century. Although it did not exercise a decisive influence on politics, it suggested that the state which had achieved German economic unification might naturally take the initiative in politics.

Unification seemed almost a certainty in 1848. Stimulated by the example of Paris, the revolutionaries scored their first successes in the western German states at the end of February, 1848. From there, the demands for constitutions, civil liberties, and a strengthened German Confederation fanned out rapidly. By mid-March, demonstrators were throwing up barricades in Berlin. Frederick William IV accepted some of the liberals' demands and appealed for calm among "ye inhabitants of my true and beautiful Berlin." His appeal came too late. Before it could be publicized, rioting broke out with redoubled violence, and more than two hundred rioters, chiefly workingmen, were killed. The mob broke into the royal palace and forced the King to go through a grotesque ceremony of saluting the corpses of the victims. Overwrought by the humiliation to himself and by the death of his subjects, Frederick William accepted all the demands of liberals and nationalists. He summoned an assembly to draw up a constitution, declared Prussia "merged in Germany," and proclaimed himself "King of the free regenerated German nation."

Drastic reform of the German Confederation now began. In May, 1848, a constitutional convention held its first session in the Church of St. Paul at Frankfurt, the capital of the Confederation. Its members,

Barricades in Berlin during the revolution of March, 1848.

popularly elected throughout Germany, represented the flower of the German intelligentsia: 18 doctors, 33 clergymen, 49 university professors, 57 schoolteachers, 223 lawyers and judges—but only one dirt farmer, and not a single laboring man. The Frankfurt Assembly lacked a broad political base, and, as events soon demonstrated, many of its members also lacked political experience and talent for practical statesmanship.

The Frankfurt Assembly had to decide the geographical limits of Germany. The Confederation included Austria proper but excluded most of the non-German Habsburg territories. Neither did it include the eastern provinces of Prussia, notably those acquired in the partitions of Poland. The Austrian issue divided the Assembly into "Big Germans," who favored the inclusion of Austria and Bohemia in the projected German state, and "Little Germans," who opposed it. The Habsburgs rejected a "Big Germany" because it would have split their domains, and so the Assembly adopted the "Little Germany" proposal.

On the question of Prussian Poland, the nationalism of the Frankfurt Assembly overcame its liberalism. By a large majority it voted to include some Prussian areas in which the Poles formed the majority of the population. The arguments advanced against the Poles in the debates revealed German nationalism at its most superheated. One orator declared that the minority of Germans had a natural right to rule the Poles, who had "less cultural content":

It is high time for us . . . to wake to a wholesome national egotism, to say the word right out for once, which in every question places the welfare and honour of the fatherland uppermost. . . . Our right is none other than the right of the stronger, the right of conquest.[*]

In contrast, the national constitution promulgated by the Frankfurt Assembly in March, 1849, was a decidedly liberal document, a combination of principles drawn from the American federal system and British parliamentary practice. The individual states were to surrender many of their

[*] Quoted in J. G. Legge, *Rhyme and Revolution in Germany* (London, 1918), 397.

powers to the German federal government. The federal legislature would consist of a lower house, elected by universal male suffrage, and an upper house, chosen by the governments and the legislatures of the constituent states. Ministers responsible to the legislature would form the federal executive. Over all would preside a constitutional monarch, the German emperor.

The Frankfurt constitution died a-borning. The Assembly elected the King of Prussia to be emperor, but Frederick William, ignoring his fine promises of March, 1848, and alarmed by Austrian opposition, rejected the offer. He called the Frankfurt constitution a "bastard" product:

> The crown is no crown. The crown which a Hohenzollern could accept . . . is not one created by an Assembly born of revolutionary seed. . . . It must be a crown set with the seal of the Almighty. . . .*

Since the major candidate for the imperial office had balked, the Frankfurt Assembly soon came to an end. It had never secured recognition from foreign governments, had never raised a penny in taxes, and had never exerted real sovereignty over Germany. But it had demonstrated that national unity would not be achieved through moral suasion.

German liberalism, too, suffered a major defeat. After the initial shock of the revolutions, the comfortably situated professional and bourgeois classes began to fear the radicalism of the workers and the lower middle class. The German princes soon either revoked or abridged the constitutions that they had granted in 1848. In Prussia, Frederick William and his conservative advisers repeatedly doctored the work of the constitutional convention summoned in 1848. The end product, the Constitution of 1850, made Prussia relatively safe for autocracy and aristocracy down to World War I (see Chapter XXII).

---
* *Ibid.*, 516-517.

The Habsburg Domains

The fate of German and Italian nationalism in 1848 rested partly with the outcome of the revolutions in the Habsburg Empire. If these revolutions had immobilized the Habsburg government for a long period, then Italian and German unification might have been realized. But Austria, though buffeted by wave after wave of revolution, rode out the storm. The success of the counter-revolution in the Habsburg Empire assured its victory in Italy and Germany.

The nature and the outcome of the Habsburg revolutions depended in turn on the complex structure of nationalities within the Austrian Empire:

NATIONALITIES UNDER HABSBURG
RULE, 1848

Nationality	Percentage of Total Population
German	23
Magyar (Hungarian)	14
Czech and Slovak	19
South (Yugo-) Slav	
Slovene	4
Croat	4
Serb	5
Pole	7
Ruthenian (Little Russian)	8
Rumanian	8
Italian	8

These national groups were not always neatly segregated geographically, each in its own compartment. For instance, in the Hungarian part of the Empire the Magyars dominated but fell slightly short of a numerical majority. Hungary contained important minorities of Slovaks, Rumanians, Croats, Serbs, and Germans. Moreover, while the bulk of the Habsburg population was rural, the German element, chiefly bureaucrats and tradesmen, predominated in most of the towns and cities throughout the Empire, even in the Czech capital of Prague and the Magyar capital of Budapest.

Nationalism developed particular force

Prince Metternich (1773-1859).

not only among Italians and Czechs but also among Magyars and Croats. Magyar nationalism won its first victory in 1844, when it secured the substitution of Hungarian for Latin as the official language of the Hungarian section of the Empire. In this overwhelmingly agricultural land, nationalism, like all other aspects of political life, was dominated by nobles and country squires who monopolized the seats in the county assemblies and the central diet. One group of Magyar nationalists aimed at the gradual modernization of Hungary's culture and economy along moderate English lines. The more extreme nationalists, however, whose spokesman was the spellbinding orator, Louis Kossuth (1802-1894), regarded the linguistic reform of 1844 as

but the first in a series of revolutionary projects cutting all ties with the Vienna government. Magyar nationalists bitterly opposed the satisfaction of the growing national aspirations of their Slavic subjects, like the Croats whose national awakening had begun when their homeland became the Illyrian province of Napoleon's empire.

The antagonism between Croats and Magyars revealed an all-important fact about the nationalistic movements within the Habsburg Empire. Some groups—Italians, Magyars, Czechs, Poles—resented the German-dominated government in Vienna. Others, notably the Croats and Rumanians, were not so much anti-German as anti-Magyar. Here was a situation where the central government might apply the policy of "divide and conquer," pitting the anti-Magyar elements against the anti-German Magyars, and conquering both. This was substantially what happened in 1848. A similar policy had already been used in 1846 to suppress a revolt in Galicia, the province that Austria acquired in the partitions of Poland. When the Polish landlords revolted, their exploited Ruthenian peasants rose against them and got the backing of Vienna.

Liberalism also played a significant part in the Habsburg revolutions, especially in Austria proper. The expanding middle class desired civil liberties, a voice in government, and the lifting of mercantilist restrictions on business. In Vienna, as in Paris and Berlin, the workers went further and demanded radical democratic reforms. From 1815 to 1848, the Habsburg government virtually ignored the grumblings and protests that arose in almost every quarter of the Empire. If Prince Metternich had had his way, he would probably have made some concessions to liberal and nationalist aspirations. But Metternich, though he enjoyed a nearly free hand in foreign affairs, did not have his way in domestic policy. He was blocked by the emperors—the bureaucratic Francis I (1792-1835) and the feeble-minded, epileptic Ferdinand I (1835-1848)—and by the vested interests of the aristocracy. The Habsburg government, though buttressed by an army of censors and spies, was at best an inefficient autocracy; Austria, Metternich accurately stated, was "administered, but not ruled."

The news of the February revolution in Paris shook the Empire to its foundations. Four separate revolutions broke out almost simultaneously in March, 1848—in Italy (as we have just seen), in Hungary, in Vienna itself, and in Bohemia. In Hungary, Kossuth and his ardent Magyar supporters forced Emperor Ferdinand to accept the "March Laws," which gave Hungary political autonomy. The March Laws instituted parliamentary government and substituted an elected legislature for the feudal Hungarian diet. They abolished serfdom and ended the immunity of nobles and gentry from taxation. But they rode roughshod over the rights of non-Magyars by making use of the Hungarian language a requirement for election as a deputy to the legislature.

Aroused by the Hungarian revolt, the workers and university students of Vienna rose on March 12. On the next day, Prince Metternich resigned from the post he had held for thirty-nine years and fled to Britain. Although the imperial government repeatedly promised reforms, rioting continued in Vienna, and by May the political atmosphere was so charged that Emperor Ferdinand and his family left the capital. Pending the meeting of a constituent assembly in July, the effective government in Vienna was entrusted to a revolutionary council.

Meanwhile, in Prague, Czech nationalists were demanding rights similar to those granted the Magyars in the March Laws. Discontent mounted with the news that the "Big German" faction at Frankfurt was contemplating the inclusion of Bohemia in a German federation. In June, 1848, the Czechs organized a Pan-Slav Congress to promote the solidarity of Slavic peoples against "Big German" encroachments. The Pan-Slav Congress set off demonstrations, in the course of which Princess Windischgrätz, the wife of the commander of the Austrian garrison at Prague, was accidentally killed (June 12, 1848). Five days later, Prince Windischgrätz, after bombarding Prague, dispersed the Czech revolutionaries and established a military dictatorship in Bohemia. The counter-revolution was beginning.

A month later (July), the Austrian army in Italy defeated Piedmont at Custozza. In September, 1848, the Vienna Constituent Assembly, which represented all the provinces of the Empire except the Italian and Hungarian, passed a great reform measure that actually strengthened the counter-revolution. It emancipated the peasants from their last remaining servile obligations, notably the requirement to work for their landlords. The peasants, the core of the Habsburg population, had achieved their main goal; they now tended to withhold support from further revolutionary activities.

The time was ripe for the policy of "divide and conquer." In Hungary, the Germans, Slovaks, Rumanians, Serbs, and Croats, all outraged by the discrimination against them in the March Laws, had risen up against the Magyars. In September, 1848, the imperial government authorized Jellachich, the governor of Croatia, to invade central Hungary. While the hard-fighting Magyars held off the forces of Jellachich, the radicals of Vienna revolted again, proclaiming their support of the Magyars and declaring Austria a democratic republic. The armies of Jellachich and Windischgrätz crushed the Vienna revolution (October 31, 1848) and executed the radical leaders.

The counter-revolution was hitting its full stride. In November, 1848, the energetic and unscrupulous Prince Felix Schwarzenberg (1800-1852), the brother-in-law of

Windischgrätz, became chief minister of the Habsburg government. Schwarzenberg engineered the abdication of the incapable Ferdinand I in December and the accession of Ferdinand's eighteen-year-old nephew, the Emperor Francis Joseph (1848-1916). Schwarzenberg declared that the promises made by the old emperor could not legally bind his successor and therefore shelved the projects of the Austrian Constituent Assembly. Schwarzenberg's high-handedness infuriated the Magyars, who fought on like tigers. In April, 1849, the parliament of Hungary declared the country an independent republic and named Kossuth its chief executive. Russia now offered Austria military assistance, for Tsar Nicholas I feared that the revolutionary contagion might spread to Russian Poland unless it was checked. Schwarzenberg accepted the Tsar's offer, and in August, 1849, Russian troops helped to subjugate the Hungarian republic.

The Lessons of 1848

The Tsar boasted in 1850 that Providence had assigned him "the mission of delivering Europe from constitutional governments." By 1850, almost the whole Continent was in the process of being delivered from the régimes of 1848. In France President Bonaparte, in Prussia Frederick William IV, and in Austria and Italy Prince Schwarzenberg guided the triumphant course of the counter-revolution. Kossuth, Mazzini, and other revolutionaries went into exile. In the early months of 1848, enthusiastic liberals had hailed the arrival of the "peoples' springtime." It had been a false spring.

Mazzini undertook to explain why. In 1850, he wrote from London:

Why, then, has *reaction* triumphed?
Yes: the cause is in ourselves; in our want of organisation; . . . in our ceaseless distrust, in our miserable little vanities, in our absolute want of that spirit of discipline which alone can achieve great results; in the scattering and dispersing of our forces in a multitude of small centres and sects, powerful to dissolve, impotent to found.

The cause is in the gradual substitution of the worship of material interests . . . for the grand problem of education, which alone can legitimatise our efforts. . . . It is in the narrow spirit of *Nationalism* substituted for the spirit of Nationality; in the stupid presumption on the part of each people that they are capable of solving the political, social, and economical problem alone; in their forgetfulness of the great truths that the cause of the peoples is one; that the cause of the Fatherland must lean upon Humanity. . . . The language of narrow nationalism held at Frankfort destroyed the German Revolution; as the fatal idea of aggrandisement of the House of Savoy [Piedmont] destroyed the Italian Revolution.[*]

The revolutionaries of 1848 had not fully learned the lessons of 1830. They frequently relied on moral exhortation and the hope of spontaneous uprisings when they would have done better to foster discipline and organization; many of them were too intellectual, too doctrinaire, or too idealistic to make practical politicians. The strength of their movement was sapped by the disputes between working-class radicals and bourgeois moderates, between the followers of Gioberti and those of Mazzini, between "Big" and "Little" Germans, and between Magyars and Slavs.

"The narrow spirit of nationalism" deplored by Mazzini was to grow ever stronger after 1848. It was to haunt the Habsburg Empire for the rest of its days and eventually destroy it. The failure of the liberals to unify Italy and Germany in 1848 transferred the leadership of the nationalist movements from the amateur revolutionaries to the professional politicians of Piedmont and Prussia. In the case of Italy, the transfer augured well, for Piedmont, alone among the Italian states, retained the moderately liberal constitution it had secured

---

[*] *Life and Writings of Joseph Mazzini* (London, 1905), III, 76-77.

in 1848. In the case of Germany, the anti-liberal Bismarck was to achieve through "blood and iron" what the Frankfurt Assembly had not accomplished by peaceful means.

Equally prophetic was the class warfare of the June Days in Paris. New demands for drastic social and economic reform were arising alongside the older demands for political liberties and constitutions. Europe was beginning to experience the challenge of the forces released by the industrial revolution. 1848 was not only the year of revolution but also the year of publication of *The Communist Manifesto* by Marx and Engels.

Reading Suggestions
on Revolution and Counter-Revolution, 1815-1850

(Asterisk indicates paperbound edition.)

GENERAL ACCOUNTS

F. B. Artz, *Reaction and Revolution, 1814-1832* (Harper, 1934). A painstaking survey of all aspects of Europe in the post-Napoleonic period from the liberal standpoint, frequently reprinted with bibliographical additions.

A. J. May, *The Age of Metternich, 1814-1848* (Holt, 1933). A useful brief introduction.

L. C. B. Seaman, *From Vienna to Versailles* (Coward-McCann, 1956). Provocative, and sometimes provoking, reinterpretations of 19th-century Europe by a bright young scholar; stimulating for those already acquainted with the facts.

SPECIAL STUDIES: THE ROMANTIC PROTEST

G. Brandes, *Main Currents in Nineteenth-Century Literature,* 6 vols. (Heinemann, 1901-1905). A monumental detailed account.

I. Babbitt, *Rousseau and Romanticism* (°Meridian). Acid evaluation by a hostile critic.

G. Boas, *French Philosophies of the Romantic Period* (Johns Hopkins, 1934). A perceptive study.

C. Brinton, *Political Ideas of the English Romanticists* (Oxford Univ. Press, 1926). A useful survey.

K. Francke, *A History of German Literature as Determined by Social Forces,* 4th ed. (Holt, 1931). An old but lively treatment, fully meeting the promise of its title.

A. N. Whitehead, *Science and the Modern World* (°Mentor). Includes a most influential and stimulating chapter appraising Romanticism.

J. Bronowski and B. Mazlish, *The Western Intellectual Tradition from Leonardo to Hegel* (Harper, 1960). Particularly valuable for bibliographical footnotes and for stressing the links between economics, politics, and intellectual history.

M. Raynal, *The Nineteenth Century: Goya to Gauguin* (Skira, 1951). Handsomely illustrated introduction to 19th-century painting.

K. Clark, *The Gothic Revival,* new ed. (Constable, 1950). Informative and entertaining essay on the neo-Gothic vogue in England.

H. R. Hitchcock, *Architecture: Nineteenth and Twentieth Centuries* (Pelican, 1958). Encyclopaedic study, giving full attention to both Europe and America.

A. Einstein, *Music in the Romantic Era* (Norton, 1947). Helpful and suggestive survey.

J. Barzun, *Berlioz and the Romantic Century,* 2 vols. (Little, Brown, 1950; *Meridian). Exhaustive study of the most characteristically Romantic composer.

SPECIAL STUDIES: POLITICAL, DIPLOMATIC, AND SOCIAL

E. L. Woodward, *Three Studies in European Conservatism* (Constable, 1929). Thoughtful essays on Metternich, Guizot, and the Catholic Church.

P. Viereck, *Conservatism Revisited* (Scribner's, 1949). Sympathetic reappraisal of Metternich as a moderate and humane conservative.

J. Lucas-Dubreton, *The Restoration and the July Monarchy* (Putnam, 1929). Perhaps the most useful detailed account of France down to 1848 available in English; conservative in tone.

F. B. Artz, *France under the Bourbon Restoration, 1814-1830* (Harvard Univ. Press, 1931). A helpful monograph; liberal in tone.

D. C. McKay, *The National Workshops* (Harvard Univ. Press, 1933). Informative study of an important facet of revolutionary France in 1848.

H. Treitschke, *History of Germany in the Nineteenth Century,* 7 vols. (McBride, Nast, 1915-1919). Colorful detailed narrative; strongly Prussian and nationalist in outlook.

A. J. P. Taylor, *The Course of German History* (Coward-McCann, 1946). A lively essay on the period after 1815; markedly critical of German nationalism.

B. King, *A History of Italian Unity, 1814-1871,* 2 vols., rev. ed. (Nisbet, 1924). Old-fashioned and rather pedestrian but still highly useful.

A. J. Whyte, *The Evolution of Modern Italy* (Blackwell, 1944). A good introduction.

A. J. P. Taylor, *The Habsburg Monarchy, 1809-1918,* 2nd ed. (Hamish Hamilton, 1948). Spirited brief treatment.

A. G. Mazour, *The First Russian Revolution, 1825* (Univ. of California Press, 1937). Excellent and authoritative monograph on the Decembrists.

C. M. Woodhouse, *The Greek War of Independence* (Hutchinson's University Library, 1952). Lively and instructive short account.

D. Perkins, *The Monroe Doctrine, 1823-1826* (Harvard Univ. Press, 1927). Authoritative monograph on the genesis of the famous doctrine.

P. Robertson, *Revolutions of 1848: A Social History* (Princeton Univ. Press, 1952). Detailed and colorful survey of the chief revolutions.

R. Postgate, *Story of a Year: 1848* (Oxford Univ. Press, 1956). A lively and well-illustrated chronicle.

L. B. Namier, "1848: The Revolution of the Intellectuals," *Proceedings of the British Academy,* XXX (1944). A long and important essay, castigating some of the 'liberals' for their illiberal attitudes.

H. Ausubel, *The Making of Modern Europe*, Vol. II (Dryden, 1951). Includes several useful essays on the material covered by this chapter, notably a reappraisal of the German revolution of 1848 by F. Meinecke.

B. Shafer, *Nationalism, Myth and Reality* (Harcourt, Brace, 1955). Valuable introduction to modern nationalism, with bibliography.

C. J. H. Hayes, *Nationalism: A Religion* (Macmillan, 1960). Summary of a lifework on this important subject.

SOURCES

H. E. Hugo, ed., *The Romantic Reader* (Viking, 1957). Excellent cross-section of early 19th-century literature, with a very helpful introduction.

I. Silone, ed., *The Living Thoughts of Mazzini* (Longmans, Green, 1939). Good selection from the prolific writings of the democratic nationalist.

J. C. Legge, ed., *Rhyme and Revolution in Germany: A Study in German History, Life, Literature, and Character, 1813-1850* (Constable, 1918). An admirable collection, doing full justice to its title.

Note: Virtually all the landmarks in Romantic literature mentioned in the text of this chapter are available in inexpensive paperbound editions.

The Impact
of the
Economic
Revolutions

CHAPTER XX

I: The Industrial
Revolution

O<small>N MAY</small> 1, 1851, in London, Queen Victoria opened the "Great Exhibition of the Works of Industry of All Nations." The first of many "world's fairs," this international exposition displayed the latest mechanical marvels in a setting that was itself a marvel of engineering—the Crystal Palace, a structure of iron and glass stretching like a mammoth greenhouse for more than a third of a mile in Hyde Park. To the visitors who thronged the Crystal Palace it was evident that Britain was the workshop of the world. The London exhibition marked neither the beginning nor the end of the industrial revolution. Machines and factories had already begun to change the face of Britain in the late eighteenth century (see Chapter XVI), and in the century since 1851 they have altered profoundly not only Britain and other western nations but also many other countries on the globe.

In the mid-nineteenth century it was plain that revolutionary changes in technology and business organization were exerting a revolutionary impact on society and politics. Industrialism bound nations closer together by stimulating international exchange and by lowering the barriers of

Opposite. T<small>HE</small> L<small>OOM</small>, *by Vincent van Gogh (1853-1890); Dutch, painted 1884; Rijksmuseum Kröller-Müller, Otterlo, the Netherlands. A compassionate reminder of the human aspects of industry; executed in the artist's somber earlier style before he moved to France.*

distance through improved transport and communication. Yet it heightened international tensions by fortifying nationalism with economic ambition and by inspiring a bloodless war for markets and raw materials. Businessmen demanded national policies that would foster economic development, and they sought the political rights that would give them a voice in determining those policies. Industrialism raised standards of living and enabled increasing numbers of men to enjoy the decencies and comforts of existence. Yet it aggravated problems of unemployment, low wages, and bad living and working conditions. Industrial workers clamored for the right to work, the right to organize, to strike, and to vote.

The rise of industry and labor inspired divergent schools of social and political thought. One school believed in the kind of liberalism preached by the exponents of laissez-faire and practiced by the July Monarchy in France. What was good for business was necessarily good for labor, too. If a worker wanted economic security and political status, he should win them through his own efforts, by becoming rich enough to obtain them. Another school of liberals, however, believed that the state should occasionally assist the workers. Some workers were satisfied by this prospect of gradual, moderate reform, but others favored the more drastic but still peaceful changes of the type recommended by Louis Blanc and his fellow advocates of Utopian socialism. Still others accepted revolutionary socialism, the violent and inevitable class war predicted by Marx and Engels.

In short, many of the great economic and political issues that are still very much with us today came to the fore more than a century ago. Industrialism created a new labor problem and intensified the older

Industrial marvels on display at the Great Exhibition, London, 1851.

farm problem. It sharpened the differences between the champions of relatively free international trade and the economic nationalists who demanded protective tariffs. It divided liberals into the opponents and the defenders of the benevolent or welfare state. It created a radical wing of the working class, soon to be split between the rival schools of Utopian and Marxian socialism. It altered the course of human history even more radically than did a great political upheaval like the French Revolution of 1789. The forces that produced these momentous changes fully deserve to be recognized by history as the Industrial Revolution.

The Causes of Industrialism

The background of the industrial revolution extends deep into the western past. The factors that prepared Europe and America for industrialism included, obviously, the capitalism of the Renaissance and the colonialism and mercantilism of the sixteenth and later centuries. Less obviously, they also included the political, religious, scientific, and intellectual forces that shaped the early modern world. The rise of the competitive state system, the Protestant stress on hard work, the brushing aside of tradition by the scientists of the seventeenth century and by the *philosophes* of the eighteenth—all played their part in creating a society ready for sweeping economic changes. Although the ultimate causes of the industrial revolution involved a wide range of human activities, its immediate causes were largely economic. Four interlocking developments, beginning in the eighteenth century, directly produced the industrial revolution of the nineteenth: (1) the increasing application of power-driven machinery to the processes of production; (2) the more efficient production of coal, iron, and steel; (3) the construction of railroads and other swift methods of transport and communication;

and (4) the expansion of banking and credit facilities.

A hundred years ago, cotton was the king of mechanized industries. Beginning with the spinning jenny in the 1760's, the use of machinery gradually spread to many phases of cotton manufacturing. In 1793, the American Eli Whitney devised the cotton "gin," an engine that separated the fibers of the raw cotton from the seeds and enabled a single slave to do what had previously required the hand labor of fifty slaves. Meanwhile, British inventors perfected a power-driven loom for weaving cotton thread into cloth. By 1830, Britain operated more than 50,000 power looms, and cotton goods accounted for half of her exports. The British census of 1851 listed more than half a million workers employed in cotton manufacturing alone.

Advances in mechanical engineering made this rapid expansion possible. Earlier, for instance, the difficulty of securing exactly fitting parts had hampered the use of machines like Watt's steam engine. Then British engineers studied the precision techniques used by watchmakers. They devised a lathe that turned screws of almost perfect regularity, and they developed machines for sawing, boring, and turning the pulley blocks used by British vessels in the Napoleonic Wars. Eli Whitney, meantime, was undertaking important experiments at his arms factory in Connecticut. He explained that he planned to "make the same parts of different guns, as the locks, for example, as much like each other as the successive impressions of a copperplate engraving." In other words, Whitney was utilizing the concept of standardized parts, one of the basic principles of today's assembly lines.

Many American and British manufacturers, however, ignored the revolutionary implications of Whitney's experiments. The tempo of mechanization, though quickening, was held back by the survival of handicraft techniques; it was dependent on the appearance of new inventions. For example, the mechanization of the woolen and clothing industries did not come until the 1850's, when Britain produced a machine for wool-combing and the American, Isaac Singer, popularized the sewing-machine.

An early Singer sewing machine, 1854.

Coal and Iron

Coal ranked with cotton as an industry that pioneered in the solution of technical problems. Steam engines pumped water from the mines; ventilating shafts and power fans supplied them with fresh air; and safety lamps gave miners protection against dangerous underground gases. The coal output of Britain, then the world's leading producer, rose steadily from about 16,000,000 tons in 1816, to 30,000,000 in 1836, and 65,000,000 in 1856.

The increased consumption of coal resulted chiefly from the expansion of the iron industry, which used large quantities of coal to make the coke needed for smelting. The efficiency of smelting advanced rapidly after the development of the blast furnace (1828), in which fans provided a blast of hot air to intensify the action of the hot coke on the iron. Thanks to the blast furnace, Britain produced iron strong enough for use in bridges and in factory buildings. Yet the best grade of iron lacked the tremendous strength of steel, which is iron purified of all but a minute fraction of carbon by a process of prolonged, intensive heating. Steel for industrial purposes could be made in the early 1800's, but only by ruinously expensive methods. Then in 1856 Bessemer, an Englishman of French extraction, invented the converter, which accelerated the removal of impurities by shooting jets of compressed air into the molten metal. A decade later, Siemens, a German living in England, devised the "open-hearth" process, which utilized scrap as well as new iron, and which handled larger amounts of metal than the converter could. The inventions of Bessemer and Siemens lowered the cost of making steel so substantially that the world output increased tenfold between 1865 and 1880.

Transport and Communication

The railroad consumed large amounts of iron and steel. The revolution in transport began early in the nineteenth century with the growth of canals and hard-surfaced roads. During the century's first three decades many hundreds of miles of canals were dug in Europe and in North America, and highway construction was improved by the Scot, McAdam, who devised the durable road surface of broken stones that still bears his name. Commerce, however, still needed a means for the overland shipment of heavy items like coal and iron; the railroad furnished the solution. In the 1820's, methods of rolling rails and constructing solid roadbeds were already known; only mechanization remained to be accomplished. Then George Stephenson and others put the steam engine on wheels and created the locomotive. In 1830, Stephenson's "Rocket" demonstrated its power by running twelve miles in fifty-three minutes on the new Liverpool and Manchester Railway, the first line to be operated entirely by steam. The railroad building boom was soon in full swing: Britain had 500 miles of track in 1838, 6,600 miles in 1850, and 15,500 in 1870.

Steam also revolutionized water transport. Fulton's steamboat, the "Clermont," made a successful trip on the Hudson River in 1807, and soon steamers plied the inland waterways of the United States and Europe. Ocean-going steamships, by contrast, long proved uneconomical to operate because of the inefficiency of the marine engine. When the Scot, Samuel Cunard, inaugurated the first regular transatlantic steamer service (between Liverpool and Boston in 1840), the coal required for the voyage took up almost half of the space on his vessels. Consequently, only passengers and mails went by steamship; most freight was still handled in sailing ships, like the beautiful and efficient American clippers. Finally, in the 1860's, the development of better marine engines and the substitution of the screw propeller for the cumbersome paddle wheel forecast the eventual doom of the commercial sailing vessel. All these improvements in transport by sea and land greatly aided industry by facilitating shipments of raw materials and finished products and by opening almost the whole world as a potential market.

Meanwhile, communications were also experiencing radical improvements. A beginning was made in 1840, when Great Britain inaugurated the penny post: to send a letter from London to Edinburgh, for instance, now cost only a penny, less than one-tenth of the old rate. More dramatic was the utilization of electricity for ultra-swift communication. An impressive series

of "firsts" started with the first telegraph message, from Baltimore to Washington in 1844. Then came the first submarine cable, under the English Channel in 1851; the first transatlantic cable, 1866; and the first telephone, 1876.

Banking and Capital

The exploitation of all these new inventions and discoveries required a constant flow of fresh capital. Here the older commercial community supported the young industrial community. Tobacco merchants of Glasgow provided the funds that made their city the foremost industrial center of Scotland, and tea merchants in London and Bristol financed the ironmasters of South Wales. Bankers played such an important role that Disraeli, the British politician, listed the Barings of London and the international house of Rothschild among the great powers of Europe. In the early nineteenth century each of the five Rothschild brothers, sons of a German Jewish banker, established himself in an important economic center—London, Paris, Frankfurt, Naples, and Vienna. The Rothschilds prospered because, in an age of frequent speculation, they avoided investment in unduly risky undertakings, and because they facilitated investment by residents of one state in the projects of other states. The Paris Rothschild, for instance, negotiated the investment of British capital in the construction of French railroads during the 1840's.

Banks further assisted economic expansion by promoting the use of checks and banknotes in place of specie. During the Napoleonic Wars the shortage of coins forced some British mill-owners to pay their workers in goods; the British government empowered local banks to issue paper notes supplementing the meager supply of coins. But, whenever financial crises occurred—and they came frequently before

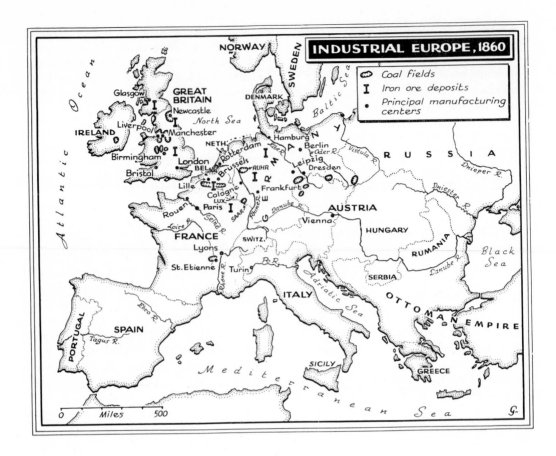

Map caption / labels:

INDUSTRIAL EUROPE, 1860

Legend:
- Coal fields
- I Iron ore deposits
- • Principal manufacturing centers

1850–dozens of local banks failed, and their notes became valueless. Parliament therefore encouraged the absorption of small shaky banks by the larger and more solid institutions, and in 1844 it gave the Bank of England a virtual monopoly of the issuing of banknotes, thus providing a very reliable paper currency. It also applied, first to railroads and then to other companies, the principle of limited liability, indicated by the familiar "Ltd." after the names of British firms. In the early industrial revolution the shareholders in most British companies had unlimited liability: they might find their personal fortunes appropriated to satisfy the creditors of an unsuccessful company. The practice of limiting each shareholder's liability to the value of his shares encouraged wider public investment by diminishing the risk.

The Timetable of Industrialization

Fiscal legislation was only one factor among many accounting for the industrial leadership of Britain in the nineteenth century. She possessed large and easily available deposits of coal and iron; the geographical compactness of the British Isles made shipments from mine to smelter and from mill to seaport short and cheap. Britain had a large reservoir of potential factory labor in the marginal farmers, driven off the land by the enclosure movement, and the Irish, emigrating from their poverty-ridden and overcrowded island. The commercial and naval leadership gained by Britain in the eighteenth century and fortified by the Napoleonic Wars paved the way for her industrial leadership. It facilitated the search for raw materials and markets, and the profits from overseas trade and the empire swelled the capital available for investment in industry. The Napoleonic Wars themselves stimulated demand for metal goods and the invention of new machines. And the construction of great docks along the lower Thames during the wars entrenched London in its position as the greatest economic center in Europe.

The tangible signs of Britain's economic predominance were evident on every hand about 1850—in the teeming London docks, in the thriving financial houses of the City, in the exhibits at the Crystal Palace, in the mushrooming industrial cities of the Midlands and the North of England, and in other quarters of the globe as well. British capital and thousands of skilled British workers participated in the construction of French railroads. American trains ran on rails rolled in British mills. Cotton goods made in Lancashire clothed a sizable part of the world's population.

Yet Britain, even in the heyday of her leadership, did not monopolize inventive skill. France, for example, devised the chlorine process of bleaching cloth and the Jacquard loom for weaving intricate patterns. Germany led the world in agricultural chemistry and in the utilization of the valuable by-products of coal. And from the United States came Eli Whitney and the cotton gin, Morse and the telegraph, Singer and the sewing machine, and Cyrus McCormick, whose reaper (1831) was the first of many agricultural machines developed in America.

The timetable of industrialization de-pended on much besides inventions; factories required raw materials, large amounts of capital and skilled labor, and a favorable political climate. The presence of all these elements made Britain the workshop of the world in the nineteenth century. But when other countries, notably the United States and Germany, began to enjoy a favorable combination of industrial requisites, Britain lost the advantage of her head start. Although the textiles of New England had been flourishing since the early 1800's, the exploitation of rich agricultural resources dominated the American economy until the time of the Civil War. Germany's industrialization awaited the stimulus provided by the successful completion of political unification in 1871.

Since 1900, the industrial revolution has marched steadily on. Oil and electricity have ended the dominance of coal; aluminum and the alloys have challenged that of steel; rayon and other synthetic fibers have partly displaced cotton and wool; automobiles, trucks, and airplanes have partly superseded the railroad. Industry has indeed revolutionized our world and our lives. It has created great corporations, which are virtually powers in their own right; it has made possible the newspaper, television, and other media of mass communication; it has devised assembly-line methods of mass production applicable to many fields of human endeavor. The full nature and the full consequences of the industrial revolution, especially since 1900, will become more evident in later chapters of this book. In this chapter, we shall stress its economic and social consequences in the nineteenth century.

II: Economic and Social Consequences
of Industrialization

The Agricultural Revolution

Improvements in industry brought improvements in farming, thus accelerating the agricultural revolution that had begun in the eighteenth century (see Chapter XVI). Factory-made implements like the reaper and the steel plow improved the cultivation of old farmlands and permitted the opening of new lands, like the North American prairie. The mechanical cream-separator raised the dairy industry to a big business. Railroads and steamships sped the transport of produce from farm to market. The processes of canning, refrigeration, and freezing, all industrial in origin and all first applied on a wide scale during the last third of the nineteenth century, permitted the preservation of many perishable commodities.

Farmers found a steadily expanding market in both the raw materials consumed by the mills of industry and the food required by teeming new factory towns. International trade in farm products increased rapidly during the second half of the nineteenth century. The annual export of wheat from the United States and Canada rose from 22,000,000 bushels in the 1850's to 150,000,000 in 1880. Imported flour accounted for one-quarter of the bread consumed in Britain during the 1850's and for one-half in the 1870's. Denmark and the Netherlands increasingly furnished the British table with bacon, butter, eggs, and cheese; Australia supplied its mutton and Argentina its beef.

Germany now partly assumed Britain's old role as the pioneer of scientific agricul-ture. German experimenters, shortly after 1800, extracted sugar from beets in commercially important quantities, thus ending Europe's dependence on the cane sugar of the West Indies. In the 1840's the German chemist, Liebig, published a series of influential works on the agricultural applications of organic chemistry. Plant growth, Liebig argued, depended on three basic elements—nitrogen, potassium, and phosphorus. But the production of crops and fodder leached these elements from the soil; unless they could be returned to it, formerly fertile lands might go the way of "the once prolific soil of Virginia, now in many parts no longer able to grow its former staple productions—wheat and tobacco." Liebig's gloomy predictions did not generally prove to be accurate, for his teachings promoted the wide use of fertilizers—guano from the nesting islands of sea-birds off the west coast of South America, nitrate from Chile, and potash from European mines.

Farming progressed and prospered in the nineteenth century as never before. Yet the agricultural revolution exacted a price, sometimes a very high price. Faced with the competition of beet sugar, the sugar-cane islands of the West Indies went into a prolonged depression. In the most industrialized countries the social and political importance of agricultural interests began to decline. Farming was no longer the principal occupation of Englishmen in the nineteenth century, and land was no longer the almost universal yardstick of wealth and political power. The manufacturers and merchants of Britain scored a decisive victory over the landed gentry in the campaign to repeal the Corn Laws, the tariffs on the importation of the wheat and other cereals which the English term collectively "corn." The powerful Anti-Corn Law League protested that the tariffs "artificially enhance the price of food," and "prevent the exchange of the products of industry for the food of other countries." Free trade was the remedy prescribed by the Anti-Corn Law League, and free trade came when Parliament repealed the Corn Laws in 1846. The decisive factor was the disastrous attack of black rot that ruined the Irish potato crop two years running and made the importation of cheap grain imperative to prevent the worsening of an already disastrous famine in Ireland (see also below, p. 235). Great Britain thus abandoned the attempt to be self-sustaining in food.

British demonstration against the Corn Laws.

Changes in Population

As a matter of fact, the population of the British Isles was growing so rapidly that self-sufficiency was virtually impossible. The number of inhabitants in England and Wales more than tripled during the course of the nineteenth century, from about 9,000,000 in 1800 to 32,500,000 in 1900. In some predominantly agricultural countries, too, the rate of increase almost matched that of industrial Britain. The Russian population, then mostly rural, rose from about 36,000,000 in 1800 to about 100,000,000 in 1900.

The most important social change flowing from the industrial revolution was not the increase of the population but the alteration of its structure and balance. Wherever mines and factories were opened, towns and cities appeared. Large areas of once-rural England became urban England, and a similar transformation was beginning in the lowlands of Scotland around Glasgow, in the northern French plain around Lille, in the German Rhineland, and along the rivers of the northeastern United States. The growth of an urban population caused a rise in the numbers and influence of the two social classes that form the backbone of an industrial society. These are the businessmen and the workingmen. Industrialists, bankers, managers, and promoters of every sort joined the already established capitalists to form the modern middle class or bourgeoisie. Millhands, railwaymen, miners, clerks, and a host of other recruits swelled the ranks of wage-earning laborers.

The impact of capital and labor upon the life of industrial nations was becoming increasingly evident by the middle of the nineteenth century. Some of the signs pointed to steady material progress—the wonders of the Crystal Palace, or the conquest of space by the railroad, the steamship, and the telegraph. Other signs, however, portended serious dislocation and violent change. The repeal of the Corn Laws buried an old agrarian way of life in Britain. The industrial depression of the late 1840's suggested an alarming pattern for economic slumps. By throwing hundreds of thousands out of work it aggravated social discontent, and in Paris, where its effects were intensified by the political events of the Revolution of 1848, it led to the class warfare of the "June Days" (see Chapter XIX).

Now it is essential for the student of history to fix his attention on *both* the peaceful and the disruptive social effects of the industrial revolution. Unemployment and the other miseries of industrial labor have produced some of the most sordid pages of modern history, but they do not tell the whole story. The slums of the ugly new factory towns a hundred years ago were often horrible indeed, yet they sometimes represented a positive improvement over the rural slums in which the grandparents of the millhands had lived. Too often, whitewashed or vine-covered country cottages concealed behind their picturesque exteriors a contaminated water supply, a total lack of sanitary facilities, and an appalling incidence of infant mortality and tuberculosis. In the cities, infant mortality dropped because of improvements in medicine and sanitation. Adults lived longer because they had better hospital facilities, ate a more balanced and nourishing diet, and observed a higher standard of personal cleanliness. The industrial revolution increased the supply of fresh food and permitted the use of cheap and washable cotton clothing in place of woolens which were seldom, if ever, laundered.

The Aspirations of the Middle Class

Both the businessmen and the workingmen nourished grievances—and aspirations. A revealing view of middle-class complaints and hopes is given in a famous parable published by the French Utopian socialist, Saint-Simon, in 1819. Saint-Simon supposed that France suddenly lost fifty of her best mechanical engineers, architects, doctors, bankers—and so on through a long list comprising the three thousand leading men in business, science, and the arts. These men, Saint-Simon stated, are "the most useful to their country"; "the nation would become a lifeless corpse as soon as it lost them."

Let us pass on to another assumption. Suppose that France preserves all the men of genius that she possesses in the sciences, fine arts and professions, but has the misfortune to lose in the same day Monsieur the King's brother [and many other members of the royal family]. Suppose that France loses at the same time all the great officers of the royal household, all the ministers (with or without portfolio), all the councillors of state, all the chief magistrates, marshals, cardinals, archbishops, bishops, vicars-general, judges, and, in addition, ten thousand of the richest proprietors who live in the style of nobles.

This mischance would certainly distress the French, because they are kind-hearted, and could not see with indifference the sudden disappearance of such a large number of their compatriots. But this loss of thirty-thousand individuals, considered to be the most important in the State, would only grieve them for purely sentimental reasons and would result in no political evil for the State.

These suppositions underline the most important fact of present politics: . . . that our social organization is seriously defective. . . .

The scientists, artists, and artisans, the only men whose work is of positive utility to society, and cost it practically nothing, are kept down by the princes and other rulers who are simply more or less incapable bureaucrats. Those who control honours and other national awards owe, in general, the supremacy they enjoy, to the accident of birth, to flattery, intrigue and other dubious methods. . . .

These suppositions show that society is a world which is upside down.[*]

To the men of the middle class, society indeed seemed upside down. In the Britain

* Saint-Simon, *Selected Writings*, F.M.H. Markham, ed. (New York, 1952), 72-74.

of the 1820's the new industrialists had small opportunity to mold national policy. Booming industrial cities like Manchester and Birmingham sent not a single representative to the House of Commons. A high proportion of businessmen belonged not to the Church of England but to non-Anglican Protestant chapels; nonconformists, as these dissenters were now termed, still suffered discrimination when it came to holding public office or sending their sons to Oxford or Cambridge. Even in France, despite the gains made in 1789, the bourgeois enjoyed as yet only the second-class citizenship sketched by Saint-Simon.

The middle classes very soon won the place in the sun which they felt they deserved. In Britain, the gradual process of reform gave them substantially all they wanted. The high spot, higher even than the repeal of the Corn Laws, was the Reform Bill of 1832, which extended the suffrage to the middle class (for details, see Chapter XXI). In France, as we have already seen, the bourgeois had their revolution in 1830 and got their citizen-king. In Belgium, the revolution of 1830 marked a very great advance in the power of the middle class. Elsewhere the movements of 1830 and 1848 had less favorable results, yet even at their most disappointing they represented a step forward in the political evolution of the middle class.

The Grievances of the Working Class

The grievances of workingmen were more numerous than those of their masters, and they were more difficult to satisfy. The difficulties may be illustrated by the long struggle of laborers to secure the vote and the right to organize and to carry on union activities. In Britain, substantial numbers of workers first secured the vote in 1867, a generation after the enfranchisement of the wealthier middle class. In France, universal male suffrage was tried for a brief period starting in 1848; it became permanent only with the establishment of the Third Republic after 1870.

During most of the nineteenth century, labor unions and strikes were regarded as improper restraints on the free operation of natural economic laws. Hence the specific ban on such combinations, as they were termed, imposed by the British Combination Acts at the close of the eighteenth century. Continental governments imposed similar restrictions, as in the Le Chapelier Law passed by the French National Assembly in 1791 (see above, p. 108). It took labor a long time to win legal recognition of union activities—until 1890 in Germany, for instance, 1867 in Austria, and 1872 in the Netherlands. In France, the July Monarchy repressed strikes with great brutality; the Le Chapelier Law was relaxed in the 1860's and finally repealed outright in 1884. In Britain, Parliament modified the Combination Acts early, in the 1820's, but did not repeal them until 1876.

Labor's drive for political and legal rights, however, was only a side issue during the early days of the industrial revolution. Many workmen faced more pressing problems: they had to find jobs and to make ends meet on inadequate wages. The modern western world has always experienced the business cycle, with its alternations of full employment and unemployment. The industrial revolution intensified the cycle. Boom periods became more hectic, and general depressions, like that of the late 1840's, became more frequent and more severe. Factories at first made little attempt to provide a fairly steady level of employment in both boom times and slack times. When a batch of orders came in, machines and men were worked to capacity until the orders were filled. Then the factory simply shut down to await the next batch.

A century and more ago labor sometimes got such low wages that a family man might

Child labor in a United States shoe factory, about 1840.

have to put both his children and his wife to work as a matter of sheer economic necessity. Humanitarian tradition probably exaggerates the extent to which industry exploited and degraded women and children, probably tends to view the exceptional instance of extreme hardship as the average situation. Nevertheless, exploitation and degradation did occur. Just as one lynching is a shocking thing, so it is a shocking thing to encounter one example of the kind here recorded in the testimony of a factory worker, Samuel Coulson, before a British parliamentary committee in 1831-32:

At what time in the morning, in the brisk time, did those girls go to the mills?
In the brisk time, for about six weeks, they have gone at 3 o'clock in the morning, and ended at 10, or nearly half-past, at night.

What intervals were allowed for rest or refreshment during those nineteen hours of labour?
Breakfast a quarter of an hour, and dinner half an hour, and drinking a quarter of an hour.

Was any of that time taken up in cleaning the machinery?
They generally had to do what they call dry down; sometimes this took the whole of the time at breakfast or drinking, and they were to get their dinner or breakfast as they could; if not, it was brought home.

Had you not great difficulty in awakening your children to this excessive labour?
Yes, in the early time we had them to take up asleep and shake them when we got them on the floor to dress them, before we could get them off to their work; but not so in the common hours.

What was the length of time they could be in bed during those long hours?
It was near 11 o'clock before we could get them into bed after getting a little victuals, and then at morning my mistress used to stop up all night, for fear that we could not get them ready for the time....

So that they had not above four hours' sleep at this time?
No, they had not.

For how long together was it?
About six weeks it held; it was only done when the throng was very much on; it was not often that.

The common hours of labour were from 6 in the morning till half-past eight at night?
Yes.

With the same intervals for food?
Yes, just the same.

Were the children excessively fatigued by this labour?
Many times; we have cried often when we have given them the little victualling we had to give them; we had to shake them, and they have fallen to sleep with the victuals in their mouths many a time.

Did this excessive term of labour occasion much cruelty also?
Yes, with being so very much fatigued the strap was very frequently used.

. . .

What was the wages in the short hours?
Three shillings a week each.

When they wrought those very long hours what did they get?
Three shillings and sevenpence halfpenny.

For all that additional labour they had only sevenpence halfpenny a week additional?
No more.*

Excessively long hours, low pay, and subhuman working conditions were the most general grievances of early industrial workers. Many plants tolerated conditions hazardous to their employees. Few had safety devices to guard dangerous machinery, and cotton mills maintained both the heat and the humidity at an uncomfortably high level because threads broke less often in a hot, damp atmosphere. Many workers could not afford decent housing, and if they could afford it, they could not always find it. Some of the new factory towns were reasonably well planned, with wide streets and space for yards and parks. Some even had a copious supply of good water and arrangements for disposing of sewage. But in rapidly growing London the Thames soon became an open sewer so foul that riverside dwellers were reluctant to open their windows. Fantastic numbers of human beings were jammed into the overcrowded slums of Lille in France and of Liverpool and Manchester in England.

Lord Shaftesbury, an English reformer of the 1840's, predicted that, unless conditions were improved, Lancashire would soon be-

London slums. Woodcut after Doré.

come "a province of pigmies." The industrial nations also threatened to remain nations of semi-literates. Until they made provisions for free public schools, during the last third of the nineteenth century, educational facilities were grossly inadequate. In England, as often as not, only the Sunday school gave the millhand's child a chance to learn his abc's. The millhand himself, if he had great ambition and fortitude, might attend one of the adult schools known as "mechanics' institutes." No wonder that in the 1840's one-third of the men and one-half of the women married in England could not sign their names on the marriage register and simply made their mark. And no wonder that Disraeli, the Tory reformer, wrote of Britain as "two nations"—the rich and the poor.

* Bland, Brown, and Tawney, *English Economic History: Select Documents* (London, 1915), 510-513.

III: The Responses of Liberalism

The Classical Economists

Faced with the widening cleavage between rich and poor, nineteenth-century liberals at first held to the doctrine of laissez-faire.

Suffering and evil are nature's admonitions; they cannot be got rid of; and the impatient attempts of benevolence to banish them from the world by legislation . . . have always been productive of more evil than good.[*]

Such was the argument advanced by liberals in the British Parliament against the first piece of legislation proposed to safeguard public health. The thinkers who advanced these ideas in the early nineteenth century are known to history as the classical economists; to their enemies they were the architects of the "dismal science." The most famous of them were two Englishmen, Thomas Malthus (1766-1834) and David Ricardo (1772-1823).

"Dismal science" is hardly too strong a term for the theories of Malthus. Though educated for the ministry, Malthus became perhaps the very first professional economist in history. In 1798, he published the famous *Essay on the Principles of Population*, a dramatic warning that the human species would breed itself into starvation. In the *Essay*, Malthus formulated a series of natural laws:

The power of population is indefinitely greater than the power in earth to produce subsistence for man.

Population, when unchecked, increases in a geometrical ratio. Subsistence only increases in an arithmetical ratio. . . . Through the animal and vegetable kingdoms, nature has scattered the seeds of life abroad with the most profuse and liberal hands. She has been com-

paratively sparing in the room and the nourishment necessary to rear them. . . . Necessity, that imperious, all-pervading law of nature, restrains them within the prescribed bounds. Among plants and animals its effects are waste of seed, sickness, and premature death. Among mankind, misery and vice.[*]

Misery and vice would spread, Malthus believed, because the unchecked increase in human numbers would lower the demand for labor and therefore lower the wages of labor.

When the wages of labour are hardly sufficient to maintain two children, a man marries and has five or six. He of course finds himself miserably distressed. He accuses the insufficiency of the price of labour to maintain a family. . . . He accuses the partial and unjust institutions of society, which have awarded him an inadequate share of the produce of the earth. He accuses perhaps the dispensations of Providence, which have assigned to him a place in society so beset with unavoidable distress and dependence. In searching for objects of accusation, he never adverts to the quarter from which his misfortunes originate. The last person that he would think of accusing is himself, on whom in fact the whole of the blame lies. . . .[†]

The reduction of the human birth rate was the only hope that this prophet of gloom held out to suffering humanity. It was to be achieved by "moral restraint," specifically by late marriage and by "chastity till that period arrives."

Ricardo, too, was a prophet of gloom. He attributed economic activity to three main forces: there was rent, paid to the owners of great natural resources like farmland and mines; there was profit, accruing to the enterprising individuals who exploited these resources; and there were

---

[*] *The Economist*, May 13, 1848.

[*] *Essay on the Principles of Population*, Bk. I, Ch. 1.
[†] *Ibid.*, Bk. IV, Ch. 3.

wages, paid to the workers who performed the actual labor of exploitation. Of the three, rent was in the long run the most important. Farms and mines would become depleted and exhausted, but their produce would continue in great demand. Rent, accordingly, would consume an ever larger share of the "economic pie," leaving smaller and smaller portions for profit-making capitalists and wage-earning workers.

Ricardo tempered his pessimistic forecasts with many qualifications and reservations. He did not, for instance, believe that the size of the economic pie was altogether fixed, in other words, that the total wealth of mankind was irrevocably "frozen." Still, he did sketch a picture of eventual stagnation, and of man as the exploiter, the depleter, the wastrel. Adam Smith had cheerfully predicted an increasing division of labor, accompanied by steadily rising wages. Ricardo, in contrast, brought labor and wages under the Malthusian formula:

Labour, like all other things which are purchased and sold . . . , has its natural and its market price. The natural price of labour is that price which is necessary to enable the labourers, one with another, to subsist and to perpetuate their race, without either increase or diminution.

.   .   .

The market price of labour is the price which is really paid for it, from the natural operation of the proportion of the supply to the demand; labour is dear when it is scarce, and cheap when it is plentiful. . . . It is when the market price of labour exceeds its natural price, that the condition of the labourer is flourishing and happy. . . . When, however, by the encouragement which high wages give to the increase of population, the number of labourers is increased, wages again fall to their natural price, and indeed . . . sometimes fall below it.*

Ricardo's disciples hardened this principle into the "Iron Law of Wages," which

* On the Principles of Political Economy, Ch. V, in The Works and Correspondence of David Ricardo, P. Sraffa, ed. (Cambridge, England, 1951), I, 93-94.

bound workmen to an everlasting cycle of high wages and large families, followed by an increase in the labor supply, a corresponding increase in the competition for jobs, and an inevitable slump in wages. Ricardo himself, however, regarded the cycle not as an "iron law" but simply as a probability. Unforeseen factors might in the future modify its course and might even permit a gradual improvement of the worker's lot.

While it is easy to see why Malthus and Ricardo were regarded as great exponents of laissez-faire, it is more difficult to understand why they were also ranked among liberals. Yet the classical economists were indeed liberals in a sense; like the *philosophes*, they did not doubt that natural laws were superior to man-made laws. What distinguished the classical economists from their eighteenth-century predecessors was their pessimism. Adherents of the "dismal science" no longer viewed nature as the creation of the beneficent God of the deists; she was at best a neutral force and at worst a sinister one. Man himself—wasteful, careless, improvident—seemed once more afflicted with a kind of original sin. The classical economists put a new stress on the human predicament and supplied a needed corrective to the naive optimism of the *philosophes*.

Yet the classical economists, too, had their naive faith. They viewed the economy as a world-machine governed by a few simple, almost unalterable laws—Malthusian laws of population, Ricardian laws of rent and wages. The history of the last century has demonstrated the inadequacy of their view. Malthus did not foresee that scientific advances would make the output of agriculture expand at a nearly geometrical ratio. He did not foresee that the perils of increasing birthrates would sometimes be averted by the use of contraceptives, first popularized during the nineteenth century, or by recourse to emigration. Many millions of people moved from crowded

Europe to lightly populated America during the nineteenth century. The exodus from overcrowded Ireland, in particular, continued so briskly after the famine of the 1840's that by 1900 the Irish population was little more than half what it had been fifty years earlier.

Famine still haunts the world today, and neo-Malthusian writers still view with alarm each new report of higher birthrates or of droughts and other agrarian disasters. Yet shortages of food have not so far prevented a simultaneous increase in human numbers and in the standard of human existence. The size of the economic pie has expanded far beyond the expectations of Ricardo, and so have the portions that are allotted to rent, to profit and to wages.

The classical economists did not take sufficient account of the immense changes being worked by the agricultural and industrial revolutions. Nevertheless, the laissez-faire liberalism that they championed won particular approval from the new industrial magnates. The captains of industry were perhaps disturbed by Ricardo's prediction that profits would inevitably shrink; but they could take immense comfort from the theory that "suffering and evil" were "nature's admonitions." It was consoling to the rich to be told, in effect, that the poor deserved to be poor because they had indulged their appetites to excess, that whatever was, was right, or at any rate ordained by nature. To the working class, however, the vaunted freedom of laissez-faire often meant freedom to be undernourished, ill-housed, and alternately overworked and unemployed. Understandably, the poor did not like to hear that they deserved to be poor. They sometimes felt that whatever was, was wrong and needed to be remedied, if necessary by interference with supposedly sacred natural laws.

To sum up: in the face of positive social evils, the classical economists offered only the essentially negative policy of laissez-faire. They were often very earnest men, honestly convinced that letting nature take her course was the only thing to do. Yet they were open to the accusation of acting without heart and without conscience, and of advancing economic theories that were only rationalizations of their economic interests. It is not surprising that, as a practical and social political philosophy, strict laissez-faire liberalism today is almost extinct.

Utilitarianism: Bentham

The retreat from laissez-faire originated with a man who was himself the friend and patron of the classical economists—Jeremy Bentham (1748-1832). Bentham behaved precisely as popular opinion expects an eccentric philosopher to behave. He amazed his guests by trotting and bobbing about the garden before dinner, or, as he put it, performing his "anteprandial circumgyrations." In death, he directed that his body be mummified and kept at the University College of London, which he had helped to found. In life, he projected dozens of schemes for the improvement of the human race, among them a model prison and reformatory which he called the "Panopticon," because guards stationed in a central block could survey the activities of all the inmates. He coined new words by the dozen, too; some of them have been happily forgotten but others have made valuable contributions to the language, like "minimize," "codify," and "international."

Bentham submitted all human institutions and principles to the great test of utility, and denounced those which failed to measure up. The French revolutionaries' Declaration of the Rights of Man moved him to a characteristic outburst: "*Natural rights* is simple nonsense: natural and imprescriptible rights, rhetorical nonsense,—nonsense upon stilts." Bentham did not believe that natural laws determined morality:

Nature has placed mankind under the governance of two sovereign masters, *pain* and *pleasure*. It is for them alone to point out what we ought to do. . . . They govern us in all we can do, in all we say, in all we think: every effort we can make to throw off our subjection, will serve but to demonstrate and confirm it. In words a man may pretend to abjure their empire: but in reality he will remain subject to it all the while. The *principle of utility* recognizes this subjection, and assumes it for the foundation of that system, the object of which is to rear the fabric of felicity by the hands of reason and of law.

. . .

The interest of the community is one of the most general expressions that can occur in the phraseology of morals: no wonder that the meaning of it is often lost. . . . The community is a fictitious *body,* composed of the individual persons who are considered as constituting as it were its *members*. The interest of the community then is, what?—the sum of the interests of the several members who compose it.

It is in vain to talk of the interest of the community without understanding what is the interest of the individual. A thing is said to promote the interest, or to be *for* the interest of an individual, when it tends to add to the sum total of his pleasures: or, what comes to the same thing, to diminish the sum total of his pains.*

Bentham listed a dozen or so simple pleasures and pains—the pleasures of the senses and the corresponding pains, the pleasure of wealth and the pain of privation, the pleasure of skill and the pain of awkwardness, and so on. Each category was subdivided, the pleasures of the senses, for instance, into those of taste, intoxication, smelling, touch, hearing, seeing, sex, health, and novelty. And each pleasure or pain could be evaluated according to its intensity, its duration, its certainty or uncertainty, its propinquity or remoteness, its fecundity, and its purity. This "felicific calculus," as Bentham termed it, was a good

example of the eighteenth century's attempts to measure the immeasurable and to apply the exact methods of natural science to the subtleties of human behavior.

Nevertheless, Bentham was no doctrinaire *philosophe*. He dismissed the eighteenth-century theory of political contracts as a mere fiction. Ordinarily, he believed, governments could best safeguard the security of their subjects by following a hands-off policy. In social and economic matters, they should generally act as "passive policemen." Hence the close and sympathetic relationship between Bentham and the classical economists. Yet Bentham realized that the state might become a more active policeman when the pursuit of self-interest by some individuals worked against the best interest of other individuals. If the pains endured by the many exceeded the pleasures enjoyed by the few, then the state should step in. In such a situation Bentham believed the state to be, in a word of his own devising, "omnicompetent," fit to undertake anything for the general welfare. Despite his abhorrence of natural rights, Bentham reached practical conclusions not unlike those of the *philosophes;* twentieth-century theories of the welfare state owe a considerable debt to his utilitarianism.

By the time of his death, Bentham was already gaining an international reputation. He had advised reformers in Portugal, Russia, Greece, and Egypt, and his writings were to exert a broad influence, particularly in France, Spain, and the Spanish-American republics. As late as 1920, his "Panopticon" provided the plan for an American prison (in Joliet, Illinois). His most important disciples, however, were English. The next chapter will show how a group of them, the Philosophic Radicals, pressed for reforms by parliamentary legislation. Here we shall see how his most important English follower, Mill, broadened and deepened utilitarianism into a doctrine of democratic liberalism.

---

* *An Introduction to the Principles of Morals and Legislation,* Wilfrid Harrison, ed. (New York, 1948), Ch. I, 125-127.

Democratic Liberalism: Mill

John Stuart Mill (1806-1873) grew up in an atmosphere dense with the teachings of utilitarianism and classical economics. From his father, who worked closely with Bentham and was a good friend of Ricardo, he received an education almost without parallel for intensity and speed. He began the study of Greek at three, was writing history at twelve, and at sixteen organized an active "Utilitarian Society." At the age of twenty the overworked youth suffered a breakdown; as Mill relates in his *Autobiography*, he had become "a mere reasoning machine." So Mill turned to music and to the poetry of Wordsworth and Coleridge; presently he fell in love with Mrs. Taylor, a woman of warm personality, to whom he assigned the major credit for his later writings. The two maintained a Platonic friendship for twenty years until the death of Mr. Taylor at length enabled them to marry. Mill's personal history is important, for it goes far to explain why he endowed the liberal creed with the qualities which it so markedly lacked in the hands of the classical economists. He gave it warmth and compassion.

Mill's humane liberalism stands forth most clearly in his essay *On Liberty* (1859) and his *Autobiography* (1873). But it is evident, too, in his more technical works, notably *The Principles of Political Economy*. He first published this enormously successful textbook in 1848 and later revised it several times, each revision departing more and more from the "dismal science" of Ricardo and Malthus. Even the first edition of the *Principles* rejected the gloomy implications of the "iron law" of wages:

By what means, then, is poverty to be contended against? How is the evil of low wages to be remedied? If the expedients usually recommended for the purpose are not adapted to it, can no others be thought of? Is the problem incapable of solution? Can political economy do nothing, but only object to everything, and demonstrate that nothing can be done? [*]

Of course something could be done, and Mill proceeded to outline schemes for curbing overpopulation by promoting emigration to the colonies and by "elevating the habits of the labouring people through education."

This one example is typical of the way in which Mill's quest for positive remedies led him to modify the laissez-faire attitude so long associated with liberalism. Although he did not accept the socialistic solution of abolishing private property, he sympathized with the French "National Workshops" of 1848 (see Chapter XIX) and with some of the moderate socialistic projects that we shall examine shortly. He asserted that the workers should be allowed to organize trade unions, form co-operatives, obtain higher wages, and even receive a share of profits. These changes could best be secured by private enterprise, Mill believed, and not by public intervention. But he also believed that there were some matters so pressing that the state would have to step in. He read the reports of parliamentary investigating committees, like that already cited in this chapter (pp. 198-199), and he was shocked by their accounts of human degradation. So he recommended legislation to protect child laborers and to improve intolerable living and working conditions.

Where Bentham had accepted universal suffrage and universal education only as ultimate goals for the distant future, Mill made them immediate objectives. All men, he believed, should have the right to vote; all should be prepared for it by receiving a basic minimum of schooling, if need be at state expense. Moreover, women should have the same rights—for Mill was a pio-

[*] J. S. Mill, *Principles of Political Economy*, Bk. II, Ch. xiii (Boston, 1848).

neer in the movement for feminine emancipation, thanks in part to the influence of Mrs. Taylor. He also proposed the introduction of proportional representation in the House of Commons, so that political minorities might be sure of a voice and might not be overwhelmed by the tyranny of the majority.

The scheme of proportional representation and the fears that actuated it are particularly characteristic of Mill. He made protection of the individual's rights the basis of his famous essay *On Liberty:*

A government cannot have too much of the kind of activity which does not impede, but aids and stimulates, individual exertion and development. The mischief begins when, instead of calling forth the activity and powers of individuals and bodies, it substitutes its own activity for theirs; when, instead of informing, advising, and, upon occasion, denouncing, it makes them work in fetters, or bids them stand aside and does their work instead of them. The worth of a State, in the long run, is the worth of the individuals composing it; . . . a State which dwarfs its men, in order that they may be more docile instruments in its hands even for beneficial purposes—will

find that with small men no great thing can really be accomplished. . . .*

Mill's eloquent defense of the dissenting individual, however, may well appear to have undemocratic implications, for in mistrusting the opinions of the majority he seemed to favor those of the intellectual and moral élite.

At any rate, Mill did not so much reject as transform the liberalism of the classical economists. He had a more tender conscience than did Adam Smith or Ricardo or even Bentham, and he lived at a later time, when the vices of industrialism were plainer. In consequence, he found the exceptions to the rule of laissez-faire more numerous and urgent than his predecessors had ever imagined them to be. Liberalism, as we understand the term today, is the legacy not of the "dismal scientists" but of Mill and of the enlightened politicians who have shaped the western democracies over the past century.

---

* *Utilitarianism, Liberty, and Representative Government,* Everyman ed. (New York, 1910), 169 f.

IV: The Socialist Response—the Utopians

In his later years, Mill referred to himself as a "socialist." By his standard, however, most of us are at least passive socialists today. Universal suffrage for men and for women, universal free education, the curbing of laissez-faire in the interests of the general welfare, the use of the taxing power to limit the accumulation of masses of private property—all these major reforms foreseen by Mill are now widely accepted. But they are not authentically socialistic. The authentic socialist does not stop, as Mill did, with changes in the *distribution* of wealth; he goes on to propose a radical change in arrangements for the

production of goods. The means of production are to be transferred from the control of individuals to the control of the community as a whole.

Socialism—like fascism, liberalism, democracy—is one of those key words in the vocabulary of politics so heavily loaded with moral connotations that they are bound to be controversial. Everyone uses the word, yet mostly to indicate emphatic approval or disapproval of a given policy. The historian, however, attempts to use the word neutrally, for purposes of description and not of passing judgment. Historically, socialism denotes any political or economic philosophy that advocates the vesting of production in the hands of society and not those of private individuals. In practice, it usually means that the state, acting as the trustee of the community, owns major industries like coal, railroads, and steel. Socialism in its most complete form involves public ownership of almost all the instruments of production including the land itself.

Today we tend to call this complete form "communism"; a century ago, however, the terms "socialism" and "communism" were used almost interchangeably. A hundred years of history have gone into making the distinction now usually drawn between the two. The distinction is not simply one between incomplete and more complete versions of the same thing. Both present-day "socialists" and "communists" promote the collectivization of property. But today the socialists believe this should be achieved gradually and peacefully through normal political procedures and with at least some compensation for private owners. The communists believe that it should be achieved swiftly and violently, by revolution and outright seizure. Though the ends have their similarities, the means are worlds apart. This highly significant difference started with the development of two divergent schools of socialist thought in the nineteenth century, the Utopian and the Marxian.

The Utopian socialists were essentially good sons of the Enlightenment. If only men would apply their reason to solving the problems of an industrial economy, if only they would wipe out man-made inequalities by letting the great natural law of brotherhood operate freely—then utopia would be within their grasp, and social and economic progress would come about almost automatically. This is the common belief linking together the four chief Utopians of the early nineteenth century—Saint-Simon, Fourier, Robert Owen, and Louis Blanc.

Saint-Simon and Fourier

Henri, Count of Saint-Simon (1760-1825), belonged to a French noble family so old and aristocratic that it claimed direct descent from Charlemagne. Educated by *philosophes,* Saint-Simon fought with the French army in the American War of Independence. During the French Revolution he won a large fortune by speculating in lands expropriated from the Church and the *émigrés,* then lost most of it through the trickery of an unscrupulous partner. Despite his own reverses, he never lost his admiration for the businessmen and workmen elevated to prominence by industrialism. His enthusiasm reached a high pitch in his parable of the old and the new leaders of France, already quoted (see above, p. 196).

Saint-Simon would have given supreme political power to the great leaders of industry, science, and art. But he reminded them: "Christianity commands you to use all your powers to increase as rapidly as possible the social welfare of the poor!" * Saint-Simon combined the Enlightenment's respect for science with Romanticism's zeal for the community. So he proclaimed the one science transcending all others to be the application of the Golden Rule. Reform should come peacefully, through "persuasion and demonstration," and it should affect particularly the idlers, the rich drones of existing society. Since all men were brothers, even men of different nations, Saint-Simon envisaged a federation of European states. It would start with a union of the most advanced countries, France and Britain, and would culminate in the establishment of a European parliament when all states had been "organized" to the point where they merited popular representation. "Organization" was Saint-Simon's favorite word, but he seldom at-

* Saint-Simon, *Selected Writings,* F.M.H. Markham, ed. (New York, 1952), 116.

tempted to spell out precisely what he meant by it.

By contrast, his compatriot and contemporary, Fourier (1772-1837), evolved an elaborate socialist plan, carried down to the last detail. At the French textile center of Lyons, Fourier was shocked by the extremes of wealth and poverty that he observed. At Paris, he was shocked when he found that a single apple cost a sum that would have bought a hundred apples in the countryside. Clearly, he concluded, something was amiss in a society and economy that permitted such fantastic divergences. He compared the historical importance of his apple with that of Newton, and honestly believed himself to be the Newton of the social sciences. Just as Newton had found the force holding the heavenly bodies in a state of mutual attraction, so Fourier claimed discovery of the force holding the individuals of human society in a state of mutual attraction.

This force was *l'attraction passionnelle*: human beings are drawn to one another by their passions. Fourier drew up a list of passions, rather like the list of pleasures in Bentham's "felicific calculus"—sex, companionship, food, luxury, variety, and so on. It seemed obvious to Fourier that existing society thwarted their satisfaction. Society, therefore, needed remodeling, needed to be rearranged into units that he called *phalanges*, "phalanxes." Some 1800 volunteers would compose each phalanx; they would form a kind of community company, agreeing to split its profits three ways—five-twelfths to those who did the work, four-twelfths to those who undertook the management, and three-twelfths to those who supplied the capital.

Fourier's phalanx, with its relatively generous rewards to managers and capitalists, fell short of complete equality. However, it gave labor the largest share of the profits, and it foreshadowed many other features of socialist planning. Adult workers who performed the most dangerous or unpleasant tasks would receive the highest remuneration. The inhabitants of the phalanx were to live in one large building, a sort of apartment hotel, which Fourier called a *phalanstère*. The *phalanstère* would provide the maximum opportunity for the satisfaction of man's sociable passions, and it would also make the routine of daily living more efficient by substituting one central kitchen for hundreds of separate ones. The sordid features of housekeeping could be left to little boys, who (according to Fourier) loved dirt anyway and would cheerfully form special squads to dispose of garbage and refuse.

From start to finish, the phalanx bore witness to Fourier's reaction against the monotony of the ordinary worker's existence. Places of work would be made as pleasant as possible by frequent, colorful redecoration. Members of the phalanx would change their jobs eight times a day because of the human predisposition to the *passion papillonne* (butterfly passion)— "enthusiasm cannot be sustained for more than an hour and a half or two hours in the performance of one particular operation." They would work from four or five in the morning to eight or nine at night, needing only five hours of sleep, since the delightful variety of work would not tire them and the days would not be long enough to permit them to taste all the pleasures of life. Finally, the phalanxes would be largely self-sufficient units, growing and making most of the things their inhabitants required.

Hopefully expecting some millionaire to finance his phalanxes, Fourier announced that he would be in his office every day at noon. For ten years he kept his daily office hour; no rich philanthropist ever appeared. Fourier undoubtedly had many wild notions and carried the principle of uninhibited human association to the extreme of advocating sexual promiscuity, thereby identifying "free love" and Utopian socialism in the popular mind. Yet Fourier

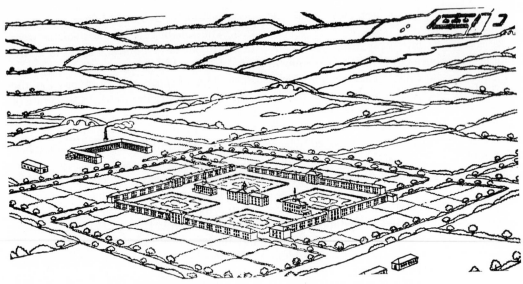

Sketch of an "Agricultural and Manufacturing Village of Unity and Mutual Co-operation," projected by the British Utopian socialist, Robert Owen, 1817.

cannot be dismissed as a mere crackpot, for he made substantial contributions to socialist theory and to social psychology. Some of his recommendations, like higher pay for dangerous jobs and devices for relieving the tedium of work, have become common practice in the modern business world.

Owen

One of the greatest Utopians was a self-made British businessman, Robert Owen (1772-1858). When he was still in his twenties, Owen took over the large cotton mills at New Lanark in Scotland. Although the former owner of the mills had been accounted benevolent by the standards of the day, conditions there shook Owen to the core. A large part of the working force consisted of children who had been recruited from institutions in Edinburgh when they were between six and eight years old. Although the youngsters did get a little schooling after hours, Owen found many of them "dwarfs in body

and mind." Adult laborers at New Lanark fared little better.

Owen set out to show that he could increase his profits and increase the welfare of his laborers at the same time. He made New Lanark over into a model industrial village. For the adults he provided better working conditions, a ten-and-a-half-hour day, higher pay, and cleaner and roomier housing. He restrained the traditional Scottish Saturday night drunk by closing down the worst resorts, making good liquor available at cheap prices, and punishing offenders who made themselves a public nuisance. As for the children, he raised the minimum age for employment to ten, hoping ultimately to put it at twelve, and he gave his child laborers time for some real schooling. Owen's educational practices were very much in the manner of Rousseau; advanced bookish subjects were avoided, while crafts, nature study, and other "practical" subjects received much attention. Education was Owen's great cure for the ailments of an industrial nation. He believed that well-educated people would make short work of the gloomy predictions of Malthus:

CHAPTER XX

All men may, by judicious and proper laws and training, readily acquire knowledge and habits which will enable them, if they be permitted, to produce far more than they need for their support and enjoyment. . . .

Mr. Malthus is however correct, when he says that the population of the world is ever adapting itself to the quantity of food raised for its support; but he has not told us how much more food an intelligent and industrious people will create from the same soil, than will be produced by one ignorant and ill-governed. It is however as one, to infinity.*

Owen inherited much of the optimism of the *philosophes;* he also inherited some of their failures and disappointments. Despite his own success as a philanthropic capitalist, few businessmen followed his example. Disappointed but not disheartened, Owen drew up plans for an idealized version of New Lanark, very much like Fourier's phalanx. He called his utopia a "parallelogram," for the buildings were to be arranged in that geometrical pattern. It was to be a voluntary organization, relatively small in size, neatly balanced between farming and industry, decidedly advanced in Owen's recommendation for the partial abandonment of conventional ties of marriage and the family. In the 1820's, Owen visited America to finance an abortive effort to set up a parallelogram at New Harmony, Indiana. The failure of this venture did not dampen his enthusiasm. He spent the rest of his career publishing and supporting projects for social reform. He advocated the association of all labor in one big union—an experiment that failed; and he sought to reduce the expenditures of workingmen by promoting the formation of consumers' cooperatives—an experiment that succeeded. He also offended many of his contemporaries by his advocacy of sexual freedom, by his Voltairean attacks on established religion, and by his enthusiasm for spiritualism.

---

* Robert Owen, *A New View of Society* (Glencoe, Illinois, 1948), 174-175.

The Early Utopians Appraised

Both Owen and Fourier attracted followers not only in their native lands but also in the United States, where religious sects were already launching ventures in communal living. The American Fourierists included many intellectuals, among them the crusading editor, Horace Greeley, and the poet, John Greenleaf Whittier. They sponsored more than thirty attempts to set up phalanxes; two celebrated ones were Brook Farm, near Boston, and Phalanx, in New Jersey. America also witnessed more than half a dozen Owenite experiments in addition to New Harmony. Like New Harmony itself, however, most of these utopias did not prosper very long; and the few that got firmly established returned to conventional ways of individual profit-taking and family life.

Owen and Fourier relied on private initiative to build from their blueprints the model communities that they so hopefully expected to become widely copied examples for the reconstruction of society. Saint-Simon, too, believed in the power of example, but with his stress on "organization" he presumably meant to give government a larger role. The early followers of Saint-Simon in France developed the strain of social Christianity in the master's teaching and formed a fantastic religious cult. Later, some of the Saint-Simonians did achieve notable feats of practical "organization"; De Lesseps, for one, promoted the digging of the Suez Canal. But it remained for another student of Saint-Simon, Louis Blanc, to recommend "organization" on a large scale by the state.

Implacable critic of the bourgeois policies of the July Monarchy, Louis Blanc (1813-1882) devised the scheme that helped to produce the controversial workshops of the Paris revolution in 1848. He first outlined his plan in a pamphlet, *The*

Organization of Labor (1839). "What proletarians need," he wrote, "is the instruments of labor; it is the function of government to supply these. If we were to define our conception of the state, our answer would be, that the state is the banker of the poor." * The government would finance and supervise the purchase of productive equipment and the formation of "social workshops"; it would withdraw its support

---

* "L'Organisation du Travail," in *The French Revolution of 1848*, J. A. R. Marriott, ed. (Oxford, 1913), I, 14. Our translation.

and supervision once the workshops were on their feet. As the workshops gradually spread throughout France, socialistic enterprise would replace private enterprise, profits as such would vanish, and labor would be the only class in society. Much of Louis Blanc's socialism is typically Utopian; he, too, relies on the workers to perfect arrangements for communal living. The real novelty of his plan lies in the role assigned to the state. With Blanc, socialism is beginning to move away from the realm of philanthropy and into the realm of politics.

V: The Socialist Response—Marx

With Karl Marx (1818-1883), who came from the Prussian Rhineland, socialism assumed its most extreme form—revolutionary communism. Where the early socialists had anticipated a gradual and peaceful evolution toward utopia, Marx forecast a sudden and violent proletarian revolution, by which the workers would capture governments and make them the instruments for securing proletarian welfare. Of all the socialists, Marx was the most dogmatic and the most cocksure. He was certain that he alone knew the answers and that the future of mankind would develop inevitably according to the pattern which he found in human history. His supreme self-confidence and his truculence and intolerance have earned him the label of the "Red Prussian."

Basic Principles

Marx found three laws in the pattern of history. First, *economic determinism:* he believed that economic conditions largely determined other human institutions—society and government, religion and art.

Second, the *class struggle:* he believed that history was a dialectical process, a series of conflicts between antagonistic economic groups. In his own day the antagonists were the "haves" and the "have-nots"—the propertied bourgeois and the propertyless proletarians, who, possessing nothing but their working skills, had nothing to fall back on in bad times and were thus at the mercy of their masters. Third, the *inevitability of communism:* he believed that the class struggle was bound to produce one final upheaval that would raise the victorious proletariat over the prostrate bourgeoisie in eternal triumph.

The Marxian philosophy of history derived from many older schools of thought. Although Marx himself was born and died in the nineteenth century, he belonged in spirit partly to the eighteenth. Both his grandfathers were rabbis, but his father was a deist and a skeptic who trained him in the rationalism of the Enlightenment. Marx early acquired the kind of faith in natural law that had characterized the *philosophes;* in his case it was faith in the natural laws of economic determinism and the class struggle. From this followed the boast made by Marx and his disciples that their socialism alone was "scientific," as opposed to the unrealistic doctrines of the Utopians.

The Romantic philosophy of Hegel (see Chapter XIX), however, provided the intellectual scaffolding of Marxism. Although Hegel had died in 1831, his influence permeated the University of Berlin during Marx's student days (1836-1841). Marx translated the Hegelian dialectic into the language of economic determinism and the class struggle. In his own day he believed that capitalistic production and the bourgeoisie comprised the thesis; the antithesis was the proletariat; and the synthesis, issuing from the communist revolution, would be true "socialism." In later years Marx summarized his relation to Hegel:

My dialectic method is not only different from the Hegelian but is its direct opposite. To Hegel, the life-process of the human brain, ...which, under the name of 'the Idea,' he even transforms into an independent subject, is the demiurgos of the real world, and the real world is only the external, phenomenal form of 'the Idea.' With me, on the contrary, the ideal is nothing else than the material world reflected by the human mind, and translated into forms of thought.

·　　·　　·

The mystification which dialectic suffers in Hegel's hands, by no means prevents him from being the first to present its general form of working in a comprehensive and conscious manner. *With him it is standing on its head. It must be turned right again*, if you would discover the rational kernel within the mystical shell.*

By the time Marx was thirty, he had completed the outlines of his theory of scientific, revolutionary socialism. He had also become a permanent exile from his native Germany. On leaving the University of Berlin, he worked for a newspaper at

Cologne in the Prussian Rhineland, then moved to Paris in 1843 after his atheistic articles had aroused the authorities against him. Exiled again, because the government of Louis Philippe feared his anti-bourgeois propaganda, he went to Brussels in 1845. Wherever he happened to be, he read widely in the economists of the past and talked with the socialists and other radicals of his own generation.

Everything Marx read and everyone he met strengthened his conviction that the capitalistic order was unjust, rotten, doomed to fall. From Adam Smith's labor theory of value he concluded that only the worker should receive the profits from the sale of a commodity, since the value of the commodity should be determined by the labor of the man who produced it. The "iron law of wages," however, confirmed Marx's belief that capitalism would never permit the worker to receive this just reward. And from reading other economists and observing the depression of the late 1840's, he concluded that economic crises were bound to occur again and again under a system that allowed labor to consume too little and capital to produce too much.

Karl Marx.

* Preface to the second edition of *Capital*, Modern Library ed. (New York, n.d.), 25. (Italics ours.)

Meanwhile, Marx began his long friendship and collaboration with Friedrich Engels (1820-1895). In many ways, the two men made a striking contrast. Marx was poor and quarrelsome, a man of few friends; except for his devotion to his wife and children, he was utterly preoccupied by his economic studies. Engels, on the other hand, was the son of a well-to-do German manufacturer and represented the family textile business in Liverpool and Manchester. He loved sports, women, and high living in general. But he also hated the iniquities of industrialism and, when he met Marx, had already written a bitter study, *The Condition of the Working Class in England*. Both Engels and Marx took an interest in the Communist League, a small international organization of radical workingmen. In 1847, the London office of the Communist League requested them to draw up a program. Engels wrote the first draft, which Marx revised from start to finish; the result, published in January, 1848, was *The Manifesto of the Communist Party*.

The Communist Manifesto

Today, more than a century after its original publication, the *Manifesto* remains the classic statement of Marxian socialism. It opens with the dramatic announcement that "A spectre is haunting Europe—the spectre of Communism." It closes with a supremely confident appeal:

Let the ruling classes tremble at a Communist revolution. The proletarians have nothing to lose but their chains. They have a world to win.
Workingmen of all countries, unite!

In the few dozen pages of the *Manifesto*, Marx and Engels rapidly block in the main outlines of their theory. "The history of all hitherto existing society," they affirm, "is the history of class struggle." Changing economic conditions determined that the struggle should develop successively between "freeman and slave, patrician and plebeian, lord and serf, guild-master and journeyman." The guild system gave way first to manufacture by large numbers of small capitalists, and then to "the giant, modern industry."

Modern industry will inevitably destroy bourgeois society. It creates a mounting economic pressure by producing more goods than it can sell; it creates a mounting social pressure by narrowing the circle of capitalists to fewer and fewer individuals and by forcing more and more people down to the propertyless status of proletarians. These pressures increase to the point where a revolutionary explosion occurs, a massive assault on private property. Landed property will be abolished outright; other forms of property are to be liquidated more gradually through the imposition of severe income taxes and the abolition of inherited wealth. Eventually, social classes and tensions will vanish, and "we shall have an association in which the free development of each is the condition for the free development of all."

"The free development of each is the condition for the free development of all" —the *Manifesto* provides only this vague description of the society that would exist after the revolution. Since Marx defined political authority as "the organized power of one class for oppressing another," he apparently expected that, in the famous phrase, "the state would wither away" once it had created a classless régime. He also apparently assumed that the great dialectical process of history, having achieved its final synthesis, would then cease to operate in its traditional form. But, readers of the *Manifesto* may inquire, is it possible for the process to be so transformed? Will not the dialectic continue forever creating economic and political theses and antitheses? Will not the state always be with us? To these questions Marx offered no satisfactory answer beyond the implication that somehow the liquidation of bourgeois capitalism would radically alter the course of history and bring the human race close to perfection.

Marx oversimplified the complexities of human nature by neglecting the non-material interests and motives of men. The history of the century since the publication of the *Communist Manifesto* has demonstrated that neither proletarians nor bourgeois have proved to be the simple economic stereotypes Marx supposed them to be. Labor has often behaved in scandalously un-Marxian fashion and assumed a markedly bourgeois outlook and mentality. Capital has put its own house in better order by eliminating the worst injustices of the factory system. No more than Malthus did Marx foresee the notable rise in the standard of living that would take place between the mid-nineteenth and mid-twentieth centuries.

Marx never made a greater mistake than when he failed to observe the growing strength of nationalism. The *Manifesto* confidently expected the class struggle to transcend national boundaries. In social and economic warfare, nation would not be pitted against nation, nor state against state; the proletariat everywhere would fight the bourgeoisie. "Workingmen have no country" and "national differences and antagonisms are vanishing gradually from day to day." In Marx's own lifetime, however, national differences and antagonisms were increasing rapidly from day to day. Within a few months of the publication of the *Manifesto*, the revolutions of 1848 were revealing the antagonism between Italians and Austrians, Austrians and Hungarians, Hungarians and Slavs, Slavs and Germans. The *Communist Manifesto* thus revealed the greatest blind spots of Marxian socialism. The communist movement in its subsequent history has often shown a comparable failure to appreciate the significance of nationalism and has made a comparable attempt to force human nature into the rigid mold of economic determinism.

Just as the *Manifesto* foreshadowed some of the weaknesses of international communism, so also it anticipated its strengths. First, it anticipated the remarkable character of communist propaganda. It supplied the earliest of those effective catch-phrases that have become the mark of the communist movement—the constant sneering at bourgeois morality, bourgeois law, and bourgeois property, and the dramatic references to the "spectre haunting Europe" and to the proletarians who "have nothing to lose but their chains." Second, the *Manifesto* anticipated the emphasis to be placed on the party's role in forging the proletarian revolution. The communists, Marx declared in 1848, were a spearhead, "the most advanced section of the working class parties of every country." In matters of theory, "they have over the great mass of the proletariat the advantage of clearly understanding the line of march, the conditions, and the ultimate general results of the proletarian movement."

Third, the *Manifesto* anticipated the equally great role to be played by the state in the revolution. Among the policies recommended by Marx were "centralization of credit *in the hands of the state*," and "extension of factories and instruments of production *owned by the state*." * Thus, despite the supposition that the state would wither away, the *Manifesto* faintly foreshadowed the totalitarian régime of the Soviet Union. And, finally, it clearly established the line dividing communism from the other forms of socialism. Marx's dogmatism, his philosophy of history, and his belief in the necessity for a "total" revolution made his brand of socialism a thing apart. Like a religious prophet granted a revelation, Marx expected his gospel to supplant all others. He scorned and pitied the Utopian socialists. They were about as

---

* Italics ours.

futile, he wrote, as "organizers of charity, members of societies for the prevention of cruelty to animals, temperance fanatics, hole-and-corner reformers of every kind."

The Later Career
of Marx

Age neither mellowed Marx nor greatly altered his views. From 1849 until his death in 1883, he lived in London. There, partly because of his own financial mismanagement, the Marx family experienced at first hand the misery of a proletarian existence in the slums of Soho; poverty and near-starvation caused the death of three of the Marx children. Eventually, Marx obtained a modest income from the generosity of Engels and from his own writings.

Throughout the 1850's Marx contributed a weekly article on British politics or international affairs to Horace Greeley's radical paper, *The New York Tribune*. He produced a series of pamphlets, of which the most famous was *The Eighteenth Brumaire of Louis Napoleon*, a study of the fall of the short-lived Second French Republic. Meantime, he spent his days in the British Museum, reading the reports of parliamentary investigating committees and piling up evidence of the conditions of miners and factory hands. Thus Marx accumulated the material for his full-dress economic study, *Das Kapital*. The first volume of this massive analysis of capitalism appeared in 1867; two further volumes, pieced together from his notes, were published after his death.

In *Das Kapital*, Marx elaborated, but did not substantially revise, the doctrines of the *Communist Manifesto*. For example, he spelled out his labor theory of value. According to Marx, the worker created the total value of the commodity that he produced yet received in the form of wages only a part of the price for which the item was sold; the difference between the sale price and the worker's wages constituted *surplus value*. This celebrated Marxian concept of surplus value represented something actually created by labor but appropriated by capital as profit.

Das Kapital goes on to relate surplus value to the ultimate doom of capitalism. It is the nature of capitalism, Marx insists, to diminish its own profits by replacing human labor with machines and thus gradually choking off the source of surplus value. Hence will arise the mounting crises of overproduction and underconsumption predicted by the *Manifesto*. In a famous passage toward the close of Volume I of *Das Kapital*, Marx compared capitalism to an integument, a skin or shell, increasingly stretched and strained from within. One day these internal pressures would prove irresistible:

This integument is burst asunder. The knell of capitalist private property sounds. The expropriators are expropriated.[*]

In 1864, three years before the first volume of *Das Kapital* was published, Marx joined in the formation of the First International Workingmen's Association. This was an ambitious attempt to organize workers of every country and of every variety of radical belief. But the First International, more a loose federation than a coherent political party, soon began to disintegrate, and it expired in 1876. Increasing persecution by hostile governments helped to bring on its end; but so, too, did the internal quarrels that repeatedly engaged both its leaders and the rank and file of its members. Marx himself set the example by his intolerance of disagreement and his utter incapacity for practical politics.

In 1889, the Second International was organized; it lasted down to the time of World War I and the Bolshevik revolution in Russia. The Second International was

---

[*] *Capital*, Modern Library ed., 837.

more coherently organized and more political in character than the First International had been. It represented the Marxian socialist parties, which, as we shall see in later chapters, were becoming important forces in the major countries of continental Europe. Among its leaders were men more adept than Marx himself at the political game. Yet the old spirit of factionalism continued to weaken the International. Some of its leaders tenaciously defended laws handed down by the master and forbade any co-operation between socialists and the "bourgeois" political parties; these were the "orthodox" Marxists. Other leaders of the Second International, however, were from the orthodox standpoint "heretics."

They, too, called themselves disciples of Marx; yet they revised his doctrines in the direction of moderation and of harmonization with the views of the Utopians. These "revisionists" believed in co-operation between classes rather than in a struggle to the death, and they trusted that human decency and intelligence, working through the machinery of democratic government, could avert the horrors of class war. Though the precise connotations have varied with the shifts of the party line, "orthodox" and "heretical" communists have persisted. The factionalism that had split the First International lived on to plague the Second and its successors in twentieth-century communism (see Chapters XXVI and XXX).

VI: Other Responses

Socialism, both Marxian and Utopian, and liberalism, both bourgeois and democratic, were the most important responses to the economic and social problems of the nineteenth century. But they were not the only responses. Nationalists revived the still lively philosophy of mercantilism, not only advocating tariffs to protect the economy at home but also demanding empires abroad to provide new markets for surplus products, new fields for the investment of surplus capital, and new settlements for surplus citizens. This neo-mercantilism will be analyzed in later chapters (XXI and XXIV). Here we shall deal with two other sets of responses—anarchism, and the reform program known as "Christian socialism" or "Christian democracy."

The Anarchists

An anarchist believes that the best government is no government at all. Most

of the recipes for socialism contained at least a dash of anarchism: witness the Marxian withering-away of the state, and the Utopians' mistrust of governments. For a few of Marx's contemporaries, however, it was not enough that the state should wither at some distant time; such an instrument of oppression should be annihilated here and now. The means to this end was terrorism, especially assassination of heads of state. These terrorists provided the stereotype of the bearded, wild-eyed, bomb-carrying radical. At the turn of the century from the nineteenth to the twentieth, their assassinations levied an impressive toll—the French President Carnot in 1894, King Humbert of Italy in 1900, and the American President McKinley in 1901. Otherwise the terrorists accomplished little except to drive the governments they hated to more vigorous measures of retaliation.

Yet anarchism, though negative and destructive in practice, did exert an important doctrinal influence on the proletarian movement. The Russian scientist and thinker, Prince Peter Kropotkin (1842-1921), made the most complete statement of its theory and ideals in his book, *Mutual Aid: A Factor in Evolution* (1902). Kropotkin foresaw a revolution that would abolish the state as well as private property and that would lead to a new society of autonomous groups whereby the individual would achieve greater self-realization and would need to labor only four to five hours a day. The most famous anarchist, however, was Kropotkin's countryman, Bakunin (1814-1876), who helped to shape the Russian revolutionary movement (see Chapter XXII) and won the attention of workers from many countries by his participation in the First International. Although Bakunin drew only a vague sketch of his utopia, he made it clear that the millennium was to be achieved through an international rebellion set off by small groups of anarchist conspirators.

Bakunin contributed to the formation of the program known as *anarcho-syndicalism*. "Anarcho" connotes its distrust of political action; "syndicalism" comes from the French *syndicat,* an economic grouping, particularly a trade union. The anarcho-syndicalists disbelieved in political parties, even Marxist ones; they believed in direct action by the workers. Direct action was to culminate in a spontaneous general strike that would free labor from the capitalistic yoke. Meantime, workers could rehearse for the great day by forming unions and by engaging in acts of anti-capitalist sabotage. These theories found their most forceful expression in a book called *Reflections on Violence* published early in our own century by the French exponent of anarcho-syndicalism, Georges Sorel.

Proudhon

The writer most frequently cited by the anarcho-syndicalists was the French publicist, Proudhon (1809-1865). "What is property?" Proudhon asked in a famous pamphlet of 1840; "property is theft." Karl Marx praised him for his "scientific" socialism, but within a few years Marx's praise had turned to contempt. A second pamphlet by Proudhon, *The Philosophy of Poverty*, elicited a Marxian rebuttal tartly entitled *The Poverty of Philosophy*, since Proudhon did not automatically accept the rightness of Marx's own views. The property that Proudhon called "theft" was not all property but unearned income, the revenues that men gained from investing their wealth rather than from the sweat of their brows. Of all the forms of unearned income, the worst, in Proudhon's view, was the "leprosy of interest," and the most diabolical of capitalists was the money-lender. Under existing conditions only those who were already rich could afford to borrow, but in the utopia envisaged by Proudhon all men would be able to secure credit. Instead of private banks and the Bank of France, there would be only a "People's Bank," lending to all without interest and issuing notes that would soon replace ordinary money. The credit provided by the People's Bank would enable each man to become a producer on his own.

Thus, where Marx foresaw a revolution in ownership of the means of production, Proudhon foresaw a "revolution of credit," a revolution in financing production. Where Marx proposed to have the proletariat liquidate the bourgeoisie, Proudhon proposed to raise the proletarians to the level of the bourgeois by making every worker an owner. Proudhon's utopia was not collectivized or socialized; it was a loose association of middle-class individualists. Because Proudhon dreaded restraints upon the individual, he opposed the social workshops of Louis Blanc and the phalanxes of Fourier; they were too restrictive. He projected, instead, a society founded upon "mutualism." Economically, mutualism would take the form of associations of producers, rather like the producers' co-operatives sometimes found in agriculture today. Politically, it would take the form of a loose federation of these associations, which would replace the sovereign, centralized state.

Proudhon's doctrines exerted a strong appeal in a country like France, with its devotion to individualism. France had tens of thousands of small businessmen on the lower fringes of the middle class, often on the edge of being pushed down into the proletariat, often denied financial credit by the bankers whom Proudhon attacked so bitterly. "Mutualism" and "federalism," furthermore, were part of the revolutionary tradition, inherited from the Girondins (see Chapter XVIII). Proudhon naturally fed the anarchist strain in anarcho-syndicalism. Yet much of his teaching contradicted the syndicalist strain. Not only did he dislike trade unions as unnatural restrictions on individual liberty; he deplored all activities suggesting class strife, including the very strikes so beloved by the syndicalists. Finally, Proudhon's hatred of bankers made him an anti-Semite, because of the number of Jews engaged in finance.

The Christian Socialists

Proudhon is usually assigned a place at the extreme of the political spectrum; by contrast, the Christian socialists occupy a position close to the Center. Historically, the Christian socialists were a small group of English reformers, drawn from the clergy of the established Church and active in the mid-nineteenth century. The Church of England, they believed, needed to put theological problems to one side and direct its efforts to ending social abuses. One of their best known leaders was Charles Kingsley (1819-1875), who wrote earnest social novels and a stream of pamphlets against the wickedness of laissez-faire. His didactic novel, *Alton Locke*, and his bitter tract, *Cheap Clothes and Nasty*, both published in 1850, exposed the "show-shops" and "slop-shops" which forced tailors and seamstresses to labor hard and long for meager pay, often in appallingly crowded and unsanitary surroundings.

Kingsley proposed the following remedies for these sweatshops:

First—this can be done. That no man who calls himself a Christian—no man who calls himself a man—shall ever disgrace himself by dealing at any show-shop or slop-shop.... Let no man enter them—they are the temples of Moloch—their thresholds are rank with human blood.

. . .

But let, secondly, a dozen, or fifty, or a hundred journeymen say to one another: 'It is competition that is ruining us, and competition is division, disunion, every man to himself, every man against his brother. The remedy must be in association, co-operation, self-sacrifice for the sake of one another.... Why should we not work and live together in our own workshops, or our own homes, for our own profit?'

. . .

And, again, let one man, or half-a-dozen men arise who believe that the world is not the devil's world at all but God's: that the multitude of the people is not, as Malthusians aver, the ruin, but as Solomon believed, 'the strength of the ruler.' ...

Let them help and foster the growth of association by all means. Let them advise the honourable tailors, while it is time, to save themselves from being degraded into slop-sellers by admitting their journeymen to a share in the profits.... Let them, as soon as an association is formed, provide for them a properly ventilated workshop, and let it out to the associate tailors at a low fair rent. I believe that they will not lose by it—because it is right. God will take care of their money. The world, it comes out now, is so well ordered by Him, that model lodging-houses, public baths, washhouses, insurance offices, all pay a reasonable profit to those who invest money in them—perhaps associate workshops may do the same....

But above all, so soon as these men are found working together for common profit, in the spirit of mutual self-sacrifice, let every gentleman and every Christian ... make it a point of honour and conscience to deal with the associated workmen, and get others to do the like. *It is by securing custom, far more than by gifts or loans of money, that we can help the operatives.*[*]

The positive doctrine of the Christian socialists was notable for its attack on materialism and its stress on brotherly love as against un-brotherly strife, on association and co-operation as against exploitation and competition. It was notable also for its optimism: if men would only act as Christians, they might solve their social problems. Indeed the Christian socialists were more Christian than socialistic and relied more on private philanthropy than on state intervention. Kingsley himself set an example for concrete improvement when he helped to launch the Working Men's College in London and promoted other activities of the type that organizations like the YMCA have made familiar.

The Catholic Response

Catholics, too, reacted against the evils of industrialism. Essentially, their program resembled that of the Anglican Christian socialists, but they called it by the more accurate name of "Christian democracy" or "social Christianity." Christian democracy formed a central part of the Catholic response to the problems of the modern world. As we shall see in later chapters, these problems bore heavily upon the Church. Anticlerical legislation threatened its position in France, Germany, Italy, and elsewhere. The Papal States and then Rome herself, after more than a thousand years of papal rule, passed to the control of the newly unified Kingdom of Italy. Science, nationalism, and the materialistic doctrines issuing from the industrial revolution were all competing for the loyalties of men. In Catholic countries the working

classes especially were drifting away from the Church.

The Church first tried to take refuge in the past. Pope Pius IX (1846-1878) issued in 1864 the *Syllabus of Errors,* which condemned many social theories and institutions that were not consecrated by centuries of tradition. Pius also condemned the materialism implicit in laissez-faire. But socially-minded Catholics were disturbed by the apparent hostility of the Pope to trade unions and democracy and by his statement that it was an error to suppose that he "can and ought to reconcile and harmonize himself with progress, liberalism, and modern civilization."

The Catholic Church, however, has not endured all these centuries by turning its back on progress, liberalism, and modernity. Pius IX was followed in the See of Peter by Leo XIII (1878-1903), who fully recognized the rapid changes being worked by science and technology. As a papal nuncio, he had witnessed them at first hand in the industrial regions of Belgium, France, and Germany. He knew that Catholicism was

Pope Leo XIII (1810-1903).

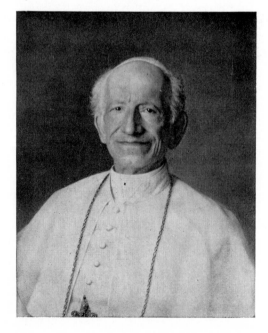

* C. Kingsley, "Cheap Clothes and Nasty," in *Alton Locke,* Eversley ed. (London, 1893), I, 103-107.

flourishing in the supposedly hostile climate of the democratic United States. Moreover, his studies of St. Thomas Aquinas convinced him that the Church had much to gain and little to lose by following the middle-of-the-road social and economic policies recommended by that great medieval Schoolman. Accordingly, Leo XIII issued a series of famous documents, notably the encyclical letter, *Rerum Novarum* ("concerning new things," 1891).

In *Rerum Novarum,* the Pope exposed the defects of capitalism with as much vigor as any socialist. Then he attacked with equal vigor the socialist view of property and the socialist doctrine of class war. He pronounced it a "great mistake" to believe

... that class is naturally hostile to class, and that the wealthy and the workingmen are intended by nature to live in mutual conflict. ... Each needs the other: Capital cannot do without Labor, nor Labor without Capital.*

Leo therefore urged the economic man to act as a Christian man of good will:

Religion teaches the laboring man ... to carry out honestly and fairly all equitable agreements freely entered into; never to injure the property, nor to outrage the person, of an employer; never to resort to violence ... ; and to have nothing to do with men of evil principles, who work upon the people with artful promises, and excite foolish hopes which usually end in useless regrets, followed by insolvency. Religion teaches the wealthy owner and the employer that their work-people are not to be accounted their bondsmen; that in every man they must respect his dignity and worth as a man and as a Christian; that labor is not a thing to be ashamed of, if we lend ear to right reason and to Christian philosophy, but is an honorable calling, enabling a man to sustain his life in a way upright and creditable; and that it is shameful and inhuman to treat men like chattels to make money by, or to look upon them merely as so much muscle or physical power.*

The state must always remain subordinate to the interests of the individuals who compose it. But this did not mean that government should adopt an attitude of laissez-faire. On the contrary, Leo repeatedly cited St. Thomas to prove that the state should indeed take measures for the general welfare. On behalf of capital, it should discourage agitators and protect property from violence. On behalf of labor, it should work to remove "the causes which lead to conflict between employer and employed." For example, it should curb exploitation by regulating child labor, limiting the hours of work, and insisting that Sundays be free for religious activity and for rest. Leo also believed that the workers must help themselves, and *Rerum Novarum* concluded with a fervent appeal for the formation of Catholic trade unions.

These Catholic unions exist today, but they are only a minority in the realm of organized labor. Neither the Christian democracy of Leo XIII nor the Christian socialism of the Anglican reformers has achieved all that the founders hoped. Yet both movements have attracted an important following and have made a real contribution to the development of a social conscience on the part of the western democracies. There is a larger element of Christian socialism than one might suspect in the British Labor party. And the Christian democrats have played an important role in the politics of many continental European states, especially since World War II. At the very least, the Anglican and Catholic reformers enriched the liberal response to the problems of industrialism and broadened the liberal appeal.

---

* *The Great Encyclical Letters of Pope Leo XIII* (New York, 1903), 218.

* *Ibid.,* 219.

Reading Suggestions
on the Economic Revolutions

(Asterisk indicates paperbound edition.)

GENERAL ACCOUNTS

W. Bowden, M. Karpovich, A. P. Usher, *An Economic History of Europe since 1750* (American Book, 1937); S. B. Clough and C. W. Cole, *Economic History of Europe*, rev. ed. (Heath, 1946); H. Heaton, *Economic History of Europe*, rev. ed. (Harper, 1948). Three useful general surveys.

T. S. Ashton, *The Industrial Revolution, 1760-1830* (Oxford Univ. Press, 1948). Clear, sound introductory account, centered on Britain.

L. Mumford, *Technics and Civilization* (Harcourt, Brace, 1934). A sweeping survey, now somewhat outdated, but still suggestive and stimulating.

SPECIAL STUDIES

P. Mantoux, *The Industrial Revolution in the 18th Century*, rev. ed. (Macmillan, 1947). A standard study of the beginnings of modern industrialism.

J. Clapham, *An Economic History of Modern Britain*, 3 vols., rev. ed. (Cambridge Univ. Press, 1930-1938). A major scholarly study of the "workshop of the world."

J. Clapham, *Economic Development of France and Germany, 1815-1914*, 4th ed. (Cambridge Univ. Press, 1936). An old book, and a good one; perhaps the most illuminating introduction to the subject.

J. L. and B. Hammond, *The Bleak Age* (*Penguin, 1947). An exposé of the social horrors wrought by industrialism.

M. C. Buer, *Health, Wealth, and Population in the Early Days of the Industrial Revolution* (Routledge, 1926). A more balanced and less gloomy account of the social consequences of economic change.

C. Brinton, *English Political Thought in the 19th Century*, new ed. (Harvard Univ. Press, 1949). Informative studies of Bentham, Mill, Owen, Kingsley, and other important figures.

J. S. Schapiro, *Liberalism and the Challenge of Fascism: Social Forces in England and France, 1815-1870* (McGraw-Hill, 1949). Suggestive essays on major thinkers.

E. Halévy, *The Growth of Philosophic Radicalism* (*Beacon, 1955). The standard study of Bentham and his Utilitarian followers.

H. W. Laidler, *Social-Economic Movements: An Historical and Comparative Survey of Socialism, Communism, Coöperation, Utopianism* (Crowell, 1949). An encyclopaedic introduction to the topics enumerated.

J. C. Schumpeter, *Capitalism, Socialism, and Democracy*, 3rd ed. (Harper, 1950). A thoughtful survey, extending down to the mid-20th century.

CHAPTER XX

E. Wilson, *To the Finland Station* (*Anchor, 1953). A sympathetic and balanced history of socialism, Utopian and Marxian.

F. E. Manuel, *The New World of Henri Saint-Simon* (Harvard Univ. Press, 1956). A significant and sympathetic reëvaluation.

F. Podmore, *Robert Owen, A Biography* (Appleton, 1924). An instructive account.

I. Berlin, *Karl Marx: His Life and Environment,* 2nd ed. (*Oxford Univ. Press, 1948). Short and excellent.

L. Schwarzchild, *The Red Prussian: The Life and Legend of Karl Marx* (Scribner's, 1947; *Universal Library). A hostile interpretation.

R. Fülöp-Miller, *Leo XIII and Our Times* (Longmans, Green, 1937). A warmly sympathetic account.

SOURCES

A. E. Bland, P. A. Brown, R. H. Tawney, eds., *English Economic History: Select Documents* (Bell, 1915). A convenient collection of source materials, including excerpts from the reports of parliamentary investigating committees.

J. S. Mill, *Autobiography; Utilitarianism; On Liberty; Representative Government* (*Liberal Arts Press; *On Liberty* also published by *Gateway Editions). Essential writings by the important Victorian liberal.

C. H. de Saint-Simon, *Selected Writings,* F. M. H. Markham, ed. (Macmillan, 1952). A most useful compilation.

The Life of Robert Owen, by Himself (Knopf, 1920). A stimulating autobiography.

K. Marx and F. Engels, *The Communist Manifesto* (*Gateway Editions).

K. Marx, *Capital* (Modern Library).

E. Burns, ed., *A Handbook of Marxism* (Random House, 1935). Excellent selections from the writings of Marx and his followers.

The Great Encyclical Letters of Pope Leo XIII (Benziger, 1903). Fundamental to the understanding of modern Catholic social thought.

HISTORICAL FICTION

C. Dickens, *Hard Times* (*Rinehart Editions). The shortest and perhaps the best of Dickens' social novels; first-rate descriptions of "Coketown" and its citizens.

Mrs. E. Gaskell, *North and South* (Dutton, 1914) and *Mary Barton* (Dutton, 1912; *Norton). Neglected but most instructive social novels by a perceptive Victorian writer.

Disraeli, *Sybil* (*Penguin). Important fictional presentation of the two nations, rich and poor, by the famous Tory statesman.

C. Kingsley, *Alton Locke* (Harper, 1850). Sentimental, but states the Christian socialist program.

E. Zola, *Germinal* (several editions). The best French novel on industrial problems; markedly more naturalistic than its English counterparts.

E. Bellamy, *Looking Backward, 2000-1887* (*Modern Library, 1951). A highly interesting adaptation of Utopian socialist views by an American of the late 19th century.

W. Morris, *News from Nowhere* (Longmans, Green, 1901). An English answer to Bellamy, advocating the destruction of machinery and the revival of medieval crafts.

The Western Democracies in the Nineteenth Century

CHAPTER XXI

WE SHALL now trace the background history of the major self-governing western states: Great Britain, France, Italy, and the United States. These are now all democracies; and though they have all had their moments—sometimes years—of lapsing from democratic standards, they are all, as the twentieth-century world goes, "old" democracies.

The smaller nations of western and northern Europe—the Netherlands, Belgium, Switzerland, the Scandinavian countries—are also part of the North Atlantic community. All these smaller states have worked out their own national variants of liberalism and democracy. In particular, the Scandinavian countries, with their homogeneous populations, their common Lutheran religion, their common traditions, and their very high rate of literacy, have sometimes surpassed the larger states in making democracy function effectively. Visitors to Copenhagen or Stockholm are impressed not only by their tidiness but also by the absence of slums and other signs of poverty. And the co-operatives of Denmark and Sweden have received much praise as the "middle way" between welfare socialism and uncontrolled economic individualism.

These smaller states have also helped to

223

maintain the balance of international politics and to shape European opinion, a role for which they are particularly well suited by their relative detachment from ambitious nationalist aspirations. In many fields their citizens have contributed proportionately more heavily to our modern western culture than their numbers would suggest. To cite only a few examples: Switzerland supplied the great historian of the Renaissance, Burckhardt, and Belgium the poet and playwright, Maeterlinck. From Finland came the composer Sibelius; from Norway, Ibsen and his modern social dramas; from Holland, the physicist Lorentz, winner of the Nobel Prize in 1902; and from Sweden, Nobel himself, the munitions king who endowed the Nobel prizes for peaceful achievement.

Spain, too, had a varied and interesting history in the nineteenth century, swinging between conservative monarchy and radical republicanism. But Spain was now a minor power, and though especially in the novel, she had a distinguished cultural achievement, we must postpone longer consideration of Spanish history until in the Civil War of the 1930's Spain once more enters the mainstream of events. We must, now, turn to the states that fate, or history, has assigned the major roles in our story. Of these in the nineteenth century, Britain was unquestionably the first, the leading power.

I: Britain, 1815-1914

The Process of Reform

In the years immediately after Waterloo, Britain went through a typical postwar economic crisis. Unsold goods accumulated, and the working classes experienced widespread unemployment and suffering. Although trade unions were forbidden by the Combination Acts, the workers none the less asserted themselves in strikes and in popular agitation that helped prepare the way for the parliamentary Reform Bill of 1832. But by the 1820's economic conditions had improved, and Britain had embarked on the first stage of those political reforms that were to make of her a democratic state.

Into this process, of course, there went economic and social drives, and the Britain of our mid-twentieth century was to be not only a very complete political democracy but also in part an economic and a social democracy. But the process of reform focused always on concrete political action. It is a process of which the British are very proud, for it was achieved without revolution and almost without violence or indeed any serious civil disturbance. The fruits of discussion, education, and propaganda were consolidated in a specific "reform bill," followed by another stage of preparatory work and another reform bill.

Parliamentary Reform

The process is most clearly marked in the great milestones of parliamentary reform that transformed the government of Britain from an oligarchy into a democracy. Britain emerged from the Napoleonic Wars with its executive, a cabinet of ministers presided over by a prime minister, wholly under the control of Parliament. The Crown was now, as the nineteenth-century political writer Bagehot was to put it, largely "decorative." On that decorative post, held for most of the century (1837-1901) by Queen Victoria, who has given her name to an age and a culture, were centered the patriotic emotions of loyal British subjects. Victoria never thought of herself as a mere figurehead; she was a determined, sensible, emotional, conventional, and intellectually unsophisticated Victorian lady.

Real power lay in the legislative branch, in the early nineteenth century by no means directly representative of the masses. The House of Lords, which for all save money bills had equal power with the lower house, was composed of the small, privileged class of peers born to their seats in the Lords, with the addition of a relatively few new peers created by the Crown from time to time. The House of Commons, its members unpaid, was recruited wholly from the gentry, the professional classes, and very successful businessmen, and was chosen by less than one-sixth of the adult male population. Both the working classes in town and country and the run of prosperous but not spectacularly successful middle-class people were excluded from the franchise. Moreover, the largely rural South, once the most populous area of the kingdom, now had more representatives than it deserved, including a large contingent from the "rotten boroughs," towns of very small population, or, as in the notorious Old Sarum, none at all. The teeming new industrial centers of the North, such as Manchester, Liverpool, Sheffield, were grossly underrepresented.

Projects to begin modernizing the structure of representation came close to being adopted in the late eighteenth century. But the wars with Revolutionary and Napoleonic France made reform impossible; in wartime and in the immediate postwar years, even moderate reformers were denounced as Jacobins. In 1819, a nervous Tory government permitted the soldiery to break up a large and peaceful mass meeting assembled at St. Peter's Field near Manchester to hear speeches on parliamentary reform. Suppression, however, was not the British way, and soon after "Peterloo" the great campaign of agitation which produced the parliamentary reform of 1832 was resumed.

In this campaign the middle class did not hesitate to appeal to the lower classes for aid by using freely the language of popular rights, and even of universal suffrage. Many popular leaders talked as if the Reform Bill would bring political democracy to England at once. Yet much of the preparation for reform was actually the work, not of liberal agitators, but of conservatives. Guided by enlightened individuals such as Canning and Robert Peel, the Tory governments of the 1820's lifted the various restrictions on civil rights imposed during the war period and the postwar crisis. They partially repealed the Combination Acts against trade unions; reformed the antiquated criminal code, so that, for example, the theft of a sheep no longer carried with it in theory a death penalty; and began the reduction in protective tariffs that was to lead to free trade. The seventeenth-century Test Act, which, though not observed, legally excluded nonconformists from public life, was repealed. So, under the name of "Catholic emancipation," were the laws that really did exclude Catholics from public life. In international politics, Canning lined Britain up as a "liberal" power against the conservative monarchies of central and eastern Europe (see Chapter XIX).

The Reform Bill itself was enacted under the leadership of the Whig Lord Grey, backed by a full apparatus of agitation and pressure groups. Tory opponents of parliamentary reform were won over—even the very Tory Duke of Wellington was converted at the last moment—until only the Tory House of Lords blocked the measure. At this climax, Lord Grey persuaded King William IV (1830-1837) to threaten the creation by royal prerogative of enough new Whig peers to put the reform through the Lords. This threat, combined with the real danger of popular violence, put the bill through on June 4, 1832.

This First Reform Bill did not bring political democracy to England. It did diminish the great irregularities of electoral districts, wiping out more than fifty rotten boroughs and giving seats in the Commons to more than forty hitherto unrepresented industrial towns. The number of voters was increased by about 50 per cent so that virtually all the middle class got the vote, but the bill by no means enfranchised the working classes.

From the new ground of the partly reformed Parliament, the agitation for a still wider suffrage went on. The middle class had won its gains, not in the name of its own admission to an oligarchy, but in the name of the right of all competent men to have the vote. With the gradual spread of literacy to the lower classes, with their gradual political awakening, the middle classes could not find very good arguments for refusing to extend the franchise; moreover, a good many of the British middle classes sincerely believed in a gradual widening of the franchise.

The Second Reform Bill came in 1867, by one of the ironies of history put through by that Tory party that traditionally stood for resistance to the widening of the suffrage. But the three decades after 1832 had produced a ground swell of agitation for more parliamentary reform, a ground swell with many cross-currents from downright radical republicanism to a resigned belief that democracy was irresistibly the wave of the future. Disraeli (1804-1881), the Tory leader in the Commons, almost certainly thought that if one party did not put through reform the other one would. With a politician's sense of reality, he decided his party might as well get the credit. Disraeli also thought that the newly enfranchised urban working class, hostile to their middle-class employers, would vote for the Tories, who were country gentle-

Benjamin Disraeli (1804-1881).

men, good responsible caretakers of the lower classes, not exploiters like the middle-class businessmen. He was proved wrong by the very first general election after the reform, for in 1868 the Tories were turned out of office.

The Second Reform Bill did not introduce full manhood suffrage. Like the first, it was a piecemeal change that brought the electoral districts into more uniformity and equality, but left them still divided into boroughs and shires as in the Middle Ages. It about doubled the number of voters in Britain by giving the vote to householders—that is, settled men owning or paying rent on their dwellings—in the boroughs. But the Reform Bill of 1867 did not give the vote in rural areas to men without the "stake" of property—that is, men who did not own a piece of real estate or even a bank account, men who were therefore felt by many upper-class Victorians to be irresponsible, willing to vote away other people's property. It did, however, give the vote to several millions of wage-earners without other sources of income.

The next reforms in the series were, more logically, put through by the Liberal party, the former Whigs under the leadership of Gladstone (1809-1898). Even these reforms of 1884 and 1885 did not introduce universal manhood suffrage or a neat democratic uniformity. They still tinkered with medieval forms, which were now pretty completely modernized. Lodgers and a few "floaters" (people whose specific "home" was hard to define in settled Victorian terms), and women were still without the vote; districts were not quite equalized; a few thousand voters with business property in one district and a home in another could vote twice; and graduates of Oxford and Cambridge could vote a second time for special university members; indeed, a university man with scattered property could, if he could get around to the polls fast enough, cast a dozen votes. Only in 1918, in a major Reform Act, was plural voting limited to two votes—a property and a university vote. Still, by 1885 Britain was clearly a political democracy, in which the majority of the people, through their representatives in the House of Commons, were politically "sovereign." Perhaps not quite, for the hereditary House of Lords had still a veto power over legislation that did not specifically appropriate money. This last limitation was removed in 1911, in a kind of codicil to the reforms of the nineteenth century, when the Parliament Act of that year ended the real power of the Lords, leaving them with no more than a delaying or suspensive veto.

William Gladstone (1809-1898) in 1866.

The Two-Party System: Liberals and Conservatives

We have outlined above the legislative landmarks in the nineteenth-century democratization of the British constitution. Now the dynamics of that process are certainly in part explicable in terms of the "class struggle." Broadly speaking, over the century the "have nots"—perhaps better, the "have littles"—gained a voice in the politics of Britain they did not have in 1815. But the central human institution of the dynamics, the *party*, clearly does not present a neat alignment of the "have littles" against the "have much." That should be clear even from the very summary account of the reform bills we have given. The Disraeli who took the "leap in the dark" of 1867 was a conservative, not a radical leader, and he hoped that the newly enfranchised workingmen would vote conservative, not radical. He was wrong in 1868, but in the longer run not wholly wrong, for after his death his party was returned to power triumphantly under the even wider franchise of 1885 for a ten-year tenure of power, 1895-1905. Some British poor and middling men obviously still continued to vote for the party of their "betters."

The fact is that the nineteenth-century British party system was not clearly based on an opposition between a possessing class and a non-possessing class. The eighteenth-century oligarchic factions of Whigs and Tories were transformed in the course of the nineteenth century into the modern mass parties of Liberals and Conservatives, both organized on a national basis, with local committees at the bottom, and making full use of party machinery for getting out the vote. The Whigs, in broadening into the Liberals, sought an electoral base ranging from the old great families, still represented in the early and middle part of the century by men like Grey and Palmerston, to the little and big businessmen, the nonconformists, the radical white-collar men, and the politically conscious workingmen. The Tories, in broadening into Conservatives, sought a base, first under Peel and then under Disraeli, from the country gentlemen, army and navy officers, and Anglican clergymen to the agricultural laborers, the small townspeople, and even some of the urban white-collar and working classes. Both parties frankly appealed to the "people"; and the Conservatives, with their "Primrose League" in memory of Disraeli's favorite flower, their appeal to love of Queen and country, their record of social legislation against the worst evils of the new factory system, did at least as good a job in building a party machine as did the Liberals. In the Victorian heyday, the librettist Gilbert was quite justified in having his guardsman sing in the operetta "Iolanthe":

> That every boy and every gal
> That's born into the world alive
> Is either a little Liberal
> Or else a little Conservative.

The Two-Party System: An Explanation

The two-party system is almost wholly confined to the English-speaking lands, to Britain, the United States, and the British Commonwealth countries. On the Continent, not only in France, Italy, and pre-Hitler Germany, but also in the little democracies of Scandinavia, Switzerland, Holland, and Belgium, the multi-party system has prevailed, and governments are generally coalitions of parties with separate organizations. English-speaking opinion probably exaggerates the defects and dangers of multi-party democracy. But it is clear that a two-party democracy does have distinct advantages in the way of stability and continuity of policy, if only because a given group can enjoy a longer, more assured tenure of power. The historian must attempt somehow to explain why the English-speaking peoples have developed this unique institution. He must seek somewhat different explanations for Britain and for the United States, for though both have two-party systems, their total political situations and traditions are far from alike.

In terms of political psychology, the two-party system means that the millions of individual voters who make up each party are in greater agreement than disagreement over what the party stands for; or at least that when they vote for a candidate they feel he stands more for what they want than for what they don't want. Each voter makes some kind of compromise *within himself*, takes something less in practice than he would ideally like. This sort of compromise the French voter of the 1880's for instance did not need to make, at any rate not to anything like the same degree as the British voter. The Frenchman could choose, from among a dozen or more platforms and candidates, the one tailored closest to his desires.

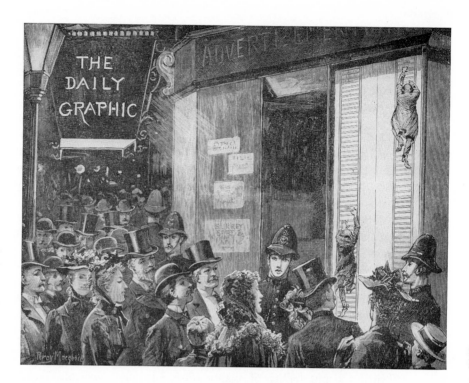

The British two-party system. London crowds outside a newspaper office watching returns from the Conservative-Liberal competition in the election of 1892.

We must still ask why Englishmen made these compromises, why they agreed more than they disagreed. The answer must be sought in the long working out of British history. One part of it lies in the relative security of the islands from external foes, in the long years in which British political habits of moderation and compromise could mature without the constant pressure of foreign wars. The immediate crisis of war may indeed promote a temporary unity in a threatened nation, like the France of 1792-1794. But long, steady exposure to war danger—and all continental states were so exposed—seems to promote psychological tendencies to seek final and extreme solutions.

This same relative isolation of Britain also contributed to the relatively mild form that the universal western struggle between feudalism and the new-model centralized state took there. In France, and on the Continent generally, the new model triumphed only in the seventeenth century, and in the form of divine-right monarchy. Continental states in the nineteenth century had only just gone through—or were still going through—the popular revolutionary modification of absolutism, and were still torn by major class antagonisms between a noble privileged class, backed usually by orthodox religion, and a middle class. In England, as we have seen in earlier chapters, that struggle had taken place a full century and a half earlier and had never been quite as bitter as on the Continent. It had left England in charge of a ruling class that was itself the product of a compromise between the old landed gentry and the new commercial classes, a ruling class that could develop within itself habits of moderation and compromise. The deep abyss the French Revolution had dug between nineteenth-century royalists and republicans and between "clericals" and "anticlericals" on the Continent did not exist in nineteenth-century England.

Thus, even more important than the fact that the Liberals and Conservatives each held together as parties whose members could sink differences in a common party action is the fact that both parties had a wide area of mutual agreement above and beyond party. To put it quite baldly, there wasn't much difference between the Conservatives and the Liberals. When one went out of power and the other came in, the ship of state tacked a bit, but it did not change direction. The Conservative Disraeli and the Liberal Gladstone were perhaps not quite shadowboxing in their heated parliamentary exchanges, but they clearly were not fighting to kill, nor perhaps even for the knockout.

To sum up, government by discussion, Her Majesty's Government and Her Majesty's Opposition equally loyal to established ways, under the shelter of the English Channel and the British navy, in a prosperous land without deep-seated class antagonisms or insuperable class barriers and rigidities—all this had developed in the British people habits of compromise, of law-abidingness, a sort of political sportsmanship. And these habits survive even in the mid-twentieth century, when Victorian geographical security has gone with the airplane and Victorian economic preponderance has gone with the rise of competing industrial nations. The British, who once cut off a king's head and drove another king into exile, have for nearly two centuries enjoyed remarkable political stability. Why these people, once thought hard to govern, have had so stable a government, is still by no means wholly understood.

Reforms
of the Utilitarians

The Reform Bill of 1832 was followed by a series of major reforms that helped make over, not merely British political life, but British economic and social life as well. The inspiration of these reforms came in large part from a small but influential middle-class group, the "Philosophic Radicals" or Utilitarians (see Chapter XX).

These disciples of Bentham and of the Enlightenment believed that men are, if once educated, impelled by rational self-interest and thus automatically do what is best for themselves and all their fellows. Under the influence of the Philosophic Radicals, English local government and the English legal system were made simpler, and were cleansed of some of the impediments to efficient government action left by the long accumulation of traditional forms, now become "red-tape." Legal procedures, for instance, which had been so complicated that the Chancery Court was many years behind its backlog of cases, were gradually speeded up. In local government, though many medieval offices remained at least in name, the essential work was done by an elective council and by elective officers with supervisory powers over the professional civil servants—including now for the first time professional "policemen." Indeed, London policemen are still called "Bobbies," after Robert Peel's innovation of the late 1820's.

The middle-class radicals, however, believed firmly that that government governs best which governs least, and they sought rather to expedite that minimum of government than to add to its tasks. They believed in education, but not in compulsory public education; private initiative would in their opinion do well what the government would do poorly and tyrannically. Large-scale government reform of British popular education had therefore to wait until 1870. Meanwhile, the private initiative preached by the Utilitarians sponsored mechanics' institutes and other means of adult and "practical" education. It also sponsored all sorts of private schools, and universities in London, Manchester, and some other British cities. These universities, resembling in many ways our American urban universities, first broke into the centuries-old monopoly of Oxford and Cambridge. Although these "provincial" or "red-brick" universities have today attained great practical and intellectual distinction, they are still socially by no means the equals of Oxford and Cambridge.

The typical Utilitarian reform, the one that stirred up public opinion most thoroughly, was the New Poor Law of 1834. This bill codified, centralized, and made more coherent a complicated system of public relief that had originated in the Elizabethan Poor Law of 1601 and earlier Tudor legislation. But it did more: it shifted the base of this relief. The old methods of home relief, "outdoor relief," had gradually come to permit supplementary payments from the parishes to able-bodied poor working on low wages, supplements for children, and in general by no means generous but still easy-going "doles" direct to families in their homes. The new system would have none of this laxness, this encouragement of men in what the Utilitarian, in spite of his belief in human rationality, rather feared was their "natural" laziness. Poor Law Unions united parishes for greater efficiency, permitted greater supervision by the central government in London, and supplied in the workhouses the "indoor relief" by which able-bodied paupers were made as uncomfortable as decency would allow. These pains, it was held, would encourage them to try to become self-supporting outside. The New Poor Law offended humanitarians in the upper classes, but from the point of view of middle-class business interests it had the decided merit of making poor relief both more efficient and more economical.

Free Trade

Greatest of these Utilitarian reforms in its long-run consequences was the repeal of the Corn Laws in 1846, after a long campaign headed by the Anti-Corn-Law League (see Chapter XX). What these pressure-group agitators wanted, and ultimately got, was a political economy in which food and other raw materials were imported from abroad without tariffs, and manufactures were exported to pay for the imports. In the long run—in another century —the difficulty for Britain would lie in the fact that other parts of the world too would become industrial workshops. In the short run, in the early nineteenth century, the difficulty was that protective tariffs in favor of English agriculture made importation of the cheapest possible foodstuffs from abroad impossible. To this difficulty the English industrialists addressed themselves in the campaign against the Corn Laws. Their victory was achieved in 1846 by the conversion of the Conservative leader Peel to their cause, and by the alliance of Peelites and Liberals that put the bill through. Britain was now a free-trade nation, the only major free-trade nation in a world that never quite lost its mercantilist (see Chapter XV, Vol. I) preconceptions and habits.

Labor
and Factory Legislation

Still another series of reforms helped make the prosperous England of Gladstone and Disraeli. These were the Factory Acts, begun in 1802 and 1819 with bills sponsored by Peel's father. Addicts of the economic interpretation of history hold that middle-class people put through reforms like those of the Poor Law and the repeal of the Corn Laws, but that the landed gentry and upper-class intellectuals, jealous of the new city wealth and outraged by the ugliness of the new industrial towns, put through reforms like those of the Factory Acts regulating hours of labor, sanitation, and the labor of women and children. It is true that many leaders of the movement to use the power of the state to regulate some part of economic life were not themselves businessmen or industrialists. They were either members of the

Tory ruling class, like the Peels, or intellectuals, like Coleridge, Disraeli, Carlyle, Ruskin, and Matthew Arnold, who preached against the horrors of working-class life in prosperous Victorian England. And it is true that the formal philosophy of the British business class was laissez-faire. But the practice was a different matter: none of the Factory Acts and similar reforms of the nineteenth century could really have gone through Parliament successfully without some support from both political parties. Moreover, neither landed gentry nor industrialists and businessmen were mutually exclusive "classes" in a neat Marxist sense. Rather, they were thoroughly mingled in education, marriage, and even in economic interests, since the gentry invested in stocks and bonds and the industrialists invested in landed estates. The elder Peel, father of the Factory Acts, was a self-made industrialist.

The Factory Acts followed a sequence not unlike the sequence of acts that reformed the suffrage. The first acts were very modest indeed; they underlined the frightful conditions they were designed to remedy. That of 1819, for instance, applied only to the cotton industry, forbade night work for children, and limited day work to twelve hours. Even so, it provided for no really effective inspection, and was violated with impunity by many employers. The Act of 1833, forbidding child labor entirely below the age of nine, and restricting it to nine hours for those below thirteen, and twelve for those below eighteen, marked an important stage by setting up salaried inspectors to enforce the law.

By the end of the nineteenth century, there was on the books a whole code of labor legislation, regulating hours of labor for everyone, giving special protection to women and children, and including provisions that made the employer responsible for workmen's compensation in industrial accidents. Then in 1911 came the great National Insurance Act, which provided through combined payments from the state, from employers and from employees, compulsory health and unemployment insurance. The "welfare state" was firmly established in Britain well before the Labor party of our own day had come to power.

Education

The same story of piecemeal but cumulative reform holds true in education. The commonly held Victorian idea that education is not properly a function of the state postponed a general education act until 1870. The issue was complicated by the wrangling of Anglicans and nonconformists, for many existing schools were controlled by a private society that made instruction in the doctrines of the Church of England compulsory. But even before 1870 a government committee had been supplementing local education boards by making grants from the national treasury (in 1860 these grants reached nearly a million pounds), by providing an inspection service, and by helping to organize teacher training. School attendance, however, was not compulsory, and the average age for leaving school was eleven years. After most workingmen got the vote in 1867, worried Tories—and Liberals—began to urge the slogan, "Educate your masters." The bill of 1870, put through under Gladstone's Minister of Education, William Forster, did not quite set up compulsory national education at the elementary level. It did permit the local school boards to compel attendance, and it did extend national aid and supervision. Church schools continued to get aid from taxes levied by the central government, however—an offense to radicals who wanted complete separation of Church and State. Non-sectarian religious instruction was given even in the equivalent of our public schools supported by local taxes, but it was not compulsory.

Beginnings were made in publicly supported schools at the secondary level, though the British "public school," which in American terms is a "private school," continued until our own day to maintain a privileged position in the British social system. In comparison with the public school systems in Germany, France, and the United States, British education on the eve of World War I was administratively complex and full of anomalies. On the whole, though, it got the job done, and the general level of popular education in the British Isles was at least as high as in the other liberal democracies.

Chartism

The most radical of major organized reform movements in nineteenth-century England was Chartism, which played a major role in the political excitements of the 1830's and 1840's, and greatly alarmed the conservative classes. The Chartists were the closest English equivalent of the radical parties which on the Continent carried on the Jacobin tradition of the French Revolution, mingled with the elements of nascent socialism. The Chartists had a formal program drawn up in a "People's Charter," calling for universal manhood suffrage, the secret ballot, abolition of property requirements for members of Parliament, payment of members, equal electoral districts, and annually elected Parliaments. Their strength lay in the new urban industrial proletariat, and especially in the more active and radical members of the proletariat, men who clearly believed that if they got the political democracy they wanted the masses would vote themselves, if not full socialism, at least a considerable degree of leveling of incomes, probably by graduated income taxes. The movement petered out in a monster petition to Parliament which was never even considered, and in the rising prosperity of the 1850's and 1860's it was effectively stifled. Yet of

the original Chartist program all but the demand for annually elected Parliaments, which soon seemed pointless even to radicals, was achieved by act of Parliament in 1918.

Foreign Policy

Nowhere does the basic unity that underlies the party strife of nineteenth-century Britain come out more clearly than in foreign relations. The strife is real enough on hundreds of concrete matters of detail; but so is the unity in the broad lines of British policy. Almost all Englishmen (an unavoidable term, which has to include Scottish, Welsh, and Ulstermen) were agreed on the fundamental position of Britain: maintain the European state-system in balance, preferably by diplomatic rather than military action, but seek no new territories in Europe; police the seas with the British navy; open world markets to British goods; maintain—and in Africa extend—the vast network of the British Empire, made up of self-governing, English-speaking lands and colonial "possessions" in lands inhabited by the darker-skinned peoples. It is certainly true that the Liberals verbally and emotionally sided in Europe with the liberal nationalist movements, that they sympathized with the struggling Italians, Greeks, and Poles, and that they disliked the old Metternichian powers, especially Russia. It is even true that a Liberal —or better, a belated Whig—foreign minister like Palmerston in mid-century pursued an active policy of near-intervention in behalf of oppressed nationalities, and that British benevolence was a factor in the attainment of Italian unity.

Yet the only European war in which Britain became involved between 1815 and 1914 was the Crimean War of 1854-56, in which France and England went to war as allies against Russia to protect Turkey and their own Near Eastern interests from Russian aggression (see Chapter XXII). This was a somewhat blundering war on both sides. But it at least checked Russian advances for a time and made the ultimate disposition of the Balkan regions of the decaying Turkish Empire unavoidably a matter for joint action by all the great powers. It was, in fact, a typical balance-of-power war in which Britain played its traditional role of taking arms against a major power that seemed about to add unduly to its lands or its "spheres of influence."

Imperial Policy

On imperial policy it seems at first glance as though British public opinion really was deeply divided. Disraeli and Gladstone were never so gladiatorially fierce as when the Conservative defended the greatness of the Empire and the Liberal attacked imperialism at home and abroad as un-Christian, illiberal, and unprofitable. And it would be absurd to maintain that in action there was no real difference between the two. Disraeli, on the one side, bought up the financially embarrassed Khedive of Egypt's controlling shares in the French-built Suez Canal (1875), thus initiating the British control of Egypt, and triumphantly made Queen Victoria Empress of India (1876). On the other side, Gladstone, in his succeeding ministry, withdrew British troops from Afghanistan in 1880, conceded independence to the Boer Republics in South Africa by the Pretoria Convention of 1881, and in 1884-1885 neglected General Gordon surrounded by rebels in the Sudan. Yet Gladstone kept British armies on the northwest frontier of India. It was under his administration in 1882 that the British actually bombarded Alexandria and monopolized control of Egypt. Gladstone did send troops to rescue Gordon, though they arrived too late, and even in South Africa the Boer Republics were freed only under the "suzerainty" of Britain. In short, Gladstone

regretted and no doubt even neglected the Empire; but he kept it (for details, see Chapter XXIV).

The Irish Problem

Much nearer home, a nationality problem grew more acute as the nineteenth century came to a close, and did draw something more than a verbal line between Conservatives and Liberals. This was the Irish problem, a problem that had beset the English in one form or another, now acute and now mild, ever since the Norman-English conquest of Ireland in the twelfth century. The English, and the Scots who came to settle in the North of Ireland province of Ulster in the sixteenth and seventeenth centuries, had remained as a privileged Protestant landowning group in the midst of a subject population of Catholic Irish peasants. For three centuries, religious, political, and economic problems in Ireland had remained unsolved. As the nineteenth century opened the English attempted to solve the political problem by a formal union of the two kingdoms, with Irish members admitted to the British Parliament, in which they were of course a minority. On January 1, 1801, began the United Kingdom of Great Britain and Ireland. In the prevailing temper of nineteenth-century Britain, it was quite impossible to deny the Irish natives all political rights; and indeed, beginning with the Catholic Emancipation Act of 1829, which allowed Irish voters to elect Catholics to office, most of the various reforms we have outlined above were extended to Ireland. The Irish, led by Daniel O'Connell, the "Great Emancipator," organized politically to press for reforms and, eventually, for home rule of the kind the dominions were to achieve (see Chapter XXIV). They sought not only for political home rule, but also for land reforms, and for disestablishment of the Anglican Church in Ireland—

that is, abolition of a state church supported by taxes levied on both members and non-members of the church.

Irish hatred for the English was fanned by the disastrous potato famine of the 1840's, when blight ruined a crop essential to the Irish food supply. Although the beginnings of modern transportation by railway and steamship existed, the British government was not organized for prompt and efficient relief measures, nor was the kind of international organization for such relief afforded nowadays by the Red Cross yet in existence. The result was a medieval famine in the heart of modern western civilization, in which tens of thousands died of starvation, and other tens of thousands were forced to migrate, mostly to the United States. The immigrants added to British difficulties, for they carried their inevitable hatreds with them, and formed pressure groups, like the Fenian Brotherhood organized in New York in 1858 to raise funds to aid Irish resistance and to make trouble generally for the British wherever they could. Indeed, the existence of these British-hating Irish-Americans was to be for nearly a century a serious problem for those directing American foreign policy, notably in the first World War.

British governments made piecemeal reforms. The Anglican Church in Ireland was disestablished in 1869 and in the next year an Irish Land Act began a series of agrarian reforms that were designed to protect the tenant from "rack-renting"—the extraction by the landlord, often an absentee member of the British "garrison," of as high a rent as the tenants could pay. The reforms were neither far-reaching nor rapid enough to satisfy the Irish. Moreover, the emotional strength of Irish nationalism grew with the spread of elementary education and the usual literary and cultural forms of national self-consciousness. The Irish question was not just a matter of land, or of religion, but also of a peculiarly intense form of underdog awareness of cultural differences and of nationality. Then in the 1870's a brilliant Irish leader arose, Charles Parnell, himself a Protestant descendant of the "garrison," but a firm Irish patriot. Under the leadership of Parnell in the British Parliament, the Irish nationalists were welded into a firm, well-disciplined party which, though it held less than a hundred seats in the House of Commons of the now United Kingdom, could often swing the balance between Liberals and Conservatives.

The critical step came when in 1885 Gladstone was converted to Home Rule, and introduced his first Home Rule Bill. This bill provided for a separate Irish parliament with some restrictions on its sovereignty, and of course under the Crown. Gladstone's decision split his own Liberal party in something like the way Peel's conversion to Free Trade had split the Conservatives in 1846. A group led by Joseph Chamberlain, who had begun political life as the reform leader of the great city of Birmingham, seceded under the name of "Liberal Unionists." In effect, they joined the Conservative party, which was often known in the next few decades, so great were the passions aroused in Great Britain by this proposed cutting loose of Ireland, simply as the "Unionist" party. Gladstone lost the election brought on by the split, and Home Rule was dropped for the moment.

Agitation continued in Ireland. It became more bitter when Parnell, involved in a divorce scandal, was dropped by the virtuous Gladstone and by some of his own Irish followers. In 1892, however, Gladstone won a close election on the Irish issue —or, rather, he obtained enough English seats to get a Second Home Rule Bill through the Commons with the aid of eighty-one Irish nationalists. The bill was defeated, however, in the Conservative House of Lords, and was dropped once more. The Conservatives, when they came in for their ten-year reign in 1895, sought to "kill Home Rule by kindness," carrying several land reform bills that furthered the process of making Ireland a land of small peasant proprietors.

But Ireland was now beyond the reach of kindness, and Irish problems were no longer—if they ever had been—largely economic and administrative. Irish nationalism was now a full cult, nourished by a remarkable literary revival in English and in Gaelic which produced writers like W. B. Yeats, John Synge, and Lady Augusta Gregory. Irish men and women everywhere —including definitely the Irish-Americans —were keyed to a pitch of emotional excitement. They would be satisfied with nothing less than an independent Irish nation.

The Liberals, back in power after 1905, found they needed the votes of the Irish nationalists to carry through their proposal for ending the veto power of the Lords. After some soul-searching, the Liberals struck the bargain: Home Rule in return for the Parliament Act. They introduced in 1912 a Home Rule Bill which—the Parliament Act in 1911 having destroyed the veto power of the Lords—was placed on the books as a law. It never went into force, however, for as Home Rule seemed about to become a fact the predominantly Protestant North of Ireland, the province of Ulster, bitterly opposed to separation from Great Britain, was organized to resist by force of arms. The Home Rule Bill as passed carried the rider that it was not to go into effect until the Ulster question was settled. The outbreak of war in 1914 made such a settlement out of the question, and the stage was set for the Irish Revolution of the 1920's (see Chapter XXVIII).

The Threat to Free Trade

As Great Britain approached the twentieth century, then, new problems arose to disturb the underlying serenity and assurance of the Victorian Age. The South African and Irish troubles, the rising international tensions that were to lead to World War I (see Chapter XXV), and the difficulties of adjusting the new distribution of national income made necessary by the rise of the "welfare state," confronted the British people all at once. Though here as always in history we must avoid the temptation to seek a single underlying cause, there was undoubtedly one major factor at work. The long lead Britain had gained in the industrial revolution was being lost as other nations acquired the technical skills of large-scale production. Germany, the Low Countries, Switzerland, the United States, and in a measure all the West, were competing with Britain on the world market.

Under such conditions, it was natural that some Britishers should come to doubt the wisdom of the Free Trade policies that had won the day in 1846. For the Germans and others were not only underselling the British abroad; they were actually invading the British home market. Why not protect that market by a tariff system? Few Britishers were foolish enough to believe that the home islands, already by the 1880's too densely populated to feed themselves and constitute a self-sufficient economy, could surround themselves with a simple tariff wall. But the Empire was world-wide, with abundant resources, with thousands of square miles of agricultural lands. Within it the classical mercantilist interchange of manufactures for raw materials could still in theory provide a balanced economic system. Britain could still be, if not the workshop of the world, at least the workshop of a quarter of the world, the British Commonwealth and Empire.

The same Joseph Chamberlain who led the secession from the Liberals on the question of Home Rule for Ireland also led a secession on an issue of more fundamental importance. He became a protectionist and imperialist. He gave special importance to the establishment of a system of imperial preference through which the whole complex of lands under the Crown would be knit together in a tariff union. Many Conservatives, never wholly reconciled to Free Trade, welcomed the issue, and the new Unionist party made protection a major plank in its program. Liberal opposition, however, was still much too strong, and there was opposition also in Conservative ranks. Chamberlain, reversing the aims but imitating the methods of Cobden and the Anti-Corn Law League of the 1840's, organized a Tariff Reform League. In 1903, he made in cabinet sweeping proposals that would have restored moderate duties on foodstuffs and raw materials (largely to give a basis for negotiating with the dominions, which already had tariff systems of their own) and on foreign manufactured goods. But the Conservative leader, Balfour, did not dare go so far, and Chamberlain resigned with his bill unpassed. Indeed, Chamberlain, who had already split the Liberal party on Home Rule, now split the Conservatives on tariff-reform. The new Liberal government after 1905 continued the policy of Free Trade. The rift Chamberlain had made in the old Liberal party was, however, never really repaired. Its right wing was driven to Toryism; its left wing to the Labor party.

The Welfare State

The Liberals were, however, committed to another policy as contrary to the classical philosophy of laissez-faire as was protectionism. This was the welfare state—social security through compulsory insurance managed by the state, and in part financed by the state, minimum-wage laws, progressive taxation on incomes and inheritances, compulsory free public education, public works and services of all kinds. The dramatic point in the working out of the program was the "People's Budget" of 1909, introduced by a new figure on the political stage, a Welshman, the Liberal Chancellor of the Exchequer, Lloyd George (1863-1945). This budget, which frankly proposed to tax the rich to finance the new welfare measures, and also the rising naval costs brought on by the armament race with Germany (see Chapter XXV), was clearly no ordinary tax measure. It was a means of altering the social and economic structure of Britain. Its opponents rightly called it "not a budget, but a revolution." It passed the Commons, but was thrown out by the Lords, even though it was a "money bill." The Liberals went to the country for the second time in 1910 and after a close and exciting election were able to put through the Parliament Act of 1911, which took away from the Lords all power to alter a money bill, and left them with no more than a delaying power of not less than two years over all other legislation. The Liberal program of social legislation was saved. It was saved under conditions strongly reminiscent of 1832, for the new king, George V (1910-1936), had promised Prime Minister Asquith that if necessary he would create enough new peerages—which might have meant several hundred—to put the Parliament Act through the House of Lords. As in 1832, the threat was enough, and the Peers yielded.

But was it a *Liberal* program? The dissenting Liberals who had followed Joseph Chamberlain out of the party in the 1880's thought not, and it was normal enough for Chamberlain's two sons, Austen and Neville, who played an important part in twentieth-century politics, to think of themselves as Conservatives. For what happened in the generation after 1880 was a major change in the political orientation of British parties. The Liberals, who had believed that that government governs best which governs least, and least expensively, had come to believe that the state must interfere in economic life to help the underdog, had come to adopt Lloyd George's plan for redistributing the national wealth by social insurance financed by taxation of the rich and well-to-do. And the Conservatives, who in the mid-nineteenth century had stood for factory acts and at least mild forms of the welfare state, were now in large part committed to a laissez-faire program against government "intervention," a program astonishingly like that of the Liberals of 1850. Whatever the future verdict of historians on the "welfare state" of the twentieth century, they will note that Great Britain was the first great democratic society to institute such a state.

The Labor Party

One factor in this change had been the growth of the British Labor party, which originated in a number of groups formed in the late nineteenth century. Labor, though never perfectly unified, had developed by 1905 into a party able to command fifty-three seats in the Commons. It wanted the welfare state, and indeed some Laborites wanted a socialist state in which at least the major industries were nationalized. Part of the motivation for the Liberal program of social legislation was a desire to forestall Labor. Just as in 1867 the Tories had "walked away with the Whigs' clothes" and had given the workingman the vote, so in 1911 the Liberals stole Labor's clothes and gave the

workingman social security. But these tactics worked no better in the twentieth century than in the nineteenth, and the workingmen on the whole stuck by the Labor party. The Liberal party began a long decline, hastened by the upsetting effects of World War I, by the addition of many new working-class voters by the Reform Act of 1918, and no doubt by many other factors.

Not all the motivation of the Liberals in these early years of the twentieth century was, however, mere fear of Labor. In part, their conversion from laissez-faire to social security was a positive one, a sincere belief that the logic of their democratic assumptions must drive them to raise the general standard of living in Britain by state action. Something broadly analogous was happening throughout the democratic West—in France, in the smaller democracies, and, a few decades later, in the United States. An important part of the bourgeoisie in all these countries swung over, not to doctrinaire socialism, but to programs of social legislation put through by the usual machinery of change under a wide democratic suffrage. The English Chartists back in the early nineteenth century had had the apparently naive belief that universal suffrage would pave the way to greater social and economic equality. In the long run, events were to prove that the Chartists were far from being entirely wrong. The welfare state began in a democracy.

II: France—Second Empire and Third Republic

The Coup d'État of 1851

A century ago France seemed to many English-speaking critics, as she seems to many today, a rather uncertain member

of the community of nations ruled by the democratic decencies—that is, government by discussion, peaceful alternation of "ins" and "outs" through the working of the party system, and the usual freedoms of the "rights of man." The democratic revolution, so optimistically begun in 1848 (see Chapter XIX), had by 1852 brought still another Bonaparte to the throne of France in Napoleon III, nephew of the first Napoleon. (Note that "Napoleon II," son of the first Napoleon by Marie Louise, never really ruled, any more than did the son of Louis XVI, the "Louis XVII" who died in prison during the great French Revolution.) As President of the Second Republic, Prince Louis Napoleon had soon quarreled with the National Assembly, which refused to amend the Constitution of 1848 to allow him a second term of office. Fearful of radicals and socialists, the Assembly also whittled down the universal male suffrage of 1848 and thus enabled the Prince President to maintain that he was acting as the champion of persecuted popular democracy.

The *coup d'état* of December 2, 1851, artfully timed for the sacred Bonapartist day of Napoleon's first coronation (December 2, 1804) and the greatest Napoleonic victory, the battle of Austerlitz (December 2, 1805), was a stereotyped affair. Controlling the army, Louis Napoleon and his fellow conspirators found it easy to purge the Assembly and make way for a popular vote on a new constitution. Even the expected street fighting on the barricades of Paris, which broke out on December 3, proved to be no wholesale bloodletting. It left victims enough as martyrs, however, and, politically more important, it enabled the President to pose as the champion of order against a largely imaginary socialist plot. Napoleon quickly got himself approved by a plebiscite, which by 7,500,000 votes to 640,000 gave him the right to draw up a new constitution. Napoleon III's use of his strong presidential office to destroy the Second Republic left its mark on the Third and Fourth Republics; French republicans came to fear a strong president of the American type, and devised institutions which, until De Gaulle in 1958 apparently overcame this fear in many (see Chapter XXX), tended to keep the French executive weak and divided.

The plebiscite was accompanied by skillful propaganda, but it was not crudely a work of force. Though many opponents of Napoleon simply did not vote, it seems that at least a very substantial majority of Frenchmen over twenty-one really were willing to try another dictator. There were many reasons why men voted "yes." Almost all were weary of the struggles of the last three years. Many were frightened by the specter of socialism, now for the first time under that name a definite factor in western politics. For nearly three decades the full force of fashionable French literature had been at work making the Napoleonic legend, and identifying the name of Napoleon with the "pooled self-esteem" of French patriotism. Many a man voted "yes" not to Louis Napoleon, nor to any approval of dictatorship for itself, but to the music of the "Marseillaise," the cannon of Austerlitz, to all the glories of France.

Napoleon III (1808-1873).

The Second Empire, 1852-1870: Domestic Developments

The new constitution set up a lightly veiled dictatorship very much like that of Napoleon I. The "chief of state" (he became formally "emperor" on the sacred date, December 2, in 1852) had full authority; he was responsible only to the nation. He governed through ministers, judges, and a whole bureaucracy, in the appointment of which he had the final voice. The popularly elected assembly, the *Corps Législatif*, was filled with "official" candidates sent up by influence of the efficient appointed officials in the provinces. It had no power to initiate or amend legislation; it had only a veto, which in the first few years it rarely used. Yet Napoleon III insisted that he was no mere tool of the possessing classes, no conservative, but an agent of real reform, an emperor of the masses, a kind of continental equivalent of the "Tory democrat" that Disraeli in England was claiming to be. This claim indeed has been made by almost all our recent dictators, from Stalin to the Peróns; they all claim to be *real* democrats, real protectors of ordinary men who in the classical western democracies, they insist, are actually victims of capitalist exploitation. Napoleon III has sometimes been seen as the first of these modern dictators, as a "proto-fascist"; and the careful student of his career can learn much that throws light on our own problems today.

Certainly by comparison with later social legislation in Germany, Britain, or Scandinavia, Napoleon's concrete achievements in direct benefit of the workers were slight. He did carry through a great program of public works, notably in Paris, where his prefect Haussmann cut through the medieval mazes of streets those broad straight avenues which all the world knows so well, and which, incidentally, can be easily swept by gunfire and make street fighting that much more difficult. And he did help with housing and encourage workers' mutual aid societies. But the legal code of labor in France in 1860 was less "modern" than that of England. The standard of living of French labor in the growing cities was well behind that of Britain, and behind that of Germany and the smaller democracies. French labor did indeed benefit from the general prosperity that came to France in the 1850's as it came to Great Britain, but the gains in wages were at least partly counter-balanced by rising prices. France lagged as a welfare state.

It was the bourgeoisie that made most out of the Second Empire. Napoleon's government encouraged improvement in banking facilities, helped the great growth of French railways by state guaranties, and in general furthered the rise of industry in the two decades after 1850. That rise was, especially in large-scale heavy industries, definitely inferior to that of the British and to the already growing German industry. But it was in absolute terms a very real rise. Paris grew into a major metropolitan area, and centers like Lyons and Rouen in textiles, Clermont-Ferrand and St. Etienne in metallurgy, and many other cities came to have genuine industrial economies, with all the problems of slums, trade unions, and other signs of modernity. Yet there remained then as under later French governments an adhesion to older methods of doing business, to small firms often under family control, to luxury trades in which handicraft skills remained important in spite of the machine, all of which meant that in quantitative terms of actual production France fell behind the industrial West. In the '60's she lost her Continental leadership in iron and steel production to the new Germany, and was subsequently far outdistanced by the burgeoning economy of the United States. Her growth in population, too, fell well behind that of the others. At the end of the nineteenth century, she was not much more than 50 per cent more populous than at the beginning—and this with almost no emigration. Britain, in spite of a large emigration, had about tripled her population, and Germany, too, was growing rapidly. Even Italy, with slender natural resources and less industry than France, was growing in population faster than France, and was to outstrip her in our own times. It must be confessed that the reasons for this demographic weakness of nineteenth- and early twentieth-century France remain a problem for the sociological historian. In view of the actual fecundity of the kindred French-Canadian stock, it would seem that "race" factors depending on biological inheritance must be ruled out.

The Second Empire: Foreign Policy

Yet the France of the Second Empire was still a very great power, and the extent of her comparative decline was by no means clear to contemporaries. Although the French gained little from the Crimean War, they did at least have the satisfaction of playing host to the postwar congress at Paris in 1856. And the Paris Exposition of 1855, a counterpart of the famous London exhibition of 1851, was a great success that showed Napoleon III at the height of his power. He had pledged himself to use that power for peace, but he allowed himself, partly through a romantic interest in "oppressed nationalities," partly from age-old motives of prestige, to become involved in a war against Austria for the liberation of Italy. French armies won victories in this war of 1859; characteristically, in these modern times of "publicity," the names of the French victories of Magenta and Solferino were taken up into dressmaking, cookery, and urban real estate.

In 1860 the Italians took things into their own hands and set about organizing the whole peninsula, including papal Rome, into an Italian kingdom. Napoleon depended too much on Catholic support at home to be able to permit the extinction of papal territorial power; moreover, the too great success of his plans was threatening the European balance of power. He therefore temporized, permitting the union of most of Italy under the house of Savoy, but protecting the Pope's temporal power with a French garrison in Rome, leaving Venetia still in Austrian hands, and taking Nice and the French-speaking part of Alpine Savoy away from Piedmont as a reward for his services. He thus managed to offend most Italians, and liberals everywhere, as well as most of his own Catholic supporters at home.

To make matters worse, in 1861 Napoleon began a wild adventure in Mexico, supporting with French arms and men an expedition to put the Austrian prince Maximilian on an imperial throne. The Europeanized Mexican upper classes were in part willing to support this venture, for like most Latin Americans of the nineteenth century, their cultural ideal was France. But from the start the Mexican people resented the foreign intruder, and Maximilian had to rely heavily on French support to penetrate to Mexico City, where he was proclaimed Emperor in June, 1863. The United States, engaged in the Civil War, could do nothing at the time against what Americans regarded as an infraction of the Monroe Doctrine. But after peace had been restored in the United States, the American government protested strongly. The rival of Maximilian, the republican leader Juarez, had no difficulty in defeating the Mexican supporters of Maximilian, once Napoleon under American pressure had abandoned them. The unfortunate Maximilian fell before a firing squad in 1867. This unsuccessful venture was the last attempt made by a European power to install a new government in any of the Americas in defiance of the Monroe Doctrine.

The "Liberal Empire"

Napoleon had come to power, as we have seen, on a platform of national unity against the extreme demands of the social revolutionists of 1848. But in spite of the plebiscite, it became more and more clear that if France had a national unity, it was not of the monolithic, totalitarian sort, but a unity that had to be worked out in the open competition of modern western political life—with parties, parliamentary debate, newspapers, in short, with government by discussion. Napoleon could not in fact be a symbolic head of state, above the struggle, nor even a final umpire. He could not be a republican, though much of France was republican; he could not be a legitimate monarchist, though much of France, and particularly the conservative France which held authoritarian views, was loyal to the legitimacy of the Bourbons, or the somewhat dubious legitimacy of the Orléanists. He could not even be a good devout Catholic, in spite of the orthodoxy of his wife, the Empress Eugénie, for his Bonapartist background was heavily tinged with the anticlericalism of the eighteenth century, and his bungling of the Italian problem had deeply offended clericals. He could only head an "official" party, relying on the manipulative skills of his bureaucrats to work the cumbersome machinery of a parliamentary system designed, like that of Napoleon I, as a disguise for dictatorship.

As the pressure of genuine party differences rose, in reflection of genuine moral, social and economic group interests, Napoleon slowly abandoned the measures of repression he had begun with, and sought to establish himself in something like the position of a constitutional monarch. An act of 1860 gave the Legislative Assembly power to discuss freely a reply to the address from the throne, and throughout the 1860's these powers were extended in the name of the "Liberal Empire." Gradually, political life in France took on a pattern of parliamentary government, with a Right, Left, and Center. As a result of the general election of 1869, the government was faced with a strong legal opposition, thirty of whom were declared republicans. On July 12, 1869, Napoleon capitulated, and granted the Legislative Assembly the right to propose laws, and to criticize and vote the budget. Partial ministerial responsibility seemed just around the corner as Napoleon entrusted the government to the head of the moderates, Emile Ollivier. A plebiscite in May, 1870, overwhelmingly ratified these changes.

It is at least possible that the Second Empire might thus have been converted into a constitutional monarchy. The changes had indeed been wrung from the Emperor by popular agitation, not merely political but also economic in the form of strikes. It is quite as possible that the radical republican ground swell would have gone on to submerge the Empire in any case. But the disastrous defeats of the French armies in the Franco-Prussian War into which Napoleon was maneuvered by the skill of Bismarck (see Chapter XXII) put an end to the experiment of the Liberal Empire. On September 4, 1870, after the humiliating capitulation of Sedan, a Parisian mob forced a rump Legislative Assembly to decree the fall of the Empire, and at the classic center of French republicanism, the Paris City Hall, the Third Republic was proclaimed.

The Birth of the Third Republic

The government of the new Republic was too good a child of 1792 to give up the war against the national enemy. A government of national defense tried to continue the struggle, but the miracle of Valmy (see Chapter XVIII) was not to be repeated. In October, General Bazaine surrendered a

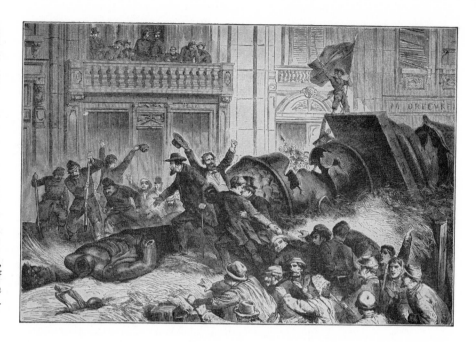

The Paris Commune, 1871. Destruction of the Vendôme column commemorating Napoleon I.

large French force at Metz, and the disorganized elements of other French armies were helpless before the powerful German forces. An exhausted nation, sick of the war, chose in February a National Assembly that met at Bordeaux and sued for peace. The special circumstances of that election, however, placed on the new Republic an additional handicap. For meanwhile Paris, besieged by the Germans, had resisted desperately until starvation forced its surrender in January, 1871. Even under pressure of the siege, Parisian radicals tried to seize power and revive the old Paris Commune, or city government, of 1792. These radicals could not stomach the capitulation that the rest of the country seemed to be preparing. In the elections to the National Assembly, their intransigence helped to turn the provincial voters toward conservative candidates pledged to make peace—and to restore, not the Republic, but the old monarchy.

This new Assembly, on March 1, 1871, voted to accept a peace ceding Alsace and a substantial part of Lorraine to Germany and paying an indemnity of five billion francs (about $1,000,000,000). Then the Paris National Guard, which had not been disarmed by the Germans, went over to the radicals, and the Paris Commune was set up. Marxist legend has consecrated the Commune of 1871 as the first major socialist government. The Communards were in fact rather Jacobins, radical anticlericals and highly patriotic republicans who wanted a society of small independent shopkeepers and artisans, not the abolition of private property. In any case, they had no chance in the besieged city to introduce sweeping social reforms. But their revolutionary aspect alarmed the rest of France, and their refusal to accept the peace was a challenge the National Assembly had to meet. To the horrors of the first siege by the Germans were added the horrors of a new siege by the government of the National Assembly, which gathered its troops at Versailles and in the "Bloody Week" of May 21-28 advanced through the barricades to clear the city.

The Third French Republic was thus born in foreign and in civil war, and began with a heritage of unresolved cleavages. Indeed, it was not at all clear in 1871 that there was a Third Republic at all. More than half the members of the new National Assembly were monarchists, anxious to undo the formal declaration of a republic made in republican Paris right after Sedan. But now we encounter one of those concrete events that are the despair of those who seek the clue to history in vast impersonal forces beyond the play of human personality. About half the monarchist deputies were pledged to the elder "legitimate" Bourbon line represented by the Count of Chambord, grandson of Charles X, and the other half to the younger Orléanist line that had come to the throne in 1830, represented by the Count of Paris, grandson of Louis Philippe. Chambord might have become in fact what he was to his supporters, King Henry V, had he been willing to make the slightest concession to Orléanist sentiments and accept the revolutionary blue, white, and red tricolor flag that Louis Philippe had himself accepted as the flag of France. But he insisted on the white flag and gold lilies of Bourbon, which for millions of Frenchmen meant complete repudiation of all that had happened since 1789. Chambord did not, of course, act just for a white flag and against a tricolor one; behind these symbols lay real motives tied up with all French history. He meant to be king, not just a Victorian symbol; but no one could be that sort of king in France at that moment.

In the resulting stalemate, the republican minority was able to maintain itself, and slowly gather strength. Thiers, the elder statesman of the Orléanist monarchy, who had been a leader in the opposition to Napoleon III, was recognized as "President of the Republic" and carried through the final settlement with Germany. He was succeeded in 1873 by Marshal MacMahon, a soldier and a monarchist, who was elected to hold the government together while the monarchist majority made peace between Bourbons and Orléanists. That peace was never made, as Chambord continued to insist on the white flag, and in 1875 a series

of constitutional measures formally established the Third Republic.

The Constitution of 1875

These laws, known collectively as the Constitution of 1875, provided for a president elected by an absolute majority of Senate and Chamber of Deputies sitting together as a National Assembly, the usual ministers, and a bicameral legislature elected by universal manhood suffrage. The Senate was chosen by indirect election, the Chamber of Deputies by direct election; all legislation had to pass both houses, though only the lower could initiate finance bills. The critical point was that of the responsibility of the ministers. Had the president been able to dismiss them, a new Napoleon III might easily have arisen to destroy the Republic. MacMahon attempted to exercise this power when on May 16, 1877, he dismissed the anticlerical premier, Jules Simon, and got the conservative Duke of Broglie to form a cabinet. But the Chamber was now really republican—or at least anti-monarchist—and voted "no confidence" in Broglie by a big majority. MacMahon was thus forced to dissolve the Chamber and call for a new national election—which he could do constitutionally. In the new elections the republicans, though losing some seats, still retained a good majority in the Chamber, and could now force the president to name a republican premier. Disgruntled, MacMahon resigned in 1879 and was succeeded by a conservative republican, Jules Grévy. This crisis of the *Seize Mai* (May 16) set a precedent for the Third Republic: no president thereafter dared to dissolve the Chamber, and the presidency became a ceremonial office, made fun of in the press and on the stage. But at any rate, nine years after its establishment in name, the Third Republic had at last become a fact.

It was in form a kind of republican transposition of constitutional monarchy, with an ornamental president instead of an ornamental king. The real executive, as in England, was the ministry, in effect a committee responsible to the legislature—indeed to the Chamber of Deputies, which soon became the focus of political action, leaving the Senate little real power. The Chamber, reflecting the political habits of the ideologically divided country, was composed not of two, but of a dozen or more parties, so that any ministry had to be supported by a coalition subject to constant shifting in the play of personalities and principles. The result was a marked instability of ministries. The "life expectancy" of a ministry under the Third Republic was hardly a year.

Yet such a figure is misleading. A French ministry under the Third Republic—and indeed under the Fourth Republic—did not usually resign and give way to a totally different ministry with totally different policies. Instead, its personnel was shifted a bit, a compromise or so was made with certain parliamentary groups, and the new ministry carried on much as did the old. For instance, Briand, the great champion of collective security (after the war of 1914-1918), headed ten different cabinets at various times between 1909 and 1926; Delcassé, the architect of France's entente with England, served as foreign minister continuously through several cabinets and seven years (1898-1905). And in our own day two individuals from the same party, Schuman and Bidault, alternated in the foreign ministry through a dozen cabinets of the Fourth Republic. Moreover, the day-to-day task of governing was carried on by a civil service, by experts in the law courts and in the educational system as well as in the executive department. This permanent personnel, or "bureaucracy" subject only to broad policy control from above, preserves a basic continuity in French political action.

The system was highly democratic, for it could work only by means of constant and subtle compromises. These, the essence of democratic government, were made in France—and in most of the democratic world outside the English-speaking countries—by the several parties in open debate and voting in the legislature *after* an election. In the English-speaking countries, these compromises are made *before* an election, *within* each of the two major parties, often in the privacy of the famous smoke-filled room. Probably the English-speaking method both conceals antagonisms and encourages the habit of willing compromise more effectively than does the continental method. But neither method will work if the underlying antagonisms are really intense, beyond compromise. For example, the American two-party system obviously failed to avert the Civil War, had indeed begun in the 1850's to break down into a plural-party system.

Boulanger and Panama

Bitter antagonisms did indeed threaten the Third French Republic between 1879 and 1914, but they did not destroy it. For one thing, the Republic's opponents on the Right and on the Left could never get together. On the Right, although the royalists eventually patched up their quarrels between Bourbon and Orléanist, and although they had some support in literary circles, they could not recover the strength they had dissipated in the 1870's. Nor could the Bonapartists make serious gains in public opinion, though they survived as a political group into the twentieth century. The Catholics, though they feared the anticlerical orientation of many republicans, were after the accession of Pope Leo XIII in 1878 encouraged to develop their way of life by frank acceptance of the freedom of worship that the Constitution of the Republic offered them. The out-and-out Rightist enemies of the Republic were forced to do violence to their own conservative and legitimist principles and to seek some new man who would win over the floating discontent always present in a modern industrial state and set up a dictatorship.

In the 1880's, they hoped that they had found such a man in General Boulanger, an ambitious soldier who had as minister of war catered to French desire for revenge on Germany. But the Boulangist movement was founded on a man of straw. The Gen-

General Boulanger (1837-1891).

eral cut an impressive figure in public appearances, and in by-elections to fill vacancies caused by deaths or resignations in the Chamber he showed he could command a popular following. But from the point of view of many traditional conservatives he had compromising origins and radical friends, and, as it became clear that Boulanger in power might rush the country into war, his following threatened to desert him. In January, 1889, he swept a by-election in Paris, but his nerve failed when he

was faced with the need to resort to the classic technique of the *coup d'état*. Instead of seizing power by force of arms, he sought refuge with his mistress. The government now took courage and threatened to try him for treason; Boulanger fled to Brussels and committed suicide on the grave of his beloved in 1891. The Republic had surmounted its first great crisis.

Boulanger's cause had gained strength from a scandal in republican ranks. Daniel Wilson, President Grévy's son-in-law, was implicated in the selling of posts in the Legion of Honor. The opposition press made out that the government was riddled with graft. More fuel went on the fire in the early 1890's, when there burst into publicity one of those crises of corruption, graft, and racketeering that seem endemic in modern western societies. This was the Panama scandal which was brought on by the failure of De Lesseps' attempt to duplicate in Panama his success in building the Suez Canal. It involved accusations of criminal corruption against ministers, deputies, financiers, and an unfortunate Jewish banker, Reinach, who either committed suicide or was murdered just before his trial. And indeed, as in the somewhat comparable Crédit Mobilier scandal in the United States in 1873, it was established that ministers and deputies had accepted financial reward for backing the shaky Panama company. Bad as it was, the Panama scandal was to pale before the Dreyfus affair. For with this famous affair a force that was to trouble the Western world for decades to come first really attained dramatic intensity. This was anti-Semitism.

The Dreyfus Case

Dreyfus, a Jew and a captain in the French army, was the almost accidental victim of an espionage intrigue and of the anti-Semitism then prevalent in France, especially in military and Catholic circles.

Accused of selling military secrets to the Germans, he was railroaded into trial as a scapegoat and was convicted of treason in 1894. Colonel Picquart, an intelligence officer, became convinced that the document on which Dreyfus had been convicted was a forgery, and that the real traitor was a disreputable adventurer of Hungarian blood but of French birth, Major Esterhazy. Picquart was quietly shipped off to Africa by his superiors, who wished to let sleeping dogs lie. But the Dreyfus family, by independent investigation, arrived at the conclusion that Esterhazy was the traitor, and sought to reopen the case. Esterhazy was tried and acquitted, but the affair was now too public for such silencing. In 1898, the famous novelist Zola brought matters to a crisis by publishing his open letter, "J'Accuse." Zola accused the military leaders, one by one, of sacrificing an innocent man deliberately in order to save the reputation of the army.

France was now divided into Dreyfusards and Anti-Dreyfusards; the former defended in Dreyfus the Republic, the latter attacked it. Almost all the far Left, which had hitherto held aloof from the affair as just one more example of the rottenness of the bourgeois state, now rallied to the Third Republic. Dreyfus was brought back from his prison on Devil's Island in French Guiana, and was retried in the midst of a frenzied campaign in the press and on the platform. The military court, faced with new evidence brought out by the suicide of Colonel Henry, the real forger of the most incriminating of the original documents used to convict Dreyfus, again found Dreyfus guilty of treason, but with the almost incredible qualification—in a treason case—of "extenuating circumstances." This attempt at face-saving saved nothing. Dreyfus was pardoned by the President of the Republic in 1899, and in 1906, after the tensions had abated, he was acquitted and restored to the army with the rank of major.

The Dreyfus affair presents a remarkably well-documented case study in social psychology. The simple juridical issue—was this man guilty or not guilty of treason—never wholly disappeared in the mass hysteria. Many Frenchmen who did not like Dreyfus or Jews or who did revere the Church, Army, and the whole apparatus of the Right, none the less sought to make up their minds solely on the basis of the facts. Yet many on both sides worked themselves up to a point where the question of Dreyfus' guilt was wholly submerged in this great confronting of the "two Frances"— the France of the Republic, heir to the great revolution and the principles of 1789, on the one hand, and, on the other, the France of the monarchy, of Throne and Altar, which had never really reconciled itself to the great revolution. For the ordinary person, the open admission of forgery by Colonel Henry and his subsequent suicide were enough; he now thought Dreyfus innocent. But for the violent Anti-Dreyfusard, Henry's act made him a hero and a martyr; he had died for his country! A paper was circulated in Paris asking for a memorial to Henry:

> Colonel Henry's Devotion to his Country.
> Public subscription for a monument to be raised to him.
> When an officer is reduced to committing a pretended forgery in order to restore peace to his country and rid it of a traitor, that soldier is to be mourned.
> If he pays for his attempt with his life, he is a martyr.
> If he voluntarily takes his life,
> HE IS A HERO.*

These were months of real mass hysteria, in which both sides were swayed by emotions far too strong for reason to control.

The Republic after Dreyfus

With the victory of the Dreyfusards, the Republic moved to the Left and pun-

* F. C. Conybeare, *The Dreyfus Case* (London, 1898), 298.

ished the Church for its support of the army and the Anti-Dreyfusards. The triumphant republicans in a series of measures between 1901 and 1905 destroyed the Concordat of 1801 between Napoleon I and the Pope which had established the Roman Catholic Church in a privileged position in the French state (see Chapter XVIII). The Catholic teaching orders were forced to dissolve, and some 12,000 Catholic schools, which had been formidable rivals of the state school system, had to close down. The state was no longer to pay the clergy, and private corporations organized by the faithful were to take over the expenses of worship and the ownership and maintenance of the churches. The Catholics refused to accept this settlement, and the churches remained technically government property.

But, though the separation had been carried out amid great bitterness, though the debates had revived the ferocious language of the 1790's, there was no recourse to the violence of the past. Catholicism was not proscribed, and somehow or other worship continued in churches that were not the full legal property of the faithful. Catholic education was indeed severely hindered, but there was no formal persecution. The separation did not really alter the fundamental social position of the Church in France. The upper classes, and the peasantry of the north, northeast and west, remained for the most part loyal Catholics; many of the urban middle and working classes, and many peasants in parts of the south, southwest, and center remained what they had become over the last few centuries, indifferent Catholics or outright and determined secularists.

The indifferent Catholics and the anti-clericals formed the backbone of the central supporting party of the Republic, the Radical Socialists, who were not socialists at all but petty bourgeois, French Jeffersonians. Indeed, the French Republic of the early twentieth century was a typically bourgeois state. It made certain concessions to demands from the workers for social security and better living conditions, but not nearly so many as the British constitutional monarchy was then making, nor indeed so many as the only partly constitutional German monarchy had made already. Trade unions in France were legal, but they had hard sledding against the reluctance of French workers to pay dues and accept union discipline. Moreover, good democrats, like Clemenceau and Briand, had no scruples about using force against strikers.

France remained fundamentally in the early twentieth century what she had been since 1789, a land of small farm-owning peasants, very conservative in their farming methods, and of relatively small family-controlled industries, very conservative in their business methods. There were some elements of big industry by the early 1900's, and French steel production at that time was actually growing faster than that of Britain, Germany, and the United States. None the less, great industry was not typical of the French economic scene, which was backward in comparison with the achievements of the industrial giants just mentioned, but at the same time well balanced by old-fashioned standards of the nearly self-sufficient national economy.

The Third Republic had weathered the storms of domestic differences at bottom because, though some Frenchmen disliked it intensely, and though many Frenchmen felt toward it that distrust of the "government" not unknown in the American democracy, most Frenchmen felt it somehow to be the embodiment of *la patrie*, the fatherland. Differences did arise among them, notably on questions of colonial policy. The great expansion of French power in Africa, Indo-China, and Oceania which made the world empire of France second only to Britain's was the work of a determined minority (see Chapter XXV). Many Frenchmen viewed their colonies with antagonism or apathy.

France since 1870 had often seemed dangerously divided on matters of domestic and imperial concern; yet on foreign policy the Third Republic was essentially united. Disagreement on the big question of foreign policy concerned details of timing, not ultimate aims. France wanted revenge for 1870; France wanted Alsace-Lorraine back. In the complex workings of international politics from 1870 to 1914, the foreign ministries of the Third Republic, shifting though their top elected personnel was through the workings of the multi-party system, none the less brought France to a position of strength through alliances in which revenge on Germany became possible. Democracies are sometimes held to be at a disadvantage in the conduct of foreign relations in comparison with states under strong monarchic or dictatorial control. Soon after the war with Prussia, democratic France was isolated, and imperial Germany was the center of a marvelous system of alliances; yet by 1914, democratic France was firmly allied with a powerful Britain and a Russia powerful at least for the moment, and imperial Germany, save for a weak Austro-Hungarian ally, was essentially isolated.

III: Italy, 1848-1914

Italian national unity, which seemed after the events of 1848-49 (see Chapter XIX) as far away as ever, was triumphantly achieved between 1859 and 1870. The Kingdom of Italy that began to emerge after 1860 had a constitution very much like that of the Third French Republic, with an ornamental king instead of an ornamental president. The ministry was responsible to a lower house which in practice developed a multi-party system rather like that of France. At first, a property qualification severely limited the suffrage; after 1881, this qualification was low enough —a direct tax of 19 lire, or about $4.00—so that the electorate numbered over 2,000,000. What amounted to full universal manhood suffrage was not, however, introduced until 1912.

Cavour and the Completion of Unification

The architect of Italian unification was Cavour (1810-1861), who became the chief minister of Piedmont in 1852. Though of aristocratic origin himself, and trained for the highly conservative career of an army officer, Cavour enthusiastically supported the economic revolutions and the aspirations of the business classes. He visited France and England as a young man and was deeply influenced by their economic accomplishments and by their economic and political ideas and institutions. Back in Piedmont, he applied the newest agricultural methods to his family estates and promoted the introduction of steamboats, railroads, industries, and banks in order to prepare Piedmont for leadership in unified Italy. Cavour was a good, moderate, mid-nineteenth-century liberal.

But Cavour was also a superlatively adept practitioner of the realistic diplomacy often called *Realpolitik*. As the chief minister of Piedmont, he set about cultivating French and English support, bringing Piedmont into the Crimean War on their side against Russia. He got no immediate award, for England was unwilling to take steps that would offend Austria. But, though bitterly disappointed, he put a good face on his defeat, and finally persuaded Napoleon III that the Austrian hold in northern Italy was an anachronism, a flying in the face of the principle of nationality. In 1859, France and Piedmont went to war with Austria, and won bloody victories at Magenta and Solferino in June. Sympathetic nationalist risings broke out in Tuscany and the Papal States. But the threat of Prussian help to Austria alarmed Napoleon, who held a conference with the Emperor of Austria, Francis Joseph, at Villafranca (July, 1859) and arranged a compromise by which Lombardy was to go to Piedmont but Venetia to remain Austrian, and the rest of the peninsula to remain divided. Cavour resigned in bitter protest.

He had, however, already won. A wave of popular agitation in the smaller states of northern and central Italy brought almost bloodless revolutions and plebiscites demanding annexation to Piedmont. Cavour came back into office to accept the annexations, and to take advantage of the promising situation developing in the Papal States and the South. For in May, 1860, a most successful expedition had set out for Naples and Sicily under the command of a radical, indeed republican, nationalist agitator, the romantic red-shirted Garibaldi. Cavour deeply distrusted Garibaldi's radicalism, which he feared might make Italy a republic and might so alarm the powers that they would intervene to undo Cavour's own annexationist achievements. For these reasons, Cavour sought first to prevent the departure of Garibaldi's expedition, and then, after this had proved impossible, to control its progress and exploit its success in the interests of his own policy. Garibaldi and his thousand "redshirts" had relatively little trouble in overcoming the feeble opposition of the Bourbon Francis II in Sicily. Recruits swarmed to his flag. Popular opinion throughout the West, even in cautious England, was overwhelmingly on the side of this romantic adventurer. Garibaldi, who had announced his loyalty to the King of Piedmont, Victor Emmanuel, now

Giuseppe Garibaldi (1807-1882).

crossed the Straits of Messina to the mainland with the approval of the British minister, Lord Palmerston, and continued his victorious march. Cavour, alarmed lest Garibaldi bring on a crisis with Napoleon by taking Rome, sent Piedmontese troops into the Papal States. They disposed of the papal forces easily, and occupied all save the area about Rome itself. King Victor Emmanuel soon joined forces with Garibaldi near Naples and assured the triumph of Cavour's policy. Meanwhile, in plebiscites, Naples and Sicily voted for union with the North.

The upshot of all these rapidly unrolling events was the proclamation of the Kingdom of Italy with Victor Emmanuel of Savoy at its head, and with Florence as its capital, in March, 1861. Cavour died in June, but what had seemed impossible only two short years ago at Villafranca had now been realized. Rome, under French occupation, and Venetia, still held by Austria, kept the new kingdom from the territorial completion the patriots wanted.

Venetia and Rome soon came easily into the kingdom in the play of international politics, and cost Italy little in bloodshed. Venetia came as a reward for Italy's siding with Prussia in the brief war of 1866 that saw Prussia defeat Austria; Rome came when the war of 1870 with Prussia forced Napoleon III to withdraw from papal territory (see Chapter XXII). On October 2, 1870, Rome was annexed to the Kingdom of Italy, and became its capital. All the peninsula, save for Trieste and Trent in the North, was now under one rule. These two small bits of *Italia Irredenta* (Italy unredeemed) were of no small importance, for Italian patriots remained unreconciled to Austrian possession of them, and went to war against Austria and her German ally in 1915 largely to obtain them.

Assets and Liabilities of United Italy

The new kingdom started out with the asset of favorable public opinion throughout the non-Catholic segments of the western world. Italian national unity seemed a natural and desirable thing, and it had been achieved without very much bloodshed, with a mixture of Garibaldian romance and Cavourian realism. Within the kingdom the enthusiasm that had brought the *Risorgimento* (resurrection) to fruition was now in the service of united Italy. Italians were a frugal, hard-working people, and in the north they made promising beginnings in the new industry of the machine age.

Yet striking liabilities impeded the new Italy. The Italians had, like the French, a division between Catholics and anticlericals—better, anti-Catholics—difficult for a modern American to understand. Still, the division was perhaps less sharp than in France; there were in Italy more middle-of-

the-roaders in practice. On the other hand, ardent Italian Catholics were embittered by the circumstances of the final drive for union, the annexation of the Papal States without the Pope's consent, the "Roman question." Italy lacked coal and iron; in terms of modern economic competition, she was a "have-not" country, a shocking discovery that the Italians made in the years following unification. Much of mountainous central Italy and all southern Italy were really marginal to nineteenth-century western civilization, with a poverty-stricken, illiterate peasantry rooted in age-old local ways utterly different from those of modern urban life, and with a small feudalistic aristocracy to whom a man like Cavour was really quite incomprehensible. Neapolitans and Sicilians resented the new political preponderance of North Italians in the unified kingdom, much as American Southerners resented Yankee "carpetbaggers" after the Civil War. If one spoke of the "two Italies," the division would be that between the already somewhat industrialized North, especially the thoroughly "modern" Po Valley, and the rural, impoverished South, still "medieval."

Moreover, at least half of Italy lacked experience in self-government. It had no tradition of government by discussion, of law-abidingness, of comfortable middle-class compromise. Italy was not indeed the land of mixed stereotypes—sunny gaiety, dark passions, music, and *banditti*—which northern Europeans and Americans believed it to be. It was a land of deep-seated class antagonisms, regional variations, fervent localism, a whole inheritance from the past which made democratic government very difficult.

The Roman question became a chronic rather than a critical one. The Pope, who refused to accept the legality of the new kingdom, simply stayed in the Vatican Palace as a "prisoner." The Vatican remained the center of the world-wide organization of the Roman Catholic Church, and in no important sense was the Pope impeded in the exercise of his powers over the faithful throughout the world. Within Italy, the Church forbade Catholics to participate in politics and urged a Catholic boycott of the new state. Gradually, in fact, Catholics did take an increasing part in politics, but the Roman question itself remained unsettled until 1929, when Mussolini and Pope Pius XI agreed to set up the Vatican City as a sovereign state of 108 acres.

The new kingdom made appreciable economic progress. Railroads, built and managed by the state, were pushed rapidly into the backward South, a brand-new merchant marine brought the new Italian flag onto the seven seas, and an army and navy gave it standing as a power. Even the national finances seemed for a time under conservative leadership to be sound. In the political field, the 1880's brought a letdown, the growth of parliamentary corruption, the beginning of a long era of unashamed political opportunism. Meantime, the industrial proletariat was small, labor inadequately organized, and the socialists were both too small and too rent by divisions to constitute a dynamic instrument of opposition and reform. Moreover, as recent economic historians insist, the very economic progress of the North, made in part at the expense

of a South both exploited and neglected, increased regional differentiation and helped build up the social tensions that were to affect twentieth-century Italy very seriously indeed.

Finally, Italy was now launching itself on a career of imperial aspiration which seems a good example of the desire to keep up with the Joneses. Since France—the envied "Latin" sister—and Britain had empires, since a great power had to have an empire, and since Italy, or rather the guiding groups in Italy, wanted to be a great power, some way of territorial expansion had to be found. The conventional economic explanations of the imperialist drive hardly make sense for the Italy of the 1880's and 1890's, a nation with no important exportable capital, with no need for colonial markets, and with plenty of domestic difficulties. True, Italy had a rapidly expanding population that found relatively few economic opportunities at home, especially in the South. But, since other countries had such a head start in empire-building, what was left open to Italian seizure was very little indeed. And even these leftovers were not suitable for colonial settlement by Europeans. They were the poorer parts of Africa, hardly worth the difficulty of exploitation.

Even so, the effort to take Ethiopia (then called Abyssinia) drained the resources of the government, and was halted by the disastrous military defeat inflicted by the Abyssinians on the Italian expeditionary force at Adowa in 1896. The general depression of the 1890's, a bank scandal, and the Adowa failure cast a shadow on the

last years of the century. Grave bread riots broke out in Milan in May, 1898, the "*fatti di Maggio*" (deeds of May), and in 1900 King Humbert was assassinated by an anarchist. The accession of a new king, Victor Emmanuel III, who was believed to have liberal leanings, gave new heart to many, and the years just before the outbreak of World War I were on the whole years of comparative quiet and prosperity, of partial reconciliation with the Church, and of the final establishment of universal suffrage. Parliamentary democracy seemed at last to be sending down solid roots. And in the years 1890-1914 the vast emigration to North and South America—the number of emigrants exceeded half a million in the peak year of 1913—almost canceled out the serious economic difficulties attendant on the high Italian birth rate and lack of new industrial employment.

Yet the men who ran Italy could never quite content themselves with a position, say like that of a Mediterranean Sweden, quite outside the competition for empire and quite outside the "great powers." Italy was not a great power, but her leaders, and their millions of followers, wanted very much to make her one. Pushed out of Abyssinia, and forced by the increasing tensions of international politics to yield to the French in Tunisia, Italy finally got from the other great powers a free hand in poverty-stricken and parched Tripoli, a fragment of the old Turkish Empire in North Africa now known as Libya. In 1911, she went to war with Turkey over Tripoli, thus stimulating the cycle of Balkan wars that were to develop into World War I.

IV: The United States

World War I was also to mark the full participation in the international balance of another relative newcomer to the family

of nations, the United States. The simplest and in many ways the most important fact of her brief national history is that in a little over a century the United States secured in terms of actual power a position like that of the great states that have filled these pages for many chapters—Austria, France, England, and the rest. The United States came to be a "great power," despite words and even sentiments that placed her outside international competition, in "isolation." Two simple sets of statistics point up this fact. In 1790, the United States comprised 892,000 square miles, and in 1910 3,754,000 square miles; even more important, the population of the United States was 3,929,000 in 1790, and 91,972,000 in 1910. The 1910 population was greater than that of either of the most powerful European states, Germany and Great Britain, indeed second only to that of Russia. And, still more important, American industrial and agricultural capacities were already greater than those of any other single country.

The Federal Union

The land that had become so powerful in a brief century was in the late eighteenth century almost empty beyond the Alleghenies, save for a few Indians of Stone Age culture; yet millions of square miles were as suited to intensive human use as any in Europe. Most interested observers knew this at the end of the American Revolution, and they expected the central parts of the North American continent to fill up with white men eventually. But most of them, including Americans like Jefferson, did not believe that the process would be as rapid as it in fact was. Moreover, all but the most sanguine felt that the developed and fully peopled continent could not possibly come under one political rule. They felt that it must be divided—as indeed the South American continent came to be—into a number of independent nations on essentially the European model. Indeed, the most pessimistic or merely hostile observers did not believe that the thirteen

Atlantic seaboard colonies gathered together to fight the British could possibly maintain their own union. Here is a sample prediction from the eighteenth century:

As to the future grandeur of America, and its being a rising empire under one head, whether republican or monarchical, it is one of the idlest and most visionary notions that ever was conceived even by writers of romance. The mutual antipathies and clashing interests of the Americans, their difference of governments, habitudes, and manners, indicate that they will have no centre of union and no common interest. They never can be united into one compact empire under any species of government whatever; a disunited people till the end of time, suspicious and distrustful of each other, they will be divided and subdivided into little commonwealths or principalities, according to natural boundaries, by great bays of the sea, and by vast rivers, lakes, and ridges of mountains.[*]

Yet hold together the former colonies did. Though the union was often sorely tested, once in the bloodiest war Americans have yet fought, it is a central fact of history that the United States did not go the way of the Latin American states. Why the United States held together cannot be explained by any single factor. Geography was certainly kinder to her than to the Latin Americans, for the Appalachians were no real barrier at all; the Rockies were not the barrier the Andes are; and the Mississippi Valley, unlike that of the Amazon, was a help rather than a hindrance to settlement and communications. The railroad and the telegraph arrived just in time to enable goods and ideas to move fast and far enough to hold Americans together. The communications and transportation network already developed by 1860 enabled the North to count on the West in the decisive struggle of the Civil War. The sheer size of the new republic after the acquisition of the Mississippi-Missouri Valley by purchase from Napoleon in 1803 seemed

[*] Josiah Tucker, Dean of Gloucester, quoted in John Fiske, *The Critical Period of American History, 1783-1789* (Boston, 1888), 57-58.

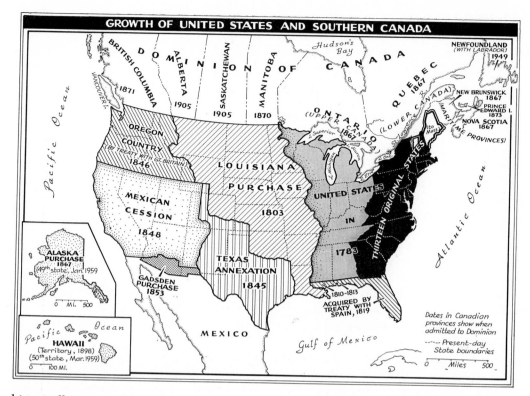

historically compatible with a loosely held empire of many tongues and peoples, like those of ancient Persia or Rome, but not with a unified nation-state. The achievements of modern technology in effect reduced sheer size to manageable proportions. After the first transcontinental railway was completed in 1869, Californians could get to the federal capital at Washington more quickly than New Yorkers could in 1801.

Yet it will not do to emphasize purely material factors in the holding together of the United States. The resistance to Britain had helped forge a genuine national patriotism. The colonists, in spite of contrasts between seventeenth-century "Puritan" New England and "Cavalier" tidewater South, in spite of Dutch and German elements in the middle colonies, brought with them one language and one law, one basic culture. Almost all the colonies had "frontiers"—in the new American sense of the word, not a guarded line with custom houses as in

Europe, but free areas on their western edges where a lively population was winning new lands from the wilderness. This frontier population was a powerful force for unity, for it had little attachment to the older centers of colonial (now state) group-consciousness, and it had great confidence in its own "manifest destiny" to keep pushing westward with the blessing and patronage, and without more than the remote control, of the new federal government.

Americans gained their independence from Britain in a civil war and a social revolution that were rather mild affairs compared, to say, with the French Reign of Terror. And, after the more committed Loyalists had left for Canada or Britain, Americans took up national life without any seriously alienated minorities. They achieved at the Philadelphia convention of 1787 and in the campaign for adoption during the next two years a federal constitution that set up a central government with the essential attributes of all governments—the ability to tax individuals (not just to ask for monies as contributions from constituent states), to control armed forces, and to maintain a monopoly of foreign relations. The new constitution, in short, set up a sovereign federal state, not a mere league of sovereign states. On the whole, this result was achieved under conservative groups anxious to preserve their economic and social privileges, afraid that democracy in separate, quasi-independent states would go too far. But this conservative conclusion to the American Revolution gave the infant federal state a safer start. Finally, the threat that British control of Canada seemed to offer put a limit on domestic divisions. The United States grew up in its earliest years aware of the need for union against a possible foreign danger.

The new republic entered the world war of the Napoleonic period in 1812. Neither the French nor the British really tried to observe the freedom of commerce that the United States claimed as the right of a neutral, but the British, who were by 1812 masters of the sea, seemed to be infringing neutral rights more seriously than the French. Moreover, American expansionists, the "war hawks," saw a possible prize in Canada to be wrested from England, and no such prize to be got from France. The American attempt to invade Canada failed, not only from ineptness, but from the determined resistance of the Canadians. In isolated combats on the seas, the United States won victories that made up for her failures on land, and helped bolster national pride. The war on the whole was a stalemate, in which the United States experienced no important gains or losses. From the Mexican War of 1846-1848, a war in which the United States, however much harassed by a Mexican government angry at the loss of Texas to rebellious Yankee settlers, was clearly the aggressor, we gained an enormous block of territory from Texas to California.

Civil War and Reconstruction

The great test of the new republic has been called the "Civil War" by the Northerners and the "War between the States" by the Southerners. War broke out in 1861 after long years of sectional strife within the union between North and South. The Civil War was really an abortive nationalist revolution, the attempt of the Confederate states to set up a separate sovereign nation. The South was predominantly agricultural, with a society based on plantation slavery and on a single major crop, cotton, much of which was exported abroad. The North was increasingly industrial, with a society based on free labor and on independent farm owners.

To the conflict of economic interest was added, as almost always in human affairs, a conflict of ideals, of ways of life. That conflict was not as deep-seated, as irreconcilable, as it seemed to be to the generation that went to war in 1861—or the South, like Ireland or Poland, would presumably have tried again to free itself. But the fires of conflict were fanned especially by the question of slavery, which seemed immoral to many in the North and which seemed the order of nature to many in the South. They were fanned also by writers and preachers on both sides, the Northerners thinking of themselves as heirs of the Puritans, the Southerners as heirs of the Cavaliers. With the secession of South Carolina and its sister states, antagonism reached the point of open war.

In retrospect, the victory of the North has an air of inevitability, especially since by 1861 the middle and upper Mississippi Valley was bound firmly to the North by economic and cultural ties. In population—especially since the South could not, did not dare, use the Negroes as soldiers—and in industrial resources above all, the North was greatly superior. Yet, aided by a very able

Ruins at Charleston, South Carolina, at the close of the Civil War.

corps of officers, by the advantages in morale that accrue to determined underdogs, and by the disastrous early overconfidence of the North, the South won initial victories that gave its cause great momentum. But the North thwarted the efforts of Confederate diplomats to secure British intervention and was able to improvise a naval force that gradually established a blockade shutting off the South from importation of necessary war materials. In the long run, Northern strength in men and materials wore the Southern armies down.

The striking thing about the Civil War is not that the North won it finally in the field, but that the South accepted the verdict of battle as final, that the Union in which Americans today have grown up should be so firm and final. The "Road to Reunion" after 1865 was indeed no easy one, and in the first years of the Reconstruction period after the war it appeared to many an almost impossible one. With the assassination of Lincoln by the fanatical Booth in 1865, the one great moderate who might have lessened the vengefulness of the Northern radicals was lost. The South was occupied by Northern soldiers, the illiterate Negroes were enfranchised, and Northern "carpetbaggers" and Southern "scalawags"—and many sincere idealists

who believed they could bring liberty and equality to a "misguided" South—combined to bring what seemed a reign of terror to old Confederates.

Yet even in these early days the Civil War did not end, as such wars have often ended, in wholesale reprisals, executions, and exile. Northerners had sung during the war, "We'll hang Jeff Davis to a sour apple tree"; but after the war Jefferson Davis, President of the Confederacy, was not hanged on a sour apple tree or anywhere else. He was imprisoned for two years, and then lived quietly for another thirty, of course writing a book to justify his career. The fate of Davis measures the miracle of reunion. There were extremely few political refugees of the kind that often attend defeated causes. The soldiers of the South returned, often to devastated homes and lost fortunes, but they returned home under amnesty. Gradually the crusading fervor of the North wore off, and the Southerners, reinforced by new men, some of them immigrant Northerners, took over control in their states. Slavery, abolished by Lincoln's proclamation in 1863, was never restored, but the Negroes were in effect disenfranchised, "white supremacy" was restored, and the race question in the New South took on forms familiar to us today.

The end of the attempt to make radical reforms in the South was clear when a disputed presidential election in 1876 saw the Republican Hayes win over the Democrat Tilden after some very unprincipled politicking. No doubt conservative, business-conscious Northerners were anxious to get back to normal conditions, and quite willing to compromise with like-minded Southerners at the expense of race equality and other high ideals. Still, the final abandonment of idealistic reconstruction seems largely a usual, to-be-expected letdown of the energies behind a great crusade. In a sense, the crusade was renewed in 1954 with the decision of the Supreme Court against segregated public schools.

The South of the later nineteenth century was in part a "New South," which is one of the basic reasons why the region has come to accept the Civil War as ended, with due sentimental compensations in wistful feeling for the past. Slowly in the late nineteenth century, more rapidly in the twentieth, it has built up its own industries, taken steps to free itself from cotton monoculture and to integrate its economy and its society with the rest of the country. The South remained throughout this period a relatively backward area, with its own special problems of poverty, illiteracy, and race difficulties, but it was not an alien land, not an oppressed nationality eager to revolt.

The end of Reconstruction left the Democratic party in control of what came to be called the "solid South." This was a natural development, for it was the Republican party that had guided the North during the war, and that had tried to carry through Reconstruction. This fact has worked to strengthen the American two-party system, since with so solid a block secure for the Democrats, the Republicans have been forced either to make compromises among themselves to preserve their own party unity, or to lose power; and the Northern Democrats have been forced to make compromises with their Southern wing. The fact that the presidency, the great prize of political action, could be obtained only by securing a majority of the Electoral College meant also that a careful balancing of regional interests had to be maintained; a minority party could get nowhere in American politics.

This is not, of course, the whole explanation for the fact that the United States, like Britain, has long maintained a two-party system. It is striking that the two-party system has endured so firmly in both countries despite the great differences between the American political machinery of checks and balances among executive, legislative, and judiciary and the British political machinery centered in an omnipotent Parliament. It is tempting, though intellectually inadequate, to see in both countries an underlying habit of political compromise with common roots in a long past of government by discussion.

Economic and Social Development

In 1865, the American economy was in many senses still "colonial"—that is, it produced in the main foods and other raw materials to be exchanged abroad for manufactured goods and, in financial terms, it was dependent on foreign money markets (chiefly London). But by 1914 the United States had been transformed into a great industrial nation, with its agriculture already to a high degree mechanized, and with financial resources so great that after World War I New York was to take over in part the place of London as a world financial center. This transformation could not have taken place, certainly not at the rate it did, without the existence of abundant manpower, of great and still almost untouched natural resources, and of the traditions of individual initiative and freedom of enterprise—which in part were certainly a product of the "frontier." Europe played a significant role in American economic growth by furnishing investment capital and, above all, by sending forth a steady flow of emigrants.

This great expansion in national wealth was achieved in a climate of opinion that supported overwhelmingly the view that the federal government should not interfere directly with business enterprise beyond maintaining public order, enforcing contracts, exercising some control over the actual coinage of money—and maintaining a protective tariff. Nor, of course, were the state and local governments supposed to go beyond such appropriate limits. This view we have already met in the classical economists who followed Adam Smith in Britain and in some of the continental states. It is a view that in the West has generally accompanied the first stages of the industrial revolution. But this revolution came relatively late to the United States, and for this if for no other reason a belief in free enterprise, in a minimum of government interference in economic activities, maintained itself more firmly in the twentieth century there than in the other parts of the western world.

This belief was reinforced by the Fourteenth Amendment to the Constitution, passed in 1866 and aimed to protect the freed Negroes in the South from state action to deprive them of civil rights. The Amendment contained the famous "due process" clause: "nor shall any state deprive any person of life, liberty, or property without due process of law." In the great era of free enterprise that followed the Civil War, the Supreme Court of the United States interpreted the celebrated clause to mean that state governments should not deprive businessmen—including corporations as "persons"—of property by regulating wages, prices, conditions of labor, and the like.

Immigration since the 1890's had brought in millions of aliens from eastern and southern Europe, men and women ignorant of American ways, and readily exploited by unscrupulous or merely conventional employers. These immigrants were hard to organize in labor unions; moreover, they and their children, uprooted, scorned, though they might be, readily absorbed the American beliefs that no man is a proletarian by nature, that there is always room on top. Yet even at the height of this "Gilded Age" or "Age of the Robber Barons" there was a movement toward the welfare state. Apparently there never was a time when laissez-faire was a universally accepted principle (except for the tariff), and wistful businessmen who nowadays look back to the nineteenth century in America as free from the curse of government interference are simply inventing a myth.

Much the same forces that had produced the Factory Acts in Britain gradually brought to the United States minimum-wage acts, limitation of child labor and women's labor, sanitary regulation, control of hours of labor, and workman's compensation. Characteristically, and in spite of the Fourteenth Amendment, these measures were taken at the state rather than at the national level, and they varied greatly in the different states. The state of Wisconsin early established a reputation for advanced social legislation, but many of the older northeastern states played an important part in the movement. By the early twentieth century, public opinion was ready for increased participation of the national government in the regulation of economic life.

Theodore Roosevelt, a Republican, president from 1901 to 1909, promised to give labor a "square deal" and to proceed vigorously with "trust-busting," attacks on the great trusts or combinations that had come to monopolize important sectors of the American economy. Although Theodore Roosevelt did not always fulfill his promises, his administration did assail the trusts in railroads and tobacco and did press the federal regulation of great corporations. A federal prosecution of the Standard Oil Company begun in 1906 resulted in 1911 in a Supreme Court decision dissolving the great holding company. Some of the separated parts familiar today, such as Esso (Standard of New Jersey), Socony-Vacuum (Standard of New York), and Calso (Standard of California), are in fact "bigger" than was the dissolved parent company of John D. Rockefeller. Yet the work of the radicals of 1900, particularly the "muckrakers" who wrote exposés of questionable business practices for popular magazines, was clearly not in vain. American "big business" was in the 1950's bigger than it was in the days of Theodore Roosevelt. But, to put the matter nicely and in good terms, it was aware of its responsibilities to the public—or, to put it not so

nicely, it was afraid of what might happen to it if it followed the advice of one of the great nineteenth-century "robber barons," Cornelius Vanderbilt, "The public be damned!" In short, big business in the United States is ultimately, as in democratic theory it must be, under the control of public opinion. This is a "realistic," not an "idealistic" statement: American public opinion is not at bottom hostile to the existence of wealthy inividuals, but it does resent excessive exploitation by big corporations.

During the first administration of Woodrow Wilson (1913-1917), a Democrat, the process of regulation gained momentum. The Federal Reserve Act of 1913, for example, gave federal officials more control over banking, credit, and currency. Approval of such measures was not, of course,

An 1899 cartoon warning the trusts of impending doom. Like Belshazzar unmindful of the handwriting on the wall, the tycoons prepare to feast on "the nation," being served by Miss Liberty, and champagne, being poured by Uncle Sam. Among the diners are: Carnegie (steel trust), Huntington (railroads), Rockefeller (oil), Armour (meat), Hanna (shipping), and, dwarfed by these powerful personalities, President McKinley.

unanimous, since Americans differ loudly and widely about almost everything from metaphysics to sports. But, save for the Civil War, they have usually been willing in the end to differ no more than vocally, to accept varieties of belief and action where they appeared harmless or unavoidable, to conform to the law with no more than occasional violence. To outsiders, and to many native critics, American life in the decades between the Civil War and 1917 often seemed one great brawl, a more-than-Darwinian struggle for wealth and power. Yet this apparently anarchistic society achieved extraordinary material things--bridges, dams, railroads, great cities—which required the co-operation of millions of men and women disciplined to a common task. This paradox of the co-existence in the United States of "rugged individualism" and social cohesion still disturbs and puzzles many commentators on the American scene.

In spite of the more than usual dose of distrust of "government" common in western—perhaps in human—tradition, government has in the United States come to play a larger and larger part in the lives of all. Although this is true of local and state governments too, it holds more especially of the federal government. The gradually increasing importance of the federal government, and the gradually decreasing initiative of state governments, are as objectively clear in the period 1789-1917 as is the material growth of the United States in population and wealth.

The Myth of Isolation

Quite as objectively clear, though still the subject of infinite debate among Americans, is the emergence of the United States as a great international power. The United States was never literally "isolated." From the very beginning, this country had a Department of State, our senior depart-ment, and the proper apparatus of ministers, consuls, and, later, ambassadors. The United States was involved in the world war of the Napoleonic era, and by the Monroe Doctrine of the 1820's took the firm position that European powers were not to extend their existing territories in the Western Hemisphere. This was no mere negation, but an active extension of American claims to a far wider sphere of influence than the continental United States. Although Americans took no part in the complex nineteenth-century balance-of-power politics in Europe, they showed an increasing concern with a balance of power in the Far East, where they had long traded. After the brief war of 1898 with Spain, a war that broke out in Cuba, always a close concern of the United States, Americans found themselves directly involved with the newly annexed territories of the Philippine Islands, Hawaii, Puerto Rico—in short, with what looked to outsiders, and to many Americans, like an American empire.

Theodore Roosevelt, who owed his rapid political rise partly to his military leadership of the "Rough Riders" in the Spanish War, was a vigorous imperialist. He pressed the building of the Panama Canal, upheld the Far Eastern interests of the United States, and advocated a larger navy. This new "navalism," which also had assertive spokesmen in Britain and Germany, derived many of its doctrines from the writings of an American officer, Captain Alfred T. Mahan. Mahan's book, *The Influence of Sea Power upon History* (1890), and his later works assigned navies a place of pre-eminent importance in determining power status and found an influential audience both at home and abroad. Americans as individuals had long been active in work for better international organization, world peace, a world court.

Furthermore, over these many decades of expanding wealth and trade, the United States had come to take full part in international commercial relations. In these relations she had, save when the federal government was blockading the Confederacy, stood out firmly for rights to trade even though there was a war on somewhere, stood out for the "rights of neutrals." This fact alone would probably have brought the United States into the world war of 1914-1918, as it had brought her eventually into the world war of 1792-1815. But in 1917 America was, as she had not been in 1812, a great and active participant in the world state-system.

Reading Suggestions
on the Western Democracies in the Nineteenth Century

(Asterisk indicates paperbound edition.)

BRITAIN

E. Halévy, *A History of the English People in the Nineteenth Century,* 2nd rev. ed., 5 vols. (P. Smith, 1949-1951). The classic detailed study; does not cover the entire period.

E. L. Woodward, *The Age of Reform* (Clarendon, 1938), and R. C. K. Ensor, *England, 1870-1914* (Clarendon, 1936). Two full and very useful volumes in the *Oxford History of England.*

D. Thomson, *England in the Nineteenth Century* (*Penguin, 1950). An excellent short account.

P. Magnus, *Gladstone: A Biography* (Dutton, 1955). A sound study of the great Victorian Liberal.

A. Briggs, *The Age of Improvements* (Longmans, Green, 1959). A general history of England, 1783-1867, which lives up to its apt, and not wholly ironical title.

Note: See also titles cited for Chapter XX.

FRANCE

D. W. Brogan, *The French Nation from Napoleon to Pétain, 1814-1940* (Harper, 1957). A brilliant essay by a writer who knows first-hand the great Western democracies of Britain, France, and the United States. A bit severe on the third Republic as a political structure.

A. Guérard, *France: A Modern History* (Univ. of Michigan Press, 1959). Actually a splendid general history of France from Cro-Magnon man to De Gaulle with most useful critical bibliographies.

A. Maurois, *The Miracle of France* (Harper, 1948). A general survey by a Frenchman with great literary gifts.

A. Guérard, *Reflections on the Napoleonic Legend* (Scribner's, 1924). Interesting study of the magnetic attraction exerted by Bonaparte after his death.

F. A. Simpson, *The Rise of Louis Napoleon,* 3rd ed. (Longmans, Green, 1950), and *Louis Napoleon and the Recovery of France,* 3rd ed. (Longmans, Green, 1951). The most detailed study in English; goes only to 1856.

J. M. Thompson, *Louis Napoleon and the Second Empire* (Blackwell, 1954). A useful synthesis, based on detailed scholarly works.

A. Guérard, *Napoleon III* (Harvard Univ. Press, 1943). A spirited attempt to picture the emperor in the attractive role of "Caesarean democrat."

D. W. Brogan, *France under the Republic* (Harper, 1940). A witty, perceptive, but allusive history of the Third Republic.

D. Thomson, *Democracy in France: The Third and Fourth Republics*, 3rd ed. (Oxford Univ. Press, 1958). A brilliant essay of interpretation; assumes basic factual knowledge on the part of the reader.

R. Soltau, *French Political Thought in the Nineteenth Century*, new ed. (Russell & Russell, 1959). A good survey, though perhaps unfair to the conservative thinkers.

G. Chapman, *The Dreyfus Case: A Re-assessment* (Viking, 1956). The most searching treatment of the "Affair" available in English; neglects the historical results of the case.

G. Bruun, *Clemenceau* (Harvard Univ. Press, 1943). A first-rate brief biography of the redoubtable politician of the Third Republic.

S. B. Clough, *France: A History of National Economics, 1789-1939* (Scribner's, 1939). A valuable treatment of topics often hard to find information on; the notes are most helpful.

ITALY

D. Mack Smith, *Italy: A Modern History* (Univ. of Michigan Press, 1959). A sound and detailed study, actually confined to "modern" history. Good reading suggestions.

A. J. B. Whyte, *The Making of Modern Italy* (Blackwell, 1944). One of the very few good accounts in English.

B. King, *A History of Italian Unity*, 2 vols., rev. ed. (Nisbet, 1924). An old account, but still informative.

D. Mack Smith, *Garibaldi* (Knopf, 1956). Brief and up-to-date; the best biography available in English.

D. Mack Smith, *Cavour and Garibaldi, 1860: A Study in Political Conflict* (Cambridge Univ. Press, 1954). Important monograph; essential reading for a full understanding of the two men.

A. J. B. Whyte, *The Political Life and Letters of Cavour, 1848-1861* (Oxford Univ. Press, 1930). Useful introduction.

B. Croce, *A History of Italy, 1871-1915* (Clarendon, 1929). By a distinguished philosopher of history; thoughtful, but controversial because of its severe judgments on Italian parliamentary leaders.

THE UNITED STATES

O. Handlin and others, eds., *The Harvard Guide to American History* (Harvard Univ. Press, 1954). An indispensable handbook for the study of American history, with full leads to the literature of the subject.

R. Hofstadter, W. Miller, D. Aaron, *The United States: The History of a Republic* (Prentice-Hall, 1957). A readable account, well illustrated.

R. B. Morris, ed., *Encyclopaedia of American History* (Harper, 1953). A standard reference work.

S. E. Morison and H. S. Commager, *The Growth of the American Republic*, 4th ed., 2 vols. (Oxford Univ. Press, 1950-1951). One of the very best textbooks.

C. A. and M. A. Beard, *The Rise of American Civilization* (Macmillan, 1936). A famous popular account, written from the standpoint of the economic interpretation of history.

O. Handlin, *Chance or Destiny: Turning Points in American History* (Little, Brown, 1955). Most readable general essay by a distinguished scholar.

L. Hartz, *The Liberal Tradition in America: An Interpretation of American Political Thought since the Revolution* (Harcourt, Brace, 1955). Provocative survey that has stirred up considerable controversy.

R. Hofstadter, *The American Political Tradition* (°Vintage), and C. Rossiter, *Conservatism in America* (Knopf, 1955). Complimentary studies, emphasizing the liberal and conservative strands respectively.

HISTORICAL FICTION

B. Disraeli, *Coningsby* (Dutton, 1911, Everyman ed.). Significant for its statement of the enlightened Conservative political position. Should be supplemented by the same author's *Sybil* for the Victorian "condition of England" problem.

A. Trollope, *The Prime Minister* (Oxford Univ. Press, 1951, World's Classics ed.). Probably the best novel on Victorian politics.

E. Zola, *The Downfall* ("La Débacle") (Appleton, 1902). Good novel of the French defeat in 1870; by the famous naturalistic writer.

A. Bennett, *Old Wives' Tale* (Modern Library). Contains a superb account of life in Paris under the siege of 1870-1871.

R. Martin du Gard, *Jean Barois* (Viking, 1949). Sound novel about the crisis of the French conscience over the Dreyfus affair.

W. D. Howells, *The Rise of Silas Lapham* (many editions). One of the best fictional introductions to American middle-class life in the late nineteenth century.

U. Sinclair, *The Jungle* (Viking, 1946). A famous exposé of the bad conditions in the meat-packing industry of Chicago about 1900.

M. Kantor, *Andersonville* (°Signet, 1957). Grim and realistic novel of the American Civil War based on detailed research; considered by many critics the best single work of fiction on the subject.

M. Mitchell, *Gone with the Wind* (Macmillan, 1936; °Pocket Permabooks). Important for its faithful reflection of widely held Southern attitudes toward the War between the States.

Central and Eastern Europe:

To the Outbreak of World War I

CHAPTER XXII

I: Introduction

IN THIS CHAPTER, we shall deal with Germany (1850-1914), the Habsburg Monarchy (1850-1914), and Russia (1825-1914). These three empires were partners in crime in the partitions of Poland of the late eighteenth century, and firm allies in the Metternich system of European balance after 1815. After 1850, they passed through periods of mutual affection and hatred. In 1914 all went to war, with Germany and Austria-Hungary as allies against Russia. Internally they had much in common, although each followed its own peculiar development. In contrast with the countries of western Europe, these were the lands of autocratic monarchy and relatively powerless parliaments appearing on the scene relatively late. In 1914, all three were still "empires," a title that only the tottering Ottoman state also claimed in Europe.

II: Germany, 1850-1914

In 1914, the militarist and nationalist German Empire was a powerful, unified industrial state with a highly educated, obedient, and competent population. By supporting the Balkan policies of its ally,

Opposite. I AND THE VILLAGE, *by Marc Chagall (1889-1960); Russian, painted 1911; Museum of Modern Art, New York City. The eternal Russian countryside interpreted by an émigré, who had recently arrived in Paris and employed the most advanced French experimental techniques (discussed below, p. 330).*

Austria-Hungary, it helped to plunge the entire world into the first of the twentieth century's wars of mass slaughter. Germany had emerged as a great continental power only after 1850, although for more than 1400 years millions of Germans had been living in the heart of Europe under a variety of political regimes. The militarism, the authoritarianism, the whole social and cultural tone of the Germany of 1914 were determined by the fact that it was the Kingdom of Prussia that had achieved German unification. Characteristic Prussian attitudes had overcome other German ways of looking at society, and had imposed themselves on non-Prussians. The Prussian triumph was complete by 1871.

Between 1850 and 1871, and especially after 1862, Prussia moved with ever-accelerating speed from triumph to triumph. Doubters and protesters were silenced or dazzled by the glitter of each new achievement; moral objections were regarded as unpatriotic. Otto von Bismarck, who directed policy, spoke of respect for legality and decency as "humanitarian twaddle" and proclaimed an era when "blood and iron" alone would decide. The ends seemed so desirable and were being gained so rapidly that even stern moralists could tell themselves that this time they need not examine the means. They shook their heads and voted the government new subsidies.

The creation of imperial Germany was above all the work of Bismarck (1815-1898). Brilliant, unscrupulous, ruthless, a genius at maneuver and at concealing his real intentions, Bismarck was often bewilderingly inconsistent in his policies. Sometimes he pursued two apparently contradictory policies at the same time, until the moment came when he had to make a final decision on which policy to follow. His intense loyalty to the Prussian Crown, however, did not falter during his long years in office, although after his dismissal by William II in 1890 he felt that his work was being undone and he often tried to embarrass the Emperor and his own successors in the government. He could not endure criticism of himself. At different periods, he loathed liberals, Catholics, and socialists, and despised his intellectual inferiors even when they belonged to his own class, the Prussian landed nobility: the Junkers, who believed firmly in their own privileges, monopolized commissions in the Prussian army, and dominated the administrative services of the Prussian state. Whatever Bismarck's policy of the moment, force lay at its roots. Influential before 1862, he towered over Prussia from 1862 to 1871, and over the German Empire thereafter until 1890. Yet his efforts could not have succeeded had they not met with general approval from the German people, who had hungered for unity since before 1848.

Prussia and the German Confederation, 1850-1859

The first major question facing the statesmen of Central Europe after the Revolutions of 1848 was whether Prussia or Austria would dominate the German Confederation. Indeed, in a broader sense, this was a question of what form the Confederation would now take. A creation of the Congress of Vienna (see Chapter XIX), it had been temporarily shaken and split by the developments of 1848, and now needed to be rebuilt. The "Big German" solution favored federation with Austria; the "Small German" solution favored separation from Austria or even from South Germany. The "Small German" program meant Prussian domination of the non-Austrian German states, and therefore became Bismarck's goal.

The period after 1848 opened with a defeat for a Prussian "Small German" solution. King Frederick William IV, who had refused to accept the imperial crown "from the gutter" when it was offered by the

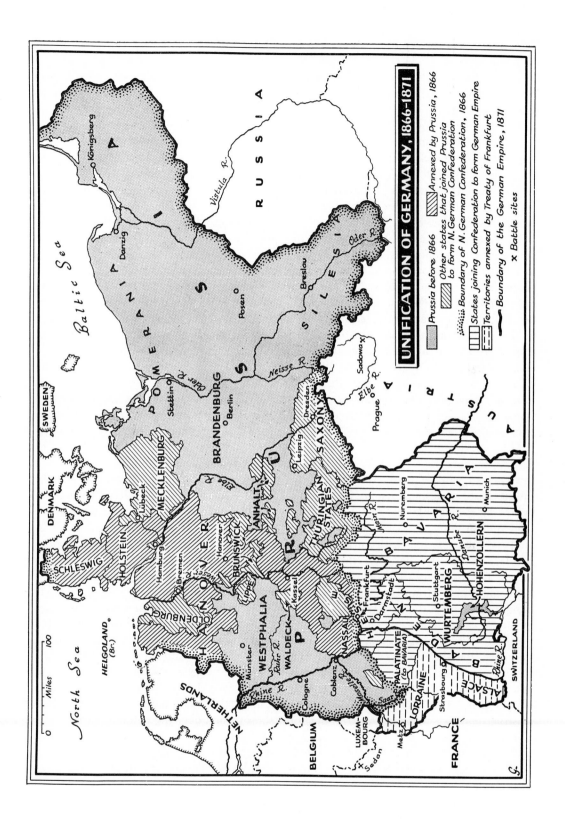

UNIFICATION OF GERMANY, 1866-1871

Prussia before 1866
Annexed by Prussia, 1866
Other states that joined Prussia to form N. German Confederation
Boundary of N. German Confederation, 1866
States joining Confederation to form German Empire
Territories annexed by Treaty of Frankfurt
Boundary of the German Empire, 1871
x Battle sites

Frankfurt Assembly (see Chapter XIX), none the less cherished the hope that the German princes might offer it to him. Taking advantage of Austria's pre-occupation with the remnants of the revolution of 1848, and overriding his own Prussian conservatives, who wished simply to strengthen their own state, Frederick William IV formed the Erfurt Union of Princes, an agreement to pool military resources. This union was designed to lead to Prussian political as well as military dominance.

The Austrians managed to bring Russian pressure to bear on Prussia. The Tsar opposed the unification of the Germans no matter under whose auspices. At Olmütz, in November, 1850, the Prussians renounced the Erfurt Union, and reluctantly agreed to the revival of the Confederation. This episode is known as the "humiliation" of Olmütz, a term that shows how bitterly many Prussians resented it. Yet Bismarck himself defended the treaty, and as a result was sent as Prussian representative to the Diet of the Confederation.

Although Bismarck made a speech approving Olmütz, he took every occasion at the Diet to work against Austria, and to thwart Austrian designs. As one facet of his policy, he strove to keep Prussia neutral in the Crimean War (1854-56), in which England and France fought with Turkey against Russia, and Austria harassed rather than helped the Russians (see below, p. 280). Realizing that Austrian behavior was alienating Russia, and that Russian friendship would be valuable later when Prussia came to grips with Austria, Bismarck frustrated the more liberal Prussians who hoped that Prussia would enter the war against Russia and thus line up with the West. He was counting on a military showdown with Austria, and on pushing Austria out of Germany, which he felt was too small for both powers. With this purpose in mind, he also wooed the French Emperor Napoleon III, despite the horror that many Prussians felt over dealings with a Bonaparte, whom they regarded as the heir of the French Revolution.

Simultaneously, during the 1850's, both the constitutional and the economic foundations of future Prussian development were laid. The Prussian Constitution of 1850 lasted down to the end of World War I. It provided for a bicameral legislature: a hereditary upper house including the nobles and royal appointees, and an elected lower house. But the method of electing this lower house made it certain that the popular will would be frustrated. Electors were divided into three classes, according to the size of the taxes they paid. The 4 per cent of the electorate who paid high taxes selected one-third of the representatives. The 14 per cent of middle taxpayers selected another third, and the remaining 82 per cent of low taxpayers selected the last third. The preponderant power of the wealthy is clear.

Even so, the lower house had very little to do beyond approving the budget. Policy questions were decided in the upper house, or still more often by the king and his personal circle of military and political advisers. The king appointed his ministers, could veto any bill he disapproved, and had a fixed sum of money at his disposal for expenses. He had a special "military cabinet" for army affairs that reported neither to the ministers nor to the legislature. Practically speaking, the king and the Junkers ran Prussia.

With its possessions in western Germany, including the Ruhr, Prussia had the richest coal deposits in Europe. She now began to build the iron and steel industry without which her future political and military triumphs would have been impossible. Alone among the continental nations, the Prussians turned over the planning of their new railway system to the army general staff, which laid out the lines with an eye to rapid and efficient mobilization and transportation of troops and military supplies in time of war.

Bismarck Comes to Power

Indeed these military concerns led directly to the beginning of Bismarck's undisputed domination of Prussian policies. King William I, who succeeded Frederick William IV in 1861, was above all a soldier. His minister of war, Roon, a friend of Bismarck's, easily persuaded the King that an army reorganization was necessary. He wanted to increase the number of conscripts called in each year from 40,000 to 63,000, and to lengthen the term of their service from two to three years. Behind Roon's military projects lay a political motive: to keep the army as conservative as possible, and to make it as big as possible, so that it might serve as counterweight to any liberal or revolutionary tendencies in the state. A prolonged political crisis arose over these aims in 1861 and 1862, when the Prussian parliament refused to vote the budget. At the very height of the crisis, Roon summoned Bismarck back to Berlin, and the King, convinced that here was a man who did not care about parliaments, appointed Bismarck to the key posts of prime minister of Prussia and minister of foreign affairs.

On the fallacious principle that there was a "gap" in the constitution that permitted the government to collect taxes even when the budget had not been approved by parliament, Bismarck now collected and spent revenue quite illegally. Again and again he dissolved the parliament, called new elections, faced another hostile house, and then repeated the process. He suppressed hostile newspapers in defiance of a constitutional proviso that the press should be free. He indicted an opposition deputy, himself a judge and a loyal Prussian, in spite of the constitutional provision that deputies could not be indicted for anything they said on the floor of the house. Yet after four years (1862-1866) of this unconstitutional behavior he got away with everything in the end, because of the glittering successes he scored by his unorthodox daring in foreign policy.

Since Bismarck intended to overthrow the German Confederation as it was then constituted, he opposed Austrian efforts to reform it. Austria wished to create an assembly of delegates chosen by the parliaments of the member states, in addition to those named by the princes, and a directorate of six monarchs. Bismarck prevented William I from attending a congress of princes called by Austria to discuss these proposals, and thus wrecked the congress (1862). In 1863, he kept Austria out of the *Zollverein*, the German Customs Union (see above, p. 178). He also consolidated his good relations with Russia during the Polish revolt (see below, p. 302) by concluding the Alvensleben convention, which allowed the Russians to pursue fleeing Poles onto Prussian territory and capture them there. Thus Bismarck wooed the Russians a

Prince Otto von Bismarck (1815-1898).

second time, as he had during the Crimean War.

The Schleswig-Holstein Question, 1863-1865

When the King of Denmark died in late 1863, the celebrated Schleswig-Holstein question gave Bismarck further opportunities. The Prime Minister of England once remarked that only three men had ever understood this complex problem, and that one was dead and one insane, while he himself, the third, had forgotten all about it. In brief, the duchies of Schleswig and Holstein at the southern base of the Danish peninsula had been ruled by the King of Denmark, but not as part of Denmark. A fifteenth-century guarantee assured the duchies that they could never be separated from each other. Yet Holstein to the south was a member of the German Confederation; Schleswig to the north was not. Holstein was mostly German in population; Schleswig was mixed German and Danish. In 1852, Prussia had agreed in an international conference on an heir who would succeed both to the Danish throne and to the duchies. At the same time, Prussia had joined the other powers in recommending that Denmark and the duchies should be united by a constitution. But, when the constitutional union of Denmark and the duchies was attempted, the duchies resisted, and the Danes tried to incorporate Schleswig. German patriots objected. The Prussians and Austrians wanted the duchies to have special representation inside the Danish parliament, and insisted that Schleswig should *not* be incorporated into Denmark. None the less, the King of Denmark in 1863 followed a policy that supported annexation.

Into this situation Bismarck now moved to win the duchies for Prussia. He wanted both the prestige that Prussia would gain and the valuable commercial port of Kiel in Holstein. First he maneuvered Prussia and Austria together into a victorious war against Denmark (1864), although Austria had no real interest in the duchies. Then he quarreled with the Austrians over the administration of the duchies. At the Convention of Gastein, 1865, it was decided that Prussia was to administer Schleswig and that Austria was to administer Holstein. But this arrangement provided only a temporary halt in Bismarck's drive against Austria.

War with Austria, 1866

Bismarck kept nagging Vienna about Austrian behavior in Holstein. He tried and failed to tempt France into an alliance. But he did succeed in lining up the Italians, who secretly obliged themselves to go to war on the side of Prussia if Prussia fought Austria within three months. This was contrary to the constitution of the German Confederation, which forbade members to ally themselves with a foreign power against other members. So distressed was William I at this illegality that he lied flatly when the Austrian Emperor asked him if such a treaty existed. Finally, Bismarck suddenly proposed that the German Confederation be reformed, and that an all-German parliament be elected by universal suffrage, which everybody knew he hated.

Bismarck probably advanced this proposal for universal suffrage in order to make it appear that his quarrel with Austria rested on a less sordid ground than the mere Schleswig-Holstein question. Yet the proposal also reflected his calculation that enfranchisement of all Germans would weaken the Progressive party, heir to the liberalism of 1848, and would produce many conservative and royalist votes from the peasantry. He had seen how Napoleon III had risen to imperial power in France on the strength of universal suffrage. And he had been influenced by conversations with Ferdinand Lassalle, a German socialist, who argued that universal suffrage would weaken the middle classes. Bismarck had hoped that the Austrians might try to throw his plan out, but the other members of the Confederation asked Prussia to propose a full plan of reform. Austria now laid the Schleswig-Holstein question before the Diet of the Confederation. Bismarck ordered Prussian troops into Holstein, and declared that Austrian motions in the Diet were unconstitutional. He had succeeded in provoking war with Austria. It was an all-German civil war, since Bavaria, Württemberg, Saxony, and Hanover (the four other German kingdoms) and most of the lesser German states sided with Austria.

The war lasted seven weeks, and was virtually decided in less than three. The Austrians had to commit a substantial part of their forces against Italy. Skillfully using their railway network, the telegraph, and superior armaments, the Prussians quickly overran northern Germany, invaded Bohemia, and defeated the Austrians at Königgrätz (Sadowa). This battle has been referred to as a Gettysburg won by the secessionist Prussians. As the rapid German civil war continued, the Prussians defeated the Bavarians and entered Frankfurt, seat of the German Confederation. The states of Hanover, Hesse-Cassel, and Nassau were all annexed to Prussia and their dynasties were expelled. Schleswig-Holstein and the free city of Frankfurt were also taken over.

Bismarck successfully opposed the generals, and even his king, who wished to punish Austria severely. Except for the cession of Venetia to Italy, Austria suffered no territorial losses as a result of the Peace of Prague (1866), but she did pay a small indemnity. Most important from Bismarck's point of view, Austria had to withdraw forever from the German Confederation, which now ceased to exist. Germany north of the Main River was to join a new North German Confederation to be organized by Prussia. However, it was stipulated that the German states south of the Main were to be free to form an independent union of their own. But Bismarck had previously concluded secret treaties of alliance with the most important South German states—Bavaria, Württemberg, and Baden—who promised to put their armies at the disposal of the King of Prussia in case of war. So the proposed South German union could never come into existence. Bismarck thus broke the Peace of Prague before it had been concluded, a real piece of diplomatic skill. Bismarck's gentle treatment of Austria was not just a matter of generosity. He was convinced that Prussia would need Austrian help in the future. Now that he had expelled Austria from Germany, imposed a "Small German" solution, and elevated Prussia to the position of dominance, he had scored his point.

Now Bismarck was free to turn to the Prussian parliament, with which he had been feuding for four years. He asked for an "indemnity," that is, a certification that all the revenue he had illegally collected and illegally spent, ever since the parliament had refused to pass the budget in 1861, had in fact been legally collected and legally spent. The deputies were so dazzled by the feats of arms against Denmark and Austria, and by the enormous new acquisitions of power and territory, that they voted the indemnity, and awarded Bismarck personally a cash gift of roughly $300,000. The indemnity marked an important defeat for parliamentary government.

The North German Confederation

An assembly elected by universal manhood suffrage now debated and adopted a constitution for the new North German Confederation, of which the Prussian king was president. The draft that Bismarck submitted is eloquent testimony to his determination to "kill parliamentarism through parliament." The future parliament (*Reichstag*) was to have no power over the budget, and the ministers were not to be responsible to it. Instead, a Federal Council (*Bundesrat*), consisting of delegates from the member states and voting according to instructions from their sovereigns, would reach all key policy decisions in secret, and would have veto power over any enactment of the Reichstag. A chancellor would preside over the Bundesrat but would not have to explain or defend its decisions before the Reichstag. Since Prussia now had not only its own votes in the Bundesrat, but those of the newly annexed states, Bismarck's plan in effect made it possible for the king of Prussia to run Germany.

This plan was only slightly modified so that the future chancellor would have to sign every act undertaken by the king of Prussia as president of the Confederation. But the executive was in no way made "responsible" to the Reichstag. Bismarck's plan also specified that, beginning five years later in 1872, the size of the army would be fixed by law, and that the Reichstag would have a vote on the budget. However, Bismarck, who became chancellor, saw to it that the debate on the military budget did not take place every year, but that sums were appropriated for long periods in advance.

Showdown with France

During the next four years, the power of the new Prussian-dominated German state began to make itself felt. Increasing uneasiness reigned in Europe. As long as Bismarck needed the benevolent neutrality of Napoleon III, he had hinted that he might not object if Napoleon took Belgium. Now the gullible Napoleon found that Bismarck no longer remembered the matter. Hoping to be compensated for his assistance in making peace between Prussia and Austria, Napoleon III made unscrupulous attempts to acquire Luxemburg by purchase from the King of Holland. Again he was frustrated by Bismarck. Suddenly confronted with the new Germany, many members of the French public and press hoped to get "revenge for Sadowa," and became strongly anti-German. The German press responded in kind. Napoleon III strove to create an alliance with Austria and Italy in order to thwart further Prussian expansion. But the Austrians shied away from a true commitment, and the Italians were unable to reach an agreement with the French because of the Roman question (see above, p. 251).

When the Spaniards ousted their queen in 1868, one of the candidates for the throne was a Hohenzollern prince whom Bismarck secretly backed by discreetly bribing influential Spaniards. Because of family dynastic practice, it was necessary to secure the consent of the reluctant King William I of Prussia, and this Bismarck finally extracted without hinting that war with France might result. Napoleon, also deep in Spanish intrigue, feared that a Hohenzollern on the Spanish throne would expose France to a two-front attack. French diplomatic pressure was exerted directly on King William, and the Hohenzollern candidate withdrew. At this moment, Bismarck seemed to be defeated.

But the French, overstimulated by their success, now demanded that William publicly endorse the withdrawal of the candidacy and promise never to allow it to be renewed. William, who was at Ems, courteously refused, and sent a telegram to Bismarck describing his interchange with the French ambassador. Bismarck then abridged this famous Ems telegram and released it to the press and all the European chanceries. He made it seem that William had thoroughly snubbed the French ambassador, and that the ambassador had been "provocative" to the King. Public opinion in Germany was now inflamed, and Bismarck set out to bait the French still further by unleashing a violent campaign against them in the German press and boasting of his prowess in editing the Ems despatch. The French reacted as Bismarck had hoped: they declared war on July 19, 1870.

Within six weeks the Germans had advanced into France, bottled up one French army inside the fortress of Metz, defeated another at Sedan, and captured Napoleon III himself. The protracted siege of Paris followed, ending in surrender early in 1871. A new French government had to sign the treaty of Frankfurt. Bismarck forced the French to pay a billion-dollar indemnity, to cede the rich province of Alsace and about two-fifths of Lorraine (which the German military wanted as a defense against possible future French attack), and to support German occupying forces until the indemnity had been paid.

The German Empire

Even before this peace had been imposed, King William of Prussia was proclaimed Emperor of Germany in the great Hall of Mirrors in Louis XIV's palace at Versailles. Bismarck had to make a few unimportant concessions to the rulers of the South German states to secure their entry into the new empire, but he never had to consult the Reichstag, which simply hastened to send its own deputation begging the King to accept the Crown. The proclamation took place in a ceremony of princes and soldiers. When a constitution for the new empire was adopted, it was simply an extension of the constitution of the North German Confederation of 1867.

As Chancellor of the German Empire from 1871 to 1890, Bismarck became the leading statesman in all Europe. He felt that Germany had no further need for territory or for war. As a nineteenth-century realist with no dream of world-empire, he felt that his limited goals had been attained. As diplomat, he henceforth worked for the preservation of Germany's gains against threats from abroad, especially the threat that haunted him most: foreign coalition against Germany (see Chapter XXV). As politician, he worked for the preservation of the Prussian system against all opposing currents.

Bismarck's chancellorship falls naturally into two periods: (1) a period of free trade, co-operation with the Liberals, and opposition to the Catholics (1871-1878); and (2)

A Prussian battery before Paris during the Franco-Prussian War.

a period of protective tariffs, co-operation with the Catholics, and opposition to the socialists (1878-1890).

Domestic Developments, 1871-1878

At home, a multitude of economic and legal questions arose as a result of the creation of the new empire. Working with the moderate Liberal party in the Reichstag, Bismarck put through a common coinage and a central bank, co-ordinated and unified the railroads and postal systems, and regularized the legal and judicial systems. In 1871, the Reichstag voted to maintain 1 per cent of the population under arms for three years. In 1874, Bismarck, simply by threatening to resign, forced the Reichstag to fix the size of the army at 401,000 for a seven-year period, until 1881. In 1880, a year before the period expired, he forced an increase to 427,000 for another seven years, to 1888. The privileged position of the army made a military career ever more attractive, and served as a constant spur to German militarism.

But the great drama of the 1870's in Germany was furnished by Bismarck's attack on the Roman Catholic Church, the *Kulturkampf* ("battle for civilization"). The "Syllabus of Errors," published by the Vatican in 1864 (see Chapter XX), denounced the toleration of other religions, secular education, and state participation in church affairs. Then in 1870 the Vatican Council, the first general council of the Church to meet since the Council of Trent in the Reformation period, adopted the dogma of papal infallibility. This dogma asserted that the judgments of the pope on faith and morals were infallible. To many non-Catholics this seemed to say that no state could count on the absolute loyalty of its Catholic citizens.

In Germany, the Catholics were a large minority of the population. They had formed a political party, the Center, that quickly became the second strongest party in the Empire. The Center defended papal infallibility and wished to restore the pope's temporal power, which had been ended by the unification of Italy. The Center not only had many sympathizers in the Catholic Polish provinces of Germany but also sponsored a labor movement of its own, which seemed to pose a social threat. Catholic peasant and workman, priest and nobleman, all opposed the Protestant urban middle class and the Prussian military predominance in the state. Bismarck identified his clerical opponents with France and Austria, the two nations he had defeated in making the new Germany.

In collaboration with the Liberals, Bismarck put through laws expelling the Jesuits from Germany, forbidding the clergy to criticize the government, and closing the schools of religious orders. In Prussia, civil marriage was now required, appropriations for the Catholic Church were stopped, and priests were forced to study at secular universities. The Pope declared these laws null and void, and summoned all good Catholics to disobey them. Catholic services stopped in towns and villages, and many Catholics were deprived of their sacraments.

Bismarck never appreciated that the Church thrives on persecution. By declaring that he would not "go to Canossa," he summoned up for Protestant Germans the picture of the German Emperor Henry IV humbling himself before the Pope in 1077. But Bismarck in the end had to go to Canossa, and repealed in the eighties most of the anti-Catholic measures he had passed in the seventies. By then he needed the support of the Center party against his former allies the Liberals, whose demands for power he found exorbitant, and against the growing menace of the Social Democrats. Moreover, the Protestant Church itself and many of the conservative Prussian nobility had grown alarmed over the excesses of the anti-Catholic campaign.

Domestic Developments, 1878-1890

Indeed, in 1877 and 1878 Bismarck had begun a gradual shift in policy, dictated in the first place by the need for more revenue. The Empire got its money in part from indirect taxes imposed by the Reichstag on tobacco, alcohol, sugar, and the like. The rest came from the individual states, which controlled all direct taxation and made contributions to the imperial budget. As military costs mounted, the government's income became insufficient, and Bismarck did not want to increase the Empire's dependence on the states by repeatedly asking them to increase their contributions. He wanted the Reichstag to vote higher indirect taxes, but its Liberal members naturally suspected that if they acceded he might do to them what he had formerly done to the Prussian parliament. They suspected that he might govern without them if a dispute arose, and depend on the money he would collect from the higher taxes they had granted him. Therefore they wanted some sort of guarantee before they untied Bismarck's hands.

Basically, German tariff policy had been one of free trade, with little protection for German goods. But after a financial panic in 1873, the iron and textile industries put pressure on Bismarck to shift to a policy of protection that would help them compete with England. Moreover, an agricultural crisis led conservatives to abandon their previous support of free trade, and to demand protection against cheap grain from eastern Europe. In 1879, Bismarck put through a general protective tariff on all imports, a move on which his former allies, the Liberals, were split.

In order to avoid granting the constitutional guarantees demanded by the Liberals, Bismarck gradually abandoned the *Kulturkampf*. The Catholic Center favored his protectionist policy; moveover, the less-ening of the clerical threat in France and the conclusion of a firm German alliance with Austria in 1879 (see Chapter XXV) removed the foreign causes for the attack on the Church. Bismarck therefore secured the support of the Center as well as that of the conservatives. Thus he was able to avoid making concessions to the Reichstag, and thus he launched Germany on an era of protection. The protectionist policy spurred still further the rapid and efficient growth of industry, especially heavy industry. Politically, the conservative Protestant agrarian forces now grew stronger, and gained many urban votes. But Bismarck never entirely trusted the Center, and strove successfully to remodel the Liberals into a stanchly conservative industrialist group.

While he was easing the *Kulturkampf* and swinging to protection in 1878-1879, Bismarck also began to proceed against the Social Democratic party. The Marxists Liebknecht and Bebel had founded this small party in 1869; in 1875, they enlarged it, much to Marx's own disgust, by accepting the followers of Lassalle, an apostle of non-violence. The German Social Democrats were not nearly so revolutionary as their own Marxist phraseology suggested, and had no doubt inherited some of Lassalle's willingness to make a deal with the existing regime. They did not threaten the state, as Bismarck pretended to think, but they had many supporters among intellectuals and former liberals, and a substantial trade-union following. They polled half a million votes in 1877, about 10 per cent of the total electorate. These revisionist Social Democrats were prepared to concentrate their efforts on improving working conditions rather than on revolution. But Bismarck always needed an enemy against whom he could unify his supporters; besides, he had been deeply impressed by the Paris Commune (see Chapter XXI), and believed that something similar might occur in Germany.

Using as a pretext two attempts by alleged Social Democrats to assassinate William I, Bismarck called a general election in 1878 and rammed through the Reichstag a bill making the Social Democratic party illegal, forbidding its meetings, and suppressing its newspapers. Individual socialists could even be expelled from their domiciles by the police. Abandoning their alleged principles, the Liberals supported this law, but they would not allow Bismarck to make it a permanent statute. He had to apply to the Reichstag for its renewal every two or three years; it was renewed each time, until just before Bismarck's own downfall in 1890. Interestingly enough, Social Democrats were still allowed to run for the Reichstag, and their votes increased during the years when they were suffering legal disabilities.

But Bismarck felt that "a remedy cannot be sought merely in repression of Socialist excesses—there must be simultaneously a positive advancement of the welfare of the working classes." As a result, all during the 1880's, the government put forward a series of bills in favor of the workers: in 1882 compulsory insurance against illness, and in 1884 against accidents. The sickness insurance funds were raised by contributions from both workers and employers; the accident insurance funds were contributed altogether by the employers. In 1889, old-age and invalidism insurance followed, with employers and employees contributing equally, and with an additional subsidy from the state. The German system of social security as developed initially under Bismarck did not reduce the Social Democratic vote, but it did provide much that the worker desired.

William II

Bismarck's faithful William I died at the age of ninety in 1888, and his son, Frederick III, already mortally ill, ruled

Emperor William II (1859-1941).

for only about three months. The next emperor was Frederick's son, William II, a young man of twenty-nine whose advent his father had greatly feared because of his immaturity, impulsiveness, and conceit. William I had allowed Bismarck to act for him, but William II was determined to act for himself. This determination underlay the subsequent controversy between him and Bismarck.

On his accession, William loudly proclaimed his sympathy with the workingman. When the anti-socialist law came up for renewal, the Emperor supported a modified version that would have taken away the power of the police to expel Social Democrats from their residences. Bismarck opposed the measure, hoping that the Socialist Democrats would indulge in excesses which would give him the excuse to suppress them by armed force. As a result,

CHAPTER XXII

there was no anti-socialist law after 1890. Other differences arose between the Chancellor and the Emperor over relations with Russia and over procedure in reaching policy decisions. Finally, in March, 1890, William commanded Bismarck to resign.

Although four chancellors succeeded him during the years before the outbreak of war in 1914, none of them can be compared with Bismarck in ability and influence. The years 1890-1914 are truly the years of William II. Energetic but unsteady, pompous and menacing but without the intention or the courage to back up his threats, emotional and vacillating, William was ill-suited to govern any country, much less the militaristic, highly industrialized, imperial Germany with its social tensions and its lack of political balance.

Domestic Tensions, 1890-1914

Party structure reflected the strains in German society. The Liberals, a party of big business, usually had little strength in the Reichstag, although many industrialists were on intimate terms with the Emperor personally. The great landowners banded together in protest against a reduction in agricultural duties which was included in a series of trade treaties concluded between Germany and other continental European countries between 1892 and 1894. In 1894, they organized the Agrarian League, which spearheaded all conservative measures and became enormously powerful in German politics. In 1902, they forced a return to protection.

The electoral strength of the Social Democrats increased during William's reign from 1,500,000 to 4,250,000, and embraced one-third of the voting population by 1914. Freed from interference by the removal of the anti-socialist law, they organized trade unions, circulated newspapers, and successfully brought pressure on the regime for more social legislation. The party had no immediate plan for a revolution, although its radical wing expected, especially after the Russian revolution of 1905 (see below, p. 305), that a revolution would come. The moderate or "revisionist" wing, which expected no open conflict between capital and labor, felt that by allying with the middle class to attain a majority in the Reichstag the Social Democrats might eventually overthrow the militarist regime. This the radical wing scornfully dismissed as mere temporizing.

As the Social Democrats became more powerful, the government allied itself more closely with the Catholic Center. Between 1895 and 1906, and again between 1909 and 1914, a coalition of conservatives and the Center formed the majority group in the Reichstag. The coalition did not wish to see any increase in the powers of parliament. Yet left-wingers within the Center party occasionally called for a liberalization of the system and for tactical purposes would even ally with the Social Democrats.

Meanwhile, issues of military, colonial, and foreign policy began to complicate the internal politics of Germany. The size of the army rose from 479,000 in 1892 to 870,000 in 1913. And for the first time Germany sought a big navy after Admiral Tirpitz became minister of the navy in 1897. The Emperor issued a series of warlike and grandiose statements hailing Germany's "future on the waters," and he and Tirpitz planned a high-seas fleet to supersede the naval forces that had been designed for coastal defense and for the defense of commerce. The navy boom was at least partly intended to supply a market for the expanding steel industry. A Navy League, ostensibly a private organization but constantly hand in glove with the regime, spread propaganda on behalf of the new fleet. The first rather modest naval law of 1898 provided for a navy that was doubled by the second law of 1900.

But the army and navy were only the most obvious weapons of world power. Bismarck's saturated country seemed saturated no longer. The Colonial Society thrived as Germany seized lands in the Far East and in Africa (see Chapter XXIV), despite the drain on the budget (for the colonies were never profitable), and despite scandal after scandal (for the Germans were often brutal colonial administrators). "Pan-Germans" planned the great Berlin-Baghdad railway to the Near East and cried shrilly for more and more adventure and conquest.

William's naval and colonial policies embittered Germany's relations with Great Britain. In 1896, the Emperor himself sent the Boer President Kruger a telegram congratulating him on his having repelled the Jameson Raid (see below, p. 350), and hinting that Germany would have been willing to intervene on the side of the Boers against Britain. Again in 1908, he gave an interview to a London newspaper, the *Daily Telegraph*, in which, with monumental indiscretion, he protested his friendship for Britain, yet at the same time declared that the English had been ungrateful to him in not acknowledging that his own military plans, sent to them in secrecy, had enabled them to win the Boer War. Of course there was nothing in his claim.

The *Daily Telegraph* affair aroused a storm of protest against William in Germany itself, and the Emperor had to apologize and promise to do better in the future.

This episode illustrates the dangerous instability of the man who was all-powerful in a mighty military state. Moreover, it also reveals the general uneasiness that underlay the apparently smooth and prosperous surface of William's Germany. The protest against the anachronistic system under which Germans lived and labored, and against the external bombast and internal insecurity of the regime, was expressed in the enormous vote of the Social Democrats in 1912.

In 1913-1914, a German army officer in the Alsatian town of Saverne (Zabern) wounded a lame shoemaker with his sword, and the commanding officer of the German garrison illegally arrested and jailed townspeople who protested. The bitter resentment of the Alsatians was echoed by a tremendous number of Germans who had become resentful over the outrageous and unrestrained behavior of their military. By a vote of 293 to 54, the Reichstag passed a resolution of censure against the government. Even more interesting is the sequel, for William decorated the guilty officer, who was acquitted by a court-martial. The Saverne affair proved that the German public was still capable of feeling discomfort over the excesses of their Prussian masters, but it also proved that even a public expression of disapproval had little effect on these masters—the Emperor, the Junkers, and the military.

III: The Habsburg Monarchy, 1850-1914

Character of the Empire

The extraordinary empire of the Habsburgs has been called ramshackle, heterogeneous, and anachronistic. And much scorn has been poured upon it for its incompetence, its smugness, its stupidity, and its failure to keep up with modern times. No doubt these charges are largely justified. But in recent years voices have been raised mourning the Empire's disappearance, and regretfully echoing a nineteenth-century Czech patriot's celebrated remark that if the Empire did not exist it would be necessary to invent it. These expressions of longing come not only from reactionaries, monarchists, and clericals lamenting a past hopelessly beyond recovery. They can be heard from the lips of old men in Tito's Yugoslavia and in the "people's republics" of Rumania, Poland, and Hungary. These old men remember with longing a regime which they felt in their youth to be oppressive and unfair.

Perhaps these sentiments are not so much praise for the Habsburgs as blame for the communists who now rule much of the former Habsburg territory, and for the extreme nationalist or fascist regimes that preceded the communist triumph. In any case, it is depressing to reflect that the problem of the national hatreds and rivalries that haunted and finally destroyed the Habsburgs is with us still in modified form today, and that this same problem still causes suffering and threatens war.

Emperor Francis Joseph (1830-1916).

During the entire period from 1850 to 1914, the Emperor Francis Joseph sat on the Habsburg throne. Simple in his personal life and immensely conscientious, he worked hard at his desk, reading and signing state papers for hours every day. But he was without fire or imagination, uninterested in books dealing with current problems, or even in newspapers, devoted to the rigid court etiquette prescribed for Habsburgs, inflexibly old-fashioned and conservative, and selfish in the old Habsburg way, always ready to dismiss a minister of whose further usefulness he was not convinced. He was intensely pious. He loved to hunt. His mere longevity inspired loyalty, but it must be admitted that he was a dull fellow, in every sense of the term. His decisions usually came too late, and conceded too little. His responsibility for the course of events is large.

Political Experiments, 1850-1867

We may divide the period of Habsburg history between 1850 and 1914 into unequal portions by using the convenient date 1867, when the Empire became the dual monarchy of Austria-Hungary. After the suppression of the Revolution of 1848, there was a decade of repression usually called the "Bach period," from the name of the Minister of the Interior, ending in 1859 with the war against Piedmont and France (see Chapter XXI). Then came eight years of political experimentation from 1859 to 1867, punctuated by the war of 1866 with Prussia.

In 1849 all parts of the Empire were for the first time unified and directly ruled from Vienna by German-speaking officials. In 1855, the state signed a concordat with the Catholic Church giving clerics a greater influence in education and in other fields than they had enjoyed since the reforms of Joseph II. Because the repressive domestic policies of the Bach system required expensive armies and policemen, the state went into debt. Instead of investing in railroads and industry, Austria spent its money on enforcing the Bach system. These expenditures left it at a disadvantage compared with Prussia. Then, during the Crimean War, instead of repaying Tsar Nicholas I for Russia's aid in subduing the Hungarian revolution, Austria "astonished the world by her ingratitude." Not only did Francis Joseph fail to assist the Russians, he actually kept them in fear of an attack by occupying the Danubian principalities (modern Rumania). In 1857, Austria experienced a severe financial crisis partly as a result of this long mobilization.

The defeat of 1859 at the hands of the French and Italians, and the loss of Lombardy with its great city of Milan, brought about the end of the Bach system. War continued to threaten, and the nationalities inside the Empire, especially the Magyars, could not be kept in a state of smoldering discontent which would render their troops unreliable. Several solutions were now tried in an effort to create a structure that would withstand the domestic and foreign strains, but which would not jeopardize the Emperor's position. Francis Joseph made no effort to consult the people. Instead, he listened first to the nobles, who favored a loose federalism, and then to the bureaucrats, who favored a tight centralism.

First, a constitutional change in 1860, the "October Diploma," set up a central legislature to which the aristocratic provincial assemblies throughout the Empire were to send delegates, and which would deal with economic and military questions. All other problems were to be left to the provinces. This, however, did not satisfy the most important non-German province in the Empire—Hungary. Except for the great magnates, the Magyars were still discontented and continued to press the demands for autonomy that they had made in 1848. But Francis Joseph, who hated the

thought of abandoning the uniformity of the Bach system even though he was ready to soften its rigor, opposed the Magyar wishes for special treatment. He was leaning on the aristocracy in the hope that they could hold off liberalism.

On the other hand, the German liberals and bureaucrats of Austria felt that the October Diploma went too far and gave the Magyars too much. To them it seemed that the Empire was being dismembered on behalf of the nobility, who dominated the provincial assemblies. The "February Patent" of 1861 was actually a new constitution in line with their views. It proclaimed a more centralized scheme. The imperial legislature took over most of the powers the October Diploma had reserved for the provincial assemblies or diets.

Great landowners, town chambers of commerce, townsmen, and peasants formed the four classes of electors to these provincial diets, and there were tax qualifications for all members of the last two classes. As in the Prussian constitution of 1850, the class or "curial" system was highly discriminatory, and worked to disfranchise the peasants. Moreover, in regions like Bohemia, where the town population was heavily German and the countryside population heavily Czech, it worked to benefit the rich and the Germans. Yet it continued until 1907, favoring the Germans and hurting the Czechs.

Naturally, the Magyars objected to this second solution even more than to the first, and flatly refused to participate. To the applause of the Germans in Vienna, including the liberals, Hungary was returned to authoritarian rule. Czechs and Poles also eventually withdrew from the central parliament and left only a German rump. Disturbed, the Emperor suspended the February Patent; he began to negotiate with the Magyars, who were represented by the intelligent and moderate Francis Deák, but the negotiations were interrupted by the war with Prussia in 1866.

The Austrian defeat at Sadowa (see above), the expulsion of Austria from Germany, and the loss of Venetia seemed to threaten the entire Habsburg system. Francis Joseph resumed negotiations with the Magyars, with the help of the great Magyar noble, Andrássy, and of Beust, who had become Austrian foreign minister. In 1867, a formula was found which was to govern and preserve the Habsburg domains down to the World War of 1914-1918.

The Dual Monarchy, 1867

This was the famous *Ausgleich*, or "compromise," which created the "dual monarchy" of Austria-Hungary. The Hungarian constitution of 1848 was restored, and the entire Empire was reorganized on a strict partnership basis. Austria and Hungary were united in the person of the emperor, who was always to be a Catholic legitimate Habsburg, and who was to be crowned King of Hungary in a special ceremony in Budapest. For foreign policy, military affairs, and finance, the two states had joint ministers appointed by the emperor. A customs union subject to renewal every ten years also united them. Every ten years the quota of common expenditure to be borne by each partner was to be settled. A unique body, the "delegations," made up of sixty members from the Austrian and sixty members from the Hungarian parliament, meeting alternately in Vienna and in Budapest, was to decide on the common budget. After the budget had been approved, it had to be ratified by the full parliaments of both countries, and signed by the emperor-king. The delegations also had supervisory authority over the three joint ministers, and might summon them to give an account of their activities. In practice, the delegations seldom met, and were almost never consulted on questions of policy. The system favored Hungary, which had 40 per cent of the population but never paid more than one-third of the expenses. Every ten years, when the quota of expenses and the customs union needed joint consideration, a new crisis arose.

Otherwise, Hungary and Austria were separate states. As King of Hungary, Francis Joseph appointed cabinet ministers, professors, bishops, civil servants, and other officials. He was obliged at least once a year to summon the Hungarian legislature, which had an upper house of hereditary peers and a lower house elected by an elaborate system with more than fifty types of voters. However, qualifications regarding economic status and nationality made the Hungarian lower house entirely undemocratic; the voters never totaled more than 6 per cent of the population. For its part, Austria retained the parliament and the seventeen provincial assemblies provided by the February Patent of 1861. According to the new Austrian constitution of 1867, the authority of the emperor somewhat resembled that of other constitutional monarchs, with the fundamental exception that he could legislate by himself when parliament was not in session. Since he could dissolve parliament at will, he enjoyed a very large discretion and was potentially a strong personal ruler.

The dual structure of Austria-Hungary was unique in Europe, and indeed in history. Because of it, many domestic developments in the two parts of the monarchy may be considered quite separately. Yet one overwhelmingly important and complicated problem remained common to both halves of the monarchy: the problem of the national minorities that had not received their autonomy. Some of these minorities (Czechs, Poles, Ruthenes) were largely in Austria; others (Slovaks, Rumanians) were largely in Hungary; the rest (Croats, Serbs, Slovenes, all of them south Slavs) were in both states. These nationalities were at different stages of development and of national self-consciousness. Some of them were sub-

NATIONALITIES IN CENTRAL AND EASTERN EUROPE

About 1914

—— Political boundaries, 1914
--- Boundary between
   Austria and Hungary
Abbreviations:
Ger. - Germans ; Mag.-Magyars;
Gr. - Greeks ; A. -Armenians;
   Swed. - Swedes
(Many scattered national
   minorities are not shown)

ject to pressures from fellow-nationals living in states outside the dual monarchy.

The Austrian constitution of 1867 provided that all nationalities enjoy equal rights, and guaranteed that each might use its own language in education, administration, and public life. Even the Hungarians in 1868 abandoned on paper the fierce Magyar chauvinism of Kossuth and the superpatriots of 1848 (see above, p. 182), and put on the statute books a law that allowed the minorities to conduct local government in their own language, to hold the chief posts in their counties, and to have their own schools. But in practice, neither the Austrian nor the Hungarian statute was respected. The nationalities suffered varying degrees of discrimination and even persecution. Since the nationality problem was common to Austria and to Hungary, and since it brought down the entire dual monarchy in the end, after the disastrous defeats of World War I, we must examine it in some detail.

CHAPTER XXII

The Czechs

After 1867, the highly nationalistic Czechs felt that they were entitled to an *Ausgleich* on the model which the Magyars had obtained. They talked of the lands of the Crown of St. Wenceslaus (who died in 929), by which they meant the provinces of Bohemia, Moravia, and Austrian Silesia, as possessing rights comparable to those that the Magyars had successfully claimed for the lands of the Crown of St. Stephen (997-1038). Not only was this argument historically unsound, but the Czechs never had the power or the opportunity that the Magyars had to bring pressure on the Austrians. Czech deputies boycotted the Austrian parliament in the hope that Francis Joseph would consent to become King of Bohemia in Prague as he had become King of Hungary in Budapest.

In 1871, the Emperor did indeed offer to be crowned as King of Bohemia. The Bohemian diet, from which all the Germans had withdrawn in a fury, drew up proposals that would have produced a triple instead of a dual monarchy, with arrangements quite parallel to those enjoyed by the Magyars. The rage of Austrian and Bohemian Germans, the opposition of Magyar politicians, who predicted chaos, and a Slavic uprising in southern Austria forced Francis Joseph to change his mind. Deeply disappointed, the Czech nationalist leaders returned to passive resistance.

By 1879, when the Czech deputies returned to the Vienna parliament, they were divided into moderate "old Czechs" and radical and impetuous "young Czechs." In the 1880's and 1890's, each time the Czechs won cultural or political gains, the German extremists bitterly opposed them, in turn only strengthening the Czech extremists and weakening the moderates. A statute requiring all judges in Czech lands to conduct trials in the language of the petitioner led to the development of an experienced body of Czech civil servants, since many Czechs knew German already while Germans usually had to learn Czech. In 1890 the government and the "old Czechs" had tentatively agreed on an administrative division of Bohemia between Germans and Czechs, but the "young Czechs" rioted in the Bohemian diet, and Prague was put under martial law, which lasted until 1897. When a new law was passed requiring that all civil servants would have to be bilingual after 1901, the Germans in the Vienna parliament threw inkwells, blew whistles, and forced out the ministry, while Czech extremists began to talk ominously about a future Russian-led Slavic showdown with the Germans. All moderation vanished in the waves of noise and hatred. No Austrian parliament could stay in session, and the government had to be conducted by decree.

Under the stress of prolonged agitation, and influenced by the apparent triumph of constitutionalism in Russia (see below, p. 306), Francis Joseph finally decided to reform the franchise. In 1907, all male citizens of the Austrian lands were now enfranchised and could vote for deputies of their own nationality. Of the 516 deputies in the new parliament, 233 would be German and 107 Czech, a figure almost proportional to the census figures.

Yet in 1913 the Bohemian diet was dissolved by a *coup*, and in 1914 Czech deputies in the Austrian parliament refused to allow national business to proceed. Thus World War I began with both parliament and the Bohemian diet dissolved, and with the Emperor and ministers ruling by themselves. Perhaps chief among the many causes for this general parliamentary breakdown was the failure to give the Czech provinces the self-government they had vainly sought since 1867. Most Czechs did not wish to cut loose from the Empire and establish a separate state of their own. Amounting to about 23 per cent of the Austrian population, the Czechs formed a hard core of discontent.

Yet, from the economic and cultural points of view, the Czechs were by far the most advanced of the Slavic peoples in the dual monarchy. By 1900, the famous Skoda armament works had become the largest in the Empire and the rival of Krupp in Germany. Porcelain and glassware, lace and beer, sugar and the tourist trade, made the Czech middle class rich and Czech craftsmen famous. Laboring conditions were bad, however, and the Czech Social Democrats were weakened by their refusal to work with their German opposite numbers.

Czech nationalism was fostered by an active Czech-language press, by patriotic societies, by Czech schools, and by the famous *sokols* ("hawks"), a physical-training society with strong nationalist leanings. At the ancient Prague University learned Czech scholars taught, of whom Thomas Masaryk, married to an American, became the most famous. Professor of philosophy and student of Slavic culture, but a lover of the West, Masaryk deeply influenced generations of students, and upheld democratic ideals in politics. Historians studied the heroic past of the Czechs, and poets, novelists, and musicians glorified it for the popular audience. Deprived of their national autonomy and exposed to German bias though the Czechs were, they can hardly be regarded as a persecuted minority. They had their language and their freedom to develop under Austrian domination.

Poles and Ruthenians

Of all the minorities in Austria, the Poles (18 per cent of the population) were the most satisfied, the only contented Poles in Europe. Most of them lived in Galicia, where they formed the landlord class and generally oppressed their peasants, especially the backward Ruthenians (Ukrainians). Like the Czechs, the Galician Poles asked for provincial self-government on the Magyar model, and like the Czechs,

they were denied. But they had their own schools, and Polish was the language of administration and the courts. The Poles enjoyed favorable financial arrangements, and after 1871 there was a special ministry for Galicia in Vienna. Since they hated Russia, Pan-Slavism never tempted them as it did the Czechs; they were not even very much interested in a future independent Poland.

The contrast between this generous treatment and the brutality suffered by the Poles living in Prussian and Russian Poland led Poles everywhere to look to Austrian Galicia as the center of national life and culture. Polish refugees from tyranny elsewhere took refuge in the cities of Cracow and Lemberg. Here were splendid Polish universities, noble families living grandly as they always had in Poland, and opportunities to serve the Crown in the provincial administration. The universities trained generations of Poles who were available later for service in independent Poland. Polish literature and the study of Polish history flourished. Though slowly, industrialization began, and a promising petroleum industry was launched. Only the Ruthenians and the Jews suffered discrimination and hardship.

The Poles eliminated Ruthenians from the Galician diet and until 1907 kept them from the imperial parliament. The Ruthenians themselves were divided into an older pro-Russian generation, and a younger generation of Ukrainian nationalists, often fanatical, who hated Poles and Russians alike and who hoped for their own autonomous status within the monarchy. In 1908, a Ukrainian assassinated the Polish governor of Galicia after a horrible instance of Polish police brutality.

Other Minorities in Austria

The other minorities in Austria were far less numerous. Less than 3 per cent of the population was Italian in 1910; about

4½ per cent was Slovene; and less than 3 per cent was Serb and Croat. The Italians of the south Tyrol and Istria, where their center was the seaport of Trieste, were far more important than their numbers warranted, however, because of the existence of the Kingdom of Italy across the monarchy's frontier. Almost all of them wanted to belong to Italy, and Italy regarded their lands as *Italia Irredenta* (see Chapter XXI). Of all the Austrian minorities, the Italian steadily proved itself the most anxious to get out of the Habsburg Monarchy altogether.

Among the south Slavs in Austria proper, the Slovenes were the most contented. Scattered in six provinces, and often living at odds with their German or Italian neighbors, they usually made only local demands, like that for lecture courses in Slovene at Graz University. The Croats in Austria (mostly in Dalmatia) were fewer and less disaffected than those in Hungary, and the Serbs in Austria were far fewer and less disaffected than the Serbs in Hungary and in the separate province of Bosnia. Yet both Serbs and Croats in Austria were divided into groups that preferred autonomy within the Empire and groups that hoped one day to join an independent south Slav state (Yugoslavia).

Minorities in Hungary: Slovaks, Rumanians, South Slavs

In Hungary, minority problems were even more acute. Magyar behavior toward other national groups grew increasingly outrageous as moderate counsels vanished in the face of short-sighted demagoguery. The Slovaks, the Rumanians, and the Serbs and Croats living in Hungary proper were the worst victims of a deliberate policy of Magyarization, but even the Croatians of Croatia, whose province had its own constitutional special status, suffered. The Magyar aim was actually to destroy the na-

tional identity of the minorities and to transform them into Magyars. The weapon they used was language.

It is difficult to understand the passionate attachment felt by the backward peasant peoples of southeastern Europe for their own languages. Yet, deprived of economic opportunity and sometimes of complete religious freedom, these peoples in the nineteenth century found in the languages they talked a living proof of national identity. The Magyars too, who made up only 55 per cent of the population of their own country exclusive of Croatia, had a fanatical devotion to their own language, an Asian tongue quite unrelated to the German, Slavic, or Rumanian languages of the minorities. They tried to force it upon the subject peoples, particularly in education. All state-supported schools had to give instruction in Magyar, from kindergartens to universities. The state postal, telegraph, and railroad services used only Magyar.

The Slovaks, numbering about 11 per cent of the population of Hungary, were perhaps the most Magyarized. Poor peasants for the most part, the more ambitious of them often became Magyars simply by adopting the Magyar language as their own. As time passed, a few Slovaks came to feel a sense of unity with the closely related but far more advanced Czechs across the border in Austria. The pro-Czechs among the Slovaks were usually liberals and Protestants. Catholic and conservative Slovaks toward the end of the century found their leader in a priest, Father Hlinka, who wanted Slovak autonomy. After Czechoslovakia had been formed in 1918, the Hlinka movement continued to be anti-Czech, and became pro-Hitler in the 1930's.

The Rumanians, who lived in Transylvania, amounted in 1910 to 16½ per cent of the population of Hungary, and possessed a majority in Transylvania itself. For centuries they had been downtrodden by the Magyars, and had had to fight to achieve recognition of their Orthodox religion. Indeed, largely in the hope of receiving better treatment, many of them had become "Uniates," accepting the supremacy of Rome but otherwise preserving their own liturgy. Despite laws designed to eliminate the use of the Rumanian language, and a great deal of petty persecution, the Rumanians stoutly resisted assimilation. For redress of grievances, many looked to Vienna, which before the *Ausgleich* had often been a source of assistance against the Magyars, but which was now committed to give the Magyars a free hand. These Rumanians hoped that Transylvania might again be made autonomous, as it had once been in the past. They pressed for the enforcement of the liberal Hungarian nationalities law of 1868. They wanted their language and their church to have equal standing with other languages and other churches.

But when in 1892 the Rumanians petitioned Vienna on these points, their petition was returned unopened and unread. When they circulated the petition widely abroad, their leaders were tried and jailed. It was little wonder that many Transylvanian Rumanians ceased to look west to Vienna for help that never came and began to look south and east across the Carpathians to Rumania, where their fellow-nationals had a kingdom of their own and a strong wish to annex the whole of Transylvania.

Under Magyar rule, some Serbs and Croats lived in Hungary proper and others in Croatia. In 1910, those in Hungary totaled about 600,000, of whom two-thirds were Serbs. Living in a compact mass in the southern and western frontier regions, these were the inhabitants of the old Habsburg "military frontier" against the Turks. They were transferred to Magyar rule in 1869, and they resented it. The Serbs especially disliked Hungarian administration, and looked to the independent kingdom of Serbia to the south. But a far greater menace to Hungarian unity was provided by Croatia proper.

Croatia

The Croats, though connected since the eleventh century with the Crown of Hungary, had become strongly nationalistic under the impact of the Napoleonic occupation, and had fought on the side of the monarchy against the Magyar revolutionaries of 1848. None the less, Francis Joseph, as part of the *Ausgleich* settlement, handed them back to the Magyars. Croatian nationalists were deeply disappointed. Led by the Roman Catholic Bishop Strossmayer, a man of deep intelligence, high culture, and liberal views, they had hoped for an autonomous Croatia and Dalmatia inside the Empire, which would serve as a nucleus to attract all the other southern Slavs. But instead, the Magyar moderates, led by Deák, worked out in 1868 an *Ausgleich* of their own between Hungary and Croatia.

All military and economic affairs were to be handled in Budapest by a special cabinet minister for Croatian affairs. Representatives from the Croatian parliament at the Croatian capital of Zagreb would sit in Budapest whenever Croatian affairs were under discussion. Croatian delegates would be part of the Hungarian "delegation" of the dual monarchy. The Croatian language could be spoken by Croat representatives at the sessions of any body they attended, and the language of command in the Croatian territorial army would be Croatian. The Croats would control their own educational system, their church, their courts and police, but all taxes would be voted by Budapest and collected by agents of Budapest. Although the Croats were far better off than any national minority in Hungary, this "compromise" did not satisfy them.

The "Party of the Right," the ancestor of Croat extremism in our own day, wanted a completely autonomous Croatia, and scorned as inferior the Serbs and other non-Catholic south Slavs, whom Strossmayer had hoped to attract. Further problems were created in Catholic Croatia by the existence of a Serb Orthodox minority (more than a quarter of the population), which spoke the same language as the Croats, and which was racially indistinguishable from them. But the Orthodox minority worshipped in different churches, and was therefore subject to religious discrimination.

For twenty years at the close of the nineteenth century the Hungarian-appointed governor cleverly fostered this Serb-Croat antagonism by using the Serbs for local offices. He received the support only of those Croats who had become Magyar-speaking, usually great landowners or government officials.

By 1903, Serbs and Croats were beginning to co-operate against Hungarian rule, and to spread pro-Slav propaganda in Dalmatia. In 1905, Croats asked Vienna for Dalmatia and for electoral reforms, but professed that they wanted to observe faithfully the arrangement of 1868 with Hungary. Serbians endorsed these Croatian demands, though some Serbs hoped for union with independent Serbia, and some Croats still hoped for complete independence.

In spite of these hopeful signs, the hopes of the moderates were dashed by the fearfully unpopular Railway Servants Act (1907), which forced all railroad workers to speak Magyar. Croats began to boycott Hungarian-made goods; the Croatian diet refused to collaborate with the new governor, who in 1909 arrested fifty-odd Croats and Serbs and charged them with plotting to unite Croatia and Bosnia with Serbia. The evidence was ridiculously inadequate, and the defendants, though condemned, obtained a reversal of the sentences on appeal to a higher court. But these Zagreb trials gave the Slavic press a splendid opportunity to denounce the policy of the dual monarchy.

In the same year, 1909, a celebrated Austrian historian, Friedjung, charged in the Vienna press that the Croatian and Serbian politicians in Croatia were plotting with Serbians in Serbia. Friedjung was eventually forced to admit that his documentary sources, which in all probability had been fed to him by the Vienna foreign office, were forgeries. The Zagreb trials and the Friedjung case, coming only five years before the assassination of Francis Ferdinand by a Bosnian Serb and the outbreak of war, demonstrate the incompetence of the dual monarchy in dealing with its own loyal south Slav inhabitants. In 1912, 1913, and 1914, Bosnian students tried to assassinate the Hungarian governor of Croatia. These were ominous rehearsals for the crime of June 28, 1914, which led to world war and not merely to internal crisis.

Bosnia-Herzegovina

In the dual monarchy the region of Bosnia-Herzegovina had a special status. By the 1870's, these two provinces had been part of the Ottoman Empire for about four centuries. Although entirely south Slav from the ethnic point of view, the population included in 1879 about half a million Moslems, half a million members of the Orthodox Church, and perhaps 150,000 Catholics, as well as a few Jews. Under Turkish rule, those who accepted Islam enjoyed economic advantages. Most of the Orthodox Christian population consisted of peasants working on the estates of Moslem landlords and looking across the frontiers to Serbia in hope of liberation. Some of the Catholics were educated in Strossmayer's seminary, and leaned toward eventual absorption in his south-Slav state, but almost nobody wanted to join the Habsburg Monarchy as it was then constituted.

The Herzegovinian uprising of 1875 against the Turks precipitated a general Balkan Slavic attack on the Turks. Russia too went to war against the Turks, but first the Austrian and Russian foreign ministers reached an agreement on the future status of the two provinces. But they later disagreed on what the agreement had been. At the Congress of Berlin in 1878 (see below, p. 302), the Austrians obtained the right to occupy the provinces, but not to annex them.

From 1878 to 1908, the forces of the monarchy occupied Bosnia and Herzegovina. The sovereignty of the Turkish sultan was recognized throughout this period, but in fact the provinces were ruled from Vienna, though not as part of either Austria or Hungary. Instead, they were put under the common Austro-Hungarian minister of finance.

The discontent of the Orthodox Serbs of Bosnia was fanned by propaganda from Serbia itself. Patriotic Serbs considered that the first logical step toward creating a greater Serbia would be to incorporate these provinces inside their own frontiers, and they resented the decision of the Congress of Berlin that had allowed Habsburg occupation. However, so long as the occupation was not turned into annexation, the Serbs preserved the hope that the provinces might some day become theirs, and meanwhile flooded them with agents and plotters. The Moslems, though favored by the Habsburg authorities, never reconciled themselves to the ending of Turkish rule, and the Catholics hoped to join Croatia.

Thus these provinces perpetually threatened to create an explosion. The more intelligent observers in Vienna pressed for some sort of an all-south-Slav solution, not unlike that of Strossmayer. This would have put Dalmatia, Croatia, and Bosnia-Herzegovina together into a south-Slav kingdom under Francis Joseph, with the same status as Hungary—a triple rather than a dual monarchy. The advocates of this solution,

known as "trialists," met the fiercest kind of hatred from the Magyars.

However, the Young Turk Revolution of 1908 caused the adventurous Austrian foreign minister Aehrenthal to fear that the status of the provinces might be changed. Fortified by a previous secret agreement with Russia, Aehrenthal simply annexed the two provinces in October, 1908, and announced that they would be given a diet of their own. This move precipitated a major European crisis (see below, p. 385), which threatened world war, but eventually subsided, leaving the Serbs bitterly resentful. Serbian ambition to acquire the provinces now seemed permanently checked. The humiliation of Serbia, the disappointment of Russia, the solidarity of Germany with Austria-Hungary as revealed by the crisis, helped set the stage for the catastrophe of 1914. The discontent of the population of Bosnia, when added to the discontent of the Czechs and Italians in Austria, and of the Slovaks, Rumanians, Croats, and other south Slavs in Hungary, goes far to account for the wartime weaknesses and postwar disintegration of the dual monarchy.

Yet the minority question, critical though it was, does not provide the entire answer. We must now briefly consider the Austrian-German and Hungarian majorities, both in their separate development and in their critical relationship to each other. Only then can we see that even the two ruling groups were subject to divisive forces that crippled them individually and together.

Austrian Society and Politics, 1867-1914

From the earliest days of the *Ausgleich*, the Austrian liberals fought the clerical conservatives. They legalized civil marriages, secularized all but religious instruction, canceled the concordat of 1855 after the proclamation of papal infallibility in 1870, and taxed church property (1873). These measures were the Austrian counterpart of the German *Kulturkampf,* but they were much milder, since Austria was 90 per cent Catholic and did not share the Protestant Prussian suspicion of the Vatican. The liberals were discredited by the financial crash of 1873, during which it was revealed that some of them had accepted bribes in return for voting in favor of charters for shady and unstable new companies. From this period dates the earliest political anti-Semitism in Austria, since some Jewish liberals were involved in the scandals and served as convenient scapegoats. Economic advance during the early years of the monarchy had brought the usual increase in the working class, which after the crash turned toward socialism in both its Marxist and its milder forms.

The Austrian nobles, who often owned great estates which they ruled almost like independent potentates, were on the whole frivolous in their tastes, and took little interest in the problems of the nineteenth and twentieth centuries. They squandered their incomes on high living and gambling. Yet they supplied almost all the political leadership that the nation got. The large size of their estates was one fundamental reason for the small size of the average peasant holding, and made it necessary even for landowning peasants to try to obtain part-time employment on a noble's property. The peasants' standard of living and level of literacy were extremely low, yet the influence of the clergy kept them subservient to their masters, loyal to the dynasty, and almost contented with their lot.

The middle class of town-dwellers and men of business, so familiar in western Europe, came later and was smaller in number in Austria. The wealthier tried to imitate the aristocracy's mode of life and to buy their way into the charmed circle. Others joined the professions, which they found overcrowded and badly paid. The unemployment of intellectuals is an extremely dangerous matter politically.

Among the bourgeoisie there were many Jews. Numbering 5 per cent of the total population of Austria, the Jews (except for very few) could not be nobles, peasants, members of the clergy, bureaucrats, or army officers. So they were forced to enter trade, the professions, and the arts, where they often prospered and distinguished themselves. What we mean when we refer loosely to pre-war "Viennese" life, with its charm and gaiety, its cultivation, its music, its cafés, its high reputation in medicine and science, was the life of a society very largely Jewish or part-Jewish. Conversion, intermarriage, and assimilation were not uncommon among the upper-middle-class Jews.

Anti-Semitism, fanned by the continued migration of poorer Jews from regions of eastern Europe where oppression had rendered them squalid and uncouth, was general among the non-Jews of Austria. But we must distinguish between the social anti-Semitism of most aristocrats, which was often simply a form of snobbery, and the serious political anti-Semitism of the lower middle classes, often the unsuccessful competitors of the Jews in the world of small shop-keeping. Partly out of religious prejudice, partly out of distaste for the liberal politics usually preferred by the middle-class Jews, the clericals inveighed against them. One response among the Jews to the swelling chorus of anti-Semitism was Zionism (sponsorship of a Jewish state in Palestine), which originated in the dual monarchy.

The stresses and strains inherent in this social structure, aggravated by the problems of the national minorities, produced in the late nineteenth century two important new political movements among the Germans of Austria: Pan-Germanism and Christian Socialism. In the early 1880's, even moderate Austrian Germans wanted to hand over the Slavic lands of Austria to the Hungarians to rule, and then, stripped to the German core, to unite economically with Germany. The Pan-Germans were more radical and more violent. They opposed the Habsburg dynasty. They opposed the Catholic Church, and led a noisy movement called "Away from Rome" (*Los von Rom*). They demanded that Austria become Protestant and unite politicaliy with Germany. They were furiously anti-Slav and anti-Semitic. They adored Bismarck and Wotan, but Bismarck did not encourage them. Their leader, Schönerer, himself a convert to Protestantism, was elected to the Austrian parliament in 1873 from the same district that later gave birth to Adolf Hitler. But the pan-Germans never managed to become more than an extreme vocal minority.

The Christian Socialists, on the other hand, became the most important Austrian political party. Strongly Catholic and loyal to the Habsburgs, they appealed at the same time to the peasant and the small businessman by favoring social legislation and by opposing big business. They too were violently anti-Semitic. At first skeptical of the value of Christian Socialism, the clergy later made the movement its own, and especially in the country prevailed on the people to vote for its candidates. The most famous single Christian Socialist was the perennial Mayor of Vienna after 1895, Karl Lueger, the idol of the lower middle classes of the capital. For years he sponsored public ownership of city utilities, parks, playgrounds, free milk for schoolchildren, and other welfare services. Lueger always catered to his followers' hatred of Jews, Marxian socialists, and Magyars. Hitler, who saw Lueger's funeral procession in 1910, hailed him in *Mein Kampf* as the greatest statesman of his times. It is impossible to understand the doctrines of German Nazism in this century without understanding the social and racial structure of the Habsburg Monarchy in which Hitler

grew up, and especially the doctrines and the appeal of Pan-Germanism and Christian Socialism.

To the Pan-Germans and the Christian Socialists, the Austrian Social Democrats, founded in 1888, responded with a Marxist program calling for government ownership of the means of production and for political action organized by class rather than by nationality. But the Austrian Social Democrats were not revolutionaries, and set as their goals such political and social gains as universal suffrage, secular education, welfare legislation, and the eight-hour day. They were usually led by intellectuals, many of them Jewish, but they were followed by an ever-increasing number of workers.

On the nationality question, Social Democratic leaders strongly urged a reform in the direction of democratic federalism. Each nationality should have control of its own affairs in its own territory; in mixed territories, minorities should be protected; and a central parliament should decide matters of common interest. Cultural autonomy for the nationalities of a multi-national state was by no means an impractical or doctrinaire Marxist idea. Its practicality was later attested by the Soviet Russians, faced as they were with a similar problem and much influenced by the thinking of Austrian Social Democrats on the question. Otto Bauer, a doctrinaire Marxist, tried to explain away national antagonisms in the Empire as a manifestation of class warfare. But the program of another Social Democrat, Karl Renner, who lived to be chancellor of the Austrian Republic when it was founded in 1919 and again when it was re-created in 1945, might have averted the necessity for the foundation of any republic at all. A believer in the dual monarchy, Renner advocated treating the nationalities as if they were churches, and allowing each citizen to belong to whatever one he chose. Each of these "national associations" would have its own schools, and disagreements among them would be settled by a high court of arbitration. Who is to say that if these views had been adopted, the monarchy might not have been preserved?

Hungarian Society and Politics, 1867-1914

In Hungary, the social structure was somewhat different. The great landed nobility, owning half of Hungary in estates of hundreds of thousands of acres apiece, were a small class numerically. Loyal to the dynasty, sometimes kind to their tenants, and socially contemptuous of all beneath them, they were often intelligent and discriminating, yet more often just as frivolous and empty-headed as their Austrian counterparts. But Hungary had a much larger class of country gentlemen, the squirearchy, whose holdings were far smaller and whose social position was lower, but whose political influence as a group was even greater. After the emancipation of the serfs in 1848, and during later periods of uncertain agricultural conditions, many members of the gentry became civil servants or entered the professions. The peasantry suffered from small holdings, insufficient education, primitive methods of farming, and a low standard of living.

The Magyars were country folk, and the towns for centuries had been centers for Germans and Jews. But during the nineteenth century, the towns became steadily more Magyar, as members of the gentry and peasantry moved into them. The Jewish population grew enormously during the same period, mostly by immigration from the north and east. In Hungary, many Jews were converted and assimilated and became strongly Magyar in sentiment and behavior. When they grew rich enough, they bought land and titles, and became gentry. But here too they were greatly disliked, especially among the poorer city pop-

ulation, and in the countryside, where they were associated with money-lending and tavern-keeping, two professions that kept the peasant in their debt. Yet though anti-Semitism existed in Hungary, it never gained as many followers or became as important a political movement as in Austria.

At the bottom of the social pyramid was a small class (never more than 20 per cent of the population) of industrial workers in the cities, mostly in the textile and flour-milling industries. Wages were low, and living and working conditions were abominable, like those in Russia rather than those in the West. Yet more and more welfare measures were passed toward the end of the century. Because of its feebleness and lack of self-consciousness, this class could not be organized into an effective socialist party.

The Catholic Church was immensely powerful and rich in Hungary as in Austria, but in Hungary Catholicism was the faith only of about 60 instead of 90 per cent of the population. Some Hungarian magnate families and many of the gentry had never returned to Catholicism after the Reformation. They remained Calvinists. Several hundred thousand Germans, chiefly in Transylvania, were Lutheran. And in Transylvania also there were Magyar Unitarians. Clericalism could never become in Hungary the dominant force it was in Austria.

Thus, because of its differing social and religious structure, Hungary could not produce strong parties like the Austrian Social Democrats and Christian Socialists. Austria had a relatively liberal franchise before 1907 and universal manhood suffrage thereafter. Hungary, in contrast, never really changed its law of 1874, by which only about 6 per cent of the population could vote. Moreover, Magyars of all shades were pretty well united in their determination to subjugate the national minorities in Hungary. Internal political or social issues,

Parliament building in Budapest.

therefore, did little to determine Hungarian political alignments. The only real issue, and the chief source of Magyar political differences, was the question of Hungary's position in the dual monarchy.

Hungarian opponents of the *Ausgleich* were in the early days organized into two groups. The Kossuthists favored complete independence; a slightly more moderate party called the "Tigers" wished to improve the position of Hungary inside the monarchy by securing for the Hungarians control over their own army, over diplomatic service, and over finances, and by limiting the tie with Austria to the person of the monarch. When the great Deák passed from public life, one of the Tigers, Coloman Tisza, abandoned his opposition to the *Ausgleich*, joined the pro-*Ausgleich* Deákists, and came to power in 1875, to govern as prime minister for the next fifteen years.

Thereafter, this merger of the Tigers and Deákists dominated Hungary except for the period from 1905 to 1910, and stayed in power largely by electoral manipulation. Called the Liberals, this group resisted any reform of the franchise and agrarian conditions, or of the treatment of the minorities.

Kossuthists maintained their opposition to the *Ausgleich*. They wanted Magyar used as the language of command for all Hungarian troops in the army, and agitated against Austria. In 1902, when the government refused their demands, they began to filibuster, and effectively paralyzed the Hungarian parliament. The Emperor refused to yield to pressure. Coloman Tisza's son, Stephen, became premier in 1903, and worked through the increasing storm to preserve the *Ausgleich*. When he tried to limit debate in order to permit the accomplishment of official business, the Kossuthists wrecked the parliament chamber. In 1905, Tisza was defeated by an opposition coalition including the Kossuthists, who now won a majority. When Francis Joseph refused to meet the demands of the new majority and appointed a loyal general as premier, the Kossuthists screamed military dictatorship and urged patriots not to pay taxes or perform military service.

This struggle between the partisans of dualism and those of independence moved only the ruling caste of Magyars, and bore no relation to the sentiments and needs of the larger part of the population. To mitigate the struggle, Francis Joseph had only to threaten to decree universal suffrage for Hungary, as he intended to do in Austria. This would open the gates to the discontented minorities, and would encourage social and economic change. Under this threat, the opposition coalition eventually yielded (1906) and voted the necessary economic and military laws. They obtained the right to revise the franchise themselves, a task they had every interest in putting off.

In 1910, the younger Tisza won a victory in the elections by the time-honored methods of corruption and intimidation. He dropped the separatists' demands, which had been convulsing the country for more than a decade. Hungary got no bank, no separate army, and no substantial franchise reform. Kossuthists had to be removed by force from parliament, and gag-rule had to be imposed. Tisza was kept busy fighting sabre duels with the Kossuthist leaders. In this atmosphere, Hungary received the news that the heir to the throne had been assassinated.

IV: Russia, 1825-1914

Character of the Empire

The third and largest of the great eastern European empires, Russia, took far longer, as was its way, to catch up with the political and social developments elsewhere in Europe. Thus there was no parliament in Russia until after the revolution of 1905, and even then the tsardom was able to weaken and eventually to dominate the new representative body. Serfdom did not disappear until 1861, and agrarian problems were in some ways intensified by the liberation of the peasants. Each time reform came, in the 1860's and in 1905 and 1906, it came as a direct result of military defeat abroad, which rendered reform absolutely essential. Thus the reforms of Alexander II (1855-1881) were inspired by Russia's defeat in the Crimean War (1854-56), and the revolution of 1905 was made possible by Russia's failure in the Russo-Japanese War (1904-1905). During most of the nineteenth and early twentieth centuries, even after the reforms, the Russian tsars claimed for themselves the same autocratic rights that Peter the Great and his Muscovite predecessors had exercised. Thus the Russian people experienced long periods of reaction: the entire reign of Nicholas I (1825-1855), and a protracted period from 1866 through 1904, including the last fifteen years of Alexander II's reign (1866-1881), the whole of Alexander III's (1881-1894), and the first ten years of Nicholas II's (1894-1917), the last of the tsars.

The failure to adjust willingly to the currents of the times and the attempt to preserve autocratic rule produced unparalleled discontent in Russia. Disillusioned and angry intellectuals in the 1830's and 1840's gave way to proponents of social change in the 1850's and early 1860's, and then to determined revolutionaries and terrorists in the late 1860's and the years that followed. Although Marxist literature was known early in Russia, and Marxist political groupings existed after 1896, the Marxists were by no means either the most numerous or the most effective of Russian revolutionaries. Native non-Marxist revolutionary parties long performed the killings and other acts of violence that convulsed the regime and won the support of large groups of Russians. It was only Lenin's transformation of the Marxist doctrines and his adaptation of Marx to the Russian scene that made it possible for his Bolsheviks to emerge as an important threat. And it was only Lenin's supreme tactical skill and boldness that enabled him to bring his Bolsheviks, still a minority, to power during the revolution of 1917, a movement that was itself made possible by Russian losses in still another war. There was nothing inevitable about the triumph of the Bolsheviks (see Chapter XXVI).

Amid the official attempts to preserve sixteenth-century patterns, Russia experienced the impact of nineteenth- and twentieth-century industrialization. New resources were developed, thousands of miles of railroads were built, and factories sprang up, engaged in both heavy and light industry. A new laboring class thronged the cities, as elsewhere in Europe, but it lived and worked under conditions far worse than those in any other country. The native Russian revolutionaries looked to the peasants, in traditional Russian fashion, to provide them with their base, and they considered peasant problems paramount. The Marxists, on the other hand, true to the teachings of their master, recruited their following among this new proletariat, and focused their attention on its problems. But they deliberately relied for their tightly organized leadership almost exclusively on a little body of intellectuals and theorists.

Despite censorship and an atmosphere of repression, Russia experienced during the nineteenth century an amazing literary flowering. Poets, novelists, and playwrights produced works that rank with the greatest of all time. Like a sudden blossoming of orchids on an iceberg, the Russian literary renaissance cannot easily be explained. The literary talents of the Russian people had long lain dormant, and now awoke in an expression of unparalleled vigor and beauty.

Nicholas I (1825-1855)

Coming to the throne amid the disorders of the Decembrist Revolution (see above, Chapter XIX), Nicholas I (1825-1855) himself personally presided over the investigation of the revolutionaries and prescribed their punishment. He used their confessions as a source of information on the state of Russian opinion. Nicholas I has been more resoundingly damned by liberals, both Russian and foreign, than has any other tsar. They have portrayed him as a kind of scarecrow of an autocrat. Reactionary and autocratic though he was, literal-minded and devoted to military pursuits, he was perhaps not such an inflexible tyrant as he has been made out.

Nicholas I worked hard at the business of the state, and firmly believed that the imperial word was sacred. Although he despised all constitutions, he honored the liberal constitution which his elder brother Alexander had granted to the Poles (see above, p. 171) until the Poles themselves revolted. He believed that his own autocratic power had been ordained by God; the autocrat could not, even if he wished, limit his own authority. Naturally such a man loathed the thought of revolution anywhere, and was perfectly prepared to cooperate abroad with the Metternich system. At home, he was prepared to make changes and improvements, but not to touch the fundamental institution of the autocracy.

CHAPTER XXII

Though he was uneasy over the dangers inherent in serfdom, he was afraid to reform it in any serious way, because he feared that concessions would stimulate revolution among the peasants. Nicholas leaned heavily on the nobility as a class, referring to its members as his "benevolent police-chiefs."

So personal was Nicholas' rule that his own chancery or secretariat became the most important organ of Russian government. He enlarged it by creating several sections, including a notorious "third section" for political police activity, which spread rapidly and kept Russian political life under surveillance. This enormous expansion of the Tsar's own secretariat did not result in the abolition of any of the older organs of government. Consequently, bureaucratic confusion became very great, paper work was multiplied, and much injustice was done through sheer incompetence. Although the Russian laws were collected, under the direction of Speransky (see above, Chapter XVII), for the first time since 1649, the collection was not a true codification or modernization.

In the field of education, Nicholas favored the improvement of technical schools, but was deeply worried about the possibility that subversive foreign ideas might penetrate into the universities. After the Revolutions of 1848 in Europe, his reactionary minister of education, Uvarov, abolished the study of philosophy in the University of St. Petersburg, because, as he said, the usefulness of the subject had not been proved, and it might do harm. Uvarov formulated Nicholas' policies under the three heads of Autocracy, Orthodoxy, and Nationality: the unlimited power of the monarch, the sanctity of the Russian Church, and the adoption of policies in accordance with the "Russian national character." The result was a police-state, complete with censorship and terror, yet not nearly so efficient as a twentieth-century despotism.

We have already seen Nicholas putting down the Polish revolution of 1830 and intervening in 1849 to restore Hungary to the Habsburgs (see Chapter XIX). He believed in dynastic friendships, and counted on the alliance with Prussia and Austria without realizing that conflicting national interests were more important than friendships between monarchs. Thus he failed to see that Prussia would combat his own efforts to thwart the unification of Germany, and that Austria's interests conflicted with his own in southeastern Europe. It was partly Nicholas' failure to see the weaknesses of his own system of alliances that led him into the disastrous Crimean War.

Czar Nicholas I calming St. Petersburg riot caused by the cholera epidemic of 1831.

The Crimean War

Like other Russian leaders before him, Nicholas confidently expected the collapse of the Ottoman Empire. Russia wished to protect the Orthodox subjects of the sultan, and also had important economic interests at stake. The great Russian wheat-producing areas in the south were being developed in earnest, and Odessa on the Black Sea had become a great commercial port for the grain trade. Nicholas hoped to establish a Russian sphere of influence in the Balkans, and even to take possession of Istanbul itself. We have already witnessed his intervention in the Greek War of the 1820's (see Chapter XIX). When the governor of Egypt, Mehemet Ali, revolted against the Ottoman Sultan in 1832 and threatened Istanbul, Nicholas landed a Russian army and got credit for saving the sultan's capital.

In 1833, the Turks paid the bill for these services by signing the Treaty of Unkiar Skelessi with Russia. Nicholas took the Ottoman Empire under his protection, and the Turks agreed to close the Straits (the Bosporus and Dardanelles) to the warships of any nation. Alarmed at the preponderance that the treaty gave to Russia in an area of the world vital to British imperial and commercial interests, British diplomacy turned its efforts to undoing it. The next time Mehemet Ali revolted, in 1839, the British were able to put him down with their fleet before he came within distance of a Russian land force. In 1841, all the other important powers joined Russia in guaranteeing the integrity of Turkey, thus putting an end to the exclusive position obtained by Russia at Unkiar Skelessi.

During the next twelve years (1841-1853), Nicholas tried to reach an agreement with Britain on what should be done with Ottoman territory if Turkey collapsed. The British did not believe that such collapse was imminent, and they hoped to prevent Russia from doing anything to hasten it. The two parties misunderstood each other. By 1853, the Tsar mistakenly felt that Britain was not opposed to Russian domination of Turkey, and Britain mistakenly believed that the Tsar would not act in Turkey without consulting her.

Then a dispute arose over whether the Roman Catholics, backed by Napoleon III, or the Orthodox clergy, backed by the Tsar, should have the right to perform certain functions in the Christian "Holy Places" in Palestine, which was still part of the Ottoman dominions. This trivial dispute was the immediate cause of the Crimean War. But the underlying cause was the Tsar's wish to re-establish the exclusive Russian position of the Treaty of Unkiar Skelessi, and the British unwillingness to permit him to do so. Nicholas coupled a demand for this exclusive position with the demand that the Turks settle the dispute over the Holy Places amicably. The latter demand was possible; the former was not. When Nicholas occupied the Danubian principalities to enforce his demands, the situation became even tenser. And so, after many months of elaborate diplomatic negotiations in which all the powers strove to work out a suitable formula to avoid war, the drift toward war proved too strong to be checked.

Famous as the occasion of the charge of the Light Brigade, and of Florence Nightingale's pioneer efforts to save the lives of sick and wounded soldiers, the Crimean War consisted mostly of the English and French siege of the great Russian naval base at Sebastopol in the Crimea. Military operations on both sides were inefficiently conducted, but eventually the Russians were compelled to surrender. In the Peace of Paris of 1856, Russia was forbidden to fortify the Black Sea coast or to maintain a fleet there. This made it impossible for the Russians to defend their own shores or to conduct their shipping in security. It now became the paramount object of

Russian foreign policy to alter the Black Sea clauses of the treaty. Not only had Russia lost the war, but Prussia had not helped her, and Austria had been positively hostile (see above, p. 280). Nicholas did not live to see the total failure of his policy. He died during the war, and was succeeded by his son Alexander II (1855-1881).

Alexander II and Reform

By this time a very substantial segment of Russian public opinion favored reforms, in reaction to the long period of repression at home and failure abroad. Moreover, the economic developments of the early nineteenth century had rendered the system of serfdom less and less profitable. In the south, where land was fertile and crops were produced for sale as well as for use, the serf tilled his master's land usually three days a week, but sometimes more. In the north, where the land was less fertile and could not produce a surplus, the serfs often had a special arrangement with their masters called "quit-rent." This meant that the serf paid the master annually in cash instead of in work, and usually had to labor at home as a craftsman or go to a nearby town and work as a factory hand or small shopkeeper to raise the money. It is probable that about a quarter of the serfs of all Russia paid quit-rent by 1855. Neither in the south nor in the north was serfdom efficient in agriculture. As industries grew, it became clearer and clearer to factory owners who experimented with both serf and free labor that serf labor was not productive. Yet free labor was scarce, and the growing population needed to be fed. Many estates were mortgaged to state credit institutions, because of inefficient management and the extravagance of the landlords. Serfdom had become uneconomic.

But this fact was not widely realized among Russian landowners, who knew only that something had gone wrong somewhere. They wished to keep things as they were, and they did not as a class feel that emancipation was the answer. Yet the serfs showed increasing unrest, and cases of revolt rose in number. Abolitionist sentiment had now spread widely among intellectuals. Conscious of the unrest, Alexander II, though almost as conservative as his father, determined to embark on reforms, preferring, as he put it, that the abolition of serfdom come from above rather than from below. Through a cumbersome arrangement in which local commissions made studies and reported their findings to members of the government, an emancipation law was eventually formulated and proclaimed early in 1861.

A general statute declared that the serfs were now free, laid down the principles of the new administrative organization of the peasantry, and prescribed the rules for the purchase of land. A whole series of local statutes governed the particular procedure to be followed in the different provinces. All peasants, crown and private, were freed, and each peasant household received its homestead and a certain amount of land, usually the amount the peasant family had cultivated for its own use in the past. The land usually became the property of the village commune, which had the power to redistribute it periodically among the households. The government bought the land from the proprietors, but the peasants had to redeem it by payments extending over a period of 49 years. The proprietor retained only the portion of his estate that had been farmed for his own purposes.

This statute, liberating more than 40 million human beings, has been called the greatest single legislative act in history. There can be no doubt that it acted as an immense moral stimulus to peasant self-respect. Yet there were grave difficulties. The peasant had to accept the allotment, and since his household became collectively responsible for the taxes and redemption

Ceremony during emancipation of Russian serfs.

payments, his mobility was not greatly increased. The commune took the place of the proprietor, and differing local conditions caused great difficulty in administering the law. Moreover, the peasants in general got too little land, and had to pay too much for it. They did not get important forest and pasture lands. The settlement, however, was on the whole surprisingly liberal, despite the problems it failed to solve and despite the agrarian crises that developed in part as a result of its inadequacies.

The end of the landlords' rights of justice and police on their estates made it necessary to reform the entire local administration. By statute, in 1864, provincial and district assemblies, or *zemstvos*, were created. Chosen by an elaborate electoral system that divided the voters into categories by class, the assemblies none the less gave substantial representation to the peasants. The assemblies dealt with local finances, education, medical care, scientific agriculture, maintenance of the roads, and similar economic and social questions. Starting from scratch in many cases, the *zemstvos* made great advances in the founding of primary schools and the improvement of public health. They brought together peasant and proprietor to work out local problems. They served as schools of citizenship for all classes, and led tens of thousands of Russians to hope that this progressive step would be crowned by the creation of a central parliament, or *duma*. Despite the pressure that such men tried to bring on the government, the duma was not granted, partly because after the first attempt on the life of the Tsar in 1866 the regime swung away from reform and toward reaction.

But before this happened, other advances had been made. The populations of the cities were given municipal assemblies, with duties much like those of the *zemstvos* in the countryside. The Russian judicial system and legal procedure, which were riddled with inequities, were reformed. For the first time, juries were introduced, cases were argued publicly and orally, all classes were made equal before the law, and the system of courts was completely overhauled. Censorship was relaxed, new schools were encouraged, the universities were freed from the restraints that Nicholas had imposed on them, and the antiquated and often brutal system of military service was modernized and rendered less severe.

Yet, despite all these remarkable advances accomplished in a relatively few years, Alexander II became the target for revolutionaries in 1866, and terrorist activity continued throughout the seventies until the assassins finally killed the Tsar in 1881. It is impossible to understand these developments without taking a brief look at Russian intellectual life under Nicholas and Alexander.

Russian Intellectual Life

Early in Nicholas' reign, Russian professors and students, influenced by German philosophers, were devoting themselves to passionate discussions on art, philosophy, and religion. Many intellectuals outside the universities followed suit. These were the first groups known as the "intelligentsia," a peculiarly Russian class. By the 1830's, they were beginning to discuss Russia's place in the world, and especially its true historical relationship to the West and the proper course for it to follow in the future. Out of their debates there arose two important opposing schools of thought: the "Westerners" and the "Slavophiles" (friends of the Slavs).

The Westerners stated their case in a famous document called the "Philosophical Letter," published in 1836, though written earlier. Its author, Chaadaev, lamented the damaging effect of Byzantine Christianity and the Tartar invasions upon Russian development, and declared that Russia had made no contribution to the world. He hailed Peter the Great's efforts at westernizing Russia as a step in the right direction. He regarded the Roman Church as the source of much that was fruitful in the West of which Russia had been deprived. Nicholas I had Chaadaev certified as insane, and commanded that he be put under house arrest with a physician visiting him every day. Yet, despite scorn and censorship, the Westerners could not be silenced. They continued to declare that Russia was a society fundamentally like the West, but

that history had delayed its full development. Russia should now catch up. The implication was that the time had come for Russia to emerge from a period of absolutism and to enter upon the paths of parliamentary government and constitutional monarchy already trodden by the West.

In response, the opponents of the Westerners, the Slavophiles, vigorously argued that Russia had its own national spirit, like the *Volksgeist* that Herder (see Chapter XIX) had discovered in the Germans. Russia was, they maintained, essentially different from the West. The Orthodox religion of the Slavs was not legalistic, rationalistic, and narrow like the Roman Catholicism of the West, but substantial, emotional, and broad. The Slavophiles violently attacked Peter the Great for embarking Russia on a false course. The West ought not to be imitated but opposed. The Russian upper classes should turn away from their Europeanized manners, and look for inspiration to the simple Russian peasant who lived in the truly Russian institution of the village commune. Western Europe was urban and bourgeois; Russia was rural and agrarian. Western Europe was materialistic; Russia was deeply spiritual. Like the Westerners, the Slavophiles attached fundamental importance to the national religion, and made it the center of their arguments; but they praised where the Westerners damned. The Westerners' views had democratic and constitutional political implications; the Slavophiles' views had anti-constitutional and anti-democratic implications.

It is very important, however, to realize that this does not mean that the Slavophiles embraced the "nationality" doctrine of Nicholas I, or that they approved of his regime. These were not the chauvinist nationalists who appeared later. They opposed the tyranny and the bureaucratic machine of Nicholas I as bitterly as did the Westerners. But they wanted a patriarchal, benevolent monarchy of the kind they fancied had existed before Peter the Great, instead of a constitutional regime on the western pattern. Instead of a central parliament, they looked back with longing to the feudal Muscovite assembly, the *zemski sobor*, and to other institutions of the tsardom before Peter. Extremists among them went about the streets dressed in the old boyars' robes that Peter had made illegal. Many intellectuals shifted back and forth between the hotly debating camps, and few ever adopted in full the ideas of either side.

Alexander Herzen (1812-1870), for example, began his intellectual career as a Westerner and a devotee of French culture. The illegitimate son of a nobleman brought up in his father's house, he was charming, engaging, and highly intelligent. Like most Russians, he was not a good interpreter of western society, however, and was deeply fascinated with the thought that its structure might be rotten and doomed. The failure of the Paris revolution of 1848, which he saw as an eye-witness, convinced him that this was true, and he now became a revolutionary socialist. At the same time, he became convinced that the Westerners' thesis must be wrong: how could Russia in a short time pass through the stages of development which the West had taken centuries to experience but which Russia had missed? So Herzen became a Slavophile. As a revolutionary, he preached the destruction of existing institutions, and as a Slavophile he looked to Russia, with its peculiar institution of the peasant commune, the *mir*, to provide an inspiration for all Europe. Herzen became an influential publicist and issued a Russian-language paper in London which was widely read by Russian intellectuals. His memoirs provide perhaps the best picture preserved to us of the intellectual ferment of the age of Nicholas.

Michael Bakunin (1814-1876) reached roughly the same conclusions as Herzen at roughly the same time. But he was a practical anarchist tactician who loved violence, not a peaceful man of letters (see also Chapter XX). He enjoyed participating in revolutions, and had a long career in and out of jail in most of the countries of Europe. He looked forward to a great revolution spreading perhaps from Prague to Moscow and thence to the rest of Europe, followed by a tight dictatorship; beyond this he was entirely vague about the future. Atheism was a fundamental part of his program—not a casual part, as it always was to the Marxists. In his long career, Bakunin was to exert from abroad a considerable influence on Russian radicals.

Nihilism, Populism, Terrorism

In the 1860's, and especially after the emancipation in Russia, the Russian "intelligentsia," like intellectuals elsewhere in Europe, reacted against the romanticism of their predecessors. Suspecting idealism, religion, and metaphysics, they turned now to a narrowly utilitarian view of art and society. As one of these young men said, a pair of shoes to him was worth more than all the madonnas of a great Renaissance painter. All art must have a social purpose, and the bonds holding the individual tightly to society must be smashed. Away with parental authority, with the marriage tie, with the tyranny of custom. For these people the name "nihilist" (a man who believes in nothing) quickly became fashionable. The portrait of a nihilist was drawn by the great novelist Turgenev in Bazarov, the hero of his novel *Fathers and Sons*. Rude and scornful, obstinate and arrogant, Bazarov was actually accepted as a model by intellectual leaders of youth in revolt against established ways of behavior. Yet nihilism as such was not a political movement. The nihilists enjoyed shocking their parents by calling for an end to the old moral system, advocating, for instance, the extermination of everybody in Russia over the age of 25.

In the 1860's, many of these young Russian intellectuals went to Switzerland, where the proper Swiss bourgeoisie were scandalized at the men with their hair cut long and the girls with their hair cut short, at their loud voices and insolent behavior. The standard cartoonist's picture of a Russian revolutionary dates from the first startled glimpse which the Swiss had of the nihilists, who at the time had not even begun to be interested in political revolution. Herzen himself was shocked by their behavior. He died in 1870, his intellectual leadership forfeit. But Bakunin understood them, and influenced many of them during their stay in Switzerland. Bakunin urged them to go back to Russia and preach an immediate revolution to the peasants.

Also present in Switzerland were two other important Russian revolutionary thinkers: Lavrov and Tkachev. Lavrov (1823-1900) taught his followers that as intellectuals they owed a great debt to the Russian peasant, whose labor for many generations had enabled their ancestors to enjoy leisure and had made their own education possible. More gradual in his approach and more realistic in his estimates of the Russian peasant than Bakunin, Lavrov advised the nihilist students first to complete their education and then to return to Russia and go among the peasants, educating them and spreading among them propaganda for an eventual, not an immediate, revolution of the masses. On the other hand, Tkachev (1844-1886) taught that no revolution could ever be expected from the peasant masses, but that it would have to come from a tightly controlled small revolutionary elite, a little knot of conspirators who would seize power. Though not very influential at the time, Tkachev was important in Lenin's later thinking.

Under the impact of these teachers, especially Bakunin and Lavrov, Russian nihilism turned to a new kind of movement, which is called "populism." Young men and women, swept by idealistic fervor, decided to return to Russia and live among the peasants. When a government decree in 1872 actually summoned them back, they found that a parallel movement had already begun at home. About three thousand young people now took posts as teachers, innkeepers, or store-managers in the villages. Some tried to spread revolutionary ideas, others simply to render social service. Their romantic views of the peasantry were soon dispelled. The young populists did not know how to dress like peasants or how to talk to peasants. Suspicious of their talk, the peasants often betrayed them. The populists became conspicuous, and were easily traced by the police, who arrested them in droves. Two famous mass trials were held in the 1870's, at which the general public for the first time learned about the populist movement. After the trials, the populists who remained at large decided that they needed a determined revolutionary organization. With the formation of the "Land and Liberty" society in 1876, the childhood of the Russian revolutionary movement was over.

The revolutionaries had been stimulated by Alexander II's grant of reforms. So great had the discontent become that it is doubtful whether any Russian government could have proceeded fast enough to suit the radicals, who had come to believe in violent overturn of the regime and were not satisfied with piecemeal and gradual reform. Stemming from John Stuart Mill and from western Utopian socialists like Fourier and Robert Owen (see Chapter XX), Russian socialism was not yet greatly influenced by Marx. In some ways it was almost Slavophile, not urban but rural, not evolutionary but revolutionary, not a mass political party but a conspiracy. Its members lived underground and developed a conspiratorial psychology. They proposed to overthrow a bourgeois society before one ever got started. The movement became more and more radical, and in 1879 those who believed in the use of terror as a weapon separated from the others and founded the group called the *People's Will;* the anti-terrorists called themselves the *Black Partition.*

The members of the People's Will now went on a hunt for Tsar Alexander II himself. They shot at him and missed. They mined the track on which his train was traveling, and blew up the wrong train. They put dynamite under the dining room of the palace, and exploded it. But the Tsar was late for dinner that night, and eleven servants were killed instead. They rented a cheese-shop on one of the streets along which he drove, and tunneled under it. Finally they killed him (March, 1881) with a crude hand-made grenade, which blew up the assassin too. The supreme irony was that Alexander II had that day signed a document designed to summon a consultative assembly, which everybody expected to lead to further constitutional reform. His successor, the reactionary Alexander III (1881-1894), refused to confirm the document, and Russia was left to stagnate in a renewed repression. The terrorists were rounded up and punished, and their organization was smashed. Despite their occasional high-flown claims to enormous popular support, they had never numbered more than a mere handful of people, and their movement had been a failure.

Foreign Policy under Alexander II

In foreign policy, Alexander II made an uneven record. In Europe, the Russians successfully repressed the Polish uprising of 1863. They seized the opportunity provided by the Franco-Prussian War of 1870, and simply tore up the Black Sea provisions of the Treaty of Paris, declaring unilaterally that they would no longer be bound by them. This was an illegal act, to which the powers later reluctantly gave their assent. It was another illustration of the immorality in international affairs that Bismarck had made fashionable.

In 1877, the Russians went to war against Turkey on behalf of the rebellious Balkan Christians of Bosnia, Herzegovina, and Bulgaria. By the peace of San Stefano, dictated early in 1878 to the defeated Turks, Russia obtained, contrary to her previous agreements, a large independent Bulgarian state, which Russian policy-makers hoped to turn into a useful Balkan satellite. But the powers at the Congress of Berlin later in the same year reversed the judgment of San Stefano. They permitted only about one-third of the planned Bulgaria to come into existence as an autonomous state, while another third obtained autonomy separately, and the rest went back to Turkey. Russian public opinion resented the powers' depriving Russia of the gains scored in the Russo-Turkish War. Bitterness ran particularly high among those who hoped to unite all Slavs in a kind of federation, the Pan-Slavs (not to be confused with the Slavophiles).

Meanwhile, in Asia, encroachments begun under Nicholas I against the Chinese territory in the Amur River valley were regularized by treaty in 1860. Russian settlements in the "maritime province" on the Pacific Ocean continued to flourish. In Central Asia, a series of campaigns conquered the native Turkish khanates, and added much productive land to the crown. Here, however, the advance toward the northwest frontier of India brought Russia into a region of great interest to Britain, and fanned hostile public opinion in Britain.

The Reaction, 1881-1904

The reign of Alexander III and the first ten years of the reign of his son, Nicholas II, formed a quarter-century of consistent policies (1881-1904). Both tsars loathed liberalism as expressed in the earlier reforms, and were determined that there would never be any more of it. Yet a peasant bank set up under Alexander III made the redemption payments easier for the peasants to pay. And a few pieces of labor legislation enacted under the influence of Bismarck's example made working conditions a bit more tolerable—for example, hours were shortened for women workers. Offsetting these measures were the establishment of a special bank that extended credit to the impoverished nobility, the re-institution of rigorous censorship, and the institution in the countryside of so-called "rural leaders" or "land captains" in place of the elected justices of the peace of Alexander II. Election procedure for the *zemstvos* and for the city assemblies was made far less democratic. Now there began a vigorous persecution of the minority nationalities, a policy called "Russification," and quite in line with the "nationality" of Nicholas I's formula. The Finns, Poles, Ukrainians, Armenians, and Jews all suffered discrimination, varying from loss of their own institutions, which the Finns had enjoyed, to outright government-sponsored massacres in the case of the Jews. On his accession, Nicholas II referred to all hopes for a change as "senseless dreams."

These years were notable also for the steady growth of the Russian railroad network, largely built and owned by the state. The Donets coal basin was exploited for the first time; the Baku oil fields came into production; steel and cotton output soared. In 1892, there came to the Ministry of Finance a self-made railroad man, Witte, who for the next twelve years was personally responsible for the ever-mounting economic progress. Witte began the Trans-Siberian railroad, put Russia on the gold standard, attracted much foreign capital, especially French, for investment, and balanced the budget, in part through government monopoly of the sale of vodka. The railroad

network doubled in length between 1894 and 1904, and the need for rails stimulated the steel industry. Correspondingly, the number of urban workers multiplied, and strikes called in protest against wretched working conditions mounted in number. In 1897, the working day was fixed by the state at eleven hours for adults, and other provisions were adopted to improve and regularize conditions. These, however, were difficult to enforce.

Under the circumstances, many of the young generation of revolutionaries now turned to Marxist "scientific" socialism, preaching the class struggle and predicting the inevitable downfall of capitalism. A small clandestine group of "intelligentsia," formed in 1894-1895 at St. Petersburg, proposed to overthrow the regime, working with all opponents of the class system. The members of the group included Lenin, a vigorous young intellectual of upper-middle-class origin, whose brother had been executed for an attempt on the life of Alexander III. In 1898, this group and others formed the Social Democratic party, which in 1900 began to publish its own newspaper. Within party ranks, grave dissension sprang up over the question of organization. Should the party operate under a strongly centralized directorate, or should each local group of Social Democrats be free to agitate for its own ends? In the tradition of Bakunin and Tkachev, Lenin insisted on the tightly knit little group of directors at the center. At the party congress of Brussels and London in 1903, the majority voted with him. Lenin's faction thereafter was called by the name Bolshevik, meaning majority, as against the Menshevik (minority) group, which favored a loose democratic organization for the party. Both groups remained Social Democrats, or SDs, as they were often called.

Meanwhile, the non-Marxist revolutionaries, who were the direct heirs of the People's Will tradition, also organized a political party. They were the Social Revolutionaries, or SRs, with their own clandestine newspaper. Where the SDs as Marxists were interested almost exclusively in the urban workers, the SRs as populists were interested in the peasantry. Their chief aim was to redistribute the land, but they continued in their terrorist ways. They assassinated several cabinet ministers, using as their slogan the cry, *We don't want reforms, we want reform.*

A third political grouping was that of the moderates and liberals, not SD or SR in orientation, but mostly veterans of the *zemstvos* and intellectuals indignant over the government's policies of repression who favored only such measures as compulsory free private education and agrarian reform. The regime stupidly made no distinction between these men and the die-hard terrorists or the rabid Marxists. Thus the moderates also gradually organized and had their own clandestine paper favoring a constitution and a national parliament for Russia. In 1905, they took the name Constitutional Democrats, and were thereafter usually referred to as Kadets, from the Russian initials KD. Faced by this political activity among its radical and moderate opponents, the government only tightened the reins, and by 1904 had adopted the view that a short victorious war was all that would be necessary to unite the country.

The Russo-Japanese War

Trans-Siberian railway construction made it desirable for the Russians to obtain a right of way across Chinese territory in Manchuria. They took the initiative in preventing Japan from establishing herself on the Chinese mainland after her defeat of China in 1895, and then required the Chinese in exchange to allow the building of the new railroad. In 1897, they seized Port Arthur, the very port they had earlier kept

out of Japanese hands. Further friction with the Japanese took place in Korea, where both powers had interests. Then, after the Boxer Rebellion of 1900 in China (see Chapter XXVIII), the Russians kept their troops in Manchuria after the other nations had withdrawn theirs. Although the Russians promised to withdraw their forces by stages, they failed to do so, largely because Russian foreign policy fell into the hands of shady adventurers, some of whom had a lumber concession in Korea and wanted war with Japan. After it became apparent that the war party had got control in Russia, the Japanese without warning attacked units of the Russian fleet anchored at Port Arthur in February, 1904. The Russo-Japanese War had begun.

Far from their bases and taken by surprise, the Russians none the less stabilized a front on land. But their fleet, which had steamed all the way around Europe and across the Indian Ocean into the Pacific, was decisively defeated by the Japanese in the battle of Tsushima (May 27, 1904). To the Russian people, the war was a mysterious, distant political adventure of which they wanted no part. Many intellectuals opposed it, and the SRs and SDs openly hoped for a Russian defeat, which they expected would shake the government's position. Alarmed at the growing unrest at home, the Russian government was persuaded by President Theodore Roosevelt to accept his mediation, which the Japanese also actively wished.

Witte, the go-getting businessman who had opposed the war from the first, was sent to Portsmouth, New Hampshire, as Russian representative. Here he not only secured excellent terms for Russia, but also won a favorable verdict from American public opinion, which had previously been strongly pro-Japanese and had thought of Russians as either brutal aristocrats or bomb-throwing revolutionaries. By the Treaty of Portsmouth (1905), Russia recognized the Japanese protectorate over Ko-

Workers fighting on the barricades in Moscow, 1905.

rea, ceded Port Arthur and the southern half of Sakhalin Island, together with fishing rights in the North Pacific, and promised to evacuate Manchuria. Russian prestige as a Far Eastern power was not deeply wounded or permanently impaired by the defeat or by the treaty. Yet the effect of the defeat in Asia was to transfer Russian attention back to Europe, where a world crisis had already begun (see Chapter XXV).

The Revolution of 1905

The most important immediate result of the Russo-Japanese War was its impact on Russian domestic developments. While it was still going on, Plehve, the reactionary minister of the interior, was assassinated by an SR bomb in July, 1904. His successor was a moderate. The *zemstvo* liberals, the future Kadets, were encouraged, and held banquets throughout Russia to adopt a series of resolutions for presentation to a kind of national congress of *zemstvo* representatives. Although the congress was not allowed to meet publicly, its program—a constitution, basic civil liberties, class and minority equality, and extension of *zemstvo* responsibilities—became widely known and approved. The Tsar temporized, issued so vague a statement that all hope for change was dimmed, and took measures to limit free discussion.

Ironically, it was a police agent of the government itself who struck the fatal spark. He had been planted in the St. Petersburg factories to combat SD efforts to organize the workers and to substitute his own union. He organized a parade of workers to demonstrate peacefully and to petition the Tsar directly for an eight-hour day, a national assembly, civil liberties, the right to strike, and a number of other moderate demands. When the workers tried to deliver the petition, Nicholas left town and ordered the troops to fire on the peaceful demonstrators, some of whom were carrying his portrait to demonstrate their loyalty. About a thousand workers were killed on "Red Sunday" (January 22, 1905). This massacre made revolutionaries out of the urban workers. Strikes multiplied, the moderate opposition joined with the radical opposition, and university students and professors demanded the same reforms as wild-eyed bomb-hurlers.

Amid mounting excitement, the government at first seemed to favor the calling of a *zemski sobor*, consultative, not legislative, in the old Russian pattern rather than the western parliamentary one, but still a national assembly of sorts. But then even this project was whittled away, as the timid, vacillating, and unintelligent Nicholas II listened to his reactionary advisers. Under the impact of delays and disappointments, demonstrations and outbreaks occurred during the summer of 1905. In October, the printers struck. No newspapers appeared, and the printers, with SD aid, formed the first "soviet" or workers' council. When the railroad workers joined the strike, communications were cut off between Moscow and St. Petersburg. Soviets now multiplied. Of the one formed in St. Petersburg, Lenin declared that it was "not a workers' parliament, nor an organization of proletarian autonomy, but a combat organization pursuing definite ends."

This reflects the Bolsheviks' view of the soviet as an instrument for the pursuit of their program of armed revolt, for the establishment of a provisional government, for the proclamation of a democratic republic, and for the summoning of a constituent assembly. This program, put forth by the most "extreme" of the revolutionaries of 1905, differed relatively little from the program of the most moderate liberals, who would, however, have kept the monarchy, and striven to obtain their ends by persuasion and pressure rather than by violence. At the time, and for years to come, the Bolsheviks, like other Marxists, accepted the

view that it was necessary for Russia to pass through a stage of bourgeois democracy before the time for the proletarian revolution could come. They were therefore eager to help along the bourgeois revolution.

Nicholas was faced, as Witte told him, with the alternatives of imposing a military dictatorship and putting down the opposition by force, or of summoning a truly legislative assembly with veto-power over the laws. The Tsar finally chose the latter course, and in October, 1905, issued a manifesto that promised full civil liberties at once, and a legislative assembly or *duma* to be elected by universal suffrage. In effect, this famous October Manifesto put an end to the autocracy, since the duma was to be superior to the tsar in legislation.

Yet the issuance of the October Manifesto did not meet with universal approval or even end the revolution at once. On the Right, a government-sponsored party called the "Union of the Russian people" demonstrated against the manifesto, proclaimed its undying loyalty to the autocrat, and organized its own storm troops, or "Black Hundreds," which killed more than 3,000 Jews in the first week after the issuance of the manifesto. The armies returned from the Far East, and proved to be still loyal to the government. Thus the soviets of 1905, unlike those of 1917 (see Chapter XXVI), included only workers, and no soldiers. On the Left, the dissatisfied Bolsheviks and SRs made several attempts to launch their violent revolution, but failed, and the government was able to arrest their leaders and eventually to put them down after several days of street fighting in Moscow in December, 1905. In the Center, one group of liberals, pleased with the manifesto, urged that it be used as a rallying point for a moderate program. These were the Octobrists, so called after the month in which the manifesto had been issued. The other groups, the Kadets, wished to continue to agitate by legal means for further immediate reforms. But the real fires of revolution had burned out by the opening of the year 1906.

The Dumas, 1906-1914

Suffrage for the Duma was universal, but voters chose an electoral college which then selected the 412 deputies. Although SRs and SDs boycotted the elections out of discontent over the indirect election system, many of their number were elected. The Kadets were the strongest single party. Quite against the expectation of the government, the peasants' vote was not conservative, but highly liberal. But even before the first Duma had met, Witte was able to reduce its powers. He secured a large French loan, which made the government financially independent of the Duma, and issued a set of "fundamental laws," which the Duma was not to be competent to alter. The Crown was to continue to control war and foreign policy; the minister of finance was to control loans and currency. The tsar's council of state was transformed by adding members from the clergy, nobility, the *zemstvos*, the universities, and chambers of commerce. It became a kind of upper house, which had equal legislative rights with the Duma, and could therefore submit a rival budget, for example, which the government could then adopt in preference to that of the Duma. Finally, the tsar could dissolve the Duma at will, provided he set a date for new elections. When it was not in session he could legislate by himself, although his enactments had later to be approved by the Duma.

The first Duma, the "Duma of Popular Indignation," met between May and July, 1906. It addressed a list of grievances to the Tsar, asking for a radical land reform that would give the peasants all state and church land, and part of the land still in private hands. The government flatly re-fused to accept this attack on property, and after some parliamentary skirmishing the Duma was dissolved. The Kadet membership, maintaining incorrectly that the dissolution was unconstitutional, crossed the frontier into Finland, and there issued a manifesto urging the Russian people not to pay taxes or report for military service unless the Duma was recalled. Its authors were soon tried and declared ineligible for office; so future Dumas were deprived of the services of this capable Kadet group of moderates.

With the dissolution of the first Duma there came to power as chief minister the highly intelligent and conservative Peter Stolypin, who stayed in office until 1911, when he was assassinated. Together with Witte, he was the leading statesman of the last period of tsarist Russia. Stolypin put through a series of agricultural laws which enabled the peasants to free themselves from the commune. A peasant wishing to detach his property could demand that he be given a single tract, which meant that the scattered strips assigned to other families would also be consolidated so that each would obtain a single plot. This program Stolypin called the "wager on the strong and sober"; he was encouraging the initiative and enterprise of individual Russian peasants who had the will to operate on their own as successful small farmers. His program accomplished much of what he hoped for. It is estimated that about a quarter of the peasant households of European Russia (almost 9,000,000) emancipated themselves from the communes during the years between 1906 and 1917. Only war and revolution kept the process from going still further. Lenin and others who hoped for revolution were deeply suspicious and afraid of Stolypin's agrarian reforms. They rightly feared that the peasant grievances would be removed, and understood that no revolution in Russia could in the end succeed without the peasants.

Simultaneously with his agrarian program, Stolypin carried on unremitting war against terrorists and other revolutionaries. He showed no hesitation in acting in the most unconstitutional fashion when it suited him. He did everything he could to interfere with the elections to the second Duma, but the SRs and SDs were well represented, and the Duma itself (March-June, 1907) would not work with the government. It was dissolved because it refused to suspend the parliamentary immunity of the SD deputies, whom Stolypin wanted to arrest.

After the dissolution of the second Duma, the government quite illegally altered the election laws, cutting the number of delegates from the peasants and national minorities, and increasing the number from the gentry. By this means the government got a majority, and the third Duma (1907-1912) and the fourth (1912-1917) lived out their constitutional lives of five years apiece. Unrepresentative and limited in their powers though they were, they were still national assemblies. In their sessions the left-wingers could be heard, and could question ministers like any other members. The Dumas improved the conditions of peasant and worker, and helped strengthen national defense as the World War drew closer. Their commissions, working with individual ministers, proved extremely useful in increasing the efficiency of government departments. The period of the third Duma, however, was also notable for the continuation of "Russification," and the Finns in particular lost their remaining rights (1910).

Under the fourth Duma, the government, with Stolypin dead, tended more toward reaction. The Leftists organized busily for another revolution, working in unions, cooperatives, evening classes for workmen, and a whole network of other labor organizations. A vast web of police spies challenged them at every turn. Meanwhile, the imperial family drifted into a very dangerous situation, as the fanatically religious and autocratically minded empress fell more and more under the sway of a half-mad, wholly evil, dirty, ignorant, and power-hungry monk from Siberia. This man, Rasputin, had the mysterious ability, possibly hypnotic, to stop the bleeding of the young heir to the throne, who suffered from hemophilia. Since the Empress had enormous influence on her beloved husband, Nicholas II, Rasputin became in a real sense the ruler of Russia, much to the horror of a great many loyal supporters of the imperial house, and greatly to the detriment of the rational conduct of affairs in an enormous twentieth-century state. At the moment when the World War began, Russia was in the throes of a major crisis precipitated by the government's reactionary policies, the scandal of Rasputin's influence, and the indignation of the loyal Duma. There was a threat of revolution, then, even before 1917.

V: Conclusion

Parliamentary government was, as we have seen, a comparative stranger to the three eastern European empires. The King of Prussia, with Bismarck's help, used his extraordinary military system to conquer and unify Germany. He imposed on all non-Austrian Germans the Prussian system of autocracy almost undiluted by a weak and subservient parliament, and backed by the army and the Junkers. The Habsburg emperor, though faced after 1907 with an Austrian parliament elected by universal suffrage, in 1914 still made virtually all policy decisions by himself. The Hungarian parliament was never genuinely representative, and the emperor successfully used universal suffrage as a threat to quell Magyar separation. The tsars, forced at last by defeat in wars to grant a modified constitution in 1905, were still able to hamstring their own central legislative body, and to wield a preponderant personal influence in politics.

In all three countries, none the less, for the first time in their history, modern political parties during this period coalesced around principles. As in the West, the governments collaborated with parties or coalitions of parties, but always faced an opposition. What a party stood for was determined largely by the peculiar circumstances of the country that gave it birth. Yet certain parallels reached across national boundaries. Although no group in Russia can be compared with the German Catholic Center, the Austrian Christian Socialists do resemble it in many ways. No group in either Germany or Austria is comparable with the Russian populists (Social Revolutionaries). Yet German Liberals, Austrian Liberals, and Russian Kadets or Octobrists can perhaps be roughly equated. So can the Pan-Germans with the Pan-Slavs. The Social Democrats were Marxist in all three countries, but increasingly less revolutionary in Germany and Austria-Hungary, and increasingly more so in Russia.

All three countries during this period experienced an economic boom and an occasional depression; the industrial revolution struck them late, but with terrific impact. By the turn of the twentieth century, Germany had made such advances that its steel production surpassed that of England, and was second in the world only to that of the United States. Though far behind Germany both in resources and in technology, Austria-Hungary too was becoming rapidly industrialized. In Russia, transport and industry boomed.

Yet in all three countries, the landed nobility continued to exercise political influence quite out of proportion to their numbers. Everywhere the existence of a new and underprivileged class of urban workers stimulated intellectual leaders to form Marxist political groups, to preach the class struggle, and, except in Russia, to strive for immediate improvements in conditions rather than for the violent overthrow of the regime. Last of all the European countries, Russia emancipated her serfs in 1861, and began a new era of agrarian experiment and unrest. In Germany, protection was the great agrarian issue after the late 1870's. In Austria-Hungary, the peasants suffered with docility.

All three countries had minority problems of varying seriousness. Germany persecuted the Poles and, after 1871 and less severely, she persecuted the Alsatians and Lorrainers. More and more, Russia persecuted the Finns, Poles, Ukrainians, and Armenians. In Austria-Hungary alone, however, the minority problem proved fatal. German anti-Slav sentiment in Austria, and Magyar mistreatment of all non-Magyars in Hungary, alienated potentially loyal subjects, and finally helped explode the state from inside. In all three countries the Jews created a special problem and suffered different degrees of discrimination and persecution.

In Germany, a combination of circumstances led first to an assault by the government on the Catholic Church and then to an alliance between the government and the Catholic political party. In the Habsburg Monarchy, a milder anticlericalism had its day, but the Church retained its hold on the population and continued to exercise enormous political influence. In Russia, the Orthodox Church as usual played almost no role in the cultural development of the people. But one group of influential intellectuals attacked it as the source of Russia's troubles, while another group hailed the Church as the true source of Russia's strength and the fountainhead of all national virtue.

So it was that the main currents of the time flowed with uneven force over the Germans, Austrians, and Russians. Nationalism, materialism, militarism, imperialism, clericalism, constitutionalism, landlordism, and socialism were all experienced to a varying degree by all the countries. What determined each country's answer to social pressure, however, was its own peculiar past and its own peculiar character.

Reading Suggestions
on Central and Eastern Europe

(Asterisk indicates paperbound edition.)

GENERAL ACCOUNTS

R. C. Binkley, *Realism and Nationalism, 1852-1871* (Harper, 1935). Though this volume, in the "Rise of Modern Europe" series, develops a somewhat implausible thesis about the possibilities of "federative polity," it provides an often illuminating discussion of the period indicated.

C. J. H. Hayes, *A Generation of Materialism, 1871-1900* (Harper, 1941). Another volume in the "Rise of Modern Europe" series, this does some penetrating probing beneath the surface of an apparently successful era, particularly in Germany.

A. J. P. Taylor, *The Struggle for Mastery in Europe, 1848-1918* (Clarendon, 1954). The first volume to be published in "The Oxford History of Modern Europe"; crisp and provocative.

SPECIAL STUDIES: GERMANY

R. Flenley, *Modern German History* (Dutton, 1953) and K. S. Pinson, *Modern Germany, Its History and Civilization* (Macmillan, 1954). Two textbooks, of which Pinson's is the longer and Flenley's perhaps the more useful.

A. J. P. Taylor, *The Course of German History* (Coward-McCann, 1946). A lively essay on the period since 1815, with strong, but not unreasonable, anti-German overtones.

F. Meinecke, *The German Catastrophe* (Harvard Univ. Press, 1950). A useful antidote to Taylor, by a very great German historian.

T. Veblen, *Imperial Germany and the Industrial Revolution*, new ed. (Viking, 1954). An old, brilliant, and still very important analysis by a great American sociologist.

J. H. Clapham, *The Economic Development of France and Germany, 1815-1914*, 4th ed. (Cambridge University Press, 1936; reprinted 1955). A somewhat out-of-date but still instructive introduction to the subject.

F. Darmstaedter, *Bismarck and the Creation of the Second Reich* (Methuen, 1948). A valuable study.

E. Eyck, *Bismarck and the German Empire* (Allen and Unwin, 1950). Translation and condensation of a large standard work in German.

A. J. P. Taylor, *Bismarck: The Man and the Statesman* (Knopf, 1955). A provocative and often hostile re-evaluation.

E. J. Passant, *A Short History of Germany, 1850-1945* (Cambridge Univ. Press, 1959). An up-to-date general survey.

H. von Treitschke, *History of Germany in the 19th Century,* 7 vols. (Humanities Press, 1915-1919), and *Origins of Prussianism,* ed. by E. and C. Paul (Humanities Press, 1942). Celebrated detailed studies emphasizing the period before 1870; strongly Prussian in tone and sympathy.

SPECIAL STUDIES: THE HABSBURG MONARCHY

A. J. May, *The Hapsburg Monarchy, 1867-1914* (Harvard Univ. Press, 1951). Concise general account.

A. J. P. Taylor, *The Habsburg Monarchy, 1809-1918,* 2nd ed. (Hamish Hamilton, 1948). A spirited brief treatment.

R. A. Kann, *The Multinational Empire,* 2 vols. (Columbia Univ. Press, 1950). A monograph, arranged nationality by nationality, and discussing national sentiments and the government's efforts to deal with them.

O. Jászi, *The Dissolution of the Habsburg Monarchy* (Univ. of Chicago Press, 1929). From a rare point of view, that of the liberal Magyar.

R. W. Seton-Watson, *German, Slav, and Magyar* (Williams and Norgate, 1916). By the greatest British authority on southeast Europe, the author of many other valuable studies of the area.

E. Wiskemann, *Czechs and Germans* (Oxford Univ. Press, 1938). A good case history of national antagonisms.

SPECIAL STUDIES: RUSSIA

H. Seton-Watson, *The Decline of Imperial Russia, 1855-1914* (Praeger, 1952). The only sound work in English covering virtually all the period dealt with in this chapter.

G. T. Robinson, *Rural Russia under the Old Regime,* 2nd ed. (Macmillan, 1949). A splendid monograph on the peasant question.

R. Hare, *Pioneers of Russian Social Thought* (Oxford Univ. Press, 1951). Chapters, varying in value, on the chief non-Marxist thinkers of nineteenth-century Russia.

N. V. Riasanovsky, *Russia and the West in the Teaching of the Slavophiles* (Harvard Univ. Press, 1953). A useful study of one side of the chief intellectual controversy of the period.

D. Footman, *Red Prelude* (Yale Univ. Press, 1945). A good biography of Zhelyabov, populist and terrorist.

B. Pares, *The Fall of the Russian Monarchy* (Jonathan Cape, 1939). An excellent study of the period 1905-1917; by an authority who was frequently on the spot.

A. Herzen, *My Past and Thoughts,* 6 vols. (Chatto and Windus, 1924-1927). The classic picture of nineteenth-century Russia, by its most distinguished rebel.

S. Witte, *Memoirs* (Doubleday, 1921). The somewhat apologetic memoirs of the man who did most to industrialize imperial Russia.

B. D. Wolfe, *Three Who Made a Revolution* (Dial Press, 1948; °Beacon). A fine triple study of Lenin, Trotsky, and Stalin; with emphasis on the period before 1914.

A. Lobanov-Rostovsky, *Russia and Asia,* rev. ed. (G. Wahr, 1951). A useful introductory survey.

B. H. Sumner, *Russia and the Balkans, 1870-1880* (Clarendon, 1937). A monograph including a helpful discussion of Panslavism.

HISTORICAL FICTION

T. Mann, *Buddenbrooks* (°Pocket Books). Inexpensive reprint of a long novel about a family in imperial Germany.

G. Hauptmann, *The Weavers, Hannele, The Beaver Coat* (°Rinehart, 1951). Three plays that convey some of the flavor of nineteenth-century Germany.

R. Musil, *The Man without Qualities* (Coward-McCann, 1953). A novel steeped in the atmosphere of pre-1914 Vienna.

M. Jókai, *Eyes Like the Sea* (Putnam, 1901). Fictionalized autobiography of a romantic Hungarian novelist, the author of many novels that give insights into Magyar nationalism.

N. Gogol, *The Inspector General* (many editions), and *Dead Souls,* George Reavey trans. (Oxford Univ. Press, 1957—The World's Classics; °Rinehart Editions). Brilliant satirical play and novel.

I. Turgenev, *Fathers and Sons* (sometimes called *Fathers and Children*—many editions), and *Smoke* (Dutton, 1949; °Everyman). Superb contemporary realistic fiction reflecting Russian intellectual and political life.

F. Dostoevsky, *The Brothers Karamazov* (Modern Library, 1937), and *Crime and Punishment* (Modern Library, 1932). Famous novels depicting the turbulent life of Russian intellectuals in the mid-nineteenth century; more romantic in tone than Turgenev's works.

The Portable Chekhov (°Viking, 1947). A selection from the short stories and plays of A. Chekhov, a skillful portraitist of the upper classes in tsarist Russia.

L. Tolstoy, *Anna Karenina* (°Modern Library). A celebrated novel set in late nineteenth-century St. Petersburg and the countryside.

The Intellectual Revolution

THE SOURCES for the intellectual history of the nineteenth century—the great books and the ephemeral books, the articles, stories, advertisements, sermons, paintings, sculptures, all the accumulated symbols of culture—have been preserved in bewildering quantity. The late century seems, in our present retrospect, to have presented samples of almost all varieties of human thought and feeling, of all western "styles." A detailed catalogue of these varieties would be dull and confusing. Here we shall center on one main theme—the qualifications, emendations, even repudiations, made by the late nineteenth century in the western heritage of the Enlightenment, that heritage of optimistic faith in simple, static, reformist "reason" and a simple "natural law" ruling men and matter. The most striking of these emendations was made by Darwin.

I: Darwinism

The Origin of Species

Darwin's *On the Origin of Species by Means of Natural Selection* (1859) is one of the books that mark a revolution in

Opposite. EMILE ZOLA, *by Edouard Manet (1832-1883); French, painted 1868; the Louvre, Paris. The cultural revolution of the later nineteenth century in one picture! The subject is the naturalistic novelist, Zola (see below, p. 323), who defended the artistic rebels of the day. On the wall may be seen both an example of the Japanese art then coming into vogue and the unconventional nude "Olympia" by the same artist, which created a scandal in 1865 (on Manet, see below, p. 329).*

Charles Darwin (1809-1882) photographed about 1855.

preserved in Noah's ark during a great universal flood that took place some time after the Creation.

Now Darwin was by no means the first to find a discrepancy between the historical and scientific record and the accepted Biblical explanation. The men of the Enlightenment had felt compelled by the facts of the record to give up the Biblical explanation. Some of them had gone so far as to conceive the record as a very long evolutionary process in which no God, at least no personal, Christian God, had a hand, but only the impersonal forces of Nature or the deist's "watchmaker God" (see Chapter XVII). But they had arrived at no satisfactory explanation of how Nature or the watchmaker God had done the job; they had no theory of how organisms had evolved. This Darwin gave the world.

Darwin's Theories

One of his clues he found in the work of the economist Malthus (see Chapter XX). In his *Essay on Population*, Malthus had pointed out that organisms—including man—tended to multiply to a point where there simply was not food enough for them all. In the intense competition for food, some of these organisms did not get enough, and died. This was the germ of the conception Darwin phrased as the *struggle for existence*. He next asked himself what determined that certain individuals would survive and that others would die. Obviously the surviving ones got more food, better shelter, better living conditions of all sorts. If they were all identical organisms, the only explanation—apart from the intervention of a supernatural being or force—would have to be mere chance. But it was clear from observation that individual organisms of a given species are not identical. Variations appear even at birth. Thus in a single litter of pigs there may be sturdy, aggressive piglets and a runt. The runt, even if a sentimental

intellectual history. Like all important revolutions, the Darwinian was no bolt from the blue. Into Darwin's work had gone long years of preparation, not merely those of Darwin's own life, but those of his predecessors and colleagues in the scientific study of what was then called natural history and is now called biology. The set of facts before him was the long record of the hundreds of thousands of years of organic life on earth. Already well established by geologists like Sir Charles Lyell and by paleontologists, this record told of the rise, development, sometimes of the disappearance, of thousands of different forms of plant and animal organisms, or *species*. The record contradicted an important part of the commonly accepted theory men of the West had about the past of organic life. The Bible in the Book of Genesis described all forms of life as begun in the space of a single week by a Creator about 6,000 years ago. And this same religious account furthermore stated explicitly that all existing men and animals were descended from single pairs of each species farmer tries to protect it, is likely to get shoved aside in suckling by his sturdier brothers, and starve. In the wild state, in free competition, the runt is almost certain to die. In the struggle for existence, the runt is proved unfit.

Here is the second of Darwin's key phrases, the *survival of the fittest*. The organism best endowed in its variations to get food and shelter lives to procreate young that will tend to inherit these favorable variations. The variations are slight indeed, but over generation after generation they are cumulative; finally an organism so different from the long-distant ancestor is produced that we can speak of a new species. This new species has *evolved*. It has evolved by the working of *natural selection*. Man as a plant and animal breeder has long made use of this process, and has hastened and indeed guided it for his own purposes by *artificial selection,* by breeding only the best strains—"best," of course, from a human point of view. But man has been doing this with domesticated plants and animals for but a tiny period of geological time, and with but few species. Over the eons, natural selection has been the working force; *and for man himself,* according to the Darwinian system, natural selection alone has been at work, since man has yet to breed his own kind as he breeds his domestic plants and animals.

Darwin held that the variations in individuals of the same species at birth are accidental, and that they are generally transmitted through inheritance. Those biologists who developed his doctrine, notably the German Weismann, did not—and this is a very important point—believe that the evidence showed that variations produced in an individual organism in the course of its life could be transmitted to its offspring. Thus, orthodox Darwinism denies the inheritance of "acquired characteristics." Obviously, a man with an amputated leg will not produce one-legged children. Experimenters have docked the tails of genera-

tions of laboratory rats, but the rats are still born with long tails. Efforts by such Russian geneticists as Lysenko to show that environmental changes can be transmitted to offspring have not yet convinced most scientists.

Today, a century after the publication of the *Origin of Species,* Darwin's work as a biologist is still accepted in most of its larger outlines. Later work, however, has found that variations of importance in the evolutionary process are probably not so much the numerous tiny ones Darwin emphasized, but rather bigger and much rarer ones now known as "mutations." Scientists have begun to study the effect of various forms of radiation on such mutations. A still much-disputed geological theory holds that catastrophic crustal movements in the past have so radically altered environment as to wipe out whole species and speed up the evolution of others. Emphasis on either mutations or on extensive crustal movements tends also to be emphasis on the sudden and catastrophic rather than on the gradual—perhaps an attitude typical of our mid-twentieth century, for even science involves human "attitudes."

Darwin believed that what he called "sexual selection"—that is, the ability of the fittest individual to attract and mate with fittest individuals of the opposite sex and thus produce the fittest offspring—was a very important factor in natural selection. Although sexual selection is by no means wholly discarded by geneticists today, many of them do not accept Darwin's version of it. The actual mechanism of heredity we know much better than Darwin did, thanks to the work of an Austrian monk, Gregor Mendel, in the late nineteenth century, and many, many successors up to the present day.

The Effect on Theology

The *Origin of Species* stirred up a most heated theological controversy. It added fuel to a fire kindled earlier by historical and linguistic scholarship with its practice of applying the same standards to the Bible that the scholar would apply to Homer, or to the old Norse and Germanic epics. Fundamentalists, both Protestant and Catholic, simply stuck by Genesis and damned Darwin and all his work. But the Catholic Church and many Protestant bodies eventually took at least a neutral attitude toward Darwinism, which they viewed as a scientific biological hypothesis neither necessarily correct nor necessarily incorrect. The great majority of Christians tacitly or openly accepted sufficient modification of Genesis to accommodate themselves to the scientist's time-scale, and adjusted the classic theological arguments from first cause, design, and the like to a God who worked his will in accordance with organic evolution; and they accepted the assimilation of the Biblical account, at least in part, with other fallible histories. In short, they were willing to grant that the *men* who wrote the Bible were not in-

fallible. Moreover, it was quite clear to reflective men that nothing Darwin or any other scientist or scholar could produce would give ultimate answers to the kind of problem set by the existence of God. It was quite clear to them that since God's eye is now on the sparrow, it must once have been on the dinosaur. Christians can be Darwinians: millions of them are. But Darwinism, if taken over wholesale into a philosophy of life, remains a denial of any supernatural intervention in the planning and running of the universe, remains a support for secularism.

The Effect on Social and Economic Attitudes

The cosmological or theological conflict had pretty well run its course by the beginning of the twentieth century. More important in the long run was the use men made of some of Darwin's basic concepts—or at least, of his more smoothly coined phrases—in debates on matters moral, economic, and political. The blanket term, "Social Darwinism," which covers all these transfers of ideas from biology to the social sciences and human relations, takes in a very wide range of persons and ideas. Darwin himself was a biologist, not a "Social Darwinist." He did not write as a social scientist.

The central idea that social and political thinkers took over from Darwin was that of competition among individuals and groups of individuals. This was of course a conception already central in their thinking, but Darwin buttressed it with the prestige of the natural sciences. The majority of these late nineteenth-century thinkers interpreted the human struggle as a struggle for the means of livelihood. There is, they were sure, among men a human "struggle for life." The variations that counted here were the variations that brought success in economic competition—the variations

An 1871 anti-Darwinian cartoon by Thomas Nast. The defrauded gorilla, pointing to Darwin at right: "That man wants to claim my pedigree. He says he is one of my descendants." Mr. Bergh (founder of the Society for the Prevention of Cruelty to Animals): "Now, Mr. Darwin, how could you insult him so?"

that produced inventors, business organizers, even perhaps political, artistic, and professional leaders. Darwin's work in natural history came to confirm the economist's doctrine of laissez-faire and the nineteenth-century liberal's doctrine of individual freedom for a man to do what his capacities permitted.

Formal economists did not indeed make much use of, or have much need for, Darwin. The classical economists had already brought the arguments for laissez-faire to their height (see Chapter XX). On the whole, for the rest of the century, the economists were to temper somewhat the rigor of the doctrine of competition among individuals. But the average successful middle-class person in the West took Darwin to heart. Here was scientific confirmation of the middle-class notions that the universe was designed to reward hard work, thrift, intelligence, and self-help and to punish laziness, waste, stupidity, and reliance on charity. Above all, the middle-class person of the time took Darwin to confirm the notion that the poor were poor because they were unfit, badly designed for living. The work of Darwin confirmed the complementary notion that attempts by private charity or by state action to take from the rich and moderately well-to-do and give to the poor were useless and quite contrary to nature, shocking efforts to reverse the course of evolution. If a man cannot earn enough to feed himself, it was argued, he had better die; lowlier organisms too incompetent to feed themselves certainly die off, to the greater good of the species. Herbert Spencer (1820-1903), an ardent British evolutionist, summed it up neatly:

Of man, as of all inferior creatures, the law by conformity to which the species is preserved, is that among adults the individuals best adapted to the conditions of their existence shall prosper most, and the individuals least adapted to the conditions of their existence shall prosper least.... Pervading all Nature we may see at work a stern discipline which is often a little cruel that it may be very

kind.... The ultimate result of shielding men from folly is to fill the world with fools.[*]

Spencer himself, if it came to that, could not have stood by while the unemployed and their families starved to death. He had an almost maniacal hatred of the state, of local government as well as national; he held out even against compulsory sewers in cities. But even Spencer could not transfer to the struggle for existence among human beings the fine ruthless freedom of the jungle, of what Tennyson called "Nature red in tooth and claw." He was against all forms of government provision for what we now call social security. But what government may not do he believed the ethically sound individual will do as charity. The rich and well-to-do will take care of the poor voluntarily—not enough to spoil them, not enough to frustrate the designs of evolution by letting them prosper and propagate their kind, but enough to prevent their starving or freezing to death.

In his *Principles of Ethics*, Spencer discovered that the softer emotions promoted by Christianity and the other higher religions—kindness, dislike of cruelty, love—were also in accord with the intentions of the laws of the universe as summed up in evolution. Mutual extermination might be the law for tigers, but not for human beings. Indeed, Spencer and many other Social Darwinists held that the altruistic moral sentiments that impel us toward charity are the highest achievement of the evolutionary process, and that a society with many altruists is thereby shown to be the fittest for survival.

Eugenics

The Social Darwinists were, then, faced with this primary difficulty. Darwin

[*] Herbert Spencer, *Principles of Ethics* (London, 1879-1893), section 257; *Social Statics* (London, 1851), p. 149; *Autobiography* (London, 1904), II, 5.

seemed to have shown that the unmitigated struggle for life within a given species, and among rival species, was the law of the universe; but human history, and human feelings, showed that men could not in practice look on with indifference while their fellow men starved to death. One way out of the dilemma was that of Spencer, a sort of humanized and mitigated struggle in which the incompetent were shelved but not destroyed. Many who held this view accompanied it with a faith in what came to be called eugenics. For them the question was not so much the elimination of the unfit but the deliberate encouragement of the production of the fit. Darwin had begun his *Origin of Species* with a consideration of the extraordinary success men had had with artificial selection in the breeding of plants and animals. Why not do the same thing with human beings? Since, according to strict Darwinian theory, acquired characteristics were not transmitted by heredity, no amount of manipulation of the social environment, no amount of wise planning of institutions, would alter human beings. Therefore, the only way to secure permanent improvement of the race was by deliberate mating of the fit with the fit.

The eugenicists, however, ran at once against the fact that man, though he domesticates plants and animals, is still himself a "wild" animal. The individual human being in choosing a mate is no doubt influenced by a great variety of motives, which the social scientist or even the practical man in human relations still understands only imperfectly. For no master human breeder, not even an understandable master principle or idea, decides who shall mate with whom. So far, the eugenicists have had little success with the positive side of their program. On the negative side, they have urged that the obviously unfit, the idiots, the feeble-minded, the insane, be prevented, even if necessary by compulsory sterilization, from having children. Some few American states have passed laws for such compulsory sterilization, but only a tiny handful of human beings, not enough to affect in the slightest the general course of human physical evolution, have undergone this treatment. Moreover, the eugenicists have aroused the opposition of many Christians who believe that it is wrong to tamper with God's human creations.

"Racism"

By far the commonest way out of the dilemma facing the Social Darwinists lay in the obvious notion that it is not so much among individual human beings that the struggle for existence really goes on, as it is among human beings organized in groups, as tribes, "races," or territorial states. The struggle that counts is not the struggle, say, among individual Englishmen to survive, but the struggle between the entity England—or Great Britain—and its rivals. The struggle for existence among men is now lifted from the biology of the individual to the politics of the group. And for the nineteenth century the group had to be the nation-state, perhaps kindred nation-states that could be organized for the struggle as one bloc of states, such as the "Nordic" or the "Latin," or perhaps at the very widest the Caucasian or white peoples in competition with the colored peoples, yellow, brown, or black. This struggle had an ultimate form: war. The group that defeated another group in war had thereby shown itself to be fitter than the beaten group, and it had a right—indeed in evolutionary terms, which usually have moral overtones, a *duty*—to eliminate the beaten group, seize its lands, and people them with its own fitter human beings. The English imperialist Cecil Rhodes held that a world wholly and exclusively peopled with Anglo-Saxons would be the best possible world.

CHAPTER XXIII

The idea of a Chosen People was of course not a new one in Darwin's time. But there is no doubt that Darwin's work, however little he may have meant it to be, was a most important element in the special forms that competition among organized states took in the latter half of the nineteenth century, and right on to our own day. Darwinism came too late to do more than prop up the philosophy of laissez-faire in economics. But Darwinism came at just the right time to intensify the struggle among organized human groups in international politics.

The particular groups or states that were to benefit as the elect of evolution in this special political sense varied with the aims, sympathies, and actual citizenship of the individual who was seeking to promote an ultimate evolutionary victory. Britain, Germany, the United States, the Latins, the Slavs, the Nordics, the whites, even indeed the Christians, were all defended as the true elect of evolution. Most of the writers who preached this kind of political evolution proceeded from the assumption that at bottom the men of a given group had certain physical traits in common, traits that gave them their superiority, and that could not possibly be transmitted to men of another group. Most of these writers, in short, were "racists" who believed that in fact *homo sapiens* had already evolved into what were really separate species. A black skin, for instance, was for them a sign of innate inferiority. The blacks would simply have to go the way of the dinosaurs, into extinction. Evolution had spoken.

There were indeed all sorts of half-way stations proposed by these writers. Few of them quite dared to preach what has in our own day been christened *genocide*—that is, the actual wholesale murder of "inferior" and beaten "races." We had to wait for Hitler for this. Most of them, though perhaps they held that in the long run the inferior peoples would in fact die out, were willing to see the inferiors duly subjected to the superiors, to have the less fit peoples serve as hewers of wood and drawers of water for their masters. Indeed, some Social Darwinists applied their theories to a new form of caste organization, which came to be known as "élitism." For them, the distinction between superior and inferior was not always one of race or even of existing state organizations, but one that applied to a cross section of the whole human race. The fit were not limited to any one race, but they were still marked out by the rigid hand of biological inheritance. They were the master group, the élite, the "supermen;" and they should everywhere band together against the dull average men, and dutifully exploit them. The German, Friedrich Nietzsche (1844-1900), who gave currency to the phrase "superman," was a subtle and difficult thinker, who disliked Darwin as a grubbing Englishman. Still Nietzsche's influence among the half-educated who admired him in the late nineteenth and early twentieth centuries was to further racist and élitist causes.

Theories of the evolution-guided superiority of certain groups were not limited to Europe. In the United States, the innate, unchangeable superiority of whites to blacks was an article of faith among many whites in the North and almost universally in the South. This faith was greatly bolstered by Darwinian anthropologists and biologists. The notion that the degree of blondness, and other readily visible traits, such as long-headedness and tallness, measured suitableness for citizenship in a great democracy helped dictate the American immigration act of 1924, which encouraged immigrants from northwestern Europe, and very seriously discouraged those from southern and eastern Europe. The American, Madison Grant, in his *The Passing of the Great Race*, published in 1916, asserted that the Nordics—the tall, long-headed, light-haired peoples of northern Europe— were "a race of soldiers, sailors, adventurers and explorers, but above all, of rulers, organizers and aristocrats." Grant continued confidently and picturesquely:

Before leaving this interesting subject of the correlation of spiritual and moral traits with physical characters we may note that these influences are so deeply rooted in everyday consciousness that the modern novelist or playwright does not fail to make his hero a tall, blond, honest and somewhat stupid youth and his villain a small, dark and exceptionally intelligent individual of warped moral character. So in Celtic legend as in the Græco-Roman and mediæval romances, prince and princess are always fair, a fact rather indicating that the mass of the people were brunet at the time when the legends were taking shape. In fact, 'fair' is a synonym for beauty.*

The title of Madison Grant's book, however, betrays an anxiety that is never far from the surface even in the most confident of these Social Darwinists. Grant feared that his "great race," gifted summit of evolution though it was, was paradoxically not going to survive. The lower races were breeding faster; democratic equalitarianism was lopping off the best and encouraging the worst. Somehow evolution was going wrong. Degeneration, not progress, was the mark of the times. Like those other "scientific" determinists, the Marxists, the Social Darwinists believed that men of good will had to set to work with pen and tongue to help along the predetermined process and keep it on the right track.

A New
Historical Determinism

Darwinian science no more than Newtonian science really answered the great questions about good and evil, about the ends of human life, that men have been asking and answering ever since we have had historical records. Darwinian science, and indeed the physics, chemistry, and other sciences that flourished in the nineteenth century, recast for many the

* Madison Grant, *The Passing of the Great Race,* 4th rev. ed. (New York, 1921), 229.

whole frame of reference in which these questions were asked. Do not mistake. Traditional Christianity, as well as many other transcendental and supernatural faiths, survived Darwin as they had survived Newton. Many men continued to believe that a God, or gods, not bound by the laws men discovered in laboratory experiments and in other systematic observations, guided their steps and gave meaning to their lives in this world and in the other world after death. But with the spread of popular education, especially in the West, great numbers came to believe that no such God or gods existed, that the material universe of science and common sense went on its regular ways in accordance with laws or uniformities which men might eventually understand completely, and which they were already beginning to understand quite well. And in its turn, this "materialist" view of the universe had repercussions on all but the most determined and fundamentalist of the supernatural faiths; at the very least, they pared down the scope of divine action, cribbing and confining it.

Darwin's work and that of many other scientists, in combination with the work of historians and philosophers and men of letters, worked a major change in the way men looked at their universe. It is an undue simplification to say that the Newtonian universe was static, the Darwinian dynamic, but the generalization is a good rough working approximation. The eighteenth-century Enlightenment was certainly feeling its way far more than its later Romantic critics admitted toward a view of the universe as developing, progressing, evolving. But, as one can see from the work of so typical a *philosophe* as Voltaire, the eighteenth century had no good explanation of the way change came about. This explanation Darwin provided for natural history, and the Romantic historians and their fellow workers in other fields provided it for human history.

CHAPTER XXIII

Today we are still in the climate of opinion set for us in the late nineteenth century. We still believe, to a greater or less degree, in what has been labeled "historicism"—that is, in the doctrine that the course of history in the widest sense shows a regular, if bewildering, unfolding that has "determined" everything now existing and that will determine everything in the future. The wildest believer in this doctrine had to admit that since he could not in fact understand the whole process in the past, he could not wholly understand the present or wholly predict the future, could not "extrapolate" a curve he couldn't yet plot accurately. Still, the clue lay in the past, out of which the present has developed as the oak has developed from the acorn.

The Christian and Hebraic (and Moslem) calendar made the earth 6,000 years old, but the Darwinian calendar envisaged millions of years for organic life alone. It might seem, therefore, that historicism, especially when reinforced by the emphasis Darwin put on the immense reaches of time, would confirm conservative opposition to rapid change, or at least encourage in men a certain resignation in the face of the slow-moving process of evolution on this earth. And so it did for some men. Darwin's grandson, Sir Charles Galton Darwin, published in 1953 a book entitled *The Next Million Years*. He concluded that, since it is now held that it takes about a million years for a species to evolve, it will be a million years before evolution produces a creature any better adapted than man; and that therefore for the next million years we shall have a history much like that of the last few thousand, with wars, revolutions, pestilence, the rise and fall of thousands of Egypts, Romes, Britains, and Americas.

But historicism in the nineteenth and twentieth centuries has had for others a quite different consequence. It has served to convince impatient and hopeful men that they had really mastered the secrets of the universe, that they understood as their misguided predecessors had not just where the forces of history were leading. They could, then, help the process instead of hindering it, perhaps even hasten it! Marxism is the classic example of this faith in historical determinism, but nationalism, racism, and a host of others all drew nourishment from it. The extraordinary speeding-up of technological improvements lent strength to this view that moral and political improvement could also be speeded up. The doctrine of Evolution, then, though logically you can argue that it should have lessened the force of utopian faiths, did in fact increase them. People thought of the sureness of evolution and forgot its slowness.

II: Literature and the Arts

The Victorian Age

It is risky to generalize about the literature and the art of the later nineteenth century. But these years do largely deserve to be called the "Victorian Age." This age has not the neatness of style we can find in ancient Athens or Renaissance Italy or Elizabethan England. We can evoke a Victorian drawing room, where Maud or Mélanie in ringlets and crinolines, surrounded by whatnots, bric-a-brac, plush hangings, and Landseer engravings, reads Tennyson, Longfellow, or Heine, or plays Liszt on the pianoforte. But so much went on outside that drawing room!—not only in the lives of peasants, workers, and businessmen, but even in art and letters. Maud or Mélanie might indeed have been reading

Dickens or Balzac, but these writers hardly fitted the drawing room. Nor would Thoreau and Melville, Zola and Dostoevski. It is quite certain that the girls would not have been reading Marx.

For the safest thing we can say about the formal culture of the second half of the nineteenth century is that it had wide variety, that indeed it was very *eclectic*. We may also add that a great deal of this formal culture, especially its more "serious" work, was now, more clearly than ever before in western history, produced and cultivated by men and women in conscious revolt against the tastes of the politically and economically dominant class of their time—that is, the middle class. Unless Maud and Mélanie were very advanced young women indeed, they did not like much of what a hundred years later we single out as important in Victorian art and literature. If they were ordinary middle-class young

women, they read sentimental novels now forgotten save by the social historian, and they lived in a culture to which the derogatory overtones that the word "Victorian" still often has for us apply well enough.

Their fathers and brothers, indeed, were often so concerned with industry and trade that they had no time for literature and the arts, which they tended to leave to their womenfolk. Or if they did have wider concerns, these concerns were rather with political and social problems, with the material betterment of their class, and—to be fair—with that of the working class too. But most of these middle-class men felt that the most that could be done for the workers was to raise their standard of living slowly under existing capitalist laissez-faire. They held that Church and State should join to restrain by law and by religion of an essentially puritanical cast the lack of self-restraint these middle-class men found too characteristic of their inferiors. For with these Victorians laissez-faire "liberalism" was a strictly economic matter; in morals they believed firmly that organized institutions should interfere to restrain the populace from the drunkenness, idleness, and loose living they were supposedly inclined to. Libertarians in economics, the educated, middle-class Victorians were most certainly authoritarians in morals.

The Realistic Novel

In literature, the later nineteenth century was a great period for the novel. Here the accepted label for the novel of the time is "realism," in contrast with the Romanticism of the earlier part of the century. Yet as one usually finds in examining these sharp contrasts between the cultural attitudes of succeeding generations in the modern West, the realists are quite obviously children of the Romanticists. The Romantic of 1830, fleeing this ugly world for an idealized Middle Ages, when knighthood was in flower and there were no sooty

Balzac, by Rodin.

factories, or writing of the idyllic Indian tribes of America, can indeed look very different from the realist of 1860, analyzing with fascination and disgust the men and women of the mill towns, the slums of the great cities, the unidyllic countryside of peasant labor. Yet both romantic and realist are individualists, and both are in firm revolt against middle-class respectability. Both deny the older "classical" ideals of aristocratic measure, of a "natural" law of decency and decorum. Both are obsessed with the analysis of the uniquely individual human soul. In our contemporary jargon, both "psychologize."

The Englishman Dickens (1812-1870) and the Frenchman Balzac (1799-1850) were both writing in the period we label "Romantic." Both revel in exaggerations, both pour themselves out freely in undisciplined torrents of words, both achieve an effect of unreal intensity—Romantic traits, surely. Yet both are thoroughly immersed in the world of their time, both are in many ways realists. On the other hand, the leading French realist of the later nineteenth century, Flaubert (1821-1880), wrote one of his novels, *Salammbô*, about an ancient and, in spite of his great efforts at historical accuracy, not very real Carthage. And in his masterpiece, *Madame Bovary*, which analyzes the romantic longings of a small-town doctor's wife, Flaubert betrays a most ambivalent feeling toward his heroine. Indeed, he once said, "*I am Madame Bovary.*" Flaubert hated the bourgeois world he wrote about quite as much as did the escapist writers of an earlier generation.

Nevertheless, there remains a difference between the writing of the second half of the century and that of the first. The realists did abandon the Romantic pursuit of the ideal and the remote and chose subjects close to their own lives. They did generally avoid tempestuous extremes and concentrate on the quieter folk. They did pay great attention to choosing the right word, the word that should stand exactly for the experience, the emotion depicted, and not rouse all sorts of irrelevant overtones. We may take as good realists the Englishman Trollope and the Russian Turgenev. Trollope (1815-1882) wrote dozens of novels about Victorian clergymen and politicians and country gentlemen, carefully observing the English decencies, never raising his voice or his style, but imparting understanding, sympathy, and a suitable, modest irony. Turgenev (1818-1883) wrote about his fellows with classic restraint, skirting delicately the depths of the Slavic soul (see Chapter XXII). Or we may take William Dean Howells (1837-1920), who in the *Rise of Silas Lapham* and other novels sought to apply realism to the American scene.

The Naturalistic Novel: Zola

Howells seemed to later critics a representative of what they called the "genteel tradition." They accused him of omitting the more unpleasant facts of life, of softening the crudities of the new industrial civilization. For as the twentieth century drew near the realists were confronted with a rebel generation that found them not "realistic" enough. This school rose first in France, where they took for themselves the name of "naturalists." Their leader, Emile Zola (1840-1902), shows clearly the influence of the scientific revolution inspired by the work of Darwin. For Zola was not content with the realist's aim to reflect the life around him with simple accuracy; he sought to arrive at laws of human development, much as the biologist seeks for laws of organic development.

The novel was to Zola an instrument of scientific generalization. He would do for society, for men in their relations with other men, what Darwin had done for natural history. He would show what men are like, of course, but he would also show how they came to be what they are, and even what they were going to be. He called his great series of novels about a family under the Second Empire, the Rougon-Macquart, the "natural history" of a family.

Zola's work points up one of the tendencies not only of the late nineteenth-century novel, in those days the spearhead of literature, but of other forms of literature as well. The literature of the time, and to a great extent of the twentieth century too, is overwhelmingly a literature of discontent, of protest against things-as-they-are. Now it is quite true that from the ancient Greek philosophers and the Hebrew prophets on, many great thinkers have held that their times were peculiarly out of joint. They had to protest against the abuses of their age, had to stir their fellows into bettering their ways. But there are certainly periods when the intellectuals are *relatively* conformist, *relatively* well disposed to the existing government and society—the Augustan Age in Rome, the Elizabethan Age, and the Age of Louis XIV, for example. And there are ages when the intellectuals, even though they are bitterly against things-as-they-are, write with hope and confidence of what is to come—as in the eighteenth-century Enlightenment. We have already noted that the Romantic movement has its pessimistic side. With the second half of the nineteenth century there sets in a strain of pessimism—at least among many leading writers—that has continued to this day. It is by no means the only strain in modern western literature, and it is by no means a strain of unrelieved pessimism. Writers on the Left, notably the socialists, are obliged by their creed to hold that somehow mankind will win through to a better society.

The Literature of Pessimism and Protest

The pessimists reacted against the eighteenth-century doctrine of the natural goodness of man. Certainly "nature" and

Caricature of George Bernard Shaw by Max Beerbohm.

"natural" as they figure in the work of a Zola carry very different connotations from these words as the eighteenth, and even the early nineteenth, centuries used them. Nature by the late nineteenth century apparently made most men greedy, selfish, combative, not very bright, and extremely addicted to a variety of irregular sexual relations which brought out to the full their other bad traits. Sometimes, as with the English novelist Thomas Hardy (1840-1928), this pessimism is built up from a series of incidents in private lives into a grand cosmic irony not without its consoling side. But for the most part these writers are concerned directly with the cruelties, stupidities, the downright insanities of ordinary people.

In France, De Maupassant (1850-1893),

324

a master of the short story, wrote sparely and simply, after the manner of his master Flaubert, about the tragedies and comedies of ordinary life; but the tragedies, or at least the ironies, prevail. In Russia, Chekhov (1860-1904), a medical man by training, used the prose drama and the short story to show how life harasses us all. Ibsen (1828-1906) in Norway, Brieux (1858-1932) in France, and George Bernard Shaw (1856-1950) in England all helped to develop the characteristically late-nineteenth-century form of the drama, the "problem play." The problem was sometimes one of wide moral and political concern, as in Ibsen's *Enemy of the People* or Shaw's *Man and Superman,* but it was very often concerned mainly with the stupid tangles of men's private, and in particular their sex, lives. Ibsen shocked his contemporaries in his *Doll's House* by having his heroine rebel against the "doll-house" atmosphere that her husband had created for her. His *Ghosts* scandalized his contemporaries by bringing to the stage the problem of syphilis.

The problem play, the problem novel, the problem short story spread through all the literatures of the West. They spread with the usual speed to the United States, where by the end of the nineteenth century the "genteel tradition" was already scorned by the bright young men, and the novelists Stephen Crane (1871-1900) and Theodore Dreiser (1871-1945) were bringing out the harsh realities of war, business, and love. It took a while for the extremes of "naturalism" to gain the United States, and it was not until our own day, and then of all places in the South of magnolia and roses, that William Faulkner and Erskine Caldwell and their many followers really plumbed the depths of human perversities behind the Anglo-Saxon four-letter words they used so freely.

Most of this realistic or naturalistic writing, even when it is by no means of Marxist inspiration, is hostile to the middle classes.

The bourgeois is no longer just the Philistine the Romantic disliked, the puritanical conformist, the stuffy enemy of sweetness and light. He is still that, but he is also the rapacious titan of industry, the jingoistic nationalist, authoritarian browbeater of his children, the tasteless addict of "conspicuous consumption" (a phrase of the American economist, Thorstein Veblen), the hypocritical practitioner of a "double standard" of sexual morality, and worse. Flaubert, who began so much, may be said to have begun this with his unfinished *Bouvard et Pécuchet*, in which he makes his two bourgeois "heroes" run the gamut of human futility, failing ludicrously in their effort to educate themselves. In England, Samuel Butler (1835-1902) in *The Way of All Flesh* set the pattern, since followed freely, for the novel in which the writer-son blames all on the tyrannical male parent. Shaw found a simple phrase to sum up what was wrong—"middle class morality." Ibsen's *Enemy of the People* is ironically named; the real enemy of the people is the people themselves, not the misunderstood leader who would bring them better things.

Even where the writers are not embittered, even where their main concern is to balance good and evil as, one suspects, they are balanced in life, the middle class does not often come out well. English novelists like H. G. Wells, Galsworthy, and Arnold Bennett, French novelists like Anatole France, Spanish novelists like Pio Baroja, and most writers of tsarist Russia find something wrong with the middle classes. An epitome, a bit more kindly than usual in Europe, of this attack on the middle classes is afforded by an American, who wrote in the 1920's, chronologically rather later than the period with which we are here concerned, but quite in its "style." Sinclair Lewis' *Main Street* and *Babbitt* are realistic rather than naturalistic novels, and George Babbitt is almost a hero without ironic quotation marks. Still, Babbitt came to sum up for thousands of American intellectuals what was wrong with a naive materialistic civilization. The novels of Sinclair Lewis sold by the hundred thousands, so that it is clear that "George Babbitt" himself in real life must have relished, or at least read, these satires on his way of life. Indeed, since many of the writers we have been dealing with were able to sell their works in a mass market, one is forced to conclude that a good portion of the middle classes in the West were in revolt against their own shortcomings.

Not all that was written between 1850 and the outbreak of war in 1914 was a literature of scorn or protest. The daughters of the Maud or Mélanie with whom we began could about 1900 read the standard conventional fare, historical novels, novels of escape, novels of true love. They could even find in writers like Kipling men who, if not exactly convinced that this was the best of possible worlds, were at least convinced that the English middle classes were the least bad of the lot. They could, in short, read for pleasure and edification, and go on with the serious business of life.

Poetry

Few writers tried to make poetry "naturalistic" in Zola's sense. Nor, on the other hand, was the late nineteenth century a period in which the epic or the grand philosophical poem, like Wordsworth's *Prelude,* flourished. Poets did attempt the drama in verse, but these dramas remained poetry to be read in the study, not plays for the boards. Tennyson, who can stand very well for the more conventional Victorian poets, tried the epic in his *Idyls of the King,* based on the legends about King Arthur's court, and he tried the philosophical poem, such as *In Memoriam,* and several "closet" dramas. But he perhaps succeeded best in his shorter lyrics.

In England Tennyson, in America Long-

fellow and his New England colleagues, in France Victor Hugo, wrote the staple poetry the late nineteenth century liked and read a great deal. These poets deserve the tag, "household words." In form, their work differs little from the norms set by the earlier Romantic movement, and their subjects are love, death, nature, patriotism, faith, doubt, and longing, the eternal lyric repertory. And they sometimes came down into the arena to deal with politics, as in Whittier's anti-slavery poems, and in James Russell Lowell's "Biglow Papers," poems in Yankee dialect on the crisis of the Civil War. The spiritual crisis brought on by loss of Christian faith in a scientific age is evident in many poems of Matthew Arnold and Arthur Hugh Clough, as well as Tennyson. Even the horrors of the industrial revolution are apparent in Thomas Hood's "Song of the Shirt":

> With fingers weary and worn,
>   With eyelids heavy and red,
> A woman sat in unwomanly rags,
>   Plying her needle and thread—
>   Stitch! stitch! stitch!
> In poverty, hunger, and dirt,
>   And still with the voice of dolorous pitch
> She sang the 'Song of the Shirt!' [*]

Yet in these very same years poetry went far along the road that brought it to our times, when the serious poet usually writes difficult, private, metaphysical, psychological, or at the very least, weighty experimental verse for a handful of initiates. Poetry for the Romanticist was indeed the reflection of his own inner world, but he hoped it would not prove by any means a private world. He wanted to be read, perhaps even by the Philistines, as indeed he was. In the second half of the nineteenth century, the French Parnassians deliberately sought the seclusion of perfect form, of polished verse fit for but few, of "art for art's sake." Still later, with Symbolists like Mallarmé,

---

[*] Thomas Hood, *Poetical Works,* Epes Sargent, ed. (Boston, 1855), 147.

they went on to very difficult verse indeed, in which the meaning had to be wrung with effort from symbols nested one within another, in which the harmonies, like those of modern music, are by no means at once apparent to the untrained listener. Significantly, when twentieth-century poets went back for precedents to their literary "fathers" or teachers, they did not go to Tennyson, Hugo, Longfellow, or Kipling, but to late Victorian poets hardly known to their contemporaries, like the English Gerard Manley Hopkins and the American Emily Dickinson. Here is a passage from Hopkins:

> Across my foundering deck shone
> A beacon, an eternal beam. | Flesh fade,
>   and mortal trash
> Fall to the residuary worm; | world's wild-
>   fire, leave but ash:
>   In a flash, at a trumpet crash,
> I am all at once what Christ is, | since he
>   was what I am, and

> This Jack, joke, poor potsherd, | patch,
>   matchwood, immortal diamond,
>   Is immortal diamond.*

Yet the historian must not be so interested in the origins of what becomes good literature for the few as to forget what the many read. Even as late as the early twentieth century, it was not Hopkins, not Mallarmé, not Emily Dickinson who were recited at parties, on the stage, or in formal ceremonials all over the West—it was still Hugo, Heine, Longfellow, or newer poets like A. E. Housman or even Robert Service and Edgar Guest.

Painting

In Victorian literature, then, there was a popular and conventional, but not vulgar, level of writing represented by men

* Gerard Manley Hopkins, *Poems*, 3rd ed. (New York, 1948), 112.

"La Parade" ("Sideshow"), by Georges Seurat, who originated pointillism, an extreme development of impressionism characterized by a technique for applying colors in tiny dots according to a rigidly systematic plan.

"La Grenouillière" ("The Frog Pond"), an impressionist painting by Claude Monet.

like Hugo and Tennyson. In painting, there was a similar level, represented by artists whose work now fills many galleries—the Fontainebleau school in France; Watts, Burne-Jones, and Rossetti in England; George Inness, and later Winslow Homer and John Singer Sargent in the United States; and many, many others throughout the West. The *avant garde,* the advanced innovators in art, the rebels, gave the paintings of these men the derogatory label "academic." Actually, the academic painters were technically very skillful, for they had the advantage of the long tradition of western painting since the Renaissance. They could mirror man and nature faithfully, in a sense more faithfully than their great rival for the patronage of the many, the camera. They were perhaps realists, but they were not naturalists in Zola's sense. They rather avoided the shambles of the industrial revolution, and to their *avant garde* opponents they seemed too much concerned with the pretty in nature and with the aristocratic or striking in portraiture.

The first great innovators in later nineteenth-century painting were the French impressionists. This school once had to content itself with separate salons, for the academics would have none of it. But it is now safely enshrined as "classic." The impressionists, too, show one of the cross-fertilizations between science and art, but in a rather subtler way than does the naturalist movement in fiction. One of the things science does is to show us that the "real" world is not what the hasty eye finds, that things are not what they seem. The impressionists were not content with the camera eye of the academics. Light, they learned from the physicists, was not a simple thing, but a complex that the eye puts together from the prismatic reflections of nature. So they proposed to break up light into its constituent colors and then allow the viewer's eye to reassemble them. They painted landscapes for the most part, and they built up their trees and flowers and buildings and skies from thousands of little dabs of color, so that the result, when seen from a few feet away, is hardly more than

A landscape by Cézanne (near Aix-en-Provence, with Mont Sainte Victoire in background).

a formless mesh of color, but seen from an adequate distance does indeed take the form of a landscape, a landscape flooded in light.

The great master of the impressionist school, Claude Monet (1840-1926) was a prolific painter, whose work is well represented in public museums. Monet repeatedly painted the same subjects, notably Rouen Cathedral and the lily pond in his own garden, to show how they varied in appearance at different times of day and under changing conditions of light. Light interested many other painters, like Turner in England, who specialized in marine pictures (see illustration on p. 132), and the Anglicized American, Whistler, who did misty scenes in London and, incidentally, was very ashamed of the fact that he had been born in Lowell, Massachusetts.

Even with the Frenchman Manet (1832-1883), who began as a realist and retained a certain harshness associated with the realistic temperament, we find another great artist breaking with the "realism" of the camera. Manet's famous "Death of Maximilian" completely destroys the Renais-sance idea of perspective, placing the firing squad almost on top of its victim, and abandons "fact" by making the executioners not Mexican soldiers (which they were) but French Zouaves. Manet uses "real" objects for his own purposes, as occasions for effects of color and composition which are *his*. These effects are, for the purposes of the artist, to be preferred as truer to the realities of the universe and nature as men *ought* to see them than is all that seems to the layman's eye to be real, natural. To put it another way: these apparently distorted effects are truer, more real, than what the ordinary man, whose vision is science-spoiled, commonsense-spoiled, schoolmarm-spoiled, sees as "real" or "natural." Some such feeling that the artist sees more and more profoundly than any mechanical device, or than any person with just conventional, or just "scientific," or just "rationalistic" training is common to modern art in almost all its forms.

Some of the best work of the middle of the century was done in drawing and engraving, where new methods of reproduction made prints available to all. Here again the French are at their best, severe moralists in the Voltairean tradition, as in the caricatures of Daumier (see illustrations on pp. 169 and 174) and Forain.

Toward the end of the century the *avant garde* turned to another technique, somewhat more difficult than impressionism to describe. The great figure here is another Frenchman, Cézanne (1839-1906). This painter, too, wanted to go beyond the smooth techniques of the academics, but he found impressionism too fuzzy, too obsessed with light. The impressionists had to him lost the sense of shape, lost the three dimensions of the real world—at least, of the "real" world of human binocular vision. He proposed to put them back, not with the classic, flowing perspective inherited by the academics from the Italians, but with blocks, chunks of color blended into a result that is after all realistic. From Cézanne there stemmed in a sense much of twentieth-century painting. Cubism, which is the exaggeration of Cézanne's insistence on hard three-dimensionality, is most obviously in his debt, but so too are Abstractionism and even Surrealism. Cézanne's work and that of two of his contemporaries, the Dutchman Van Gogh and the Frenchman Gauguin, were once thought wild, private, and unprofitably experimental. But they are now popular in museums and in countless inexpensive reproductions. Neither the artist nor the sociologist understands this process, by which the once outrageous innovation becomes an established classic, well enough to be sure whether a given contemporary work will or will not survive. Indeed, the purchase of *contemporary* art for private or public collections remains one of the most speculative of human ventures: the odds are heavily against the investor. All art connoisseurship, including that of rare books, is in terms of economics about as risky a business as there is, though as usual in speculation in our culture, the successful connoisseur and collector wins great prizes.

The Other Arts

The nineteenth century was not a great period for sculpture. An age that had mastered the industrial arts so well produced monumental statues aplenty. The most famous for Americans is the Statue of Liberty in New York harbor, the work of the French sculptor Bartholdi, a gift from the Third French Republic to the American Republic. But the statues of statesmen and warriors that adorn public places everywhere in the West are so conventionally realistic that we hardly accept them as human beings. Sculpture in the large at least would appear to be an aristocratic art, designed for the palace and the formal garden. Its nineteenth-century civic use seems at its best—or least bad—in Paris, in the decoration of the great Arc de Triomphe, a delayed memorial to the Grand Army of Napoleon I, and in the new Opéra and many other buildings. Toward the end of the century, Frenchmen like Rodin (see illustration, p. 322) and Maillol began a break with the formal statuary of their time, simplifying and strengthening the contours of their men and women, treating their subjects with less academic convention and more power. It should be noted that inexpensive, small-scale copies of the great sculpture of antiquity and the Renaissance now became common, and many a Victorian drawing room in Europe and in Europe overseas boasted a plaster Venus or a bronze Mercury. Museums in various parts of the world could all afford large plaster casts. Some direct acquaintance with the great artistic achievements of the past was now available to a very wide general public.

Indeed the nineteenth century knew almost too much of the past of the arts and was too eclectic and derivative in its tastes. Certainly this eclecticism weighed heavily on the architect. Somewhere in the West in these years someone built something in almost every style that had ever been used. Western men built Chinese pagodas, Egyptian pyramids, Greek temples, and, especially in America, Gothic universities. In the United States buildings were typed for style: banks, those solid institutions, went back to Greece and Rome, at least for their fronts; churches and universities relied on Gothic; public buildings went in for the Renaissance, duly modified by the reigning taste in the Paris Ecole des Beaux-Arts (School of Fine Arts); private citizens went in for anything that pleased them for their own houses, modified perhaps a bit by the traditions of their region. Individual architects worked on a historic style that they adapted in their own way. Thus the American Richardson revived the Romanesque, the early medieval predecessor of Gothic, with its round arches and its solidarity, achieving certainly a style of his own, which

The first skyscraper: the Home Insurance Building in Chicago.

can be seen in Trinity Church in Boston—and in many railroad stations on the Boston and Albany.

Two broad styles may be found in the confusion of nineteenth-century architecture. One style, for public buildings, was basically Renaissance, with pediments, balconies, sometimes with domes, and with friezes and other decorations. This style varies somewhat from nation to nation. French public buildings, under the influence of the Beaux-Arts, looked at least vaguely like a chateau in Touraine; German buildings kept a touch of the huddled Middle Ages; and British buildings, much imitated in Boston, New York and Philadelphia, were simpler, more in the manner of Palladio. The other style, for private homes, was represented in Europe by the "villa," and in America by the residence, often a "mansion," that the successful businessman built for himself on Elm Street. In the United States this style was at its most flaunting in the mansions of the 1870's, the "era of General Grant." These were big houses, for families were large, domestic servants were plentiful and cheap, and building costs were relatively low. They ran to high ceilings, for the bourgeois wanted nothing to remind him of the low rooms of his peasant past. Today they look too tall for their width, and their lines seem much too broken by little towers, porches, scrollwork, all sorts of decorative devices. But they had the latest comforts, if they were in a town large enough—gas light, bath and water closet, and central heating, though western Europeans came rather slowly to this last innovation.

In architecture, as in sculpture, true innovation began toward the end of the century. In structural steel, men now had a way of emancipating themselves from the limitations that had so taxed the Gothic builders; they could now go almost as high as they pleased. They began to do so in the United States, where the first "skyscraper," the Home Insurance Building in Chicago, was put up in 1885. Although some later skyscrapers ended up in Gothic towers, abundantly decorated, the general tendency imposed by the materials was toward simplicity of line. This taste for simplicity began to spread, and with the twentieth century the way was open for modern "functional" architecture. Structural steel should remind us that some of the most satisfying work of the late nineteenth century was not primarily meant for beauty, but very often achieved it. The great bridges of the time, for example, the Firth of Forth Bridge in Scotland, and Brooklyn Bridge, are still handsome as well as impressive and useful.

In the minor arts of furniture, household decoration, and clothing, the Victorian Age seems to us now most characteristic and most ugly. Although it is hard to believe that men will ever collect "antiques" of the 1870's as they now collect the work of earlier periods, horsehair sofas and marble-topped tables are nowadays coming into the trade in antiques. So, we return to the Victorian drawing room with which we began. It was an incredibly heavy and incredibly dark room, for the height of the windows was canceled by the dark carpets, upholstery, and hangings, and by the mahogany or walnut furniture. And it was cluttered with what were known as *objets d'art*. Our taste in interior decoration today is different from that of the Victorians in part because in our society domestic labor is scarce and expensive; the mere job of dusting the bric-a-brac of a nineteenth-century house would be too much for the modern housewife.

Yet we must as always note that qualifying "in part." Simplification of interior décor was probably helped along, but not initiated or simply "caused," by scarcity and high cost of domestic labor. Even at levels of high art as well as at those of taste and fashion, human beings—modern western human beings at least—tend to rebel against the ways of a preceding generation. Reaction against Victorian decorative arts, a

movement for simplification, starts in England with William Morris (1834-1896) in full Victorian times, and is in full swing by the 1890's with Voysey and Mackintosh in England, *art nouveau* France, and the Secession in Austria. Already, the "functional" chair is in sight.

Music

One great art remains to be discussed—music. Now though in music there is no such obvious commonsensical basis in "Nature" as the camera eye gives the representational arts, it is not misleading to take the established "classical" eighteenth-century tonality and forms, say from Bach through Haydn and much of Mozart, as a kind of norm or "law" which nineteenth-century composers revolted against, sought to go beyond.

Part of this revolt deserves the old label "romantic": the composer sought to move his hearers, to tears, to rapture, to ecstasy, by startling novelties, by unique and overpowering orchestra sonorities, by "programme music" in which the sounds were deliberately tied to other parts of human experience—i.e., suggested bird songs, waterfalls, wind in the pines, a thunderstorm—or even in the *Sinfonia Domestica* (1904) of the German Richard Strauss, the mild bedlam of child-rearing and household routines. The old forms—sonata, symphony, concerto—were by no means abandoned; they were, rather, exceeded, burst.

In the late nineteenth century itself, the supreme achievement in music seemed clearly to be Richard Wagner's (1813-1883). After the usual struggle of the innovating artist to get a hearing, Wagner by the 1870's had become the heir of Beethoven. He set out to make opera the supreme synthesis of the arts, with drama, music, scenery all fused in one great transcendence of this dull world of ordinary living. He gave up the routine recitative—the relatively undramatic passages "explaining" the action—interlarded with arias in which the singer or singers dropped what action there had been and advanced boldly to the front of the stage to launch into song. He sought rather to combine music and action in a realistic and dramatic whole. His characteristic device was the *Leitmotiv,* a definite and recognizable melodic theme associated with a given character or symbolizing an element in the drama. These

Daumier caricature. How the public feels after listening to the music of the future by Wagner.

themes he wove together for both voices and orchestra into a continuous flow of music. He chose epic subjects: the four operas of the *Ring of the Nibelungen,* in which he drew on the Teutonic myths, by no means without thought for Teutonic greatness; *Parsifal,* on the theme of the Holy Grail; *Tristan and Isolde,* a drama of fated love and death taken from the Arthurian legends. Wagner's operas call for robust voices, which in turn call for barrel-chested tenors and huge sopranos ill-suited to concepts of romantic love or indeed of heroism. In our time Wagner's popularity

has suffered because of his Victorian heaviness, his inordinate lengths, and the great noise he makes. Nietzsche once wrote aptly that Wagner's music *sweats.* Moreover, he has suffered—the musical purist often thinks he has suffered unjustly—from the associations of his life and work with German nationalism, racism, even Nazism.

Yet Wagner deserves his fame as a composer. His break with the norms of the classical past, his orchestration, his chromaticism, his desperate efforts to *transcend,* to express the inexpressible, or at least the extraordinary, are a landmark in the road that leads from the *Well-Tempered Clavichord* to our contemporary atonality. Even the Frenchman Debussy (1862-1918), who found Wagner too noisy, too unbridled, too *German,* and who sought to capture in his music a French sense of quiet measure, followed Wagner in this revolt against classical tonality.

Again, as in poetry, nineteenth-century music had its popular successes, free from *avant garde* difficulties. "Popular" music in most of the West was tuneful, and inclined to nostalgia, not unpleasant tears, conventional sentiment; here the work of the American Stephen Foster (1826-1864) is a superior sample indeed. Light music flourished, in the tuneful operettas of Offenbach, like *La Belle Hélène,* based on the legend of Helen of Troy, in the waltzes of Johann Strauss and Waldteufel, and for Anglo-Saxons in the gently, never bitterly or agonizedly, satirical operas of Gilbert and Sullivan.

The Arts in Review

We shall make three broad generalizations about the arts (in their widest sense, to include literature) in the nineteenth century, ever mindful of the difficulties of the undertaking, especially for historians, who nowadays are rarely trained in the arts. Nor shall we forget that the old Latin tag, *De gustibus non est disputandum* (tastes are not to be disputed) ought really to go: there is no use disputing except about tastes.

First, there is, as we have already noted, an amazing range and variety in nineteenth-century arts. This is a century that did not even build its public buildings in a single style. The patron—better yet in this century of the great market, the customer—could pick from the styles of centuries. Popular magazines, inexpensive reprints of older books, serializations of new works, the beginnings, especially in the United States, of circulating libraries, inexpensive (as well as expensive) reproductions of works of art, in short, the new technical and economic resources of a society on its way to democratic equalities, meant that much was available in all the arts. The reader could shift from Dickens or Tennyson to Homer or Chaucer, go frankly common with "penny dreadfuls" or "dime novels," or turn to the difficulties of innovators like Mallarmé, or Browning, held in those days to be a difficult poet. No doubt there were individuals with tastes so broad, or so undiscriminating, as to dip into all these. There were of course standards—conventional, classical, and "academic"—of good and bad in the arts, and most of these standards were dinned in firmly in the current "classical" or "liberal" education. The nineteenth-century college student, unlike the twentieth-century one, was in his formal education carefully shielded from the contemporary in the arts.

Second, by the end of the nineteenth century there is a very clear rift, the origins of which go back several centuries, between the tastes of the few and those of the many, or in current American terms, between the tastes of the "highbrows," or "longhairs," or intellectuals, and the tastes of the rest of the people. Now these terms must not be taken to indicate the existence of two totally different groups, two circles that never intersect. Nevertheless, it is clear that from the point of view of the sociologist of

knowledge, there had come to be by the end of the nineteenth century what some have called the "alienation of the intellectuals;" to this theme we shall have to return, for it must be one of the concerns of anyone who deals with contemporary western culture.

Third, there is accentuated in the nineteenth century a tendency in a sense constant in western art: the revolt of one cultural generation against the ways of its parent generation. Again, we are not here dealing with absolutes: the rebels of the "naughty 'nineties," the members of the "lost generation" of the 'twenties of our own century, did not think-and-feel in ways totally alien to the ways of their parents. Moreover, the phenomenon we are here discussing is almost wholly limited to the "highbrows," to high art, and is, save at the level of trivial changes of fashion, hardly noticeable in popular art. No doubt the great innovators do eventually, if they are great enough, get translated, adapted, even accepted, by a wider public. Still, the gap remains. The few are indeed, as we have just noted, innovators: like Gerard Manley Hopkins, or Monet, Manet, or Cézanne, or Wagner or Debussy, they produce something new, strange, something that widens, changes, the possibilities of human experience. They are, in short, *avant garde*—in popular language, "moderns." For those who come to share their widened experiences, they are successful innovators, men and women who add to the great cumulative culture of mankind quite as clearly as do the great scientists and inventors; for those who do not share their experiences, they are usually wild men, profitless rebels against the eternal verities, the eternal beauties, morally and politically undesirables to boot, and what they are trying to do can't and shouldn't be done. We shall come again to this point in a final chapter, for the problem of "modern" art is one of the many we have inherited from the nineteenth century.

III: Philosophy

Idealism and Realism

The art and literature of the later nineteenth century furnish samples of almost the full range of human attitudes toward the world. The formal philosophy and the less formal view of life taken by ordinary educated people varied quite as widely, and we can find as many different schools in metaphysics and ethics as we can find in literature and art. The philosophical school of idealism was born in its modern form in the Germany of Kant and Hegel (see Chapters XVII and XIX). In the later nineteenth century it continued to thrive in the land of its birth; it made converts in the Oxford School of T. H. Green, Bradley, and Bosanquet, and in the American philosopher, Josiah Royce; and it even penetrated into the Latin countries. The philosophical opposite of idealism, now christened "realism," was at least as widespread. Modern realism, though as a philosophy it attempted to answer questions the scientist does not try to answer *in so far as he is a scientist,* had its roots in the same soil as modern science and the scientific rationalism of the eighteenth-century *philosophes,* and was a product of the Enlightenment.

The American philosopher, William James (1842-1910), found two terms to sum up this polar antithesis of idealism and realism that runs through western philosophical tradition. Men are, wrote James, by disposition either "tender-minded" or "tough-minded." They are either tough-mindedly convinced that the world of sense-experience is the *real* world or tender-mindedly convinced that the world of sense-experience is somehow an illusion, or at any rate an imperfect, changing, and therefore unreal copy or reflection of the *real* world which is in our minds—imperfectly—and perfectly in God's mind.

One might conclude that, since the later nineteenth century was a period of great material progress, deeply concerned with this world of the senses, then on the whole the "tough-minded" would prevail over the "tender-minded." Yet this was by no means true in formal philosophy, where the tender-minded were quite numerous and articulate. Perhaps the ordinary unreflective man leans toward the tough-minded side, if only because common sense urges upon him the presence of the world of sense-experience, the world of matter. But there are no reliable statistics on this point, and to the extent that Christianity forms an inescapable underpinning for the world-view of western men, not even common sense can altogether dispose of the world of the tender-minded, of concepts like "soul," "spirit," and "other world."

Dynamism and the Cult of the Will

Certain common denominators, however, underlay the formal thought of the later nineteenth century. Here, too, Darwinism left its mark. The thought of the period had a dynamic historical and evolutionary cast that not even the tender-minded could avoid. The idealist, following Hegel, believed that above the whirl and change of this world of the senses there was an unchanging, perfect world of the Absolute. But he also believed that this imperfect world was being slowly drawn toward that other world, developing by ways he could only incompletely understand, but developing, growing, evolving. On the other hand, the nineteenth-century realist no longer held that his reason could give him a neat mathematical formula for the good life; he too thought that everything grows, that even what is made according to human plans must take account of nature's mysterious ways of growth.

A second and related note in the thought of the period is an emphasis on will, often capitalized into Will, on doing, on the life-force that makes the "struggle for existence." The word appears everywhere, even as a title—Schopenhauer's *World as Will and Idea*, Nietzsche's *Will to Power*, William James' *Will to Believe*. It appears but slightly disguised in the French philosopher Henri Bergson's "creative evolution" and "élan vital" and in Bernard Shaw's "life-force." It appears as an insistence that knowing is not a passive registering, but a creative *doing*, in the work of the Italian Benedetto Croce. It lies behind the use of the word "myth" by the French anarcho-syndicalist, Georges Sorel, and the German Hans Vaihinger's phrase, the "philosophy of the as-if." For both these latter thinkers, the great ideas, the great abstractions of Right and Wrong, are not mere attempts of the mind to understand the world; indeed they are quite false if taken as analytically descriptive of this world. But they are, rather, the guides our desires, our wills, set up for our action. They are fictions, myths, "as-if," but all the more *real* for being such. The Italian idealist philosopher Croce summarized: true knowing is doing, making.

The pragmatism of William James, somewhat unfairly described by its critics as the philosophy that nothing succeeds like success, is clearly one of these philosophies of the will. To James, himself "tough-minded," reality is no Absolute as in the idealist tradition; indeed, reality is nothing fixed and certain. Reality is what works for us human beings; truth is what we want to believe. James thought he had saved himself from the obvious danger of this line of thought—that is, making reality and truth

purely subjective, purely a matter of the individual's judgment—by granting that not everything we want is practical, that not all our desires "work." If my will to believe tells me I can make a broad jump of three hundred feet, experience, the "pragmatic" test, will prove that I cannot. But to many of James' critics, he had by no means saved himself from subjectivism. Pragmatism remained to these critics a doctrine dangerously erosive of traditional values, leading either to an exaltation of mere vulgar success, or to a silly belief in believing for the sake of believing.

The Revolt against Reason

The cult of the will brings us to a major current in the broad stream of later nineteenth-century thought, to the center

William James in 1907.

of nineteenth-century repudiation of the thought of the eighteenth, a repudiation never universal, and more evident among the creative writers, artists, intellectuals, than among ordinary educated men and women. This was an intensification of the revolt against reason already initiated by the Romantics earlier in the century; it may be called "anti-intellectualism," "irrationalism," or, more exactly, "anti-rationalism." Even this last term is somewhat misleading, for it stresses negation, whereas the attitude it describes is also an affirmation. There seems, however, to be no better term for the attitude than anti-rationalism.

One further caution. This anti-rationalism is one of the "roots" of contemporary totalitarianism, and especially of fascist and Nazi totalitarianism (see Chapter XXVII). But it is by no means a simple synonym for totalitarianism. It is a much broader and more inclusive term. It is quite possible to have been influenced by anti-rational currents and remain a good, if not altogether orthodox, democrat and individualist. It is quite possible to be a Marxist totalitarian and reject a great deal, especially in its psychological core, of modern anti-rationalism. Indeed, the Marxist is in an important sense a naive, almost an eighteenth-century rationalist: get the economy to work perfectly, he says, and men will behave themselves perfectly.

The basic position of anti-rationalism, and one for which it is heavily indebted to the Romantic movement, is a rejection of the eighteenth-century Enlightenment's belief that the ordinary human being is naturally reasonable. To the extent that it rejects the Enlightenment, anti-rationalism is indeed a negation, as the "anti" implies. But it has its positive side—the belief that if men can accept and understand their true, complex nature, their irrationality, and their dependence on forces beyond their immediate control, they can win their way to a richer life than the rationalists ever planned for them.

The Chastened Rationalists

Broadly speaking, there are two kinds of anti-rationalism, which shade into one another: the moderate and the extreme. Moderate anti-rationalism at bottom is trying to salvage as much as possible of the eighteenth-century belief in human rationality. Such on the whole is the attitude of modern psychology from Freud (see Chapter XXXII) and William James on. This psychology seeks to aid human reason by pointing out the difficulties under which it must work. Reason, these thinkers maintain, is limited by men's instincts or "drives," by their biological inheritance of animality, so much emphasized by the evolutionists, and by their sociological inheritance of custom and tradition, so much emphasized by historians and by the school of Edmund Burke (see Chapter XIX).

To use a metaphor from John Locke, which he in turn derived from the slogan of the Cambridge Platonists, "the mind of man is the light of God," moderate anti-rationalists regard human reason as a flickering candle, not as the great white universal light it appeared to be to *philosophes* like Condorcet. *But they do not wish to extinguish this candle.* On the contrary, they wish to keep it alive, to nurse it along into greater and greater brightness. This process, in keeping again with the views of the evolutionist, they regard as inevitably long and slow, likely to be hindered rather than helped by ambitious plans to hasten it. These moderate thinkers were not so much anti-rationalists as they were disillusioned or chastened rationalists.

The Extreme Anti-rationalists

By contrast, the second kind of anti-rationalism would actually put out the candle of human reason. For the extreme anti-rationalists reason is not just feeble; it is bad. It is for them, so to speak, a mistake evolution has made—a wrong turning, from which the human race must somehow retrace its steps to a sounder life of instinct, emotion, and faith. Thomas Hardy, the English novelist, put the position clearly in the remark, "Thought is a disease of the flesh." There was a strong dose of this extreme anti-rationalism in the Nazi movement. Hitler himself distrusted reason as a degenerate French invention. Good Germans, he hoped, would come to think with their blood, with their German folk inheritance. This is the attitude reflected in the cry of a Spanish falangist general in 1936:

"Down with intelligence and long live death!" Extreme anti-rationalism may also be found at the bottom of some of the wilder movements in modern art, which want to do away with all the rules of grammar or harmony or perspective, and write or compose music or paint from the heart—or the guts—without regard for "meaningless forms."

The position of these extremists is strongly rooted in the Romantic movement, with its emphasis on the heart as against the head, on fresh instinct as against stale logic, on "the desire of the moth for the star," on always wanting more, more, more. (See Chapter XIX.)

IV: Political and Social Thought

Many of the extreme anti-rationalists turned violently against democracy, which seemed to them to rest on an altogether false estimate of what human beings were really like. The democrat believes at bottom that the ordinary man can be freed from the weight of erroneous traditions, habits, and prejudices. Once he has the real facts before him, he can attain by free discussion among his fellows a series of decisions that will be incorporated in acts and institutions under which all men can live happily. But if you hold that most, or even many, men are by nature incapable of fair, dispassionate thinking and discussion, if you hold that the load of tradition, habit, and prejudice cannot by any system of education be lifted from them, if in short you hold that men are by nature irrational, you will at least have to revise drastically your notions of democracy, or reject them.

The extreme anti-rationalist rejected the notions of democracy. The German philosopher Nietzsche, who did most of his work in the 1880's, will do as a sample of such

political thinkers in this period. Nietzsche wrote mostly in short aphoristic passages, which are hard to systematize and are often quite contradictory. But the central line of his thinking led to the concept of a new aristocracy, to the "superman" (in German, *Uebermensch*). Nietzsche's followers, who were numerous throughout the West in the two decades before 1914, insisted that he meant a new *spiritual* aristocracy. The supermen would be above the petty materialism and national patriotism of the middle classes. Nietzsche's opponents, who were also many, held that he was just another preacher of Nordic superiority, that his supermen were, as he put it in one of his famous passages, "the blond beasts" who had so often terrorized Europe. Certainly some of his German followers took him at his word, and held that he meant the real live Germans to be his supermen.

At any rate, Nietzsche was clearly an enemy of democracy, which he held to be second only to its child, socialism, as a society in which the weak unjustly and unnaturally ruled the strong. Here are some of his aphorisms, from which the reader can judge for himself:

Democracy represents the disbelief in all great men and in all élite societies: everybody is everybody else's equal. 'At bottom we are all herd and mob.'

I am opposed to Socialism because it dreams ingenuously of 'goodness, truth, beauty, and equal rights' (anarchy pursues the same ideal, but in a more brutal fashion).

I am opposed to parliamentary government and the power of the press, because they are the means whereby cattle become masters.*

Clearly Nietzsche hoped that the herd, the slaves, the masses would, in spite of their crass materialism, somehow recognize the true masters, the new enlightened despots.

Nietzsche is frankly attacking, from what he thought was a fundamental position, the values associated with the democratic inheritance of the eighteenth-century Enlightenment. But even those thinkers we have already noted (see Chapters XIX and XX) as defenders of that inheritance were in the nineteenth century influenced by romantic and anti-rationalist doubts as to the natural goodness and reasonableness of ordinary men and women, as to the beneficent workings of a free market, the "invisible hand" of laissez-faire economics, and much else of conventional, established, no longer innovating liberalism. John Stuart Mill in the mid-century had worried over the "tyranny of the majority." Walter Bagehot, a good English liberal much influenced by Darwin, pointed out in his *Physics and Politics* (1872) how strong was the accumulated force of habit and tradition, which he called the "cake of custom," how hard it was to persuade men to rational action. By the end of the century, liberals throughout the West were facing the problem of revising their attitudes toward life to conform with the new emphasis on the tough network of habit, custom, and prejudice.

---

* Friedrich Nietzsche, *The Will to Power*, A. M. Ludovici, trans. (London, 1910), II, 206.

Already by 1914 the broad lines of the social attitudes of our own time were being laid out. One line goes toward some kind of revolutionary élitism, toward the seizure of power by a minority that believes itself to have the formula whereby the gifted few can put order into a society threatened with chaos because of attempts to make decisions by counting heads, no matter what is inside them. The variety of these specific formulas is, however, very great, for the late nineteenth century was in its political and ethical ideas at least as eclectic as it was in architecture. Some make race the mark of the élite, and go so far as to preach world rule for their chosen race. Others make class the mark of the élite, and seek to achieve the "dictatorship of the proletariat." Indeed, as Marxian socialism developed in Lenin's hands the élitist implications, which were never very much hidden in the work of that truculent and impatient hater of human beings as they are, Karl Marx, come out openly as the doctrine that the enlightened minority must seize power and rule dictatorially for a while, at least. Others dream of a brand-new élite, such as Nietzsche's supermen, to be created by a kind of new religion. Others look to eugenics to make possible the breeding of such a new élite—though it must be confessed that in spite of their appeal to natural science, these are among the most impractical of the lot.

A second line goes toward a more flexible form of élitism, one that tries to conserve as much as possible of democratic values. On the whole, English Fabianism and continental revisionist socialism deserve this classification. The leaders of these movements wanted no violent overturns, no seizure of power. They believed in gradualness, even in the basic democratic counting of heads. But there was in all of them a strong touch of doubt as to the political capacity of the ordinary man. They were not for the extension of New England town-meeting democracy to the millions of the modern state. They hoped they could persuade the millions to elect legislators who would listen to the wise planners who had studied the social sciences, who could devise the wise new institutions that would make human life so much better. Above all, the planners themselves would by no means disdain what the anti-rationalists had taught them about the irrationality of ordinary men; they would make full use for good ends of what they could learn from the "practical" politician, the advertising man, the skilled professional manipulator of human beings; they would be Machiavellians, but Machiavellians on the side of the angels.

A third line seeks to preserve and protect what they consider a good, or at any rate an existing, élite from democratic drives toward equality, especially in the form of state intervention in economic and social life to promote security for all. This is substantially the line followed by men like the American sociologist William Graham Sumner, by the English philosopher Herbert Spencer, and by many others throughout the West. They are not unfairly labeled conservatives, for they sought to preserve in its broad lines an established order. But they were not simply routine, unphilosophical conservatives who opposed any changes at all. They had a definite philosophy, strongly influenced by the spirit of the times, by the anti-rationalism we have here outlined. Their basic position was a distrust of the instrument of thought applied unsparingly to human society, and in this they go back to Burke and indeed to philosophical conservatives throughout the western tradition.

But they are clearly children of their age, above all in their concrete fears of "socialism." Most of them believed in progress, and most of them prized material plenty, peace, industrial society. They held, however, that on the whole the existing middle classes, the existing leaders of a business world, the existing—or rather, the recently existing— network of Victorian habits and morals, were the best insurance that progress would continue. Above all, they feared planners and planning, at least in political positions. They distrusted the state. At bottom, they were good Darwinians, who believed that the evolutionary process depended on the struggle for life among competing individuals fettered as little as possible by planned human attempts to "rig" the struggle. They believed that social evolution could not be hastened, and that attempts to hasten it, no matter how well meant, would in fact retard it by limiting actual human variation and initiative. They are by no means altogether without sympathizers among us today, but it must be admitted that theirs has not, so far, been the "wave of the future." The Herbert Spencer who thought compulsory sewage disposal in cities was an interference with the "right" of the individual to conduct his own private struggle against typhoid fever would be even more uncomfortable in the mid-twentieth century than he was in the late nineteenth. Indeed, he is little read today.

Reading Suggestions
on the Intellectual Revolution

(Asterisk indicates paperbound edition.)

GENERAL ACCOUNTS

C. Brinton, *Ideas and Men* (Prentice-Hall, 1950). The later chapters of this general survey of intellectual history are also available in an inexpensive reprint: *The Shaping of the Modern Mind* (*Mentor).

R. C. Binkley, *Realism and Nationalism, 1852-1871* (Harper, 1935), and C. J. H. Hayes, *A Generation of Materialism, 1871-1900* (Harper, 1941). These two volumes provide fairly full coverage of the topics treated in this chapter.

J. T. Merz, *A History of European Thought in the 19th Century.* 4 vols. (Blackwood, 1912-1928). Misleadingly named, for it deals with philosophy and scientific thought only. (For further reading suggestions see Chapters XIX and XX.)

F. S. Marvin, *The Century of Hope*, 2nd ed. (Oxford Univ. Press, 1927). A bird's-eye view of general cultural history, somewhat old-fashioned now.

G. H. Sabine, *A History of Political Theory*, rev. ed. (Holt, 1955). The 19th-century portions of this general account are the best in this field. For more on socialism in the 19th century, see reading suggestions for Chapter XX.

K. S. Latourette, *Christianity in a Revolutionary Age: A History of Christianity in the 19th and 20th Centuries* (Harper, 1958–). Two already published volumes (1960) cover Europe in the 19th century very thoroughly: three more will finish the work with full attention to the rest of the world.

H. D. Aiken, *The Age of Ideology: The 19th Century Philosophers* (*Mentor, 1957). A volume of selections with introduction and interpretations in the useful series "Great Ages of Western Philosophy."

SPECIAL STUDIES: DARWINISM

C. Darwin, *On the Origin of Species by Natural Selection* (Modern Library, 1936, * New American Library), and *Journal of Researches into the Geology and Natural History of the Various Countries Visited during the Voyage of H.M.S.* Beagle *round the World* (Dutton, 1908. Everyman ed.; *Bantam). Respectively, Darwin's classic exposition, and his often fascinating report on the *Beagle* expedition that provided some of the evidence for his theories.

J. Barzun, *Darwin, Marx, Wagner* (Little, Brown, 1941; *2nd ed., Anchor). An interesting study; finds common denominators in men usually catalogued as quite different.

H. Spencer, *The Man versus the State*, A. J. Nock, ed. (Caxton, 1940). A representative work by a whole-hearted Social Darwinist.

M. R. Davie, ed., *Sumner Today* (Yale Univ. Press, 1940). Selected essays by William Graham Sumner, the most famous American Social Darwinist.

W. Bagehot, *Physics and Politics* (*Beacon, 1956). An early and suggestive adaptation of Darwinism to the political realm; very good reading, unlike the work of some other Social Darwinists.

B. Kidd, *Social Evolution* (Macmillan, 1898, and later editions). A now almost forgotten best-seller, very characteristic of late 19th-century Social Darwinism.

R. Hofstadter, *Social Darwinism in American Thought* (°Beacon, 1955). Interesting study of the ultimate impact of Darwin's theories.

C. Zirkle, *Evolution, Marxian Biology, and the Social Scene* (Univ. of Pennsylvania Press, 1959). A controversial treatment of a controversial subject.

SPECIAL STUDIES: LITERATURE AND THE ARTS

G. M. Young, *Victorian England: Portrait of an Age* (Doubleday, 1954; °Anchor). A brilliant evocation.

E. Wilson, *Axel's Castle, A Study in the Imaginative Literature of 1870-1930* (Scribner's, 1931; °same publisher). A suggestive study.

G. Brandes, *Main Currents in Nineteenth-Century Literature,* 6 vols. (Heinemann, 1901-1905). A valuable detailed study.

J. C. Sloane, *French Painting between the Past and the Present: Artists, Critics, and Traditions from 1848 to 1870* (Princeton Univ. Press, 1951).

M. Raynal, *The Nineteenth Century: Goya to Gauguin* (Skira, 1951). A superbly illustrated volume on painting.

S. Giedion, *Mechanization Takes Command* (Oxford Univ. Press, 1948). Interesting account of the effects of industrialism on the arts.

P. H. Láng, *Music in Western Civilization* (Norton, 1941), and C. Gray, *History of Music,* 2nd ed. (Knopf, 1947). Two very different and helpful histories of music.

H-R. Hitchcock, *Architecture: Nineteenth and Twentieth Centuries* (Pelican, 1958). A massive detailed study.

NOVELS AND DRAMAS

G. Flaubert, *Madame Bovary* (many editions). The classic novel of French realism.

E. Zola, *Germinal* (many editions) and *L'Assommoir* (translated under several titles). Two characteristic novels by the great French exponent of naturalism.

S. Butler, *The Way of All Flesh* (many editions). A good example of gloomy naturalism in the novel, English-style.

S. Lewis, *Babbitt* (Harcourt, Brace, 1949), and *Main Street* (Harcourt, Brace, 1950). Novels that are important documents of American social history in the early twentieth century.

E. Bellamy, *Looking Backward, 2000-1887* (°Modern Library, 1951); H. G. Wells, *A Modern Utopia* (Scribner's, 1905); and W. Morris, *News from Nowhere* (Longmans, Green, 1901). Three contrasting visions of Utopia in the light of science and industrialism.

H. Ibsen, *Six Plays: A Doll's House, Ghosts, An Enemy of the People, Rosmersholm, Hedda Gabler, The Master Builder* (°Modern Library). Six pioneering dramas by a master of late nineteenth-century realism.

E. Brieux, *Damaged Goods,* preface by G. B. Shaw (Fifield, 1914). The famous play about venereal disease.

G. B. Shaw, *Man and Superman* (°Penguin), and *Back to Methuselah* (Oxford Univ. Press, 1947. World's Classics). Two of Shaw's many plays that discuss aspects of the modern intellectual revolution.

IA ORANA MARIA

Nineteenth-Century Imperialism

CHAPTER XXIV

I: The Movement in General

IN THE *Oxford English Dictionary,* which tries to find the earliest possible example of a definition, the editors can go no further back than 1881 for "imperialism: the principle of the spirit of empire; advocacy of what are held to be imperial interests." The word is new; what it stands for is in part very old indeed—as old as human war and conquest. Yet there were some important new elements in the imperialism of western peoples in the nineteenth century, as the very form of the word suggests. An "ism" is a belief, a set of principles that men hold consciously as a guide to living. Nineteenth-century imperialism was in almost every country a major part of political life, with goals, methods, and advocates known to all who were concerned with politics. And since by 1900 almost all of western and central Europe, the United States, and indeed all the outposts of European culture enjoyed high literacy and widespread public discussion, imperialism took its place with liberalism, conservatism, nationalism, socialism, and a host of other "isms" as a subject of universal debate. Perhaps no important "ism" seems to us now, a mere half-century after the heyday of this imperialism, about 1900-1910, to be

343

quite so outdated. Indeed, we now use as a smear word the term "colonialism" rather than "imperialism."

The Economic Aspect

Carefully defined, another element, the economic, may be said to distinguish nineteenth-century imperialism from early forms of imperialism. No doubt the material, acquisitive, motive runs through all forms of territorial expansion from prehistoric times to the present. It is clear in the earliest days of Spanish and Portuguese expansion in the quest for gold, silver, and profits. But, as the nineteenth century wore on, imperialist nations were responding to economic pressures in a new form. Liberal, and especially Marxist, economists and sociologists no doubt exaggerated this new element, but there is a basis of truth in their arguments.

According to these economic critics of imperialism, capitalists and industrialists in the older countries began to discover in the nineteenth century that they were unable to market at home all they could produce. But, being capitalists, they could not bring themselves to solve their difficulties by paying proportionately *less* of the total product of society in interest, dividends, and other payments to their own kind of people, the upper classes, and paying *more* in wages, pensions, bonuses, and the like to their workmen. Instead of sharing the wealth and creating at home the mass purchasing power and the mass market they needed, they preferred to turn to the non-western world, to markets abroad, to the exploitation of dependent peoples. This attempt to bolster the capitalist system meant competition among the great western industrial powers for land and peoples to exploit. Lenin, in his *Imperialism as the Latest Stage of Capitalism* (1917), stressed the need to use the finance-capital that was rapidly accumulating, rather than the need

for markets. The great bankers, according to Lenin, drove the willing politicians into the search for dependencies, a search that marked what he termed the inevitable "last stage of capitalism."

No one who has studied this great nineteenth-century expansion questions that economic pressures were among the motivations of the men who carried it out. Furthermore, as we have already seen, leading industrial powers in both America and Europe were experiencing an increasing demand for higher tariffs by the late 1800's. In the United States and Germany, and even in free-trading Britain, industrialists wanted protection against foreign competitors. This was an era of neo-mercantilism, reviving and "streamlining" the older mercantilist doctrines of Colbert and others. Colonies as well as tariffs entered into the strategy of the neo-mercantilists, as they had done in the case of the old.

The Powers Involved

The year 1870 is a convenient dividing line between the more active age of imperialism that was to come and the less active age that had preceded. The period from 1815 to 1870 saw a partial decline in imperial fortunes, as most of Spain's American colonies gained their independence, and as Britain took the first steps leading to the virtual independence of Canada (see below, p. 367). In this same period, however, the French established themselves in Algeria, and the British extended their rule in India. The dividing line of 1870 does not mark a sharp break in the history of imperialism, but rather the acceleration of a movement that had never ceased.

The successful competitors in nineteenth-century imperialism, those who brought new lands under their flags, were Great Britain, which already in 1815 had a great empire, France, Germany, Italy, and the United States. Even little Belgium, itself a "new" nation in 1830, acquired a tremendous piece of tropical Africa, the Congo, 900,000 square miles in area in comparison to the homeland's 11,775 square miles. Russia did not expand overseas, and indeed parted with her vast but thinly inhabited possession in North America when the tsarist government sold Alaska to the United States in 1867. But she began the effective settlement of the great areas east of the Urals, and began to push into the borderlands of the Middle and Far East, toward Persia, India, and China.

In the process of expansion, the expanding nations inevitably rubbed up against one another in all sorts of competition, from the merely economic to actual shooting war. Almost every great international conflict of the nineteenth century, save for the mid-century duels between Prussia and Austria and between Prussia and France, had a direct concern in imperialist rivalries outside Europe. Imperial competition is a complicated story, then, woven into the whole fabric of international relations in the nineteenth century. We shall note briefly the major areas of inter-European rivalries and then summarize the growth of the major empires over the century.

The Areas Involved

The Monroe Doctrine (see Chapter XIX), toward which European nations were increasingly respectful as the strength of the United States increased, helped to keep both American continents free from further actual annexation by outside powers. So, too, did the British navy, for British policy was here to support the *status quo*. Toward the fateful year of 1914, the competition between Britain and Germany for markets and for fields of investment in South America grew intense, and was one of the many factors that brought these powers to war. Since no state was strong enough to take from Britain her older

colonies, throughout the nineteenth century British problems in both colonies of settlement and colonies of exploitation were limited to the British system itself. The Americas and the lands of the British Empire were then, on the whole, outside the scramble.

A major field of imperialist rivalry and penetration was the Near or Middle East, essentially the widespread lands under varying degrees of Turkish control, and Persia. In earlier chapters (XIX and XXII) we saw how the Balkans and the Straits became major issues in nineteenth-century diplomatic history. The whole "Eastern Question," as it is sometimes called, revolved around the problem of what was to be done with these old lands, which were peopled almost wholly by Moslems. They were backward lands by nineteenth-century western standards, mostly with poor rainfall and farm lands exhausted by centuries of primitive agriculture. They were poor also in natural resources (for their great wealth in petroleum was not really known or very important until the twentieth century). England, France, and Russia were in active competition over the Near East early in the nineteenth century, and they were later joined by Italy and Germany.

Africa was the scene of the most spectacular imperial rivalry. In 1815, except for the nominally Turkish lands of North Africa, the little Dutch settlement at the Cape of Good Hope (taken over by the British in 1815), and a string of Portuguese, Spanish, French, and British "factories" or trading posts along the old Portuguese exploration route that went back to the fifteenth century, Africa was untenanted by Europeans and, in the interior, almost unexplored. It was peopled by Negro races, long subjected to the horrors of the slave trade, and often living at the level of primitive tribesmen. The slave trade was pretty well abolished in many areas by mid-century, and exploration was pretty well under way. Then in the latter half of the century

Chinese painting of the arrival of one of the first English steamers and her passengers at Canton, about 1840.

French help, defeated an Italian army at Adowa and secured a respite in independence until the Italians tried again under Mussolini.

The Far East, too, was a major scene of imperialist rivalries. European powers strengthened their hold on older colonies and acquired new ones in Southeast Asia—the mainland areas of Burma, Indo-China, and Malaya, and the island groups between Australia and the mainland. But the ancient, thickly populated, highly civilized Chinese Empire was never subjected, as was Africa, to actual partition and direct annexation. China was, however, not well enough organized politically or industrially to stand up against European penetration, and was by the end of the century subjected to a rough, *de facto* partitioning among Britain, France, Germany, and Russia. Each power, operating from certain treaty ports as centers, was able to exercise a degree of control—basically economic—over considerable areas. Rivalry among these European powers, and the rising power of the United States, which was exercised in favor of the "Open Door" policy of permitting as much free trade in China as was possible and of preserving Chinese sovereignty, served to counterbalance Chinese weakness, and kept China throughout this period on the list of independent nations.

Finally, Japan kept herself isolated from the rest of the world for two centuries, from the mid-seventeenth to the mid-nineteenth. This compact island empire was closed to foreigners during the period when the European powers slowly strengthened their small holds in China. Then in 1853 the American naval officer, Perry, induced Japan to open her ports to outside trade. By adopting some western ways, particularly economic ways, Japan was able not merely to preserve her real independence during the late nineteenth century but actually to begin her own imperial expansion on the mainland of Asia after winning a brief war with China in 1894-1895 (see below, p. 363).

the great powers—Britain, France, and Germany—with Portugal, Italy, and Belgium tagging along, succeeded in blocking out in territorial units under their respective flags almost the whole of the continent. The only exceptions were the small Republic of Liberia, which had been set up by American anti-slavery groups as a land for emancipated American Negro slaves (though very few of them went there), and the mountainous and backward inland state of Abyssinia (now known as Ethiopia). And Abyssinia, coveted by Italy, had a very narrow escape. In 1896, the Abyssinians, under their Emperor Menelek and with

CHAPTER XXIV

II: The British Empire

We may now move on through the imperial record, country by country. Nineteenth-century Britain retained and, with the help of emigrants from the mother country, developed the great areas that were suitable to white colonization—Canada, Australia and New Zealand, and South Africa. This section focuses on Britain's imperial possessions in Africa and Asia. The development of self-government in Canada, Australia, and New Zealand will come more appropriately at the close of this chapter, in our survey of the results of nineteenth-century imperialism.

South Africa

In 1815, Britain had just acquired from the Netherlands Cape Colony at the southern tip of Africa. Cape Colony was inhabited by a few Dutch and French Huguenot colonists and was suited, in spite of a relatively low rainfall, to European living. As Britishers moved in, the older colonists, known in their own Dutch vernacular as Boers, grew more and more discontented. The adoption of English as the sole official language, the abolition of slavery throughout the Empire in 1834, the attempts of the government at London to protect the native blacks, and other measures of Victorian liberalism went against the grain of the patriarchal Boers, who were fundamentalist Christians for whom slavery was ordained of God and for whom liberalism was the work of the devil. Between 1835 and 1837, some ten thousand Boers moved north overland in the "Great Trek," a heroic folk migration that bulks even larger in contemporary nationalist South African feeling than do the comparable sagas of covered-wagon days in American tra-

dition. After some confused three-cornered fighting among Boers, British, and native Zulus, the Boers established two virtually independent South African states—the Transvaal and the Orange Free State. Well inland, on territory suitable for grazing but not for intensive agriculture, these thinly populated states lived on for a time hardly noticed by the outside world.

The British in South Africa noticed them, of course, and many of the British wished to add these lands to the Empire. They settled from the sea another British province to the east, along the Indian Ocean side, known as Natal. In the course of the century, Cape Colony and Natal, which together had a black population heavily outnumbering the British and remaining Boers combined, acquired the self-governing rights that British colonies of settlement in Canada, Australia, and New Zealand were also acquiring. British South African leaders for the most part wanted to bring the Boer Republics under the British flag. But as the London home government swung between Tory and Liberal domination, it also swung between a policy of imperialist expansion and the "Little Englander" policy of leaving the Trekkers alone. In 1852, by the Sand River Convention the British acknowledged the independence of Transvaal. But in 1877 they reversed themselves and annexed it as a step toward the federation of all South Africa under the British Crown. The Boers revolted in 1880 and the Liberal Gladstone, then in power, lived up to his principles by making at Pretoria in 1881 a treaty with the Boers which re-established Transvaal as independent, though under the "suzerainty" of Great Britain.

The British were already filtering up through the semi-desert country to the west

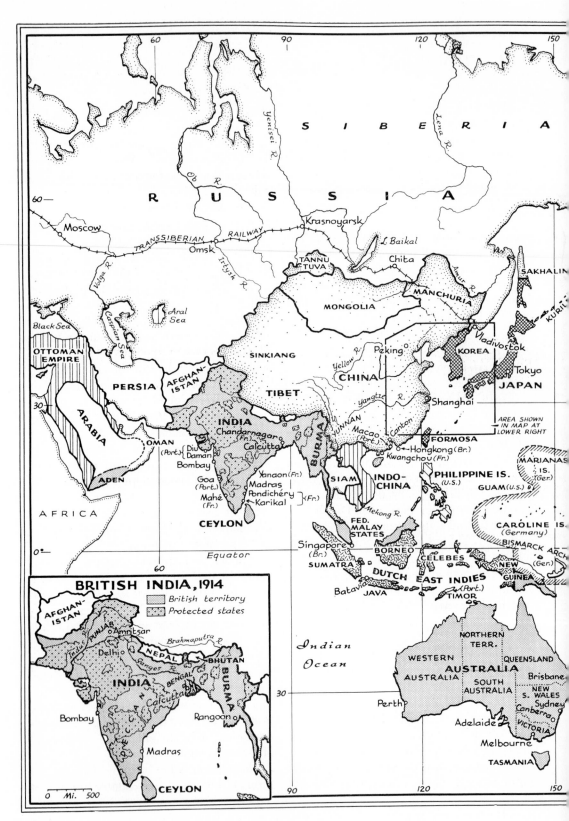

SIBERIA

RUSSIA

Moscow   Krasnoyarsk

TRANSSIBERIAN   RAILWAY
Omsk   L. Baikal
                    Chita   SAKHALIN

TANNU
TUVA   MANCHURIA
        MONGOLIA   KURIL

Aral
Sea   Vladivostok
Black Sea   KOREA
                SINKIANG   Peking   Tokyo
OTTOMAN   Yellow R.   JAPAN
EMPIRE   CHINA
        PERSIA   AFGHAN- TIBET   Shanghai
                 ISTAN   AREA SHOWN
ARABIA   IN MAP AT
        OMAN   INDIA   Chandarnagar(Fr.) LOWER RIGHT
        (Port.) Diu   Calcutta   FORMOSA
                 Daman   Macao(Port.)
                 Bombay   YUNNAN Canton Hongkong(Br.)
        ADEN   Goa   Yanaon(Fr.) BURMA   Kwangchou(Fr.)
                 (Port.) Madras SIAM INDO- PHILIPPINE IS. MARIANAS
AFRICA   Mahé   Pondichéry CHINA (U.S.)   IS.
                 (Fr.) Karikal (Fr.)   GUAM(U.S.) (Ger.)
                 CEYLON   FED.
                              MALAY   CAROLINE IS.
                              STATES   CELEBES (Germany)
        Equator Singapore BORNEO   BISMARCK ARCH.
                 (Br.)   NEW (Ger.)
                 SUMATRA   DUTCH EAST INDIES GUINEA
                 Batavia JAVA   (Port.)
                                    TIMOR

Indian
Ocean   NORTHERN
                                    TERR.
                              WESTERN   QUEENSLAND
                              AUSTRALIA AUSTRALIA
                                    SOUTH   Brisbane
                                    AUSTRALIA NEW
                                              S. WALES
                              Perth   Sydney
                                              Canberra
                                    Adelaide VICTORIA
                                    Melbourne
                                    TASMANIA

BRITISH INDIA, 1914

British territory
Protected states

AFGHAN-
ISTAN   PUNJAB Amritsar
        Delhi Brahmaputra R.
             NEPAL BHUTAN
        INDIA BENGAL BURMA
             Calcutta
Bombay   Rangoon

Madras

0 Mi. 500   CEYLON

348

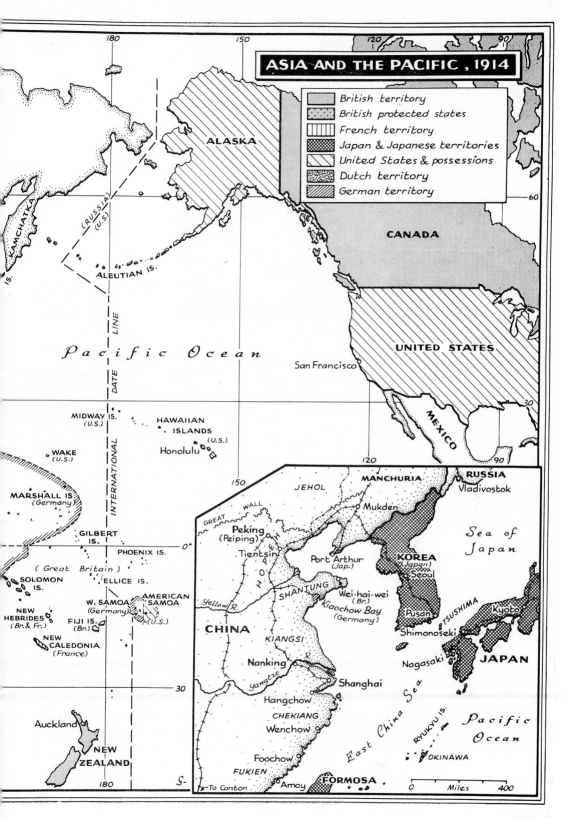

ASIA AND THE PACIFIC, 1914

	British territory
	British protected states
	French territory
	Japan & Japanese territories
	United States & possessions
	Dutch territory
	German territory

ALASKA
(RUSSIA) (U.S.)

KAMCHATKA

IS.

ALEUTIAN IS.

CANADA

Pacific Ocean

UNITED STATES

San Francisco

MEXICO

MIDWAY IS.
(U.S.)

HAWAIIAN
ISLANDS
(U.S.)

WAKE
(U.S.)

Honolulu

MARSHALL IS.
(Germany)

GILBERT
IS.

PHOENIX IS.

(Great Britain)

SOLOMON
IS.

ELLICE IS.

NEW
HEBRIDES
(Br. & Fr.)

W. SAMOA
(Germany)

AMERICAN
SAMOA
(U.S.)

FIJI IS.
(Br.)

NEW
CALEDONIA
(France)

INTERNATIONAL   DATE   LINE

Auckland

NEW
ZEALAND

G-

JEHOL

MANCHURIA

RUSSIA
Vladivostok

GREAT   WALL

Mukden

Peking
(Peiping)

Tientsin

Port Arthur
(Jap.)

KOREA
(Japan)
Seoul

Sea of
Japan

Wei-hai-wei
(Br.)

SHANTUNG

Kiaochow Bay
(Germany)

Pusan

TSUSHIMA

Kyoto

HOPEH

Yellow R.

CHINA

KIANGSI

Shimonoseki

Nanking

yangtze   R.

Shanghai

Nagasaki

JAPAN

Hangchow

CHEKIANG

Wenchow

East China Sea

Pacific
Ocean

RYUKYU IS.

OKINAWA

Foochow

FUKIEN

To Canton

Amoy

FORMOSA

0   Miles   400

349

Paul Kruger (1825-1904) seated in front of his Pretoria residence.

of the Boer Republics when the discovery of gold and the development of the diamond industry in these republics undid Gladstone's work. The Transvaal was no longer just a poor and isolated grazing country; it offered a great source of wealth that tempted quite a different kind of settler. The region about Johannesburg, the famous Rand, filled up with adventurers of a dozen nations, all looking to Britain to protect them from the conservative Boers, to whom they were undesirable *Uitlanders* (outlanders, foreigners).

The Boer War and After

The inevitable conflict came to a head with the Jameson Raid of December 29, 1895—midsummer in South Africa. The British in South Africa were now under the leadership of Cecil Rhodes, prime minister of Cape Colony, a determined and articulate imperialist who had made a quick fortune consolidating the chaotic diamond industry. The raid itself, under a follower of Rhodes, Dr. Jameson, was an invasion of Transvaal from British territory to the west, and was planned to coincide with a rising of Uitlanders in Johannesburg. But the rising did not take place, and the President of Transvaal, Kruger, had no trouble in defeating Jameson's handful of invaders. The famous "Kruger telegram," in which the German Kaiser congratulated the Boer President, was one of the critical steps in sharpening the Anglo-German rivalry that led to world war in 1914 (see Chapter XXV). Its immediate effect in South Africa was to harden Boer resistance and to lead in 1899 to the outbreak of war between Britain and the two Boer Republics.

The war, following the pattern of British wars in modern times, went badly at first for the British, who did not have enough troops immediately available to put down determined men who had been brought up in outdoor life and who were fighting on their own ground. Western opinion generally sided with the underdog Boers, and in Britain itself many Liberals and Laborites strongly opposed the war as rank imperialism. But in the long run the overwhelming strength of the British prevailed. By the middle of 1900 the British had won in the field, but they needed another eighteen months to subdue the desperate guerrilla bands into which Boer opposition dissolved. In 1902, by the Treaty of Vereeniging, the Boers accepted British rule, with the promise of ultimate self-government. This promise the British fulfilled speedily. In 1910 there came into being a Union of South Africa, uniting Cape Colony, Transvaal, Orange Free State, and Natal in a state in which the central government was stronger than the provinces. English and Afrikaans, as the South African Dutch dialect had come to be called, were set up as equally official languages.

On the eve of World War I, South Africa was among the self-governing British dominions. British and Boer seemed to be well on the way to composing their long quarrel, and to be ready to collaborate in setting up a new outpost of the West. But there were ominous signs even then. The Boers had by no means been Anglicized, and they were still fundamentally opposed to their partners in empire. And the two European elements together were in a minority of one to four as compared with the non-Europeans—the native blacks, the East Indians (who had come in numbers as immigrants, especially to Natal), and the "colored" peoples of mixed blood. The seeds of the current troubles in South Africa were clearly present even in the hopeful days immediately after the establishment of the Union.

Egypt

At the opposite end of Africa, Britain during the last half of the nineteenth century took over from the French the control of Egypt, nominally a vassal state of the crumbling Ottoman Empire. French influence there, already strong in the eighteenth century, was increased by Napoleon's expedition (see Chapter XVIII); indeed, a degree of French cultural influence persists among the Egyptian upper classes and intellectuals to this day. Under French supervision, a private company built between 1859 and 1869 the Suez Canal, which united the Mediterranean with the Red Sea and shortened the sea trip from Europe to India and the Far East by thousands of miles. The British had bitterly opposed the building of this canal under French patronage; but now that it was finished, the canal came to be considered an essential part of the "lifeline" of the British Empire.

Accordingly, the British took over Egypt and with it Suez. They carried out this action skillfully and slowly, threatening at crucial moments to use force, but not using it on any large scale. The decisive step in the process was the purchase by the British under Disraeli of 176,000 shares of stock in the Suez Canal Company. These shares had originally been assigned to the ruler of Egypt, the Khedive, as the price of his consent and co-operation in the canal project. The Khedive, a great and unwise spender, was heavily in debt to European financiers by 1875, and he sold his shares for a good price. The largest block of Suez stock was now in British hands.

Disraeli purchases the Suez Canal shares held by the Khedive of Egypt.

THE LION'S SHARE.

*German view of British
imperialism in Africa.*

By the eve of World War I, Britain exercised virtual sovereignty over Egypt. The Khedive and his government remained, and on paper Egypt was still a separate state. But a British Resident was always at hand to exercise firm control, especially over foreign relations. Under this British regime—the word "protectorate" is the usual term—much was done to modernize Egypt. The standard of living of the masses in Egypt was by no means raised to anything like that of the European masses. But the great dam at Aswan on the Nile, finished in 1902, was the first of a series of public works that added to the total productive power of the country, improved public health, lowered the mortality rate, and strengthened the numbers and prosperity of the middle class. Modernization also meant the beginnings of a wider literacy, of an educated middle class, and indeed of an intellectual class that earned its living by the written or spoken word. Most of these people responded by hating the British and by nursing a constantly growing nationalism—"Egypt for the Egyptians." We shall encounter this pattern again elsewhere.

The Rest
of British Africa

In between South Africa and Egypt the British pieced out their African possessions throughout the century. At its end, they had the lion's share of the continent. They had only 4,000,000 square miles out of over 11,000,000, but they controlled 61,000,000 people out of not much over 100,000,000. A mere listing of these holdings would be a dull and unenlightening catalogue. They can be found, usually colored red, in any good atlas of the turn of the century and on a famous British postage stamp of late Victorian times (see map, Chapter XXXI). A good sample of these colonies is Nigeria, in which the great administrator Sir Frederick (later Lord) Lugard worked out the characteristic British method of colonial government in tropical Africa that was known as "indirect rule."

The colony and protectorate of Nigeria, centering around the great river Niger, was formally put together from earlier West African colonies in 1914. Northern Nigeria was ruled by Moslem emirs of the Fulani race whose culture was superior to that of the subject and exploited Negroes; southern Nigeria was inhabited by numerous heathen tribes that had long been harassed by slave raids. The British had first to subject the Fulani by force, a process that was completed late in the nineteenth century.

They then applied, as a French statesman put it, "with method but not with system," what came to be called indirect rule. Emirs and chieftains were confirmed in their separate rules, subject to the banning of internal warfare, the abolition of slavery, and similar measures imposed from above. A British Resident supervised the rule of the leading chiefs, with district Residents (later Commissioners) to supplement the work in the local subdivisions. But native law, native religion, and native traditions, in so far as they did not conflict violently with western standards, were carefully maintained. The British staff was never large; Lugard complained that in 1903 he had only one British administrator on the average for every 400,000 natives. But somehow the handful of imperial officials were able to ensure the peace. Slowly, much too slowly for impatient idealists, railroads, roads, improved agriculture, commerce, and education—the externals at least of western civilization—began to appear in Nigeria. Early in this century the first African Negro students began to appear in British universities. By mid-century, there was already a western-educated class in West Africa, using English as their chief language.

Other British Spheres

In the Americas, Britain maintained her colonial dependencies in the Caribbean, in Bermuda and the Bahamas, and, on the mainland, in British Honduras and British Guiana. Limited self-government of the seventeenth-century kind, which some of them had lost in the mid-nineteenth century, was only gradually granted them in the twentieth. These were all tropical or semitropical lands, with a relatively small planter class and with large Negro or mixed lower classes. These lands suffered gradual impoverishment as a result of certain economic developments, notably the great competition offered to the staple cane sugar of the region by the growth in temperate climates of the beet-sugar industry, together with an increase in population beyond the limited resources of the region.

By 1914, the British West Indies had already become a "problem area."

In the Pacific and in Southeast Asia, Britain in the nineteenth century added some red dots on the map of her empire, and especially in Malaya she developed the great industries of rubber and tin that were to be major factors in her economy after World War I. She took an important part in the process of opening China to western trade by means of treaty-port concessions and spheres of influence. Indeed, Britain took one of the great steps in breaking down Chinese attempts to keep off the foreigner, for in 1841 she waged what has come to be called invidiously but not unjustly the "Opium War." This war was brought on by a Chinese attempt to control the opium trade in which British merchants had an important stake. By the Treaty of Nanking in 1842, Britain acquired Hong Kong and secured the opening of five ports, including Canton and Shanghai.

India:
Political Organization

In China, however, Britain was but one, though the most important, of the Great Powers scrambling for empire in that densely peopled land. In India her victory over France in 1763, confirmed by her victory in 1815, left her in sole control over a subcontinent of Asia, for the remnants of French and Portuguese possessions there hardly counted. India was the richest of Britain's overseas possessions, the center and symbol of empire, as the imaginative Disraeli realized when in 1876 he had Queen Victoria proclaimed Empress of India.

In 1763, India was already a great and well-peopled land, but not, in the western sense, a single *nation*. It was a vast congeries of races and religions, ranging from the most cultivated and philosophic Brahmins to the most primitive tribesmen, still in the Stone Age. As the nineteenth century began, the two main methods of British control had already become clear. The richest and most densely populated regions, centering on the cities of Calcutta, Madras, Bombay, and on the Punjab, were maintained under direct British control. The British government did not annex these lands directly; they were first administered as the property, so to speak, of the English East India Company, a chartered enterprise surviving from the great days of mercantilism in the seventeenth and eighteenth centuries. The company in its heyday, led by empire-makers like Clive and Warren Hastings, had taken on enormous territories, and made treaties like a sovereign power. Hastings was prosecuted for "high crimes and misdemeanors" in a famous trial of the late eighteenth century. But what he acquired the British kept.

In the nineteenth century the company was regarded by most economists and political thinkers as a shocking anomaly, and the India Office of the central government in London gradually took over the real control and administration of British India. The trading monopoly of the company had long since been undermined. In 1857, the company's native army of Sepoys rebelled. As usual in such major uprisings, the rebellion was brought on by a number of causes. But the basic cause was that the soldiers, Hindu, Moslem, and others, all had come to fear that British ways were being imposed on them to the destruction of their own ways. The Sepoy Rebellion was put down, but not before several massacres of Europeans had occurred, and not without a serious military effort by the British. The mutiny meant the end of the English East India Company. In 1858, the British Crown took over the company's lands and obligations, announcing that no further annexations were sought in India.

The rest of India—roughly a third of its area and a fourth or a fifth of its population —came to be known as the "feudal" or "native" states. These were left nominally under the rule of their own princes, who might be the fabulously rich Sultan of Hyderabad or Gaekwar of Baroda, or merely a kind of local chieftain. The "native" states were actually governed by a system of British Residents somewhat like the system we have just seen in Nigeria. The India Office never hesitated to interfere with the succession, or to disallow acts of princes, or even to assume direct rule for a time when it was thought necessary. The "native" states add many picturesque notes to a detailed history of India, but in the long run the distinction between direct and indirect rule in India did not mean very much in practice.

India: "The Meeting of East and West"

The years between 1763 and 1919 in India are a fascinating record of what Arnold Toynbee, the philosopher of history, calls "contacts between civilizations." Indeed, anyone who wants to understand the great contemporary problem of relations between the West and the rest of the world—to use clear terms, between white peoples and colored peoples—will do well to learn all he can of this great meeting of East and West in the subcontinent of India.

In material terms, many phases of the British rule in India are readily measurable. In 1864, the British *Statesman's Year Book* gave the population of India as about 136,-000,000, and in 1904 close to 300,000,000. Although the latter figure includes additional territories, in Burma and elsewhere, it is clear that nineteenth-century India saw a significant increase in total population. In 1901, nearly 15,000,000 males out of a total of 150,000,000 were literate in some language; one out of ten could read and write, a low rate of literacy by western standards, but already a high one by contemporary Asian standards. It is characteristic of Indian society that the comparable figures for women in the same census of 1901 show that only one out of one hundred and fifty could read and write.

Such statistics are plentiful, and what they show is an India on the eve of World War I with thousands of miles of railroads, telegraph lines, universities (teaching in English), hospitals, factories, and great and busy seaports. But, in proportion to the total population, India did not have these advantages to anything like the extent that even the poorest of European countries had them. Statistics show a native ruling class sometimes fantastically rich, and an immense peasant class for the most part living as their ancestors had lived, on the edge of starvation. A middle class was just beginning to form, and, like all the middle classes formed in non-European lands under European penetration, it had proportionately far more aspirants to genteel white-collar professional posts than to posts in commerce, engineering, and industry, to say nothing of scientific research.

The total wealth of India certainly increased under British rule in this century and a half, and in 1914 it was spread more widely among the Indian populations, save for the most primitive areas, than it had been in 1763. Proportionately less and less wealth went directly from an "exploited" India to an "exploiting" Britain. The familiar Englishman of the seventeenth and eighteenth centuries, the "nabob" who made a fortune in India and retired with it to comfort, and perhaps to a peerage, in England, almost ceased to exist as the nineteenth century wore on. Anglo-Indian economic relations took on more and more the form of trade between a developed industrial and financial society in Britain and a society geared to the production of raw materials in India. In this trade, native Indians took an increasing part if only as middlemen, and toward the end of the century native industries, notably textile manufac-

turing, financed for the most part with British capital, began to arise in India.

Throughout the century, of course, a large number of British—small in proportion to the total population, but numbering in the thousands—were basically supported by the Indian economy; they "lived off India." Some of them were private businessmen, but the greater number were military and civilian workers, the latter the celebrated Indian Civil Service who "ran" India. Yet natives were gradually working their way into positions of greater responsibility, into both private and public posts at the policy-making level.

Of the British ruling class in India one very important fact is now plain: it did not, like the English and Scots who went to Ireland in early modern times, really take root in India. Britain—one must be careful not to say "England," for the Scots played a conspicuous role in India as they did throughout the Empire—was always "Home," always the place where one hoped to end one's days. Though son not infrequently followed father in the Indian army or civil service, or even in business, these "Sahibs" as a whole never became fully adjusted to life in India. The spiritual climate was perhaps an even greater barrier than the physical climate. Here is a letter from an Englishwoman in Madras in 1837:

It is wonderful how little interested most of the English ladies seem by all the strange habits and ways of the natives. . . .

I asked one lady what she had seen of the country and the natives since she had been in India. 'Oh, nothing!' said she: 'thank goodness, I know nothing at all about them, nor I don't wish to: really I think the less one sees and knows of them the better!' [*]

The natives, too, often found the gap between East and West too great to be bridged. Another Englishwoman writes in 1913:

---

[*] Hilton Brown, ed., *The Sahibs* (London, 1948), 225.

Coming home we saw a native cooking his dinner on a little charcoal fire, and as I passed he threw the contents of the pot away. Surprised, I asked why. 'Because,' I was told, 'your shadow fell on it and defiled it!' *

Yet the work of raising the economic basis of Indian life was in large part the work of the British. They were often overbear-

---

* *Ibid.*, 230.

ing, insensitive, white men at their worst in their dealings with the natives. But they were, more often than the doctrinaire liberal will admit, men devoted to the task of bettering the lot of their charges, men who made a real effort to understand them. Some of them studied with western scholarly methods the past and present of Indian culture and society, thus laying the foundations on which Indian scholars now build.

III: The Other Empires

The French:
North Africa

The British victory in the "Second Hundred Years' War," capped by their defeat of Napoleon in 1815, had stripped France of all but insignificant remnants of her former empire. Yet during the nineteenth century France succeeded in building up a new colonial empire second in area only to that of the British. France, despite her frequent revolutionary changes in government, maintained an imperialist policy that added between 1824 and 1914 close to three and a half million square miles to the lands under the tricolor flag, and some fifty million people, almost all non-European. The figures for area are indeed somewhat misleading, for a million and a half square miles are included in the Sahara Desert, which is almost uninhabited.

Little of this second French colonial empire was suitable for settlement by Europeans. The great exception was French North Africa, including Tunisia, Algeria, and Morocco. As the provinces of Africa and Mauretania, these lands were once flourishing parts of the Roman Empire; after France took them over, they reached

a greater degree of material prosperity than they had enjoyed for nearly eighteen centuries. These lands, which have a typically Mediterranean climate, were inhabited chiefly by Berber and Arab peoples of Moslem faith. Though the total native population increased greatly under French rule, something over a million European colonists moved in. In majority French, but with sizable groups of Italians and Spaniards, these colonists took some land from the natives, though they added to the total arable acreage by initiating irrigation projects and other improvements. They remained, however, an alien group.

The French got a toe-hold in North Africa in 1824 through an expedition against the Algerian pirates, with whose Tripolitan counterparts, incidentally, the United States had fought in 1801. The French stayed on, increasing their control over Algeria and adding protectorates over Tunisia to the east in the 1880's and over Morocco to the west in the early twentieth century. Britain gave the French a free hand in Morocco as compensation for their exclusion from Egypt (see above, p. 382).

Especially in Algeria and Tunisia, the French promoted European settlement while trying what they thought was reasonably hard not to antagonize the natives. They called their policy one of "assimilation," in contrast with the British policy of hands off and indirect rule. They hoped, they explained, to assimilate Africans into French civilization, making them ultimately into good children of the eighteenth-century Enlightenment, good citizens of the Republic founded on the principles of 1789. They hoped to create an empire of "100,000,000 Frenchmen," more than half of them overseas, and to draw on abundant native manpower to fill up the ranks of the Republic's armies.

In the military sense, the policy of assimilation worked out somewhat as the French had hoped; in the main, however, assimilation was difficult and only partially successful. The French, always desirous of spreading their culture, did indeed assimilate part of the native ruling classes. Under the Third Republic they made Algeria politically a part of France itself, organizing it into three departments and giving them representatives to the Chamber of Deputies, with a franchise open to the relatively small group of Europeanized natives as well as to colonists. In Morocco, the French took a somewhat different tack. They sought, in part successfully, to open this backward land to French business and to the international tourist trade. Their urban center of Casablanca became a great modern city. And, without quite admitting the fact, they really abandoned assimilation for something close to the British policy of indirect rule. In 1912, the very able colonial administrator, Marshal Lyautey, began to organize turbulent Morocco, applying the "splash of oil" policy—that is, he pacified certain key centers by establishing firm working relations with the natives and then let pacification spread over the surface of Morocco like a splash of oil on water. The sultan and his feudal subordinates were maintained in Morocco, relatively free to carry on many of their age-old ways, but stripped of real power.

The French: Tropical Africa

In 1815, the British had left France her small posts in West Africa at the mouth of the Senegal River, together with the slight foothold France had obtained in the seventeenth century on the great island of Madagascar off the East African coast. By 1914, the French had been very successful in the partition of Africa, perhaps at bottom because the British pre-

French victory near Algiers, 1830.

ferred French to German aggrandizement, especially after 1870. By 1914, at any rate, France numbered in Africa alone nearly as many inhabitants as in her home territories (about 39,000,000).

Except in North Africa, these people were almost all Negroes of primitive material culture who were for the most part untouched by either Islam or Christianity. Except in certain coastal towns, where their administration and business were concentrated, the French had not by 1914 achieved very much toward assimilating or westernizing these vast districts. Most of their attempts to hasten the economic development of their African lands by organized joint-stock companies failed miserably.

It is quite possible that France spent more on these African colonies than she gained from them. Indeed, one of the stock arguments of nineteenth-century anti-imperialists was that colonies did not "pay" the mother country, and the French African colonies were one of their favorite exhibits. One economist—an Englishman, to be sure, and presumably unmoved by much that moves Frenchmen—concluded that in 1892 French gains from colonial trade were 16,000,000 francs, whereas net government expenditures for the colonies were 174,000,000 francs. For 1915, he made an even more discouraging estimate.[*] Such figures, however, seem not to have discouraged any of the great powers in their imperialist efforts. Obviously the simplest form of the economic interpretation of history, the notion that political entities are moved by simple bookkeeping concepts of governmental economic profit and loss, does not hold true for nineteenth-century imperialism.

Again, though French colonies in tropical Africa had by no means been modernized even in material conditions by 1914, every-where a beginning had been made. Everywhere the tricolor went, there also went the beginnings of medicine and hygiene, modern methods of communication, industry, and agriculture, and formal education for at least a few natives. In justifying the policy of assimilation, the French claimed for themselves, in contrast with the British, a lack of race prejudice, a willingness to accept the blacks as equals. This contrast is underlined by the English author whose figures we have just quoted:

Of course, it is true that the French also attempt to understand the native and in the main to give him freedom to produce as he pleases. The Frenchman actually tends much more to be a 'good fellow' with the natives than does the Briton, who is much more aloof. But this greater democracy does not seem to inspire a greater degree of confidence. Somehow, the Briton is more apt to succeed in instilling in the native confidence in the results of producing by the system that he recommends.[*]

Although there is some truth in the claim for greater French toleration, the deed is not quite up to the word. The French in Africa did not often marry Negroes; but intermarriage is in this real world an unreal test of racial equality. Negroes very rarely *commanded* white Frenchmen in military or civilian activity. Both at home and in Africa, on the other hand, once the Negroes seemed firmly under control, the French went a long way toward encouraging Negro art and folkways, in keeping with a policy very close to the ideal delineated by Lugard for Nigeria. The British, however, especially in the twentieth century, edged toward some kind of assimilation; African Negro undergraduates in British universities took on a lot more of Britishness than just their fine standard English accent. The contrast between British and French African policies was far from complete—there were many similarities.

---

[*] Constant Southworth, *The French Colonial Venture* (London, 1931), 122.

[*] *Ibid.*, 193.

CHAPTER XXIV

The French: Asia

In Asia, the French took over in the nineteenth century lands that came to be called French Indo-China. These lands included two rich rice-growing deltas (around Hanoi in the north and Saigon in the south), inhabited by peoples culturally and in part racially related to the Chinese. They also included Cambodia, culturally related to India, and the primitive mountain peoples of Laos. French experience here on the whole ran parallel to imperialist experience elsewhere in Southeast Asia, though the Anglo-Saxon fondness for nagging the French has tended to create the impression that the French did far worse in Indo-China than did the Dutch in Java or the British in Malaya. Slow but real material progress was made, though the basic problem of poverty among the masses remained unsolved. Native nationalist movements, nourished by educated natives with jobs of less dignity and authority than they believed should be theirs, rose in strength as the years went on. France also took part, from her base in Indo-China, in the struggle for control of China proper. The French sphere of influence was southern China, in particular the province of Yunnan adjoining Indo-China, and in 1898 the French got a lease on a port in Kwangchou Bay.

The Germans

We can be brief in listing the colonial acquisitions of the other powers. Germany and Italy came late to the imperial scramble, as they came late to national unity. Nevertheless, Germany was clearly a great power, and Italy aspired to be one; hence, both sought to acquire the token colonies, at least, that seemed necessary to that dignified status. This is the familiar policy of "keeping up with the Joneses." Germany in 1914 had three really large pieces of tropical and subtropical Africa—the Kameruns (Cameroons), German Southwest Africa, and German East Africa—and the smaller Togoland, close to a million square miles in all. These were not rich or well-developed areas, and their total contribution to the German economy was almost negligible. The German achievement on the whole was not greatly different from that of other European powers in Africa; it was neither morally nor economically much better or much worse. In the Pacific, the Germans picked up some small islands, and a large, primitive territory on the island of New Guinea. Germany took part in the attempted partition of China; her ninety-nine-year lease was on Kiaochow Bay.

The German drive for colonies was quite self-conscious; it was well organized in a pressure group with all the fixings of modern propaganda. Bismarck himself, who cared little for the prestige of colonies, was obliged to give way and consent to African ventures. His successors went further, and William II helped Germany to enter one of the most confused and dangerous fields of imperialist expansion, the Near East. On the eve of World War I, the German "Berlin to Baghdad" push was well under way, and the Germans had supplanted the British as patrons of the Turks.

The Italians and Belgians

Italy, condemned to the role of weakest of the great powers, got very little, even out of the partition of Africa. Tunis, which she coveted, went instead to France. Italy's major imperial effort centered on the African lands at the southern end of the Red Sea, but after her defeat by the Abyssinians under Menelek in 1896 she had to content herself with a few thousand square miles, most of it desert, in Eritrea and Somaliland. Italian efforts to add to this inadequate empire by taking Tripoli from its nominal Turkish suzerains succeeded, but these same efforts led to the Italo-Turkish war of 1911, which was in a sense the real beginning of World War I (see Chapter XXV). The Italians had so little to work with it is hard to assess their success or failure.

Little Belgium, largely through the enterprise of her King Leopold II (1865-1909), managed to acquire a large piece of equatorial Africa. This project began as the Congo Free State, with all sorts of noble ideals of co-operative European civilizing missions in Africa; but it ended up in 1908 as simply the Belgian Congo. Nineteenth-century scandal about forced labor and native exploitation in the Congo called Leopold's experiment to the attention of the world and provided liberal anti-imperialists with fresh arguments. But the Belgians, who had long since moderated Leopold's policies, retained until 1960 a legal hold on a restive Congo seeking independence (see Chapter XXXI).

The Americans

To the horror and indignation of many Americans, to the delight of others, the United States at the very end of the century joined the great powers and acquired overseas lands. In 1898, we waged a brief and successful war with Spain, for which the immediate cause was the still mysterious sinking of the American battleship *Maine* in the harbor of Havana, Cuba. The Spanish-American War left the United States in control of the remnants of the Spanish Empire in America (the Caribbean islands of Cuba and Puerto Rico) and the

President Theodore Roosevelt and Panama.

archipelago of the Philippines off the coast of Asia. Meantime, the United States also acquired Hawaii (1898) and part of the Samoan Islands in the Pacific (1899). Then in 1903 American support of a revolution in Panama, then a part of Colombia, assured the independence of a new republic and direct American control of the zone of the projected Panama Canal.

The Americans withdrew from Cuba, leaving her as an independent republic, though subject under the Platt Amendment of 1901 to what in foreign eyes always seemed American "protection." The Platt Amendment, named from its proposer, Senator Orville Platt of Connecticut, limited Cuban control of its foreign policy and its national debt, and gave the United States the formal right to intervene to preserve Cuban independence. It was resented bitterly by Cuban patriots as an infringement of Cuban sovereignty, and was given up by the United States in 1934. The rest of her acquisitions the United States kept for the time, though in the Philippines she had to put down an armed rising by Filipinos who wanted immediate independence. American anti-imperialists attempted to upset the somewhat anomalous arrangement under which their government kept lands without strict authorization from the American Constitution. But a Supreme Court decision in the so-called "Insular Cases" (1901) held that territory might be subject to American jurisdiction without being incorporated constitutionally in the United States of America. Under this decision, Americans began the process of training the Filipinos for eventual independence. Meanwhile, the United States, too, had an empire, which on the maps was duly colored as an American "possession."

The Japanese

One more empire was being formed during the decades before World War I,
the only empire to be created by a people of non-European stock—the Japanese. Even during their isolation (see Volume I, Chapter XIV), the Japanese had maintained an interest in western developments, particularly in technology, and had imported western books through the trading station that the Dutch were allowed to maintain at Nagasaki. More important, in 1853 the basic political and economic structure of Japan had long needed overhauling. An oligarchy of the feudal type ruled, but its ineffective government, its grasping tax-collection, and the economic misery resulting all made it widely unpopular. Discontent was growing, especially among two important social classes. One was the urban middle class of merchants and craftsmen. Although the industrial revolution had not yet reached Japan, the country already had populous cities, notably Tokyo (then called Yedo or Edo). The urban middle class, somewhat like the French bourgeoisie on the eve of 1789, wanted political rights to match their increasing economic power. The other discontented class may be compared roughly with the poorer gentry and lesser nobility of Europe under the Old Régime. These were the *samurai* or feudal retainers, a military caste now threatened with impoverishment and political eclipse. The *samurai* dreaded the growth of cities and the subsequent threat to the traditional domination of agriculture and the landlords; many of them also resented the fact that they were largely excluded from positions of power by the prevailing oligarchical regime. These social pressures, more than any outside western influence, forced the modernization of Japan.

Economically, the transformation proceeded rapidly. By 1914, much of Japan resembled an advanced western country. She, too, had railroads, fleets of merchant vessels, a large textile industry, big cities, and big business firms. The industrialization of Japan was the more remarkable in view of her meager supplies of many essential raw materials. But she had many important assets. As a glance at the map will show, her geographical position with respect to Asia is very like that of the British Isles with respect to Europe. Japan, too, found markets for her exports on the continent nearby and used the income to pay for imports. The ambitious Japanese middle class, supplemented by recruits from the *samurai*, furnished aggressive business leadership. A great reservoir of cheap labor existed in the peasantry, a large and submissive class. The peasants, who needed to find jobs away from the overcrowded farms, were inured to a very low standard of living, and were ready to work long and hard in factories for what seemed by western standards indecently low wages.

Politically, Japan appeared to undergo a major revolution in the late nineteenth century and to remodel her government along western lines. Actually, however, the change was by no means so great as it seemed. A revolution did indeed occur, beginning in 1868 when the old feudal oligarchy crumbled under the pressure of the discontented elements. Authority and prestige were restored to the position of emperor ("mikado"), a largely forgotten office whose incumbents had for years had no real power. In 1889, the emperor bestowed a constitution on his subjects, with a bicameral diet composed of a noble House of Peers and an elected House of Representatives.

The architects of these changes, however, were not democrats. They were aristocrats, ambitious young *samurai*, supported by allies from the business world and determined to make Japan over from above as they wished. The result was to substitute a new oligarchy for the old; a small group of aristocrats dominated the emperor and the state. The constitution of 1889, rather like that of the German Empire, provided only the outward appearances of liberal parliamentary government. The ministry was responsible not to the

Japanese portrait, about 1853, of the American Commodore Perry, who opened Japan to Western trade, thus ending Japan's two centuries of isolation.

diet but to the emperor, and hence to the dominant ruling class. The diet itself was scarcely representative; the right to vote for members of its lower house was limited to a narrow electorate, including the middle class but excluding the peasants and industrial workers. As Sir George Sansom, a British expert on Japan, has observed, she had no trouble in accepting western "things," but a great deal in handling western "ideas."

Japan began her expansion by taking from China, after a brief war in 1894-1895, the island of Formosa, which she annexed, and the piece of Asiatic mainland closest to Japan, the peninsula of Korea, whose independence China was forced to recognize as a preliminary to eventual Japanese annexation. But Russia, too, had designs on Korea; the results of this rivalry were the Russo-Japanese War of 1904-1905 and a second great Japanese victory (see Chapter XXII). Japan now secured unchallenged preponderance in Korea, which she annexed in 1910, special concessions in the Chinese province of Manchuria, and the cession by Russia of the southern half of the island of Sakhalin, to the north of the main Japanese islands. She had expanded in the classic European way.

By 1914, the Japanese overseas empire was undergoing rapid economic development by emigrants from the home islands. But the harsh treatment of the subject peoples by their new masters was preparing the way for later troubles in the Far East. So, too, were the grandiose projects for taking over China formulated by Japan's rulers, whose heads had been turned by their spectacular string of successes.

IV: The Debate Over Imperialism

In the nineteenth century all the western countries, even monarchical states like Germany, had a wide range of free public opinion, and some kind of parliamentary government by discussion. The kind of expansion we call imperialism, therefore, had to be defended articulately, since it was attacked articulately. The defense and attack are both important parts of the intellectual history of our times, for the debate, under greatly changed conditions, still goes on in mid-twentieth century.

Pro: The Argument from Social Darwinism

One central argument for the defense borrowed heavily from the Social Darwinists (see Chapter XXIII). Europeans both in Europe and in their "colonies of settlement," so ran the argument, were able to beat non-Europeans in war. By this very fact they had shown that they were in terms of evolution and progress more fit to survive than were the non-Europeans. Eternal competition is the price of survival and the best always survive—or *ought* to survive, for these theorists of imperialism had already begun to worry a bit. White men, this argument insisted, are simply better specimens of *homo sapiens* than are colored men; Anglo-Saxons (or Germans, or Slavs, or Latins, depending on the writer's origins) are simply better specimens than other white men.

An imperialist like Cecil Rhodes, to judge from much that he wrote and said, very likely dreamed of a world which in the fullness of time and evolution would be peopled entirely by Anglo-Saxons. Their breed would actually be improved over their ancestors of 1900, after the inferior peoples had died out—or had been killed off. But these were very distant views indeed. The prospect of ruddy Kentish farmers actually established in freeholds along the Congo was too unrealistic at the end of the nineteenth century. More fashionable imperialistic doctrine held that throughout the tropical world, the superior white men would put order and prosperity into the lives of colored men, would as trustees of civilization give up the comforts of Europe to rule in discomfort in the hot countries. Some imperialists thought that this benevolent rule of white men in the tropics would last indefinitely, since in their opinion non-whites were totally unable to undertake tasks of leadership and to assume moral responsibility.

Pro: The Argument of Duty

Other European imperialists, however, took the attitude that, though the non-whites could not run their own affairs then, they could ultimately learn to do so. For the present and for a good many years to come, whites would have to educate them on the spot; someday—the length of time judged necessary varied with the temperament of the judge—these non-whites would have matured sufficiently to take over responsibilities now confined to whites. These are not responsibilities of *ownership,* but rather responsibilities of *trusteeship.* Kipling put the case comfortably enough— for white men—in his famous poem:

> Take up the White Man's Burden—
>   Send forth the best ye breed—
> Go bind your sons to exile
>   To serve your captives' need;
> To wait in heavy harness,
>   On fluttered folk and wild—
> Your new-caught, sullen peoples,
>   Half-devil and half-child.*

---

* "The White Man's Burden," from "The Five Nations," *Rudyard Kipling's Verse, 1885-1932* (London, 1933), 320.

This argument of trusteeship was by all odds the most popular defense of imperialism, particularly among Anglo-Saxon peoples.

Yet the historian, aware of the complexities of human nature, will be wary of the notion that the ethical arguments of the imperialists were insincere. Many a European both in and out of the colonies of exploitation really believed in the trusteeship theory, and really did his best to live up to it. The Christian missionary is a major factor in the nineteenth-century expansion of the West. Indeed, Kenneth Latourette's long and thorough history of the expansion of Christianity has a final volume entitled *The Great Century* for the nineteenth century. More formal converts to Christianity were made all over the world in this century, so often labeled the century of materialism, than ever before.

How thorough the conversion of the colored peoples was is a difficult problem. In areas of primitive culture, whole tribes nominally accepted Christianity but continued many of the immemorial ways of their heathen past. In India, China, and Japan, old civilized countries with deep-rooted religious faiths of their own, Christianity did not win over anything like a majority of the people. Nevertheless, the missions did succeed in the course of the century in building up devoted native followers, of whom the most intelligent or most enterprising were often sent to Europe or the United States to complete their education.

Pro: The Defensive Argument

Finally, the imperialist philosophy of 1900 was by no means based on an unworried sense of white supremacy. Western civilization is one of the most worrying of all civilizations. Many publicists regarded imperialism as essentially defensive. The whites, outnumbered in a harsh world, had to organize themselves and hold the non-whites off. There was talk of the "yellow peril" and of white "race suicide." The writings and speeches of such apparently confident imperialists as Rhodes, Kipling, the German Emperor Wilhelm II, and Theodore Roosevelt sounded this curious note of fear and uncertainty. We are the best, but really we are a little too good for this world; we cannot breed fast enough.

One further aspect, or variation, of the defensive argument involved the importance of naval bases and coaling stations. Here the appetite tended to grow by eating: first, the French could argue that security of the homeland required control of North Africa, but presently the far-off holdings in Indo-China demanded a string of bases along which the navy could operate to protect the empire.

Con: Anti-Imperialist Arguments

Against imperialism, opponents marshaled a great many arguments. To the Social Darwinists the anti-imperialists replied by denying that the struggle for existence applied to human groups in the way it applied to plants and animals. It is precisely by sublimating the crude conflict of kill-or-be-killed into the higher rivalry for cultural excellence, they argued, that human societies transcend the struggle for life. Each group, each race, has something to contribute to the total of civilization, and the deliberate destruction or suppression of any group lames and lessens the others, prevents the true working out of evolution—that is, *cultural* evolution—among human beings as contrasted with mere animals. The anti-imperialists also brought forward very prominently the economic argument we have already noted (p. 344). They worked hard to show that in fact, es-

pecially in Africa, colonies did not "pay," that the imperialist appeal to self-interest in the homeland was a delusion, the dishonest work of propagandists for the privileged minority in the homeland and in the colonies who *did* profit personally from imperialist ventures.

From this point the anti-imperialists went on to maintain that support at home for colonial expansion rested therefore on the ordinary man's vicarious satisfactions from national achievements. The ordinary man liked to see his country figure in the world atlas as an imperial power. He liked to think of Britain's empire on which the sun never set; or, if he was a Frenchman, of the tangible evidence that France was still a great power, still carrying on her *mission civilisatrice;* or, if he was an Italian, that at last Italy too was a nation, and behaving as nations should. The anti-imperialists were on the whole not very successful in their attempts to use ridicule and irony against behavior that they found irrational. But their conviction that human action ought to be rational and devoted to the greatest good of the greatest number placed them firmly in the liberal tradition.

So strong was the anti-imperialists' belief that they were right—in spite of the growth of empires all about them—that in Britain the school of "Little Englanders," much influenced by laissez-faire economics, came to the comforting assurance that imperialism was impossible. The colonies, they held, must inevitably drop away from the mother country—to use their favorite stereotype—like ripe fruit from a tree. Why not then avoid getting into the futile process further by *not* taking any more of Africa or China? Why not hasten the inevitable by giving up the empire?

Not all the anti-imperialists were liberals or idealists. Indeed in France some of the most vehement were the extreme nationalists who wanted *revanche* (revenge) on Prussia for the French defeat in the war of 1870. These *revanchards* were not sorry for the Negroes; they opposed French colonialism because it distracted French energies from what they thought was the sole proper national business—getting ready to beat the Germans.

What sank into the mind and feelings of the ordinary westerner as a result of the anti-imperialist arguments was an uneasy awareness that somehow the practice of imperial expansion did not square with the best avowed intentions of democracy. Particularly in the United States, the feeling grew that imperialism and colonialism were contrary to the ideas of liberty and equality, even if the imperialists honestly claimed to be following the "trusteeship" principle. America took over an empire in 1898, but not without vigorous protests from numerous groups of anti-imperialists, and not without specific promises from the government that it would "free" dependents the moment they were capable of self-rule. This opposition of Americans to colonialism, especially when practiced by themselves, is one of the important factors in the world situation of the mid-twentieth century, and we shall return to it in later chapters.

V: The Colonies of White Settlement

Thus far our account of the nineteenth-century expansion of Europe has been limited largely to the "colonies of exploitation," the protectorates, and the spheres of influence held by Europeans. No such account is at all complete, for the most striking thing about this expansion was that it involved an actual transplantation of Europeans to "colonies of settlement" on a scale incomparably greater than in the previous three centuries since Henry the Navigator and Columbus.

The colonies of settlement were originally very thinly inhabited lands. Australia, indeed, was almost empty; and the whole native Red Indian population of America north of the Rio Grande was almost certainly in 1800 not over a million. The European settlers simply overwhelmed these primitive peoples. In Tasmania, a large island to the south of the Australian mainland, the natives were totally wiped out, and in Australia itself they were very nearly wiped out. In the United States the Red Indians were so far eliminated that many an American grew up in the later nineteenth century without ever seeing a redman except in a Wild West show.

In most of Latin America, however, the native Indian stock, far from being wiped out, persisted; the upper class, politically and economically, was drawn from European "creole" stock; and a great many people of mixed European and Indian and Negro blood filled the lower social ranks. In the far south of the continent, in the Argentine, Uruguay, and Chile, conditions resembled more nearly those in the United States, and these twentieth-century nations are now almost wholly European in stock largely from the Iberian peninsula and Italy.

The expansion of Europe into the Americas was also an expansion of Africa. By 1850 the leading European powers had pretty generally got the slave trade under control; but the nucleus of Negroes brought into both North and South America by the trade in the earlier centuries continued to grow. Despite handicaps of race barriers, strongest in the United States, the Negroes multiplied; by 1900, for example, there were some 9,000,000 of them in the United States.

Canada: Background of Revolt

Apart from the extraordinary growth of the United States, the most important phase of the nineteenth-century movement of Europeans overseas is the growth of what is now called the British Commonwealth of Nations, or, more correctly, simply the Commonwealth. Doubtless it is an oversimplification to claim that the British learned their lesson from the American Revolution, and that consequently in Canada, Australia, and South Africa they were wise enough to abandon the policies of George III and Lord North. But the formula is fundamentally sound. The first laboratory for this experiment in a new kind of "colonialism" was Canada (see map on p. 255).

The rebellious thirteen colonies of North America had wanted to add a fourteenth, and had tried hard to win Canada. But a complex of causes all contributed to leaving Canada in British hands at the peace in 1783. The French Canadians in Quebec distrusted the new Protestant power growing up to the south; the American rebels had grave difficulties keeping up an army to cope with the British in the United States itself; America's French ally did not wish the new country to be too strong. Later, as we have seen in Chapter XXII, the United States failed in the War of 1812 to reverse the verdict of 1783.

Upper Canada (Ontario), which was mainly British in stock, and Lower Canada (Quebec), which was mainly French, and the Maritime Provinces of Nova Scotia, New Brunswick, and Prince Edward Island were at first quite separate British "colonies," as the American thirteen had once been. Each had an apparatus quite like the old American one—a royal governor appointed by the Crown, a council appointed by the governor, and an elected assembly based on a more or less popular franchise. But just as in the thirteen colonies during the preceding century, the arrangement bred conflicts between the assemblies and the royal government. In 1837, revolts broke out in both Upper and Lower Canada, with popular leaders like Mackenzie and Papineau arrayed against the governor and his followers, and with essentially the same kind of constitutional and financial grievances that the thirteen colonies had had sixty years before.

Canada: Durham and A New Status

The revolt of 1837 was a military fiasco, and it is probable that public opinion in both provinces was against the rebels; there was a fear that too close an imitation of the American Revolution would lead to absorption by the United States. But the British government was alarmed, and sent out as governor-in-chief of all the British North American provinces the Earl of Durham, a young lord of Whig antecedents and Utilitarian leanings. Durham, feeling that he was not properly supported from London, resigned after less than a year in Canada. But the famous report he made to the British Parliament on his return in 1839 became the cornerstone of the new British imperial structure of dominions, a constitutional document that Durham's admirers have sometimes ranked with Magna Carta.

The Durham Report proposed the union of Upper and Lower Canada and the establishment of responsible government—that is, a popularly elected legislature with ultimate authority—for both the union and each of the separate provinces. The report is still of great interest. Durham had all the average Englishman's insensitivity to things French, and it is an understatement to say that he never understood the Québecois of Lower Canada. But he was true to his principles—even these French Canadian Catholics must have their own responsible government. As he wrote:

The maintenance of an absolute form of government on any part of the North American Continent can never continue for any long time, without exciting a general feeling in the United States against a power of which the existence is secured by means so odious to the people; and as I rate the preservation of the present general sympathy of the United States with the policy of our Government in Lower Canada as a matter of the greatest importance, I should be sorry that the feeling should be changed for one which, if prevalent among the people, must extend over the surrounding Provinces. The influence of such an opinion would not only act very strongly on the entire French population, and keep up among them a sense of injury and a determination of resistance to the Government, but would lead to just as great discontent among the English. . . . Nor would their jealousy be obviated by the selection of a Council from the persons supposed to have their confidence. It is not easy to know who really possess that confidence; and I suspect that there would be no surer way of depriving a man of influence over them than by treating him as their representative without their consent. . . .*

The actual realization of Durham's recommendations was achieved with due British slowness. The first step, the Union Act of 1840 passed by the British Parliament, though it did unite Upper and Lower Canada, was at the very least unspecific on the critical point of responsibility—that is, on whether an administration defeated in the legislature had to resign or not. Nearly a decade later, under the governorship of Lord Elgin, the principle was quietly established in practice, never to be withdrawn. Nor was the next step unduly hurried. The British North America Act of 1867 achieved in principle the union of all the British provinces in North America, except Newfoundland, oldest of all, whose separatist tendencies were so strong that it did not join Canada until 1949. The act of 1867, itself basically due to formal Canadian initiative at a meeting of the "Fathers of Confederation" at Charlottetown, set up the Dominion

---

* Sir Reginald Coupland, *The Durham Report* (Oxford, 1954), 155-156.

of Canada by the union of Ontario, Quebec, and the Maritime Provinces, with provision for the admission of territories in the west as provinces on something like the pattern for admission of the western states in the United States. There were still many survivals of the former "colonial" status of Canada, from the bestowal of titles, especially knighthood with its unrepublican and undemocratic "Sir," to the possibility of judicial appeal from Canadian courts to the Privy Council in Westminster. Above all, the relation of Canada to Britain in terms of international affairs, armed forces, right of secession, and much else was not yet spelled out, and was not to be spelled out formally until the Statute of Westminster in 1931 (see Chapter XXVIII).

The Extension of Dominion Status

The individual provinces of Australia had common British origins and had relatively short lives as separate territorial units —the oldest, New South Wales, dates only from 1788. But, in spite of these facts, these provinces developed their local differences and separateness, symbolized by the fact that they used differing gauges for their railroads. They gained the essentials of self-government in the Australian Colonies Government Act of 1850, but federal union of New South Wales, Victoria, Queensland, and the others was not achieved until the Commonwealth of Australia was formed in 1901. The influence of the American example is clear in the constitution of the Commonwealth, which provides for a senate with equal membership for each of the six states, a house of representatives apportioned on the basis of population, and a supreme court with something close to the American power of judicial review. But in Australia as in the other British dominions, the parliamentary system of an executive (prime minister and cabinet) dismissible

by vote of the legislative body was retained; the American "presidential" system was deliberately rejected.

Australia, like Canada, was essentially an empty country in 1800, and like Canada it filled gradually with immigrants, mostly from Britain. Perhaps the head start of the United States, with its great attraction for British and European immigration, slowed down the growth of these British dominions. But the process, though slow, was steady, and by 1914 all the dominions, including the quiet islands of New Zealand, traditionally most "English" of them all, were prosperous, democratic societies just settling down from the last of the pioneer stage. Their narrative history is most interesting, but we cannot go into it here, nor into the fascinating and illuminating subject—insufficiently pursued—of the likenesses and unlikenesses of the corporate personalities of these new countries and the United States, all offsprings of the "frontier."

The Commonwealth in Review

In the nineteenth century, Americans pushing west and Russians pushing east added millions of square miles to their respective lands as colonies of settlement. Although in both, and especially in America, this process of the "frontier" had important effects on their national character, it did not create great immediate problems concerning the "independence" of the settlers. The British, however, went thousands of miles overseas for their colonies of settlement. They found very soon that these colonies could not be treated as the long tradition since Columbus prescribed—that is, as mere outposts of the mother land with no political self-rule, held in strict mercantilist economic leading strings. Nor could they be, if only because of the separating seas, simply added as they filled up as a territorial continuation of the mother land, as

Australia grows up. Lord John Russell, a British statesman, measures the growth.

Siberia was added to Russia and the territories of the American West to the federal Union. By 1914, the British at home and the citizens of their overseas colonies of settlement had worked out something new in political configurations, unprecedented in man's brief history.

Canada, Australia, New Zealand, and South Africa were indeed by 1914 wholly self-governing. They could and did even levy customs dues on imports from Britain. They had the beginnings of military forces of their own, and of course complete control of that clear attribute of "sovereignty" —their own internal police. Men were even

beginning to speculate about whether they were not in possession of that other clear attribute of sovereignty—the right to conduct foreign relations, both diplomatic and military. For example, could Canada be at peace with a country with which Great Britain was at war?

The test came in 1914. All the dominions went to war against Germany and her allies. Even the dubiously loyal Union of South Africa went to war against the sender of the Kruger telegram; we are bound to record that the always land-hungry Boers had their eyes on the German colonies in Africa, and especially on the big empty colony of German Southwest Africa, right adjacent to the Union. The government of each dominion, however, went through the formal process of declaring war, just as "sovereign" countries do. Yet the relation between Canada, for instance, and Great Britain was something different from the relation between two such sovereign countries as the Argentine and Spain. The dominions had not quite set up wholly for themselves, or, to revert to the favorite cliché of the nineteenth-century Little Englander, they had not dropped off like ripe fruit. The nature of the tie between the dominions and Britain was not clear then, and it must be admitted it is not fully clear now. But it exists, and to it also we shall return in a chapter on imperialism in our own day. (See Chapter XXXI.)

VI: The Results of Imperialism

The broad general results of this long phase of European expansion down to 1914 may now be summarized.

First and most obviously, in the nineteenth century almost the whole planet was affected by the process. The white man was almost everywhere by 1914, and white explorers not infrequently found that the tin can, that ubiquitous symbol of the West, had got there ahead of them.

Second, the expansion of Europe was accompanied by a numerical expansion of the whole human race. Between 1800 and 1900 the population of the world just about doubled, from some 800,000,000 in 1800 to some 1,600,000,000 in 1900. European white stock did indeed account for the most spectacular part of the rise, but non-whites in Asia and elsewhere also increased. We do not sufficiently understand human population growth to say flatly that the expansion of Europe *caused* the growth of population among non-European peoples in the nineteenth century. But it did bring to many areas of the world some increase of law and order, some increase in material production and improvements in transportation and distribution, health and sanitation—factors that probably contribute to population growth. And, with such exceptions as the native Australian "Blackfellows" and some North American Indians, European expansion did not usually mean the physical extermination of non-European peoples.

Third, we may say with no reservations whatever that by 1914 it was quite clear that "natives" were beginning to reject the claims of white supremacy. Among the more civilized and long-established peoples in the Near East and Asia the educated classes were already developing a sense of nationalism. They took over from the West that particular form of group consciousness that is attached to a territorial political unit and that is shared, in principle at least, by all who live within the unit. This nationalism was a new thing outside Europe, and a very important one for us today, for

it has gone on increasing and developing. In the early twentieth century, it was most evident in Japan and, to some extent, China, and in advanced "colonial" nations like Egypt and India, though there were signs of it almost everywhere.

This new phenomenon was not the same thing as simple hostility to whites, or to particular nations among the whites. It was an organized political faith—in short, modern "patriotism." Naturally, Egyptian, Indian, and Chinese patriots were first of all concerned with getting rid of their European imperial masters; their attitudes were those of oppressed nationalistic groups everywhere, even in Europe itself. After all, the most striking and most successful rebellion of early 20th-century nationalist movements against an imperial "master" was that of very European and very white Ireland against the British. These "colonial" peoples were touchy, addicted to nursing grievances imaginary as well as real, eager to seize on any national trait that could be glorified, admiring, hating, and envying their masters. Above all, they were organized on a new principle taken from the West, a principle that is ultimately perhaps more destructive of their own traditional cultures than anything else that has come to them from the West. This is the equalitarian and leveling, if not democratic, spirit inherent in the secular religion of nationalism. In theory at least nationality transcends the dividing lines of profession, social class, and even caste. The fellah, the Egyptian peasant whose ancestry reaches back through the centuries, could claim to be as good an Egyptian as the aristocratic pasha—indeed a better one, since he was uncorrupted by European culture. People began to talk and write of "Arab" nationalism; yet the "Arabs" were not exactly a race, nor a people nor any specific political-territorial entity—at most, "Arab" referred to a language, a culture, and to a part of those who held the Moslem faith.

Fourth, and in spite of the gloomy economic conclusions of anti-imperialists, there seems no doubt that over the century the homelands of Europe gained in total wealth from their expansion overseas. Indeed, raw materials from overseas were necessary to maintain the standard of living in thickly populated countries like Britain, Germany, Belgium, and the Netherlands. Theoretically, these raw materials could have come into European lands in free trade with free countries overseas; actually they came in part from imperial expansion. In purely empirical terms, the imperialism of the nineteenth century does seem to confirm Professor Webb's analysis (see Volume I, Chapter XIV): The expansion of Europe was a great demographic and economic bonanza, a dynamic material growth never before attained by man.

Finally, imperialist rivalries, especially after 1870, exacerbated the normal rivalries among the European great powers, and were thus a major factor in the complex of causes that brought on general war in 1914. This is particularly true of the Anglo-German rivalry, which, unlike that of France and Germany or of Austria and Russia, had no long historical background. This Anglo-German rivalry was everywhere by 1900—among commercial travelers of both nations, trying to sell machinery in Peru; among missionaries trying to convert the heathen in Africa; among army officers, naval officers, editors, organizers, all seeking to make German influence more important than British somewhere or to keep British influence more important than German. The rivalry extended even to the academic world and to that world in the United States. There were those who regarded the Rhodes Scholarships for study at Oxford (1904) as a British attempt to counterbalance the great prestige that the German universities, and especially their degree of Ph.D., had acquired in America during the latter nineteenth century.

Reading Suggestions
on Nineteenth-Century Imperialism

(Asterisk indicates paperbound edition.)

GENERAL ACCOUNTS

W. L. Langer, *The Diplomacy of Imperialism, 1890-1902*, 2nd ed. (Knopf, 1951). A classic detailed study of a particularly hectic period of the imperial scramble; also includes a valuable discussion of the forces making for imperialism.

J. A. Hobson, *Imperialism, A Study* (Nisbet, 1902). Perhaps the most famous attack on imperialism.

V. I. Lenin, *Imperialism, The Highest Stage of Capitalism* (International Publishers, 1939). The classic expression of the communist interpretation of imperialism.

B. Kidd, *The Control of the Tropics* (Macmillan, 1898). A good example of the serious defenses of imperialism offered at the end of the nineteenth century.

J. A. Schumpeter, *Imperialism and Social Classes* (Noonday, 1955; *Meridian). A valuable essay on imperialism from the standpoint of the economist and sociologist.

E. M. Winslow, *The Pattern of Imperialism* (Columbia Univ. Press, 1948). A study of the forces, especially political, making for modern imperial expansion.

K. S. Latourette, *A History of the Expansion of Christianity*, 7 vols. (Harper, 1937-1945). Volumes 5 and 6 of this major work concern the expansion of Christianity into the non-European world, 1800-1914.

SPECIAL STUDIES: AFRICA

L. Woolf, *Empire and Commerce in Africa* (Allen & Unwin, 1919). A detailed and highly critical account from a left-wing point of view.

H. H. Johnston, *The Opening Up of Africa* (Holt, 1911. Home University Library). Sympathetic popular account by the author of many other works on Africa.

H. L. Hoskins, *European Imperialism in Africa* (Holt, 1930. A Berkshire Study). Handy introductory manual.

R. L. Buell, *The Native Problem in Africa* (Macmillan, 1928); and H. A. Wieschoff, *Colonial Policies in Africa* (Univ. of Pennsylvania Press, 1944). Two solid and helpful studies.

C. W. de Kiewiet, *A History of South Africa, Social and Economic* (Clarendon, 1941), and E. A. Walker, *A History of South Africa*, 2nd ed. (Longmans, Green, 1940). Two good studies of the area.

B. Williams, *Cecil Rhodes* (Constable, 1921). Probably the best book on the famous empire-builder. But for a different estimate, see G. S. Millin, *Cecil Rhodes* (Harper, 1933).

B. Williams, *Botha, Smuts, and South Africa* (Macmillan, 1948. Teach Yourself History series). Introduction to the period following the Boer War.

F. D. Lugard, *The Dual Mandate in British Tropical Africa*, 3rd ed. (Blackwood, 1926). Significant detailed account of British colonial policy in action.

H. R. Rudin, *Germans in the Cameroons, 1884-1914: A Case Study in Imperialism* (Yale Univ. Press, 1938). Good study of the topic indicated.

L. de Lichtervelde, *Léopold of the Belgians* (Century, 1929), and L. Bauer, *Leopold the Unloved, King of the Belgians and of Wealth* (Little, Brown, 1935). Vindicating and attacking, respectively, the great exploiter of the Congo.

SPECIAL STUDIES: ASIA

J. T. Pratt, *The Expansion of Europe into the Far East* (Sylvan Press, 1947). Excellent introduction to the subject.

D. E. Owen, *Imperialism and Nationalism in the Far East* (Holt, 1929. A Berkshire Study). Handy brief introductory manual.

K. S. Latourette, *The Development of China*, new ed. (Houghton Mifflin, 1956). A good survey.

A. C. Lyall, *The Rise and Expansion of British Dominion in India*, 5th ed. (Murray, 1914). Sympathetic account.

R. Coupland, *Britain and India, 1600-1941* (Longmans, Green, 1941). Very brief introduction by an authority on imperial questions.

G. Sansom, *The Western World and Japan, A Study in the Interaction of European and Asiatic Cultures* (Knopf, 1950), and *Japan, A Short Cultural History*, rev. ed. (Appleton-Century, 1943). Two indispensable works by a great authority on Japan.

S. N. Fisher, *The Middle East: A History* (Knopf, 1959). A solid detailed account, emphasizing the nineteenth and twentieth centuries.

K. S. Latourette, *A History of Modern China* (*Penguin Books).

E. O. Reischauer, *Japan, Past and Present* (Knopf, 1946). Helpful and reliable brief introduction.

B. H. Sumner, *Tsardom and Imperialism in the Far East and Middle East, 1880-1914* (British Academy, 1944). Good short account.

Cambridge History of India, Vols. V and VI (Cambridge Univ. Press, 1929). A new edition of these standard detailed volumes is in preparation.

V. H. Smith, *The Oxford History of India*, 3rd ed. (Oxford Univ. Press, 1958). This fully rewritten book, edited by Percival Spear, is an excellent brief but detailed account of the whole history of India, with a new Part III on British India by Dr. Spear.

H. Brown, ed., *The Sahibs: The Life and Ways of the British in India as Recorded by Themselves* (Hodge, 1948). An illuminating compilation.

SPECIAL STUDIES: THE BRITISH EMPIRE AND DOMINIONS

J. H. Rose and others, eds., *The Cambridge History of the British Empire*, 7 vols. (Macmillan, 1929-1940). This solid work, more useful for facts than for interpretation, has separate volumes on such major areas as India, Canada, and Australia and New Zealand.

P. Knaplund, *The British Empire, 1815-1939* (Harper, 1941). An authoritative and scholarly survey by an American specialist.

C. E. Carrington, *The British Overseas: Exploits of a Nation of Shopkeepers* (Cambridge Univ. Press, 1950). An advanced and detailed study from a British point of view.

C. P. de T. Glazebrook, *Canada: A Short History* (Oxford Univ. Press, 1950). A good brief survey.

R. Coupland, ed., *The Durham Report* (Clarendon, 1946). The famous document that in a sense marks the beginning of the development of the British Commonwealth.

G. Greenwood, ed., *Australia: A Social and Political History* (Praeger, 1955). Good collaborative work, with bibliographies.

H. Belshaw, ed., *New Zealand* (Univ. of California Press, 1947). An informative volume in this publisher's United Nations Series, with good historical and geographical essays.

J. B. Condliffe, *New Zealand in the Making*, and *The Welfare State in New Zealand* (both Macmillan, 1959). These books provide a good economic history of 1792-1957.

SPECIAL STUDIES: OTHER SUBJECTS

S. H. Roberts, *History of French Colonial Policy, 1870-1925*, 2 vols. (King, 1929). Detailed and substantial study.

D. W. Brogan, *France under the Republic* (Harper, 1939). Contains a brief and illuminating treatment of French imperialism.

M. E. Townsend, *The Rise and Fall of Germany's Colonial Empire, 1884-1918* (Macmillan, 1930). A useful account.

J. W. Pratt, *America's Colonial Experiment* (Prentice-Hall, 1950). A valuable survey of the American empire.

D. Perkins, *Hands Off: A History of the Monroe Doctrine* (Little, Brown, 1941). A useful popular account by a leading specialist.

HISTORICAL FICTION

R. Kipling, *Kim* (many editions) and *Soldiers Three* (many editions). Famous works by the even more famous champion of imperialism.

N. Coward, *Cavalcade*, in *Play Parade* (Garden City Publishing, 1933). A patriotic play and a sentimental tribute to old imperial glories.

S. Cloete, *The Turning Wheels* (Houghton Mifflin, 1937). A novel about nineteenth-century Boers.

O. Schreiner, *The Story of a South African Farm* (Benn, 1930). An older novel about South Africa.

A. Gide, *The Immoralist* (*Vintage). A novel in which the European hero is thoroughly corrupted by North Africa.

E. M. Forster, *A Passage to India* (many editions). A celebrated and astringent novel about the British in India.

L. Hémon, *Maria Chapdelaine* (Macmillan, 1940; *Image). The best-known novel about rural French Canada.

Hugh McLennan, *The Precipice* (Duell, Sloan & Pearce, 1948). One of the few good psychological studies of relations between English-speaking and French-speaking Canadians.

H. H. Richardson, *The Fortunes of Richard Mahony* (Readers Club, 1941). A series of novels about modern Australia by an Australian.

H. Rider Haggard, *King Solomon's Mines* (Longmans, Green, 1926). A splendid example of the rousing novel of imperialist adventure.

The First World War

CHAPTER XXV

I: Introduction

ON June 28, 1914, the Habsburg Archduke Francis Ferdinand, heir to the throne of Austria-Hungary, and his wife were assassinated in the streets of Sarajevo, capital of the recently (1908) annexed provinces of Bosnia and Herzegovina, which had been occupied by Austria-Hungary since 1878 (see Chapter XXII). The assassin, Princip, was a Serbian nationalist. Bosnia had long been coveted by the Serbs, and, as we have already seen, many of its Serb and Croat inhabitants longed for a more effective expression of their nationalist aspirations than they had achieved under Habsburg rule. The Austro-Hungarian government, alarmed by the ambitions of Serbian nationalists, took the occasion of the assassination to send a severe ultimatum to Serbia. The Serbian government's refusal to accept the ultimatum in its entirety led to an Austrian declaration of war on Serbia, on July 28. Within the week, the great states of Europe were engaged in a general war—the Central Powers (Austria-Hungary and Germany) against the Allies (Serbia, Russia, France, and Britain). Princip's revolver was eventually to kill some ten million men.

This was the first general war, the first war to involve most of the members of the world state-system, since the wars of the French Revolution and Napoleon a century

Opposite. IMPROVISATION NUMBER 30, *by Wassily Kandinsky (1866-1944); Russian, painted 1913; the Art Institute of Chicago. Kandinsky called this his "cannon picture," executed, appropriately enough, on the eve of World War I. Both the painting and its official title are representative of early twentieth-century abstractionists and their efforts to achieve expression through nonrepresentational means.*

earlier. There had indeed been wars enough, foreign and civil, in the century between. They were, however, save for relatively minor wars like the Crimean War of 1853, wars between two parties, like the Franco-Prussian War of 1870, the bloody American war between North and South in 1861-1865, and a whole series of colonial wars against rebellious natives.

In 1914 a great many people in Europe and America felt that this sort of general war was all but impossible. These people, predominantly liberal intellectuals, had been alarmed by the series of crises we shall shortly describe, crises that showed how close a general war might be. But they had followed hopefully the movements for international peace and co-operation—the Red Cross, the international labor movements, and the Hague conferences of 1899 and 1907, which, though they failed to achieve their avowed purpose of armaments limitation, did set up a tribunal for the arbitration of international disputes, the "world court."

World War I was long, bloody, and destructive. The shock of its outbreak, vastly increased by the strains of the war itself, and above all by the failure of the postwar peace settlement, brought on in the 1920's a most extraordinary discussion of the causes of the war. This discussion was by no means limited to professional historians. It was carried on in the press and on the platforms by all the agencies that touched public opinion. Most of it was designed to "revise" the verdict of the Versailles Treaty of 1919, in which the victorious Allies declared Germany and Austria-Hungary solely responsible for precipitating the war of 1914. The beaten Germans, penalized in the peace, had obvious reasons for trying to prove themselves innocent of war guilt. But important currents in public opinion in Great Britain, the United States, and even in France also flowed into this "revisionist" movement. So far did revisionism go in the 1920's that some American historians parceled out varying portions of the guilt among the victors and vanquished alike, with the confidence of schoolmasters handing out merits and demerits.

We cannot be so confident today. From our further perspective, the question of war guilt in 1914 fades out into a question of historical causation, and into the fact of historical tragedy. We can say with the English writer, George Meredith:

> In tragic life, God wot,
> No villain need be! Passions spin the plot.
> We are betrayed by what is false within.[*]

No one power or group of powers caused the war of 1914. Its causes lie deep in the history of the state-system of western civilization, and, more particularly, in its history since 1870. The dramatic date of the assassination of Francis Ferdinand, June 28, 1914, serves as a dividing line between the ultimate, or long-term, factors and the proximate, or short-term, factors.

---

[*] *Modern Love,* XLIII.

II: Causes of the War

The Shift in the Balance of Power

In the long term, an obvious factor that made war more likely was the unification of Germany and Italy. The creation of these two new major states in the 1860's and 1870's altered the always delicate balance of power in the European state-system. The efforts of statesmen during the next forty years to adjust the system and to take account of the two new powers and their claims proved ultimately unsuccessful. The older established powers were by no means willing to give up their own claims. We have seen that ever since the modern European—or, better, the western—state-system developed out of medieval fragmentation the separate units, the states, have tried to grow. They have tried to grow in wealth, in prestige, and, most conspicuously of all, in territory. In the second half of the nineteenth century, with the principle of national sovereignty well established, with even the smaller states like Switzerland and Sweden generally accepted as not to be swallowed, there was little territory in Europe that could be easily disposed of for the purpose of making adjustments. Unification had closed Germany and Italy, which as recently as 1815 had been classic areas for "compensation." Only southeastern Europe, the Balkan lands of the obviously weakening Turkish Empire, remained in the late nineteenth century as possible pickings for ambitious powers. Even there, the growth of national feeling in states like Rumania, Serbia, Bulgaria, and Greece made sheer annexation difficult. Nevertheless, Russia and Austria-Hungary both had ambitions in the Balkans; behind them, aiming rather at domination of Turkey and the Near East, came Germany and Great Britain. Finally, as we have noted in Chapter XXIV, much of Africa, Asia, and Oceania had been partitioned among the great powers amid intense rivalry. It seemed always possible to re-do this partitioning.

Meantime, influenced by their rivalries in Europe and abroad, the great powers were also choosing sides in a series of alliances and agreements. By the early years of the twentieth century two camps existed—the Triple Alliance of Germany, Austria-Hungary, and Italy, and the Triple Entente of France, Britain, and Russia. The system, as many people at the time saw clearly, had grown so tightly organized that there was almost no free play left, and

with the wisdom of hindsight we can now see that after 1900 almost any crisis might have led to war. Sarajevo was the one that did.

This state of international politics was christened by an English liberal, Lowes Dickinson, "the international anarchy." It was, however, no chaos, but a highly organized rivalry, "anarchical" only in the sense that there was no higher authority to put a stop to the rivalry. In concrete instances, two or more powers wanted the same piece of land, as a territorial addition or as a sphere of influence. France and Great Britain both wanted Egypt; France and Germany both wanted Morocco; Russia and Austria-Hungary both wanted control over the Balkans; Russia and Japan both wanted Manchuria; and so on around the map. Compromises were made, lands and spheres of influence were shared, but in the long run there simply wasn't enough to go around.

The Role of Public Opinion

We have in this outline used the shorthand of names like "Great Britain" or "Germany." But these are mere symbols, as colored blobs on a map are symbols, for millions of human beings whose desires somehow do add up into the actions of states, did add up to the war of 1914. In no state were the millions all in agreement. There were Germans who wanted no bit of Africa or any other piece of land. There were Englishmen who, far from being content with Britain's place in the world, wanted more, wanted Britain to be for the whole round world what Rome had been for the Mediterranean world in the first centuries of the Christian Era, hoped eventually to eliminate all but Englishmen (and perhaps Scotsmen) in a fine Darwinian struggle. There were everywhere in Europe at least a few absolute pacifists, men who were determined under any conditions to refuse to fight, men who once war broke out became "conscientious objectors." We must not think of the war and the events that led up to it as simply the work of a few men at the top in each nation, the professional soldiers, the villainous diplomats in frock coats and striped trousers. In all the countries, there was a spectrum that ran from the militarist to the pacifist, through all shades of opinion.

But the outbreak of the war saw in each belligerent nation a broad national public opinion in support of the government. In 1914 some men marched to war convinced that war was a beneficial thing; the bands played, the crowds shouted, and war, perhaps for the last time in our day, seemed romantic as well as necessary. Here is the account of a young German on the last train out of Switzerland before the outbreak of war:

An elderly gentleman was sitting in our compartment. He began to talk to us at once, as if we were intimate acquaintances. On the back of his hotel bill he had added up the numerical strength of the European armies and balanced them against each other. He compared the two totals and assured my mother that the spiritual qualities of the German troops compensated for the numerical superiority of the Russians. For in this war spiritual qualities alone would decide the day, and

Germany's spiritual qualities were the best in Europe. As a university professor he knew that our youth were ready for the fray, and full of ideals. At last the hour had come when our people could enter on its great world mission. . . .*

German Aspirations

The Germans were led by their Kaiser, William II, who had come to the throne in 1888. The "revisionist" historians have been able to show that in the hectic five weeks after the assassination at Sarajevo the Kaiser, contrary to world opinion at the time, did not work steadily for war, that indeed he tried to prevent war. But he cannot be even partially absolved for the long-term, for the ultimate, causes of the war. In the decisive years between 1888 and 1914 he was the posturing, aggressive leader of patriotic expansion, the "White Knight" leading his people to glory (see also Chapter XXII). He was perhaps more of a figurehead, less of an actual maker of policy than the world took him to be, but still a willing and effective figurehead for expansionists.

German ambitions and German fears

---

* Ernst Glaeser, *Class of 1902*, Willa and Edwin Muir, trans. (London, 1929), 171-172.

Berlin crowds singing "Deutschland über Alles," 1914.

produced an intense hatred of Britain, a hatred mixed with envy and a sense of inferiority, a hatred that focused on the English upper classes, perfectly tailored, serene in effortless superiority, the favorite children of fortune. Many a German tourist, perhaps quite accidentally given an Italian hotel room inferior to that given a traveling Englishman, would come home burning with indignation at this personal evidence that Germany was being denied its place in the sun. In the German navy, in the years before the war, there was a simple toast in the officers' mess: *Der Tag* (The Day). Everyone knew that this was the day of the declaration of war between Germany and Britain. These feelings are all condensed in the famous "Hymn of Hate" of the German poet Ernst Lissauer:

We will never forego our hate,
Hate by water and hate by land,
Hate of the head and hate of the hand,
Hate of the hammer and hate of the Crown.
Hate of the seventy millions choking down.
We love as one, we hate as one,
We have one foe and one alone:
England! *

British Aspirations

Few Englishmen returned this hate; the English were still on top. Yet as the years wore on, the expensive race between Britain and Germany in naval armaments continued; in incident after incident German and British diplomats took opposite sides; and—this seemed especially important to the hard-headed—German wares of all sorts undersold British wares in Europe, in North and South America, and in Asia. Englishmen began to think that someone ought to teach these ill-mannered Germans a lesson. Moreover, they had begun to worry about their own position of prosper-

---

* Ernst Lissauer, "A Chant of Hate Against England," trans. by Barbara Henderson, in Burton E. Stevenson, comp., *The Home Book of Verse*, 3rd ed. (New York, 1918), II, 2549-2550.

ity and leadership. In India, the greatest possession of the English, it was clear already that great concessions toward self-government would have to be made to the natives. Close at home the Irish question was in one of its most acute phases, with Ulster in arms against the proposed Home Rule. Englishmen were worried about their obsolescent industrial plants, their apparent inability to produce goods as cheaply and as efficiently as the Germans; they were self-critical about their failures as salesmen abroad, their stodgy self-satisfaction.

A great many Britishers thought of themselves as good liberals and good internationalists, anxious to preserve the peace and the decencies of international life. Many were radicals and Labor party men committed to pacifism. The coming of war in 1914 was to show how thoroughly almost all these men identified Great Britain and righteousness. As for the bulk of the conservatives, they were as nationalist as in any other great country. In Britain, their nationalism attached itself to the Empire, to the "White Man's Burden," to a whole set of symbols that the Germans found intolerable.

The Other Belligerents

In democratic France as in democratic England there was a wide spread of opinion on international politics. A numerous socialist Left was committed to pacifism and to the concept of a kind of international strike of workers at the threat of actual war. A more moderate group also opposed conventional patriotic aggressiveness toward the foreigner. Both among the men who conducted French foreign relations and among the general public, however, there remained right down to the eve of the Great War the embittered patriotism of the beaten. Frenchmen wanted *revanche*, revenge for the defeat of 1870. They wanted Alsace-Lorraine back. For all these years, the statue representing Strasbourg among the cities of France in the Place de la Concorde in Paris was draped in black. With the warmest patriots, the organizers of patriotic societies, the editors of patriotic journals, this feeling for revenge was obsessive.

By the opening decade of the 1900's many observers thought that the new generation was losing its desire for revenge, that Frenchmen had at last decided to accept the verdict of 1870. But French diplomatists continued to preserve and strengthen the system of alliances against Germany, and in the excited weeks of July, 1914, it was clear that the French were ready for war.

In the other major belligerents, too, the ultimate decisions of governments won much popular support. Russians were filled with the "pooled self-esteem" of nationalism, were convinced that God and the right were on their side. Italians saw in war the chance to get *Italia Irredenta* (Trent, Trieste, and their surrounding lands) and still more territory from the Habsburg Monarchy. In the dual monarchy, as we have seen (see Chapter XXII), the loyalty of subject nationalities could scarcely be counted on; but the dominant Germans of Austria and Magyars of Hungary welcomed the opportunity to put the troublesome Slavs in their place for good and all.

The Era of Bismarck, 1871-1890

The road to Sarajevo starts in 1871, at the Treaty of Frankfurt, where France was obliged to cede Alsace and Lorraine to the new German Empire. It was no straight road, but one of many twists and turnings, and few historians would now maintain that 1871 made 1914 inevitable. We cannot follow the road in detail, but we must map its main course.

For some twenty years Bismarck was its

chief engineer. In fairness to the Iron Chancellor, it must be said that during his last twenty years in office he sought peace, and indeed obtained it. Powerful elements in the new empire made it impossible for him to grant to France the same kind of generous peace he had given Austria in 1866. Yet Bismarck did try to salve the wound he knew France had suffered; he encouraged her to expand her empire in North Africa by the acquisition of Tunis in 1881, even though this offended the Italians, who also coveted Tunisia. But he feared a French attempt at revenge, and sought to isolate her diplomatically by building a series of alliances from which she was excluded. Germany, he insisted, was now a "saturated" power, and wanted nothing more in Europe; and in a famous phrase he insisted that all the Balkans were not worth "the bones of a single Pomeranian grenadier." Above all, he sought to keep on good terms with both Austria and Russia, and, what was much more difficult, to keep both these powers on good terms with each other. Since both wanted predominance in the Balkans, Bismarck's task was formidable.

He laid the cornerstone of his diplomatic system by a defensive alliance with Austria-Hungary in 1879, an alliance that held right down to 1918. And he was able to make a secret treaty, the so-called League of the Three Emperors, which bound Germany, Russia, and Austria together. The three powers agreed to act together in dealings with Turkey, and to maintain friendly neutrality should any one of them be at war with a fourth power other than Turkey. Next, working skillfully on Italian annoyance over the French expansion in Tunis, Bismarck secured an alliance among Germany, Austria-Hungary, and Italy, directed chiefly against France. This was the famous Triple Alliance of 1882, often renewed, which on paper still existed in 1914.

On this series of tightropes Bismarck maintained a precarious balance through the 1880's. Chief in his mind was the dan-

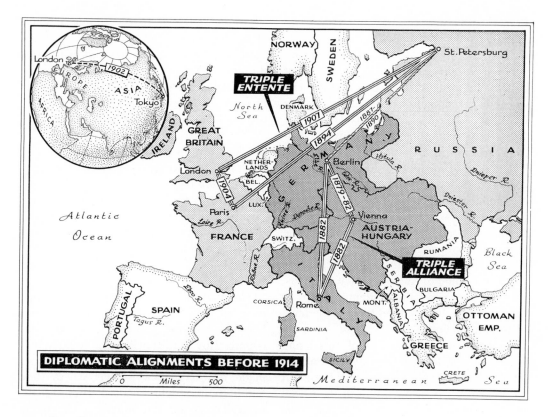

DIPLOMATIC ALIGNMENTS BEFORE 1914

ger that the Russians, always fearful of Austrian schemes in the Balkans, would desert him and ally themselves with France, still a great power and anxious to escape from the isolation that Bismarck had designed for her. In 1887, Russia did refuse to renew the League of the Three Emperors, but Bismarck was able to repair the breach for the moment by a secret Russo-German agreement known as the Reinsurance Treaty. The two promised each other neutrality in case either was involved in a war against a third power; but this neutrality was not to hold if Germany made an "aggressive" war against France or if Russia made an "aggressive" war against Austria. Since Russian nationalist agitation continued against both Austria and Germany, Bismarck in 1888 made public as a warning to Russia the terms of the Austro-German alliance, and allowed the main terms of the Triple Alliance to be known informally.

Formation of the Triple Entente, 1890-1907

Then in 1890 the young Emperor William II dismissed Bismarck. The Emperor's advisers, headed by Baron von Holstein, persuaded him not to renew the Reinsurance Treaty with Russia, in spite of Russian desire for such renewal. Shortly afterward, what Bismarck had worked so hard to prevent came about. After lengthy negotiations, Russia and France in 1894 came together in an alliance that ended French isolation. It was formally a defensive alliance, in which each was to come to the aid of the other if Germany or Austria made "aggressive" war against either, and it was accompanied by the necessary military agreements between the two general staffs. Against the Triple Alliance there now stood, quite openly, a Dual Alliance of

France and Russia. England as yet remained technically uninvolved.

The next great stage in the tightening network of alliances was to bring Great Britain in against the Central Powers. Britain had long kept her hands free on the Continent, refusing formal alliances. In the 1890's, she maintained as to Europe what came to be called a policy of "splendid isolation." But in the two decades after the accession of Kaiser William II Britain was to commit herself to a formal alliance with Japan and to an "understanding" (in French, *entente*) with France and Russia. What chiefly drove Britain to these actions was the naval race with Germany and the rapid worsening of Anglo-German relations, a worsening even more evident perhaps at the level of public opinion than at the level of formal diplomacy.

A good concrete instance of this rising hostility is the Kruger telegram of 1896, in which the Kaiser congratulated President Kruger of the Boer Republic of Transvaal on the defeat of the Jameson raid (see p. 350). It may be that the Kaiser and his circle hoped at bottom that this gesture would be taken by the English government as a kind of polite and permissible diplomatic blackmail, an evidence of how great a nuisance the German government could be to the British if it were not on their side. But the British press took the telegram as an unbearable insult, and the German press replied angrily to British anger.

It was fear of Russia rather than fear of Germany, however, that inspired Britain to make the first break with formal isolationism, the alliance with Japan in 1902. The outbreak of war between Russia and Japan hastened negotiations between Britain and France. In the Anglo-French Entente of 1904 France gave England a free hand in Egypt, England gave France a free hand in Morocco, and various outstanding difficulties between the two in other parts of the world were ironed out. More important, the base was laid for general collaboration between the two in international affairs. Only six years previously, in 1898, there had been a grave flare-up of the traditional colonial rivalry between France and England when a French column was met by a British column at Fashoda in the disputed Sudan territory of the upper Nile Valley. Fashoda caused quite as big an outbreak of fury in the French and the British press as the Kruger telegram only two years before had caused in the German and the British press. Yet Fashoda left wounds much less deep than the Kruger telegram; the contemporary press is not always a faithful guide to the climate of public opinion, let alone to that of professional diplomacy.

The final stage in aligning the two camps came in 1907 when Russia, chastened by her defeat at the hand of Japan and encouraged by the French, came to an agreement with Great Britain. Both countries made concessions in regions where they had been imperialist rivals—Persia, Afghanistan, Tibet—and the British at last made some concessions toward the Russian desire to open up the Straits. The agreement was scarcely based on any genuine sympathy between the two peoples, for the British, notably, had been Russophobic for well over a century. Nevertheless, it did round out the Triple Entente against the Triple Alliance.

A Decade of Crises, 1905-1914

The last decade before 1914 was a series of crises and local wars, any one of which might have spread into a world war. First came a deliberate theatrical gesture from the Kaiser, when in 1905 he made a ceremonial visit to Tangier in Morocco as a way of telling the world that the Germans would not accept the Anglo-French assignment of Morocco to France. The net effect was to tighten the entente between France

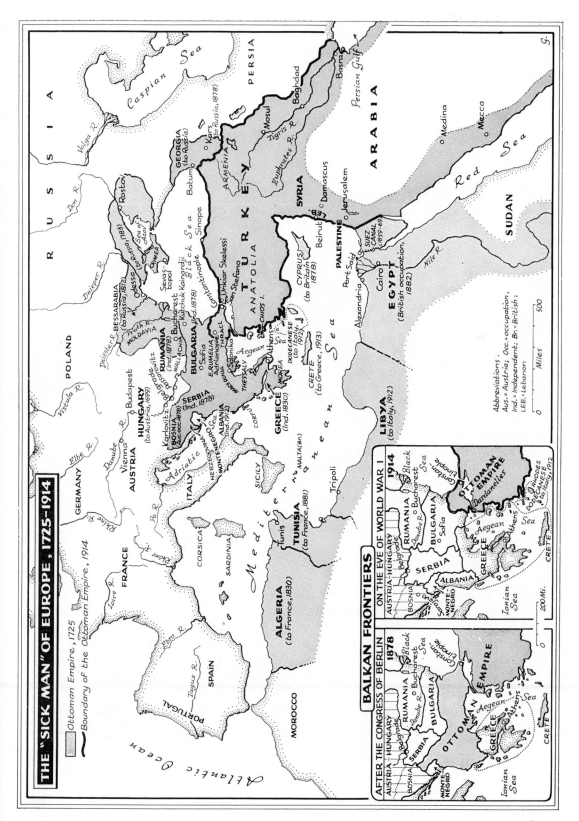

THE "SICK MAN" OF EUROPE, 1725-1914

Ottoman Empire, 1725
Boundary of the Ottoman Empire, 1914

BALKAN FRONTIERS
ON THE EVE OF WORLD WAR I

AFTER THE CONGRESS OF BERLIN **1878**

AUSTRIA–HUNGARY

1914

Abbreviations:
Aus. = Austria; Occ. = occupation;
Ind. = Independent; Br. = British;
LEB. = Lebanon

0   Miles   500

0   200 Mi.

and Britain, for the British indicated clearly to the French that they would support them. Indeed at this time there began the informal military and naval conferences between the British and the French that the French, at least, believed "committed" the British to armed support if the Germans attacked. Although the French Foreign Minister, Delcassé, a partisan of firm policy toward the Germans, was forced out of office, even this partial victory did the Germans no good. French public opinion was infuriated by this intervention in their domestic politics. In the end, a general international conference at Algeciras in Spain (1906) backed up the French, who went ahead with their plans for a protectorate in Morocco. At Algeciras American diplo-

Turkey Gobblers after their rations.

matic influence was used on the side of France; the United States, too, was beginning to emerge from its own variety of isolationism.

A "second Moroccan crisis" in 1911 heightened tensions, and brought the possibility of a general war home to most Frenchmen. The Kaiser sent a German gunboat, the *Panther*, to the Moroccan port of Agadir as a protest against French occupation of the old city of Fez. In ensuing negotiations, well-publicized in the press, the Germans finally agreed to leave the French a free hand in Morocco, but only at a price the French considered blackmail: part of French Congo was ceded to Germany.

In the Balkans, a decisive turn of the road toward Sarajevo came in 1908. Austria formally proclaimed the annexation of the old Turkish provinces of Bosnia-Herzegovina, which she had occupied since 1878. Austria's decisive act infuriated the Serbs, who wanted to add Bosnia to their state. It also infuriated the Russians, all the more since few Russians knew that their diplomat Izvolski had in fact made an informal agreement with the Austrian minister Aehrenthal in September, 1908, to accept the annexation of Bosnia-Herzegovina in return for Austrian support of an agreement permitting Russian warships to use the Straits. In the event, Austria did the annexing, but Russia did not get her use of the Straits. This wound to Russian pride was profound.

War now broke out on the edges of Europe. In 1911, the Italians sent troops to Tripoli, the poorest part of North Africa, but at least a part that had not yet been taken from the Turks by other Europeans. Then in 1912 war spread to the Balkans. Nationalist revolutionaries called the "Young Turks" had risen successfully against the Sultan in 1908. The Young Turks wanted the modern industrial achievements of the West, they wanted its political apparatus of representative government, and they wanted above all to

have Turks respected, admired, and feared as members of a thoroughly modern *nation*. Some of their intellectuals followed the nineteenth-century Romantic pattern back into the past, where they found, not the nomad Turks of history, but fine sturdy "Turanians" from the inspiring steppes of Central Asia. There was even a "Pan-Turanian" movement, strangest of the "Pan" movements, which sought to group Magyars, Turks, and the Turkish peoples of Central Asia, who were all only distantly related to each other, as children of a common destiny. No wonder the Habsburgs were alarmed! It began to look as if those who hoped to divide up Turkey had better hurry while the dividing was good. In the hurry, the world got swept into the War of 1914, the preliminary stages of which were the Balkan Wars.

In the first of these wars, in 1912, an alliance of Bulgaria, Serbia, and Greece beat the Turks, and started the process of dividing up most of European Turkey. But here Austria imposed an absolute veto on granting Serbia territories that would give her access to the Adriatic Sea. Meanwhile, the victors quarreled among themselves, and in the Second Balkan War (1913) the Greeks and Serbs, joined by the Rumanians and the all-but-beaten Turks, readily defeated the Bulgarians. Turkey got back some of her territory in Europe. But the Balkans were in a state of uncertainty and bad blood when Francis Ferdinand was assassinated.

The Final Crisis,
July-August, 1914

There are millions of words in print about the proximate causes of World War I in the six weeks between the assassination on June 28 and the general spread of war on August 4, when Britain came in against Germany. Thanks to the end of the rule of Hohenzollern, Habsburg, and

Romanov houses as a result of the war, the secret archives were thrown open much sooner than would be normal. And in the pressure of debate in the 1920's, over the question of war guilt even the victorious countries, Britain, France, and the United States, opened their archives to a surprising extent. These are weeks for which documents, often telegrams, can be dated by the hour and minute. These are weeks in which messages are constantly crossing

Princip, immediately after the assassination at Sarajevo, June 28, 1914.

each other, confusing things hopelessly. These are weeks in which professional diplomatists and statesmen, egged on by an excited—and it must be said often *irresponsible*—press, nevertheless tried for the most part to master the crisis without recourse to war.

The diplomats and statesmen were drawn into war because almost all of them believed that they faced an alternative worse than war, a defeat or loss of face for their nation. Austria believed correctly, though positive proof was then lacking, that the Serbian government had some foreknowledge of the plot of the assassin Princip and should therefore have given her warning. For this reason, and also because she wished to check the Serb agitation that had long been unsettling the Yugoslav peoples living in the dual monarchy, Austria decided to make stiff demands on Serbia after the assassination of Francis Ferdinand. Before doing so, however, she consulted her German ally, who promised to support whatever policy Austria might adopt toward Serbia. This German response has become famous as a diplomatic "blank check," duly signed by Germany in advance with the precise amount to be filled in later by Austria.

Thus encouraged, the Austrian government, on July 23, sent Serbia an ultimatum to be answered within forty-eight hours. The ultimatum made many separate demands, which added up to an insistence that Serbia and Serb propagandists keep their hands off Habsburg territories and populations, now and in the future. Most of the demands the Serbs accepted, at least in principle; but they refused to accept two of them, which would have permitted Austrian police or military men to take, on Serbian soil, an actual part in a Serbian investigation of Princip's plot. Probably Serbia had some assurance that Russia was willing to give her a kind of "blank check," and would assist her if the partial refusal of the ultimatum led to war. The Serbian reply, therefore, was a little less virtuously honest than it seemed to be to most of the world in July, 1914. Still, the Austrian ultimatum appears to have been couched in terms deliberately unacceptable to the Serbs, and the Serb reply seems to have been a base for more consideration than it got from the Austrians. Because the Serbs had not accepted the whole of the ultimatum, Austria declared war on July 28, after turning down as inconsistent with national honor a European conference proposed by the British foreign minister, Sir Edward Grey.

From this declaration of war on, the German diplomatists, backed by William II and actually resisting the German military men, tried to hold back their Austrian ally. It is impossible to clear William from responsibility for the German "blank check," which had emboldened Austria and had perhaps been designed by Germany to do just that. Now, however, the Germans certainly tried to revoke the check and made a last effort to stop the spread of the war. Since Russia was beginning the full mobilization of her armies, the Kaiser, on July 29, told Tsar Nicholas II in a personal telegram of the German attempt to get the Austrians to compromise. Apparently this telegram served to get full Russian mobilization modified into partial mobilization and to get direct Austro-Russian talks resumed on July 30. For a brief moment it looked as if the crisis might be overcome.

But mobilization was not easy in Russia, a country of long distances, poor communications, and bureaucratic red tape, and the Russian military feared that their enemies would get the jump on them. In perhaps the most crucial decision of this hectic last week, the Russian government, probably against the deeper inclinations of the Tsar himself, decided to renew general mobilization. Germany at once insisted that all Russian mobilization cease, and, when it continued, ordered her own at 4:00 P.M. on August 1, and declared war on Russia at 7:00 P.M. the same day. France, meantime, had determined to stand by her Russian ally, now evidently about to be attacked, and had also mobilized at 3:55 P.M. on August 1. Germany declared war on France on August 3.

Britain was still wavering. Although her entente with France did not legally bind the two nations together, it had led, as we have just seen, to the very close co-ordination of defense plans by the French and British military and naval staffs. Perhaps,

then, Britain would have come into the war anyway. What made her entry certain was the German violation of the neutrality of Belgium, which both Britain and Prussia had joined with other powers to guarantee in 1839. The German military were determined to take decisive action in the West and to knock France out of the war before the Russians could get their vast but slow-moving armies into action. Accordingly, German plans called for a sweep through a corner of Belgium to avoid the heavily fortified and hilly terrain in northeastern France. On August 2, the Germans had notified Belgium that they intended to march through her territory, though they promised to respect her territorial integrity in the peace to come.

Belgium rejected this demand, and appealed to the other guaranteeing powers. Sir Edward Grey, though opposed in the British cabinet by two pacifists, seized firmly on this ground of action, and on August 4 Britain declared war on Germany. The German chancellor, Bethmann-Hollweg, informed of this action, let slip the phrase that Britain had gone to war just for a "scrap of paper"—the treaty of 1839 that guaranteed Belgium against invasion. This unhappy phrase, seized upon by the press of the world, not only solidified British opinion in favor of the war but was responsible more than any other single factor for the charge of war guilt laid against Germany.

The Entry of Other Powers

By August 6, when Austria declared war on Russia, all the members of the Triple Alliance and the Triple Entente had come to blows, with the exception of Italy, who, however, had never really been a good ally of Austria because of the Irredentist issue. Italy, refusing to consider herself bound by the Triple Alliance, de-

Two advertise-
ments that ap-
peared in New
York City
newspapers,
1915. The
sinking of the
British liner,
Lusitania, by
a German
submarine
(May, 1915)
claimed more
than one thou-
sand lives,
some of them
American.

to cut off the food and raw materials that came to the British Isles from overseas, and without which their peoples would have starved. This unrestricted submarine war-fare meant sinking American ships that Americans held were quite legally bringing such supplies, *not* contraband of war, to England and France. On April 6, 1917, the United States completed the roster of great powers involved in the conflict by declaring war on Germany.

Dissident Americans, then and since, have declared that the United States was enticed into the war by the wicked few—by sentimental lovers of England or France; by bankers who had lent money to the Allies and wanted to protect their invest-ments; by silly idealists who agreed with President Wilson in wishing to "make the world safe for democracy"; and, of course, by scheming Allied diplomatists, corrupt Europeans who held a strange fascination over American "babes in the wood."

Deep-seated sentiments among many good Americans in 1916-1917 rebelled against our jeopardizing American ideals by involving ourselves in the conventional—and wicked—European struggle for power. Even today, after a second general or world war in which American participation aroused much less opposition at home (see Chapter XXIX), it is difficult for the his-torian to discuss objectively the causes of our entrance into this so-called First World War. The historian must indeed note that ever since what Americans call King Wil-liam's War and Europeans usually call the War of the League of Augsburg (1688-1697) (see Chapter XV, Vol. I) we as colonists or as an independent nation have sooner or later got drawn into every major general war in the western state-system. In purely empirical terms, it may be argued that the normal expectation is for the United States to enter into any great world war. And in more disputable general terms, such as we have brought out in Volume I, Chapter XIII, it may be argued that in the

clared her neutrality. The Central Powers of Germany and Austria-Hungary, then, stood against the Allies—Russia, France, Britain, and Serbia. Japan came in on the side of the Allies late in August, and Tur-key came in on the Austro-German side in November, 1914. After competing terri-torial offers from both Allies and Central Powers, Italy finally joined the Allies in May, 1915.

As the war turned into a stalemate, on both Western and Eastern fronts in the winter of 1916-1917, the Germans made the desperate decision to try to get at Great Britain by the only way that seemed available. They would use their submarines western (now world) state-system a general or world war never breaks out unless there is an aggressor nation whose activities do in fact threaten the independent existence of all other nations. The United States, in this view, went to war in 1917 for a very deep-seated reason indeed: the possible victory of Germany threatened our very existence as an independent, but committed and co-operating, participant in an international order.

More specifically, in 1917 the United States insisted that the existing international order gave Americans the right to travel and to trade freely with neutrals and, in dealings with belligerents, to be limited only by well-known principles of international war forbidding actual transport of munitions, or other *direct* forms of aid to belligerents. This is the doctrine of "freedom of the seas," which would indeed have allowed Germans to search American vessels, but which quite clearly did not permit German submarines to sink American vessels on sight and without notice. The German decision to undertake unrestricted submarine warfare was in western historical precedent a completely adequate and normal justification of and explanation for our declaration of war. But, we must repeat, behind this reason lay a widespread though by no means universal feeling among many Americans, a feeling especially strong in those persons most concerned with our foreign relations, that a German victory would mean a world-order in which the kind of America we wanted could not be secure.

Jefferson had indeed in 1807 abandoned the doctrine of freedom of the seas, and had in the Embargo Act simply forbidden American vessels to trade either with the French or the British side. In 1917, we should have had to put an embargo on all American shipping to most foreign ports, or else put up with German torpedoing of American ships, and the drowning of American citizens. Neither course would seem to have been acceptable to a majority of Americans in 1917. Since many of the Latin-American states followed the lead of the United States, there were all-told from 1914 through 1918 something over sixty separate declarations of war or severances of relations. It was indeed a world war.

III: The Course of the War

Resources
of the Belligerents

As the opposing nations lined up in 1914, the Allies (British, French, Russians, and others) had an overwhelming superiority in total population and resources. The Central Powers (Germany, Austria-Hungary and Turkey) had in their own continental lands not over 150,000,000 people; Britain, France, Russia, and Italy in their own continental lands had at least 125,000,000 more people than their enemies. Moreover, in their overseas possessions, which included the 315,000,000 people of India, the Allies had many millions more. As for material resources, the Central Powers had, especially in Germany, admirably organized industries and enough coal and iron to fight a long war. But here too the statistics were overwhelmingly in favor of the Allies. Moreover, though German submarines and, in the early days, surface raiders were able to interrupt seriously Allied lines of communication overseas, on the whole the Allies were still able to get from these overseas sources indispensable food and other supplies. And when in 1917 a beaten Russia, in the throes of a revolution, ceased to be of aid, the Allies gained the great resources of the United States.

In the long run, much as in the American Civil War, the side with the most men and materials wore down its enemies and won the war. But it was by no means the uneven struggle that the statistics of total population and material resources would indicate. Again as in our Civil War, the weaker side had initially important advantages, won great victories, seemed indeed at critical moments on the point of final victory. Not until the very last months before the armistice of November, 1918, could the Allies really feel confident of victory.

Geography gave Germany and Austria the advantages of being side by side, and of having interior lines of communication, which enabled them to make rapid transfers of troops from one threatened front to another. Though the Germans and Austrians did not always see eye to eye, they did speak the same language, and had for long been firmly allied. Most important of all, Germany in particular was more ready for war than were her enemies. She had an efficiently organized military machine and a good stock of munitions, her industry could be readily geared to war, her plans were complete, her people were united in support of the war, and they enjoyed the great psychological advantage of being on the offensive, of carrying the war to the enemy. Indeed, no important part of the war was ever fought on German soil; it ended, with important results for later history, with the German army still in being, with the soil of the German Fatherland still uninvaded.

By contrast, geography separated the western Allies from Russia. German control of the Baltic and Turkish control of the Straits proved throughout the war a serious obstacle to communication between Russia and her allies, who had to take roundabout and difficult routes through Archangel in Arctic waters and even through Vladivos-tok on the Pacific at the end of the long, slow, single-track Trans-Siberian railway. For the Allies, transfer of troops between eastern and western fronts was militarily almost impossible, even had it been politically possible. It was not, however, politically possible, and here is one of the greatest weaknesses of the Allies.

Russia, Britain, and France had only recently come together, as "friendly" powers and not as close allies. Each of them was a strongly marked nationality, having many sources of conflict with the others. They had no long tradition of mutual co-operation, no common language. France and England were democracies, and though the peoples of both rallied firmly to the national cause in 1914, they were of recent years unused to the kind of firm, centralized, political and military control that is necessary in war. As for unified military planning and administration, it was never achieved between Russia and the western Allies. Even among Britain, France, and the United States on the Western Front, it was not achieved until the French General Foch was appointed commander-in-chief in 1918, and then only imperfectly, for full merging of staffs was not achieved.

Finally, of the three great Allied powers in 1914, only France was ready with a good big land force, and France, with only 39 millions of people against Germany's 65 millions, was the weakest of the Allies in manpower. Britain was indeed prepared on the sea, and her navy was an invaluable asset; but it could not be of direct use against the German army. Russia had universal military service and an army great in numbers. But she had vast distances to overcome, an inadequate railway system, a relatively undeveloped heavy industry, an army whose morale had been shaken by the recent defeat at the hands of the Japanese, a people whose morale had been shaken by the recent abortive revolution, a military and a political organization riddled with inefficiency and corruption.

The Western Front: German Offensive

The Germans had a plan, the so-called Schlieffen plan, which they immediately put into execution. It called for a holding operation on the left, with a strong right wing that was to advance swiftly through Belgium, take Paris, and then fall on the rear of the French armies. While this great enveloping movement in the west swiftly eliminated France, relatively weaker German forces, it was planned, would hold down the slow-moving Russians. With France beaten, the Germans could turn their full force against the Russians and beat them. Then there would be only the British left, and the future would take care of them.

The German plan almost succeeded. It failed for two reasons, to which a great number of separate tactical factors contributed. In the first place, the German chief of staff, Moltke, had seriously modified the Schlieffen plan by weakening the critical right wing, partly in order to send divisions to the east, which, ironically, arrived there too late to participate in the defeat of the Russians. By the time the German right wing neared Paris, it had too few divisions to take the capital and then roll up the French army to the eastward. In the second place, the French, with help from the Belgians and British, exploited the German weakness at the critical moment and stopped the drive short of its goals. The Germans lost the first great battle, known as the Battle of the Marne.

The German advance, which had been almost continuous since August 2, had been stopped. In the next few weeks the opposing forces engaged in what came to be called the "race for the Channel," with the Germans trying to outflank the Allies and get the Channel ports, thus shutting the short sea passage to future British reinforcements. They failed here, too, and throughout the war the ports of Calais and Boulogne, and indeed a small south-

French soldiers in the trenches near Verdun.

western corner of Belgium, were to remain in Allied hands—a valuable military advantage.

By the autumn of 1914 the Western Front was thus stabilized. For over three hundred airline miles between the Channel and the Swiss border of Alsace near Basel, hundreds of thousands of soldiers faced each other in a continuous line that was full of bends called "salients." Both sides "dug in" and formed a series of rough fortifications. The central feature of these fortifications was a series of parallel trenches deep enough to conceal a man standing upright. As time went on, these trenches were greatly improved; they were supplied with parapets, machine-gun nests, and an elaborate network of approach trenches and strong points, until the whole front became one immense fortification. Thousands of local actions in the four years of trench warfare shifted the lines here and there, and a series of partial break-throughs occurred on both sides. But on the whole the lines held, and the actual fighting in the west was confined to an extraordinarily narrow, though very long, field.

On this Western Front the ultimate decision was reached; but there were many other fronts. Some of them were disparagingly called "the side-shows" by those who advocated concentrating in the west. Yet in perspective we can now see that they all played a part in determining the final result. Since, over the long pull, the Germans had fewer men and resources, the dispersal of energies that these "side-shows" called for, and the continuous need to bolster their Austrian and Turkish and Balkan allies, were major factors in their defeat. For the sake of clarity, we shall here take up these other fronts separately and briefly, but the reader must never forget that for the belligerents the war was a whole; its wide-flung theaters were mutually dependent, with each one influencing the others.

The Eastern Front

The Eastern Front, where the Russians faced both the Germans and the Austrians, was no mere side-show. Millions of men were involved on both sides, and had the Russians not held out, as they did, until the end of 1917 the Allies in the west could never have withstood the reinforcements that the Germans and Austrians would have been able to send to France and Italy. The war in the east was more a war of movement than the war in the west. But even in the east there were long periods of stalemate, especially during the winters, periods when the opposing armies faced each other in long lines of improvised fortifications in trench warfare much like that in the west.

The Russians began well. Against the exposed Austrian salient of Galicia (Austria's share of the eighteenth-century partitions of Poland), the Russians threw in vast masses of men. They pushed the Austrians out of Lemberg (later the Polish Lwów, now the Russian Lvov), and by the end of September, 1914, they had reached the northern ends of some of the passes leading into Hungary through the Carpathian Mountains. Against the Germans, who also had to defend in East Prussia a salient surrounded on the east and south by Russian territory, the Russians won the Battle of Gumbinnen, in August 1914, and so alarmed the German general staff that the Germans felt obliged to reorganize their eastern command. General von Ludendorff, under the nominal command of his senior, Von Hindenburg, and aided by a brilliant junior, Von Hoffmann, turned successively against the two Russian armies, which were attempting a pincers movement. Late in August, at Tannenberg, the Germans decisively defeated a Russian army under Samsonov, who committed suicide. And early in September they won another decisive victory against the Russians at the

Masurian lakes, thus clearing East Prussia of Russians.

The Germans' hard-pressed Austrian allies to the south were by now clamoring for help, and the Western Front was still demanding men. Hindenburg and his aides had to do their best with what they had. In a series of hard-fought battles in Poland they succeeded in relieving the pressure on the Austrians. The end of the year 1914 found the Austrians still hanging on in Galicia, and found the Germans in a good position to push eastward from East Prussian and Polish bases. In two great joint offensives in May and July, 1915, the Central Powers won substantial successes; they inflicted severe losses on the Russians from which the Russians never really recovered. At the end of the year 1915 the battle line ran roughly from near Riga, deep in the Baltic provinces of Russia, to the eastern edge of Galicia at Tarnopol and Czernowitz.

In 1916, the Russians, with a new commander, General Brusilov, undertook a great new offensive against the Austrians in the south. The Russian need to bolster their failing morale would probably have made some action necessary, but the Russians were also being pressed by the Western Allies to do something to help the Italians, who were threatened by the Austrians in the region of Trent. It seems likely that the Brusilov offensive was begun too soon, without adequate preparation, It scored a striking success at first; in places, the Russians drove the Austrians back some eighty miles, and they took large numbers of prisoners. But once more the Germans came to the rescue; with fresh troops transferred from the west, they halted Brusilov before he had won a decisive success.

It was from the backwash of this defeat that the Russian Revolution, which began early in March, 1917, was born. In the moderate phase of that uprising, before the Bolshevik revolution of November, 1917, Brusilov undertook one last desperate offensive. But he was soon checked, and the way was open for the Bolsheviks to carry out their promise to make peace. By the end of 1917, Russia was out of the war. She was forced by the Central Powers to sign the extraordinarily punitive Peace of Brest-Litovsk (March, 1918), by which she lost her Polish territories, her Baltic provinces, the entire Ukraine, Finland, and some lands in the Caucasus. The Caucasian lands went to Turkey; most of the others came under what proved to be the temporary domination of Austria and Germany.

The Italian Front

In April, 1915, Italy concluded with Britain, France and Russia the secret Treaty of London, which promised the Italians their long-sought-for Trent and Trieste, and other lands at Austrian and Turkish expense. In May, the Italians formally declared war on Austria-Hungary (they did not declare war on Germany until August, 1916), and a new front was added along the Austro-Italian frontier at the head of the Adriatic. Much of this front was too mountainous for effective action, and it was pretty much confined to some sixty miles along the Isonzo River. For two years there was a series of bloody but indecisive actions along this river that at least pinned down several hundred thousand Austrian troops. Then in the late autumn of 1917, with Russia already beaten, came the blow that very nearly knocked Italy out. Once again the Germans supplied the propulsive force. Ludendorff, now in supreme command, sent six German divisions to the Isonzo. The Germans and Austrians broke through at Caporetto, and sent the Italians into a retreat across the Venetian plains, a retreat that was really a rout. French and British reinforcements were hastily rushed across the Alps, but what did most to stop the Austro-Germans was probably the grave difficulty, under modern conditions of warfare, of supplying mass armies of infantry in rapid advance. The Italians were finally able to hold along the line of the Piave River, almost at the Po.

The Dardanelles

One of the most important of the "side-shows," the Dardanelles campaign of 1915, not only proved in its failure to be a bad blow to the morale of the Allies, but was to have important repercussions in World War II. With the entry of Turkey into the war in November, 1914, and with the Western Front capable of being held against the Germans by the French alone, a group of British military and political leaders advanced the idea that British strength should be put into amphibious operations somewhere in the Aegean area. A steady drive could also be made overland toward Vienna and Berlin through territory where the Central Powers were not expecting an attack in force. The great exponent of this "Eastern Plan" was Winston Churchill, First Lord of the Admiralty. The British decided to try the plan. The point of attack chosen was the Dardanelles, the more westerly of the two straits that separate the Black Sea from the Aegean. The campaign is sometimes known as the "Gallipoli campaign" from the long narrow peninsula on the European side of the Straits which was one of the keys to the whole action. Here Allied victory would have had the additional advantage of opening communication with Russia via the Black Sea.

In March, 1915, the British and French fleets tried to force the Straits, but they abandoned the attempt somewhat prematurely when several ships struck mines. Later landings of British, Australian, New Zealand, and French troops at various points on both Asian and European shores of the Dardanelles were poorly co-ordinated and badly backed up. They met with fierce and effective resistance from the Turks—a junior officer named Mustafa Kemal greatly distinguishing himself—and in the end they had to be abandoned. Russia remained sealed in by the Straits all during the war. But Churchill continued to believe that the Dardanelles plan had failed, not because it was a bad plan, but because it had not been carried out with determination. And in the Second World War he was to revive, against American military opinion, something of his old plan, which became known as the plan to strike at the "soft underbelly" of the Axis.

The Balkan Fronts

Serbia's part in the crisis that produced the war meant that from the start there would be a Balkan front. In the end there were several such fronts, and no Balkan state remained uninvolved. The Austrians failed here also, and although in December, 1914, they did manage to take the Serbian capital, Belgrade, they were driven out again. Bulgaria, wooed by both sides, finally came in with the Central Powers in the autumn of 1915. The Germans sent troops and a general, von Mackensen, under whom the Serbs were finally beaten. The remnant of their armies was driven to take refuge on the island of Corfu in neutral Greece.

To counter this blow in the Balkans, the Allies had already landed a few divisions in the Greek city of Salonika, and had established a front in Macedonia. The Greeks themselves were divided into two groups. One was headed by King Constantine, who at bottom was sympathetic with the Central Powers, but who for the moment was seeking only to maintain Greek neutrality. The other was a pro-Ally group headed by the able old politician Venizelos. Although the Allies rode roughshod over formal notions of Greek neutrality, Venizelos did not get firmly into the saddle until June, 1917, when Allied pressure

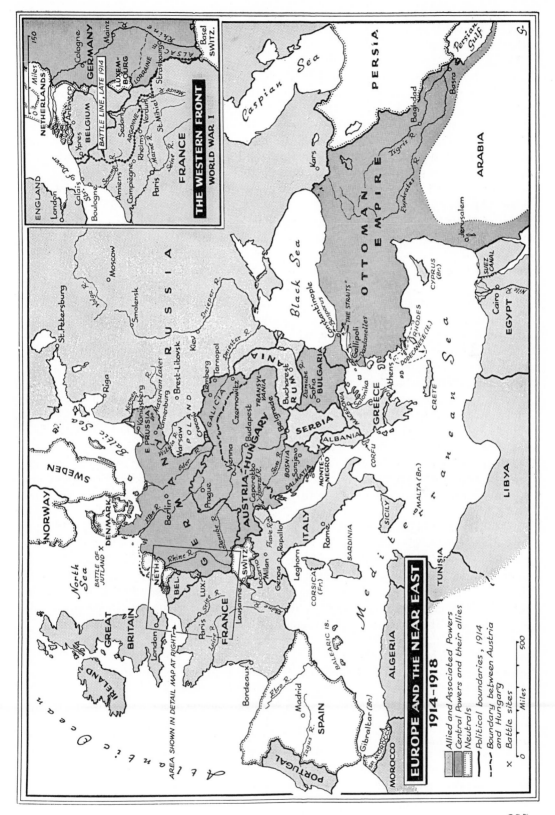

THE WESTERN FRONT
WORLD WAR I

EUROPE AND THE NEAR EAST
1914–1918

Allied and Associated Powers
Central Powers and their allies
Neutrals
Political boundaries, 1914
Boundary between Austria
and Hungary
× Battle sites

0   Miles   500

compelled King Constantine to abdicate in favor of his second son, Alexander.

Meanwhile Rumania, whom the Russians had been trying to lure into the war, finally yielded to promises of great territorial gains at the expense of Austria-Hungary and came in on the Allied side late in August, 1916, at a time most inopportune for the Rumanians. Stiffened by German help, the Austrians swept through Rumania and by January, 1917, held most of the country. When the Russians made the separate Peace of Brest-Litovsk with the Germans in March, 1918, the Rumanians were obliged to make cessions of territory to Bulgaria, and to grant a lease of oil lands to Germany.

In spite of the formal accession of Greece, the Macedonian front remained in a stalemate until the summer of 1918, when, with American troops pouring rapidly into France, the Allied military leaders decided they could afford to build up their forces in Salonika. The investment paid well, for under the leadership of the French general, Franchet d'Esperey, the Allied armies on this front were the first to break the enemy completely. The French, British, Serbs, and Greeks began a great advance on September 15, 1918, all along the line from the Adriatic to the Bulgarian frontier. They forced the Bulgarians to conclude an armistice on September 30, and by early November they had crossed the Danube in several places. The armistice in the west on November 11 found the tricolor of France, with the flags of many allies, well on its way to Vienna. This hark-back to Napoleon helped inspire in the French a somewhat unfounded confidence that they were once more the dominant nation on the continent of Europe.

The Near East and the Colonies

A whole series of fronts throughout the world was involved in what we may call the colonial "clean-up," the subduing of the German overseas empire and of the outlying parts of the Turkish Empire. The Turks, trained and in part officered by German experts, often resisted effectively. In Mesopotamia, in April, 1916, in a blow to British prestige as bad as the Dardanelles defeat, they forced the surrender of the British general, Townshend, who had landed at Basra from India in 1915 and had marched up the Tigris-Euphrates Valley. But the Turks were never able to take the Suez Canal, nor to advance far into Russian Armenia. Moreover, the British were able to play on the Arabs' dislike for their Turkish suzerains. In a series of desert campaigns the romantic Colonel T. E. Lawrence, an Englishman who knew the Arabs intimately, played a leading part. By the end of 1917, the British held Baghdad and Jerusalem. In September, 1918, a great British offensive in Palestine was so successful that on September 30 the Turks concluded an armistice which took them out of the war.

These campaigns, fought in the lands that had been the cradles of western civilization, were of great importance in making the world we live in today. For from them came not only the independent Arab nations (Syria, Lebanon, Iraq, Jordan, Saudi Arabia, Egypt) but also the Jewish national state of Israel, to which these Arab states are so hostile. In November, 1917, in the Balfour Declaration, the British promised "the establishment in Palestine of a national home for the Jewish people." This promise bore fruit in the mandate of 1922 from the League of Nations, by which such a state was set up under British protection under the name of Palestine.

In the overseas colonies the Germans, though cut off from the homeland by the British navy, fought well. In German East Africa they actually managed to hold out to the bitter end in a series of skillful campaigns, so that they still had forces in the field in East Africa on Armistice Day, 1918.

But elsewhere they were fighting with inadequate bases and with inadequate forces, so that by the end of 1914 the British, Australians, South Africans, French, and Japanese had pretty well taken over the German overseas possessions. The Allies had won the "colonial war." Only years later, however, did the most important result of that war become clear: the subject races had learned that their rulers were by no means invulnerable.

The War at Sea

This brings us to a most important front—the war at sea. In the long pull, British sea power, reinforced by the French and later by the Italian and the American navies, once more proved decisive. The Allied command of the sea made it possible to draw on the resources of the rest of the world, and in particular to transfer with surprisingly few losses large numbers of British and American troops to the crucial Western Front. Quite as important, sea power enabled the Allies to shut Germany and her allies off from overseas resources. The Allied blockade slowly but surely constricted Germany, limiting not merely military supplies for her armies, but food supplies for her civilian population. At the end of 1918, many Germans were suffering from malnutrition, an important factor in the German willingness to surrender without fighting to the bitter end.

Yet the war at sea was not easy for the Allies. The submarine, which the Germans had invested in heavily, proved every bit as dangerous as British alarmists before the war had feared. When the Germans launched their unrestricted submarine warfare, they made dangerous inroads on the merchant ships that were essential to the very life of Britain. By the end of 1917, some 8,000,000 tons of shipping had been sunk by the Germans, most of it by submarines. And at one point in 1917 the Brit-

ish had barely enough food reserves to last a month. The submarine menace was eventually overcome by a series of measures co-ordinated between the Allies and the Americans—extensive use of the convoy system, attack on the submarines by depth bombs, constant anti-submarine patrols, and development of small, fast "sub-chasers." But we might wonder what would have happened in 1916-1917 (and again in 1942-1943) if the Germans had contented themselves with holding actions on land and had put all their productive fighting energies into the submarine. This they did not do in either war. Temptation for quick land success was too great.

The navy of surface vessels that the Germans had built up since the 1890's—and that, as we have seen, was so important in the growth of Anglo-German hostility—never played a really decisive part in the war itself. German surface-raiders caused severe damage in the first year, but they were finally swept off the seas. Once, however, the main German fleet threw a very bad scare into the British. This was the famous Battle of Jutland, which has been refought over and over again by naval historians. Fought in the North Sea on May 31 and June 1, 1916, this running battle resulted in the sinking of twice as much British as German tonnage, and showed how good the German navy was. But the German admiral, Scheer, was forced to run into port before the British capital ships, for which he was no match. Although Jutland was a tactical victory for the Germans, the strategic victory remained with the British, for never again did the German surface navy seriously threaten British command of the sea in European waters. At the war's end the German high command attempted to get the fleet out in a heroic last stand. It was the German sailors' refusal to take the ships out—their mutiny, in fact—that gave a critical push to the German revolution which led to the Armistice of 1918.

Aerial dogfight during World War I.

The Western Front: Allied Victory

This war also saw the beginnings of air warfare. German lighter-than-air machines, the Zeppelins, raided London many times in 1916-1917, and both sides made airplane bombing raids on nearby towns. But the total damage was relatively light, and had no decisive effect on the final result. The airplane was of more importance in scouting, and especially in spotting for artillery; in spite of its short range in those days, it also proved useful as a means of locating submarines. The fighter plane was greatly improved during the war, and the base was laid for the development of the air forces we now know. Indeed, the airplane made greater strides in these four years of war than it had made since the Wrights first flew at Kitty Hawk in 1903.

Although the great new invention of the airplane did not itself alter traditional warfare, a new type of warfare was indeed developed, especially on the great Western Front, the warfare of the trenches. The machine gun, the repeating rifle, and fast-firing artillery, with the guidance of spotter planes, could pour in such deadly fire that it was almost impossible for either side to break through the opposing trench systems on a wide front. Both sides tried to break through in the two years after the Marne, and both sides suffered losses of a kind that had never been suffered before.

Two new weapons almost broke the deadlock. The first was poison gas, which was first used by the Germans in shells in October, 1914, with disappointing results. Then in April, 1915, the Germans used chlorine gas discharged from cylinders. The overwhelmed French broke in a line five miles wide, leaving the line completely undefended. But the Germans had not prepared to follow through, and the gap was closed once the gas had dispersed. Meanwhile the experts developed a simple countermeasure, the gas mask, which became part of the equipment of every soldier on both sides. The age-old balance of attack and defense was once again reestablished.

The second new weapon came much nearer to producing decisive success. This was the tank, a sort of armored land battleship for which plans had been made back in the Renaissance by the fertile Leonardo da Vinci. But Da Vinci's tank remained a mere sketch for lack of propulsive power. In the second decade of the twentieth century, however, the internal-combustion engine was ready to do what horses could not do. The tank was a British invention that had been nursed along in its infancy by the always adventurous Winston Churchill. But the new weapon was used too soon, in inadequate numbers and before adequate mechanical tests had been made, in the British Somme offensive of 1916. Even so, nine tanks led or accompanied the infantry triumphantly through the German lines to the capture of Flers. Had the tanks been withheld for a few more months, and backed up with careful planning, they might have broken the German lines on a wide front. The Germans naturally took up the tank at once, and were soon producing their own.

The technique of attack in the west gradually developed over the years, and in the end broke the defensive stalemate. Long and careful artillery preparation, known as a "barrage," literally flattened out a section of the enemy defenses and the "no man's land" in front of them, and forced the enemy to retire to rear trenches. Then, accompanied or preceded by tanks, the infantry edged in while the artillery barrage was lifted and focused on the next enemy line. It was a slow and costly process, which did not work on a wide scale until 1918. Then the Germans, with the Russians out of the fight, made a last and almost successful effort to break through, trying to separate the British from the French. With the failure of the last German push in the summer, Foch ordered a general attack. French, British, and American armies had all broken the German lines by early autumn, and were just gaining freedom of action in the open country when the Germans surrendered. The Germans later maintained that they were not beaten decisively in the field. Most experts, how-ever, now think that had the war gone on the Germans could not have stopped an Allied invasion in 1919.

Morale
on the Fighting Fronts

The long narrow battle lines of the four-year trench war were the scene of a concentrated destruction hardly equaled in the war of 1939-1945, except by the atomic bomb at Hiroshima; at some points in France the top soil was blown completely away by shellfire, producing a desert that is still visible today. The war, however, was not unique, unprecedented, or unlike all other wars, as many an excited publicist at the time declared. It produced military heroes and military scapegoats, great generals and generals who failed. As with the Confederacy in the American Civil War, the defeated Germans seem to have had the most-praised generals, the Ludendorffs, the Mackensens, the Hoffmanns. The old traditional chivalrous warfare, the warfare of athletic heroes, was continued, and even heightened in the air, where the "aces" of the highly individualistic duels between planes were the Rolands of a machine age. And in many of the fronts on land, and in the war at sea, the age-old melodrama of

A British one-man tank.

war lost none of its reality. Lawrence in Arabia was no disgrace to the tradition of Sir Walter Scott or even, in the eyes of good patriotic Englishmen, to the tradition of Homer.

Yet especially on the Western Front, this war seemed to many of its participants an unheroic nightmare of blood and filth. Sensitive young intellectuals, who in earlier times would never have had to fight, survived to write bitterly about their experiences—in war novels like *Under Fire*, by the Frenchman Barbusse, or *All Quiet on the Western Front* by the German Remarque, and in war poems like those of Siegfried Sassoon and Wilfred Owen. But this literature cannot be trusted fully as an accurate reflection of what the millions of common soldiers who were not intellectuals felt about the war. We know simply that they stood it in stints in the front lines separated by rest leaves for four years. But for most of them the dullness, the discomforts, and the brief terror of battle must have tested their patriotism and worn out their sense of adventure.

The Home Fronts

These soldiers and sailors were, for the most part, not professionals; they were civilians, "drafted," lifted from civilian families unused to the ways of the military. Behind the front, on the production lines, subject to the unheroic but harassing strains of rationing and all sorts of limitations in daily living, subject also to the constant prodding of war propaganda, the families too were part of this great "total war." They too stood it, though in France in 1917, after the bloody failure of a great offensive under General Nivelle, civilian and military discontent, fanned by politicians, came almost to the point of breaking French morale. And in Germany, the collapse that resulted in the armistice of November 11, 1918, though it obviously had many com-

London air-raid warning during World War I.

plex causes, looks like a general failure of morale, a psychological collapse under intolerable spiritual and material pressures.

For the Germans, still influenced by nineteenth-century ideas about the rights of the individual and laissez-faire economics, were slow to organize their society for total war. They failed notably to ensure the proper and equitable distribution of food supplies, so that as 1918 wore on whole sectors of the urban population began to suffer from malnutrition. Nor were finances and war production managed with that perfection of techniques that most of the world had already come to expect of the Germans. Rationing, strict control of production, price control, systematic use of the resources of conquered countries, these and many other measures were employed by the Germans, but not with the care, decisiveness, and long preparation that were to characterize them in the conflict of 1939-1945.

All countries engaged in the war, the democratic western Allies as well as the autocratic Central Powers, sooner or later felt obliged to introduce drastic wartime economic planning, which anticipated in some sense the more collectivistic economy of today. Everywhere there was compulsory military service. Even in Britain, proud of its long devotion to the rights of the individual, the famous Defense of the Realm Act—known with wry affection as DORA—clamped down severely on the Englishman's sacred right to say and do what he liked, even if he did not seem to be giving aid and comfort to the enemy. In the United States, all sorts of men, including the famous "dollar-a-year men," business executives who were working for the government for the first time, flocked to Washington and helped build up an enormous new central government, which regulated the economy as it had never been regulated before. And of course all the belligerents engaged in the war of propaganda, or, as it came to be called in the next great war, in psychological warfare.

The Allies won the battle of the production lines, in which the United States played a major if not a decisive part. We have already noted that in material resources the Allies had a marked potential superiority over the Central Powers; this superiority they were eventually able to realize to the full. Had the Germans not given up when they did, and had the Allies staged the all-out offensive in the west they had planned for the spring of 1919, it seems certain that they would have overwhelmed the Ger-

mans. Allied production was slow in getting started. There were mistakes, bottlenecks, and experiments like that of the tanks which failed at first because of undue haste. At the beginning the Allies were often at cross-purposes in production as well as in actual military strategy. Nevertheless, by the end of 1917 the Allied military machine was adequately, indeed in some ways wastefully, supplied.

The Role of Propaganda

The Allies also won the most critical phase of the war of propaganda. They sought to convince the neutral world, especially the neutrals of western civilization, the United States, Latin America, and the Swiss, Dutch, Scandinavians, and Spanish, that the Allies were fighting for the right and the Central Powers for the wrong. It was not a complete victory, for important groups in all these countries remained "pro-German" to the end, and Spain on the whole was probably throughout the war pro-German, or at least anti-French and anti-English. Still, it seems that a majority of the neutral West was early convinced that the cause of the Allies was just. This conviction was strengthened from the very start by the traditional liberalism of France and Britain in contrast with the traditional autocracy of the German and the Austrian empires, though the presence of the autocratic Russian Empire on the Allied side somewhat handicapped Allied propagandists. The conviction was greatly strengthened in the early days of the crisis of 1914 by the intransigence of the Austrians toward the Serbs, and in particular by the blundering phrase of Bethmann-Hollweg, that Britain had gone to war for a mere "scrap of paper."

The sense of Allied rightness was strengthened by early Allied propaganda, which was often one-sided and unfair. Notably, it accused the Germans of frightful atrocities in Belgium. The Germans did indeed impose rigorous military controls on conquered populations, but little in their record was worse than is usual, and perhaps inevitable, in all warfare. Allied propaganda also simplified and falsified the complex chain of causation that produced the war, making it appear that the Germans and the Austrians were wholly responsible for the outbreak of the war, that the "predatory Potsdam gang" had planned the whole thing from the beginning, and that Serbs, French, Russians, and British had been wholly innocent of deed or word that might have brought on the war. This propaganda backfired shortly after the war; revulsion against its unfairness had much to do with the widespread acceptance of the extreme revisionist thesis that on the whole

World War I poster, calculated to appeal both to Americans' patriotism and their anti-German sentiments.

Germany, in particular, had been quite guiltless of starting the war.

Political Repercussions

Except in Russia, the four years of war saw no major changes in political structure. The Central Empires retained until their collapse their incompletely responsible parliamentary governments, and the parliaments on the whole were reasonably submissive. And in spite of the inevitable strengthening of the executive in wartime, France, Britain, and the United States carried on their democratic institutions. In the United States the critical presidential election of 1916 came just before American entrance into the war, and resulted by a narrow margin in the return of the incumbent, Woodrow Wilson. In Britain and France the democratic process brought to power in the midst of wartime crisis two strong men—Lloyd George and Clemenceau—who carried through with great vigor the prosecution of the war, and who, though their fame was dimmed in the troubled years after the war, remain in historic memory as great national heroes of their respective countries.

In Britain the skillful but indecisive Liberal leader Asquith proved unable to master events, even though he widened his government into a coalition in May, 1915. In December of that year he was succeeded by another Liberal, Lloyd George, the architect of Britain's social insurance system (see Chapter XXI), who had also proven himself an admirable organizer of war production. Under Lloyd George the coalition really worked, and his position as war leader was to remain unchallenged. We shall meet him again at the peace negotiations, as we shall meet his French counterpart, Clemenceau. The "Tiger," as Clemenceau was known to his friends and enemies alike, came to power at the end of 1917, at a time when defeatism threatened both the military and the internal strength of France. Clemenceau took firm command of the war effort and disposed of the disaffected politicians with the decisiveness—and disregard for the peacetime "rights of man"—of an old Jacobin.

IV: The Peace Settlements

As in Westphalia in 1648, at Utrecht in 1713, and at Vienna in 1815, the warring powers gathered in a great meeting to make the peace settlement. This time they met at Paris—or, rather, in suburban Paris. They met at Versailles to settle with the Germans, at St. Germain to settle with the Austrians, at Neuilly to settle with the Bulgarians, at the Grand Trianon (in the park of Versailles) to settle with the Hungarians, and at Sèvres to settle with the Turks. But peace congresses almost never meet in a world that is really at peace. There are always aftermaths, local wars and disturbances, lesser diseases that follow the great bout of illness. The aftermaths of 1918-1919 were particularly numerous and acute, and conditioned the whole work of the peace congresses. To them we must turn briefly before we consider the actual settlements.

The Aftermath of World War

The sorest spot was Russia, now in 1919 in the throes of civil war and foreign invasion. No sooner had the Germans been forced to withdraw from the regions they had gained at Brest-Litovsk (see above, p. 393) than the Allies sent detachments to various points along the rim of Russia—on the Black Sea, on the White Sea in the far north, and on the Pacific (for details see Chapter XXVI). The Allies still hoped to restore in Russia, if not the monarchy, at least a moderate democratic republic. Their dread of final Bolshevik success (the term "Bolshevism" was then almost universally used, instead of communism) and of the possible spread of Bolshevism westward, added to the tensions at Versailles and confirmed the conservative position Clemenceau and Lloyd George were taking.

And Bolshevism was indeed spreading westward. The German revolution of November, 1918, had been carried out under socialist auspices. But all through the winter of 1918-1919 there were communist riots and uprisings, and in Bavaria in April a soviet republic was proclaimed. The government of the new republic of Germany put these communist uprisings down, but only by an appeal to the remnants of the old army and to officers thoroughly hostile to the new republic. In the break-up of the Austro-Hungarian monarchy in the autumn of 1918, the successor states—Czechoslovakia, Austria, Hungary, Yugoslavia, Rumania —which had been formed in whole or in part out of the former Habsburg lands, were disturbed by all sorts of social and economic troubles. In Hungary, Bela Kun, who had worked with Lenin in Moscow, won power by means of a socialist-communist coalition, and then elbowed out his socialist colleagues and set up a communist dictatorship. In August, a Rumanian army that had invaded Hungary forced Bela Kun to flee. Finally, all through the Germanies groups of ex-soldiers, the *Freikorps*, were roving about, stirring up trouble, and threatening the overthrow of the German Republic (for details, see Chapter XXVII).

In the Near East the Allies had even worse troubles to face. Greece, which had been so hard to drag into the war, was now in full cry against the Turks. Her nationalists had revived the old hope of a restored Byzantine Empire, with the Greeks once more in command of the Straits. Her armies, not without Allied encouragement, landed at Smyrna in Asia Minor in the spring of 1919 and marched off in the track of Alexander the Great. The French and the British, to whom control over different parts of the former Turkish Empire had been assigned, began at once having trouble with their new Arab subjects—or wards. The Jews were already pressing for the establishment of a national home in Palestine in accordance with the Balfour Declaration, and the Arabs were already opposing them.

In India the aftermath of war was bad indeed. The universal epidemic of influenza —actually a pandemic—in 1918 (which most public-health experts believed killed more people than were killed in battle) had been especially disastrous in India. Indians had fought well as professional soldiers during the war on the Allied side; educated Indians thought their country was ripe for much more self-rule. The disorders of 1918-1919 culminated in the Amritsar massacre of April, 1919, in which a British general, reverting to old-time methods, ordered his soldiers to fire on an unarmed crowd, killing or wounding some 1600 people. Amritsar shocked world opinion, added to the odium the Allies were already acquiring among liberals everywhere, and knitted India more closely together in opposition to the British. In China the weakening of Russia had been taken by the Japanese as a signal to renew their ambitious plans in the north of China, and indeed the American troops sent to Vladivostok in Siberia (see Chapter XXVI) were there less to oppose the Bolsheviks than to oppose the Japanese.

So the world was in turmoil and disorder when the Allies, great, small, and middle-sized, assembled in Paris to make the peace. The problems that faced the peacemakers were world-wide, complex, and often insoluble—insoluble in the sense that no decision on a given problem, say the disposition of the Adriatic port of Fiume which was claimed by Italians and Yugoslavs, could possibly satisfy all the major groups concerned, to say nothing of the minorities. Yet the world hoped, and indeed expected, from the peacemakers more than it had in any previous crisis. Public opinion in the eighteenth and nineteenth centuries had built up a tremendous faith in the possibility of a peaceful, just, and happy world. This war had been a war to "make the world safe for democracy," a "war to end war." It had produced in the American President Wilson a man who could phrase skillfully the hopes of men, and who as he journeyed to Paris after the Armistice appeared to be the heroic savior and hope of mankind.

These liberal dreams and expectations were, however, by no means the sole tenants of men's minds. All men were not Wilsonians. There were, inevitably, the selfish, the disillusioned, the narrow, the jingoists, and the professionals who had made promises to the Italians and the Rumanians, who had planned all sorts of compensations and adjustments. There were, more important, the plain ordinary men and women who wanted peace and security but who also wanted national glory and the punishment of the wicked Germans who, they believed, had put them through those four years of hell. There were, in short, thousands of conflicting hopes and fears, all of them embodied in living human flesh, not just the abstractions they must seem to be on the printed page.

The Fourteen Points

The more generous of these hopes were in 1918 clearly embodied in one man and in one text. Woodrow Wilson, on January 8, 1918, in an address to the American Congress, had announced the famous Fourteen Points, which were widely accepted by people in Allied and even in enemy countries as a platform for the peace to come, but were also widely misunderstood and subject to the most divergent interpretations. Here is the whole of this most important document:

I. Open covenants of peace, openly arrived at, after which there shall be no private international understandings of any kind but diplomacy shall proceed always frankly and in the public view.

II. Absolute freedom of navigation upon the seas, outside territorial waters, alike in peace and in war, except as the seas may be closed in whole or in part by international action for the enforcement of international covenants.

III. The removal, so far as possible, of all economic barriers and the establishment of an equality of trade conditions among all the nations consenting to the peace and associating themselves for its maintenance.

IV. Adequate guarantees given and taken that national armaments will be reduced to the lowest point consistent with domestic safety.

V. A free, open-minded, and absolutely impartial adjustment of all colonial claims, based upon a strict observance of the principle that in determining all such questions of sovereignty the interests of the populations concerned must have equal weight with the equitable claims of the government whose title is to be determined.

VI. The evacuation of all Russian territory and such a settlement of all questions affecting Russia as will secure the best and freest cooperation of the other nations of the world in obtaining for her an unhampered and unembarrassed opportunity for the independent determination of her own political development and national policy and assure her of a sincere welcome into the society of free nations under institutions of her own choosing; and, more than a welcome, assistance also of every kind that she may need and may herself desire. The treatment accorded Russia by her sister nations in the months to come will be the acid test of their good will, of their comprehension of her needs as distinguished from their own interests, and of their intelligent and unselfish sympathy.

VII. Belgium, the whole world will agree, must be evacuated and restored, without any attempt to limit the sovereignty which she enjoys in common with all other free nations. No other single act will serve as this will serve to restore confidence among the nations in the laws which they have themselves set and determined for the government of their relations with one another. Without this healing act the whole structure and validity of international law is forever impaired.

VIII. All French territory should be freed and the invaded portions restored, and the wrong done to France by Prussia in 1871 in the matter of Alsace-Lorraine, which has unsettled the peace of the world for nearly fifty years, should be righted, in order that peace may once more be made secure in the interest of all.

IX. A readjustment of the frontiers of Italy should be effected along clearly recognizable lines of nationality.

X. The peoples of Austria-Hungary, whose place among the nations we wish to see safeguarded and assured, should be accorded the freest opportunity of autonomous development.

XI. Rumania, Serbia, and Montenegro should be evacuated; occupied territories restored; Serbia accorded free and secure access to the sea; and the relations of the several Balkan states to one another determined by friendly counsel along historically established lines of allegiance and nationality; and international guarantees of the political and economic independence and territorial integrity of the several Balkan states should be entered into.

XII. The Turkish portions of the present Ottoman Empire should be assured a secure sovereignty, but the other nationalities which are now under Turkish rule should be assured an undoubted security of life and an absolutely unmolested opportunity of autonomous development, and the Dardanelles should be permanently opened as a free passage to the ships and commerce of all nations under international guarantees.

XIII. An independent Polish state should be erected which should include the territories inhabited by indisputably Polish populations, which should be assured a free and secure access to the sea, and whose political and economic independence and territorial integrity should be guaranteed by international covenant.

XIV. A general association of nations must be formed under specific covenants for the purpose of affording mutual guarantees of political independence and territorial integrity to great and small states alike.*

* Woodrow Wilson, *War and Peace: Presidential Messages, Addresses, and Public Papers*, R. S. Baker and W. E. Dodd, eds. (New York, 1927), I, 159-161.

The fourteenth point, the germ of the League of Nations, was especially dear to Wilson.

Opposing Hopes and Promises

The hopes and promises that opposed and contradicted the Fourteen Points were not neatly embodied in a single document. We may classify them roughly in three categories: the previous diplomatic commitments made by the Allies; the immediate and widespread popular hopes fanned by Allied propaganda and confirmed at the last moment by some Allied statesmen; and—much more difficult to pin down—the long-established habits and traditions that had become part of the dominant policies and trends of each nation, big and little.

In the first category, the most difficult of the diplomatic commitments was the contradictory set of promises made to both Italy and Serbia by the original Entente, including Russia, about the disposal of Habsburg lands. And there were other commitments, especially in the Balkans, that were very difficult to sort out. In the second category were the promises, widely believed by the British and French peoples, that Germany would be made to suffer to the full for her war guilt. She would have to pay the whole cost of the war in reparations, her war criminals would be punished, she would be rendered incapable ever again of assuming the role of the aggressor. In some vague way, everything would shortly be much better for everybody.

Finally, in the third category were the deeply rooted drives of the various nations—French drives for revenge against Germany, for restoration of French hegemony in Europe, and, no doubt inconsistently but very humanly, for security; the Italian Irredentist drive; the British longing for a Victorian serenity and economic leadership well armored against German commercial competition; and the nationalist aspirations of the new states of Central Europe that had at last been released from long frustration. And by no means the least important was the old and firmly held American tradition that Americans call "isolationism," the desire to be free from European alliances and entanglements.

The Process of Peacemaking

The Peace Conference met formally on January 18, 1919. Nearly thirty nations involved in the war against the Central Powers sent delegates. Russia was not represented. None of the victorious great powers—Britain, France, the United States—was in a mood to invite the Bolsheviks, now in power in Moscow, to the peace table; and no Russian government-in-exile was strong enough to get such an invitation. The defeated nations took no part in the deliberations; they were simply notified of the final terms and asked to sign. The Germans, in particular, were given but the slightest chance to comment on or criticize the terms offered them. Very soon the German publicists coined a term for the treaty—"*Diktat*," the imposed, the dictated peace. The Germans' anger over this failure of the Allies to negotiate with their new and virtuous republic was to play a large part in the ultimate rise of Hitler.

Although a few western liberals were from the first disillusioned by the exclusion of Communist Russia and the Central Powers from the Peace Conference, the conference did get off to a good start. Wilson's reception in Europe had been extremely enthusiastic. People everywhere were still rejoicing over the end of the nightmare. The Fourteen Points seemed already a realized peace; and for the future, it was held, the proposed association of nations, working together in the freedom of parliamentary discussion, would soon eleminate the costly burdens of armament. Wilson's hopeful phrases sounded in press and pulpit, and none more loudly than his "open covenants openly arrived at." To many a liberal these words meant that the peace would be made in a sort of big, idealized New England town meeting, in which the representatives of all the powers, big and little, would have their free say in public, in which decisions would ultimately be taken by majority vote, in which the caucus, the smoke-filled room, the backstairs intrigues would all be missing.

These liberals were almost at once disillusioned, for the conference soon fell into the familiar pattern of centuries. The small nations were excluded from the real negotiations; the business of the conference was carried on in private among the political chiefs of the victorious great powers—the Big Four of Wilson, Lloyd George, Clemenceau, and Orlando (it was really a Big Three, for Italy was not strong enough to impose her Orlando, who was a much less striking character than his colleagues). Decisions were made in the traditional way of diplomacy, with all the pressures, chicanery, intrigues, compromises, and plain horse-trading that go on when leaders get together in private. Public opinion was consulted only indirectly, as each statesman sought to make sure that he had at least a majority of the politically important elements of his own nation behind him in his demands.

The hopeful members of the general public were by no means the only ones who grew disillusioned as the Paris Conference went the way of the Vienna Congress a hundred years before. The professional diplomatists of the little and middle-sized powers had probably never really expected that they would be treated on equal terms, but the completeness of their exclusion from the real work of the conference annoyed them, and angered their people back home. More important, all the major powers had brought with them large staffs of experts, economists, political scientists, historians, career men in many fields. These bright young men were sure they knew better than their elders how to solve the problems of human relations, were confident that they would do the real work and make the really important decisions. They drew up report after report, some of which went up through devious channels to Clemenceau or Lloyd George or Wilson. But they did not make policy. The disillusion of

Paris crowd after the Armistice, 1918.

Lloyd George, Clemenceau, and Wilson in Paris during the peace negotiations, 1919.

the young experts was great and long-lived, and since many of them were quite articulate they did much to discredit the work of the conference, especially among liberal intellectuals everywhere.

Wilson and his experts were gradually badgered into accepting harsher peace terms. The reparations bill against Germany was lengthened; Poland, Italy, and Japan made claims to lands that clearly were not theirs; the victors more and more openly showed that they proposed to behave as victors in war habitually have behaved. Wilson gave way or compromised on a dozen points, and then chose to stand fast against the weakest of the Allies. He would not let the Italians have the Adriatic seaport of Fiume, which had once been the sole seaport of Hungary. They might have neighboring Trieste and their coveted Trentino, where they could rule over German or Slavic-speaking minorities, indeed,

in some areas, majorities; but Fiume they might not have. Fiume was indeed a difficult case. It was Italian-speaking and historically was linked with the great past of Venice; but it had never been part of modern Italy, and it had *not* been promised to Italy in the secret treaties of 1915. The Italian delegation left the conference in anger, but Wilson was immovable. The fate of Fiume was not settled at the conference; only in 1924, by treaty with Yugoslavia, did the city go to Italy in return for Susak, a port right next door that served the Yugoslavs quite adequately for the next two decades.

But Wilson did get his new international organization, the cornerstone of his plans for a better world. The covenant of the League of Nations was an integral part of the Treaty of Versailles. The League was no true supranational state, but a kind of permanent consultative system composed of the victors and a few neutrals. The way was left open for the Germans and the Russians to join the League, as they later did. But in 1919-1920 Wilson's League looked to many liberals a lot like Metternich's and Castlereagh's old Congress system of 1815, by no means worth the sacrifices Wilson had made to obtain it. The League had an assembly in which each member-state had one vote, and a council in which the five great powers (Britain, France, Italy, the United States, and Japan) had permanent seats, and to which four other member-states were chosen by the assembly for specific terms. A permanent secretariat, to be located at Geneva, was charged with administering the affairs of the League. In its working out, as we shall see (Chapter XXIX), the League never fulfilled the hopes of the liberals. It did not achieve disarmament, nor did its machinery of peacemaking prove capable of preventing aggression. The great powers simply went on their usual ways, using the League only as their policy-makers—their heads of state rather than their diplomatists—saw fit.

CHAPTER XXV

The Territorial Settlement

Central to all the work in Paris was the problem of territorial changes. Here, peacemakers were confronted not merely, as at most peace conferences in our western society, with the claims of the victorious Allies but also with the claims of the new nations that had sprung up from the disintegrating Austrian, Russian, and Turkish empires. They had to try to satisfy the eternal land hunger of those who run nations, without violating too obviously another great Wilsonian principle, the "self-determination of peoples." This principle was hard indeed to apply in much of Central Europe, where peoples of different language and national self-consciousness were mixed together in an incredible mosaic of unassimilated minorities (see map on p. 282). The result was to multiply the number of "sovereign" nations in this world. Nationalism, which some hopeful people had thought was on the wane, was now fanned to intense new life in a dozen states.

France received Alsace-Lorraine back from Germany. Clemenceau also hoped both to annex the small but coal-rich Saar Basin of Germany as compensation for French coal mines destroyed by the Germans during the war, and to detach from Germany the territory on the left (or west) bank of the Rhine, thereby strengthening French security and setting up a Rhineland republic that might become a French satellite. Both French hopes, opposed by Wilson and Lloyd George, went unrealized. The Saar was to be separated from Germany for fifteen years as an international ward supervised by the League of Nations. At the end of the fifteen-year period a plebiscite would determine its future status; meanwhile, its coal output was to go to France. The Rhineland remained part of the German Republic, though it was to be demilitarized and occupied for a time by Allied soldiers.

Belgium was given some small towns on her German border. Italy gained her Irredenta of Trent and Trieste, indeed in generous measure, for thousands of German and Slavic-speaking peoples were included within her new boundaries. Poland, erased from the map as an independent state in 1795, was now restored and given lands that she had had before the partitions of the eighteenth century and that contained important minorities of Germans and other non-Polish peoples. The old Habsburg Empire was entirely dismembered. The heart of its German-speaking area was constituted as the truncated Republic of Austria, which was forbidden to join itself to Germany, and the heart of its Magyar-speaking area became a diminished Kingdom of Hungary. The Czech-inhabited lands of Bohemia and Moravia were joined with Slovakia and the Ruthenian lands of the Carpatho-Ukraine further east in the brand-new "succession state" of Czechoslovakia. This new state faced the problem of a large and discontented Sudeten German minority.

Another "succession state" was Yugoslavia, officially the Kingdom of Serbs, Croats, and Slovenes, which, as its full name suggests, represented a great expansion of pre-war Serbia to include the south Slav territories of the Habsburgs. Rumania, too, profited by the break-up of the old dual monarchy by receiving the former Hungarian lands of Transylvania. Rewarded also with Bessarabia, a Russian province that the Bolsheviks could not defend, Rumania emerged with doubled territory. In the southern Balkan Peninsula, Greece received all of Thrace, at the expense of Turkey and Bulgaria.

Out of the former tsarist domains held at the end of the war by the Germans there were set up, in addition to Poland, the "Baltic republics" of Estonia, Latvia, and Lithuania. Once Europe had settled down, plebiscites were provided for to determine certain other territorial adjustments, notably whether certain parts of East Prussia

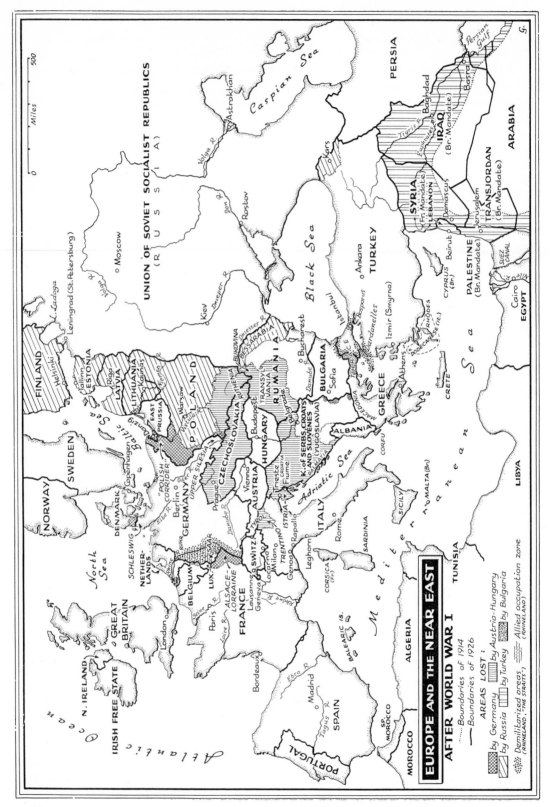

EUROPE AND THE NEAR EAST
AFTER WORLD WAR I

AREAS LOST:
Boundaries of 1914
Boundaries of 1926

by Germany | by Austria-Hungary
by Russia | by Turkey | by Bulgaria

Demilitarized areas, | Allied occupation zone
(RHINELAND, "THE STRAITS") | (RHINELAND)

and Silesia should go to Poland or remain German. The new Polish state had been granted access to the Baltic Sea through the so-called "Polish corridor," a narrow strip of land which had once been Polish, and which terminated in the almost wholly German city and port of Danzig. The Poles wanted Danzig, but the Allies compromised by setting up a Free City of Danzig and by giving the Poles free trade with the city. Even so, the Polish corridor now separated East Prussia from the rest of Germany, and Germans had to cross it in sealed trains.

Outside Europe, the Near East presented the most acute problems. By the Treaty of Sèvres the Turks were left in Europe with no more than Constantinople and a small strip of land around it, and in Asia with only their homeland of Anatolia. Mesopotamia and Palestine were given as mandates—a term we shall shortly explain —to Britain, while Syria and Lebanon were given as mandates to France. The Greeks were to hold Smyrna and nearby regions in Asia Minor for five years, and then submit to a plebiscite. But the Treaty of Sèvres never went into effect, though it was duly signed by the Sultan. In Anatolia a group of army officers led by Mustafa Kemal revolted against the government at Constantinople and galvanized the Turkish people into a new national life. The Turks drove the Greek army out of their country and set up a Turkish republic with its capital not at Constantinople but at Ankara in the heart of Anatolia. With this new government the Allies were finally obliged to conclude the Treaty of Lausanne in 1923. The new peace transferred the Smyrna area and eastern Thrace from Greek to Turkish control and was in general more advantageous to the Turks than the Treaty of Sèvres had been.

This treaty embodied in dramatic form a principle new in part in the West—the formal transfer of populations. True, peoples had been evicted by conquerors before; witness among other instances the eviction of the French Acadians from Nova Scotia by the British in the eighteenth century, or the settling of our Indians in Indian Territory, now part of the state of Oklahoma. But here was an almost complete exchange: Greeks in Turkey were moved to Greece, Turks in Greece were moved to Turkey. No very significant discontented national minorities were left. Each government was to take care of the transferred populations, and though much hardship occurred, on the whole the plan worked.

The Mandates

For the rest of the world the old straightforward annexing of the overseas territories of defeated powers, as practiced in 1713, 1763, and 1815, seemed no longer possible in 1919. Liberal opinion both in Europe and in America had already been offended to the bursting point, and Wilson himself would never have permitted outright annexations. The consequence was the mandate system, whereby control over a given territory was assigned to a particular power by the League of Nations, which undertook periodic inspections to see that the terms of the mandate were being fulfilled. This system was designed by its proponents as a means of educating colonial peoples, leading them into the ways of democratic self-government, and preparing them for eventual independence. Under it the former German overseas territories and the non-Turkish parts of the Ottoman Empire were now distributed. Of Germany's African possessions East Africa (now called Tanganyika) went to Britain; Southwest Africa went to the Union of South Africa; and both the Cameroons and Togoland were divided between Britain and France. In the Pacific, the German portion of New Guinea was given to Australia, western Samoa to New Zealand, and the Caroline, Marshall, and Mariana island groups to

Japan. In the Near East, as we have seen, France thus secured Syria and Lebanon, while Britain took Palestine and Mesopotamia.

The mandate system may seem to have been a way of disguising annexation, the hypocritical tribute of reactionary vice to progressive virtue. And so to a man like Clemenceau it probably was. The Japanese quite openly annexed and fortified their new Pacific islands in defiance of the terms of their mandate. But to many of the men who put through the idea of mandates the system really was what it professed to be, a nursery for eventual nationhood. For the most part the mandatory powers did make some show at least of treating mandated territories in a way that would prepare them for eventual freedom. And many of them are now indeed "free."

The Punishment of Germany

After land transfers, the most important business of the Peace Conference was reparations, which were imposed on Austria, Hungary, Bulgaria, and Turkey as well as on Germany. It was, however, the German reparations that so long disturbed the peace and the economy of the world. The Germans were made to promise to pay for all the damage done to civilian property during the war, and to pay at the rate of five billion dollars a year until 1921, when the final bill would be presented to them. They would then be given thirty years in which to pay the full amount. The amount was left indefinite at Versailles, for the Allies could not agree on a figure. But the totals suggested were astronomical. It was clear from the first that the payments would ultimately have to be in goods—German goods in competition with the goods of the Allies. A Germany prosperous enough to pay reparations could not be the weak and divided nation that men like Cle-

menceau really wanted. Thus from the very start the "realists" at Versailles—Lloyd George and Clemenceau—cherished quite inconsistent hopes for the future.

The Versailles settlement also required Germany to hand over many of her merchant ships to the Allies and to make large deliveries of coal to France, Italy, and Belgium for a ten-year period. Furthermore, a whole miscellany of articles in the treaty was directed toward the disarmament of Germany on land, on sea, and in the air. The German army was to be limited in size to 100,000 men, and the western frontier zone, extending to a line 50 kilometers (about 30 miles) east of the Rhine, was to be completely "demilitarized"—that is, to contain neither fortifications nor soldiers. In addition, the Allies could have armies of occupation on the left bank of the Rhine for fifteen years, and perhaps longer. The treaty forbade Germany to have either submarines or military planes and severely limited the number and size of surface vessels in her navy.

Last, and by no means least important, Article 231 of the Treaty of Versailles obliged Germany to admit that the Central Powers bore sole responsibility for starting the war in 1914. Here is the article that was to cause so much history to be written—and made:

The Allied and Associated Governments affirm, and Germany accepts, the responsibility of Germany and her allies for causing all the loss and damage to which the Allied and Associated Governments and their nationals have been subjected as a consequence of the war imposed upon them by the aggression of Germany and her allies.

The Settlement Evaluated

To the Germans, Versailles was of course a cruel and humiliating peace, the *Diktat*, the great national grievance on which Hitler was to play so skillfully. To liberals of the time and later it seemed an unsound, revengeful peace, above all disastrous in its unrealistic reparations policy. In our present world of cold and hot wars, Versailles almost arouses nostalgia. It was at least a settlement, and one that in the best moments of the 1920's seemed a basis for slow improvement in international relations (see Chapter XXIX).

The League it set up was potentially a means by which a new generation of international administrators might mitigate the old rivalries of nations. The reparations could be, and indeed were, scaled down to something more reasonable. The new succession states were based on a national consciousness that had been developing for at least a hundred years. Though the theorist might protest at the "Balkanization of Europe," the creation of more weak and discontented little states like those in the Balkans, the fact remains that it would have been hard to deny national independence, or at least autonomy, to the Czechs, the Poles, the Baltic peoples, and the south Slavs. Germany, though she certainly was not treated generously, was at least not wiped off the map, as Poland had been in the eighteenth century. She was not even actually demoted to a second-rate position in the world. She remained, as she was shortly to prove, a first-rate power. In the long series of settlements under our modern western state-system, which goes back to the Italian wars of the fifteenth century, Versailles looks nowadays like neither the worst nor the best, but like a typical compromise peace.

It was, however, too much for the American people, who were not used to the harsh needs of international compromise. But it is an oversimplification to argue that this was solely a matter of American idealism turning away in disgust from a settlement that was all too spotted with unpleasant realities. The final American refusal to ratify the Treaty of Versailles, like all great collective decisions, was the result of many forces. Politics certainly played an important part, for the Republicans had won control of both the Senate and the House of Representatives in the congressional elections of November, 1918. The President of course was still Wilson, a Democrat, and Wilson made no concessions to the Republicans either by taking a bipartisan delegation of Democrats and Republicans to Paris with him or by accepting modifications in the treaty which would have satisfied some of his Republican opponents. The Senate thereupon refused to ratify the treaty.

It is, however, extremely unlikely that even a much more pliable and diplomatic American president than Wilson could have secured from the Senate ratification of another important treaty involved in the proposed settlement. This was the project of a defensive alliance among France, Britain, and the United States into which Wilson had been pushed as part of the price of getting France to give up her proposals for a separate Rhineland republic and for annexation of the Saar. With the United States out, Britain refused a mere dual alliance with France against a German attack. France, still seeking to bolster her security, patched up a series of alliances with the new nations to the east and south of Germany—Poland, and the "Little Entente" of Yugoslavia, Czechoslovakia, and Rumania, a rather unsatisfactory substitute.

The peace thus left France with an uneasy hegemony in Europe, a hegemony dependent on the continued disarmament and economic weakening of Germany, on the continued isolation of Russia, and on the uncertain support of her new allies. Moreover, France had been disastrously weakened by the human and material losses of the war, and her position of leadership, though it alarmed the British with their long memories of French rivalry in the past, was an unreal thing. In reality, Germany was the strongest nation in Europe, and the Great War had checked, but not halted, her attempt to dominate the Continent and indeed the world. The next

German attempt was to draw both Britain and America back from the isolation into which they attempted to withdraw after the collapse of the system planned at Paris in 1919.

A most important matter, however, was not directly touched by the Versailles settlement: Russia, or the Union of Socialist Soviet Republics (U.S.S.R.), the formal name of the new communist state, did not figure in the great treaties. Yet in many senses the most important result of World War I was the emergence of this new-old Russia, her strength and capabilities in the long run increased by the stimulus of successful revolution.

Reading Suggestions
on the First World War

(Asterisk indicates paperbound edition.)

THE BACKGROUND: GENERAL ACCOUNTS

Q. Howe, *A World History of Our Own Times*, Vol. I (Simon & Schuster, 1949). Survey from 1900 to 1918 by a capable and opinionated publicist.

A. J. P. Taylor, *The Struggle for Mastery in Europe, 1848-1918* (Clarendon, 1954). A crisp and suggestive survey.

S. B. Fay, *The Origins of the World War*, 2nd ed. (Macmillan, 1932). A fully documented account by an American scholar; somewhat sympathetic to Germany.

B. E. Schmitt, *The Coming of the War, 1914*, 2 vols. (Scribner's, 1930). Another well-documented scholarly account; somewhat sympathetic to Britain.

H. E. Barnes, *The Genesis of the World War: An Introduction to the Problem of War Guilt* (Knopf, 1926). An extreme statement on the "revisionist" position on war guilt.

M. von Montgelas, *The Case for the Central Powers, An Impeachment of the Versailles Verdict* (Knopf, 1925). Representative of the German "revisionist" school.

L. Albertini, *The Origins of the War of 1914*, 2 vols. (Oxford Univ. Press, 1952-1953). By an Italian scholar; stresses the role of Italy.

N. Mansergh, *The Coming of the First World War* (Longmans, Green, 1949). A brief popular survey from 1878 to 1914.

THE BACKGROUND: SPECIAL STUDIES

W. L. Langer, *European Alliances and Alignments, 1871-1890*, 2nd ed. (Knopf, 1950). A detailed scholarly survey, favorable to Bismarckian diplomacy.

W. L. Langer, *The Diplomacy of Imperialism, 1890-1902*, 2nd ed. (Knopf, 1951). Includes much material pertaining to the shifting alliances of the European powers.

L. C. B. Seaman, *From Vienna to Versailles* (Coward-McCann, 1956). Interesting essay in interpretation by a young British scholar.

E. M. Carroll, *French Public Opinion and Foreign Affairs, 1870-1914* (Century, 1931), and *Germany and the Great Powers, 1866-1914: A Study in Public Opinion and Foreign Policy* (Prentice-Hall, 1938). Scholarly studies in a significant area of research.

R. J. S. Hoffman, *Great Britain and the German Trade Rivalry, 1875-1914* (Univ of Pennsylvania Press, 1933). A helpful monograph.

E. L. Woodward, *Great Britain and the German Navy* (Clarendon, 1935); A. J. Marder, *The Anatomy of British Sea Power* (Knopf, 1940); and B. Brodie, *Sea Power in the Machine Age* (Princeton Univ. Press, 1943). Three useful studies of the important question of naval power.

E. N. Anderson, *The First Moroccan Crisis, 1904-1906* (Univ. of Chicago Press, 1930), and I. C. Barlow, *The Agadir Crisis* (Univ. of North Carolina Press, 1940). Two useful monographs on the issue of Morocco in pre-war diplomacy.

E. M. Earle, *Turkey, The Great Powers, and the Bagdad Railway* (Macmillan, 1923). Scholarly account of another major issue of pre-war diplomacy.

A. F. Pribram, *Austrian Foreign Policy, 1908-1918* (Allen & Unwin, 1923). Balanced statement from the Austrian standpoint.

P. Renouvin, *The Immediate Origins of the War* (Yale Univ. Press, 1928). Scholarly account from the French point of view.

G. P. Gooch and H. Temperley, eds., *British Documents on the Origins of the War, 1898-1914*, 12 vols. (His Majesty's Stationery Office, 1926-1938). Representative of the great collections of diplomatic documents published by the governments of the major belligerents after World War I.

Outbreak of the World War: German Documents Collected by Karl Kautsky (Oxford Univ. Press, 1924), and *German Diplomatic Documents, 1871-1914*, 4 vols. (Methuen, 1928-1931). English translations of some of the vast number of German diplomatic documents.

THE BACKGROUND OF THE WAR: AMERICAN POLICY

T. A. Bailey, *A Diplomatic History of the American People*, 4th ed. (Appleton-Century-Crofts, 1950), and S. F. Bemis, *A Diplomatic History of the United States*, 3rd ed. (Holt, 1950). Two standard surveys.

W. Millis, *The Road to War: America, 1914-1917* (Houghton Mifflin, 1935). Readable journalistic account, highly critical of Wilson's policy.

C. C. Tansill, *America Goes to War* (Little, Brown, 1938). Scholarly treatment, also critical of Wilson's policy.

C. Seymour, *American Diplomacy during the World War*, 2nd ed. (Johns Hopkins Univ. Press, 1942). Sympathetic toward Wilson's policy.

THE WAR

W. S. Churchill, *The World Crisis*, 6 vols. (Scribner's, 1923-1931). Detailed survey by the famous British statesman.

C. R. M. Cruttwell, *History of the Great War* (Clarendon, 1934). Perhaps the best one-volume history.

J. E. Edmonds, *A Short History of World War I* (Oxford Univ. Press, 1951). A brief account by an official British military historian.

Note: There are many detailed military histories of World War I. The problems that arose on the home front have been the subject of a large number of special studies published under the auspices of the Carnegie Endowment for International Peace. Some idea of their scope may be had by consulting *Economic and Social History of the World War: Outline of Plan, European Series* (Carnegie Endowment for International Peace, 1924). Another useful collection of special studies has been published by the Hoover Institute of War, Revolution, and Peace at Stanford University.

THE PEACE

H. R. Rudin, *Armistice, 1918* (Yale Univ. Press, 1944). The standard monograph.

H. W. V. Temperley, *A History of the Peace Conference of Paris,* 6 vols. (Frowde, Hodder and Stoughton, 1920-1924). The standard detailed account; by a British scholar.

H. G. Nicolson, *Peacemaking, 1919* (Constable, 1933). A good shorter account; by a British expert on diplomacy.

P. Birdsall, *Versailles Twenty Years After* (Reynal & Hitchcock, 1941). Balanced reappraisal by an American scholar.

T. A. Bailey, *Wilson and the Peacemakers* (Macmillan, 1947). Sound study of America's role.

J. M. Keynes, *The Economic Consequences of the Peace* (Harcourt, Brace, 1920), and E. Mantoux, *The Carthaginian Peace; or, the Economic Consequences of Mr. Keynes* (Scribner's, 1952). Respectively, the most famous attack on the Versailles settlement and a thoughtful study of the results of that attack.

HISTORICAL FICTION

E. Childers, *The Riddle of the Sands* (Nelson, 1913), and H. H. Munro ("Saki"), *When William Came* (Lane, 1914). Two unusual novels, written before the outbreak of the war and predicting what it might be like. Childers' is a story of intrigue and adventure, and "Saki's" is a forecast of the German occupation of Britain.

J. Romains, *Verdun* (Knopf, 1939). Excellent and balanced novel about French troops on the western front, 1914-1916.

H. Barbusse, *Under Fire* (Dutton, 1917) and E. M. Remarque, *All Quiet on the Western Front* (Lion Books). Two famous novels, by a Frenchman and a German, respectively, reflect the horror aroused in intellectuals by trench warfare.

J. Dos Passos, *Three Soldiers* (Modern Library, 1941) and E. Hemingway, *A Farewell to Arms* (many editions). Two American novels about the war, indicative of the post-war disillusionment of the "lost generation."

e. e. cummings, *The Enormous Room* (Modern Library, 1941), and A. Zweig, *The Case of Sergeant Grischa* (Viking, 1928). Novels about prisoners of war and the eastern front, respectively.

C. S. Forester, *The General* (Little, Brown, 1947). Astringent novel about the "brass" in World War I.

J. Buchan, *Greenmantle* (Nelson, many eds.). A novel of espionage indicating that the war contained its ingredient of high adventure in addition to blood and guts.

What Price Glory? in M. Anderson and L. Stallings, *Three American Plays* (Harcourt, Brace, 1926). A famous play showing that the war had its rowdy side.

CHAPTER XXV

Communist Russia, 1917-1941

CHAPTER XXVI

I: Introduction

O N JUNE 22, 1941, Adolf Hitler's German armies poured over the frontier of his Russian ally and began a rapid advance toward Moscow, toward the major Russian industrial centers, and toward the most productive Russian agricultural centers. The Russia Hitler invaded was no longer the Russia into which Napoleon had sent the *grande armée* a hundred and twenty-nine years before or the Russia whose millions of embattled soldiers had perished in the First World War against the Germany of William II and his Habsburg allies. It was no longer the Russia of the tsars. Since 1917 it had been the Russia of the Bolsheviks. Yet it was still Russia.

Along with the tsars, the nobility and the bourgeoisie had gone down to ruin after the communist revolution of 1917, and the clergy as a class had suffered almost as much. A small, tightly knit, conspiratorial group of fanatical Marxist revolutionaries had seized power and for the next twenty-four years had striven to make Russia over. Drawn mostly from the peculiarly Russian class of the intelligentsia, and declaring themselves to be the representatives of the industrial proletariat, the Bolsheviks had worked gigantic changes, especially in the years after 1928. Industry, proceeding under forced draft, had expanded enormously, and the proportion of the population employed in industry had risen to almost 50 per cent; the proportion engaged in agriculture had also fallen correspondingly.

The peasant had been a victim of serfdom until 1861, had been subject to the initiative-destroying domination of the commune until 1906, and had then been encouraged by Stolypin to make himself a free farmer (see Chapter XXII). Now, under the Bolsheviks, he found himself subjected to new and grievous pressure. Agriculture had been collectivized and the age-old longing of the peasant for private property in land had been ruthlessly suppressed.

These staggering social and economic changes had not been accomplished without internal friction. Inside the government, personal rivalries, plots, counter-plots, fake plots, and charges of plots had produced repeated purges extending down through the ranks of the population. The choking conspiratorial atmosphere which the Bolshevik rulers had breathed during their long years of underground preparation for a seizure of power now enveloped the citadels of power. Personal rivalries for domination of the machinery of the state were cloaked beneath the Byzantine theological language of doctrinal controversy over fine points in the sacred writings of Marx and Lenin. Yet the controversies had immediate significance in the formulation and choice of government policies. The Communist party, the secret police, and the army had become the interlocking agencies which ran the state at the bidding of the dictator. The dictator himself, Stalin, had made his own career possible chiefly through the ruthless use of his position as Secretary of the Communist party.

The foreign policy of the communist state had passed through a brief period in which ideological considerations had seemed occasionally to outweigh national interest in the old sense. It had then returned to the pursuit of traditional Russian ends, coupled with the objective of promoting eventual world-revolution. But in furthering Russian aims abroad the Bolshevik leaders were now in possession of an instrument more flexible than any the tsars had ever commanded. This was the Communist International, or Comintern, a federation of the Communist parties in the individual countries of the world. These parties could often be used as promoters of purely Russian ends rather than strictly communist ends. With the shifting stresses and strains of international politics during the late 1920's and 1930's, the "line" of the Comintern shifted often and bewilderingly, but always in accordance with the aims of the Soviet foreign office. Usually the majority of communists elsewhere in the world fell meekly into position, and loudly proclaimed when necessary the opposite of what they had proclaimed the day before.

Yet the changes during the first twenty-four years of the Soviet period, vast though they were, could not conceal the continuities between the new Russian system and the old. The dictator of 1941, the revered leader of his people, for whom his followers made increasingly grandiose claims, was not unlike the tsar of 1917 in his assumption of autocratic power. The individual Russian of 1941, despite his sufferings under the new system, had remained deeply patriotic, ready to sacrifice himself for his country, even under a government he hated. The peasant of 1941 still yearned hopelessly for his land; the worker struggled for economic advancement and social security. Bureaucrats, managers, intellectuals, and artists, all in the service of the state, formed in 1941 a new élite which replaced but did not differ greatly from the old privileged class. A police force superior in efficiency to those of Ivan the Terrible, Peter the Great, and Nicholas I, but not different in kind, in 1941 exercised thought control over all citizens, and terrorized even prominent members of the system itself.

More and more, Stalinist communism

had taken on the trappings of a religion, with its sacred books, its heresies, its places of pilgrimage, its doctrinal quarrels. Thus the old Russian orthodoxy had by 1941 not been replaced but rather modified. Russian nationalism, too, asserted itself ever more insistently and crudely, until finally, in the war that Hitler began, the government encouraged the cult of traditional heroes of earlier times, and even glorified Ivan the Terrible himself, a symbol no longer of "feudal" domination but of the Russian national spirit. The early revolutionary departures from accepted standards in Russian marriage, family life, and education, had by 1941 all been abandoned in favor of a return to conventional bourgeois behavior. This chapter will trace in some detail the vast changes here summarized and will attempt to demonstrate the survival of the old Russia beneath the veneer of the new.

II: The Russian Revolution of 1917

The Immediate Background

Ridden by domestic crisis though Russia was in 1914 (see Chapter XXII), the country greeted the outbreak of World War I with demonstrations of national patriotism. The Duma supported the war, and did yeoman service in organizing Red Cross activities. The left-wing parties—the radical agrarian SRs (Social Revolutionaries) and the Marxist SDs (Social Democrats)—abstained from voting war credits, but offered to assist the national defense. By 1917 more than 15,000,000 Russians had been drafted into the armies. Losses in battle were staggering from the first; the Russians suffered more than 3,800,000 casualties during the first year of war. On the home front, criticism was aroused by the inadequate handling of the supply of munitions, and by mid-1915 the Center and Left groups in the Duma were urging moderate reforms, such as the end of discrimination against minority nationalities and an increase in the powers of the *zemstvos*, the local assemblies. The Empress Alexandra took the lead in opposing all such measures, and kept urging her weak husband, Tsar Nicholas II, to act more autocratically. When Nicholas took personal command of the armies in the field and prorogued the Duma (autumn, 1915), she became virtually supreme at home. The supremacy of the Empress meant also the supremacy of her favorite, the unscrupulous adventurer Rasputin.

With the Empress and Rasputin in con-

Rasputin.

trol, a gang of shady adventurers, black-mailers, and profiteers bought and sold offices, speculated in military supplies, put in their own puppets as ministers, and created a series of shocking scandals. Confusion, strikes, and defeatism mounted at home during 1916, while the armies slowly bled to death at the front. Even the conservatives had begun to denounce Rasputin publicly, and in December, 1916, he was poisoned, shot several times, and ultimately drowned, all in one nightmare evening, by a group of conspirators closely related to the imperial family. Despite repeated warnings from moderates in the Duma that the government itself was preparing a revolution by its failure to create a responsible ministry and to clean up the mess, the Tsar remained apathetic. Relatives of the imperial family and members of the Duma began independently to plot for his abdication. In the early months of 1917 all conditions favored a revolution, but the revolutionaries were not prepared.

The March Revolution

On March 8, strikes and bread-riots broke out in the capital, and four days later Romanov rule, which had governed Russia since 1613, was doomed. Yet this revolution of March, 1917, has been well called leaderless, spontaneous, and anonymous. SRs and both Bolshevik and Menshevik factions of SDs (see above, p. 303) were genuinely surprised at what happened. Indeed, the Bolshevik leaders were either abroad in exile, or under arrest in Siberia. The determining factor in the overthrow of the Tsar was the disloyalty of the garrison of Petrograd (the new Russian name given to St. Petersburg during the war). Inefficiency had led to a food shortage in the capital, though actual starvation had not set in. When the Tsar ordered troops to fire on striking workers, only a few obeyed, and on March 12, in revulsion against the order, the troops joined the strikers, broke into the

arsenals, and began to hunt the police, who quickly disappeared from the scene. The Duma lagged behind the revolting troops and workers in estimating the situation, and the Tsar lagged behind the Duma. By March 14, when the Tsar had finally decided to appoint a responsible ministry, it was too late; the cabinet had vanished. Troops ordered to put down the revolt simply melted away and joined the rebels.

A Soviet of workers and soldiers, modeled on the 1905 Soviet of workers (see above, p. 306), but now including soldiers as well, was formed by leftists released from prison by the enthusiastic mobs. The Soviet proceeded to organize a workers' militia, to create a food-supply commission, and to issue newspapers. Its fifteen-man executive committee became the policy-makers of the revolution. The Soviet located its headquarters across the hall from the Duma, which had not dissolved as ordered, but remained in session. The Marxists among the Soviet leaders still believed in the necessity of a preliminary bourgeois revolution, and did not yet regard the Soviet itself as an organ of power. They favored the creation of a provisional government, in which they would not participate, but to which they would offer limited support. They put themselves at the disposition of the Duma, and asked that it temporarily run the country. Thus the Duma, a limited assembly elected by a restricted franchise, was literally forced by the Soviet into the position of leading the revolution.

Negotiations between the Soviet and a Duma committee brought a provisional government into existence. Despite the widely differing social and economic aims of Soviet and Duma, both agreed to grant political liberties immediately and to summon a constituent assembly, which was to establish the future form of government by giving Russia a constitution. The provisional government was composed mainly of Kadets (Constitutional Democrats) and other moderates and was headed by the

Russia in revolution. Workers and soldiers invade the Duma.

liberal Prince Lvov, chairman of the union of *zemstvos* and of the Red Cross. It included also one radical member of the Soviet, Alexander Kerensky, Minister of Justice, a clever labor lawyer and member of the Duma also, who accepted office despite the understanding that members of the Soviet would not do so.

After some abortive efforts to save the dynasty in the person of the Tsar's brother, Nicholas finally abdicated, and his brother refused the throne because of the popular hatred of the family. Under pressure from the Soviet, the provisional government arrested Nicholas II and the Empress on March 20. The Duma had thus accepted the mandate given it by the revolutionaries. Had it accepted instead its dismissal at the hands of the Tsar and gone home, it seems probable that the monarchy would have been preserved at the cost of some liberal concessions. But moderate reformers were now in power, and Russia embarked on the troubled months between March and October, 1917.

The Provisional Government

The provisional government is usually regarded as having been a total failure.

Measured by the final results, such a view is perhaps justified. But the judgment of history must take into consideration the dreadful difficulties that faced the provisional government. These were not only immediate and specific, but general and underlying. Russian moderates had had no experience of authority. They were separated by a great cultural gulf from the lower classes. Their opportunity to rule now came to them in the midst of a fearful war, which they felt they had to pursue while reconstructing and democratizing the enormous and unwieldy Russian Empire.

Moreover, the Soviet possessed many of the instruments of power, yet refused to accept any responsibility. Workers and soldiers in the capital supported the Soviet, while in the provinces the new governors appointed by the provisional government had no weapon except persuasion to employ against the local peasant-elected soviets, which multiplied rapidly. Present-day critics of the provisional government often denounce its failure to suppress its revolutionary opponents, but they overlook the fact that the provisional government did not possess the tools of suppression. The Petrograd garrison, for instance, by agreement with the Soviet, could not be removed or disarmed. The support given by the Soviet to the provisional government has been compared to the kind of support that is given by a hangman's noose.

The two great specific issues facing the provisional government were agrarian discontent and the continuation of the war. The peasants wanted land, and they wanted it immediately. The provisional government, however, made up as it was of responsible liberals, believed in acting with deliberation and according to law. It refused to sanction peasant seizure of land, despite increasing disorder in the countryside. Instead, it appointed a commission to collect material on which future agrarian legislation was to be based—an act totally inadequate to the emergency.

As to the war, the members of the government felt in honor bound to their allies not to make a separate peace. Moreover, most of them still unrealistically hoped that Russia might win, and gain the territories which the Allies had promised. But the Soviet subverted discipline in the armies at the front by issuing a "declaration of the rights of soldiers," which virtually put an end to the authority of officers over enlisted men. Although the Soviet made it as hard as possible for the government to pursue the war, it did not sponsor a separate peace. Even the Bolshevik members of the Soviet, who now began to return from exile, demanded only that Russia participate in general peace negotiations, which, they urged, should begin at once.

Lenin and Bolshevism

The most important of the returning Bolshevik exiles was Lenin. His real name was Vladimir Ilyich Ulianov, but in his writings he used the pen-name Lenin, to which he sometimes prefixed the initial N., a Russian abbreviation for "nobody," in order to tell his readers that he was using a pseudonym. This "N." has given rise to the mistaken but still widely held idea that Lenin's first name was Nikolai (Nicholas). Son of a provincial official and intellectual, Lenin became a revolutionary in the late 1880's and, as we have already seen (p. 303), took a chief role in the early years of the SDs as the leader of the party's Bolshevik wing. He had returned to Russia from abroad for the Revolution of 1905, but he left Russia once more in 1908, and stayed abroad until 1917.

When the news of the March Revolution reached Lenin in Switzerland, he made desperate efforts to get back home. Finally, through the Swiss Social Democrats, he made contact with the German general staff, which felt that it would be a good investment to see that Lenin reached Russia, where he might disrupt the Russian war effort against Germany. Thus it was that the German military transported Lenin across Germany from Switzerland to the Baltic in the famous sealed railroad car. He arrived at the Finland Station in Petrograd on April 16, 1917, a little more than a month after the March Revolution.

Most Russian Social Democrats had long regarded a bourgeois parliamentary republic as a necessary preliminary to an eventual socialist revolution and socialist society. For this reason they were prepared to help in transforming Russia into a capitalist society, though not without grave doubts that the bourgeois capitalists might be as bad as the tsar and the landlords, or that the masses might be "deluded" into accepting the new system. They favored the creation of a democratic republic, at the same time believing that complete political freedom was absolutely essential for their own future rise to power. Despite the Marxist emphasis upon the industrial laboring class as the only proper vehicle for revolution, Lenin early realized that in Russia, where the "proletariat" embraced only about 1 per cent of the population, the SDs must seek other allies. At the time of the Revolution of 1905 he began to preach the need for limited alliances for tactical purposes between the Bolsheviks and the SRs, who commanded the support of the peasantry. When the alliance had served its purpose, the SDs were to turn on their allies and destroy them. Then would come the socialist triumph.

Instead of a preliminary bourgeois democratic republic, Lenin called in 1905 and later for an immediate "revolutionary-democratic dictatorship of the proletariat and the peasantry," a concept that seems to us self-contradictory, and is surely vague. Lenin's view, however, was not adopted by most Bolsheviks. Together with the Mensheviks they continued to believe and urge that a bourgeois revolution and a parliamentary democracy were necessary first steps.

Because Lenin did not trust the masses to make a revolution (by themselves, he felt, they were capable only of "trade-union consciousness"), he favored a dictatorship of the Bolshevik party over the working class. Because he did not trust the rank and file of Bolshevik party workers, he favored a dictatorship of a small élite over the Bolshevik party. And in the end, because he really trusted nobody's views but his own, he favored, though never explicitly, his own dictatorship over this élite. Another future Russian leader, the brilliant intellectual Leon Trotsky, early warned that in Lenin's views one-man dictatorship was implicit.

Trotsky, for his part, voiced an opinion of his own, held by neither Mensheviks nor Bolsheviks. The bourgeoisie in Russia, he argued, was so weak that the working class could telescope the bourgeois and socialist revolutions into one continuous movement. After the proletariat had helped the bourgeoisie achieve its revolution, he felt that the workers could move immediately to power. They could nationalize industry and collectivize agriculture, and, although foreign intervention and civil war were doubtless to be expected, the Russian proletariat

would soon be joined by the proletariats of other countries, which would make their own revolutions. Except for this last point, Trotsky's analysis accurately forecast the course of events. Between 1905 and 1917, Lenin himself accepted Trotsky's view from time to time, but warned that it endangered political democracy.

Lenin had been deeply depressed by the failure of 1905, and by the threat posed by Stolypin's agrarian reforms. He almost despaired when the socialist parties of Europe went along with their governments in 1914 and supported the war. To him this meant the end of the second socialist International, for the Social Democrats had failed to recognize the war as the "bourgeois-imperialist" venture that it appeared to Lenin to be. He preached defeatism as the only possible view for a Russian SD to follow.

Lenin's greatest talent was not as an original thinker but as a skillful tactician. He often seemed able to judge with accuracy just what was politically possible in a given situation, and he was not afraid to gamble. Thus, even before he returned to Russia in April, 1917, he had assessed some of the difficulties facing the provisional

Lenin.

government, and had determined that the masses could take over. Immediately upon his arrival, he hailed the world-wide revolution, proclaiming that the end of imperialism, "the last stage of capitalism," was at hand. Ignoring the positions previously taken by Bolsheviks and Mensheviks alike, he demanded now that all power immediately be given to the soviets. His speeches sounded to the SDs themselves like the ravings of a madman.

Almost nobody but Lenin felt that the loosely organized soviets could govern the country, or that the war would bring down the capitalist world in chaos. In April, 1917, Lenin called not only for the abandonment of the provisional government and the establishment of a republic of soviets but for the confiscation of estates, the nationalization of land, and the abolition of the army, of government officials, and of the police. These demands fitted the mood of the people far better than the cautious and well-meant efforts of the provisional government to bring about reform by legal means. Dogmatic, furiously impatient of compromise, entirely convinced that he alone had the truth, Lenin galvanized the Bolsheviks into a truly revolutionary group waiting only the moment to seize power.

The Coming of the November Revolution

The months from March to November, 1917, before the Bolsheviks came to power, can be divided into a period between March and July, during which revolution deepened, a feeble reaction from July to September, and a new quickening of the revolutionary current from September to the final uprising in November. In the first period, the government faced a crisis, because the Kadet ministers wished to maintain the Russian war aim of annexing the Straits, while the Soviet wanted a peace "without annexations or indemni-

ties." Out of the crisis Kerensky, now war minister, emerged as the dominant leader. He failed to realize that it was no longer possible to restore the morale of the armies, which were dissolving under the impact of Bolshevik propaganda. A new offensive ordered on July 1 collapsed, as soldiers refused to obey orders, deserted their units, and rushed home to their native villages, eager to seize the land. Ukrainian separatism also plagued the officials of the government. The soviets became gradually more and more Bolshevik, as Lenin and Trotsky worked tirelessly at recruitment and organization. Although the June congress of soviets in Petrograd was less than 10 per cent Bolshevik in make-up, the Bolshevik slogans of peace, bread, and freedom won overwhelming support.

Yet an armed outbreak by troops, who had accepted the Bolshevik slogans, found the Petrograd Soviet unwilling and unable to assume power. While the mob roared outside, the Soviet voted to discuss the matter two weeks later and meanwhile to keep the provisional government in power. A regiment loyal to the Soviet protected it against the working class! The government declared that Lenin was a German agent, and, as his supporters wavered, raided the newspaper offices of *Pravda* ("Truth," the Bolshevik paper); Lenin had to go into hiding to avoid arrest. This episode of mid-July is what is known among Bolsheviks as "playing at insurrection." Though shots had been exchanged and overt action had been embarked upon, there had been no revolutionary follow-through. Power had not been seized, probably because Lenin felt that the Bolsheviks did not have enough support in the provinces.

Now Kerensky became premier. The government hardened its attitude toward the Ukrainians, but could not come to a popular decision on either land or peace. General Kornilov, chosen by Kerensky as the new commander-in-chief of the armies, quickly became the white hope of all conservative groups, and in August plotted a *coup,* intended to disperse the Soviet. His attitude toward the provisional government was uncertain, but, had he succeeded, he would probably have demanded a purge of its more radical elements. The plot, however, was a failure, because railroad and telegraph workers sabotaged Kornilov's movements, and because his troops simply would not obey him. The Bolsheviks, adopting the slogan "We will fight against Kornilov, but will not support Kerensky," threw themselves into preparations for the defense of Petrograd, which proved to be unnecessary. By September 14, Kornilov had been arrested, and the affair ended without bloodshed. The threat from the Right helped the Bolsheviks greatly, and sentiment in the Petrograd and Moscow soviets now for the first time became predominantly Bolshevik.

The Kornilov affair turned the army mutiny into a widespread revolt. Instances of violence multiplied. As peasants refused to pay rent, pastured their animals on the landlords' land, and often burned the manor house and killed its owner, so the soldiers moved from disobedience to the murder of their officers. Orderly and legal reform had attracted nobody. The peasants could not be convinced that the nobility owned less than a quarter as much land as the peasants, and that rash action only retarded progress. As disorder mounted in the countryside, the Bolsheviks tightened their hold over the soviets in the cities.

Lenin returned to Petrograd on October 20, soon thereafter the Bolsheviks got control over a Military Revolutionary Committee, originally chosen to help defend Petrograd against the advancing Germans, and now transformed, under the guidance of Trotsky, into a general staff for the revolution. Beginning on November 4, huge demonstrations and mass meetings were addressed by Trotsky, and on November 7 the insurrection broke out.

In Petrograd, the revolution had been well prepared and proceeded with little bloodshed. Kerensky escaped in a car of the American Embassy. The Military Revolutionary Committee, as an organ of the Petrograd Soviet, simply took over. The Bolsheviks called a second congress of soviets, and when the Mensheviks and right-wing SRs walked out, Trotsky called them the refuse that would be swept into the garbage-can of history. Co-operating with the left-wing SRs and adopting their land program, Lenin abolished all property rights of landlords and transferred the land thus affected to local land committees and soviets of peasant deputies. Though Lenin did not in the least approve of the system of individual small holdings which this decree put into effect, he recognized the psychological advantage which the adoption of the SR program would gain him. He also urged an immediate peace without annexations or indemnities, and appealed to the workers of Germany, France, and England to support him in this demand. Finally, a new cabinet, called a Council of People's Commissars, was chosen, with Lenin as President, and Trotsky as Foreign Commissar.

As Commissar of Nationalities the Bolsheviks installed a younger man, a Georgian, named Joseph Djugashvili, who had been a successful organizer of bank rob-

Kerensky (in car) reviewing troops.

Bolshevik sailors firing on civilians, Petrograd, July 3, 1917.

beries in the days when the party treasury was filled in this way, but whose role had otherwise been relatively obscure. He had taken the name Stalin, which suggests a steel-like hardness. Under Lenin's coaching, Stalin had also become the party authority on minority questions and had published a pamphlet on the subject in 1913.

Outside Petrograd, the revolution moved more slowly. In Moscow there was a week of street-fighting between Bolshevik Reds and Whites, as anti-Bolshevik forces were already known. Elsewhere, in factory towns, the procedure was usually fast, in non-industrial centers usually slower. Most of Siberia and of Central Asia came over, but Tiflis, the capital of Georgia, went Menshevik and passed resolutions calling for a constituent assembly and the continuation of the war. The reason for the rapid and smooth success of the Bolsheviks was that the provincial garrisons opposed the war and willingly allied themselves with the workers. Local Military Revolutionary Committees were created in most places and held elections for new local soviets. Naturally there was much confusion at first, but surprisingly little resistance to the

consolidation of the authority of the new regime. Gradually the town of Rostov-on-Don, near the Sea of Azov, became the main center of resistance, as Kornilov and other generals, together with a number of the leading politicians of the Duma, made their way there.

This initial triumph of the revolution did not mean that the population of Russia had been converted to Bolshevism. By cleverly sensing the mood of the people, Lenin had opportunistically given the Bolsheviks a set of slogans around which the people could rally, although some of the slogans did not at all correspond with the true Bolshevik views. As we shall shortly see, the Russian people was in fact strongly anti-Bolshevik. But the Bolsheviks had triumphed, and the democratic hopes for freedom of the press and other freedoms were now doomed to disappointment.

Deprived of competent civil servants, the new regime worried along through an atmosphere of continued crisis. Late in November, 1917, an agreement was reached with the Left-Wing SRs, three of whom entered the government, and peace negotiations were begun with the Germans. The

CHAPTER XXVI

revolution proper was over. Lenin was in power.

The Constituent Assembly

It is of great interest to record that the Bolsheviks now permitted elections for a constituent assembly. Lenin had no use for this sort of democratically chosen parliament, which he considered "inferior" to the soviet. Yet, probably because he had so long taunted the provisional government with delaying the elections, he seems to have felt compelled to hold them. The Russians for the first and last time in their history had a completely free election, under universal suffrage. Lenin himself accepted as accurate figures showing that the Bolsheviks polled about one-quarter of the vote. The other socialist parties, chiefly the SRs, polled 62 per cent. As was to be expected, the Bolshevik vote was heaviest in the cities, especially Moscow and Petrograd, while the SR vote was largely rural.

Disregarding the majority cast for his opponents, Lenin maintained that "the most advanced" elements had voted for him. It was of course only his opinion that made those who had voted Bolshevik more "advanced" than those who had voted SR or Kadet. He allowed the constituent assembly to meet only once, on January 18,

1918. Lenin dissolved it the next day by decree, and sent guards with rifles to prevent its ever meeting again. The anti-Bolshevik majority was naturally deeply indignant at this pure act of force against the popular will, but there was no public outburst, and the delegates disbanded. In part, this was because the Bolsheviks had already taken action on the things that interested the people most—peace and land—and in part because of the lack of a democratic parliamentary tradition among the masses of the Russian people.

In spite of the many years of agitation by intellectuals and liberals for just such a popular assembly, Russia did not have the large middle class, the widespread literacy, the tradition of debate, and the respect for the rights of the individual which seem to be an essential part of constitutionalism. Yet it is surely extreme to decide that there was no chance for constitutional government in Russia in 1917-1918. Was the constituent assembly "an attempt to transplant an alien concept of government to a soil where it could never flourish"? Or was it "a noble experiment incorporating a sound principle but doomed by the crisis into which it was born"? The fact that Lenin had the rifles to prevent the constituent assembly from fulfilling the function which the popular will had assigned to it does not answer the question either way.

III: War Communism and NEP, 1917-1928

War Communism

The first period of Soviet history, which runs from the end of 1917 to the end of 1920, is usually called the period of "war communism," or "military communism." The term itself of course implies

that the main features of the period were determined by military events. Civil war raged, and foreign powers intervened on Russian soil. But the term is also somewhat misleading. This was a period of militant as well as military communism, symbolized early in 1918 by the change of the party's name from Bolshevik to Communist. At the same time the capital was shifted from Petrograd, with its exposed location on the western fringe of Russia, to the greater security of Moscow, in the heart of the country.

Flushed with victory in Russia, the Bolsheviks firmly believed that world-revolution was about to begin, probably first in Germany, but surely spreading to Britain and even to the United States. This view led the Bolsheviks to hasten the construction of a socialist state in Russia, and to take a casual attitude toward their international affairs, since they expected that relation with capitalist states would be very temporary. Although the actions of the Russian government during this period were later described almost apologetically as emergency measures, this is only partly true. Many of the decisions that were taken in part under the spur of military pressure were also regarded as leading to a new society.

A supreme economic council directed the gradual nationalization of industry. Sugar and petroleum came first, and then in June, 1918, a large group including mines, metallurgy, and textiles was nationalized. By 1920, all enterprises employing more than ten workers (more than five, if motor power was used) had been taken over by the state. The state organized a system of barter, which replaced the free market. Internal trade was illegal; only the government food commissary could buy and sell; money disappeared as the state took over distribution as well as production. It appropriated the banks, repudiated the tsarist foreign debt, and in effect wiped out savings. Church and State were separated by decree, and judges were removed from office and replaced by appointees of the local soviets.

The government subjected the peasantry to ever more arbitrary and severe requisitioning. It mobilized the poorer peasants against those who were better off, called *kulaks* (from the word meaning "fist" and

used to apply to usurers, as if to say "hard-fisted"). By calling for a union of the hungry against the well-fed, the regime deliberately, and not for the last time, sowed class hatred in the villages and stimulated civil war in the countryside. It should be remembered that by western European standards even a Russian *kulak* was often wretchedly poor. The decree forming the first secret police, the "Cheka" (from the initials of the words meaning "extraordinary commission"), was issued in December, 1917, only a few weeks after the revolution and long before any intervention from abroad. Terror became a weapon in the civil war.

Before the Communist government could function at all, peace was necessary, as the army had virtually ceased to exist. Negotiations between the Russians and the Germans and Austro-Hungarians at Brest-Litovsk dragged on into 1918, the Russians hoping that revolution would break out in Germany, and the Germans demanding enormous territorial cessions, which they increased as the Russians delayed. Finally, on March 3, 1918, the Russians signed the Peace of Brest-Litovsk, which deprived them of the entire Ukraine, the Baltic provinces, Finland, and some Caucasian lands. It cost Russia one-third of its population, 80 per cent of its iron, and 90 per cent of its coal. Many communists resigned rather than accept the peace, and the Left SRs quit the government. The Germans overran the Ukraine and the Crimea, and installed a highly authoritarian regime, against which the communists continued to agitate. The Whites, with German help, put down the Reds in Finland.

Civil War

During the months following Brest-Litovsk, disorder in the countryside as a result of requisitioning and class warfare was swelled by the outbreak of open civil

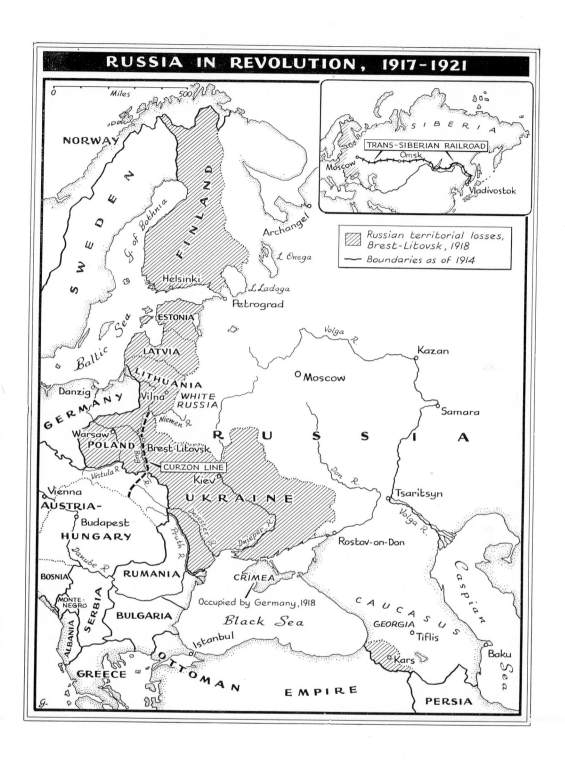

RUSSIA IN REVOLUTION, 1917-1921

TRANS-SIBERIAN RAILROAD

Moscow · Omsk · Vladivostok

SIBERIA

Russian territorial losses,
Brest-Litovsk, 1918
Boundaries as of 1914

Miles
0   500

NORWAY

SWEDEN

FINLAND

G. of Bothnia

Archangel

L. Onega

Helsinki

L. Ladoga

Baltic Sea

ESTONIA

Petrograd

LATVIA

LITHUANIA

Danzig

Vilna

WHITE RUSSIA

GERMANY

Warsaw

POLAND

Brest-Litovsk

CURZON LINE

Niemen R.

Bug R.

Vistula R.

Vienna

AUSTRIA-

Budapest

HUNGARY

Kiev

UKRAINE

Dniester R.

Dnieper R.

Prut R.

Danube R.

BOSNIA

MONTE-NEGRO

SERBIA

ALBANIA

RUMANIA

BULGARIA

GREECE

Istanbul

OTTOMAN   EMPIRE

CRIMEA

Occupied by Germany, 1918

Black Sea

Volga R.

Moscow

Kazan

Samara

RUSSIA

Don R.

Tsaritsyn

Rostov-on-Don

Volga R.

CAUCASUS

GEORGIA

Tiflis

Kars

Caspian Sea

Baku

PERSIA

429

war. During the war a brigade had been formed inside Russia of Czechs resident in the country and of deserters from the Habsburg armies. When Russia withdrew from the war, it was decided to send the Czech brigade across Siberia by rail, and then by ship across the Pacific, through the Panama Canal, and across the Atlantic to France, to fight the Germans there. On the rail trip across Siberia, the Czechs got into a brawl with a trainload of Hungarian prisoners, and one of the Hungarians was killed. This obscure quarrel on a Siberian railway siding between members of the unfriendly races of the Habsburg Empire precipitated civil war in Russia. When the Soviet government tried to take reprisals against the Czechs, who numbered fewer than 35,000 men, the Czechs seized a number of the towns of western Siberia. The local soviets were unprepared, and the SRs were sympathetic to the Czechs. Local anti-Bolshevik armies came into being. It was under threat from one of them in July, 1918, that a local soviet decided to execute the Tsar and his entire family rather than lose possession of them. All were murdered.

By late June, 1918, the Allies had decided to intervene in Russia on behalf of the opponents of Bolshevism. The withdrawal of Russia from the war had been a heavy blow to them, and they hoped to re-create a second front against the Germans in the east. The idea of a capitalist "crusade" against Bolshevism, popularized by Soviet and pro-Soviet historians as the sole motive for the intervention, was in fact a far less impelling motive. Moreover, the Allies had been at war a long time, and their populations were war-weary. So they viewed with disfavor communist efforts to stimulate revolution in all the capitalist nations of the world.

Out at the eastern end of the Trans-Siberian Railroad in Vladivostok, the Czechs overthrew the local soviet in June, 1918, and by early August British, French, Japanese, and American forces had landed.

The assignment of the Americans was to occupy Vladivostok and to safeguard railroad communications in the rear of the Czechs. Of the Allies, only the Japanese had long-range territorial ambitions in the area. In effect, the Bolshevik regime had now been displaced in Siberia; the SRs disbanded the soviets and re-established the *zemstvos*, calling for "all power to the constituent assembly." There were three anti-Red governments of varying complexions in three different Siberian centers. Elsewhere, in August, 1918, a small British and American force landed at the White Sea port of Archangel. An SR assassin killed the chief of the Petrograd Cheka, and Lenin himself was wounded.

The regime now sped its military preparations. As Minister of War, Trotsky imposed conscription, and, by a mixture of cajolery and threats of reprisals against their families, secured the services of about 50,000 tsarist officers. The Red Army, which was Trotsky's creation, grew to over 3,000,000 strong by 1920. Its recapture of Kazan and Samara on the Volga in the autumn of 1918 temporarily turned the tide in the crisis that seemed about to engulf the Soviet state.

The German collapse on the Western Front permitted the Bolsheviks to repudiate the Treaty of Brest-Litovsk, and to move back into parts of the Ukraine, where they faced the opposition of a variety of local forces. Elsewhere, the opposition consisted of three main armies. General Denikin led an army of Whites, which moved from Rostov-on-Don south across the Caucasus and received French and British aid. Admiral Kolchak's forces in western Siberia overthrew the SR regime in Omsk, and Kolchak became a virtual dictator. General Yudenich's army, including many former members of the German forces, operated in the Baltic region, and threatened Petrograd from the west. Allied unwillingness to negotiate with the Bolsheviks was heightened by the successful Red *coup* of Bela Kun in Hungary (see Chapter XXVII), which seemed to foreshadow further spread of revolution.

In the spring of 1919, the Reds defeated Kolchak, and by winter took Omsk. In 1920, the Admiral was arrested and executed. Though the Reds also reconquered the Ukraine, mutinies in their own forces prevented them from consolidating their victories and from moving, as they had hoped to do, across the Russian frontiers and linking up with Bela Kun in Hungary. In the summer of 1919, Denikin took Kiev and struck north, advancing to within two hundred and fifty miles of Moscow itself. But his position was weakened by the repressive character of the regime he brought with him and by his recognition of Kolchak as his superior officer, together with the poor discipline of his troops and his own rivalry with one of his generals, Baron Wrangel. Yudenich advanced to the suburbs of Petrograd, but the Reds by the end of 1919 were able to defeat the White threat everywhere, though Wrangel retained an army in the Crimea. Trotsky now called for the militarization of labor to reconstruct the ravaged country; labor battalions were formed, but recovery was long delayed.

In any case, even after the defeat of the Whites, the Reds in 1920 had to face a new war with the Poles, who hoped to keep Russia weak and to create an independent Ukraine. After an initial retreat, the Red armies nearly took Warsaw, from which they were repelled only because the French chief of staff, General Weygand, assisted the Poles. The Reds, eager to finish off the Whites, and persuaded that there was after all no hope for the establishment of a communist regime in Poland, concluded peace in October, 1920. The Poles obtained a large area of territory in White Russia and the western Ukraine. This area was not inhabited by Poles but had been controlled by Poland down to the eighteenth-century partitions. It lay far to the east of the "Curzon line," the ethnic frontier earlier proposed by the British foreign minister, Lord Curzon. The Reds then turned on Wrangel, who had erupted from the Crimea and had established a moderate regime in the territory he occupied. He was forced to evacuate, assisted by a French fleet, in November, 1920. The White movement had virtually come to an end.

Why the Counter-revolution Failed

Many factors accounted for the Whites' failure and the Reds' victory. The Whites could not get together on any political program beyond the mere overthrow of the Reds. They adopted a policy of "non-

Truckload of revolutionists at time of overthrow of Kolchak government in Vladivostok, 1920.

anticipation," which meant that some future constituent assembly would settle the governmental structure of Russia. Their numbers included everybody from tsarists to SRs, and they disagreed so violently on the proper course for Russia to follow that they could agree only to postpone discussion of these critical problems.

Moreover, their movement was located on the geographical periphery of Russia—in Siberia, in the Crimea, in the Ukraine, in the Caucasus, and in the Baltic. But the Whites never reached an understanding with the non-Russian minorities who lived in these regions. Thus they ignored the highly developed separatist sentiments of the Ukrainians and others, to which the Bolsheviks were temporarily willing to cater.

Further, the Whites could not command the support of the peasantry. Instead of guaranteeing the results of the land division already carried out with Bolshevik sanction, the Whites often restored the landlords and undid the land division. During the war the peasantry on the whole grew sick of both sides. This attitude explains the appearance of anarchist bands, especially in the south. Then too, the Whites simply did not command as much military strength as the Reds, who outnumbered them in manpower and who had inherited much of the equipment manufactured for the tsarist armies. Holding the central position, the Reds had a unified and skillful command, which could use the railroad network to shift troops rapidly. The Whites, moving in from the periphery, were divided into at least four main groups, and were denied effective use of the railroads.

Finally, the intervention of the Allies on the side of the Whites was ineffectual and amateurish. It may even have harmed the White cause, since the Reds could pose as the national defenders of the country and could portray the Whites as the hirelings of foreigners. In the light of hindsight, it seems safe to say that either the Allies should have mounted a full-fledged military operation against the Reds, or, if this was impossible (as it probably was, in view of the condition of their own armies after the end of the First World War), they should have stayed out of Russia and allowed the civil war to burn itself out. It is still sometimes argued, however, that, although the Reds won the civil war, the Allied intervention helped keep them so heavily engaged inside Russia that they could not sponsor successful revolutions in other countries. This point of view may well have some justification.

NEP ("The New Economic Policy")

Since 1914, Russia had been deeply involved in fighting and crises. By early 1921, with the end of the civil war, famine was raging and sanitation had broken down. Family ties were disrupted, human beings were brutalized, and class hatreds were released on an unparalleled scale. Industry was producing at a level of about one-eighth of its pre-war output, and agricultural output had decreased by at least 30 per cent. Distribution approached a breakdown. The communist regime appeared to be facing its most serious trial of all: the loss of support in Russia.

A large-scale anarchist peasant revolt broke out in early 1921, and lasted until mid-1922. Lenin remarked that this revolt frightened him more than all the Whites' resistance. But the decisive factor in bringing about a change in policy was the mutiny at the Kronstadt naval base near Petrograd in March, 1921. Formerly a stronghold of Bolshevism, Kronstadt now produced a movement of rebellious anarchists who called for "soviets without communists" to be chosen by universal suffrage and secret ballot, for free speech and free assembly, for the liberation of political prisoners, and for the abolition of requisitioning. Except for the last item and for the phraseology of the first, the program was ironically similar to that of all liberals and socialists in tsarist Russia. The Kronstadt movement seems to have expressed the sentiments of most Russian workers and peasants. Had the government been concilatory, there might have been no bloodshed; but Trotsky went to war against the rebels, and defeated them after a bloody fight.

This episode led directly to the adoption of the "New Economic Policy," always referred to by its initials as NEP. But the underlying reason for the shift was the need for reconstruction, which seemed attainable only if militant communism were at least temporarily abandoned. Lenin himself referred to "premature" attempts at socialization. It was also necessary to appease the peasants, and to ward off any further major uprisings. Finally, the expected world revolution had not come off, and the resources of capitalist states were badly needed to assist Russian reconstruction. Concessions to foreign capitalists were now possible; indeed, the adoption of NEP coincided with the conclusion of an Anglo-Russian trade treaty. Abroad, NEP was hailed as the beginning of a Russian "Thermidor," a return to normality like that following the end of the Terror in the French Revolution (see Chapter XVIII).

Under NEP the government stopped requisitioning the whole of the peasant's crop above a minimum necessary for subsistence. The peasant had still to pay a very heavy tax in kind, but he was allowed to sell the remainder of his crop and keep the money. The peasant could sell his surplus to the state if he wished, but he could also choose to sell it to a private purchaser. Peasant agriculture became in essence capitalist once more, and the profit motive had reappeared. Lenin imitated Stolypin by guaranteeing the peasant permanency of tenure. The whole system tended to help the *kulak* grow richer, and to transform the poor peasant into a hired, landless laborer.

Elsewhere in the economy under NEP the state retained what Lenin called "the commanding heights"—heavy industry, banking, transportation, and foreign trade. In domestic trade and in light industry, however, private enterprise was once more permitted. This was the so-called "private capital sector" of the economy, in which workers could be paid according to their output, and factory managers could swap some of their products in return for raw materials.

Lenin himself described NEP as a partial return to capitalism, and urged the communists to become good businessmen. Yet NEP was never intended as more than a temporary expedient. Lenin believed that it would take a couple of decades before the Russian peasant could be convinced that co-operative agriculture would be the most efficient. He also argued that a temporary relaxation of government intervention would increase industrial production and give the Russians a useful lesson in entrepreneurship.

Economic recovery was indeed obtained. By 1926-1927, industrial production was back at pre-war levels, although agriculture had not kept pace. But NEP was bitterly disliked by leading communists, who were shocked at the reversal of all the doctrines they believed in. By 1924, private business accounted for 40 per cent of Russian domestic trade, but thereafter the figure fell off. Those who took advantage of the opportunities presented by the NEP were known as NEPmen. They were often persecuted in a petty way by hostile officials, who tried to limit their profits, tax them heavily, and drag them into court on charges of speculation. The *kulak* had essentially the same experience. Thus the government often seemed to be encouraging private enterprise for economic reasons and simultaneously to be discouraging it for political reasons.

Within the Communist party, one group favored the increase of the private sector and the extension of NEP, as a new road toward the socialist goal. These were the so-called "Right deviationists." Their opponents favored the ending of concessions, the liquidation of NEPmen and *kulaks,* and a return to Marxist principles at home and the fostering of world revolution abroad—in short, the pressing of the "socialist offensive." These were the "Left deviationists," who included Trotsky. In the Center stood men who attacked both deviations, the Right as an abandonment of communism, the Left as likely to lead to a disruption of the worker-peasant alliance.

The Struggle for Power: Stalin versus Trotsky

But the big question of NEP was not the only one to agitate the communist leaders in the early twenties. Lenin suffered two strokes in 1922, and another in 1923, and finally died in January, 1924. During the last two years of his life he played an ever lessening role. Involved in the controversy over NEP and the other controversies was the question of the succession to Lenin. Thus an individual communist's answer to the question of how to organize industry, what role to give organized labor, and what relations to maintain with the capitalist world depended not only upon his estimate of the actual situation but also upon his guess as to what answer was likely to be politically advantageous. From this maneuvering the Secretary of the Communist party, Joseph Stalin, was to emerge victorious by 1928.

The years between 1922 and 1928, especially after Lenin's death, were years of a desperate struggle for power between Stalin and Trotsky. Lenin foresaw this struggle with great anxiety. He felt that Trotsky was abler, but feared that he was overconfident, and inclined to make decisions of his own. He felt that Stalin had concentrated enormous power in his hands, in his role as party secretary, and feared that he did not know how to use it. When he learned that Stalin had gone counter to his orders in smashing the Menshevik Republic of Georgia instead of reaching an accommodation with its leaders, he wrote angrily in his testament that Stalin was too rude, and that his fellows should remove him from his post as general secretary. At the moment of his death, Lenin had published a scathing attack on Stalin, had broken off relations with him, and was about to try to relegate him to the scrapheap. Trotsky's suggestion that Stalin poisoned Lenin is not based on any evidence, but it is clear that Lenin's death rescued Stalin's career, and that, far from being the chosen heir, as he later claimed, he did not enjoy Lenin's confidence at the end.

During these years Trotsky argued for a more highly trained managerial force in industry, and for economic planning as an instrument that the state could use to control and direct social change. He favored the mechanization of agriculture and the weakening of peasant individualism by encouraging rural co-operatives, with even a hint of the collective farms where groups of peasants, in theory, would own everything collectively, rather than individually. As Trotsky progressively lost power, he championed the right of individual communists to criticize the regime. He referred to the policies of Stalin and his other increasingly powerful enemies as "bureaucratic degeneration," and came to the conclusion that only through the outbreak of revolutions in other countries could the Russian socialist revolution be carried to its proper conclusion. Only if the industrial output and technical skills of the advanced western countries could be put at the disposal of communism could Russia hope to achieve its own socialist revolution. This is the famous theory that socialism cannot succeed within the boundaries of one country: either world revolution must break out, or Russian socialism is doomed to inevitable failure.

Leon Trotsky (1879-1940).

The opponents of Trotsky's "left deviation" found their chief spokesman in Nikolai Bukharin. A man who never held such responsible administrative posts as Lenin or Trotsky or Stalin, and who had often shifted his position on major questions, Bukharin none the less took a consistent line during these years; as editor of *Pravda* he was extremely influential. A strong defender of NEP, Bukharin softened the rigorous Marxist doctrine of the class struggle by arguing that since the proletarian state controlled the commanding heights of big capital, and since big capital would win, socialism was sure of success. This view is not unlike the "gradualist" position taken by western European Social Democrats. Bukharin did not believe in an ambitious program of rapid industrialization; he favored co-operatives, but opposed collectives. In foreign affairs he was eager to co-operate abroad with non-communist groups who might be useful to Russia. Thus he sponsored Soviet collaboration with Chiang Kai-shek in China and with the German Social Democrats.

In his rise to power, Stalin used Bukharin's arguments to discredit Trotsky and to eliminate him. Then, partly because Bukharin's policies were failing, Stalin adopted many of Trotsky's policies, and eliminated Bukharin. Original Stalinist ideas, however, developed during this process. Stalin was not basically an intellectual or a theoretician; he was a party organization stalwart. He adopted theoretical positions partly because they seemed to him the ones most likely to work, and partly because he was charting his own course to supreme power. He came to favor rapid industrialization, and to understand that this meant an unprecedentedly heavy capital investment. At the end of 1927, he suddenly shifted from his previous position on the peasantry, and openly sponsored collectivization. This shift arose because of his concern that agricultural production was not keeping pace with industry. He declared that the balance could be redressed only if agriculture, like industry, was transformed into a series of large-scale unified enterprises.

In answer to Trotsky's argument that socialism in one country was impossible,

Stalin maintained that an independent socialist state could exist. This view did not at all imply the abandonment of the goal of world revolution, as has often been thought. Stalin always maintained that the socialist state (Russia) should be the center of inspiration and assistance to communist movements everywhere; Russia would help them and they would help Russia. But, in his view, during the interim period before the communists had won elsewhere it was perfectly possible for Russia to exist as the only socialist state, and indeed to grow more socialist all the time. In international relations this doctrine of Stalin made it possible for the Soviet Union to pursue either a policy of "peaceful coexistence" with capitalist states, when that seemed most profitable, or a policy of militant support of communist revolution everywhere, when that seemed most profitable. Stalin's "socialism in one country" also struck a responsive chord in the rank and file of Russian communists, who were disappointed in the failure of revolutions elsewhere. It also meant that Russia, not the West, was to be the center of the new society. Stalin's doctrine reflected his own Russian nationalism rather than the more cosmopolitan and more western views of Trotsky.

The Struggle for Power: Stalin's Victory

Analysis of the rival theories competing for acceptance in Russia in the twenties helps explain the alternatives before the communist leadership. It does not explain how Stalin won. To understand this we must move from the realm of theory and political platforms to the realm of practice and political power. At the end of the civil war, Stalin was Commissar of Nationalities. In this post he dealt with the affairs of 65,000,000 of the 140,000,000 inhabitants of the new Russian Soviet Republic. He managed the destiny of the Asians whom he, as one of them, understood. Their local Bolshevik leaders became his men; where they did not, as in his native Georgia, he ruthlessly crushed them. Though a Georgian, he identified himself with Russian nationalism in the interests of a centralized Bolshevik state.

It was Stalin who took charge of creating the new Asian "republics" which enjoyed the appearance of local self-government, programs of economic and educational improvement, and a chance to use their local languages and develop their own cultures. It was he who in 1922 proposed and guided the adoption of a new Union of Socialist Soviet Republics as a substitute for the existing federation of republics. In the U.S.S.R., Moscow would control war, foreign policy, trade, and transport, and would co-ordinate finance, economy, food, and labor. And on paper it would leave to the republics home affairs, justice, education, and agriculture. A Council of Nationalities, with an equal number of delegates from each ethnic group, would join the Supreme Soviet as a second chamber, thus forming the Central Executive Committee, which would appoint the Council of Peoples' Commissars—the Government. To this constitutional reform Stalin pointed as an achievement equal to Trotsky's military organizational work during the civil war.

Stalin was also Commissar of the Workers' and Peasants' Inspectorate. Here his duties were to eliminate inefficiency and corruption from every branch of the civil service, and to train a new corps of civil servants. His teams moved freely through all the offices of the government, observing and recommending changes, inspecting and criticizing. In creating this post Lenin had hoped to clean house, but the ignorance and the lack of tradition that rendered the tsarist and Bolshevik civil service incompetent and corrupt operated in Stalin's Inspectorate as well. Although the Inspectorate could not do what it was established to do, it did perform another role. It gave Stalin control over the machinery of government. Lenin attacked Stalin's work in the Inspectorate just before he died, but by then it was too late.

Stalin was also a member of the Politbureau, the tight little group of party bosses elected by the Central Committee, which included only five men throughout the civil war. Here his job was day-to-day management of the party. He was the only permanent liaison officer between the Politbureau and the Orgbureau, which allocated party personnel to their various duties, in factory, office, or army unit. In addition to these posts, Stalin became general secretary of the party's Central Committee in 1922. Here he prepared the agenda for Politbureau meetings, supplied the documentation for points under debate, and passed the decisions down to the lower levels. He controlled party patronage—that is to say, all party appointments, promotions, and demotions. He saw to it that local trade unions, co-operatives, and army units were put under communist bosses responsible to him. He had files on the loyalty and achievement of all managers of industry and other party members. In 1921, a Central Control Commission, which could expel party members for unsatisfactory conduct, was created; Stalin, as liaison between this commission and the Central Committee, now virtually controlled the purges, which were designed to keep the party pure.

In a centralized one-party state, a man of Stalin's ambitions who held so many key positions had an enormous advantage in the struggle for power. Yet the state was so new, the positions were so much less conspicuous and so much more humdrum than the Ministry of War, for instance, held by Trotsky, and Stalin's manner was so generally conciliatory, that the likelihood of Stalin's success did not become evident until it was too late to stop him. Inside the Politbureau he formed a three-man team with two other prominent Bolshevik lead-

ers, the demagogue, Zinoviev, and the expert on doctrine, Kamenev. Zinoviev was chairman of the Petrograd Soviet and boss of the Communist International; Kamenev was Lenin's deputy and president of the Moscow Soviet. All three were old Bolsheviks, in contrast to Trotsky, who had been a Menshevik and an independent member of the intelligentsia.

The combination of Stalin, Zinoviev, and Kamenev proved unbeatable. The three put down all real and imagined plots against them by the use of the secret police. They resisted Trotsky's demands for "reform," which would have democratized the party to some degree and strengthened his position while weakening Stalin's. They initiated the cult of Lenin immediately before his death, and kept it burning fiercely thereafter, so that any suggestion for change coming from Trotsky seemed almost an act of impiety. They dispersed Trotsky's followers by sending them to posts abroad. They prevented the publication of Lenin's "testament," so that the rank and file of the party would not know about Lenin's doubts concerning Stalin. They publicized all Trotsky's earlier statements in opposition to Lenin, and did not hesitate to "revise" history in order to belittle Trotsky. They were confident, and rightly so, that Trotsky was too good a communist to rally around him such anti-Bolshevik groups as old Mensheviks, SRs, and NEPmen.

Early in 1925, Stalin and his allies were able to force the resignation of Trotsky as Minister of War. Soon thereafter the three-man team dissolved; Stalin moved into alliance with Bukharin and other right-wing members of the Politbureau, to which he began to appoint some of his own followers. Using all his accumulated power, he beat his former allies on all questions of policy, and in 1926 they moved into a new but powerless alliance with Trotsky. Stalin now (1926) deposed Zinoviev from the Politbureau, charging him with intriguing in the army. Trotsky was the next one to be expelled from the Politbureau, and Zinoviev was ousted as president of the Comintern.

In 1927, differences of opinion over Stalin's foreign policy in England and in China (see below, p. 451) led to public protests by the opposition. And these in turn led to the expulsion of the opposition from the party itself. Refusing to renounce his views, Trotsky was deported to Siberia, the first stage in a long exile that took him to Turkey, Norway, and Mexico, where he died in 1940 at the hands of an assassin armed with an ice-pick. The others recanted and obtained a new lease on life. Stalin's victory was virtually complete.

IV: Stalin's Supremacy:
Russian Internal Affairs, 1928-1941

The Communist party congress that expelled Trotsky in December, 1927, also brought NEP to an end and proclaimed that the new "socialist offensive" would begin in 1928. The thirteen years between 1928 and 1941 were to see almost incredible changes in the domestic life of Russia—collectivized agriculture, speedy industrialization, forced labor, the great purges and the extermination of all political opposition, the building of an authoritarian state apparatus, and a "retreat" to bourgeois standards in almost every department of social and intellectual life.

Collectivized Agriculture

In 1928, the failure of the peasants to deliver to the cities as much grain as had been required seemed to underline the dangers inherent in the land divisions of 1917 and in the concessions of NEP. Farm productivity on the small individual holdings was not high enough to feed the city population. Food prices for the workers were high, yet the *kulaks* wanted further concessions. Grain was hoarded. Stalin had often inveighed against "fanning the class struggle in the countryside," and had denied the intention of collectivizing agriculture rapidly or on a mass scale. The government economic plan issued during 1928 set a figure of 20 per cent of Russian farms as the *maximum* to be collectivized by 1933. Yet during 1929, Stalin embarked on immediate full-scale collectivization, declared war on the *kulaks*, and virtually put an end to individual farming in Russia.

The government did not have the money or the credit to import food. Further, no governmental machinery is adequate to force peasants to disgorge crops that they are hiding. Therefore, the government enlisted on its side the small peasants; in exchange for their assistance in locating and turning over the *kulaks'* crops, they would be promised a place on a collective farm, to be made up of the *kulaks'* land and equipped with their implements. Probably a good many of the subsistence farmers (about 20 per cent of the number of private farms, possibly 5,000,000 households) more or less welcomed this opportunity. Initial encouraging reports led Stalin to go full speed ahead. The *kulaks*, he declared in late 1929, were to be liquidated as a class. There were about 2,000,000 households of them, perhaps as many as 10,000,000 people in all. They were now to be totally expropriated, and at the same time barred from the new collectives. Since no provision was made for them, this move turned collectivization into a nightmare.

Peasants now were machine-gunned into submission; *kulaks* were deported to forced labor camps or to desolate regions in Siberia. In desperate revolt against the command to join collectives, the peasants burned crops, broke plows, and killed their cattle rather than turn them over to the state. More than half the horses in all Russia, 45 per cent of the cattle, and two-thirds of the sheep and goats were slaughtered. Russian livestock has never since caught up with the losses it suffered because of the excesses of collectivization. Land lay uncultivated, and over the next few years famine took a toll of millions of lives. As early as March, 1930, Stalin showed that he was aware of the ghastly mistakes he had made. In a famous statement on "dizziness with success" he put the blame on local officials who had been too eager to rush through the program. By contradicting his own orders of a few months before he managed to escape some of the hatred that would otherwise have been directed at him. As usual, many Russian peasants disliked the man they could see, the local official, and were willing to exculpate the "little father" in the capital.

Fifty per cent of Russian farms had been hastily thrown together into collectives during this frightful year. Only an additional 10 per cent were added during the next three years, so that by 1933 60 per cent in all had been collectivized. The number rose again later in the 1930's, until by 1939 more than 96 per cent of Russian farms were collectivized. In 1941, there were 250,000 collectives, 900,000,000 acres in extent, supporting 19,000,000 families. Yet the excesses of the early "dizziness with success" were never repeated.

The 1930's also brought a modification of the original rules governing collectives. Originally collectives had been of two main types: there was the *sovkhoz*, or soviet farm, not strictly a collective at all but a state-owned enterprise, operated by the government and worked by hired laborers who were government employees; and there was the *kolkhoz*, or collective farm proper. The *sovkhozes* were designed as centers of government research and development in agriculture, and were often very large in size. But they were mostly brought to an end by Stalin in the 1930's, when he ordered some forty million acres originally allotted to them to be distributed among the *kolkhozes*. As of 1941, the *sovkhozes* occupied no significant area of land.

The *kolkhoz* itself was also originally of two types: the commune, in which all the resources of the members without exception were owned together, and the *artel*, or co-operative, in which a certain amount of private property was permitted to the members. After Stalin's modifications of the system in the thirties, the *artel* became the overwhelmingly predominant form of collective farm. In an *artel* each family owned its homestead, some livestock, and minor implements; these could be left by will to the owner's descendants. But most of the work was done on the collectively operated land. Each collective had its own managing board, responsible to the government, which supervised the work of the peasants, who were organized in brigades, each under a brigadier. Like factory laborers paid on a "piece-work" basis, peasants were remunerated according to their output, which was measured by the artificial unit of the "labor day." One day's work in managing a farm might be, for example, assessed at three labor days, while one day's work weeding a vegetable patch might be assessed at only half a labor day.

Each *kolkhoz* turned over to the government a fixed amount of produce at fixed rates, and the total of all these amounts was designed to guarantee the feeding of the urban population, especially workers in heavy industry and members of the Red Army. In addition, the *kolkhoz* paid further taxes to cover government expenses for local construction and education. Any surplus might be sold by the peasant directly to the consumer, without the participation of any middleman. Private resale was regarded as speculation and was subject to punishment. After 1934, the government obtained at least two-thirds of its revenue by the resale on the markets at a large profit of farm produce bought at low fixed prices from the *kolkhoz*. This government profit was known as the "turnover tax."

The government assisted and controlled the *kolkhoz* through the supply of mechanical equipment furnished by the Machine Tractor Stations. The collectives could not own their own tractors, but rented them from the stations, paying in exchange a fee ranging up to perhaps 20 per cent of the crop. The stations were important centers for political surveillance, and included staff members who were agents of the regime. By the decision when and to whom to allot tractors and how many tractors to allot, administrators of the Machine Tractor Stations could directly affect the success of a collective; their good will was therefore of the utmost importance to the management.

In general, the aim of collectivization was to reorganize farming so as to ensure food for the industrial labor force, which was being increased by recruitment from the farms themselves. Collectivization certainly increased the total food supplies at the disposal of the government and released farmers for work in industry. But it seems certain that the over-all rise in agricultural production was small, and that in many cases the yield per unit decreased.

Industrialization

Intimately related to the drive in agriculture was the drive in industry. Here, too, Stalin had viewed with scorn the grandiose plans of the "superindustrializers" and as late as 1927 had proposed an annual increase rate in industrial production of only 15 per cent. But just as he shifted to the frantic pace of collectivizing agriculture, so he first gradually, then suddenly, shifted to forced draft in industry also.

In 1928 began the era of the Five-Year Plans, each setting ambitious goals for production over the next five years. In 1929 and 1930, Stalin appropriated ever higher sums for capital investment, and in June, 1930, he declared that industrial production must rise by 50 per cent in the current year, a fantastic and impossible figure. Under the First Five-Year Plan, adopted in 1928, annual pig-iron production was scheduled to rise from 3,500,000 tons to 10,000,000 tons by 1932, but in that year Stalin demanded 17,000,000 tons instead. It was not forthcoming, of course, but Stalin's demand for it was symptomatic of the pace at which he was striving to transform Russia from an agricultural to an industrial country.

Part of the reason for this rapid pace lay precisely in the collectivization drive itself. Large-scale farming, to which Stalin was committing Russia, must be mechanized farming. Yet there were only 7,000 tractors in all Russia at the end of 1928. Stalin secured 30,000 more during 1929, but this was nowhere near a beginning. Industry had to produce millions of machines, and the gasoline to run them. Since the countryside had to be electrified, power stations were needed by the thousands. And literally millions and millions of peasants had to be taught how to handle machinery. But there was nobody to teach them, and no factories to produce the machinery. The output of raw materials was inadequate, and the plants to process them were not there.

Another part of the reason for the drive to industrialize lay in the tenets of Marxism itself. Russia had defied all Marx's predictions by staging a proletarian revolution in a country almost without a proletariat. Yet despite the communists' initial political successes, Stalin felt that "capitalism had a firmer basis than communism in Russia, so

View of automated con-veyer assembly line in Gorky Machine Tool Plant in Kiev.

long as it remained a country of small peasants." The communists felt that the world proletariat expected them to industrialize Russia, but even more they were determined to create as a support for themselves the massive Russian proletariat which as yet did not exist. Further, Stalin was determined to make Russia as nearly self-sufficient as possible, in line with his theory of socialism in one country. Underlying this was a motive at least as intense as any dictated by Marxist doctrine—Russian nationalism.

The strength of this motive is revealed in a speech that Stalin made in 1931:

To slacken the pace means to lag behind, and those who lag behind are beaten. We do not want to be beaten. No, we don't want to. . . . Old Russia . . . was ceaselessly beaten for her backwardness. She was beaten by the Mongol Khans, she was beaten by Turkish Beys, she was beaten by Swedish feudal lords, she was beaten by Polish-Lithuanian gentry, she was beaten by Anglo-French capitalists, she was beaten by Japanese barons; she was beaten by all—for her backwardness. For military backwardness, for cultural backwardness, for political backwardness, for industrial backwardness, for agricultural backwardness. She was beaten because to beat her was profitable and went unpunished. . . . We are fifty or a hundred years behind the advanced countries. We must make good this lag in ten years. Either we do it or they crush us.[*]

Whatever one may think of this quotation as history (and it omits all Russia's *victorious* wars), it reveals that Russian national self-interest as interpreted by Stalin required the most rapid possible industrialization. And it is of interest that ten years afterward the Germans did attack, something Stalin could of course not have predicted so accurately, but something that he seems to have sensed.

Stalin seems also to have felt that he had only to keep a fierce pressure on the management of industry, and the desired commodities and finished goods would be forthcoming in the desired quantities. The goals of the First Five-Year Plan were not attained, although fulfillment was announced in 1932. Immediately, the second plan, prepared by the state planning commission, went into effect, and ran until 1937; the third was interrupted only by

———

[*] Quoted in Isaac Deutscher, *Stalin* (New York, 1950), 328.

Hitler's invasion. Each time the emphasis was on the elements of heavy industry—steel, electric power, cement, coal, oil. Between 1928 and 1940 steel production was multiplied by four and one-half, electric power by eight, cement by more than two, coal by four, and oil by almost three. Similar developments took place in chemicals and in machine production. Railroad construction was greatly increased, and the volume of freight carried quadrupled with the production of new rolling stock.

By 1940, Russian output was approaching that of Germany, although Russian efficiency and the Russian standard of living were far lower. What the rest of Europe had done in about seventy-five years Russia had done in about twelve. Enthusiasm was artificially whipped up by wide publicizing of the high output of individual workers called "Stakhanovites," after a coal miner who had set production records. "Stakhanovites" and "heroes of labor" were richly rewarded, and the others were urged to imitate them in "socialist competition."

All this was achieved at the expense of dreadful hardships, yet eyewitnesses report that many of the workers were as enthusiastic as if they had been soldiers in battle, as indeed in a sense they were. Valuable machinery was often damaged or destroyed by inexperienced workers right off the farm. The problems of repair, of replacement, of achieving balance between the output and consumption of raw materials, of housing workers in the new centers, of moving entire industries thousands of miles into the Ural region and Siberia, were unending and cost untold numbers of lives. An American eyewitness estimates that Russia's "battle of ferrous metallurgy alone involved more casualties than the battle of the Marne."

Administratively, the Russian economy was directly run by the state. The Gosplan, or state planning commission, drew up the Five-Year Plans, and supervised their fulfillment at the management level. The Gosbank, or state bank, regulated the investment of capital. An economic council administered the work of various agencies: its major divisions were metallurgy and chemistry (iron and steel, non-ferrous metals, chemicals, rubber, alcohol); defense (aviation, armaments, munitions, tanks, ships); machinery (heavy machines, medium machines, machine tools, electrical industry); fuel and power (coal, oil, electric power); agriculture and procurement; and consumer's goods (grain, meat and dairy products, fisheries, textiles, light industry). Under iron and steel, for example, there functioned the production trusts controlling their own mines as well as blast furnaces and rolling mills. These were the so-called "combinats," or great production complexes like that at Magnitogorsk in the Urals. In each plant, as in each collective, the manager was responsible for producing the quota set for him within the maximum cost allowed him. He was consulted on production targets, and had considerable leeway in selecting his staff and allocating labor and raw materials. He was bound to render a rigid accounting to the government, which of course fixed the price he must pay for his raw materials.

The Social Impact

The social effects of the economic program were dramatic. Urban population rose from about 18 per cent in 1926 to about 33 per cent in 1940. The number of cities with a population between 50,000 and 100,000 doubled, and the number of cities with a population exceeding 100,000 more than quadrupled. The largest cities, Moscow and Leningrad (the new name for Petersburg-Petrograd after the death of Lenin), almost doubled in size, and among smaller cities, to take just one example, Alma Ata in Siberia grew from 45,000 to 230,000 between 1928 and 1939. The entire social picture was radically altered.

The relative freedom to choose one's job which had characterized the NEP period disappeared. Individual industrial enterprises signed labor contracts with the *kolkhozes* by which the *kolkhoz* was obliged to send a given number of farm workers to the factories, often against their will. Peasants who had resisted collectivization were simply drafted into labor camps. In the factories, the trade unions became simply another organ of the state. The chief role of the unions was to achieve maximum production and efficiency, to discourage absenteeism and poor work. Trade unions might not strike, or engage in conflict with management. All they could do was administer the social insurance laws, and seek improvements in workers' living conditions by negotiation.

Thus in the U.S.S.R. the old privileged classes of noble landlords, already weak at the time of the revolution, ceased to exist. The industrial, commercial, and financial bourgeoisie, which was just coming into its own at the time of the revolution, was destroyed after 1928, despite the temporary reprieve it had experienced under NEP. Most of the old intelligentsia, who had favored a revolution, could not in the end stomach Stalin's dictatorship, and many of them emigrated. Of the million and a half émigrés from Russia after the revolution, only a very small number (contrary to the general view in the West) were cousins of the Tsar. Those of the old intelligentsia who remained were forced into line with the new Soviet intelligentsia, which Stalin felt to be a very important class. All were compelled to accept the new Stalinist dogma and to drop their interest in the outside world. The new intelligentsia was expected to concentrate on technical advance, and on new administrative devices for speeding up the transformation of the country.

Although the effect of these social changes would presumably have been to level all ranks, Stalin set himself against the old Bolshevik principles of equality.

The Marxist slogan, "From each according to his capacity, to each according to his needs," was shelved in favor of a new one, "From each according to his capacity, to each according to his work." Where Lenin had allowed none of the members of the government to earn more than a skilled laborer, Stalin set up a new system of incentives. A small minority of bureaucrats and skilled laborers, factory managers, and successful *kolkhoz* bosses earned vastly more than the great majority of unskilled laborers and peasants. Together with the writers, artists, musicians, and entertainers who were willing to lend their talents to the services of the regime, these men became a new élite, separated by a wide economic and social gulf from the toiling masses. They had a vested interest in furthering a regime to which they owed everything, and without which they would be nothing.

Soviet propagandists declared that this was a temporary situation. They described the present society in the Soviet Union as "socialist," while regarding "communism," not yet achieved, as the goal toward which the U.S.S.R. was still moving. Yet, just as the "withering away" of the state, which the Marxists predicted, was instead replaced under Stalin by the enormous swelling of state power and state machinery, so the equality predicted by the Marxists was replaced by a new caste system. The means of production were publicly owned in the Soviet Union, as the Marxists had urged. But the power of the state, the birth of a new élite, the brutalization of millions of human beings, and the ruthless use of force after the revolution had been achieved were all the contributions of Stalin.

The Purge Trials

Stalin's program was not achieved without opposition. The crisis of 1931 and 1932, when industrial goals were not being met and the countryside was being swept by starvation, created discontent inside the regime as well as outside. A small number of officials circulated memoranda advocating Stalin's deposition as General Secretary, an act which the party had every right to perform. Stalin jailed them for conspiracy, and one leading Bolshevik committed suicide. It is widely believed that Stalin's own wife reproached him at this time with the ravages that the terror was working, and that she too committed suicide. At one moment, but only at one, we are told, Stalin's self-confidence wavered and he offered to resign, but nobody in the Politbureau dared accept the offer, and the moment quickly passed. His attack against those he believed to be his enemies took the form of the famous purges, which began in 1934 and continued at intervals until 1938.

These purges remain the most mysterious episode in Soviet history. They are often compared with the Jacobin Terror of the French Revolution, when the revolution "devoured its children." But, in contrast to the rapid appearance of the Terror in France, the purges did not begin for seventeen years after the Russian Revolution. Members of the opposition had been demoted, expelled from the party, and even exiled, as in the case of Trotsky, but nobody had been executed. There is an entirely credible story that the Bolshevik leaders had agreed among themselves early in their career never to start guillotining each other. Yet, when the terror began in Russia, it was even more drastic than it had been in France. Moreover, unlike Robespierre, Stalin managed to survive.

From exile, Trotsky continued to attack Stalin in a journal called *The Bulletin of the Opposition.* Clever as always, he scored telling points against Stalin, and his words were carefully read by Soviet officials. Yet the older generation of communists, though they may have hated Stalin, made no move against him. A younger group, however, seemingly more restless and convinced that Stalin had abandoned Lenin's program, found the model for conspiracy in the heroes of the terrorist movement who had assassinated Alexander II (see Chapter XXII). They were apparently prepared to use terrorism against Stalin and his henchmen. Even within the Politbureau men loyal to Stalin grew restless at his ruthlessness, and urged him to relax the pressure; Sergei Kirov, boss of Leningrad, took the lead.

Stalin at times seemed to yield to this urging, as when he ordered more gentle treatment for rebellious *kulaks* in June, 1932, and limited the powers of the political police. But at other times he seemed to be taking the opposite course, as when he issued a decree making an entire family responsible for the treason of any of its members. On the whole, however, tension relaxed during 1932-1934. Kirov proclaimed a new era of lenience at a party conference, and former leaders of the opposition, including Bukharin, were appointed to help draft a new and liberal constitution.

Then on December 1, 1934, Kirov was assassinated by a young terrorist communist in Leningrad. Although the story that Stalin himself had plotted the assassination cannot be confirmed, it is clear that Stalin now determined to strike at the opposition. The assassin was executed. Accused of complicity, Zinoviev and Kamenev were jailed, and forced to admit that they had plotted to restore capitalism. Yet the drafting of the new "democratic" constitution went on. Stalin became ever more withdrawn, ever more autocratic, ever more resolved to destroy the old Bolsheviks, as Ivan the Terrible had destroyed the old nobility. After an interlude during 1935 and early 1936, during which Stalin said that "life had become more joyous," the purges proper began.

The official story was that Trotskyite agitation abroad was linked with the murder of Kirov, and the alleged plans for the murder of Stalin. A series of public political trials took place. In the first (1936), Zinoviev, Kamenev, and fourteen others admitted these charges and were executed. In the second (1937) seventeen other leading Bolsheviks declared that they had knowledge of a conspiracy between Trotsky and the German and Japanese intelligence service, by which Russian territory was to be transferred to Germany and Japan. All were executed. Then (June, 1937) came the secret liquidation of the top commanders in the Red Army, who were accused of conspiring with "an unfriendly foreign power" (Germany) with a view to sabotage. All were executed after an announcement that they had confessed. The last of the public trials took place in March, 1938, as twenty-one leading Bolsheviks, including Bukharin, confessed to similar charges and were executed.

But these public trials and the secret trial of the generals give only a faint idea of the extent of the purge. Every member of Lenin's Politbureau except Stalin and Trotsky was either killed or committed suicide to avoid execution. Two vice-commissars of foreign affairs and most of the ambassadors of the diplomatic corps, fifty of the seventy-one members of the Central Committee of the Communist party, almost all the military judges who had sat in judgment and had condemned the generals, two successive heads of the secret police, themselves the leaders in the previous purges, the prime ministers and chief officials of all the non-Russian Soviet Republics—all were killed or vanished. A list of those who disappeared reads like a "who's who" of high officialdom in state and party throughout the twenties and thirties. Literally thousands were executed or disappeared without a trace. The public trials probably included only those who were willing to confess, whether guilty or not. The rest were condemned privately and quite without due process of law.

Although it is clear that many of those who were executed opposed Stalin, the

Vishinsky at the time he was government prosecutor during the purge trials, 1938.

charges against them were certainly not true. Had they been true, the great conspiracy involving almost everybody but Stalin himself would surely have accomplished more than the assassination of Kirov. It is altogether unlikely that any of the top communists conspired with Hitler, little though they loved Stalin. Some who confessed may have felt so great a loyalty to the cause of communism, however perverted, that they sacrificed themselves for Stalin's soviet state. Some doubtless hoped to save their families, or even themselves, and a few leaders were spared the death penalty to encourage confessions from the others. Many may have hoped that the confessions were so ridiculous that nobody could believe them.

What Stalin apparently wanted was to destroy utterly all possibility of future conspiracies. So he trumped up charges against anybody who conceivably could become a member of a regime that might replace his own. Despite the enormous upheaval of the purges, no breakdown took place in the state. New bureaucrats were found to take the places of the old. The new Stalin-trained officials, uncultivated but competent, now manned all top-level positions.

The Authoritarian State

In the midst of the purges, in 1936, Stalin proclaimed the new constitution, the "most democratic in the world." By its provisions nobody was disfranchised, as priests and members of the former nobility and bourgeoisie had previously been. Civil liberties were extended, but even on paper these were never more than a sham, since the constitution provided that they could be modified in the "interest of the toilers." The fact that the U.S.S.R. was a one-party state prevented elections from being anything but an expression of unanimity. The right to nominate candidates for the Supreme Soviet belonged to Communist party organizations, trade unions, co-operatives, youth groups, and cultural societies; but all were completely dominated by the party. The party picked the candidates, and no more than one for each post was ever presented to the voters. The party controlled the soviets, and the party hierarchy and government hierarchy overlapped and interlocked.

Every citizen was eligible for membership in the party on application to a local branch, which voted on his application after a year of trial. Communist children's organizations fed the youth groups, which in turn fed the party. The party was organized both territorially and functionally in pyramidal form, with organizations at the bottom level in factory, farm, and government office. These were grouped together by rural or urban local units, and these in turn by regional and territorial conferences and congresses. The party organizations elected the All-Union party congress, which selected the Central Committee of the party, and which was in theory the highest policy-making organ, though actually no party congress was held between 1939 and 1954. The Central Committee selected the Politbureau. At each level of the party pyramid there were organizations for agitation and propaganda, for organization and instruction, for military and political training. The party exercised full control over the government, which simply enacted formally what the party had decided upon. The Five-Year Plans, for example, were party programs that went into effect even before they were formally adopted by the government.

The highest organ of the government was the Supreme Soviet, made up of two houses —a Soviet of the Union, based on population, and a Soviet of Nationalities, elected according to national administrative divisions. In theory, the Supreme Soviet was elected for a term of four years. The Supreme Soviet itself did little; it appointed a presidium which issued the decrees and carried on the work of the Supreme Soviet between sessions. It also appointed the Council of Ministers (long called the Council of People's Commissars). This cabinet, rather than the Supreme Soviet or its presidium, enacted most of the legislation, and was thus the legislative as well as the executive organ of the Russian state. The chairmanship of the Council of People's Commissars, the chairmanship of the Politbureau, and the General Secretariat of the Communist party were all posts held by Stalin, who in addition served as Commissar of Defense, chief of the State Defense Council, which ran the country during wartime, and Generalissimo. Similar overlapping of party and government posts was the regular practice.

In 1924, Stalin's constitutional reform had created the new Union of Soviet Socialist Republics, including the enormously large Russian Federative Republic, the Ukraine, White Russia, Georgia, Armenia, and Azerbaidjan, and three central Asian Soviet Socialist republics: Uzbekistan, Turkmenistan, and Tadjikistan. In 1936, Kazakh and Kirghiz republics were added, making a total of eleven. As a result of the annexations of the Baltic states and of Finnish and Rumanian territory in 1940, five more republics were created: Lithuania, Latvia, Estonia, Karelia, and Moldavia. These sixteen "Union" republics differed widely in population. Within the huge Russian republic were sixteen "autonomous" republics, and numerous other subdivisions, all called "autonomous." The larger SSR's had similar subdivisions.

Each of the Union republics and autonomous republics had a government patterned exactly on that of the Soviet Union, except that the supreme soviet of each republic was unicameral and not bicameral, since it lacked a chamber of nationalities. Many complaints have been heard in recent years about the way in which "Great-Russian chauvinism" has permeated official policy toward the individual minority republics. Although this soviet descendant of tsarist Russification policy has always been a menace, it is widely believed that in the years before World War II, the chief objective was not to try to Russify the nationalities but to communize them. With this end in view, the party permitted and encouraged local nationalities to revive their culture, study their past traditions, and use their own language. Like every other cultural manifestation permitted in the U.S.S.R., these national cultural achievements were "managed." Not only was it impossible for anti-Soviet or anti-communist material to appear in print or in any of the plastic arts, but, as everywhere, all artistic effort was closely supervised and had to serve the regime positively. The value of "cultural autonomy" under these circumstances is of course highly debatable.

Although the Stalin constitution specifically gave each republic the right to secede, this provision was pure window-dressing. The central government was overpoweringly stronger than the government of any one republic, which in any case was often not even made up of natives. Although each

of the sixteen republics was in 1944 given its own foreign office by an amendment to the constitution, this amendment was never intended to give them autonomy in this critically important field. Actually, it seems simply to have been a device for securing representation of the Ukraine and White Russia in the United Nations. The representatives of these two republics to the United Nations have never been anything but extra Soviet delegates; the first Ukrainian delegate to the U.N. was not even a Ukrainian, but a Russian who was once Soviet ambassador to the independent Ukraine of the revolutionary era.

The Russian Thermidor?

The period between 1934 and 1941, notable for the purges and for the constitutional development of Stalin's one-party state, is also called by many shrewd observers of revolutions the true Russian

Stalin.

"Thermidor," as distinct from NEP. The term "Thermidor" has come to mean a period in which a revolution has burnt itself out, and the prevailing mood shifts from messianic enthusiasm to one of desire for normality. In revolutionary France, the shift was signalized by the fall of Robespierre and the Jacobin regime and the advent of the Directory, a different government with different objectives, policies, and personnel, which was in turn succeeded by Napoleon's dictatorship (see Chapter XVIII). In the U.S.S.R. the striking fact was that Stalin stayed in office throughout: he was in effect the Russian Robespierre, Directory, and Napoleon all rolled into one. If we accept the parallel, the Russian Thermidor was a managed and manipulated Thermidor, involving no real liberalization of the regime or relaxation of controls. Yet perhaps the parallel is not entirely valid, since Stalin resembled Napoleon far more than he did the weak Directory.

In any case, the period of the late 1930's saw a wholesale retreat from many ideas of the revolution. Simultaneously with the purges and the new constitution, the bread ration was raised, the *kolkhoz* was reformed to permit the individual farmer to own his homestead, new medals and titles were awarded to leading workers in plants and to scientists, engineers, and military men. In the Red Army traditional tsarist distinctions between officers and men were restored, and marshals were named for the first time. Thus, without relaxing political control, Stalin introduced an element of relaxation into the daily life of the rank and file, at the very height of his Terror. The standard of living went up as the production of consumer's goods was encouraged, and as workers were invited to spend their earnings on little luxuries previously unavailable.

Simultaneously, the state rediscovered Russia's great past. The standard communist teaching had been that proletarians have no fatherland; the very name of Russia had almost been abandoned. Now, in contrast, officially controlled organs of opinion editorialized that one should love one's own country, and hailed the heroes of the tsarist era. Alexander Nevsky, who had defeated the Teutonic knights; Dmitri Donskoi, who had defeated the Tartars; Peter the Great; Kutuzov, who had defeated Napoleon; even Ivan the Terrible— all were praised to the skies. The reputations of the great literary figures of the nineteenth century underwent a similar rehabilitation. This retreat to Russian nationalism reached its climax during World War II, when the Marxist *Internationale* itself was dropped as the national anthem.

The old Bolsheviks had attacked the family as the backbone of the old order, had made marriage difficult and divorce easy, had drawn no distinction between legitimate and illegitimate children, and had encouraged promiscuity and abortions. Stalin's state now rehabilitated the sanctity of marriage, denounced the seducer, made divorces very hard to get, declared the family essential to the state, and encouraged children to obey their parents. Doubtless the shift came in part as a result of the falling birthrate and increasing juvenile delinquency, but it was none the less part of the abandonment of radicalism.

The early Bolsheviks had destroyed the old school system, abolished homework and examinations, and allowed children to administer the schools collectively with their teachers. Attendance fell off, the schools became revolutionary clubs of youngsters, and the training of teachers was neglected. The universities deteriorated, since anybody aged sixteen could enroll in them. Degrees were abolished, and technical training was stressed to the exclusion of other subjects. Under NEP, this chaotic situation was modified, and the basic problem of increasing literacy was seriously tackled. But the subjects of ordinary school curricula were replaced by the so-called "project" system with heavy emphasis on labor problems and Marxist theory. The teachers had little to do except memorize texts, and quiz the children to test their mastery of them. The Communist party itself took over the universities, purged the faculties, and compelled the students to spend one week in three at work in factories—a system that helped neither the student nor the university, and cannot have increased industrial production by very much.

The "thermidorean reaction," as might have been expected, changed this system drastically. Training of teachers improved, their salaries were raised, and regular ranks in the civil service were established for them. The old pre-revolutionary system of admissions and degrees in the universities was restored, as was the pre-revolutionary school curriculum. Examinations and homework re-appeared; discipline was enforced on school children. The emphasis on political education was reduced, and co-education was abandoned. Fees for tuition were restored for secondary schools, the Russian counterpart of the American high school or the French *lycée*. These tuition fees made higher education difficult to obtain except for children of the new élite or unusually talented students who were able to win state scholarships. Literacy rose to about 90 per cent, if we may believe Soviet figures.

The educational reforms certainly made books, theaters, museums, and libraries available to many more Russians than ever before. Newspapers and periodicals multiplied, and the regime's respect for science and learning was genuine. But the regime's attitude was narrowly utilitarian and thoroughly intolerant. All cultural activities were measured by their positive contribution to the state. Education became indoctrination. Systems of ideas that might rival communism were not allowed to compete, since the government could always silence those who might be their spokesmen. In this respect the Soviet regime was even more authoritarian than that of a ruler like Tsar Nicholas I (see Chapter XXII).

Under Nicholas I, censorship prevented the writer from saying certain things, but it did not positively prescribe what he must say. It was a negative, not a positive censorship, and it left a margin of personal freedom that permitted some of the greatest works of all literature to be written in Russia. The Soviet censorship, on the other hand, was positive, and required of all artists that they constantly praise the new system, and devote their talents to publicizing its merits. The party line extended into all cultural fields, even music, where talented composers had to apologize abjectly for failing to produce communist symphonies, whatever they may be. The creative artist did not know from day to day whether his efforts would win him a Stalin prize or a sentence to a Siberian labor camp.

Neither did the scientist or scholar. Sciences like physics and genetics involve philosophical presuppositions. Soviet biologists, for example, have been punished for accepting standard western scientific principles that simply cast doubt on the possibility of creating a new biological race in one generation. The defenders of the "new Soviet man" stoutly proclaimed that it *is* possible. In the humanities even the students of word-roots and early linguistic development were victimized, and historians and social scientists steered a particularly perilous course.

The Russian Thermidor came last of all, and doubtless very reluctantly, to modify the traditional communist position on religion. Here militant atheism had been the policy of the early Bolsheviks. They jailed and sometimes executed bishops and priests; they sponsored an atheist society and a museum of anti-religious propaganda. Behind this attitude lay more than the standard Marxist feeling that religion was the opium of the masses; in Russia, the Orthodox Church had always been a pillar of tsarism, and had held back the intellectual advance of the country. Many years of attacks on religion, however, failed to eradicate Orthodoxy from among the people. When in 1937 Hitler built a Russian church in Berlin, and took every occasion to speak kindly of the Orthodox Church, Stalin moved in the religious field also. Declaring that Christianity had contributed to past Russian progress, the government called off its anti-religious propaganda and enlisted its own atheist society to rehabilitate the Church. Church-going became respectable once more, although members of the party were not encouraged to profess religion. As a result, when war came, the leading church dignitaries supported the regime enthusiastically, although Hitler won a number of Ukrainian clerics to his side. In 1943, Stalin received high churchmen; the government lowered taxes on church property, lifted the curfew for Easter, and appointed a new Patriarch, on whose subservience the regime could count.

Viewed together, the changes of the Thermidor period seem to have had a double purpose. They were designed in part to retain popular loyalty during a period when the party itself was being disrupted by the purges. But they were also designed in part to strengthen the country to meet an expected attack from Germany. However far the return to old and popular forms and ideas was carried, it was always the regime that took the lead. And never at any moment did Stalin relax his firm control over all departments of national public and private life.

V: Soviet Foreign Policy, 1918-1941

Foreign Office and Comintern, 1918-1928

During the period of "war communism," the Bolsheviks had a chance to reflect upon their previously firm conviction that the world revolution was to be expected in the immediate future. The communist states in Bavaria and in Hungary proved to be short-lived (see Chapter XXVII); everywhere the moderates triumphed. As the civil war drew to a close, Lenin and his followers realized that to rebuild a shattered Russia it would be necessary to deal with the capitalist world. In the Foreign Office they had two competent men: Chicherin, a learned aristocrat turned Bolshevik, and Litvinov, his shrewd and able chief assistant. These two and their staff now became diplomats in the service of the Soviet state, like diplomats in the service of other states.

But the idea of world revolution was of course not abandoned. Lenin in 1919 founded the Third International, known thereafter as the Comintern. It issued what amounted almost to a new Communist Manifesto, summoning communists all over the world to unite against the "bourgeois cannibals" of capitalism. Zinoviev was put in charge, and his chief assistants were also Russians. Labor, socialist, and anarchist parties in Bulgaria, Norway, Italy, and Spain began to adhere to the new organization, although many withdrew in disgust when it became clear that the Bolsheviks were establishing a dictatorship in Russia with secret police and an army. Yet the Comintern continued to operate side by side with the Foreign Office, and during the next few years often in seeming contradiction to it. This duality gave Russian foreign policy a unique aspect. The maintenance of the Comintern aroused suspicion abroad, and made capitalist states reluctant even to recognize the new Russia.

The Foreign Office concluded a trade treaty with England in 1921, at the beginning of the NEP period, which bound Russia not to stir up the peoples of the British Empire by any means, and re-opened trade between the two countries. Similar treaties were concluded between Russia and Poland, the Baltic States, Scandinavia, Germany, and Italy. A truce had been arranged between the communist and capitalist worlds. In 1922, the Russians were invited to an international economic conference at Genoa. The British and French were convinced that NEP meant a return to capitalism, and had worked out a scheme for investment in Russia as part of a program for the postwar economic reconstruction of Europe. Not only did the Russians reject this plan, but they signed with defeated Germany the Treaty of Rapallo (April, 1922), which provided for the renunciation of all claims for reparations and implied a German willingness to recognize Bolshevik nationalizations. This recognition the other powers, especially France, were unwilling to grant because of the large amounts of capital they had invested in Russia before the revolution. Rapallo relieved Russian isolation, and brought German technical knowledge to the service of the Bolsheviks. They permitted the Germans to build and operate armament and aircraft factories on Russian soil in defiance of the Treaty of Versailles.

In 1923, at Lausanne, Russia lost a dispute with Britain over international regulation of the Straits, and further friction with Britain arose over Afghanistan. But Britain recognized the Soviet regime in 1924, despite Trotsky's description of the mild Laborite Ramsay MacDonald as a "Christian Menshevik" whose country was full of cockroaches—a comment that illustrates some of Russia's difficulty in getting along with the rest of the world. Later in the same year, 1924, the so-called "Zinoviev letter" was published in England. It purported to instruct the British Communist party in the techniques of revolution, and it may or may not have been genuine; but the "Zinoviev letter" influenced the British voters to return a Conservative government, which denounced the treaties with Russia. In 1927, a raid on the offices of a Russian firm doing business in London produced further evidence of communist agitation in England, and the government now broke relations with Russia altogether. The Anglo-Russian council of trade unions set up by the communists collapsed when the Russians criticized British moderation in the general strike of 1926. Meantime, the United States had no diplomatic relations with the Soviet regime, and did not recognize it until 1933.

During the years 1918-1927, the Comintern compiled a record of failure. First, the Russians failed to keep in line the leaders of the Italian Left in a conference at Leghorn in 1921, and thus contributed handsomely to the success of Mussolini in the next year. They failed in Bulgaria to collaborate with a liberal agrarian regime, and allowed the triumph of a fascist group in 1923. Most important, they failed in Germany, where a revolution actually threatened during 1923 as a result of French occupation of the Ruhr (for details of these events, see Chapter XXVII). After Lenin's death, the feud between Stalin and Trotsky was reflected in the Communist parties of other countries and cost the Comintern heavily.

The Russians failed in Poland, where they helped Pilsudski to dictatorial power in 1926, after which he turned against them. They failed in the Moslem and colonial world. But their greatest failure came in China (see also Chapter XXVIII), where in 1923 the Chinese nationalist revolutionary leader, Sun Yat-sen, agreed to take communist advice and received one of the

Comintern's best men, Borodin. Borodin helped Sun re-organize his political party, the Kuomintang, and admitted communists to it, although this alienated the right-wing supporters of the national party. In March, 1926, Sun having died, his brother-in-law Chiang Kai-shek led a *coup* against the government, and began to arrest communists. It is often argued that, had Stalin at that moment broken with Chiang and proceeded to sponsor a Chinese communist revolution, he might well have won China. Indeed Trotsky analyzed the situation that way at the time. But Stalin in his own analysis went back to a theory that the Bolsheviks had not espoused since Lenin's return to Russia in April, 1917: the theory that a bourgeois revolution must precede a socialist revolution, and that all the communists could and should do in China was to help Chiang achieve this first revolution. The eventual result was a series of massacres of Chinese communists by Chiang, and a loss of prestige for Stalin and for Russia.

Indeed Stalin had apparently never really believed in the effectiveness of the Comintern as an instrument of world revolution. When he came to sole power, he could not abandon it, however, because of the criticism he would have aroused, and because he sought to dilute and eventually to eradicate the largely Trotskyite sentiments of communists in other countries. He therefore applied to the Comintern the same techniques he had used against the party at home, and established full control over it through use of the Russian delegation. This delegation was responsible to the Politbureau, and as the representative of the only successful revolutionary country it enjoyed great prestige. Successively, the Comintern was influenced to denounce the enemies of Stalin: Trotsky and the Left in 1924, Bukharin and the Right in 1928. Thereafter there was no divergence between the Comintern and the Foreign Office.

Stalin and the West, 1928-1939

Simultaneously with the adoption of the "new socialist offensive" at home, Stalin swung the Comintern leftward into a new period of militant revolutionary activity. The Social Democrats of western countries were denounced now as "social fascists" and as the most dangerous enemies of communism. The communists were going to bring about revolutions by themselves. Yet Stalin's personal belief in the possibility of revolution elsewhere seems to have been small. "One Soviet tractor is worth more than ten good foreign communists" is a remark quoted as typical of the views of Stalin's entourage in the days of the First Five-Year Plan; it reflects his real contempt for the rest of the world and his deeprooted Russian nationalism.

This lack of real interest in the behavior of communists abroad and the failure to understand the true play of forces inside other countries led directly to the triumph of Hitler in Germany in 1933 (see Chapter XXVII). The communists in Germany, who had been instructed by the Comintern that the Social Democrats and not the Nazis were their worst enemies, fought the Nazis in the streets, but allied themselves with them in the Reichstag. They believed that a Nazi triumph would very soon be followed by a communist revolution. Thus even after Hitler came to power, the Russians renewed their nonaggression pact with Germany.

Yet the shock of realization that Hitler had meant precisely what he said about liquidating communists, and the fear that the U.S.S.R. itself might be in danger, soon led Stalin to modify Russian policy in the direction of collective security. After Hitler had refused to guarantee the Baltic states jointly with Stalin, Russia entered the League of Nations in September, 1934. The Soviet delegate, Litvinov, now became the most eloquent defender of universal disarmament and punishment for aggressors. Soon afterwards, the Russians began to negotiate for an "eastern Locarno" security pact to balance the agreement reached by the western European nations at Locarno in 1925 (see below, p. 540). Although no such structure could be created because of Polish and German hostility to the U.S.S.R., Russia did sign pacts with France and Czechoslovakia in 1935 providing for consultation, under the terms of the League, in the event of aggression, and for mutual aid, if the League certified that aggression had occurred. Soviet aid to Czechoslovakia, if the Czechs became victims of aggression, was to be delivered only if the French, who were bound to the Czechs by a long-standing alliance, honored their obligations first.

In view of the shift in Soviet foreign policy, the Comintern also shifted its line. In 1935 the recent deadly enemies, the Social Democrats and bourgeois liberals of the West, were to be warmly embraced as allies against the fascist menace. Communists were to take the lead in forming "popular fronts" against fascism, and might properly welcome anybody, no matter how conservative in other ways, who would stand together with them on this principle. Revolutionary propaganda and anticapitalist agitation were to be soft-pedaled. The communists in all the countries of the world led the fight for the defense budgets that they had previously sabotaged. Georgi Dimitrov, the Bulgarian communist, hero of the Reichstag fire trial (see below, p. 484) and a symbol of antifascist courage and wit, was made boss of the Comintern. Inside the Soviet Union the adoption of the "popular front" strategy was probably not unrelated to the purges, since the "Right deviationists" were anxious to reach an accommodation with the fascist states, and the "Left deviationists" insisted on the steady pursuit of world revolution.

This was the period when popular front governments came to power in France and Spain, and when some people in the West with bright hopes and little knowledge of the Soviet Union naively accepted the communists as their true brothers in arms against the menace of Hitler. However effective the "popular front" may have been as a tactic with western individuals, the purges inside Russia disillusioned western governments. A state that had to exterminate its top civil and military personnel for the crime of collaborating with the enemy did not make an attractive ally. If one believed the purge charges, one regarded a Soviet alliance as of doubtful value; if one did not believe them, how could one trust Stalin? On Stalin's side, western appeasement of Hitler and Mussolini (see Chapter XXIX) doubtless disillusioned him with the West.

Russia and the western European bloc each assumed that the chief purpose of the other was to turn the full force of Hitler's forthcoming attack away from itself and in the opposite direction. That Hitler intended to attack, nobody could doubt. On September 12, 1936, in a speech at Nuremberg, he specifically declared once more that

if I had the Ural mountains with their incalculable store of treasures in raw materials, Siberia with its vast forests, and the Ukraine with its tremendous wheatfields, Germany under National Socialist leadership would swim in plenty.[*]

There was, then, much reason for the West to hope that the attack would be directed against the U.S.S.R.; this Stalin was determined to avert.

Soviet intervention in the Spanish Civil War (see below, Chapter XXVII) is an interesting demonstration of Stalin's real position. General Francisco Franco, who led an army revolt against the republican government of Spain in 1936, soon obtained aid from Mussolini and Hitler. The Russians, though reluctant to intervene in Spain at all because of their anxiety to

---

[*] A. Hitler, *My New Order*, R. de Sales, ed. (New York, 1941), 400.

prove their respectability to the western powers, realized that a failure to help the Spanish republic would cost them support all over the world. But their aid was too little and came too late, and consisted largely of police agents who devoted themselves to fighting Spanish anarchists and Trotskyites. The Russians hoped that the western powers would intervene also, feeling that if they did so they would be irrevocably committed to continue the fight against Hitler on other battlefields. But western neutrality in Spain helped convince Stalin that a western alliance could not be counted upon.

A still more important factor here was the western appeasement of Hitler, which reached its climax in the Munich agreement of Britain, France, Germany, and Italy in September, 1938 (see also Chapter XXIX). From the Russian point of view, the Munich cession of Czech lands to Hitler, and the French failure to support Czechoslovakia and thus make operative the Russo-Czech alliance, could have only one purpose—to drive Hitler east. Stalin was apparently ready to support the Czechs if the French did too; when they did not, he seems to have decided that he had better sound out Hitler for an understanding. Thus a truly operative alliance

between Stalin and the West proved impossible between 1935 and 1939.

When the British and French realized that appeasement had failed to stop Hitler, they sought reluctantly for a firmer alliance with the U.S.S.R. From March to August, 1939, Stalin kept open both his negotiations with the West and his slowly ripening negotiations with the Germans, which at first seemed to be concerned only with a trade agreement. The British and French mission, when it finally arrived in Moscow, was not composed of sufficiently high-ranking men to inspire Russian confidence. Moreover, the western powers naturally refused to turn over to Stalin the territories that he wanted as a bulwark against Germany—Finland and the Baltic republics of Estonia, Latvia, and Lithuania.

The growing eagerness of the Germans to secure a nonaggression pact gave Stalin the opportunity he sought to divert the war from Russia. In May, 1939, Litvinov was dismissed as foreign minister because he was Jewish and could therefore not negotiate with Germans; he was replaced by Molotov. In the pact Molotov eventually reached with Hitler late in August, 1939, both powers undertook to remain neutral toward each other in the event of war. A secret additional protocol provided for a

A BRITISH IDEA OF A RENDEZVOUS OF THE DICTATORS

After the Hitler-Stalin pact, August, 1939.

division between Germany and Russia of Poland, which Hitler was about to attack. At worst, this put Russia's frontier farther west in the event of a subsequent German attack. The Russians lived up to the economic clauses of the agreement to the letter, although the Germans did not. The publication of the Hitler-Stalin pact necessitated an abrupt shift in the world communist line, which had remained staunchly "popular front." Now it was once more necessary for puzzled communists to denounce liberals and Social Democrats as enemies. They had to call the war that Hitler launched against Poland within a few days an "imperialist war," in which there was no difference between the two sides and in which communists should not get involved.

Stalin and the Second World War

Stalin overrated the military power of the Poles to resist Hitler, and thus miscalculated the course of the first weeks of war. Faced with the complete collapse of Poland, he marched into the eastern portion. Disturbed by the lull ("the phony war") on the western fronts, he probably feared that Hitler would turn against him at once. This might well have happened had Hitler been able to secure peace with France and England, as he strove to do. During the lull, in December, 1939, came Stalin's attack on Finland, which, unlike the Baltic states, had refused to grant him strategic bases. The attack on the Finns by Stalin aroused a storm of anti-Russian sentiment in the West. Both Britain and France supported the recruitment of armies of volunteers, and considered air-raids against Russian targets in support of the Finns. The League of Nations expelled Russia. Despite severe setbacks to the Russian troops, the war against the Finns was won by the spring of 1940 before the west-

ern allies had been able to give them effective aid.

And in the spring of 1940, Stalin's second major calculation went awry. Like many observers, he apparently expected France to hold out a long time and had believed that, even if Hitler eventually defeated the French, Germany would be greatly weakened. Now instead came the lightning German operations in the west, and the war on the Continent was over. Only the British held out (see Chapter XXIX). Preoccupied with the security of his western frontiers, Stalin simply seized the three Baltic republics and staged rigged plebiscites in which the Latvians, Estonians, and Lithuanians asked to be included in the Soviet Union. He demanded of Rumania in June, 1940, the province of Bessarabia, whose loss after World War I the U.S.S.R. had never recognized, and also northern Bukovina, which had formerly been Habsburg, not Russian, territory, but which had a large Ukrainian population and was strategically valuable. Parts of these territories were annexed to existing SSRs and parts were incorporated into the new Moldavian SSR. The Germans had expected Russian seizure of Bessarabia, but not of northern Bukovina; they permitted the seizure, however, telling the Rumanians that they could expect no help from Hitler. But that was as far as Hitler's co-operation with Stalin in eastern Europe went. The re-annexation of Bessarabia had given the U.S.S.R. the mouths of the Danube, controlling an important artery. The Russians seemed to be moving into southeast Europe, a region in which the Germans were not prepared to let them operate alone.

Only a few weeks after the Russian seizure of Rumanian territory, Hitler asserted his own southeastern interests by forcing the Rumanians to cede territory to Hungary (August, 1940) and then guaranteeing the new Rumanian frontiers, a guarantee that could apply only against the U.S.S.R. Soon afterwards, German troops appeared in Finland, "to reinforce the German armies in Norway," Hitler explained. And in the autumn of 1940 German troops entered Rumania proper, "to guard the Rumanian oil-fields against British sabotage." These maneuvers on his new frontiers deeply disquieted Stalin, as well they might have.

In October, 1940, Italy attacked Greece, and open war had spread to the Balkans. In November, when Molotov went to Berlin, Hitler tried to dazzle him with grandiose offers of an enormous future Soviet sphere of influence extending through Persia to the Persian Gulf and Indian Ocean, and including India, after the British Empire was destroyed. Each time this luscious bait was held out, Molotov tried to bring the discussion back to southeast Europe and Finland, and to establish Russia's sole rights in this sphere. This the Germans would not allow. After the failure of the conversations, Hitler ordered preparations for an attack on the U.S.S.R.

In the spring of 1941, the Germans had to rescue the Italians from the Greek campaign, which had bogged down in Albania. This rescue was preceded by the movement of German troops into Bulgaria, which the U.S.S.R. regarded as essential to its own defense. Then came an unsuccessful German effort to win Yugoslavia without war, and swift victorious German campaigns in Yugoslavia and Greece (March-May, 1941). Germany alone ruled supreme in the Balkan region, and, though the Yugoslav and Greek resistance had delayed the German timetable, Hitler was able to launch the invasion of the U.S.S.R. on June 22, 1941. Stalin must have known it was coming; indeed the western powers had warned him. But he seems to have hoped against hope to the end. A few weeks before it came, Stalin, proudly calling himself an Asiatic, had secured a neutrality pact with Japan, Hitler's ally. The Japanese, deeply engaged in China, and intending to go to war with the United States, wished as much as did the Russians for insurance against a war on two fronts.

VI: Conclusion

Karl Marx, who scorned and disliked Russia, would have been utterly dumbfounded had he lived to see that backward agricultural land, almost without a proletariat, produce the only successful European communist revolution. Although much ink has been spilled in an effort to discover why a Marxist revolution took place in the country where, in theory, the conditions were least favorable, the problem is not really so difficult. Two possible general solutions suggest themselves: either Marx was wrong, or what happened in Russia was not a Marxist revolution at all. Or perhaps both these answers are partly right. It seems clear that Marx did not correctly estimate the revolutionary force latent in the Russian peasantry; since Marx died in 1883, he could not foresee the full inadequacy of the tsarist regime, the extent of tensions created by World War I, or the feebleness of the provisional government of 1917. But it also seems clear that to bring the Bolsheviks to power it took Lenin's appreciation of the importance of the peasantry, his grasp of the immediate situation, his willingness to risk everything, and his luck at being in the right place at the right time with the right weapons.

On the other hand, the revolution was not wholly Marxist. Once the Bolsheviks were in power, of course, it was inevitable that the succession of real situations they faced should modify their Marxist-Leninist theories. Thus civil war and foreign intervention brought chaos from which NEP provided a necessary respite. And in Stalin there came to power an amalgam of Marxist, Russian nationalist, and power-hungry politician such as nobody could have foreseen. Moved by a combination of motives, Stalin proceeded hastily and brutally to make over Russia in a decade. Although he fell short of his goal, his program had created an industrial state not totally unprepared for the blows that Hitler was to deal it. Slaves of the state though they were, collectivized by force, industrialized by force, purged, terrorized, and struggling by the million to exist in forced labor camps, the Russians in World War II succeeded, with much help from the United States, in defeating Hitler and his allies.

How much the loyalty of Russians to Stalin was due to the failure of the German invaders to treat them well, and how far Hitler with a different policy might have won their support are questions with which we cannot deal here. The Russians were facing a coalition of fascist states—Germany, Italy, Hungary, Rumania, and others grouped together in an alliance called "the Axis powers" (from the German-Italian "Axis"), a coalition pledged to the utter destruction of communism. We turn now to the history of these powers and of the fascist form of totalitarian doctrine they embraced.

Reading Suggestions on Communist Russia

(Asterisk indicates paperbound edition.)

GENERAL ACCOUNTS

E. H. Carr, *A History of Soviet Russia*. Six volumes of this work, still in progress, have so far appeared (Macmillan, 1950-1960). The only attempt at a complete history of the Soviet Union from original sources; Carr is a somewhat uncritical admirer of Lenin, and his work must be used with care.

B. Moore, Jr., *Soviet Politics: The Dilemma of Power* (Harvard Univ. Press, 1950). An illuminating analysis of the relationship between communist ideology and Soviet practice.

R. N. Carew Hunt, *The Theory and Practice of Communism* (Macmillan, 1951). An excellent introduction to the subject.

M. Fainsod, *How Russia Is Ruled* (Harvard Univ. Press, 1953). An analysis of the Soviet system in 1953, firmly rooted in the historical background. New edition to appear in 1960.

W. W. Rostow and others, *The Dynamics of Soviet Society* (°Mentor, 1954). Attempt by a group of scholars to determine why the Russians behave as they do.

SPECIAL STUDIES

W. H. Chamberlin, *The Russian Revolution, 1917-1921*, 2 vols. (Macmillan, 1935). Still the standard work on the subject.

L. Trotsky, *The History of the Russian Revolution*, 3 vols. (Simon and Schuster, 1932). A brilliant and biased study by one of the leading participants.

B. D. Wolfe, *Three Who Made a Revolution* (Dial, 1948; °Beacon). Excellent triple study of Lenin, Trotsky, and Stalin.

D. Shub, *Lenin* (Doubleday, 1948; °abridgment available, Mentor). The best biography of Lenin in English.

I. Deutscher, *The Prophet Armed, The Prophet Unarmed* (Oxford Univ. Press, 1954 and 1959). Biography of Trotsky, by an admirer.

I. Deutscher, *Stalin: A Political Biography* (Oxford Univ. Press, 1949). The most complete account in English.

J. Maynard, *Russia in Flux* (Macmillan, 1948). Enlightening though sometimes far-fetched attempts to show basic continuities between the old and new regimes; by a British civil servant in India who made Russian studies his avocation.

C. Brinton, *The Anatomy of Revolution,* 2nd ed. (Prentice-Hall, 1952; °Vintage). Comparison of the Russian revolution with the French revolution of 1789 and the English seventeenth-century revolution.

M. Fainsod, *Smolensk Under Soviet Rule* (Harvard Univ. Press, 1959). A uniquely important study, based on a huge collection of captured documents, of the actual workings of the communist system in Smolensk in the 1930's.

H. Schwartz, *Russia's Soviet Economy,* 2nd ed. (Prentice-Hall, 1954). Good introduction to the subject.

N. Timasheff, *The Great Retreat* (Dutton, 1946). An account of the social changes in Russia during the Soviet period.

R. Pipes, *The Formation of the Soviet Union* (Harvard Univ. Press, 1954). Excellent monograph on the question of national minorities in Russia, 1917-1923.

J. W. Wheeler-Bennett, *Brest-Litovsk, The Forgotten Peace* (Macmillan, 1938). Excellent monograph on the Peace of Brest-Litovsk.

L. Fischer, *The Soviets in World Affairs,* 2nd ed. (Princeton Univ. Press, 1951). The only study of Soviet foreign policies up to 1929.

M. Beloff, *The Foreign Policy of Soviet Russia,* 2 vols. (Oxford Univ. Press, 1947, 1952). A solid study covering the years 1929-1941.

F. C. Barghoorn, *The Soviet Image of the United States* (Harcourt, Brace, 1950). How the U.S.S.R. looks at the U.S.A.; by a former representative of the American Department of State.

E. Lyons, *Assignment in Utopia* (Harcourt, Brace, 1937). An American journalist records his disillusionment with Soviet communism.

R. H. Crossman, ed., *The God That Failed* (Harper, 1950). Brief statements by Arthur Koestler, Stephen Spender, Ignazio Silone, and other intellectuals recording their disenchantment with communism.

V. A. Kravchenko, *I Chose Freedom* (Scribner's, 1946). The most celebrated of many works by ex-Soviet officials and citizens who preferred the West to the U.S.S.R.

HISTORICAL FICTION

A. Koestler, *Darkness at Noon* (Modern Library, 1946; °New American Library). A famous novel, presenting in fictional form a keen analysis of the attitudes of the Old Bolsheviks whom Stalin purged.

V. Serge, *The Case of Comrade Tulayev* (Doubleday, 1950). Another excelent novel of the purges.

G. Blunden, *The Room on the Route* (Lippincott, 1947). Perhaps the most vivid fictional portrayal of the impact of terror on the ordinary person.

A. Tolstoy, *Road to Calvary* (Knopf, 1946). Translation of a Stalin Prize Novel about the revolution and civil war.

The Rise of Fascism, 1918-1939

CHAPTER XXVII

I: Introduction

IN THIS CHAPTER we shall deal with the rise of fascism in Europe in the period between the two great wars. By 1939, authoritarian governments of the Right were in firm control of Italy, Germany, Spain, and all the countries of eastern and southeastern Europe except Russia. The process by which these regimes came to power differed widely from country to country, as did some of the external features of the regimes. At first glance, fascism is more complex and more difficult to understand than communism, a doctrine whose development can be traced from Marx through Lenin before its followers were able to put it, or something like it, into practice in Russia. Unlike communism, fascism has no such line of theoretical development. Its proponents often seem to have acted first and worried about doctrine later, devising theories to meet the needs of the moment.

Fascism has been called the revolution of the classes of order. Political parties on the Continent have often represented the interests of the various social classes; when those interests have seemed to be about evenly balanced in a parliamentary state, a long and indecisive political tug-of-war has often ensued. For example, let us assume that a revolution from the Left threatens or can be made to seem to threaten. Then the middle classes, so the theory runs, seize power and take refuge in their own form of extremism—fascism, that is, nationalism tricked out with a few radical phrases to win mass support, and draped in mystical garments. This formula can be applied to Mussolini's rise to power in Italy in 1922, to Hitler's rise to power in Germany in 1933, to Franco's rise to power in Spain in 1936-1939, and to many of the eastern European dictators. Yet the formula takes us only so far. Only a study of the different circumstances in each of the different countries can give it body and meaning.

Economic depressions played a role in the rise of almost every dictator: the postwar depression in Italy, and elsewhere the world-wide depression of 1929 and later. We notice, moreover, a certain similarity in the externals of fascism everywhere— colored shirts, private armies, mass hypnotism, special salutes, special war cries and ceremonies, mystical glorification of the nation, and a vast program of conquest. The dictator's program is justified by references to "have" and "have-not" nations; his own nation is always a "have-not," always oppressed.

Fascism is just as violent in its hatred of democracy, liberalism, and parliamentary institutions as in its professed dislike of communism. Indeed fascism shares communism's abhorrence of constitutional procedure, its disregard of the individual human being, and its insistence that the state is supreme. Fascism persecutes its enemies, both real and fancied, with the same ruthlessness we have observed in Stalin's Russia. Censorship, political police, concentration camps, the rule of the bludgeon, the end of legal protection—all these practices are common to both fascism and communism.

When Mussolini ruled in Rome, public buildings everywhere carried the admonition to loyal Italians, "Believe, fight, obey" *(Credere, combattere, obbedire)*. Presumably this was intended to be inspiring. Yet all it really means is: Believe (what Mussolini tells you), fight (for Mussolini and his backers), obey (Mussolini). When put this way, the formula is seen to subvert all religion and all human decency. Yet many an idealist was taken in by it, under the stress of the unbearable pressures on individuals generated by the tension of the years between the wars.

II: Italy and Fascism

The Setting

Although Italy was a member of the victorious Allied coalition, she finished the First World War with a sense of defeat. Six hundred and fifty thousand of her men had been killed and one million wounded. Industry slumped immediately after the war, and within a few months 10 per cent of the industrial workers were unemployed. Prices rose rapidly, and wages failed to keep up. The promised pensions for wounded veter-

ans and families of the killed were long delayed. Strikes and disorders became frequent. Many of the young men released from the armies with no trade but war and no job to go to drifted restlessly and discontentedly, fit prey for leaders with glittering promises.

Perhaps most important, the Italian government itself, hoping to influence the peace negotiations, began to spread propaganda among the Italian people to the effect that their wartime allies were robbing them of the Slavic lands in Dalmatia, across the Adriatic, promised to Italy by the secret Treaty of London (see above, Chapter XXV) in exchange for Italy's entrance into the war. This arrangement the United States had never agreed to, and now would not accept. Although the Allied leaders at the Paris Peace Conference remained unaffected by the storms of protest

D'Annunzio.

arising from Italy, the Italian people did come to believe that they had shed their blood in vain. Popular sentiment in Italy, especially in the army, swung toward extremists of one sort or another.

Some Italians hysterically supported Gabriele d'Annunzio, a short, bald nationalist poet and romantic novelist who formed a band of volunteers. They seized the city of Fiume, the Adriatic seaport over which Croatians and Hungarians had long disagreed (see above, p. 408). Referring to

the "stench of peace," and denouncing Woodrow Wilson, d'Annunzio declared that the time for heroic individual action was at hand. Fiume had actually not been awarded to Italy even by the Secret Treaty of London, but d'Annunzio felt that Italy must have it, and that was enough. He ran his own government in Fiume until the end of 1920.

D'Annunzio patterned his regime there upon that of an imaginary medieval commune in a poem by Italy's romantic poet Carducci (1835-1907). Modeling himself consciously upon the governor of the commune in the poem, d'Annunzio would appear on the balcony of the city hall, address an inspirational harangue to the crowd, and ask for its unanimous consent for whatever he wished to do. This his listeners would grant, raising their right hands high, as the imaginary citizens of Carducci's commune had done. Some of d'Annunzio's followers wore black shirts. When d'Annunzio asked them to whom Fiume belonged they would shout *A noi*, "to us," and when he asked them to whom Italy belonged, they would give the same answer. Indeed, he planned to lead his followers from Fiume to Rome, and thence out into the world to conquer it, presumably with daggers, which he preferred to mechanized weapons. He drafted the Statutes of Fiume, a constitution in which he made a conscious attempt to organize society along the lines he imagined to have existed in the guilds and artisans' corporations of the Middle Ages.

In November, 1920, the Italian government signed the Treaty of Rapallo with Yugoslavia, by which Fiume was to become a free city. Italian forces drove d'Annunzio out, and into retirement in a villa on the Italian lakes. But the techniques of force, the haranguing of the mob from the balcony, the straight-arm salute, the black shirts, the rhythmic cries, the plans for conquest, and the "corporative" scheme of the Statutes of Fiume served as precedent and inspiration for Benito Mussolini, founder of Italian fascism.

In the first four years after the end of the war, Mussolini created and brought to power a new political force in Italy. In October, 1922, he was summoned to office by King Victor Emmanuel III (1900-1947); from then on he gradually created a totalitarian state of which he was the sole, undisputed ruler. Suppressing all opposition at home, and threatening the peace abroad, the fascist state in Italy served in some degree as model for the Nazis in Germany, for the Falangists in Spain, and for totalitarian regimes in virtually all the European successor states of the Habsburg and Ottoman empires. Eventually, Mussolini was forced, largely by his own propaganda, into an alliance with Hitler. In 1940, this alliance took Italy into World War II, and in 1945 it brought Mussolini himself to an ignominious death, upside down on a communist partisan gallows, with his mistress beside him.

Mussolini: Early Career

Mussolini was born in 1883, in the Romagna, a province of central Italy famous for its political extremists, and for the violence with which they express themselves. His father was an ardent socialist who had begun his career as an anarchist under the influence of Bakunin (see above, p. 300). Trained as an elementary-school teacher, Mussolini was already a passionate socialist by the time he was eighteen. He spent some time as an agitator among Italian emigrant laborers in Switzerland (1902-1904) and in Austria (1909) but was expelled by the police. Back in Italy, he was imprisoned for opposing the war against Turkey over Tripoli (1911). In 1912, he became editor of the most important Italian socialist newspaper, *Forward (Avanti).*

When World War I began, Mussolini was at first vigorously opposed to Italy's entry. But then, during 1914, he changed his mind. First he favored "relative neutrality," meaning that socialists should leave themselves free to support Italian entry if such a course seemed likely to prove favorable to them. When the Italian Socialist party refused to follow this idea, he resigned as editor of *Avanti.* Soon afterward (November, 1914), he founded his own newspaper, *The People of Italy (Il Popolo d'Italia)* in Milan, and began to advocate an immediate Italian declaration of war on the side of the Allies. For this the Socialist party expelled him.

But these bare bones of a biography reveal only the externals. As a socialist, Mussolini before 1914 was a passionate left-winger. He was an apostle of violent social revolution and a bitter opponent of milder evolutionary and reformist doctrine. He urged that a small, well-knit armed minority should seize power and establish a dictatorship. He loathed militarism, was himself a draft-dodger, and urged soldiers to desert the army. He hated monarchy, and savagely attacked in his writings all the crowned heads of Europe, especially the Italian House of Savoy. He was a vigorous atheist, urged workers to stay away from church, and scorned the teachings of Christ. As an international revolutionary he opposed nationalism, and even referred to the Italian flag as "a rag to be planted on a dunghill."

Yet he was to repudiate almost all these positions, and as fascist chieftain to substitute almost the exact opposites. As a fascist, he attacked bolshevism and all left-wing movements; he made his peace with the monarchy and the Church; he became a militant nationalist, a mystic patriot, and a rabid militarist. The repudiation of the views he had held so long and advocated so skillfully is not nearly so astonishing as it seems. From the first, Mussolini did not much care for programs; what he wanted was to rule.

A complete opportunist, he could shift his line on any question at a moment's notice if it seemed advantageous. For example, after the war, though he was now a fascist, he at first supported a radical program of social change, indistinguishable from the program he would have advocated had he still been a socialist. He favored the action of the Italian workers in the fall of 1920, when they occupied the factories in a kind of sit-down strike. Yet, within a year, he was using the fears which this strike had aroused in the middle classes to argue that he was the only possible bulwark against "bolshevism." About certain matters, however, he was consistent: he always hated parliaments and he always loved violence.

Mussolini's switch from isolationism to interventionism in the war in 1914 was the first of his important shifts. It may be that as a revolutionary socialist he had come to feel that only war could produce in Italy the conditions necessary to a revolution. It may be that his affection for violence got the better of his socialist doctrines, and that he pleaded for action simply for the sake of action. After his expulsion from the Socialist party, he agitated furiously for war, speaking to groups of similarly minded young men called *fasci* or groups (the image is of a bundle of rods, a symbol of office in the Roman Republic of antiquity). Soon after Italy did enter the war in 1915, Mussolini was conscripted and sent to the front. He was badly wounded in 1917 by an Italian mortar shell that exploded during practice, and he spent several months in the hospital. When he got out, he continued to edit his newspaper, spewing forth a mixture of extreme revolutionary and extreme nationalist propaganda.

Mussolini: Rise to Power

In March, 1919, Mussolini founded the first *fasci di combattimento* ("groups for combat"). There was no sign as yet to indicate that by October, 1922, the leader

of this small movement would become the most powerful man in Italy. In 1919, he called for every kind of revolutionary violence—seizure of the land, attacks on the factories, shooting of storekeepers who charged high prices, expropriation of mines and transports, and war by the vanquished "proletarian" nations against the victorious capitalists who had kept Italy from annexing Dalmatia. He now maintained that socialism was too conservative; his movement, far from setting itself against a revolution, was in the vanguard of those who were crying for one.

Yet in Italy a revolution along Bolshevik patterns was most unlikely, if not impossible. The peasants were not very revolutionary, for they already held much of the land except in the extreme south. And the industrial workers, though often discontented, knew that a revolution could be starved out because the country needed to import most of its raw materials. The Socialist party was overwhelmingly in the hands of moderates, and in 1919 Catholics founded the Popular party (*Partito Populare Italiano*), designed to compete with the Socialists for the votes of the lower classes, who now had universal suffrage.

In the postwar disorders the peasants seized without consent of the landowners less than one-tenth of 1 per cent of the arable land in Italy. The leaders of the Socialist party and the General Confederation of Labor voted down the proposals of anarchist and communist extremists to turn the workers' occupation of the factories into a revolution. The government waited for the workers to grow tired. This they did in less than a month (September, 1920); then they left the occupied factories and went home.

Yet the actual state of affairs is often less important than what influential sections of society persuade themselves to believe is the actual state of affairs. Although the danger of revolution was small, the fear of revolution was great. Thus, during 1920 and 1921 the industrialists and landowners, squeezed by taxation and inflation, became bitter. Shopkeepers and tradesmen wanted street disorders to end, food prices to be regulated, and the co-operative food stores of the Socialist and Catholic parties to be put out of business as competitors. In particular, professional men and others with fixed incomes suffered as prices and wages went up and salaries lagged behind. The police grew tired of suppressing local disorders and of being repaid with insults. Ex-servicemen, insulted by anarchists and communists for their war records, naturally grew more patriotic.

All these groups identified the forces they did not like as Bolshevik, and accepted as an article of faith the myth of an impending Bolshevik revolution. After a series of fascist-socialist street fights and riots, these "anti-Bolsheviks" began to look to Mussolini's fascist bands as the defenders of their interests. D'Annunzio's defeat left Mussolini as his natural heir. The Left opposition to Mussolini was weakened when the communists split off from the Socialist party in 1921. The *fasci* grew enormously, from 30,000 in May, 1920, to 100,000 in February, 1921, to more than 300,000 at the time of the "March on Rome" in October, 1922. No longer were they merely squads of discontented and idle youths with vaguely revolutionary and nationalist ideas. Now, says one fascist of the period, "the sons and hangers-on of the bigwigs" poured into the organization:

They had come into the Fascio for their own ends. . . . If they met men in working clothes, they fell on them and began beating them. Their mentality was on a par with that of the Communists, who had beaten and murdered anybody who was decently dressed. One saw . . . the well-known surly and rapacious faces of war profiteers . . . and we were obliged to accept their money because we needed it to stifle an evil worse than they.[*]

[*] Umberto Banchelli, *Memorie di un Fascista,* quoted by G. Salvemini in *The Fascist Dictatorship* (New York, 1927), 67-68.

The liberal parliamentary leaders of Italy felt that the fascist bands were teaching the Left a useful lesson. They encouraged the commanding officers of the army to issue rifles and army trucks and gasoline to the fascists and even assigned army officers to command their operations. The police were encouraged to look the other way during disorders started by the fascists, and local judges were urged to help by releasing arrested fascists. Mussolini's newspaper was circulated free to the soldiers in the army as a "patriotic" sheet.

A campaign of terror now began against the socialists and Christian Democrats, as the fascist squadrons cruised around Italy in trucks, burning down labor-union offices, newspaper offices, and local Socialist party headquarters, and beating up and sometimes murdering labor leaders or local anti-fascist politicians. The *fasci* forced duly elected officials to resign. The torch, the cudgel, and the famous castor-oil treatment were all characteristic weapons. It is estimated that 2,000 people, anti-fascist and fascist, policemen and innocent bystanders, died by violence between October, 1920, and October, 1922.

The "March" on Rome

In the elections of May, 1921, Mussolini and thirty-four other fascists were elected to Parliament, along with ten Nationalists, their political allies. The momentum of the fascist movement was now too great to be slowed down. Mussolini abandoned his anti-monarchical views, and fascism became a political party (November, 1921) as a necessary step in the drive for power. Too late, the government became alarmed and tried to take measures against the fascists, but the squads were too strong, the police too accustomed to collaborating with them, and the politicians themselves as yet unaware that a tightly directed armed mob could really take over the state. Inside the royal family, the King's cousin, the Duke of Aosta, had become a fascist sympathizer, as had many army generals, the entire Nationalist party, and the leading industrialists.

In the fall of 1922 it was clear that the army would not resist a fascist *coup* in Rome itself. When a decree of martial law was presented to the King, he refused to sign it, probably influenced by his knowledge that the army would not fight the fascists and that the Duke of Aosta would gladly take his crown. The refusal of the King to declare martial law greatly heartened the fascists. Now, as the fascists "marched" on Rome, mostly by storming railroad trains and stealing free rides, the King (October 29, 1922) telegraphed Mussolini in Milan to come to Rome and form a cabinet. Mussolini arrived by sleeping-car the next morning.

Fascism, which had begun as a patriotic anti-Bolshevik movement, and had then turned into an anti-labor movement in the service of the industrialists and landowners, had finally come to power as a conspiracy against parliamentary government in the service of a military clique. Just before taking office, Mussolini announced:

Our program is simple: we wish to govern Italy. They ask us for programs, but there are already too many. It is not programs that are wanting for the salvation of Italy but men and will-power.*

The Fascist Dictatorship

Mussolini now moved gradually to turn his premiership into a dictatorship. A month after coming to office, he obtained dictatorial powers that were to last only until the end of 1923. Although the constitution theoretically remained in force, Mussolini proceeded to take over the administration. He created a Fascist Militia almost 200,000 strong, which owed complete allegiance to him. He enlarged the regular army, and required its members to take an oath of personal loyalty to him. Before his dictatorial powers expired, he secured from Parliament by pressure a new electoral law. This law provided that the political party which received the largest number of votes in a general election, if that number amounted to at least one-

---

* Quoted by H. Finer, *Mussolini's Italy* (New York, 1935), 152.

Mussolini and fascisti during the "march" on Rome, October, 1922.

quarter of the vote, should automatically receive two-thirds of the seats in Parliament. The rest of the seats would be divided proportionately. This law made certain the fascists' domination of future parliaments. Indeed, in the election of April, 1924, the fascists actually polled 65 per cent of the vote cast; but this figure reflects a widespread use of intimidation and terrorism at the polls. The first all-fascist cabinet was now appointed. Meanwhile, local administration was made secure by the appointment of fascist prefects and subprefects in the provinces; these officials pursued the enemies of fascism with the same weapons of murder and mayhem that had been used before Mussolini's March on Rome.

Early in 1924, the leader of the opposition to Mussolini, the socialist Giacomo Matteotti, published a book called *The Fascists Exposed*, in which he detailed many of the outrages the fascists had committed on their way to power. It seemed probable that further revelations were in store, exposing some of Mussolini's cabinet members as corrupt. On June 10, 1924, Matteotti was "taken for a ride" in true gangster style and murdered. The crime was traced to members of Mussolini's immediate circle. This scandal rocked Italy, and for a moment it even seemed possible that Mussolini would fall. But he dismissed from office those who were involved, and pledged himself to restore law and order. Actually, he delayed trying the guilty men until March, 1926, and even then they all got off lightly.

What really helped Mussolini over the crisis, ironically enough, was the departure of most of the opposition deputies from Parliament. They declared that they would not return until the Matteotti murder had been solved and the government had been shown to be innocent. Far from making things harder for Mussolini, as they had intended, their departure actually made things easier. Mussolini simply denied his own guilt, imposed a rigid press censorship, and forbade the opposition to meet. Most of the deputies never did return to Parliament, and in 1926 their seats were declared forfeit.

Though the Matteotti crisis continued into 1925, Mussolini simply tightened the screws. A series of laws called the "most fascist laws" *(legge fascistissime)* tightened control over the press, forbade secret societies like the Freemasons, whom Mussolini had loathed ever since his socialist youth, and extended the control of the central government to all the cities and towns by depriving them of their elected officials, who were replaced by officials appointed from Rome. Opponents of the regime were arrested and transported into exile on desolate islands off the Italian coast. Early in 1926, Mussolini was empowered to govern by decree. Three attempts on his life led to a new law providing the death penalty for action against the King, the Queen, or Mussolini. All opposition political parties were abolished in the same year, and the Fascist party was left as the only legal political party in Italy.

More and more the Italian state and the Fascist party were brought into co-ordination. Mussolini was both the *Duce* (leader) of the fascists and the *capo di governo*, the chief of state. At one moment he also held eight cabinet posts simultaneously. The members of the Fascist Grand Council, a "politbureau" numbering roughly twenty of the highest party functionaries, all appointed by Mussolini, held all the important posts in the administration not held by Mussolini himself. In 1928, the Grand Council was given important constitutional duties: preparing the lists of candidates for election to the Chamber, advising Mussolini, and proposing changes in the constitution or the succession to the throne. The Grand Council thus became a kind of third house, above the other two houses of Parliament, the Senate and the Chamber.

The Corporative State

Indeed, Mussolini planned to change the principles of the western parliamentary system. He believed that the interests of labor and capital could and must be made to harmonize with the over-riding interests of the state. Instead of a political system as we understand it, he accepted the idea that representation should be based on economic interests organized in "syndicates." Such an idea was not new: the French syndicalist, Georges Sorel (see above, p. 216) had already argued in this vein. But Sorel believed in class warfare, and in government by syndicates of workers only. Mussolini, following the Italian nationalist syndicalist, Rossoni, believed in capitalism, class-collaboration, and producers' syndicates as well as workers' syndicates.

In 1925, fascist labor unions were recognized by employers as having the sole right to negotiate labor contracts. Then, in April, 1926, the state officially recognized producers' and workers' syndicates in each of six areas—industry, agriculture, commerce, sea and air transport, land and inland waterway transport, and banking—plus a syndicate of intellectuals, making thirteen syndicates in all. Each syndicate could bargain and reach contracts, and could assess dues upon everyone engaged in its own economic field, irrespective of membership in the syndicate. Strikes and lockouts were both forbidden. When labor conditions did not improve, a "charter of labor," promising insurance and other benefits, was issued in 1927. In 1926, the syndicates were put under the control of a special Ministry of Corporations; Mussolini was the minister.

In 1928, the system of parliamentary representation was changed in accordance with fascist syndicalism. A new electoral law provided for a new Chamber of Deputies (400 instead of 560 members). The national councils of the thirteen syndicates could nominate a total of 800 candidates. Each syndicate had a quota, half to be selected by the employers and half by the employees. Cultural and charitable foundations could nominate 200 more candidates. When the total list of 1,000 was completed, the Fascist Grand Council could either select 400 of them, or strike out names and add names of its own, or even substitute an entire new list. The voters would then vote in answer to the question: "Do you approve of the list of deputies selected by the Fascist Grand Council?" They could vote "Yes" or "No" on the entire list, but they could not choose from among the candidates. If a majority voted "Yes," the list was elected; if not, the procedure was to be repeated. Despite the highly touted role of the syndicate, all the power obviously lay with the Fascist Grand Council. Universal suffrage was abolished even for this very limited form of election. Payment of a minimum tax or dues to a syndicate was required of each voter; women could not vote. In 1929, the elections under this system produced a "yes" vote of 8,519,559 and a "no" vote of 137,761.

Between 1930 and 1938 several constitutional steps were taken which seemed to move the syndicates into the center of the stage. Representatives from the syndicates and the government were now formed into a Council of Corporations, which was to act as a co-ordinating committee, settle disputes between syndicates, assist production, and establish the fascist corporations themselves, which had not yet been created. The Council was divided into seven sections corresponding to the seven syndicate areas, and in 1931 each of these sections of the Council was simply declared to be a corporation. In 1933, it was announced that the whole corporate system would be revised; and in 1934 the new elections (which of course returned the Fascist Grand Council's list of candidates) produced a "suicide" Chamber of Deputies, which was expected eventually to put an end to its own existence. Its replacement was to be a new "revolutionary assembly," which Mussolini called into existence in the fall of 1934. The assembly, also called the Central Committee of Corporations, contained 824 members, representing twenty-two newly created corporations. The Fascist party, as well as employers and employees, was represented on each corporation.

But it was not until 1938 that the last step was taken, when the "suicide chamber" ended its existence and replaced itself with the Central Committee of Corporations, which was now called the Chamber of Fasces and Corporations. There was nothing left of the old parliamentary constitution that had been set up by Cavour except the Senate, nominally appointed by the King but actually subservient to Mussolini, who on one occasion had the King appoint forty fascist senators all at once. This new structure, the corporative state, was influenced by d'Annunzio's strange medieval ideas, and by Mussolini's own wish to produce new political and economic forms. But in spite of much oratory by fascist sympathizers about the corporative state and its virtues, it does not appear that the new bodies ever had very much to do with running the economic or political life of Italy, which remained firmly under the direction of the fascist bureaucracy.

Other Fascist Domestic Policies

During the thirties, the fascist version of the planned economy made its appearance in Italy. The government issued or withheld permits for factory construction. In agriculture, a concerted effort was launched to make Italy more nearly self-sufficient. This effort was dramatized with the "Battle of Wheat," in which the Italians were treated to contests, prizes, and personal appearances by Mussolini. In 1932, official figures reported that wheat produc-

tion had risen to a point where it could supply 92 per cent of the nation's normal needs, and the drive was enlarged to include other cereal products. The government subsidized steamship and air lines, encouraged the tourist trade, and protected Italian industries by means of high tariffs on foreign products. Marshes were drained and land was reclaimed; the incidence of malaria was reduced. Enormous sums were spent on public works, and great strides were made in the development of hydroelectric power. The trains, at least so thousands of tourists reported, ran on time; many argued that "there must be something in this man Mussolini." Yet Italy's weakness in essential raw materials proved to be insuperable.

The state reached into the life of the individual at almost every point. Though Italy was overpopulated, and had for decades relieved the situation only by mass emigration, Mussolini made emigration a crime. He encouraged people to marry and have the largest possible families: he reduced their taxes, extended special loans, taxed bachelors, and extended legal equality to illegitimate children. He hoped in this way to swell the ranks of his armies, and to strengthen his claim that Italy must expand abroad. Children, the future party members, were enrolled in a series of youth movements, beginning at the age of six. The textbooks in the schools, the books in the libraries, the professors in the universities, the plays on the stage and the movies on the screen were all made vehicles of fascist propaganda. The secret police, OVRA (from the initials of the Italian words for "Vigilance Organization against Anti-Fascist Crimes"), endeavored to discover and suppress all opposition movements.

In 1929, Mussolini settled the Roman question (see Chapter XXI) by entering into the Lateran Treaty with the papacy. This treaty recognized the independent state of Vatican City and thus restored the temporal power of the pope, though on a greatly reduced scale. Mussolini also recognized Catholicism as the state religion, and promised to halt anti-papal propaganda. He gave up the right to tax contributions to the Church or the salaries of the clergy, and paid $105,000,000 to compensate the papacy for the Italian occupation of papal territories since 1870. A concordat further regulated the relations between Church and State. Religious marriages were legalized, and religious instruction was extended in schools. The Church agreed not to engage in politics in its newspapers and periodicals.

Yet, despite the fact that many church officials viewed the fascist movement sympathetically, difficulties arose after these agreements had been concluded. In an encyclical, Pope Pius XI (1922-1939) indicated his disapproval of Mussolini's "relentless" economic policies and of the corporations as "serving special political aims rather than contributing to the initiation of a better social order." Mussolini now charged that the Church's "Catholic Action" clubs were engaged in politics, and dissolved them. The Pope denied the charges, and denounced the Fascist party's practice of monopolizing the time and education of the young. In 1931, however, a further agreement was reached, and the clubs were re-opened.

Fascist Foreign Policy and Its Consequences

Since Mussolini's foreign policies form an integral part of the international relations leading up to World War II, we shall discuss them more fully in Chapter XXIX. Here we may simply point out that his extreme nationalism, his love of panoply and parades, and his militarism were the logical extensions of his domestic ideas and accomplishments. Mussolini's wish to re-create the glories of ancient Rome impelled him to undertake a policy of adventure in the Mediterranean, which he called *Mare Nostrum* (Latin for "our sea") as a sign that he was the heir to the Caesars. This policy began in 1923, when five Italians working for the League of Nations were assassinated as they marked out the new frontier between Albania and Greece. Mussolini bombarded and occupied the Greek island of Corfu, and refused to recognize the League's right to intervene. Only British pressure led to a settlement of the matter.

Later, Mussolini's policy of adventure led him to military aggression in Ethiopia, in Spain, and in Albania (which he dominated during the 1920's and occupied in April, 1939). It drove him into an alliance with his fellow-fascist, Hitler, and led him to voice loud claims against the French for Corsica, Tunisia, Nice, and Savoy. And it alienated Italy from her natural allies, France and Britain. Thus, Mussolini's grandiose fascist ideology first spurred Italy to win self-sufficiency, to rebuild her seaports, and to create a merchant fleet and navy. But the same ideology ultimately separated her from the only powers who might have saved her from the disaster toward which Mussolini was driving.

The German alliance was also responsible for a striking new departure in fascist domestic policy. This was the official adoption of anti-Semitism, which took place in 1938. With only 70,000 Jews, most of whom had long been resident, Italy had no "Jewish problem." Italian Jews were entirely Italian in their language and sentiments, and could be distinguished from other Italians only by their religion. Many of them were prominent in the fascist movement, and many were anti-fascist. There was no widespread sympathy in Italy for the government's adoption of Hitler's racial policies. Yet Hitler's dominating influence led Mussolini to expel Jews from the Fascist party, and to forbid them to teach or attend school, to intermarry with non-Jews, and to obtain new licenses to conduct businesses.

In summing up Mussolini's career, we may turn to a quotation from an article that he himself wrote in 1920 to denounce Lenin. In reading it, substitute Mussolini for Lenin, Italy for Russia, fascist for communist, and you will have a clear idea of fascism:

Russia is a state . . . composed of men who exercise power, imposing an iron discipline upon individuals and groups and practicing 'reaction' whenever necessary. . . . In the Russia of Lenin there is only one authority: his authority. There is only one liberty: his liberty.

There is only one opinion: his opinion. There is only one law: his law. One must either submit or perish. . . . Russia . . . swallows up and crushes the individual and governs his entire life. . . . Whoever says state necessarily says the army, the police, the judiciary, and the bureaucracy. The Russian state is the state *par excellence*. . . . It has *statized* economic life . . . and formed a huge army of bureaucrats. At the base of this pyramid, . . . there is the proletariat which, as in the old bourgeois regimes, obeys, works, and eats little or allows itself to be massacred. . . .*

---

* Mussolini on Lenin in 1920, quoted by G. Megaro, *Mussolini in the Making* (Boston, 1938), 325-326.

III: Germany and the Weimar Republic, 1918-1933

In Germany, where Hitler was eventually to acquire power far greater than Mussolini's, the advent of fascism came later than in Italy. The German experiment with democracy lasted fifteen years after the end of World War I. Two days before the armistice of November 11, 1918, the Social Democrats proclaimed a republic in Germany. On July 31, 1919, this republic adopted a constitution drawn up by a national assembly at Weimar; it is therefore known as the "Weimar Republic." The Weimar Constitution was never formally abandoned, but after Adolf Hitler became chancellor on January 30, 1933, Germany was in fact a dictatorship.

It is convenient to divide the history of Germany between World Wars I and II at 1933, at the moment when Hitler took office as chancellor. Between 1918 and 1933, there are three shorter periods: the period of political threats from Left and Right and of mounting economic chaos, from 1918 to the end of 1923; the period of political stability, fulfillment of the Versailles Treaty requirements, and seeming economic prosperity, from 1924 to late 1929; and the period of economic depression and mounting right-wing power, from late 1929 to January, 1933.

The Impact of Defeat

For the overwhelming majority of the German people, defeat in 1918 came as a great surprise. The military authorities who ran the German Empire during the last years of the war had failed to report to the public German reverses on the battlefield. No fighting had ever taken place on German soil, and the Germans had got used to thinking of their armies as in firm possession of the foreign territories they had overrun. Now these armies came home intact. It is often argued that the Allies committed a grave blunder by their failure to march to Berlin and demonstrate to the German people that they had actually been defeated. Schooled in reverence for their military forces, the Germans could not grasp the fact that their armies had lost the war. Moreover, the Allies, under the leadership of Wilson, simply refused to deal with the Supreme Command of the German armies. Field Marshal von Hindenburg, as supreme commander, was never required to hand over his sword to Marshal Foch, or to sign the armistice. Rather, it was the civilian politicians who had to bear the odium. In this way the Allies unintentionally did the German military caste a great favor.

Before the ink was dry on the armistice agreement, the generals, led by Hindenburg himself, were explaining that the German armies had never really been defeated. This was exactly what the public wanted to believe, and the harsh facts—that Ludendorff and Hindenburg had insisted on surrender because the armies could no longer fight—were never effectively publicized. So the legend that Germany had somehow been "stabbed in the back" by civilians, by liberals, socialists, communists, and Jews, took deep root and became almost an article of faith among many Germans. This legend was widely disseminated by politicians, especially by those who had a stake in the old Prussian system—the monarchists, agrarians, industrialists, and militarists. All through the period of the Weimar Republic, these groups remained hostile toward it; their hostility ranged from political opposition to conspiracies to overthrow the government.

The Allies added another error by including the celebrated "war-guilt" clause in the Treaty of Versailles. The German signatories were obliged to acknowledge what none of them believed, and what subsequent historians would disprove: that Germany alone had been responsible for the outbreak of the war. The war-guilt clause made it harder for the German public to acknowledge defeat and the evils of the past system, to sweep away the militarists, and to bend to the task of creating a virile republic. Instead, it led many Germans to dissipate their energies in denying war-guilt, in hating the enemies who had saddled them with the charge, in bewailing the sell-out of their generals,

and in waiting for a chance to show by force that they had been right all the time.

Postwar Political Alignments and Activities

This strengthening of the anti-republican forces of the Right was further increased by the threat to stability from the Left. Responsibility for launching the republic and for preventing disorder fell upon the "majority socialists," made up of Social Democrats and right-wing Independent Socialists, and led by the Social Democrat, Ebert. The Social Democrats were a moderate group. For example, they made no attack on agrarian property, and they allowed the Junkers to maintain intact their estates and the social and political position that went with them. The Social Democrats, true to their reformist tradition, concluded with the industrialists collective bargaining agreements that guaranteed the eight-hour day, rather than trying to launch a serious movement for nationalizing German industry.

But to the left of the Social Democrats agitation for a proletarian revolution on the Russian pattern was carried on by the left wing of the Independent Socialists and the Communist "Spartacists" (named for Spartacus, the leader of a slave revolt in ancient Rome). Unable to operate effectively through soviets, the Left tried to stage a revolution in the winter of 1918-19, but Ebert called in the army to stop it. The generals used not only regular units but also newly formed volunteer units, or "Free Corps," made up mostly of professional soldiers, who were embittered by Germany's recent military defeat and were violently opposed to democracy.

Now the right wing of the Independent Socialists withdrew from the government, and sole responsibility thenceforth rested with the Social Democrats, who put their man Noske into the war ministry. As the civil strife continued, the communists attempted a *coup*, which Ebert, Noske, and the troops put down. Cavalry officers murdered the two chief leaders of the communists after peace had been restored, at the cost of more than a thousand casualties. Meanwhile, in Catholic Bavaria, disorders led to the brief emergence of a Soviet republic, which was liquidated in May, leaving Bavaria the home of a sort of permanent red-scare. The Bavarian local authorities, throughout the entire life of the Weimar Republic, encouraged the intrigues of monarchists, militarists, and nationalists. It was in Bavaria that Free Corps assassinations were planned, and it was there that Hitler got his start.

In this way the forces of the German Right, ostensibly crushed by the war, were given a powerful new lease on life by the Allies. Meantime, Germany still had an army, the *Reichswehr*, limited in size to 100,000 men, consisting chiefly of officer cadres, magnificently trained and able to take over the command of far larger numbers if and when troops became available.

The political constellation of the new Germany did not consist solely of Social Democrats and extremists of Right and Left. The old parties of imperial Germany (see Chapter XXII) reappeared, often with new labels. The right wing of the old Liberals now emerged as the People's party, including the more moderate industrialists, with a platform of private property and opposition to socialism. Its leader was Gustav Stresemann. Former Progressives and left-wing Liberals now formed the new Democratic party, a genuine middle-class republican and democratic group, including many of Germany's most distinguished intellectuals. The Catholic Center party reemerged with its name and program unchanged. It accepted the Republic, rejected socialism, and favored social legislation under pressure from its left wing of trade-union members, but it opposed far-reaching reform under pressure from its right wing

of aristocrats and industrialists. The Social Democrats, the Democrats, the Center, and the people's party represented those groups which, though not all enthusiastic, were willing to try to make the new state work. On the Right, the former Conservatives reemerged as the National People's party or Nationalists, dominated by the Junkers as before. The Nationalists had the support of some great industrialists, of most of the bureaucrats, and of a substantial section of the lower middle class, which hoped to return to the good old days of the monarchy. The Nationalists did not accept the Republic.

The Weimar Constitution, 1919

When the Germans voted for a national constituent assembly in January, 1919, the parties supporting the Republic won more than 75 per cent of the seats (see table on p. 473), with the Social Democrats alone obtaining nearly 40 per cent. The assembly met in Weimar, elected Ebert to be President of Germany, and formed a government that reluctantly signed the Treaty of Versailles after a delay of some months. The assembly then adopted the new constitution. The new Germany was still a federative state, but the central government had great authority to legislate for the entire country. The president might use armed force to coerce any of the states which failed to obey the constitution or national laws. The cabinet was responsible to the lower house, or *Reichstag*, which was to be chosen by universal suffrage of all citizens (including women) over twenty.

The president, who was to be elected every seven years by the entire people, was given considerable authority. He was empowered to make treaties, appoint and remove the cabinet, command the armed forces and appoint or remove all officers, dissolve the Reichstag, and call new elections. Further, he could take any measure

GERMAN ELECTIONS TO THE WEIMAR ASSEMBLY AND REICHSTAG, 1919-1933

(Number of seats obtained by the major parties, arranged with the Left at the top, the Right at the bottom)

	Jan. 1919	June 1920	May 1924	Dec. 1924	May 1928	Sept. 1930	July 1932	Nov. 1932	Mar. 1933
Communists	— [a]	2	62	45	54	77	89	100	81
Independent Socialists	22	81	— [b]						
Social Democrats	163	112	100	131	152	143	133	121	125
Democrats	74	45	28	32	25	14	4	2	5
Center	71	68	65	69	61	68	75	70	74
People's party	22	62	44	51	45	30	7	11	2
Nationalists	42	66	96	103	78	41	40	51	52
Nazis			38	20	12	107	230	196	288

[a] The Communist party boycotted the elections to the Weimar constituent assembly.
[b] In these and succeeding elections the Independent Socialists had merged with the Social Democrats.

he deemed necessary to restore order when it was threatened, and might temporarily suspend the civil liberties that the constitution granted. Yet the Reichstag could order such measures repealed. Inside the cabinet, the chancellor was a real prime minister, with responsibility for planning policy. The constitution also provided for popular initiative: one-tenth of the electorate could bring in a bill or propose an amendment to the constitution. On the economic side, the constitution provided that the government might socialize suitable enterprises, but guaranteed private property and the right of inheritance.

Several other contradictions reflected the conflict of interest between the Social Democrats and the middle-class parties. But the powers of the president and the introduction of proportional representation were perhaps the two chief weaknesses. The powers of the president made dictatorship a real possibility. Proportional representation required that votes be cast for entire party lists of candidates, and thus prevented independent voters from "splitting the ticket," and independent politicians from obtaining office. This system encouraged small splinter parties to multiply.

Right and Left Extremism, 1920-1922

In 1920, pressure from the Right loomed as the most serious threat to the Republic. In March, 1920, a *coup* (in German, *putsch*) drove the government from Berlin for several days. The commander of the Berlin military district, supported by Ludendorff and the Free Corps leaders, hoped to bring to power an East Prussian reactionary official named Kapp. Ebert managed to defeat this "Kapp *putsch*" by calling a general strike that paralyzed Germany. Because the old monarchical judicial system still existed, the men arrested and tried for the Kapp *putsch* all got off with extremely light sentences, whereas left-wingers brought before the courts were very harshly punished.

As an immediate outgrowth of the strike called by the government, a communist revolt took place in the Ruhr. In pursuit of the communists, German troops entered the area, which had been demilitarized by the Versailles Treaty; this action in turn led to French military intervention and a brief occupation of the Ruhr and Frankfurt

(April-May, 1920). In the elections of June, 1920, the electorate began to support the extremists of Right and Left. The Democrats and Social Democrats lost strength.

In April, 1921, when the Allies presented the bill for reparations, which totaled 132 billion gold marks, the politicians of the Right favored simple rejection of the terms, while the Weimar parties realistically decided that the threat of invasion made this course impossible. Again, the moderates had to take responsibility for a necessary decision that was sure to prove unpopular, and that they themselves did not approve. The minister for reconstruction, Walter Rathenau, a Democrat and a successful industrialist, hoped that a policy of "fulfillment" might convince the Allies that Germany was acting in good faith, and might in the long run lead to concessions. An intensely patriotic German, Rathenau was also a Jew, and drew the particular venom of the anti-Semitic nationalist orators.

The secret terrorist groups of the Right began a campaign of assassination. The first important figure to be murdered (August, 1921) was Matthias Erzberger, the Catholic Center politician who had signed the armistice, and a leading moderate. His assassins escaped through Bavaria. When one of them was caught, the courts acquitted him. Next, after some hesitation, the League of Nations awarded to Poland a substantial area of the province of Upper Silesia, containing much wealth and many German inhabitants, which all Germans felt to be rightly theirs. This action aroused the Right still further. Rathenau was killed in June, 1922, by men who believed in the "stab-in-the-back" theory, and thought that by murdering a Jew they could avenge the "betrayal" of the German army.

Hitler: Early Career

During the months between the assassination of Erzberger and that of Ra-

thenau a new and ominous element had emerged among the welter of right-wing organizations in Bavaria. This was the "National Socialist Party of the German Workers" founded by Adolf Hitler, the son of an obscure, illegitimate Austrian customs official, whose real name had been Schicklgruber. Born in 1889, Hitler early quarreled with his father, and seems always to have felt bitter and frustrated. In 1907, he was rejected by the Vienna Academy of Fine Arts, where he wished to study painting. He became an odd-job man, selling an occasional water-color, but always hovering on the edge of starvation. It was during these years that his hatred of the Jews began. As we know (see Chapter XXII), lower-middle-class Vienna at the time was deeply devoted to its anti-Semitic demagogue, Mayor Lueger, whom Hitler admired. Because Karl Marx himself had been of Jewish origin and because many Viennese Jews were socialists, Hitler associated socialism with the Jews, and lumped both together as somehow responsible for his own personal troubles and for the ills of the world.

There were plenty of nineteenth-century theorists, German and others, from whose works Hitler drew support for his anti-Semitism. The French Count Joseph Arthur de Gobineau (1816-1882) had laid the pseudo-scientific foundation for modern anti-Semitism, and for theories of "Nordic" and "Aryan" supremacy. One of his most influential readers was the great German composer, Richard Wagner (see Chapter XXIII). Wagner's son-in-law, the Englishman Houston Stewart Chamberlain (1855-1927), wrote a long and turgid book called *The Foundations of the Nineteenth Century*, which glorified the Germans and assailed the Jews; for example, one section was devoted to a "demonstration" that Christ himself had not been of Jewish origin. Chamberlain furiously opposed democratic government and, interestingly enough, capitalism. Thus he provided Hitler with a congenial mixture of racism, nationalism, anti-democratic thought, and radicalism.

Although Hitler owed much to earlier nationalists and racists, he worked out a twentieth-century adaptation of their nineteenth-century ideas. After he had read their books, he came to hate Vienna as a cosmopolitan and Jewish community, and moved to Munich in 1913. In 1914, he enlisted in the German army and fought through the war as a corporal. He won the iron cross for bravery, but was regarded by his commanding officer as too "hysterical" to deserve a commission. After the war, he had come back to Munich, where, as might have been expected, he loathed the new republic and the "Bolsheviks," admired the Free Corps, and decided to become a politician.

Ludendorff had moved to Munich, and become the center of the reaction. Hitler was employed as a political education officer for the troops. While engaged in this work, he discovered a small political group that called itself the "German Workers' Party." This group combined nationalism and militarism with a generous amount of radicalism. Hitler joined the party in 1919 and soon proved himself to be a far abler politician than any of his colleagues. He urged intensive propaganda for the union of all Germans in a greater Germany, for the elimination of all Jews from political life, a state guarantee of full employment, the confiscation of war profits, the nationalization of trusts, the encouragement of small business, and a land-grant to the peasantry. The seemingly radical character of his program caused many Germans otherwise sympathetic to hesitate before giving Hitler money. As early as 1920, he began to reassure them by saying he opposed not "industrial capital" but only "Jewish international loan capital."

Hitler was an extremely successful orator, with almost hypnotic gifts of capturing a crowd. By 1921, he had made himself the absolute leader, the *Fuehrer* (compare with *duce*), of the party, and in the same year he strengthened himself by founding the SA (*Sturmabteilung*, or storm-troops), brown-shirted units largely recruited from the Free Corps. The storm-troopers wore armbands with the swastika emblem, patrolled mass meetings, and performed other services for the leader. Their commander was a notorious pervert, Captain Roehm, who was also political adviser to the commander of the infantry stationed in Bavaria. Like the Italian fascists, the German Nazis (so-called from the pronunciation of the German word *National*, which is the first word of the party's name) thus had illegal and unofficial access to government supplies of arms through army sympathizers. Besides Roehm, Hitler's closest collaborators included Hermann Goering, a wartime aviator who had shot down twenty Allied planes, but who found himself restless in peacetime, and took on the job of giving the SA a military polish; Rudolf Hess, his Egyptian-born lieutenant and private secretary; and Alfred Rosenberg, a Baltic German distinguished for fanatical hatred of Jews and Bolsheviks, and first editor of the party newspaper.

Hitler and his Nazis were still a very minor political force in 1922 when the middle-of-the-road parties attempted to strengthen the Republic. After the assassination of Rathenau, Stresemann's People's party moved away from the Nationalists, who were now tainted by murder, and entered into a collaboration with Center and Democrats. So tense was the political situation that the scheduled presidential elections were postponed to 1925.

The Inflation, 1922-1923

Political maneuvers to meet the increasing threat from the Right, however, were largely nullified by the increasing economic problem posed by steadily growing

Inflation in Germany. A banknote for 2,000,000,000,000 marks.

inflation, which in 1922 and 1923 reached unheard-of extremes. Inflation is a complicated economic phenomenon, and no mere list or description of its causes can really tell the full story. But the single chief cause for the runaway inflation in Germany after 1921 was probably the failure of the German government to levy taxes with which to pay the expenses of the war. The imperial regime had expected to win, and to make the losers pay Germany's expenses by imposing huge indemnities. So it paid for only about 4 per cent of the war costs by means of taxation. As defeat neared, the government borrowed more and more money from the banks. When the loans came due, the government repaid them with paper money that was not backed by gold. Each time this happened, more paper money was put into circulation, and prices rose; each rise in prices naturally led to a demand for a rise in wages, which had to be paid with more paper money. The inflationary spiral was under way. Instead of cutting purchasing power by imposing heavy taxes, the government permitted buyers to compete with each other for goods in short supply, thus speeding up the whole process of inflation.

Many other forces helped inflation along. The German gold shortage, which deprived the government of the gold with which to back its currency, was itself due to several factors. Since Germany had had to pay in gold for goods bought abroad during the war, she had stripped herself of her gold supply; the rich sent great sums out of Germany for fear that the government would attach them to pay reparations. Raw materials were in short supply; industry was disorganized; and credit was curtailed. The armies of occupation had to be maintained at German expense, and reparation payments had to be made. Nationalist Germans maintained that these expenses, especially reparations, were the cause of inflation; but, though reparations certainly helped the process, they were by no means solely responsible for it. The total sums involved in reparations were never great enough to affect the German currency until long after the inflation was under way. Indeed, the inflation was partly due to the industrialists' wish to avoid paying reparations, and to clear their own indebtedness by letting the currency become worthless.

The following timetable shows how bad the situation had become by the end of 1922. When the war was over, the mark, normally valued at 4.2 to a dollar, had fallen to 8.4. In January, 1921, it was 45; by December, 160. By September, 1922, it was 1,303, and at the end of the year it was 7,000. In these months, the government begged for a moratorium on reparations payments and for a foreign loan. But the French were unwilling. They had already paid billions for the rebuilding of areas that the Germans had devastated during the war, and they wanted the Germans to pay the bill. As a guarantee, the French demanded the vitally important German industrial region of the Ruhr. Despite British opposition, the French occupied the Ruhr in January, 1923, after the Germans had defaulted on their reparations payments. The French intended to run the mines and factories for their own benefit, and thus make up for the German failure to pay reparations.

The Germans could not resist with force, but they declared the occupation of the

Ruhr illegal, and ordered the inhabitants to embark on passive resistance—to refuse to work the mines and factories or to deliver goods to the French. This order the people of the Ruhr obeyed. Local tension in the occupied area became serious when the French took measures against German police and workers, and when German Free Corps members undertook guerrilla operations against the French.

But the most striking result of the French occupation of the Ruhr was its effect upon the already desperate German economy. Not only was the rest of Germany cut off from badly needed goods from the occupied area, but the Ruhr inhabitants were idle at the order of the German government and had to be supported at government expense. The printing press struck off ever-increasing amounts of ever-more-worthless marks. Now the exchange went from thousands of marks to the dollar to millions, to billions, and, by December, 1923, well up into the trillions.

The Consequences of Inflation

Such astronomical figures are meaningless except in terms of the personal and social consequences. A student set off one afternoon for the university with his father's check in his pocket to cover a year's tuition, room, board, and entertainment. When he arrived the next morning after an overnight journey, he discovered that the money he got for the check would pay for one short streetcar ride! Life-time savings were rendered valueless; people trundled wheelbarrows full of marks through the street in an effort to buy a loaf of bread. Those who lived on fixed incomes were utterly ruined, and the savings of the investing middle classes were wiped out. Real property took on fantastic value. The story is told of two brothers, one frugal and the other spendthrift, who had shared equally in a fortune inherited from their father. The frugal one had invested his money; the spendthrift had bought a fine wine-cellar, which he had proceeded to drink up. When inflation came, all the frugal brother's investments would not buy him a haircut, but the spendthrift found that the empty bottles in his cellar were worth billions on billions of marks apiece, and that he was rich again. Under such circumstances speculation in real estate flourished, and skillful speculators made immense fortunes.

For the German worker inflation did not mean the liquidation of his savings, because he usually had none. It did mean a great drop in the purchasing power of his wages, so great that he could no longer afford the necessities of life. His family suffered from hunger and cold. Since the financial position of the labor unions was destroyed, they were no longer able to help the workers, who gave up their membership in droves. The great industrialists, however, gained from the inflation, in part just because it did cripple the labor unions, but still more because it wiped out their indebtedness, and enabled them to absorb small competitors and build giant business combines.

Politically, inflation greatly strengthened the extremists of both Right and Left. The middle classes, although pushed down to the economic level of the proletariat, still possessed the middle-class psychology. In status-conscious Germany, they would not adhere to the working-class parties of Social Democrats or Communists. Disillusioned, they would not adhere to the moderate parties that supported the Republic—the People's party, the Center, and the Democrats. So the Nationalists, and Hitler's Nazis above all, reaped a rich harvest. The hardships of the working class led many workers to turn away from the Social Democrats to the Communists. But Soviet Russian restraint on the leaders of the German party prevented any concerted revolutionary drive until the fall of 1923, by which time poor organization and strong governmental repressive measures had doomed their efforts.

With the country seething in crisis, Stresemann as chancellor in the fall of 1923 proclaimed that because of the economic dislocation Germany could not keep up passive resistance in the Ruhr. He ordered work to be resumed and reparations to be delivered once again. Political troubles multiplied when the Right refused to accept the new policy. At the height of the agitation in Bavaria, Hitler in early November, 1923, broke into a right-wing political meeting in a Munich beer-hall, and announced that the "national revolution" had begun. At gun-point he tried to get other local leaders to support him in a march on Berlin. They agreed, but let him down when they learned that the national government was prepared to put down the Nazis. Although Ludendorff himself joined the Nazi demonstration in Munich, as he had joined the Kapp *putsch* of 1920, troops broke up the demonstration with only a few casualties.

Ludendorff and Hitler were tried in proceedings that have become famous as the most striking example of the Weimar judicial system's partiality for men of the Right. Ludendorff was respectfully acquitted. Hitler was allowed to use the dock as a propaganda platform for his ideas, and was sentenced to the minimum term for high treason: five years. He actually spent eight months in comfortable confinement, during which time he wrote large portions of *Mein Kampf* (*My Battle*), the famous bible of the Nazis.

The End of Inflation, 1923-1924

Communist disorders and the Nazi beer-hall *putsch* marked the last phase of the inflation period. A couple of weeks before Hitler's effort, the government had given extraordinary financial powers to Hans Luther, minister of finance, and Hjalmar Schacht, banker and fiscal expert. All printing of the old currency was

stopped. A new bank was opened to issue new marks, which were simply assigned the value of the pre-war mark (4.2 to the dollar). The new currency was backed not by gold but by an imaginary "mortgage" on all Germany's agricultural and industrial wealth, a psychological gesture that won public confidence. It took one trillion of the old marks to equal one of the new. Simultaneously, rigorous economy was put into effect in every branch of the government, and taxes were increased. The public protested loudly, but the measures remained in force until they had accomplished the intended effect. The cure for inflation produced serious hardships too. Prices fell, and over-expanded businesses collapsed. Unemployment rose sharply, wages stayed low, and workers labored long hours.

During 1924, the Allies contributed to the ending of the crisis in Germany by formulating the Dawes Plan, named for Charles G. Dawes, the American financier and later vice-president under Calvin Coolidge. The plan recommended the evacuation of the Ruhr by the French, the establishment of a special bank to receive reparations payments, gradually rising annual payments for the first five years, and an international loan to finance the German deliveries in the first year. The Nationalists violently attacked the proposals as a sinister scheme to enslave Germany to foreign masters. In the Reichstag elections of May, 1924, the Nationalists scored impressive gains, as did the Nazis and the Communists, while the moderate parties all suffered (see table on p. 473). But a coalition managed to win acceptance of the Dawes Plan in August, 1924, by the device of promising the Nationalists representation in the cabinet. When new elections were held in December, the Nazis and Communists suffered losses, and the Social Democrats and moderates gained. A Center-People's party—Nationalist coalition took office early in 1925 and governed Germany. One wing of the Nationalists, however, led by the enormously rich industrial press and film magnate, Alfred Hugenberg, who had made a fortune during the inflation, opposed all co-operation with the Republic. Though Germany had moved appreciably to the Right, foreign policy remained in the conciliatory hands of Stresemann, who remained foreign minister through all governments between November, 1923, and his death in October, 1929.

Recovery at Home, 1924-1929

During these less-troubled middle years of the Weimar Republic economic recovery proceeded steadily, until, in 1929, German industrial output exceeded that of 1913. First-rate German equipment, coupled with superb technical skill and a systematic adoption of American methods of mass production, added up to a highly efficient industrial machine. This "rationalization" of industry increased production but brought with it over-borrowing and some unemployment. "Vertical trusts," which brought together in one great corporation all the parts of an industrial process from coal and iron mining to the output of the finished product; and cartels, associations of independent enterprises that controlled sales and prices for their own benefit, were characteristic of the German system. The emphasis was always on heavy industry, which meant that continued prosperity would depend upon a big armaments program.

All through this period, reparations were paid faithfully, with no damage to the German economy. Indeed, the money that flowed out in reparations was greatly exceeded by the money that flowed into Germany from foreign, especially American, investors. Dependence on foreign capital, however, which would cease to flow in time of depression, made German prosperity artificial.

In 1925, after President Ebert died, a presidential election was held in which three candidates competed. The Catholic Center, the Democrats, and the Social Democrats supported the Center leader, Wilhelm Marx. The Nationalists, People's party, and other right-wingers joined in support of Field Marshal Hindenburg, then seventy-seven years old. The Communists ran their own candidate, and thus contributed to the election of Hindenburg, who won by a small plurality. Abroad, the choice of a man so intimately connected with imperial militarist Germany created dismay; but until 1930 Hindenburg acted entirely in accordance with the constitution, to the distress of most of the nationalist groups. The domestic issues of this period all aroused great heat, but were settled by democratic process. In the elections of 1928, the Social Democrats were returned to power, and the Nationalists and Nazis were hard hit (see table on p. 473). All in all, prosperity encouraged moderation and a return to support of the republic.

"Fulfillment" Abroad, 1925-1930

In foreign affairs, this middle period of the Weimar Republic was one of gradually increasing German participation in the system of collective security. Thus in 1925 Germany signed the Locarno treaties, which took the French armies out of the Rhineland, substituted a neutral zone and a frontier guaranteed by Britain and Italy, and set up machinery for the arbitration of disputes between Germany and her neighbors. These treaties did not, however, guarantee to Poland and Czechoslovakia the eastern frontiers of Germany. In 1926, Germany was admitted to the League of Nations, with a permanent seat on the League's Council. In 1929, Germany accepted the Kellogg-Briand Pact, which outlawed aggressive war (see below, p. 519).

In 1929, a new reparations plan named after the American, Owen D. Young, chairman of the committee which drew it up, substantially reduced the total originally demanded by the Allies. The Young Plan also established lower rates of payments than those under the Dawes Plan and allowed the Germans a greater part in their collection. Before June, 1930, the Rhineland was evacuated by the Allies, four years ahead of the date set by the Treaty of Versailles. Although many of these gains for Germany were accomplished only with so much preliminary difficulty that they were robbed of their sweetness, and although the German Nationalists, Nazis, and Communists thoroughly opposed them all, still German foreign policy was generally calculated to reassure the rest of the world.

The Impact of the Depression, 1929-1931

But even before the last achievements of this "period of fulfillment," the depression had set in to knock the foundations out from under prosperity and moderation. Unemployment rose during 1929. After the American stock-market crash in October, foreign credits, on which prosperity had so largely depended, were no longer available to Germany. Short-term loans were not renewed, or else were recalled. Tariff barriers were hurting foreign trade. Hunger and want reappeared.

Although unemployment insurance cushioned the first shock for the workers, the lower middle classes, painfully recovering from the inflation, had no such barrier between them and destitution. Their desperation helped Hitler, whose fortunes during the years of fulfillment had fallen very low, although he had attracted a number of new followers who were later to be important in his movement. Paul Joseph Goebbels, publicist and journalist, proved to be a master of mob psychology and an effective orator. Heinrich Himmler, a mild-mannered but ruthless chicken-farmer, took charge of the élite black-shirted SS (*Schutzstaffel*, defense corps), which was formed as a special guard of honor. The SS, with a higher standing than the SA, and with special membership requirements of "racial purity," was later to become the nucleus for the Gestapo, or secret police. Hitler also recruited Joachim von Ribbentrop, champagne salesman and party ambassador to the German upper classes.

The government fell in 1930 over a disagreement on a question of unemployment insurance benefits. Hindenburg appointed to the chancellorship Heinrich Bruening, a member of the Catholic Center party. Bruening would have liked to support parliamentary institutions and to continue Stresemann's policies of fulfillment, but he was to find it impossible to do either. President Hindenburg, now eighty-two, had come more and more under the influence of General Kurt von Schleicher, an ambitious political soldier who had intrigued himself into the President's favor. Hindenburg was now itching to rule by decree, as the constitution authorized him to in an emergency. By failing to pass Bruening's economic program, the Reichstag gave Hindenburg the opportunity he wanted. Bruening went along, partly because he felt that a genuine emergency existed, but partly because he was determined to keep his bitter political rivals, the Social Democrats, from replacing him in office.

The budget was declared in effect by presidential decree; when the Reichstag demanded that the decree be abrogated, the Reichstag was dissolved and new elections were called. The electoral campaign was notable for a running series of street fights between Communists and Nazis. When the votes were counted (September, 1930), these two extreme parties made great gains at the expense of all the moderates (see table on p. 473). The Nazis' Reichstag representation rose from 12 to 107, and the Communists' from 54 to 77. Bruening had to carry on against the wishes of the electorate; supported only by Hindenburg, he now turned authoritarian.

In order to avoid a new government in which Nazis would participate, the Social Democrats decided to support Bruening. When the Reichstag met, Nazis and Communists created disorder on the floor, but they voted together in opposition to government measures. These measures passed only because the Social Democrats voted for them. In 1931, Bruening made an effort to arrange an Austro-German customs union which would co-ordinate the tariff policies of the two countries and help them both fight the depression without affecting their political sovereignty. Whether such an arrangement between two countries that were both suffering from unemployment would actually have succeeded cannot be decided; nor can we be sure whether the impulse for Germany and Austria to unite politically might not have proved overpoweringly strong. At any rate, the whole project raised in the minds of the Allies, especially the French, the specter of a "greater Germany," and the scheme was vetoed by the World Court. The collapse of the great Austrian bank, the *Kredit-Anstalt,* deepened the depression, despite a British loan to Austria in 1931, and despite the one-year moratorium on reparations payment procured for Germany by the American President Herbert Hoover.

The Republic in Danger, 1931-1932

Now Nazis, Nationalists, the veterans organization of the Steel Helmets (*Stahlhelm*), the Junkers' Agrarian League, industrialists, and representatives of the former princely houses formed a coalition against Bruening. This coalition had great financial resources, and a mass backing, chiefly Nazi. It had its private armies in the SA, in the *Stahlhelm*, and in other semi-military organizations. Because the Left was split, and the Communists in effect acted as political allies of the Right, nothing stood between this new right-wing coalition and a political victory except the person of Hindenburg, who controlled the army, and by virtue of the Weimar Constitution was able to keep Bruening in office. Early in 1932, the great industrialist, Fritz Thyssen, invited Hitler to address a meeting of coal and steel magnates. Hitler won their financial support by convincing them that if he came to power he would be their man. Though some of Hitler's followers were now impatient for a new *putsch*, he curbed them, believing that the Nazis could come to power legally.

In the elections of March, 1932, Hitler ran as the candidate of the Nazis and Hindenburg as the candidate of the Center, Social Democrats, and other moderate

Soup-kitchen for the unemployed, Berlin, 1931.

parties. The Nationalists nominated a *Stahlhelm* man, and the Communists of course ran their own candidate. Hitler polled 11,338,571 votes, and Hindenburg polled 18,661,736, only four-tenths of 1 per cent short of the required majority. In the runoff election, the Nationalists backed Hitler, whose total rose to 13,400,000 as against Hindenburg's 19,360,000. The eighty-four-year-old Marshal, re-elected as the candidate of the moderates, was, however, no longer a moderate himself, but the tool of the Junkers and the military.

Although the government now ordered the Nazi SA and SS disbanded, the decree was not enforced. In April, 1932, the Nazis scored impressive victories in local elections, especially in all-important Prussia. Bruening was unable to procure in time either an Allied promise to extend the moratorium on reparations payments or permission for Germany to have equality in armaments with France. Schleicher, who was now deeply involved in intrigue against Bruening, worked on Hindenburg to demand Bruening's resignation. This Hindenburg did on May 29, 1932, the first time a president had dismissed a chancellor simply because he had lost personal confidence in him. Bruening's successor was Franz von Papen, a rich Catholic nobleman and a member of the extreme right wing of the Center, who installed a cabinet composed of nobles. Papen was Schleicher's man—or so Schleicher thought.

The Center disavowed Papen, who had the real support of no political party or group, but whom the Nazis temporarily tolerated because he agreed to remove the ban on the SA and SS. Papen called new Reichstag elections, on the theory that the Nazis had passed their peak, that they would obtain a decreased vote, and that then they could be chastened and would co-operate in the government. In foreign policy Papen succeeded where Bruening had failed, as the Allies scrapped the Young Plan and required Germany to pay only three billion gold marks into a fund earmarked for general European reconstruction. Instead of being bound for many decades to pay reparations, Germany was now freed from all such obligations.

The election of July 31, 1932, gave the Nazis 230 seats and made them the biggest single party in the Reichstag; the Communists gained also, chiefly at the expense of the Social Democrats. The Democrats and the People's party almost disappeared, while the Nationalists suffered, and the Center scored a slight gain (see table on p. 473). Papen had gained no support in the new Reichstag. He wanted to take some Nazis into the government, but the Nazis demanded the chancellorship, which Hindenburg was determined not to hand over to Hitler. Papen now planned to dissolve the Reichstag and to call new elections. By repeating this process, he hoped to wear down Hitler's strength each time, until he brought Hitler to support him and accept a subordinate place. As Papen put pressure on the industrialists who had been supporting Hitler, the Nazi funds began to dry up, leaving Hitler seriously embarrassed. The elections of November 6, 1932, bore out Papen's expectations. The Nazis fell off from 230 seats to 196; and, although the Communists gained substantially and ominously, Papen too won some support (see table on p. 473). Now the Nazis were really desperate. Goebbels wrote in his diary:

Received a report on the financial situation of the Berlin organization. It is hopeless. Nothing but debts and obligations, together with the complete impossibility of obtaining any reasonable sum of money after this defeat.[*]

Hitler: Rise to Power, 1932-1933

Had Papen been permitted to continue his tactics, it is possible that Hitler

---

[*] Quoted by S. William Halperin, *Germany Tried Democracy* (New York, 1946), 511-512.

might have been kept from power. But Papen resigned as a matter of form because he could not count on majority support in the Reichstag. It was generally expected that Hindenburg would reappoint him, but Schleicher, who was jealous of Papen, intrigued against the reappointment. Angry with Schleicher and sorry to lose Papen, Hindenburg forced Schleicher himself to take the office on December 3, 1932. Now the backstairs general was chancellor, but he had no political support whatever, and had alienated even Hindenburg. He lasted in office only about eight weeks before Hitler was appointed chancellor.

Schleicher did score a great diplomatic success by winning a five-power declaration that recognized in principle Germany's right to parity in armaments. At home, he made every effort to appeal to all shades of opinion, except the extreme Left. But this attempt in itself alienated the implacably anti-labor industrialists and the Junkers. The tortuous Papen, eager for revenge, intrigued with these enemies of Schleicher. Early in January, 1933, Papen met Hitler at the house of the Cologne banker, Baron Kurt von Schroeder. The industrialists, who had temporarily abandoned Hitler, now agreed to pay the Nazis' debts. Hitler, in turn, no longer insisted on the chancellorship for himself, thus leading Papen to hope that he would come back into office with Hitler's backing. Hindenburg, too, was enlisted. When the President refused to give Schleicher the authority to dissolve the Reichstag at its first new session, which

Hindenburg and Hitler at the time the latter became chancellor.

would surely have voted him down, Schleicher had no choice but to resign (January 28, 1933).

But Hitler had now raised the ante and demanded the chancellorship for himself. Papen consented, provided Hitler undertook to govern in strict accordance with parliamentary procedure. Papen was to be vice-chancellor, and still thought he could dominate the government, since only three of its eleven ministers would be Nazis. He therefore persuaded Hindenburg to take Hitler as chancellor. But Papen underestimated Hitler. Though Hitler swore to Hindenburg that he would maintain the constitution, the Weimar Republic was doomed from the moment Hitler came to the chancellor's office on January 30, 1933.

IV: Germany under Hitler, 1933-1939

The Nazi Dictatorship

Hitler's first weeks in power were devoted to transforming his chancellorship into a dictatorship. He dissolved the Reichstag and called for new elections. During the campaign, opponents of the Nazis were intimidated by violence and threats, and were denied radio time and free use of the press. Yet a Nazi victory in the election still did not seem sure. On February 27, 1933, fire opportunely broke out in the Reichstag building. Hitler pointed to it as a sample of the disorders that the Communists were likely to instigate. Hindenburg issued emergency decrees suspending free speech and the free press, and thus made it even easier for the storm-troops to use terror against their political opponents. It is now generally supposed that the Nazis themselves set the Reichstag fire, but they convicted and condemned to death a Dutch communist named Vanderlubbe, who apparently was mentally deficient.

Despite their campaign the Nazis won only 44 per cent of the votes, which gave them 288 seats in the Reichstag (see table on p. 473). Using the SA as a constant threat, Hitler bullied the Reichstag. Except for 94 Social Democrats (the Communists were denied their seats), all members voted for the famous Enabling Act (March 23, 1933). This act conferred dictatorial powers upon the government, and suspended the constitution. The act was renewed in 1937 by a subservient Reichstag, and again in 1943.

Now Hitler could act as he chose, unimpeded by the laws. He instituted a Ministry of Propaganda under Goebbels. He stripped the state governments of the powers they had had under Weimar, and made Germany a strongly centralized state (April, 1933) by appointing governors from Berlin who had the power to override the state legislatures. When President Hindenburg died in August, 1934, at the age of eighty-seven, Hitler assumed the office of president as well as that of chancellor, but he preferred to use the title *Der Fuehrer* (the leader) to describe himself. This new move was approved by a plebiscite, in which Hitler obtained 88 per cent of the votes cast.

Political parties which opposed Hitler were forced to dissolve. The government banned Communists and Socialists (May, 1933); the Nationalists dissolved themselves (June, 1933); the government put an end to the Catholic parties (July, 1933), and all monarchist groups (February, 1934). The *Stahlhelm* was incorporated into the Nazi party (June, 1933) and was deprived of its identity (November, 1935). As early as July, 1933, the Nazis were declared to be the only legal political party in Germany.

The appeal of the Nazis to the German people lay in part in their denunciation and repudiation of the "disorderly" parliamentary system. A strong man who got things done struck a responsive chord in the public. In the last elections, November, 1933, there were no opposition candidates, 92 per cent of the electorate voted Nazi, and there were only two non-Nazi deputies in the chamber of 661. As in fascist Italy and communist Russia, youth groups fed the party, which soon had a powerful regional organization all over Germany and among Germans abroad.

Within the Nazi party itself, however, a difficult situation was created by those who had believed Hitler's more radical pronouncements on social and economic questions. Many of these Nazis were concentrated in the SA, whose members, most of them from the lower middle classes, were also distressed by the way in which Hitler had treated their organization. The SA had made possible his rise to power, but now it was rather an embarrassment to him, no longer quite respectable, and certainly not in favor, as were the SS and especially the army.

On June 30, 1934, Hitler ordered and personally participated in the celebrated "blood purge," or, as he himself called it, "the night of the long knives." Roehm himself, founder and leader of the SA, was shot, and so were, by Hitler's own admission, seventy-three others, including Schleicher and his wife. Other estimates of the casualties run as high as 1,000. In any case, after June, 1934, there was no further opposition to Hitler.

Racism and Political Theory

Within a few days after the passage of the enabling law, Hitler struck the first of his many blows against the Jews, whom he had so long denounced. In a country of approximately 60,000,000 people, the Jews counted less than 1 per cent of the population (something under 600,000), not including part-Jewish Germans. The Jews had become leading members of the professions and the arts, and had made outstanding contributions to German culture. Since most Jews were assimilated and patriotic Germans, many of them would probably have become Nazis if they had been permitted. They would have supported Hitler in everything but anti-Semitism. Instead, anti-Semitic doctrines required their ruthless elimination.

The businesses and professions of the Jews were boycotted; they were forbidden to hold office (April, 1933), although a temporary exception was made for veterans of World War I. In the "Nuremberg laws" of September 15, 1935, a Jew was defined as any person with one Jewish grandparent. All such persons were deprived of German citizenship. Intermarriage between Jews and non-Jews was forbidden as "racial pollution." Jews might not fly the national flag, write or publish, act on stage or screen, teach in any educational institution, work in a bank, exhibit paintings or give concerts, work in a hospital, enter any of the government's labor or professional bodies, or sell books or antiques. They were not eligible for unemployment insurance or charity; and the names of Jews who had died for Germany in World War I were erased from war memorials. Many towns and villages, under the spur of government-sponsored propaganda, refused to permit Jews to live inside their precincts.

In November, 1938, a Jewish boy of seventeen, driven to desperation by the persecution of his parents, shot and killed a secretary of the German embassy in Paris. Two days later, organized German mobs looted and pillaged Jewish shops all over Germany, burned and dynamited synagogues, and invaded Jewish homes to beat up the occupants and steal their possessions. The state then compelled the Jews to restore the damaged properties, and to pay an enormous fine. Jews were forced to take special names, to wear yellow stars of David, and to belong to a Reich "Union of Jews." Although some Jews managed to leave Germany, it was usually at the cost of abandoning all their possessions; yet they were the lucky ones. All these measures and many others (for example, "cows purchased from Jews may not be serviced by the communal bull") designed to drive the Jews into ghettos and starvation were but the prelude to the physical extermination in gas-ovens to which they were to be subjected by the Nazis during World War II. What distressed many horrified western observers almost more than the actions themselves was the failure of any substantial number of highly educated and "civilized" non-Jewish Germans to register any form of protest.

Enthusiasm for "racial purity" had its positive as well as its negative side. The blond, blue-eyed ideal "Nordic types" were urged to mate with each other early and to have many children. German motherhood was made the object of paeans of praise. And, to keep the race pure, sterilization was introduced, supposedly for the prevention of the inheritance of disease. The functioning of such a law depended upon the condition of the medical and legal professions, which soon fell into the hands of charlatans. Medical experimentation of horrifying cruelty and of no conceivable scientific value was practiced during the war on human beings of "inferior" races—Jews, Poles and other Slavs, and gypsies. These practices were the direct outcome of Nazi pseudo-scientific "eugenic" legislation.

The Bases of Foreign Policy

In the field of foreign affairs, German racism justified the incorporation of all territory inhabited by Germans, including Austria, the western borderlands (Sudetenland) of Czechoslovakia, Danzig, the Polish corridor, and other less important places. And the doctrine of "living-space" (*Lebensraum*) justified the incorporation of non-German areas—the rest of Czechoslovakia, Poland, and all southeastern Europe, as well as large areas of Russia. Hitler felt that what the Germans needed, they were entitled to take, since they were a superior people.

Some German intellectuals looked back with longing upon the Holy Roman Empire of the Middle Ages, the first *Reich*. Now that the war had ended the second *Reich* of William II, they hoped to behold a third one, incorporating the old territories, no matter who now lived in them. This is the meaning of Hitler's use of the term "Third Reich," to describe the Nazi state, which he proclaimed would last a thousand years. A "scientific" basis for the *Lebensraum* theory was supplied by the teachers of "geopolitics," chief among whom was Karl Haushofer, professor of geography, retired major-general, and teacher of Hitler's close friend, Rudolf Hess. Haushofer declared that Britain and France were decadent, that small powers must disappear (except for Switzerland and the Vatican City), that Germany, preserving its master-race pure, must possess the will to power, and expand ruthlessly, occupying the "heart land" of Eurasia, from which the world could be dominated.

Another school of thought in Germany argued that Germany's future lay in an alliance with Russia in which Russia's inexhaustible manpower would be joined with Germany's industrial output and military techniques for purposes of conquest. This notion had been strong in German army circles in tsarist days, and continued to exist after the Bolshevik Revolution, especially after the Treaty of Rapallo (see above, p. 451) concluded between Germany and the Soviet Union in 1922. Outside the army, other Germans retained the Bismarckian attitudes of hostility to the West and to Poland and of friendship toward Russia, whatever the color of her regime.

Now that Russia was Bolshevik and the active sponsor of the German Communist party, some German nationalists who were in any case as violently anti-liberal and anti-parliamentarian as the Stalinists, felt sympathetic to communism. Among the German Marxists, communists included, there existed a strong nationalistic feeling, which, at its most extreme, brought them quite close to the nationalists.

Officially, both communists and those nationalists who were essentially conservative condemned their views. But Hitler "presented nationalism in a proletarian disguise and captured the imagination of his followers." Where neither communists nor nationalists could attract the support of the all-important lower middle class, Hitler's "national socialism" succeeded, in large part because of its leader's skill in tricking nationalism out in the Marxist phrases that had become part of the general German vocabulary.

Legal and Economic Policies

Hitler entirely revamped the judicial system of Germany, abandoning traditional legal principles, and substituting "folk" justice, which, Hitler said, subordinated the individual totally to the people (*Volk*). So mystic a doctrine meant in practice that whatever Hitler wanted was German law. People's Courts (May, 1934) were established to try all cases of treason, a crime that was now extended to include a wide variety of lesser offenses, such as circulating banned newspapers. Hitler appointed all the judges of the People's Courts. Concentration camps were established for enemies of the regime, who could be immured or executed by the headsman's axe, without appeal. In fact, they could not even have defense counsel of their choice, but had to accept counsel approved by the courts. The Gestapo (*Geheime Staatspolizei*, Secret State Police) was established in April, 1933, in Prussia, and a year later was extended to all of Germany. It had a free hand in opening private correspondence, tapping wires, and spying on individual citizens.

All economic life was brought under the regime. In agriculture, the Nazis aimed at the largest possible measure of self-sufficiency, and, of course, at political control over the peasantry. The Junkers were protected, and no effort was made to divide their vast estates. In 1933, a special law protected farms of less than 312 acres against forced sale and attachment for debt, an act that won the small farmer to Hitler. But the government determined the production required of farms, and fixed farm prices and wages, and fees for dis-

tributing farm products. Unused land was put under cultivation, and private citizens were required to grow vegetables in greenhouses. This was part of Hitler's preparation for war. By 1937, Germany was 83 per cent self-sufficient in agriculture, a rise of 8 per cent since the Nazis had come to power. Fats and coffee were perhaps the two most important deficiencies remaining.

In industry, taking a leaf out of Stalin's book, Hitler proclaimed a Four-Year Plan in 1933 and a second one in 1936. The first was aimed chiefly at economic recovery and at ending unemployment. Labor camps for men and women helped decrease unemployment, as did rearmament and a program of public works. By 1936, unemployment had dropped from about 7,000,000 to less than 1,500,000. The second plan was designed to prepare for war, and especially to make Germany blockade-proof. Output of raw materials was increased and the materials were distributed first and foremost to armament and other war industries; labor was allocated with similar ends in view; and prices and foreign exchange were controlled. Goering was made boss of the plan.

Under his direction fell the new Goering

Hitler greeted by heiling Germans.

Iron Works, designed to make up for the loss of the rich iron resources of Alsace-Lorraine, which had yielded three quarters of Germany's iron. To this end, low-content ores were worked, and the government absorbed the higher costs. Output went up in two years more than 50 per cent. Germany's gifted scientists were enlisted to make up for other deficiencies by devising successful but expensive synthetic products. Important in this field were the distillation of motor fuel from coal, and the production of synthetic rubber. The state also built strategic highways, the *Autobahnen,* excellent modern expressways.

The Nazis abolished all labor unions in 1933, and employers' associations in 1934. To replace them, a "Labor Front" was established under Dr. Robert Ley, including all wage-earners, salaried persons, professionals, and employers. Strikes and lockouts had been forbidden. Workers were assured of jobs so long as they quietly accepted the entire system. The Labor Front in one of its aspects was a huge spy organization constantly on the alert for anti-Nazis in the factories; it could reduce their pay, fire them, or put them in jail. An adjunct to the Labor Front was the "Strength through Joy" organization, which provided paid vacation trips for German workers to resorts or tourist centers, and which sponsored concerts and other entertainments.

As the second Four-Year Plan went into effect, the worker found himself increasingly immobile. He had a work-book, detailing his past training and positions held, and he could not get a new job unless the state decided it would be more suitable for him. All graduates of secondary schools had to register with the employment authorities. Men and women of working age were liable to conscription for labor. Just before the war, all agricultural and mining and certain industrial workers were frozen in their jobs. On the side of capital, the big cartel became the all-pervasive feature of German industrial organization—a system of profitable monopoly under state control. The interlocking directorate made the system even tighter than it looked. Six industrialists, for example, held among them one hundred and twenty-seven directorates in the largest corporations, were presidents of thirty-two, and all held government posts besides. The Minister of Economics sat at the top of the economic pyramid, authorizing plant expansion, controlling imports and exports, fixing prices, establishing costs, and allocating raw materials.

Religion and Culture

The Christian churches, both Protestant and Catholic, posed a problem for the Nazis. Extremists among Hitler's followers had always been in favor of a return to paganism and the old German gods celebrated by Wagner's operas. Hitler himself, born a Catholic, had once declared that Germany was his only God. Yet office brought sobering second thoughts, since Germany was after all nominally a Christian country. In the hope of avoiding state domination, the Lutheran ministry in 1933 organized a national synod, which the Nazis almost immediately took over by appointing their own bishop. The efforts of extreme Nazis to purge the Bible and to abandon the crucifix led to discontent. The dissidents, led by Pastor Martin Niemoeller, objected to Nazi theology and efforts at control. But Niemoeller also pledged his loyalty to Hitler, made no objections to Nazi racism, and went to a concentration camp solely out of determination to resist dictation over the Lutheran Church. The "confessional" movement he led probably did not extend beyond about 15 per cent of the Protestant clergy.

In July, 1933, Hitler and the German Catholics reached a concordat guaranteeing freedom of worship and permitting religious instruction in the schools. Catholics were to be allowed to form youth groups, and to appoint professors of theology. But the Nazis did not live up to these terms. They interfered with the circulation of Catholic magazines, persecuted the youth groups, and insulted Catholic priests in their press as members of the "black international." On the other hand, the Catholic Church found much to oppose in the teachings to which Catholic children were exposed in the Hitler youth groups. Cardinal Faulhaber of Munich denounced the Nazi violation of the concordat in 1933, but his action only intensified the struggle. Thus in the case of the Protestants, a national church sponsored by the Nazis met with some opposition, while in the case of the Catholics, the Nazis acted as Bismarck once had done and conducted a genuine *Kulturkampf* (see Chapter XXII). Not that millions of Catholics, both clerical and lay, did not support the regime wholeheartedly, persecutions of the Jews and all. They did; and no voice was raised from among the clergy of either major Christian sect to protest against Nazi racism or militarism.

The Nazi process of *Gleichschaltung* (coordination) was applied in every portion of the national life, including education and the arts. One of the leading Nazi officials once remarked, "When I hear the word culture, I reach for my revolver," a revealing and not untypical reflection of the extreme Nazi attitude. Hitler's own artistic views were simple in the extreme: he preferred nudes, the more luscious and Germanic the better, and this taste he strove to impose on the nation, denouncing most modern and experimental trends in art as non-Aryan. The school curriculum, especially history, could no longer be taught with that "objectivity" which was a "fallacy of liberalism," but had to be presented to the student in accordance with the Nazi doctrine of "blood and soil." Nazi racial doctrines, the great past achievements of Germany, the development of the military spirit, and physical culture—these were the cornerstones of the new education.

V: The Failure of Parliamentarism in Spain and Eastern Europe, 1918-1939

In the troubled years between the wars, non-democratic authoritarian governments emerged not only in Germany and Italy but also in Spain, in the succession-states to the Habsburg Empire (with the exception of Czechoslovakia), and in the other states of eastern and southeastern Europe.

Spain: The Background

Spain is so different from the other countries of Europe, and its politics are so complicated, that foreigners are tempted to draw dangerously misleading parallels. The developments leading to the establishment of the Franco regime are meaningless unless we keep in mind the special geographic, economic, cultural, and social background against which they took place. In Spain, local feeling in town and village and province is intense; only occasionally has some common cause united the Spanish people. Politically, this has meant that separatism is often an issue, particularly in Catalonia and in the Basque provinces of the north. Although Spain approaches economic self-sufficiency in both agriculture and industrial raw materials, the soil is poor, the system of farming is backward, and the rural areas are heavily overpopulated. Poverty is endemic, which means that discontent is everywhere.

Religion, the driving force that united Spaniards against the Moslems in the Middle Ages, and against the Protestants in the sixteenth and seventeenth centuries, has played an extraordinarily large part in the national life. But early in the nineteenth century, the Catholic Church in Spain decided to lead against liberalism the same kind of struggle it had led against its earlier enemies. So in most parts of Spain the Church became identified with the landowners. Loss of faith became very widespread. Catholic sources report that by the 1930's only minute fractions of the population attended Mass. With the same devotion and passion they had once shown for the Church, the lower classes in Spain adopted one or another of the modern revolutionary doctrines.

When the Spaniards turned to revolutionary doctrine, it was chiefly in Bakunin's anarchist beliefs and later in Sorel's syndicalism that they found ideas they could cling to. Anarchism (and anarcho-syndicalism) really took hold in Spain, and in Spain alone. The industrial workers of Catalonia and the miserable peasants of Andalusia were anarchist; they wanted to destroy the state utterly rather than conquer and use it. Despite a long history in Spain, anarchism, which at its peak numbered a million to a million and a half adherents, could only harass governments but could not overthrow them, and its positive achievements were limited to securing by means of strikes an occasional increase in wages. It was deeply puritanical in tone, and fanatically anti-Catholic. Shrewd observers have likened it to a Christian heresy that takes all too literally the social teachings of the New Testament. Its adherents turned against the Church with all the fanaticism with which they had once supported it, because they felt that the Church had let them down. The burning of churches and the killing of priests, with which Spanish revolutions have always been marked, have been the work chiefly of anarchists.

But Spain also had an increasingly substantial Marxist Socialist party, with its own federation of trade unions parallel to that of the anarchists. The socialists drew their first strength from the urban workers of Castile and from the mining and steel-producing centers of the north. When Spain became a republic in 1931 (see below), the socialists added many rural supporters and the party numbered a million and a quarter in 1934. The socialists were moderates who had refused to adhere to the Comintern in 1920, but who had joined the revived Second International a few years later. Dissidents founded a small Communist party, from which there were soon Trotskyite deviations. Catalonians had their own socialist formation, and the Church itself supported labor unions of its own in the north, where it had not become identified with the landlords. The socialist doctrine that each should be rewarded according to his needs fits with the traditional Spanish contempt for success and property. In fact, Spain is essentially a country that has never accepted the capitalist system or the industrial revolution any more than it has accepted the Protestant Reformation.

Carlism, the doctrine of the extreme Right, is another vivid illustration of Spanish maladjustment to the outside contemporary world. Founded in the nineteenth century as a movement supporting Don Carlos, a pretender to the throne, Carlism is more interesting as a sweeping repudiation of modern society. It calls for the restoration of the Inquisition, regards the railroad and the telegraph literally as inventions of the devil, and rejects the Copernician theory of the universe. Carlism has its lower-class devotees, too, especially among the rebellious farmers of Navarre in the north.

Birth of the Spanish Republic

King Alfonso XIII, a constitutional monarch strongly ambitious for absolute power ruled over Spain until 1923. He was supported by a government based on electoral corruption and intimidation, in which "liberals" and "conservatives" took orderly turns at office, and in which the real power rested with the local political bosses. Not having participated in World War I, Spain was spared much of the ensuing anguish. Yet wartime trade with the combatants had built up Spanish industry and by making war-profiteers had increased the tension between rich and poor.

In 1923 General Primo de Rivera, acting with the approval of Alfonso, proclaimed martial law, imposed censorship, and persecuted political opponents. His dictatorship lasted until 1930, but lost its popularity after 1926. He spent too much on public works, and was caught in the depression. Moreover, he did not fulfill the promises for a constituent assembly and political reform. Rivera got the socialists to participate in his regime, and put through appropriate labor legislation in the hope of weakening the anarchists. But, since he depended on the army and the landowners, he could not institute agrarian reform. He also alienated the Catalonians, and his repressive measures deprived him of middle-class support.

After Primo de Rivera's resignation and death in 1930, King Alfonso soon restored the constitution. Municipal elections (April, 1931) resulted in a victory for the republicans, representing the lower middle classes of the towns, small tradesmen, intellectuals, teachers, and journalists. The King left the country without abdicating. Elections to a constituent assembly in June, 1931, brought in a great republican-socialist majority, and in November the assembly forbade the King's return and confiscated his property. Spain was a republic. The monarchy, having stood only for clergy, army, and aristocracy, had failed.

The assembly went ahead to adopt a new constitution in December. This provided for a responsible ministry, a single-chamber parliament, and a president to be chosen by an electoral college consisting of parliament and an equal number of electors chosen by popular vote. It was clear that the army would rise against the Republic whenever the opportunity was presented, and that the army would have the support of the Church and the large landowners. Moreover, although the Republic temporarily had socialist support, it did not have the support of the anarchists. From the first, danger threatened both from the Right and from the Left.

Crisis of the Spanish Republic, 1933-1936

The first crisis arose over a new constitutional statute defining the position of the Church. The assembly rejected a moderate proposal which would have preserved the Church as a special corporation with its own schools, and which might have proved acceptable to most Catholics, even though the Cardinal-Primate of Spain had already denounced the Republic. Instead, a measure was passed that closed church schools and ended state grants to the Church after two years. This hurt education badly, and lost the republicans many supporters, especially among the lower clergy itself. Although the Republic secured much Catalan support by a grant of autonomy, it failed to act decisively on agrarian reform.

The anarchists expressed their dissatisfaction by major risings (1933), which the government put down by force. The jails were full, and unemployment was as high as ever. Repression of the anarchists lost the Republic much Left support, but of course failed to gain it that of the Right, which came back strongly in the elections of November, 1933, as the largest party in parliament. Now the government helplessly swung to the Right, and much of its previous legislation, especially legislation affecting the Church and the working classes, remained a dead letter. The Church and monarchists put forward a young man named Gil Robles as their leader. His views were strongly fascist, and he especially admired Dollfuss, the Austrian chancellor (see below).

On the Left, the socialists no longer collaborated with the government. Grown more revolutionary, they now engaged in strenuous competition with the anarchists for the loyalty of the Spanish workers. Strikes and disorders multiplied. In October, 1934, the socialists called a general strike in protest against the inclusion of three of Robles' followers in the government. Catalonia declared itself an independent republic, and was deprived of its autonomy. The coal-miners of the Asturias in the north staged a revolt, joined in by both anarchists and socialists, which was put down with the loss of more than 3,000 lives. The government's use of Moors (Moslems from North Africa) against Spaniards was deeply resented; the Moors had been dispatched by the new minister of war, General Francisco Franco.

Thus the Right in turn lost its public support; and now the Left, under the impact of the Asturias uprising, and influenced by the line of the Comintern (see above, p. 453), united in a "Popular Front" for the elections of February, 1936. For the first time, anarcho-syndicalists went to the polls and voted for a common list with republicans, socialists, and communists. The Left won a considerable victory, perhaps largely because it promised an amnesty for men involved in past outbreaks. Catalan autonomy, land reform, and anticlerical measures were of course the first order of business. The moderate Republican, Azaña, was elected president.

But moderation was now out of fashion on the Left. The Popular Front was a coalition *for election purposes only.* Instead of entering Azaña's cabinet, Largo Caballero, leader of the left wing of the socialists, now "played at revolution." He was hailed by *Pravda* as a new Lenin, and acted as if he intended to seize power. Yet he could not have made good this threat, since he had no force with which to back it up. The route to power for left-wing revolutionaries would open up only if the Right attempted a military *coup,* if the government then armed the workers to fight it, and if the workers then won.

On the Left also, and for the first time, the Spanish Communist party in 1936 emerged as a considerable element. Under Primo de Rivera's dictatorship the communists had been so insignificant that he had not even taken the trouble to suppress their newspaper. But their participation in the Asturian uprising and the Popular Front gained them political strength despite their numerical weakness (3,000 members). Oddly enough, they were more moderate in their immediate aims than the socialists, because they felt the need for a long preliminary period of Popular Front co-operation to increase their own power, and because this was Stalin's "respectable" period.

Simultaneously in 1936, on the Right, there emerged, also for the first time, the *Falange* (phalanx), a party founded in 1932 by the son of Primo de Rivera. The founder was an orthodox fascist on the Italian pattern ("harmony of all classes and professions in one destiny") but was not opposed to agrarian reform or other socialist programs. The Falange had the usual paraphernalia. Its symbol was a bunch of arrows and a yoke; its slogan was *Arriba España* ("Upward, Spain"); its program called for national expansion in Africa, the annexation of Portugal, the building of an empire in South America; it had youth groups and a private army. Although the

Franco reviews Italian troops in 1939 victory parade in Madrid.

Falange polled relatively few votes in the election of 1936, most of Gil Robles' right-wing support went over to it after the Popular Front victory. Through the spring of 1936 the Falange worked for a counter-revolution with army, monarchist, clerical, and Carlist groups. Everybody knew a military *coup* against the government was in the offing. In July it came, under the military leadership of General Franco.

The Spanish Civil War, 1936-1939

The Spanish Civil War (1936-1939) was the first act in the conflict that was to ripen into World War II. Decisively aided by Germany and Italy, Franco's forces pushed on to eventual victory, with the capture of the republican strongholds of Madrid and Barcelona in 1939. During the war, the functions of the weak republican government were usurped by a series of workers' committees, and then a Popular Front regime under Largo Caballero came to office in September, 1936. In government territory, terror reigned, at first the work of anarchists, and, after their suppression, of the communists, who, with Russia behind them, ruthlessly worked against their rival leftist parties in the regime. The rebels made Franco chief of staff in November, 1936. In their territory also terror took its toll, as men of all sorts connected with the Republic were killed. After the Franco triumph, the prisons were filled and the executioner was kept busy.

With all its fascist trappings, the Franco regime, the only fascist regime to survive World War II, still depended after the war upon the same classes that had supported the Spanish monarchy—the landowners, the army, and the Church. It was presumably opposed by the poor in city and country alike. But the fear of a new civil war, which lay heavily on all classes, prevented open opposition.

Eastern Europe

The triumph of the Right in one form or another in eastern Europe is explained partly by the lack of a firm parliamentary tradition; partly by the failure to solve grievous economic problems, especially after the great worldwide depression of 1929; and partly by a popular fear of Bolshevism, sometimes quite out of proportion to any serious threat, but skillfully played upon by unscrupulous leaders. Perhaps as important as all the other factors put together was the initial impression created by the successes of Mussolini and Hitler. The way to get ahead in the world, at least after 1935, seemed to be to put on a uniform, proclaim a doctrine of extreme nationalism, and launch a war of nerves against your neighbors by loudly voicing your claims, and by threatening to make them good by violence.

After the depression, the economic pressures exerted by Germany, whose industrial economy complemented the agrarian economy of these states, enabled her to dominate their foreign trade, especially in the Balkan area. To show how these factors operated, we shall now examine three case-histories—Austria, Hungary, and Yugoslavia.

Austria

The Austria that was left at the end of World War I had an almost purely German population of about 8,000,000, about 2,000,000 of whom lived in the former imperial capital of Vienna. Long the great market for an enormous hinterland and the supplier of industrial finished goods to the agricultural provinces, Vienna was now cut off from its former territories by political boundaries and tariff walls. Between 1922 and 1925, Austrian finances were under direct League of Nations supervision; a League loan and reconstruction policies brought a measure of recovery. But what might have represented one road to economic salvation—union of Austria with Germany—though voted by the assembly of the new Austrian republic in March, 1919, was forbidden on political grounds by the Allies in the Treaty of St. Germain (September, 1919). These two problems, economic survival and union with Germany, were complicated by the continuation in even more violent form of the basic political struggle of imperial Austria: Social Democrats against Christian Socialists (see Chapter XXII). The Social Democrats were a gradualist reformist, but Marxist, party with strong urban support, especially in Vienna itself. The Christian Socialists were a conservative clerical party with a mass following in the countryside and among the urban lower middle classes, and counted many priests among their leaders.

In the mid-twenties, the two hostile parties, usually almost evenly balanced in the parliament, organized private armies: the Christian Socialists, the *Heimwehr* (home guard), and the Social Democrats, the *Schutzbund* (defense league). Their mutual hostility was increased by the relief and workers' housing measures undertaken by the Social Democratic municipal government of Vienna. These measures were financed by taxing the rich. After 1930, when a treaty was signed with Italy, Mussolini more or less overtly supported the Christian Socialists, who grew more and more fascistic in their outlook. The failure of Bruening's plan for a customs union with Germany and the related collapse of the Vienna *Kredit-Anstalt* bank (see above, p. 481) increased tension in 1931, and in September, 1931, the *Heimwehr* tried its first fascist *coup,* which failed. Efforts in 1932 to organize a Danubian economic cooperation scheme—an alternative to Austrian union with Germany, and favored by France—were rendered futile by Italian and German opposition. After Hitler came to power in early 1933, many Christian Socialists became openly Nazi.

The Christian Socialist chancellor, Engelbert Dollfuss, however, strove to curb the Nazis. To this end he suspended parliamentary government in March, 1933, and in effect ended parliamentary democracy. He forbade the wearing of uniforms by political groups, and tried to expel Nazi agitators. In retaliation, Hitler made it prohibitively expensive for German tourists to visit Austria, and thus destroyed one of the most lucrative sources of Austrian income. In the face of Nazi-inspired disorder, Dollfuss banned the Nazi party (June, 1933). But, instead of burying the hatchet and uniting with the Social Democrats against Hitler, Dollfuss pursued them too. He banned all parties except his own "Fatherland Front," a union of all right-wing groups except the Nazis, and raided Social Democratic headquarters, precipitating a workers' riot. The government then bombarded with artillery the workers' new apartment houses, in which the Social Democratic leaders had taken refuge (February, 1934). The Social Democratic party was broken, but the Vienna workmen were permanently alienated and were united in opposition to the regime. Dollfuss had to depend more and more upon Italy to support him against the threat from Hitler. He established himself as a fascist dictator (April 30, 1934), but was assassinated in July by the Nazis. It was only Italian troop concentrations on the frontier that led Hitler to disavow this attempted *coup*.

Dollfuss' successor, Schuschnigg, was committed to the same policies. But Mussolini's desire to win Hitler's support for Italian aggression in the Mediterranean weakened Schuschnigg. The Austrian chancellor made plans looking toward a Habsburg restoration, tried to concentrate armed power in his own hands rather than those

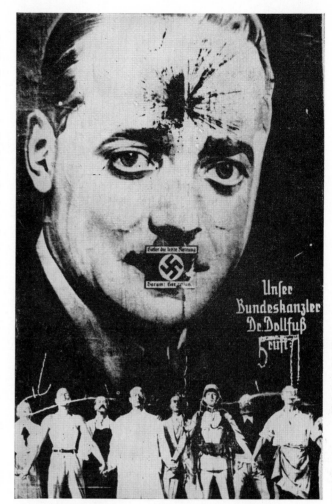

Poster of Chancellor Dollfuss and representative Austrians defaced by Nazis, 1933.

of the *Heimwehr,* and strove to create an understanding with France and her allies to replace the one with Italy. But he failed in the face of German aggression. In February and March, 1938, Hitler increased the pressure on Schuschnigg, who was subjected to the first of the famous series of grim interviews between Hitler and statesmen of smaller countries. The Fuehrer demanded and obtained privileges for the Nazis in Austria. When the predictable Nazi disorders broke out, Schuschnigg desperately tried to win working-class support, but it was too late.

The final move that precipitated armed German invasion of Austria was Schuschnigg's announcement that a plebiscite would be held on the question of Austrian independence. Hitler marched in, installed a Nazi chancellor, put Schuschnigg in jail, and began the extension of the Nazi system to Austria. In April, 1938, he held a plebiscite on the question of Austrian union with Germany and obtained a 99.75 per cent vote of *Ja*. Mussolini had to bow in 1938 to what he had prevented in 1934, and Austria, increasingly fascist since 1930, had become a mere province of Nazi Germany.

Hungary

On October 31, 1918, eleven days before the Armistice, Count Michael Karolyi became prime minister of Hungary, after the country had already severed its ties with Austria. One of the richest of the great magnates, Karolyi was also a democrat, pro-Ally, and imbued with Wilsonian ideas. He proved his own sincerity as a social reformer by handing over the 50,000 acres of his own estate to be divided among the peasants, and by preparing a land-reform law. He made every effort to reach a compromise with the national minorities, but understandably enough they would no longer trust any Magyar. The French commander of the Allied armies did not assist Karolyi, and demanded that the Hungarians withdraw from Slovakia. In March 1919 Karolyi resigned, in protest over the loss of Transylvania.

Thwarted nationalism now combined with a growing radicalism, stimulated by the news of Bolshevik activities in Russia brought by returning Hungarian prisoners of war. A left-wing government took over, more and more dominated by Bela Kun, Lenin's agent, a Hungarian-born Jew. He put through revolutionary nationalization decrees and installed a soviet political system by bloody-handed terrorist methods, especially in the countryside, where the peasants resented the delay in giving them the land. The Allies could not tolerate a Bolshevik régime in Hungary. The Rumanians invaded and drove Kun out; during 1919 and part of 1920 they occupied the country and stripped it of everything they could move. Meanwhile, under French protection, a counter-revolutionary government was formed, and returned to Budapest, where Admiral Horthy, a member of the gentry, became regent and chief of state (March 1, 1920). Hungary was now a kingdom without a king, Horthy an admiral without a fleet. Twice the Habsburg King Charles tried to regain the throne, but was frustrated largely because Hungary's neighbors objected. The new counter-revolution gave free rein to a "White Terror" directed largely against the Jews but also against Magyar workers and peasants.

The Treaty of Trianon (June, 1920) confirmed Hungary's losses: a small strip of land to Austria, Transylvania to Rumania, Slovakia to Czechoslovakia, and Croatia and other Serb and Croat territories to Yugoslavia. Thereafter in Hungary the most important political issue was "revisionism," the effort to revise the treaty and get these lands back. No tourist who visited Budapest could escape the huge statue of Hungary mourning the lost provinces, north, east, south, and west, or the great map laid out in flowerbeds in the public park showing in different-colored blossoms the far-flung territories relinquished but still claimed by the Magyars. The national motto was now "*Nem, nem, soha*" (No, no, never).

The rank and file of Hungarians, however, were relatively indifferent to revisionism as an issue, as they had always been indifferent to the nationalist questions that agitated their rulers, the great magnates, and the gentry. But Hungary had no land reform; the great estates remained intact; and magnates and gentry retained their dominant position. Behind a thin screen of parliamentary government, an authoritarian dictatorship governed the country on behalf of the old ruling groups. It was helped by a swollen bureaucracy, and it became more and more fascist in character as the years went by.

For ten years (1921-1931) Count Bethlen as prime minister was the real power in the country, which he ran as if nothing had changed since 1914. The peasants were effectively disfranchised as they had always been; the Social Democrats were tolerated as a trade-union party; and the upper house of magnates was re-established. The League of Nations helped economic recovery by a loan and a reconstruction plan (1923-1926), and in 1927 a treaty with Italy began an intimate relationship between Hungary and Mussolini. The depression and the financial crisis of 1931 drove Bethlen from office. He was succeeded by the strongly nationalist and fascist-minded Gömbös, who was pro-German as well as pro-Italian, and who permitted the first Nazi-like organizations to form. Of these the Arrow Cross was the strongest, but it remained on the fringes of power until almost the end of World War II, largely because Hitler got what he wanted in Hungary without it.

Following Gömbös' death in 1936, his successors were all men of the same stripe. The Italians supplied arms to the Hungarians; Hitler favored their revisionism along with his own. After Austria had fallen to Hitler, he had Hungary in his pocket, and when he broke up Czechoslovakia in March, 1939, the Hungarians seized the extreme eastern portion, Ruthenia, and a small part of Slovakia. To pursue revisionism, the Hungarians had to follow Hitler, since he alone offered the opportunity to re-draw the map as they felt it should be drawn. So, before war broke out, they had withdrawn from the League, and had enacted anti-Semitic laws in the Nazi pattern. But because Hitler needed Rumania too, he would not give the Magyars all of Transylvania. Ironically enough, the price they paid for espousal of revisionism between the wars was the Soviet-dominated régime installed in Hungary after World War II.

Yugoslavia

In the new "Kingdom of the Serbs, Croats, and Slovenes," proclaimed in December, 1918, there came together for the first time in one state the former south-Slav subjects of Austria and Hungary and those of the former independent Kingdom of Serbia. This was in most respects a satisfied state from the territorial point of view; revisionism therefore was not an issue. But, as the name of the new state shows, it faced the serious problem of creating a governmental system that would satisfy the aspirations of each of its nationality groups. Over this problem democracy broke down and a dictatorship was established. The dictatorship was not of the fascist type, although, as German power waxed, important politicians in the country became convinced that the future lay in Hitler's hands, and responded accordingly. The rank and file of the population, by and large, were peasants deeply devoted to freedom, although unskilled in western forms of parliamentarism. They opposed fascism, and, when they got the chance, ousted the politicians who sought to align them with it.

Serbian political ambitions had helped to start the war. The Serbs were more numerous than Croats and Slovenes together (approximately six million to three and a quarter million Croats and a few over one million Slovenes in 1931). Many Serbs felt that the new kingdom, which their Serbian king ruled from his Serbian capital of Belgrade, should be that "greater Serbia" of which they had so long dreamed. Orthodox in religion, using the Cyrillic alphabet, and having experienced and overthrown Ottoman domination, many Serbs tended to look upon the Croats as effete subjects of the Habsburgs who were lucky to get the chance to live in the same state with them. Roman Catholic in religion, using the Latin alphabet, and having opposed Germans and Magyars for centuries, many Croats felt that the Serbs were crude easterners who ought to give them a full measure of autonomy within the new state. Thus the issue was posed: Serb-sponsored centralism against Croat-sponsored federalism. The Slovenes, more conciliatory and less numerous, sometimes acted as balance wheel to keep the political machinery moving. But the Serbs forced the acceptance of their answer to the constitutional question. This brought about dictatorship, alienated large numbers of Croats, bred extremism among them, and contributed greatly to the benefit of the country's enemies and to its own sufferings during the second war.

The Croats, under their peasant leader Radich, boycotted the constituent assembly of 1920, and the Serbs put through a constitution providing for a strongly centralized state. In the 1920's both sides generally refused to compromise, although occasionally temporary understandings were reached. When a Serb deputy shot Radich dead on the floor of parliament in June, 1928, a crisis arose that terminated only when King Alexander proclaimed a dictatorship in January, 1929. Alexander made every effort to settle the problem by wiping out all vestiges of old provincial loyalties. There was to be no more Serbia or Croatia, but new artificially created administrative units named after the chief rivers that ran through them. The whole country was renamed Yugoslavia, as a sign that there were to be no more Serbs and Croats. But it was still a Serbian government, and the Croats could not be made to forget it. Elections were rigged by the government, and all political parties were dissolved. Croat leaders spent much time in jails, which, like most Balkan jails, were highly uncomfortable. This dictatorship of King Alexander passed no racial laws, elevated no one political party to exclusive power, and had no colored shirts, special songs, or other fascist paraphernalia. But it was unmistakably authoritarian and anti-democratic.

One result was the strengthening of Croat extremists, who had wanted an independent Croatia in the days of the Habsburgs, and who now combined this program with terrorism, supported from abroad by the enemies of Yugoslavia—Italy and Hungary. The Croat extremists were called *Ustashi* (rebels), and their leader, Ante Pavelich, was subsidized by Mussolini. He was deeply involved in the assassination of

Assassination of King Alexander of Yugoslavia at Marseilles, 1934.

Alexander at Marseilles in October, 1934. Under the regency of Prince Paul (Alexander's cousin) the dictatorship continued. As German economic power in the Balkans grew, leading politicians grew enamored of Germany, and some efforts were made to bring Yugoslav policies into line with those of the Axis. But these policies met with such unconcealed popular opposition that they were never pursued very far. In the summer of 1939, on the very eve of war in Europe, an agreement was finally reached with the Croats that established an autonomous Croatia. But by then it was too late, since the Croats were not satisfied with the boundaries of their own province.

Though the Yugoslavs in 1941 bravely resisted German invasion, they did not have the military power to hold Hitler's armies back. When the conquering Germans and Italians split the country up, they turned Croatia over to the extremist Croat Pavelich, head of the Ustashi, who carried out horrifying massacres of Serbs and Jews. The innocent men, women, and children suffering death and torture at the hands of Pavelich's forces owed some of their anguish to the short-sightedness of Serbian politicians who had failed to solve the problem of Croat autonomy within a peaceful Yugoslavia, and who had thus stimulated the extremists.

Other Authoritarian Regimes

The case-histories we have been considering are unique in detail, yet they furnish interesting parallels to developments elsewhere in eastern Europe. Thus in Poland, Pilsudski led a military *coup* against the democratic government in 1926, and exercised a military dictatorship that became ever more authoritarian, especially after the depression. This *coup* was made possible largely because of the government's failure to grant concessions to Lithuanians and other national minorities, and

to deal with the economic problems left by the years of war and occupation. Tension was heightened when Germany denounced a trade treaty and precipitated a crisis in the Polish coal industry. The violent hatreds that divided the political parties made it even easier. Once he had won power, Pilsudski turned to the great landowners and big industrialists, and built his government on their support and on that of his military clique.

In Rumania it was the deep entrenchment of corruption in political life that initially jeopardized the parliamentary system, as the party in power usually rigged elections without shame. In addition, there was widespread anti-Semitism, which was adopted as the chief program of the "Iron Guard," a Rumanian Nazi party. Greenshirted and wearing bags of Rumanian soil around their necks, the Guard began a program of assassinating moderate politicians early in the 1930's. Economic dislocation and peasant misery brought about by the worldwide agricultural depression strengthened the Guard and other fascist groups. To head off a Guardist *coup*, King Carol of Rumania installed his own fascist dictatorship in 1938. Although the Guardist leaders were "shot while trying to escape," Rumania could not avoid German pressure. After Hitler had acceded to Russian seizure of Bessarabia and Northern Bukovina, and had given Hungary northern Transylvania (August, 1940), Carol had to leave the country, and Hitler's man, Marshal Antonescu, took over, with Iron Guard support.

In Bulgaria, always a strongly pro-Russian country, the genuine threat of communism was a serious problem. Moreover, Bulgaria, like Hungary, was revisionist because of her failure to gain the Macedonian territory given by the peace treaties to Yugoslavia and Greece. The issue was exacerbated by the presence in the country of thousands of Macedonian refugees, who tended to join revolutionary terrorist societies. Bulgaria, an equalitarian country with no minorities problem, no rich land-owners, no aristocracy, and no great industries, none the less produced political cleavages even more violent than those in countries where economic inequality prevailed. Unparalleled ferocity has marked its political life. In the early twenties, a peasant politician, Stamboliisky, gave the country a period (1920-1923) of reasonably popular government. But even he curbed the press as he fought both Macedonian terrorists and communists. His imposition of high income taxes alienated the bourgeoisie, and his conciliatory policies toward Yugoslavia infuriated the army. In 1923, right-wingers murdered him and installed a strongly authoritarian régime. From then on, communist plots and bomb outrages and Macedonian terrorist strife racked the country. After 1930, the Italian marriage of King Boris led to a rapprochement with Mussolini. In 1934, a military *coup* brought a group of army officers to power; they dissolved the political parties and tried their hands at a dictatorship of their own. But this development was successfully countered in 1936 by King Boris himself, who, like Alexander of Yugoslavia and Carol of Rumania, imposed a royal dictatorship, which lasted from then until his mysterious death during World War II.

In Greece between the wars, the main issues were whether the country should be a monarchy or a republic, and how to overcome the economic difficulties consequent on the transfer of 1,250,000 Greeks from Turkey. On the constitutional question, the population wavered, voting for a monarchy in 1920, for a republic in 1924, and for a monarchy again in 1935, always by enormous majorities. Economic dislocation brought strength to communism among the refugees and in labor groups. The political exuberance for which Greece is celebrated made the regular conduct of parliamentary government impossible. The inter-war period was punctuated by a whole series of

coups by generals, some republican, some monarchist, all more or less authoritarian, but most of them ineffective and none especially bloodthirsty. The last of these was the most fascist, General John Metaxas, who became dictator in August, 1936. Metaxas abolished political parties, instituted censorship and political persecution of his opponents, launched a program of public works, and imitated the Nazis in other ways. But when the Italian invasion came from Albania in October, 1940, Metaxas ordered resistance, which was the beginning of Greece's heroic showing in World War II.

Fascism in Review

None of these régimes in eastern Europe was fascist in the full sense of the term. In Italy and Germany the régimes rested, at least initially, upon the popular support of a substantial proportion of the people, even though that support was kept alive by the technique of artificial stimulation. In eastern Europe, on the other hand, the dictatorships rested on the police, the bureaucracy, and the army, and not on the support of the peasant masses. To an eastern European politician of almost any complexion an election was an occasion for bribery, intimidation, and promises that he had no intention of trying to fulfill. The hope placed by some western liberals in peasant parties proved in the end illusory.

Thus the growth of anti-democratic governments of the Right in Europe during the period between the wars strikingly reveals the difficulties in the way of moderate parliamentary régimes in countries without parliamentary traditions. This does not mean that the western liberal tradition is not for export. But a liberal constitution on paper and a liberal franchise are in themselves no guarantee that a régime on western models can become stabilized. The postwar economic agony had scarcely disappeared before the depression of the late twenties and early thirties struck. Under these circumstances men turned to extremists of the Left and Right. But the fear of communism, combined with the seductive nationalist propaganda of the Right, brought about fascist victories in Italy and Germany. Thereafter, the triumph of the Right elsewhere was assured, and a new world war was inevitable.

Reading Suggestions on the Rise of Fascism

(Asterisk indicates paperbound edition.)

THE ROOTS OF FASCISM

A. Cobban, *Dictatorship: Its History and Theory* (Scribner's, 1939). Highly suggestive survey, reaching well back into history.

P. Viereck, *Metapolitics: From the Romantics to Hitler* (Knopf, 1941). A survey of the background in German political thought.

C. J. Hayes, *A Generation of Materialism, 1871-1900* (Harper, 1941). Contains a concise and corrosive section on the seedtime of fascism.

Note: The titles listed above present differing views on the origins of fascism, a subject still much debated by historians. Further titles bearing on the subject may be found in the reading suggestions for Chapter XXIII.

ITALY

G. Megaro, *Mussolini in the Making* (Houghton Mifflin, 1938). An unequaled study of Mussolini's early career.

H. Finer, *Mussolini's Italy* (Holt, 1935) and H. A. Steiner, *Government in Fascist Italy* (McGraw-Hill, 1938). Two very solid studies by expert political scientists.

G. A. Borgese, *Goliath: The March of Fascism* (Viking, 1938), and G. Salvemini, *Under the Axe of Fascism* (Viking, 1936). Lively works by important anti-fascist Italians.

G. Salvemini, *Prelude to World War II* (Doubleday, 1954). A survey of Mussolini's foreign policy, by one of his most implacable enemies.

GERMANY

A. Hitler, *Mein Kampf* (Reynal and Hitchcock, 1939). A complete English translation of the Nazi bible, the basic work to be read for an understanding of the movement.

A. Hitler, *My New Order,* R. de Sales, ed. (Reynal and Hitchcock, 1941). Speeches after the Führer's coming to power.

A. L. C. Bullock, *Hitler: A Study in Tyranny* (Oxham's, 1952; *abridgment, Bantam). The best biography.

S. W. Halperin, *Germany Tried Democracy* (Crowell, 1946). A reliable history of the Weimar Republic, 1918-1933.

R. G. L. Waite, *Vanguard of Nazism* (Harvard Univ. Press, 1952). A good study of the "Free Corps" movement.

J. W. Wheeler-Bennett, *Wooden Titan* (Morrow, 1936), and *Nemesis of Power* (St. Martin's Press, 1954). Two first-rate studies, the first dealing with Hindenburg, and the second with the role of the German army in politics from 1918 to 1945.

F. L. Neumann, *Behemoth: The Structure and Practice of National Socialism* (Oxford Univ. Press, 1944). The best work on the subject.

K. Heiden, *History of National Socialism* (Knopf, 1935), and S. H. Roberts, *The House That Hitler Built* (Harper, 1938). Two older and still useful studies of the Nazis.

F. von Papen, *Memoirs* (Dutton, 1953). An apologetic autobiography by the scheming right-wing politician.

E. Wiskemann, *The Rome-Berlin Axis* (Oxford Univ. Press, 1949). A study of the formation and history of the Hitler-Mussolini partnership.

R. Fischer, *Stalin and German Communism* (Harvard Univ. Press, 1948). A study of the role played by the communist movement in the history of Germany between the wars.

Note: Some of the titles listed under the reading suggestions for Chapter XXVIII deal with international relations during the inter-war period and will illuminate Nazi foreign policy.

OTHER COUNTRIES

G. Brenan, *The Spanish Labyrinth* (Macmillan, 1943) (*Cambridge University Press, 1960). A useful study of the Spanish Civil War against its historical and economic background.

C. Bowers, *My Mission to Spain* (Simon & Schuster, 1954); C. J. Hayes, *Wartime Mission to Spain, 1942-1945* (Macmillan, 1945); and Lord Templewood (Sir Samuel Hoare), *Complacent Dictator* (Knopf, 1947). Three differing views of Franco and the Spanish problem, by three ambassadors, the first two American, the last British.

G. E. R. Gedye, *Betrayal in Central Europe* (Harper, 1939). A careful journalist's account of Austria and Czechoslovakia.

H. Seton-Watson, *Eastern Europe between the Wars, 1918-1941* (Cambridge Univ. Press, 1946). A useful account dealing with all the eastern European countries except Greece and Albania.

R. L. Buell, *Poland: Key to Europe* (Knopf, 1939). A helpful survey.

R. West, *Black Lamb and Grey Falcon* (Viking, 1941). A highly subjective account of Yugoslavia, loaded with political bias, but fascinating and informative reading.

HISTORICAL FICTION

I. Silone, *Bread and Wine* (*Penguin, 1946; *New American Library), and *Fontamara* (Smith and Haas, 1934). Two good novels on rural Italy under fascism; by a distinguished anti-fascist writer.

C. Levi, *Christ Stopped at Eboli* (Farrar, Straus, 1947; *Universal Library). An anti-fascist Italian doctor and painter writes movingly of his exile in a remote and poverty-stricken southern Italian village.

H. Fallada, *Little Man What Now?* (Simon & Schuster, 1933; *Ungar), and E. Remarque, *Three Comrades* (Little, Brown, 1937; *Popular Library). Two touching novels of depression-ridden Germany.

E. von Salomon, *"Der Fragebogen"* (*The Questionnaire*) (Doubleday, 1955). One of the plotters against Rathenau, a strong sympathizer with authoritarian movements, tells his life story satirically, against the background of American military government in post-1945 Germany.

E. Hemingway, *For Whom the Bell Tolls* (Scribner's, 1940). A characteristic Hemingway novel, set in the Spain of the Civil War.

The Democracies, 1919-1939:

Domestic and Imperial Problems

CHAPTER XXVIII

Opposite. EMPLOYMENT AGENCY, *by Isaac Soyer (1907-); American, painted 1937; Whitney Museum of American Art, New York City. The patience and desperation of ordinary people trapped in the Great Depression.*

I: Introduction

THE central fact—or irony—of politics between the two world wars is that the war "to make the world safe for democracy" seemed to have made it in effect a difficult and dangerous place for democracy. Idealists like President Wilson had expected that the collapse of the old Romanov, Habsburg, and Hohenzollern empires would automatically insure an increase in the number of democratic states. But instead, as we have just seen, much of Europe came under régimes that were hostile to liberal democracy. Even Italy, which had appeared to be evolving toward a democratic constitutional monarchy, turned fascist. In the 1920's and 1930's, then, the core of democracy remained in the great North Atlantic powers—Britain, France, and the United States—and in the smaller states of the Low Countries and Scandinavia.

The upsurge of communism and fascism created grave problems in international relations for the three great democracies. At times in the 1920's it looked as if they might successfully overcome these problems and bring the world back to peaceful habits. But in the 1930's the great worldwide depression, the advent of Hitler, and the aggressions of fascist states in the West and of an expansionist Japan in the Far East rapidly darkened the international scene.

With the outbreak of another general war in 1939, it was clear that the two decades since 1919 had been at best a twenty years' truce, a truce broken with increasing frequency by international troublemakers.

Certainly the totalitarian aggressors bore the major responsibility for the unleashing of a second world war. Yet a far from minor factor in the deterioration of the twenty years' truce was the relative weakness of the peaceful democracies themselves. In the 1920's Britain, France, and the United States became preoccupied with their own domestic problems. In the early 1930's their preoccupation increased as a result of the urgent crisis of the depression. But this was the very time when international problems demanded equally urgent attention. International trade was steadily shrinking in the face of the depression and of mounting tariff barriers; the prospects for peace were steadily fading before the saber-rattling and actual saber-wielding of the enemies of democracy. Faced with two equally urgent sets of problems, the democracies turned first to the domestic ones, and then discovered that the international situation was rapidly moving toward war.

Nor was this all. During the twenty years' truce the democracies faced a third set of problems, not as yet so urgent as the other two, but of very great potential importance. This third set involved imperial issues—the relationship between the great democracies and the non-western peoples, many of whom were still under colonial rule or some other form of control by demo-cratic mother countries. Particularly in Asia and the Middle East, the non-western peoples were beginning to assert their nationalism and to demand the loosening of old imperial ties. This formidable political movement did not reach full intensity until the years following World War II when a long procession of former colonies, protectorates, and mandates began to join the ranks of independent states (see Chapter XXXI). But the nationalist movements that have brought these newcomers into the family of nations since 1945 grew steadily in the 1920's and 1930's.

The three sets of problems—domestic, foreign, and imperial—faced by the democracies during the twenty years' truce were interconnected and interrelated in countless ways. We shall underline some of these interrelations, as we have shown the links between the internal and external policies of the communist and fascist states. But, in order to point up the main issues, we shall also separate national, international, and colonial problems in a fashion that may oversimplify the complexities of real life. Our survey emphasizes first the chief domestic problems of the democracies in the inter-war years and then considers the growing conflict between their colonialism and the nationalism of the non-western world; in Chapter XXIX we shall analyze their foreign policies, as distinguished from their imperial policies. We begin here with an examination of the crisis confronting Britain on the home front after November, 1918.

II: Great Britain

The Postwar Depression

Save for trifling losses from German Zeppelin raids and coastal bombardments, the British Isles suffered no direct material damage in World War I. But the British armed forces lost about seven hundred and fifty thousand men killed in action, and about a million and a half wounded. The casualties of the Empire and the Commonwealth as a whole came to nearly a million killed and over two million wounded. The economic losses of the mother country had been grave indeed—the almost incalculable difference between the actual cost of destructive war and what might otherwise have been productive effort.

The national debt after the war was ten times that of 1914. Many British investments abroad, returns on which had been a major factor in Victorian prosperity, had had to be liquidated. Forty per cent of the great British merchant fleet, the income from which had helped to balance Britain's international accounts and pay for her imports, had been destroyed by enemy action. The whole fabric of international trade on which Britain depended was torn in a thousand places in 1918, and could not be rapidly restored in the unsettled conditions that prevailed in the postwar world. And, finally, to supplement the war production of Britain and France, the industrial plants of the United States, of Canada, and even of India had been called on, and had received a stimulus that made them in peacetime more effective competitors of the British. In the 1920's, the industrial plant of the Germans, nourished in part by loans from America, once more took up the rivalry that had so alarmed the British before the war.

In short, victorious Britain faced in an aggravated form the basic economic difficulty that we analyzed in Chapter XXI. The country that had been in Victorian days the "workshop of the world" had now lost its head start and could no longer give full employment to its millions of workers. And yet those workers were in no mood to accept a lower standard of living. They had made great gains in social security before the war, and they had fought the war in the hope of still better things to come. In the "khaki election" held just after the Armistice of 1918 they had been promised a "land fit for heroes"; they had

been promised that the defeated enemy would through reparations pay the costs of the war, and give Britain a new start.

This hope was very early disappointed. No substantial reparations came through, economic difficulties soon began to accumulate, and by 1921 there were already almost a million unemployed. In that same year the British government, faced with the rising cost of living, increased the very meager unemployment payments. These payments, soon given the derogatory name of the "dole," were strictly speaking not old-fashioned poor relief, but payments on unemployment insurance policies that had been part of Lloyd George's social legislation of prewar days. However, large-scale unemployment continued, and some young workers never acquired employment status. Unemployment insurance could not be maintained on a sound actuarial basis, and the payments became in fact a form of poor relief.

The Great Britain of the 1920's experienced no equivalent of the "Coolidge prosperity" that the United States was to enjoy. We must not exaggerate: the British economic decline was not catastrophic. London, Manchester, and Liverpool did not become ghost cities, though some of the gravely depressed areas, like the coal-mining regions of South Wales, did begin to show real signs of decay. What happened was rather a *relative* decline, the comparative slowing up of an economy geared to dynamic growth, with a working population conditioned psychologically to a slowly rising standard of living and a middle class similarly conditioned to traditional comforts. Moreover, this was the twentieth century, the century of the newspaper, the movie, the radio. The British were well aware, for instance, that Americans had automobiles, radios, and a lot else; they, too, wanted those things.

Britain was, then, suffering from ills characteristic of economic old age. The coal industry is a good concrete illustration of these ills. There was still a lot of coal in Britain; but much of it was costly to mine, since the most easily and cheaply worked seams were being exhausted. The industry was badly organized, with many small and inefficient mines running at a loss, and with machinery and methods that were antiquated in comparison with American and the best continental standards. Productivity per man-hour over the whole industry was low. Worst of all, perhaps, the 1920's saw the rapid rise all over the industrialized world of major competitors of coal—oil, and electricity based on water power—and the consequent decline of British coal exports. Since the British Isles had no petroleum, and no very great potential in hydroelectric power, coal, the historic basis of British industrial power, simply had to be mined. The workers were unionized and were in no mood to accept cuts in wages; the owners did not want to run their business at a loss. A strike in March, 1921, after the government had rejected Labor party proposals for making permanent the wartime nationalization of the industry, focused national attention on this critical problem. The strike was settled in July, but only by the government's consenting to pay subsidies to cover increased wages.

The Conservative and Labor Programs

Against the background of economic depression, British domestic politics during the twenty years' truce displayed a fairly clear class basis. The Conservatives, still often called Tories, tended to get the support of aristocrats and of middle-class people who wanted to attack new problems with traditional methods and with a minimum of government intervention. The Labor party tended to get the support of trade unionists and of intellectuals from all classes who demanded that the government intervene more vigorously in the economic field. We must not oversimplify, however; not every reformer necessarily voted Labor nor every stand-patter Tory. Yet economic issues did sharpen the differences between the two major British parties.

The first casualty in the struggle between Labor and the Conservatives was the old Liberal party, which was ground to a mere husk between the two contending groups. The Conservatives, who had won the lion's share of seats in the "khaki election," decided in 1922 to withdraw their support from the coalition government headed by the Liberal Lloyd George. In the ensuing elections the Conservatives won, and the Liberals, split between the followers of Lloyd George and those of the more orthodox Asquith, lost heavily. Labor won 142 seats—more than the Liberals did —and became for the first time His Majesty's Opposition.

Both Conservatives and Labor realized the underlying difficulties of Britain's position. Both were fully aware that twentieth-century Britain had to sell enough goods and services abroad—enough manufactured goods and shipping, insurance, banking, and tourist services—so that the income from them would buy food for her people and much of the raw materials for her factories. But the parties were not agreed on how to achieve this necessary task. Broadly speaking, the Conservatives wanted to retain private industry, with government and other technical experts helping to make it efficient. But they were thwarted by high tariffs in the United States and elsewhere, by the drive to economic self-sufficiency all over the world, and by the difficulties of trade with communist Russia.

The state of world trade drove the Conservatives more and more to the solution Joseph Chamberlain (see Chapter XXI) had advocated earlier: protective tariffs against competing foreign goods, and the knitting of the Empire and Commonwealth, with their vast variety of resources, into a largely self-sufficient trade area by "imperial preference" agreements. Such agreements would give raw materials from the colonies and dominions preferred treatment in the British market in return for preferred treatment of British manufactures in the colonial and dominion markets. In theory, at least, the scheme could have worked, for the Commonwealth and Empire of the nineteen-twenties—one-quarter of the world's land and people—had the requisite natural resources and offered a potential market capable of supporting the British Isles in the style to which they were accustomed. In practice, however, the great snag was the unwillingness of the constituent parts of the Empire and Commonwealth to accept for themselves the role of producers of raw materials in exchange for British manufactured goods and British services. The self-governing dominions, loyal though they had been during the war, were in no mood to assume a role essentially like that of colonies in the old mercantilistic days. They were looking toward independent nationhood, and they wanted what seems to go with nationhood in our world—their own industries. This was also true of what was potentially the richest unit in the Empire, India.

The Labor solution was nationalization —that is, government purchase and operation of key industries with just compensation to their private owners, rather than seizure without compensation as in Soviet Russia. The key industries were transportation, power, coal, steel, perhaps even textiles, cutlery, pottery, machine tools—all the industries that seem to thrive best on large-scale organization. A good many Laborites wanted nationalization simply because, as socialists, they believed that profits, rent, and interest paid to "capitalist" private owners were forms of worker-exploitation, and that under nationalization these forms of exploitation would cease. But many of their leaders knew that even nationalized industries would still face the fundamental problem of selling enough

goods abroad to keep the economy going. They argued, therefore, that nationalization would enable British industries to produce more cheaply and efficiently. It would do away with wasteful competition and with the inefficient firms so conspicuous in the coal industry, for instance. It would, they fondly believed, force into productive work both unnecessary managerial and selling staffs, and stockholders and other investors who lived without working.

Moreover, Labor supporters believed that, once nationalization had been achieved, the British workmen would take a new attitude toward their work. Knowing that they were now the *real* owners of their own industries, they would put their hearts into their work, abstain from feather-bedding, absenteeism, and similar practices, and raise production to a point where the goods of Britain could undersell those of her capitalist rivals in world markets. This belief was reinforced by the somewhat paradoxical faith in free trade that the Labor party had inherited from the Liberals, and by its high hopes for improved international relations. Consequently, Labor was hostile to the Conservative policies of protective tariffs and imperial preference.

Postwar Politics

In the twenty years between the wars neither the Tories nor the Laborites were able to carry out their full platform. Labor itself, though it came to power briefly in 1924 and in 1929, with its leader Ramsay MacDonald as prime minister, never had a parliamentary position firm enough to nationalize any industry. The Conservatives, by no means unanimous on the degree of economic self-sufficiency they wanted for the Empire, were decisively held up by the refusal of the Commonwealth countries to go much further than to accept certain limited imperial preferences.

Despite the wider cleavage between the

Volunteers lining up for government service during British general strike, 1926.

two parties, British politics still retained many of the amenities of Victorian parliamentary life. The House of Commons, even though it now included workingmen and others who by no means spoke with an "Oxford accent," was still one of the best clubs in the world. For a few weeks in 1926 some 2,500,000 trade-union members attempted a general strike in support of the coal-miners, who were already on strike in protest against a cut in their wages. The general strike failed, but during its brief course fundamental British attitudes were revealed. Thousands of men from the middle and upper classes volunteered to keep essential services operating, and in Plymouth a soccer team of strikers played a team of police. Britain, despite mounting tensions, remained a land of general law-abidingness, where the class struggle that the Marxists talked so much about seemed to have come thoroughly under the control of the parliamentary decencies.

In 1928, almost unnoticed, the last step was taken in the *political* democratization of Britain that had begun in 1832. In 1918, in preparation for the "khaki election," the government had put through a reform bill which eliminated all the old exceptions to universal male suffrage and gave the vote to all men over twenty-one. Culminating a long and spectacular campaign in which "suffragettes" had demonstrated, marched, orated, and even gone to jail in behalf of women's rights, the bill also gave the vote to women. But, with almost a caricature of British caution, it set the voting age for women at thirty years, thus insuring that there would always be more male than female voters. The distinction was too irrational to stand up, especially after experience had demonstrated—as it also did in the United States—that women divide politically about the way men do. In 1928, a measure known irreverently as the "bill for flapper suffrage" gave women the vote at twenty-one.

Although the dole, depressed industries, and other signs of economic ill-health persisted, Britain did experience a measure of recovery in the late 1920's. But then the great depression, the signal for which was given by the New York stockmarket crash in October, 1929, began its spread around

CHAPTER XXVIII

the world. Britain, already weakened, was one of the first to be engulfed. Faced by a serious deficit, and unwilling to try to meet it by cutting the dole and other social services, the second Labor government of Ramsay MacDonald resigned in August, 1931.

It gave way to a coalition of Conservatives, Liberals, and right-wing Laborites headed by the same MacDonald. This coalition cabinet put through reductions in the dole and the social services. Late in 1931 it took the decisive step, a hard one in view of Britain's traditional financial leadership and devotion to the gold standard, of going off the gold standard and letting the pound fall in value. In 1932, it made the first move away from free trade by enacting protective tariffs, and in the same year Britain ceased payment on her war debts to the United States, except for a few "token" payments. These measures did little to help the unemployed or to strike at the roots of British economic troubles. But they did stem the depression sufficiently to enable the coalition to win two general elections in 1931 and 1935.

Yet the coalition government was in fact dominated by Conservatives, and after the 1935 election the Conservative leader, Stanley Baldwin, took over the post of prime minister. Gradually the British economy pulled out of the worst of the depression, although—some economic theorists might say *because*—Baldwin did nothing beyond keeping the budget in balance. By 1936, however, Mussolini's and Hitler's aggressions were beginning to demand British attention. The economic question and the social question, by no means solved, faded before the threat of another war.

Settlement of the Irish Question

The years between the wars were of great importance for Ireland. The outbreak of war in 1914 put off the threatened revolt against Home Rule in Ulster (see Chapter XXI), but the Irish were hardly reliable partners in the war. In 1916, the faction furthest removed from the Ulster rebels, the Irish nationalists, got German aid and staged an armed rising in Dublin. The British put down this "Easter rebellion," but not before they had created a fresh and effective set of Irish political martyrs. The British government did not dare extend conscription to Ireland until April, 1918, and the attempt made then led the Irish nationalists to boycott the British Parliament and to cease attending its sessions.

In 1919, Home Rule as decreed in 1914 was not enough for the nationalists of Ireland. The Home Rulers of prewar days had yielded to more extreme rebels, the Sinn Fein (meaning in Gaelic, "ourselves alone"), who wanted complete independence. The years 1919-1921 were filled with violence, ambushes, arson, and guerrilla warfare, as the Irish, who now had their own illegal parliament, moved into full revolution. The British, tired from their long war, were not in a state of mind to use force effectively; the Irish, on the other hand, were admirably organized and full of fight.

Yet the immediate upshot of the violent phase of the revolution was a compromise, for the Sinn Fein split in two. A moderate wing, led by Arthur Griffith and Michael Collins, was willing to accept a compromise in which Protestant Ulster would remain under direct British rule and the Catholic counties would be given dominion status. A radical wing, led by Eamon de Valera—exceedingly Irish in spite of his Spanish surname—insisted that the whole island achieve complete independence as a republic. The moderates negotiated with the British, and in 1921 obtained for the twenty-six counties of southern Ireland dominion status under the name of the Irish Free State. The Free State had its own parliament, the Dail, and was completely self-governing; it merely accepted the British Crown as symbolic head. The six Protestant counties of Ulster maintained their old relationship with Britain, which now became officially the United Kingdom of Great Britain and Northern Ireland.

This settlement was unacceptable to De Valera and the more extreme revolutionaries, and the Irish revolution now became a civil war between partisans of the Free State and partisans of a republic, with the old round of burning, ambush, and murder. But the Irish, too, were beginning to tire of violence. When the moderate leader, Michael Collins, a man much closer to earth than De Valera, was assassinated by a republican, public opinion turned away from the extremists. Meantime the Free State was gradually settling down. De Valera, after refusing to sit in the Dail because he would have had to take an oath of loyalty to the king, changed his mind and decided to bring his fellow republicans into the national parliament in 1927.

From then on, almost in the manner of illogical and compromise-loving England. the Irish Free State gradually and peacefully got what the extremists had been killing and burning for. De Valera's party won a plurality in the Dail in 1932, and a majority in 1933; thereupon it proceeded to abolish the oath of loyalty to the Crown and to cut most of the slender threads that still tied the Free State to England. In 1939, Catholic Ireland was so free from British domination that she could declare and maintain her neutrality throughout World War II. In 1949, the final step was taken when Britain recognized her as the fully independent Republic of Eire (Gaelic for "Ireland").

The Commonwealth of Nations

No such secession took place elsewhere among the British possessions in the years between the two world wars. On the contrary, definite constitutional recognition

De Valera taking the salute of the Irish Republican Army, Western Division, in County Clare, autumn, 1921.

of the essential independence of the dominions seemed to make them more loyal, though at the cost of any central British authority over their economic policies, and, at least in law, over their foreign policies. The capstone of a long process that had begun with the Durham Report nearly a century before (see Chapter XXIV) was the Statute of Westminster of 1931. This spelled out the new relations between the dominions and the mother country that had been negotiated in an imperial conference five years earlier. The preparatory report of 1926 anticipated the gist of the Statute of Westminster by declaring that Britain and the dominions

... are autonomous communities within the British Empire, equal in status, in no way subordinate one to another in any aspect of their domestic or external affairs, though united by a common allegiance to the crown and freely associated as members of the British Commonwealth of Nations.

That phrase "freely associated" means also "able freely to choose to be dis-associated." In other words, the right of a state to secede, which Americans fought a great civil war to decide is *not* a part of the United States Constitution, *is* a part of the constitution of the British Commonwealth of Nations. And the twenty-six counties of Southern Ireland in effect took advantage of this right to set up their republic quite outside the Commonwealth.

The new status acquired by the dominions in 1931 was symbolized by a change in terminology. Henceforward they were no longer to be considered parts of the British Empire but free members of the British Commonwealth of Nations. In this new relationship Britain would have to *negotiate* with Canada or Australia about tariffs, trade conditions, immigration, and the like, just as if they were foreign countries. Although Britain was unable to build a self-sufficient economic unity out of her dominions, still in 1939, as in 1914, the dominions all came into the war on Britain's side. They made this decision even though they had the legal right to follow the example of Ireland and remain neutral.

One dominion, however, came close to remaining neutral: the Union of South Africa. In the 1930's many Afrikaners, the non-English white citizens of the Union, took a sympathetic view of Hitler's activities, partly because his contempt for dark-skinned "races" coincided with their own beliefs. Some even began to press for a separate republic. The great Boer leader, Jan Smuts, on the other hand, was firmly pro-British and anti-Nazi and succeeded, by a fairly narrow margin, in aligning the Union on the British side in World War II. Meanwhile, in the British Empire, as distinguished from the Commonwealth, clouds were gathering; in India particularly, as we shall see, the movement for independence was gaining impressive strength. Yet these problems of Empire and Commonwealth were for the British people during the interwar years of relatively secondary importance compared to the really urgent issues of domestic and foreign policy.

III: France

The Impact of the War

In France, both World War I and the postwar difficulties caused more serious dislocation than they did in Britain. In the war itself, France lost proportionately more in human lives and in material damage than did any other major belligerent. Two million Frenchmen in the prime of life were

War devastation in northern France. The town of Béthune, May, 1919.

either killed or so seriously mutilated as to be incapable of normal living. In a land of only 39,000,000, and with an already low birth rate, it is likely that this human loss impaired the French potentiality for achievement in all phases of civilization. Many of the men who would have been statesmen, industrialists, scientists, and artists in the 1930's were killed off in 1914-1918. Three hundred thousand houses and twenty thousand factories or shops were destroyed. In a land of conservative economic organization, where work was done slowly and without large-scale automatic machinery, this material setback would be long felt. Psychologically, the feeling of victory by no means compensated for the traumatic losses of the four years of struggle.

France set as her goal the laming of her recent enemy, Germany, in every possible way. She tried to extract reparations to the last possible sum, undeterred by the arguments of economic theorists that Germany could not pay. But she insisted even more on keeping Germany down, isolated in international relations, and without the physical means of fighting. In a pinch, most Frenchmen would probably have been willing to forego reparations in order to deprive Germany of the economic plant necessary for modern war. They would have preferred this to collecting reparations from a rich and productive Germany.

In the postwar years, however, French statesmen attempted to follow both policies and failed. The culmination came in January, 1923, under the premiership of the conservative Raymond Poincaré, when French and Belgian troops occupied the great German industrial region of the Ruhr in an effort to make Germany pay full reparations. The Germans replied by passive resistance (see Chapter XXVII). By 1925, it was clear that the Ruhr occupation had brought no gains to France, and the new French government, chosen after the failure of Poincaré's policy, withdrew the troops.

Meanwhile, the French were undergoing inflation. The inflation resulted in part from the cost of rebuilding the devasted areas—a cost that drained government finances and that was only partly covered by German payments. It resulted also from the high cost of maintaining armed forces—for the French dared not disarm—from the general disorder of international trade, and from the staggering debts piled up during the war by the French government, which, like the imperial German government, had preferred loans to taxes. By the mid-1920's the franc had slipped from its prewar value of 20 cents to a dangerous low of about 2 cents. In the crisis, Poincaré was recalled to power to "save the franc." In 1926, he initiated new taxes and stern measures of economy which, together with the gradual restoration of normal international trade after the French withdrawal from the Ruhr, stemmed the decline of the franc. In 1928, it was officially revalued at 3.92 cents.

The French inflation, though mild compared with the German, nevertheless caused economic and social dislocation. Frenchmen who had lent their government francs worth 20 cents now found themselves deprived of four-fifths of their loans. This very considerable repudiation fell with particular severity on the middle class, especially the lower middle class, the *petite bourgeoisie*. The greatest sufferers were those living on their savings or on relatively fixed incomes—on pensions, for example, or on the return from bonds, or even on the contents of the wool sock in which the suspicious French peasant traditionally hoarded his cash. Bourgeois people naturally fear pauperization, fear being pushed

down into the ranks of the proletariat, and the French were no exceptions. Inflation thus weakened a social class that had long been a mainstay of republicanism in France and added to the social tensions that form the central theme of French domestic history in the period between the two world wars.

Social and Political Tensions

During World War I, the French had temporarily put aside the great political and social conflict they had inherited from 1789. After the war, the "sacred union" of political parties that had carried France through the struggle soon dissolved, and the traditional conflict was resumed. This is sometimes termed the conflict between the "two Frances"—the republican France of the Left, and the royalist, or authoritarian France of the Right. The conflict was not quite a simple Marxian class struggle between rich and poor, capitalist and proletarian, though it was certainly in part such a struggle. On the Right were the wealthier classes, many of them openly hostile to the very existence of the parliamentary state. They were reinforced by conservative peasants and by small businessmen and investors, who were not hostile to the Third Republic as such but who were determined to resist any attempt to extend the social services of the "welfare state." As a result of this right-wing resistance, France lagged behind Britain, Germany, Sweden, and other European states in providing measures of social security.

On the Left were the champions of the welfare state, the Socialists and the Communists, backed by the more radical workers, by many white-collar people, especially in the government service, and by some intellectuals. The effectiveness of the Left was hampered by the postwar split between the Communists, who followed the

Moscow line, and the Socialists, who did not, and by a comparable schism within the major trade-union organization, the C.G.T. (*Confédération Générale du Travail* —General Confederation of Labor). Still nominally part of the Left, but actually in the political middle and not anxious to go far toward the welfare state, was the misleadingly named Radical-Socialist Party, long the political bulwark of the Third Republic. The Radicals were strong among the peasants of southern France, and among white-collar workers and smaller professional men.

Religious difficulties further embittered French politics. French Leftists, including the Radicals, were anticlerical by tradition. After the war they rashly attempted to introduce anticlerical measures into strongly Catholic Alsace. Alsace had not been affected by the separation of Church and State carried through in France after the Dreyfus crisis (see Chapter XXI), since it had then belonged to Germany. In the long run, the government was obliged to make compromises on the Alsatian question and on other clerical issues. After bitter public debate, it finally decided in the mid-1920's to resume diplomatic relations with the Vatican, which had been broken off at the time of the separation.

In the late 1920's, the years of increased prosperity that followed the revaluation of the franc, the Third Republic seemed to be getting the better of its internal difficulties. Indeed, the world economic crisis that began in 1929 was late in striking France, and for a while in 1930 it looked as though the French economy, less devoted to large-scale industry than that of the United States, Britain, or Germany, might weather the crisis much more easily. But France, too, depended on international trade, particularly on the export of perfumes, wines and brandies, Paris gowns, and other luxuries. By 1932, the depression had struck, and the government was in serious economic and political difficulties.

The Stavisky Case and the Popular Front

The political crisis came to a head in February, 1934, as a result of the Stavisky case, a financial scandal reminiscent of the Panama scandal of the 1890's (see above, p. 246). Stavisky, a shady promoter and swindler who had all sorts of connections with important public figures of the Third Republic, was caught at last in a fraudulent bond issue of the municipal pawnshop of Bayonne. The full details have never emerged, but Stavisky's suicide—or murder —in December, 1933, rocked France. On the extreme Right, royalists, enjoying the freedom of a democratic society, had long been organized, notably in a pressure group known as the *Action Française*, and were gaining recruits among upper-class youth. The *Camelots du Roi* ("The King's Henchmen"), strong-armed squads of the *Action Française*, went about beating up Communists, who in turn responded by violence. Less fascist in character, yet also supporting the Right, was a veterans' organization, the *Croix de Feu* ("cross of fire"—the reference is to war), organized by Colonel de la Rocque. During the agitation following the Stavisky case, the *Camelots du Roi* and the *Croix de Feu* took part in riots against the government that broke out in Paris in February, 1934. The Left countered with a brief general strike; France seemed to be on the eve of revolution.

Once more, however, as in the time of Dreyfus, the republican forces rallied to meet the threat, and once more after the crisis had been surmounted France moved to the Left. The February crisis itself was overcome by a coalition of all parties save royalists, Socialists, and Communists. But the franc was again falling in value. The conservative premier, Flandin, attempted to cut back government expenditures by measures similar to those that had worked a decade earlier under Poincaré; this time they did not work. The forces of the Left responded by forming the so-called Popular Front, made up of the Radical-Socialist, Socialist, and Communist parties, and backed by the C.G.T., which had temporarily healed the schism between Communists and non-Communists. Their victory in a general election in May, 1936, led to the formation of a Popular Front ministry under the leadership of the Socialist Léon Blum.

The Popular Front came to power in part as a kind of French equivalent of the American New Deal. The workers, the white-collar men, the government employees, even many of the peasants and shopkeepers, were now convinced that the classical formulas of economic retrenchment were not the remedy for the ills of France. They wanted a direct attack on the stronghold of retrenchment, the Bank of France, still a private institution dominated by the "two hundred families" alleged to control the French economy. They wanted more equal distribution of wealth by government spending; in short, they wanted the "welfare state."

Other factors entered into the victory of the Popular Front. Mussolini had begun his Ethiopian adventure, and Hitler his rearmament; many a Frenchman in 1936 voted Left as a protest against the compromises that French politicians had been making with the dictators. Finally, these were the years when Russia, just admitted to the League of Nations, seemed to be pursuing a course of collaboration with the West against the threat of Nazi Germany. Moscow therefore urged the French Communists to give up their old policy of constant opposition and to co-operate with their hated enemies, the Socialists.

It was a bad time for a French New Deal. The nation was bitterly divided between partisans and enemies of the Popular Front; business and farming classes were traditionally reluctant to pay income taxes, which would have to be raised to meet the costs

Demonstrators in the Stavisky riots, Paris, February, 1934.

of social services; the economy was not geared to labor-saving devices. The Blum cabinet had an ambitious program—a maximum work week of 40 hours; partial nationalization of the Bank of France, the railroads, and the munitions industry; compulsory arbitration of labor disputes; and measures of social welfare. Although Blum achieved most of this program on paper, everything conspired to block its successful execution. The Communists did not really co-operate, for they refused to participate in the Blum cabinet and sniped at it from the sidelines in the Chamber and in the press. Businessmen took fright at the mushrooming membership of the C.G.T. and at the "sit-down" or "stay-in" strikes of French industrial workers in June, 1936.

Moreover, as the anti-democratic régimes in Germany, Italy, and Spain went on to new victories, France was driven to expensive rearmament. Capital, however, was rapidly leaving the country to be invested or deposited abroad, and the monied class would not subscribe to the huge defense loans that were essential if the French armed forces were to be put in shape to face the war that began to seem inevitable. Blum was obliged to call a halt in March, 1937. The Popular Front now disintegrated, and the C.G.T. lost millions of its newly recruited members and suffered a new schism between Communists and anti-Communists.

Divided France

The morale of the French sagged badly after the collapse of the Popular Front. Under the mounting tensions of 1938 and 1939, the Radical-Socialist premier, Daladier, kept France on the side of Britain in opposition to the Rome-Berlin axis, and various measures of retrenchment—including virtual abandonment of the 40-hour week—kept the French economy from collapse. But the workers took very badly the failure of the Popular Front, and as late as November, 1938, a general strike almost came off, and was combated by putting the railway workers under military orders. The "have" classes, on the other hand, were outraged by the fact that Blum's experiment had been made at all; many of them were convinced that their salvation lay in a French totalitarian state—"better Hitler than Blum," as their despairing slogan went. The France that was confronted with war in 1939 was not only inadequately prepared in terms of materials; it was psychologically and spiritually divided, uncertain of what it was fighting for. An American historian of France, commenting on this failure of the French spirit in the 1930's, summarized:

It is a tragedy when a great man loses his strength and his personality; it is a catastrophe when a nation loses its assurance. To me the tragic pathos of the French problem can be summed up in a remark made by my hostess in a Parisian pension in 1937 when she called my attention to the notice about the air-raid shelter for the neighborhood. 'Over there [in Germany],' she said with a choke in her voice, 'the shelters will be safe; ours will be faulty.' She wanted to be proud of the nation for which her husband had given up his life in 1916; she wanted to believe in the community that had given her nurture, but she had lost faith and with it her nerve. These simple words are dramatic evidence of the failure of the *élan vital* of a great people.[*]

Many Frenchmen before 1940 relied on their great empire to restore the flagging *élan vital* of the mother country. Colonial troops, particularly from Senegal and North Africa, had helped to replenish the diminished ranks of the army during World War I. Enthusiasts spoke of France as a nation not of just the 40,000,000 at home but of 100,000,000 Frenchmen, including the population of the colonial territories. But this was stretching the facts too far.

---

[*] J. B. Wolf, "The Elan Vital of France: A Problem in Historical Perspective," *Modern France*, E. M. Earle, ed. (Princeton, 1951), 31.

Economically, the Empire as a whole did advance in the 1920's and 1930's, yet only small native elite groups—only a relative handful of Indo-Chinese or Senegalese or Algerian Arabs, for instance—were assimilated as Frenchmen or desired such assimilation. What the colonial populations were beginning to desire was some sort of home rule or independence. Although some leaders of the French Left urged concessions to native aspirations, little was in fact conceded, and French imperial policy in the 1920's and 1930's continued along traditional lines. Perhaps no policy pursued then could have prevented the disintegration of the French Empire that occurred after World War II, but the old-fashioned policy that prevailed did nothing to reconcile native nationalists to their French overlords.

IV: The United States

Neither the human nor the material losses of the United States in World War I were at all comparable with those of Britain and France. American casualties were 115,000 dead and 206,000 wounded; the comparable French figures were 1,385,000 dead and 3,044,000 wounded *in a population one-third as large*. Moreover, in purely material terms, the United States almost gained from the war. Heavy industries were greatly stimulated by Allied war orders; the war put the growing financial center of New York at least on equal terms with that of London; the dollar had begun to dethrone the monarch of the nineteenth century, the pound sterling. The Allies had borrowed from the American government, but until 1933 some interest came in on these loans. Moreover, the stimulation of American industry resulting from these loans exceeded the loss from the final repudiation of war debts in the early 1930's. The United States, then, came out of the war almost unscathed, victorious, and prosperous.

Isolationism

Yet in some ways the American revulsion against the war in 1919 and the years following was as marked as that of Britain, France, and defeated Germany. On the level of party politics, that revulsion helped to unseat the Democrats, who, under President Wilson, had controlled the federal government since 1913. The Republicans won the presidential elections of 1920, 1924, and 1928. Three successive Republicans occupied the White House—Harding (1921-1923), Coolidge (1923-1929), and Herbert Hoover (1929-1933).

On the level of policy and public attitudes, American revulsion against war took the form of *isolationism*, the desire to withdraw from international politics. This isolationism was by no means universal among Americans. Some historians feel that the drives and attitudes of millions of men had already made isolationism certain in 1919. Others feel that a slight shift in the words and deeds of men in high places could have changed the final decision and could have brought America into the League of Nations. If, as we have already seen, the Democratic President Wilson had been willing to meet Republican opposition in the Senate by a few concessions, then perhaps the Treaty of Versailles, League of Nations and all, might have achieved the two-thirds majority in the Senate the Constitution requires for treaties. Or if someone on the Republican side, with skill and prestige, had been able to put through the notion of a bipartisan foreign policy, then with patience and good will the United States might have been brought into the League. Public opinion, say those who take this view, was not against our carrying on the task we had begun in 1917; only a noisy minority in the country as a whole, and the little group of obstinate senators at the top, wanted us to withdraw.

Yet those who remember the years right after 1918 find it hard to deny that the country was swept by a wave of desire to get back to "normalcy," as President Harding later termed it, ungrammatically. A great many Americans felt that they had done all they needed to do in beating the Germans and that further direct participation in the complexities of European politics would simply involve American innocence and virtue that much more disastrously in European sophistication and vice. The not uncommon American reaction against its "strong" presidents took the form of repudiating all of Wilson's work at Paris as un-American. Furthermore, as the months of negotiation went on with no final decisions reached, Americans, always an impatient people, began to feel that sheer withdrawal was about the only effective action they could take.

The Treaty of Versailles, containing at Wilson's insistence the League of Nations, was finally rejected in the Senate on March 19, 1920. The United States remained technically at war with Germany until July, 1921, when a resolution making a separate peace was passed by Congress and signed under the presidency of Harding. American isolationism was expressed in these years in other concrete measures. The Fordney-McCumber Tariff of 1922 and the Smoot-Hawley Tariff of 1930 set successively higher duties on foreign goods, and emphasized America's belief that her high wage scales needed to be protected from cheap foreign labor.

Yet the United States continued all through the 1920's to insist that the debts owed to her by the Allied powers be repaid. It is true that these were refunded in a series of agreements, and that in the closely related problem of German reparations Americans on the whole cast their weight on the side of a general scaling-down of German obligations. But Congress paid little heed to the argument, so convincing to most economists, that European nations could not repay save through dollars gained by sales of their goods in the American market, and that American tariffs continued to make such repayment impossible. Congressmen tended to reduce the complexities of international debts to President Coolidge's simple dictum: "They hired the money, didn't they?"

The spirit of isolationism also lay behind the immigration restrictions of the 1920's, which reversed the former American policy of almost free immigration. The act of 1924 set an annual quota limit for each country of 2 per cent of the number of nationals from that country resident in the United States in 1890. Since the heavy immigration from eastern and southern Europe had come after 1890, the choice of that date reduced the flow from these areas to a mere trickle.

The Road to Internationalism

Yet during this era of partial isolationism the United States by no means withdrew entirely from international politics. Rather, as an independent without formal alliances, she continued to pursue policies that seemed to most Americans traditional, but that in their totality gradually lined her up against the chief perturbing nations of the years between the two world wars. Even before the drift of her commitments against Germany, Italy, and Japan became clear in the 1930's, Americans had in fact engaged themselves. In 1928, the Republican Secretary of State Kellogg submitted to the great European powers a proposal for a renunciation of war. Incorporated with similar proposals from the French Foreign Minister Briand, it was formally adopted in August of that year as the Pact of Paris, commonly known as the Kellogg-Briand Pact. It was eventually signed by twenty-three nations, including the United States. It is now the fashion to decry the Pact as futile, and it is certainly true that it did not prevent World War II. Yet by this action the United States expressed a concrete concern over the peace of the world.

In a hundred ways the United States was at work laying the foundations for the position of world leadership it reached after World War II. American businessmen were everywhere; American loans were making possible the revival of German industrial greatness; American motors, refrigerators, typewriters, telephones, and other products of the assembly line were being sold the world over. In the Far East, the United States as early as 1922 took the lead in the Nine-Power Treaty that committed her and the other great powers, including Japan, to respect the sovereignty and integrity of China. If President Roosevelt in 1941 resisted the Japanese attempt to swallow China and other Far Eastern territory, he was simply following a line laid down under President Harding.

Boom—and Bust

In domestic affairs, the Coolidge era (1923-1929) has now become legendary. These were years of frantic prosperity; nearly everybody played the stock market and the value of stocks rose to fantastic heights. They were the years of "prohibition," the ban on the manufacture and sale of alcoholic beverages, enforced, in theory, by the Volstead Act of 1919 under the Eighteenth Amendment to the Constitution. And so they were also the years of the speakeasy and the bootlegger. They were the years of the short skirt—the shortest, probably, in all western history, if we except the Scottish kilt—of sex appeal, the Charleston, and other forms of "sin." They were years which, like the "naughty nineties" of the nineteenth century, we look back on with a sort of reproving envy, years that now look colorful and romantic.

But the Coolidge era was by no means completely summed up in novels of the jazz age, like *The Great Gatsby* of F. Scott Fitzgerald, or even in Sinclair Lewis' half-satirical *Babbitt* and *Main Street*. It was an era of marked industrial progress, of solid advancement of the national plant and productive capabilities. It was an era of the steady spreading in the United States of standards of living heretofore limited to the relatively few, standards of living that seemed to intellectuals vulgar and inadequate, but that were nevertheless a new thing in the world. These were the years when, if you had a servant, you could no longer take her for granted, but had to take some pains to keep her satisfied. They were years for which, at their best, the right symbol is no Hollywood character, no intellectual, no great pioneer of industry, nor even a gangster, but rather President Coolidge himself, sober, plodding, unimaginative.

At its most glamorous, the era ended with the onset of the great depression in the autumn of 1929. During the preceding year, Wall Street had enjoyed an unprecedented boom. Speculators by the millions were playing the market in the hope of quick resale of stocks at huge profits; they bought shares "on margin," paying only a fraction of their cost in cash, and often borrowing the money to pay that small fraction. Not only stocks but many other purchases were financed on borrowed money. Credit had swollen to the point where it was no longer on a sound basis in a largely unregulated economy. Eventually, shrewd investors began to sell their holdings in the belief that the bubble soon would burst. The result was a disastrous drop in stock values, beginning in October, 1929, and continuing almost without let-up to 1933. Both the speculators and the lenders from whom they had borrowed money were ruined.

The immediate cause of the depression, then, was the stock-market crash. About the more deep-seated causes the economic physicians are not even today wholly agreed. Some of them believe that a capitalist society inevitably produces business cycles oscillating from the highs of prosperity to the lows of depression; that these cycles are of various lengths, short, medium, and long; and that an unusual number of cyclical lows coincided in the late 1920's to make the depression particularly serious. Others, not uninfluenced by Marx, hold that under American capitalism the troughs of a depression are bound to be deeper each time, if only because of the great scale of the American economy.

This much seems certain: Coolidge prosperity was very unevenly distributed among the various parts of the American economy and American society. Agriculture, notably, suffered a kind of permanent depression throughout the 1920's. At the close of World War I, farmers commanded very high prices for their produce and enjoyed an apparently insatiable market at home and abroad. They expanded their production—and borrowed to finance the expansion— often at a reckless rate. Then, as "normalcy" returned in the early 1920's, the foreign market dried up, the home market shrank, farm prices fell rapidly, and the inevitable foreclosure of farm mortgages began. Wage-earning workers, though not hard hit like the farmers, gained but little increase in their purchasing power during the 1920's. The worker did often raise his standard of living, by purchasing a house or a car, but he did it on credit, by assuming the burden of a heavy mortgage or by financing a purchase on installments to be paid over a long period. The "big money" of the Coolidge era went chiefly to business, above all to big business.

The great depression was very severe in many countries throughout the world, but nowhere was it worse than in the United States. Its effects may be measured by the round figure of 16,000,000 Americans unemployed at the low point in the early 1930's —something like one-third of the national labor force. In terms of what economists call the "gross national product" the United States Department of Commerce sets for 1929 the figure of $103,828,000,000; for 1933, however, the same department sets a figure of only $55,760,000,000.

The most remarkable thing about this grave crisis in the American economy is that it produced almost no organized movements of revolt, no threat of revolution. The intellectuals of the 1930's did indeed turn to "social consciousness," and Marxism made some converts among writers and artists. But the bulk of the population showed no serious signs of abandoning their fundamental belief that the way out lay through the legal means provided by existing American institutions. Even before the election of Franklin D. Roosevelt in 1932, local authorities and private charities, helped out by the establishment early in 1932 of the federal R.F.C. (Reconstruction Finance Corporation) to release frozen assets, did a good deal to soften the worst sufferings of the unemployed. The Republican administration of President Hoover, however, was generally committed to the philosophy of laissez-faire; aside from the R.F.C., it did little to cushion the effects of the depression. People who wanted a more vigorous attack on economic problems voted for the Democrats in 1932; most significantly, they did not vote in very important numbers for the socialist or communist presidential candidates. In the crisis of a great depression the American two-party system evidently continued to meet basic political needs.

The New Deal

The victory of the Democrats in 1932 seemed to give them a clear mandate to marshal all the resources of the federal government against the depression. The Democratic president, Franklin Roosevelt (1933-1945), took office on March 4, 1933, in the midst of a financial crisis that had closed the banks all over the country. He at once summoned Congress to an emergency session, and declared a bank holiday. Gradually the sound banks reopened, and the New Deal began. Subsequently, under improving economic conditions, the American business community mostly turned with great bitterness against Roosevelt and all his works. But in those early months of 1933 the mere fact that a national administration was trying to do something about the situation was a powerful restorative to national morale. The nation emerged from the bank holiday with a new confidence, echoing the phrase from Roosevelt's inaugural address that there was nothing to fear "but fear itself."

The New Deal was in part a series of measures aimed at immediate difficulties and in part a series of measures aimed at permanent changes in the structure of American society. The distinction between its short-term and its long-term measures is in a sense arbitrary, for the men who carried both through were never quite clear in their own minds exactly what they were trying to do. What must chiefly interest us is the implications of their work. In the perspective of western history, the New Deal is the coming to the United States, under the special pressures of the great depression, of those measures—"socialist" to some of their opponents—that we have already seen in European countries like Great Britain and imperial Germany. They are best summed up in that value-charged term, the "welfare state."

The short-term measures of the New Deal aimed by releasing the dollar from its tie with gold to lower the price of American goods in a world that was abandoning the gold standard. They aimed to thaw out credit by extending the activities of the R.F.C. and by creating such new governmental lending agencies as the Home Owners' Loan Corporation. They aimed to relieve unemployment by public works on a

Franklin D. Roosevelt.

large scale, to safeguard bank deposits by the Federal Deposit Insurance Corporation, and to regulate speculation and other stock-market activities by the Securities and Exchange Commission. The historical significance of many of these innovations rested in the fact that they were undertaken not by private business or by state or local authorities but by the federal government. There was one exception to the rule of widening federal activity: the Twenty-first Amendment to the Constitution repealed the Eighteenth and abandoned the increasingly unsuccessful federal efforts to enforce prohibition.

The long-term measures of the New Deal were, of course, more important. The Social Security Act of 1935 introduced to the United States on a national scale the unemployment allowances, old-age pensions, and other benefits of the kind that Lloyd George had brought into Britain. Somewhat more equal distribution of the national wealth resulted from increased federal taxation, especially taxes on individual and corporate incomes. Congress passed a whole series of acts on labor relations, the net effect of which has been to strengthen and extend the role of organized labor in American economic life. A series of acts on agriculture, though leaving the business of farming still in the hands of several million individual farmers producing for sale in a cash market, nevertheless regulated crops and prices to a degree that would have been incomprehensible to a nineteenth-century farmer. And finally— the showpiece of the New Deal—a great regional planning board, the Tennessee Valley Authority, has used government power to make over the economic and social life of a relatively backward area by checking the erosion of farmlands, by instituting flood control, and by providing cheap electric power generated at government-built dams.

More than twenty-five years after the bank holiday of 1933, Americans were still debating the New Deal. It unquestionably left the United States a society very different from that pictured by the classical economists. No real society has ever quite corresponded to the theoretical extreme of free enterprise, in which every man sells and buys what he wants—or can—and in which the man who cannot "earn" a living quite simply dies. But in the sense in which the United States of, say, 1870 was close to such a society, the United States of the New Deal and after is quite far from such a society. The rush of free competition has been tempered by government regulation, because it has become clear that in such competition much that men prize would in fact be competed out of existence. Most Americans have come to see the need for government regulation in the conservation of natural resources. Even here, however, when it comes to the overgrazing of pasture lands or the farming methods that lead to soil erosion, some Americans are still reluctant to have the government interfere with their "rights."

When the question at stake is the distribution of wealth, rather than its actual exhaustion, Americans are often unwilling to accept limitations on free enterprise. On this issue, even after the New Deal, the champions of government regulation and private initiative still do battle. The Marxist indictment of a competitive society, that under it the rich tend to become richer and the poor to become poorer, is not wholly true. But the last two hundred years of western history suggest that without some government regulation the modern scramble for wealth tends to produce a society pyramidal in structure. With a few men of great wealth at the top, the pyramid spreads out through the well-to-do to a broad base of human beings just able to scrape along. In our western society, however, the political power democracy gives to that numerous broad base has over the years been used to alter the very shape of the social pyramid. "Soak-the-rich" taxation and government aid to the poor have flattened it out, cutting it down at the top and pushing it up from the bottom. Indeed, the figure may no longer be a pyramid, but something approaching diamond-shaped, widest in the middle. It is not yet in any human society a straight line, representing absolute social and economic equality.

There is, then, in modern America a leveling, both up and down. The great baronial mansions of the Hudson Valley, of Newport, even of California, are too expensive to maintain, and are being turned into museums or put to institutional use. The worst of the urban slums are being slowly demolished to make way for modern housing projects. The very rich still exist, at least in Texas, but the number of the very poor is diminishing. Meanwhile, the total national product has increased. It is not merely that a fixed national income is being more evenly distributed; despite the complaints of conservatives that the leveling process is destroying incentives to hard work and invention, the gross national product has increased greatly since the depth of the depression in 1932-1933. There is more to be shared.

It must be noted that the American society that emerged from the New Deal can by no means be accurately described as "socialistic." The United States of the mid-twentieth century is rather a "mixed economy," in which individual economic activity—that of the worker as well as that of the entrepreneur or manager—is indeed regulated and restricted, but not entirely controlled, by government. The United States still displays an extraordinary range of economic activity, from the "socialistic" Post Office to enormous private industries that are themselves societies, almost governments, with administrative problems and bureaucracies of their own, and on down to small independent businessmen, who are often the best examples of almost pure free enterprise.

Confident America

Although Americans still argue about the New Deal, it seems evident that the measures taken by the Roosevelt administration, combined with the strength of American institutions and culture, pulled the United States at least part way out of the depression. These measures also restored a high degree of confidence to Americans. The intellectuals, whose role in modern America has generally been in opposition to the men of business, in the 1920's had found the United States a hopelessly crass and vulgar society. But in the 1930's, though some intellectuals flirted with Marxism, many of them turned to support the new American way marked out by the New Deal.

The onset of war in Europe found Americans, as we shall see in the next chapter, anxious not to jeopardize in war their still precarious prosperity, anxious to remain neutral if Europe should persist in going to war. But the United States was not, like the France of 1940, a tired, skeptical land, divided fundamentally into mutually hostile classes. Roosevelt and his Republican opponents had been for some time exchanging insults: the "economic royalists" fought back at "that man in the White House." Yet in the pinch of the international crisis of 1939-1941 it became clear that, although the nation was not completely united, at any rate it was not pathologically divided. As so often in American history, the violence of verbal politics masks a very basic unity. When the war came to the United States in 1941, Americans were largely ready for it psychologically and—what is really remarkable in a western democracy —not too unready for it militarily.

When the war came, moreover, the United States had already made many efforts to enlist the support of the Latin-American states. In 1930, before the so-called "Roosevelt Revolution" in American diplomacy, President Hoover's State Department issued the Clark Memorandum, specifically stating that the Monroe Doctrine does not concern itself with inter-American relations but is directed against outside intervention in the affairs of the Western Hemisphere. The United States was no longer to land the Marines in some Central American republic at the drop of a hat but was trying to strengthen hemispheric solidarity. And so, on the foundations of the Clark Memorandum, President Roosevelt built his celebrated "Good Neighbor" policy toward the other American nations (for details on Latin America, see Chapter XXXI).

Meantime, what may be called American imperial policy was likewise undergoing some liberalization, notably with respect to the Philippines. When the United States had annexed the islands at the close of the Spanish-American War (see Chapter XXIV), a stubborn Filipino insurrection broke out in protest, and it took American forces three years (1899-1902) to subdue the rebels. Filipino nationalism, though partially disarmed by the conciliatory measures taken by the United States after the suppression of the rebellion, none the less continued to hope for eventual freedom. In the 1930's American officials negotiated with Filipino leaders with the aim at first of bestowing a rather dilute kind of dominion status on the islands. But by the outbreak of World War II the negotiations had advanced to the point where it was evident that the Philippines would soon gain at least nominal independence.

V: The Loosening of Imperial Ties

The Filipino insurrection of 1899 was a portent. Even before 1914, there were signs that many of the more advanced "colonial" peoples were already chafing under imperialism. Native nationalist movements were creating trouble for the British in Egypt and India, for the French in Morocco and Algeria, and for all the imperial powers in China. The First World War itself speeded up the process of rousing national consciousness among the "natives" of the various empires, and at its end there was no doubt that the hold of the West had been loosened. Psychologically, the experience of the war gave a lift to non-western peoples; they had often rendered important services to their white masters, and their leaders had widened their knowledge of the West. The Arab peoples of the old Ottoman Empire had raised armies of their own and had fought with European aid for their own freedom from Turkish rule.

French colonial troops and British Indian troops had taken part in the conflict, sometimes in Europe itself.

The very spectacle of the masters quarreling among themselves did something to lower the prestige of the West among subject peoples. Moreover, the Allies had fought the war in the name of democratic ideals of self-determination for all peoples, and in their propaganda against the Central Powers they had stressed their opposition to imperialism. The fifth of Wilson's Fourteen Points asserted that in disputed claims to colonial territories "the interests of the populations concerned must have equal weight" with the interests of the colonial powers. It is true that the Allies did not give up any of their territories in 1919, and did indeed add to them under the mandate system (see Chapter XXV). To many of the subject races, as to liberals in the West itself, the mandate was simply a disguise for the old imperialism; but it is surely significant that a disguise seemed necessary to the imperialist powers. The West now appeared to be committed to a process of at least gradual emancipation of the colonial dependencies.

It was in the Far East that old imperial ties were most clearly loosened during the inter-war years. China, as we shall soon see in more detail, was engaged in a great struggle to free herself from the tutelage of the western colonial powers. The conflict in China, however, was much more than a simple conflict between oriental nationalists and occidental imperialists. Almost from the start it was complicated by two additional elements—increasing communist intervention in Chinese politics, and the increasing threat to Chinese independence from an expansionist Japan. It is scarcely an exaggeration to say that China faced the prospect of simply exchanging one set of imperial overlords for another.

Japan

Alone among non-western peoples, the Japanese experienced the industrial revolution and were able to maintain themselves as a fully independent major political entity during the great age of imperialism (see Chapter XXIV). More than that, as the twentieth century opened, Japan was clearly a great power, a full but somewhat unwelcome participant in the struggle for imperial position. As we have seen, the Japanese made these impressive accomplishments without radically altering their traditional oligarchical and absolutist political structure.

In the decade after World War I, it looked as though Japan might achieve a gradual liberalization of her political institutions. The cabinets of the 1920's included many men from the business class who favored vigorous expansion abroad but who also granted some measures of cautious liberalism at home. The suffrage was gradually extended, and in 1925 all men received the right to vote. For the first time, political parties, western-style, began to put down roots, especially in the urban population, and seemed likely to give new vitality to the Diet, the not very powerful central representative assembly of Japan. Trade unions also took shape and began to win a following.

Japan, however, did not evolve into a parliamentary democracy on the western model during the twenty years' truce. By the early 1930's, political power was falling more and more into the hands of army and navy officers, many of them descended from the feudal *samurai* class (see above, pp. 361-362). This officer clique hated the prospect of liberal civilian government and envied and mistrusted the business class. They found a potent political weapon in the institution of the emperor, who was supposed to possess the kind of political infallibility that westerners associate with a divine-right monarch. Putting their own words into the emperor's mouth, the admirals and generals used his pronouncements to further their own ends. And, to make doubly sure, they assassinated or terrorized the chief spokesmen of nascent Japanese liberalism.

The consequence was the progressive clamping of a military dictatorship on Japan during the 1930's. Although popular elections continued to be held, their results were disregarded, and the Diet lost its recently acquired vitality. Businessmen supported the new régime out of fear or out of anticipation of the huge profits to be secured from its adventures abroad. A cult of emperor-worship, known as state Shinto, was concocted out of a rather innocuous traditional Japanese religion to focus popular loyalties on the divine mission of the emperor and to insure popular submission to the will of the men who ruled in his name. A corps of ruthless agents, picturesquely named "thought police," hounded

"*Rule Japannia. Very nice, yes!—so long as honourable foreign ladies continue to sit apart.*" Cartoonist Low comments on Japan's profiting by British and American failure to pursue a coordinated Far Eastern policy during the 1930's.

anyone suspected of harboring "dangerous thoughts." In short, Japan now had a government that exploited many uniquely Japanese traditions but in its operations also bore a striking resemblance to the totalitarian governments of Europe.

Nowhere was the parallel with European totalitarianism more marked than in the foreign policy of Japan between the two world wars. Like Hitler's Germans or Mussolini's Italians, the Japanese claimed to be a "have-not" nation. They, too, pointed to their steadily growing population—and did all they could to encourage its further growth. They, too, harped on the overcrowding of the homeland, its inadequate resources, and its restricted markets. Behind these arguments lay real economic problems of sustaining the Japanese economy in the face of the depression and the worldwide disruption of international trade, problems of providing food and work for the 60,000,000 Japanese of 1930. In seeking to solve these problems by imperial expansion, the militarists of the 1930's were following a pattern that had already been set by the West. And they were also following the path marked out by the Japanese officers and politicians who had secured Formosa in 1895 and annexed Korea in 1910. During

World War I Japan had tried in vain to subjugate China; by World War II she had apparently almost succeeded in doing so. To follow the course of this Japanese imperialism we must turn to the history of its chief victim, China.

China: The Revolution of 1911-1912

By 1900, the Chinese Empire was far gone in political decay. Nominally independent under the rule of its Manchu dynasty, it had lost much of its effective sovereignty through concessions of naval bases and economic and political privileges to the European powers and Japan. Following China's defeat by Japan in 1895, European imperialists engaged in a hectic scramble for further concessions. The Germans leased Kiaochow, the French Kwangchou Bay, the Russians Port Arthur, and the British Wei-hai-wei (see also Chapter XXIV). In 1899, the American Secretary of State, John Hay, sought to end the scramble by getting the powers to accept the principle of the "Open Door," whereby all foreign goods could be marketed in China on equal terms, with no special favors to any one power. Although the interested states subscribed to Hay's policy in principle, the Open Door meant little in practice.

Meantime, a formidable reaction to the outburst of imperialist activity was gathering within China itself. The hard-pressed Manchu government encouraged the formation of an anti-foreign nationalist secret society called the Boxers. The result was the Boxer Rebellion of 1900, in which more than 200 foreigners, mainly missionaries, were slain. The foreign powers, including the United States, used troops to protect their nationals and property against the Boxers. In 1901 they obliged the Manchu government to pay an enormous indemnity and to grant them further rights that, of course, further impaired Chinese sovereignty.

The next Chinese rebellion, the revolution of 1911, was directed against the Manchu régime that had proved so incapable of resisting the encroachments of imperialism. In this revolution a factor operated that may often be found in the whole process of national self-assertion by non-western peoples. The movement is directed against the West—against westerners themselves or against native governors who seem to be the agents of the West. But it is a movement inspired at least in part by western ideas and examples, a movement that could scarcely have come into being without the influence of the West.

The Chinese revolution of 1911 was comparatively bloodless in its early stages. It was sealed by the abdication on February 12, 1912, of the six-year-old Manchu Emperor, Pu-yi. From the start, the two chief revolutionary groups displayed conflicting ideas about the nature of the new society that would replace the discarded Manchu régime. One group soon formed the Nationalist party, the Kuomintang, led by Sun Yat-sen and many young intellectuals who had studied and traveled in the West. Its leaders wanted a democratic parliamentary republic of China modeled on the western

political system, though preserving as far as possible the basic Chinese family and village structure, on which western industrial society was to be grafted. The other group, whose leader was Yuan Shih-k'ai, wanted a strong central government basically authoritarian in structure, with authority not in the hands of an emperor and the traditional and highly conservative Chinese mandarin bureaucracy, but in the hands of strong men capable of achieving the modernization of China from above.

Sun Yat-sen.

A struggle for power broke out between the assembly elected after 1911 and Yuan Shih-k'ai. The party of Sun Yat-sen was defeated, and by 1914, after a "purge" of the Kuomintang members of the assembly, Yuan Shih-k'ai issued a constitutional compact that put him in the presidential office for ten years. Sun Yat-sen and his followers had failed to turn China into a western parliamentary democracy. Sun was, however, a gifted leader, and the ideas for which he stood, though they never got firmly rooted in China, have never quite disappeared. Sun remains somewhat paradoxically the great hero of the Chinese revolution of 1911.

Yuan's subsequent career bears some resemblance to that of another military reformer, Oliver Cromwell. Faced with continuing opposition, not only from the republicans of the Kuomintang but also from the monarchists, Yuan decided to follow the age-old Chinese pattern and set himself up as the first of a new dynasty of emperors to follow the Manchus. A revolt caused him to revoke his plans, and early in 1916 he reorganized the republic with a military cabinet. He died on June 6, 1916, leaving the new republic enmeshed in another age-old Chinese political pattern—the dissolution of all but the shadow of central control and the assumption of real power by regional strong men. A new era of provincial "war-lords" had begun.

In the years of crisis following 1911, China also faced the aggressive attempts of Japan to take over the Far Eastern imperial interests of European powers now at war among themselves. Early in 1915, the Japanese presented in secrecy to the Chinese government the "Twenty-One Demands," which amounted to a demand for something close to a protectorate over China and for all sorts of concrete concessions. The Chinese republic, now at the nadir of its strength, countered by declaring war against the Central Powers, thus securing at least the nominal protection of two of the Allies, Britain and France. The Japanese did not feel able to defy western objections, and so contented themselves with taking over Kiaochow and other German concessions in the Shantung peninsula. At the end of the war, the victorious Allies, with the United States in the lead, acted to check the ambitions of their recent military partner, Japan. At the Washington Conference of 1922 (see also Chapter XXIX) Japan was forced to sign the Nine-Power Treaty guaranteeing the independence of China. This rebuff to Japan was one of the first events in the long chain that aggravated the hostility of Japan toward the United States, and ended, two decades later, in the attack on Pearl Harbor.

China between the World Wars

The details of Chinese history between the two world wars are extraordinarily complex. The main elements during this twenty-year period were the Kuomintang, the Communists, and the Japanese invaders. The Kuomintang, after the death of Sun Yat-sen in 1925, came under the leadership of Chiang Kai-shek, an army officer trained in Japan and the brother-in-law of Sun Yat-sen. The Nationalists of the Kuomintang were engaged in a constant and often very unsuccessful struggle to set up an effective central government against the power of provincial "war-lords." They were also often locked in battle with the Communists and the Japanese.

All three of the main forces fought in word and deed for the allegiance—or at any rate for the passive acceptance—of nearly five hundred million Chinese, for the most part peasants, and for the most part illiterate. For the most part, too, the masses of China were so far from sharing western attitudes toward the state that it is hardly an exaggeration to say that they felt toward politics as we westerners feel toward the weather—that it is something beyond human control. In transforming the Chinese into a nation in the western sense, the indispensable step was something more than building railroads and factories or promoting the study of modern science instead of the Chinese classics. It was getting the Chinese peasant to regard himself as an individual Chinese citizen.

This indispensable process was beginning in the 1920's and 1930's. It goes far to explain why the Japanese, when they renewed their aggression in 1931, were virtually beaten from the start in the attempt to become the true masters of China. In an earlier age one can readily imagine the Japanese as military conquerors in China setting up a new dynasty, foreign in origin, but very soon thoroughly absorbed by the Chinese. That this age-old pattern was not followed in the 1930's shows that China herself was changing, that here too the modern expansion of the West, the spread of western ways and ideas, was altering her traditional way of life.

The Japanese attack came in September, 1931, on Manchuria, an outlying northern province of China that was a particularly tempting target for Japanese aggression. Manchuria had good resources of coal and iron; it adjoined Korea, already a Japanese possession; and it had never been fully integrated into the structure of Chinese government and looked, therefore, as though it could easily be pried loose. Moreover, the Japanese regarded themselves as the natural successors of the Russians, whom they had driven from Manchuria in the Russo-Japanese War of 1904-1905. By 1932, the Japanese were strong enough in Manchuria to proclaim it a puppet state, which they called Manchukuo, under a puppet ruler, Pu-yi, who as a boy had been the last emperor of China.

The Chinese responded to Japan's aggression in Manchuria by a very effective boycott of Japanese goods; the Japanese countered by carrying the war to the great Chinese port of Shanghai. Given the weakness of the Kuomintang government, effective Chinese resistance would have required full support from stronger outside powers. Neither the western powers nor the League of Nations gave China more than verbal support (for details, see Chapter XXIX); the Chinese had to give up their boycott of Japanese goods, and the Japanese remained in Manchuria. Tension between China and Japan persisted, however, and the Japanese soon decided to attempt the absorption of all the rest of China. Their invasion came in

July, 1937, without a formal declaration of war.

In a purely military way the Japanese did very well. By October, when the key southern Chinese city of Canton fell, they had taken the strategic points of the coastal area and the thickly peopled lower river valleys. Chiang Kai-shek took refuge with his army and his fellow politicians of the Kuomintang in the interior province of Szechwan. There he set up his capital at Chungking; and there, protected by distance and a ring of mountains, receiving western aid through India by the Burma Road and, when that was closed, by air, the Nationalist government held out until the end of World War II and the collapse of Japanese imperialism.

Yet the Japanese, even at the height of their success, had achieved no more than the stretching across China of a string of garri-

Chiang Kai-shek at the time of the Japanese invasion of China.

sons, and the control of great cities like Shanghai and Peiping. They held the railroads, subject to guerrilla attack, but away from the relatively sparse lines of modern communication they were helpless. Many a Chinese village in the area nominally Japanese never changed its ways during the occupation. Nowhere did the Japanese win over the acquiescence, to say nothing of the loyalty, of the Chinese people.

The Nationalists of the Kuomintang led the resistance to the Japanese from the beginning, yet they, too, ultimately failed to win the full loyalty of the Chinese people. This was partly a military matter. Chiang's armies were never able to stand on equal terms with the Japanese. They lacked a good base in modern industrial society, and, as the Japanese early seized the few industrial cities of China, Chiang was always relatively badly off in terms of logistics. In the long exile in Szechwan, moreover, the morale of the Nationalists decayed. The ordeal, far from purifying and strengthening them, emphasized their alienation from the masses of the Chinese, their corruption and intrigue, their inability to live up to the early promise of Sun Yatsen and the Kuomintang. For it was not the Nationalists, but the Communists, who succeeded in capturing and harnessing the human emotions and aspirations, the binding power that will hold men together in society with the tightness modern material culture demands. It was the Communists, not the Nationalists, who apparently came to stand to most Chinese for what made them Chinese; the Communists came to embody Chinese "nationalism."

The Chinese Communists

The Chinese Communist movement began in the early 1920's. It was inspired by direct contacts with the Comintern in Moscow, guided by Soviet agents, and encouraged at first by leaders of the Kuomin-

tang. Sun Yat-sen hoped that the example and advice of the successful Russian party might help to strengthen his own faltering party organization. For a time, the Chinese Communists were no more than the left wing of the Kuomintang. Soon, however, the inevitable breach occurred between them and the more conservative elements among the Nationalists, led by Chiang Kaishek.

The Communists lost out badly in this early struggle for power. In 1926, Chiang's forces began a campaign of persecution and assassination against them; in 1927, the Communists were expelled from the Kuomintang. An important reason for this setback was the failure of the Chinese Communists to get effective support or help from Moscow. The years 1926 and 1927 were the years of the Trotsky-Stalin feud in Russia, and the conflict between these two titans was intensified by their differences over the "correct" Chinese policy of the Soviet Union (see above, p. 452). Stalin, who was rapidly gaining the ascendancy, believed that China was not ripe for a proletarian revolution; therefore, he did nothing to succor his Chinese comrades.

During the next two decades, down to the end of World War II, the relative strength of Communists and Nationalists underwent a gradual and decisive shift. Both parties, it should be noted, were in a sense totalitarian. Both were organized on the one-party pattern, which left no place for an opposition; neither of them was geared to the give-and-take of western party politics. The Communists, driven about over much of China during the 1930's, ended up with a base in the region of Yenan in the north; their strategic position somewhat resembled that of Chiang in his southern base of Szechwan. But there was an important difference. In the long years of Japanese occupation, Chiang remained in Chungking with his army and his bureaucracy. The Communists, on the other hand, managed to string their network of organized armies and local councils in and around the Japanese in the north; they extended their apparatus right down to the sea and up through Manchuria. By 1945, the Communists were ready for a successful conflict with the Kuomintang (see Chapter XXXI).

Southeast Asia

The great turning point in the recent history of the Far East has been World War II, with its aftermath of Communist victory in China, of French withdrawal from Indo-China, British from Burma, Dutch from the East Indies, and American from the Philippines. Before World War II there were few clear signs of the spectacular changes to come in Southeast Asia, that part of the Far East stretching east from India and south from China through the islands of Indonesia. But good observers during the twenty years' truce noted the slow growth of nationalist opposition to imperial rule, particularly in Indo-China and the Netherlands East Indies. They saw that the British-controlled Malay peninsula, with its characteristic colonial economy of rubber and tin production, was peculiarly dependent on the economic health of the West and peculiarly vulnerable in a major depression.

India

In India, by contrast, World War I marked a crucial turning point. India made important contributions to the British armies, particularly to their victory over the Turks. Educated Indians, growing in numbers and long exposed to the kind of ideas we call liberal, received the full impact of Allied propaganda in favor of the war to save the world for democracy. Monetary inflation and other war dislocations favored the growing agitation for

self-government. Already in the war period the British Viceroy, Lord Chelmsford, and his experts, both British and Indian, were working toward a plan of reform. Public opinion not only in India but throughout the world was sharpened in favor of the Indians by what seemed to be a throw-back to the crude days of imperial force when, in April, 1919, British troops fired on demonstrators at Amritsar (see above, p. 404).

The Amritsar massacre, however, was an exception. One basic fact about India after World War I was the still relatively serene British rule with its slow but steady acclimatization of Indians to western material things like railroads and hospitals and to western ideas like equality and freedom. A second basic fact, growing out of the first, was the growing Indian demand for the termination of British colonial rule. A third basic fact, conditioning the second, was the existence of tension between Hindus and Moslems, which we must now examine in some detail.

A large Moslem minority, about a quarter of the total population, had grown up in the seven hundred years since the first invasion of India by Moslem peoples. In the Indus Basin and part of the Punjab in the northwest, and in part of Bengal in the east, the Moslems were actually a majority; elsewhere they lived scattered among the Hindus and other non-Moslems. Though some of the Moslems belonged to the aristocratic classes, the bulk were peasants, and on the whole the Moslem community was outstripped financially and industrially by the Hindu community. Although some Moslems, especially in the upper classes, were proud descendants of conquering tribes, for the most part the Moslems and the Hindus were roughly of the same racial mixtures, both really native Indians.

Yet Moslems and Hindus felt—and feel—toward each other (we are talking in terms of average members of the two communities) in a way exceedingly difficult for most westerners to understand. A friendly British observer has summed it up in this manner:

What are the things which keep Muslims and Hindus apart, which make them feel that they are different races and nations, which keep them permanently potentially on edge with each other? The first perhaps is the doctrinal issue of idolatry. The Muslim has borrowed from the Semitic races both his passionate rejection of polytheism and his passionate hatred of idolatry. . . . The worship of many gods, the portrayal of the divine in human form, is something to him which is less than human, the mark of the beast. It has, I think, no counterpart in the West; for it is far stronger than our ideas of good form or fair play or the behaviour of a gentleman. . . . The ramifications of these emotions are widespread through the whole realm of Hindu-Muslim relations because of the ubiquitous working of the Hindu doctrine of incarnation. So much in Hinduism is divine. The Muslim does not mind a Hindu not eating beef, for example, but he does object to his worshipping the cow. In times of irritation there is consequently a strong urge to kill a cow out of sheer bravado.

On the side of social custom the chief irritant among Muslims is the caste system in general and the claims of the Brahmins in particular. These claims offend the strong Muslim sense of equality and repel by their exclusiveness. The Muslim taboo of pork is another sore point in social relations, for though it is not a food of caste Hindus any more than of Muslims, its defiling effect makes it an easy subject for provocation. So, too, does the Muslim prohibition of music in worship. Pork in the mosque or music outside are certain ways of provoking a Hindu-Muslim riot.

But the mental anguish of mutual relations is not all on the Muslim side. Hindus suffer acutely in the ceremonial sphere. Hindu feelings about the cow are as untranslatable into Western terms as are Muslim feelings about idolatry, and they are no less strong. A Hindu may literally turn sick at the sight or smell of beef. Muslim practice in the matter of food seems to the typical Hindu to be impure, dirty, and degraded, something beneath the level of man. He cannot understand, on the other hand, what he calls Muslim fanaticism on the subject of idolatry. Orthodox Hindu and Muslim individuals can be, and often are, very good friends, but they usually take good care that their intercourse avoids these danger areas.[*]

It is not surprising, therefore, that after serious attempts to bring Hindu and Moslem into a unified resistance movement against the British, two separate bodies grew up in the twentieth century—the Indian National Congress and the All-India Moslem League. Immediately after World War I the two bodies did often succeed in presenting a common front against the British, but as time went on their mutual opposition, indeed their irreconcilability, tended to increase rather than diminish.

In spite of these difficulties, the Indian drive for self-government and independence went on steadily from the end of World War I. For the Hindus, the Congress party was held together effectively and given extraordinary influence over the masses by one of the great leaders of the twentieth century, Mahatma Gandhi (1869-1948). Gandhi was not a Brahmin (a member of the highest Hindu caste) but a member of the *bania* or shopkeeping caste. Educated as a lawyer at Oxford and therefore familiar with the West, trained during his youth in politics in South Africa with its Indian minority, Gandhi was admirably equipped to deal with both British and Hindus. Among his own people he appealed by his simple and austere personal life, his fasts, and his exiguous native costume. He worked out the technique of insurrection called "non-violent non-co-operation," which appealed to the fundamental Hindu belief that force is illusory and therefore ineffective. Characteristic measures sponsored by Gandhi were the organized Indian boycott of British goods and the Mahatma's own resistance through hunger-strikes.

Other Congress leaders, especially at the local level, were willing to use more clearly western methods of agitation, propaganda,

[*] Percival Spear, *India, Pakistan, and the West* (London, 1949), 89-91.

and, it must be admitted, rather violent non-violence. Concession after concession was wrung from the British, and as the Indians gained political experience in provincial self-government and in the civil service, dominion status appeared to be just around the corner. This was the situation at the outbreak of World War II. By the time the war was over, however, it was evident that the mutual antagonism of Hindus and Moslems might well require the formation not of a single unified India but of two separate states (see Chapter XXXI).

The Middle East

The European powers had a long history of attempts to secure an imperial stake in the Near East—or Middle East, to use the roughly equivalent term that gained currency in World War II. The Middle East refers essentially to Persia and to the Asian and African lands that were still nominally part of the decaying Ottoman Empire at the opening of the twentieth century. At that time, the Middle East was still a poverty-stricken region. But by 1914 the first discoveries of petroleum had been made, discoveries that have gone on and on until today the Middle East contains the largest proved reserves of oil in the world. The whole of the area was not to share in this new wealth: the major fields were found in southwestern Persia, in the river valleys of Iraq (ancient Mesopotamia), and along the Persian Gulf.

The new-found riches of the Middle East did not lessen the interest of the European powers in the region during the twenty years' truce. And in the 1930's, as American experts began to worry about the depletion of oil reserves in the Western Hemisphere, the United States entered the Middle East in something more than its older roles of Protestant missionary and benevolent educator at the American colleges in Beirut (Lebanon) and Istanbul. American oil

India on the brink of independence: Gandhi and crowd, 1945.

companies joined with British, Dutch, and French companies in developing and marketing Middle Eastern petroleum.

In the inter-war years, then, the Middle East was an area of increased economic imperialism. It was not, however, an area of the cruder sort of political imperialism, although the western powers maintained sufficient control to insure the orderly exploitation of oil resources. As we have seen in Chapter XXV, at the close of World War I the Arab territories of the old Ottoman Empire were administered as western mandates, not annexed as western colonies. The French got the mandates for Syria and for Syria's half-Christian neighbor, Lebanon. The British, who already held a protectorate over Egypt, got the mandates for Palestine and Iraq. The only Arab state of significance enjoying anything like full independence was Saudi Arabia, which occupied the bulk of the desert Arabian peninsula. It was an essentially medieval state, the personal creation of a remarkable tribal chieftain, a latter-day feudal warrior, Ibn Saud (1880-1953).

The postwar arrangements, which brought so much of the Arab world under a dilute form of imperial control, did not satisfy the aspirations of Arab nationalists. In these nationalist movements the usual ingredients—western education, hatred of westerners, desire to emulate them—were mixed with a common adherence to Islam, and a vague but real feeling of belonging to some kind of common Arab "nation." Arab nationalism was already being focused on the special problem of Palestine, for by the Balfour Declaration of 1917 the British had promised to open this largely Arab-populated territory as a "national home for the Jewish people." The immigration of Jews into Palestine during the years between the wars caused repeated clashes between Arab nationalists and Jewish nationalists or Zionists. The seeds were being sown for the Palestine problem of our own day (see Chapter XXXI).

The French made few concessions to Arab nationalism; in fact, they infuriated the Syrians by bombarding their capital of Damascus in the course of quelling an insurrection in 1925 and 1926. The British attempted a more conciliatory policy by granting some of their wards nominal independence and substituting the ties of alliance for the older imperial ties. In 1922 Egypt was proclaimed an independent state under King Fuad, though the British retained the right to station troops in the country and insisted that westerners resident there continue to enjoy special privileges. In 1936, an Anglo-Egyptian agreement provided for the eventual termination of foreigners' privileges and for the eventual withdrawal of British troops; Egypt, however, continued to be closely allied with Great Britain. Meantime, the British were following rather similar policies in Iraq and in Transjordan, the half-desert area east of Palestine. Until World War II it looked as though Britain might

have found a way of leading the Arabs gradually to independence and retaining their friendship. But the exacerbation of the Palestine problem after the war and the rapid intensification of Arab nationalism were to blast any hope that the Arabs would remain grateful and loyal "old boys" of the British imperial school.

In the meantime, the former master of the Middle East, Turkey, was undergoing a political renaissance. The losses suffered by Turkey as a result of World War I reduced her territory for the first time to a cohesive national unit, the largely Turkish-populated lands of Anatolia (or Asia Minor). To defend this Anatolian core against threatened additional losses to the Greeks and to the victorious Allies, the Turks at once launched an ardent nationalist revival extending much farther the reforms begun by the Young Turks before 1914 (see above, p. 385). The leader of this new political revolution was a highly gifted army officer, Mustafa Kemal (1881-1938), who forced the expulsion of the Greek forces from Anatolia and negotiated more favorable terms with the Allies at Lausanne in 1923 (see above, p. 411). Under his guidance, the old Ottoman Empire was abolished in 1922, and in its stead the Republic of Turkey was proclaimed, with a constitution modeled on western parliamentary lines. To point up the new orientation of the republic, Kemal moved its capital from cosmopolitan Istanbul, on the western edge of Turkish territory, to Ankara in the heart of Anatolia.

Kemal also imposed rapid, wholesale, and sometimes ruthless measures of westernization. Women received the vote and, at least in theory, were emancipated from traditional Moslem restraints. The whole fabric of social and political life was removed from the highly conservative influence of Islam, again in theory at least. An advanced European law code was introduced; Sunday, not the Moslem Friday, was made the weekly day of rest; even the

Turkish language was drastically reformed by the requirement that it employ a western alphabet—a move of major importance, for only a fraction of the Turkish people had ever been able to master the old Ottoman Turkish, with its heavy content of Persian and Arabic words, and with its difficult Arabic script. All Turks were now required to take surnames in the western manner, and Kemal himself appropriately took that of Atatürk, "Father of the Turks." By the time of his death in 1938 Atatürk had indeed revolutionized his country, even though westernization was only just beginning to trickle down to the grass roots of Turkish society. And he had insured its independence of the West, as Turkish neutrality during World War II was soon to demonstrate.

The example of Turkey was followed, though less sweepingly and less effectively, by the other traditionally independent major state of the Middle East—Persia, or, as it has been officially styled since 1935, Iran ("Land of the Aryans"). The Iranian revolution began in 1906 in response to the imperialist encroachments by Britain and Russia that were making Persia a kind of Middle Eastern China. The political structure inherited from the Middle Ages was gradually altered in the direction of limited monarchy, with an elected parliament and with the Shah as a constitutional ruler. Since the political transition was far from smooth, the Iranian revolution proved to be an arrested or abortive one. The country, with its highly powerful class of wealthy landlords and its millions of poor peasants and restless tribesmen, did not adapt itself readily to modern western political institutions. The nearest Iranian equivalent of Atatürk was Reza Shah, an able army officer and a feverish but erratic modernizer who lacked Kemal's sense of the possible. Reza Shah seized the Iranian throne after World War I and lost it in 1941 when his pro-Nazi sympathies led Britain and Russia to send in troops and force his abdication. The fate of Reza Shah served as a reminder that the British and the Russians still kept some of their old interests in Iran, where they had often competed for concessions and for spheres of influence in the past. It also showed that some of the seemingly sovereign states of the non-western world were not yet strong enough to maintain their independence against the might of the great powers. By the time of World War II imperial ties had been loosened, but they were by no means severed or dissolved; the revolution against imperialism was yet to come (see Chapter XXXI).

Reading Suggestions
on the Democracies, 1919-1939:
Domestic and Imperial Problems

(Asterisk indicates paperbound edition.)

BRITAIN AND FRANCE

R. Graves and A. Hodge, *The Long Weekend* (Faber & Faber, 1940). A lively social history of Britain during the inter-war years.

G. E. Elton, *The Life of James Ramsay MacDonald* (Collins, 1939), G. M. Young, *Stanley Baldwin* (Hart-Davis, 1952), and K. Feiling, *The Life of Neville Chamberlain* (Macmillan, 1946). Biographies of three important British statesmen.

C. R. Attlee, *The Labour Party in Perspective,* 2nd ed. (Gollancz, 1949). A review of the inter-war period in Britain by the Labor leader.

D. Brogan, *France under the Republic* (Harper, 1940). Still one of the most informative introductions to French history in the 1920's and 1930's.

D. Thomson, *Democracy in France,* 3rd ed. (Oxford Univ. Press, 1958). A most stimulating essay in interpretation for those already acquainted with the basic facts.

E. J. Knapton, *France since Versailles* (*Holt, 1952, A Berkshire Study). Handy little manual.

A. Werth, *The Twilight of France, 1933-1940* (Harper, 1942). Condensation of several longer studies by an able foreign correspondent.

THE UNITED STATES

Four volumes in the "Chronicles of America Series" (Yale Univ. Press) provide good coverage of the period: H. U. Faulkner, *From Versailles to the New Deal* (1950); D. Brogan, *The Era of Franklin D. Roosevelt* (1951); A. Nevins, *The United States in a Chaotic World* (1950); and A. Nevins, *The New Deal and World Affairs* (1950).

D. Perkins, *The New Age of Franklin Roosevelt, 1932-1945* (Univ. of Chicago Press, 1957). A sympathetic but by no means uncritical survey.

F. L. Allen, *Only Yesterday* (*Bantam Books), and *Since Yesterday* (Harper, 1940). Lively social histories of the 1920's and 1930's, respectively.

F. Perkins, *The Roosevelt I Knew* (Viking, 1946), and R. E. Sherwood, *Roosevelt and Hopkins,* 2 vols. (*Bantam Books). Perhaps the best of the books about Franklin Roosevelt by the people who worked with him.

F. Freidel, *Franklin D. Roosevelt* (Little, Brown, 1952, 1954, 1956). Three volumes of this detailed and careful biographical study have appeared so far.

A. M. Schlesinger, Jr., *The Crisis of the Old Order, 1919-1933* and *The Coming of the New Deal* (Houghton Mifflin, 1957, 1959). The first two volumes in "The Age of Roosevelt" by a prominent young American historian favorable to the New Deal but also objective in his judgments.

J. M. Burns, *Roosevelt: The Lion and the Fox* (Harcourt, Brace, 1956). A stimulating though rather limited estimate of Roosevelt the politician.

ECONOMIC DEVELOPMENTS

J. K. Galbraith, *The Great Crash, 1929* (Houghton Mifflin, 1955). A well-written study of the Wall Street slump by a prominent American economist.

P. Einzig, *The World Economic Crisis, 1929-1932* (Macmillan, 1932); H. V. Hodson, *Slump and Recovery, 1929-1937* (Oxford Univ. Press, 1938); H. W. Arndt, *The Economic Lessons of the Nineteen-Thirties* (Oxford Univ. Press, 1944). Other useful books on the great depression.

CHAPTER XXVIII

J. Schumpeter, *Capitalism, Socialism, and Democracy*, 3rd ed. (Harper, 1950); J. M. Keynes, *The End of Laissez-Faire* (Woolf, 1926). Thoughtful essays by two major economic thinkers.

D. A. Shannon, ed., *The Great Depression* (*Prentice-Hall, 1960). A useful collection of source readings, stressing the social consequences of economic ills in the United States.

OTHER TOPICS

E. Fischer, *The Passing of the European Age* (Harvard Univ. Press, 1943). Defense of the thesis that leadership in western civilization has passed from Europe to other continents.

E. O. Reischauer, *Japan, Past and Present*, 2nd ed., rev. (Knopf, 1956). An excellent introductory account.

L. Fischer, *Gandhi* (*New American Library, 1954). A sympathetic biography.

P. Spear, *India, Pakistan, and the West*, 3rd ed. (Oxford Univ. Press, 1958). Illuminating brief introduction.

R. Symonds, *The Making of Pakistan*, 3rd ed. (Faber & Faber, 1951). Informative survey of Moslem India.

J. K. Fairbank, *The United States and China*, rev. ed. (Harvard Univ. Press, 1958). One of the most reliable and informative introductions to the whole controversial subject of recent Chinese history.

K. S. Latourette, *A History of Modern China* (*Penguin). A good brief account.

S. N. Fisher, *The Middle East: A History* (Knopf, 1959). Well-balanced survey, packed with facts.

G. L. Lewis, *Turkey* (Praeger, 1955). Lively summary of the Atatürk revolution and its consequences.

Sir Harry Luke, *The Old Turkey and the New* (Bles, 1955). Perceptive essay on the contrasts between the Ottoman Empire and the Turkey of Atatürk.

S. H. Longrigg, *Syria and Lebanon under French Mandate* (Oxford Univ. Press, 1958). Detailed study of the very mixed record of French rule in the Levant.

Note: Many titles useful for the history of the non-western world during the twenty years' truce will also be found in the reading suggestions for Chapter XXXI.

FICTION

E. Waugh, *A Handful of Dust* (New Directions, 1945). Corrosive novel satirizing English society in the inter-war years.

H. Spring, *Fame Is the Spur* (Viking, 1940). A politician is corrupted by ambition; largely parallels the career of Ramsay MacDonald.

W. Holtby, *South Riding* (Macmillan, 1936). Good social novel of industrial England.

A. Gide, *The Counterfeiters* (Knopf, 1927). Mordant study of the French middle class by an eminent novelist.

F. Scott Fitzgerald, *The Great Gatsby* (many editions). A celebrated picture of "flaming youth" in the American Jazz Age.

J. Steinbeck, *The Grapes of Wrath* (many editions). The famous novel about exiles from the Oklahoma "dust bowl" of the 1930's.

E. O'Connor, *The Last Hurrah* (Little, Brown, 1956). An affectionate portrait of a political boss in a big American city.

E. Hemingway, *The Sun Also Rises* (*Bantam Books). Often considered the best novel about the "lost generation" of American expatriates.

A. Malraux, *Man's Fate* (Modern Library, 1936). Excellent novel about Chinese communist revolutionaries in the 1920's.

The Second World War

CHAPTER XXIX

GENERAL or world wars in our state-system are usually born of a previous war, or, perhaps better, of a previous peace settlement that fails to solve certain important problems. We have already been obliged in seeking the origins of the First World War to go back to 1870, to Bismarck, to the "rape of Alsace-Lorraine" and the consequent rise of the spirit of revenge among Frenchmen. We shall now have to go back to 1919 and the grave difficulties that arose in the attempt to carry out the settlement of Versailles. So troubled were international relations for the twenty years after 1919, so closely in time did the Second World War follow on the First, that the interval between the two has been christened the "twenty years' truce." And it is not impossible that historians in the future will actually consider the two wars really one war, as they now consider the wars of the French Revolution and Napoleon essentially one war. Though to the purist historian the first world wars were perhaps those of Louis XIV, for the present, we must use the accepted terms, World War I (1914-1918) and World War II (1939-1945). Such usage has at least the advantage of pointing up by the use of roman numerals the close relationship of these two wars.

Opposite. WITHDRAWAL FROM DUNKIRK, *by Richard Eurich (1903-); English, painted 1940; National Maritime Museum, Greenwich, England. An old-fashioned but graphic picturization of the evacuation of British forces from the Continent in the dark summer of 1940—a heroic retreat that became a national epic.*

539

I: International Politics, 1919-1932

During the first part of the twenty years' truce, international leadership of the democratic world rested with Britain and France. Though supported in principle and often in practice by the United States, they were increasingly unable to stem the rise of powers hostile to liberal democracy—Italy, Germany, Spain, Russia, Japan. In the end, the beaten perturber of 1918, Germany, once more waged aggressive warfare against the major Allies of 1918. This time Germany allied with two of its former enemies, Italy and Japan, each disappointed with its share of the spoils of victory in 1918.

Why was the peace settlement of 1919 followed in twenty years by a second great war? Why was it so unlike the last great settlement, that of 1815 following the Napoleonic wars, which had inaugurated a long period of general peace, interrupted only by localized wars? Nazi Germany maintained that the second war was the direct and inevitable result of the *Diktat*, the dictated peace of Versailles that ended the first war. Supported by most Germans and many German sympathizers, the Nazis claimed that Germany was humiliated by the war-guilt clause, stripped of territories and colonies that were rightfully hers, saddled with an astronomical and unpayable reparations bill, denied the normal rights of a sovereign state in armaments—in short, so badly treated that simple human dignity made revolt against the *Diktat* and its makers a necessity. Now something of this is true. The settlement of Versailles did saddle the new German Republic with a heavy burden in part dictated by revenge and fear toward the old German Empire. A wiser Allied policy would perhaps have tried to start the new government off without too great a burden, as the Allies in 1815 did

with the France of Louis XVIII (see Chapter XIX).

The "Era of Fulfillment"

But the *Diktat* thesis is very far from containing the whole truth. What breaks down the argument that the iniquities of Versailles *alone* explain the second war is the "era of fulfillment." In spite of the Treaty of Versailles, the Germans and their former enemies did manage to come together in the 1920's.

The great landmark of the "era of fulfillment" was a general treaty negotiated in October, 1925, at Locarno in Switzerland. Germany there agreed with France and Belgium on a mutual guarantee of their common frontiers; Britain and Italy agreed to act as guarantors—that is, to provide military aid against the violator if a violation of the frontiers occurred. Germany affirmed her acceptance of the western frontier drawn for her at Versailles, and France, for her part, affirmed the new moderate direction that her German policy had taken since the failure of her occupation of the Ruhr.

The "Locarno spirit" of reconciliation endured for the next several years. It was nourished by the general prosperity of both the French and the Germans and by the constructive policies of their respective foreign ministers, Briand and Stresemann. In 1926 Germany was admitted to the League of Nations, an event that seemed to signify not only the restoration of Germany to international respectability but also German acceptance of the peaceful purposes and duties of League membership. These hopeful impressions received confirmation when Germany signed the Kellogg-Briand Peace Pact of 1928 (see above, p. 479). In 1929, the French consented to withdraw the last of their occupation troops from the Rhineland during the forthcoming year, thus ending the Allied occupation of Germany at a date considerably in advance of the one stipulated in the Versailles Treaty.

Meantime, other international developments were bolstering the "Locarno spirit." The great world-wide organization planned by Wilson, the League of Nations, began its operations in 1920. We shall soon see that the League was never able to impose its will on a determined and defiant aggressor. Yet the record of the League during the 1920's was by no means one of unmitigated failure. In the first place, the League became a going concern. Its Council, dominated by the great powers, and its Assembly, representing all its members, met regularly at the League's "capital," the Swiss city of Geneva. Second, the League played a direct part in the peaceful resolution of two crises that, had they not been resolved, might well have led to little wars —in 1920 a dispute between Sweden and Finland over some Baltic islands, and in 1925 a frontier incident in the Balkans involving Greece and Bulgaria.

The United States, though not a member of the League, took a leading part in furthering one of the League's chief objectives —disarmament. Soon after the first war the United States invited the other principal sea powers to consider the limitation of naval armaments. Meeting in Washington during the winter of 1921-1922, the naval conference achieved an agreement establishing a ten-year "holiday" in the construction of capital ships (battleships and heavy cruisers). The agreement also set the allowed tonnages of capital ships at a ratio of 5 for the United States, 5 for Britain, 3 for Japan, and 1.67 each for France and Italy.

A conference at London in 1930, however, had less success in limiting "non-capital" ships, including submarines. The partial failure of the London naval conference was a portent. Two years later, after long preparation, the League itself convoked a meeting to address the still more pressing problem of limiting military arma-

Delegates to the Washington disarmament conference, left to right: Prince Tokugawa (Japan), Balfour (Britain), Hughes (United States), Briand (France), van Karnebeek (Netherlands), Schanzer (Belgium), and Count d'Alto (Italy).

ments. Not only the League members, but also the United States and the Soviet Union, sent representatives to Geneva. The Geneva disarmament conference of 1932, however, accomplished nothing. It was wrecked above all by a renewal of Franco-German antagonism, by the German demand for equality in armaments with France, and by the French refusal to grant the demand.

The Failure of "Fulfillment"

In 1932, then, the "Locarno spirit" was dead, and the "era of fulfillment" had ended. There is one very obvious factor in any explanation for the failure of the hopes aroused in the 1920's—the world depression that began in 1929. In Germany itself the depression was a last straw, a decisive factor in putting Hitler in power. In the democracies, too, it had heavy consequences for the peace of the world, for the depression sapped their morale and made them less confident. But the great worldwide depression is no more in itself a *sole* explanation of World War II than is the *Diktat* of Versailles.

Another factor that was unsettling to international politics was Soviet Russia. In the eyes of the western nations, Russia was a revolutionary power that could not really be trusted, that could not be fully integrated into the international state-system. The Soviet Union was the center of a revolutionary faith hated and distrusted by the politicians of the West, who feared, by no means without justification, communist agitation among their own peoples. Westerners simply could not trust a Marxist government which was based on the belief that all western "capitalist" democracies were destined to collapse and become communist after a violent class war.

Still another basic factor that led to the second war was the continuing failure of the three great western democracies, Britain, France, and the United States, to present anything like a united front. Americans of internationalist sympathies have probably exaggerated the results of the sudden American withdrawal into isolationism in 1919. It is hard to believe, especially in light of the rivalry and cross-purposes that Britain and France displayed *within* the League of Nations, that formal American membership in the League would have helped the situation greatly. Still, the isolation of the United States undoubtedly exacerbated French fears and the French sense of weakness, and pushed France toward the sort of intransigence that was illustrated by her disastrous intervention in the Ruhr in the mid-1920's (see p. 512).

More serious was the failure of France and Britain to work together effectively. France, exhausted and in this decade with a declining population, endeavoring to play the part of a first-rate power but supported only by second-rate resources, lived in perpetual fear of a revived Germany. She sought not only to carry out to the full the economic and political measures of the Versailles Treaty that aimed at weakening Germany and keeping Germany weak. She sought also to make up for Russia's defection as her eastern ally against Germany. This she did by making alliances, beginning in 1921, with the smaller states to the east of Germany—Poland, Czechoslovakia, Rumania, and Yugoslavia. All of them wanted French protection against the possible restoration of the Habsburg Empire, from which they had gained so much territory, and all of them except Poland were informally linked together as the "Little Entente."

To a Britain whose statesmen knew well the long story of Anglo-French conflicts from the Hundred Years' War to Napoleon, the France of the 1920's seemed once more aiming at European supremacy, seemed once more an active threat to the traditional British policy of preventing any such supremacy. Although it is now plain that the French were animated rather by fear than by ambition, and that they could never again be major aggressors, it is true enough that many of their statesmen seemed to be falling into old ways, or at least old words, of aggression. The mistaken British diagnosis was at least understandable.

Finally, something of the old British isolationism had survived the war, and made the British—and especially their dominions—unwilling to commit themselves firmly to guarantees to intervene with force in continental Europe. Britain did indeed accept Locarno, but in the previous year the dominions had played a large part in her rejection of the more sweeping "Geneva protocol" urged upon her by France, which would have committed its signatories to compulsory arbitration of international disputes.

The difficulties of the Anglo-French partnership also go far to explain the weaknesses of the League of Nations. The effectiveness of any piece of machinery is bound to hinge on the skill and co-ordination of the mechanics who operate it. The League lacked a means of enforcing its decisions. And it was somewhat top-heavy, since the fully representative Assembly counted for less than did the smaller Council, where Britain and France took a preponderant role. When these two mechanics disagreed, therefore, the machinery scarcely operated at all. One example of the way in which the grand purposes of the League suffered from Anglo-French friction is the rejection of the Geneva protocol. Another is the Corfu

incident of 1923, when Mussolini for a time defied the League and set a sinister precedent for the later use of gangster tactics by the dictators (see Chapter XXVII). In the midst of the Corfu crisis the League was crippled by Anglo-French discord over the Ruhr policy of France.

The Aggressors

The Corfu incident underlines the presence of one more element, the most important of all, in the rapid deterioration of the twenty years' truce. This, of course, was the fact of aggressions by Italy, Germany, and Japan. In Chapter XXVII we saw how the ruthlessly ambitious programs of fascism and Nazism steadily led Mussolini and Hitler to a foreign policy of adventure and aggression. In Chapter XXVIII we saw how the somewhat similar totalitarian policies of the Japanese militarists led them to begin the seizure of China by their occupation of Manchuria in 1931. With this background of underlying tensions—the punitive features of the Versailles settlement, the disastrous effects of the depression on the Locarno spirit, the continuance of the revolutionary focus in Russia, the defensive attitude of the western democracies and their mutual mistrust, the new aggressive faiths of fascism and nazism, and the rise of imperialist Japan—we may now proceed to the actual steps along the road to a second world war.

II: The Road to War, 1931-1939

The First Step: Manchuria, 1931

It is now clear that the first step along the road to war was the Japanese

seizure of Manchuria in 1931. Stimson, President Hoover's Secretary of State, responded to the seizure by announcing that the United States would recognize no gains made by armed force. Stimson hoped that Britain and the other democracies might follow this American lead, but his hopes were largely disappointed. The League of Nations did send out a commission headed by the British Earl of Lytton, and the subsequent Lytton Report condemned the Japanese act as aggression. Neither the United States nor the League, however, fortified its verbal protests by effective action; force was not met by force. Japan, refusing to accept the Lytton Report, withdrew from the League of Nations in March, 1933, making the first formal breach in the League's structure.

The Second Step: German Rearmament, 1935-1936

The next breach in the League's structure, and the next step toward war, were made by Germany. In October, 1933, Hitler withdrew from the League, thereby virtually serving notice on the world of his aggressive intentions. On March 16, 1935, he denounced the clauses of the Treaty of Versailles that limited German armaments and set about the open rebuilding of the German armed forces.

The response to this unilateral and hence illegal act set the pattern for the next few years. On April 17, 1935, the League of Nations formally condemned Germany's repudiation of treaty obligations—and Germany continued to rearm. In May, 1935, France hastily concluded with the Soviet Union a treaty of alliance against German aggression—and Germany continued to rearm. In June, 1935, the British, realistically and short-sightedly—for their action seemed like desertion to the French—signed with rearming Germany a naval agreement limiting the German navy to one-third the size of the British, and German submarines to 60 per cent of those of Britain.

It is hardly surprising that Hitler's next act drew no more than the customary protests from the signatories of Locarno. This was the "reoccupation" of the Rhineland

in March, 1936—that is, the sending of German troops into the western German zone that had been demilitarized by the Treaty of Versailles. Britain and France once more did nothing, although many military critics thought then—and still think—that united British-French military action in 1936 could have nipped Hitler's career of aggression in the bud.

The Third Step: Ethiopia, 1935

Meanwhile the Italians struck in Ethiopia. In that pocket of old Africa a "sovereign" state had precariously maintained itself, largely because its imperial neighbors, Britain, France, and Italy, would neither agree to divide it nor let any one of the three swallow it whole. The Italians, who wanted it most, had lost the disastrous battle of Adowa to the native Ethiopians in 1896. This humiliation rankled with the fascists, who felt they had to show the world that there was more than rhetoric in their talk about a revived Roman Empire.

In 1934, a frontier incident at Ualual in desert Italian Somaliland—or in Ethiopia, for both sides claimed the place—put the matter before the international politicians. France and Britain were characteristically quite ready for appeasement of Italy, partly because they hoped to align Mussolini with them against Hitler. They offered him almost everything in Ethiopia, including those concrete economic concessions naive people think are the essence of imperialism—and wars, and indeed everything in human events. But since Ethiopia was a member of the League, the French and the British insisted that its formal independence be observed. This Mussolini would not accept, and in October, 1935, his troops began the invasion of Ethiopia. Airplanes, artillery, and tanks made the difference between 1896 and 1935. This time the underdog was not the winner. Poison gas finished the task early in 1936, and the King of Italy acquired the coveted title of Emperor of Ethiopia. Once more there was an emperor —of sorts—in Rome!

The League of Nations had already formally condemned the Japanese aggression in Manchuria and the German denunciation of the disarmament clauses of the Treaty of Versailles. In 1935, it at once declared that Italy, by invading Ethiopia, a League member, had violated her obligations under the Covenant of the League. Now the League made the momentous decision to test its power to move from words to deeds. In this it had the full and hearty accord of most of its members, and was urged on by the British, less vocally by the French, and strongly by Haile Selassie, the rightful Emperor of Ethiopia. On October 11, 1935, fifty-one member nations of the League voted to invoke against Italy the famous Article 16 of the League Covenant. which provided for economic sanctions against a member resorting to war in disregard of its covenants.

The sanctions thus invoked failed. There were loopholes; oil, for instance, was not included in the list of articles barred from commerce with Italy, which had only meager stockpiles of this vital war material. There was much mutual recrimination among members of the League over what articles should be placed on the prohibited list and over the fact that Britain and France did nothing to check Italian movements of troops and munitions through the Suez Canal, which Britain then in fact controlled. Germany was no longer in the League, and was wholly unbound by its decision. No major power applied these sanctions rigorously: to that extent, it is true that the method of economic sanctions was not really tried.

The Ethiopian fiasco was a disastrous blow to the League, which from now on was helpless in high international politics. Its special services as a group of trained international civil servants, its "functional groups," dealing with labor problems, international police matters like the drug traffic and prostitution, and much else, persisted, however, to be absorbed after World War II by the United Nations. But for the rest of the 1930's the League was hardly even a formal factor in the increasing tensions. No one was surprised or greatly concerned when Italy, copying Japan and Germany, withdrew from the League in December, 1937.

The Fourth Step:
The Spanish Civil War, 1936-1939

The next step after Ethiopia on the road to war is of great psychological and moral interest. No doubt the later direct aggressions of Hitler in Czechoslovakia and Poland were the politically decisive steps. But the Spanish Civil War (for details, see Chapter XXVII), which broke out in July, 1936, was the emotional catalyst that divided millions of men and women all over the western world. It is still, in spite of the passing of years, a kind of great collective Dreyfus case, a test of conscience and loyalty for our time.

The Spanish Civil War was fought between a fascist Right and a democratic Left, with Catholics, monarchists, and just plain conservatives also on the Right, and with socialists, communists, and anarchists also on the Left. It was a quasi-religious war, waged with the great violence and with the consecrated devotion that mark wars of principle. No one can say for sure how the struggle would have ended if it had remained a purely Spanish one, as the American Civil War had remained a purely American one. Certainly the Loyalists would have been in a much stronger position if the democratic powers had followed the usual practice in international law of sending arms to the *de jure* government of Spain. Such speculation, however, is use-

"Honest, Mister, there's nobody here but us Spaniards." Franco's explanation to Chamberlain and Daladier.

less. Almost from the very start the Spanish Civil War engaged, not merely the vicarious emotional participation of the West, not merely individual foreign enlistments, but the active though never wholly open intervention of other nations. This intervention was decisive and effective on the part of the fascist powers, Italy and Germany; it was less determined and effective on the part of communist Russia; and feeblest of all on the part of Britain and France. Early in 1939, with the fall of Barcelona, the Civil War was in effect over. Once more a fascist group had won.

Meantime, dizzy with success, Mussolini was going on to other adventures. In October, 1936, he signed a pact with Hitler, thereby formally establishing the Rome-Berlin "Axis" and committing fascist Italy to alliance with Nazi Germany. Mussolini gave strong support to Franco's rebellion in Spain. And, late in 1938, he orchestrated a public outcry in Italy for the French to hand over certain territories. He wanted not only Nice and Savoy, which had been ceded to Napoleon III during Italian unification negotiations almost a century earlier, but also the Mediterranean island of Corsica, which had been French since the days of Louis XV in the eighteenth century, and Tunisia, which had never been under Italian rule and had been French

since 1881. These outrageous demands came to nothing, but they did not exactly improve relations between France and Italy. Finally, on Good Friday (April 7), 1939, Mussolini attacked Albania, long coveted by the Italians, and quickly subjugated this backward little Balkan state. For a few years, Victor Emmanuel was to be King of Albania as well as Emperor of Ethiopia.

The Fifth Step: "Anschluss," 1938

The immediate origins of World War II lie, however, neither in Italian nor in Spanish fascist aggression, but in the mounting series of German aggressions. Hitler had begun the open rebuilding of German armed forces in 1935. Three years later, he felt strong enough to undertake the first enterprise of expansion, an enterprise which, like all he undertook, he insisted was no more than a restoration to Germany of what the *Diktat* of Versailles had deprived her. Austria, German in language and tradition, had been left a mere fragment by the disruption of the Habsburg Empire. Ever since 1918 there had been a strong movement among Austrians for annexation (*"Anschluss"*) to Germany proper. This movement had been strenuously opposed by the victors of the first war, and especially by France, but agitation for *Anschluss* kept on, nourished by Nazi propaganda and, in 1934, an attempted *Putsch*.

Hitler carefully laid the ground for the success of the next Nazi attempt. The pact with Italy that formally established the Rome-Berlin "Axis" (October, 1936) disarmed Mussolini's opposition to *Anschluss*. Early in 1938 Hitler began what turned out to be his standard technique of softening his victims for the final blow. He unleashed a violent propaganda campaign by press, radio, and platform against the alleged misdeeds of the government of independent Austria. In February, 1938, he summoned the Austrian Chancellor Schuschnigg to his Bavarian retreat at Berchtesgaden, where he let loose a bullying tirade against the hapless Schuschnigg. In March, Hitler moved his troops into Austria and made *Anschluss* a fact.

Hitler now had six million more German-speaking nationals in the fold; and in the union of Austria and Germany he had achieved something that no Habsburg and no Hohenzollern had been able to do in modern times. But he showed no signs at all of being content with what he had gained. Almost at once he went to work on the acquisition of the Sudeten Germans of Czechoslovakia.

The Sixth Step: Czechoslovakia Dismembered, 1938-1939

The Czechoslovak republic was the only state in central or eastern Europe where parliamentary democracy had achieved a resounding success after World War I. The republic faced a difficult problem of national minorities, but it had the good fortune to inherit some of the most highly developed industrial regions of the old Habsburg Empire. Its economy, consequently, was far better balanced between industry and agriculture than was that of the other states of eastern Europe. This healthy economy was mirrored in the social structure, where a working balance was maintained among peasants, middle classes, and industrial workers. The period immediately after the war, as well as the great depression of the 1930's, times of great suffering elsewhere, affected Czechoslovakia very lightly. Yet these advantages could hardly have preserved democracy in the republic had it not been for the enlightened policies of Thomas Masaryk, liberator and president of his country until his resignation at the age of 85 in 1935.

Even the enlightened Czech regime, however, could not keep the country from ultimately being smashed by outside pressures working on its sensitive minorities. The Sudeten German minority of 3¼ millions, feeling, as Germans, superior to Slavs, resisted the new republic at every turn, even when the Prague government made concessions to satisfy their just grievances. Sudeten extremists early turned to Hitler, but even moderates and socialists among the Sudetens were more or less pan-German in their views. From 1933 on, Nazi agitation, supported by Hitler with men and money, became increasingly serious in Czechoslovakia. Early in 1938, having secured Austria, Hitler decided to push the Czech affair next. Henlein, his Sudeten agent, made demands on the Prague government for what amounted to complete Sudeten autonomy. The summer of 1938 was spent in negotiations and in mutual propaganda blasts. The Czechs relied heavily on their French allies and on the friendly, though not formally allied, British. But by the spring of 1938, it seems clear now, Britain and France had agreed not to defend the territorial integrity of Czechoslovakia.

By the autumn of 1938, Hitler was ready for action. On September 12 he made a violent speech at Nuremberg, insisting on self-determination for the Sudeten Germans. This was the signal for widespread disorders in Czechoslovakia and for the proclamation of martial law by its government. The situation was now a full-fledged European crisis that called for the personal intervention of men at the very top of their states. The British Prime Minister, Neville Chamberlain, made two preliminary visits to Hitler in Germany in an effort to moderate German demands, and finally persuaded Hitler—with the help of Mussolini —to call a full conference of the four great western powers. This conference—Hitler, Mussolini, Chamberlain, and Daladier for France—met in Munich on September 29, 1938. Russia was not invited; her exclusion was to complete her abandonment of the "Popular Front" policy (see Chapter XXVI).

Munich was a sweeping victory for Hitler. Czechoslovakia was partially dismembered; her Sudeten rim-lands were turned over to Germany; the Czechs were obliged to hand over Teschen and certain other areas to the Poles; the whole economy and transportation system were lamed; the defense of her frontiers was made impossible by the loss of the border mountains and their fortifications; and Slovakia was given autonomy within a federal state, emphasized by the official change in spelling from Czechoslovakia to Czecho-Slovakia. The Czech leaders had felt it impossible to resist the Germans without the aid of the French and British; their people acquiesced bitterly in the settlement of Munich. The Germans had played fully on the differences between the more industrialized Czechs and the still largely agricultural Slovaks. But even had the country been strongly united, the laming blow of Munich would have ruined its morale. Hitler acted quickly. In the very next spring, before the final lines of demarcation set at Munich had actually been drawn, he summoned the Czech President, Hacha, to Germany for another of those ghastly interviews, in which he announced that the fate of the Czech people "must be placed trustingly in the hands of

Chamberlain, Daladier, Hitler, Mussolini, and Ciano (Mussolini's son-in-law) at Munich, September, 1938.

the *Fuehrer*." In March, 1939, Hitler marched his army into the remaining fragments of Czechoslovakia, meeting no real resistance.

The most respectable defense that can be made of Munich and appeasement rests on the argument that the West was buying time to prepare for a war which it knew to be inevitable but for which it was not yet ready. Chamberlain may have thought so; but Winston Churchill and others have pointed out most cogently that the democracies were in a stronger military position relative to that of Germany in September, 1938, than in September, 1939. It also seems likely that Chamberlain and Daladier, as well as millions all over the world, believed, or hoped, that the acquisition of the Sudeten Germans would satisfy Hitler, that after Munich he would behave as Bismarck had behaved after Sedan, and that he would settle down and try to preserve the balance of power. Some westerners even hoped that Hitler would perhaps ally with them against communist Russia or obligingly get himself so entangled in eastern Europe that he would bring on a Russo-German war. Hitler's words and deeds, however, had given no real foundation for the belief that he would now "play ball" with the West. And we now know that he had as early as November 5, 1937, announced to his close advisers his unalterable intention of destroying Czechoslovakia and moving on into Poland and the Ukraine.

The actual destruction of old Czechoslovakia in March, 1939, seems not to have surprised anyone. Indeed the curious mixture of resignation, condemnation, and resolution with which this action was greeted in the West marks a turning point. The days of appeasement were over. Munich had proved to be an epoch-making event, a catalyst for both professional western diplomatists and statesmen, and for western opinion generally. Hitler's next aggression would not lead to a Munich. We can never be quite sure whether Hitler and his aides

thought they could take their next step without bringing on a general war. In public and semi-public, Hitler, Goering, and the other leaders made no secret of their feeling that the British and French were decadent, spineless, inefficient societies, quite unable to summon the courage needed to resist an inspired and rejuvenated Germany. Yet there is good evidence that Hitler expected at least a local war with Poland this time, and that he was quite prepared to face involvement with the French and the British.

The Final Step: Poland, 1939

Poland was inexorably his next victim. The Polish corridor dividing East Prussia from the rest of Germany was an affront to great-power psychology. So, too, was the separation from Germany of the Free City of Danzig, on the edge of the Polish corridor. Danzig was thoroughly German in language and tradition. Germans, even quite enlightened Germans, thought of the Poles, as indeed of all Slavs, as inferior people who would benefit from capable German supervision. Hitler began his Baltic adventure in March, 1939, when he took the port town of Memel from Poland's northern neighbor, Lithuania.

The critical issue in the tense half-year that led up to the outbreak of war on September 1, 1939, was not at all the possibility that Poland, unsupported by Britain and France, would undergo the same fate as Czechoslovakia. The British government publicly supported Poland by signing a pact of mutual assistance with her in April. Indeed, in the midst of the final week of crisis, Chamberlain's foreign minster, Lord Halifax, sent a telegram to Hitler himself in which he made a pathetic appeal to the lessons of history:

It has been alleged that if His Majesty's Government had made their position more

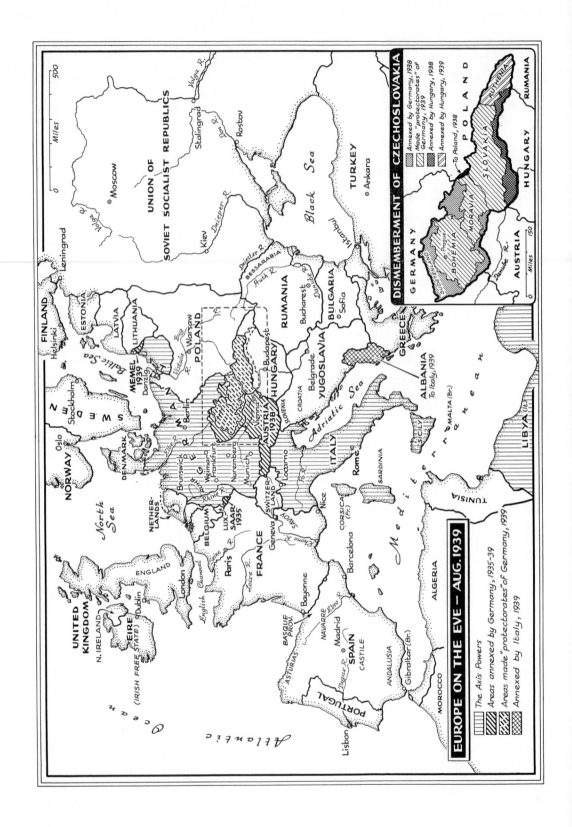

EUROPE ON THE EVE — AUG. 1939

The Axis Powers
Areas annexed by Germany, 1935–39
Areas made "protectorates" of Germany, 1939
Annexed by Italy, 1939

DISMEMBERMENT OF CZECHOSLOVAKIA

Annexed by Germany, 1938
Made "protectorates" of Germany, 1939
Annexed by Hungary, 1938
Annexed by Hungary, 1939
To Poland, 1938

clear in 1914 the great catastrophe would have been avoided. Whether or not there is any force in that allegation, His Majesty's Government are resolved that on this occasion there shall be no such tragic misunderstanding. If the need should arise, they are resolved and prepared to employ without delay all the forces at their command. . . . I trust that Your Excellency will weigh with the utmost deliberation the considerations which I have put before you.[*]

The real critical point at issue was the attitude of Russia. Hitler had an almost obsessive fear of a war on two fronts, a war against major powers to the east and to the west of the kind on which Germany had embarked in 1914. He was in fact to be drawn within two years into just such a war. Even if he had been faced in 1939 by the united front of Britain, France, and Russia in support of Poland, it is perfectly possible that he could not have restrained himself and his followers. One is tempted to see the Nazi top command as driven on by some abnormal and obsessive motivation and quite oblivious to ordinary considerations of self-interest. Hitler perhaps could no more keep his hands off Poland than an alcoholic can keep his hands off liquor. But, as events developed, Hitler was able to seize Poland without fear of Russian intervention. Indeed, he was able to arrange with Stalin a partition of Poland quite recognizably on the model of the eighteenth-century partitions.

Why did the Russians make their about-face? They had been deeply hurt by their exclusion from the negotiations over the Czechoslovakian crisis of the year before, an exclusion that they blamed primarily on the British and the French. From the failure of the western powers to stand up to German violations of the Versailles Treaty ever since 1934, the Russians had drawn conclusions at least as disparaging to the western will to fight as those drawn by Hit-

* Documents on British Foreign Policy, 1919-1939, E. L. Woodward and R. Butler, eds. (London, 1954), 3rd series, Vol. II, No. 145.

ler. In particular, they deeply distrusted the British Tories under Neville Chamberlain, for they believed that in many ways Tory Britain was more fundamentally hostile to communist Russia than even Nazi Germany was.

The Russians' mistrust of the West was not dispelled by the diplomatic mission that Britain and France sent, belatedly and grudgingly, to negotiate with Russia in this critical summer of 1939. The western powers proposed a mutual assistance pact, but the efforts of their negotiators were inept and halfhearted. Moreover, Chamberlain's government made a tactless choice of negotiators. One of them, Ironside, had been involved in the British intervention against the Reds at Archangel in the early beleaguered days of the Bolshevik state—he had, indeed, been made a peer under the title "Baron of Archangel and of Ironside"; another was a mere functionary of the Foreign Office. The Russians like to deal with top people; they like to be made to feel important. Significantly, Hitler, who was also negotiating with Russia at the time, put Foreign Minister Ribbentrop himself on the job. So the Anglo-French overture to Moscow came to nothing. The Russian leaders had apparently reached the conclusion that the West was a broken reed, that if they themselves did not come to terms with Hitler he would attack them anyway.

Finally, the Russians were quite as distrustful of the Polish government as of anyone else. The western, especially the French, policy of encouraging the smaller powers of eastern Europe to act as counterweights to *both* Germany and Russia now bore its natural fruit. The Polish government would not accept Russia as protector; it would not, in these hectic months of negotiations, consent to the passage through Polish territory of Russian troops in case of war with Germany. The Russians were tempted by the opportunity to recover lands in eastern Poland that they had lost in World War I and its aftermath. To the horror of the West, they signed at Moscow on August 23, 1939, a nonaggression pact with Germany, the "Hitler-Stalin pact," a cynical about-face of two supposedly irreconcilable ideological enemies (see the Low cartoon, p. 454). A week later, the German army marched into Poland. On September 3, Britain and France honored their obligations, and declared war on Germany. The twenty years' truce was at an end.

Democratic Policy
in Review

It is not really difficult to understand why the democracies behaved as they did in these years. Britain, France, and the United States were the victors of 1918, and by the very fact of their victory they were on the defensive. Wisdom and luck might have made their defense more effective than it was, but nothing could have altered the fact that they were on the defensive. In the long past of our state system, the defensive has always proved a difficult position, has always been—perhaps

from the very nature of western culture with its drives toward change—at a disadvantage against aggression. This disadvantage seems by no means associated with democracies as such. Absolute monarchies have suffered quite as much from the difficulties of the defensive, as the failure of Metternich shows (see Chapter XIX).

In the years between the two world wars, the normal tendency of the victors to relax was no doubt increased by some of the facts of democratic life. The western democracies were committed to an effort to secure for every citizen some minimum of material comforts; they were committed to the pursuit of happiness. Their normal tendency was to produce butter rather than guns. Their totalitarian opponents may well have been quite as "materialistic" as they, but for them the butter was to be attained in the future, and by means of the guns. In short, the German, Japanese, and Italian governments were able to get their societies to tighten their belts in order to make military preparation possible. On the other hand, it was exceedingly difficult for democratic governments to get such sacrifices from their citizens until war actually broke out.

III: The Nature of the War

The first world war of our century had, in its main theater, the Western Front, been one long siege. Since the military experts tended to fight it over and over again in their planning, both France and Germany in the 1930's built two confronting lines of fortifications on their common frontier. The Maginot Line, on the French side, and the Siegfried Line, on the German, were far more formidable than the improvised trenches of the war of 1914-1918. So it is not surprising that on the outbreak of hostilities in September, 1939, most peo-

ple expected first, that the war would be decided primarily in the area between France and Germany, and second, that it would be a closely confined war of siege in the West, with at most diversional activity in other parts of the world.

But the war itself showed once more the perils of prediction in great human affairs. As Germany was joined by her Axis partners, Italy and Japan, and as the United States entered it, this second world war became much more truly a world war than the first had been. It was decided in Russia, in the Pacific, even in the Mediterranean, quite as much as in the West. And it turned out to be one of the most extraordinarily open wars of movement in history. Indeed, the armies of the British Montgomery and the German Rommel in North Africa moved through the desert with the freedom of nomad hordes of old; but the gasoline engine had replaced the horse.

It was also a war in which for the first time the airplane played a major role, a role foreshadowed in the fighting waged in Ethiopia and Spain during the 1930's. Over the water, the airplane, both land-based and carrier-based, soon established itself as a central factor in naval warfare; in the opinion of many experts, it had made the great warship obsolete. Over the land, the airplane soon established itself as an essential arm of the fire power of land armies, an arm that needed and in the end got careful integration with the ground forces. But even in this war the airplane did not live up to the advanced billing given it by its more imaginative proponents; it did not become the *sole* means of warfare, superseding all others. Air power by itself proved inadequate in the great test of 1940, when the Germans tried to reduce Britain from the air.

Aerial bombardment—toward the end of the war carried on by German pilotless aircraft and rocket missiles—did indeed bring the horrors of warfare back to the civilians of the cities. Military experts had been inclined to believe that civilians could not possibly stand aerial bombardment, and that any country whose cities were subject to a few such bombardments would be obliged to sue for peace. Yet European and Asian civilian populations proved able to stand up to months of bombardment. German civilian deaths from air bombardment have been estimated at about 500,000. Organized systems of shelter, partial dispersal of populations, the obvious but not previously noted fact that much of the space of modern cities is made up of streets, parks, gardens, churches, and other public buildings not used at night (when much of the bombing was done)—all combined to make it possible for the people of heavily bombed cities like Berlin and Tokyo to endure what were in effect front-line conditions.

Yet at the very end of the war a technical innovation was introduced that may indeed have altered radically the character of war, may indeed make any future war so unendurably destructive that it will at least be brief. This was the atomic bomb, developed in secrecy by American and British experts, and first used on the Japanese city of Hiroshima on August 6, 1945. A single bomb destroyed something over half the city. Somewhat less material damage was done by a second and somewhat different bomb dropped on Nagasaki, a hilly city, three days later. But over a hundred thousand people were killed in the two cities by the two bombs, an incidence of death that seems to justify fully the fears that the atomic bomb and its still more frightful hydrogen bomb successors have aroused in our own generation.

IV: Early Successes of the Axis

Polish and Finnish Campaigns

The first campaign of World War II reached a by no means unexpected conclusion. No one had seriously supposed that isolated Poland could possibly stand up for long against the German armed forces, or that Britain and France could possibly get into action rapidly enough to help their

Polish ally decisively. Yet the speed of the German conquest surprised almost everyone. The German air force, the *Luftwaffe,* soon gained absolute command of the air, and used it to disrupt Polish communications and to spread terror with its dive bombers. Special German task forces, fully motorized, swept through and around the more primitively armed Poles. This was what the Germans called a *Blitzkrieg,* or lightning war. The German word was later simplified by the English into "blitz," and was used by them to apply to the German air bombardment of Britain in the years 1940-1941.

Anxious to get his share of Poland, Hitler's new collaborator, Stalin, hastened to push the Russian armies in from the east on the hapless Poles. He also established Russian military bases in the Baltic republics of Estonia, Latvia, and Lithuania, which had been created out of Russian provinces at the close of World War I. "Mutual assistance" pacts between giant Russia and the tiny Baltic states were to be the entering wedge for their full occupation by Russia in 1940 and their amalgamation, as constituent republics, into the Union of Socialist Soviet Republics—a title officially without the word "Russia."

Fear of Germany, or an imperialistic desire to expand, or both, also drove the Russian leaders into a war with neighboring Finland for bases in the Baltic (November, 1939). The Russians, who had perhaps miscalculated the strength of their little opponent, did rather badly at first. By March, 1940, however, they had worn down the Finns; they secured their bases and annexed Finnish lands very close to the great Russian city of Leningrad. It seems quite possible that this "winter war" with Finland had a major effect in encouraging Hitler to his fateful decision of 1941 to make war on Russia. The German military experts drew from Russian difficulties in this war conclusions extremely disparaging to Russian capabilities.

"Phony War" and Blitzkrieg in the West

Meanwhile in the West what the British called the "phony war" was pursuing its uneventful course. The French and the British duly mobilized as in 1914, and as in 1914 the British sent a few divisions to the Continent. But the Germans refused to repeat the pattern of 1914. Occupied in Poland, they did nothing in the West. Occasionally a French patrol from the Maginot Line would exchange shots with a German patrol, but for the most part the troops exercised, ate, slept, and went on leave as though they were merely in training.

The Germans, however, had no intention of sitting out a defensive war in the West. But not even modern warfare is wholly emancipated from the weather. The German general staff was not prepared to begin a decisive campaign in the West with the winter ahead. They waited until spring, and in April they made sure of their northern flank, as they had not in 1914, by making a sudden sea and air invasion of neutral Denmark and Norway. Denmark, totally unprepared, was occupied almost without resistance. Norway, also unprepared, made a brave showing. But neither the British nor the French were able to help her with more than token forces, and by the end of April important Norwegian resistance was broken. The Germans now had admirable bases for air and submarine action against the British.

The great blow was struck, without warning, on May 10, 1940, when the German armies, brilliantly supported in the air, invaded the Low Countries. Holland, spared in 1914, was this time invaded so that the Germans might make doubly sure of their northern flank. A carefully planned attack on the key Belgian fort of Eben Emael, an attack that had been rehearsed on a dummy of the fort set up inside Ger-

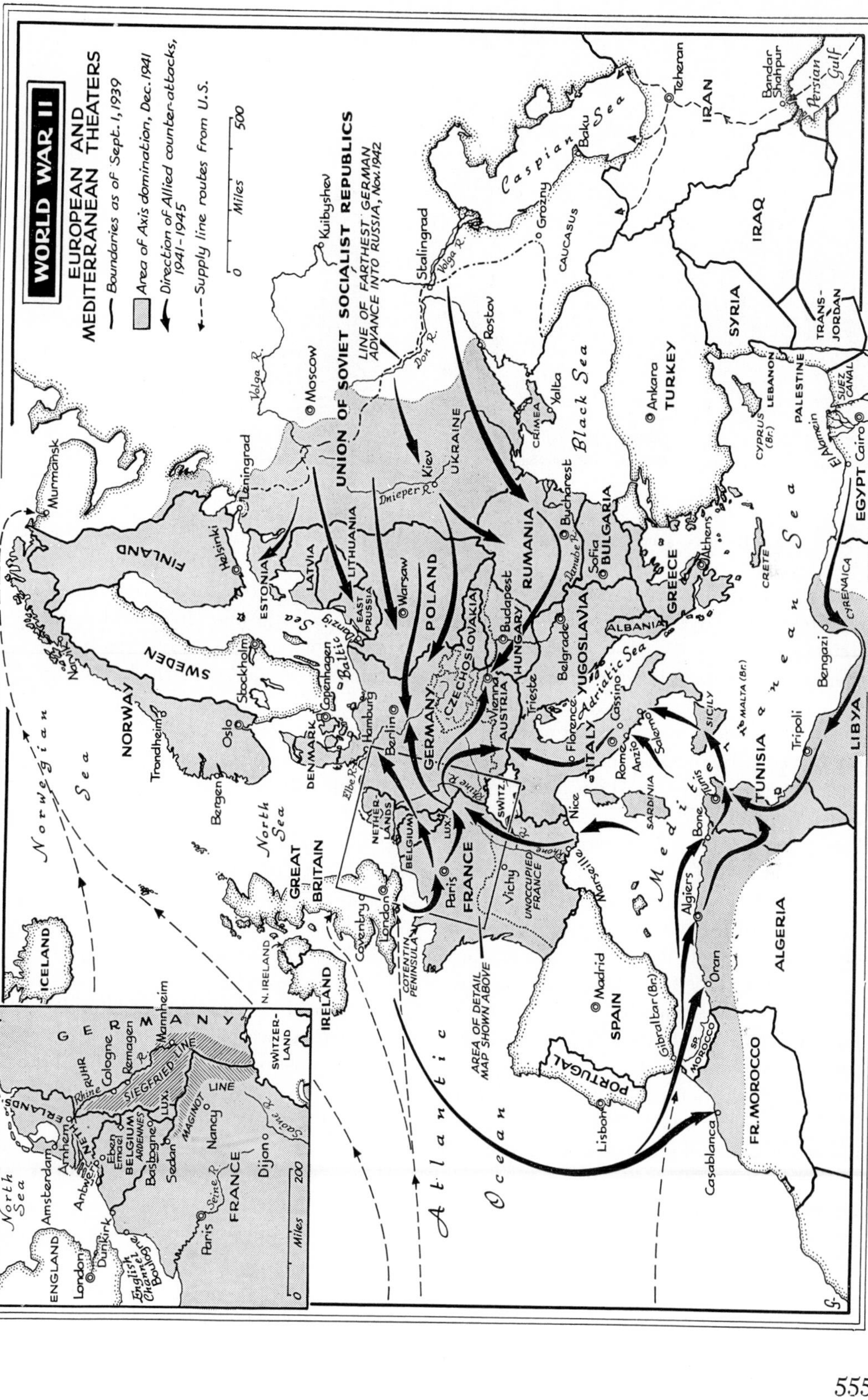
WORLD WAR II
EUROPEAN AND MEDITERRANEAN THEATERS
Boundaries as of Sept. 1, 1939
Area of Axis domination, Dec. 1941
Direction of Allied counter-attacks, 1941-1945
Supply line routes from U.S.
0 Miles 500
UNION OF SOVIET SOCIALIST REPUBLICS
LINE OF FARTHEST GERMAN ADVANCE INTO RUSSIA, Nov. 1942
Murmansk
Leningrad
Moscow
Kuibyshev
Stalingrad
Volga R.
Don R.
Rostov
Grozny
CAUCASUS
Baku
Caspian Sea
Teheran
IRAN
Bandar Shahpur
Persian Gulf
IRAQ
SYRIA
TRANS-JORDAN
LEBANON
PALESTINE
SUEZ CANAL
Cairo
EGYPT
El Alamein
CYPRUS (Br.)
TURKEY
Ankara
Black Sea
Yalta
CRIMEA
UKRAINE
Kiev
Dnieper R.
RUMANIA
Bucharest
Danube R.
BULGARIA
Sofia
GREECE
Athens
CRETE
ALBANIA
YUGOSLAVIA
Belgrade
Adriatic Sea
HUNGARY
Budapest
CZECHOSLOVAKIA
Vienna
AUSTRIA
Trieste
POLAND
Warsaw
EAST PRUSSIA
LITHUANIA
LATVIA
ESTONIA
FINLAND
Helsinki
Danzig
Baltic Sea
SWEDEN
Stockholm
NORWAY
Oslo
Bergen
Trondheim
Narvik
Norwegian Sea
DENMARK
Copenhagen
Hamburg
Berlin
GERMANY
Elbe R.
Rhine R.
NETHERLANDS
BELGIUM
LUX.
SWITZ.
FRANCE
Paris
Vichy
UNOCCUPIED FRANCE
Rhone R.
Nice
Marseille
ITALY
Florence
Rome
Anzio
Cassino
Salerno
SICILY
SARDINIA
MALTA (Br.)
Mediterranean Sea
TUNISIA
Tunis
Bone
Tripoli
LIBYA
Bengazi
CYRENAICA
ALGERIA
Algiers
Oran
SP. MOROCCO
FR. MOROCCO
Casablanca
Gibraltar (Br.)
SPAIN
Madrid
PORTUGAL
Lisbon
GREAT BRITAIN
London
Coventry
North Sea
N. IRELAND
IRELAND
ICELAND
COTENTIN PENINSULA
AREA OF DETAIL MAP SHOWN ABOVE
Atlantic Ocean
ENGLAND
London
English Channel
Boulogne
Dunkirk
Antwerp
Amsterdam
Arnhem
NETHERLANDS
Eben Emael
BELGIUM
ARDENNES
Bastogne
Sedan
MAGINOT LINE
Nancy
Dijon
Saone R.
Seine R.
Paris
FRANCE
LUX.
SIEGFRIED LINE
RUHR
Cologne
Remagen
Rhine R.
Mannheim
GERMANY
SWITZERLAND
0 Miles 200

Churchill giving the Victory sign to British servicemen, 1943.

many, was at once successful, and opened the way into the Low Countries.

In the era of weakness in the 1930's, both the Belgians and the Dutch had been extremely anxious to avoid compromising themselves by planning for joint resistance with Britain and France against a possible German attack. They were now to suffer the full consequences of their own policy of attempting to appease Hitler. For the crucial failure to hold the Germans in actual battle was in the Low Countries. We cannot be sure that a carefully co-ordinated plan among French, British, Belgians, and Dutch would have stopped Hitler. But clearly the lack of such co-ordination was a major factor in the German success. Indeed, though much has since been written against the "Maginot mentality," it is a fact that the Germans did not take the French Maginot Line by frontal assault, but outflanked it at the critical point where it tapered off along the Franco-Belgian border in the hilly region of the Ardennes.

Through the Ardennes the Germans poured their best motorized troops into France. In a blitzkrieg that once more capitalized on the "lessons of 1914," the Germans resisted the temptation to turn at once on the prize of Paris, but instead drove straight through northern France to the Channel, where the port of Boulogne fell on May 26, a little over two weeks after the start of the campaign. By this stroke the Germans separated the British, Belgian, and part of the French troops from the bulk of the French armies to the south. Shortly afterward the French replaced General Gamelin with General Weygand as commander-in-chief. Meanwhile in Britain Neville Chamberlain had resigned after an adverse vote in the Commons on May 8 as a result of failure in Norway. He was succeeded as prime minister by Winston Churchill. The British act was of major importance, comparable to the replacing of Asquith by Lloyd George in World War I. Chamberlain was neither a man of action nor an appealing or heroic figure; Churchill was to prove himself all this and more. Under him the British made a united front in the crisis.

The new leaders, in a desperate last moment, attempted to work out a plan for pinching off the adventurous German motorized thrust by a concerted attack from north and south. But the Belgians, badly disorganized, decided to capitulate, and

CHAPTER XXIX

neither the French nor the British could rally themselves to carry out the movement. In the last days of May and the first days of June the British did indeed achieve the miracle of the successful withdrawal of some 215,000 British and 120,000 French soldiers by sea from the beaches around Dunkirk at the northern tip of France. With useful protection from the Royal Air Force, an extraordinary flotilla of all sorts of vessels, including private yachts and motorboats, got the men off, though almost all their equipment had to be abandoned. Dunkirk was a courageous action, and one that did much to help British morale. But from German documents that fell to the Allies after the final defeat of Germany it is pretty clear (though the point is still controversial) that the miracle of Dunkirk was possible largely because Hitler himself decided not to press home the destruction of the British forces penned on the coast, on the ground that Britain was no longer a real threat. At the last moment, Hitler too gave in to the lure of Paris, and decided to push the attack on the French homeland at once. Here he was wholly and rapidly successful. The French under Weygand could not rally, and the Germans marched southward almost unopposed. The clear signal to the world that the rally of 1914 at the Marne would not be repeated was given on June 13, when the French declared Paris an "open city" and evacuated it without fighting.

"The Fall of France"

The battle of France was thus decided by mid-June. But the French might yet try to defend the south, or, failing that, use their navy and merchant marine to get as many men as possible across the Mediterranean into French North Africa. There, based on their great empire overseas, they might have continued with British aid the fight against the Germans. Some of the French leaders wished to do this, and in the crisis Winston Churchill made to the French the extraordinary offer of a complete governmental union of the two countries to continue the struggle. His offer was not accepted.

On June 16, Reynaud was supplanted by Marshal Pétain as prime minister, in what amounted to a kind of *coup d'état*. Pétain and his colleagues were determined on peace at any price, and this they got. On June 22, 1940, an armistice was signed at Compiègne at the spot where the armistice of November 11, 1918 had been signed. By this armistice the French withdrew from the war, handed over three-fifths of France, including the whole Atlantic and Channel coasts, to German occupation, and retained under strict German supervision no more than the central and Mediterranean regions. This "unoccupied France" was ruled from the little resort city of Vichy, where Pétain set up a French form of authoritarian, anti-democratic state of which he was "chief." History has labeled his government simply "Vichy France." To most Frenchmen it was a German-imposed rule.

Some few of Pétain's collaborators were pro-German, convinced that totalitarianism was inevitable. But it is now clear that for most of them, even for men like the "collaborator" Laval, a dominant figure at Vichy, and indeed for Pétain himself, the important motive in those bewildering June days of 1940 was simply a desire to make terms with the inevitable. They were absolutely sure that Hitler had won the war. They did not believe that Britain had any chance of successfully resisting the German war machine that had crushed France. In this belief they were followed at first by the great majority of Frenchmen.

The new Vichy government attempted to remake France along conservative, indeed monarchist, lines that had not been practical politics since the *Seize Mai* of 1877 (see Chapter XXI). Symbolic of why the Vichy régime failed is its attempt to substitute for the great slogan "Liberty,

Equality, Fraternity" a new trinity of "Labor, Family, Fatherland." Even an outsider can see that the new slogan lacked fire. More concretely, the Vichy régime from the start was compromised by its association with the hated Germans; born of defeat, it could do little in the few years it had to live before it died in the Allied victory.

Even in the bad days of June, 1940, a few Frenchmen, led by General Charles de Gaulle, who was flown out to London at the last moment, refused to give up the fight. De Gaulle, with British aid, set up a French National Committee with headquarters in London. A nucleus of French soldiers taken off the beach at Dunkirk, and a stream of refugees who came out of France by all sorts of means in the next few years, made up the "Free French" or "Fighting French." At home in France the "Resistance movement" gradually formed underground to prepare for eventual liberation. North Africa, strongest of the French colonies, remained under the control of Vichy. But some parts of the colonies rallied to the Free French from the start. Notably in Equatorial Africa, under the leadership of the great Negro governor, Félix Eboué, a most useful base for Allied operations was secured from the first.

Hitler's elation after the armistice with France, 1940.

Weak as these fighting French groups were in the early days, they were at least a rallying point. They were able to set up an effective radio center in England from which they conducted a skillful propaganda campaign against Vichy and the Germans, beamed across the Channel to the homeland, where, we now know, it achieved a large audience.

On June 10, Hitler's ally Mussolini had brought the Italians into the war against France and Britain, too late to affect the outcome of the battle of France. But this "stab in the back" as Franklin Roosevelt called it, further outraged American opinion, already alarmed by the Nazi successes. And Italy was now irrevocably engaged in the struggle, anxious to secure some kind of success that would offset the great gains of her German ally. The war, up to this time confined to northern and western Europe, now spread to the Mediterranean.

The Battle of Britain

The Germans, for all their miracles of planning and execution, had not really worked out a way to deal with Britain. Hitler seems to have believed that with France out of the war Britain would see the light and make a separate peace, a peace of compromise in which Germany would dominate the continent of Europe and Britain would continue satisfied with her overseas empire. This division of the spoils, Hitler reiterated in public and private, should be eminently satisfactory; he did not threaten the British Empire. Yet for over four centuries Britain had gone to war rather than accept the kind of one-power domination over western and central Europe that Hitler exercised after the fall of France. The British, therefore, paid no attention at all to his peace feelers.

Hitler was counting heavily on the possibility that German submarines could eventually cut off British supplies of food and raw materials from overseas, and thus

London during the "blitz."

starve her into submission. But at best this must take a long time, and Hitler was impatient. The obvious thing to do was to attempt a landing in England. But the Germans had made no real preparation for amphibious warfare; they had no specially designed landing craft. Moreover, the German air force and the German navy were at odds over the best way of combining for an invasion across the Channel. A hastily assembled flotilla of miscellaneous vessels was badly damaged by British aircraft, and early in August, 1940, Hitler and Goering, his air marshal, made the fateful decision to try to do the job from the air.

The Battle of Britain that followed had two main phases. First, in August and September the Luftwaffe attempted in daylight bombing attacks to wipe out British airports and fighter planes. The Royal Air Force, admirably organized and directed, and using the new detection apparatus called radar to spot the attackers early, proved just barely strong enough to check the Germans. In the critical actions of September 15-21, German official records now available show 120 planes lost (the British at the time claimed 268). This was, however, a rate of loss Goering felt the Germans could not stand. In one of his im-

perishable phrases, Churchill said of the British fighter pilots, "Never ... was so much owed by so many to so few."

The second phase began in the autumn of 1940. The Germans sought by night bombing of major British industrial centers to destroy British production and to terrify the civilian population so that the government would be obliged to sue for peace. Neither aim was successful. Even at Coventry, an important center of the automotive industry, though grave damage was done, the industry was by no means knocked out. As for civilian morale, it is clear that these bombings strengthened the British will to resist. Civilian defense measures proved adequate to protect both persons and property from that extreme of destruction which might indeed have broken the will to resist. By winter, when the weather gave the British some respite, the Battle of Britain had been won.

Mediterranean and Balkan Campaigns

Hitler now faced the possibility of a long stalemate, something that conquerors like Napoleon in the past have rarely been able to face. Like Napoleon turning to Egypt in 1798, Hitler turned at first to the obvious strategy of getting at Britain through her Mediterranean lifeline to India and the East. His ally Mussolini, already itching to expand in the Mediterranean, in October, 1940, invaded Greece from Albania—with no success. Just how far Hitler himself wanted to invest in action in this theater is not clear. Certainly he toyed with the idea of a campaign against the British fortress of Gibraltar through Spain, to be coördinated with Axis attacks in the eastern Mediterranean to clear that sea of the British. But the Spanish dictator Franco wanted too high a price from the French for his consent to a German march through Spain, and Hitler was unwilling to risk driving Vichy France, which still controlled French North Africa, too far. In the upshot, the Germans had to be content with backing up Mussolini in Greece and with an attack on Egypt from the Italian colony of Libya. Efforts to rouse native action against the British and French in the Near East were suppressed without grave difficulty by British and Free French action, and Turkey stood obstinately neutral.

Nevertheless, the German commitment to help the Italians in Greece took valuable German divisions away from another task in the spring of 1941, and as the Germans attempted to move overland through Yugoslavia they were involved in a costly guerrilla war. The British did their best to back up their Greek allies, but once more they were not strong enough. German air power crippled British naval power in the waters around Crete, and by June the Axis had conquered the Greek mainland and the islands.

The Invasion of Russia

The other task for which the German forces were to be used in the spring of 1941 was the conquest of Russia. Hitler had

firmly resolved not to repeat what he thought was the fateful mistake of Germany in 1914; he would not engage in a war on two fronts. Yet by his invasion of Russia in June, 1941—an invasion delayed for a perhaps decisive two months by the Balkan adventure—he committed himself to just such a war. Russia was indeed a tempting goal. The Nazi plan had always looked to the fertile areas of Poland and South Russia as the natural goal of German expansion, the *Lebensraum* (see p. 486) of German destiny. With the precedents of successful blitzkrieg in Poland, western Europe, and now Greece, Hitler and his military experts believed that they could beat the Russians in a single campaign before winter set in. It was quite clear that neither Britain nor the United States—even though the latter should enter the war—could land armies in Europe in 1941. An attack on Russia, then, Hitler seems to have told himself, would not *really* create two fronts. Indeed, once Russia was conquered, as in Hitler's mind it was sure to be, the Germans would have no trouble disposing of Britain, and, if necessary, the United States.

Russia was not conquered in 1941. But it was a very close thing, closer perhaps than the Battle of Britain. Hitler's plan almost worked. There really was a successful Blitzkrieg. Within two months the Germans were at the gates of Leningrad, and in the south they had conquered the Ukraine by the end of October. Hundreds of thousands of Russian troops had been killed or taken prisoner. In sheer distance, the German armies had pushed more than twice as far as they had in France.

Yet, as the Russian winter closed in, the Germans had taken neither Moscow nor Leningrad. Russian heavy industry had been in part transferred to the remote Urals, and existing plants there and in Siberia had been strenghened. The United States was beginning to send in supplies. The vast resources of Russian manpower were still adequate for Russian needs. The government had not collapsed, and national spirit was high. Moreover, the Germans had shown once more, as they had in the Battle of Britain, that their boasted planning was far from perfect. Their troops were not sufficiently equipped to stand the rigors of a Russian winter. Confident that one summer and autumn would be enough to finish the business, the German planners had left the winter to take care of itself. Indeed, in winter fighting between December, 1941, and May, 1942, the Russians regained much useful ground.

American Policy

Meanwhile, the Germans had fallen into a second fatal involvement. Impressed with what he thought were the disastrous failures of German policy in World War I, Hitler had sought to keep out of war with the United States. Although the United States had a strong isolationist sentiment, and even a handful of Axis sympathizers, American opinion had from the very beginning of the attack on Poland in 1939 been far more nearly unanimous against the Germans and Italians than it had been against the Central Powers in 1914. With the fall of France in 1940, anti-Axis sentiment grew stronger, reinforced by a feeling that if Hitler had his way in Europe the United States would be marked out as his next victim.

Between June, 1940, and December, 1941, the Roosevelt administration, with the consent of the Congress and with the general —though not unanimous—backing of American public opinion, took a series of steps "short of war" in aid of Britain and later Russia. By conventional nineteenth-century standards of international relations, these steps were far from being in accord with America's technical status as a neutral; they would have given Hitler ample legal justification for declaring war against the United States. The American government transferred to the British fifty "over-age" destroyers in exchange for Atlantic naval bases in British colonies, supplied the British with all sorts of arms, and used the American navy to help get these supplies across the Atlantic. Above all, in March, 1941, by the so-called "Lend-Lease Act" the United States agreed to supply materials needed for defense, including foodstuffs, to "any country whose defense the President deems vital to the defense of the United States." Supplies at once began rolling into England, and later to other allies in the struggle against the Axis, without the unfortunate complications produced by the war-debt methods employed during World War I.

This help went, as we have just noted, even to communist Russia. The "cold war" of the 1950's between Russia and the United States produced currents of opinion in this country which held that we should never have helped Russia in 1942-1945. But the historian knows that in great wars of coalition the wise rule is: help your allies even if you don't like them, even, indeed, if you don't trust them. Strict adherence to this doctrine by Roosevelt and Churchill clearly helped prevent among Britain, the United States, Russia, and the Free French the kind of actual back-stabbing and desertion that characterized the failure of Europe to defeat, or even contain, the revolutionary French and Napoleon between 1792 and 1812 (see Chapter XVIII).

Yet Hitler still did not let himself get involved in war against the United States. He had, however, firm commitments to aid Japan. And Japan, controlled by a militarist group, had taken advantage of the fall of France and the Netherlands and the weakness of Britain to speed up vastly the policy of expansion in Asia that she had begun in Manchuria as far back as 1931. She early took advantage of the fall of France to penetrate into French Indo-China. She continued to press her campaign on the mainland of China. The American government, which had never in the days of technical peace in the 1930's been willing to accept Japanese conquests in China, did not now abandon its policy of opposition to what it considered Japanese aggression. It is indeed highly likely that had the American government been willing to allow Japan a free hand to do what she liked in the Far East there would have been no Pearl Harbor. But short of such complete abandonment of the previous American policy in the Far East, it is unlikely that the United States could have kept out of war with Japan.

Pearl Harbor and After

In the summer and autumn of 1941, the American government took steps to freeze Japanese credits in the United States, to close Japanese access to raw materials, and to get the Japanese to withdraw from China and Indo-China. Negotiations toward these ends were going on between the Japanese and the Americans when on December 7, 1941, the Japanese without warning struck with carrier-based airplanes at the American naval base at Pearl Harbor in Hawaii. Grave damage was done to ships and installations, but American power in the Pacific was by no means destroyed. Moreover, the psychological effect of the "day of infamy" on American public opinion was to produce in a nation of many millions an almost unanimous support for war against Japan. And the consequence was the immediate declaration of war against Japan by the United States. Germany and Italy honored their obligations to their Axis partner by declaring war against the United States on December 11. The war was now literally and fully a world war.

Although the United States was incomparably better prepared than she had been in 1917, she was still at a disadvantage. Against Germany she could for the moment do no more than continue, indeed increase, aid to Britain and Russia by Lend-Lease and take full part in the struggle against the German submarines. Against Japan she was almost as powerless. Her Pacific outposts of Guam, Wake Island, and the Philippines fell in rapid succession to Japanese arms. Nor could the British and the exiled Dutch governments protect their colonies in Southeast Asia. By the spring of 1942, the Japanese had taken Malaya from the British and Indonesia from the Dutch, and had virtual control of Siam and Burma. They seemed poised for an attack on Australia.

A Japanese navy air view of United States ships bombed during the attack on Pearl Harbor.

V: The Victory of the United Nations

The Turning Points

There were several turning points in the struggle. The earliest was a series of naval actions in which Japanese expansion was stopped. In these actions, carrier-based airplanes played a decisive role. On May 7, 1942, in the battle of the Coral Sea in the southwest Pacific, Allied sea and air power halted a possible Japanese invasion of Australia and its protecting islands. In June, American sea and air power dispersed a Japanese fleet that was aiming at the conquest of Midway Island. Although the Japanese landed on American territory in the Aleutians, they never seriously threatened Hawaii or mainland Alaska.

In the West, the Americans and the British were as yet unwilling to respond to Russian pressure for a "second front" on the European mainland. But they were able in November, 1942, to effect a series of landings in French North Africa. Secret negotiations with anti-Axis elements among the French in North Africa were not completely successful, and the landings in Morocco were sharply though briefly resisted by the Vichy French. None the less, the Allies were rapidly established in force in Morocco and Algeria.

The Libyan segment of the long North African coast had been held by the Germans and their Italian allies since the beginning of the war in the Mediterranean, and there had been seesaw campaigns in these desert areas, campaigns that recaptured some of the adventure, even romance, of wars of old. At the time of the North African landings, the British under General Montgomery were holding a defensive line inside the Egyptian frontier, but on October 23, 1942, the British started on an offen-sive which was planned to co-ordinate with that of General Eisenhower, commander of the Allied forces in French North Africa, in the classic maneuver of catching the enemy in a vise. The Germans responded quickly to the threat, and succeeded in re-inforcing their African armies through Tunis, which was delivered to them by the Vichy authorities. The planned expulsion of the Germans and Italians from North Africa was thus delayed, but the vise closed slowly. In May, 1943, Free French, British, and American troops took the last Axis strongholds of Tunis and Bizerte, and accepted the surrender of some three hundred thousand Axis troops.

The North African campaign had clearly been a turning point. The Allies had successfully made large-scale amphibious landings, and they had annihilated one of the most renowned of Axis forces, commanded by one of the few German generals to strike the imagination of the world, Rommel, the "desert fox." North Africa was by no means a great central operation, but it was nevertheless a major campaign in which the Allies gained confidence and prestige.

The great turning point on land was, however, the successful Russian defense of Stalingrad, a defense that turned into an attack in the same month (November, 1942) that saw the Allied landing in North Africa. After their check in the winter of 1941-42, the Germans had turned their Russian summer offensive of 1942 away from Leningrad and Moscow, and toward the oil-rich regions of southeastern European Russia. The Germans were already beginning to suffer oil shortages, partly because of Allied bombing, but even more because, though they held the oil fields of Rumania, they simply did not have oil enough for the ravenous demands of mechanical warfare. This push toward the Russian oil fields carried the Germans a prodigious distance inside Russia, over a thousand miles from their original starting point. But again it failed, falling just short of the really rich oil fields of Grozny and Baku. Russian distance and Russian manpower, and the Russian ability to take punishment, were too much for these overextended Germans. Their armies were pinched off at Stalingrad, and early in 1943 the Russians started the long march that was to take them to Berlin two years later.

The Battle of Supply

A much less spectacular turning point than the engagements in the Coral Sea, in North Africa, and at Stalingrad was the Allied victory in the battle of supply. Yet this victory was of even greater importance, since naval and military successes ultimately depend on supplies. Even for Russia, an important source of supplies was the United States. But the United States was separated from its allies—and its enemies—by water, and all but the most precious and least bulky supplies, which could go by air, had to move across the seas. If the Germans could stop this movement, or even reduce it greatly, they might still be able to win in spite of the overwhelming resources of the Allies. They made important improvements in their submarines, notably the schnorkel, a device that enabled submarines to travel submerged for great distances. Submarine crews and commanders were well trained and resourceful. But there were not enough submarines, and the countermeasures of the Allies—radar, co-ordination of naval vessels and aircraft, the convoy system, and others—slowly reduced the proportion of sinkings.

Early in 1942, after Pearl Harbor, the rate of sinkings had been really dangerous, and German submarines had operated close to the Atlantic coast of the United States. But by the end of 1942 the statistics showed a turn of the tide, and in the summer of 1943 the Allies were confident enough to announce publicly that the number of sinkings from U-boat action in the first half of 1943 was only a quarter of what it had been in the first half of 1942.

The Axis on the Defensive

In the last two years of the war, the Axis powers were on the defensive. Both in Europe and in Asia the coalition forces attacked with land forces along definite lines of march; these were "campaigns" of the traditional kind. But the way for these armies was made easier by two new factors in warfare, air power and modern propaganda, or "psychological warfare." These new methods did not "win" the war by themselves, but they were useful adjuncts, and they undoubtedly hastened the process. Air bombardment, at least until the atomic bomb at Hiroshima, was never quite the perfect annihilation that the prophets of air power had preached. The Germans put some of their key production underground. Allied "precision" bombing rarely reached perfection. But as the superior Allied air power grew, as it was used systematically to destroy enemy capabilities in critical materials like ball bearings and oil, and as American airplanes dropped incendiary bombs on the relatively flimsy Japanese cities, it did much to destroy the Axis will and power to resist.

On Germany and Italy the attack by land was pressed in three directions—by the Russians from the east, and by the British, French, Americans, and the other Allies from the south and from the west. In the south the Allies moved over to Sicily in a successful amphibious operation (July, 1943) within two months of their final victory in North Africa, and from

Sicily they moved in another six weeks across the Straits of Messina to the mainland of Italy. Yet the Italian campaign was never quite the great success the Allies hoped it would be in these earlier days. The Allied victories of the summer of 1943 were, however, sufficient to put Italy itself for the most part out of the war. High officers of the Italian army and others close to the king, helped by dissident fascist leaders, engineered a *coup* in July which brought about the fall and imprisonment of Mussolini and the beginnings of negotiations between the Allies and the new government headed by Marshal Badoglio.

But the Germans were quite unwilling to abandon the peninsula, perhaps as much for reasons of prestige as for military reasons. A detachment of German troops rescued Mussolini from his Apennine prison (September, 1943), and set him up as the head of a "Fascist Republic." The former *Duce* continued in this post until he was executed by partisans in April, 1945. Meantime, Italy had a civil as well as a foreign war on her hands. It is likely that the majority of the Italian people, never really taken in by Mussolini's posturing as an imperial Roman, had never liked the war and were now heartily sick of it. Still, many were politically active in Italy in 1943-1945, and of these the fascist-Axis group was far less strong than the pro-Allied group. Italy came naturally enough into the United Nations. The war in Italy went on. In June, 1944, the Allies succeeded, after particularly severe fighting around Cassino, in breaking through to Rome, and by August they were in Florence. They did not really penetrate any farther until the final collapse of the Germans in the early months of 1945.

The Defeat of Germany

The great Allied push in the west, it was finally decided at the Teheran conference of Churchill, Roosevelt, and Stalin (December, 1943), would be in France. After meticulous preparation, the long-awaited landings in France began on June 6, 1944. The Allies had chosen the Norman coast at the base of the Cotentin (Cherbourg) peninsula, and seem thereby to have gained some initial advantage of surprise, for the German high command believed the landings would come farther north and east along the Channel coast. The Germans had in their four years of occupancy fortified the French coastline with great thoroughness. But the Allies had also had those four years for study, invention, and planning. In the test, Allied landing craft, amphibious trucks, naval and air support—by now the Luftwaffe had almost been driven from the skies—artificial harbors, and a well-organized supply system proved sufficient to gain a beachhead for the land forces. From this beachhead, a little over a month after "D-Day," they were able to break out at Avranches and sweep the Germans back across the Seine in a great flanking movement led by the American General Patton's Third Army.

A long-planned auxiliary landing on the French Mediterranean coast and a march north up the Rhone-Saône valleys was launched on August 15, 1944, and met very little resistance. Everywhere the French, by now well organized for resistance, welcomed the liberating forces, some of whom were French and French colonials fighting as heirs of the Free French of 1940. Paris, a symbol rather than a mere place, was liberated toward the end of August after its inhabitants had staged an uprising, barricades and all, in the style of 1848, against the German garrison.

The Germans were beaten, but not disorganized. In July, 1944, an attempt to assassinate Hitler and to pave the way for negotiations was made by conservative elements, both military and civilian. But Hitler survived the bomb intended for him, and the Nazis retained their firm grip on the German state. The Allies were en-

Coast Guard photograph of the landing operations during the invasion of Normandy.

couraged by their rapid successes in July and August to try to destroy the German armies before winter, or to cut them off from their homeland. Patton's mechanized troops ran out of fuel, however; the new German pilotless planes and rockets delayed the full use of Antwerp as a port of supply; and by late autumn it was clear that the Germans had retired in good order to their own Siegfried Line.

From the east, the Russians had been pushing on relentlessly ever since the turning of the tide at Stalingrad. In the campaign of 1943, while the western Allies were busy in Italy, the Russians won back most of their own territories that had been lost in 1941 and 1942. They kept up the pressure during the winter, and started an early spring campaign in the south. By the au-

tumn of 1944, the Russians had been able to sweep through half-hearted resistance from Hitler's Balkan satellite governments to a juncture with the Yugoslav communist guerrillas under Tito, and were ready for the attack on Hungary. In the center and north, they had recovered all their own territory, and were ready to attack Germany itself from the east.

The year 1945 saw the rapid conclusion of the Battle of Germany. The Russians had not stopped for winter, but had pressed on through Poland to menace Berlin early in March. The western Allies broke through the Siegfried Line in February, crossed the Rhine, and entered the heart of Germany. Early in February, 1945, the leaders of the three great Allied powers, Stalin, Churchill, and Roosevelt, met at Yalta in the Crimea and confirmed final plans for the conquest of Germany. It was plain that the Germans, whose key industries had been so riddled from the air that they no longer could support their armies adequately, and whose manpower had been reduced to the very bottom, could not hold out for long. But the Allied planners were anxious to prevent, or at least to check, the race to be the first to arrive in Germany; and they wanted to arrange peacefully for demarcations between the parts of Germany that each ally was to occupy. The decision to give the Russians the honor of taking Berlin is one that, with many other decisions reached in the conference at Yalta, has since been severely criticized in the West. At the time, however, it seemed a natural decision, a legitimate recognition that during the two years of successful offensive against the Germans the Russians

had worn down many more German divisions than had the western Allies.

The Russians fought their way into a Berlin already pulverized by the air power of the western Allies. Hitler went down to his death, as he had long promised, in a Germanic funeral pyre at his Berlin headquarters. Though his body was never found and identified, there can be no serious doubt concerning his fate.

The Allied advance into Germany revealed for the first time the full ghastliness of Nazi treatment of slave laborers from conquered lands, of political opponents, and of Jews, Poles, and other German-styled "inferior" peoples. One after another, the concentration camps were liberated—Auschwitz, Belsen, Buchenwald, Dachau, Nordhausen, and others. And the world was appalled at the gas ovens that had claimed so many victims, at the piles

Bodies of Gestapo victims at Nordhausen concentration camp.

of emaciated corpses not yet cremated, and at the pitiful state of the prisoners who had survived. This was one of the horrors of war whose reality exceeded the grimmest expectations of Allied opinion.

By May 8, 1945, Churchill and Truman (who had become the American president on Roosevelt's death in April) were able to announce the end of German resistance, the day of victory in Europe, V-E Day. It was symbolic of difficulties to come that Stalin was offended because the western Allies had accepted from some of the German army leaders a formal surrender at Rheims in France. He chose to announce separately, on Russia's part, the final victory over Germany, and not until the next day.

The Defeat of Japan

V-J Day, the day of victory in Japan, was now the great goal of Allied effort. Russia had carefully refrained from adding Japan to its formal enemies as long as Germany was still a threat. Britain and the United States, on the other hand, were anxious to win Russia as a formal fighting ally against the Japanese. This natural desire—natural in the sense of historical precedent, for coalitions in the past have usually sought to rally as many allies as possible—was responsible for many of the concessions made to Russia in the last months of the German war.

The two years of Allied successes against Germany had also been two years of Allied successes against Japan. The attack on Japan had been pressed home in three main directions. First, in a process that the American press soon christened "island-hopping," the American navy drove straight toward Japan from the central Pacific. One after another, the small island bases that stood in the way were reduced by American naval forces, which used both air support and the amphibious methods that were

being worked out simultaneously in Europe and North Africa. The names of these islands are now a part of the litany of American arms—Tarawa, Eniwetok, Kwajalein, Iwo Jima, Okinawa.

Second, in a series of operations calling for the close co-operation of air, sea, and land forces the Americans and Australians, with help from other Commonwealth elements, worked their way up the southwest Pacific through the much larger islands of the Solomons, New Guinea, and the Philippines. The base for this campaign, which was under the command of the American General MacArthur, was Australia and such outlying islands as New Caledonia and the New Hebrides. The start of the campaign goes back to the first major offensive step in the Far East, the dramatic and difficult seizure of Guadalcanal in the Solomons by the United States Marines on August 7, 1942. These campaigns involved jungle fighting of the hardest sort, slow and painful work. But by October, 1944, the sea forces had won the great battle of the Philippine Sea and had made possible the successful landing of MacArthur's troops on Leyte and the reconquest of the Philippine Islands themselves from the Japanese.

The third attack on the "Greater East Asia Co-Prosperity Sphere" of Japanese expansion came from the south, in the "CBI" —the China-Burma-India Theater. No brief narrative can do justice to the complex interweaving of events in this theater, where the main effort of the Allies was to get material support in to Chiang Kai-shek and the Chinese Nationalists at Chungking (see Chapter XXXI) and, if possible, to damage the Japanese position in Burma, Thailand (Siam), and Indo-China. After Pearl Harbor, when the Japanese seized and shut the famous "Burma Road," the only way for the Allies to communicate with Chiang's Nationalists was by air. It is perhaps true that the western Allies did not invest an overwhelming proportion of their resources in this CBI Theater, but they did

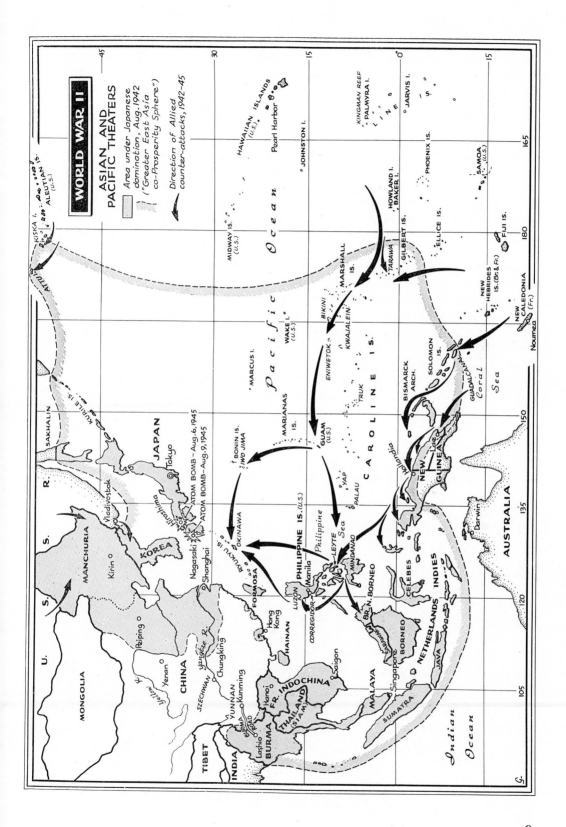

WORLD WAR II

ASIAN AND PACIFIC THEATERS

Area under Japanese domination, Aug. 1942 ("Greater East Asia co-Prosperity Sphere")

Direction of Allied counter-attacks, 1942-45

help keep the Chinese formally in the fight. And, as the final campaign of 1945 drew on, the British, with Chinese and American aid, were fighting three Japanese field armies in this CBI Theater.

The end came in Japan with a suddenness that the Allied peoples, perhaps even the Allied governments, hardly expected. From the Pacific island bases, American airplanes inflicted crippling damage on Japanese industry in the spring and summer of 1945; the Japanese fleet had been almost destroyed; submarine warfare had brought the Japanese economy near to strangulation; and there was impressive evidence of the declining morale of Japanese soldiers. None the less, American decision-makers were convinced that only the use of the atomic bomb could bring a quick decision and avert the very heavy casualties likely in the proposed invasion of the Japanese home islands. The result was the dropping of the first atomic bomb, on Hiroshima, August 6, 1945. On August 8, the Russians, who had agreed to come into the war against Japan once Germany was beaten, began an invasion of Manchuria in full force. Faced with what they felt was certain defeat, the Japanese government, unlike the German, decided not to make a last-ditch stand in their own country. On September 2, after brief negotiations, the Japanese made formal surrender at Tokyo. Japan gave up its conquests abroad, and submitted to American military occupation. Contrary to the desires of part of Allied opinion, however, the Emperor of Japan was not dethroned. Purged of most of its militarists, the Japanese government continued to rule under Allied—actually American—supervision.

The Allied Coalition

The "Grand Alliance," known in its last years as the "United Nations," had mustered overpowering strength against Germany, Japan, Italy, and such collabo-

View of Hiroshima after the first atom bomb was dropped, photographed from hospital buildings about one mile from center of explosion.

Giraud, Roosevelt, de Gaulle, and Churchill at Casablanca, January, 1943.

rators as the Axis powers could secure in the Balkans, Southeast Asia, and western Europe. Britain, Russia, and the United States were the heart of the Allied coalition. But Nationalist China, for all its inefficiencies, had occupied the attention of hundreds of thousands of Japanese soldiers, and the resources of the French Empire and the French resistance movements at home and abroad had been most useful. The United Nations had been able to count on the resources of Latin America, and Brazil had been an active member of the alliance. In this truly global war, Brazilian troops had fought in Italy, which at the end had been the most cosmopolitan of theaters. There American (including Japanese-American, or Nisei), French imperial, British imperial, pro-Allied Italian, Polish, and other troops had fought, in addition to the Brazilians. At the very end of the war, even Argentina was brought into the United Nations coalition, when she declared war

on Germany and Japan on March 27, 1945.

The instruments of continuing Allied union were the conferences of the "Big Three"—Churchill, Roosevelt, and Stalin—with their political and military advisers and experts, and the more frequent Anglo-American conferences. Even before the United States entered the shooting war, Roosevelt and Churchill met off Newfoundland and issued the Atlantic Charter, on August 14, 1941, in which they declared for the freedom of the seas, equality of access to economic opportunity, abandonment of aggression, and the restoration of rights to conquered peoples. The Atlantic Charter has been attacked as no more than another empty assertion of impossible ideals, but the true realist sees in it an important step in rallying world opinion against the Axis. Later, formal conferences —between Roosevelt and Churchill at Casablanca (January, 1943) and Quebec (August, 1943), and among the "Big Three" at

Teheran (December, 1943) and Yalta (February, 1945)—brought to a head consultations that had been steadily carried on at lower political and military levels. From July 17 to August 17, 1945, a final great conference at Potsdam near conquered Berlin brought Britain, Russia, and the United States, with two new figures, President Truman and Prime Minister Attlee, together to confirm in general the Yalta decisions.

There were always grave military and political matters to be ironed out. It was not easy to maintain even the Anglo-American collaboration, which was perhaps the closest military collaboration between two major sovereign powers ever achieved. For the actual direction of operations in the field, the British and Americans decided to set up, not just the sort of supreme command the Allies painfully achieved late in World War I under Foch (see p. 390), but a complete intermeshing of staffs. All down the line, an American in command always had a Britisher as his second, and a Britisher in command always had an American as his second. In the pinch, and in spite of normal national jealousies, the arrangement worked. An anecdote about General Eisenhower from North African days relates that he sent an American officer home, not because he called his immediate superior a so-and-so, but because he called him an *English* so-and-so. At the highest level, the Combined Chiefs of Staff, in close touch with top American and British government officials, did the over-all planning. The Russians were never brought into such close military co-operation, and in the field the Russians always fought on their own.

Political Issues

A political issue that bulked large at the time with liberals seems not to have seriously divided the Allies during the war itself. This is the issue of "unconditional surrender." Here recent history had an overpowering influence on the policy adopted. Hitler had simply followed widespread German opinion in insisting that in World War I Germany had not really been defeated in the field, but had been betrayed by the false promises of Wilson's Fourteen Points into surrendering while still undefeated. This time the Allied leaders were determined to give the Germans no excuse for a future rallying point of this sort. The Germans must be beaten unmistakably, and Allied troops must enter Berlin as conquerors. There must be no political negotiation at all, simply unconditional military surrender. There was some opposition to this policy during the war, at least in lands of free political expression like Britain and the United States. This opposition rested partly on humanitarian grounds, but also on the belief that the prospect of unconditional surrender would inevitably stiffen the German will to resist, and would unite the nation behind Hitler instead of allowing Allied psychological warfare its full effect by promising anti-Nazi elements some reward for deserting the Nazi cause. In retrospect, it does not seem that Hitler would ever have negotiated with the Allies; and after the failure of the attempt to kill him with a bomb in July, 1944, there was little chance that the Germans themselves would overthrow the Nazi government.

Another political problem made a much clearer rift between the British and the Americans. The underlying issue was just how far anti-German elements in France, Italy, and other occupied lands must go in proving that they were good honest democrats in order to secure the backing of the democratic western powers. Here the difference in the underlying tone of American and British policies was evident in the views of Roosevelt and Churchill. Roosevelt was convinced that if the Allies did not interfere to support scheming conservatives and reactionaries in the occupied lands, but instead allowed their peoples to choose their form of government freely, then they would choose democracy. Churchill was much less idealistic. He was eager to use any elements that were hostile to the Germans, even if their hostility was quite recent, and he had little faith in the capacity or desire of peoples like the Italians for Anglo-Saxon democracy. Therefore he was quite willing to back Badoglio and the monarchists in Italy; Roosevelt kept insisting that the Italians wanted and needed a republic, yet the opposition was not a clear one between American support of democratic or Leftist elements and British support of conservative, monarchist, Rightist elements. We were hard on Badoglio and soft on Vichy; the British were hard on Vichy, soft on Badoglio.

In French politics the issue was further complicated by Roosevelt's suspicions of de Gaulle, whose firm resistance in June, 1940, had made him the inevitable leader of the French movement for liberation. To Roosevelt, de Gaulle seemed a potential man on horseback, no better than Boulanger or Napoleon III. To Churchill, de Gaulle seemed indeed difficult, a man obsessed with the need to restore the greatness of France, but an indispensable ally. As it turned out, the Gaullists, in collaboration with the organized French resistance in the homeland, did take over the civilian administration of French territory as it was liberated, and France by free popular vote restored in the Fourth Republic a form of government essentially like that of the Third. In Italy, the liberated people voted the establishment of a republic. What had threatened at one time to be a serious difficulty between American policy and British policy was resolved by the action of the liberated people themselves.

But the political issue that has bulked largest since World War II was by no means so clear an issue during the war itself. This is the problem of Russian domination in eastern and southeastern Europe. It is easy to say that at Yalta the western powers took much too soft a line with the Russians, allowed them to push their armies much too far westward, and relied foolishly on Russian promises to permit free elections in Poland, Hungary, Czechoslovakia, and the Balkans. This criticism may be supplemented by the old British motif of the "soft under-belly," by maintaining that the western powers should have struck as soon as possible, perhaps in 1943, from the Mediterranean into the Danube Valley in order to have arrived there ahead of the Russians. Proponents of these criticisms present us with an Iron Curtain that would then have been drawn far to the east of where it now is, with an eastern and a southeastern Europe that would now be democratic and on the side of the West rather than on the side of the Russians.

The chief trouble with this argument is that it fails to take into account two basic facts. First, most of the small eastern European countries had no real tradition of western-style democracy; most of them had moved toward fascist totalitarianism before World War II (see Chapter XXVII). Second, during the war itself it was by no means clear to western leaders, or to western public opinion, that the Germans and the Japanese would be beaten so readily. Even leaders like Churchill, who seems never really to have trusted the Russians and who was to coin the phrase "the Iron Curtain" soon after the war, did not dare risk losing the aid of Russian manpower and material resources during the war itself. Even in 1945, at Yalta, with Japan still very much in the fight, appeasement of the Russians seemed absolutely essential, not only to Roosevelt, who hoped the Russians would collaborate with us in the post-war world, but also to Churchill who seems to have had little hope of such collaboration from the Russians.

In the Far East, political problems seemed less serious—at least in wartime. There was general agreement that the Chinese Nationalists, however corrupt and inefficient their government was, had to be supported against the Japanese. Nor did the final decision to accept the continuance on the throne of the Japanese emperor arouse serious opposition in the West. The critical decisions on the Far East were rather the work of the troubled period after V-E and V-J days, when to the bitter disappointment of most western peoples it became clear that the peace was likely for some time to be no more than a continuation of war. Indeed, there was no peace, and these years deserve a term that was soon coined, the years of "cold war." The once "colonial" peoples throughout the world were now roused against "imperialism."

In sum, as we all know now, and as we shall see in more detail in the next three chapters, the great war of 1939-1945 ended indeed, but there was no peace. From our own western point of view, and in plain language, the defeat of the perturbers, the aggressors, the villains, Germany and Japan, was *almost immediately* followed by the rise of a new perturber, a new villain, Russia, which had already given clear indications of its perturbing power. And indeed, it is easy to go on to the conclusion that just because the Germans and Japanese were beaten in the way they actually were,

the present menace of Russia—pretty clearly a greater menace than the old German menace—was helped, was in fact made possible, by that defeat; from there it is a fatally easy step to the dangerous conclusion that Russia, not Germany, was our enemy all along.

Yet the wise student of history will not readily jump to the conclusion that any other Allied policy, and in particular a different American policy at Yalta and Potsdam, could have either prevented the rise of Russia, or produced a virtuous, cooperative, democratic Russia. We are still far too close to World War II to understand its many ramifications. The historian who sticks to his last can do no more than conclude that in the perspective of modern western history the sorely tried western statesmen at Yalta and Potsdam, in the midst of a hot war, were using time-honored methods to win that war as quickly and as decisively as possible: and in particular, with the long record of failures of coalitions in the past before them, they were determined to hold together their extraordinary and by no means "natural" coalition, known hopefully as the United Nations, until *both* the mainstay powers of the Axis coalition were beaten. This they did.

Reading Suggestions
on the Second World War

(Asterisk indicates paperbound edition.)

GENERAL ACCOUNTS

W. S. Churchill, *The Second World War*, 6 vols. (Houghton Mifflin, 1948-1953). Magisterial account by a chief architect of Allied victory; the first volume reviews international affairs between the wars.

Q. Howe, *A World History of Our Own Times, Vol. II* (Simon & Schuster, 1953). Survey by a capable and opinionated American publicist.

E. H. Carr, *The Twenty Years' Crisis* (Macmillan, 1946). A stimulating review of inter-war diplomacy by a capable and opinionated Englishman.

J. F. C. Fuller, *The Second World War* (Duell, Sloane, and Pearce, 1949), and C. Falls, *The Second World War*, 2nd ed. (Methuen, 1948). Two succinct and very useful military accounts. Both are written from a British viewpoint.

F. Pratt, *War for the World: A Chronicle of our Fighting Forces in World War II* (Yale Univ. Press, 1950). A good succinct American account.

United States Army in World War II (Dept. of the Army, 1947–). The official history, in many detailed volumes, to be found in library catalogues under the general title above, or under "United States: Department of the Army."

S. E. Morison, *History of United States Naval Operations in World War II* (Little, Brown, 1947–). Twelve volumes have appeared, and the set will soon be completed. Official but detached and professional history, with full attention to political and diplomatic problems, and to the work of other branches of the armed forces.

C. Wilmot, *The Struggle for Europe* (Harper, 1952). Highly controversial study, critical of the American high command.

SPECIAL STUDIES

F. Gilbert and G. A. Craig, eds., *The Diplomats, 1919-1939* (Princeton Univ. Press, 1953). A helpful symposium.

A. Wolfers, *Britain and France between Two Wars* (Harcourt, Brace, 1940). A solid analysis of the foreign policies of the two powers.

S. R. Smith, *The Manchurian Crisis, 1931-1932* (Columbia Univ. Press, 1948). Monograph on the crisis that marked the watershed between the post-war and the pre-war periods.

J. W. Wheeler-Bennett, *Munich: Prologue to Tragedy* (Macmillan, 1948), and L. B. Namier, *Diplomatic Prelude, 1938-1939* (Macmillan, 1948). Good studies of the last international crises before World War II.

W. L. Langer and S. E. Gleason, *The Challenge to Isolation, 1937-1940* (Harper, 1952), and *The Undeclared War, 1940-1941* (Harper, 1953). Solid studies of America's role.

C. C. Tansill, *Back Door to War: The Roosevelt Foreign Policy* (Regnery, 1952). Representative work of the "new revisionists," a school of writers who castigate Roosevelt for allegedly pushing America into war.

H. F. Armstrong, *Chronology of Failure* (Macmillan, 1940); "Pertinax" (André Géraud), *The Gravediggers of France* (Doubleday, 1944); M. Bloch, *Strange Defeat* (Oxford Univ. Press, 1949). Three perceptive studies of the French defeat in 1940.

A. J. Liebling, ed., *The Republic of Silence* (Harcourt, Brace, 1947). Excellent collection of materials pertaining to the French resistance movement.

A. Weber, *Farewell to European History; or, the Conquest of Nihilism* (Kegan Paul, Trench, Trubner, 1947). A German sociologist reviews—and regrets—his country's part in the crises of World War II.

D. L. Gordon and R. Dangerfield, *The Hidden Weapon: The Story of Economic Warfare* (Harper, 1947). A very good popular account by trained experts.

H. Feis, *Churchill, Roosevelt, Stalin* (Princeton Univ. Press, 1957). A fascinating and very fair-minded account of the relations among these three leaders during the war.

There are already many memoirs from the great actors in this war. Two essential contrasting ones are D. D. Eisenhower, *Crusade in Europe* (Doubleday, 1948) and B. L. Montgomery, first Viscount Montgomery, *Memoirs* (World, 1958).

N. Mailer, *The Naked and the Dead* (*Bantam, 1954); I. Shaw, *The Young Lions* (*New American Library). Characteristic examples of the American novel of World War II.

H. P. M. Brown, *A Walk in the Sun* (Knopf, 1944; *New American Library). Unusually good novel about the Italian campaign.

N. Monsarrat, *The Cruel Sea* (*Pocket Books); H. Wouk, *The Caine Mutiny* (Doubleday). Two justly popular novels about the naval aspects of World War II.

A. J. Guérard, *Maquisard* (Longmans, Green, 1948). Good novel about the French resistance.

Fitzroy Maclean, *Escape to Adventure* (Little, Brown, 1950). Not fiction, but true adventure; an antidote to Mailer's book above.

CHAPTER XXIX

The West
and Russia
in the
Contemporary
World

CHAPTER XXX

I: The "Cold War"
—The International
Aftermath

THE FRENCH still call their national history since 1789 "contemporary
history." Behind this usage, which must
seem strange to an American, there lies a
principle valid for us: the French feel that
the great issues, the great problems, stemming from the events of 1789 have still not
received even the compromises, the partial
solutions, we expect here on earth for such
problems. If the term "contemporary" be
so understood, it is clear that events all
over the world since 1945 must be considered "contemporary history"—and indeed are likely to have to be so considered for some time. For in international
politics alone, the rivalry between coalitions led respectively by the United States
and the Soviet Union, which we noted
briefly at the end of Chapter XXIX, and
the revolt of former "colonial" or otherwise
dependent peoples we shall study in Chapter XXXI, are still very critical problems,
still apparently far from the kind of solution that enables the historian to set up a
landmark, an end of a period. We must
now trace further the history of international politics since 1945, a history that

577

is dominated by the rivalry of the United States and Soviet Russia, a history that, just because it is so very "contemporary," just because we are all so immersed in it, cannot be treated with the completeness, the relative accuracy, the objectivity, the historian strives for.

The Aftermath of War

By now the reader will realize that the great ills of general war take many years to clear up, that they are never neatly cured by a formal peace. As we have seen in earlier chapters, it took a long time to repair the damage done to European nations by World War I. In France, for instance, the human losses were so great that full recovery was impossible. The total damage of World War II greatly exceeded that of the earlier war because of its far-flung battlegrounds, the mass executions in Nazi concentration camps, the casualties suffered by civilians through air attacks, starvation, and disease. The total number of human deaths resulting from the war has been estimated at 22,000,000, more than half of them civilians, a total at least double that of World War I. It should, however, be noted that if the deaths from the epidemic or pandemic of influenza among civilians in 1918 are counted as part of the casualties of World War I, the total human losses in the two wars are much more nearly equal, were indeed probably somewhat *greater* in the First than in the Second World War. No major epidemic accompanied World War II; and even in theaters of war of relatively primitive sanitation, new medical knowledge kept deaths from disease at a low figure. Material damages to property, however, have for the Second World War been estimated in excess of $2,000,000,000,000 (two thousand billion), many times that for the First. These tragic losses cannot in our time be fully repaired. But they were at least offset in many countries during the decade following 1945 by a high birth rate and by brisk programs of economic reconstruction and modernization. Our world of the 1960's is materially richer than it was in 1939.

Of all the problems created by modern wars, perhaps the knottiest is that of reconstructing international politics. As we shall see, after 1945 a widespread revolution swept the colonies and dependencies of the European states. Imperial ties were severed or loosened, and new independent states appeared in many areas formerly under western control. In the world as a whole, a new international alignment developed after the defeat of the Axis aggressors. The rival states of the United States and Soviet Russia faced each other in a struggle that has been called the "cold war."

Since 1945 there has been a series of crises in almost all parts of the world, save for Russia and the United States themselves, in which these two powers have taken opposite sides. The list is formidable: Greece, Trieste, Berlin, Korea, Indo-China, Suez (indeed the Middle East generally and chronically), and others of less note (see Chapter XXXI). Moreover, in countries like France and Italy communist and other political parties openly pro-Russian struggle with openly pro-American parties; in other parts of the world, notably in Latin America, proscribed communist groups intrigue in the interest of Moscow; in the great forum of the United Nations, the United States and Russia are almost constantly on opposite sides of the debate.

New Elements and Old

New elements entered into the postwar situation. Atomic and hydrogen bombs, guided missiles, the very real possibility of bacteriological warfare and other horrible weapons for the first time made concrete and plausible the threat that a new general war might wipe out the human race— or at the very least might destroy the physical and the moral bases of civilization, and reduce what is left of mankind to something like another Stone Age. This amounts to the statement that the age-old balance between attack and defense, and, more important, between human ability to destroy and human ability to build and repair, has in fact been so altered that attack and destruction will be paramount. The experts in physics and allied fields are by no means in agreement as to whether the new weapons, if used without restriction, would set up such lethal reactions—from, for instance, radiation—that human life on earth would be wiped out. The experts in human relations are in even less agreement as to the likelihood that such weapons will actually be used without restriction. Fear of total collapse of our civilization is undoubtedly widespread, especially among the kind of people known as "intellectuals," vocal people who can and do express this fear. How far such fear spreads among the many in our world we do not clearly know. At any rate, there has so far been no collective despair strong enough to turn the many away from work and play. Ours is still a remarkably productive material civilization.

Further, the existence of only one system of states related in international politics—the actuality of One World—was new. Ever since Columbus, civilization had been building up to this One World, and after 1945 what had once been rhetoric became fact. There were still out-of-the-way pockets on the earth where the inhabitants had no direct concern with international politics, but by and large all organized political units were either in the western camp or in the Russian, or else they were wavering between the two.

The actual leaders of the rival camps were new to that position. In the world wars of Napoleon and the Kaiser, Britain and either France or Germany had been the centers of the opposing groups. Now the United States and Russia became the unquestioned focal points of world power. Although Russia had been an important element in international politics since Peter the Great, and although the United States had been active in international politics in spite of strong isolationist theories ever since it had been founded, neither state assumed international leadership until the 1940's.

But it is a grave mistake to simplify the situation, as some publicists do, into one where only the United States and Russia count as superpowers, and where all the rest of the world can be neglected. Great as these two states are in manpower and in production, actual and potential, the two together have no more than an eighth of the total population of the globe. And, although, thanks especially to the extraordinary productive capacity of the United States, the two together have a much greater proportion of the world's present productive capacity, they still have less than the potential of the rest of the world combined. Neither state is, in fact, materially autarkic, self-sufficient. The leaders of both have shown by their actions that they do not regard their rivalry as a simple duel of rival autarkic units, but rather as a competition for the active allegiance of the rest of the world. Each is in fact the head of a great coalition, which each has sought to extend, or at least strengthen. And neither coalition is a perfect monolithic block; members of each coalition can and do try to go their own way.

Indeed, if their rivalry breaks into a general war, that war will probably be decided in favor of the side that does win the allegiance of the strongest combination of countries. In short, any such war will be a war of coalitions. In a sense, then, the future of the world depends on whether those who are neither Russian nor American can decide that the Soviet Union or the United States is in fact the aggressor. The present rivalry between these two states is indeed a rivalry for the heart and soul of mankind.

This kind of rivalry, we repeat, is not

new. It has in its current form, however, a depth and intensity attributable to a new combination of elements. Eighteenth-century wars, for instance, were largely struggles for sheer power, sheer territorial and other material gains, with perhaps a touch of emotional nationalism among the politically conscious as an added incentive. With the wars of the French Revolution and the nineteenth century, nationalism entered in more forcefully, spread to all classes, and remains, along with the struggle for power, a major element in the present situation. But the present struggle between the United States and Russia seems even more deep-seated than the nationalist wars of old. It is a struggle to make prevail over this earth one way of life, one set of ideals and basic beliefs, to the exclusion of the other. This profound struggle, we must note, is underestimated and vulgarized if it is called a struggle over "ideologies."

To sum up: there are both in Russia and in the United States, and among the peoples lined up with each, many who feel strongly that at least *in the long run* Russian communism and western democracy cannot as actual going societies live together on this earth. The historian will not by any means conclude from this analysis that war between the two coalitions is inevitable; he must conclude that adjustments between the two systems will be difficult to make, that something like an "armed truce" or a "cold war" is likely to last for some time, and that the threat of a World War III is by no means unreal, by no means the work of neurotic alarmists.

The Communist Bloc in Europe

Concretely, the years following the end of the war in Germany and Japan saw the alignment of most of the world either on Russia's side or on that of the United States. After Yalta and Potsdam (see Chapter XXIX), the Russians disregarded what western statesmen believed were firm commitments to allow the countries of eastern Europe and the Balkans to choose freely their own form of government—and presumably to align themselves with the West if they wished.

Violating the peace treaties reached in 1946 with Hungary, Rumania, and Bulgaria, and relying everywhere in eastern Europe on Soviet troops, the Russians built up, by familiar methods of one-party politics, with rigged elections, proscriptions, pressures of all sorts, the solid bloc of satellite lands known as the Iron Curtain countries. Beginning early in World War II, the Russians simply absorbed, as constituent republics of the U.S.S.R., part of Finland, the whole of Estonia, Latvia, and Lithuania, and parts of Poland and Rumania as well as the extreme eastern end of old Czechoslovakia. At the close of the war, they annexed part of East Prussia, so that Königsberg, sacred to Germans as the home of the great philosopher Kant, was now Kaliningrad, renamed for a high Soviet official. In eastern and southeastern Europe they organized "people's republics," dependent states with communist governments, in Poland, Czechoslovakia, Rumania, Hungary, Bulgaria, and Albania.

Their troops formally occupied about one-third of Germany, roughly between the Elbe and the Oder rivers, where they also organized a satellite East German Republic. The parts of Germany lying east of the Oder, save for the sections of East Prussia directly annexed to the U.S.S.R., they handed over to their Polish satellite. Here a wholesale transfer of population removed the Germans into either East Germany or exile, and replaced the Germans with Poles. Finland became part of the Russian security system, but has subsequently enjoyed distinctly more autonomy than the satellites and has retained its prewar political institutions. Austria, divided between the occupying forces of East and

West, was detached from Germany, and Hitler's first major territorial gain, the *Anschluss*, was undone. Berlin, to the east of the dividing line between the Soviet and the Allied zones in Germany, was occupied in separate zones by Russia, the United States, Great Britain, and France, but was left completely surrounded by the territory of the Soviet-dominated East German state. No peace treaty could be reached with Germany or Austria.

Around the periphery of this newly built satellite empire, the Russians conducted probing operations against those areas not yet in their power. One of the most serious came in Greece, where, during World War II, a communist-dominated guerrilla movement had already once attempted to seize control, and had been thwarted only by British troops and Winston Churchill's determination not to allow Greece to go communist. In 1946, the Greek communists tried again, backed this time by the Soviet-dominated governments of their northern Balkan neighbors. Simultaneously, Stalin exerted pressure on the Turks to gain concessions in the Straits area. Now President Truman proclaimed that countries feeling the threat of communist aggression could count on help from the United States. Under this "Truman doctrine," he sent American military aid to Greece and Turkey. The threat to the Turks evaporated, and by 1949, after severe fighting, the Greeks had put down the communist rebellion.

In Germany, the lack of any western-controlled connection between Berlin and West Germany was serious; for here, on April 1, 1948, the Russians began one of the most bitter phases of the "cold war." By shutting off the land routes from the west into Berlin, they attempted to force the western Allies to turn Berlin wholly over to them. The Allies stood firm, however, and achieved the almost incredible feat of supplying a great metropolitan area wholly by air. In the six months of the blockade, Allied aircraft flew over 2,300,000 tons of coal, food, and other necessities into western Berlin. They also set up their own counterblockade of Russian-occupied eastern Berlin. On September 1, the Russians gave up, and Berlin returned to its sufficiently abnormal status of joint occupation. But Soviet determination to oust the western powers from Berlin remained unaltered, and would be reiterated in 1958 (see below, p. 613).

Just as Tsarist Russian governments, when balked in Europe, had turned to Asia for political and military adventure, the Soviet Union, during the years immediately following the failure of operations in Greece and Germany, kept the pressure on the West by acting through its allies, the newly victorious Chinese communists, whose activities in Korea, Vietnam, Tibet, and elsewhere we shall shortly note (see below, p. 614, and Chapter XXXI).

Yugoslavia

But, in addition to their defeats in Greece and Berlin, the Russians found themselves, in 1948, faced with rebellion from a country that had seemed the most loyal of all their newly acquired European satellites; and this rebellion, Stalin felt, threatened their whole European position. Yugoslavia, which had overthrown a pro-German government in 1941, had remained throughout World War II a theatre of intense guerrilla action against the Germans and Italians. There were two main groups of guerrillas, the Chetniks, led by General Mikhailovich, representing the conservative Serb domination over the south Slav kingdom, and the Partisans, led by Joseph Broz, better known by his underground communist nickname, Tito. As the war continued, the communist-dominated Partisans gained ground against the Chetniks, who seem to have preferred to compromise with the German and Italian occupying forces

EUROPE, 1960

	NATO countries { North Atlantic Treaty Organization
	Communist bloc
◎	Capital cities

Map labels:

Reykjavik, Keflavik, ICELAND
Norwegian Sea
Narvik, Bodo, NORWAY, SWEDEN
Trondheim, Bergen, Oslo, Stockholm, Göteborg
FAEROE IS. (Den.)
SHETLAND IS.
Skagerrak, Baltic
DENMARK, Copenhagen, Gdansk (Danzig), Szczecin
Inverness, SCOTLAND, Edinburgh
UNITED KINGDOM, N. IRELAND
North Sea
Belfast, IRELAND, Dublin, Limerick
Liverpool, WALES, ENGLAND, London, Southampton
NETHER-LANDS, The Hague, Amsterdam
Hamburg, Bremen, Berlin (JOINT OCC.)
GERMAN FEDERAL REPUBLIC (WEST GERMANY)
GERMAN DEMOCRATIC REPUBLIC (EAST GERMANY)
Wroclaw, SILESIA, PO-
Bonn, Frankfurt, Prague, CZECHOSL-
CHANNEL IS. (Br.)
Cherbourg, Brest, Nantes
Brussels, BELGIUM, LUX., SAAR, Nancy, Paris
Seine R., Rhine R., Danube R.
Munich, Linz, Vienna, AUSTRIA, HU-
FRANCE, Loire R., Geneva, Lyon, Bern, SWITZ.
Bay of Biscay, Bordeaux, Bayonne, Garonne, Toulouse
Rhône R., Turin, Milano, Venice, Trieste, Zagreb, YUGO
Nice, RIVIERA, Genoa, Po R., Adriatic, Split
Oporto, ANDORRA, Marseille, Florence, ITALY
Lisbon, PORTUGAL, Ebro R., Madrid, SPAIN, Barcelona
CORSICA (Fr.), Rome, Bari
Tagus R., Valencia, BALEARIC IS., SARDINIA, Naples, CAPRI
Guadalquivir R., Granada
Cadiz, Gibraltar (Br.)
Palermo, Bizerte, SICILY, MT. ETNA, Catania
Casablanca, Rabat, MOROCCO, Oran, Algiers, ALGERIA, Tunis, TUNISIA, MALTA (Br.)
Mediterranean
IFNI (Sp.)
SAHARAN PROVS.
Tripoli
LIBYA

Atlantic Ocean

40, 30, 20, 10, 0, 10
60, 50, 40, 30, 20, 10

rather than continue a war in alliance with communists. By 1943, Britain and the United States, with their eyes fixed on the paramount need to beat Hitler, decided to support Tito with supplies. When the Russians entered Belgrade in October 1944, they helped put their fellow-communist Tito in control.

Once in power, Tito installed his own communist government, abolished the Yugoslav monarchy, and aped his Soviet masters in all his policies more faithfully than any of the Russians' other subordinates in satellite Europe. Yet in June, 1948, the world learned with surprise that the U.S.S.R. had quarreled with Yugoslavia, and expelled Tito's régime from the propaganda union of communist parties known as the Cominform (Communist Information Bureau), successor to the Comintern (see above, p. 450). The Soviet satellites swung into line. They broke their economic agreements with Yugoslavia, unloosed great barrages of anti-Tito propaganda, and stirred up border incidents. The Yugoslavs published the secret correspondence with Moscow that had led to the break, from which we learn that Soviet arrogance and insistence on penetrating the Yugoslav army and security organizations had aroused Yugoslav national feeling, never very far below the surface. Stalin, for his part, suffered from the misapprehension that he could bully the Yugoslavs into submission. "I will shake my little finger," he said, "and there will be no more Tito."

But Tito remained in power, accepting the aid that was quickly offered him by the United States. Washington saw that a communist régime hostile to Stalin was a new phenomenon that could not help embarrassing the Russians. Gradually Yugoslav communism evolved a modified ideology of its own, declaring that Stalin was a heretic and Tito and his followers the only true Leninists. Tito decentralized the economy, beginning in the factories, where workers' committees now began to participate actively in the planning. From the economy, decentralization spread to the local government apparatus, then to the central government, and finally to the Yugoslav Communist Party, now rechristened "League of Yugoslav Communists." Though the régime admitted its past outrageous excesses, the police continued to be a powerful force. Tito gradually abandoned agricultural collectivization, which, as always, was most unpopular with the peasants.

The Yugoslav régime, however, remained a communist régime, suspicious of the western capitalists who were helping it, and including men who hoped for an eventual reconciliation with the U.S.S.R. So long as Stalin lived, that proved impossible. In their fear of the spread of the new "national" communism to the other satellites,

Tito (extreme right), wartime leader of Yugoslav partisans, at his mountain headquarters.

the Soviets directed the other east-European régimes in a series of ferocious purges, executing leading communists for "Titoism," and thus terrorizing anyone who might hope to establish any sort of autonomy within the communist bloc. When Stalin died in 1953, his heirs gave high priority to healing the breach with Yugoslavia, and eliminating the weakness it had created in their European position (see below, p. 612).

China

To the east, China with its half-billion inhabitants emerged in 1949 as an ally of Russia (for details, see Chapter XXXI). Inevitably, this turn of events aroused great bitterness in the United States. The bitterness was expressed not only in the refusal of the United States to recognize Communist China, but also in the reproach that the American government, and particularly the Department of State, had so bungled relations with China that the Reds won by default—if not by the positive encouragement of fellow-traveling Americans.

These events are so recent that it is foolish to hope that they can be judged with detachment. But this much can be affirmed: once the negotiations of the American General Marshall for a Communist-Nationalist understanding had failed after the close of World War II, the Chinese Nationalist government could have been maintained on the mainland of China only by all-out American support, including almost certainly the use of American troops. It is most unlikely that in 1948-49 any American government would have felt it had the support of American public opinion in committing the country to an active war in China.

Since then, however, the United States has supported with her navy and with economic aid the Chinese Nationalist government on the island of Formosa, retroceded to China by Japan, which had seized it in 1895. The Formosa government, benefiting from American naval support, was able to hold on to some small islands, the Quemoy group, only a few miles from the communist-controlled mainland. The communist government has from time to time shelled these islands with conventional artillery, chiefly to keep the world reminded of their determination to do away with what they consider the anomaly of the Formosa government's pretensions to be China's real, legitimate government. Important currents of opinion among our European allies and among liberals in this country oppose the American policy of supporting the government of Chiang Kai-shek on Formosa, but so far we have held to our policy under both Democratic and Republican administrations. The United States has also successfully opposed all efforts to gain for Communist China admission to the United Nations, where in 1960 the seat for China was still held by the Formosa government.

The "Free World"

After World War II, the United States assumed the leadership of the "free world," the coalition opposed to the great Russian coalition. On this western side are Great Britain and the Commonwealth of Nations (which includes India and Pakistan), France and the French Community, western Europe generally, West Germany, Greece, Turkey, parts of the Middle East, Latin America, and the recent enemy Japan. In organized productive activity, in potential material resources, even, thanks to the inclusion of the Indian subcontinent, in actual population, this coalition is stronger than the Russian bloc. Even in geopolitical terms, though the solid land mass of the communists may at first glance seem to have the advantage over the scattered lands of the free world, modern sea and air power has helped to knit the free world together in a military sense.

Soon after 1945 the United States took the lead in developing measures to strengthen the non-communist states, particularly in Europe, against possible communist aggression from without or subversion from within. Notably, in 1947 America sponsored the Marshall Plan (named for the Secretary of State, General Marshall) to accelerate economic recovery from the damage and disruption of World War II and thus to rectify conditions on which communists might otherwise have thrived. In 1949, the United States sponsored the North Atlantic Treaty Organization, "NATO," a defensive alliance including not only the states on the European and American shores of the North Atlantic but also Iceland, Italy, Greece, and Turkey.

The central problem of the free world since 1945, however, has been not so much military as political: whether the free world really is united against the communist bloc, whether it has the political and moral resources to hold together. The "free world" is by no means uniformly free. Doctrinaire liberals in the West complain that some of the states lined up with them —Franco's Spain, Portugal under the milder dictatorship of Salazar, Pakistan—are totalitarian and anti-democratic; that the Argentine Republic, though no longer under Perón, is still, as are some other Latin-American countries, a semi-dictatorship, and a military one at that; that throughout the Middle East it is not the miserably oppressed people, but only the exploiting members of the upper classes who support the West; that in parts of Africa America's allies, the British, French, Portuguese, still hold some Negroes in colonial subjection; that semi-feudal Ethiopia is a caricature of a free country. To this liberal indictment the candid observer has to reply that it is in part true. If he is content to take a simple realistic position, the observer can remark that in an international crisis like the "cold war" the enemy of your enemy is in fact your friend. The important thing is that Franco, Salazar, Trujillo, and other surviving dictators are at least bitterly opposed to the communists.

This brings us to another central aspect of the problem of international relations since World War II. The war thrust the United States into a position of leadership. How well equipped has she shown herself for that position? Events since 1945 have shown that Americans lack the kind of experience that peoples like the Romans and the British acquired over the long years of their leadership. Americans are idealistic, impatient, anxious for quick results; they could learn much wisdom from the old French proverb—"The best is often the enemy of the good." But events have also shown the assets of Americans. Though they have continued to have difficulty with the color line in the United States, they have also done much since World War II toward ending the segregation of Negroes in schooling, in the armed services, and elsewhere. In relations with peoples of darker skin overseas, further, the Americans seem to be a trifle less overbearing than their British predecessors, even though many of our GI's did call all Koreans "gooks." They are not, like the Germans, burdened with a belief in crude racist theories. Though they find it hard to understand the religious views of people like the Hindus, for instance, they are used to the practice of religious toleration.

The democratic coalition led by the United States of course has been subject to nationalistic stresses and strains—the pride, the economic interests, the long traditions that make Englishmen or Frenchmen or Germans or Luxemburgers want some things that other members of the coalition do not want. But we have already seen that the Russian bloc suffers from comparable stresses. Communist difficulties, however, cannot really come out into the open, save for such an exceptional instance as the break between Tito and Stalin, or in actual rebellion, as in East Germany in 1953 or Hungary in 1956 (see below, pp. 612-613). Western difficulties can and do come out steadily into the open.

In most of the free world it is possible for ordinary interested citizens to consider in public, in the schools, in the press, in political meetings, the problems that confront them. They can attempt to assess their weaknesses objectively, in the firm democratic conviction that they can understand and overcome these weaknesses. This, it is clear, the communists, even after the relaxation of controls following Stalin's death, cannot do. Rigorously controlled from above, they cannot learn the truth about the West—or about themselves. The experience of two world wars has shown that, in spite of the inconvenience and dangers of such openness of disagreement, in the long run full and fair discussion leads to better results than does suppression. This freedom of the free world is an asset, not a liability.

Old international tensions and disputes involving free nations have been settled, or at least eased, by difficult and sometimes painful negotiations. For one example, in 1954 the Italian Republic and Tito's Yugoslavia agreed to partition the area of Trieste, so long disputed between Italians and Yugoslavs. Another strategic and hotly disputed territory had its status defined in 1956. This was the Saar (see Chapter XXV). At the close of World War II, the French had occupied—and hoped to annex—this important coal-mining area lying on their northeastern frontier, even though its population was largely German. West Germany disliked this prospect, and in 1956, after prolonged negotiations, and after it had become clear that the Saarlanders wanted to return to Germany, the French agreed to hand back the Saar. This Saar settlement marked a step toward the easing of traditional Franco-German bitterness, a bitterness that had only recently been exacerbated by the brutal Nazi conquest of France.

In some ways, however, the West is handicapped by the fact that the Russians have a new, aggressive, revolutionary faith with special appeal to underdog groups everywhere. They have something of the proselyting strength that helped Napoleon as the heir of the great French Revolution. They can and do promise the downtrodden something new. All this need not mean that the West should be driven into a kind of conservative defensiveness, like Metternich after 1815 or the western democracies after 1918. It does mean that the western nations must be constantly aware of such a danger, that they must not let themselves appear, especially in the less advanced countries of Asia and Africa, or in Latin America, to be backing up the established order at all costs, to be resisting all social and economic changes. Underdeveloped countries have applauded statements like that of President Truman in his inaugural address in 1949, when he promised backward areas help in the task of raising their standard of living. Since 1945, the western states have begun to understand that they must make their own democratic faith in reality what it has always been in ideal, a gospel of advance all along the line.

The Neutrals

We have hitherto written as though the contemporary world were *either* communist *or* democratic, at least in sympathy; and in a sense this is so. But the formula *either-or* is not quite accurate. There are neutrals in this world, though the mere fact that ardent pro-westerners have coined a new, depreciatory term for them, "neutralists," is surely significant. There are always, even in advanced countries, the politically indifferent individuals who simply don't care about politics; and in large parts of the world there are millions too poor and too ignorant to be able to share political emotions. But among the politically conscious, we may distinguish two groups of neutrals. First, in France, England, and indeed throughout the free western world, there are those who refuse to line up either with the United States or with Russia. They are not by any means all motivated in the same way. Some are idealist intellectuals, often old-fashioned socialists, who feel, like Mercutio in *Romeo and Juliet,* "a plague o' both your houses"; for them, both the United States and the Soviet Union are on a bad track, both expansionists, both vulgar materialists. Of these "alienated" intellectuals we shall have more to say in Chapter XXXII. Others are men who remember when France, or Britain, or Germany was a first-rate power. They cannot bring themselves to accept leadership from either the United States or Russia; they still hope to bring back leadership to *their* nation. But so far, these neutrals have not swung the balance away from the western bloc in Europe or in Latin America.

The other group of neutrals seems now a much more important force in the world. They are centered in the world of non-European stock, and in that world they are centered in India. Indeed in the Indian leader Nehru the neutrals have a figure who in the 1950's attained world stature. To the leaders of western policy, Nehru has often seemed an enemy, a difficult, prideful man, who is really playing the Russian game. Yet it is not impossible that in the future historians may record that Nehru was after all "neutral" on our side. Meanwhile, we can but note that in India, and to a degree throughout the non-European world, there are many who refuse to line themselves up either with Russia or with the United States.

The United Nations

In spite of the open clash between communists and the free world in Korea,

in spite of semi-open or guerrilla warfare elsewhere in the East, in spite of the Iron Curtain, there has existed since World War II an international organization in which both communist and non-communist countries meet in at least nominally peaceful discussion. This is the United Nations. Formed of active opponents of the Axis during World War II, the United Nations (hopefully, perhaps significantly, in the singular) was broadened and endowed with a charter in a great general meeting in San Francisco in 1945. By 1950, it had sixty member-nations, including Russia (with extra votes, for the Ukrainian and White Russian republics of the U.S.S.R.), the Soviet satellites of Poland and Czechoslovakia, and the maverick communist state of Yugoslavia. The former enemy nations were denied entrance at that time, as were Rumania, Bulgaria, Albania, Spain, and

Premier Nehru at an All-India Congress party meeting.

The U.N. Security Council in session.

Ireland, since either American or Russian opposition prevented their admission.

In 1955, however, a most complex bit of maneuvering occurred in which countries like Canada took an important part, thus proving that the U.S.A. and the U.S.S.R. did not monopolize international politics. This resulted in the admission of sixteen new members to the United Nations, raising the total membership to seventy-six. Some of the new members were clearly sympathetic with the western bloc—Austria, Ireland, Italy, Portugal, and Spain; some were Russian satellites—Albania, Bulgaria, Hungary, Rumania; and others, many of them former imperial wards of the West, generally belonged to the ranks of the neutrals—Ceylon, Jordan, Libya, Nepal, Finland, and two components of old French Indo-China, Cambodia and Laos. This membership "deal" was a typical compromise not wholly satisfactory either to the United States or to Russia. Japan was finally admitted in 1956. Ghana, the former British colony of the Gold Coast in Africa, was admitted in 1957 after it became an independent state within the Commonwealth. As former "colonial" states become independent they will almost certainly be admitted to the United Nations, which at the beginning of 1960 had 81 members.

The United Nations is the direct successor of the League of Nations, and its structure is almost the same as that of the League. Like the League, the U.N. represents a conference of sovereign states, a meeting of diplomats, not a world government in any way. The U.N. has a General Assembly, which can make recommendations on many issues of international interest; here each member-state has an equal voice. And it has a Security Council to deal primarily with threats to the security of states. This council has eleven members, five of whom—Nationalist China, France, Great Britain, the U.S.S.R., and the U.S.A.—are permanent members; the other six are elected for two-year terms by the General Assembly.

The key fact about the organization of the U.N., the fact that has made it for the most part simply a great international forum, is the veto power of the permanent members of the Security Council. For all save matters of procedure, the five permanent members must be unanimous if a vote is to pass the Security Council. Thus any one of the "Big Five" has the right of absolute veto in the Council. This veto was incorporated in the charter of the U.N. primarily in deference to the U.S.A. and the U.S.S.R., both of whom sought to safeguard their independence of action and to avoid being forced by the U.N. to follow policies of which they did not approve. The veto, however, has been employed almost exclusively by Russia. The result has been to cripple the effectiveness of the Security Council, but a by-product not paralleled in the history of the League of Nations has been the increased significance of the General Assembly, which became, in the phrase of the late Senator Vandenberg, "the town meeting of the world"—but, note carefully, a town meeting that can only debate, not govern.

Like the League of Nations, the U.N. has special functional councils and agencies. The list of these agencies is very long and includes, among many others, the Trusteeship Council to supervise the remaining former mandated colonial territories, the Economic and Social Council, the International Court of Justice or "World Court," UNESCO (the U.N. Educational, Scientific, and Cultural Organization), the World Health Organization, the Food and Agriculture Organization, and the International Bank for Reconstruction and Development (the World Bank). The U.N. has its own permanent staff of civil servants, and has its headquarters in a dramatic new building on

U.N. promotes world health: disinfecting Arab refugees.

the East River in New York City. Many critics hold that this transfer of the world capital from neutral Switzerland, the home of the old League, to the greatest city of the most powerful member-state was a mistake. It gives color, they hold, to the accusation that the U.N. is simply a device to further American imperialism.

The Record of the United Nations

It is still far too early to appraise the value of the U.N. Impatient advocates of a world-state are fond of pointing out that the U.N. is no more than a diplomatic gathering, that it has no "teeth" of its own, that it had to borrow the American army in the Korean crisis, that it must be transformed into a real government with the power to act directly on individuals, not just on states. These advocates of world government make much of the parallel with the United States Articles of Confederation from 1781 to 1789, in which the thirteen states were loosely organized under a Congress that had no taxing power, no police power, and no judicial power over the member-states. They call for an international duplicate of the American Constitution of 1789, which set up a federal government with these direct powers over citizens of the United States. In 1789, however, the thirteen former colonies had a common language, common political institutions and traditions, obvious common interests of many kinds. The eighty-odd nations of the U.N. today have hardly the beginnings of such things in common. It looks as if a world government today were quite impossible unless it is to be imposed by force.

But the United Nations does exist, and its very existence is for all but the most impatient idealist a promise of something better. In its first decade of operations, the U.N. was not able to solve big problems like the "cold war" or the international control of atomic weapons. But it did arrange the partition of Palestine and keep the Israeli-Arab "little war" from becoming a major conflict (see Chapter XXXI). It did act forcefully, with United States help, against the aggression of North Korea in 1950—a single achievement quite surpassing any achievements of the League of Nations. It did put its own force in 1956 into Egypt to intervene between the Egyptians and the Israelis.

Finally—a major accomplishment of the U.N. too often overlooked—some of its special agencies have made a most promising start in aiding the underdeveloped, disease-ridden, famine-threatened countries of the globe. The World Bank gave them loans to finance basic projects like electric generating stations. The World Health Organization mobilized the medical resources of the world to nip in the bud a cholera epidemic menacing Egypt. And W.H.O. also launched campaigns to immunize European and Asian children against tuberculosis and to curb malaria in Italy, Greece, and many other lands. Experts from the Food and Agriculture Organization have gone to overcrowded states like Italy and India to advise farmers in ways to increase their output and make more food available. In these and other ways the U.N. has executed its charter's pledge "to promote social progress and better standards of living."

International Relations in Perspective

To summarize: in the long perspective of this book, and especially in the perspective of the Enlightenment of the eighteenth century, it has to be written that in the second decade after the defeat of Germany and Japan in 1945, there is not yet what men commonly have called peace. The reader will of course know that peace in 1713, or 1815, or even 1926 (after Locarno) did not mean there were no international rivalries, no armaments, no alliances, no threats of possible war. But peace did mean then at least a lessening of tension; it did mean that men could relax, could use such a phrase as the one that President Harding made famous in 1920: "back to normalcy." How far the world still is from such a relaxing of tension can be very concretely symbolized: in two great cities, Berlin and Jerusalem, barbed wires and sentry boxes set up within each city separate one section from another. In May 1960 the failure of a long-planned "summit conference" when Russia announced, and the American government confessed, that American planes flew intelligence missions over Russia, made it clear that metaphors about "living on the edge of a volcano" were not mere rhetoric. The "Berlin problem" seemed to defy solution (see below, pp. 613-615).

Yet the state of international politics must not be painted in too black colors. If the aggressor since 1945 has been the communist bloc, then at least the western democracies have not given the aggressor the freedom of play which all too often such aggressors—and notably in the very recent past Hitler, Mussolini, and the Japanese imperialists—have been given by the powers they were seeking to undermine. The leading nations of the West, the United States, Britain, France, West Germany, Italy, all do have a very great degree of freedom of the press. A complete outsider sampling that press might well be bewildered, for somewhere he would find almost all conceivable judgments on western policy in international relations since World War II. He would find that policy described as outright militarism, as an attempt by the United States to conquer the world; and he would find that policy described as the rankest kind of "appeasement," as complete failure to stand up to the Russians and the Red Chinese and their satellites; and he would find many judgments in between these extremes. But it looks as though a fair-minded observer would conclude that the West had so far succeeded in "containing" the communist bloc, as, once the fact of Russian aggression became clear in 1946-47, the West under American leadership set out to do. This is surely not "appeasement."

Moreover, the United Nations, where representatives from both blocs must by its very constitution meet periodically, is still in being, and still offers a means of arriving at those compromises which are as essential in international as in domestic politics. And, as we have already noted briefly and shall see more clearly in the next section, the purely *material* damage of World War II had ten years later been more than made up. There were still poverty, malnutrition, shocking material conditions in many parts of the world; there were domestic problems that the conscientious man of good will could feel to be at least as horrendous as was the threat of World War III in international politics; and yet in general the economist would have to say in the second decade of the "cold war" that men generally were more "prosperous," and the whole human race more numerous by millions than they were before 1939.

II: The Postwar History
of the Major Free-world States

If one could look at the history of the various nations of the western world since 1945 with a mind wholly free from concern with international relations, and unworried by the problems of taste, morals, and religion that disturb so many thoughtful people, one might even dare use a nineteenth-century word like "progress." In command over nature, over material resources, that great leap forward that began with the modern age, and was hastened in the economic revolutions, has since 1939 actually accelerated. In our political and social life, where progress is not so readily measurable, at the very least our democratic ways of life display continuity with those of our fathers. Concretely—and again omitting the fears suggested by the atomic bomb and the possibilities of World War III—the child born almost anywhere in the free democratic West since World War II can look forward to a longer life span than that of his parents, to a longer time in formal education, to a higher real income, to

more leisure, to more continuous employment, to greater security in illness and old
age. He, or she, for reasons not quite clear
to scientists, is even likely to attain an inch
or two more in height than the parents. We
may spell all this out in a brief survey of
the major nations of the West.

The United States

The most obvious fact about the
United States since 1945 is its long and
great economic prosperity. But perhaps the
most important, and to some observers the
most surprising, development in recent history has been the way in which the American people have been willing to assume the
responsibilities, the burdens, that have
come their way in international politics. At
the end of World War I we cut ourselves
as free of "foreign entanglements" as we
could, and some of our European allies
feared at the end of World War II that we
might do so once more. But we have on
the contrary, after a rather abrupt cutting
off of Lend-Lease in 1945, continued to
render substantial economic aid to our allies. And we have taken on treaty obligations, notably in NATO, which are basically
old-fashioned alliances. In 1919 we refused
to join the League of Nations; in 1945 we
were the heart and soul, the organizers, of
its successor, the United Nations. It is not
that isolationists were suppressed; indeed
they still exist, and command great newspapers and a solid representation in Congress. But they are in a minority, a minority
that has hardly been able to block a single
measure of foreign policy.

All in all, this change from isolationism to
full international leadership is one of the
most remarkable changes of our time. A
well-organized movement against any of
our numerous treaty commitments since
the Marshall Plan of 1947, *if it had had the
majority of the American people behind it,*
could have succeeded in spite of the fact

that since the end of World War II official
Republican and Democratic party policies
have been on the whole in "bipartisan"
agreement on our participation in international politics.

Indeed, the political history of the
United States since 1945 is a good confirmation of what we have already said (see
above, Chapter XXI) about the basic agreement that must be shared by both parties
in the two-party system that prevails in
the English-speaking countries. Harry Truman, Democrat, who as vice-president had
succeeded to the office on the death of
Franklin Roosevelt in 1945, was elected
over the Republican Thomas Dewey in
1948 in an election that caught the experts
by surprise, for the advance polls indicated
the election of Dewey. In 1952, however,
General Eisenhower, Republican, with his
immense personal popularity, was elected
president over the Democratic candidate,
Adlai Stevenson, and carried his party to a
majority in Congress. Now by tradition
the Republicans are (comparatively) conservative, the party of business; and the
Democrats are (comparatively) liberal or
radical, the party of the working man, the
"little fellow." Those parentheses are important. In fact, the victorious Republicans after 1952 left intact the essentials of
Democratic legislation since Franklin Roosevelt's victory in 1932: the system of social
security, which the Republicans actually
extended, the Tennessee Valley Authority,
and a whole complex set of federal agencies, the main task of which was to "intervene" in the economic life of the nation, as,
for instance, the federal purchase of farm
surpluses to keep up the income of farmers.
The Republicans did this, even though their
official philosophy stressed free enterprise
and condemned government regulation.
And they also retained the great armed
forces—including the draft—we had had to
build up since 1940, and the foreign policy
we have outlined above.

In 1954, the Supreme Court of the

United States handed down a decision that is sure to figure as a major one in the history books of the future. Segregation in public schools—specifically, the existence of separate schools for whites and for Negroes in the southern and border states and in the District of Columbia—was declared contrary to the law of the land. Notably in the District of Columbia, in Maryland, Kentucky, Missouri, and in a few districts elsewhere, like the "atomic city" of Oak Ridge in Tennessee under federal control, steps were taken at once to implement this decision. In the rest of the South, the decision evoked an opposition that carrried the historian's mind back to the long struggle over Reconstruction after 1865. Significantly, not even the bitterest southern opponent of desegregation talked about secession; but there was much talk about what amounted to nullification (the right claimed by South Carolina in 1832, when it declared unconstitutional the tariff acts of Congress). The majority of southerners were clearly determined to "get around" the decision somehow or other, and such American precedents as the Volstead Act implementing the Eighteenth Amendment suggest the likelihood that they will for the time succeed. Six years after the original decision of the Supreme Court, none of the core states of the old South—South Carolina, Georgia, Alabama, Mississippi, and Louisi-

Little Rock. A white student jeers at a 15-year-old Negro girl as she attempts to enter Central High School.

ana—had integrated a single public school.

Relatively unnoticed, another innovation has been made in the structure of the American political society. The United States, regretting its experiment in "imperialism" after the Spanish-American War of 1898, had taken up a firm position in foreign policy in favor of the emancipation of dependent peoples everywhere. Not unmindful of world opinion and of proverbs like "practice what you preach," we freed the Philippines, which on July 4, 1946, became a sovereign state, though still rather in the American orbit. Our relatively small Pacific island possessions we could justify on the grounds of military necessity. Alaska in 1958, Hawaii in 1959, long denied by federal "politics" the statehood they were anxious to get, became full-fledged states, raising the number of states to fifty.

There remained the large and populous island of Porto Rico, which was in fact a colonial dependency, in a singularly anomalous relation to the United States. Only a minority of its inhabitants really wanted independence on the Philippine model, if only because the economic advantages of free trade with and free immigration to the United States were so great for the island, which had a very high birth rate. We arrived at a compromise that probably owed something to British precedents in their Commonwealth. Porto Rico, now Puerto Rico in good Spanish, in 1952 became an *Estado Libre Associado,* or *Commonwealth,* with its own constitution, its own self-government, but still a part of, or "associated with," the United States.

The economy of the United States, which had proved more than equal to the task of carrying on the Second World War, continued its upward course in the years after 1945. There were mild "recessions" in 1948, 1953, and 1958, but nothing the most pessimistic commentator could call a real depression. Indeed, by the mid-fifties even a few Marxists were beginning to express their doubts about the inevitable "bust" their theories told them must always follow a capitalist "boom." And on the other side, orthodox western economists were beginning to assert that the United States had in fact licked the problem of the business cycle, that we had so many "built-in safeguards" in our social insurance, our banking and corporation laws, our ability—and willingness—to undertake public works at the first sign of depression, that though we should have recessions, we should never have a depression like that of the thirties. The historian, by training and disposition cautious, can hardly yet pronounce on this question; he can merely record the fact of the great prosperity, and its extension to almost all parts of the nation, and to almost all social classes.

Socially, the American drive toward some very concrete forms of equality has continued since the Second World War. It is not quite true that in the traditional sense of the word there are no "classes" in the United States in mid-twentieth century, but it is almost true. In polls, the overwhelming majority of Americans refuse to call themselves "upper class" or "lower" or "working class"; if they *must* use a label, something like 90 per cent will choose "middle class." In terms of sheer income, we still have some very rich men in spite of graduated income taxes and inheritance taxes. And we still have, in part but not wholly because of the low economic status of many Negroes, some very poor, who are not well fed or well housed. Indeed, in terms of actual real income, some nations of western Europe are closer to rough equality than we are. And yet both in terms of the career open to talents—the absence of barriers to social mobility—and in terms of what we may loosely call the social atmosphere, the United States remains the land where the social ideals of democracy are most nearly realized. The Negroes are indeed an exception, though not wholly so; in the arts, in the fields of entertainment and sports, and within their own community in all fields, the gifted Negro can rise.

As we shall see in the last section of this chapter, democracy in the United States has by no means been accepted by intellectuals inside and outside the country at the values given it in our last few paragraphs. The commonest of complaints against the atmosphere, the "style" set by mid-twentieth-century democracy in the United States, is foreshadowed in the fears of men like Alexis de Tocqueville and J. S. Mill (see Chapter XX) concerning the "tyranny of the majority." Americans, so it is claimed, tend to be actually more and more *alike*, conformists instead of equals; they tend to eat the same frozen and packaged foods, look at the same television programs, ride in the same cars, live in the same ranch houses, and so on at great length. They have even made their part of this great continent of such a sameness that a French or English traveler can write that if you have seen one American city you have seen them all. And, worse from the point of view of the intellectual critic, they have, he says, jealously tried to keep down individuals and groups who do not conform to the general standards of mediocrity. American society, he holds, may be on the way to a kind of democratic totalitarianism of equal, average, conforming individuals. The historian trying to be objective must insist that the reality is not quite so simple. Above all, he must point to the rich and varied group life in contemporary America. The very intellectuals who so dislike the "average" American are wholly free to attack him, wholly free to avoid him—with a little effort, perhaps—wholly free to eat their own unfrozen foods, and read their own "little magazines," attend their own "little theatres," and avoid looking at television.

The historian must also record what can now be seen as one of the crisis-provoked periods of partial suppression of "civil rights" in the 1950's, a period that will always be associated with the name of the late Senator McCarthy of Wisconsin. The cold war had inevitably made the existence of believers in communism in the United States difficult. The pattern for dealing with such problems had been set in our own history as early as the era of the French Revolution (the Jacobins frightened the possessing classes in those days at least as much as communists did in the twentieth century). What opponents of the process called "witch-hunts," and proponents called "security measures," were undertaken against individuals in responsible positions, especially in education, defense industries, and government, who might be pro-communist—that is, pro-Russian.

We are still much too near the McCarthy episode to judge its place in American history; and indeed the average liberal will regard the term "episode" as an underestimate of the importance of a crisis he considers to have been a threat to American democracy. But it must be insisted that when the gifted and irresponsible English publicist Bertrand Russell wrote of a "reign of terror" in the United States in the early 1950's he was grossly exaggerating, from the point of view of a historian. Grave injustices were indeed done to many individuals who were in no sense traitors. The term "communist" was unfairly extended by McCarthy and his imitators and admirers to include many barely "left of center." McCarthy himself was an unscrupulous demagogue. But if one compares the French reign of terror in 1792-94 or the Russian "purge" trials of the 1930's, one is struck with the really enormous differences. No blood was shed in this country, the prisons were not filled, and the ordinary citizen went on his way just as he always had. McCarthyism was a bad symptom in the American body politic; but it has apparently not proved chronic. Even before his death in 1957, McCarthy no longer even made the headlines.

Americans are indeed a worrying peo-

ple. The announcement that the Russians had in October 1957 succeeded in putting up a rocket which orbited around the earth (in Russian, *sputnik*, literally a satellite, a traveler-with) had immediate repercussions in America, and undoubtedly worried more people than did McCarthyism. Our publicists began to blame our educational system, our fondness for consumers' goods, silly rivalry among Army, Navy, and Air Force, and much else for our failure to keep up with the Russians in the conquest of space. The worry over our excessively "permissive" education, over our unwillingness to make the young go through the rigorous training of science, persisted even after we sent up our own satellites into space in 1958. Much of such experimental work in both countries is necessarily secret; but to an unexcited observer it looked in 1960 as if we and the Russians were about even in preparation for conquering space, even though the Russians had been the first to hit the moon with a rocket.

Finally, and more positively, it must be repeated that the "tyranny of the majority" has hitherto not prevented a really amazing proliferation of all sorts of groups in the United States. The intellectual critic, who can sometimes manage to attack what he has just claimed does not exist, complains that we are a "nation of joiners." Clearly, we don't all join the same groups. Even at the level of "serious" organizations, and discounting the innumerable ones based on hobbies, sports, artistic interests, and the like, one is struck with the evidence of what must be called American "multanimity." The gamut of "pressure groups" alone, from say the Anti-Saloon League to the organized distillers or brewers, from the anti-vivisectionists to the prestigeful American Medical Association, from organized labor through organized farmers to the National Association of Manufacturers, is sufficient to bewilder observers from abroad. In religion, our multanimity is even more striking; somewhere in the United States—

in the Los Angeles area if nowhere else—there must be gathered together representatives of almost all of what William James called the "varieties of religious experience." In the arts, the conventional, the average, the thing that satisfies the man in the street —and it isn't by any means always the same thing—exists side by side with the wildest extremes of "modernism." Indeed, the observer who takes the trouble to look at the whole of American culture is likely to worry rather over how such a huge assemblage of varied human beings can hold together than over the tendency toward a "tyranny of the majority."

Canada

As in the First World War, Canadian troops fought in the Second World War from the start, and proved a most important factor in the great coalition against the Axis. Since 1945, Canada has enjoyed an economic growth and prosperity proportionately even greater than that of the United States. A great deal of capital from the United States poured in, and much was raised at home and in Britain. Canada, though still producing vast amounts of raw materials from farm, mine, and forest, came in these decades to be a great industrial nation, exploiting her remarkable hydroelectric resources and her oil and mineral wealth. In the mid-fifties Canada took the lead in carrying out a long-discussed plan for a canal from the Great Lakes to the lower St. Lawrence, a canal deep enough to accommodate ocean-going ships, and producing in addition important hydroelectric power. In the United States, vested interests along the Atlantic seaboard, foreseeing competition from the new seaway in the lucrative midwest trade, had long succeeded by typical pressure-group lobbying methods in preventing American participation in the scheme. It is indicative of Canada's independent nationhood that she was able to announce her intention of going ahead with the scheme—which could be done, though imperfectly, entirely on Canadian territory—without the United States if necessary. Faced with this prospect, the United States joined Canada in a collaborative development, work began in 1954, and the canal was opened in 1959.

Politically, postwar Canada has been one of the stablest of western nations. Although in the provinces other parties have held power, in the federal government the Liberals, first under Mackenzie King, who died in 1948, and then under Louis St. Laurent, were in power from 1935 to 1957. In that year the Conservatives—significantly, they are known formally as the Progressive Conservative Party—won a close victory, which in a 1958 election became a landslide. The new Prime Minister, Mr. Diefenbaker, secured 208 out of a total of 265 seats in the House of Commons.

In its socio-economic structure the Dominion conforms to the general western pattern in that it preserves great freedom of the press, the "career open to talent," and in terms of the contrast of laissez-faire *versus* government regulation, a mixed economy in which the mixture perhaps is somewhat stronger on the side of private enterprise than on that of government participation and regulation. The English-speaking and the French-speaking peoples of this bilingual nation continued in relations essentially unchanged since the war (see Chapter XXXI).

Western Europe

The old geographical term "Western Europe" has by the development of the cold war been turned into a political, indeed a cultural, term. It is used fairly freely to indicate those nations of Europe outside Russian domination, outside the Iron Curtain, some of which, like Greece and Turkey, are certainly not geographically part of Western Europe. We must take up some of the postwar developments in the most important of these countries. But first it must be noted that, although the form of the "sovereign" state and many of the bundle of sentiments we call "nationalism" have been preserved in the region, there have been since 1945 real attempts to bring some sort of functional unity to the region. There have been, in short, attempts to organize a free "Europe" on a level above the nation-state. To date, the most far-reaching in actual practice has been the realization of the Schuman Plan. Under this plan, France, West Germany, Italy, and the three "Benelux" nations of Belgium, the Netherlands, and Luxembourg have in effect created for their coal and iron industries a free market area in which a joint administrative body can make certain final and binding decisions *without the participation of any governmental agency of any one of the six nations*. At least on paper, this Coal and Iron Union means that *some* part of the sacred "sovereignty" of each nation has been given up. In the late 1950's the same "six nations" took the lead in plans for a broad free market or customs union to include much of free Europe. The British, however, continued to hold off from all such plans, though by 1960 they had helped organize a looser union, called the "Outer Seven" (Austria, Denmark, Norway, Portugal, Sweden, Switzerland, the United Kingdom) in contrast with the "Inner Six" named above. The Six and the Seven may eventually come together; at the moment they are rivals.

On various other levels, this kind of cooperation has gone on, short of theoretical abdication of "sovereignty," but actually involving the give-and-take of compromise well beyond the older, purely diplomatic, ways. Such in military affairs is NATO, the North Atlantic Treaty Organization, which, however, was threatened by the increasing tendency of Europeans to believe that post-Stalin Russia did not intend to make war.

Such in economic affairs is the Organization for European Economic Cooperation, which began in 1947 to implement the American Marshall Plan for economic recovery. And such in general politics is the Council for Europe, which has indeed no "teeth," no power of making law, but is a kind of federal consultative parliament for western Europe, to which governments send official representatives. It meets at Strasbourg, a city delicately poised between France and Germany. In summary: for the "whole-hog" European federalist who wants a United States of Europe on the American model, what has been done toward European unity since 1945 is very little; for the historian who knows how deep-seated are the nationalist habits of thought and mind in Europe, what has been done since 1945 toward transcending the limitations of those habits is a very great deal. It may well be that not much more than was done in the 1950's is at present possible, given the strength of national traditions. Here, as with desegregation in American schools (see p. 594), the impatient reformer has to face what seems to be a lesson of history: continuous reform, with no lulls, is more than human beings can take.

Great Britain

The United Kingdom of Great Britain and Northern Ireland seemed to many, especially to Americans, to have undergone a revolution late in 1945. A general election held in July, 1945, gave results exactly opposite to those of the famous "khaki election" of 1918 (see Chapter XXVIII). Though Churchill was far more of a national hero than even Lloyd George had been, a nation that was determined on radical changes threw out Churchill and his Conservative party and returned a Labor party pledged to a measure of "socialism" —not, be it carefully noted, communism. The new prime minister was Clement Attlee, himself by no means a proletarian, but a middle-class British gentleman and high-minded social worker. Under the Labor cabinet, the government proceeded to take over, with due compensation to the owners, the coal industry, the railroads, and some parts of commercial road transportation, and began to nationalize the steel industry. Britain already had a well-developed system of various social insurances; this was now capped by a system of socialized medical care for all who wished it, a system strongly opposed at first by the medical profession. The educational system was partly reformed in an effort to make education more democratic, and to lengthen the required period of compulsory education. In accordance with Labor party philosophy, various parts of the old empire were given independence, like Burma, and others were granted dominion status—that is, national independence within the extraordinary British multi-national system (see Chapter XXXI).

Yet the nature and extent of this British "revolution by consent" were greatly misunderstood, especially by American conservatives. We can now see clearly that the new Britain was more like than unlike the old one and the rest of the free West. What came out of the changes after the Labor party victory of 1945 was an economy pushed a little more toward collectivism than before, but still very much indeed a "mixed" economy. Coal and railroads, nationalized, did not become great state trusts run by bureaucrats on the Russian model, but rather public corporations with a structure not unlike that of great private industries in the West, and run by a board not by any means wholly under either bureaucratic or political thumbs. Great sectors of the economy remained in private hands, under no more than the kind of government regulation common even in the United States, which itself had a "mixed economy." Proof of the essential moderation of this British revolution is afforded by the conduct of the Conserva-

tives, who with Churchill still at their head were returned to power in 1951. The nationalization of steel, which had begun, was indeed stopped; but otherwise the victorious Conservatives kept intact the "socialism" of their opponents, including the national health scheme of socialized medicine, to which even the medical profession had become pretty well reconciled. There are of course Englishmen who think that their country has taken quite the wrong track since 1945, and who would like to restore the old ways of private enterprise and laissez-faire; but there are not enough of them, apparently, to win elections and dominate Parliament. Even the Conservative sweep in the elections of 1959, almost doubling its majority under the popular prime minister Harold Macmillan, did not result in such a return to full private enterprise.

In American—and, it must be added, in German—eyes, the British have not since the war proved resilient enough to keep up with the extraordinary pace of economic improvements through technological innovation. A symptom: the British motor-car industry, which immediately after the war was in a good position to gain a big share of the world market, in the 1950's saw its lead reduced, until the Germans, especially with their inexpensive, standardized light car, the *Volkswagen*, took over the lead. In all the various indices of production, the British are definitely behind the Germans and the Americans. But they are still a great industrial people, suffering from the fact that just because they were the *first* to industrialize in the modern manner their plant tends toward obsolescence, and, more important, their ways tend to be set, hard to change rapidly. The British, for instance, are usually, in the opinion of Americans who are used to high-pressure methods, ineffective salesmen. But, it must be admitted that as the decade of the 1960's began the British economy was prosperous.

The British were the last of the major

western nations to feel themselves able to give up rationing and other belt-tightening measures the war had made necessary. Britain, more than any other great nation, had completely outgrown its ability to raise enough food to supply its inhabitants. The British had to export manufactured goods to get money to import the food they needed; but they also had to limit those imports, to raise all they possibly could on home lands. The British people therefore put up with many restrictions in what they rather mildly called an "austerity program." By the mid-fifties most of these restrictions had been lifted and by the 1960's the British consumer could buy whatever he could afford. Yet the British people still faced a kind of chronic fear that in this harsh world they could not quite compete with younger peoples, that they could not sell enough to buy enough in the world market for their crowded population which —this is of major importance—was not, like the masses of Asia, used to a bare minimum of existence, but on the contrary to a high standard of living.

To all these troubles was added a widespread awareness of the fact that Britain, which only a lifetime ago was the leading nation of the world, now saw herself stripped of some of her empire, with the rest uncertain, playing what American editorial writers liked to call "second-fiddle" to her former colonial possession, the United States. No wonder the British felt they were suffering undeservedly, and had what a witty commentator called a "Job complex." British leaders can still hardly forget their former supremacy, and still, quite naturally, cannot accept deferring to the United States. Yet in spite of all these psychological difficulties, the British have been true, often under much strain, to the American alliance. The Franco-British invasion of Egypt in 1956 (see Chapter XXXI) looked at first like a complete break between Britain and the United States; but though the alliance was surely badly strained, it has

survived, and in the Berlin crisis of 1959 and at the collapse of the summit conference in May, 1960, proved strong enough to hold in spite of the somewhat diverging views of the British, the Americans, and—a remarkable combination—the Franco-Germans. Prime Minister Macmillan in various diplomatic journeys, including one to Russia in February and March, 1959, had restored something of the old diplomatic prestige and initiative to Britain.

France

If to the British the events of the last war and its aftermath seem to have been hard on their pride, on the French these years inflicted what the psychologists call a trauma. Complete defeat by the Germans; occupation by the hated foe; economic exploitation by the Germans to the point where the French government was almost bankrupt; liberation which, in spite of the admirable part played in it by the Fighting French and the French Resistance movement, was still clearly the work of American and British arms; the grave postwar difficulties of trying to hold together an empire whose peoples were in revolt— all these were elements in a picture of drastic decline. To complete the picture must be added the fact that France had not since the mid-nineteenth century kept pace with the leading industrial nations in production, in finance, above all in population. American editorial writers, if they tended to rub in British weaknesses, were much shorter with the French; even "second-rate power" seemed to many of them an exaggeration—France, according to them, had ceased to count in international affairs, was a "tenth-rate power." This was, of course, grossly exaggerated, for in the first postwar decade (1946-1956) France made a striking economic recovery.

The French government in exile, led by General de Gaulle, very easily re-established in 1944 in liberated France the old republican forms of government. Frenchmen called this state the Fourth Republic; but after de Gaulle, disappointed by his failure to attain real power, retired from politics in 1946, the Fourth Republic began to look exactly like the Third. Cabinets lasted on an average only a few months; to the old splinter parties was added a Communist party of renewed strength, openly dedicated to revolutionary change; the problems of the old empire, now known as the French Union, seemed insoluble, and Algeria in particular, where active rebellion of Moslem partisans began in 1954, was a running sore; there was indeed economic progress, but there was also inflation, and a sharp sense of grievance among the workers.

Yet the French people struggled on, by no means in the depth of existentialist despair that seemed to overcome their intellectuals. North Africa proved to be the last straw. In 1958, in the midst of a crisis that saw a threatened military *coup d'état* in Algeria, de Gaulle emerged from retirement and with skill and luck—only later historians can judge how much of each—managed a bloodless, or almost bloodless, revolution. The French people in a free election ratified these changes, and the Fifth Republic, with the power of the executive very greatly strengthened and the power of the legislature to overthrow the executive greatly lessened, began its life. De Gaulle created a good impression in the free world by permitting the overseas territories to vote for independence if they liked: only Guinea voted to leave the French Union. The "Union" was slowly loosened into the "Community" (see Chapter XXXI). Algeria, which the French regarded not as an overseas colony, but as an integral part of France, continued in these first years of the Fifth Republic to present very grave difficulties. Generally speaking, however, de Gaulle was off to a good start in that he had not behaved like the fascist revolutionaries of the 1920's and 1930's: he had avoided outright Caesarism,

and had maintained the forms of a democratic republic. Only time could tell whether he would preserve the spirit of a democracy.

The French still seemed to such relatively serene nationalists as the Americans touchy and difficult. President de Gaulle in 1959 refused to permit American installations for atomic weapons on French soil unless the French were given full information about atomic techniques and could join the United States and Britain in the exclusive "club" of western atomic powers. (Russia of course had her own atomic industry.) In February, 1960, in spite of many protests, and a specially bitter one from independent Ghana, the French exploded an atomic bomb of their own in the Sahara. But there were signs that the French had begun to feel that nationalism was not enough. It was a Frenchman, Robert Schuman—he came by his German name naturally enough, for he was born an Alsatian—who fathered the plan for a Coal and Steel Union. Another Frenchman, Jean Monnet, from the impeccably French town of Cognac, has been a mainstay of plans and actual work for the economic union of Europe. Just how far from the intransigent nationalism of Clemenceau (see Chapter XXV) the France of the 1950's had come is evident from French willingness to give up trying to

Rapprochement between former enemy states. Charles de Gaulle of France and Konrad Adenauer of Germany.

make the Saarlanders French, and to accept their political and cultural union with Germany in return for some of the unsentimental coal of the Saar. France is perhaps the clearest example of an abated nationalism in the modern world. She may, in spite of de Gaulle's often-expressed concern for her "grandeur," prove to be the leading state in the uniting of Europe.

De Gaulle came through a serious crisis in January and February, 1960, with increased prestige. He had announced his refusal to treat with Algerian rebels (the National Liberation Front) as heads of state, but did promise a free plebiscite, once order had been re-established, as to the future status of Algeria. Against this proposal, which they feared might if carried out result in the independence of Algeria, some of the European settlers rose and erected barricades in the cities of Algiers and Oran. In a broadcast de Gaulle insisted that the French army do its duty and put down the revolt. After a few days the rebels dispersed, and de Gaulle had passed one more bitter crisis (see also Chapter XXXI).

West Germany

Germany in the second decade after the end of Hitler's aggression remained one of the great enigmas of our time, if only because, in the sense in which we had got used to thinking of Germany, there was no such land. Eastern Germany and a good deal of the heartland of Germany in Thuringia and Saxony were a satellite "people's republic" inside the Iron Curtain; there was constantly threatened Berlin, divided between American, British, and French zones of occupation, within which there was full freedom of movement, and a Russian zone; and there was West Germany, a federal republic with its capital at the old university town of Bonn, and by the early 1950's fully integrated as an independent state into the western coalition. These divisions

seemed unnatural and unstable, a state of affairs that could not possibly last. Yet the western powers and Russia had in some fourteen years been unable to come to any agreement on the terms under which Germany could be re-united. There was no formal joint treaty of peace.

The western powers, convinced that in a free vote of all Germans a united nation on the western side would emerge, have attempted to get a great plebiscite. The Russians, aware that they would lose out under such conditions, refuse. Their East Germany is in population and resources notably inferior to West Germany. Added to these difficulties is the fact that Russia annexed to herself part of old East Prussia, and compensated her new Polish satellite with the rest of the old regions won by the Germans from the Slavs in part centuries ago. Poland as resuscitated reaches west as far as the Oder-Neisse line, and includes the big city of Stettin, which became the Polish Szczecin.

If it could be considered merely in itself, as a finality, the West German Federal Republic would be set down as one of the great successes of the postwar period. West Germany was not badly treated by the Allied occupiers, if only for the reason that these powers knew as early as 1946 that they would need the Germans on their side against the Russians. An innovation in international procedure was the postwar trial of Nazi leaders for "war crimes." Goering, second to Hitler, was convicted and condemned to death, as were eleven other leaders; others received lesser penalties. Many westerners, including the distinguished American Senator Robert Taft, held that these trials were not legal, were based on *ex post facto* "law," and were nothing more than the thinly disguised "woe to the vanquished" of old. Nevertheless, the Nuremberg trials seem not to have burned deeply into the souls of Germans. Similarly, the whole process called "de-Nazification"—that is, the elimination of ardent Nazis of the lower echelons from public life—though it gave rise to a great deal of discussion in Germany and outside, though on the whole it appeared to western liberals to have erred on the side of clemency, seemed after more than a decade to have left no major wounds. There were of course in Germany "irreconcilables," but the temper of West Germans was, most observers concluded, surprisingly free from bitterness toward the West; and though some westerners with sharp memories of two German aggressions continued to harbor doubts as to German friendship with the West, on the whole westerners seem to have concluded that this time West Germany would not relapse and could be trusted not to desert the West for Russia. Sporadic outbreaks in the winter of 1959-1960—swastikas painted on walls, scurrilous anti-semitic inscriptions—set off similar manifestations in Europe and America, but seem to have been the work of a few fanatics, spreading through our world of mass-communication like any other fashion rather than a serious manifestation of renewed Nazism.

Very great economic prosperity no doubt helped create the new state of mind. Great numbers of refugees came into West Germany from the Russian occupied areas. Indeed, after fourteen years they continued to come from East Germany in smaller numbers. At first, these refugees added to the woes of West Germany, and the camps and relocation centers for the refugees taxed everybody concerned. But in the long run these refugees have added to a productive labor force which comes closer to the Americans in actual performance than that of any other great nation, and in some fields exceeds American productive standards.

The government of the Federal Republic, first set up in 1949 with a democratic "fundamental law" greatly influenced by the western powers, but apparently acceptable to the Germans, became wholly "sovereign" in the 1950's. In Konrad Adenauer, who became Chancellor in 1949, the West Germans have had a political leader of great firmness and moderation, who managed to remain acceptable in the democratic sense to all but the extreme German nationalists and the extreme left, and yet enjoyed the increasing admiration of the western powers.

Adenauer, a Christian Democrat, maintained himself in power largely by the votes of his own party. Indeed, West Germany since the war has come close to two-party politics. The main opposition, the Social Democratic party, has not yet held power federally, though it has won a majority in the city-state of Hamburg, and has supplied the remarkable mayor of free Berlin, Willy Brandt. Adenauer has no potential successor of his own party who has anything like his popular appeal, and in spite of his age—he was born in 1876—continued to hold power into 1960. The normal swing of politics, always assuming no catastrophic break, should sooner or later bring the Social Democrats into power in the federal government. They seem at least as committed against Russia as the British Labor party, and their accession to power should not affect the western alliance system.

The Other Western Countries

In Italy, a plebiscite in 1946 showed 54.3 per cent of the voters in favor of a republic, and with its establishment the House of Savoy ceased to rule. This is a rare thing among plebiscites, a close and honest vote. It might seem that so close a division would augur ill for the stability of the new republic, and so in the long run it may. But the history of Italy since World War II has been encouraging for those who hope for the spread of democracy in the West. It is true that the Communist party was strong in Italy in those years, true also that the old heritages (see Chapter XXI) of backwardness in the South, of parliamentary splinter groups and squabbling, of tension between Catholics and anti-Catholics, were not written off at once. Still, Italy shared in the postwar economic revival, enjoyed a cultural upswing especially marked in the novel and in the cinema, and managed to "contain" her own communists. For many Americans who feel the need for a European love, Italy supplanted France as an object of affection. Certainly among American and British intellectuals, there was a sharp turn away from Paris toward Rome and Florence and Venice. Most Italians seem relieved that they no longer had to aspire to imperial greatness.

For the rest, Spain under Franco and Portugal under Salazar survived the fall of the Rightist totalitarian dictators at the end of the war. Under pressure of the cold war, the United States, in spite of strong protests from liberals and radicals at home, granted economic help to Franco in return for air bases in Spain. It seems clear that the standard of living of the Spanish masses remains low, that they have not shared the economic advances of the last few decades to the extent usual in the West. It seems clear that there is much suppressed opposition to Franco in Spain. Yet beyond a few student demonstrations, there was little actual evidence of the always threatened fall of the dictator. The problem of succession to Franco, who was born in 1892, would seem still unsolved.

In a work of this scope, we cannot even touch on the recent domestic history of many smaller nations of great interest in themselves, and of great importance to the true democrat, who does not measure importance merely by size. Suffice it to note that the smaller nations of Western Europe, Portugal excepted, have continued to maintain democratic forms of government; that they continue to make contributions to our common western artistic and scientific inheritance; and that their representatives in the United Nations and in various regional groupings are frequently figures of great distinction, their total influence in such activities a useful corrective to the policies of the great powers. The new Republic of Ireland, for instance, has played an important part in the U.N. since its admission in 1955. Most of the small nations, save Switzerland, always proud of its legal neutrality, and Sweden and Finland, too close to Russia, are actively on our side as members of NATO.

III: The U.S.S.R. in the Postwar Period

Russia to the Death of Stalin

Just as Russian history under the tsars falls naturally into epochs that begin and end with the reigns of individual rulers, so the history of the Soviet Union since the end of World War II divides naturally in March 1953, with the death of Stalin. So powerful an autocrat had he been that the mere weight of his personality continued to dominate Soviet society for some time after his death: things could not change overnight. But change they did.

At the end of the war, although Russia had enormous armies mobilized, and had occupied, annexed, or turned into satellites many areas of Europe, it was essentially a weak and vulnerable giant. Not only had enemy attacks and occupation caused incalculable devastation and left millions of survivors destitute, but Russia's capitalist ally, the United States, had invented and used a secret weapon so decisive as to make war against its possessor impossible for a power that did not possess it. In the years during which the Soviet Union had no atomic bombs and the United States had them (1945-1949), any Russian ruler would have felt uneasy. Stalin, ruthless conspirator and dictator that he was, who liked nothing so much as the destruction of an enemy, and who regarded all the capitalist world as his enemy, knew that if he had been the sole possessor of the atomic bomb, he would have used it. And he attributed to his rival the strategy that he himself would have pursued. At one blow, all the technological advance of the Soviet period, undertaken to bring Russia up to the industrialized West, especially the United States, seemed to have been wiped out. Thus the prime goal of Stalin's policies after the war was to catch up once again, and to put the U.S.S.R. back into the running as an industrial power in possession of the new atomic weapon. Thanks in part no doubt to scientific information given the Russians by spies in the West, but thanks also to the high level of Russian science and technology, and to their capacity to concentrate their investments, the Russians achieved this by 1949.

Yet the effort imposed severe strains. At precisely the moment when the destructive war ended, and the people, whose low standard of living had been driven even lower, were longing for new housing, and a few creature comforts, Stalin decreed continuing austerity. The only way he knew to attain it was to continue and even to heighten the tension and terror characteristic of his régime. The rhythm of temporary relaxations of terror and its sudden renewal kept even the most important functionaries of the state awake at night. As Stalin grew older, the secrecy, censorship, and conspiratorial miasma at the top of the

Soviet state all intensified. Abroad, this preoccupation was reflected in events we have already examined: the cold war, with its operations in Greece, Berlin, Korea, its massive propaganda against the West and the Marshall Plan and NATO in France and Italy, and its fight against the schismatic Yugoslavs. At home, it took the form of demands for ever greater conformity in artistic and literary work. It also led to the introduction of something quite new to the U.S.S.R. and the Russian people, official anti-Semitism.

In his fear of the West, Stalin moved against that group of Soviet citizens who had the closest contacts with the western world, the Jews. The press began to denounce long lists of "rootless, homeless cosmopolitans," who always proved to have Jewish names, thus fanning the strong traditional anti-Semitism of the Russians and Ukrainians. The government closed Jewish cultural organizations, and stopped publications in Yiddish, imposed religious restrictions, and eventually began a series of arrests and purges and deportations of prominent Jews, often those who had been active in organs of the régime itself. Government service, the army, the professions, the universities, all experienced purges. Propaganda reached its peak with the publicity given an alleged "Doctors' Plot" in which Jewish doctors were accused of plotting to poison Stalin. When Stalin died, the stage seemed set for a full-scale anti-Semitic drive reminiscent of Hitler. Fear of the West, and detestation of Zionism—many Soviet Jews wanted to live in Israel, and gave the first Israeli ambassador to the U.S.S.R. a tumultuous welcome on her arrival—did not alone explain Soviet anti-Semitism. Partly it was a sentiment that the Soviet leaders felt personally, despite their long years of preaching cultural autonomy for nationalities. Partly it was the recognition that the population at large could be expected to welcome anti-Semitism at a moment when there was little else for them

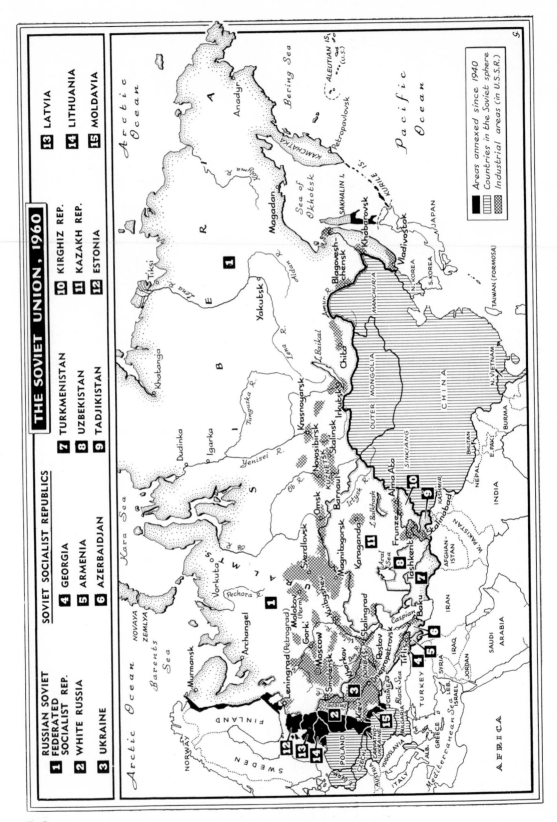

THE SOVIET UNION, 1960

SOVIET SOCIALIST REPUBLICS

1 RUSSIAN SOVIET FEDERATED SOCIALIST REP.
2 WHITE RUSSIA
3 UKRAINE
4 GEORGIA
5 ARMENIA
6 AZERBAIDJAN
7 TURKMENISTAN
8 UZBEKISTAN
9 TADJIKISTAN
10 KIRGHIZ REP.
11 KAZAKH REP.
12 ESTONIA
13 LATVIA
14 LITHUANIA
15 MOLDAVIA

Areas annexed since 1940
Countries in the Soviet sphere
Industrial areas (in U.S.S.R.)

to approve of in government policies. In any case, its adoption provided Stalin's heirs with a further embarrassment and a knotty problem.

As Stalin grew older, it became a favorite game in the West to speculate on his succession, and on the forces that would be released at the moment of his death. Would it be the Communist party, or the Secret Police, or the army—the three agencies in the U.S.S.R. that had power of their own— that would emerge supreme? Would it be some combination of two of these against the third? Was this or that member of the Politburo identified with one or another of these three chief agencies? Would there be a bitter personal rivalry that might disrupt the whole machinery of Soviet government, something comparable to the struggle between Stalin and Trotsky for the succession to Lenin?

Since the Death of Stalin: Khrushchev's Rise

When the great moment actually came, there was at first no evidence of disunity or personal rivalry within the Politburo. Georgi Malenkov, personally close to Stalin, succeeded him as Premier, but surrendered his Communist party secretaryship to Nikita Khrushchev. It was thus clear from the beginning that nobody would immediately inherit all of Stalin's power, and the fact that it would be shared was underlined almost at once by the pronouncements that came from the régime, denouncing the "cult of personality" (i.e., Stalin's former one-man rule), and proclaiming a "collegial" system (i.e., government by committee). But before the end of 1953 there came the official announcement that the dreaded chief of the Secret Police, and Politburo member, Beria, always regarded as a potential heir of Stalin, had been executed for treason. The observer might interpret this move, so remi-

niscent of the purges of Stalin's own era, as an indication that the members of the Politburo were circling around each other with their knives out, or that the Communist party and the army had indeed united to thwart a bid for power on the part of the Secret Police. The emergence of the war hero, Marshal Zhukov, into positions of some political importance gave color to this view as, perhaps, did the rise to even higher eminence of the "political" general, Bulganin.

But all expectation that a "free-for-all" among the remaining members of the inner circle would ensue, or that the régime might be shaken by personal rivalries, was in error. True, Malenkov vanished from the top post of Premier, to be succeeded by Bulganin, but Malenkov, though he admitted grievous errors, was at first simply demoted to a lower cabinet post, and remained in the Politburo. Some indication as to the real locus of power might perhaps be found in the fact that the errors confessed by Malenkov (especially the effort to concentrate collective farms into enormous "agrogorods" or agricultural towns, which had indeed failed) were actually Khrushchev's errors, for which Malenkov now had to take responsibility. Yet, though Khrushchev was certainly very powerful, his fellow-members of the Politburo had great influence, and showed no outward signs of fearing him as all had feared Stalin. On the whole, it appeared that the transfer of power had actually gone quite smoothly in the U.S.S.R., and that among the rulers, in the happy phrase of George Orwell's *Animal Farm*, "all were equal, but some were more equal than others."

At a Party Congress, held early in 1956, Khrushchev made a speech in which he not only carried the attack on the "cult of personality" to new heights, but openly denounced Stalin by name, emotionally detailing the ghastly acts of personal cruelty to which the psychopathically suspicious nature of the late dictator had given rise.

The Hungarian revolt. Head of statue of Stalin toppled in downtown Budapest.

Khrushchev thus echoed what western observers of the U.S.S.R. had been saying for years. As the details of the speech were leaked out to the Soviet public, there was of course some distress at the smashing of the idol they had worshiped so long; but a good many of them had no doubt all along suspected that Stalin was something less than god-like. So the widespread disorders that some observers were predicting failed to materialize.

But outside the U.S.S.R., the sudden deflation of Stalin and the admission of so many past injustices proved far too strong a brew for the citizens of some of the satellites to swallow. Anti-communist riots by workers—supposedly the pillars of any communist state—in Poznan, Poland, in June 1956, were followed by severe strikes, demonstrations, and upheavals in the rest of Poland a few months later. Polish national sentiment was declaring itself, but the uprising remained within the grip of one wing

of the Communist party, that led by Wladislaw Gomulka, who had been purged for alleged Titoism in 1951. Not even the presence in Warsaw of Khrushchev himself and other members of the Soviet Politburo prevented the rise of Gomulka to power, although at one moment the Russians seem to have contemplated using their army to impose their will by force. Because the new government in Poland was, after all, a communist government, however, they allowed it to remain in power.

In Hungary, however, the movement went further. Starting, like the Polish uprising, as a movement within the Communist party, and spurred by the outspoken writings of many communists who loathed the restraints of Stalinism, the Hungarian movement brought Imre Nagy, a communist like Gomulka, into office as Premier. But then the popular hatred for communism as such got out of hand, and heroic young men and women flew to arms in Budapest in the hope of ousting the communists and of taking Hungary altogether out of the Soviet sphere. They even denounced the Warsaw Pact, the Russian alliance of eastern European satellites set up by Moscow to oppose NATO. It was then that Khrushchev ordered full-fledged military action. In November, 1956, Soviet tanks and troops, violating an armistice, swept back into Budapest and put down the revolution in blood and fire. A puppet government led by Janos Kadar was installed in Hungary. More than 150,000 Hungarian refugees fled to Austria to be resettled in various western countries. Despite the Soviet charges that the uprising had been trumped up by the western "imperialists" and "fascists," the West in fact had played no part at all, not daring to help the Hungarians for fear of starting the world war that everybody knew must be avoided.

These momentous events of 1956 in eastern Europe gave Khrushchev's opponents at home an opportunity to unite against his policies. Within the Politburo they had a majority. But Khrushchev was able to rally to his support the larger body of which the Politburo is the inner core, the Central Committee of the Communist Party of the U.S.S.R. A veteran party worker, with supporters in all key party posts, he repeated Stalin's performance after the death of Lenin (see above, pp. 436-438) and emerged from this greatest test not only unscathed, but with his powers immeasurably enhanced. Now the Soviet press denounced the "anti-party group" of Malenkov, Molotov, and Kaganovich, three of the members of Stalin's own entourage. In Stalin's own day this would have led them to the execution-block, or would have been reported only after they were safely dead. Khrushchev, however, acted differently. All three were expelled from the Politburo and removed from their high posts, but all three were given minor positions at a safe distance from Moscow. Molotov, for example, became Ambassador to Outer Mongolia.

Not long after, Premier Bulganin followed them; he had sided with them against Khrushchev, and took the consequences. Men of Khrushchev's own choosing replaced them. Together with the downgrading of Zhukov, this seemed to complete Khrushchev's succession to Stalin's position of undisputed power.

Since the Death of Stalin: Domestic Policies

Yet there were certain differences. Khrushchev, already in his sixties, could hardly hope for Stalin's quarter of a century of dictatorship. Moreover, in the course of making himself supreme, he had already embarked on certain policies very difficult to reverse. After 1953 he had released millions of captives from prison and from slave-labor camps. Almost everybody in Russia had a relative or a friend now freed. All of them that could took jobs, some even government jobs. Within a year or two Soviet society at every level except at the very top of the bureaucracy had absorbed these sufferers from tyranny who would be the first to oppose its reimposition. Moreover, the Secret Police, from being the largest single "employer" of labor and a power almost independent in the state, had been curbed. Its chief, Beria, was the only Soviet leader to have been executed since Stalin's death. Its influence was cut down, and subordinated to that of other institutions. Though fear had not disappeared, it had diminished, and by 1960 western travelers had greatly increased in numbers in the U.S.S.R., while Soviet citizens were far less afraid to talk to them. The spectacle of thousands of Muscovites flocking eagerly through the 1959 American exposition, and freely asking questions of American guides, would have been unthinkable under Stalin.

As always, economic development remained central to the thinking of the Soviet leadership. Malenkov's initial program to increase the consumer goods for which the Soviet people longed proved impossible to realize at the same time as the great industrial advances demanded by the fifth five-year plan (1951-55). Forced to choose, Khrushchev at the end of 1954 proclaimed, like Stalin, the priority of heavy industry. The sixth plan (1956-60), setting more ambitious goals than ever before, aimed specifically at catching up with the United States, now the sole remaining industrial rival of the U.S.S.R. in the world. But the huge expenses involved in the Polish and Hungarian outbreaks (a billion dollars' worth of credits to eastern Europe alone) forced the Soviet government to shelve the plan. By the end of 1958 they announced a new seven-year plan, to run until 1965. Starting from base figures of 500 million tons of coal, 55 million tons of steel, and 113 million tons of oil, it called for continued and steady increase; the production of oil was actually scheduled to double in seven years.

In agriculture, good weather had helped Khrushchev win, at least temporarily, a gamble of plowing under the virgin lands of the Asian steppes, risky because drought would have meant disaster. By 1958, much amalgamation had taken place among the collective farms: they had decreased in number from about 250,000 to about 78,000, and the average size had increased greatly, to about 4500 acres. In 1958, accordingly, a new law called for the gradual abolition of the MTS (Machine Tractor Stations; see above, p. 440), because no single MTS could now efficiently serve many of the huge new collectives, each of which was to buy its own machinery. The MTS would gradually become mere Repair and Technical Stations, servicing the machines owned by the collectives. The seven-year plan called for an increase in intensive farming rather than a further extension of development of new lands, though the investment rate for the Asian areas was high. Though the plan promised consumer goods, one

might anticipate that the targets were as usual too high, and that the Soviet citizen would in 1965 still be very short of housing, household devices, cars, and other consumer goods familiar to Americans, nor would he eat nearly as well or dress nearly as well as the average American. Yet the Soviet economy had achieved great successes.

Most spectacular were the successes achieved by the application of the economy to technological advance in the field of weapons and rocketry. It was the U.S.S.R. that successfully launched the first earth-satellite (Sputnik—1957) and that first reached the moon with a rocket (1959). Heavy payloads soared aloft before the American engineers got their lighter ones off the ground. Though inter-continental missiles were apparently more readily available to Moscow than to Washington in 1960, American bases in Europe and Africa made our own shorter-range weapons equally dangerous to the U.S.S.R. Each power had enough nuclear weapons and means of delivering them to destroy the other, and itself at the same time. Under the impact of the Soviet technical advance, Americans were reconsidering their own educational system, and calling for more emphasis on scientific research.

In art and letters, the Soviet achievement remained strikingly less successful. Few would doubt that the atmosphere of a totalitarian dictatorship—especially when headed by a man so little educated in his tastes as Stalin, and so determined to force upon art the positive expression of loyalty to the régime—helps to stifle the cultural initiative in a people known to be as gifted in these fields as any in the world. Except for some Soviet music, such as that of Shostakovich, an occasional novel, like Sholokhov's *And Quiet Flows the Don*, for instance, and the stunning performances of traveling ballet artists, most western critics would in 1953 have maintained that the giants of the Russian nineteenth century—Tolstoy, Dostoevsky, Chekhov—had found no worthy successors. Here too the problem facing Khrushchev was how to manage a relaxation of the absolute standards imposed by Stalin and at the same time not permit a cultural revolution in which the government and society would be fair game. Both the Polish and the Hungarian uprisings had begun with the writers.

Three novels may serve as indices of Khrushchev's efforts and their results. The first, *The Thaw* (1955), written by the veteran propagandist for the régime, Ilya Ehrenburg, hailed the relaxation of coercive measures over artists as loudly as Ehrenburg himself had once favored and applied them. The second, *Not by Bread Alone*, written by Vladimir Dudintsev, precipitated a storm when it was published in the Soviet Union in 1956 because it presents in its hero a competent and enthusiastic engineer whose invention of a new pipe-casting machine is thwarted at every turn by the entrenched bureaucrats. The government-controlled writers agencies denounced Dudintsev, who was forced to retract his views and mend his ways, but not before his readers had got a memorable literary glimpse of the Soviet industrial system. The third novel, *Dr. Zhivago* (1958), by Boris Pasternak, a famous poet long in disgrace with the Stalinists, became a *cause célèbre* throughout the world.

Pasternak, who for many years had confined himself to translating Shakespeare, took advantage of the "thaw" to offer for publication his novel of the Russian revolution. Loose and episodic, full of coincidence and perhaps of symbolism, it tells the moving life-story of a Russian doctor, who, through all the agonies of war and revolution, affirms the freedom of the individual human soul. Many readers felt that Pasternak was writing in the great Russian tradition of the nineteenth century, and that they were hearing once more the voice of a major Russian artist. Accepted for publication in Russia, a manuscript of *Dr. Zhivago* was sent abroad to Italy to be published. Then the Russian censors changed their minds. Pasternak was forced to request that the manuscript in Italy be returned to him, but the publisher refused. Russian, Italian, English, and other versions of the novel appeared abroad, and aroused such great admiration that the Nobel Prize Committee in 1958 awarded to Pasternak its prize for literature. Honored and touched, he accepted. But then the Soviet régime revealed that it was hardly safe to defend individual human freedom in a Soviet novel. Amidst vile language—he was called a pig and a traitor—Pasternak's fellow writers, dutifully following the régime's lead, denounced him. Threatened with exile if he accepted the prize, he rejected it, as a deeply patriotic Russian. The Nobel prize for literature was denounced as a capitalist invention, although the same week a Soviet physicist was allowed to accept the Nobel prize for physics.

Apparently in part at least because the entire world was looking on at this recrudescence of Stalinism, Pasternak suffered no further harm. Gradually he was rehabilitated, and his most vociferous enemies silenced. But his case revealed the limits of the "thaw." His Jewish origin, his intellectualism, his proclamation of individualism touched hostile chords in Khrushchev himself and in other prominent Soviet officials that made it impossible to publish *Dr. Zhivago* in the U.S.S.R. The acclaim it received in the West only made things worse for its author at home. And it was no accident that Khrushchev in the fall of 1959 chose Sholokhov, no friend of Pasternak, though himself at times in some difficulties with the régime, as his companion for his visit to the United States. In literature only limited freedom could be tolerated. Similarly, in art, modern painting and western abstract works were much discussed but still under official disapproval. The biggest black-market item in Moscow in 1959 was jazz records from the United States.

After Stalin: Foreign Policy

Khrushchev continued the vigorously aggressive foreign policies of Stalin, pursuing the same ends by all the same means. Perhaps the chief new feature was the extension of Soviet activity to the Middle East to a degree not before attempted. Here the Russians had the advantage of being able to deal with Gamal Abdel Nasser, the new ruler of Egypt and an inveterate enemy of the West, which he associated not only with past colonialism but with support for Israel. Czechoslovak and Russian arms flowed to Egypt, and Russian technicians followed. Perhaps the high point of Soviet influence was reached during the Suez affair in 1956 (see Chapter XXXI). When the United States joined the U.S.S.R. in denouncing the British and French attack, however, it became impossible for Nasser to lump all the western powers together. Soon Nasser began to learn that Russian influence usually followed Russian favors. What really disillusioned him was the revolution in Iraq during the summer of 1958, when it became clear that Soviet-sponsored communists were opposing Nasser's own pan-Arab aims. Prompt American intervention in Lebanon and British intervention in Jordan in 1958 may have temporarily countered the threat of the spread of Soviet influence beyond Iraq. As the months passed, however, communist influence in Iraq itself seemed to be growing, while in Iran—scene of abortive Soviet probes in 1946—instability prevailed. The Soviet Union, then, scored some, but by no means decisive successes in the Middle East. Here and in other "undeveloped" areas, notably Africa, the U.S.S.R. was seriously challenging the West as the supplier of economic and technological aid. A new chapter in the cold war had opened.

In Europe, Soviet influence seemed relatively stable until the Polish and Hungarian uprisings. Indeed, before these took place,

Khrushchev had made a great effort to heal the breach with Tito. In May, 1955, he went in person to Belgrade, and not only publicly apologized for the quarrel, taking the blame upon the U.S.S.R., but openly agreed that "differences in the concrete forms of developing socialism are exclusively matters for the people of the country concerned," which seemed to approve of Tito's position. Relations between Tito and Moscow were temporarily improved, although the Yugoslavs never abandoned their ties to the West. Khrushchev even went so far as to declare that many prominent victims of the "Titoist" purges had been executed wrongly, and abolished the Cominform, the body that ostensibly had started the quarrel with Tito. But in making these admissions and healing the quarrel Stalin had started, Khrushchev had opened the door to the Polish and Hungarian troubles that soon began; Soviet behavior in Hungary showed Tito and the rest of the world how limited was Khrushchev's willingness and ability to permit free choices to other communist states. Tito denounced the Soviet intervention against Nagy, though he was frightened by the wholly anti-communist character that the Hungarian revolt subsequently took on, and failed to oppose the decisive Soviet military actions that put an end to the uprising.

For a second time, relations between Moscow and Tito were strained. They were patched up again in the summer of 1957; the Soviets once more hoped that Tito would again accept Moscow's leadership among communist parties. But when in November the Russians invited representatives of all the communist parties to Moscow to celebrate the fortieth anniversary of the Russian Revolution, and produced a declaration of twelve communist parties denouncing "revisionism"—as Tito's views had come to be known—Tito flatly refused to sign. Indeed he published his own counterprogram declaring that each communist nation should make its own decisions freely.

The old quarrel was renewed for the third time. Tito would not re-enter the discipline of a world-communist union led by Russia. Khrushchev's efforts had failed. Moreover, the Poles signed the declaration with obvious reluctance, and Gomulka continued to insist on autonomy for his government in internal and party affairs.

The harshness of the onslaught against revisionism and Khrushchev's acceptance of defeat in his efforts to win the Yugoslavs by softness reflected Chinese influence. After the Polish and Hungarian revolts, the Chinese communist leaders had been invited to visit those countries, and lay down the line; they now showed both a great anxiety to play a role in formulating world communist ideology, and a strong preference (probably for internal reasons) for Stalinist orthodoxy and repression. By the spring of 1958, the Chinese and Khrushchev himself had declared that Stalin's original denunciation of the Yugoslavs back in 1948 had been correct after all. In June 1958, the Soviet government underlined this decision in grim fashion when it announced the executions of Imre Nagy and other leaders of the Hungarian uprising, in violation of solemn promises of safe-conduct. The executions probably were intended also to serve as a warning to Gomulka not to try to extend Polish independent behavior too far. Soon after, Gomulka did denounce revisionism, and criticized Nagy and the Yugoslavs both, but in a tone far milder than that employed by the Russians and Chinese.

All the eastern European satellites were bound together in the "Council for Mutual Economic Aid" (Comecon) established in 1949, which took measures to standardize machinery, coordinate economic policies, and issued blasts against western European efforts at cooperation like the Common Market and Euratom. The Asian communist régimes also collaborated. Yugoslavia never was a member, and after 1958 was no longer invited to send observers. By

the fall of 1959, Khrushchev had not solved a dilemma that indeed seemed essentially insoluble: how to maintain totalitarian authority over the European satellites while simultaneously trying to relax Stalinist methods.

But the central concern of Soviet foreign policy in Europe remained Germany. In East Germany (DDR, *Deutsche Demokratische Republik*) it had created its most industrially productive European satellite, now fully geared into the Comecon, and expected to make a long-term contribution to the development of the communist world. Except for a brief but violent workers' riot in East Berlin in 1953, the German communist puppets had succeeded in repressing the population's hatred for Soviet and communist rule. Moreover, strategically the DDR was of great importance to the U.S.S.R.: control over East Germany enabled the Russians to keep Poland surrounded, and helpless to achieve more than a token autonomy. Yet full domination over this important satellite was impeded by the fact that the United States, Britain, and France each retained a zone of occupation in Berlin, deep in the heart of the DDR, and accessible by subway from East Berlin. Every year, thousands of East Germans showed how they felt about communism by escaping into West Berlin. For those who stayed behind in the DDR, West Berlin provided an example of prosperity and free democratic government that acted more effectively on their minds than any mere propaganda.

This situation accounted for Khrushchev's determination to get the western powers out of Berlin. The method he proposed was thoroughly Stalinist: he threatened to sign a peace treaty with the puppet government of East Germany—never recognized by the West—to turn over to it the communications to Berlin, and to support it in any effort it might then make to cut these communications and force the western powers out. Western refusal to accept this high-handed and unilateral abrogation of agreements concluded during World War II led to a prolonged diplomatic crisis during 1959, in which the U.S.S.R. several times postponed a final date of decision, but made no real concession to the western view.

All the powers had come to realize that no problem was more critical. The West could hardly permit the U.S.S.R. to recreate the conditions it had fought during the airlift of 1948. Nor could it accept the suggestion that, once western troops were removed, Berlin would be a "free city." Defenseless and surrounded by communist territory, Berlin and its 2,000,000 "free" citizens, it feared, would soon be swallowed up. This would be an intolerable defeat. Moreover, the negotiations proposed by the U.S.S.R. whereby the DDR would thereafter "confederate" with the West German Federal Republic aroused the gravest doubts. How could a state that was a full member of the western system of NATO federate with one that belonged to the Soviet system of the Warsaw Pact, a state that stood for free capitalist development federate with one completely communized, a parliamentary state responsibly governed by a multi-party system with checks and balances federate with a communist totalitarian state? It seemed probable that Khrushchev did not believe in the possibility of the confederation he was proposing, and hoped instead that any possible union of the Germanies would be discredited, and that the DDR, with full control over Berlin would emerge as a permanent Soviet satellite.

In Middle Eastern and European foreign policy, then, Khrushchev, down to 1960 was as tough as Stalin, despite his relaxation of domestic terror. In Asia, the question was complicated by western inability to determine exactly how much of a role the U.S.S.R. still played, and how far Communist China had been given, or had taken, a free hand. Certain episodes—such as the Chinese bombardment of Quemoy in 1958, their savage conquest of Tibet, and the

timing of the communist movements in Laos in 1959—aroused the suspicion that the Chinese were acting independently of Moscow. The Tibetan venture brought the Chinese to the Indian border, and in some cases, apparently, across it; the Indians not only sympathized with the Tibetan Buddhists who were being slaughtered and exiled but found their own security threatened, and could take no comfort from the

Khrushchev in America.

harsh answers the Chinese gave to their protests. Yet it could hardly be to Moscow's interest to shift the balance of India's neutrality toward the West. Similarly, the Laos operations, which aroused the United States and her allies in South East Asia, came at a moment when Khrushchev was striving to negotiate directly with the United States, and seemed to be a deliberate Chinese effort to prevent such negotiations.

These matters are still "current events," rather than history. No historian can yet comment on them with enough information and responsibility. Yet the series of visits between Moscow and Washington—Mikoyan and Kozlov, Khrushchev's two deputies visiting the United States, and Vice-President Nixon visiting Moscow—was now culminating in the dramatic, highly publicized, and unprecedented tour by Khrushchev himself in America.

The scheduled "summit conference" of Khrushchev with Eisenhower, Macmillan, and de Gaulle, however, failed dramatically as Khrushchev out-Stalined Stalin in bitter denunciations of the United States for "spying" on Russia in high-altitude airplane flights (May, 1960). Eisenhower's visit to Russia was cancelled, and the cold war grew hot again. But Soviet intransigence towards the West seemed likely to stop short of aggressive war. Indeed, Russian policy might yet soften toward the West, thus reflecting a rising fear of the huge, over-populated, frantically industrializing Chinese state, and a wish to come to terms with the West in the face of a long-range threat more frightening than a capitalist-communist agreement.

Stresses
within the Communist Bloc

The communist bloc, as we have seen, is a vast area, a set of contiguous states, occupying the "heartland" of the great Eurasian continent, from Leipzig to Vladivostok and Peiping. How solid a bloc it will prove to be is one of the great unsolved problems of our time. Since the end of World War II it has been subject to two interrelated stresses. First, all its constituent states, including the two giants, Russia and China, have faced the internal problems set by the communist revolutions of which they are the children. The communist philosophy makes great promises to men—promises of peace, material abundance, the good life for all. In the communist states these prom-

ises have not yet been fulfilled. Perhaps they can be partially fulfilled, enough to maintain the populations in a reasonable state of contentment; perhaps they can be softened and compromised; perhaps the populations can be made to accept such substitutes as nationalism. And perhaps not. The people may be tempted to relax, to try, even in their totalitarian societies, to influence their government toward compromises with the West. It is significant that, though the Soviet Union continued after the war the pre-war five-year plans, some emphasis was placed on consumer goods, the sort of things that the ordinary person purchases for his own use. The "pursuit of happiness" may yet move communist societies closer to our own.

We may be somewhat more certain of a second possible weakness in the communist bloc. The units of the bloc are after all nation-states, some of them with long histories as self-conscious, independent states and societies. Not even the magic of communism can at once master the nationalistic forces that in the past prevented the merging of such self-conscious states and societies into perfectly unified blocs or into super-states or into true federal unions. It would be rash to predict that Rumania, Czechoslovakia, or China will go "Titoist" and follow the Yugoslav example of breaking with Moscow in some future crisis; Poland, however, seems to have broken off part way; and Finland has somehow contrived to maintain its independence. It would be simple historical common sense to assert that the present Russian communist coalition is by no means immune from the stresses and strains that have always made coalitions hard to hold together. Peoples with any traditions of, or even aspirations toward, independence are inevitably hard to handle. The events of the autumn of 1956 in Poland and Hungary underlined these stresses. Moreover, an eventually industrialized China, with a population more than twice that of the

U.S.S.R., might well consider itself entitled to occupy a more significant power position in the communist coalition than at present. Westerners should not, of course, overemphasize the difficulties the Russians face; above all, they must not think of a Russian-Chinese quarrel, a Polish revolt, as "inevitable." But neither should they feel that the Russian bloc is a monolith, unchanging, a perfect coalition.

Communists outside the Russian Bloc

Beyond the U.S.S.R. itself and its bloc of communist countries, communism under Russian inspiration has been at work, in varying degrees of strength, all over the world. That strength is hard to measure country by country for the period since 1945. In some parts of the world, such as Malaya and Indo-China, the communists soon became organized fighting groups with partisan (guerrilla) armies in the field. In other parts, such as Spain, the communists have been outlawed, but they most certainly exist as an active underground movement. In still other areas, as in France and Italy, they are a legally organized party taking part in elections for legislative bodies.

The contemporary struggle in international relations between the Russian and the American "coalitions," we must insist, is by no means unprecedented, save perhaps in its worldwide scope. It is *in part* a balance-of-power struggle basically of the sort we have encountered frequently in earlier centuries. The really crucial question of our time is this: is the communist bloc inspired by quasi-religious ideas and sentiments to an uncompromising crusade to make the whole world one communist society? History unfortunately cannot give for this problem the kind of answer the scientist or engineer expects to get for his problems. It does indeed look to us as though the Russians are still crusaders as well as conventional aggressors. The historian can only add that in the past intolerant, uncompromising, self-sacrificing, crusading fervor has never lasted very long in any large human group.

He can, however, be more reassuring on one very important phase of the current international struggle. Communism in very many parts of the western world, including the United States itself, has to be—or its devotees think it has to be—a conspiratorial or quasi-conspiratorial movement. Many otherwise sensible people are alarmed by this conspiratorial aspect of a movement they hate and fear. Yet the record of our civilization is clear. Conspiracy as such, the melodramatic underworld of secrecy and skullduggery, though it may commit all sorts of evil deeds from assassination to theft of atomic "secrets," can at most trigger an explosion *among explosive materials,* as did Princip's revolver shot at Sarajevo (see Chapter XXV). It cannot explode materials not suitable for explosion. No stable, successful, contented society is going to explode. Communism as conspiracy does not really threaten the West; communism as a world-religion, or as a substitute for such a religion, in the long run can threaten the West only if it is a better religion than our own.

Reading Suggestions
on the West and Russia in the Contemporary World

(Asterisk indicates paperbound edition.)

H. W. Gatzke, *The Present in Perspective: A Look at the World since 1945* (Rand McNally, 1957). An excellent brief survey of our "grave new world."

A. J. Zurcher, ed., *Constitutions and Constitutional Trends since World War II*, 2nd ed. (New York Univ. Press, 1955). A very good, up-to-date collaborative account.

G. Myrdal, *An International Economy: Problems and Prospects* (Harper, 1956). An able study by a professional economist with wide international experience.

L. Fischer, *This Is Our World* (Harper, 1956). A subjective and most suggestive journalist's survey of the trouble spots of the globe.

H. A. Kissinger, *Nuclear Weapons and American Foreign Policy* (Harper, 1957; *Anchor). An important document in the debate on foreign policy.

G. F. Kennan, *Russia, the Atom, and the West* (Harper, 1958). A brief, pithy, controversial contribution to the same debate.

C. M. Eichelberger, *U.N.: The First Ten Years* (Harper, 1958). Good short account.

A. J. Zurcher, *The Struggle to Unite Europe, 1940-1958* (New York Univ. Press, 1958). A succinct up-to-date account of an important movement.

M. Salvadori, *NATO: A Twentieth Century Community of Nations* (Van Nostrand, 1957; *Anvil). With documents and interpretations.

E. Wilson, *Red, Black, Blond, Olive* (Oxford Univ. Press, 1956). Interesting studies of four societies—a New Mexico Pueblo, Haiti, Russia, Israel.

THE DEMOCRACIES

The following volumes in the "American Foreign Policy Library" series, D. C. McKay, ed. (Harvard Univ. Press), provide good introductions to the areas treated: C. Brinton, *The United States and Britain*, 2nd ed. (1948); D. C. McKay, *The United States and France* (1951); H. S. Hughes, *The United States and Italy* (1953); F. D. Scott, *The United States and Scandinavia* (1950).

G. Kennan, *Realities of American Policy* (Princeton Univ. Press, 1954). By a thoughtful exponent of a realistic policy.

F. L. Allen, *The Big Change* (Harper, 1952). Perceptive essay on American social history since 1900, emphasizing the change from old-fashioned capitalism to what Allen argues is today socially responsible capitalism. On this theme see also Editors of Fortune, *USA: The Permanent Revolution* (Prentice-Hall, 1951), and M. Salvadori, *The Economics of Freedom* (Doubleday, 1959).

C. Brinton, *The Temper of Western Europe* (Harvard Univ. Press, 1953). A cautiously optimistic evaluation.

F. Williams, *Socialist Britain* (Viking, 1949) and C. Palmer, *The British Socialist Ill-Fare State* (Caxton, 1952). A defense and a critique of Labor's postwar reforms.

G. Wright, *The Reshaping of French Democracy* (Reynal & Hitchcock, 1948). Lively study of constitution-making in 1946.

A. Werth, *France: 1940-1955* (Hale, 1956). An informative though not always balanced analysis by a journalistic expert.

H. Luethy, *France against Herself* (Praeger, 1955; *Meridian). Perceptive study of divided France by a Swiss.

D. Schoenbrunn, *As France Goes* (Harper, 1957). A readable, balanced account by a first-rate journalist.

M. Grindrod, *The Rebuilding of Italy, 1945-1955* (Royal Institute of International Affairs, 1955). Sound contemporary history.

J. Hampden Jackson, ed., *A Short History of France: From Early Times to 1958* (Cambridge Univ. Press, 1959). A collaborative work by British experts, covering the whole of French history, but with much emphasis on the latest period.

J. P. Warburg, *Germany: Key to Peace* (Harvard Univ. Press, 1953). An instructive survey.

W. Fleisher, *Sweden: The Welfare State* (Day, 1956). An objective examination of a small democracy.

COMMUNISM AND THE COLD WAR

(See also books recommended under Chapter XXVI.)

D. J. Dallin, *The New Soviet Empire* (Yale Univ. Press, 1951). Survey from an anti-Soviet standpoint.

G. A. Almond, ed., *The Appeals of Communism* (Princeton Univ. Press, 1954). An interesting symposium.

W. Leonhard, *Child of the Revolution* (Regnery, 1958; *Gateway). Revealing account by a defecting East German Communist official.

M. Einaudi and others, *Communism in Western Europe* (Cornell Univ. Press, 1951). A very illuminating examination of French and Italian communists.

R. L. Wolff, *The Balkans in Our Time* (Harvard Univ. Press, 1956). An informed account of an important area.

H. L. Roberts, *Russia and America: Dangers and Prospects* (Harper, 1956; *New American Library). A valuable summary.

Z. K. Brzezinski, *The Soviet Bloc Unity and Conflict* (Harvard Univ. Press, 1960). A sound and detailed study of the relationships between Moscow and the other communist states, including China, Poland, Yugoslavia, and Hungary.

C. J. Friedrich and Z. K. Brzezinski, *Totalitarian Dictatorship and Autocracy* (Harvard Univ. Press, 1956). Systematic examination of totalitarian institutions.

W. Z. Laqueur, *The Soviet Union and the Middle East* (Praeger, 1959). A pioneering investigation of a new and important subject.

R. Walker, *China Under Communism* (Yale Univ. Press, 1955).

NOVELS (ALL DISCUSSED IN THE TEXT)

I. Ehrenburg, *The Thaw*, trans. Manya Harari (Harvil, 1955).

V. Dudintsev, *Not by Bread Alone*, trans. E. Bone (Dutton, 1957).

B. Pasternak, *Dr. Zhivago*, trans. Max Hayward and Manya Harari (Pantheon, 1958; *Signet).

The Revolt against Imperialism

CHAPTER XXXI

I: Introduction: Causes and Nature of the Revolt

THE FIRST WORLD WAR had brought a gradual loosening of the imperial ties binding non-western peoples to the great colonial powers of the West (see Chapters XXV and XXVIII). The Second World War greatly accelerated and intensified this process. In many cases, during the years after 1945, imperial ties were more than loosened: they were cut to ribbons. Not only were the empires of vanquished Italy and Japan dismantled after 1945, the imperial possessions of the victors and the nominal victors—the British, Americans, French, and Dutch—suffered major amputations. In Asia, the Middle East, and Africa newly independent states began to emerge—India, Pakistan, Burma, Indonesia, the Philippines, Syria, Lebanon, Israel, Libya, the Sudan, Tunisia, Morocco, and still others. By 1960, fifteen years after the close of World War II, the list of newcomers to the world's sovereign states, already impressively long, was continuing to grow rapidly. Meantime, states like China, Iran, and Egypt, that had long been sovereign in name but in practice were often subject to some degree of control by the im-

619

perial powers, vigorously asserted their independence. The nationalism of the non-western world was coming of age.

What caused this great revolt against imperialism after World War II? One important answer is provided by the war itself. In the Second World War, as in the First, the western democracies often relied on colonial troops, with a consequent boost to the self-esteem of the peoples providing the troops. In both wars the propaganda of the democracies to show the justness of their cause fostered ambitions for the basic democratic rights of self-government and self-determination. In both wars inflation and other economic dislocations such as rationing, shortages, and the enjoyment of war profits by the few rather than the many, heightened these ambitions and swelled the sense of grievance on the part of non-western peoples.

But the second war, unlike the first, destroyed the magic invulnerability of the West, for the western possessions in the Far East did fall before the attacks of non-western conquerors, the Japanese. The final defeat of Japan apparently did little to offset the immense damage done to western prestige. Moreover, two of the great imperial powers, the French and the Dutch, were only by courtesy numbered among the victors of World War II, with almost fatal consequences for their prestige. Nationalist leaders in the non-western world also knew that British power had been seriously weakened by the tremendous drain of the war, and that the outcome of the British election of 1945, in which the somewhat anti-imperialist Labor party defeated the resolutely imperialist Conservatives, promised liberalization of British policy. Nationalist leaders further knew that the real victors in the war were the United States and the Soviet Union, each in its very different way outspokenly anti-colonial.

In the long perspective of history, however, the Second World War was the im-mediate, not the ultimate, cause of the colonial revolt. The deeper causes must be sought in the five-hundred-year record of western expansion, and in the western tra-dition itself. The mainsprings of western culture—Christianity and the secular faiths of progress, democracy, and nationalism—provided little nourishment for imperialist policies. The West could not conceal from the educated natives its own great ethical and political writings. Indeed, it often laid before them with pride the Christian Bible, the American Declaration of Independence, the French Declaration of the Rights of Man, even the Communist Manifesto. It was hardly possible to keep on telling the natives that "all men are created equal" really meant that "white men are created the superiors of colored men." In terms of ideals and ideology, western imperialism carried within itself the seeds of its own failure—or, more positively, its own trans-figuration into self-determination for all peoples.

The great instrument for the spread of western ideas to non-western peoples was the education, both formal and informal, provided the natives by the West itself. In the nineteenth century, this education owed a great deal to the efforts of Christian missions, though toward the end of the century it became more secular as a result of increasing participation by the governing powers themselves. Almost every-where formal education was limited to a comparatively small number of natives. In India, the sons of rajahs went to Oxford, and so too did bright boys from the slowly rising middle classes; by the twentieth century western education in India itself was beginning to assume the western form of "careers open to talents." Some non-Europeans turned against this western educa-tion and took refuge in a reaffirmation of the values of their traditional culture, of Hinduism or Islam, for example. But for the most part, the educated natives came to feel that their lands could become truly

Mustafa Kemal Atatürk at ninth anniversary celebration of the founding of the Turkish Republic, 1932.

independent only by imitating the West, by learning its industrial, technological, and military skills.

The educated classes throughout the world of western imperialism emphatically wanted independence. Many were by the twentieth century revolutionaries; some became great admirers of the Bolshevik revolution in Russia, and a few received training in the techniques of revolution in Moscow itself. A great many westerners made the mistake of assuming that these nationalist revolutionaries were a totally unrepresentative minority of the native populations, and that the great colonial masses, illiterate and poor, did not really follow their own native educated class but asked nothing better than to be ruled by the kindly whites. Of course the subject races have always had their share of "Uncle Toms" (a term used in scorn by American Negroes for their fellows who appear too submissive toward the whites). But the "Uncle Toms" have not given their stamp to non-western populations. The urban masses, and then, more gradually, the peasant masses, began to share the feelings

of nationalism and to demand that the foreigner must go.

The imperialist powers themselves followed policies that greatly aided the ripening of nationalism. Almost everywhere they penetrated they brought enough sanitary engineering, enough medicine, enough law and order to lower the death rate and to enable the native population to grow as it had never grown before. But that very growth made more mouths to feed, and the fact of population pressure became increasingly obvious to the educated and uneducated alike. Furthermore, education gave the natives some of the white man's special magic, his control over material things and over the elaborate machines of the modern world; the natives began to acquire scientific knowledge and engineering skills. Thereby, they came to feel more and more the white man's equal, less and less willing to accept a subordinate position in things of the spirit now that, in material things, they were drawing even.

In the world outside the West the things of the spirit often assume transcendent importance. It has been said that nationalism

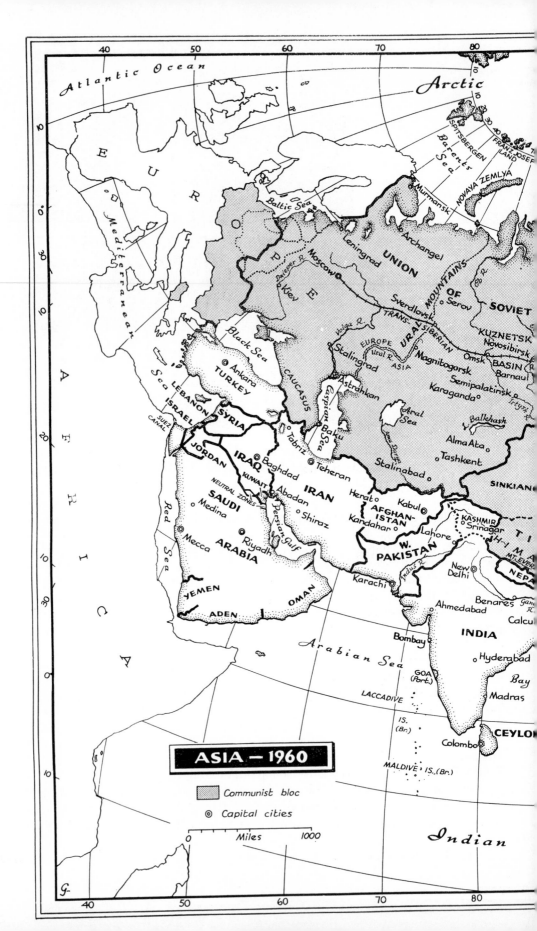

ASIA – 1960

Communist bloc
⊚ Capital cities

Miles 1000

is a kind of secular religion, and the validity of this interpretation has been borne out time and again in the Turkey of Atatürk and his successors, in the India of Gandhi and Nehru, in Communist China, and elsewhere. Resistance to foreign imperialism, real or imagined, and exaltation of one's native land have become articles of faith, commanding the kind of devotion that a religion requires of its followers. We shall see that when the Iranian government nationalized the properties of the Anglo-Iranian Oil Company it sacrificed the material to the spiritual, as it were, for it gave up badly needed oil royalties to obtain nationalistic satisfaction.

Many westerners, bewildered by such apparently irrational behavior, have refused to believe that nationalist "extremists" were the only native political force of any substance. Somewhere there must be "moderates" who would in good season subdue the extremists and turn to the sweet reasonableness of compromise. With some exceptions, this western belief has proved thoroughly illusory: in a crisis, the moderates have vanished, for they have joined the ranks of the extremists. No westerner should really be surprised by this, for the moderates have often been the victims of revolution, as in the France of 1792-1794 and the Russia of 1917-1919. The extremism of the nationalist revolutionaries of yesterday and today is, then, by no means without historical precedent. And, if the precedent is not ready at hand, it can always be invented, as it was in the era of Atatürk by the Turkish nationalists who devised a "new" history of their own. They sought to demonstrate, on extremely flimsy evidence, that everything ancient and worthwhile, including the alphabet, came from the Hittites and Sumerians and other very early peoples who, they alleged, were really Turks.

The extremes to which non-western nationalism may go are not always merely picturesque. Very recent history has recorded the Mau Mau terror in Kenya, the recurrent outbreaks between Hindu and Moslem in India, the many outrages against French individuals in Morocco and Algeria, the equally outrageous French reprisals, the implacable hatred of Arab for Israeli—this catalogue of violence could easily be made longer. It must also be noted that these non-western nationalisms often express high ambitions and ideals; they are striving to create nations, not to preserve nations already firmly rooted. To cite merely one example: since 1945 there has been much talk of an Arab "nation" stretching across North Africa and the Middle East from the Atlantic to the Indian Ocean. The reality is that this vast Arabic-speaking realm is fragmented into a dozen separate political units, and that in most of them traditional loyalties to religious sects, to village, family, or tribe, and to social class are still very strong. Yet it is also clear that there is a growing yearning for Arab nationhood and that loyalties to entities outside religion, family, and class are beginning to develop. This forging of new loyalties—or, to change the metaphor, this adolescent stage of nationalism—is one more reason why the revolt against imperialism is indeed a revolution.

II: Asia

Defeated Japan

In the Far East, the Second World War witnessed the spectacular rise and fall of imperialist Japan. The "Greater East Asia Co-Prosperity Sphere" of Japan showed at its peak many obvious analogies with Napoleon's system of satellite states and even more with that of Hitler. The Japanese employed methods of rule that were directly patterned on western precedent; they relied chiefly on the time-honored device of setting up puppet native governments, and exploiting for their own benefit the economic resources of the conquered lands. Their empire disintegrated in the atomic blast of Hiroshima. It had never been cemented by the loyalty of its component parts.

Yet the Japanese started with at least one very great asset: they were an Asian people, a colored people, not westerners with the burden of white supremacy to carry. They could come as the emancipators of Asians and Pacific islanders, and their propaganda sounded this note most vigorously. Yet, Asians though they were, they did not endear themselves to their fellow Asians and they never converted more than a minority in each conquered land. Their armies looted and committed atrocities; the Japanese abroad behaved like any other master race and did not conceal their feelings of superiority over the natives. Time might have taught the Japanese a lesson in social psychology, and they might have been able with time to consolidate their grandiloquently named "co-prosperity sphere"; but time they did not have.

The end of World War II saw Japan reduced to her own islands, stripped of her overseas possessions. The overwhelming part played by the United States in the defeat of Japan insured that the military occupation and the subsequent peace of 1952, whereby Japan regained formal independence, would be almost wholly an American concern. Though there was a strong current in American opinion that demanded the deposition of the Emperor, he was left on his throne, deprived of his divine status, and subjected to the close control of General MacArthur and the forces of occupation. Americans found to their astonishment that on the surface at least the Japanese people, far from taking the occupation with hostility, seemed almost to admire their occupiers. They seemed not to understand what democracy meant—apart from baseball and some other American folkways—but they appeared very anxious to learn. Their behavior roused a good deal of speculation about national psychology, some of which appealed to the rigorous early toilet-training of Japanese children to explain the national willingness to obey a master.

We are dealing here not only with history, but also with a very problematic present. The Japanese have not had a democratic society or a democratic political organization in the past, and it is by no means certain that they will firmly establish a democracy of the western type, although they have made a promising start since 1945. If a well-developed industrial economy is an indispensable base for the development of democracy, the Japanese have already a great advantage over all other non-western peoples. We must, however, beware of the simple conclusion that, because Japan took over industrialism from the West, she will automatically become thoroughly westernized. Sir George Sansom, a wise western observer who knows Japan well, writes:

Thus, while it may be said that the introduction of power-driven machinery brought to bear upon Japanese life a strong influence of Western origin, this is true only with qualifications.... Printing and binding machinery, for example, increases the number and circulation of books and newspapers, of which the contents may well be such as to spread ideas critical of foreign countries. . . .

It is true that Western clothing, food, transport, and communications, as well as Western ideas, have enlarged and diversified Japanese life, but they have not necessarily changed its essential character. The cumulative effect of industrialization upon a people whose material culture is simple must destroy much of what is indigenous; but the impact of an advanced Western culture upon an advanced Eastern culture may, despite far-reaching superficial changes, succeed in producing resistance, or even hostile reactions in matters of vital import—in the totality of a people's feelings about life and society.[*]

Poor though the Japanese peasant and laboring classes are by American standards, they are far ahead of other non-western peoples. And grave though the population problem is, with some 90,000,000 people living in 147,000 square miles, it is not so desperate as it is in the crowded farmlands of India or Java or Egypt. Japan must, however, find foreign markets for her industrial production if she is to maintain and improve her national standard of living. Her position is singularly like that of Britain: she must export or die.

Finally, the growth of the tension between the United States and Russia has made Japan an American ally, an island outpost off the eastern edge of the Communist land-mass. For Japan to be an effective ally, the United States must find a way to help her obtain in the free world the markets she needs. But, as the Japanese recover their strength, they may well try to regain their old markets in China, even though it is now Communist, and may even renew their old aspirations to great-power status.

Communist China

The Second World War produced a major shift in the balance of power in the Far East. As Japan went down, China rose, a Communist China, antagonistic to the "imperialists" of the West, particularly Americans. As we have already seen, in Chapter XXVIII, by the late 1930's the Communists were engaged in a struggle for power, a virtual civil war, with the Nationalists of the Kuomintang, headed by Chiang Kai-shek. During World War II, the United States backed the Nationalist government at Chungking and, when the war ended, hoped to be able to reconcile the Nationalists and the Communists and make China a democratic, pro-American state. In such a state the Communists would have been a legal party and a large one, as in France or Italy, but not a majority group. In 1946, the American negotiator, General Marshall, however, failed in his attempt to bring the two parties to a working agreement.

After Marshall's return to the United States in January, 1947, the result of the renewed Chinese civil war was never seriously in doubt. The Communists received very effective support from the Soviet Union, including war material that the Japanese had surrendered to the Russians in Manchuria. The Kuomintang government was weakened by its own ebbing morale, by its dwindling popular support, and by an ever-mounting inflation that had gathered force during the war and further ravaged an economy already ruined by the long Japanese occupation. Late in 1949, the Nationalists, driven from the mainland, transferred their government to the island of Formosa (Taiwan), which Japan had relinquished in 1945. The Communists, lacking naval strength, could not pursue Chiang and the Nationalists.

---

[*] G. B. Sansom, *The Western World and Japan* (New York, 1949), 497-498.

China, then, by 1950 had gone Communist and formed part of the great Soviet bloc. Americans, in the face of the total failure of their China policy, began a bitter debate over the reasons why the Communists had been able to unite China under their control. A decade later, this controversial question has not become a historical question, for no one as yet can command either the perspective or the documents needed for a fair appraisal. The historian can, however, warn against any explanation of the Communists' success that rests on the notion that a few conspirators, a few wicked men, with perhaps a few misled ones, brought about the Communist victory. Wicked men and conspirators were indeed active in China, but they were powerless to accomplish anything on the scale here involved without the assistance of what we call "social forces," "economic needs," and "morale." These may be vague terms, but they represent millions upon millions of human beings. We must now try to spell out their meaning in China.

The Communists had used the long struggle against Japan from 1937 to 1945 to broaden their base of operations and to widen their popular appeal. They made a successful effort to bring their soldiers into good relations with the peasants, and to make soldiers and peasants alike aware that they could act together. China was a land where the soldier was traditionally regarded as the lowest of human beings, a destructive force like a flood or a typhoon. Against such a traditional view the Communist slogan— "the soldiers are fish and the people water" —came as a really revolutionary stroke. This characteristic Chinese aphorism was at once understood to mean that the army rested on popular support and confidence. Again, the Communists were able to bridge the traditional gap in China between the intellectual and the ordinary person. Communist success here was facilitated in the 1940's by the uprooted state of mind of Chinese intellectuals, who were searching for new beliefs and hopes. Most of them seemed to find the lift they sought in the Communist program, with its almost religious stress on "liberation" of the common man, especially the peasant, through economic, social, and political revolution.

The historian, of course, cannot predict what will come of the Communist régime in China; he can, however, record what appear to be the most striking accomplishments of the régime during its initial years in power and point out some of the major problems it is likely to face in the immediate future. The Communists run China through a most elaborate totalitarian structure, largely patterned on the Russian model. The handful of men at the top exert authority by means of the army, the intricate hierarchy of the regular governmental administration, and the equally intricate structure of the Communist party. In addition, a host of special organizations—trade unions, federations of women, of youth, of students, of intellectuals, and the like— claim membership in the millions or tens of millions. At the base are the "communes," to which both the urban and rural masses are being assigned, and which seem to aim at the maximum of controlled collective effort not only in working but also in living and thinking.

To many westerners this wholesale imposition of the "party line," this molding of a collective personality, is the most outstanding and alarming characteristic of Red China. A distinguished American expert, Professor Fairbank, has studied the question and reached these conclusions:

The Communist achievement in organization, among a people so recently famous for their lack of it, has depended upon the inspiring, coercing or manipulating of individual personalities. . . . When American P.O.W.'s in Korea 'confessed' to germ warfare and collaborated with their Chinese captors, they were responding to techniques developed through use with Chinese of all sorts, including Party members. As a result of these methods capitalists and rich peasants smilingly gave their property to the state, professors scathingly denounced their Western bourgeois education, middle school students devotedly gave their lives to party work.

These diverse phenomena represent the real Communist effort at revolution, to change Chinese thinking and behavior. This is far more significant than the material efforts in technology and industry and at the same time is a prerequisite for their material success. Though very diverse, thought reform generally has had certain common features: control of the environment, both of the person physically and of the information available to him . . . ; the stimuli both of idealism and of terror, intermixed; and a grim psychological experience, undergone with guidance through successive phases and intensified by the manipulation of one's sense of guilt and shame. The Chinese slang term "brainwashing" imparts perhaps too much mystery to a process faintly visible elsewhere in religious crusades of the past, only now more thoroughly organized. Modern psychologists can explain how privation, prolonged insecurity and tension, combined with exhausting fatigue and repetitive indoctrination, can shatter the individual's sense of inner identity and create pressures from which the only escape for many is submission to authority and acceptance at least temporarily of new attitudes and concepts. This coercing of the human mind, quite different

Shanghai Electrical Machinery Works in Communist China.

in degree from the mild voluntary form of American advertising methods, is still only partially understood and exploited. . . . Perhaps it is not surprising that in China, where the practical art of human relations has been more fully developed than anywhere else, these psychological methods should be most advanced.[*]

In economic policy the Communist Chinese have generally followed Soviet precedent. Red China, too, has its ambitious five-year plans for industry and its complementary program of agricultural collectivization, introduced soon after lands expropriated from large owners had been redistributed to the peasants. Chinese leaders have repeatedly claimed that "a great leap forward" in economic productivity has already been taken, and that greater and greater leaps will inevitably follow. Some westerners have taken these claims at face value and assume that Red China should already be numbered among the industrial giants. But the evidence available suggests that, although the Communist Chinese have made substantial gains in productivity, they still have a very long way to go to catch up with the major economic powers. The Soviet Union reached economic goals similar to those set by their Chinese brethren, but only at a very high price in human misery and with advantages that China does not enjoy. The economy of China in 1948 was more primitive than that of Russia in 1917; the Chinese themselves had less education and were less familiar with modern economic techniques; and, above all, the Chinese population was four times larger than that of Tsarist Russia. Red China, with more than 600,000,000 inhabitants, is the most populous country in the world; traditionally, these swarming masses have suffered appallingly from flood, drought, and starvation. For the Communist régime to control these natural calamities, feed its growing population, and mod-

[*] J. K. Fairbank, *The United States and China*, new ed. (Cambridge: Harvard University Press, 1958), 291-292.

ernize its economy, all at the same time, will be a formidable undertaking indeed.

Another aspect of the Chinese Communist régime has aroused keen interest in the West—its relationship with the Soviet Union. After World War II all legal traces of China's old subjection to the West vanished, notably extraterritoriality—the right of certain European states to try their own nationals in China by their own courts and their own law. The old ties between China and the West were replaced by new ties with Soviet Russia. Many westerners believe that this development marked a defeat for Chinese nationalism, that China has simply moved out of the imperial orbit of the West and of Japan and into that of the Soviet Union. Many Chinese, on the contrary, apparently find in their Communist régime the fulfillment of their national aspirations. They seem to view Russia as a partner rather than as an overlord, to believe that the Soviet Union can supply western technology without imposing western imperial controls. Down to 1960, at any rate, there has been more evidence to support the second view than to confirm the first. The Russian-Chinese relationship has in fact seemed to be a reasonably effective partnership, although the U.S.S.R. does act as the senior partner and the Chinese have shown some indications of pursuing a more independent role than that usually assigned to a junior partner.

The Korean War

In Communist Chinese relations with the West a major crisis developed early when the "cold war" (see Chapter XXX) became "hot" in June, 1950. The scene of the fighting, Korea, is a peninsula at the eastern extremity of Asia, bordering on Manchuria and Siberia, and close to Japan. Tsarist Russia had hoped to penetrate the area, but these hopes withered with the Russo-Japanese War of 1905 and Japan's annexation of Korea in 1910. In 1945, at the close of World War II, Russian troops occupied the northern part of Korea and American troops occupied the southern part. The country was divided in the middle by a line along the 38th parallel of latitude; a Communist-inspired North Korean People's Republic was set up on one side, and an American-inspired South Korean Republic on the other. When all American forces except for a few specialists were withdrawn from South Korea, the North Koreans marched in to unite the nation under Communist control.

Instead of appeasement, in the tradition of the 1930's, America at once moved troops into Korea. It was a close call, but American troops got there soon enough to halt the North Korean drive and then to push the enemy back well north of the 38th parallel toward the frontier of China. At this point, Communist China, apparently alarmed by events, entered the war, and the fighting moved southward. By 1951, the line of battle had been stabilized roughly along the old boundary between North and South Korea. After prolonged negotiations, an armistice was finally concluded in July, 1953.

The United States carried on its defense of South Korea in the name of the United Nations and received small but valuable detachments of troops from some of its allies. Although the American government wanted to limit the war to the defense of South Korea, the United Nations commander on the spot, the American General MacArthur, concluded that it was necessary to press the war into Communist China. American officials, and in particular America's allies, feared that such a step would bring Russia actively in on the Chinese side and might precipitate World War III. In consequence, General MacArthur was recalled by order of President Truman in April, 1951.

The Korean settlement by no means ended the tension between Communist

China and the United States. The American government continued its refusal to recognize Red China, and serious friction developed over Formosa, which the Communists seemed determined to capture and the United States seemed equally determined to keep out of Communist hands. Antagonism between China and the United States also arose over the question of Southeast Asia, where the Communists sought to turn native nationalism and anti-colonialism to their own advantage.

Southeast Asia

World War II set off a really major political explosion in Southeast Asia. The Japanese conquest and occupation destroyed belief in the invincibility of the white nations, and in 1945 the western powers were by no means able to pick up where they had left off. Moreover, the United States was in the process of granting independence to its own imperial wards, the Filipinos. In 1949, consequently, the Dutch abandoned the attempt to retain a stake in their former colony, the Netherlands East Indies, and recognized its independence as the Republic of Indonesia. Britain gave Burma independence outside the Commonwealth (1948) and the Federation of Malaya independence within the Commonwealth (1957); the great port of Singapore at the tip of Malaya, with its largely Chinese population, secured a special autonomous status (1958). France, meanwhile, made rather more limited concessions to the component states of Indo-China—Vietnam, which included the populous and fairly prosperous coastal areas; and Cambodia and Laos in the more primitive hinterland. But the French did not go far enough or fast enough to prevent their involvement in a lengthy Indo-Chinese war (1945-1954), during which native rebels received Chinese Communist support. Increasingly hard-pressed, the French agreed to partition Vietnam in 1954: the northern half went Communist, and the southern half went to a rather weak native government under the protection of France and the United States.

Although the revolution against colonialism made rapid headway in Southeast Asia, the newly independent nations of the area have scored much less impressive gains in their attempts to solve their basic problems. One great problem is economic. This area, so long cast in the colonial role of producing rice, spices, rubber, tin, and other raw materials, finds it hard to achieve economic independence without western assistance. Many of its peoples regard with suspicion the aid offered by their former masters; yet, if they do not take it, they may drift into economic chaos and possibly into the Communist orbit. Only two states in the area—Thailand (Siam) and the Philippine Republic—joined with Pakistan to participate in the Southeast Asia Treaty Organization (SEATO), sponsored by the West in 1954 as a counter to Communist penetration. For a time that penetration looked most ominous, as the Communists supported a troublesome guerrilla rebellion in the Philippines and waged a stubborn jungle war in Malaya, where they profited by the sympathy of a part of the large Chinese population. By the late 1950's the Communist threat appeared to have been checked, yet the political instability of the Southeast Asian states suggested that the threat might always recur.

The brief history of the Republic of Indonesia furnishes a case study of the difficulties experienced by these states in founding stable political institutions. In the 1950's Indonesia attempted to run its government along generally western parliamentary lines, but almost everything went wrong. The economy was disrupted by inflation and shortages, by administrative corruption and the black market, and by the expulsion of experienced Dutch businessmen. The Moslems, comprising the bulk of the population, were unable to form coherent, responsible political parties and splintered into factions. The outlying islands, resentful of domination by the capital island of Java, rebelled against the central government. Everywhere the high expectations kindled by the achievement of independence were disappointed. In the face of a situation approaching anarchy, the Indonesian President, Soekarno, began to speak of the need for "guided democracy" and for the creation of indigenous, rather than borrowed, political institutions. In 1959 and 1960 Soekarno initiated "guided democracy" by suspending the ineffectual parliamentary régime and vesting authority in himself and in the army and an appointive council. Although this particular experiment got off to a lame start, it conforms to a general pattern we shall encounter in other parts of the non-western world where political machinery imported from the West has also broken down.

India and Pakistan

At the end of World War II, the victory of the British Labor party, pledged to grant India self-government, made Indian emancipation a certainty. But the deep-seated tension between Moslems and Hindus (see Chapter XXVIII) now assumed critical importance. When the Hindus' Congress party and the All-India Moslem League faced the need to make a working constitution for India, they found themselves in complete disagreement. The Moslems had long been working for a partition into separate Hindu and Moslem states, and this was in the end reluctantly accepted by the Hindus. In 1947, Hindu India and Moslem Pakistan were set up as self-governing dominions within the British Commonwealth.

Pakistan ("land of the pure," a name coined by Moslem students in Britain in the 1930's) is a state divided into two parts, widely separated by intervening Indian territory—the larger, West Pakistan, in the northwest, and the smaller and more densely populated, East Pakistan, in East Bengal. The rest of the former British Indian Empire became the Republic of India by virtue of its constitution of 1950. Pakistan, with its 90,000,000 people and its relatively poorly developed industry, is weaker than India with its more than 400,000,000, and at first kept closer political ties with the British Commonwealth.

The partition was not achieved without violence. In view of the way races and religions are geographically mingled in the subcontinent, it could not result in a complete separation of Hindus in one state and Moslems in another. The line of partition between India and West Pakistan evoked bitter fighting between members of the two communities, and many thousands of lives were lost. It resulted in a wholesale transfer of populations as Hindus moved from Pakistani territory into India and Moslems moved from Indian territory into Pakistan. Still a source of trouble between India and Pakistan is the mountainous region of Kashmir, an important tourist center. Kashmir, though mainly Moslem in population, was at the time of partition ruled by a Hindu princely house which turned it over to India. India has continued to occupy most of Kashmir, to the great economic disadvantage of Pakistan. The United Nations sought to determine the fate of Kashmir by arranging a plebiscite, but down to 1960 it failed to secure the needed approval of both parties.

Generally, however, both India and Pakistan have come to accept partition, although it has obliged both to maintain military establishments that strain their limited resources. Both have settled down to the arduous work of forging new nation-states, and both have done well in the business of international politics. India, in particular, has undertaken the difficult and risky task of setting up as mediator not only between

Indian village. Boys' school in background, village elders sitting in the center.

East and West but between Communism and the democratic world—a task flattering to national self-esteem.

In domestic politics the two states went through sharply contrasting experiences. The chief architect of Pakistani independence, Jinnah (see Chapter XXVIII), died in 1948. Deprived of its leader, the young state floundered in its attempts to make parliamentary government work and to attack pressing economic problems. In 1958, a *coup d'état* liquidated the parliamentary régime and gave full powers to the army commander, Ayub Khan. The new régime began by attacking administrative corruption and the black market, distributing land to the peasants, and instituting a program of "basic democracies" to train the population in self-government at the local level. By 1960 the pace of Pakistan's "basic democracies" appeared markedly brisker than

that of Indonesia's "guided democracy."

Newly emancipated India suffered a grievous loss when Gandhi was assassinated by an anti-Moslem Hindu fanatic in 1948. But Nehru, Gandhi's "younger brother," as he was termed, at once assumed full leadership. Under the guidance of Nehru, who was already a seasoned politician, and aided also by the long experience of British administration, India accomplished a feat almost without precedent in the non-western world. It successfully inaugurated a genuine parliamentary democracy of the western type and conducted free and hotly fought elections, based on universal suffrage, among voters who were in the main illiterate and rural. Understandably, Indians are very proud of their accomplishment.

Both countries have had to cope with formidable economic problems—Pakistan

CHAPTER XXXI

with poverty and lack of industry, and India with poverty and lack of sufficient agricultural output to sustain her enormous population. India faces in an acute form the population pressure that bears so heavily on many other non-western countries. There are now over 400,000,000 people in the Republic of India, approximately 8,000,000 are added annually, and this population is periodically threatened by famine and by actual death through starvation. In 1950, the government launched the first in a series of five-year plans for economic development. These plans stress undertakings by the state but also allot a role to private enterprise, for India has a "mixed" economy, both socialist and individualist. Under the five-year plans, private industry has expanded, irrigation and flood-control works have been started, transport and communications improved, and a beginning made on the enormously difficult and significant task of educating hundreds of millions of peasants in new and more efficient ways of working the land. The West has helped by furnishing technical experts, money, and the surplus grain needed to avert the threat of famine. Though not uniformly successful, the plans have invigorated Indian life and permitted a modest increase in employment opportunities and average incomes. Experts estimate, however, that even with a modernized economy India will find it hard to support a population much in excess of its present numbers. Although birth control is abhorrent to the traditional ways of Hinduism, the government has sponsored a campaign for its practice.

Hinduism in Review

Hinduism is a unique and all-important element in the new Indian republic. More than that, it throws much light on the essential differences between East and West, and in particular on the kind of

setting in which the great drama of non-western political awakening is being played. Hinduism is an immensely complex and ancient way of life for which the word "religion," in its western connotation, is not adequate (see also Chapter XXVIII). It has no church organization in the Christian sense, no clear-cut theology, no established Bible. Of the three major developed cultures that the West has encountered in its expansion over the world, Hinduism is furthest from ours. In comparison, Islam is actually a relative of Christianity, and Chinese society, in spite of its traditional unwestern family structure, has affinities with the utilitarian or worldly strain in the West.

For Hinduism, this world of sense-experience is an illusion, but an illusion that has somehow to be overcome. Death is essential to the overcoming, but death is not enough. Each living man, indeed each living thing, is a soul alienated by the very fact of living from the ultimate, universal soul which is peace, absence of struggle and desire, ineffable non-being. The holiest of men by turning away entirely from the world, by living without desire—but not by any such simple solution as suicide—can perhaps attain this non-being in the end. But most human beings are now living out in this world the consequences of a sinful life as another personality in the past. Indeed, the most sinful of men who have lived in the past have been punished by reincarnation as animals or even as insects (which is why the most orthodox of Hindus will harm no living thing). And even among men, their sins in past incarnations are reflected by their status, their *caste*. The poor, the humblest, are such because their sins have been greater; they cannot improve their lot in the western sense, for they can only slowly in subsequent incarnations redeem their wickedness by living as holy a life as possible.

Hindu society, with its caste system, its innumerable tabus, and its lack of any basis for belief in material progress, found grave difficulties in the way of adopting western culture. That the Hindus have adopted as much as they have is testimony of the penetrating power of the West. For instance, it is quite impossible to preserve literal untouchability in modern India. The lowest Hindu group, actually below and outside the caste system, were called "untouchables" because even their shadow would corrupt a caste-Hindu. No one can keep untouchable in an Indian railroad car. Many Hindu intellectuals have indeed been so far westernized that they have no real basis for calling themselves Hindus; but even for them, and much more for the uneducated, the long accumulation of habits, feelings, and ingrained attitudes cannot be quickly altered.

For example, India confronts in a complex form the problem of language that affects many other non-western nations. Since the country contains ten major linguistic regions, each with its own distinctive tongue, English is the only language commonly understood by most educated Indians. English is also virtually indispensable for its modern scientific vocabulary, yet its use is often attacked as an ignoble concession to colonialism. The new official language, Hindi, cannot provide the needed technical vocabulary; moreover, it is strongly opposed in some regions as an instrument of Hindu persecution of religious minorities, and regional pride in language bolsters regional pride in politics. The central government shows signs of meeting these complexities by compromise, sanctioning the continued use of English as the instrument of higher education, yet working steadily to subordinate regionalism to centralization. In these and manifold other ways the brave new Republic of India is trying hard to mold a modern nation-state out of its often intractable human material.

III: The Middle East

The Middle East, too, has experienced revolutionary changes since 1945. These changes have been first and foremost political: the increasing assertion of national independence by the Middle Eastern states, and their mounting antagonism to the West. Other major issues have arisen, all linked to the central fact of the Middle Eastern political revolution—oil, communism, Arab hostility to the new Jewish national state of Israel, and Arab yearning for some kind of pan-Arab unity. We shall survey each of these problems in turn.

Political Changes

The Middle Eastern mandates obtained by France and Britain after World War I (see Chapter XXV) collapsed after World War II. Syria and Lebanon won their full independence from the French, and the British withdrew from Palestine. The new state of Israel took over western Palestine, and the eastern part was annexed by Transjordan, which now styled itself, after its ruling dynasty, the Hashimite Kingdom of Jordan. The Sudan, located in Africa to the south of Egypt but linked by language and interests to the Arab world, emerged into independence after a half-century of joint administration by Britain and Egypt. Many other old imperial ties between the Middle East and the West have been severed since World War II, notably in two countries traditionally under British influence, Egypt and Iraq.

Revolution broke out in Egypt in 1952,

634

directed both against the British and against the traditional ruling groups among the Egyptians themselves. Although Britain had taken real steps toward freeing Egypt from her tutelage before World War II (see Chapter XXVIII), she did not move fast enough to satisfy Egyptian nationalists. During the war, furthermore, she offended them deeply by forcing King Farouk to dismiss a cabinet sympathetic to Nazi Germany. After the war, Farouk, once a very popular monarch, lost prestige both because of his well-publicized appetite for high living and because of his personal involvement in a scandal concerning the provision of defective supplies to the Egyptian army. From Farouk and his palace clique the odor of corruption and scandal spread through the upper levels of the government.

The revolution, when it came on July 23, 1952, was the work of a group of young army officers, whose closest historical relatives appear to be such military revolutionaries as the Young Turks of the early twentieth century. In some policies the new government of Egypt's strong man, Gamal Abdul Nasser, followed a path paralleling that marked out by Turkey's strong man, Atatürk (see Chapter XXVIII). It abolished the monarchy and drew up a republican constitution. It encouraged the emancipation of women and pared down the traditionally large role of the conservative courts of religious law without, however, making the kind of frontal assault on Islam that Atatürk had attempted. In practice, the régime was rather markedly dictatorial: only one party was tolerated, elections were closely supervised, and press campaigns were orchestrated by the picturesquely named "Ministry of National Guidance." Nasser justified this absolutism on the basis of his own disillusionment at the popular reaction to the events of July, 1952:

Before July 23rd, I had imagined that the whole nation was ready and prepared, waiting for nothing but a vanguard to lead the charge against the battlements, whereupon it would fall in behind in serried ranks, ready for the sacred advance towards the great objective. And I had imagined that our role was to be this commando vanguard. . . .

Then suddenly came reality after July 23rd. The vanguard performed its task and charged the battlements of tyranny. It threw out Farouk and then paused, waiting for the serried ranks to come up. . . .

For a long time it waited. Crowds did eventually come, and they came in endless droves—but how different is reality from the dream! The masses that came were disunited, divided groups of stragglers. . . . At this moment I felt, with sorrow and bitterness, that the task of the vanguard, far from being complete, had only begun.

We needed order, but we found nothing but chaos. We needed unity, but we found nothing behind us but dissension. We needed work, but we found behind us only indolence and sloth. . . .

In addition to all this, there was a confirmed individual egotism. The word "I" was on every tongue. It was the solution to every difficulty, the cure for every ill. I had many times met eminent men—or so they were called by the press—of every political tendency and color, but

Nasser being greeted by fellow Egyptians after announcing nationalization of Suez Canal, 1956.

when I would ask any of them about a problem in the hope he could supply a solution, I would never hear anything but "I."

Economic problems? He alone could understand them; as for the others, their knowledge on the subject was that of a crawling infant. Political issues? He alone was expert. No one else had gotten beyond the a-b-c's of politics. After meeting one of these people, I would go back in sorrow to my comrades and say, "It is no use. If I had asked this fellow about the fishing problems in the Hawaiian Islands, his only answer would be 'I.'" *

Discounted for its rhetorical exaggerations, this passage nevertheless reveals much about the difficulty of establishing stable and responsible régimes in the new world of non-western nationalism.

Economically, Nasser's Egypt confronts a single overriding fact: it is perhaps the most overpopulated state in the world, struggling to support 25,000,000 people in a land that is 95 per cent desert. The revolutionary government, therefore, started an ambitious program of social and economic improvements. To increase agricultural output it projected new irrigation schemes, including a high dam in southern Egypt to impound more of the Nile's flood waters. To provide more jobs—and to bolster Egyptian national pride—it accelerated the pace of industrialization. It lowered the death rate by expanding welfare services and sought, with little initial success, to check the very high birth rate (approximately double that of the United States) by a cautious campaign promoting the practice of birth control.

Though pressing domestic problems were very far from being solved, Nasser's government also made a series of spectacular moves in foreign policy. Starting in 1955, it concluded a series of agreements with Communist states for the purchase of arms, for the financing and construction of the High Dam, and for the sale of Egypt's chief

export, cotton. In July, 1956, openly defying the West, Egypt nationalized the Suez Canal, up to then operated by a company under British and French control. A major international crisis resulted. At the end of October, Israel invaded the Sinai peninsula, to the east of the canal, in reprisal for Arab raids on her territory, and Britain and France began to land troops in the area of the canal itself. The war was nipped in the bud when the Soviet Union threatened to send "volunteers" to defend Egypt, and when both the United States and a majority of United Nations members vigorously disapproved the invasion. In due course, a United Nations Emergency Force moved into the troubled areas, the canal (which had been blocked during the fighting) was reopened, and the canal company accepted Egypt's offer of a financial settlement.

Early in 1958 Nasser pulled one more surprise by proclaiming the merger of Egypt and Syria into the United Arab Republic. The two components of the new U.A.R. were not geographically contiguous but separated by the states of Israel, Lebanon, and Jordan. Their rather unlikely union seems to have been dictated by the fear, both on Nasser's part and on that of moderate Syrian leaders, that the chronic instability of Syrian politics might precipitate a *coup* by Communists or fellow-travelers. The Republic of Syria, during its dozen years of independence, had made solid economic progress but had also piled up an impressive record of political confusion; once it experienced three *coups* in a single year.

In 1958 revolution came to the U.A.R.'s eastern Arab neighbor, Iraq. During World War II, Iraq, like Egypt, produced a nationalist and pro-Nazi régime and was forced by Britain to change her ways. After the war, the tough Iraqi politician, Nuri as-Saïd, brought his country into alignment with the West, particularly Britain, and inaugurated a development program of dams, oil refineries, and other public works,

---

* Gamal Abdul Nasser, *Egypt's Liberation* (Washington: Public Affairs Press, 1955), 32-36.

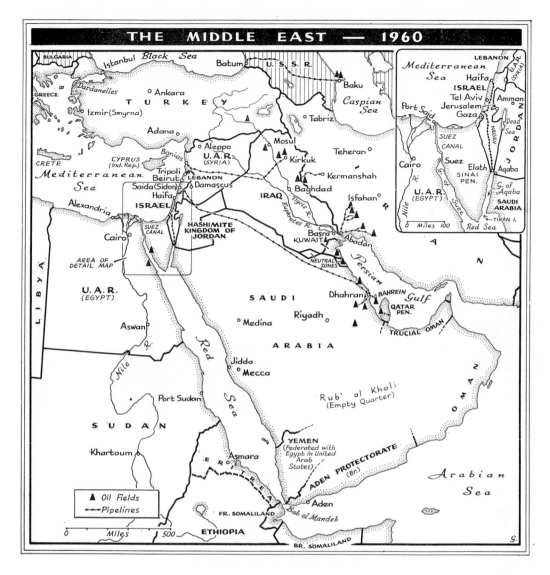

THE MIDDLE EAST — 1960

▲ Oil Fields
←→ Pipelines

0   Miles   500

financed by royalties from the western-controlled Iraq Petroleum Company. Iraqi nationalists, however, far from being won over, agitated against Nuri's vigorous repression of his political opponents, denounced him as a tool of the imperialists, and claimed that the benefits of his development program would go only to the wealthy few and not to the impoverished many. On July 14, 1958, a conspiracy of nationalistic army officers in Baghdad overthrew the old régime and executed both Nuri and the inoffensive and insignificant young king.

The Iraqi revolutionary government, unlike that of Egypt, made a very shaky beginning in the face of repeated local revolts and of the threat of massive infiltration by communists. In 1960 it looked for the first time as though the revolutionary leader, General Qasim, might be on the way to easing these chronic problems and establishing his régime on more solid foundations.

After World War II, Turkey remained the most reliable of the West's allies in the Middle East. Fortified by American military and economic aid against possible Russian designs on her eastern provinces and the Straits, she settled down to work out the full consequences of Atatürk's reforms. The government expanded industry, built roads and schools, and pushed ahead with the essential task of bringing the Atatürk spirit of westernization to the peasants, who make up three-quarters of the population. Some of the secularist policies of Atatürk were dropped to propitiate the large element of conservative Moslem opinion. Religious instruction was restored in the schools, and the call to prayer, banned under Atatürk, was sounded once more in Arabic from the minarets and often amplified by a public address system. Turkey remains, by western standards, a poor country, importing more than she can afford to, dependent on western economic aid. By Middle Eastern standards, however, the achievement of the Turks is impressive.

By 1950, when the Turks enjoyed their first really free elections and power shifted from Atatürk's Republican party to the Democrats, it appeared the Turkish democracy had come of age. The Democrats, however, under Prime Minister Menderes, became increasingly arbitrary as their tenure in office lengthened, muzzling the press and persecuting the Republican opposition. In May 1960 student riots led to an army *coup* which overthrew Menderes in the name of democracy; the future of Turkish politics remained uncertain.

Oil

Turkey's chronic difficulty in paying for imports stems in large measure from her lack of oil, for she must buy abroad most of the petroleum that she uses. This example illustrates the first major fact about the oil of the Middle East. The major discoveries have not been made throughout the region but have been concentrated in its southeastern quarter: in the Tigris-Euphrates valley of Iraq, in the adjacent area of southwestern Iran, and along the Persian Gulf in Saudi Arabia and Kuwait. In the 1950's the little British-protected sheikhdom of Kuwait became the largest single producer in the whole area. These oil resources have been developed by European and American companies, operating under the close supervision and protection of their national diplomatic services. Westerners have not simply taken the oil, as the Spaniards took the precious metals from the New World; they have paid for it, perhaps not so much as they would have at home, but with mounting royalty payments to the Middle Eastern states.

The mushrooming development of Middle Eastern oil after World War II created many problems. First, after 1945, the cheap and easily exploited oil of the Middle East supplied the great bulk of the expanding market in central and western Europe. Whence the alarm of Britain and France, in particular, at the time of the Suez crisis of 1956 over the temporary disruption of the pipeline from Iraq to the Mediterranean and the temporary blocking of the canal itself to the passage of tankers. Whence also their interest in the rapid development of alternative cheap sources of supply, especially in the recently discovered fields of Libya and the Sahara. As of 1960, however, the Middle East possessed about two-thirds of the world's proved reserves of petroleum.

Second, a chronic issue of contention arose over the division of profits between the western companies and the countries in which the oil was produced or through which it passed in pipelines on its way to the Mediterranean. This issue caused an acute crisis in Iran, where the Anglo-Iranian Oil Company and the Iranian government had a long history of mutual antagonism and bitter negotiations. In 1951, under the leadership of an ardent nationalist, Mossadeq, the government nationalized the properties of Anglo-Iranian. Mossadeq's policy won wide support among his countrymen for its bold defiance of the West, but a world-wide boycott of nationalized Iranian oil caused a disastrous drop in revenues and an acute economic crisis in Iran. The issue was finally resolved after a *coup* in Teheran, the capital, had driven Mossadeq from office and into jail (1953). Although Iranian oil remained nationalized, the government now paid western companies to assist in the exploitation and marketing of its oil. Elsewhere in the Middle East the demand for higher royalties and the threat of nationalization have continued to worry the western companies.

Third, the oil-producing countries themselves have put their royalties to widely divergent uses. In Saudi Arabia, much of the oil money has gone to support conspicuous consumption on the part of the very numerous royal family and its retainers. In neighboring Kuwait, the Sheikh, acting on British advice, has invested part of his immense wealth in schools, hospitals, and very costly installations for providing this waterless country with fresh water distilled from the saline Persian Gulf. In Iran, following the resumption of oil revenues after the fall of Mossadeq, the government has invested some of the income in ambitious projects, particularly a plan to rehabilitate the oil-producing province of Khuzistan on the model of the American Tennessee Valley Authority. The existence of oil-financed development schemes does not, however, insure the popularity of the sponsoring government: witness the 1958 revolution in Iraq, where elaborate projects did nothing to endear the rulers to the ruled.

tion of the old tsarist drive into the area. Middle Eastern nationalists, already highly mistrustful of the West, have seemed to fear the imperialism they know more than the communist imperialism they are just starting to know. Although westerners often assume that Islam immunizes its adherents against atheistic Marxism, many Middle Eastern Moslems appear to have reconciled their religious beliefs and communism. The communist appeal has particularly attracted the social groups that may be bracketed as the intellectuals—students, teachers, lawyers, journalists, bureaucrats in routine jobs. These are men who feel themselves to be the natural leaders of their countries, but they have been frustrated by the entrenched position of the traditional ruling classes, and frustrated also because they have in a sense been educated beyond the social and economic capacity of their countries to assimilate them.

All of this, however, does not mean that communism will inevitably take over the Middle East. Down to 1960, at any rate, local communist groups have been repressed, sometimes brutally, by the governments in power, even by the revolutionary régimes in Egypt and Iraq, which have accepted extensive aid from the Soviet Union. It is, moreover, quite possible that the new revolutionary governments will succeed in relieving the frustrations of the intellectuals and enlisting their allegiance. Finally, the Russians themselves, notably in their dealings with Iran since World War II, have proved to have as heavy a hand with the natives, to be as crude imperialists, as any of the western nations.

Communism

The revolutions and general instability affecting many of the Middle Eastern states constitute one of the factors making them possible targets for communist penetration. Another factor is the Soviet resump-

Israel

A more obvious danger to the peace of the Middle East has been the chronic warfare, both "cold" and "hot," between the Arabs and Israel. In the course of the half-century preceding World War II, Zionism (that is, Jewish nationalism) attracted support among many Jews throughout the world, especially among the often-persecuted Jewish communities in Russia and eastern Europe. The Zionist hopes of creating a new state on the site of the ancient Jewish homeland received a great lift from the Balfour Declaration of 1917 and the subsequent British policy of admitting Jewish immigrants into Palestine (see Chapter XXVIII). Hitler's persecutions and World War II made the problem of increased Jewish immigration to Palestine critical. At the same time, Britain, the mandatory power, wished to protect its great interest in the Middle East by cultivating the friendship of the Arab states. But within Palestine itself the flooding Jewish tide was submerging the Arabs, who had long been settled there and felt that this was *their* homeland.

Worn out with fruitless efforts to secure a compromise between Arabs and Jews, the British withdrew from Palestine in 1948, and the Jews at once proclaimed the new state of Israel and secured its recognition by the United Nations. The Israelis now had to fight to maintain their state. In the ensuing war, the total resources in manpower of the Arab states were far greater than those of Israel, but the dissensions among the various Arab states, their military inefficiency, and the better technical equipment and morale of the Israelis resulted in a victory for the Jews. A truce, but not a formal peace, was patched up under the auspices of the United Nations. Israel did not secure the whole of Palestine, but did obtain the better part, a long, narrow strip along the Mediterranean, with some eastward projections, one of which took in part of Jerusalem, the spiritual capital of Judaism. The "old city" of Jerusalem, however, including the Wailing Wall and the site of Solomon's temple, remained in the hands of Jordan and thus under the control of the Arab enemy.

In the course of the Arab-Israeli struggle,

most of the Palestinian Arabs, numbering nearly a million, fled from Israel to the surrounding Arab states. Although the United Nations organized a special agency to extend relief to the refugees and to arrange for their permanent resettlement, relatively few have in fact been resettled. The Arab states have been either unable or unwilling to absorb them, and many refugees have insisted on remaining in depressing camps, for they view resettlement as an abandonment of their cherished conviction that the Israelis will soon "be pushed into the sea" and that they themselves will return to their old homes. This unsolved problem of the Palestinian refugees has sharpened the hostility between Arab and Israeli. The results since 1948 have been a most uneasy truce, frequently broken in frontier incidents by both sides, and Arab harassment of Israel in many ways, notably by an economic boycott and by Egypt's refusal to allow ships carrying Israeli goods to pass through the Suez Canal.

Israel faces not only a grave problem in external relations but also grave internal problems. It cannot trust its Arab minority, numbering about 200,000, approximately one-tenth of the population. It has continued to admit as many Jewish immigrants as possible, some of them of advanced western culture, but others, from North Africa and Yemen, still largely living in the Middle Ages. The welding of these disparate human elements into a single nationality is a formidable task, on which the Israelis have made a promising beginning. Immigration, however, has greatly swollen the total population of Israel, which now contains about a million more people than it did before World War II and in an area not much bigger than Connecticut. Much of that area is mountainous, with a thin rocky soil and inadequate rainfall, and some of it is sheer desert. The Israelis have applied talents and training derived from the West to make the best use of their limited resources, but they have not been able to attain a balanced economy, particularly a balanced trade. They must still depend on outside aid, especially from their many sympathizers in the United States.

The dependence of Israel on western support, indeed the very existence of Israel, have profoundly affected relations between the Arab states and the West. To most Arabs Israel appears to be a western creation, deliberately set up in their midst to spite them and to thwart their own economic development. It is hard for anyone who has not heard an Arab plead his case to imagine the passion with which he argues it or the overwhelming influence that he ascribes to Jewish voters, Jewish journalists, and Jewish financiers in the shaping of American policy. In such an atmosphere, it has been difficult for the western nations, most of all for the United States, to retain cordial relations with Arabs who are in any case very sensitive nationalists.

Arab Unity—and Disunity

The Arab states are united in their hatred of Israel. They are also formally united in the Arab League, created in 1945 and having as members both the independent Arab states of the Middle East—Lebanon, Jordan, Iraq, Saudi Arabia, Yemen, the United Arab Republic—and three Arab states of North Africa—Libya, Tunisia, and the Sudan. This league gives its members some sense of common purpose, even though it has achieved little in any concrete way. Many Arab intellectuals and some Arab politicians, notably Egypt's Nasser, have nursed pan-Arabic schemes and dreamed of a great Arab nation stretching from Morocco all the way to the easternmost tip of the Arabian peninsula.

Realization of this pan-Arab dream seems a long way off, despite the merger of Syria and Egypt into the United Arab Republic. The U.A.R. itself got off to a rather hesitant start, as the Syrians faced the hard problem of adjusting themselves to the political and economic controls imposed by their dominant Egyptian partners. Nasser's success, moreover, alarmed other Arab groups, particularly the Christians of Lebanon, who fear the loss of their jealously guarded rights, and the Iraqi nationalists grouped around General Qasim, who also has aspirations to pan-Arab leadership. Politically, a single Arab nationalism is only an ideal goal; the present reality is a multitude of often conflicting Arab nationalisms.

Culturally, the word "Arabic" is clear and exact only in reference to a language, and even there it applies both to the classical language of the Koran and to a variety of modern colloquial tongues. There is no Arab race, for the Middle East and North Africa have long been an extraordinary melting pot of peoples. And there is no single Arab religion, for, although most Arabs are Moslems, some adhere to one or another of a wide and fascinating range of Christian sects. Within Islam itself, moreover, there is a great gap between the ardent puritanism of Saudi Arabia and the much milder beliefs and practices of many urban Moslems, and between the relatively broad-minded Sunni Moslems and the minority of narrow, gloomy Shi'ites. In civilization, the Arab world covers a very wide range from Saudi Arabia, where oil flows in a land still very medieval, to cosmopolitan and sophisticated cities like Cairo or Beirut, the capital of Lebanon.

IV: Africa

During the ten years following World War II the nationalist revolutions sweeping the non-western world scored their greatest victories in Asia and the Middle East. In the later 1950's the revolutionary spotlight shifted to Africa. The political emancipation of this backward continent moved forward with astonishing and constantly accelerating speed, as old colonies, protectorates, and mandates began to vanish almost overnight, to be replaced by independent or at least autonomous states. Strange new political labels began to appear—Ghana, Mali, Malagasy, and many others.

The chronological listing of the many separate steps in the emancipation of Africa would probably increase the bewilderment of the general reader. Here, therefore, striving for clarity without undue simplification, we shall treat separately the four great areas into which the continent may be divided. First, there is "black" Africa, the largest of the four, including most of the western half of the continent, straddling the Equator, tropical in climate, unattractive for European settlement and in consequence almost wholly Negro in population. Second, there is "white" Africa, the Union of South Africa, more temperate in climate and hospitable to Europeans, scene of an acute crisis between a long dominant white minority and an increasingly desperate Negro majority. Third, there is British Central and East Africa, lying across the Equator but with highland areas suitable for European settlement, so that the critical problem—white minority *versus* Negro majority—is rather like that of South Africa. And finally, there is North Africa, from which we may omit Egypt, which is essentially part of the Middle East. In the heart of North Africa—Algeria—as at the other end of the continent, we again find acute tension between a European minority and a suppressed majority, in this instance between the *colons* (the European settlers) and the native Algerian Arabs.

"Black" Africa

At the beginning of the great European expansion, in the mid-nineteenth century, the Negroes of tropical Africa were everywhere at a far lower stage of culture, as culture is conventionally rated, than were the Chinese, the East Indians, and the peoples of the Middle East. They were also at a far less efficient level of economic and political organization. Yet this most primitive part of Africa is precisely the one where independence or something close to it has been attained most rapidly. The explanation of this sudden leap forward may be found in part in the operation of forces that we have encountered elsewhere in the non-western world. The white rulers brought with them sanitation, engineering, law and order, the beginnings of economic development, and above all the schooling which kindled in the minority of educated natives the inevitable aspirations for self-rule. And the explanation may also be found in the rigors of tropical life, for only a relative handful of Europeans settled in "black" Africa. It has been easier for the colonial powers to drop their imperial reins in Negro Africa than in more temperate areas where the white man has put down deeper roots and developed more vested interests.

As we have seen in Chapter XXIV, most of Negro Africa did not come under effective European rule until the second half of the nineteenth century. Two or three generations have sufficed to construct and

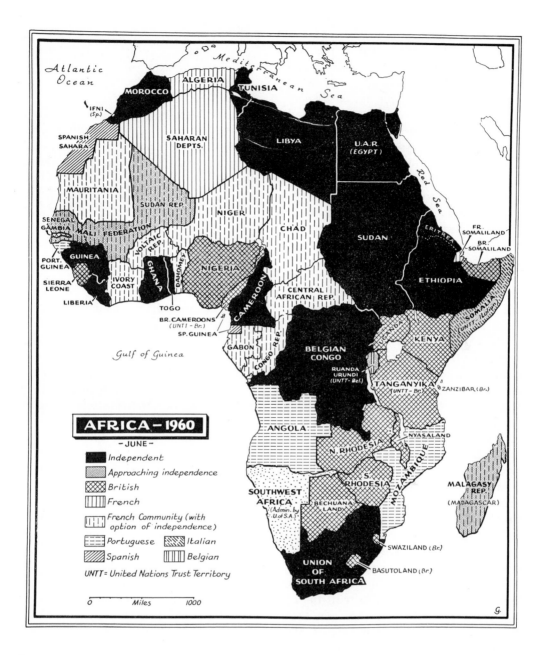

AFRICA — 1960

— JUNE —

- ■ Independent
- ▨ Approaching independence
- ▧ British
- ▥ French
- ▥ French Community (with option of independence)
- ▤ Portuguese   ▨ Italian
- ▧ Spanish   ▥ Belgian

UNTT = United Nations Trust Territory

0 — Miles — 1000

dismantle these vast tropical empires. The seeds of change were planted in the years between the two world wars with the beginnings of articulate native nationalisms. During World War II and the immediate postwar years, the policies of the imperial powers themselves began to change. Some English leaders, particularly from Labor, talked of the possibility of "black" domin-

ions, and some Frenchmen recommended abandoning their traditional policy of assimilating the natives into Frenchmen (see above, p. 357) and transforming their empire into a union or community of partially self-governing units. The actual process of dismantling African empires—to phrase it more positively, the transfer of power from white rulers to the Negroes they had ruled

—started in the early 1950's. The Gold Coast, a British West African possession whose most important export was not gold but cocoa, obtained sizable grants of self-government. But these did not satisfy native nationalists who demanded complete independence and declared dominion status to be outmoded. Accordingly, negotiations were undertaken and in March, 1957, the Gold Coast emerged as the state of Ghana, named after a kingdom that had thriven in the area during the Middle Ages, and enjoying independence and membership both in the United Nations and in the British Commonwealth of Nations.

Ghana has set a pattern not only for other British possessions in "black" Africa but also for those of France and Belgium. As of 1960, only Portugal continued to administer her tropical African territories— Angola on the west coast and Mozambique on the east—in the old colonial way. In the course of 1960 two territories far larger than Ghana were scheduled to achieve nationhood, British Nigeria and the Belgian Congo. The example of the Congo was particularly dramatic, for it had been only yesterday, almost literally, that most Belgians were looking forward to the indefinite enjoyment of this unusually rich and productive colony. Then, at the close of the 1950's, the upsurge of native nationalism burst loose, accompanied by bloody riots. For the immense French possessions in West Africa and Equatorial Africa a great turning point came in 1958 with the constitution of the Fifth Republic (see above, p. 601). The constitution offered these former colonies the alternatives of complete independence or the status of autonomous republics linked to the mother country in the French Community. Since only Guinea on the west coast immediately chose the first alternative, a dozen new republics now joined the French Community. By 1960, however, it was evident that some of the republics wanted the Community liberalized along the lines of the British Com-

President Kwame Nkrumah of Ghana meets President Habib Bourguiba of Tunisia.

monwealth so that its members might exercise full independence rather than simple home rule. The future development of the Community seemed to be foreshadowed when the federation of Mali (see below, p. 645) and the Malagasy Republic, on the great island of Madagascar off southeastern Africa, obtained the desired promotion in status early in 1960.

The road to political emancipation in tropical Africa, though it has been traversed swiftly, has not been entirely smooth, and it is not likely to be free of obstacles and dangers in the immediate future. There have been serious riots and massacres, Africans against Africans more often than black against white, both in the Belgian Congo and in the Cameroun Republic, northwest of the Congo. Indeed, Cameroun, part of the old German Cameroons mandated to France in 1919 (see above, p. 411) and later made a United Nations trust territory, gained independence on January 1, 1960, amid scenes of disorder and civil strife that scarcely augured well for the stability of the infant republic. The bloody rites of pagan religion, feuds between rival tribes, clashes between rival nationalist organizations, and the resentment of the primitive villager against the superior education and superior airs of the urban administrator are all forces making for unrest and violence.

The brand-new African states have fashioned their constitutions on democratic models, but like the one old-established republic of tropical Africa, Liberia, and like so many other non-western nations, they have copied the form rather than the spirit. The political pattern of the immediate future is likely to be that of the single-party state, dominated by a strong man like Nkrumah of Ghana or Sekou Touré of Guinea. Negro Africa shares two other problems with emerging nations in other parts of the non-western world. The first is the problem of its fragmentation into many political sovereignties corresponding to old colonial divisions. Whether any sort of pan-African movements will face as many hazards as the pan-Arab movement has encountered is a question that only the future will answer. As of 1960, "black" Africa has made at least a beginning toward the formation of larger entities. Two components of old French West Africa, the Senegal and Soudan Republics, have formed the federation of Mali, and Guinea and Ghana are linked in a loose confederation. The second problem is economic development. In a society still economically colonial—with raw materials produced by a labor force barely emancipated from slavery or something like it, still largely uneducated, and with a very low standard of living—there is a real danger that political progress will greatly outdistance economic growth. Under these conditions the politically emancipated masses may become ripe for agitation by communists or other troublemakers.

"White" Africa

Over the past century or so, the whites in Africa have pushed northward from the Cape of Good Hope for several thousand miles as true settlers. In the Union of South Africa, in Rhodesia on the Central African plateau, and in the Kenya highlands of East Africa they live—or try to live—as their more fortunate fellow Europeans who settled the relatively empty continents of North America and Australia live. They have tried to make new homes as farmers, grazers, businessmen, professional men. But there is this great difference: in Africa they have not been able to push aside the natives, as Americans pushed aside the Red Indians, and as the Australians pushed aside the Blackfellows. Everywhere the whites are in a minority, dependent on the Negroes for cheap labor on farms, in mines, and in other essential services. The living conditions of the black masses are bad, as in the Negro slums around the South African metropolis of Johannesburg. In addition, what happened almost everywhere in the colonial world, except among the Polynesians of the Pacific, has happened in Africa: the native population has grown steadily in numbers. More important, the Negroes have increasingly refused to accept the role forced on them by their white masters, that of the docile servant, a twentieth-century helot.

In the years since World War II the Union of South Africa has become the most dramatic center of race conflict, the place where the old, unregenerate feeling of white supremacy comes up most clearly against subject peoples already stirred by western examples. According to the statistics for 1958, there were in the Union 11,500,000 non-Europeans and 3,000,000 Europeans, a ratio of almost four non-Europeans to one European. The non-Europeans included nine and a half million Bantu Negroes, about a million and a half Colored (that is, of mixed European and non-European blood), and almost half a million Asians, chiefly Indian shopkeepers. The statistics, no doubt for reasons of political tact, do not divide the Europeans into "British" and "Afrikaners" (the older term for these descendants of the Dutch and French Huguenots was "Boers"). Political parties in South Africa, however, are organized by nationality, and to judge by party votes the Afrikaners outnumber the British in three of the four provinces of the Union—the Cape, Transvaal, and the Orange Free State; only in Natal is the white minority preponderantly British.

These five elements—Afrikaners, British, Bantu, Asian, Colored—exist as quite self-conscious, propaganda-making groups, sometimes mutually exclusive in their aims. Of the five, it is the Afrikaners who have increasingly put their stamp on the policies of the Union during the past generation. During the 1930's, as we have seen in Chapter XXVIII, the Afrikaners developed pro-Nazi sympathies. In World War II, the Union came close to declaring its neutrality, as many Afrikaners would have wished; and its actual participation was comparatively limited. After the war, in 1949, the Union annexed the former German colony of Southwest Africa. It made this annexation after refusing to convert its League of Nations mandate into a United Nations trusteeship. Politically, Southwest Africa supports the Nationalist Afrikaner party, since it has attracted Afrikaner rather than British immigrants. Meanwhile, the gap between British and Afrikaner increased; in British-dominated Natal, there were vigorous threats of secession from the Union.

This Afrikaner-British hostility, this return after the hopeful first years of the Union to the emotions that made the Boer War, soon focused on the question of curtailing the already very meager rights of non-Europeans. To the Afrikaners, the British were not sufficiently firm toward the blacks but were too "soft" and too "liberal." Actually, the average South African of British descent was by no means without a sense of what he called the "color bar," by no means anxious to turn the Union over to a black majority. Although not together in their thinking, the Afrikaner-British difference here was one more of degree than of kind.

The Afrikaners got their way by winning elections, and in the years since World War II have pushed through extreme measures to insure white supremacy. They have cut down the rights of the Colored, and have imposed on the Negroes measures of rigid segregation in almost all possible fields of human relations. The native policy of the Afrikaners is known as *Apartheid*— literally, apartness, separation. Behind *Apartheid* there is simple race prejudice of a kind familiar to Americans. Yet the Afrikaners also believe, as some Americans believe, that whites and blacks can develop in separate but adjacent groups, intertwining but never mingling. They believe that the whites can dominate political life, while the blacks get some of the benefits of mod-

Police disperse African women after a demonstration in Durban, South Africa.

ern economic and technological progress and continue to live in their own very separate quarters. In South Africa the policy of *Apartheid* is more rigorously separatist than the corresponding policy of segregation in the United States. It has been tightened in recent years, in contrast to the loosening of the American policy of segregation. Above all, *Apartheid* is set as an aim in a land where, unlike the United States, the blacks outnumber the whites more than three to one.

It is quite clear that the Bantu majority does not accept *Apartheid* as a blueprint for the future. Their extremist leaders at least would like to sweep both whites and Asians out of South Africa altogether. In the late 1950's, Bantu discontent began to take on ominous proportions; violent demonstrations occurred against government restrictions on the making of alcoholic beverages by Negroes and against proposals to restrict the education of Bantus, thus denying them the possibility of the career open to talent. In the early months of 1960, new demonstrations erupted, provoked by regulations requiring the Bantus to carry identifying passbooks in order to facilitate police enforcement of segregation. The Afrikaners rode out the immediate crisis by recourse to violent repression, but at the cost of opening new dissensions among the whites and of alienating world opinion, including opinion in Britain and the rest of the Commonwealth. Many Afrikaners claimed they would leave the Commonwealth and institute a separate republic rather than mitigate *Apartheid;* some of them asserted they would never surrender but would fight on and on in the cause of white supremacy until some more-than-Wagnerian twilight of the gods. To the outsider, this Afrikaner intransigence is almost incomprehensible. Even though the whites command tanks, planes, and the other modern weapons of repression, they are utterly dependent on black labor; the Bantus, too, possess a weapon of potentially great power—the strike, the refusal to perform vitally needed work for their masters. But the difficulties of South Africa go deeper into the human heart than economics can ever go.

Central and East Africa

Stretching north from the Union of South Africa is the Central African Federation comprising the two Rhodesias, Southern and Northern, and Nyassaland. Britain established the Federation in 1953 as a step along the road to the eventual self-government of these territories. The road has proved to be difficult because of the tensions between native nationalists and European settlers. The natives, dissatisfied with receiving only token representation in the government of the Federation, are pressing for full political rights. This would mean bringing the whites under black rule, something that few whites have been prepared to accept up to now. Most of the whites live in Southern Rhodesia, the richest part of the Federation, but even there they comprise less than 10 per cent of the population. As of 1960, defenders of white supremacy were threatening the secession of Southern Rhodesia from the Federation and its possible merger with the neighboring Union of South Africa. Meantime, officials in the Colonial Office in London were working hard to find a formula that would somehow manage both to allay white fears and to satisfy Negro aspirations.

The Colonial Office was also struggling to solve the similar problem facing the British East African colony of Kenya, where native nationalism had already employed underground methods that struck terror into the heart of the white man. Kenya is on the Equator, but through it runs the mountain spine of Africa; there are thousands of square miles of rolling grass and forest lands with an excellent climate for Europeans. Realizing this was white-man's

Young Kikuyu suspected of Mau Mau terrorism in Kenya.

What the Mau Mau did was spread terror by murder, not only of occasional isolated white farmers but also of their own more peaceful and conservative fellow tribesmen. Here we may observe a dramatic and tragic example of a difficulty that confronts many new nations of Negro Africa—the elimination in a few years of customs and folkways of old standing. The Mau Mau forced reluctant fellow tribesmen to take an oath backed by full tribal fear of the gods of the oath; if a man goes back on the oath, the Kikuyu believe, the gods will take vengeance not only on the foreswearer himself but also on his family. Many moderate Kikuyu were emancipated on the surface from the tribal religion, but not enough at heart to risk the Anglo-Saxon procedure of reporting to the police an oath extracted from them by force. A few really convinced Christian Kikuyu held out against Mau Mau at the risk of their lives; a few still loyal to the old pagan religon held out quite as courageously, for they, too, were morally outraged by the Mau Mau campaign.

Caught in the Mau Mau net, however, was the great mass of the tribe. These were Kikuyu who were torn between the old and the new, no longer secure in the complex institutions of the tribe (primitive people have complicated, not simple, institutions), and yet by no means secure in the competitive individualistic life of the West. They were fundamentally handicapped in that life by the lack of economic opportunity. It was the "average" Kikuyu who supported the Mau Mau. It was the young Kikuyu who needed but could not afford a motor bike with a seat behind for the girl whom he was courting (they did not court that way in the old days); it was the tenant Kikuyu who, lacking land of his own, saw no possibility of surviving in old age; it was the Kikuyu who wanted his children to be educated but could not afford the school fees.

Late in 1952, the Kenya government de-

country, the British government followed ample imperial precedent and decided to reserve some five million acres for European settlement. The Europeans came, a few tens of thousands of them, and largely with native labor developed big farms.

The natives continued to grow in numbers (there are now more than six million of them). Those living in the highlands were pushed aside into native reserves that they rapidly outgrew. The lands that they had sold to the British they could not have realized they were alienating forever, for their whole land system was quite unlike the white man's. (This is a familiar pattern in American dealings with Red Indians, too.) But in fifty years of British colonial rule the natives learned much; now they too wanted *tyledees* (title deeds), wanted the land back.

The main native tribe in the highland regions, the Kikuyu, responded to the growing pressure by developing a secret society known as the Mau Mau. The Mau Mau were a daring and fanatical minority among the Kikuyu, and their goal was the extermination or at least expulsion of the whites. Among uneducated tribesmen they could not use the methods of direct propaganda familiar among pressure groups in the West.

clared a state of emergency, and help was flown from Britain. Two years later, the immediate crisis was apparently surmounted, and white Kenyans were once again calling attention to the tourist attractions and economic opportunities of their land. Nevertheless, although native terror had been repressed, native grievances and demands endured. London responded with a plan to groom Kenya for home rule under arrangements that would first give both blacks and whites a share of authority and eventually permit the full political ascendancy of the Negroes. The European settlers, faced with the prospect of being outnumbered in politics as they are in the total population, have been reluctant to go along. They argue that a Negro government must pledge itself to respect the sanctity of white property and to maintain the exclusively white schools in which European children are educated. They also argue that no native government could honor such pledges and that the Negroes are far from being ready for self-government. Before long, however, it seems probable that the settlers will have to come to terms with the natives, and that the democratic way of counting all heads equally, white or black, will prevail.

The other regions of British East Africa —Uganda and Tanganyika (the former German East Africa)—also won political concessions in the 1950's and also experienced the complaints of native nationalists over the slowness of progress toward self-rule. Because of the absence of large European vested interests, however, they escaped the complications of inter-racial tensions. Further north, meantime, the British relinquished their stake over the Sudan (not to be confused with the Soudan Republic in former French West Africa), which lies between Uganda and Egypt and controls the middle reaches of the Nile valley. This meeting place of Negro and Arab Africa had been placed under joint Anglo-Egyptian rule after its reconquest from the

Dervishes in the 1890's (see Chapter XXIV). In 1953, after decades of often deadlocked negotiation, Britain and Egypt agreed to the independence of the Sudan. Born on January 1, 1956, the young Republic of the Sudan presently eased its most urgent problem in foreign relations when it sanctioned Egyptian construction of the High Dam (see above, p. 636), which would inundate the Nile valley in the northern Sudan. In domestic politics, it soon followed a familiar non-western pattern: government by parliament and parties proved unworkable, and in 1958 an army *coup* established a military régime.

One other European empire in Africa has not only shrunk but actually vanished since World War II—the Italian. The war restored independence to Ethiopia, which then proceeded, under United Nations auspices, to establish a federation with Eritrea, the former Italian outpost on the Red Sea. On the horn of Africa (the northeastern tip of the continent), former Italian Somaliland became a United Nations trust territory, administered by Italy and scheduled to secure full sovereignty on July 1, 1960 as Somalia. Somalia has thus followed in the steps of the North African component of Italy's short-lived empire, Libya. When Libya gained nationhood in 1952 with the blessings of the United Nations, many observers questioned the wisdom of bestowing sovereignty on this immense but unpromising area, lightly populated and largely desert. Yet Libya has survived, thanks in large measure to American and British aid; and, thanks to recent discoveries of oil, its economic future no longer seems entirely bleak.

North Africa

Since World War II, of course, international attention has been riveted not on Libya but on the revolution unfolding further west in French North Africa, reaching from Tunisia on the Libyan frontier through Algeria to Morocco on the Atlantic coast. Some of the revolutionary forces at work here parallel those we have already encountered in the Middle East—growing nationalism on the part of Arabic-speaking native majorities, greatly influenced by the general political ferment in the Arab world; threats of communist penetration; unsuccessful attempts by the imperial power to continue old policies and maintain its old position. The crisis has been compounded by the presence of two other factors. First, over the past century Frenchmen and other Europeans have settled in North Africa as *colons*, particularly in Algeria where their numbers exceeded one million by the 1950's, somewhat more than 10 per cent of the total population. The *colons* have a rich economic stake to protect; many of them cling to the old nineteenth-century imperial ideology and oppose concessions to native nationalism as rigidly as their South African counterparts, the Afrikaners. The second factor has been legal. Morocco and Tunisia, while they seemed colonies for all practical purposes, were in fact French protectorates and retained at least shadowy native governments during the decades of French domination. Algeria, by contrast, has increasingly—and, it would seem, most unrealistically—been treated as no mere colonial outpost but as an integral part of France, a trans-Mediterranean extension of the mother country.

This difference in legal status has made it easier for the French to relax their hold on Morocco and Tunisia. Faced by mounting native unrest in both protectorates and at the same time by a deteriorating situation in Indo-China, the French government at first attempted repression. Then in 1956 it overrode violent objections by the *colons* to give Morocco and Tunisia virtually complete independence. Since then the French have relinquished most of the remaining ties binding their former wards. Partly for this reason, the leaders of newly emancipated Morocco and Tunisia have pursued more moderate policies and shown less vindictiveness against the old imperial master than has been common among the Arab states of the Middle East.

In Algeria, however, moderation and compromise have failed—or, more exactly, have not even been attempted until very recently. Instead, there have been chronic rebellions by native nationalists, chronic intransigence on the part of *colons*, and finally, starting in 1954, a full-dress war which proved even more costly to the French treasury and to French prestige than the earlier war in Indo-China. In May, 1958, the *colons* and their sympathizers among the French armed forces in Algeria rebelled against the Fourth Republic in defense of the settlers' interests. Their uprising played a pivotal role in the collapse of the Fourth Republic and the establishment of the Fifth (see above, p. 601). In October, 1959, de Gaulle, President of the Fifth Republic, promised the native Algerians an eventual free choice in determining their political future, if they would first agree to cease fighting.

Neither nationalists nor *colons* heeded de Gaulle's appeal for pacification. The *colons* rose again early in 1960, again with some support from the army, this time to vilify de Gaulle, whom they had called their saviour less than two years earlier. Although de Gaulle's government put down the new rebellion, it also appeared to yield to the pressure of *colons* and army by stiffening its policy toward the Algerian Arabs. So, in the spring of 1960, the Algerian "drama" (as the French call it) continued its tragic course, as the apparently irresistible force of native nationalism continued to collide with the apparently immovable object of *colon* resistance.

V: The Americas and the British Commonwealth

Latin America
and the Caribbean

At first glance it may seem absurd to include parts of the western hemisphere in the non-western world. Most of the Latin-American republics have enjoyed independence for a century or more. Together with the remnants of old colonial empires in the Caribbean, they have closer bonds of language, religion, and culture with the great nations of the West than do any of the new states in Africa or Asia. Populated by a mixture of Indian, Negro, and white Creole stock, many of them have advanced substantially toward the establishment of multi-racial societies.

Yet a second look shows that the peoples of the western hemisphere south of the United States have long been struggling with the kinds of problems we are considering in this chapter. Economically, they are seeking to diversify their undertakings, to go beyond their traditional and essentially colonial role of serving as supplier of such foodstuffs as bananas, sugar, coffee, and beef and such raw materials as oil, nitrates, and minerals. They are seeking to end their almost total dependence on commodities that fluctuate widely and frequently in price on the world market and to lay a more stable economic base on which to raise the standard of living of their still impoverished masses. Politically, the parallels with the rest of the non-western world are often striking. There have been the same denunciations of western colonialism (in this case usually "Yankee imperialism"), the same emergence of dictatorial régimes, enlightened or repressive, the same round of *coups* and revolutions, the same promises of utopia so easy to make and so hard to fulfill. In what may be termed the anatomy

of non-western revolutions, many comparisons may be found between Cuba after Castro's uprising of 1958-1959 and the Egypt of Nasser or the Iraq of Qasim.

Since World War II the old colonial possessions in the West Indies and in Guiana on the mainland of South America have experienced significant political changes. Here France has abided by her old policy of assimilation and made French Guiana and the islands of Guadeloupe and Martinique into overseas departments of the mother country. The Dutch, by contrast, have given their islands and their share of Guiana (Surinam) substantial home rule. The British, with the most extensive and scattered possessions, have encountered the most difficult problems. They soon curtailed the initial measures of self-government in British Guiana because of the threat that communists or fellow-travelers might dominate local politics. A West Indian Federation, the nucleus of a possible future Caribbean dominion, ran into heavy weather as soon as it was launched, largely because of the mistrust between overcrowded Jamaica, its most important member, and the smaller British islands. Finally, as we have already seen (above, p. 594), the American island of Puerto Rico acquired the unique status of a commonwealth closely associated with the United States. Judged by the standards of the world of 1960, the revolution against imperialism has been proceeding relatively slowly in the Caribbean.

Three Latin-American
Revolutions

The history of the Latin-American republics in the twentieth century has been

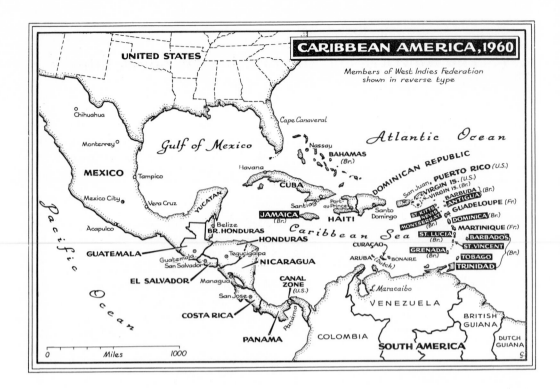

The following is a list of place names and labels appearing on the map:

CARIBBEAN AMERICA, 1960

Members of West Indies Federation shown in reverse type

UNITED STATES

Chihuahua

Cape Canaveral

Monterrey

Gulf of Mexico

Nassau

Atlantic Ocean

BAHAMAS (Br.)

MEXICO

Tampico

Havana

DOMINICAN REPUBLIC

PUERTO RICO (U.S.)

Mexico City

Vera Cruz

CUBA

San Juan, VIRGIN IS. (U.S.)

VIRGIN IS. (Br.)

BARBUDA (Br.)

Acapulco

YUCATAN

Santiago

Port au Prince

Santo Domingo

ST.KITTS

NEVIS

ANTIGUA

GUADELOUPE (Fr.)

Belize

BR. HONDURAS

JAMAICA (Br.)

HAITI

MONTSERRAT (Br.)

DOMINICA (Br.)

Caribbean Sea

MARTINIQUE (Fr.)

HONDURAS

CURAÇAO (Dutch)

ST. LUCIA (Br.)

BARBADOS

GUATEMALA

Guatemala

San Salvador

Tegucigalpa

ARUBA (Dutch)

BONAIRE

GRENADA (Br.)

ST.VINCENT

TOBAGO (Br.)

NICARAGUA

EL SALVADOR

Managua

CANAL ZONE (U.S.)

TRINIDAD

San Jose

Maracaibo

VENEZUELA

Pacific Ocean

COSTA RICA

Panama

BRITISH GUIANA

PANAMA

COLOMBIA

SOUTH AMERICA

DUTCH GUIANA

0   Miles   1000

studded with "revolutions," many of them actually no more than abrupt shifts of power from one ruling strong man or clique to another. In a book of this kind it is impossible and unprofitable to survey all of them. We shall, however, examine two that have proved to have far-reaching implications—the Mexican revolution of 1911, and the Perónista movement in Argentina—as well as a third that may follow suit, the Cuban revolution of Fidel Castro.

In Mexico the overthrow of Napoleon III's puppet emperor, Maximilian, in 1867 (see above, Chapter XXI) marked an apparent victory not only for the Monroe Doctrine but also for Mexican nationalism and liberalism. For the latter, however, it did not prove to be a lasting victory. In 1876 power was seized by Porfirio Díaz, a ruthless, efficient, and sometimes enlightened dictator, who dominated the country for the next thirty-five years. Díaz enforced law and order, punctually met payments on foreign debts (non-payment of

which had occasioned the venture of Napoleon III), won high respect abroad, and attracted the investment of much foreign capital in his country. But he also catered almost exclusively to the interests of foreign investors and the large Mexican landowners; agitation by laborers for redress of legitimate grievances was suppressed; many peasants lost their stake in the land and were reduced to being peons, hardly better than serfs, on large agricultural estates.

Popular discontent with the Díaz régime finally boiled over in 1910, and the dictator fled abroad in the next year. The acute phase of the revolution thus begun lasted for the almost unprecedented span of thirty years. The 1910's, '20's, and '30's were decades of intermittent violence and insurrection and of revolutionary reformers who turned into wealthy dictators; they were also decades of radical social and economic experimentation. The Catholic Church, long regarded by many Mexicans as opposed to economic and political reform and

SOUTH AMERICA, 1960

⊙ *Capital cities*

PANAMA CANAL

Cartagena

Caracas

VENEZUELA

Medellin

Bogotá

COLOMBIA

Orinoco R.

Georgetown

Paramaribo

DEVIL'S ISLAND

GUIANAS

Cayenne

(Br.) (Dutch) (Fr.)
1781 1667 1626
1803

*Dates here show when territories
were acquired by powers concerned*

Quito

ECUADOR

Guayaquil

Iquitos

Negro R.

Manaos

Amazon R.

Belem
(Pará)

Fortaleza

Natal

Amazon R.

Purus R.

Madeira R.

B R A Z I L

Tapajos R.

Recife
(Pernambuco)

Araguaia R.

Tocantins R.

Callao

PERU

Lima

Cuzco

L. Titicaca

La Paz

São Francisco R.

FEDERAL
DISTRICT

Brasilia

Salvador
(Bahia)

Arequipa

BOLIVIA

Sucré

Tacna

Arica

Belo Horizonte

Antofagasta

GRAN CHACO

PARAGUAY

Paraguay R.

Parana R.

São Paulo

Rio de Janeiro

Santos

Asuncion

Tucuman

A N D E S   M T S.

Cordoba

Parana R.

Porto Alegre

CHILE

Valparaiso

Santiago

Mendoza

URUGUAY

Buenos Aires

Montevideo
de la Plata

ARGENTINA

Colorado R.

Bahia Blanca

Pacific Ocean

Atlantic Ocean

FALKLAND IS.
(Br.)

Str. of Magellan

Punta Arenas (Magallanes)

0   Miles   800

Cape Horn

G.

*Area shown in map of
Caribbean America*

U.S. OF MEXICO

REPUBLIC OF HAITI

UNITED
PROVINCES OF
CENTRAL AMERICA

GREAT COLOMBIA

GUIANAS

PERU

EMPIRE OF
BRAZIL

BOLIVIA

PARAGUAY

CHILE

URUGUAY

ARGENTINE
CONFEDERATION

LATIN
AMERICA
1828

After the Wars
for Independence

0   Miles   2,000

653

unconcerned with the welfare of the masses, was the target of extreme anticlerical measures. The foreign oil companies, American and British, suffered expropriation of valuable concessions. All this did not make for harmonious relations with the United States, and at one point early in the revolution (1916) President Wilson sent troops into Mexico to retaliate for a Mexican incursion into the American state of New Mexico. The revolutionary governments gave labor unions extensive privileges and power, expropriated great estates to emancipate the peons, and began a vigorous program of educating the large and neglected population of native Indians. A remarkable cultural awakening took place, based on native traditions and crafts, and Mexican painters like Rivera and Orozco (see illustration facing p. 619), won international fame.

The Mexican revolution, however, stopped short of installing a fully socialistic régime, and by World War II seemed to be entering the Thermidorean stage. The course of Mexican history since 1945 has confirmed this impression. Like many revolutions, the Mexican appears to have lost much of its extremism, its radical dogmatism, its determination to realize for all the promises of Liberty, Equality, and Fraternity. Postrevolutionary Mexico is in part at least reconciled to the need for foreign capital, for the good opinion of North Americans, and above all for patience in the long task of raising the standards of her masses.

At the other extremity of Latin America, the Argentine Republic has not faced Mexico's problem of a large and backward Indian population, since it is peopled almost entirely by European immigrants and their descendants. Although independent for 150 years (since 1810), Argentina had until the middle of the twentieth century a typical colonial economy, exporting beef and grain and other raw materials to Europe and importing manufactured goods. The economy was based on a social system that gave power to a small landlord class. The beginnings of industrialization, and especially the growth of the Argentine capital, Buenos Aires, into a great metropolis of nearly 5,000,000, increased the numbers of working-class and middle-class people and increased also popular dissatisfaction with the aristocratic régime. Mussolini and Hitler won admirers in many circles in Argentina; democratic elements generally looked to France and to the radical French republican tradition. The United States, to phrase it mildly, was rather envied than admired.

President Juan D. Perón and Eva Perón salute crowds after his second inauguration, 1952.

Argentina sat out World War II, coming in on the Allied side only at the very end.

After the war, in the national election of 1946, a newcomer to Argentine politics rose to prominence, Colonel Juan Perón. Perón became a dictator on the fascist European model—that is, he contrived to hold power by the kind of appeal and by the methods that we have analyzed in Chapter XXVII for Mussolini, Hitler, and Franco. Perón, however, never established himself quite as firmly as did his European counterparts, and in 1955 he went down before a characteristic Latin-American military *coup d'état*. Many factors accounted for his fall. In searching for support, Perón was driven more and more to appeal to the poorer masses, the *descamisados* ("shirtless ones"), and thus lost much of his following in the conservative upper classes. Moreover, after the death of his actress wife Eva, who seems to have been much brighter than her husband, he quarreled with the Roman Catholic Church and put through anticlerical measures that cost him further support. Finally, Perón never solved the grave economic and financial problems arising out of his country's essentially colonial position; indeed, his extravagant spending on public works and welfare projects virtually bankrupted Argentina. Although it is hazardous to generalize on the basis of Latin-American experience, his fall suggests two tentative conclusions. First, a great weakness of the Nazi-fascist formula was its attempt to solve social problems by a modern form of the old Roman "bread and circuses," which simply won't work in the twentieth century. Second, the overthrow of Perón without outside interference shows that dictators can be unseated from within, even in modern times of mass propaganda, if they lose the support of the military.

Unlike post-Mussolini Italy or post-Hitler Germany, Argentina since Perón has found it hard to adjust to a more constitutional government. The military régime established after the 1955 *coup* gave way, as it had promised, to a duly elected civilian government in 1958. The new government, beset by drastic economic problems, has applied the drastic remedy of enforcing measures of economic austerity. It has cut down imports, withdrawn costly subsidies that kept prices low, and permitted inflation without increasing wages. In the long run, the economy of Argentina may become healthier and more stable, and so may its political life. But in the short run the Perónistas, the supporters of the fallen dictator, are making political capital out of the discontent aroused by economic austerity and have placed the constitutional government in a precarious situation.

Cuba, too, faces the problems of economic colonialism. Politically sovereign since the Spanish-American War (see above, p. 361), Cuba emerged as an economic dependency of the power responsible for her independence, the United States. American companies controlled many of her sugar plantations, her chief natural resource; the United States supplied the bulk of her imports and the tourist dollars that helped to pay for them. In accordance with the usual pattern in such economic situations, little of Cuba's national wealth was shared by the majority of the population. In 1952, the Cuban government, which had never been noted for honesty or liberalism, fell into the hands of an especially corrupt and ruthless dictator, Batista. On January 1, 1959, Batista fled before an insurrection led by a former student leader, still a young man in his early thirties, Fidel Castro. Castro had gained a wide popular following and, of most immediate importance, had undermined Batista's hold over the army.

The Cuban revolution is much too recent for historians to make more than a provisional evaluation of its meaning. Their task is made still harder because the revolution has put a severe strain on Cuban-American relations, with Castro charging the United States with plotting counter-revolution and the American press—though not, significantly, the American government—countering with charges of deep communist penetration of the Castro government. The central fact appears to be that Castro is bringing to Cuba the kinds of changes that the Mexican revolutionaries brought to their country between 1910 and 1940, and that he is trying to apply them very rapidly indeed. He has seized American-owned sugar plantations, given farms to landless peasants, and spent lavishly on projects for social welfare. He has sought to offset the loss of American tourists and other sources of dollar income by finding new markets for Cuban products elsewhere, including the communist states. This is, in short, a revolution against what many Cubans believe to be American economic imperialism.

Canada

To judge by a few of the nationalistic statements made by Canadian leaders since the advent of the Progressive Conservative government in 1957 (see above, p. 597), one might almost conclude that Canada, too, is in the throes of a revolution against American imperialism. The facts, however, scarcely support such a conclusion. Canada's rapid economic development depends heavily on investment by Americans. And Canadian assertions of independence are directed toward Britain as well as toward the United States; they reflect the usual desire on the part of self-confident human groups to insist on their national identity. Contrary to an opinion still prevalent in the United States, Canada is in no sense ruled by Great Britain. She is a fully sovereign state, tied to the mother country by no juridical bonds, though an active and loyal member of the British Commonwealth. Those who determine her national consciousness think of themselves not as an appendage of Britain or the States but rather as an influential mediator between the States and Britain.

It is true that Canada is not all of one piece. The French Canadians speak their own language, and in their Province of Quebec possess special privileges, in education for example, for which the United States affords no real parallel. There are French Canadians who cherish the kind of irredentist national feelings that cause so much trouble in other quarters of the world. To judge by the extremist French-Canadian press and by some campaign speeches, one might well believe that in Canada the problem of nationality is as acute as it is between Afrikaners and British in South Africa, or between Ulstermen and the men of Eire in Ireland. In neither world war have the French Canadians been exactly enthusiastic for the Allied cause, and in both they have had to be very carefully managed by the federal government. But the majority of French Canadians are loyal to the existing government, and ready to work with the English-speaking majority. They cannot sensibly hope to make all Canada French; as devout Catholics, they cannot want reunion with a France that since 1789 has had so strong a republican and anticlerical cast; and from a possible partition of Canada into separate English-speaking and French-speaking nations they are held back by a fear of absorption into the United States, which they know would make an end to their special privileges.

New Zealand and Australia

In New Zealand, smallest of the old dominions, the advance of social legislation has continued, capped as early as 1941 by a national scheme for socialized medicine, anticipating that of the mother country by several years. New Zealand still has a partly colonial economy, exporting butter, wool, and frozen meat, and importing finished goods, still for the most part from Britain itself. But it has enough home industry to preserve its self-respect. The islands, with their 100,000 square miles, are not yet crowded by their 2,000,000 total population, and the original natives, the Maoris, are not in the position of straitened peoples like the Kikuyu in Kenya, or the Navahos in the United States. They have produced military and political leaders and professional men, and seem to be in the midst of as successful a process of peaceful and dignified westernization as has yet been recorded.

In Australia, there are no minority problems. The Commonwealth has had to overcome some provincial separatism (railroad gauges vary from province to province, for instance), but Australian states are hardly more basically differentiated than are, say, those of the American West. Twentieth-century Australia, too, is in a large degree a welfare state. Organized labor has worked, as it did in England, through a political Labor party which has had its terms of power in the federal as well as in state governments. But Australia today is well short of full socialism. This society, newer than the United States, still has a greater touch of frontier boisterousness. In both world wars, American troops seemed to neutral observers positively quiet and disciplined, positively devoted to spit-and-polish, in comparison with their Australian allies.

Modern Australia shares with New Zealand a very serious problem. The two together are but a handful of whites on the edge of the overcrowded Far East. Both participate in the Colombo Plan, an organization sponsored by the British Commonwealth by which the wealthier members help to finance the development of the impoverished non-communist states of South and Southeastern Asia. But both Australia and New Zealand have maintained rigorous policies of excluding all save white immigration. Both are relatively thinly settled, with a combined population of only a little over 12,000,000. Both still fear the rise of a power in Asia that might reach out and overwhelm them, although the decisive defeat of Japan in World War II has quieted their worst apprehensions. In terms of international relations, both must rely on the United States as their ultimate defender. But this does not imply that they will cut themselves off from Britain, a step for which emotionally and even economically they are not prepared.

The Nature of the British Commonwealth

The British Commonwealth as a whole has had a very important development in recent decades. Its constitutional structure was fixed in 1931 by the Statute of Westminster (see above, p. 511). Its membership has been enlarged since 1945 by the admission of India, Pakistan, Ceylon, Malaya, and Ghana, states that are quite unlike the other dominions and not British in any ordinary sense of the word. India, in fact, insists on using the term Commonwealth without that adjective British. The statement in the Statute of Westminster that the members are "autonomous communities" is not mere rhetoric and is, if anything, an understatement. A member can set up tariffs against other members, regulate immigration by citizens of other states in the Commonwealth, have its own diplomatic services, make treaties with states both inside and outside the Commonwealth, raise and use its own armed forces, have its own flag, and much else.

Yet surely the Commonwealth itself is not just an imaginary entity. In juridical language, the "Crown" remains as a stated link among the dominions. But this term is an extraordinarily rarefied abstraction. Canadians may dutifully put the Queen on their postage stamps. They do indeed cheer visiting British royalty; but in these days so do Americans. Canadians now legally, and very carefully, call themselves "Canadian citizens" and not "British subjects." In India, the Crown seems to be nothing as flesh-and-blood as a Queen, but a complete abstraction.

Yet the Commonwealth has held together in two great wars and has to date managed to retain India with its past of bitter rebellion and South Africa with its deep-seated racial tensions. Perhaps nothing more than convenience and habit holds the Commonwealth together. These are, however, powerful forces, especially when they take the form of economic and strategic convenience and democratic habits. The Commonwealth nations have expressed their habits and traditions in actual institutions. They have a solid backlog in law, in the practice of parliamentary and party government, in education and in political ideas, in the unspoken assumptions and folkways of their peoples. This obviously applies to the older dominions, the white ones. On the surface, especially in terms of folkways, it might appear obviously *not* to apply to a country like India. Yet British ways have sunk deep roots into Indian life, especially among the new ruling classes.

The British Commonwealth has no common federal organ of government. "Imperial Federation"—a scheme for the establishment of federal executive, legislative, and judicial organs—was much talked and written about in the late nineteenth and early twentieth centuries. Nowadays Imperial Federation is hardly even seriously contemplated. Despite the lack of formal central institutions, the business of the Commonwealth does get done by means of regular conferences among British and dominion prime ministers and their staffs, and among administrators and experts of all sorts. Such conferences are the meetings, not of mere diplomats, but of conscious political partners. Hopeful men, especially in the Commonwealth, like to believe that this rather informal type of association not only has proved its strength but also can be expanded to include other colonies when they are ready for self-government, as the examples of Ghana and Malaya have already suggested. And there are some who believe that the British Commonwealth can set a better pattern for a possible world federation than can any other scheme yet devised.

VI: Conclusion

In the brief period since World War II, the status of colonial peoples has altered more than in any period since the modern expansion of Europe began in the fifteenth century. As a result of this revolution, the size of western colonial empires has shrunk dramatically. The British have given up Burma, Ceylon, India, Pakistan, Malaya, Palestine, and Ghana, and have started to make concessions elsewhere. The French, next to the British the most important traditional imperial power, have had to accept the transformation of most of their colonies into sovereign or near-sovereign units of the French Community. The Americans have liberated the Philippines voluntarily, the Dutch have given up Indonesia reluctantly, and the Belgians are withdrawing from the Congo. As of 1960 only the Portuguese empire seemed relatively unaffected by the winds of revolutionary change.

Some westerners still despise non-westerners, call them "wogs," "gooks," or other derogatory names, and believe that they are still essentially Kipling's "lesser breeds without the law" and quite incapable of handling modern western machines and techniques. The shallowness of this belief has been shown up repeatedly. The Iranians, contrary to western expectations, managed to extract and refine petroleum on their own during the days of Mossadeq; Nasser, contrary to western expectations, has managed to keep the Suez Canal dredged and operating since its nationalization. In the Far East, above all, the once-despised orientals have proved to be virtually the military equals of western powers. Witness the Japanese victory over Russia in 1905 and the string of Japanese successes in their early campaigns in World War II. The West has also experienced such effective types of resistance as the nonviolence of Gandhi, the savage terror of the Mau Mau, and the guerrilla tactics of communist-led rebels in Indo-China and Malaya. This dramatic equalizing or near-equalizing of westerner and non-westerner in the test of physical force has revolutionized the international balance. It has enlarged the communist bloc, notably by the addition of China, and it has created a new neutral bloc, centered on India, to which many of the new Asian, African, and Middle Eastern nations seem to be gravitating (see above, p. 588).

The revolution against imperialism that we have just examined is an unfinished revolution. It is almost certain to spread rapidly in the coming years; how rapidly we can only guess. Yet, as of 1960, western imperialism, though obviously in full retreat, is not finished or dead. As we have repeatedly seen, most of the new nations and some of the older ones still have essentially colonial economic status; it will take time to loosen the ties that bind them to the buyers of their raw materials and the suppliers of their imported manufactures. Further, it is by no means clear that experiments in a new kind of tie between the western homeland and former colonies, like the French Community and particularly the British Commonwealth, are foredoomed to failure. The loose tie that binds the Commonwealth is not much like the old imperial tie, but it may conceivably prove sufficient to keep the Commonwealth a going concern. Finally, even the former imperial preserves that have won full sovereignty have been shaped in part by the expansion of the West. They could not escape the wide movements of western men, western things, western ideas and western ideals. The West will not inherit the earth; but it has already set its stamp on the non-western world.

Reading Suggestions
on The Revolt against Imperialism

(Asterisk indicates paperbound edition.)

GENERAL ACCOUNTS

V. M. Dean, *The Nature of the Non-Western World* (*New American Library, 1957). Informative general introduction.

R. Emerson, *From Empire to Nation* (Harvard Univ. Press, 1960). Comprehensive account of the rise to self-assertion of Asian and African peoples.

R. Linton, ed., *Most of the World* (Columbia Univ. Press, 1949). A good survey of the peoples of Africa, Asia, and Latin America.

J. Strachey, *The End of Empire* (Random House, 1960). The decline of imperialism reviewed by a left-wing British Laborite.

F. S. C. Northrop, *The Meeting of East and West* (Macmillan, 1946); B. Ward, *The Interplay of East and West* (Norton, 1957); A. J. Toynbee, *The World and the West* (Oxford Univ. Press, 1953); D. Jerrold, *The Lie about the West* (Dent, 1954). Wide-ranging interpretations of basic problems in the relations between the western and non-western worlds.

B. Rowland, *Art in East and West* (Harvard Univ. Press, 1955). A valuable comparative study.

M. Zinkin, *Asia and the West* (Institute of Pacific Relations, 1953). An instructive survey; by the author of more specialized studies of the area.

G. McT. Kahin, ed., *Major Governments of Asia* (Cornell Univ. Press, 1958). China, Japan, India, Pakistan, and Indonesia are the governments surveyed.

E. O. Reischauer, *The United States and Japan*, new ed. (Harvard Univ. Press, 1957). Admirable survey by a leading authority on Japan.

H. Borton, *Japan between East and West* (Harper, 1957). Informative essays by various experts.

J. K. Fairbank, *The United States and China*, new ed. (Harvard Univ. Press, 1958). Perceptive appraisal of the communist revolution in China.

K. S. Latourette, *The American Record in the Far East, 1945-1951* (Macmillan, 1952); H. Feis, *The China Tangle* (Princeton Univ. Press, 1953). Two balanced evaluations of American-Chinese relations during the critical years after World War II.

C. Dubois, *Social Forces in Southeast Asia* (Harvard Univ. Press, 1959). Valuable introduction to a subject hard for westerners to understand.

G. McT. Kahin, *Nationalism and Revolution in Indonesia* (Cornell Univ. Press, 1952). Good analysis of the transformation of the Netherlands East Indies into an independent republic.

T. G. Spear, *India, Pakistan, and the West*, 3rd ed. (Oxford Univ. Press, 1958: Home Univ. Library); W. N. Brown, *The United States and India and Pakistan* (Harvard Univ. Press, 1953). Useful introductory accounts.

V. M. Dean, *New Patterns of Democracy in India* (Harvard Univ. Press, 1959). A sympathetic and balanced survey of the major problems confronting the Indian republic.

W. C. Smith, *Islam in Modern History* (*New American Library, 1959). Instructive study of another topic hard for westerners to understand; useful for both Asia and the Middle East.

SPECIAL STUDIES: THE MIDDLE EAST

The Middle East: A Political and Economic Survey, 3rd ed. (Royal Institute of International Affairs, 1958). A most useful reference work.

G. Lenczowski, *The Middle East in World Affairs*, 2nd ed. (Cornell Univ. Press, 1956). An informative survey of developments since World War I.

G. Lewis, *Turkey* (1955); N. A. Ziadeh, *Syria and Lebanon* (1957); F. Stoakes and S. H. Longrigg, *Iraq* (1959); T. Little, *Egypt* (1958). Useful general accounts in the series, "Nations of the Modern World" (Praeger).

R. N. Frye, *Iran* (*Holt, 1953). Good short background study.

G. Antonius, *The Arab Awakening* (Khayat's College Book Co-operative, 1955). Pioneering study of the genesis of modern Arab nationalism.

H. Z. Nuseibeh, *The Ideas of Arab Nationalism* (Cornell Univ. Press, 1956). Academic but informative analysis.

C. Issawi, *Egypt at Mid-Century* (Oxford Univ. Press, 1954). A first-rate detailed study stressing social and economic problems.

"Caractacus," *Revolution in Iraq* (Gollancz, 1959). By no means detached or un-prejudiced, but instructive because of its sympathetic insight into Iraqi nationalism.

D. Peretz, *Israel and the Palestine Arabs* (Middle East Institute, 1958); W. R. Polk and others, *Backdrop to Tragedy: the Struggle for Palestine* (Taplinger, 1959). Balanced accounts of the controversial Arab-Israeli conflict.

W. Frank, *Bridgehead* (Braziller, 1957). Impressionistic but perceptive study of the chief problems confronting Israel.

G. Lenczowski, *Oil and State in the Middle East* (Cornell Univ. Press, 1960). Valu-able survey of the major problems connected with Middle Eastern oil.

W. Z. Laqueur, *Communism and Nationalism in the Middle East* (Praeger, 1956) and *The Soviet Union and the Middle East* (Praeger, 1959). Detailed and objective studies of a topic of central importance.

SPECIAL STUDIES: AFRICA

W. M. H. Hailey, ed., *An African Survey*, rev. ed. (Oxford Univ. Press, 1957). A standard work of reference.

T. L. Hodgkin, *Nationalism in Colonial Africa* (New York Univ. Press, 1957). An informative introduction.

C. W. de Kiewiet, *The Anatomy of South African Misery* (Oxford Univ. Press, 1957); G. M. Carter, *The Politics of Inequality: South Africa since 1948* (Praeger, 1958). Valuable studies by American scholars with wide knowledge of the subject.

L. S. B. Leakey, *Mau Mau and the Kikuyu* (Day, 1954). The indispensable book on the subject.

G. Tillion, *Algeria: the Realities* (Knopf, 1958), and M. K. Clark, *Algeria in Turmoil* (Praeger, 1959). Two differing interpretations of the North African "drama."

L. Kuper, *Passive Resistance in South Africa* (°Yale, 1960). Instructive study of an important weapon in the hands of oppressed peoples.

SPECIAL STUDIES: THE AMERICAS AND THE BRITISH COMMONWEALTH

P. E. James, *Latin America*, 3rd ed. (Odyssey, 1959). An up-to-date general survey.

D. Perkins, *The United States and the Caribbean* (1947); A. P. Whitaker, *The United States and South America: the Northern Republics* (1948), and *The United States and Argentina* (1955); H. F. Cline, *The United States and Mexico* (1953). Help-ful introductions to specific areas of America "south of the border."

G. Grady, *Democracy in the Dominions*, 2nd. ed. (Univ. of Toronto Press, 1952). Valuable study of a topic seldom treated—the comparative institutional history of the various dominions.

SOURCES AND FICTION

G. A. Nasser, *Egypt's Liberation* (Public Affairs Press, 1955). Brief and illuminating essay on the Egyptian revolution by its leading figure.

M. Makal, *A Village in Anatolia* (Vallentine, Mitchell, 1954). Invaluable insights into rural Turkish life; by a young Turkish schoolteacher.

W. O. Douglas, *Strange Lands and Friendly People* (Harper, 1951), and *West of the Indus* (Doubleday, 1958). A justice of the Supreme Court reports on his travels in the non-western world.

E. Huxley, *The Flame Trees of Thika* (Morrow, 1959). Memories of an East African childhood.

P. H. Newby, *The Picnic at Sakkara* (Knopf, 1955). Illuminating novel of a British professor involved with Egyptian nationalists.

A. Paton, *Cry, the Beloved Country* (Scribner's, 1948). The classic novel about the plight of South African Negroes.

H. Bloom, *Episode in the Transvaal* (Doubleday, 1955). Exciting novel of racial tension in South Africa.

N. Saghal, *Prison and Chocolate Cake* (Knopf, 1954). Informative novel about India by an Indian.

R. Godden, *The River* (Little Brown, 1946; *Compass Books). Sensitive novel about India by an Englishwoman.

G. Greene, *The Quiet American* (Viking, 1956; *Compass Books). Satirical portrait of a "do-gooder" in Vietnam.

W. J. Lederer and E. Burdick, *The Ugly American* (Norton, 1958; *Crest Books). Fictionalized exposé of the vices (and virtues) of Americans coping with the non-western world.

Man's Fate in the Twentieth Century

CHAPTER XXXII

Opposite. THREE MUSICIANS, *by Pablo Picasso (1881-); Spanish, painted 1921; courtesy of the Philadelphia Museum of Art. An arresting example of the wide-ranging experiments in new forms of expression made by the giant of twentieth-century art (see also below, p. 680).*

I: The Intellectual Revolution Continues

THE old truism about the difficulty of seeing the whole forest when attention is fixed on the separate trees holds especially for contemporary intellectual history. Among the countless "ideas" that come to our attention through the printed or the spoken word, through symbols, diagrams, pictures, even through musical sounds, it is almost impossible to distinguish those ideas which are characteristic of our age, which give it its flavor or style, which establish its "climate of opinion." Indeed, it is tempting to conclude that this very *variety* of ideas, spread abroad among countless millions through all the channels of mass communications, is the distinguishing mark of our time. There is, moreover, a further difficulty confronting the historian of contemporary thought and feeling. As we shall note later in this chapter, in our time the gap between the culture of the few—let us frankly use the Americanism, the "highbrows"—and the culture of the many, who are not necessarily "lowbrows," just not highbrows—this gap is especially wide and deep. The historian who relied wholly on evidence from the work of "serious" modern poets or artists would come to quite different conclusions from one who rested on evidence from the "comic" strips, popular music, or the works of Norman Vincent Peale.

Yet this variety of tastes and beliefs, even this gap between the highbrows and the rest of the people, has been discernible in its modern form ever since printing and widespread literacy bore their fruits in the eighteenth and nineteenth centuries. We in the twentieth century are still struggling with specific problems of religion, philosophy, society, taste, and man's fate generally that were set for us by the Enlightenment of the eighteenth century, though some, of course, were set far back in pre-history. More especially, we are continuing the intellectual revolution begun by the Romanticists and Darwin (see Chapters XIX and XXIII). It may well seem in further perspective that the generation that flourished just before and just after the first World War made even more decisive changes in the temper of western thought than did the Darwinians.

Psychology: Freud

Under leads from the biological sciences, the nineteenth century came to put particular emphasis on *process*, on the dynamics of change in time. The twentieth century, under leads from psychology, has come to put particular emphasis on the role of the unconscious in human thought and action, on the irrationality—or at least non-rationality—of much human behavior. Foremost among the thinkers responsible for this emphasis was Sigmund Freud (1873-1939). Freud was a physician, trained in Vienna in the rationalist medical tradition of the late nineteenth century. His interest was early drawn to mental illness, where he soon found cases in which patients exhibited symptoms of very real organic disturbances, but for which no obvious organic causes could be found. Under analysis, as Freud's therapeutic treatment came to be called, the patient, relaxed on a couch, is urged to pour out what he can remember of his earliest childhood, or indeed infancy. After many such treatments the analyst can hope to find what is disturbing the patient, and by making him aware of what that is, hope to help him.

Had Freud merely contented himself with this kind of therapy, few of us would have heard of him. But from all this clinical experience he worked out a system of psychology that has had a very great influence, not only on psychiatry and psychology, but on some of our basic conceptions of human relations. Freud starts with the concept of a set of "drives" with which each person is born. These drives, which arise in the unconscious, are expressions of the "id." Freud never tried to locate the id physiologically; he used the term, which in Latin means "this [thing]," to avoid the moralistic overtones in words like "desires." These drives try to get satisfaction and pleasure, to express themselves in action. The infant, notably, is "uninhibited"—that is, his drives well up into action from the id without restraint from his conscious mind. But by no means without restraint from his parents or nurse—and there's the difficulty. The infant finds himself frustrated. As he grows, as his mind is formed, he comes to be conscious of the fact that some of the things he wants to do are objectionable to those closest to him, and on whom he is so dependent. He himself therefore begins to repress these drives from his id.

With his dawning consciousness of the world outside himself, he has in fact developed another part of his psyche, which Freud at first called the "censor," and later divided into two phases which he called the "ego" and the "superego." The ego is the individual's private censor, his awareness that in accordance with what Freudians call the "reality principle" certain drives from his id simply cannot succeed.

664

The superego in a way is what common language calls "conscience"; it is the individual's response as part of a social system in which certain actions are proper and certain actions improper.

There is no doubt a simplification, but perhaps not a misleading one, if the matter is put this way: the ego is—or better, is meant to be—the servant of the id, rejecting, modifying, or permitting its drives in accordance with what the ego judges is so, the "reality principle," the "facts"; the superego too is the servant of the id, or better, guardian, often a tyrannical guardian, acting in accordance with what the superego judges ought to be the "right," the proper thing to do. Or, more simply, the ego deals with nature, including human nature; the superego deals with culture, which can only be human culture. Both ego and superego act to curb, restrain, "suppress" the individual.

Now these drives of the id, and indeed in most of its phases the dictates of the

Sigmund Freud.

superego, are for Freud a sort of great reservoir of which the individual is not normally aware—that is, they are part of his "unconscious." In a mentally healthy individual, enough of the drives of the id succeed so that he feels contented. But even the healthiest of individuals has had to repress a great deal of his drives from the id. This successful repression the Freudians account for in part at least by a process they call "sublimation." They think that the healthy individual somehow finds for a drive suppressed by ego or superego, or by both working together, a new and socially approved outlet or expression. Thus a drive toward sexual relations not approved in one's circle might be sublimated into the writing of poetry or music, or even into athletics.

With the neurotic person, however, Freud held that drives, having been suppressed, driven back down into the unconscious, find no suitable other outlet or sublimation, and continue, so to speak, festering in the id, trying to find some outlet. They find all sorts of outlets of an abnormal sort, symptoms of illness in great variety. They display themselves in all sorts of neuroses and phobias, which have in common a failure to conform to the "reality principle." The neurotic individual is "maladjusted." And if the failure to meet the reality principle is really complete, the individual is insane, "psychotic," and lives in an utterly unreal private world of his own.

Freud, at least in his earlier years, did indeed hold that the id is wholly, or almost wholly, sexual in nature. But even from the first, he gave to "sexual" so broad a meaning that it quite transcended what most of us mean by the term. One of his favorite early terms for the contents of the id, so to speak, is libido, from the Latin for desire, with strong overtones of "lust." He claimed to have found evidences of sexuality even in the behavior of infants. Now our western society frowns on these earlier manifestations of sexuality. Mothers in Freud's day, for instance, would try hard to prevent the child's sucking its thumb, in Freudian terms an obvious, and harmless, form of eroticism. Other forms of infantile sexuality meet with even stronger disapproval, and often with stern punishment from parents. The infant and later the child are therefore obliged to repress their sexuality. In the neurotic person, Freud believed, this repression is the main source of his difficulties. As an adult, he finds it impossible to achieve normal sex relations, and "regresses" to earlier stages of eroticism. Since "irregular" manifestations of sexuality are very strongly condemned by our society, the individual driven to them by his unconscious either suppresses them, or, if he indulges in them, feels a great sense of guilt. Either way, according to Freud, he may end as a neurotic.

Freud's therapy rested on the belief that if the individual neurotic could come to understand why he behaved as he did he could not infrequently make a proper adjustment and lead a normal life. But here Freud parted company with the rationalist tradition of the eighteenth century. He held that there was no use preaching at the individual, reasoning simply with him, telling him the error of his ways, pointing out what was unreasonable in his behavior. Reason could not get directly at the unconscious, where the source of his trouble lay. Only by the long slow process of psychoanalysis, in which the individual day after day sought in memories of his earliest childhood for concrete details, could the listening analyst pick from this stream of consciousness the significant details that pointed to the hidden repression, the "blocking" that came out in neurotic behavior. Freud gave special importance to the dreams of the patient, which he must patiently describe to the analyst; for in dreams, Freud thought, the unconscious wells up out of control, or but partly controlled, by the ego. Once the patient, however, got beneath the surface of his conscious life, and became aware of what had gone wrong with his hitherto unconscious life, he might then adjust himself to society.

The Implications of Freudianism

What is important for us in the wider implications of Freud's work, his part in the broad current of contemporary modifications of eighteenth-century rationalism, is first this concept of the very great role of the unconscious drives—that is, the unthinking, the non-rational, in our lives. Ordinary reflective thinking is for the Freudian a very small part of our existence. We are back at the metaphor of reason as a flickering candle, or to use another well-worn metaphor, of reason as simply the small part of the iceberg that shows above the water, while submerged down below is the great mass of the unconscious. Much even of our conscious thinking is, according to the Freudian, what psychologists call "rationalization," thinking dictated, not by an awareness of the reality principle, but by the desires of our id. One can get a good measure of the difference between eighteenth-century rationalism and Freudian psychology by contrasting the older belief in the innocence and natural goodness of the child, Wordsworth's "mighty prophet, seer blest," with the Freudian view of the child as a bundle of unsocial or antisocial drives, as in fact a little untamed savage.

But second, and most important, note that the Freudians do not wish to blow out the candle of human reason. They are moderate, not extreme, anti-rationalists; they are chastened rationalists. Their whole therapy is based on the concept, which has Christian as well as eighteenth-century roots, that "ye shall know the truth, and the truth shall make you free." Only, for the Freudian, truth is not easily found, cannot be distilled into a few simple rules

Pavlov playing gorodki, a Russian folk game.

which many others find absurd or offensive, by maintaining that for the Freudian too there is, though difficult to find, a way out, a form of salvation, in the full self-knowledge that comes from successful psychoanalysis.

Freud, to whom religion was an "illusion," was himself a cult-leader. His faithful disciples still form an orthodox nucleus of strict Freudian psychoanalysts. Other disciples parted with the master, notably the Swiss Jung (1875–   ) who did believe in religion, and whose great popular phrase was the "collective unconscious," and the Austrian Adler (1870-1937) who rejected the master's emphasis on the sexual, and coined the familiar phrase, "inferiority complex." The Freudian influence on imaginative writing, indeed on philosophy and the arts generally, was and remains very great indeed, though usually dispersed, vague, indirect, and very hard to summarize. Negatively, the life work of this nineteenth-century-trained scientist went in these "humanistic" fields to reinforce the reaction against nineteenth-century scientific and rationalistic materialism; positively, Freud's work helped all sorts of modernisms, strengthened the revival of intuition, "hunch," sensibility, and, perhaps paradoxically, a Stoic or existentialist rejection of bourgeois optimism.

of conduct which all men, being reasonable and good, can use as guides to individual and collective happiness. It is on the contrary very hard to establish, and can be reached only by a long and precarious struggle. Many will not reach it, and will have to put up with all sorts of maladjustments and frustrations. The Freudian is at bottom a pessimist, in that he does not believe in the perfectibility of man. Indeed, there are those who see in the Freudian concept of human nature something like a return to the Christian concept of original sin. They continue the parallel,

Psychology: Behaviorism

It need hardly be said that in this multanimous century of ours the Freudians hold no monopoly of the field of psychology. Indeed, the eighteenth-century tendency to regard human nature, if not as wholly rational, at least as wholly malleable by those who could manipulate the human and non-human environment, still had representatives in mid-twentieth century. Yet at least one of these "behaviorist" tendencies in psychology had its own flareback to reinforce pessimism over the possibilities of immediate reform of the human condition. The Russian psychologist Pavlov (1849-1936), Nobel prize-winner in 1904, has given us the now familiar term "conditioned reflex." Pavlov's laboratory dogs, after being fed at a given signal, came to water at the mouth at this signal, though no food was within sight or smell. The "natural"—that is, inborn—response of watering at the mouth would ordinarily come only when the dog's senses showed him actual food; Pavlov got the same response artificially by a signal that certainly did not smell or look like food to the dog. The upshot was clear evidence that training or conditioning can produce automatic responses in the animal that are essentially similar to the kind of automatic responses the animal is born with.

Pavlov's experiments had important implications for the social scientist. They confirmed eighteenth-century notions about the power of environment, of training and education, in the sense that environment can be manipulated to produce specific responses from organisms. But—and this is a bitter blow to eighteenth-century optimism—they suggested that once such training has taken hold, the organism has, so to speak, incorporated the results almost as if they had been the product of heredity, not environment, and further change becomes very difficult, in some instances impossible. Pavlov, after having trained some of his dogs, tried mixing his signals, frustrating and confusing the dogs by withholding food at the signal that had always produced food for them. He succeeded in producing symptoms of a kind close to what in human beings would be neurosis.

Now the cautious social scientist does not, of course, take over Pavlov's conditioned reflexes and apply them uncritically to all human behavior. He does not assume, for instance, that the Vermonter voting the straight Republican ticket is behaving quite like the dog watering at the mouth as an accustomed bell is rung. Even in Vermont,

voting Republican is not quite a conditioned reflex. But the cautious social scientist will hold that concepts like that of the conditioned reflexes do throw light on a great deal of habit-determined human conduct. For the anti-rationalist, Pavlov's work was further demonstration that a very great deal of our behavior is not determined, or even greatly influenced, by what goes on in the cerebral cortex, the part of our brain that "thinks."

Socio-political Thought

We have in the foregoing already edged over naturally enough from psychology to the wider field of man's behavior as a political animal. In what are sometimes optimistically called the social or behavioral sciences, the twentieth century has continued to develop the critique of our eighteenth-century inheritance of belief in the basic reasonableness and goodness of "human nature." Once more, let us reemphasize, first, that this "revolt against reason" is better and more fully to be described as a revolt against reason as exemplified in popular concepts of what science is and does. Second, that many thinkers in this revolt did not attack such scientific reason as such in its own fields of established sciences, but simply urged that there are other valuable ways of using the human mind. And third, that though many of these thinkers were anti-rationalists, and almost always "élitists," fascists, racists, reactionaries hostile to the democratic tradition, others were what we have called "chastened rationalists," thinkers who wished to salvage what they could of the eighteenth-century basis of the democratic tradition (see Chapter XXIII).

The specific programs, the emotional allegiances, the "values" of twentieth-century thinkers in this broad field we may hesitantly call "sociological" were varied indeed. And yet most of them, certainly the great ones, do have in common a sense of the subtlety, the complexities, the delicacy —and the toughness and durability—of the ties that bind human beings together—and hold them apart—in society. Indeed, that last sentence of ours, with its coupling of opposites in tension, is typical of this twentieth-century approach to problems of man in society; compare an incidental and therefore significant remark tossed off by Arthur Koestler, "for we are moving here through strata that are held together by the cement of contradiction." * Or, as the Swiss writer Denis de Rougemont puts the same kind of challenge to our conventional notions of what makes sense, tensions between two terms that are *true, contradictory, and essential."* † The distinguished American sociologist, Talcott Parsons, in his *The Structure of Social Action* (1937) finds in the work of many different thinkers, such as the German Max Weber, the Frenchman Durkheim, the Englishman Alfred Marshal, the Italian Pareto, and others, a common aim to put the study of man in society on a basis that takes full account of the difficulties of "objectivity" in such study, and gives full place to our contemporary awareness of the place of the subjective and the non-rational in human life.

Pareto

We may here speak for a moment about Pareto (1848-1923), not because he was the greatest or the most influential thinker, for he was not, but because the work of this scientifically trained engineer is such a clear example of the difficulties of thinking about men as we think about things. Pareto tried hard to establish a genuine *science* of sociology; but it was a sociology very different from that of his only slightly older contemporary

* A. Koestler, *The Invisible Writing* (Boston, 1954), 349.

† D. de Rougemont, *Man's Western Quest* (New York, 1957), 116.

Herbert Spencer (see Chapter XXIII). Pareto in his *The Mind and Society* (original Italian edition, 1916) is concerned chiefly with the problem of separating out in human actions the rational from the non-rational. What interests Pareto is the kind of action that is expressed in words, ritual, symbolism of some kind. Buying wool socks for cold weather is one such action. If they are bought deliberately to get good socks at a price the buyer can afford, this is rational action in accord with the doer's interests; it is the kind of action the economist studies statistically. If, however, they are bought without regard for price by a sentimental lover of England who buys imported English socks in order to do his bit to help England, then clearly something else, something the economist has to disregard in his price statistics, has come into play. This "something else" is the substance of Pareto's study.

Pareto distinguishes part of such social action as *derivations*, which are close to what most of us know as rationalizations. These are the explanations and accompanying ritualistic acts associated with our religion, our patriotism, our feelings for groups of all kinds. Prayer, for instance, is for Pareto a derivation; he was, like so many of this period, a materialist, at bottom hostile to Christianity, though he approved of it as means of social concord, and was fascinated by its hold over men. It is irrational, or non-rational, to pray for rain, because we know as meteorologists that rain has purely material causes quite beyond the reach of prayer. These derivations are indeed a factor in human social life, but they do not really move men to social action.

What does move men in society, and keeps them together in society, says Pareto, are the *residues*. These are expressions of relatively permanent, abiding sentiments in men, expressions that usually have to be separated from the part that is actually a derivation, which may change greatly and even quickly. Pagan Greek sailors sacrificed to Poseidon, god of the sea, before setting out on a voyage; a few centuries later, Christian Greek sailors prayed, lighted candles, and made vows to the Virgin Mary just before sailing. The derivations are the explanations of what Poseidon and the Virgin respectively do. They vary. The believer in the Virgin thinks his pagan predecessor was dead wrong. The residues are the needs to secure divine aid and comfort in a difficult undertaking, and to perform certain ritual acts that give the performer assurance of such aid and comfort. The residues are nearly the same for our two sets of sailors. Both the pagans and the Christians have the same social and psychological needs and satisfy them in much the same ways, though with very different "explanations" of what they are doing.

Two of the major classes of residues Pareto distinguishes stand out, and help form his philosophy of history. These are first the residues of persistent aggregates, the sentiments that mark men who like regular ways, solid discipline, tradition and habit, men like the Spartans, the Prussians, or any rigorously disciplined military class. Second, there are the residues of the instinct for combinations, the sentiments that mark men who like novelty and adventure, who invent new ways of doing things, who like to cut loose from the old and the tried, men not easily shocked, men who hate discipline, men like most intellectuals and inventors—and many entrepreneurs and businessmen. In societies of many individual members, men influenced largely by one or the other of these major residues tend to predominate and to characterize that society. Like most philosophers of history, Pareto is far from clear on just how a conservative society where the residues of persistent aggregates predominate changes into another kind of society. But he does have this conception of a pendulum swing, even a struggle of thesis and antithesis.

The nineteenth century in the West was in Pareto's mind a society in which the residues of instinct for combinations played perhaps the greatest role of which they are capable in a human society. The nineteenth century was a century of competition among individuals full of new ideas, inventions, enterprises, convinced that the old ways were bad, that novelty was the great thing to strive for at the expense of everything else. It was a society notably out of equilibrium. It had to run toward the other kind of residues, toward the persistent aggregates, toward a society with more security and less competition, more discipline and less freedom, more equality and less inequality, more uniformity and less variety. It had to go the way some writers hold that we are going in the twentieth century.

Pareto's final general conception is that of an equilibrium in a society. It is an equilibrium constantly disturbed, at least in western society, but constantly renewed by a sort of natural healing force not to be supplanted by the efforts of any social physician or planner. Pareto does not entirely rule out the possibility that human beings by taking thought may in little ways here and there change social arrangements in such a way that what they plan turns out to be a reality. But the overwhelming emphasis of his work is that change in human conduct as a whole must be distinguished from change in human ideas and ideals. Since man is what he is, and, in our western culture, since the residue of instinct for combinations is so widespread, there is bound to be change in many fields of human interest. Fashion and all its commercial dependents can almost be said to be change for change's sake. But for Pareto there was also a level of human conduct where change is very slow indeed, almost as slow as the kind of change the geologist and the evolutionist study.

This level of human conduct where change is very slow is the level of the residues. At most, Pareto held, the skilled political leader can manipulate the derivations in such a way that some residues are made relatively inactive, and others are activated. He cannot possibly produce new residues or destroy old ones. You must not expect human beings to be consistently unselfish, sensible, devoted to the common good, kindly, wise. Above all, you must not expect that any institution, any law, any constitution, any treaty or pact, will make them so. But Pareto goes a bit beyond this position. Planning, except for limited and always very concrete ends, is dangerous. Not only is it very likely that a big, ambitious, legislated change will not achieve the results the planners planned; it is likely to produce unpredictable and perhaps unfortunate results. Until we know more of social science, Pareto holds, the best thing to do is to trust to what the upstart intellectual arrogantly condemns as the irrational side of human nature. We must believe that the ingrained habits of the human race are, even by evolutionary standards, more useful to survival than the impertinent logic of the reformers.

The Planners and Persuaders

Yet the abiding influence of the newer psychological and sociological approach to the study of man in society has by no means been in the Paretan and conservative direction of letting ill enough alone. Those who want to influence human behavior, all the way from the microcosmic field of personal consumer-choices to the macrocosmic field of international relations, have been willing to make use of the new insights into human nature. From the latest piece of "motivational research" to show the cigarette manufacturer how to overcome the effects on his customers of recent medical research on the causes of lung cancer to the high-minded efforts of proponents of world-government to devise some symbol, visual, musical, concrete, that

will supplant nationalist symbols, such as patriotic hymns, flags, and the like, hard-working planners are busily engaged in trying, often successfully, to change even our habits, even our prejudices. To use Pareto's now little-used terminology, they are seeking, not to change our behavior by appealing to our "reason" in the plain sense of that word; they are trying to "activate" certain of our sentiments, our residues, or "de-activate" others, or both. These planners and persuaders, aware of how scientific technologists in non-human fields have applied the famous aphorism of Francis Bacon, "Nature is not to be conquered save by obeying her" (in the original Latin, *natura non vincitur nisi parendo*), have apparently decided to apply in human affairs the aphorism, *human* nature is not to be guided save by obeying it.

In the field of serious political and social thought, this characteristic twentieth-century emphasis on the psychology of motivation has been appealed to not only by conservatives or "reactionaries" like Pareto and others, including both Mussolini and Hitler, who had pretensions to philosophy, but also by many who were democrats, or at least "progressives," at heart. An early example of this latter type of political thinker is Graham Wallas, a British leftist, whose *Human Nature in Politics* (1908) was a most influential book. Wallas, campaigning as a Progressive for a seat in the London County Council, discovered by experience that the voters he canvassed were more pleased and influenced by little tricks of baby-kissing, chit-chat, and personal flattery than by appeals to reason or even to self-interest. Something of the same emphasis on the need to go beyond abstractions in politics appears in the earlier writings of the American Walter Lippmann, whose *Preface to Politics* appeared in 1913. It has, of course, always been known to practicing politicians.

There remains, especially among American intellectuals, a strong current of thought-feeling that refuses to descend into Machiavellian strategy, even—indeed most of all—in a righteous cause. It still seems to these good children of the eighteenth-century Enlightenment that reason and high ethical principles must and will prevail together, and that to appeal to the "lower" elements in nature so emphasized by modern psychology is no way to rise above the evils of existing society. Such opinions are by no means commonly held, or, at any rate, not commonly put into practice, by active politicians, and one of the many gaps that seem in our society to widen rather than to narrow in these days is the old gap between the idealistic "theorist" and the "practical man" who wants to get things done.

Yet the intellectual leaders of mid-twentieth century progressive political thought are increasingly forced to the conclusion that more has to be done in the way of planning. Notably, they urge, we must plan in the whole sector of our production economy which does not turn out such consumers' goods as motor cars, television sets, cosmetics and a myriad others, but does turn out such essentials as education, social service, housing, hospital care, scientific research, and public transportation. The planners know also that in a democracy plans cannot simply be imposed on those planned for, as to a great degree they can in a totalitarian state like Russia. They are paying great attention to the problems, on which modern thinking in the field of the social sciences does throw some light, of how to get the many to want and ask for—and pay for—what the planners think the people really need, and *ought* to want.

Philosophy

In the field of formal—which nowadays tends to mean also university-supported—philosophy the mid-twentieth century displays once more its variety. It is safe to say that in the West at least there are today representatives of almost every philosophical system, from extreme idealism to extreme materialism and complete skepticism, that has ever existed; and even in the communist countries, one suspects that there are lurking idealists ready to come out in the open if official Marxist materialist metaphysics are ever relaxed. The currents of voluntarism, pragmatism, psychologism we noted earlier (see Chapter XXIII) still flow, no doubt a bit diminished. From such nineteenth-century sources as Nietzsche and the gravely disturbed and disturbing Danish theologian, Kierkegaard (1813-1885), there has developed a philosophy known as "existentialism." The existentialists are somewhat harried Stoics (see Volume I, p. 91) who find this existing reality of mid-twentieth century all there is, and pretty depressing, but are determined to face this reality as heroically as possible. We are, no doubt, quite unfair to them in this brief characterization. They are sensitive artists and intellectuals in revolt but not in despair. Their noblest representative, though not formally one of the existentialist group, the French novelist and philosopher, Albert Camus (1913-1960) is perhaps destined to be remembered as a classic of our age. Finally, formal philosophical idealism, which a generation ago seemed, save for Croce, to be languishing everywhere, has proved of recent years to have considerable vitality, perhaps basically in forms we may call Neo-Kantian, as with the late German philosopher, Ernst Cassirer (1874-1945).

The most original, and in a sense most typical and vital, philosophic movement of our century bears clearly and paradoxically the stamp of the "revolt against reason." It looks to an outsider as if the movement called variously logical analysis, logical positivism, and, in one of its phases, symbolic logic, accepted most of the strictures the new psychology made on old-fashioned rationalism, and then went ahead to insist that, although only a tiny bit of human experience could be brought under rubrics of rational thought, that tiny bit was indeed to be protected and explored carefully. This somewhat varied school can be considered as beginning early in the twentieth century in Vienna, the city of Freud. But such distinguished pioneers of the school as Ludwig Wittgenstein (1889-1951) and Rudolf Carnap (1891–) emigrated, the first to England, the second to the United States. Logical analysis could hardly flourish in Hitler's Germany or in Stalin's Russia. It is skeptical of too much to flourish in any but a very free and many-minded society.

The American physicist, P. W. Bridgman, put the school's basic position clearly in various writings. Where, on the pattern of scientific practice, a problem can be answered by the performance of an "operation" and the answer validated by logical and/or empirical tests, knowledge can be achieved; where, however, as in such problems as whether democracy is the best form of government, whether a lie is ever justifiable, or whether a given poem is a good one or a bad one—in short, almost all the great questions of philosophy, art, literature, history—no such "operation" is possible, the problem is *for the logician* "meaningless."

Most of these logical positivists would admit that non-logical methods for getting at such problems, though they could not result in the kind of finally accepted answers the scientists expect to get, are nonetheless for normal human living, useful and indeed necessary. Some of the *popularizers* of this philosophy, however, pretty explicitly held that all mental activity save logical analysis and empirical verification is at least inferior mental activity, or more likely, nonsense, a waste of time, or worse. A distinguished American popularizer, Stuart Chase, in his *Tyranny of Words* (1938) proposed to clarify our thinking by substituting "blah-blah" for terms that have no

such good logical or "operational" clearance. Thus the famous French revolutionary slogan, "Liberty, equality, fraternity" would come out simply as "Blah-blah, blah-blah, blah-blah." Approaching their problems very differently from the way Freud and Pareto did, these logical analysts nevertheless came to a similar conclusion about the reasoning capacity of most human beings: most human beings, they conclude, are at present incapable of thorough, persistent, successful logical thinking, and they cannot be taught to do this kind of thinking in any foreseeable future. Clearly, this is a position only with difficulty logically reconcilable with the American democratic tradition.

Once more we encounter the sharp tensions of modern intellectual life. Since these logical analysts seemed to set up the practices of science, as they understood them, as the sole right way of thinking, many of those devoted to the arts and the humanistic studies generally turned in revenge to the denunciation of science as a narrowing, dangerous, use of the mind. Anti-scientism is as characteristic of our age as scientism.

Probably the most widespread philosophical movement of our century developed outside of, or on the margin of, formal professional philosophy. This movement may be called "historicism," the attempt to find in history an answer to those ultimate questions of the structure of the universe and of man's fate the philosopher has always asked. At bottom, the transfer of Darwinian concepts of organic evolution from biology to this great, sweeping field of philosophical questions contains the essence of twentieth-century historicism: once the traditional Judaeo-Christian concepts of a single creation in time, a God above nature, and the rest of the traditional world-view were abandoned, men in search of answers to their questions about these ultimates had to fall back on the historical record. Man is not made by God, but by nature, which amounts to saying that *man makes himself* in the course of history. We get our only clues as to man's capacities here on earth, clues as to how he ought to behave, clues as to that future that so concerns him, from the record of the past.

But "clues" is a modest and misleading word here. Many of the thinkers who appealed to history found much more than indications of what *might* be, much more than the always tentative, never dogmatic or absolute "theories" the scientist produces in answer to the less-than-ultimate questions he asks. Many of these philosophers of history, to simplify a bit, found in what they held to be the course of history a substitute for the concepts of God or Providence. They found in the record of the past substantially the equivalent of what Christians found in revelation—the explanation of man's nature and destiny, his *end* in the sense of a teleology or an eschatology. Paradoxically, they found in history something quite outside and beyond history.

Of these historicisms, the most important and the most obviously a substitute for Christianity is of course Marxism, which we have dealt with elsewhere (see Chapter XX). The theological parallels are plain, and have been frequently noted by non-Marxists: for God, absolute and omnipotent, the Marxist puts the absolutely determined course of Dialectical Materialism; for the Bible, he puts the canonical writings of Marx-Engels, with the addition, for the orthodox of the Soviet Union and its satellites, of those of Lenin; for the Church, the Party; for the Christian eschatology of divine judgment and heaven or hell, the revolution and the "classless society."

But Marxism, if the most rigorous, is only one of the historicisms of our time. The German, Oswald Spengler (1880-1936), produced in his *Decline of the West,* published just at the end of World War I, a characteristic specimen. Spengler

found from the historical record that societies or civilizations have, like human beings, an average life-span, a thousand years or so for a civilization being the equivalent of seventy years or so for the individual. He traced several non-western civilizations, but in the West he found three main ones, a Hellenic from 1000 B.C. to about the birth of Christ, a Levantine from the birth of Christ to about 1000 A.D., and our own modern western, which began (according to him) about 1000 A.D and was, therefore, due to end about 2000 A.D. We cannot here analyze his work at length. Spengler had real insights, but his work as a whole, most historians would say, is simply not history —it is metaphysics, or if you like a coined word, meta-history. There are critics who explain Spengler simply; he saw Germany was about to be defeated, and he therefore consoled himself by believing western civilization was about to end.

Better known nowadays than Spengler's is the work of the English historian, Arnold Toynbee (1889–   ) whose great ten-volume *Study of History* (1934-1954) has been very neatly condensed by D. C. Somervell into two manageable volumes. Toynbee is worth studying as a symptom of the intellectual difficulties of historicism and of our age. He has a Christian background, a careful training in historical scholarship, and a strong family tradition of kindly humanitarian service. World War I marked him with a great hatred for war, and a conviction that nationalism, which he once declared to be the real if unavowed religion of our western society, is the villain of the piece. His great system is an attempt to trace the causes of the rise and fall of societies in the past, and owes a good deal to Spengler. But Toynbee is a gentle English Christian humanist, not a German romantic racist brought up on Nietzsche. He does, like the majority of contemporary philosophers of history, conclude that our western society is facing a very serious challenge, that in terms of the cyclical rise

CHAPTER XXXII

and fall of societies he has traced it looks as if we were about to give ourselves the "knock-out blow." But he refuses to give up hope. The facts of historical development may, he holds, indicate destruction for us; but we may transcend history, and under the influence of a revived, or new, or Buddhist-influenced Christianity of gentleness and love, pull ourselves out of the hole.

Historicism has, again quite characteristically in our culture, given rise to bitter protests and to its opposite. Almost all professional historians, in the West nowadays mostly conventionally democratic in their values, simply give these philosophers of history the cold shoulder. Independent existentialists like Camus (who did not consider himself an existentialist) are firm in their contention that, though we may not neglect history as a record of human experience, we must find in ourselves something—salvation, perhaps—quite beyond history. And as for the logical analysts, history is far too lacking in precise data to make it a subject worth their while.

The Sciences

No general history can deal substantively with the history of science and technology in the twentieth century. Each science, each branch of each science, has continued in this century its cumulative course. The co-operation (not without rivalry) among "pure" scientists, applied scientists, engineers, bankers, businessmen, and "government" has produced in all phases of human control over material things the kind of exponential increases that send the lines of our graphs quite off the paper. Man's attained rate of travel is no doubt an extreme example, one not achieved in the same degree for instance in such fields as those of medicine and genetics. But in 1820 the fastest rate was still 12 to 15 miles an hour; railroads made it 100 miles or so by 1880; piston-engined airplanes made it 300 miles or so by 1940; jet planes broke the sound barrier only yesterday in 1947, making speeds of close to 1000 miles per hour possible; and now rockets have carried mammals and will soon carry living men in space free of our atmosphere at speeds of thousands of miles an hour.

Each science is of course highly specialized, and the active scientist usually is supreme master of only part of a given science. Indeed, one of the great worries of our numerous contemporary worriers is well expressed in the old tag that has modern specialists knowing more and more about less and less. But the tag really is an old one—and, like most such tags, partly true and worth our attention, yet not quite borne out by any catastrophic break in our culture. For the fact is that at a broad, non-specialist's level of understanding most educated men in the West have a very good idea of what modern science is trying to do, and how it does it.

Einstein in 1931.

The wider implications of modern science as its ways of work and its general concepts affect our world-views is a subject no general history can neglect. In the broadest sense, there can be no doubt that, though many practicing scientists are good Christians, the scientific attitude toward nature and natural laws, the scientific attitude of skepticism toward the supernatural, has added powerfully to the modern drive toward rationalism, positivism, materialism. Science continues to promote the world-view we have seen arising in early modern times, and culminating in the Enlightenment of the eighteenth century (see Chapter XVII). Indeed, many scientists have managed to make of the pursuit of scientific knowledge itself a kind of religion.

More particularly, the great event of the twentieth century has been the revolution in physics symbolized for the public in the figure of the late Albert Einstein (1879-1955). The concepts of relativity, a space-time continuum, and quantum mechanics freed physics from the "Newtonian world-machine" and helped the very great modern innovations in the field, innovations that worked together with the late nineteenth-century discoveries of the phenomena of radiation (X-rays, the researches of the Curies, Roentgen, and others) to make possible our contemporary developments in fields like electronics. Einstein's theories on the equivalence of mass and mechanical energy, his concept of time as the fourth dimension and the representation of gravitation as a field (compare "magnetic field") rather than a force secured wide public attention, if not always comprehension. From all this a few laymen came to the conclusion that since the apparently rigid world of mechanical causation of classic physics had broken down, since there was associated with the name of the distinguished German physicist Werner Heisenberg an "indeterminacy principle" familiar to practicing scientists, the common-sense law of cause-and-effect had in fact been repealed, and the universe was once more a fine free space in which anything could happen. This of course is not true, and the work of Newton has not been so much contradicted by modern physics as supplemented. Heisenberg's principle resulted from close work on the particle called an electron. An individual electron observably jumps from one orbit to another without evident and predictable sequence. Yet *statistically* the behavior of many, many electrons together is predictable, as predictable as it was in Newton's day. It is quite likely that misunderstood doctrines of "relativity" in physics, misapplied to ethics and aesthetics, did have a part in the fashionable doctrines of moral and aesthetic relativism of only yesterday.

The development of astronomy has been largely influenced by that of physics. To the layman, such modern astronomical concepts as that of a finite but expanding universe, of curved space, and perhaps above all the almost inconceivable distances and quantities, light years, galaxies, and the like, have made astronomy the most romantic of sciences. And these distances and quantities *are* almost inconceivable: a light year is the distance traversed by light in one year, or roughly 5,880,000,000,000 miles; our own Milky Way Galaxy has some thirty thousand million stars and nebulae, in the form of a disk with a diameter of about 100,000 *light years*. Recent developments in rocketry have made our moon seem attainable by actual human flight instead of merely by flight of the science-fiction imagination.

Chemistry, on the other hand, in spite of the marvels of synthesis it produces, has less attraction for the imagination. Yet in our daily living it is surely the science of chemistry that touches us most closely, in our foods, our medicines, our clothing, almost all the material objects we use.

Chemistry has also aided the very great gains that have been made in the twentieth century in the pure biological sciences and in their applications to medicine and public health as well. Not only in the United States and the rest of the West, but all over the world, infant mortality, many contagious diseases, even undernourishment, have been so far conquered that the average expectancy of life at birth has gone up as much as twenty years in advanced nations since 1900. Even in the economically backward areas of the globe, more children are born and more live, so that the population problem has become acute, and is still unsolved. It is significant, however, that the actual extreme limits of the human life span have not yet been significantly affected. It does not seem that a limit of something like 110 to 120 years for human life, historically known to have prevailed for centuries, has yet been exceeded.

There remains one more major problem which the progress of twentieth-century science has sharpened, a problem closely related to that of specialization in science and learning. There is in some senses a widening gap today between those who pursue what we call "humanistic" studies and those who pursue scientific studies. It is by no means difficult philosophically to reconcile these two pursuits; the poet and the physicist have, as creative human beings, more in common than we others usually can see. But the fact remains that from the point of view of the sociologist the two groups in our cultural life do clash, the scientists finding the humanists fuzzy-minded, sloppy intellectually, and clearly inferior, the humanists finding the scientists limited, pedestrian, cold, inhuman, and quite unable to manage the Frankenstein monster of modern technology they have created. Fortunately, there are good men who are at work mediating between these two sides, men who incline to the belief that the opposition is by no means one rooted in the facts of life and human nature.

In sum, the very great achievements of modern science and technology have raised many problems for our western democracy: the overriding problem presented by the fact that hydrogen bombs, missiles, and biological warfare have made the destruction of the human race no mere bit of rhetoric, nor a theological doctrine like that of Judgment Day, but a possible situation confronting even rationalistic common sense; the problem of humanizing science; the problem of overpopulation; the problems of educating scientists and endowing scientific research; and many other problems. Yet the fact remains that science and technology seem to be the deciding factors that have raised the masses far enough beyond misery and near-starvation to make possible what we Americans call democracy. And perhaps even more important, the continuing very great vitality of western civilization—a vitality as real in the arts as in the sciences—is at its clearest in the magnificent achievements of modern science. Modern science rightly worries the worriers, but it should also console them, for it shows man still in a light reflected long ago by the Greek Sophocles:

What a thing is man! Among all wonders
The wonder of the world is man himself

. . .

Man the Contriver! Man the Master-mind.*

Literature and the Arts

In the field of imaginative literature, music, painting, the fine arts, and the arts generally, we invent new styles and attitudes yet by no means wholly destroy what the past has left us. Here, as for all our culture, the contemporary historian has to note the great variety of tastes and standards that have piled up. But he must also note that there appears in mid-twentieth century with special sharpness another characteristic of

* Sophocles, *Antigone*, John Jay Chapman, trans. (Boston, 1930), lines 332-340.

our time, the wide and deep gap between the art—in the broad sense of "art" to include letters, music, architecture—of the few, or "highbrow" art, and the art of the many, or popular art. Bridges between the two there are, usually built on highbrow initiative from the highbrow side toward the lowbrow side. A good example is the fashion among the cultivated few for some phases, at least, of American popular music, or jazz. For many French intellectuals, as difficult, as refined, as remote from the masses as any intellectuals have ever been, "le jazz hot" is the only cultural achievement of the United States. Every now and then, if only briefly, some contributor to that most popular form of popular art, the American comic strip, gains a following among the highbrows, or at least, among undergraduates.

Yet there are other connections between highbrow and popular arts, perhaps also in tastes and even in morals. For instance, the initiative for modern frankness about such matters as sex undoubtedly came from the few. The males, at least, of the lower classes—to use a term no good American would use—have always been verbally frank in such matters. But in the nineteenth century the famous four-letter words were never printed, and they were never used by ladies, nor even by women. Freudian and other influences among the highbrows about 1900 began a process of dissolving Victorian decencies in the name of honest realism. This process has surely penetrated in our day to the many, though it is still true that most popular and public art (furtive pornography is another thing), with the exception of "cheesecake" and novels of the Mickey Spillane kind, is a good deal more reserved about matters sexual than is highbrow art. Yet here again we must note the blurring class lines in contemporary America; the tremendous sale in 1959 of the unexpurgated *Lady Chatterley's Lover* by D. H. Lawrence would indicate that the book was read by many who would make no claim to the status of intellectual.

Moreover, though the masses in the West are by no means in a state of despair, nor in a state of unprofitable idleness and dependence like the urban masses in imperial Rome, popular culture in the mid-twentieth century does have a stamp of big-city slickness, surface cynicism, and an addiction to vicarious violence and cruelty. But it must be remembered that modern technology has made the existence of a popular culture of this sort exceedingly evident. Most of such culture in the past was never recorded and preserved, or, if it was, has been selected out and sometimes prettified as "folk-lore." Even so, the ferocious tales of Norse or Greek "mythology" would indicate that Mickey Spillane is not without his predecessors.

High Art: Literature

Once more, imaginative writing in the twentieth century makes no striking break with that of the late nineteenth. Poetry and literary criticism remain, as they had begun to be in the 1890's or even earlier (see Chapter XXIII), difficult, cerebral, and addressed to a very small, if fit, audience. An occasional poet, like the American, Robert Frost, breaks from the privacy of the little magazines and the limited editions to wide popularity and a place enshrined in old-fashioned anthologies. But Frost is no more esoteric in form or substance than Wordsworth. More remarkable and more symptomatic, there are signs that T. S. Eliot, born in St. Louis, but as an adult wholly Anglicized, an abstruse and allusive poet, an intellectual of intellectuals, is also attaining a wider audience. The figure of speech with which he began "The Love Song of J. Alfred Prufrock" in 1917, which once seemed strange, "advanced," is now tame enough for any anthology:

Let us go then, you and I
When the evening is spread out against
    the sky
Like a patient etherised upon a table.*

The novel remains the most important form of contemporary imaginative writing. Critics have long bemoaned its exhaustion as an art-form, but the novel does not die. It is quite impossible here for us to give

James Joyce.

even a thumb-nail sketch of the contemporary novel. It is not even wise of us to attempt to indicate writers likely to be read in the twenty-first century. It may be that a novelist like the American, J. P. Marquand, disliked by the pure highbrow because he writes best-sellers, will survive better than such a favorite of the pure as William Faulkner, who writes existentialist novels about darkest Mississippi. The late Thomas Mann (1875-1945) seems already

---

** T. S. Eliot, *Complete Poems & Plays* (Harcourt, Brace, 1952), 3.

enshrined as a classic; but Mann, who began with a traditionally realistic novel of life in his birthplace, the old Hanseatic town of Lübeck, never really belonged to the *avant garde*. He is typical of the sensitive, worrying, class-conscious (his class was that of the artist-intellectual, no mere Marxist class) artist of the age of psychology.

More useful for us here, since it illustrates one of the problems of all modern art, is the career of the Irishman, James Joyce (1882-1941). Joyce began with a subtle, outspoken, but formally conventional series of sketches of life in the Dublin of his youth, *Dubliners* (1914), and the novelist's inevitable, and with Joyce undisguised, autobiography, *Portrait of the Artist as a Young Man* (1916). Then, mostly in exile on the Continent, he wrote what may well prove a classic, the experimental novel *Ulysses* (1922). This novel is an account rather than a narrative of twenty-four hours in the life of Leopold Bloom, a Dublin Jew. It is full of difficult allusions, parallels with Homer, puns, rapidly shifting scenes and episodes, and is written without regard for the conventional notions of plot and orderly development. Above all, it makes full use of the recently developed psychologies of the unconscious as displayed in an individual's "stream of consciousness." The last chapter, printed entirely without punctuation marks, is the record of what went on in the mind of Bloom's Irish wife as she lay in bed waiting for him to come home. What went on in her mind was in large part too shocking for the early century, and *Ulysses*, published in Paris, long had to be smuggled into English-speaking countries. It is still not exactly welcomed in Ireland.

Ulysses, though it took attentive reading, and even for those most fully abreast of the *avant garde* culture was often puzzling, is still a novel in English. Joyce's final big work, long known as simply "Work in Progress," but published as *Finnegan's Wake* (1939), is one of those works of radical experimentation about which, like many modern paintings, the ordinary educated layman simply has to say that it means nothing, or very little, to him. The continuities and conventions of narration and "plain English," not wholly flouted in *Ulysses,* are here almost wholly abandoned. There are words, and even sentences; but *meaning* has to be quarried out by the reader and may when quarried turn out to be quite different from what Joyce intended. But there are keys to *Finnegan's Wake*—we cite one in our reading list for this chapter—and the reader who wants to try to get at this interesting experiment in modern art can get his start there. Here is the beginning and ending of *Finnegan's Wake:*

rivverrun, past Eve and Adam's, from swerve of shore to bend of bay, brings us by a commodius vicus of recirculation back to Howth Castle and Environs.

. . . . .

. . . A gull. Gulls. Far calls. Coming, far! End here. Us then. Finn, again! Take. Bussoftlhee, mememormee! Till thousendsthee. Lps. The keys to. Given! A way a lone a last a loved a long the *

Note once more: such writing may well be a blind alley, but the traditions of western invention—we use that word in a very broad sense—insist that it may not be declared a blind alley until it has been well explored.

High Art: The Fine Arts

It is, however, the fine arts, painting perhaps in first rank, but with sculpture, architecture, and the minor decorative arts all included, that confront the ordinary cultivated westerner with the problem of "modernism" in its most clear form. The process of getting beyond the camera eye and Renaissance ideas of perspective— in general, "realism"—which we began to trace in Chapter XXIII has gone on right

---

* J. Joyce, *Finnegan's Wake* (New York, 1959), 3, 628.

to this day. Indeed, painting done today can be almost—not quite—sharply divided into two groups: that done traditionally, academically, representational painting of the kind that surprises and puzzles no one though it still pleases many; and the many kinds of experimental or non-representational, or simply "modern," painting. The variety of these experiments is great indeed. Most of them have been made by the great figure of contemporary painting, Pablo Picasso (1881–   ).

A native Spaniard, and an adopted Frenchman, Picasso has in his long life painted in many "styles" or "periods." The paintings of his "Blue Period," for instance, executed in the first years of our century, exemplify Expressionism, the attempt to express in art such highly subjective emotional states as grief and despair. These pictures are said to have been influenced by the work of El Greco, the sixteenth-century master; certainly, both artists convey a sense of concentrated emotion by exaggerating human proportions. Around 1905, Picasso, stimulated in part by primitive Negro art, turned to more daring innovations, striving, as Cézanne had striven (see above, p. 329), to transfer to the two dimensions of a picture the three dimensions of the real world. Sometimes he used the techniques of Abstractionism, the reduction of figures to a kind of plane geometry, all angles and lines. Sometimes he used those of Cubism, the reduction of figures to a kind of solid geometry, all cubes, spheres, and cones. Sometimes he even glued onto a picture bits of real objects—paper or the caning from a chair—in the process called *collage* ("paste-up"). The picture reproduced at the beginning of this chapter shows that Picasso fused and refined these techniques to create great art. In the range and inventiveness of his work Picasso calls to mind the masters of the Renaissance. On the one hand, he has done many portraits that are almost classical in style, as in the work of his "White Period" following World

War I. On the other hand, he has continued radical experimentation not only on canvas but also in sculpture, in ceramics, and in "constructions" of wood and other materials that might be called the sculptor's counterpart of *collage*. Most disturbing to the ordinary viewer, perhaps, are Picasso's recurrent efforts, stemming from Cubism, to show the human figure from two or more angles simultaneously—whence the apparently misplaced eyes and the anatomical distortions and rearrangements in many of Picasso's pictures.

Most remote from this world of sense experience as organized by common sense is the work of various kinds of abstract painters, paintings which are sometimes elaborate patterns of lines and colors, sometimes geometrical, sometimes apparently mere random daubs. It all means something, if only to the painter; but that meaning cannot be seized by the uninitiated. You have to learn to understand modern painting.

The conservative worried by modern art can perhaps take some comfort in the fact that the most extreme manifestation of this art is now some forty years past, and has never been quite equaled in its extraordinary defiance of all conventions, all rules, all forms. This extreme manifestation, perhaps more important sociologically than artistically, was the protest made by a very alienated group of intellectuals, the Dadaists, the "angry young men" of World War I and its aftermath. They reacted against a world so much sillier than their Dada that it could slaughter thousands in warfare. Here are some characteristic passages from an account of Dada written by a sympathetic observer:

In Berlin as elsewhere we notice the persistent desire to destroy art, the deliberate intent to wipe out existing notions of beauty, the insistence upon the greatest possible obliteration of individuality. Heartfield works under the direction of Grosz while Max Ernst and Arp sign each other's paintings at random.

. . . .

In the first New York Independents' exhibition, 1917, he [Marcel Duchamp] entered a porcelain urinal with the title *Fontaine* and signed it R. Mutt to test the impartiality of the executive committee of which he himself was a member. By this symbol Duchamp wished to signify his disgust for art and his admiration for ready-made objects.

. . . .

At an exhibition in Paris among the most remarkable entries sent by the poets was a mirror of Soupault's entitled *Portrait of an unknown*. . . . Certain paintings by Duchamp supposed to be in this exhibition were replaced by sheets of paper marked with numbers which corresponded to the Duchamp entries in the catalog. Duchamp, who had been asked to take part in the exhibition, had just cabled from New York: "Nuts." *

Again we must repeat what we have said before: it is perfectly possible that in the long run of history the directions taken in the contemporary fine arts by those we now think of as leaders, pioneers, will prove stale and unprofitable. But no one who has not made an effort to understand these arts is justified in condemning them out of hand. And one hostile position the disgruntled conservatives in these fields often take seems quite untenable: this is the labeling of such modern art as "pedantic," "decadent," as a sign of exhaustion, death, lack of creative power. Quite the contrary, this art is alive, inventive, dynamic, an attempt to extend the confines of human experience, an attempt quite as remarkable, though in its results not so readily assessed, as that of modern science and technology. The historian must note that the extreme traditionalists, doing exactly what their forefathers have done, are much more vulnerable to the accusation that their work is a sign of exhaustion and decay.

This remark holds even more strikingly true in architecture. The twentieth century has seen the growth of the first truly origi-

* Georges Huguet in *Fantastic Art, Dada, Surrealism*, A. H. Barr, Jr., ed. (Museum of Modern Art, 1936), 23, 19, 33.

Frank Lloyd Wright, Kaufmann house in Bear Run, Pennsylvania (1936-39).

nal style in architecture since the end of the eighteenth century. "Modern" or "functional" architecture is no revival of a past style, no pastiche of elements of such past styles, no living museum of eclectic choice, like most of nineteenth-century architecture. It prides itself on its honest use of modern materials, its adaptation to modern living, its dislike of waste space and over-display. There is in modern architecture a certain touch of austerity, even puritanism, that should confound those who think that our age is sunk in lush sensuality. In the long run, mid-century modern architecture will probably seem to have carried its dislike for ornamentation, especially external or-

namentation, rather too far. There are already signs that architects are beginning to tire of vast expanses of plain glass, and steel.

"Modern" music, unlike "modern" painting or architecture, has never quite crystallized into a distinctive style. The twentieth century has produced a great many attempts to extend the frontiers of classical music—by using scales other than the conventional one, by stressing dissonance and discord, and by borrowing the insistent rhythms of popular jazz. A generation ago, the general public came to identify these innovations most closely with the Russian, Igor Stravinsky (1882—   ), who on the eve of World War I composed two ballet scores, *Petrouchka* and *The Rite of Spring*, that were far removed from the polite and formalized ballet of tradition. Stravinsky may prove to be the musical counterpart of the successful artistic pioneer Picasso; significantly, however, although Stravinsky has continued experimental compositions, none of his later works has equaled his great ballets in impact or popularity.

In sum: all the "creative" modern arts are complex and difficult, and as of this moment far from being "understanded of the people." The very evident gulf between the tastes of the many and the tastes of the few may be an indication of a dangerous side of our democratic society. Certainly this is a subject on which no one is justified in taking an attitude of "holier than thou." But here the complete prevalence of the popular side, the elimination of the art of the few, seems most unlikely. It would seem that contrasting sets of standards and tastes, and the consequent great variety of works of art of all kinds, are one of the marks of our democratic society.

For it is fact that the two great attempts to put across a really totalitarian society in this century, that of Stalin in Russia and that of Hitler in Germany, were marked by very successful efforts to suppress highbrow culture, especially in art and in philosophy. Science, as we now know, flour-ished in Nazi Germany, and continues to flourish in a Russia which bans Boris Pasternak's novel, *Dr. Zhivago*. Russia was in most ways the most extreme example. This great socio-economic experiment, it may seem somewhat paradoxically, banned experiment in the arts and in the whole range of humanistic culture, at least after the accession of Stalin to power. Soviet architecture was even more atrociously monumental than the worst of nineteenth-century commercial architecture. Until Pasternak's novel, sent out of Russia in manuscript for translation into Italian under communist patronage, came in 1958 to widespread attention, no piece of Soviet writing really struck the imagination of the West. This failure cannot justly be laid to western censorship or banning; it is simply that the crude propaganda literature of Communist Russia did not greatly interest even fellow-traveling western highbrows. Things got worse under Stalin, when such promising beginnings as Soviet movies—those of Eisenstein, for instance—and the more daring music of Russian composers like Shostakovich came under what one has to call censorship by bourgeois taste. For it is quite clear from the Russian experience that when the proletariat gets power, it wants, and in the arts at least gets, about what the conventional bourgeois of an earlier generation thought desirable and lovely.

II: The Temper of Our Times

Modern western man is acutely conscious of what may be called, a trifle imprecisely, the spirit of the age, the temper of the time, the climate of opinion. In the United States we incline to believe that each recent decade has had a character of its own, from the naughty 'nineties to the fearful 'fifties. For the present, and the im-mediate past, we have a number of popular phrases—The Age of Anxiety, The Aspirin Age, The Age of Longing, The Age of Conformity, The Age of Suspicion, even The Age of Tranquilizers.

These phrases all have in common a tone of pessimism, mildly seasoned with the shrug-it-off, laugh-that-we-may-not-weep, not very profound cynicism which is a mark of our urban democratic culture. And it surely is also a mark of our age that its serious, its highbrow, culture is to an extraordinary degree pessimistic about the present state of man, gloomy and fearsome about the future, though by no means in agreement either on diagnosis of what is wrong with our culture or in prognosis of its development. Here is a dignified and eloquent sample from the late Albert Camus' speech of acceptance of his Nobel Prize in 1958:

...As the heir of a corrupt history that blends blighted revolutions, misguided techniques, dead gods, and worn out ideologies, in which second-rate powers can destroy everything today, but are unable to win anyone over; in which intelligence has stooped to becoming the servant of hatred and oppression, that generation [Camus' own], starting from nothing but its own negations, has had to re-establish both within and without itself a little of what constitutes the dignity of life and death. Faced with a world threatened with disintegration, in which our grand inquisitors may set up once and for all the kingdoms of death, that generation knows that, in a sort of mad race against time, it ought to re-establish among nations a peace not based on slavery, to reconcile labor and culture again, and to reconstruct with all men an Ark of the Covenant. Perhaps it can never accomplish that vast undertaking, but most certainly throughout the world it has already accepted the double challenge of truth and liberty, and, on occasion, has shown that it can lay down its life without hatred. That generation deserves to be acclaimed wherever it happens to be, and especially wherever it is sacrificing itself.[°]

Let us note that, although from Plato, even from Ikhnaton on, our serious literary and artistic culture has always shown a strain of pessimism, our own intellectual leaders are, first, more than usually appre-

hensive and censorious and second, more than usually aware of the gulf between their way of living, their standards of value, and those of their fellow citizens. Just one sample: here in a recent work is a well-known American writer complaining that most Americans confuse "normal" with "average," and suggesting that we need a genuine synonym for "average":

Fortunately, such a genuine and familiar synonym does exist. That which is "average" is also properly described as "mediocre." And if we were accustomed to call the average man, not "the common man" or still less "the normal man," but "the mediocre man" we should not be so easily hypnotized into believing that mediocrity is an ideal to be aimed at.[°]

Now the historian, in attempting by comparative study of similar phenomena in different times and places to arrive at workable generalizations, has great difficulty with this problem of what is the "normal" or "usual" relation between intellectual classes—the writers, artists, scholars, teachers, preachers, and their followers —and other classes, even within our western culture. Such study simply isn't well enough developed to permit measurement, graphs, quantitative generalization. Qualitatively, we may risk the assertion that the gravity and extent of the gap between the way American intellectuals, and to a degree western intellectuals generally, think-and-feel and the way the rest of western society thinks-and-feels—the phenomenon we may call in shorthand "the alienation of the intellectuals"—this phenomenon may well be a grave symptom of weakness in our society.

Yet the degree of alienation of the intellectuals is hard to measure, and we may have exaggerated it in the passage above. American intellectuals complain bitterly about the impossibility of the good life in the machine age, but they for the most part

° Reprinted with the permission of Alfred A. Knopf, Inc., from Albert Camus' Speech of Acceptance upon the award of the Nobel Prize for Literature, December 10th, 1957, translated by Justin O'Brien. Copyright © 1958 by Alfred A. Knopf, Inc.

° J. W. Krutch, *Human Nature and the Human Condition* (Random House, 1959), 93.

use the machines with apparent satisfaction. They find fault with our business civilization, but a great many of them do a very good business in it, and the rank-and-file are not in terms of income as badly off as they think they are. They often regard themselves as a scorned and victimized minority in a hostile society of Babbitts, but a distinguished California sociologist has recently argued that they are in fact well regarded:

While he [the American intellectual] may feel himself neglected and scorned, his work poorly valued by the community, the community places him fairly high when polled on the relative status of occupations. In one such study of the ranks of ninety-six occupations, conducted in 1947 by the National Opinion Research Center of the University of Chicago, college professors ranked above every non-political position except that of physician; artists, musicians in a symphony orchestra, and authors ranked almost as high. . . . [In another poll in 1950] professors came out fourth among twenty-four categories, and thirty-eight per cent of those polled placed them definitely in the "upper class." *

At any rate, it is clear that the great majority of Americans, and even the great majority of Europeans, are not as cosmically worried, not as pessimistic about man's fate, as are the intellectuals. Indeed, it seems likely that the many in western society still adhere basically to the eighteenth-century belief in progress, moral as well as material. A recent candidate for the American presidency could say in a campaign speech, which by its very nature must be what hearers want to hear, "It is an article of the democratic faith that progress is a basic law of life." † In fact, one of the reproaches the intellectuals make to the many in the West is that the many appear on the whole quite contented with their

material prosperity, their gadgets, their amusements, their American-style "classless society," a society where one man is really as good as another, where all have a high level of consumption, not the Utopian, theoretical Marxist heaven of an unrealized "classless society."

Yet the pessimism of the intellectuals is understandable. The almost-Utopia which many of the thinkers of the Enlightenment believed was just around the corner in the eighteenth century is not here yet. Let us, in conclusion, briefly review that eighteenth-century basis of our western democratic faith, and see what our intellectual guides are making of that faith now, two hundred years later.

The Optimism of the Enlightenment

As we have pointed out (see Chapters XVII, XX, and XXIII), there grew up among western men in the early modern centuries, and there came to full bloom in the eighteenth and nineteenth centuries, a view of man's fate here on earth which was essentially new. This is the view that all men may rightly expect to be happy here on earth. As St. Just, the youthful colleague of Robespierre in the French Revolution, put it, "Happiness is a new idea in Europe"; or as Jefferson, with his gift for phrasing, put it, one of the rights of man is the "pursuit of happiness." Of course men have presumably always sought happiness here on earth. In historic Christianity, however, they did not really expect it here on earth, but only in an afterlife in heaven; indeed, Christianity had an overtone of belief that happiness in heaven was in part at least a reward for suffering here on earth.

The *philosophes*, the eighteenth-century thinkers who set the broad terms of this modern optimistic world-view, meant by happiness a condition or state in which

---

* S. M. Lipset, *Political Man* (New York: Doubleday, 1960).

† Adlai Stevenson, quoted in C. A. Chambers, "Belief in Progress in Twentieth Century America," *Journal of the History of Ideas* (April, 1958), 221.

Reading Suggestions
on Man's Fate in the Twentieth Century

(Asterisk indicates paperbound edition.)

PHILOSOPHY AND PSYCHOLOGY

E. Jones, *The Life and Work of Freud*, 3 vols. (Basic Books, 1953-1957). The standard work.

R. L. Schoenwald, *Freud: The Man and His Mind* (Knopf, 1956), and P. Rieff, *Freud: The Mind of the Moralist* (Viking, 1959). Two good modern studies emphasizing Freud's place in our contemporary culture.

B. F. Skinner, *Science and Human Behavior* (Macmillan, 1956). A clear and extreme statement of contemporary behavioristic psychology.

D. D. Runes, ed., *Twentieth-Century Philosophy* (Philosophical Library, 1942). Essays by distinguished philosophical writers covering the field pretty completely.

M. G. White, *The Age of Analysis: Twentieth-Century Philosophers* (*Mentor, 1955). Excerpts and comments, very well chosen.

R. Harper, *Existentialism: A Theory of Man* (Harvard Univ. Press, 1949). A sympathetic introduction to a "movement" not quite philosophically respectable.

W. Kaufman, ed., *Existentialism from Dostoevsky to Sartre* (*Meridian, 1956). Instructive selections from the existentialists, together with helpful critical comment.

P. W. Bridgman, *The Way Things Are* (Harvard Univ. Press, 1959). A distinguished physicist sets down a chastened statement of a contemporary positivist's point of view.

POLITICS AND SOCIOLOGY

H. S. Hughes, *Consciousness and Society: The Reorientation of European Social Thought, 1890-1930* (Knopf, 1958). A superb and unique study of the intellectual history of the early twentieth century, broader than its title might indicate.

W. Y. Elliott, *The Pragmatic Revolt in Politics: Syndicalism, Fascism, and the Constitutional State* (Macmillan, 1928). A prescient study still most pertinent.

T. Parsons, *The Structure of Social Action*, 2nd ed. (Free Press, 1949). A landmark in American sociological thinking.

R. D. Humphrey, *Georges Sorel: Prophet Without Honor* (Harvard Univ. Press, 1951). A suggestive study of an anti-intellectual.

V. Pareto, *The Mind and Society*, 4 vols. (Harcourt, Brace, 1935). A major work in general sociology, hardly to be read quickly. A good though difficult brief exposition of Pareto's thought is L. J. Henderson, *Pareto's General Sociology* (Harvard Univ. Press, 1937).

J. H. Meisel, *The Myth of the Ruling Class: Gaetano Mosca and the 'Elite'* (Univ. of Michigan Press, 1958). An illuminating study of an important thinker too little known in this country.

G. Wallas, *Human Nature in Politics* (Constable, 1908). A pioneer study in political psychology.

K. R. Popper, *The Open Society and Its Enemies* (Princeton Univ. Press, 1950). A major work on the problems of modern democracy.